CALIFORNIA
WORKERS'
COMPENSATION
CLAIMS AND BENEFITS

2007 SUPPLEMENT

By

David W. O'Brien, B.E., J.D.

Workers' Compensation
Administrative Law Judge, Retired

Legal Editor
Jason C. Hilfrink, B.S., J.D.
Erica S. Willis, B.A., J.D.

Edited by
Sean R. Weber

FS&K Publishing™
23801 Calabasas Road, Suite 2025
Calabasas, California 91302-1547
Tel: (818) 206-9234 • Fax: (818) 591-3672
info@FSKPublishing.com • FSKPublishing.com

ISBN 0-9749024-1-1

PREFACE

The State of California has, over the years, enacted laws establishing programs designed to alleviate the hardships experienced by workers of this state in times of distress. These programs are structured in such a way as to render assistance expeditiously, inexpensively, and effectively, with the goal of reducing to a minimum the suffering caused to workers in certain situations.

The distress toward which a certain body of these laws is directed is distress that may be visited upon a worker and, in many cases, upon his or her family, when he or she becomes unable to work and needs an income and/or is in need of medical care due to an on–the–job injury. Assistance for the worker comes from the Workers' Compensation Insurance Program.

This book is a concise and realistic explanation of the Workers' Compensation Insurance Program and designed in such a way as to introduce the reader to the basic provisions of the program by use of extensive quotes from the Labor Code and case law.

To more readily assist our readers, we have produced a separate book for the State Disability Insurance Program and the Unemployment Insurance program.

Case citations have been carefully selected and those that are given are not always intended to constitute authority for, or against, the conclusions drawn or the analysis given, but may be intended to refer the reader to an authority that discusses the general subject matter or the specific subject of analysis in more detail.

If the reader is using cases in this book to support a Petition or Writ of Review, it is important to check the official cases to be certain that they are "published" opinions inasmuch as an "unpublished" appellate court case may not be cited in any action or proceeding before an appellate court, except where the opinion is relevant under the doctrines of law of the case, res judicata, or collateral estoppel. See California Rules of Court, Rule 977. However, cases denied Writ of Review have no stare decisis effect as to appellate courts, but they are citable authority as to the holding of the Appeals Board. This is consistent with the well–established principle that contemporaneous administrative construction of a statute by the agency charged with its enforcement and interpretation, while not necessarily controlling, is of great weight; and courts will not depart from such construction unless it is clearly erroneous or unauthorized. *State Comp. Ins. Fund. v. Workers' Comp. Appeals Bd.* (1995) 37 Cal. App. 4th 675, 683 [43 Cal. Rptr. 2d 660, 60 Cal. Comp. Cases 717]; *Wings West Airlines v. Workers' Comp. Appeals Bd.* (1986) 187 Cal. App. 3d 1047, 1053 at fn. 4 [232 Cal. Rptr. 343, 51 Cal. Comp. Cases 609]; *Ralphs Grocery Co. v. W.C.A.B.* (1995) 38 Cal. App. 4th 820 [45 Cal. Rptr. 2d 197, 60 Cal. Comp. Cases 840]; and *Venega v. W.C.A.B.* (1998) [63 Cal. Comp. Cases 277]; *Lara v. W.C.A.B.* (1995) 60 Cal. Comp. Cases 840. See also *Consumers Lobby Against Monopolies v. Public Utilities Com.* (1975) 25 Cal. 3d 891, 902–905 [160 Cal. Rptr. 124]; *Clotherd v. W.C.A.B.* (1992) 225 Cal. App. 3d 455, 462 [275 Cal. Rptr. 130]. See also *Tenet/Centinela Hospital Center v. W.C.A.B. (Rushing)* (2000) 65 Cal. Comp. Cases 477.

Citations from the California Workers' Compensation Reporter are now included inasmuch as the Reporter is a properly citable authority, especially as an indication of contemporaneous interpretation and application of workers' compensation law. See *Griffith v. W.C.A.B.* (1989) 54 Cal. Comp. Cases 145.

I have continued my initial goal, in this twelfth edition, as well as this 2007 Supplement of setting forth sufficient facts and language used in leading cases from the Supreme Court, Courts of Appeal, and Workers' Compensation Appeals Board, so that rarely will the reader have to seek out the case itself to fully understand the reasoning of the Court or Board.

Realizing that in certain instances the reader must have the precise language of a code section at hand, we have added throughout these books direct quotes from a number of pertinent code sections.

Finally, I hope I have succeeded in my goal of sorting out and bringing to our readers' attention those endless laws and cases of which we all must be aware in the field of Workers' Compensation.

To sort out is not enough. I hope I have placed the cases and codes in those places you will logically look to see if there is law on the issue under study.

—DAVID W. O'BRIEN, Esq.

SPECIAL NOTICE

I have returned to self–publishing this book, and no longer are my prior publishers involved. I will be forever indebted to them for their fine work in publishing and promoting my book over the past years. In addition, I would like to thank Lawrence I. Stern, Esq. for all of his assistance.

Because the Appeals Board and the Administrative Director have made such massive changes in their rules and regulations, I recommend that all readers consult and review the new rules and regulations. Though every effort was made to remove the old rules and regulations from the text of this twelfth edition and 2008 Supplement, the voluminous nature of the changes lends to the possibility of error.

Please also note that due to anticipated changes by the Court Administrator in the forms to be used in Workers' Compensation practice, no form book has been included with this text.

DEFENSE PRO, INC.
CHARTS

I want to thank Defense Pro, Inc. for their generosity in permitting me to print their Charts that can be found in Appendix M. The information contained in the charts is extremely valuable to the workers' compensation community. You may telephone Defense Pro, Inc. at (877) 374–3744.

ABOUT THE AUTHOR

David W. O'Brien, a member of the California and New Hampshire bars, received his Bachelor of Education from Plymouth State University in 1950 and the degree of Doctor of Law from the University of San Francisco in 1960. He is admitted to the U.S. District Courts, Districts of New Hampshire and California. He is also a member of the American Bar Association.

Retired Workers' Compensation Administrative Law Judge O'Brien served as a Workers' Compensation Judge with the California Workers' Compensation Appeals Board, as an Administrative Law Judge with the California Unemployment Insurance Appeals Board, as a Deputy Commissioner of Corporations for the State of California, and as a Senior Counsel for the State Compensation Insurance Fund. He has also devoted many years to the private practice of law as both a defense and plaintiff attorney, serves as an expert witness in civil cases and is a Certified Administrator for Self–Insurance Plans.

During the Korean War, Judge O'Brien served as a special agent in the Counter Intelligence Corps.

Judge O'Brien is also the author and publisher of *"California Unemployment and Disability Compensation Programs,"* 10th Edition, as well as a pamphlet entitled *"Know the Facts–California Workers' Compensation Insurance–Employee Rights and Responsibilities"* (in English and Spanish) approved by the Administrative Director for use in educating employees as to their rights and responsibilities in the event of an industrial injury. Judge O'Brien also produces a series of educational home study audio tapes approved by the Administrative Director for ongoing Qualified Medical Evaluator's education.

Judge O'Brien is now associated with Floyd, Skeren & Kelly, a Limited Liability Partnership, 23801 Calabasas Road, Suite 2025, Calabasas, California, 91302, (818) 715–0018, FAX (818) 591–3572 and email email@fsklaw.com

Intentionally blank

TABLE OF CONTENTS

APPENDIX A
PRE–DESIGNATION OF PERSONAL PHYSICIAN; REQUEST FOR CHANGE OF PHYSICIAN; REPORTING DUTIES OF PRIMARY TREATING PHYSICIAN; PETITION FOR CHANGE OF PRIMARY TREATING PHYSICIAN

APPENDIX B
MEDICAL PROVIDER NETWORK (MPN); INDEPENDENT MEDICAL REVIEWER

APPENDIX C

APPENDIX D

APPENDIX E

Intentionally blank

§ 3.0   ADMINISTRATION

Page 18, Column 1, first paragraph, delete chart and insert the following:

GOVERNOR
Hon. Arnold Schwarzenegger
State Capitol Building
Sacramento, CA 95814
Tel: (916) 445–2841
Fax: (916) 445–4633
Website: www.governor.ca.gov
Email: governor@governor.ca.gov

LIEUTENANT GOVERNOR
Hon. John Garamendi
Capitol Office:
State Capitol Building, Room 1114
Sacramento, CA 95814
Tel: (916) 445–8994
Fax: (916) 323–4998
Website: www.ltg.ca.gov
Email: Lt.Governor@ltgov.ca.gov

Southern California Office:
300 South Spring Street, Suite 12702
Los Angeles, CA 90013
Tel: (213) 897–7086
Fax: (213) 897–7156

INSURANCE COMMISSIONER
Hon. Steve Poizner
Sacramento Office
300 Capitol Mall, Suite 1700
Sacramento, CA 95814
Tel: (916) 492–3500
Fax: (916) 445–5280
Website: www.insurance.ca.gov
Email: comissionerpoizner@insurance.ca.gov
General Tel: (800) 927–4357

San Francisco Office
45 Fremont Street, 23rd Floor
San Francisco, CA 94105
Tel: (415) 538–4010
Fax: (415) 904–5889

Los Angeles Office
300 South Spring Street, South Tower
Los Angeles, CA 90013
Tel: (213) 346–6464
Fax: (213) 897–9051

§ 3.1   Department of Industrial Relations

Page 19, Column 1, fourth paragraph, delete chart and insert the following:

DEPARTMENT OF INDUSTRIAL RELATIONS
(DIR)

DIRECTOR
Hon. John Rae
455 Golden Gate Avenue
San Francisco CA 94102
Tel: (415) 703–5050
Fax: (415) 703–5059
Website: www.dir.ca.gov
Email: info@dir.ca.gov

§ 3.2   Division of Workers' Compensation–Administrative Director

Page 19, Column 1, eighth paragraph, delete chart and insert the following:

DIVISION OF WORKERS' COMPENSATION
ADMINISTRATIVE DIRECTOR
Hon. Carrie Nevans
1515 Clay Street
17th Floor
Oakland, CA 94612
Tel: (510) 286–7100
Fax: (510) 286–7144
Website: www.dir.ca.gov/dwc
Email: dwc@dir.ca.gov
Recorded information: (800) 736–7401

Page 21, Column 1, first paragraph, delete chart and insert the following:

DIVISION OF WORKERS' COMPENSATION

ADMINISTRATIVE DIRECTOR
Hon. Carrie Nevans
1515 Clay Street, 17th Floor
Oakland, CA 94612
Tel: (510) 286–7100
Fax: (510) 286–7144
Website: www.dir.ca.gov/dwc
Email: dwc@dir.ca.gov
Recorded information: (800) 736–7401

COURT ADMINISTRATOR
Hon. Keven Star
1515 Clay Street
17th Floor
Oakland, CA 94612
Tel: (510) 286–7121
Website: www.dir.ca.gov

ASSOCIATE CHIEF JUDGES
Hon. Mark Kahn (Southern Region: Van Nuys)
Hon. Joel K. Harter (Northern Region: Sacramento)

MEDICAL DIRECTOR
Anne Searcy, M.D.

CHIEF LEGAL COUNSEL
Destie Overpeck

PROGRAMMATIC SERVICES
Angela Michael, Chief

LEGISLATION AND POLICY
Susan Gard, Chief

AUDIT UNIT
Bob Walensa, Manager

MANAGER–COMMUNICATIONS
Richard Stephens

DISABILITY EVALUATION UNIT
Blair Megowan, Manager

INFORMATION & ASSISTANCE UNIT
Bob C. Wong, Manager

INFORMATION OFFICER
Susan Gard

REHABILITATION UNIT
Otis Byrd, Manager

RESEARCH UNIT
Bill Kahley, Manager

UEBTF/SIBTF CLAIMS UNIT
Shirley H. James, Manager

WORKERS' COMPENSATION APPEALS BOARD DISTRICT
OFFICES WITH PRESIDING JUDGES

Anaheim
1661 N. Raymond Avenue, Room 200
Anaheim, CA 92801–1162
Tel: (714) 738–4000
Hon. Ellen L. Flynn

Bakersfield
1800 30th Street, Suite 100
Bakersfield, CA 93301–1929
Tel: (661) 395–2723
Hon. Robert Norton

Eureka
100 "H" Street, Suite 202
Eureka, CA 95501–0481
Tel: (707) 445–6518
Hon. Robert Kutz

Fresno
2550 Mariposa Street, Suite 4078
Fresno, CA 93721–2280
Tel: (559) 445–5051
Hon. Abel Shapiro

Goleta
6755 Holister Ave, Suite 100
Goleta, CA 93117–3018
Tel: (805) 968–0258
Hon. Robert Ebenstein

Grover Beach
1562 Grand Avenue
Grover Beach, CA 93433–2261
Tel: (805) 481–4912
Hon. Michael LeCover

Long Beach
300 Oceangate Drive, Suite 200
Long Beach, CA 90802–4339
Tel: (562) 590–5001
Hon. Joseph Rebeck

Los Angeles
320 West 4th Street, 9th Floor
Los Angeles, CA 90013–1105
(213) 576–7335
Hon. David Marcus

Marina del Rey
4720 Lincoln Blvd, 2nd Floor
Marina del Rey, CA 90292
Tel: (310) 482–3820
Hon. Robert Hjelle

Oakland
1515 Clay Street, 6th Floor
Oakland, CA 94612–1402
Tel: (510) 622–2866
Hon. Kenneth Peterson

Oxnard
2220 East Gonzales Road, Suite 100
Oxnard, CA 93036–8293
Tel: (805) 485–2533
Hon. David Brotman

Pomona
732 Corporate Center Drive
Pomona, CA 91768–1601
Tel: (909) 623–4301
Hon. J. Michael Morgan

Redding
2115 Civic Center Drive, Suite 15
Redding, CA 96001–2796
Tel: (530) 225–2845
Hon. Kathleen Ortega

Riverside
3737 Main Street, Suite 300
Riverside, CA 92501–3337
Tel: (951) 782–4269
Hon. Elena Jackson

Sacramento
2424 Arden Way, Suite 230
Sacramento, CA 95825–2403
Tel: (916) 263–2735
Hon. Joel Harter

Salinas
1880 North Main Street, Suite 100 & 200
Salinas, CA 93906–2016
Tel: (831) 443–3060
Hon. Thomas Clarke

San Bernardino
464 W. Fourth St., Suite 239
San Bernardino, CA 92401–1411
Tel: (909) 383–4341
Hon. Charles Regnell

San Diego
7575 Metropolitan Road, Suite 202
San Diego, CA 92108–4402
Tel: (619) 767–2083
Hon. Cliff Levy

San Francisco
455 Golden Gate Avenue, 2nd Floor
San Francisco, CA 94102–3660
Tel: (415) 703–5011
Hon. Susan Hamilton

San Jose
100 Paseo de San Antonio, Room 241
San Jose, CA 95113–1482
Tel: (408) 277–1246
Hon. Oliver Boyer

Santa Ana
28 Civic Center Plaza, Suite 451
Santa Ana, CA 92701–4070
Tel: (415) 558–4121
Hon. William Whiteley

Santa Rosa
50 "D" Street, Suite 420
Santa Rosa, CA 95404–4760
Tel: (707) 576–2391
Hon. James Johnson

Stockton
31 East Channel Street, Room 344
Stockton, CA 95202–2393
Tel: (209) 948–7759
Hon. David Bovett

Van Nuys
6150 Van Nuys Blvd. Suite 105
Van Nuys, CA 91401–3373
Tel: (818) 901–5367
Hon. Linda Morgan

§ 3.5 Workers' Compensation Appeals Board

Page 25, Column 2, fifth paragraph, delete chart and insert the following:

WORKERS' COMPENSATION APPEALS BOARD
455 Golden Gate Avenue, 9th floor
San Francisco, CA 94102
Tel: (415) 703–4554
Fax: (415) 703–4549
Website: www.dir.ca.gov/wcab

Mail Address:
P. O Box 429459
San Francisco, CA 94142–9459

COMMISSIONERS
Hon. Joseph M. Miller, **Chairperson**
Hon. Frank M. Brass
Hon. Ronnie Caplane
Hon. James C. Cuneo
Hon. Alfonso J. Moresi
Hon. Janice Murray
Hon. William K. O'Brien

DEPUTY COMMISSIONERS
Hon. Dennis J. Hannigan, Secretary
Hon. Rick Dietrich, Assistant Secretary
Hon. Neil P. Sullivan, Assistant Secretary

§ 3.6(A) Court Administrator

Page 26, Column 1, second paragraph, delete chart and insert the following:

Hon. Keven Star
1515 Clay Street
17th Floor
Oakland, CA 94612
Tel: (510) 286–7121
Website: www.dir.ca.gov

§ 3.13(A) Medical Director

Page 33, Column 1, thirteenth paragraph, delete chart and insert the following:

MEDICAL DIRECTOR
Anne Searcy, M.D.
1515 Clay Street, 17th floor
Oakland CA 94612
Tel: (800) 794–6900
Website: www.dir.ca.gov
Email: asearcy@dir.ca.gov

§ 3.15 State Compensation Insurance Fund

Page 41, Column 2, end of last paragraph, insert the following:

The Fund is subject to the powers and authority of the Insurance Commissioner to the same extent as other insurers transacting workers' compensation insurance, except where specifically exempted by reference. For purposes of Section 700, the Fund is deemed admitted to transact this class of insurance. Insurance Code section 11778

§ 3.16 Department of Insurance

Page 42, Column 1, first paragraph, delete chart and insert the following:

INSURANCE COMMISSIONER
Hon. Steve Poizner
Sacramento Office
300 Capitol Mall, Suite 1700
Sacramento, CA 95814
Tel: (916) 492–3500
Fax: (916) 445–5280
Website: www.insurance.ca.gov
Email: comissionerpoizner@insurance.ca.gov
General Tel: (800) 927–4357

San Francisco Office
45 Fremont Street, 23rd Floor
San Francisco, CA 94105
Tel: (415) 538–4010
Fax: (415) 904–5889

Los Angeles Office
300 South Spring Street, South Tower
Los Angeles, CA 90013
Tel: (213) 346–6464
Fax: (213) 897–9051

FRAUD DIVISION
Deputy Commissioner
Hon. Dale Banda
PO Box 277320
Sacramento, CA 95827
Tel: 916–854–5760
Fax: 916–255–3202
Website: www.insurance.ca.gov/0300–fraud
Email: fraud@insurance.ca.gov

OMBUDSMAN
Hon. Janet Burger
Ombudsman's Office
300 Capitol Mall, Suite 1600
Sacramento, CA 95814
Tel: (916) 492–3545
Fax: (916) 445–6552
Website: www.insurance.ca.gov
Email: ombudsman@insurance.ca.gov

Page 42, Column 2, last paragraph, insert the following:

Minimum Standards for Claims Adjusters

The Commissioner must and has adopted Regulations setting forth minimum standards of training and experience for claims adjusters. Insurance Code section 11761 provides:

(1) The commissioner shall adopt regulations setting forth the minimum standards of training, experience, and skill that workers' compensation claims adjusters must possess to perform their duties with regard to workers' compensation claims. The regulations adopted pursuant to this section shall, to the greatest extent possible, encourage the use of existing private and public education, training, and certification programs.

(2) Every insurer shall certify to the commissioner that the personnel employed by the insurer to adjust workers' compensation claims, or employed for that purpose by any medical billing entity with which the insurer contracts, meet the minimum standards adopted by the commissioner pursuant to subdivision (a).

(3) For the purposes of this section, "medical billing entity" means a third party that reviews or adjusts workers' compensation medical bills for insurers.

(4) For the purposes of this section, "insurer" means an insurer admitted to transact workers' compensation insurance in this state, the State Compensation Insurance Fund, an employer that has secured a certificate of consent to self–insure pursuant to subdivision (b) or (c) of Section 3700 of the Labor Code, or a third–party administrator that has secured a certificate of consent pursuant to Section 3702.1 of the Labor Code. See Appendix K for Standards Applicable to Workers' Compensation Claims Adjusters and Medical Billing Entities and Certification of those Standards by Insurers.

In implementing the above requirements, the Commissioner in Title 10, California Code of Regulations sections 2592–2592.06 requires adjusters to have knowledge in such areas as:

(1) Historical overview of the workers' compensation system.
(2) Organizational structure of the system.
(3) The workers' compensation insurance policy, its forms and endorsements, insurance principles of compensation.
(4) Concepts and terminology.
(5) Benefit provisions.
(6) Compensability.
(7) Notice requirements.
(8) Temporary disability.
(9) Permanent disability, including evaluation and rating.
(10) Death benefits.
(11) Return to work and vocational rehabilitation.
(12) Cumulative trauma.
(13) Serious and willful misconduct.
(14) Workers' Compensation Appeals Board procedures, forms, hearings, and penalties.

(15) Investigation.
(16) Fraud.
(17) Medical terminology.
(18) Knowledge and use of utilization guidelines (American College of Occupational and Environmental Medicine or other guidelines approved by the Administrative Director of the Division of Workers' Compensation.)
(19) Medical evidence.
(20) Medical dispute resolution (Qualified Medical Examiners, spinal surgery second opinions, pre–designation of physicians, independent medical reviewers, utilization review.)
(21) Fee schedules.
(22) Liens.
(23) Apportionment.
(24) Subrogation.
(25) Reserving.
(26) Ethical issues.

See Appendix L for the most "Frequently Asked Questions".

Executive Office
1515 Clay St., Room 901
Oakland CA 94612
Tel: (510) 622–3959
Fax: (510) 622–3265
Website: www.dir.ca.gov/Chswc
Email: chswc@hq.dir.ca.gov

§ 3.17 Workers' Compensation Insurance Rating Bureau

Page 43, Column 1, twelfth paragraph, delete chart and insert the following:

WORKERS' COMPENSATION INSURANCE RATING BUREAU
(WCIRB)
525 Market St. Suite 800
San Francisco, Ca 94105
Tel: (415) 777–0777
Fax: (415) 778–7272
Website: www.wcirbonline.org
Email: wcirb@wcirbonline.org

§ 3.18 Commission on Health and Safety and Workers' Compensation

Page 45, Column 1, fifth paragraph, insert the following:

COMMISSION ON HEALTH AND SAFETY AND
WORKERS' COMPENSATION

CHAIRPERSON
Hon. Christine Baker

COMMISSION MEMBERS
Hon. Angie Wei (2006 Chair)
Hon. Allen Davenport
Hon. Leonard C. McLeod
Hon. Alfonso Salazar
Hon. Kristen Schwenkmeyer
Hon. Robert B. Steinberg
Hon. Darrel "Shorty" Thacker
Hon. John C. Wilson

Intentionally blank

§ 4.0   WHAT IS AN INDUSTRIAL INJURY?

Page 53, Column 1, first paragraph, insert following '...injuries'

In *Benyamino v. WCAB* (2006) 71 Cal. Comp. Cases 899, the Court of Appeal, Fifth District, in an unpublished decision, upheld a Board's ruling holding that the applicant failed to prove by a preponderance of the evidence that her carpal tunnel syndrome was work related, as a caregiver, as it is just as likely the carpal tunnel syndrome could have been caused from her work at home as a homemaker.

The Court, in upholding the Board's denial of benefits stated:

Wilma Benyamino (Benyamino) petitions this court for a writ of review to determine the lawfulness of the decision of the Workers' Compensation Appeals Board (WCAB) denying her claim for benefits due to insufficient evidence of an industrial injury. (Lab. Code, § 5950; Cal. Rules of Court, rule 57.) We will deny the petition.

BACKGROUND

Benyamino was employed by the state Department of Social Services (DSS) as an In–Home Supportive Services caregiver to her parents. She worked approximately 30 hours per week cleaning, washing, moving objects, shopping, and providing general care. In March 2004, Benyamino filed two claims for workers' compensation benefits for injury to her hands and wrists. She alleged she sustained a specific injury on August 26, 2003, and a cumulative trauma injury over time through March 3, 2004. She later claimed the injuries were to her wrists and back.

The parties submitted the issue as to whether Benyamino's injuries arose out of and occurred in the course of employment on the parties qualified medical examinations. Benyamino relied primarily on the medical reporting of Leonard Gordon, M.D., while DSS relied on the opinion of Roland H. Winter, M.D. Benyamino also asked the workers' compensation administrative law judge (WCJ) to consider whether Dr. Winter's evaluation applied the wrong legal standard.

On May 10, 2005, the WCJ found Benyamino did not sustain an industrial injury to her wrists and back. The WCJ expressly found Dr. Winter's reports persuasive in concluding Benyamino did not sustain either a specific injury or cumulative trauma and also noted that neither physician reported she performed anything other than " 'general daily activities and use of the hands.' "

Benyamino petitioned for reconsideration. In a report to the WCAB, the WCJ explained Benyamino failed to meet her burden of proving industrial causation of the wrist injury and she offered no evidence whatsoever to support an industrial back injury. On July 20, 2005, the WCAB summarily denied Benyamino's petition for reconsideration, adopting and incorporating the WCJ's reasoning.

DISCUSSION

In reviewing an order, decision, or award of the WCAB, an appellate court must determine whether, in view of the entire record, substantial evidence supports the WCAB's findings. (§ 5952; Garza v. Workmen's Comp. App. Bd. (1970) 3 Cal. 3d 312, 317 [475 P.2d 451, 90 Cal. Rptr. 355, 35 Cal. Comp. Cases 500].) We are precluded from substituting our choice of the most convincing evidence or reweighing the evidence to decide disputed questions of fact. (§ 5953; Western Growers Ins. Co. v. Worker's Comp. Appeals Bd. (1993) 16 Cal. App. 4th 227, 233 [20 Cal. Rptr. 2d 26, 58 Cal. Comp. Cases 323].) Although we will not disturb an award merely because it is susceptible of opposing inferences, we may not accept factual findings if they are illogical, unreasonable, improbable, or inequitable considering the entire record and overall statutory scheme. (Judson Steel Corp. v. Worker's Comp. Appeals Bd. (1978) 22 Cal. 3d 658, 664 [586 P.2d 564, 150 Cal. Rptr. 250, 43 Cal. Comp. Cases 1205]; Western Growers Ins. Co., *supra*, at p. 233.)

To constitute an industrial injury, workplace events must have caused a temporary or permanent disability, death, or need for medical treatment beyond first aid. (§§ 3208.2, 5401, subd. (a).) "An injury may be either: (a) 'specific,' occurring as the result of one incident or exposure which causes disability or need for medical treatment; or (b) 'cumulative,' occurring as repetitive mentally or physically traumatic activities extending over a period of time, the combined effect of which causes any disability or need for medical treatment." (§ 3208.1.) Notwithstanding the statutory requirement to construe workers' compensation laws liberally in favor of extending disability benefits, an employee seeking benefits carries the burden of proof by a preponderance of evidence that an injury or disease arose out of and in the course of employment. (§ § 3202, 3202.5,

3208, 3600, 5705; Livitsanos v. Superior Court (1992) 2 Cal. 4th 744, 753 [828 P.2d 1195, 7 Cal. Rptr. 2d 808, 57 Cal. Comp. Cases 355].) Medical evidence that lacks convincing force and probability of truth does not establish prima facie proof of a work connection. (Wehr v. Workers' Comp. Appeals Bd. (1985) 165 Cal. App. 3d 188, 194 [211 Cal. Rptr. 321, 50 Cal. Comp. Cases 165].)

Medical evidence prepared by Dr. Gordon on July 16, 2004, suggested Benyamino had developed carpel tunnel syndrome, but that "[t]his would need to be confirmed with an electrodiagnostic study, as the provocative tests are equivocal, the Phalen's test is negative, and the Tinel's sign does produce some tingling although not in any specific distribution." The doctor concluded "[t]he causation of this problem would be from general daily activities and use of the hands." He explained Benyamino's work is "not intensely repetitive or forceful as far as the hands are concerned, and therefore this problem results from general use which would include the time she takes care of her parents." He also found "she is able to continue her usual and customary work." Four months later, on November 15, 2004, Dr. Gordon reported that Benyamino's electrodiagnostic study was negative. He therefore withdrew his conclusion she suffered from carpel tunnel syndrome and opined she suffered from "a nonspecific cumulative trauma problem."

Meanwhile, Dr. Winter reported on April 8, 2004:

"Ms. Benyamino likely has carpal tunnel syndrome. It is my opinion that this is not related to her employment, taking care of her parents. This work is non–repetitive in nature. There is a lot of variability. If she were not working at her parents' home, doing in–home care, she would likely be doing exactly the same type of work at home being a homemaker. It is certainly possible that she could get carpal tunnel syndrome, but I do not believe it is related to, caused by, or arising out of her employment."

Dr. Winter next discussed possible treatments and repeated, "I do not believe this is work–related." In an October 11, 2003, report, Dr. Winter expressly agreed with Dr. Gordon's description of work activities requiring " 'general use' " of the wrists and hands. He then explained:

"In the orthopedic literature it is somewhat controversial whether repetitive use of the wrists and hands can cause carpal tunnel syndrome. There is little controversy that 'general use' of the wrists and hands does not cause carpal tunnel syndrome.

"Ms. Benyamino's carpal tunnel syndrome certainly is not due to her 'general use' of her wrists and hands while taking care of her parents. I do not believe her current symptoms are related to, caused by, or arising out of employment.

"I agree with Dr. Gordon's recommendation, as far as treatment is concerned, but this should be obtained on a nonindustrial basis. I also agree that Ms. Benyamino can continue working her regular job."

Adopting and incorporating the WCJ's reasoning, the WCAB concluded Dr. Winter, who initially diagnosed Benyamino with carpel tunnel syndrome, "blithely fails to recognize" that the medical testing for carpel tunnel syndrome was negative "and fails to give any rationale why 'general use' would support a finding of industrial injury."

The WCAB explained Dr. Winter's "report cannot be considered substantial evidence." Adopting the WCJ's report, the WCAB concluded that Benyamino "failed to meet her burden of proving industrial causation with substantial medical evidence."

Benyamino attacks the validity of Dr. Winter's medical reporting, claiming he relied on an incorrect legal theory when he stated Benyamino's work activities were no different from her regular non–work activities and that he did not believe she sustained an industrial injury. Benyamino fails to acknowledge, however, that she carried the burden of proving a work–related injury. We agree with the WCAB that she failed to prove industrial causation with substantial medical evidence.

Benyamino relies exclusively on Dr. Gordon's two medical reports. In his first report, he diagnoses her with carpel tunnel syndrome and explains that her general use of her hands, including the time spent working, caused her injury. After medical testing confirmed she did not have carpel tunnel syndrome, he amended her diagnosis and opined she possessed a "nonspecific cumulative trauma problem," but that his prior opinions nevertheless remained unchanged. Dr. Gordon made no attempt to explain how Benyamino's general hand and wrist use caused a "nonspecific cumulative trauma injury." Moreover, a cumulative injury consists of "repetitive mentally or physically traumatic activities extending over a period of time, the combined effect of which causes any disability or need for medical treatment." (§ 3208.1, emphasis added.) Dr. Gordon did not detail any repetitive physically traumatic activities Benyamino performed as an In–Home Supportive Services worker that could have resulted in her diagnosed "nonspecific cumulative trauma injury."

Contrary to Dr. Gordon, Dr. Winter opined Benyamino "likely has carpel tunnel syndrome," but that he did "not believe it is related to, caused by, or arising out of her employment." He explained that there was "little controversy" in orthopedic literature that the general use of the wrists and hands, as those required of Benyamino's work activities, would not cause carpel tunnel. He did not find she sustained any other type of injury.

As the trier of fact, the WCAB indisputably possessed the power to resolve conflicts in the evidence and to make credibility determinations in rejecting Benyamino's claim of industrial causation. (Garza v. Workmen's Comp. App. Bd., supra, 3 Cal. 3d at p. 317.) Given the medical evidence submitted at the disability hearing, we agree the WCAB could reasonably find that Benyamino failed to prove by a preponderance of evidence that any "nonspecific cumulative trauma injury" she sustained was causally connected to her employment as a home care worker to her parents. Accordingly, we must deny the Petition for Writ of Review.... .

§ 4.2(F) Time Limitation Limits Only Number of Employers, Within One Year Preceding Date of Injury, Not Number of Years of Exposure

Page 59, Column 2, at end of final paragraph, insert following '…injury'

See *New Jersey Nets, et al. v. WCAB (Theus)* (2006) 71 Cal. Comp. Cases 859, for a case involving an NBA basketball player who's date of injury, as found by the judge, was on the last day he played for the New Jersey Nets. The judge stated, in part:

It seems to me that Labor Code § 5500.5 was created for this type of situation. Where injurious exposure is alleged over a period, only the last twelve months are liable. Apportionment to previous injurious exposure is not allowed. The courts have made inroads, but there must be a clear record that there was a prior disability and that is not present in this case. Reggie Theus had some injuries and many "dings," but he continued to work his usual and customary duties. He played all 82 games with the Nets in 1991. He was the highest scorer on the team, playing in the most arduous league in professional sports. Where was the disability? It was certainly not shown but [sic] defendant in this case. However, after leaving the Nets, there is a bright line departure from his prior twelve years. He could not get a contract. Nobody wanted him. He was relegated to playing in the Italian League as a name marquee player past his prime. It is so clear that the day in and day out toll led to this end, and the Nets were the end. Petitioner is not questioning the level of disability or the relationship to his job. Petitioner only questions whether the liability should fall where it did. The legislature created this law, knowing that in the end, things would even out. In the next basketball case, the Nets may not be within the Labor Code § 5500.5 liability zone. However, in this case the preponderance of the evidence shows that the "date of injury" was the last day with the Nets, and, indeed, his last day in the NBA. Nothing in the petition has changed that opinion.

As a further note, even if the Italian League play was considered part of the injurious exposure, that employment stopped in April of 1992, making the injurious period April 1991 to April 1992. The Nets stipulated to employment "through 1991." As such, the Nets still fall within the injurious period allowed by Labor Code § 5500.5, and since liability is joint and several, the Nets would still have the entire liability… .

§ 4.2(N) Liability Based on Period of Stressful Employment and Not the Degree of Stress

Page 63, Column 1, third paragraph, insert following '…the Degree of Stress'

Where the stress of an employee's occupation occurs throughout the employment, liability for contribution between carriers or legally uninsured employers must be determined in proportion to their respective periods of insurance coverage during the employee's period of employment. *State Compensation Insurance Fund v. WCAB* (1977) 42 Cal. Comp. Cases 919, (Writ denied); *State Compensation Insurance Fund v. WCAB* (1977) 42 Cal. Comp. Cases 921, (Writ denied). Similarly, in *C.A. Rasmussen, Liberty Mutual Insurance Group v. WCAB* (1999) 64 Cal. Comp. Cases 1395, (Writ denied) the Board ordered contribution between the two insurers during the last year of employment proportionate to their coverage.

In San *Diego Gas & Electric v. WCAB (Williams)* (2007) 72 Cal. Comp. Cases 501, the Court of Appeal, First District, upheld a Board's decision holding that Section 5500.5 does not limit the cumulative trauma period to an employee's last year of exposure but merely establishes which employers can be held liable for the cumulative trauma injury.

§ 4.2(U) Right to Contribution of the Elected Carrier Against Other Employers and Carriers Within the Period of the Cumulative Injury or Occupational Disease (One Year for Claims Filed on or After January 1, 1981)

Page 69, Column 1, fourth paragraph, insert following '…petition.'

See also *Council of Community Clinics, et al. v. WCAB (Cass)* (2005) 70 Cal. Comp. Cases 1225, for an unpublished decision where contribution was barred by the one–year statute of limitations even where a trial judge had earlier ordered mandatory arbitration on the issue.

The Court of Appeal, Fourth Appellate District, in upholding the judge's decision stated, in part:

Here, when the WCJ ordered the parties to arbitration, the Board had not yet made an award for compensation benefits and no employer was held liable under an award. In the absence of an award under which an employer is held liable, the statute's requirement that a party "institute proceedings" was not satisfied. (General Accident, *supra*, 47 Cal. App. 4th at p. 1148 [section 5500.5, subdivision (e)'s requirement that a party " 'institute proceedings' " within one year after an award necessitates a separate supplemental proceeding].) Thus, CNA was not entitled to rely on the WCJ's order for arbitration as instituting proceedings for purposes of the one–year limitations provision of section 5500.5, subdivision (e).

Because contribution is a supplemental proceeding, it must be instituted by filing a separate petition once an award has been made. (General Accident, *supra*, 47 Cal. App. 4th at p. 1148.) Nothing in the statutory language of section 5500.5 or related statutes shows the Legislature intended an order for mandatory arbitration to become a substitute for filing a petition for contribution. Indeed, a request for action by the Board, other than an application, answer or declaration of readiness, must be made by petition. (Cal. Code Regs., tit. 8, § 10450.) A party liable for an award can "institute proceedings" for the purpose of requesting contribution under section 5500.5, subdivision (e) only by filing a separate petition and must do so within one year of that award. (Footnote 3) (General Accident, *supra*, 47 Cal. App. 4th at p. 1149; Rex Club, *supra*, 53 Cal. App. 4th at p. 1472 [one–year limitation for filing a petition for contribution under section 5500.5, subdivision (e) is measured from the date of the Board's award].)

Further, preliminary acts such as agreeing to assign the matter to a particular arbitrator or designating contribution as an issue to be decided in arbitration do not qualify as instituting proceedings to determine contribution within the meaning of section 5500.5, subdivision (e). (General Accident, *supra*, 47 Cal. App. 4th at p. 1149 [joinder of another party did not satisfy section 5500.5, subdivision (e)'s one–year statute of limitations].) There is no authority for excusing an employer or its insurance carrier from actually filing a petition for contribution within one year of being held liable for payments for which contribution is sought. Once an employer is liable for an award, the formality of timely filing a petition–a document that puts on notice the party against whom contribution is claimed–is required to trigger the right to have that claim adjudicated by the Board and thereby dispel any uncertainty about the status of the potential claim for contribution. (Footnote 4) The filing of a petition within one year of an award is a relatively simple matter with which to comply, and the clear language of section 5500.5, subdivision (3), as well as case law interpreting it, clearly informs an employer that compliance is required… .

Footnote 3. The necessity of filing a petition in no way nullifies the WCJ's order to arbitrate. Rather, upon the timely filing of a petition for contribution, the proceeding would properly be before the designated arbitrator in accordance with the arbitration submittal order.

Footnote 4. The necessity of filing a petition also serves a practical purpose. If the elected employer successfully defends against a claim of liability, there would be no reason for that employer to pursue contribution from the non–elected employers. Thus, it is logical to require a petition be filed to institute contribution proceedings only after a finding of liability as to the elected employer.

Page 72, Column 1, sixth paragraph, insert following… Footnote 1

In *Majestic Insurance Company, et. al. v. WCAB (Marin)* (2005) 70 Cal. Comp. Cases 1519, the Board held that CIGA's claims for reimbursement/contribution against solvent insurance carriers for all benefits paid by itself and previously paid by insolvent insurance carrier was timely under Section 5500.5 where the claim by CIGA was filed within one year of a judge's approval of a settlement between the applicant and the solvent carrier.

Further, the Board held that CIGA had a right to reimbursement from the solvent insurance carrier for pre–insolvency payments made by the insolvent insurance carrier. The Board stated, in part:

Although Majestic argues that CIGA's lien was untimely filed on January 22, 2003, we are persuaded that CIGA's proceedings are in the nature of contribution/reimbursement, and not in the nature of lien claims. However, CIGA filed its petition for contribution/reimbursement within one year of the approved compromise and release of September 24, 2002 and this would satisfy the one year time requirement under Labor Code section 5500.5(e).

Therefore, turning to the merits of CIGA's petition, we agree that it is entitled to reimbursement for that which it paid and to the payments made solely by the insolvent carrier HIH. In *Liberty Mutual Fire Ins. Co. v. Workers' Comp. Appeals Bd. (Barineau)* (2001) [66 Cal. Comp. Cases 1108] (writ denied), the Board found that Insurance Code section 1063.2(b) allowed CIGA to be a party in interest in proceedings involving a covered claim and gives them the same rights as the insolvent insurer would have had, had it not been in liquidation. This includes the right to adjust, compromise, settle and pay a covered claim. The recovery from an insolvent insurance carrier fits within this language. Thus, the fact that CIGA has the same rights as the insolvent insurer would have had, if it had not been in liquidation, means that CIGA has the right to pursue subrogation from third parties to the same extent the insurer could have pursued subrogation, if it were not in liquidation. In *Barineau, supra*, the Board ruled, "since the proceeding for contribution is in the nature of a subrogation proceeding, if CIGA is authorized to institute subrogation proceedings, they are also authorized to institute contribution proceedings." (*Id.*, p. 1110.) We specifically note that the Court of Appeal allowed to stand the assertion that CIGA could collect through subrogation proceedings and once having done that, they could keep the funds if they have made the payments, but had to turn the funds over to the insurance commissioner if they had not. Under either circumstance, CIGA would have the right to institute subrogation proceedings and we are persuaded that the disbursement of those assets is irrelevant to the right to collect them.

Further, in *Lewis v. California Insurance Guarantee Association* (2004) 69 Cal. Comp. Cases 490, a recent Board panel decision, the Appeals Board found, based on a letter brief submitted by California Department of Insurance (citing Insurance Code §§ 1063.2(b) and 1037(b)), that CIGA was a proper party to pursue contributions on behalf of the insurer in liquidation for any pre–insolvency and post–insolvency benefits paid; that CIGA would be entitled to recover benefits paid by the insurer in liquidation prior to its insolvency, which would be placed in assets of liquidated insurer's estate; and that the benefits paid by CIGA and recovered by it could be retained by it.

On this basis, we will amend the WCJ's decision to reflect that CIGA does have standing to seek reimbursement for that portion of its lien based on pre–insolvency payments made by HIH... .

§ 4.3   Date of Injury

Page 76, Column 1, fifth paragraph, insert following '...Cases 53.)'

In *Mariposa et. al. v. WCAB (Johnson)* (2006) 71 Cal. Comp. Cases 1499, the Court of Appeal, Fifth District, in an unpublished decision stated, in part:

Filing an Application for Adjudication establishes jurisdiction with the WCAB to initiate proceedings for the collection of workers' compensation benefits. (§ 5500.) For regular benefits, WCAB proceedings may be commenced up to one year from the later of either the date of injury or the date the employer last provided temporary or permanent indemnity payments or medical treatment. (§ 5405.) Having denied Johnson's claim for workers' compensation benefits, the County did not provide temporary or permanent disability payments or medical treatment.

"For the purpose of establishing the date of injury, section 3208.1 distinguishes between 'specific' and 'cumulative' injuries." (*Bassett–Mcgregor v. Workers' Comp. Appeals Bd.* (1988) 205 Cal. App. 3d 1102, 1109–1110 [252 Cal. Rptr. 868, 53 Cal. Comp. Cases 502]; see also *Western Growers Ins. Co. v. Workers' Comp. Appeals Bd.* (1993) 16 Cal. App. 4th 227, 234 [20 Cal. Rptr. 2d 26, 58 Cal. Comp. Cases 323].) A specific injury occurs "as the result of one incident or exposure which causes disability or need for medical treatment," while a cumulative injury results from "repetitive mentally or physically traumatic activities extending over a period of time, the combined effect of which causes any disability or need for medical treatment." (§ 3208.1.)

Johnson's workers' compensation claim alleged a cumulative, not a specific, injury. The date of injury for a cumulative injury "is that date upon which the employee first suffered disability therefrom and either knew, or in the exercise of reasonable diligence should have known, that such disability was caused by his present or prior employment." (§ 5412.) Accordingly, an employee may file a claim alleging a cumulative injury up to one year after the employee either knew, or should have known, a disability was industrially related.

For statute of limitations purposes, the date of injury " 'requires concurrence of two elements: (1) compensable disability and (2) knowledge of industrial causation.' " (*Bassett–McGregor v. Workers' Comp. Appeals Bd., supra,* 205 Cal. App. 3d 1102, 1110.) "Whether an employee knew or should have known his disability was industrially caused

is a question of fact." (*City of Fresno, supra,* 163 Cal. App. 3d at p. 471.) "The running of the statute of limitations is an affirmative defense (§ 5409), and the burden of proofing [*sic*] it has run, therefore, is on the party opposing the claim." (*Kaiser Foundation Hospitals v. Workers' Comp. Appeals Bd.* (1985) 39 Cal. 3d 57, 67, fn. 8 [702 P.2d 197, 216 Cal. Rptr. 115, 50 Cal. Comp. Cases 411].) While an employer's burden of proving the statute of limitations has run can be met by presenting medical evidence that an injured worker was informed a disability was industrially caused, "[t]his burden is not sustained merely by a showing that the employee knew he had some symptoms." (*City of Fresno, supra,* 163 Cal. App. 3d at p. 471, 473.)...

As set forth in the WCJ's findings, there is no dispute that Johnson was aware his stress symptoms were work–related over more than a year before filing his workers' compensation claim. Johnson's awareness alone, however, was insufficient to begin the statute of limitations period. As the WCAB explained in adopting the WCJ's Report and Recommendation:

"The fact that Applicant may have taken sick leave on various dates, including the clinic visit on 6/18/03, during which a Physician's Assistant was of the opinion that his complaints had a 'multilevel causation factor type of illness,' which was otherwise not defined, was not found to constitute sufficient evidence to prove disability of the type that would start the running of the limitations period. Applicant continued working at his usual and customary occupation.

"Disability, for the purposes of applying LC 5412 can include temporary disability or Permanent Disability. [*Chavira v. Workers' Comp. Appeals Bd.* (1991) 235 Cal. App. 3d 463, 474.] Although the record includes copies of time sheets that show Applicant took sick leave on various dates, going back to 4/16/02, there is no adequate explanation as to the nature of any such sickness or illness for the purposes of establishing he then had a disability that would start the limitations period to run. [Exhibit Citation.] The same is true with regard to several leave request forms, most of which are checked 'Sick leave personal,' without providing further explanation. [Exhibit Citation.] There is no dispute that Applicant continued as a full time Probation Officer, in whatever capacity, until 9/10/04, when he perceived that the stress/hostile environmental problems had escalated to the point that he could not continue working. The record does not contain evidence that Applicant sustained any temporary or permanent disability, within the meaning of LC 5412, more than one year before filing the initial application."

"Cases interpreting section 5412 for statute of limitations purposes hold that the date of injury is the date upon which employment activities cause *compensable* disability, and the statute of limitations does not begin to run until the last day of employment exposure to such activities, or the compensable disability caused by such activities, whichever is later." (*State Comp. Ins. Fund v. Workers' Comp. Appeals Bd.* (2004) 119 Cal. App. 4th 998, 1002 [14 Cal. Rptr. 3d 793, 69 Cal. Comp. Cases 579] (*Rodarte*).) Temporary disability requires the employee to suffer actual wage loss, while permanent disability requires an enduring impairment of earnings capacity. (*Id.* at pp. 1002–1005.) "Medical treatment alone is not disability, but it may be evidence of a compensable permanent disability…" (*Id.* at pp. 1005–1006.)… .

§ 4.7   Psychiatric Injuries Sustained on or After July 16, 1993

Page 100, Column 2, twelfth paragraph, insert following '…the defendant]'

In *Aguirre v. WCAB* (2005) 70 Cal. Comp. Cases 1487, the Board held that an applicant's claim was barred under Section 3208.3(d) where he worked out of a union hall for six years where the standard practice of the business had required him to move from one employer to another but he did not work for more than six months for the named employer, and therefore, under the facts he failed to meet the six–month requirement.

In *CIGA v. WCAB (Fernandez)* (2006) 71 Cal. Comp. Cases 629, the Board upheld a judge's decision finding that an applicant's psychiatric injury as a compensable consequence of an orthopedic injury was not barred by Section 3208.3(h) even where applicant's specific orthopedic injury occurred before the applicant had completed six months of work for her employer, because she returned to work for a trial period after her orthopedic injury, making her total work for her employer more than six months.

The judge observed that Section 3208.3(h) does not state that the injury must occur within the six–month period. See also *CIGA, et al. v. WCAB (Norwood)* (2006) 71 Cal. Comp. Cases 808.

§ 4.7(A)   Sudden and Extraordinary Employment Conditions

Page 106, Column 2, first paragraph, insert following '…case.'

In *Matea v. WCAB* (2006) 71 Cal. Comp. Cases 1522, the Court of Appeal, Sixth District, held that lumber falling off of a rack and injuring an employee's leg constituted a *"sudden and extraordinary event of employment"* sufficient to overcome the bar on psychiatric injury claims for employees who have been employed for less than six months as set forth in Labor Code section 3208.3(d).

In holding that the above incident constituted a *"sudden and extraordinary event of employment"*, the Court looked to Webster's Third International Dictionary to define "sudden" as "happening without previous notice or with very brief notice: coming or occurring unexpectedly: not foreseen or prepared for" and "extraordinary" as "going beyond what is usual, regular, common, or customary;" and "having little or no precedent and usually totally unexpected." The Court continued, opining that events such as gas and mine explosions as well as work place violence (noted by prior

courts as examples of sudden and extraordinary events) were but examples of events that could fall within the definition.

Finally, the Court did reaffirm that the burden of proof was upon the applicant to establish that the event was *"sudden and extraordinary"*. The Court stated, in part:

The question before this court is whether Matea carried his burden of showing by a preponderance of the evidence " 'in the light of the entire record' " (Lamb, *supra*, 11 Cal. 3d at pp. 280–281) that he suffered a compensable psychiatric injury as a result of an admitted leg injury during the first six months of his employment with The Home Depot. Matea testified that his leg was injured when a rack of lumber fell on his left leg. No other testimony regarding how Matea's leg was injured was introduced at the hearing before the WCJ, but various medical reports were submitted wherein Matea further described the events leading up to his injury. The WCJ found on the record before him that Matea "was injured when a wall shelf holding up a large amount of lumber gave way without warning, which resulted in the fall of the lumber on [Matea's] leg."

The Board found, based on Matea's trial testimony, that " 'he injured his foot when a rack of lumber fell on his left leg.' " We are bound by the Board's factual findings, as they are supported by substantial evidence. (§ 5952.)

While the record is sparse and the facts are few concerning what caused the lumber to fall, we believe that all the lumber in a rack falling into an aisle and onto an employee's leg causing injury to the employee was in this case such an uncommon, unusual, and totally unexpected event or occurrence that it "would naturally be expected to cause psychic disturbances even in a diligent and honest employee." (Wal–Mart, *supra*, 112 Cal. App. 4th at p.1441, fn. 9.) As the WCJ stated, no testimony was presented regarding how often lumber falls from racks into the aisles at The Home Depot, and there was no evidence presented that such occurrences are regular and routine events. We must assume, as the WCJ assumed, that they are uncommon, unusual and totally unexpected events; otherwise, The Home Depot would have presented testimony to the contrary. Therefore, in the absence of any contrary evidence, when Matea presented evidence that he was injured as a result of all the lumber from a rack falling onto him, he met his burden of proving that he was injured as a result of a sudden and extraordinary employment condition as required by section 3208.3, subdivision (d). Accordingly, the Board erred in interpreting section 3208.3, subdivision (d), to find otherwise… . **[Editor's Note:** See Section 4.7(C) for Court's full decision of the case.]

§ 4.7(B) Psychiatric Injury Caused by Lawful, Nondiscriminatory, Good Faith Personnel Actions

Page 123, Column 1, first paragraph, insert following '...personnel action.'

In *First Bank and Trust, et al. v. WCAB (Ziegler)* (2006) 71 Cal. Comp. Cases 533, the Board upheld a judge's finding that a bank manager's psychiatric condition was not barred by Section 3208.3(h) because it was not caused by her change of position from Bank Manager to Customer Service Manager, but from the accumulation of stress (over the years of her employment, six or seven robberies occurred at the branch where she worked) as well as the workload over the years of her employment.

Counseling was not considered a "personnel action" in *County of Alameda, et al. v. WCAB (Kan)* (2006) 71 Cal. Comp. Cases 827, as it does not involve discipline or a threat of discipline.

§ 4.7(C) Psychiatric Injury Related to a Physical Injury – Compensable Consequence

Page 129, Column 2, insert following '...Footnote 12'

In holding that the falling of lumber from a rack onto an applicant's left leg was an uncommon, unusual and totally unexpected event at work, the Court of Appeal, Sixth District in *Matea v. WCAB* (2006) 71 Cal. Comp. Cases 1522, stated, in part:

INTRODUCTION

Petitioner Aaron Matea sustained an admitted industrial injury when a rack of lumber fell on his left leg. In addition to his physical injury Matea alleged a resulting psychiatric injury, but at the time of his injury he had worked for respondent The Home Depot for less than six months. California's workers' compensation system is intended to guarantee compensation to employees injured in the course of their employment, but Labor Code section 3208.3, subdivision (d) (Footnote 1) precludes compensation "for a psychiatric injury related to a claim against an employer unless the employee has been employed by that employer for at least six months." An exception to this six–month rule is provided for psychiatric injuries that are "caused by a sudden and extraordinary employment condition." (§ 3208.3, subd. (d).) In this case, the workers' compensation judge (WCJ) found that that Matea's injury was caused by "a sudden and extraordinary event." The Workers' Compensation Appeals Board (the Board) reversed that finding by the WCJ and found that it was Matea's burden to show that his psychiatric injury was caused by a sudden and extraordinary employment condition but, based on Matea's trial testimony, he did not meet his burden.

Matea has filed a timely petition for writ of review, contending that the Board erred when it reversed the WCJ's findings. In analyzing Matea's claim we must determine whether or not Matea met his burden of showing by a preponderance of the evidence that the circumstances under which his leg injury occurred constituted "a sudden and extraordinary employment condition" under section 3208.3, subdivision (d). We conclude, based on the limited record and factual findings of the Board before us, that Matea has met his burden and has established that he was injured during the first six months of his employment as a result of "a sudden and extraordinary employment condition" as required by section 3208.3, subdivision (d). Accordingly, we will annul the Board's decision.

BACKGROUND

FACTS

Eighteen–year–old Matea began working for The Home Depot in July 2001. On September 16, 2001, while working as a manager–trainee, Matea injured his left foot and ankle when all the lumber (12–foot four by fours) from a rack fell on him after the store closed. (Footnote 2)

He does not know how many pieces of lumber actually fell on his leg. He suffered a contusion and swelling but no fracture, and has been diagnosed with reflex sympathetic dystrophy (RSD). He worked in a restricted capacity after his leg injury for short periods of time. However, Matea's attempts to return to his prior position were unsuccessful and he last worked in December 2001. He reports constant pain in his ankle and foot. He also reports depression due to his belief that he is not going to improve and anxiety due to his fear of being hurt again. One psychiatrist determined that the predominant cause of Matea's pain disorder and depression was his September 16, 2001 industrial injury. Another psychiatrist found no industrial psychiatric injury...

The WCJ's Findings and Award

The WCJ filed and served his findings and award on July 6, 2005. The WCJ found in pertinent part that Matea was 100 percent permanently disabled and, although he was not employed by The Home Depot for a total of six months as required by section 3208.3, subdivision (d), his psychiatric injury was caused by "a sudden and extraordinary event. While the case is a close one, the facts here do seem to meet that definition. [Matea] was injured when a wall shelf holding up a large amount of lumber gave way without warning, which resulted in the fall of the lumber on [Matea's] leg. No testimony was presented regarding how often Home Depot has its shelves give way and dump lumber onto its aisles, but one assumes that such occurrences are quite rare, given that those aisles are open to the public."

The WCJ awarded Matea permanent disability of 100 percent, entitling him to payments at the rate of $314.40 per week beginning January 15, 2004, and continuing for life. The WCJ also awarded Matea further medical treatment reasonably required to cure or relieve him from the effects of his injury, and reimbursement for self–procured medical treatment expenses. The Home Depot filed a petition for reconsideration.

§ 4.0

The Board's Decision

The Board filed an opinion and order granting reconsideration and decision after reconsideration on September 23, 2005. The Board found that, pursuant to section 3208.3, subdivision (d), Matea's claim of psychiatric injury "is barred unless the psychiatric injury was caused by a 'sudden and extraordinary employment condition.' And since the 'sudden and extraordinary' provision negates the six–month employment requirement, which is already established herein, it is [Matea's] burden to show that the psychiatric injury was caused by a sudden and extraordinary employment condition. [P] Based on [Matea's] trial testimony, we conclude that [Matea] did not meet his burden. At the trial of January 21, 2005, [Matea] testified that 'he injured his foot when a rack of lumber fell on his left leg.' ... The Home Depot is a big–box hardware store that sells lumber to the public; the fact that [Matea], a store manager trainee, would be working in close proximity to racks of lumber is not unusual. Again, it was [Matea's] testimony that the injury of September 16, 2001 happened when 'a rack of lumber fell on his left leg.' Considering the site of employment, wherein it would have been normal for [Matea] to work in proximity to lumber racks, we conclude that a rack of lumber falling on his leg was not a 'sudden and extraordinary employment condition' within the meaning of section 3208.3, [subdivision] (d). Therefore, his claim of psychiatric injury is barred by the six–month employment requirement. Accordingly, we will reverse the WCJ's finding that [Matea] sustained an industrial psychiatric injury."

The Board rescinded the WCJ's decision and award. It found that Matea sustained a compensable injury to his left leg, but all remaining issues, including but not limited to permanent disability, were returned to the trial level for further proceedings and a new decision consistent with the Board's opinion. Matea petitioned for reconsideration.

The Board filed an opinion and order denying further reconsideration on November 3, 2005. The Board stated in part, "the Court in *Wal–Mart Stores, Inc. v. Workers' Compensation Appeals Board* [(*Wal–Mart*)] (2003) 112 Cal. App. 4th 1435[, 1441,] fn. 9[,] [5 Cal. Rptr. 3d 822] stated that the ' "sudden and extraordinary" language is limited to occurrences such as gas main explosions or workplace violence–the type of events that would naturally be expected to cause psychic disturbances even in a diligent and honest employee.' [P] In asserting that his injury was 'sudden and extraordinary' in this case, [Matea] misinterprets the [*Wal–Mart*] Court's language in Footnote 9. The injury in this case may have been a devastating injury, but it was not legally sudden and extraordinary because it was not in the nature of a gas main explosion or workplace violence or a type of event that would naturally be expected to cause psychic disturbances even in a diligent and honest employee."...

Analysis

Matea contends that a shelf full of lumber giving way, causing the lumber to fall on a worker and injuring his leg, is a "sudden and extraordinary employment condition" within the meaning of section 3208.3, subdivision (d). He argues that the Board misread the dicta in *Wal–Mart, supra*, 112

Cal. App. 4th 1435, a case that did not need to decide what constitutes a sudden and extraordinary employment condition under section 3208.3, subdivision (d), by reading the language in Footnote 9 "as if it were written into the statute." "[Section] 3202 requires the [Board] to limit the statute to its terms, and those terms are simple. It only requires the injury to be sudden (if it were not sudden Mr. Matea would not have been crushed) and extraordinary which means unusual." "To hold that the statute bars this type of injury improperly narrowly construes the statute, violates [section] 3202, as well as the plain meaning of the statute."

We agree with the court in *Wal–Mart* that the sudden and extraordinary employment condition language in section 3208.3, subdivision (d), is limited to "the type of events that would naturally be expected to cause psychic disturbances even in a diligent and honest employee." (*Wal–Mart, supra*, 112 Cal. App. 4th at p. 1441, fn. 9.) We also agree that the sudden and extraordinary employment condition language in section 3208.3, subdivision (d), could certainly include occurrences such as gas main explosions or workplace violence. However, giving the language of the statute "its usual, ordinary import" (*Dyna–Med, supra*, 43 Cal. 3d at pp. 1386–1387), in light of its legislative history, and liberally construing the statute in the employee's favor (§ 3202), we believe that the Legislature intended to except from the six–month limitation psychiatric injuries that are caused by "a sudden and extraordinary employment condition," and not by a regular or routine employment event. While the amendments to section 3208.3 eliminated an explicit distinction between "a regular and routine employment event" and "a sudden and extraordinary employment condition," in subdivision (d), we believe that the Legislature's intent in doing so was not to impose an additional limitation on what constitutes a sudden and extraordinary employment condition. (Cf. *City of Oakland, supra*, 99 Cal. App. 4th at p. 267.) Rather, the amendments to section 3208.3 in 1993 were intended to impose an additional limitation on what constitutes a compensable psychiatric injury by excepting psychiatric injuries resulting from routine physical injuries during the first six months as well as psychiatric injuries resulting from routine personnel decisions during the first six months of an employee's employment.

Webster's Third International Dictionary (1993), at page 2284, defines "sudden" as "happening without previous notice or with very brief notice : coming or occurring unexpectedly : not foreseen or prepared for." The same dictionary defines "extraordinary" as "going beyond what is usual, regular, common, or customary;" and "having little or no precedent and usu[ally] totally unexpected." (Webster's 3d Internat. Dict., *supra*, p. 807.) Gas main explosions and workplace violence are certainly uncommon and usually totally unexpected events; thus, they may be sudden and extraordinary employment conditions. However, we believe that there may also be other "sudden and extraordinary" occurrences or events within the contemplation of section 3208.3, subdivision (d), that would naturally be expected to cause psychic disturbances even in diligent and honest employees. Therefore, if an employee carries his or her burden of showing by a preponderance of the evidence that the event or occurrence that caused the alleged psychiatric injury was something other than a regular and routine employment event or condition, that is, that the event was uncommon, unusual, and occurred unexpectedly, the injury may be compensable even if the employee was employed for less than six months.

Amici curiae California Insurance Guarantee Association and American Insurance Association argue that the Legislature used the term "condition" rather than "event" in section 3208.3, subdivision (d), and contend that the Legislature thereby intended to limit the exception to sudden and extraordinary "conditions of employment" rather than to sudden and extraordinary employment "events" or "occurrences." We disagree with this contention. In subdivision (e) of the same section, which was enacted in 1993 at the same time that subdivision (d) was amended, the Legislature, in limiting claims for compensation filed after termination of employment or layoff, stated in part that the employee bears the burden of showing "one or more of the following *conditions* exist: [P] (1) Sudden and extraordinary *events of employment* were the cause of the injury. ..." (Italics added.) We believe that the Legislature intended "employment conditions" in subdivision (d) of section 3208.3 to mean the same thing as the "events of employment" condition in subdivision (e) of the same section. The Legislature simply intended section 3208.3, subdivision (d) as amended to limit claims for psychiatric injuries resulting from routine stress and routine injuries during the first six months of employment. (*Wal–Mart, supra,* 112 Cal. App. 4th at pp. 1437–1439.)

The question before this court is whether Matea carried his burden of showing by a preponderance of the evidence " 'in the light of the entire record' " (*Lamb, supra,* 11 Cal. 3d at p. 281, italics omitted) that he suffered a compensable psychiatric injury as a result of an admitted leg injury during the first six months of his employment with The Home Depot. Matea testified that his leg was injured when a rack of lumber fell on his left leg. No other testimony regarding how Matea's leg was injured was introduced at the hearing before the WCJ, but various medical reports were submitted wherein Matea further described the events leading up to his injury. The WCJ found on the record before him that Matea "was injured when a wall shelf holding up a large amount of lumber gave way without warning, which resulted in the fall of the lumber on [Matea's] leg."

The Board found, based on Matea's trial testimony, that " 'he injured his foot when a rack of lumber fell on his left leg.' "We are bound by the Board's factual findings, as they are supported by substantial evidence. (§ 5952.)

While the record is sparse and the facts are few concerning what caused the lumber to fall, we believe that all the lumber in a rack falling into an aisle and onto an employee's leg causing injury to the employee was in this case such an uncommon, unusual, and totally unexpected event or occurrence that it "would naturally be expected to cause psychic disturbances even in a diligent and honest employee." (*Wal–Mart, supra,* 112 Cal. App. 4th at p. 1441, fn. 9.) As the WCJ stated, no testimony was presented

regarding how often lumber falls from racks into the aisles at The Home Depot, and there was no evidence presented that such occurrences are regular and routine events. We must assume, as the WCJ assumed, that they are uncommon, unusual and totally unexpected events; otherwise, The Home Depot would have presented testimony to the contrary. Therefore, in the absence of any contrary evidence, when Matea presented evidence that he was injured as a result of all the lumber from a rack falling onto him, he met his burden of proving that he was injured as a result of a sudden and extraordinary employment condition as required by section 3208.3, subdivision (d). Accordingly, the Board erred in interpreting section 3208.3, subdivision (d), to find otherwise.

We do not believe that our finding of a compensable injury under section 3208.3, subdivision (d) here, on the limited record and factual findings in this case, will lead to increased claims for psychiatric injuries by employees who have been employed for less than six months. The employee still bears the burden of showing that the alleged psychiatric injury did not "derive[] from the effects of a[] ... routine physical injury" (*Wal–Mart, supra,* 112 Cal. App. 4th at p. 1438), and was not the result of the routine type of stress or employment event that all employees who work for the same employer may experience or expect within the first six months of their employment (*Hansen, supra,* 18 Cal. App. 4th at p. 1184; *City of Oakland, supra,* 99 Cal. App. 4th at pp. 265–267; *Pacific Gas & Electric, supra,* 114 Cal. App. 4th at p. 1182). Each case must be considered on its facts in order to determine whether the alleged psychiatric injury occurred as a result of sudden and extraordinary events that would naturally be expected to cause psychic disturbances even in a diligent and honest employee. (*Wal–Mart, supra,* 112 Cal. App. 4th at p. 1441, fn. 9.) Thus, our findings here are consistent with the express legislative intent of the original enactment of section 3208.3 in 1989, which was "passed in 'response to increased public concern about the high cost of workers' compensation coverage, limited benefits for injured workers, suspected fraud and widespread abuses in the system, and particularly the proliferation of workers' compensation cases with claims of psychiatric injuries.' " (*City of Oakland, supra,* 99 Cal. App. 4th at p. 265.)

DISPOSITION

The Board's opinion and order after reconsideration filed on September 23, 2005, is annulled. The matter is remanded to the Board with directions to issue a new and different order in the case consistent with this opinion. Matea shall recover costs... .

Footnote 1. All further statutory references are to the Labor Code.

Footnote 2. Pursuant to a ruling by the WCJ, the transcripts of Matea's deposition testimony attached as exhibits to The Home Depot's post–trial brief were considered admitted into evidence. During his April 8, 2002 deposition, Matea testified that his injury occurred when all the lumber fell on him as he tried to put a 12–foot four by four piece of lumber on top of the stack on a rack. Matea did not testify at his

November 18, 2002 deposition as to how his injury occurred. Matea told Dr. Carroll Brodsky, a psychiatrist, on November 17, 2002, that the 12–foot four by four pressure–treated lumber fell from an upper rack onto him as he was taking some returned lumber back to another part of the store. On December 13, 2002, Dr. Charles Borgia, an orthopedic surgeon, indicated in his report that Matea's injury occurred as he was stocking 12–foot four by four treated lumber and the lumber fell onto his left leg. On February 10, 2004, Matea told Dr. Allan Sidle, a psychiatrist, that he was pushing a cart of lumber returns when he heard a noise, like metal bending, and lumber from a rack poured down on him. Matea testified at the hearing before the WCJ on January 21, 2005 that he injured his foot when a rack of lumber fell on his left leg, and the reports of Drs. Brodsky, Borgia and Sidle were admitted into evidence at that hearing.

In *Puga v. WCAB* (2007) 72 Cal. Comp. Cases 195, the Court of Appeal, Fifth District, in an unpublished decision upheld a denial of benefits to an employee employed as a tractor driver, installer and repairer of ceiling fans in a chicken house, who fell from a ladder injuring his neck, thoracic spine and psyche, and in denying benefits distinguished *Matea, supra,* by stating:

Within approximately two months of beginning working for The Home Depot, the employee in *Matea* injured his left foot and ankle when a pile of lumber fell from a rack. (*Matea, supra,* 144 Cal. App. 4th at p. 1439.) In addition to his physical injuries, the employee reported suffering from depression from his belief that he was not going to improve and the anxiety caused by his fear of being hurt again. (*Ibid.*) The Home Depot admitted injury to the employee's leg, but contested the alleged psychiatric injury because the injury occurred within the employee's first six months of employment. (*Id.* at p. 1440.) The WCJ concluded the employee was 100 percent permanently disabled after specifically finding "his psychiatric injury was caused by 'a sudden and extraordinary event.' " (*Id.* at p. 1441.) The WCJ seemed to rely on evidence that "a large amount of lumbar gave way without warning" and that " 'one assumes that such occurrences are quite rare, given that those aisles are open to the public.' " (*Ibid.*)

Reconsidering *Matea,* the WCAB reversed the WCJ and concluded the employee did not meet his burden of proving a sudden and extraordinary employment condition under section 3208.3, subdivision (d). (*Matea, supra,* 144 Cal. App. 4th at p. 1441.) The WCAB reasoned it was "normal" and "not unusual" for an employee in big box hardware store to be working in proximity to racks of lumbar and the resulting accident, therefore, was barred by the six–month employment requirement. (*Id.* at p. 1442.) The WCAB expressly relied on the language of Footnote 9 from *Wal–Mart,* noting the injury " 'may have been a devastating injury, but it was not legally sudden and extraordinary because it was not in the nature of a gas main explosion or workplace violence or a type of event that would naturally be expected to cause psychic disturbances even in a diligent and honest employee.' " (*Ibid.*)

Reviewing the WCAB's decision in *Matea,* the Sixth Appellate District explained:

"We agree with the court in *Wal–Mart* that the sudden and extraordinary employment condition language in section 3208.3, subdivision (d), is limited to 'the type of events that would naturally be expected to cause psychic disturbances even in a diligent and honest employee.' (*Wal–Mart, supra,* 112 Cal. App. 4th at p. 1441, fn. 9.) We also agree that the sudden and extraordinary employment condition language in section 3208.3, subdivision (d), could certainly include occurrences such as gas main explosions or workplace violence. However, giving the language of the statute 'its usual, ordinary import' [citation], in light of its legislative history, and liberally construing the statute in the employee's favor (§ 3202), we believe that the Legislature intended to except from the six–month limitation psychiatric injuries that are caused by 'a sudden and extraordinary employment condition,' and not by a regular or routine employment event. While the amendments to section 3208.3 eliminated an explicit distinction between 'a regular and routine employment event' and 'a sudden and extraordinary employment condition,' in subdivision (d), we believe that the Legislature's intent in doing so was not to impose an additional limitation on what constitutes a sudden and extraordinary employment condition. [Citation.] Rather, the amendments to section 3208.3 in 1993 were intended to impose an additional limitation on what constitutes a compensable psychiatric injury by excepting psychiatric injuries resulting from routine physical injuries during the first six months as well as psychiatric injuries resulting from routine personnel decisions during the first six months of an employee's employment.

"Webster's Third International Dictionary (1993), at page 2284, defines 'sudden' as 'happening without previous notice or with very brief notice: coming or occurring unexpectedly: not foreseen or prepared for.' The same dictionary defines 'extraordinary' as 'going beyond what is usual, regular, common, or customary;' and 'having little or no precedent and usu[ally] totally unexpected.' (Webster's 3d Internat. Dict., *supra,* p. 807.) Gas main explosions and workplace violence are certainly uncommon and usually totally unexpected events; thus, they may be sudden and extraordinary employment conditions. However, we believe that there may also be other 'sudden and extraordinary' occurrences or events within the contemplation of section 3208.3, subdivision (d), that would naturally be expected to cause psychic disturbances even in diligent and honest employees. Therefore, if an employee carries his or her burden of showing by a preponderance of the evidence that the event or occurrence that caused the alleged psychiatric injury was something other than a regular and routine employment event or condition, that is, that the event was uncommon, unusual, and occurred unexpectedly, the injury may be compensable even if the employee was employed for less than six months." (*Matea, supra,* 144 Cal. App. 4th at p. 1448–1449.)"

The *Matea* court continued by looking to the facts surrounding the employee's injury. Relying on the WCJ's original assumption and lack of any contrary testimony presented by the employer, the court concluded the employee "met his burden of proving that he was injured as a result of a sudden and extraordinary employment condition as required by section 3208.3, subdivision (d)." (*Matea, supra,* at p. 1450.) The court cautioned, however, that "[e]ach case must be considered on its facts in order to determine whether the alleged psychiatric injury occurred as a result of sudden and extraordinary events that would naturally be expected to cause psychic disturbances even in a diligent and honest employee." (*Ibid.*)

Although the WCAB here relied on Footnote 9 from *Wal–Mart* when it concluded Puga's alleged psychiatric injury "was not caused by 'an extraordinary employment condition,' because falling off a ladder is not in the nature of a gas main explosion or workplace violence," it also concluded Puga's injury was not "a type of event that would naturally be expected to cause psychiatric injury even in a diligent and honest employee." The WCAB continued:

"During the second month of applicant's employment in this case, she had been using a ladder to install and repair ceiling fans in a chicken house. She carried the ladder to do the job and she would go up and down the ladder several times a day. [Citation.] Thus, applicant's use of the ladder was not extraordinary, as it was part of the very duties for which applicant had been employed."

In her supplemental briefing to this court, Puga argues her fall from the ladder was uncommon, unusual, and unexpected, and that Zacky Farms did not produce any evidence that this type of injury was a common occurrence for a poultry farm laborer. She attempts to bolster her claim by presenting a general job description of a poultry farm laborer from a Department of Labor dictionary of occupational titles that does not mention the use of a ladder.

Puga's own testimony refutes her claim that her regular job duties did not include regular ladder use. According to the summary of minutes prepared by the WCJ, Puga testified:

"For the second month she was installing and repairing ceiling fans in the chicken house. To do this job she carried a ladder. [P] . . . She would go up and down the ladder several times a day."

Puga was therefore engaging in her regular and routine employment activities at the time of her injury. Even construing the workers' compensation laws liberally towards extending benefits to an injured employee, like the WCAB majority, we are unconvinced Puga's injury arose out of an "extraordinary employment condition" as a matter of law under section 3208.3, subdivision (d)... .

See *CIGA v. WCAB (Tejera)* (2007) 72 Cal. Comp. Cases 482, where the Board upheld a judge's decision finding that a truck driver's injuries to have been caused by *sudden and extraordinary* conditions when his trailer jack–knifed and he was thrown to the pavement.

Although acknowledging that motor vehicle accidents are not extraordinary events for truck drivers, the judge and the Board found the events of the accidents (steering wheel broke off) not to be frequent events and therefore justified an exception.

Page 130, Column 2, second paragraph, insert following '...process rights... ." '

Each psychiatric diagnostic disorder cannot be analyzed separately to determine predominant cause.

Psychiatric injury cannot be parsed into separately diagnosable components for the purpose of establishing the predominance standard.

In *Sonoma State University, et al. v. WCAB (Hunton)* (2006) 71 Cal. Comp. Cases 1059, the Court of Appeal, First District, reversed the Appeals Board and held that separate diagnosis of psychiatric disability combined must be predominant to meet the test of Section 3208.3(e)(1) even though one of the diagnoses was caused exclusively by industrial factors. The Court stated, in part:

Workers' compensation law provides that a psychiatric injury is not compensable unless the employee can demonstrate that events of employment "were predominant as to all causes combined of the psychiatric injury." (Labor Code Section 3208.3) subd. (b)(1).) The question presented by this case is whether an employee's psychiatric injury meets the threshold for compensability where the entire psychiatric disability is not predominantly work–induced but where one (or more) of several diagnosed psychiatric conditions is entirely (or predominantly) work–induced. We conclude that a psychiatric injury cannot be parsed into separately diagnosable components for purposes of satisfying the standard set forth in section 3208.3.

II. DISCUSSION

A. Standard of Review

Although the WCAB's findings on questions of fact are conclusive (Section 5953), the construction of a statute and its applicability to a given case are questions of law that this court reviews de novo. (Rex Club v. WCAB (1997) 53 Cal. App.4th 1465, 1470–1471 [62 Cal. Rptr. 2d 393, 62 Cal. Comp. Cases 441].) An erroneous interpretation or application of the law is grounds for annulment of the WCAB's decision. (Id. At p. 1471.)

B. Governing Statute

Workers' compensation psychiatric injury claims are governed by section 3208.3. Pursuant to that section, an employee seeking compensation for a psychiatric injury must demonstrate "by a preponderance of the evidence that actual events of employment were predominant as to all causes combined of the psychiatric injury." (Section 3208.3, subd. (b)(1).) The courts have interpreted the phrase "predominant as to all causes" as a requirement that more than 50 percent of the injury's causation must be work–related. (Department of Corrections v. WCAB (1999) 76 Cal. App.4th 810, 816 [90 Cal. Rptr. 2d 716, 64 Cal. Comp. Cases 1356].) An employee who is unable to meet this threshold for establishing industrial causation has not demonstrated a compensable injury and cannot receive a workers' compensation award for the injury.

C. Interpretation of "[P]sychiatric [I]njury" as Used in Section 3208.3

Petitioners Sonoma State and Octagon Risk Services (collectively Sonoma State) argue that Huton did not meet the predominant causation threshold for compensation eligibility because work–related events had caused only 35 percent of Hunton's overall psychiatric disability. Hunton argues, and the WCAB agreed, that she did satisfy the threshold requirement because one of her diagnosed psychological disorders was wholly attributable to work–related causes and, thus, constituted a compensable psychiatric injury. The question, then, is how one defines "psychiatric injury" when calculating industrial causation under section 3208.3, subdivision (b)(1). Must the predominance of industrial factors be proven with respect to the psychiatric injury in its entirety? Or, does a separately identifiable disorder, comprising only a portion of the psychiatric disability but wholly work–related, constitute a compensable psychiatric injury? As there are no judicial precedents addressing this issue, we rely on principles of statutory construction for guidance…

Section 3208.3 was originally enacted as "part of the Legislature's response to increased public concern about the high cost of workers' compensation coverage, limited benefits for injured workers, suspected fraud and widespread abuses in the system, and particularly the proliferation of workers' compensation cases with claims for psychiatric injuries." (Hansen v. Workers' Compensation Appeals Bd. (1993) 18 Cal. App. 4th 1179, 1183–1184 [23 Cal. Rptr. 2d 30, 58 Cal. Comp. Cases 602].) At that time, the Legislature took the unusual step of codifying the underlying purpose of their enactment: "It is the intent of the Legislature in enacting this section to establish a new and higher threshold of compensability for psychiatric injury under this division." (§ 3208.3, subd. (c).) Given this clearly articulated legislative purpose, "any interpretation of the [statute] that would lead to more or broader claims should be examined closely . . . ." (PG&E, *supra*, 114 Cal. App. 4th at p. 1182.)

Section 3208.3 originally provided that a psychiatric injury was compensable if it was at least 10 percent attributable to industrial factors. (Stats. 1989, ch. 892, § 25, p. 3003.) But the Legislature further tightened the requirements for compensating psychiatric injury in 1993 by amending section 3208.3 to require that industrial factors be "predominant as to all causes combined of the psychiatric injury." (§ 3208.3, subd. (b)(1); see Stats. 1993, ch. 118, § 1, p. 1225.) This amendment was apparently intended to further combat fraudulent psychiatric claims. (Sakotas v. Workers' Comp. Appeals Bd. (2000) 80 Cal. App. 4th 262, 272–273 [95 Cal. Rptr. 2d 153, 65 Cal. Comp. Cases 366].) "In recognition of this intent, the Governor's signature message to the California Assembly contained the following language: [P] 'This package of reforms saves money by tightening the standard for stress claims in the system, the fastest growing type of claim in . . . workers' compensation.' " (Id. at p. 273.)

In Lockheed Martin Corp. v. Workers' Comp. Appeals Bd. (2002) 96 Cal. App. 4th 1237 [117 Cal. Rptr. 2d 865, 67 Cal. Comp. Cases 245], this court (Division Four of the First District Court of Appeal) considered whether the compensability standard of section 3208.3 governed not only purely psychiatric injuries, but also psychological disorders caused by work–related physical injuries. In Lockheed Martin, the WCAB had interpreted the statute narrowly to exclude from the "predominant cause" requirement any psychiatric injuries that were the result of physical injuries. (Lockheed Martin, at p. 1245.) This court reversed, holding that such an interpretation could not be squared with the Legislature's intent to "[take] aim[] primarily at phony stress claims." (Id. at p. 1249.) '[T]he potential for fraud and the problems inherent in psychiatric claims, 'notably vagueness in defining the injury and problems of establishing industrial causation and apportionment' [citation], exist no less because the alleged psychiatric injury is related to a physical injury." (Ibid., fn. omitted.)

Similarly, here, the WCAB's interpretation would undermine rather than effectuate the Legislature's purpose. Allowing each diagnosable psychological disorder to be analyzed separately for compensability would create a lower rather than a higher threshold for obtaining compensation, would result in more rather than fewer stress claims, and would provide more rather than less potential for fraud. Further, the WCAB's interpretation of the statute could lead to absurd or unfair results. If a claimant were allowed to isolate particular disorders for the purpose of establishing compensability, then a claimant with one industrially–caused disorder contributing only 10 percent to his or her psychological disability would meet the causation threshold required for compensation eligibility while a claimant with an undifferentiated diagnosis, whose injury is 50 percent attributable to industrial causes, would not meet the threshold. This interpretation would award compensation to those applicants whose experts are prompted to parse the psychological injuries into separate diagnoses even though the work–induced components are de minimis, while precluding compensation for employees whose work was a substantial factor in causing their injuries but whose experts did not or could not make compartmentalized diagnoses. We are satisfied this could not have been what the Legislature meant to do in adopting section 3208.3.

Accordingly, we hold that a claimant's psychiatric injury satisfies the standard for compensability set forth in section 3208.3 only if it is proven that events of employment were predominant as to all causes combined of the psychiatric disability taken as a whole.

III. DISPOSITION

The award of workers' compensation benefits is annulled, and the matter is remanded to the WCAB with directions to enter an order denying such benefits. The parties shall bear their own costs in the proceedings before this court… .

§ 5.0   WHO MAY COLLECT WORKERS' COMPENSATION INSURANCE BENEFITS?

§ 5.2   Employee—Definition

Page 141, Column 1, tenth paragraph, insert following '…liability company.'

In holding that illegal aliens (undocumented) come within the definition of "employees" and are therefore entitled to workers' compensation benefits, the Court of Appeal, Second District, in *Farmer Brothers Coffee v. WCAB (Ruiz)* (2005) 70 Cal. Comp. Cases 1399, stated in part:

2. Statutory Definition of "Employee"

Petitioner contends that Ruiz does not come within the definition of "employee" set forth in section 3351, subdivision (a), as "every person in the service of an employer under any appointment or contract of hire or apprenticeship, express or implied, oral or written, whether lawfully or unlawfully employed, [including aliens]."

Petitioner suggests that by including the phrase unlawfully employed, the Legislature intended to exclude illegal employees from the definition. Petitioner contends that unlawfully employed must mean only that the employer is guilty of hiring the worker in violation of federal law. (See 8 U.S.C. § 1324a.) When it is the employee who has violated the law by using fraudulent documents, petitioner reasons, he or she cannot be considered as coming within the definition set forth in section 3351, subdivision (a).

Before hiring an employee, an employer is required to examine specified identification documents, and if applicable, immigration and work authorization documents, and to report under penalty of perjury on a federal form that it has verified that the individual is not an unauthorized alien. (8 U.S.C. § 1324a(b)(1)(A).) Employers may be subject to civil or criminal penalties for failures to comply in good faith, and employees may be subject to civil and criminal penalties for using false documents. (See 8 U.S.C. § 1324a(e)(4)–(5), (f)(1); § 1324c(a)(1)–(3); 18 U.S.C. § 1546(b); Hoffman, *supra*, 535 U.S. at p. 148.).

There is no language in the statute to indicate that the Legislature intended "unlawfully employed" to have such a complex meaning or to incorporate federal immigration law, and our task in construing the statute is simply "to ascertain and declare what is in terms or in substance contained therein, not to insert what has been omitted, or to omit what has been inserted . . . ." (Code Civ. Proc., § 1858.)

The sole authority cited by petitioner to support its questionable logic is a dissenting opinion in a Pennsylvania Supreme Court case, urging the court "to announce, as a matter of public policy consistent with federal immigration law, that unauthorized aliens are not eligible for workers' compensation benefits [because] [o]ne who obtains employment in a manner contrary to federal law should not benefit from that illegal employment relationship." (Reinforced Earth Co. v. W.C.A.B., *supra*, 810 A.2d at pp. 111–112, dis. opn. of Newman, J., fn. omitted.)

The majority refused to do so, leaving that task to the Pennsylvania Legislature. (See id. at p. 105.)

In California, as in Pennsylvania, the Legislature establishes public policy. (Forman v. Chicago Title Ins. Co. (1995) 32 Cal. App. 4th 998, 1020 [38 Cal. Rptr. 2d 790].) Once it has done so, the courts may not simply fashion a policy more to their liking. (Ibid.; Cal. Const., art. III, § 3.) We therefore decline petitioner's suggestion that we insert such a policy into the statute.

In any event, assuming for discussion that the California Legislature meant "unlawfully employed" to refer only to the employer's violation of its reporting obligations under title 8 United States Code section 1324a(b)(1)(A), petitioner has failed to point out evidence that it did or did not comply with its federal reporting obligations, and our review has revealed none. Since petitioner did not dispute Ruiz's claim that he performed work at its request, it was petitioner's burden to prove that Ruiz was not an employee for purposes of the Workers' Compensation Act. (See § 3357; Schaller v. Industrial Acc. Com. (1938) 11 Cal. 2d 46, 51 [77 P.2d 836, 3 Cal. Comp. Cases 32].) Since petitioner did not prove otherwise, we assume that it did not comply with federal requirements, and therefore, petitioner's own definition of "unlawfully employed" has been met… .See Section 45.0 of this book for a discussion of procedures to establish earnings of an undocumented worker.

Page 141, Column 2, seventh paragraph, insert following '...Cases 286.'

Domestic Service Referral Agencies May Not Be Employers for Workers' Compensation Purposes.

Domestic service agencies are not deemed to be employers for workers' compensation purposes if they comply with Civil Code section 1812.5095(b)(1)–(9) and Section 1812.5095(f). Commenting on this in *An Independent Home Support Service, Inc., v. Superior Court of San Diego County* (2006) 71 Cal. Comp. Cases 1779, the Court of Appeal, Fourth District stated, in part:

On this petition for peremptory writ of mandate (petition) we are presented with the question of whether compliance with the provisions of Civil Code (Footnote 1) section 1812.5095, part of the Employment Agency, Employment Counseling, and Job Listing Services Act (Employment Agency Act) (Div. 3, pt. 4, tit. 2.91, § 1812.500 et seq.) exempts petitioner An Independent Home Support Service, Inc. (AIHSS), a referral agency that provides domestic workers to individuals and entities, from state law requirements of maintaining workers' compensation insurance for the domestic workers. We conclude that by complying with the terms of section 1812.5095 such referral agencies are deemed not to be the employers, for the purposes of workers' compensation, of the domestic workers they refer. Accordingly, we issue a writ of mandate directing the respondent Superior Court of San Diego County to vacate its order granting real party in interest State Compensation Insurance Fund's (State Fund) motion to strike references in AIHSS's complaint to Civil Code section 1812.5095, Civil Code section 1812.501, and Unemployment Insurance Code section 687.2.

FACTUAL AND PROCEDURAL BACKGROUND

(Footnote 2)

AIHSS is a domestic agency as defined in section 1812.501, subdivision (h). It provides a referral service to individuals and entities that require the services of a domestic worker, typically for an elderly or infirm family member. The company has a roster or pool of between 100 and 150 domestic workers. Patients who need home care assistance are often referred to AIHSS by hospitals at the time they discharge an individual, and, if the patient's care custodian is unable or unwilling to administer to his or her needs, the patient may call AIHSS. AIHSS will then refer a domestic worker for an interview with the patient.

The domestic worker is free to accept or decline the engagement and negotiate the hourly rate of pay. The domestic worker submits biweekly invoices to AIHSS which are approved by the care recipient. AIHSS is responsible for collecting sums due the domestic worker. Receipts are deposited in a separate dedicated trust account, and the domestic worker is paid from this account.

In February 2004 the California Department of Industrial Relations, Division of Labor Standards Enforcement (the Department) conducted an investigation of AIHSS's offices. As a result of the investigation, the Department determined that AIHSS was employing three office workers for which it had not obtained workers' compensation insurance in violation of the law. Thereafter, after a hearing before the Labor Commissioner, that determination was upheld as to two employees. As to the third, that individual was determined to be not subject to workers' compensation insurance because that employee was a shareholder, officer and director of AIHSS.

AIHSS obtained workers' compensation insurance from State Fund on behalf of the two office workers. State Fund then performed an "underwriting inspection" of AIHSS's business. As a result of the inspection, State Fund advised AIHSS it had determined that the domestic workers referred to patients by AIHSS were employees of AIHSS for workers' compensation purposes. According to AIHSS, this determination would raise its monthly workers' compensation premiums from approximately $100 per month to as high as $16,000 per month.

AIHSS appealed that determination to State Fund's San Diego District Office, asserting that the domestic workers were independent contractors, not employees, under section 1812.5095 and the test set forth in *S. G. Borello & Sons, Inc. v. Department of Industrial Relations* (1989) 48 Cal. 3d 341 [769 P.2d 399, 256 Cal. Rptr. 543, 54 Cal. Comp. Cases 80] (*Borello*). State Fund denied the appeal, finding that the domestic workers were considered employees of AIHSS for workers' compensation purposes. In doing so, State Fund did not discuss the applicability of section 1812.5095 or *Borello*.

AIHSS appealed State Fund's decision to the Insurance Commissioner. AIHSS was informed that as of June 2005 the Insurance Commissioner no longer heard appeals pertaining to a worker's status as employee or independent contractor.

AIHSS then filed a complaint against State Fund for declaratory relief, breach of contract and injunctive relief, alleging that its domestic workers were independent contractors under section 1812.5095 and *Borello*. In the complaint, they supported their allegations in part by referring to and relying on section 1812.501, subdivision (h), which defines "domestic agencies," and Unemployment Insurance Code section 687.2, which provides when a company such as AIHSS is considered an employer of domestic workers for unemployment insurance purposes.

In November 2005 State Fund filed a motion to strike all references in the complaint to Civil Code sections 1812.501, subdivision (h), 1812.5095, and Unemployment Insurance Code section 687.2. State Fund argued that these code sections were irrelevant as the Legislature did not intend that they apply to workers' compensation insurance, but only to unemployment insurance.

The court agreed with State Fund and granted the motion to strike, finding:

"These provisions pertain to the interpretation and applicability of unemployment insurance, not workers compensation, which is at issue here. The Workers Compensation Act is liberally construed to extend benefits to persons injured in their employment. [Citation.] The tests to determine whether there is an employment relationship [have] been established through case law."

This petition followed.

DISCUSSION

AIHSS asserts that its compliance with section 1812.5095 exempts it from state law requirements of maintaining workers' compensation insurance for the domestic workers it refers to patients, and therefore the court erred in granting State Fund's motion to strike. We conclude that compliance with the requirements of section 1812.5095 does exempt AIHSS from maintaining workers' compensation insurance for its domestic workers. Therefore we grant AIHSS's petition seeking to set aside the court's order granting State Fund's motion to strike. (Footnote 3)

I. Standard of Review

Because we are called upon to construe a statutory scheme, we accord no deference to the trial court's determination. Instead, we apply de novo review to the issues posed by this action. (*Radian Guaranty, Inc. v. Garamendi* (2005) 127 Cal. App. 4th 1280, 1288 [26 Cal. Rptr. 3d 464].)

II. Principles of Statutory Interpretation

"In interpreting a statute where the language is clear, courts must follow its plain meaning. [Citation.] However, if the statutory language permits more than one reasonable interpretation, courts may consider various extrinsic aids, including the purpose of the statute, the evils to be remedied, the legislative history, public policy, and the statutory scheme encompassing the statute. [Citation.] In the end, we " 'must select the construction that comports most closely with the apparent intent of the Legislature, with a view to promoting rather than defeating the general purpose of the statute, and avoid an interpretation that would lead to absurd consequences.' " " (*Torres v. Parkhouse Tire Service, Inc.* (2001) 26 Cal. 4th 995, 1003 [30 P.3d 57, 111 Cal. Rptr. 2d 564, 66 Cal. Comp. Cases 1036]; see also *Harris v. Capital Growth Investors XIV* (1991) 52 Cal. 3d 1142, 1165–1166 [805 P.2d 873, 278 Cal. Rptr. 614].)

III. Analysis

A. Section 1812.5095 Unambiguously Applies to Workers' Compensation

AIHSS asserts that the court erred in striking from its complaint references to section 1812.5095 and other relevant statutes because its compliance with the terms of section 1812.5095 meant it was deemed not to be the employer for workers' compensation purposes of domestic workers it refers to clients. We conclude that the plain language of section 1812.5095 demonstrates that it was intended to apply to workers' compensation insurance, not, as State Fund asserts and the court found, only unemployment insurance.

Section 1812.5095, subdivision (b) provides in part: "An employment agency *is not the employer* of a domestic worker for whom it procures, offers, refers, provides, or attempts to provide work, if all of the following factors characterize the nature of the relationship between the employment agency and the domestic worker for whom the agency procures, offers, refers, provides, or attempts to provide domestic work . . . ." (Italics added.) Section 1812.5095, subdivision (b) then sets forth nine different requirements that the employment agency must comply with in order for it not to be considered the employer of the domestic worker. (§ 1812.5095, subd. (b)(1)–(9).)

Of relevance to this appeal is subdivision (d) of section 1812.5095, which provides for the following written notice the employment agency must give to each domestic worker: "An employment agency referring a domestic worker to a job shall inform that domestic worker, in writing, on or before the signing of the contract pursuant to paragraph (1) of subdivision (b), that the domestic worker may be obligated to obtain business permits or licenses, where required by any state or local law, ordinance, or regulation, and *that he or she is not eligible for* unemployment insurance, state disability insurance, social security, or *workers' compensation benefits through an employment agency complying with subdivision (b)*. The employment agency referring a domestic worker shall also inform that domestic worker, if the domestic worker is self–employed, that he or she is required to pay self–employment tax, state tax, and federal income taxes." (Italics added.)

Further, subdivision (f) of section 1812.5095 provides: "An employment agency referring a domestic worker to a job shall orally communicate to the person seeking domestic services the disclosure set forth below prior to the referral of the domestic worker the following disclosure statement: [P] '(Name of agency) *is not the employer of the domestic worker it referred to you*. Depending on your arrangement with the domestic worker, *you may have employer responsibilities*.' [P] Within three business days after the employment agency refers a domestic worker to the person seeking domestic services, the following statement printed in not less than 10–point type shall be mailed to the person seeking domestic services: [P] '(Name of agency) *is not the employer of the domestic worker it referred to you. The domestic worker may be your employee or an independent contractor depending on the relationship you have with him or her*. If you direct and control the manner and means by which the domestic worker performs his or her work *you may have employer responsibilities, including* employment taxes and *workers' compensation*, under state and federal law. For additional information contact your local Employment Development Department and the Internal Revenue Service." (Italics added.)

Contrary to the contention of State Fund, and the findings of the court, nothing in the plain language of section 1812.2095 limits its application to unemployment insurance. Subdivision (b) states that a referral agency that complies with its terms is not considered the employer. Further, there is no rational reason (and State Fund posits none) why the Legislature would require the agencies to notify domestic workers that they will not receive workers' compensation benefits from the agency if section 1812.5095 did not apply to workers' compensation insurance. If State Fund's interpretation were accepted, such notices would in effect be false and would confuse domestic workers as to who was responsible for providing workers' compensation insurance. Rather, that notice and the notice required to be given to the clients hiring domestic workers were intended to make clear who was responsible for that obligation. In clear language, the Legislature mandated that (1) domestic workers be informed that the referral agency was not responsible for providing workers' compensation insurance; and (2) domestic workers and the clients hiring them be informed that one or the other of them would be responsible for workers' compensation insurance, depending upon the nature of their relationship. The plain language of section 1812.5095 demonstrates it applies to workers' compensation insurance.

Moreover, the items that the employment agencies must comply with to be deemed not the employer of a domestic worker are the same type of factors that would compel a finding that a company or individual was not the employer of a worker for workers' compensation purposes under common law tests. In order to be considered not an "employer" for purposes of section 1812.5095, employment agencies must, among other things, (1) allow the domestic worker to sign with other employment agencies and work for persons not referred by the employment agency; (2) allow the domestic worker to select or reject any work referred by the employment agency; (3) allow the domestic worker to negotiate the amount of pay for the work referred; (4) not provide training to the domestic worker; (5) allow the domestic worker to perform his or her work "without any direction, control, or supervision exercised by the employment agency with respect to the manner and means of performing the domestic work"; (6) "not provide tools, supplies, or equipment necessary to perform the domestic work"; (7) incur no obligation to pay the domestic worker if "the person for whom the services were performed fails or refuses to pay for the domestic work"; and (8) not have the power to terminate the domestic worker from his or her employment with the person to which the domestic worker was referred. (§ 1812.5095, subd. (b)(1)–(9).)...

Thus, the existing law that Assembly Bill No. 1370 sought to clarify and apply to domestic referral agencies, had, at the time Assembly Bill No. 1370 was being considered, been interpreted as holding that nurses' registries were not only not employers for unemployment insurance, but also for purposes of worker's compensation. The Legislature is presumed to be aware of existing law at the time it considers enacting a statute.

Further, the fact that the stated purpose in enacting Assembly Bill No. 1370 failed to specifically mention workers' compensation is of no moment. Regardless of the original intent in enacting section 1812.5095, the language of the statute does not, expressly or impliedly, limit its reach to unemployment insurance. The Legislature could have easily stated in subdivision (a) that domestic referral agencies were "employers for unemployment insurance purposes only." "[A] court is not authorized in the construction of a statute, to create exceptions not specifically made. If the statute announces a general rule and makes no exception thereto, the courts can make none." (*Stockton Theatres, Inc. v. Palermo* (1956) 47 Cal. 2d 469, 476 [304 P.2d 7].)

The express language of the statute reveals that if domestic referral agencies comply with its terms, they are not the employers of the domestic workers, and, as a result, are not responsible for workers' compensation insurance. Legislative intent may not be used to bootstrap a meaning

that cannot be found in the statutory language. (See *City of Sacramento v. Public Employees' Retirement System* (1994) 22 Cal. App. 4th 786, 793–794 [27 Cal. Rptr. 2d 545].) "The will of the Legislature must be determined from the statutes; intentions cannot be ascribed to it at odds with the intentions articulated in the statutes." (*People v. Knowles* (1950) 35 Cal. 2d 175, 182 [217 P.2d 1].)...

However, the statement by the Senate Rules Committee, paraphrasing subdivision (d) of section 1812.5095, is not inconsistent with that section. The word "if" only refers to the fact that a domestic referral agency is only considered not to be an employer *if* it meets certain criteria specified in the statute. Moreover, the "if" in the statement by the Senate Rules Committee modifies not only the notice as to workers' compensation, but also as to unemployment insurance and state disability insurance. Thus, to accept State Fund's argument, section 1812.5095 would also not shield domestic referral agencies from unemployment and disability insurance obligations if they did not meet the common law test defining employees versus independent contractors, and section 1812.5095 would be rendered meaningless.

DISPOSITION

Let a peremptory writ of mandate issue directing the respondent Superior Court of San Diego County to vacate its order of January 20, 2006, granting real party in interest State Compensation Insurance Fund's motion to strike references in its complaint to Civil Code section 1812.5095, Civil Code section 1812.501, subdivision (h), and Unemployment Insurance Code section 687.2. Our order of May 26, 2006, staying the trial court proceedings is vacated. Costs on the writ proceeding are awarded to petitioner... .

Footnote 1. All further statutory references are to the Civil Code unless otherwise specified.

Footnote 2. Because we are reviewing the court's grant of State Fund's motion to strike portions of AIHSS's complaint in this matter, we accept as true all material factual allegations contained therein. (*Blank v. Kirwin* (1985) 39 Cal. 3d 311, 318 [703 P.2d 58, 216 Cal. Rptr. 718].)

Footnote 3. Based upon our holding we need not consider AIHSS's contention that even if compliance with section 1812.5095 by itself did not exempt it from the responsibility of maintaining workers' compensation, the court erred in granting State Fund's motion to strike because that fact would be relevant to determining if they met the common law test for determining if it were an employer under workers' compensation law.

See also *IHSS v. WCAB (Bouvia)* (1984) 49 Cal. Comp. Cases 177.

§ 5.8(A)   Independent Contractors

Page 157, Column 2, delete third paragraph, beginning 'Business and Professions Code...' through the end of the fourth paragraph ending '...or otherwise... ' and add the following:

Business and Professions Code section 7048 provides in pertinent part:
7048.

This chapter does not apply to any work or operation on one undertaking or project by one or more contracts, the aggregate contract price which for labor, materials, and all other items, is less than five hundred dollars ($500), that work or operations being considered of casual, minor, or inconsequential nature.

This exemption does not apply in any case wherein the work of construction is only a part of a larger or major operation, whether undertaken by the same or a different contractor, or in which a division of the operation is made in contracts of amounts less than five hundred dollars ($500) for the purpose of evasion of this chapter or otherwise.

This exemption does not apply to a person who advertises or puts out any sign or card or other device which might indicate to the public that he or she is a contractor or that he or she is qualified to engage in the business of a contractor.

Page 160, Column 2, fourth paragraph, insert following '...raised here.'

See *Mendoza v. Glenn Brodeur* (2006) 71 Cal. Comp. Cases 1135, for a similar holding, where the Court of Appeal, First District, stated in part:

This personal injury case involves the overlay of workers' compensation law.

Defendant Glenn Brodeur hired plaintiff Ernesto Mendoza, an unlicensed roofer, to replace his roof. After a few hours on the job, plaintiff fell from the roof and was injured. Plaintiff contended that defendant did not provide workers' compensation insurance. In plaintiff's personal injury action, the trial court granted defendant's motion for summary judgment on the ground that plaintiff was not an employee under workers' compensation law and plaintiff had not come forward with evidence supporting a triable issue of fact for tort liability.

Plaintiff contends that summary judgment is unwarranted. We agree. Under Labor Code section 2750.5 and applicable case law, plaintiff is defendant's employee for purposes of tort liability. In the summary judgment proceedings below, which involved only an issue of law, it was premature to require plaintiff to come forward with evidence of defendant's negligence. Accordingly, we reverse...

Plaintiff contends that the trial court erred by granting the summary judgment motion because his exclusion from workers' compensation coverage under section 3352(h) does not bar him from suing in tort. Plaintiff is correct for the following reasons.

When defendant argues that plaintiff is not his employee because of section 3352(h), defendant overlooks the fact that this means that plaintiff is not his employee only for the purposes of workers' compensation. Section 3352(h) does not ipso facto preclude any employment relationship between defendant and plaintiff. Rather, because plaintiff is concededly unlicensed, section 2750.5 kicks in and creates an employment relationship. And that relationship allows plaintiff to maintain an action in tort.

We addressed a similar issue in Furtado v. Schriefer (1991) 228 Cal. App. 3d 1608 [280 Cal. Rptr. 16, 56 Cal. Comp. Cases 266] (Furtado). Schriefer hired Furtado to paint his house. It was undisputed that Furtado required a license for the painting, but did not have one. While painting the house, Furtado fell and was injured. He sued Schriefer. (Id. at pp. 1611–1612, 1616.) The trial court found that Furtado was Schriefer's employee pursuant to section 2750.5, but the court did not consider the impact of section 3352(h)– despite the dispute over whether Furtado had worked less than 52 hours. (Furtado, *supra*, at pp. 1612, 1614.)

We agreed with the trial court that under section 2750.5, Furtado could not be an independent contractor for purposes of workers' compensation law. (Furtado, *supra*, 228 Cal. App. 3d at p. 1616.) We reversed on the ground that section 3352(h) and section 2750.5 have to be construed together. "Section 2750.5 supplements the definitions of employee and independent contractor found in the workers' compensation statutory scheme. It does not purport to override those definitions." (Furtado, *supra*, at p. 1617.) We remanded so the trial court could determine whether Furtado was an employee for purposes of workers' compensation coverage, or was excluded by section 3352(h). If Furtado was found to be excluded, we held that "Furtado should be allowed to proceed with his personal injury action against Schriefer." (Furtado, *supra*, at p. 1617, [fn. omitted].)

The Court of Appeal reached a similar conclusion in Rosas v. Dishong (1998) 67 Cal. App. 4th 815 [79 Cal. Rptr. 2d 339, 63 Cal. Comp. Cases 1376] (Rosas). The Dishongs hired Rosas to do tree–trimming work which required a license that Rosas did not have. Rosas was injured while trimming, and filed a workers' compensation claim. The Dishongs' homeowners insurance carrier denied the claim under section 3352(h). Rosas then sued the Dishongs in tort, alleging general negligence and premises liability. (Rosas, *supra*, at pp. 817–818.)

The Rosas court upheld the trial court's conclusion that section 2750.5 made Rosas an employee as a matter of law for purposes of tort recovery. (Rosas, *supra*, 67 Cal. App. 4th at pp. 818–823.) The court accepted the analysis followed by the trial court: while Rosas was excluded as an employee for purposes of workers' compensation by section 3352(h), "as an unlicensed contractor performing work for which a license is required, he is deemed to be an employee for civil tort purposes and potentially entitled to recovery. (§ 2750.5)" (Rosas, *supra*, at p. 821.) The court noted that Division 3 of the Labor Code, which includes section 2750.5, is meant to apply when the workers' compensation statutes do not: "Where a worker is excluded from workers' compensation coverage under section [3352(h)], the statutory scheme provides for potential liability under division 3, including section 2750.5." (Rosas, *supra*, at p. 822.)

We thus conclude that plaintiff was an employee of defendant by operation of section 2750.5. Since plaintiff was not an employee for purposes of workers' compensation law, he can maintain an action in tort against defendant. (Footnote 4)

This brings us to the proper disposition of the summary judgment motion. As noted, the sole ground of that motion was whether section 3352(h) excluded plaintiff as an employee. It does, but only for purposes of workers' compensation. Given defendant's concession that plaintiff is unlicensed, section 2750.5 operates to allow the present tort action.

Summary judgment should not have been granted. No evidentiary burden shifted to plaintiff. Virtually the entire argument of defendant's motion was the legal impact of section 3352(h)– which, of course, overlooked the impact of section 2750.5. Defendant only noted in passing, and at the conclusion of his motion memorandum, that "[t]he evidence also establishes that no act or omission on the part of Defendant caused Plaintiff's injury." The evidence did no such thing, because there was no evidence put forward by defendant regarding the exact circumstances of the accident and injury.

Plaintiff had nothing to refute. The evidentiary issue of fault–including violation of duty, negligence, and causation–simply was not properly addressed by the motion for summary judgment. The only evidence regarding the actual injury involved only the question of control of the worksite, not fault–and even that evidence, as defendant concedes, raises a triable issue of fact.

The drastic disposition of dismissal of plaintiff's case was legally unwarranted. It was premature to require him to come forward with evidence to show a triable issue of fact when defendant had not shifted the evidentiary burden... .

Footnote 4. We note that defendant relies on Furtado, *supra*, 228 Cal. App. 3d 1608 without seeming to realize it supports plaintiff. We also note that defendant relied below on Cedillo, *supra*, 106 Cal. App. 4th 227. That case has rather complicated facts which we need not discuss in detail. But despite defendant's reliance on Cedillo, that case does rely on Rosas, *supra*, 67 Cal. App. 4th 815 and supports our conclusion that an unlicensed contractor excluded by section 3352(h) may sue in tort as an employee under section 2750.5. (Cedillo, *supra*, at pp. 234–237.)

Page 161, Column 1, seventh paragraph, insert following '...the job.'

See also unpublished decision *Heiman et. al. v. WCAB (Aguilera)* (2007) 72 Cal. Comp. Cases 314, where the Court of Appeal, Second District, held that an unlicensed contractor and property management firm that hired the unlicensed contractor were jointly and severally liable to an injured employee of the unlicensed contractor for workers' compensation and that the homeowners' association was also liable for workers'

compensation, when the Court found that the unlicensed contractor and the property management firm that hired the unlicensed contractor were dual employers of the injured employee, and that the homeowners' association and the property management firm were in a principal/agent relationship. The Court stated, in part:

Petitioner, a professional property manager, hired an unlicensed and uninsured contractor to install rain gutters on a condominium building, and an employee of the contractor was seriously injured on the first day of the job. The Workers' Compensation Appeals Board (WCAB) concluded that petitioner was the employer liable for workers' compensation. Petitioner contends that the WCAB erred because petitioner was instructed to hire the unlicensed contractor as the agent of the condominium homeowners association or the condominium owners, which were found not liable for workers' compensation under the Labor Code. (Footnote 1)

We conclude that petitioner and the unlicensed contractor were dual employers that are jointly and severally liable for workers' compensation. The unlicensed contractor employed the injured employee, and petitioner hired the unlicensed contractor as a professional property manager and the agent of the homeowners association. The homeowners association was not an owner or exempt employer under the Labor Code. Even if petitioner was the agent of the condominium owners, an agent may be liable for performing an act authorized by the principal whose rights are not imputed to the agent. Since liability for an agent's authorized act is imputed to the principal and the homeowners association was a legal entity separate from the owners, we further conclude that the liability of petitioner as agent is imputed to the homeowners association as principal.

Accordingly, the WCAB's decision is affirmed in part and annulled in part, and the matter is remanded for further proceedings consistent with this opinion...

C. Pegasus's Liability Is Unchanged By Its Agency Status.

Pegasus contends that as the agent of the Association or owners, it has the same rights or legal status as its principal under Civil Code section 2330 (Footnote 21) and is an owner and exempt employer under sections 3351(d) and 3352(h). We disagree.

Civil Code section 2330 plainly states that rights and liabilities accrue from the agent's authorized acts to the principal. The statute does not state that the principal's rights or defenses accrue to the agent. Moreover, Pegasus was the agent of the Association, not the owners, as determined by the WCAB.

It is also well established that an agent may be liable for his or her own acts on behalf of the principal whether or not the principal is liable. (See *Frances T., supra,* 42 Cal. 3d at pp. 505, 511.) For example, in *Cowell v. Industrial Acc. Com.* (1938) 11 Cal. 2d 172, 176–177 [78 P.2d 1016, 3 Cal. Comp. Cases 43] (*Cowell*), a corporate cement business, which also managed the stockholders' ranch and hired the ranch hand who was injured, was determined to be the agent and joint employer. And although liability of the county as the state's agent was not addressed in *In–Home Supportive*

Services, supra, 152 Cal. App. 3d at pages 729–730, the state as principal was determined to be a dual employer because the county hired the injured employee and both had the right of supervision and control.

In this case, Hruby was hired directly by Pegasus as the "managing agent" on behalf of the Association. Since Pegasus was also an independent contractor in the business of managing properties and Hruby had no dealings with the Association, Pegasus "was in the best position to make the determination whether the price of the contract reflected the cost of insurance for workers' compensation purposes and whether Mr. Hruby was properly licensed to perform the work" as stated by the WCAB. Moreover, the Agreement provided that Pegasus had responsibility for labor laws even though employees hired to perform maintenance or repairs would be employees of the Association. For these reasons, we conclude that Pegasus is an "employer" liable for workers' compensation under section 2750.5, and is not exempted under sections 3351(d) and 3352(h) whether the agent of the Association or the owners. (Civil Code § 2330; *Cowell, supra,* 11 Cal. 2d at pp. 176–177; *In–Home Supportive Services, supra,* 152 Cal. App. 3d at pp. 729–730.)

5. The Association Is Liable As Principal.

Throughout the proceedings, Aguilera, the Fund, Pegasus and the WCAB have taken the position that the Association is liable because Hruby who was an unlicensed contractor was hired by Pegasus as the agent of the Association. As we have already noted, we have concluded that Pegasus is an employer that is jointly and severally liable for workers' compensation under section 2750.5, *State Fund* and *Blew.* In addition, we have concluded that Hruby was hired by Pegasus as the agent of the Association, which is the principal and a separate legal entity. We have also explained that liability for an agent's authorized acts may be imputed from the agent to the principal pursuant to Civil Code section 2330, *Cowell* and *In–Home Supportive Services.* (Footnote 22)

Even if the Association was also the agent of the owners as reasoned by the WCJ, the Association may be liable for its own acts. (See *Frances T., supra,* 42 Cal. 3d at page 505.)

The owners admit the agency relationship between Pegasus and the Association but contend, as determined by the WCJ, that the Association should be deemed an owner and exempt "employer" under sections 3351(d) and 3352(h). Otherwise the owners will not benefit from sections 3351(d) and 3352(h) as the Legislature intended, "since imposing liability on the homeowner's association would necessarily impose liability on each individual homeowner."

However, we need not decide whether the Association should be deemed an owner and an exempt "employer" since we agree with the WCAB that the duties of Hruby and Aguilera were not "personal" and were in the "trade or business" of the Association contrary to section 3351(d). The owners do not address this issue.

Although under section 3351(d) an employee is a person "whose duties are incidental to the ownership, maintenance,

or use of the dwelling, including the care and supervision of children, *or* whose duties are personal and not in the course of the trade, business, profession, or occupation of the owner or occupant" (emphasis added), the WCAB's interpretation that the language defining duties should be read together rather than separately is entitled to great weight unless clearly erroneous. (See *Boehm & Assocs., supra,* 76 Cal. App. 4th at pages 515–516; *Ralphs Grocery Co., supra,* 38 Cal. App. 4th at page 828; *Nunez v. Workers' Comp. Appeals Bd.* (2006) 136 Cal. App. 4th 584, 587 [38 Cal. Rptr. 3d 914, 71 Cal. Comp. Cases 161].) We note that when the Legislature added and revised section 3351(d) (Footnote 23) and Insurance Code sections 11590 (Footnote 24) and 11591, (Footnote 25) so that homeowner liability policies would provide workers' compensation coverage for residential employees, (Footnote 26) coverage for duties performed in the business of the insured was expressly excluded. Moreover, each statute contains language or references to the other statutes that indicate the Legislature intended these statutes to be interrelated and read together. (Footnote 27)

Therefore, the WCAB's interpretation of section 3351(d), that the language defining duties should be read together, is consistent with the statutory scheme. (Footnote 28)

In addition, the WCAB's determination that the rain gutter repair and installation was not "personal" and was in the "trade or business" of the Association under section 3351(d) is consistent with the record, the Labor Code and the Davis–Stirling Common Interest Development Act. The Association managed the condominium building and provided for maintenance or repairs pursuant to the Agreement and Civil Code section 1364(a). (Footnote 29)

The services provided by Hruby and Aguilera were also for maintenance or repairs within the meaning of section 3355, (Footnote 30) and management and maintenance by the Association were provided on a regular basis under the Agreement and section 3356. (Footnote 31)

Moreover, the Association had corporate powers to finance, contract and conduct business under Civil Code section 1363(c) (Footnoted 32) and Corp. Code section 7140.

(Footnote 33)

The Association performed these functions through its officers or directors and Pegasus as the paid "managing agent" under the Agreement and the Civil Code. Consequently, the duties performed by Hruby and Aguilera were not "personal" and were in the "trade, business" of the Association, and the Association was not an owner and exempt "employer" under sections 3351(d) and 3352(h). (Footnote 34)

Therefore, the Association is liable for workers' compensation as the principal of Pegasus.

6. The Owners Are Not Liable For Workers' Compensation.

We agree with the WCJ and the WCAB that the owners are not liable for workers' compensation as either an "employer" under section 2750.5 or an employer under section 3351(d) because Aguilera did not work sufficient hours under section 3352(h). (*Cedillo, supra,* 106 Cal. App. 4th at pp. 235–236.) Even if the Association or Pegasus is the agent of the owners as suggested by the WCJ, "employer" liability for workers' compensation is not imputed to the owners as principal because of the statutory immunity provided under the Labor Code. (See *ECC Construction, Inc. v. Ganson* (2000) 82 Cal. App. 4th 572, 575–576 [98 Cal. Rptr. 2d 292] [condominium owners not personally liable under Corp. Code § 7350 for construction contract with condominium association that was nonprofit mutual benefit corporation, although association may look to members for debt].) Nor are the owners an "employer" that is liable for workers' compensation solely for being a member of the Association since generally "A member of an unincorporated association does not incur liability for acts of the association or acts of its members which he did not authorize or perform." (See *White, supra,* 17 Cal. App. 3d at page 827; *Orser v. George* (1967) 252 Cal. App. 2d 660, 670–671 [60 Cal. Rptr. 708], which is cited by *White,* and *Security–First Nat. Bk. v. Cooper* (1944) 62 CalApp.2d 653, 667 [145 P.2d 722] [*Security–First National Bank*)].) (Footnote 35)

Therefore, the owners are not liable for workers' compensation and thus benefit from sections 3351(d) and 3352(h) as the Legislature intended.

DISPOSITION

Hruby and Pegasus were dual employers of Aguilera that are jointly and severally liable for workers' compensation under the Labor Code. Pegasus was also the agent of the Association, which was a separate legal entity that is liable for workers' compensation as the principal. Pegasus and the Association were not owners or exempt employers under sections 3351(d) and 3352(h). The WCAB's decision awards Aguilera workers' compensation to be paid *solely* by Pegasus. We reject that limited conclusion and hold that Hruby is jointly and severally liable with Pegasus and the Association is also liable as Pegasus' principle. To the extent that WCAB's decision is inconsistent with our conclusion, it is annulled. The award will otherwise be affirmed.

The decision of the WCAB is affirmed in part and annulled in part, and the matter is remanded for further proceedings consistent with this opinion... .

Footnote 1. All statutory reference is to the Labor Code unless otherwise stated.

Footnote 21. Civil Code § 2330 states: "An agent represents his principal for all purposes within the scope of his actual or ostensible authority, and all the rights and liabilities which would accrue to the agent from transactions within such limit, if they had been entered into on his own account, accrue to the principal."

Footnote 22. See also Corp. Code § 18250, which was enacted in 2004 and was based on former Corp. Code § 24001 and which states: "Except as otherwise provided by law, an unincorporated association is liable for its act or omission and for the act or omission of its director, officer, agent, or employee, acting within the scope of the office, agency, or employment, to the same extent as if the association were a natural person."

Footnote 23. Section 3351(d) was added in 1975 and provided: "Any person employed by the owner of a private dwelling whose duties are incidental to the ownership, maintenance, or use of the dwelling, including the performance of household domestic service. For the purposes of this subdivision, household domestic service shall include, but not be limited to, the care and supervision of children in a private residence." Section 3351(d) was amended in 1977 to essentially its current form and § 3352(h) was added. (See fn. 4 and fn. 5, *ante.*)

Footnote 24. Insurance Code § 11590 was also added in 1975 and stated: "Except as provided in Section 11591 or 11592, no policy providing comprehensive personal liability insurance, or endorsement thereto, may be issued, amended, or renewed in this state on or after January 1, 1977, unless it contains a provision for coverage against liability for the payment of compensation, as defined in Section 3207 of the Labor Code, to any person defined as an employee by subdivision (d) of Section 3351 of the Labor Code. Any such policy in effect on or after January 1, 1997, whether or not actually containing such provisions, shall be construed as if such provisions were embodied therein."

Insurance Code § 11590 was also revised in 1977 and basically was unchanged except for the addition of the provision: "However, such coverage shall not apply if any other existing, valid and collectible, workers' compensation insurance for such liability is applicable to the injury or death of such employee."

Footnote 25. Insurance Code § 11591 was also added in 1975 and provided: "The requirements of Section 11590 shall be inapplicable to any such policy of insurance or endorsement where the services of such employee are in connection with business pursuits of the insured."

Insurance Code § 11591 was also amended in 1977 and states: "The requirements of Section 11590 shall be inapplicable to any such policy of insurance or endorsement where the services of such employee are in connection with the trade, business, profession, or occupation, as such terms are defined in Sections 3355 and 3356 of the Labor Code, of the insured."

Footnote 26. Scc *State Farm, supra,* 16 Cal. 4th at pp. 1193–1196 (son hired to work on father's residence not excluded under § 3352(a) and homeowners policy since coverage elected by insuring under § 4150 et seq.); see also *In–Home Supportive Services, supra,* 152 Cal. App. 3d at pp. 735–736.

Footnote 27. In contrast, the Supreme Court in *State Farm* concluded that insurance coverage under Ins. Code § 11590 was broader than indicated by section 3351(d) because there was no reference in these statutes to section 3352(a), which excludes residential employees employed by a parent, spouse or child. (*State Farm, supra,* 16 Cal. 4th at pp. 1194–1198.)

Footnote 28. The term "personal" in section 3351(d) may be a reference to the term "household domestic service", which was included in the 1975 version of the statute. The term "household domestic service" implies duties that are personal to the homeowner and not related to the homeowner's commercial or business activity. (See *Fernandez v. Lawson* (2003) 31 Cal. 4th 31, 36–37 [71 P.3d 779, 1 Cal. Rptr. 3d 422, 68 Cal. Comp. Cases 1021].)

Footnote 29. Civil Code § 1364(a) provides in part: "Unless otherwise provided in the declaration of a common interest development, the association is responsible for repairing, replacing, or maintaining the common areas, other than exclusive use common areas . . . ."

Footnote 30. Section 3355 states: "As used in subdivision (d) of Section 3351, the term "course of trade, business, profession, or occupation" includes all services tending toward the preservation, maintenance, or operation of the business, business premises, or business property of the employer."

Footnote 31. Section 3356 provides: "As used in subdivision (d) of Section 3351 and in Section 3355, the term "trade, business, profession, or occupation" includes any undertaking actually engaged in by the employer with some degree of regularity, irrespective of the trade name, articles of incorporation, or principal business of the employer."

Footnote 32. Civil Code § 1363(c) states: "Unless the governing documents provide otherwise, and regardless of whether the association is incorporated or unincorporated, the association may exercise the powers granted to a nonprofit mutual benefit corporation, as enumerated in Section 7140 of the Corporations Code, except that an unincorporated association may not adopt or use a corporate seal or issue membership certificates in accordance with Section 7313 of the Corporations Code.

The association, whether incorporated or unincorporated may exercise the powers granted to an association in this title."

Footnote 33. Corp. Code § 7140 states in part: " . . . a corporation . . . shall have all of the powers of a natural person, including . . . [P] (e) . . . to indemnify and purchase and maintain insurance . . . [P] (g) Levy dues, assessments . . . [P] (i) Assume obligations, enter into contracts . . . [P] (l) Carry on a business at a profit and apply any profit that results from the business activity to any activity in which it may lawfully engage."

Footnote 34. The Fund argued at oral argument that the rain gutter repair and installation was also not "personal" and in the "trade, business" of Pegasus, and is another reason why § 3351(d) and § 3352(h) do not apply to Pegasus.

Footnote 35. See also *Holmes v. Roth* (1992) 11 Cal. App. 4th 931, 934–935 [14 Cal. Rptr. 2d 315, 57 Cal. Comp. Cases 801] (mere membership does not entitle condominium owner to raise workers' compensation exclusivity as defense to doorman's negligence claim); Corp. Code § 18260, which was enacted in 2004 and is based on former Corp. Code § 24002 that is cited by *White*; Corp. Code § 18605 and § 18610 which were enacted in 2004 and codify the rule of *Security–First Nat. Bk.* and Corp. Code, § 18620.

Page 163, Column 1, fifth paragraph, insert following '…contractor…'

In *Ramirez et al. v. Nelson et al.* (2006) 71 Cal. Comp. Cases 776, the Court of Appeal, Second District, quoted the California Supreme Court in holding that a person lacking the requisite contractors' license may not be an independent contractor and stated, in part:

In this wrongful death case, a worker trimming trees was electrocuted. His parents sued the homeowners in whose trees their son was working. The jury found the homeowners were negligent, but that their negligence was not a substantial factor in the worker's death. We conclude the trial court erred in refusing a jury instruction based on Penal Code section 385.

Section 385 makes it a misdemeanor for any person, either personally or through an employee, to move any tool or equipment within six feet of a high voltage overhead line. We reverse.

FACTS

Maria Dolores Ramirez and Martin Flores ("the Floreses") are the parents of the decedent, Luis Flores.

Thomas and Vivian Nelson are homeowners. Their backyard has a number of trees, including a eucalyptus tree. Every two or three years, Southern California Edison has the eucalyptus tree trimmed so that its branches do not reach the high–voltage electrical lines that run above the tree. The electrical lines are visible to everyone.

On January 15, 2002, Southern California Edison's tree trimmers gave the Nelsons notice they would trim the eucalyptus tree the next day, but they did not do so. About three weeks later, the Nelsons orally contracted with Julian Rodriguez to trim trees in their backyard, including the eucalyptus tree. The Nelsons had used Rodriguez four or five times in the past to trim trees. Their neighbor had used him for years. The Nelsons believed Rodriguez did exceptional work trimming trees.

Rodriguez arrived at the Nelsons' home on February 14, 2002. He had a crew of four men, including Flores. Flores worked on the eucalyptus tree while other crew members worked on other trees in the Nelsons' backyard. The Nelsons neither supervised the trimming, nor did they provide the tools. The eucalyptus tree is more than 15 feet in height.

Vivian Nelson could see Flores working about half–way up in the eucalyptus tree from her kitchen window. He was working above his shoulders with a pole. She could not tell from her kitchen window from what material the pole was made.

Around noon, Vivian Nelson heard men shouting in Spanish. She looked out the kitchen window, and saw men running to the eucalyptus tree. She went out onto her deck, and saw Flores hanging in the eucalyptus tree from his safety harness. She called her husband, who called 911.

Flores had been killed by electrocution. No one saw the accident happen. After the accident, Vivian Nelson noticed that the pole Flores had been using was made of aluminum and wood.

The Nelsons did not know that Rodriguez was not licensed and had no workers compensation insurance. The Floreses' safety expert admitted, however, that the license required for tree trimming did not require the applicant to take an examination. The expert acknowledged that to obtain a license, Rodriguez "wouldn't have been required to demonstrate knowledge of any particular subject matter pertaining to tree trimmers, whether it be techniques, tools, [or] anything[]."

DISCUSSION

I.

The Floreses contend the trial court erred in refusing to instruct the jury that a violation of section 385 is negligence per se.

A statutory violation is presumed negligence per se. (Evid. Code, § 669.) The presumption arises because the statute sets the standard of care. (Casey v. Russell (1982) 138 Cal. App. 3d 379, 383 [188 Cal. Rptr. 18].)

Section 385, subdivision (b), provides: "Any person who either personally or through an employee or agent, or as an employee or agent of another, operates, places, erects or moves any tools, machinery, equipment, material, building or structure within six feet of a high voltage overhead conductor is guilty of a misdemeanor."

The Floreses argue section 385, subdivision (b), applies because Flores was an employee of the Nelsons under Labor Code section 2750.5. Labor Code section 2750.5 creates a rebuttable presumption that a contractor performing work for which a license is required pursuant to section 7000 et seq. of the Business and Professions Code is an employee rather than an independent contractor. Labor Code section 2750.5 sets forth factors in subdivisions (a), (b) and (c) that must be proved to rebut the presumption.

The penultimate paragraph of Labor Code section 2750.5 provides: "In addition to the factors contained in subdivisions (a), (b), and (c), any person performing any function or activity for which a license is required pursuant to Chapter 9 (commencing with Section 7000) of Division 3 of the Business and Professions Code shall hold a valid contractors' license as a condition of having independent contractor status." The Business and Professions Code requires to be licensed any person who contracts to trim trees 15 feet in height and above. (Bus. & Prof. Code, § 7026.1, subd. (c).) The tree that Flores was trimming at the time of his death was over 15 feet in height.

In State Compensation Insurance Fund v. Workers Compensation Appeals Board (1985) 40 Cal. 3d 5, 15 [706 P.2d 1146, 219 Cal. Rptr. 13, 50 Cal. Comp. Cases 562] (State Compensation), our Supreme Court held that the meaning of the penultimate paragraph of Labor Code section 2750.5 is clear: "[T]he person lacking the requisite license may not be an independent contractor." The court also stated: "[T]he section purports to determine status of persons as independent contractors or employees, and the language of the section does not reflect legislative intent that a contractor lacking the requisite license shall be an independent contractor for some purposes but not for others." (Ibid.)

Under State Compensation, Flores was an employee of the Nelsons for the purpose of section 385, subdivision (b). (See Rosas v. Dishong (1998) 67 Cal. App. 4th 815, 821–825 [79 Cal. Rptr. 2d 339, 63 Cal. Comp. Cases 1376] [unlicensed tree trimmer injured in a fall is employee of homeowner under Lab. Code, § 2750.5].) It does not mean, however, that workers compensation is Flores's exclusive remedy. Because Flores worked less than 52 hours for the Nelsons during the 90 calendar days immediately preceding his death, he is excluded from workers compensation. (Lab. Code, § 3352, subd. (h).) Thus the Nelsons may be liable in tort. (See Rosas, supra, at p. 821, fn. 4.)

The Nelsons' reliance on Fernandez v. Lawson (2003) 31 Cal. 4th 31 [71 P.3d 779, 1 Cal. Rptr. 3d 422, 68 Cal. Comp. Cases 1021], is misplaced. There an employee of an unlicensed tree trimmer sued a homeowner for injuries he received when he fell from a 50–foot tree. The parties assumed the injured worker was an employee of the homeowner by operation of Labor Code section 2750.5. (Fernandez, supra, at p. 34.) The question was whether the homeowner is required to comply with the California Occupational Safety and Health Act of 1973 (Cal–OSHA). (Lab. Code, § 6300 et seq.) The court held that such noncommercial tree trimming comes within the "household domestic service" exception to Cal–OSHA. (Lab. Code, § 6303, subd. (b).)

Section 385, however, contains no such exception. Contrary to the Nelsons' argument, section 385 is not a part of Cal–OSHA. Section 385 was enacted in 1947, long before Cal–OSHA. (Stats. 1947, ch. 1229, § 1.) The Nelsons point out that portions of Cal–OSHA and its implementing regulations refer to section 385. (See, e.g., Lab. Code, § 6302 & Cal. Code Regs., tit. 8, § 330, subd. (h) [exempting from reporting requirements any injury, illness or death caused by a Penal Code violation except a violation of § 385].) But reference to section 385 does not make it part of Cal–OSHA.

Nor does the unanimous opinion in Fernandez determine that Labor Code section 2750.5 does not apply to homeowners. The parties there simply assumed Labor Code section 2750.5 applied under State Compensation. At best, Fernandez contains a concurring opinion by Justice Brown. The concurring opinion criticizes State Compensation for failing to consider the ramifications of placing employer status on unsuspecting homeowners. (Fernandez v. Lawson, supra, 31 Cal. 4th at p. 42 (conc. opn. of Brown J., Baxter J. conc.).) It urges that the penultimate paragraph of Labor Code section 2750.5 means only that the unlicensed contractor, as opposed to the homeowner, is precluded from asserting independent contractor status. (Ibid.; see also State Compensation, supra, 40 Cal. 3d at pp. 16–18 (conc. opn. of Mosk, J. & dis. opn. of Lucas, J.).) Although State Compensation has been criticized, it is still the law, and we are bound to follow it. (Auto Equity Sales v. Superior Court (1962) 57 Cal. 2d 450, 455 [369 P.2d 937, 20 Cal. Rptr. 321].)

The Nelsons cite Fernandez in support of their argument that the trial court has discretion to decide whether a criminal statute imposes civil liability. But Fernandez decided that as a matter of law noncommercial tree trimming comes within the "household domestic service" exception to Cal–OSHA. It does not purport to give the trial court discretion to decide whether a criminal statute imposes civil liability.

The Nelsons point out that a statutory violation simply creates a rebuttable presumption of negligence per se. (Citing Casey v. Russell, *supra*, 138 Cal. App. 3d at p. 383.) The presumption is rebutted if the actor can show some justification or excuse for violating the statute. (Ibid.) Violation of a statute may be justified or excused where the actor neither knows nor should know of the occasion for compliance. (Id. at p. 384.) The Nelsons believe that Fernandez stands for the proposition that knowledge of Cal–OSHA is not to be imputed to homeowners. But Fernandez is based on the "household domestic service" exception to the application of Cal–OSHA, not the homeowners' lack of knowledge. Moreover, as we have stated, section 385 is not part of Cal–OSHA. There is no reason why knowledge of section 385 should not be imputed to homeowners.

The Nelsons argue that the Floreses did not prove a violation of section 385 occurred. The Nelsons' argument is based on the theory that there is no evidence Flores moved his saw within six feet of the power line.

In determining whether an instruction should be given, the question is not whether the proponent of the instruction has carried a burden of proof. Instead, the question is whether the instruction is supported by substantial evidence. (Soule v. General Motors Corp. (1994) 8 Cal. 4th 548, 572 [882 P.2d 298, 34 Cal. Rptr. 2d 607].) Here no one saw the accident occur. But the jury could reasonably conclude that the Legislature established six feet as the prohibited zone because anything outside the six–foot zone is safe. Thus the jury could reasonably conclude from the fact of Flores's electrocution, that he moved his saw within six feet of the high voltage line. This circumstantial evidence supports the instruction. Of course, on retrial the parties may introduce expert evidence on this question.

The Nelsons claim that the failure to give the instruction was harmless. They point out that the jury found them negligent without an instruction on section 385. But without an instruction on section 385, the jury would not know the Nelsons were negligent in employing Flores to move a tool within six feet of a high–voltage line. There is a reasonable probability that had the jury been so instructed, it could have found causation. Thus the error was not harmless. (9 Witkin, Cal. Procedure (4th ed. 1997) Appeal, § 438, p. 484.)

It follows from what we have said that the trial court also erred in refusing to allow the Floreses to refer to Flores as the Nelsons' employee.

II.

The Floreses contend that under Haft v. Lone Palm Hotel (1970) 3 Cal. 3d 756, 769–775 [478 P.2d 465, 91 Cal. Rptr. 745], the burden shifted to the Nelsons to prove their negligence was not the proximate cause of the accident. We consider this contention to aid the court and parties in the event of a retrial.

In Haft, a father and son were found drowned in a hotel swimming pool. There were no witnesses to their deaths. The hotel violated a statute by failing to provide a lifeguard or post a warning. The court held that the failure to provide a lifeguard to observe occurrences in the pool area deprived the plaintiffs of a means of establishing the facts leading to the drownings. Under the circumstances, the burden shifted to the defendant to prove its statutory violation was not the cause of the victims' deaths.

But here, assuming the Nelsons violated section 385, the violation did not prevent the Floreses from establishing the cause of Flores's death. In fact, nothing the Nelsons did prevented anyone from observing Flores. That no one saw the accident occur, does not by itself shift the burden of proof. The Floreses retain the burden of proof as to causation in the event of a retrial.

The judgment is reversed and remanded for further proceedings... .

Page 178, Column 2, fourth paragraph, insert following '...and 1300))'

In holding that a real estate salesperson/broker was not an employee, but an independent contractor, in *Facundo v. WCAB* (2006) 71 Cal. Comp. Cases 834, the Appeals Board stated, in part:

> Workers' compensation law requires the applicant to show that she was an employee at the time of the alleged injury. The leading case regarding determination of employment status is S.G. Borello & Sons, Inc. v. Dept. Ind. Rel. (1989) 48 Cal. 3d 341 [256 Cal. Rptr. 543, 769 P.2d 399] [54 Cal. Comp. Cases 80] ("Borello"), where the Supreme Court concluded that, despite the terms of a written contract otherwise, cucumber crop harvesters more closely resembled laborers, and thus employees, rather than skilled independent contractors.
>
> In this case, although applicant contends she is an employee as a matter of law, we note that the issue of whether a real estate salesperson is an employee for workers' compensation purposes is a factual issue that requires analysis of the circumstances of each case. (See Grubb & Ellis Co. v. Spengler (1983) 143 Cal. App. 3d 890, 895–898 [192 Cal. Rptr. 639]; Payne v. White House Properties, Inc. (1980) 112 Cal. App. 3d 465, 470–471 [169 Cal. Rptr. 373, 45 Cal. Comp. Cases 1323]; Gipson v. Davis Realty Co. (1963) 215 Cal. App. 2d 190, 207 [30 Cal. Rptr. 253]. See also, Borello, *supra*, 48 Cal. 3d at p. 349: The determination of whether an injured person is an employee or independent contractor is a question of fact.)... .

The Board next discussed the factors set out in *Borello, supra* for determining whether an employment relationship exists, including the most important factor, right of control over the mode and manner in which the work was done. The Board continued, in part:

> In this case, the employment contract (P P 9–10) clearly states that applicant is an independent contractor. Absent proof that the parties, by their actual conduct, acted like employer and employee, the contract is a material factor that cannot be overlooked. Based upon our review of the record, we conclude that applicant's trial testimony is insufficient to establish that the parties, by their actual

conduct, acted like employee and employer in this case.

With regard to the right of control, applicant's testimony does not establish that the employer controlled the mode and manner of how she sold real property. Applicant testified that the real estate agents were periodically required to answer the telephone. (See Summary of Evidence (SOE), October 24, 2004, 3:6–13.) However, there is nothing in applicant's trial testimony to indicate that she lacked discretion and control over the method and means used in selling real estate. This means that applicant was not an employee, because an employer traditionally has the right to exercise control over the manner in which the employee's job must be performed.

With regard to the right of termination, paragraph 12 of the contract did not give Valley an unlimited right of termination, and applicant did not have an unlimited right to quit. That is, applicant could terminate the agreement at any time, but she was required to complete work in progress. Valley could terminate applicant for cause, but otherwise was required to give applicant 30 days notice prior to terminating her. Also in reference to termination, applicant testified that she was required to take leads, and if she did not take them, she would not get more and would eventually be terminated. However, applicant did not testify why she thought that was the case, and applicant did not give any examples of other salespersons who were terminated for that reason. While applicant testified that she had a sales quota, she did not testify about what happened if she did not make the quota. (See SOE, January 12, 2005, 5:2–6.) The factor of the right to terminate the employment agreement does not weigh in favor of an employer–employee relationship between Valley and the applicant.

With regard to the factors of skill, and whether applicant was engaged in a distinct occupation or business, we note that real estate sales is a licensed occupation, which involves people–oriented, special skills beyond those which might be expected of just any employee. (See Borello, supra, 48 Cal. 3d at p. 356.)

With regard to the nature of the occupation, i.e., whether the work is usually done under the direction of the principal or by a specialist, without supervision, we note that applicant was paid by commission, from which deductions were taken, and she was not paid for the number of hours worked. Thus, applicant's pay depended upon her own initiative and judgment. And although Valley provided applicant with office facilities, she was responsible for administrative costs, such as workers' compensation insurance and phone costs. (See SOE, October 24, 2004, 3:13–16.)

In conclusion, we have considered the Borello factors in light of the agreement which made applicant an independent contractor, as well as her right to control the details of her work. Based on the agreement and applicant's testimony in reference to the various factors, we conclude that the evidence fails to establish that she was an employee of Valley at the time of the alleged injury. Therefore, we will affirm the WCJ's decision... .

Page 187, Column 1, third paragraph, following '...under review...'

See also *JKH Enterprises, Inc. v. Department of Industrial Relations* (2006) 71 Cal. Comp. Cases 1257, where the Court of Appeal, Sixth District, upheld a trial Court's finding that drivers for a courier service were employees for workers' compensation purposes rather than independent contractors, stating, in part:

B. The Department's Findings and Order Are Supported by Substantial Evidence

Under the substantial evidence test, the agency's findings are presumed to be supported by the administrative record and the appellant challenging them has the burden to show that they are not. (*Mann v. Department of Motor Vehicles, supra*, 76 Cal. App. 4th at p. 318.) We conclude that JKH has not met this burden.

The ultimate finding by the hearing officer in this case was that JKH's drivers, as an unskilled but integral part of its business, were functioning as employees rather than independent contractors, and, thus, JKH was required to comply with *Labor Code* Section 3700 by providing the drivers with workers' compensation coverage. The decision cited *Borello, supra*, 48 Cal. 3d 341, as primary support for this conclusion.

The California Supreme Court decided *Borello* in 1989, and it remains the seminal case with respect to the determination whether a hiree is an employee or independent contractor for purposes of the requirement of an employer to provide workers' compensation insurance. The court made several authoritative pronouncements in the case. First, the court made clear that while the common law emphasis on the hirer's degree of control over the details of the work in the determination of an employment relationship remains significant, it is not the only factor to be considered in the workers' compensation context. This is because the question of a hiree's status must be considered in light of the history and remedial and social purposes of the Workers' Compensation Act. (*Labor Code* Section 3600 et seq.; *Borello, supra*, 48 Cal. 3d at pp. 351–356.)

Unlike common law principles, the policies behind the Act are not concerned with "an employer's liability for injuries caused by his employee." (*Borello, supra*, 48 Cal. 3d at p. 352.) Instead, they concern " 'which injuries to the employee should be insured against by the employer. [Citations.] . . . .' [Citations.]" (Ibid.) Accordingly, in the workers' compensation context, in addition to the "control" test, the question of employment status must be decided with deference to the "purposes of the protective legislation." (Id. at p. 353.) "The nature of the work, and the overall arrangement between the parties, must be examined to determine whether they come within the 'history and fundamental purposes' of the statute." (Id. at pp. 353–354.) These are: "(1) to ensure that the cost of industrial injuries will be part of the cost of goods rather than a burden on society[;] (2) to guarantee prompt, limited compensation for an employee's work injuries, regardless of fault, as an inevitable cost of production[;] (3) to spur increased industrial safety[;] and (4) in return, to insulate the employer from tort liability for his employee's injuries. [Citations.] [P] The Act intends comprehensive coverage of injuries in employment. It accomplishes this goal by defining 'employment' broadly in terms of 'service to an employer' and by including a general presumption that any person 'in service to another' is a covered 'employee.' [Citations.]" (Id. at p. 354.)

Second, the court affirmed that factors other than "control" must be considered since that test, "applied rigidly and in isolation, is often of little use in evaluating the infinite variety of service arrangements." (Borello, supra, 48 Cal. 3d at p. 350.) The individual factors are not to " 'be applied mechanically as separate tests; they are intertwined and their weight depends often on particular combinations.' [Citation.]" (Borello, supra, at pp. 350–351, fn. omitted.) The factors find support in prior case law (Empire Star Mines Co. v. Cal. Emp. Com. (1946) 28 Cal. 2d 33, 43–44 [168 P.2d 686] overruled on another ground in People v. Sims (1982) 32 Cal. 3d 468, 480 [651 P.2d 321, 186 Cal. Rptr. 77]; Tieberg v. Unemployment Ins. App. Bd. (1970) 2 Cal. 3d 943, 949 [471 P.2d 975, 88 Cal. Rptr. 175]); the Restatement Second on Agency; other legislation pertaining to the contractors state license law and providing "extensive guidelines for determining whether one who operates under a required contractor's license is an independent contractor or an employee" (Borello, supra, at p. 351, fn. 5, 350–355.); and case law from other jurisdictions concerning the determination of "independent contractorship in light of the remedial purposes of . . . legislation." (Id. at p. 354, citing federal case law construing the Fair Labor Standards Act].)

The court declined to adopt "detailed new standards for examination of the issue," but stated that these factors "may often overlap those pertinent under the common law," that "[e]ach service arrangement must be evaluated on its facts, and the dispositive circumstances may vary from case to case," and "all are logically pertinent to the inherently difficult determination whether a provider of service is an employee or an excluded independent contractor for purposes of workers' compensation law." (Footnote 14) (Borello, supra, 48 Cal. 3d at pp. 354–355.)

In Borello, the court rejected the hirer's contentions about the absence of an employment relationship and concluded that the particular hirees there were employees and not independent contractors. This, despite that the employer did not exercise significant control over the details of the work, which was the growing and harvesting of cucumbers for the production of pickles. The minimal degree of control that the employer exercised over the details of the work was not considered dispositive because the work did not require a high degree of skill and it was an integral part of the employer's business. The employer was thus determined to be exercising all necessary control over the operation as a whole. (Borello, supra, 48 Cal. 3d at pp. 355–360.)

Substantial evidence in the administrative record supports the same conclusion here. As found by the Department, the functions performed by the drivers, pick–up and delivery of papers or packages and driving in between, did not require a high degree of skill. And the functions constituted the integral heart of JKH's courier service business. By obtaining the clients in need of the service and providing the

workers to conduct it, JKH retained all necessary control over the operation as a whole. Under Borello, and similar to its facts, these circumstances are enough to find an employment relationship for purposes of the Workers' Compensation Act, even in the absence of JKH exercising control over the details of the work and with JKH being more concerned with the results of the work rather than the means of its accomplishment. (Ibid; see also Yellow Cab Cooperative, Inc. v. Workers' Comp. Appeals Bd., supra, 226 Cal. App. 3d 1288, 1293–1300.) And neither JKH's nor the drivers' own perception of their relationship as one of independent contracting, or any other single factor, either alone or in combination, mandates a different result. We therefore reject JKH's contention that its lack of control over the details of the work, the drivers' use of their own cars, and the presence of the "Independent Contractor Profiles" signed by the drivers dictate but one conclusion here–that the drivers are independent contractors. This contention does not adequately take into account the comprehensive and authoritative holding of Borello.

We further reject JKH's contention that under Millsap v. Federal Express Corporation (1991) 227 Cal. App. 3d 425 [277 Cal. Rptr. 807] (Millsap), we must conclude that the administrative record here establishes only the absence of an employment relationship. First, and significantly, Millsap was deciding the question of whether an employment relationship existed for common law negligence purposes (the hirer's liability to a third party for the conduct of the hiree) and not for purposes of the Workers' Compensation Act. As Borello holds, we must decide this question with specific reference to this protective legislation, and with its history and purposes in mind. (Borello, supra, 48 Cal. 3d at pp. 352–353.) Secondly, on the facts, the hiree in Millsap, who similarly made deliveries for the hirer, was paid on a per route, "piecemeal" basis whenever he submitted invoices and the court concluded that each time he picked up packages for delivery, there was a new "contract." (Millsap, supra, 227 Cal. App. 3d at p. 432, fn. 3.) In contrast, here, the route drivers are paid on an hourly basis, all the drivers receive their pay on regularly scheduled paydays, and several of the drivers have maintained their working relationships with JKH on the same terms for at least a couple of years. In sum, because of its context and its sufficiently distinguishable facts, Millsap does not dictate a finding here that JKH's drivers are independent contractors.

Nor does the other case that JKH relies on, State Compensation Ins. Fund v. Brown (1995) 32 Cal. App. 4th 188 [38 Cal. Rptr. 2d 98, 60 Cal. Comp. Cases 91] (Brown), compel that conclusion. There, the dispute concerned the collection of workers' compensation premiums alleged to be owed by a trucking company. Thus, like Millsap, Brown was not a case in which the court was making a determination about the hiring relationship against the backdrop of the Workers' Compensation Act. Instead, the plaintiff, State Compensation Insurance Fund, raised contract claims solely for the collection of insurance premiums. Further, as a factual matter, the nature of the work in Brown–truck driving–was determined by the court to require skill, abilities, and the exercise of discretion beyond that expected or required of a general laborer. (Id. at pp. 202–203.) Also, the truck drivers were found to be engaged in a distinct occupation from that of the hirer, who functioned essentially as a "broker" of trucking services. The truck drivers made substantial capital investment in their own trucks, and they were paid on a job by job basis. The totality of these circumstances led the court to conclude that there was no employment relationship and that the truck drivers were entrepreneurial and truly independent contractors. (Id. at p. 203.) The same cannot be said here based on the facts cited in the Department's decision. And those facts are supported by substantial evidence in the record.

Finally, JKH cries foul in response to the Department's argument that its classification of the drivers as independent contractors was based on subterfuge and that this artifice was a factor tending to show an employment relationship. But substantial evidence supports the Department's argument. The record is undisputed that JKH appears to have been formed in response to a prior stop work order issued to VIP Courier and that JKH operates its delivery services in the same structural fashion, despite its incorporation and the "Independent Contractor Profiles" having been signed by JKH's drivers. Borello specifically cites the bona fides of the independent contractor classification as a factor that is relevant to the determination of an employment relationship. (Borello, *supra*, 48 Cal. 3d at p. 351, fn. 5.)

In sum, there is substantial evidence in light of the whole record to support the Department's determination that 15 of 16 of JKH's drivers were functioning as its employees rather than as true independent contractors. Even JKH concedes that there is some evidence in the record of certain factors tending to support this, though it describes this evidence as "minimal" and short of substantial. But where, as here, our review is limited to examining the whole administrative record to determine if the Department's findings and order are supported by substantial evidence, it is not our function to reweigh the evidence or the particular factors cited by the Department in support of its decision, to which we afford considerable deference. Once we conclude, as we have here, that the Department's findings are indeed supported by substantial evidence, and that those findings in turn support the Department's legal conclusion or ultimate determination, our analysis is at an end.

DISPOSITION

The trial court's order denying JKH's petition for writ of mandate and granting the Department's request for a preliminary injunction is affirmed… .

Footnote 14. These factors substantially include: (1) whether there is a right to fire at will without cause; (2) whether the one performing services is engaged in a distinct occupation or business; (3) the kind of occupation, with reference to whether, in the locality, the work is usually done under the direction of the principal or by a specialist without supervision; (4) the skill required in the particular occupation; (5) whether the principal or the worker supplies the instrumentalities, tools, and the place of work for the person doing the work; (6) the length of time for which the

services are to be performed; (7) the method of payment, whether by the time or by the job; (8) whether or not the work is a part of the regular business of the principal; (9) whether or not the parties believe they are creating an employer–employee relationship; (10) whether the classification of independent contractor is bona fide and not a subterfuge to avoid employee status; (11) the hiree's degree of investment other than personal service in his or her own business and whether the hiree holds himself or herself out to be in business with an independent business license; (12) whether the hiree has employees; (13) the hiree's opportunity for profit or loss depending on his or her managerial skill; and (14) whether the service rendered is an integral part of the alleged employer's business. (Borello, *supra*, 48 Cal. 3d at pp. 350–355.)

§ 5.8(A)(3) Exception of Nonliability of Individuals or Other Entities Who Engage the Services of an Independent Contractor, Under the Peculiar Risk Doctrine

Page 202, Column 2, first paragraph, insert following 'Property Owner'.

When the owner of land is aware of a concealed condition, in the absence of precautions and an unreasonable risk of harm to those coming in contact with it, and are aware that a person on the premises is about to come in contact with it, a jury can reasonably conclude that a failure to warn or repair the condition constitutes negligence.

In *Kinsman, et al. v. Unocal Corp.* (2005) 70 Cal. Comp. Cases 1692, the California Supreme Court addressed the issue of whether a landowner that hires an independent contractor is liable to an employee of that contractor who is injured as a result of hazardous conditions on the landowner's property. In holding that in limited situations the landowner may be liable, the high Court stated, in part:

In a series of decisions over the last dozen or so years, this court has delineated the circumstances under which the employee of an independent contractor who is injured on the job may sue the hirer of that contractor. (*Privette v. Superior Court* (1993) 5 Cal. 4th 689 [854 P.2d 721, 21 Cal. Rptr. 2d 72, 58 Cal. Comp. Cases 420] (*Privette*); *Toland v. Sunland Housing Group, Inc.* (1998) 18 Cal. 4th 253 [955 P.2d 504, 74 Cal. Rptr. 2d 878, 63 Cal. Comp. Cases 508] (*Toland*); *Camargo v. Tjaarda Dairy* (2001) 25 Cal. 4th 1235 [25 P.3d 1096, 108 Cal. Rptr. 2d 617, 66 Cal. Comp. Cases 843] (*Camargo*); *Hooker v. Department of Transportation* (2002) 27 Cal. 4th 198 [38 P.3d 1081, 115 Cal. Rptr. 2d 853, 67 Cal. Comp. Cases 19] (*Hooker*); *McKown v. Wal–Mart Stores, Inc.* (2002) 27 Cal. 4th 219 [38 P.3d 1094, 115 Cal. Rptr. 2d 868, 67 Cal. Comp. Cases 36] (*McKown*).) This case requires us to consider an issue not addressed by the previous cases: when, if ever, is a landowner that hires an independent contractor liable to an employee of that contractor who is injured as the result of hazardous conditions on the landowner's premises? Specifically, in this case we must decide whether a carpenter employed by an independent contractor that installed scaffolding for workers who replaced asbestos insulation in an oil refinery facility may sue the refinery owners for injuries caused by exposure to asbestos, when it is claimed that only the refinery owner knew the carpenter was being exposed to a hazardous substance.

We conclude that a landowner that hires an independent contractor may be liable to the contractor's employee if the following conditions are present: the landowner (Footnote 1) knew, or should have known, of a latent or concealed preexisting hazardous condition on its property, the contractor did not know and could not have reasonably discovered this hazardous condition, and the landowner failed to warn the contractor about this condition. We further conclude that under the circumstances of the present case, the jury was not sufficiently instructed that the landowner was liable in this case only for failing to warn about a *hidden* hazardous condition, and that the lack of sufficient instruction was prejudicial to defendant. We therefore reverse the jury verdict in plaintiffs' favor and remand for a new trial...

B. Landowner Liability in General and for an Independent Contractor's Employees

"[T]he basic policy of this state set forth by the Legislature in section 1714 of the Civil Code is that everyone is responsible for an injury caused to another by his want of ordinary care or skill in the management of his property...

The proper test to be applied to the liability of the possessor of land in accordance with section 1714 of the Civil Code is whether in the management of his property he has acted as a reasonable man in view of the probability of injury to others, and, although the plaintiff's status as a trespasser, licensee, or invitee may in the light of the facts giving rise to such status have some bearing on the question of liability, the status is not determinative." (*Rowland v. Christian* (1968) 69 Cal. 2d 108, 118–119 [443 P.2d 561, 70 Cal. Rptr. 97] (*Rowland*).) Applying these principles to the facts before it, in which a social guest injured his hand on a cracked water faucet, the court stated: "Where the occupier of land is aware of a concealed condition involving in the absence of precautions an unreasonable risk of harm to those coming in contact with it and is aware that a person on the premises is about to come in contact with it, the trier of fact can reasonably conclude that a failure to warn or to repair the condition constitutes negligence. Whether or not a guest has a right to expect that his host will remedy dangerous conditions on his account, he should reasonably be entitled to rely upon a warning of the dangerous condition so that he, like the host, will be in a position to take special precautions when he comes in contact with it." (*Id.* at p. 119.)

This formulation is similar to the Restatement of Torts Second, section 343, on which Kinsman in the present case partly relies. "A possessor of land is subject to liability for physical harm caused to his invitees by a condition on the land if, but only if, he [P] (a) knows or by the exercise of reasonable care would discover the condition, and should realize that it involves an unreasonable risk of harm to such invitees, and [P] (b) should expect that they will not discover or realize the danger, or will fail to protect themselves against it, and [P] (c) fails to exercise reasonable care to protect them against the danger."

"Generally, if a danger is so obvious that a person could reasonably be expected to see it, the condition itself serves as a warning, and the landowner is under no further duty to remedy or warn of the condition. [Citation] However, this is not true in all cases. '[I]t is foreseeable that even an obvious danger may cause injury, if the practical necessity of encountering the danger, when weighed against the apparent risk involved, is such that under the circumstances, a person might choose to encounter the danger.' " (*Krongos v. Pacific Gas & Electric Co.* (1992) 7 Cal. App. 4th 387, 393 [9 Cal. Rptr. 2d 124] [duty to protect against obvious electrocution hazard posed by overhead electrical wires]; see also Rest.2d Torts, § 343A [possessor of land liable for obvious danger if "the possessor should anticipate the harm despite such . . . obviousness"].)

The question before us is how these general principles apply when a landowner hires an independent contractor whose employee is injured by a hazardous condition on the premises. As we have discussed, the hirer generally delegates to the contractor responsibility for supervising the job, including responsibility for looking after employee safety. When the hirer is also a landowner, part of that delegation includes taking proper precautions to protect against obvious hazards in the workplace. There may be situations, as alluded to immediately above, in which an obvious hazard, for which no warning is necessary, nonetheless gives rise to a duty on a landowner's part to remedy the hazard because knowledge of the hazard is inadequate to prevent injury. But that is not this case, since Kinsman acknowledges that reasonable safety precautions against the hazard of asbestos were readily available, such as wearing an inexpensive respirator. Thus, when there is a known safety hazard on a hirer's premises that can be addressed through reasonable safety precautions on the part of the independent contractor, a corollary of *Privette* and its progeny is that the hirer generally delegates the responsibility to take such precautions to the contractor, and is not liable to the contractor's employee if the contractor fails to do so. We see no persuasive reason why this principle should not apply when the safety hazard is caused by a preexisting condition on the property, rather than by the method by which the work is conducted.

However, if the hazard is concealed from the contractor, but known to the landowner, the rule must be different. A landowner cannot effectively delegate to the contractor responsibility for the safety of its employees if it fails to disclose critical information needed to fulfill that responsibility, and therefore the landowner would be liable to the contractor's employee if the employee's injury is attributable to an undisclosed hazard. Nothing in the *Privette* line of cases suggests the contrary. As in *Hooker* and *McKown*, the hirer's liability in such circumstances would be derived from the hirer's rather than the contractor's negligence.

In view of the above, the usual rules about landowner liability must be modified, after *Privette*, as they apply to a hirer's duty to the employees of independent contractors. As noted, the Restatement Second of Torts, section 343, states that the landowner's duty is triggered when it "(a) knows or by the exercise of reasonable care would discover the condition, and should realize that it involves an unreasonable risk of harm to such invitees, and [P] (b) should expect that they will not discover or realize the danger, *or will fail to protect themselves against it.*" (Italics added.) In light of the delegation doctrine reaffirmed by *Privette*, the italicized phrase does not seem applicable to landowner liability for injuries to employees of independent contractors. Because the landowner/hirer delegates the responsibility of employee safety to the contractor, the teaching of the *Privette* line of cases is that a hirer has no duty to act to protect the employee when the contractor fails in that task and therefore no liability; such liability would essentially be derivative and vicarious. (See *Toland, supra,* 18 Cal. 4th at pp. 268–270 [no duty to supervise work based on the hirer's "superior knowledge" of the proper safety precautions].) (Footnote 2)

But when the landowner knows or should know of a concealed hazard on its premises, then under ordinary premises liability principles, the landowner may be liable for a resultant injury to those employees.

We therefore disagree with the Court of Appeal in the present case inasmuch as it holds that a landowner/hirer can be liable to a contractor's employee only when it has retained supervisory control and affirmatively contributes to the employee's injury in the exercise of that control. Rather, consistent with the above discussion, the hirer as landowner may be independently liable to the contractor's employee, even if it does not retain control over the work, if (1) it knows or reasonably should know of a concealed, pre–existing hazardous condition on its premises; (2) the contractor does not know and could not reasonably ascertain the condition; and (3) the landowner fails to warn the contractor. (Footnote 3)

The rule that landowners may be liable to contractors' employees for injuries resulting from latent hazardous conditions was followed in our pre–*Privette* cases. In *Markley v. Beagle* (1967) 66 Cal. 2d 951 [59 Cal. Rptr. 809, 429 P.2d 129], for example, the employee of an independent contractor, en route to repair a ventilation fan on the hirer's roof, was injured when a mezzanine railing inside the building gave way. (*Id.* at p. 955.) As the court stated:

"Plaintiff was an employee of an independent contractor engaged by the tenant who operated the restaurant to service the ventilating system. He was therefore a business invitee of the owners to whom they owed a duty of reasonable care. They knew or should have known that he would use the mezzanine to get to the fan on the roof, and the jury could reasonably conclude that . . . the owners were negligent in failing to discover the dangerous condition of the railing and to either correct it or adequately warn plaintiff of it." (*Id.* at pp. 955–956.) Nothing in the *Privette* line of cases suggests that *Markley* is no longer good law.

Abrons v. Richfield Oil Corp. (1961) 190 Cal. App. 2d 640 [12 Cal. Rptr. 271], cited by Unocal, is not to the contrary. In *Abrons*, the employee of an independent contractor was injured when an oil–saturated ditch on the property of the hirer, the Richfield Oil Corporation, caved in. The Court of Appeal affirmed the nonsuit judgment against the employee, stating: " 'The Richfield employees exercised no supervision or control of the [contractor's] employees in the course of the latter's work . . . .' . . . The appellant observed that the ground that was being excavated was 'oil saturated.' His testimony, as set forth in the settled statement, was that the 'deeper he dug the more oil saturation manifested itself and there was an oily odor within the excavation.' Braun furnished no shoring materials. No one 'from the Richfield Oil Corporation was present at any time and no one from Richfield observed the work or assisted in any way.' " (*Id.* at p. 646.) Although the *Abrons* court focused on the hirer's lack of supervision and control, the fact that is most telling from the perspective of the present issue is that the hazard in question, the oil–saturated ground, although perhaps initially concealed, soon became apparent, and the contractor nonetheless failed to take appropriate safety precautions. (Footnote 4)

Another case cited by Unocal, *Grahn v. Tosco Corp.* (1997) 58 Cal. App. 4th 1373 [68 Cal. Rptr. 2d 806, 62 Cal. Comp. Cases 1546] (*Grahn*), decided after *Privette* but before *Toland* and the other cases, resembles the present case factually and merits discussion. The employee of an independent contractor contracted asbestos–related lung disease from removing and installing insulation on defendant's jobsite in the 1970's. The plaintiff proceeded on three theories, negligent hiring, retained control, and premises liability. (Footnote 5)

As to the latter theory, the Court of Appeal held that the general negligence instruction given to the jury was prejudicially misleading. "While a hirer has a duty to maintain its premises in a reasonably safe condition for employees of an independent contractor, not every dangerous condition on the hirer's premises subjects the hirer to liability for physical harm to the independent contractor's employees. Where the operative details of the work are not under the control of the hirer and the dangerous condition causing injury is either created by the independent contractor or is, at least in part, the object of the work of the independent contractor, the duty to protect the independent contractor's employees from hazards resides with the independent contractor and not the hirer who may also generally control the premises." (*Grahn, supra,* 58 Cal. App. 4th at p. 1398.)

We find the above formulation somewhat confusing and only partly correct. It is not clear, in the context of premises liability, what it means to say that "[w]here . . . the dangerous condition causing injury is either created by the independent contractor or is, at least in part, *the object of the work of the independent contractor*, the duty to protect the independent contractor's employees from hazards resides with the independent contractor and not the hirer who may also generally control the premises." (*Grahn, supra,* 58 Cal. App. 4th at p. 1398, italics added.) If the employee of an independent contractor as part of his job, for example, burrows into ground belonging to the landowner/hirer, and is injured when he ruptures an underground storage tank containing a hazardous substance that the landowner knew was present but the contractor did not, the dangerous condition causing the injury was arguably "the object of the work of the independent contractor." (*Ibid.*) But that fact should not preclude landowner liability. What is critical in the above hypothetical is that if the landowner knew or should have known of the hazard and the contractor did not know and could not have reasonably discovered it, then the landowner delegated the responsibility for employee safety to the contractor without informing the contractor of critical information that would allow the contractor to fulfill its responsibility. Under such circumstances the landowner may be liable. Nor would it matter, as Unocal argues, that the substance was not hazardous until the employee performed a certain action that released the hazard. The landowner may be liable for any injury from a latent hazard that a contractor's employee would foreseeably encounter. (See *Rowland, supra,* 69 Cal. 2d at p. 119.)

But *Grahn*'s statement regarding the hirer's nonliability for hazards on the premises related to "the object of the work of the independent contractor" (*Grahn, supra,* 58 Cal. App. 4th at p. 1398) does point to an important limitation on a landowner's duty toward the contractor's employees. A landowner's duty generally includes a duty to inspect for concealed hazards. (See *Ortega v. Kmart Corp.* (2001) 26 Cal. 4th 1200, 1205 [36 P.3d 11, 114 Cal. Rptr. 2d 470].) But the responsibility for job safety delegated to independent contractors may and generally does include explicitly or implicitly a limited duty to inspect the premises as well. Therefore, the principles enunciated in *Privette* suggest that the landowner would not be liable when the contractor has failed to engage in inspections of the premises implicitly or explicitly delegated to it. Thus, for example, an employee of a roofing contractor sent to repair a defective roof would generally not be able to sue the hirer if injured when he fell through the same roof due to a structural defect, inasmuch as inspection for such defects could reasonably be implied to be within the scope of the contractor's employment. On the other hand, if the same employee fell from a ladder because the wall on which the ladder was propped collapsed, assuming that this defect was not related to the roof under repair, the employee may be able to sustain a suit against the hirer. Put in other terms, the contractor was not being paid to inspect the premises generally, and therefore the duty of general inspection could not be said to have been delegated to it. Under those circumstances, the landowner's failure to reasonably inspect the premises, when a hidden hazard leads directly to the employee's injury, may well result in liability... .

Footnote 1. Although the term "landowner" is used throughout this opinion, and the land in question was owned by defendant Unocal Corporation, that term is used to refer to either an owner or a possessor of land that owes some kind of duty of care to keep the premises safe. (See *Alcaraz v. Vece* (1997) 14 Cal. 4th 1149, 1155–1156 [929 P.2d 1239, 60 Cal. Rptr. 2d 448].)

Footnote 2. The rule articulated above concerns specifically an employee's injury while at work on the landowner's premises. This case does not present the question of landowner liability when the employee is on the premises but not working, as when, for example, the employee is on a part of the premises other than the jobsite.

Footnote 3. We emphasize that the proposed holding would not apply to a hazard created by the independent contractor itself, of which that contractor necessarily is or should be aware. (See *Zamudio v. City and County of San Francisco* (1999) 70 Cal. App. 4th 445, 455 [82 Cal. Rptr. 2d 664, 64 Cal. Comp. Cases 230].)

Footnote 4. Other jurisdictions have taken a variety of approaches to the issue of landowner liability to employees of independent contractors, and no single approach has emerged as dominant. In some cases, there are no special rules for liability toward contractor's employees, and general negligence rules are applied. (Roberts v. Owens–Corning Fiberglas Corp. (La.Ct.App. 2004) 878 So. 2d 631, 639, fn. 5.) Some have not rejected the peculiar risk doctrine in this context and/or have embraced the "superior knowledge" doctrine advocated by the Toland concurring and dissenting opinion discussed below. (PSI Energy, Inc. v. Roberts (Ind. 2005) 829 N.E.2d 943; Gutteridge v. A.P. Green Services, Inc. (Pa.Super.Ct. 2002) 2002 Pa. Super. 198 [804 A.2d 643, 656–658].) Other courts have endorsed rules similar to the one formulated in this opinion. (Jablonski v. Fulton Corners, Inc. (N.Y.Civ.Ct. 2002) 193 Misc. 2d 135 [748 N.Y.S.2d 634, 638] [landowner liability for defects on premises of which it had actual or constructive notice]; Plock v. Crossroads Joint Venture (Neb. 1991) 475 N.W.2d 105, 118–119 [239 Neb. 211] [employer–landowner liable to contractor's employees for latent defects known to employer but not to contractor]; Glenn v. United States Steel Corp., Inc. (Ala. 1982)) 423 So. 2d 152, 154 [employer not liable for defects that the contractor reasonably should have been aware of].) Other courts allow for recovery only on the theory that the employer has actively retained control of the jobsite and the contractor's work. (Callahan v. Alumax Foils, Inc. (Mo.Ct.App. 1998) 973 S.W.2d 488, 490; Fisher v. Lee and Chang Partnership (Tex.App. 2000) 16 S.W.3d 198, 200–201 [under Texas statute, retained control and knowledge of latent defect required for premises liability toward the contractor's employee].) In at least one jurisdiction, the landowner is not liable for injuries occurring on the premises where it has temporarily surrendered possession and control of those premises to the contractor. (West v. Briggs & Stratton Corp. (Ga.Ct.App. 2000) 244 Ga. App. 840 [536 S.E.2d 828, 832].) In other cases, the rule is not so clear. (See Jones v. James Reeves Contractors, Inc. (Miss. 1997) 701 So. 2d 774, 782–783 [stating a rule of employer liability based on actual control of contract's work, but suggesting there may be liability for latent defects].)

Another case cited by Unocal, *Grahn v. Tosco Corp.* (1997) 58 Cal. App. 4th 1373 [68 Cal. Rptr. 2d 806, 62 Cal. Comp. Cases 1546] (*Grahn*), decided after *Privette* but before *Toland* and the other cases, resembles the present case factually and merits discussion. The employee of an independent contractor contracted asbestos–related lung disease from removing and installing insulation on defendant's jobsite in the 1970's. The plaintiff proceeded on three theories, negligent hiring, retained control, and premises liability. (Footnote 5)

As to the latter theory, the Court of Appeal held that the general negligence instruction given to the jury was prejudicially misleading. "While a hirer has a duty to maintain its premises in a reasonably safe condition for employees of an independent contractor, not every dangerous condition on the hirer's premises subjects the hirer to liability for physical harm to the independent contractor's employees. Where the operative details of the work are not under the control of the hirer and the dangerous condition causing injury is either created by the independent contractor or is, at least in part, the object of the work of the independent contractor, the duty to protect the independent contractor's employees from hazards resides with the independent contractor and not the hirer who may also generally control the premises." (*Grahn, supra*, 58 Cal. App. 4th at p. 1398.)

We find the above formulation somewhat confusing and only partly correct. It is not clear, in the context of premises liability, what it means to say that "[w]here . . . the dangerous condition causing injury is either created by the independent contractor or is, at least in part, *the object of the work of the independent contractor*, the duty to protect the independent contractor's employees from hazards resides with the independent contractor and not the hirer who may also generally control the premises." (*Grahn, supra*, 58 Cal. App. 4th at p. 1398, italics added.) If the employee of an independent contractor as part of his job, for example, burrows into ground belonging to the landowner/hirer, and is injured when he ruptures an underground storage tank containing a hazardous substance that the landowner knew was present but the contractor did not, the dangerous condition causing the injury was arguably "the object of the work of the independent contractor." (*Ibid.*) But that fact should not preclude landowner liability. What is critical in the above hypothetical is that if the landowner knew or should have known of the hazard and the contractor did not know and could not have reasonably discovered it, then the landowner delegated the responsibility for employee safety to the contractor without informing the contractor of critical information that would allow the contractor to fulfill its responsibility. Under such circumstances the landowner may be liable. Nor would it matter, as Unocal argues, that the substance was not hazardous until the employee performed a certain action that released the hazard. The landowner may be liable for any injury from a latent hazard that a contractor's employee would foreseeably encounter. (See *Rowland, supra*, 69 Cal. 2d at p. 119.)... .

Footnote 5. *Grahn*'s treatment of the first two theories was disapproved of in *Camargo, supra*, 25 Cal. 4th at page 1245 and *Hooker, supra*, 27 Cal. 4th at page 214.

In concluding that the *Privette* Doctrine governs even when an injured plaintiff is not an employee of a contractor but an independent contractor of the contractor, the Court of Appeal, Second District, in *David Michael v. Denbeste Transportation, Inc.* (2006) 71 Cal. Comp. Cases 378, stated, in part:

In this work site accident case, plaintiff David Michael, a truck driver hauling hazardous waste, appeals from a summary judgment in favor of defendants Denbeste Transportation, Inc. (a hazardous waste hauler subcontractor and Michael's hirer), Chemical Waste Management, Inc. (CWM) (a hazardous waste handler and Denbeste's hirer), Aman Environmental Construction, Inc. (Aman) (the general contractor for the demolition work on the site and CWM's hirer), and Secor International, Inc. (a consultant hired by the owner of the site, but not the hirer of Michael or the other defendants).

In a line of cases from *Privette v. Superior Court* (1993) 5 Cal. 4th 689 [854 P.2d 721, 21 Cal. Rptr. 2d 72, 58 Cal. Comp. Cases 420] (*Privette*) to *Kinsman v. Unocal Corp.* (2005) 37 Cal. 4th 659 [123 P.3d 931, 36 Cal. Rptr. 3d 495, 70 Cal. Comp. Cases 1692] (*Kinsman*), our Supreme Court, in a body of law known as the *Privette* doctrine, has defined the circumstances under which an injured worker who is an employee of an independent contractor may sue the hirer of that contractor. This case presents the first impression issue of whether the *Privette* doctrine applies where the injured plaintiff is not an employee, but an independent contractor, of that contractor. We conclude that the *Privette* doctrine governs because its policies and rationale are applicable here. Accordingly, we affirm the summary judgment in favor of Aman, CWM, and Secor on the ground that they owed no duty to plaintiff as a matter of law under the *Privette* doctrine. In the unpublished portion of our opinion, we conclude that Denbeste is not entitled to summary judgment because of triable issues of fact as to whether Michael was Denbeste's employee or an independent contractor...

Assuming for purposes of analyzing the liability of Aman and CWM that Michael is an independent contractor rather than an employee with respect to Denbeste, (Footnote 5) we conclude that the *Privette* doctrine governs nevertheless. Applying the *Privette* doctrine's limitations on liability here is consistent with common law principles and public policy elucidated in *Kinsman*, including the strong policy in favor of delegation by hirers. Further, notwithstanding the exclusion of independent contractors from the mandatory workers' compensation system (*Torres v. Reardon, supra*, 3 Cal. App. 4th at p. 840), any lack of insurance coverage for Michael's injuries is not dispositive in determining application of the *Privette* doctrine. (See *Lopez v. C.G.M. Development, Inc.* (2002) 101 Cal. App. 4th 430, 444–445 [124 Cal. Rptr. 2d 227, 67 Cal. Comp. Cases 1023] (*Lopez*) [hirer of contractor not liable to injured employee of contractor under *Privette* doctrine notwithstanding failure of contractor to obtain workers' compensation insurance for its employees].)

As *Privette* explained: "At common law, a person who hired an independent contractor generally was not liable to third parties for injuries caused by the contractor's negligence in performing the work. [Citations.] Central to this rule of nonliability was the recognition that a person who hired an independent contractor had ' "no right of control as to the mode of doing the work contracted for." ' [Citations.] The reasoning was that the work performed was the enterprise of the contractor, who, as a matter of business convenience, would be better able than the person employing the contractor to absorb accident losses incurred in the course of the contracted work. This could be done, for instance, by indirectly including the cost of safety precautions and insurance coverage in the contract price." (*Privette, supra*, 5 Cal. 4th at p. 693.) Accordingly, "at common law, it was regarded as the norm that when a hirer delegated a task to an independent contractor, it in effect delegated responsibility for performing that task safely, and assignment of liability to the contractor followed that delegation." (*Kinsman, supra*, 37 Cal. 4th at p. 671.)

Michael does not contend that the duties of Aman and CWM with respect to the work site were nondelegable. Even if the duties were nondelegable, the court in *Park v. Burlington Northern Santa Fe Railway Co.* (2003) 108 Cal. App. 4th 595 [133 Cal. Rptr. 2d 757, 68 Cal. Comp. Cases 730] (*Park*) held that the *Privette* doctrine governed the issue of the liability of a generator of hazardous waste. "[A]lthough the duties imposed on the generator of hazardous waste by statute and regulation are nondelegable duties that survive *Privette*, the generator is not liable to the employee of a subcontractor who is employed to dispose of the hazardous waste unless it is shown that the generator's conduct affirmatively contributed to the employee's injuries." (*Park, supra*, 108 Cal. App. 4th at p. 610.) The court in *Park* concluded that the plaintiff did not show that any direct negligence of the generator caused his injuries or that the generator did anything which affirmatively contributed to his injuries. (*Id.* at p. 614.) And the court in *Sheeler v. Greystone Homes, Inc.* (2003) 113 Cal. App. 4th 908 [6 Cal. Rptr. 3d 683, 68 Cal. Comp. Cases 1810] stated that "the nondelegable duty rule is incompatible with the limitations on hirer liability established in *Privette* and subsequent cases." (*Sheeler v. Greystone Homes, Inc., supra*, 113 Cal. App. 4th at p. 922.)

The policy in favor of a hirer's delegation of responsibility is consistent with the policy underlying the workers' compensation laws. " 'The fundamental policy underlying the workers' compensation laws is that those hiring others to perform services should bear the risk of injuries incurred in the undertakings. When the person seeks to hire the services through a licensed independent contractor, it is *reasonable to anticipate* that the independent contractor will insure against the risk and that the cost of the insurance will be passed on as part of the price of the contract. Thus it is *reasonable to exonerate* the hirer of the independent contractor.' " (*Lopez, supra*, 101 Cal. App. 4th at p. 445.)

Under the SSP, Aman and CWM had delegated to Denbeste safety responsibilities with respect to Denbeste's "personnel." Thus, when Aman and CWM hired Denbeste, the former could reasonably anticipate that Denbeste would insure against the risk of injuries incurred in Denbeste's work. And if Aman and CWM had no duty to ascertain whether Denbeste had complied with its obligation to obtain workers' compensation insurance for its employees (*Lopez, supra*, 101 Cal. App. 4th at p. 445), they likewise should

have no duty to inquire into whether Michael was an employee or an independent contractor with respect to Denbeste. As noted, at the Filtrol site, Denbeste had employees (who were provided workers' compensation insurance) performing the same tasks as Michael.

As recognized by the trial court, in delegating responsibility for employee safety to their subcontractors, Aman and CWM "had a right to anticipate that [their] liability would not depend upon whether individuals hired by subcontractors (such as Denbeste)" were employees or independent contractors, and there is no reason why Aman and CWM "should be held to any greater liability because plaintiff is an independent contractor than it would if he were Denbeste's employee." (Footnote 6)

Michael does not identify any public policy reason why Aman's and CWM's responsibilities to him (as an independent contractor) should be greater than their responsibilities to other workers who are Denbeste's employees. Without the limitations of the *Privette* line of cases, Michael would have greater rights than a Denbeste employee. And those rights would be in derogation of the common law principle that hirers (Aman and CWM) delegating a task to an independent contractor (Denbeste) reasonably expect that in delegating such responsibility, the hirers have also assigned liability for the safety of workers engaged by that independent contractor. (See *Kinsman, supra*, 37 Cal. 4th at p. 671.) For the foregoing reasons, we conclude that the *Privette* doctrine applies to Aman and CWM.

2. No Liability Under Privette Doctrine

Under the two prongs of the *Privette* doctrine, as stated in *Kinsman* (the first prong being the concealed hazard theory and the second prong being the retained control theory), we conclude that Aman and CWM are not liable to Michael as a matter of law. Assuming that the lack of tarp racks or other fall protection can be considered a concealed hazardous condition, it reasonably cannot be maintained that the contractor (whether Denbeste or Michael) did not know and could not reasonably ascertain the condition... .

Footnote 5. The trial court noted that the parties disputed whether Michael was Denbeste's employee or an independent contractor and assumed for the sake of argument that Michael was an independent contractor. "The question of whether one engaged to perform services for another is an employee or an independent contractor is ordinarily a question of fact. However, if only one inference may be drawn from all the facts, the question is one of law." (*Torres v. Reardon* (1992) 3 Cal. App. 4th 831, 838 [5 Cal. Rptr. 2d 52].) The principal test of an employment relationship is whether the employer has the right to control the manner and means of accomplishing the result desired. (*Id.* at p. 837.) In addition, the test involves a consideration of several "secondary criteria," including whether the worker is engaged in a distinct occupation or an independently established business, whether the worker or the principal supplies the tools or instrumentalities, the method of payment, whether the work is part of the regular business of the principal, whether the worker has a substantial investment in the business other than personal services, and whether the worker hires employees to assist him. (*Ibid.*)

Although Denbeste argued in its motion for summary judgment that Michael was an independent contractor as a matter of law, the trial court declined to reach such a conclusion and assumed, without deciding, that Michael was an independent contractor.

Footnote 6. Although not discussed by the parties, Michael was not a "stranger to the work" as that term is defined in law, notwithstanding his assumed status as an independent contractor. (*Kinney v. CSB Construction, Inc.* (2001) 87 Cal. App. 4th 28, 38 [103 Cal. Rptr. 2d 594, 66 Cal. Comp. Cases 28] (*Kinney*).) Neighbors, bypassers, and visitors to the work site are considered to be "strangers to the work. "Such strangers to the work appear to fall squarely within the original rationale for the 'retained control' doctrine: they have no assured remedy from any other source; if the subcontractor is primarily responsible, the hirer is entitled to equitable indemnity; it is fair to shift the burden of the injury from the innocent stranger to the beneficiary of the work; and the imposition of liability encourages the hirer to exercise the retained control so as to make the operation safe for third parties." (*Kinney, supra*, 87 Cal. App. 4th at pp. 38–39.)

§ 5.8(A)(5)   Contractors' State License Board

Page 228, Column 2, tenth paragraph, insert following '…714–994–7450.'

Effective January 1, 2007, the Legislature amended Section 7125 of the Business and Professions Code to provide:

(a) Except as provided in subdivision (b), the board shall require as a condition precedent to the issuance, reinstatement, reactivation, renewal, or continued maintenance of a license, that the applicant or licensee have on file at all times a current and valid Certificate of Workers' Compensation Insurance or Certification of Self–Insurance. A Certificate of Workers' Compensation Insurance shall be issued and filed, electronically or otherwise, by one or more insurers duly licensed to write workers' compensation insurance in this state. A Certification of Self–Insurance shall be issued and filed by the Director of Industrial Relations. If reciprocity conditions exist, as defined in Section 3600.5 of the Labor Code, the registrar shall require the information deemed necessary to assure compliance with this section.

(b) This section does not apply to an applicant or licensee who meets both of the following conditions:

(1) Has no employees provided that he or she files a statement with the board on a form prescribed by the registrar prior to the issuance, reinstatement, reactivation, or continued maintenance of a license, certifying that he or she does not employ

any person in any manner so as to become subject to the workers' compensation laws of California or is not otherwise required to provide for workers' compensation insurance coverage under California law.

(2) Does not hold a C–39 license, as defined in Section 832.39 of Title 16 of the California Code of Regulations.

(c) No Certificate of Workers' Compensation Insurance, Certification of Self–Insurance, or exemption–certificate is required of a holder of a license that has been inactivated on the official records of the board during the period the license is inactive.

(d) The insurer, including the State Compensation Insurance Fund, shall report to the registrar the following information for any policy required under this section: name, license number, policy number, dates that coverage is scheduled to commence and lapse, and cancellation date if applicable.

(e) For any license that, on January 1, 2007, is active and includes a C–39 classification in addition to any other classification, the registrar shall, in lieu of the automatic license suspension otherwise required under this article, remove the C–39 classification from the license unless a valid Certificate of Workers' Compensation Insurance or Certification of Self–Insurance is received by the registrar prior to the operative date of this section.

(f) This section shall remain in effect only until January 1, 2011, and as of that date is repealed, unless a later enacted statute, that is enacted before January 1, 2011, deletes or extends that date.

The Legislature also amended, effective January 1, 2007, Business and Professions Code section 7125, to require the Registrar of Contractors in lieu of automatic license suspension to remove the C–39 roofing classification from any active contractor's license, even if the contractor has no employees, unless a valid Certificate of Workers' Compensation Insurance or Certificate of Self–Insurance is received by the Registrar of Contractors prior to January 1, 2007.

SEC 2. Section 7125 was added to become effective January 1, 2011 to provide:
7125.

(a) The board shall require as a condition precedent to the issuance, reinstatement, reactivation, renewal, or continued maintenance of a license, that the applicant or licensee have on file at all times a current and valid Certificate of Workers' Compensation Insurance or Certification of Self–Insurance. A Certificate of Workers' Compensation Insurance shall be issued and filed, electronically or otherwise, by one or more insurers duly licensed to write workers' compensation insurance in this state. A Certification of Self–Insurance shall be issued and filed by the Director of Industrial Relations. If reciprocity conditions exist, as defined in Section 3600.5 of the Labor Code, the registrar shall require the information deemed

(b) This section does not apply to an applicant or licensee who has no employees provided that he or she files a statement with the board on a form prescribed by the registrar prior to the issuance, reinstatement, reactivation, or continued maintenance of a license, certifying that he or she does not employ any person in any manner so as to become subject to the workers' compensation laws of California or is not otherwise required to provide for workers' compensation insurance coverage under California law.

(c) No Certificate of Workers' Compensation Insurance, Certification of Self–Insurance, or exemption–certificate is required of a holder of a license that has been inactivated on the official records of the board during the period the license is inactive.

(d) The insurer, including the State Compensation Insurance Fund, shall report to the registrar the following information for any policy required under this section: name, license number, policy number, dates that coverage is scheduled to commence and lapse, and cancellation date, if applicable.

(e) This section shall become operative on January 1, 2011.

Further, Section 11665 was added to the Insurance Code to provide:

(a) An insurer who issues a workers' compensation insurance policy to a roofing contractor holding a C–39 license from the Contractors State License Board shall perform an annual payroll audit for the contractor. The insurer may impose a surcharge on each policyholder audited under this subdivision in an amount necessary to recoup the reasonable costs of conducting the annual payroll audits.

(b) The commissioner shall direct the rating organization designated as his or her statistical agent to compile pertinent statistical data on those holding C–39 licenses, as reported by the appropriate state entity, on an annual basis and provide a report to him or her each year. The data shall track the total annual payroll and loss data reported on those holding C–39 licenses in accordance with the standard workers' compensation insurance classifications applicable to roofing operations. The first report shall be filed no later than March 1, 2008, and shall cover the data compiled for the 2005 calendar year.

(c) This section shall become operative on January 1, 2007, and shall remain in effect only until January 1, 2011, and as of that date is repealed, unless a later enacted statute, that is enacted before January 1, 2011, deletes or extends that date.

§ 5.8(D) Casual Workers Employed by Owners or Occupants of Residential Dwellings

Page 231, Column 1, first paragraph, insert following '…prior employment.'

In an unpublished decision, the Court of Appeal, Fifth District, in *Covarrubias v. WCAB* (2006) 71 Cal. Comp. Cases 585, held that the term *"employer"* in Section 3351 does not require the owner to be both an *owner* and an *occupant*. The Court stated, in part:

Ordinarily, when an employee sustains a worksite injury his exclusive remedy against his employer is provided by the workers' compensation law, and the employer is immune from a suit for damages. (§§ 3600, 3601, 3602, subd. (a).) But when the employer has not secured workers' compensation coverage or its equivalent, an injured employee may bring a civil suit against his employer. (§ 3706; Huffman v. City of Poway (2000) 84 Cal. App. 4th 975, 982–987 [101 Cal. Rptr. 2d 325, 65 Cal. Comp. Cas 1280].) If the employee establishes that he was injured in the course and scope of his employment, there is a rebuttable presumption that an uninsured employer was negligent and the employer is precluded from claiming comparative fault or assumption of risk as a defense. (§ 3708; Huang v. L.A. Haute (2003) 106 Cal. App. 4th 284, 289–291 [130 Cal. Rptr. 2d 619, 68 Cal. Comp. Cas 188].)

The key here is whether Covarrubias could show the existence of a material question of fact as to whether the statutory rebuttable presumption should apply in this case. In relevant part, section 3708 provides that its presumption "shall not apply to any employer of an employee, as defined in subdivision (d) of section 3351 . . . ." Section 3351, subdivision (d) is a classification of "any person employed by the owner or occupant of a residential dwelling whose duties are incidental to the ownership, maintenance, or use of the dwelling, including the care and supervision of children, or whose duties are personal and not in the course of the trade, business, profession, or occupation of the owner . . . ." (Italics added.) Subdivision (d) "includes in its definition of an employee persons who are hired to make repairs on a residence" (Cedillo v. Workers' Comp. Appeals Bd. (2003) 106 Cal. App. 4th 227, 235 [30 Cal. Rptr. 2d 581, 68 Cal. Comp. Cas 140]) and is "sufficiently broad as to encompass most situations where a homeowner or renter hires a plumber or carpenter to make repairs." (State Compensation Ins. Fund v. Workers' Comp. Appeals Bd. (1985) 40 Cal. 3d 5, 14 [706 P.2d 1146, 219 Cal. Rptr. 13, 50 Cal. Comp. Cas 562].) Covarrubias readily falls within the description of the class of employees who are hired to repair a residence.

Instead, Covarrubias argues that he does not fall within section 3351, subdivision (d) for a different reason. His claim is that the Hansens are not the "owner or occupant of a residential dwelling," and his employment by them takes him out of the scope of the statute. He premises his argument on a construction of the statute that requires an employer who is an "owner or occupant of a residential d0welling" to be an employer who is both an owner and also an occupant of the residence.

The argument fails as it rests upon a premise that the Legislature did not mean what it said when it chose to define an "employee" as any person employed by an "owner or occupant." (§ 3351, subd. (d), italics added.) In interpreting a statute, " ' "[t]he court turns first to the words themselves for the answer." [Citation.] We are required to give effect to statutes "according to the usual, ordinary import of the language employed in framing them." [Citations.] "If possible, significance should be given to every word, phrase, sentence and part of an act in pursuance of the legislative purpose." [Citation.] "[A] construction making some words surplusage is to be avoided." [Citation.]' [Citation.]" (Woosley v. State of California (1992) 3 Cal. 4th 758, 775–776 [838 P.2d 758, 13 Cal. Rptr. 2d 30], final brackets added; Ruoff v. Harbor Creek Community Assn. (1992) 10 Cal. App. 4th 1624, 1629 [13 Cal. Rptr. 2d 755].) By limiting its scope to owners who live on the property, a distinction the Legislature could have drawn but did not, Covarrubias's proposal would render the disjunctive "or occupant" entirely redundant. We will not ascribe such a tortuous meaning to the Legislature's plain language. The word "or" as employed in the statute means "in the alternative."

In light of this language, it is not surprising that, as Covarrubias acknowledges, there are no reported cases supporting his position that "owner" excludes owners who are not also occupants. The cases Covarrubias cites are inapposite, as none of them address this issue. And, while Covarrubias maintains that his statutory interpretation is congruent with the purpose of the workers' compensation statutes and the liberal construction accorded them (see § 3202; State Farm Fire & Casualty Co. v. Workers' Comp. Appeals Bd., *supra*, 16 Cal. 4th at p. 1196), those principles do not permit us to find ambiguity in statutory language that is clear on its face. We conclude the subdivision extends to residence owners without regard to whether they occupy the residence. The trial court therefore correctly ruled that the presumption of negligence was not available here.

While not necessary to the resolution of this appeal, the Hansens were entitled to summary judgment for another reason as well. Section 3552, subdivision (h) excepts from section 3351, subdivision (d)'s definition of "employee" any person who was employed for less than 52 hours during the 90 calendar days immediately preceding the date of the injury or who earned less than $100 during those 90 days. It is undisputed that Covarrubias falls within this category. As he was therefore not an employee for workers' compensation purposes, his only remedy was to sue in tort for negligence without the benefit of the statutory presumption–an avenue of relief he concedes is foreclosed by his inability to establish causation. The contention is not properly before us. "[A]n argument or theory will generally not be considered if raised for the first time on appeal, unless the question is one of law to be applied to undisputed fact. Thus, possible theories not fully developed or factually presented to the trial court cannot create a 'triable issue' on appeal." (Johanson Transportation Service v. Rich Pik'd Rite, Inc. (1985) 164 Cal. App. 3d 583, 588 [210 Cal. Rptr. 433]; Zimmerman, Rosenfeld, Gersh & Leeds v. Larson (2005) 131 Cal. App. 4th 1466, 1488 [33 Cal. Rptr. 3d 111].) Although Covarrubias claims he raised this theory below, he did not; the factual points he now claims to have raised in support, e.g., that the Hansens lived in Hawaii and rented out the Burlingame residence through a property manager, were in fact broached only in relation to his claim that the Hansens were not "owners" because they did not live in the house. Furthermore, this does not appear to be a question of law that can be decided based only on the few undisputed facts in the record. (See, e.g., Stewart v. Workers' Comp. Appeals Bd., *supra*, 172 Cal. App. 3d at pp. 354–355 [ownership and rental of a house for purposes of supplemental income held not a trade or business under the circumstances].) Covarrubias therefore waived this contention by failing to raise it in the trial court... .

Page 231, Column 1, fifth paragraph, insert following '...such employee.'

In explaining that employees of insured homeowners are covered under Section 3351(d) if not exempted under 3715(b), unless the homeowner is uninsured, the Court of Appeal, First District, in annulling the Appeals Board's Significant Board Decision in *California State Automobile Association Inter–Insurance Bureau v. WCAB* (2006) 71 Cal. Comp. Cases 347, stated:

The Workers' Compensation Appeals Board (Appeals Board) determined Paul Hestehauge was an employee of homeowners Wayne and Laurie Charkins for purposes of awarding workers' compensation benefits. The Charkinses' insurer, California State Automobile Association Inter–Insurance Bureau (CSAA), filed a petition for writ of review in this court challenging the Appeals Board's determination. Neither Hestehauge nor the Appeals Board answered the petition. We granted the petition and issued a writ of review. We conclude Hestehauge was not an employee of the Charkinses.

BACKGROUND

The Charkinses hired Hestehauge to paint the living room, dining room, and possibly the kitchen of their home. Their agreement was informal–nothing was put into writing. Hestehauge was visiting from his native Australia, and the Charkinses had met him through a mutual friend. Hestehauge was an experienced house painter, but he did not have a California contractor's license.

On Hestehauge's first day painting at the Charkinses' home, he fell from a ladder placed on top of a scaffold. He suffered serious injuries.

Hestehauge applied for workers' compensation benefits. He also filed a civil suit against the Charkinses. In the workers' compensation proceedings, a workers' compensation judge (WCJ) held a hearing on the threshold issue of whether Hestehauge was an employee of the Charkinses. The WCJ found he was. The Appeals Board granted a petition for reconsideration filed by CSAA, but then took nearly two years to issue a decision. Ultimately, the Appeals Board upheld the WCJ's decision.

DISCUSSION

"The operation of the workers' compensation law is predicated on the existence of an employer–employee relationship." (Hanna, Cal. Law of Employee Injuries and Workers' Comp. (Rev. 2d ed. 2005) § 3.01, p. 3–10; see Lab. Code, § 3600, subd. (a).) (Footnote 1)

Whether an employment relationship exists generally turns on the workers' compensation definition of "employee." (In–Home Supportive Services v. Workers' Comp. Appeals Bd. (1984) 152 Cal. App. 3d 720, 727 [199 Cal. Rptr. 697, 49 Cal. Comp. Cas 177] (In–Home).) The definition of employee is found in part 1, chapter 2, article 2 of the workers' compensation law (§§ 3350–3371, entitled "Employees"), with the primary inclusive and exclusive provisions contained in sections 3351 and 3352. (In–Home, at p. 727; see also State Farm Fire & Casualty Co. v. Workers' Comp. Appeals Bd. (1997) 16 Cal. 4th 1187, 1203 [947 P.2d 795, 69 Cal. Rptr. 2d 602, 62 Cal. Comp. Cas 1629] (State Farm) (dis. opn. of Werdegar, J. [sections 3351 and 3352 together set out the categories of employment relationship that do and do not bring a worker within the scope of the workers' compensation law].)

Included in the definition of employee are persons we will refer to as "residential employees." Residential employees are persons hired by the owner or occupant of a residential dwelling to maintain the dwelling or to provide personal services. (§ 3351, subd. (d).) (Footnote 2)

But the person must work at least 52 hours and earn at least $100 during the 90 days preceding the date of injury to be considered an employee. (§ 3352, subd. (h)). (Footnote 3)

Persons who do not meet this test are excluded from workers' compensation coverage. (See State Compensation Ins. Fund v. Workers' Comp. Appeals Bd. (1985) 40 Cal. 3d 5, 14 [706 P.2d 1146, 219 Cal. Rptr. 13, 50 Cal. Comp. Cas 562] [subd. (h) excludes from coverage as an employee the plumber or carpenter licensed or not who worked less than 52 hours at the residence]; Cedillo v. Workers' Comp. Appeals Bd. (2003) 106 Cal. App. 4th 227, 235 [130 Cal. Rptr. 2d 581, 68 Cal. Comp. Cas 140] [unlicensed roofer who had worked less than 52 hours and earned less than $100 was not an employee of homeowner].)

The Appeals Board concluded Hestehauge did not have the requisite earnings or hours to qualify as an employee under sections 3351, subdivision (d), and 3352, subdivision (h). That should have been the end of the inquiry.

The Appeals Board, however, at Hestehauge's urging, discovered what it believed was an alternative definition of employee in section 3715, subdivision (b). As we shall explain, section 3715 applies only to uninsured employers. It is undisputed the Charkinses were insured under a policy issued by CSAA; therefore, section 3715, subdivision (b) does not apply here.

Section 3715 is part of the scheme for punishing uninsured employers and compensating their injured employees. (See Lab. Code, part 1, ch. 4, art. 2, §§ 3710–3732, entitled "Uninsured Employers Fund.") The consequences for an employer who fails to insure are severe. (See Hanna, Cal. Law of Employee Injuries and Workers' Comp., *supra*, § 2.17, pp. 2.38–2.40.) Among the sanctions is the loss of immunity from tort liability. (§ 3706.) Section 3715 permits an employee "whose employer has failed to secure the payment of compensation" to apply for workers' compensation benefits in addition to filing a civil action. (§ 3715, subd. (a).) (Footnote 4)

Under section 3715, the Appeals Board must award benefits just as if the employer had been insured, and the employer must pay the award. (§ 3715, subds. (a) & (b).) If the uninsured employer cannot pay the award, it must be paid out of the state's Uninsured Employers Benefit Trust Fund. (§ 3716, subd. (a).)

The dual remedy provided by section 3715 applies to residential employees, albeit with different hour and dollar criteria than that found in section 3352, subdivision (h). (§ 3715, subd. (b).) (Footnote 5)

"Despite the restrictions on compensation coverage for residential workers in [section 3352, subdivision (h)], a residential worker whose employer is uninsured and whose employment meets the criteria of [section 3715, subdivision (b)] may concurrently seek workers' compensation benefits and civil damages from the employer." (1 Cal. Workers' Comp. Practice (Cont.Ed.Bar 4th ed. 2005) § 2.68(3), p. 112.) (Footnote 6)

The Appeals Board decided section 3715, subdivision (b), created an employment relationship regardless of the presence or absence of insurance. Hestehauge met test (3) in subdivision (b) because he would have earned over $100 if he had completed the painting job. Therefore, according to the Appeals Board, he was the Charkinses' employee.

The genesis of the Appeals Board's (and Hestehauge's) belief that section 3715, subdivision (b), might apply in this case is a mystery. The subdivision, in approximately its present form, was added to section 3715 in 1977 (Stats. 1977, ch. 17, § 24, p. 32), and the facts of the instant case are hardly novel. Yet the Appeals Board's decision does not cite a single instance of section 3715 being invoked as alternate ground for finding an employment relationship in an appellate decision in this state in the nearly 30 years subdivision (b) has been in effect. (Footnote 7)

Section 3715 is not even mentioned in decisions where it might have been relevant if it applied to insured homeowners. (See e.g., Cedillo v. Workers' Comp. Appeals Bd., *supra*, 106 Cal. App. 4th at pp. 234–235; Furtado v. Schriefer (1991) 228 Cal. App. 3d 1608, 1616–1617 [280 Cal. Rptr. 16, 56 Cal. Comp. Cas 266]; Stewart v. Workers' Comp. Appeals Bd. (1985) 172 Cal. App. 3d 351, 355–356 [218 Cal. Rptr. 245, 50 Cal. Comp. Cas 524]; In–Home, *supra*, 152 Cal. App. 3d 720, 741; Scott v. Workers' Comp. Appeals Bd. (1981) 122 Cal. App. 3d 979, 984–985 [176 Cal. Rptr. 267, 46 Cal. Comp. Cas 1008].)

The language of section 3715 and its placement in the part of the workers' compensation law dealing with uninsured employers leave little doubt that its application is limited to uninsured employers. Our conclusion is reinforced by the fact the Legislature requires homeowners' insurance policies to contain workers' compensation coverage (Ins. Code, § 11590), but only for residential employees as defined in subdivision (d) of section 3351. (See State Farm, *supra*, 16 Cal. 4th at p. 1197 [§ 3351, subd. (d) incorporates § 3352, subd. (h)].) It would hardly make sense to require insurers to provide coverage for residential employees, but then to leave a large number of residential employees outside the scope of that required coverage.

The Appeals Board's decision includes a lengthy discussion of the history of workers' compensation coverage for residential employees. In particular, the Appeals Board's decision relies on language in section 3715, subdivision (b), which provides: "It is the intent of the Legislature that the amendments to this section by Chapter 17 of the Statutes of 1977, make no change in the law as it applied to those types of employees covered by this subdivision prior to the effective date of Chapter 1263 of the 1975 Regular Session."

Because section 3715, on its face, does not apply to insured employers, a statement of legislative intent regarding that section would appear to have little relevance to the instant case. We will briefly comment on the statement only because the Appeals Board's decision relies so heavily upon it.

According to the Appeals Board, residential employees were covered by the workers' compensation law before 1977 if they were engaged in employment similar to that described in section 3715, subdivision (b). (See former § 3354 (repealed by Stats. 1975, ch. 1263, § 6, p. 3316, operative Jan. 1, 1977).) The Appeals Board's theory is that revisions to the workers' compensation law in 1977 were not meant to change the law as it applied to residential employees, and that the Legislature intended to preserve the pre–1977 definition of a residential employee. The Appeals Board believes the Legislature expressed this intent in the part of subdivision (b) of section 3715 quoted above.

Workers' compensation coverage for residential employees has expanded and contracted over the years. (See State Farm, supra, 16 Cal. 4th at pp. 1204–1207 (dis. opn. of Werdegar, J.); In–Home, supra, 152 Cal. App. 3d at pp. 735–736.) In 1975, the Legislature amended section 3351 by adding subdivision (d) without any reference to an exclusion for casual labor (minimum hour or dollar requirements). (See Stats. 1975, ch. 1263, § 4, p. 3314.) At the same time the Legislature added Insurance Code section 11590, which required all policies of "comprehensive personal liability insurance" to contain a provision for workers' compensation coverage for employees described in section 3351, subdivision (d). (Id., § 3, p. 3313.) These changes in the law were to take effect January 1, 1977. (Id., § 16, p. 3321.)

There apparently was some hue and cry regarding these provisions, so the Legislature revisited the issue and passed urgency legislation in early 1977 that narrowed the description of residential employee by adding the exclusion found in section 3352, subdivision (h), while at the same time revising the insurance requirements. (Stats. 1977, ch. 17, §§ 13, 17, 18, pp. 29–30.) This is the same legislation that added subdivision (b) to section 3715. (Stats. 1977, ch. 17, § 24, pp. 32–33.)

The problem with the Appeals Board's theory is that at the same time the Legislature was supposedly attempting to preserve the pre–1977 definition of residential employee

through its statement of legislative intent in section 3715, it was explicitly defining in sections 3351 and 3352 the types of persons employed in residential dwellings who would be considered employees under the workers' compensation law. A second problem with the Appeals Board's theory is that it would render section 3352, subdivision (h), meaningless in cases where there was a dispute over whether the worker met the hour and dollar requirements for residential employment. The 10 working days, $100 test set forth in section 3715, subdivision (b)(3) is a far easier test to meet, particularly because it requires only that it be "contemplated" the work will take 10 days or cost $100 (as opposed to actually worked or earned). Add in the detail that the Appeals Board interprets the test in the disjunctive (10 working days or $100), and almost all persons but the teenage babysitter working only a couple of hours potentially would be considered a homeowner's employee. (Footnote 8)

As in Hestehauge's case, there would be no need even to look at section 3352, subdivision (h).

The courts have been charged with liberally construing the workers' compensation law with the purpose of extending the benefits of the law to persons injured in the course of their employment. (§ 3202.) "This rule provides a means for resolution of ambiguities in the statutes which affect coverage. It cannot, of course, override a clear statutory expression of exclusion from coverage." (In–Home, supra, 152 Cal. App. 3d at p. 733.)

Hestehauge is excluded from workers' compensation coverage under section 3352, subdivision (h). He was not the Charkinses' employee for workers' compensation purposes.

DISPOSITION

The Order and Decision After Reconsideration of the Appeals Board is annulled... .

Footnote 1. All further statutory references are to the Labor Code, unless otherwise noted.

Footnote 2. Section 3351 provides: " 'Employee' means every person in the service of an employer under any appointment or contract of hire or apprenticeship, express or implied, oral or written, whether lawfully or unlawfully employed, and includes: . . . [P] (d) Except as provided in subdivision (h) of Section 3352, any person employed by the owner or occupant of a residential dwelling whose duties are incidental to the ownership, maintenance, or use of the dwelling, including the care and supervision of children, or whose duties are personal and not in the course of the trade, business, profession, or occupation of the owner or occupant."

Footnote 3. Section 3352 provides: " 'Employee' excludes . . . : . . . [P] (h) Any person defined in subdivision (d) of Section 3351 who was employed by the employer to be held liable for less than 52 hours during the 90 calendar days immediately preceding the date of the injury for injuries, as defined in Section 5411, or during the 90 calendar days immediately preceding the date of the last employment in an occupation exposing the employee to the hazards of the disease or injury for injuries, as defined in Section 5412, or who earned less than one hundred dollars ($ 100) in wages from the employer during the 90 calendar days immediately preceding the date of the injury for injuries, as defined in Section 5411, or during the 90 calendar days immediately preceding the date of the last employment in an occupation exposing the employee to the hazards of the disease or injury for injuries, as defined in Section 5412."

Footnote 4. Section 3715, subdivision (a), provides in relevant part: "Any employee, except an employee as defined in subdivision (d) of Section 3351, whose employer has failed to secure the payment of compensation as required by this division, or his or her dependents in case death has ensued, may, in addition to proceeding against his or her employer by civil action in the courts as provided in Section 3706, file his or her application with the appeals board for compensation and the appeals board shall hear and determine the application for compensation in like manner as in other claims and shall make the award to the claimant as he or she would be entitled to receive if the employer had secured the payment of compensation as required, and the employer shall pay the award in the manner and amount fixed thereby or shall furnish to the appeals board a bond, in any amount and with any sureties as the appeals board requires, to pay the employee the award in the manner and amount fixed thereby."

Footnote 5. The first paragraph of section 3715, subdivision (b), provides: "Notwithstanding this section or any other provision of this chapter except Section 3708, any person described in subdivision (d) of Section 3351 who is (1) engaged in household domestic service who is employed by one employer for over 52 hours per week, (2) engaged as a part–time gardener in connection with a private dwelling, if the number of hours devoted to the gardening work for any individual regularly exceeds 44 hours per month, or (3) engaged in casual employment where the work contemplated is to be completed in not less than 10 working days, without regard to the number of persons employed, and where the total labor cost of the work is not less than one hundred dollars ($ 100) (which amount shall not include charges other than for personal services), shall be entitled, in addition to proceeding against his or her employer by civil action in the courts as provided in Section 3706, to file his or her application with the appeals board for compensation. The appeals board shall hear and determine the application for compensation in like manner as in other claims, and shall make the award to the claimant as he or she would be entitled to receive if the person's employer had secured the payment of compensation as required, and the employer shall pay the award in the manner and amount fixed thereby, or shall furnish to the appeals board a bond, in any amount and with any sureties as the appeals board requires, to pay the employee the award in the manner and amount fixed thereby."

Footnote 6. One simple explanation for the Legislature's decision to use different, broader criteria to describe residential employment for uninsured employers is that this is more punishment meted out to uninsured employers. Note also that the members of this broader class are also entitled to a presumption of negligence in a civil action against an uninsured employer. (§ 3708.) More fundamentally, however, in the case of an uninsured homeowner, there will not be insurance proceeds to pay either a workers' compensation claim or a civil judgment. Under sections 3715 and 3716, the injured worker will at least have recourse to the Uninsured Employers Benefit Trust Fund if the homeowner cannot otherwise satisfy the claim or judgment.

Footnote 7. The Appeals Board cited a handful of its own decisions, but those decisions apparently yielded inconsistent results.

Footnote 8. CSAA challenges the Appeals Board's interpretation, noting the statute states the test in the conjunctive ("and"). We need not resolve the question here, but we do note the Appeals Board's analysis might provide an answer to the meaning of the statement of Legislative intent. In applying the 10 days, $100 test, the Appeals Board relied on court and administrative decisions interpreting the similar test for "casual" employment found in former section 3354. (See e.g., Daniels v. Johnson (1940) 38 Cal. App. 2d 619, 621–622 [101 P.2d 707, 5 Cal. Comp. Cas 110].) It appears the Legislature might have intended to preserve that body of law for use when section 3715, subdivision (b), was invoked against an uninsured employer.

Page 236, Column 1, second paragraph, insert following '...and notice.'

See *Allstate Insurance Company v. WCAB (Diaz)* (2007) 72 Cal. Comp. Cases 113, where the Board upheld an arbitrator's Finding and Award which found an applicant to be an employee of a residential property owner when he fell from the property owner's roof while constructing a garage/storage unit.

§ 5.9(B)   Workers Associated Under a Partnership Agreement

Page 245, Column 2, first paragraph, insert following '...Sec. 3360.'

In finding that an injured employee was not a *partner* in a partnership and therefore was entitled to workers' compensation benefits, the judge in *Rea et. al. v. WCAB (Rindon)* (2006) 71 Cal. Comp. Cases 1453, stated, in part:

"The defendant, UEF argues that under the general definition of partnership this business enterprise meets those indices for it states: "[a] partnership is an association of two or more persons to carry on as co–owners of a business for profit *whether or not the persons intended to form a partnership*."

The UEF cites the Corporations code and asserts that there is a presumption of a partnership if the person receives a share of the profits of the business. Unfortunately, citing the corporations code does not assist in analyzing the issue of a partnership in the light of the *presumption of the labor code that one who provides services for another, other than an independent contractor, or one expressly excluded herein as an employee, is presumed to be an employee.* (L.C. 3357) Had the injured worker been a hired hand it could very well be that Mr. Nickerson *and* Mr. Rindon would be held responsible for that worker's injuries as partners and/or as joint ventures and in fact could be presumed to be partners for that purpose.

However, the fact pattern here is much different. The defendant had a contractor's license as an individual contractor and was allowing Mr. Rindon to work illegally under his license as a "partner" without having obtained a partnership contractor's license. In this relationship Mr. Rindon is presumed by Labor Code Section 3357 to be an employee of Mr. Nickerson. Thus the burden of proof of the existence of a partnership/joint venture to rebut this presumption shifts to the defendant, UEF.

If the "partnership" could be created *accidentally* then the defendant, Nickerson, could have simply partnered with any number of workers in [*sic*] as partners and had them work under his contractor's license and avoided any requirement of workers' compensation insurance. The defendant, UEF, however, argues that the applicant here is obtaining the best of both worlds–a profit sharing relationship with the defendant and workers' compensation coverage that neither he nor his "partner" paid for. In this case the choice is relatively easy. In order to legally do business as a tree trimmer partnership, the defendant and applicant were required to put the license in the name of the partnership [7026.1(b)]. They never did this. By failing to put the partnership under the license, *they did not consummate their agreement to create a partnership to do tree trimming.* This avoids the risk of a licensed contractor forming undisclosed partnerships with multiple workers to avoid the requirement of workers compensation insurance yet allows that contractor to readily form a legitimate partnership by putting the contractor's license in the name of the partnership.

There was absence of other indicies [*sic*] of a partnership as well:

1. No business license as a partnership.
2. No business cards or stationary [*sic*] indicating they were a partnership. There was a stationary [*sic*] that combined the names of their separate businesses, but not indication of a partnership (after all they did not have a partnership contractor's license number).
3. No partnership bank accounts.
4. No sharing of profits and losses equally (When Mr. Nickerson did his own jobs without Mr. Rindon on the job, he did not share those earning with Mr. Rindon).
5. No filing of partnership tax return.
6. No formal dissolution of the partnership.
7. For the forgoing [*sic*] reasons it was concluded that the defendant had not met its burden to rebut the presumption that applicant was an employee

providing services to Mr. Nickerson on the date of injury...

For the forgoing [*sic*] reasons it was concluded that the defendant had not met its burden to rebut the presumption that applicant was an employee providing services to Mr. Nickerson on the date of injury... .

§ 5.9(O)(A) Determining Earnings Capacity of State Prison Inmates

Page 249, Column 1, sixth, insert following '...on appeal.'

Labor Code section 3370 provides:

(a) Each inmate of a state penal or correctional institution shall be entitled to the workers' compensation benefits provided by this division for injury arising out of and in the course of assigned employment and for the death of the inmate if the injury proximately causes death, subject to all of the following conditions:

(1) The inmate was not injured as the result of an assault in which the inmate was the initial aggressor, or as the result of the intentional act of the inmate injuring himself or herself.

(2) The inmate shall not be entitled to any temporary disability indemnity benefits while incarcerated in a state prison.

(3) No benefits shall be paid to an inmate while he or she is incarcerated. The period of benefit payment shall instead commence upon release from incarceration. If an inmate who has been released from incarceration, and has been receiving benefits under this section, is reincarcerated in a city or county jail, or state penal or correctional institution, the benefits shall cease immediately upon the inmate's reincarceration and shall not be paid for the duration of the reincarceration.

(4) This section shall not be construed to provide for the payment to an inmate, upon release from incarceration, of temporary disability benefits which were not paid due to the prohibition of paragraph (2).

(5) In determining temporary and permanent disability indemnity benefits for the inmate, the average weekly earnings shall be taken at not more than the minimum amount set forth in Section 4453.

(6) Where a dispute exists respecting an inmate's rights to the workers' compensation benefits provided herein, the inmate may file an application with the appeals board to resolve the dispute. The application may be filed at any time during the inmate's incarceration.

(7) After release or discharge from a correctional institution, the former inmate shall have one year in which to file an original application with the appeals board, unless the time of injury is such that it would allow more time under Section 5804 of the Labor Code.

(8) The percentage of disability to total disability shall be determined as for the occupation of a laborer of like age by applying the schedule for the determination of the percentages of permanent disabilities prepared and adopted by the administrative director.

(9) This division shall be the exclusive remedy against the state for injuries occurring while engaged in assigned work or work under contract. Nothing in this division shall affect any right or remedy of an injured inmate for injuries not compensated by this division.

(b) The Department of Corrections shall present to each inmate of a state penal or correctional institution, prior to his or her first assignment to work at the institution, a printed statement of his or her rights under this division, and a description of procedures to be followed in filing for benefits under this section. The statement shall be approved by the administrative director and be posted in a conspicuous place at each place where an inmate works.

(c) Notwithstanding any other provision of this division, the Department of Corrections shall have medical control over treatment provided an injured inmate while incarcerated in a state prison, except, that in serious cases, the inmate is entitled, upon request, to the services of a consulting physician.

(d) Paragraphs (2), (3), and (4) of subdivision (a) shall also be applicable to an inmate of a state penal or correctional institution who would otherwise be entitled to receive workers' compensation benefits based on an injury sustained prior to his or her incarceration. However, temporary and permanent disability benefits which, except for this subdivision, would otherwise be payable to an inmate during incarceration based on an injury sustained prior to incarceration shall be paid to the dependents of the inmate. If the inmate has no dependents, the temporary disability benefits which, except for this subdivision, would otherwise be payable during the inmate's incarceration shall be paid to the State Treasury to the credit of the Uninsured Employers Fund, and the permanent disability benefits which would otherwise be payable during the inmate's incarceration shall be held in trust for the inmate by the Department of Corrections during the period of incarceration. For purposes of this subdivision, "dependents" means the inmate's spouse or children, including an inmate's former spouse due to divorce and the inmate's children from that marriage.

(e) Notwithstanding any other provision of this division, an employee who is an inmate, as defined in subdivision (e) of Section 3351 who is eligible for vocational rehabilitation services as defined in Section 4635 shall only be eligible for direct placement services.

Attorney Referral for Inmates

Labor Code section 3371 provides:

If the issues are complex or if the inmate applicant requests, the Department of Corrections shall furnish a list of qualified workers' compensation attorneys to permit the inmate applicant to choose an attorney to represent him or her before the appeals board.

Intentionally blank

§ 6.0   WHAT ARE THE ELIGIBILITY REQUIREMENTS?

Page 294, Column 1, sixth paragraph, insert new topic following '…timely.'

§ 6.9(B)(1)   Addiction

If the proper use of medications prescribed by an authorized treating physician cause an applicant to become addicted to the medication, the employer must treat the addiction. Commenting on this in *Ballard v. WCAB* (1971) 36 Cal. Comp. Cases 34, the California Supreme Court stated, in part:

It is settled that the section must be read in the light of the rule that an employer takes the employee as he finds him at the time of the employment. Accordingly, when a subsequent injury lights up or aggravates a previously existing condition resulting in disability, liability for the full disability without proration is imposed upon the employer, and the Appeals Board may apportion the disability under the section "only in those cases in which part of disability would have resulted, in the absence of the industrial injury, from the 'normal progress'" of the preexisting disease. (E.g., Smith v. Workmen's Comp. App. Bd. [(1969)] 71 Cal. 2d 588, 592 [34 Cal. Comp. Cases 424, 78 Cal. Rptr. 718, 455 P.2d 776]; Granado v. Workmen's Comp. App. Bd. [(1968)] 69 Cal. 2d 399, 401 [33 Cal. Comp. Cases 647, 71 Cal. Rptr. 678, 445 P.2d 294]; Zemke v. Workmen's Comp. App. Bd. [(1968)] 68 Cal. 2d 794, 796 [33 Cal. Comp. Cases 358, 69 Cal. Rptr. 88, 441 P.2d 928]; Berry v. Workmen's Comp. App. Bd. [(1968)] 68 Cal. 2d 786, 789 et seq. [33 Cal. Comp. Cases 352, 69 Cal. Rptr. 68, 441 P.2d 908]; Reynolds Elec. etc. Co. v. Workmen's Comp. App. Bd. [(Buckner) (1966)] 65 Cal. 2d 438, 442–443 [31 Cal. Comp. Cases 421, 55 Cal. Rptr. 254, 421 P.2d 102]; Colonial Ins. Co. v. Industrial Acc. Com. [(Pedroza) (1946)] 29 Cal. 2d 79, 83–86 [11 Cal. Comp. Cases 243, 172 P.2d 884]; Tanenbaum v. Industrial Acc. Com. [(1935)] 4 Cal. 2d 615, 617–618 [20 I.A.C. 390, 52 P.2d 215].)

Similar rules have been applied in cases where, after an industrial injury, the workman commits suicide, and it is shown that the injury and the resulting disability were causally related to the suicide. Recovery is proper if it is shown that without the injury there would have been no suicide. (Beauchamp v. Workmen's Comp. App. Bd. [(1968)] 259 Cal. App. 2d 147, 152 et seq. [33 Cal. Comp. Cases 112, 66 Cal. Rptr. 352]; Burnight v. Industrial Acc. Com. [(1960)] 181 Cal. App. 2d 816, 822 et seq. [25 Cal. Comp. Cases 121, 5 Cal. Rptr. 786].)

There is no evidence that petitioner was addicted to drugs prior to her injury or prior to the prescription of drugs to relieve from its effects, and the record in the light of the finding of the referee adopted by the Board, does not warrant a denial of benefits. He did not find that she was not now addicted but found that she "would be considered 'addicted'" in the sense that she was an habitual user. He said she was in need of treatment, although he questioned the extent of addiction.

Although the referee was correct in limiting the employer's liability to the effects of the drugs furnished by prescription, such liability extends not only to situations where those drugs by themselves would cause addiction but also to situations where the prescribed drugs light up or aggravate a preexisting condition resulting in disability. In short, the fact that "the most likely cause" of the addiction is the preexisting "obvious life–long neurotic personality problems" does not serve to warrant denial of recovery if the addiction resulted in part from the prescribed drugs. The employer takes the employee as he finds him at the time of employment. Similarly, the finding that her problems would have culminated in addiction "even in the absence of this trauma and the treatment rendered thereafter" do not furnish a basis for denial for all recovery because even in cases where disability would follow from the normal progress of the preexisting disease apportionment is proper where the industrial injury has contributed to the disability. There is no finding that the prescribed drugs did not, along with the personality problems and the illegally obtained drugs, contribute to any part of the disability, and the findings do not support the denial of recovery.

Moreover, the referee's finding that the addiction would have occurred even in the absence of the injury and the prescribed medication is not sustained by the evidence. Dr. Malitz refers to her disability as a "manifestation of her pre–existing personality disorder," but does not state whether the industrial injury and its treatment may have also been a causative factor. It is apparent that his opinion is based upon the incorrect legal theory that petitioner cannot recover if her preexisting personality problem was a contributing cause. He states that petitioner "must accept full responsibility for any of her actions in illegally obtaining and using drugs." The decisive question is not whether her actions in illegally obtaining drugs was a causative factor or contributed to her disability; the question is not whether it was appropriate for the doctors to prescribe drugs for her or whether they were to "blame"; under the authorities discussed above, the question is whether the prescribed drugs were a causative factor in her present disability. Dr. Malitz nowhere states that her present condition was caused solely by her personality disorder and the unlawfully obtained drugs or that her present condition would have occurred absent the industrial injury and the prescribed drugs. His statements that "there would be nothing to indicate that the negligible psychic stress associated with her injury was a causative factor" is by its own terms limited only to the psychic stress.

Under the authorities discussed above, if the accident or treatment contributed to her addiction problem, petitioner is entitled to a partial recovery, and if the addiction would not have materialized but for the injury she is entitled to a full recovery notwithstanding the fact that her personality problems also were contributing factors. Dr. Malitz does not deny either of the bases of liability, and a medical report based upon an incorrect legal theory and devoid of relevant factual basis does not constitute substantial evidence. (Smith v. Workmen's Comp. App. Bd., *supra*, 71 Cal. 2d 588, 593 [34 Cal. Comp. Cases 424, 78 Cal. Rptr. 718, 455 P.2d 776]; Zemke v. Workmen's Comp. App. Bd., *supra*, 68 Cal. 2d 794, 798, 801 [33 Cal. Comp. Cases 358, 69 Cal. Rptr. 88, 441 P.2d 928]… .

In *Satloff v. WCAB* (2006) 71 Cal. Comp. Cases 452, benefits were denied to an anesthesiologist who became addicted to narcotic medications which he injected into himself from his employer's drug supply, allegedly because of stress associated with administering anesthesia to sick newborns and working with a surgeon who demeaned him.

The trial judge, in recommending that the applicant's Petition for Reconsideration of his denial of benefits be denied, observed that the cases cited by the applicant in support of his case concerned industrially induced addiction to the medications that were prescribed by the authorized treating physician pursuant to an award of medical care. Further, the judge noted that applicant failed to present substantial evidence that job stress

caused the need to engage in the use of narcotics that were the property of his employer.

§ 6.10 When is an Employee Acting in the Course of Employment (COE)?

Page 299, Column 1, seventh paragraph, insert following '…not controlling….'

In distinguishing *scope of employment* from *course of employment*, the Court of Appeal, Third District, in *Hartline v. Kaiser Foundation Hospitals* (2005) 70 Cal. Comp. Cases 1283, stated, in part:

"The rule of respondeat superior is familiar and simply stated: an employer is vicariously liable for the torts of its employees committed within the scope of the employment. [Citation.]" (Lisa M. v. Henry Mayo Newhall Memorial Hospital (1995) 12 Cal. 4th 291, 296 [907 P.2d 358, 48 Cal. Rptr. 2d 510].) The plaintiff has the burden of proof to demonstrate the negligent act of the employee was committed within the scope of employment. (Ducey v. Argo Sales Co. (1979) 25 Cal. 3d 707, 721 [602 P.2d 755, 159 Cal. Rptr. 835]; Yamaguchi v. Harnsmut (2003) 106 Cal. App. 4th 472, 482 [130 Cal. Rptr. 2d 706, 68 Cal. Comp. Cases 201].) Whether an act is within the scope of employment is a question of fact, unless the facts are undisputed and no conflicting inferences are possible, in which case the question is one of law. (Lisa M. v. Henry Mayo Newhall Memorial Hospital, *supra*, at p. 299; John Y. v. Chaparral Treatment Center, Inc. (2002) 101 Cal. App. 4th 565, 574 [124 Cal. Rptr. 2d 330].)

Under the "going and coming" rule, an employee going to or coming home from work is "ordinarily considered outside the scope of employment so that the employer is not liable for his torts." (Hinman v. Westinghouse Elec. Co. (1970) 2 Cal. 3d 956, 961 [471 P.2d 988, 88 Cal. Rptr. 188, 35 Cal. Comp. Cases 756] (Hinman).) "The 'going and coming' rule is sometimes ascribed to the theory that the employment relationship is 'suspended' from the time the employee leaves until he returns [citation], or that in commuting he is not rendering service to his employer. [Citation.]" (Ibid.)

Kaiser claimed in its motion for summary adjudication it could not be vicariously held liable under the rule of respondeat superior based on the going–and–coming rule. According to Kaiser, the undisputed evidence established Collins was going to work from her home at the time of the accident. Kaiser contended none of the established exceptions to the going–and–coming rule applied because Collins was not on a special errand for Kaiser, Kaiser did not defray Collins's travel expenses and did not compensate her for her travel time, and Kaiser did not require Collins, as a condition of her employment, commute to work in her personal car.

Hartline argued the going–and–coming rule did not preclude liability because a triable issue of material fact existed as to whether Collins was acting within the scope of employment based on the "premises rule" as explained by the court in Santa Rosa Junior College v. Workers' Comp. Appeals Bd. (1985) 40 Cal. 3d 345, 353 [708 P.2d 673, 220 Cal. Rptr. 94] (Santa Rosa).

The trial court granted Kaiser's motion for summary adjudication based on Hartline's failure to demonstrate the existence of a triable issue of material fact after Kaiser presented facts showing the applicability of the going–and–coming rule. The trial court stated: "Even if the court were to apply [the premises line] rule here, a factual predicate is 'close proximity' to the workplace, e.g., 'the parking lot used by employees.' Here, however, Collins allegedly struck plaintiff just off the street, at the entrance to the parking lot, not in the parking lot itself . . . . The 'premises line' rule, therefore, could not apply."

C. The "Premises Line" Rule

In Santa Rosa, supra, 40 Cal. 3d 345, a college instructor was killed in an accident while driving his personal car home from work. The California Supreme Court applied the going–and–coming rule, reversing the Workers' Compensation Appeals Board award of workers' compensation death benefits to the instructor's widow. The Supreme Court stated, "the facts in this case do not fit convincingly into any of the established limitations or exceptions . . . . Because [the instructor's] accident occurred miles away from the [college] campus, exceptions to the 'premises line' doctrine cannot reasonably be invoked to render the going and coming rule inapplicable." (Id. at p. 353, fn. omitted.)

Although the "premises line" rule was not applicable, the California Supreme Court in Santa Rosa explained in a Footnote the substance of the rule as it had been applied in workers' compensation law. "For purposes of applying the going and coming rule, the employment relationship begins when the employee enters the employer's premises." (Santa Rosa, supra, 40 Cal. 3d at p. 353, fn. 11.) Indeed, "injuries sustained in close proximity to the employer's premises may, in fact arise out of the employment, especially when the accident occurs in the parking lot used by employees or on public property immediately adjacent to the workplace. Recognizing this, we have defined the course of employment to include a 'reasonable margin of time and space necessary to be used in passing to and from the place where the work is to be done.' " (Footnote 2)

(Ibid.; see Lewis v. Workers' Comp. Appeals Bd. (1975) 15 Cal. 3d 559, 561 [542 P.2d 225, 125 Cal. Rptr. 353, 40 Cal. Comp. Cases 727]; see Pacific Indem. Co. v. Industrial Acc. Commission (1946) 28 Cal. 2d 329, 337 [170 P.2d 18, 11 Cal. Comp. Cases 148].)

Hartline argues the "premises line" rule, as used in workers' compensation law, should apply to this case involving respondeat superior, although no published case has previously so applied the rule. Hartline argues this result should follow from the California Supreme Court's statements (1) that the test under workers' compensation law for whether an injury arises "out of and in the course of employment" (Lab. Code, § 3600) is closely related to the test for whether an employee is acting within the "scope of employment" under respondeat superior (Hinman, supra, 2

Cal. 3d at p. 962, fn. 3), and (2) that "[i]n the 'going and coming' cases, the California courts often cite tort and workers' compensation cases interchangeably." (Ducey v. Argo Sales Co., supra, 25 Cal. 3d at p. 722.) Hartline contends public policy favors the adoption of the premises line rule for purposes of respondeat superior. Finally, Hartline contends the trial court incorrectly stated and applied the law regarding the "premises line" rule to this case.

We reject Hartline's contention that the premises line rule should apply in civil tort cases involving the going–and–coming rule for purposes of respondeat superior and, therefore, do not need to reach his last claim.

The California Supreme Court in Hinman expressly noted the workers' compensation test for whether an injury arises out of and in the course of employment is "not identical," although it is "closely related," to the test for whether an employee is acting within the scope of employment under respondeat superior. (Hinman, supra, 2 Cal. 3d at p. 962, fn. 3.) "[A]lthough worker's compensation cases can be helpful in determining the employer's vicarious liability for its employee's torts [citation], they are not controlling precedent 'when liability is predicated upon respondeat superior principles.' " (Perez v. Van Groningen & Sons, Inc. (1986) 41 Cal. 3d 962, 968, fn. 2 [719 P.2d 676, 227 Cal. Rptr. 106]; see Caldwell v. A.R.B., Inc. (1986) 176 Cal. App. 3d 1028, 1035 [222 Cal. Rptr. 494].)

In fact, " 'scope of employment' " for purposes of respondeat superior is more restrictive than " 'arising out of and in the course of employment' " for workers' compensation. (Saala v. McFarland (1965) 63 Cal. 2d 124, 128–129, fn. 3 [403 P.2d 400, 45 Cal. Rptr. 144, 30 Cal. Comp. Cases 220] [employee injured by coworker in parking lot received workers' compensation benefits as accident occurred on employer's premises, but coworker was not acting within scope of employment for purposes of tort liability].) That is, "[i]f an injury is within the 'scope of employment,' it will probably be 'arising out of and occurring in the course of employment'; however, the reverse is not true." (Church v. Arko (1977) 75 Cal. App. 3d 291, 300 [142 Cal. Rptr. 92, 42 Cal. Comp. Cases 1219] [rejects argument that the "scope of employment" for purposes of respondeat superior begins and ends with the round trip to and from the place of employment where an employee finds it convenient or even essential to use a car to travel to and from work].)

As the Court of Appeal in Blackman v. Great American First Savings Bank (1991) 233 Cal. App. 3d 598 [284 Cal. Rptr. 491], specifically cautioned: "Workers' compensation law takes a different approach to exceptions to the going–and–coming rule . . . . [Citation.] Workers' compensation and respondeat superior law are driven in opposite directions based on differing policy considerations. Workers' compensation has been defined as a type of social insurance designed to protect employees from occupational hazards, while respondeat superior imputes liability to an employer based on an employee's fault because of the special relationship. [Citation.] Further, courts heed statutory admonitions for a liberal construction favoring coverage in workers' compensation cases which are not present in respondeat superior law." (Id. at pp. 604–605; accord, Munyon v. Ole's Inc. (1982) 136 Cal. App. 3d 697, 702 [186 Cal. Rptr. 424] [Workers' Compensation Act is a shield protecting injured workers; vicarious tort liability is a sword extending tort liability beyond those directly and immediately negligent]; Anderson v. Pacific Gas & Electric Co. (1993) 14 Cal. App. 4th 254, 259–260 [17 Cal. Rptr. 2d 534, 58 Cal. Comp. Cases 120].)

We conclude the premises line rule, developed in the context of the policies behind workers' compensation, does not fit the policy justification for making employers vicariously liable for their employee's torts.

The modern justification for respondeat superior is a deliberate policy allocation of risk. (Hinman, supra, 2 Cal. 3d at p. 959.) That is, an employer's liability extends "beyond his actual or possible control over the employees to include risks inherent in or created by the enterprise because he, rather than the innocent injured party, is best able to spread the risk through prices, rates or liability insurance." (Rodgers v. Kemper Constr. Co. (1975) 50 Cal. App. 3d 608, 618 [124 Cal. Rptr. 143, 40 Cal. Comp. Cases 987] (Rodgers).) A risk is inherent in or created by an enterprise when "in the context of the particular enterprise an employee's conduct is not so unusual or startling that it would seem unfair to include the loss resulting from it among other costs of the employer's business. [Citations.] In other words, where the question is one of vicarious liability, the inquiry should be whether the risk was one 'that may fairly be regarded as typical of or broadly incidental' to the enterprise undertaken by the employer. [Citation.]" (Id. at p. 619; see Perez v. Van Groningen & Sons, supra, 41 Cal. 3d at p. 968.) "Respondeat superior liability does not attach simply because employment brought the employee and victim together at a certain time and place. [Citation.] The employee's activities must be inherent in, typical of or created by the work so that it is a foreseeable risk of the particular employment. [Citations.]" (Tognazzini v. San Luis Coastal Unified School Dist. (2001) 86 Cal. App. 4th 1053, 1057 [103 Cal. Rptr. 2d 790], italics added.) Respondeat superior assigns responsibility to the employer " 'for accidents which may fairly be said to be characteristic of its activities.' " (Rodgers, supra, at p. 618, quoting Ira S. Bushey & Sons, Inc. v. Unites States (2d Cir. 1968) 398 F.2d 167, 171.)

The risks associated with an employee's commute to and from work generally are not, absent special circumstances recognized by the exceptions to the going–and–coming rule, inherent in, typical of, or created by their work. Certainly in this case, Collins's involvement in a car accident could not fairly be said to be characteristic of her work as a physical therapist for Kaiser. Just because employers have to employ workers and workers have to get to and from their work does not mean their commute is part of the enterprise risk of the employer. The fact that this accident just happened to occur on Kaiser's premises (driveway to the parking lot) or on public property immediately adjacent to such premises (Santa Rosa, supra, 40 Cal. 3d 345, 353, fn. 11) does not change the character of such accident to a risk foreseeably related to Kaiser's particular employment of Collins or to the necessary operation of Kaiser's health care business.

Indeed, it would be an arbitrary expansion of employer liability to assign vicarious responsibility to the employer for whatever occurs on their premises or in public areas near their premises involving an employee without regard to whether such actions were actually " 'typical of or broadly incidental' " to the employer's enterprise. (Rodgers, supra, 50 Cal. App. 3d at p. 619.) Mere physical location of the employee is an insufficient nexus for purposes of vicarious liability.

The trial court did not err in granting Kaiser's motion for summary adjudication of Hartline's vicarious liability cause of action. As a matter of law, Collins was not acting within the scope of her employment when she hit Hartline and his dog with her car on her way into Kaiser's parking lot... .

Footnote 2. Footnote 11 reads in its entirety as follows: "For purposes of applying the going and coming rule, the employment relationship begins when the employee enters the employer's premises. We have reaffirmed the 'premises line' rule, stating that it 'has the advantage of enabling courts to ascertain the point at which employment begins – objectively and fairly.' (Gen. Ins. Co. v. Workmen's Comp. App. Bd. (Chairez) 16 Cal. 3d 595, 599.) However, injuries sustained in close proximity to the employer's premises may, in fact arise out of the employment, especially when the accident occurs in the parking lot used by employees or on public property immediately adjacent to the workplace. Recognizing this, we have defined the course of employment to include a 'reasonable margin of time and space necessary to be used in passing to and from the place where the work is to be done.' (Lewis v. Workmen's Comp. App. Bd. (1975) 15 Cal. 3d 559, 561, quoting Cal. Cas. Ind. Exch. v. Ind. Acc. Com. [1943] 21 Cal. 2d 751, 754.) Where the employment itself creates a danger to employees entering or leaving the premises, we have posited a 'field of risk' or 'zone of danger,' the extent of which varies from case to case, depending on the degree to which the employer's conduct contributes directly as a proximate cause of the employee's injuries. (Parks [v. Workers' Comp. App. Bd. (1983) 33 Cal. 3d 585] at p. 592. See, also, Greydanus v. Ind. Acc. Com. (1965) 63 Cal. 2d 490, 493; Pac. Ind. Co v. Ind. Acc. Com. (Henslick) (1946) 28 Cal. 2d 329, 338.) This line of cases stems from one of the earliest attempts to circumvent or soften Ocean Accident [etc. Co. v. Industrial Acc. Com. (1916) 173 Cal. 313]. (See Judson Mfg. Co. v. Ind. Acc. Com. (1919) 181 Cal. 300, 302 ['It would be a harsh and indefensible rule that would withhold compensation from an employee engaged in traversing a dangerous pathway in his employer's building on his way to his own particular place of work therein, on the ground that he had not yet entered upon the real work of his employment'].)"

§ 6.10(A)   Injured Going to or From Work (Going and Coming Rule)

Page 311, Column 1, first paragraph, insert following '...coming rule.'

See *Pettigrew v. WCAB* (2006) 71 Cal. Comp. Cases 1248.

§ 6.10(B)   Injured While on a Special Mission (Special Mission Rule)

Page 313, Column 2, seventh paragraph, insert following '...his employment....'

In *Aylworth v. WCAB* (2006) 71 Cal. Comp. Cases 948, the Court of Appeal, First District, upheld the Board's denial of benefits to a deputy sheriff injured while driving home from a union meeting. In distinguishing *Perez*, *supra*, from the instant case, the Board did not find evidence showing the union meeting *materially* benefited the sheriff's employer.

§ 6.10(E)   Injured while Using Own Vehicle

Page 333, Column 1, fifth paragraph, insert following '331 P.2d 99]).'

See also *Citadel Broadcasting, et al. v. WCAB (Nelson)* (2006) 71 Cal. Comp. Cases 517, where the Board found that applicant's injury, sustained while driving from his home to a mandatory weekly company sales meeting, was not barred under the "going and coming" rule, when applicant established that he could not have performed his sales job without his own vehicle, no company vehicle was available for his use, his employer expected him to provide a vehicle for its benefit, and defendant provided no evidence that applicant could perform his duties without a vehicle.

§ 6.10(I)   Injured while on a Trip for the Employer – Commercial Traveler

Page 347, Column 1, fifth paragraph, insert following '...stated:'

Decedent, Lloyd A. Wiseman, a vice president of a San Francisco bank, died of asphyxiation and burns in a hotel room in New York City. He was in that city on bank business, and his traveling expenses, including his hotel bills, were paid by the bank. A woman, not his wife but registered as such, was found unconscious in his room and died shortly thereafter. There was evidence that they had been drinking. Sometime between 4 and 5 in the morning of his death, Wiseman telephoned the hotel manager for help because of a fire in his room. After calling the fire department, the manager went to the room but was unable to open the door with his passkey. Firemen arrived shortly thereafter and broke into the room but were too late to save the occupants. It was the opinion of the assistant fire marshal that the fire was caused by careless smoking by either one or both of the occupants.

Petitioners, the widow and minor daughter of the employee, filed claims as his dependents with the Industrial Accident Commission for death benefits. The referee made an award in favor of petitioners, but a panel of the commission granted the employer's petition for reconsideration, vacated the referee's award and findings, and denied petitioner's claim. Their petition for reconsideration was denied, and they brought this proceeding to review the award... .

Page 347, Column 2, third paragraph, insert following '...death.'

One Justice dissented, stating:

The respondent commission made a finding that "said employee did not sustain an injury arising out of and occurring in the course of employment on October 5, 1952." The majority opinion annuls the award based upon that finding and necessarily holds, as a matter of law, that the injury was one "arising out of" and "proximately caused" by the employment. (Labor Code Section 3600.) In my opinion, the evidence clearly indicates that the injury arose out of, and was proximately caused by, an alcoholic and adulterous debauch while the employee was engaged in "a frolic of his own," and that it cannot be said, as a matter of law, that it arose out of and was proximately caused by his employment.

The authorities do not sustain the theory that every injury which is sustained by a traveling employee from the time he leaves home until his return is a compensable injury. The general rule to which petitioners allude is set forth in Dalgleish v. Holt, 108 Cal. App. 2d 561,566 [237 P.2d 553], but it is there said: "However, this rule does not embrace all activities of a commercial traveler irrespective of their connection with the purposes of the employment. The conditions essential to compensation as set forth in section 3600 of the Labor Code Apply equally to traveling employees; the status of an employee as a traveling salesman does not change a course of action which is not within the scope of the employment to one that is." In that case, as well as in the so–called Lund case (State Emp. Etc. System v. Industrial Acc Com., 97 Cal. App.2d 380 [217 P.2d 992]), upon which petitioners strongly rely, the question was held to be one of fact under the evidence presented. The most that can properly be said here is that the question was one of fact rather than of law, which question has been resolved by the commission against petitioners.

The language used in affirming the denial of a claim in Lunde v. Congoleum–Nairn, Inc., 211 Minn. 487 [1 N.W.2d 606], appears germane to the present discussion. It was there said at page 607 [1 N.W.2d]: "Basically, the argument for relator is wrong in its seeming assumption that factors of time and place are decisive. It ignores the real determinant which is the employee's activity of the moment. [Decedent's] activity of the moment was wholly his own and, as found below, beyond the scope of his employment. That a traveling salesman is within his own 'territory' does not bring all his actions away from home within the compensation act. The risks of diversions on errands and for reasons personal to him are not all occupational as matter of law…. Too reasonable is the conclusion that course of employment of both was left for the time being for a detour leading to pleasure rather than business effort." (See also Woodring v. United Sash & Door Co., 152 Kan. 413 [103 P.2d 837]; Warren v. Globe Indem. Co., (La.App.) 30 So.2d 346; Southern Casualty Co. v. Ehlers, (Tex.Civ.App.) 14 S.W.2d 111; United States Fid. & Guar. Co. v. Skinner, 188 Ga 823 [5 S.E.2d 9]; Hurley v. Lowe, 168 F.2d 553.)

It may be conceded that the illegality or immorality of the acts of an employee do not compel a denial of compensation in all cases, but they were material here for the consideration of the commission in determining whether the injury to the employee arose out of and was proximately caused solely by a purely personal activity which was not reasonably contemplated by his employment. Petitioners do not urge that the illegal and immoral conduct of decedent here was reasonably contemplated, and the commission properly concluded that it was not. It follows that as the commission could reasonably infer that the injury and death arose out of and were proximately caused solely by such purely personal and uncontemplated activity, its finding that the injury did not arise out of the employment finds ample support in the evidence. The general language of the cases involving injuries incurred by the employee while engaged in reasonably contemplated activities on the employer's premises or in accommodations furnished by the employer is therefore not in point here, and does not support the conclusion that the award of the commission should be annulled.

It seems clear that if a traveling employee should meet his death as the result of being shot by an intended victim while engaged in an illegal and uncontemplated personal activity such as an attempted robbery or an attempted rape by the employee of a guest in the employee's hotel room, such death would be held noncompensable as a matter of law. It would arise out of and be proximately caused solely by the illegal and uncontemplated personal activity rather than the employment. It seems equally clear here that the commission could and did properly determine from the evidence, as a matter of fact, that the death arose out of and was proximately caused solely by the illegal and uncontemplated personal activity of the deceased employee rather than the employment.

I would therefore affirm the award of the respondent commission denying compensation."… .

Page 350, Column 1, ninth paragraph, insert following '…encouraged it.'

In *Fleetwood Enterprises, Inc. v. WCAB (Moody)* (2005) 70 Cal. Comp. Cases 1659, a design manager (applicant) for Fleetwood was assigned to attend an RV show in Dusseldorf, Germany.

Following the show, the company employees on the trip were to visit a German RV manufacturer, and then go on to Italy to meet with a fiberglass supplier.

At the Dusseldorf airport, applicant picked up a rental car, which had been arranged by Fleetwood. The car had to be returned to Dusseldorf.

With Fleetwood's permission, applicant had arranged to have his wife meet him in Geneva after the RV show and the visit to the German manufacturer. Fleetwood's travel office handled Mrs. Moody's (applicant's wife) arrangements, as well as those for its employees. After applicant drove to Geneva to pick up his wife, the applicant and his wife, the other Fleetwood employees and their German guide traveled to Italy for the next meeting in the city of Ferrara. This visit involved not only a plant tour but also socializing with the local manufacturer's representatives and sightseeing in and near Ferrara.

When the business in Ferrara was complete, applicant's co–workers returned to the United States, leaving from Milan, Italy. The applicant and his wife, however, remained in Italy with the rental car. They traveled to Florence and Rome, staying overnight in each city (two nights in Rome), before heading north towards Germany and Dusseldorf. Soon they were involved in a vehicle accident.

At the time of the accident discussed hereafter, there were three days before their return flight, and the Moodys had no specific itinerary but intended a rambling route as the fancy took them. However, both were in fact tired of travel and testified that they would have liked to leave from Rome right then, if the vehicle had not been due in Dusseldorf.

The accident occurred about three o'clock in the afternoon after they left Rome. Their vehicle was struck by a car that had crossed the center line of the roadway.

In an attempt to establish that he was still performing job duties at the time of the accident, applicant testified that his job as design manager required him to be familiar with all updates and innovations from other RV manufacturers. Although the primary method for obtaining information about competitors was to attend trade shows, he also routinely kept an eye open for RVs made by others, both on the road and at campgrounds, often speaking with the owners to determine which features they liked or disliked. He continued this practice during the subject trip to Europe, photographing "unusual" European RVs during the post–business or vacation portion of the trip. He was particularly interested in finding examples of a "seats–on–top" feature that European manufacturers had recently brought out, and in seeing how European manufacturers coped with the smaller dimensions practical in European cities and on

European roads. Mrs. Moody confirmed that when they traveled, they looked not only at other RV's, but at any "artistic design" they thought might be adaptable for use in an RV.

During the trip, applicant used an American Express card in his name, but which was actually a Fleetwood business card. As a rule, when he used the card both for business and personal reasons, he was responsible for the personal charges. However, Fleetwood apparently paid all the charges for the subject trip and did not ask applicant to reimburse it for his post–business expenses.

After the accident, Fleetwood took charge of applicant's medical care and expenses, sending an Italian–speaking employee to Italy to assist and eventually chartering an air ambulance to expedite his return. These expenses were primarily funded through Fleetwood's *group health program* rather than workers' compensation, although Fleetwood apparently directly paid some of the extraordinary expenses and care upgrades. During the critical period, Fleetwood's representatives repeatedly assured applicant and Mrs. Moody that they would be taken care of and that whatever they needed would be provided.

The accident occurred on October 8, 1999. Applicant returned to work in April of 2000 but was laid off in November of 2002. He did not file a workers' compensation claim form until May of 2002. Fleetwood denied the claim by letter dated August 1, 2002.

The Appeals Board upheld the judge's finding of compensability, ruling that the presumption of compensability under Section 5402 was established. The trial judge found, and the Board agreed, that even if the presumption of Section 5402 did not apply, applicant had met his burden of proving that the injury was compensable.

The Court of Appeal, Fourth District, disagreed with the Board and remanded the case for further proceedings on the issue of applicability of Section 5402, but nevertheless found that the Board incorrectly determined that the applicant was in the *course and scope of his employment* at the time of his accident. In annulling the Board's order, the Court stated, in part:

In considering the finding of compensability, we are mindful of the rule that the workers' compensation laws are to "be liberally construed by the courts with the purpose of extending their benefits for the protection of persons injured in the course of their employment." (§ 3202.) Reasonable doubts as to whether an injury occurred in the course and scope of employment should be resolved in favor of the employee. (Department of Rehabilitation v. Workers' Comp. Appeals Bd. (2003) 30 Cal. 4th 1281, 1290 [135 Cal. Rptr. 2d 665, 70 P.3d 1076, 68 Cal. Comp. Cases 831].) However, these principles do not relieve the claimant of the burden of establishing the relevant facts by a preponderance of the evidence. (§ 3202.5; Wehr v. Workers' Comp. Appeals Bd. (1985) 165 Cal. App. 3d 188, 193–194 [211 Cal. Rptr. 321, Cal. Comp. Cases 165].)

To begin with, as briefly noted above (see fn. 6), we essentially disregard all evidence of what Fleetwood's representatives said concerning the accident. Fleetwood appears to have acted with commendable concern and even generosity in assisting the Moodys. However, statements or assumptions by Fleetwood employees not shown to have been fully acquainted with the facts (and certainly lacking in expertise with respect to the underlying legal principles) are of only minimal relevance and are not binding on Fleetwood. If an employer denies compensability, obviously the denial has no probative value. By the same token, the fact that an employer initially believes that an injury is compensable is not evidence of compensability unless the employer is in full possession of the facts and is competent to apply the governing law to those facts. (Footnote 9)

We turn therefore to the facts and circumstances surrounding the accident. We conclude that the evidence is susceptible only of the conclusion, fatal to applicant, that there was no continuing or resumed business purpose at the time of the accident; further, that no other factor justifies imposing liability for benefits upon Fleetwood. (Footnote 10)

As applicant argues, it is well–established that an employer's liability extends beyond the normal workplace. For example, there is no question that if applicant had been injured on the road between Dusseldorf and Ferrara, the injury would have been compensable, because a "commercial traveler" is covered at all times during a business trip. (See Wiseman v. Industrial Acc. Com. (1956) 46 Cal. 2d 570, 572 [297 P.2d 649, 21 Cal. Comp. Cases 192] (Wiseman).) (Footnote 11)

Next, although the general rule is that an injury is not considered to have been suffered in the "course and scope of employment" while the employee is en route to or from work (see e.g., Santa Rosa Junior College v. Workers' Comp. Appeals Bd. (1985) 40 Cal. 3d 345, 351–352 [708 P.2d 673, 220 Cal. Rptr. 94]; 2 Witkin, Summary of Cal. Law (9th ed. 1987) Workers' Compensation, § 192, pp. 754–755), an exception is recognized where the employee is on a "special mission" for the employer. This simply means that if the employee's commute also includes some act benefiting the employer, any injury is compensable. Thus, in Green v. Workers' Comp. Appeals Bd. (1986) 187 Cal. App. 3d 1419, 1422 [232 Cal. Rptr. 465, 51 Cal. Comp. Cases 601], an employee was told that he would be attending a trade show after his normal work hours and had to go home to obtain suitable clothing; held, an injury suffered on the way home was compensable. Finally, if a commuting employee uses a method of transportation that benefits the employer by facilitating the employee's work, an injury during the commute may be compensable. (County of Tulare v. Workers' Comp. Appeals Bd. (1985) 170 Cal. App. 3d 1247, 1253 [216 Cal. Rptr. 885, 50 Cal. Comp. Cases 435].) Applicant relies on all of these theories in several variations.

The most critical issue is whether applicant was still on a "special mission" for his employer at the time of the accident. The WCJ was persuaded by the testimony from applicant and his wife concerning their continuing interest and vigilance with respect to RV designs and elements that might be of use to Fleetwood. We will accept this testimony as true, because the WCJ and the Board are the sole judges of credibility (Western Growers Ins. Co. v. Workers' Comp.

Appeals Bd. (1993) 16 Cal. App. 4th 227, 233 [20 Cal. Rptr. 2d 26, 58 Cal. Comp. Cases 323]); and on issues relating to factual findings, our review is limited to a search of the record for substantial evidence in support of the findings. (§ 5952, subd. (d).) Nevertheless, these facts do not support a finding of compensability.

There is no evidence that Fleetwood expected or required applicant to continue photographing RV's in between admiring Michelangelo's David and the Coliseum. The fact that Fleetwood was aware of his plans and facilitated his travel arrangements is immaterial in the absence of evidence that it did so because it expected applicant to function as an employee during that portion of his trip or that it exercised any control over his route.

Applicant asserts vigorously that, as a senior management employee, he was expected to be ever–vigilant concerning competitors and potential innovations. It is true that, in a somewhat analogous situation, an employee injured while participating in specific recreational or social activities is eligible for workers' compensation benefits if he or she can show that the activity was a "reasonable expectancy" of, or "impliedly required by," the employment. (§ 3600, subd. (a)(9).) However, although it is commendable for an employee to keep his employer's business in mind at all times, such a unilateral devotion to duty cannot be permitted to expand the employer's liability for workers' compensation to a "24/7" basis. We decline to extend the concept of "course of employment" to cover applicant's every waking hour. Accepting the fact that applicant looked at RV's during his Italian holiday, this did not transform his personal vacation into a business trip. Although a trip which has components of both business and pleasure may give rise to a compensable injury, the business element must be integral to the trip. The fact than [sic] an employee performs "some tidbit of work" during a personal trip will not transform the journey into part of the "course of employment." (Bramall v. Workers' Comp. Appeals Bd. (1978) 78 Cal. App. 3d 151, 158 [144 Cal. Rptr. 105, 43 Cal. Comp. Cases 288] (Bramall).) (Footnote 12)

In this case, applicant's occasional sighting of an interesting RV was clearly no more than a "tidbit" compared to several days of sightseeing. Although, as a conscientious employee, he may have always kept an eye open for useful ideas, which was not the purpose of his trip from Ferrara to Florence to Rome. We think it can be assumed that many employees – especially "white–collar" employees – give occasional thought to their employers' business, but such attention does not mean that they are "at work" at such times. Applicant, for example, may well have thought out design possibilities while at home, or while jogging, or while out for a Sunday drive, but Fleetwood would have not been liable to pay workers' compensation benefits if he had slipped in his hallway, suffered a heart attack on the track, or been involved in a collision. A unilateral, sporadic consideration of the employer's business, at times and locations that cannot be regulated or supervised by the employer, does not expand the course of employment.

This conclusion is consistent with existing case law. In Garzoli v. Workmen's Comp. App. Bd. (1970) 2 Cal. 3d 502, 506 [467 P.2d 833, 86 Cal. Rptr. 1, 35 Cal. Comp. Cases 193] (Garzoli), the court held that a police officer who was effectively required to wear his uniform while commuting to work, and was expected by his superiors to render aid or assistance when necessary, was "in the course of his employment" during the commute. Significantly, the court observed that the fact that the officer was "on call" 24 hours a day was not sufficient to nullify the "going and coming" rule; critical was the fact that he was visibly in uniform at the time of the accident and thus realistically subject to being expected to act like a police officer if necessary. The result in Garzoli was distinguished on this basis in State Lottery Com. v. Workers' Comp. Appeals Bd. (1996) 50 Cal. App. 4th 311, 318–319 [57 Cal. Rptr. 2d 745, 61 Cal. Comp. Cases 1134], in which the court declined to find an off–duty injury to be compensable merely because the employee was "on call" at all times.

In accordance with this approach, we reject the contention that applicant's occasional focus on job–related elements resulted in a constant "course of employment." (Footnote 13)

We are also compelled to note – intending no reference to the current case – that the rule for which applicant argues is simply unacceptably rich in opportunities for fraud. Unlike the situation in Garzoli, there would be no objective, verifiable indications of the employee's availability to participate in work activities let alone his actual performance of such activities. Any injured employee would be highly motivated to claim that at the time of the injury, he was actually pondering some work–related issue. The few valid claims under such a rule would be swamped in a flood of fraudulence, inevitably tending to discredit the entire workers' compensation system. If such a rule is to be made, we will not be the ones to make it. (Footnote 14)

Applicant then cites the rule that injuries incurred during a business trip may be compensable even if the employee has deviated substantially from the expected route. Thus, in IBM Corp. v. Workers' Comp. Appeals Bd. (1978) 77 Cal. App. 3d 279 [142 Cal. Rptr. 543, 43 Cal. Comp. Cases 161] (IBM Corp.), a California employee attending a 10–day training session in Chicago was killed while returning to Chicago from a weekend visit to relatives living 60 miles away. No training sessions took place over the weekend, but the employee was paid a per diem and obviously as a practical matter had to remain in the area. Upholding the award in favor of the employee's family, the court noted that the employer must have expected some form of "leisure time activity" on the part of the employee, and noted dryly that the family visit was "certainly no more of a departure . . . than was the banker's leisure time activity in Wiseman [see Footnote 9]." (IBM Corp., *supra*, 77 Cal. App. 3d at p. 283.) The employee was obliged to remain in the Chicago area during the weekend, and he could hardly have been expected to remain holed up in his hotel room. (Indeed, as Wiseman demonstrates, even that would not necessarily preserve him from injury.) Thus, the employer's liability was properly extended to cover the injury.

However, this begs the question of whether the business trip was over in this case. We agree that if applicant had been injured during a sightseeing stop between Dusseldorf and Ferrara, the injury might well have been compensable; but that is not this case. (Footnote 15)

Here, the business trip ended in Ferrara. IBM Corp. is not controlling.

The next argument to be addressed is based on the principle, stated above, that when an employee uses a mode of transportation advantageous to the employer, even a true commute may give rise to a compensable injury. The reasoning is that because driving the car was beneficial to the accomplishment of the business purpose, applicant's injury should be compensable. (Footnote 16)

Again, we find the crucial issue to be whether the business purpose continued, or even re–emerged, through the time of the accident.

In this respect applicant's strongest argument would be that he was required to return the car to Dusseldorf and thus had a business purpose in driving north from Rome. The argument has some appeal, but we reject it. (Footnote 17)

For one thing, it would be equally arguable that the entire trip after applicant left Ferrara was a journey back to Germany and the required return of the car, and this would again impermissibly turn the entire vacation extension into a purportedly integral part of the business trip. (Footnote 18)

Furthermore, we decline to characterize applicant as a reluctant caretaker of the car when its availability was an obvious convenience to him. Although there is substantial evidence that the car did have to be returned in Germany, and that this was the arrangement made by Fleetwood before the group arrived, there is no evidence that this arrangement was for the particular benefit of Fleetwood. Given the difficulty of renting a car in Germany for a journey into Italy, it might well have seemed more reasonable for the Fleetwood group, after their stops in Germany, simply to have flown into Italy and rented a new car there. (Footnote 19)

Or, the three Fleetwood representatives could have all traveled in the car of Manfred; indeed, after applicant's wife joined the group, at times all five went in Manfred's car, albeit without luggage. (Footnote 20)

What is apparent is that the arrangement was definitely to applicant's advantage. Having a car in which to drive south from Germany to Italy allowed him to pick up his wife at a Swiss airport, not to mention the convenience of having the car "ready to go" when the other Fleetwood representatives and Manfred headed for their respective homes. And despite the testimony from applicant and his wife to the effect that they would have preferred to leave from Rome, there is no evidence that there was any concern about the Dusseldorf departure at the time arrangements were made. The only pertinent evidence suggests that this was quite satisfactory to applicant because, as noted above, they had friends in Germany who could be visited on the way back. (Footnote 21)

Furthermore, although there was some evidence that Fleetwood would expect applicant to pay for his use of the car, he told his wife that the arrangements ensured that "We won't have to pay for a car." The fact (if it be a fact) that the arrangements later became irksome to him does not mean that a matter of mutual convenience was transformed into a burden imposed by Fleetwood. (Footnote 22)

Another potent factor bearing on the conclusion that the business trip had ended, for workers' compensation purposes, is that applicant's decision to go sightseeing with his wife substantially extended his time on the trip. It does not require a degree in statistics to recognize that if X accidents are likely to occur in a period of Y days, twice as many accidents will occur in 2Y days. Here, Fleetwood legally assumed the obligation that applicant would be involved in an accident some time in a period of Y days. However, applicant's decision to extend his trip also increased the chance that he would be involved in an accident, and that risk is not properly placed on Fleetwood. We find some instruction in the Board case of Norman v. Workers' Comp. Appeals Bd. (1997) 62 Cal. Comp. Cases 87 [writ denied] (Norman), (Footnote 23) in which an employee sent to Las Vegas on business turned back due to traffic on her way home, and then was injured when she resumed her journey the next day. In denying benefits, the Board relied both on her choice to use her own vehicle, and her turn–back to Las Vegas, as constituting "substantial deviations" from the employer's purpose. It also noted that in taking these actions, she put herself at a place and time not within the employer's specifications or control.

Norman stands at least for the principle that an employer is entitled to fix the temporal spatial limitations of a business trip, and that an employee who chooses to extend the trip for his or her personal convenience will lose the protection of workers' compensation. (Footnote 24)

In this case, applicant's election to remain in Europe for his own pleasure relieved Fleetwood from any further responsibility for potential misadventures during that portion of the journey.

In a final argument, applicant also claims that the opportunity to visit Italy on his own with his wife was an "inducement" to him to "agree" to make the trip. (See Trejo v. Maciel (1966) 239 Cal. App. 2d 487, 497 [48 Cal. Rptr. 765, 31 Cal. Comp. Cases 462] (Trejo).) (Footnote 25)

While there is evidence that he found the possibility of additional travel attractive, he cites us to no evidence that he had a realistic option of refusing to go at all or that Fleetwood offered the opportunity of a personal vacation to persuade him to go. (See also id., fn. 16.) The theory is inapplicable.

In summary, we find that the Board incorrectly determined that applicant was in the course and scope of his employment at the time of the accident. The order awarding benefits is therefore annulled. However, we will remand the matter for further proceedings on the issue of the applicability of section 5402.

Petitioner to recover its costs… .

Footnote 9. Note that we are not here dealing with a situation in which an employer, for equitable reasons, might be estopped to change its position after appearing to accept liability. Nor is this a case in which an employer representative with personal knowledge of critical facts changes his position after expressing an opinion. For example, if an employer actually present when an employee was injured promptly offered benefits, this would tend to support the employee's assertion that he was performing work duties if the employer later claimed the injury occurred during noncompensable "horseplay." Here, however, the critical facts are really not disputed and the "course of employment" issue is one of law.

Footnote 10. It has occurred to this court that the emphasis on whether or not applicant was in the process of returning the vehicle at the time of the accident may have been misplaced. As we explain, applicant's Italian travels were not conducted in the scope of his employment but as a private traveler for pleasure. Fleetwood's agreement that he could use the rental car had nothing to do with his employment. Suppose that a carless employee wishes to borrow a company car to attend some weekend festivity. The employer agrees but requires him to return the car to company premises. If the employee is injured on the drive back on Monday, is the employer liable for workers' compensation benefits? We would say "No," because the agreement that the employee could borrow the car was utterly unrelated to the fact of his employment. So it is here. Fleetwood might just as well have allowed Manfred, their German connection, to use the car so long as it was returned to Dusseldorf.

We realize that the "dual capacity" doctrine has been largely abrogated by statute. (§ 3602, subd. (d); see Ashdown v. Ameron Internat. Corp. (2000) 83 Cal. App. 4th 868, 874–875, [100 Cal. Rptr. 2d 20, 65 Cal. Comp. Cases 1026].) This doctrine allowed an employee to sue for damages – that is, avoid the "exclusive remedy" rule – if the employer stood in some "conceptually distinct" relationship to the employee with respect to the injury–causing mechanism. However, the doctrine only applied in the first place if the employee's injury was also compensable under workers' compensation. (§ 3602, subd. (a); § 3600.) Thus, if applicant had "rented" a car from Fleetwood to drive while attending a RV trade show, he would now be limited to workers' compensation damages if he were injured due to a defect in the vehicle. As there was no mutual intent that applicant would be performing job duties on his Italian journey, there is no bar to considering that Fleetwood, in "lending" him the car, was not acting as his employer at all.

Under this analysis, the obligation to return the car to Dusseldorf was simply not one entered into by an employee to the benefit of his employer.

However, as this was not the theory of the case in the briefing or argument, we do not rely on it. (See Gov. Code, § 68081.)

Footnote 11. In Wiseman, a banker on a business trip to New York died in a fire in his hotel room, where he had been drinking and smoking with a woman "registered as his wife." One imagines that the real widow filed for benefits with mixed emotions.

Footnote 12. At oral argument, counsel for applicant criticized our quotation of Bramall, arguing that the reference to "tidbit of work" was inappropriate. We recognize – as did the court in Bramall – that " 'where the employee is combining his own business with that of his employer, or attending to both at substantially the same time, no nice inquiry will be made as to which business he

was actually engaged in at the time of injury, unless it clearly appears that neither directly [n]or indirectly could he have been serving his employer.' [Citation.]" (Bramall, *supra*, 78 Cal. App. 3d at p. 157.) Bramall further noted that the "dominant purpose" test for compensability had virtually been abandoned.

Bramall was a "coming and going" case, and the court simply commented that the general rule that injuries suffered in the course of a normal commute are not compensable is not overcome merely because the employee performs "some tidbit of work" at home. We believe that the phrase also accurately states the rule applicable where an employee incorporates some trivial work–related activity into a personal journey. If nothing else, the felicity of the phrase justifies its inclusion.

We also note that the case cited in this context by applicant is not controlling. In Price v. Workers' Comp. Appeals Bd. (1984) 37 Cal. 3d 559 [693 P.2d 254, 209 Cal. Rptr. 674, 49 Cal. Comp. Cases 772] (Price), the employee commonly arrived at work early, and the doors were frequently open so that he could, in fact, begin work early. On the date of injury the doors were locked, and he was compelled to remain with his car on the street. While waiting, he decided to add oil to the engine, and while doing so was struck by a passing vehicle. The Supreme Court found that, because there was no dedicated parking area, the worker was "within the 'zone of employment' " (id. at p. 567); that his early arrival conferred an affirmative benefit on the employer (ibid.); and that, given the fact that he had nothing else to do while he waited, adding oil was an act " 'reasonably contemplated by the employment.' " (Id. at p. 568.) None of these theories directly applies to this case.

Footnote 13. We caution that we are not presented with facts showing that applicant was injured, for example, while actually inspecting a foreign RV in Florence or Rome.

Footnote 14. It is also to be noted that such an approach would clearly favor "white–collar" workers over their "blue–collar" brethren, as the duties of the latter less frequently involve intellectual functions, which theoretically could be performed anywhere, at any time.

Footnote 15. Applicant also cites Trans World Airlines v. Worker's Comp. Appeals Bd. (2002) 67 Cal. Comp. Cases 1386 [writ denied], in which a flight attendant was injured visiting a "cave park" during a 36–hour layover. The park was apparently listed by the employer as an available nearby attraction, and the Board held that the worker's visit to the park was an "expected" leisure activity during the layover. Once again the distinction is that here, the "business purpose" of the trip was not merely interrupted, it was concluded.

Footnote 16. Applicant argues for the application of an even stronger version of this rule that imposes liability if the employer furnishes the transportation. (See Zenith Nat. Ins. Co. v. Workmen's Comp. App. Bd. (1967) 66 Cal. 2d 944, 947 [428 P.2d 606, 59 Cal. Rptr. 622, 32 Cal. Comp. Cases 236].) However, because our crucial finding is that the "special errand" had terminated and applicant was "on his own" at the time of the accident, the fact that the vehicle was rented in Fleetwood's name is not controlling.

Footnote 17. At oral argument, Fleetwood conceded that if the accident had occurred on the airport grounds in Dusseldorf, the injury would have been compensable on the basis that any "deviation" from his employer's business had terminated. We do not reach this issue, and we stress that our decision extends only to the facts of this case.

Footnote 18. Although the Moodys had no specific itinerary for the return from Rome to Dusseldorf, they did intend to visit friends in Germany and this supports the conclusion that their personal interests remained paramount at the time of the accident.

Footnote 19. The journey from Germany involved passing through Switzerland and one or more nights on the road with no apparent business purpose. This leisurely itinerary did, however, serve to allow applicant to travel to Geneva to pick up his wife while his companions apparently pursued other interests during the day.

Footnote 20. But Manfred did later drive the other two Fleetwood representatives to the airport (probably Milan), with their luggage and, presumably, his own; it is reasonable to suppose that applicant and his bag could also have been transported.

Footnote 21. We also note that, in an obvious effort to make the Italy trip seem like a "chore," Mrs. Moody testified that she didn't really want to go to Italy and that she would have preferred to go to Germany. However, she didn't go to Germany with applicant, because, as she also testified, she didn't want to be dragged around looking at RV's. Thus, if the Moodys' main wish was to sightsee in Germany, they had to drive back from Italy. Again, the return to Dusseldorf can only have become a job "obligation" in retrospect.

Footnote 22. While applicant testified that he and his wife would have liked to cut their trip short and return home from Rome, it cannot be assumed that they would have done so but for the need to return the vehicle. There is no evidence that their flight date or departure city could have been changed, or whether the cost of any such change would have been acceptable. Applicant merely testified that he was "not aware" of any restrictions on his ticket.

Footnote 23. While cases so reported are not controlling and do not constitute stare decisis, they are citable to show the holding of the Board. The Board's interpretation of statutes it is charged with applying is entitled to respect. (Ralphs Grocery Co. v. Workers' Comp. Appeals Bd. (1995) 38 Cal. App. 4th 820, 827 at fn. 7 [45 Cal. Rptr. 2d 197, 60 Cal. Comp. Cases 840].)

Footnote 24. Insofar as the Board relied upon the fact that, at the time of the accident, the employee was at a place that the employer could not control the decision may be inconsistent with IBM Corp.

Footnote 25. Trejo is not a workers' compensation case, but it involves some of the same principles in the context of the employer's respondeat superior liability for the torts of an employee during a journey.

Page 353, Column 2, eighth paragraph, insert following '...greater in Reno.'

In *Reynoso v. Xanuda Fire & Marine Co.,* ANA 361883, 3618 84, March 21, 2006 (34 CWCR 103 34), the Board upheld a judge's award of compensation to a field service engineer injured in an auto accident on her way to a bible class while on a three week out of town employer assignment. The Board, in support of its decision, cited *Wiseman, supra,* noting that the test is whether the accident occurred while the activity, during which the employee is injured, is one *"that an employer may reasonably expect to be incident to its request that an employee spend time away from home. An employee away from home can hardly be expected to remain holed up in a hotel room."* (Italics by author for emphasis) [**Editor's Note:** In this case, the Board found no merit in defendant's argument that Section 3600(a)(9) also precluded coverage of applicant's injury, noting that the section is inapplicable to commercial travelers because a business traveler is *"on duty"* while in the course of his or her employment while on a business trip, citing *Jimenez v. Insurance Company of the State of Penn* (2004) 32 CWCR 220.]

§ 6.10(L)   Injured While Engaged in a Recreational, Social or Athletic Activity

Page 362, Column 1, fourth paragraph, insert following '...expressed herein.'

In annulling the Board's decision that allowed benefits to a police officer who injured a leg while playing in a pickup game of basketball at a private facility, the Court of Appeal, Third District, in *City of Stockton v. WCAB (Jenneiahn)* (2006) 71 Cal. Comp. Cases 5, stated, in part:

> This case poses the question whether a police officer who injured his leg while off duty, playing in a pickup game of basketball at a private facility, is entitled to workers' compensation benefits.
>
> A workers' compensation judge (WCJ) concluded the injury arose out of and occurred in the course of the police officer's employment because, in the WCJ's view, the officer reasonably believed that "his participation in cardiovascular activities such as basketball were [sic] expected by his employer." In a two–to–one decision, the Workers' Compensation Appeals Board denied the employer's petition for reconsideration.
>
> The police officer's employer then petitioned for, and we issued, a writ of review. We now shall annul the award of workers' compensation benefits.
>
> As we will explain, when an employee is injured during voluntary, off–duty participation in a recreational, social, or athletic activity, Labor Code section 3600, subdivision (a)(9) provides that the injury is not covered by workers' compensation, unless the activity was "a reasonable

expectancy of" the employment or it was "expressly or impliedly required by" the employment. General assertions that the employer expects an employee to stay in good physical condition, and that the employer benefits from the employee's doing so, are not sufficient for worker's compensation coverage since that would impose virtually limitless liability for any recreational or athletic activity in which the employee chooses to participate–a result that would run afoul of the limitation set forth in Labor Code section 3600, subdivision (a).

Turning to the facts of this case, we conclude the evidence does not support a finding that Officer Jenneiahn subjectively believed that his employer expected him to engage in an occasional pickup game of basketball in order to stay in shape. In any event, such a subjective belief would have been objectively unreasonable under the circumstances here. Thus, it cannot be said that the specific activity during which he was injured was a reasonable expectancy of, or was expressly or impliedly required by, his employment. For this reason, the Workers' Compensation Appeals Board erred in concluding that Jenneiahn's injury was covered by workers' compensation.

FACTS

Sean Jenneiahn is employed as a police officer by the City of Stockton (the City). He engages in additional employment by officiating at high school basketball and baseball games.

The City's police department has a regulation stating that police officers shall maintain good physical condition. However, after an officer is hired, the department does not require any physical fitness tests or examinations. According to the record in this case, no officer has ever been fired or otherwise disciplined for not being physically fit.

Officer Jenneiahn was not aware of the regulation requiring physical fitness, although he remembered that the application for employment said an officer must be physically fit to do the job. Some of his training officers advised him to stay in shape, and Jenneiahn believed that officers should remain physically fit. He did so by jogging and running, doing cardiovascular workouts, and playing basketball and softball.

The City's police officers are not given time to work out while on duty. However, in the basement of the police department, the City maintains a gymnasium and workout facility that is available for officers' use. Officer Jenneiahn did not use the department's facility because he preferred to work out elsewhere when he was not on duty.

While off duty and playing in a basketball game, Officer Jenneiahn hyperextended his leg and suffered a fracture of the tibia plateau.

The facility where the injury occurred is owned and operated by the Stockton Police Officers' Association (SPOA), not by the City. The facility, which has a gymnasium, kitchen, bar, pool tables, basketball court, barbeque facility, and racquetball court, is used for a variety of social, recreational, and athletic activities. SPOA members can use it whenever they want as part of their union dues.

When the SPOA facility opened, the City's Chief of Police issued a special order strictly prohibiting officers from visiting the facility for any reason while on duty, including taking meal breaks or using the restrooms.

The basketball game in which Officer Jenneiahn was playing when he was injured was not an employer–sponsored event. In fact, it was not a scheduled event at all. The game was described as a pickup game; Jenneiahn went to the SPOA facility and got into a game with others who were there. At the time, he had not been playing very much basketball. He was staying in shape by running and officiating at basketball games. He testified that he would have been in shape regardless of whether he played basketball.

DISCUSSION

I.

The question whether workers' compensation benefits should be received for injuries suffered by an employee during off–duty recreational or athletic pursuits has arisen often.

In Liberty Mut. Ins. Co. v. Ind. Acc. Com. (1952) 39 Cal. 2d 512 [247 P.2d 697, 17 Cal. Comp. Cases 237] (hereafter Liberty Mutual), the claimant was a live–in employee at a recreational resort. When not performing his duties, he could participate in any of the recreational activities available in the area, including swimming in a pool created by a dam across a stream. He was injured while diving into the pool. Because the pool was located beyond the area under its control, the employer could not prohibit the employee from swimming in the pool. (Id. at pp. 515–516.) The California Supreme Court concluded the injury was not covered by workers' compensation because it occurred while the employee "was engaged in a personal recreational activity on his own free time in an area without the orbit of his employment and beyond the control or dominion of his employer." (Id. at p. 517.) The court observed that to hold otherwise would make compensation coverage virtually limitless. (Id. at p. 518.)

The same conclusion was reached in Fireman's Fund Etc. Co. v. Ind. Acc. Com. (1952) 39 Cal. 2d 529 [247 P.2d 707, 17 Cal. Comp. Cases 229] (hereafter Fireman's Fund), where the claimant, a live–in cook and housekeeper, was injured during a walk. It was her custom to take short walks once or twice a day, and she had been advised to do so by the employer's doctor. On the day of the injury, she informed her employer that she was going for a walk. The employer told the employee not to go too far. (Id. at pp. 530, 531.) The Supreme Court found the injury was not compensable because it occurred while the employee was "walking on a public road as an act of recreational diversion of her own free choice and when off–duty from her work." (Id. at p. 535.) The court rejected her argument that she "was following her medical adviser's recommendation as to a suitable exercise, and so was conditioning herself to perform better the duties of her employment." (Id. at p. 534.) The court explained: "[I]f such theory should be adopted as sufficient to establish the necessary causal connection with the employment, then any injury sustained by an employee in a recreational activity would be compensable." (Ibid.)

In United Parcel Service of America, Inc. v. Industrial Accident Commission (1959) 172 Cal. App. 2d 73 [342 P.2d 41, 24 Cal. Comp. Cases 170], the Court of Appeal concluded that an employee who was injured in a foot race at a company picnic was not entitled to worker's compensation because "the intangible value of improvement in the employee's health or morals that is common to all kinds of recreation and social life" is not sufficient to make an injury compensable. (Id. at pp. 74, 75, 76–77; see also State Farm Fire & Casualty Co. v. Workers' Comp. Appeals Bd. (1981) 119 Cal. App. 3d 193, 197 [173 Cal. Rptr. 778, 46 Cal. Comp. Cases 622].)

And in City of Los Angeles v. Workers' Comp. Appeals Bd. (1979) 91 Cal. App. 3d 759 [154 Cal. Rptr. 379, 44 Cal. Comp. Cases 421] (hereafter City of Los Angeles), the Court of Appeal concluded that worker's compensation did not apply to injuries suffered by a police officer while weightlifting at home in preparation for a physical fitness test. (Id. at pp. 761, 766.) The Workers' Compensation Appeals Board had found compensation was appropriate because the officer was required to undergo a physical fitness test for which he was preparing. (Id. at p. 762.) The Court of Appeal disagreed, stating: "There is a wide variety of occupations in which it is necessary for the employee to maintain or improve physical or mental proficiency in order to continue employment or qualify for advancement. The variety of activities which might be thought to serve those purposes is infinite. When the self–improvement activity is voluntary, off the employer's premises and unregulated, the employer can have little knowledge of the physical risks involved, and no opportunity to minimize or protect the employee against such risks. These circumstances strongly militate in favor of classifying such activities as personal in the absence of some connection with employment other than hoped–for personal improvement. The fact that the employer tested the fitness of the employee periodically should not by itself make a self–improvement program an industrial activity." (Id. at p. 764, fn. omitted.)

In 1978, the Legislature acted on the question by adding to Labor Code section 3600 a provision that is now subdivision (a)(9) of the section. (Footnote 1)

(Further section references are to the Labor Code, with references to subdivision (a)(9) of section 3600 cited simply as subdivision (a)(9).) Section 3600 provides generally that an injury is covered by worker's compensation benefits when, at the time of the injury, "the employee is performing service growing out of and incidental to his or her employment and is acting within the course of his or her employment" and "the injury is proximately caused by the employment, either with or without negligence." (§ 3600, subds. (a)(2) & (a)(3).) However, subdivision (a)(9) sets forth a limitation. To be compensable, the injury must be one that "does not arise out of voluntary participation in any off–duty recreational, social, or athletic activity not constituting part of the employee's work–related duties, except where these activities are a reasonable expectancy of, or are expressly or impliedly required by, the employment."

The statutory scheme was construed in Ezzy v. Workers' Comp. Appeals Bd. (1983) 146 Cal. App. 3d 252 [194 Cal. Rptr. 90, 48 Cal. Comp. Cases 190] (hereafter Ezzy). The Court of Appeal noted that what is now subdivision (a)(9) was added by the Legislature in reaction to decisions that had allowed workers' compensation for injuries suffered by employees during off–duty activities where the activities "were reasonably foreseeable or expectable in the work setting." (Id. at p. 261.) The court concluded the subdivision was "intended to draw a brighter line delimiting compensability by replacing the general foreseeability test with one of 'reasonable expectancy' of employment" (ibid.), a test that is met when the employee subjectively believes his or her participation in the activity is expected by the employer, and the belief is objectively reasonable. (Id. at p. 260.)

The claimant in Ezzy was injured while playing in a regularly scheduled league softball game sponsored by her employer's law firm. (Ezzy, supra, 146 Cal. App. 3d at p. 257.) While the Court of Appeal considered the case to be close, it found the injury was compensable because (1) the claimant, a part–time law clerk in her second year of law school, was particularly vulnerable to pressure or suggestion that she play, (2) she felt she was essentially "drafted" to play when a partner handed her a t–shirt and schedule and told her that the team would see her at the next game, (3) female employees were pressured to play so the team would not forfeit due to the league's requirement that a team have four women on the field at all times during a game, (4) the firm paid for all equipment, t–shirts, and post–game refreshments, and hosted an awards banquet for players, (5) the firm benefited through improved office cooperation, spirit, morale, and camaraderie, and (6) the firm had not posted or read to its employees the provisions of what is now subdivision (a)(9). (Id. at pp. 257–258, 263–264.)

In Hughes Aircraft Co. v. Workers' Comp. Appeals Bd. (1983) 149 Cal. App. 3d 571 [196 Cal. Rptr. 904, 48 Cal. Comp. Cases 900] (hereafter Hughes Aircraft), the Court of Appeal further considered what is now subdivision (a). Noting legislative history shows the provision's purpose is "to ensure that an employer could provide voluntary off–duty recreational, social and athletic benefits for his employee's personal use without also bearing the expense of insuring the employee for workers' compensation benefits during participation in those activities" (id. at p. 575), the court found that the Legislature intended to exclude from coverage any injuries that are only remotely work–related, so as not to deter employers from subsidizing, sponsoring, or encouraging personal employee activities of a recreational or social character. (Ibid.)

The claimant in Hughes Aircraft suffered a slip and fall injury while attending an annual off–premises, off–duty holiday party that was subsidized 90 percent by the employer. The employer organized the event to foster an atmosphere of togetherness, but attendance was wholly voluntary. An employee's position would not be enhanced by attendance, and there would not be any adverse consequence if an employee did not attend. (Hughes Aircraft, supra, 149 Cal. App. 3d at pp. 572, 573.) The Workers' Compensation Appeals Board awarded compensation based solely on its view that the employer obtained a direct benefit from the party. (Ibid.) The Court of

Appeal held "it was incorrect as a matter of law to conclude that the existence of a direct benefit to the employer could be used to circumvent the express terms" of now subdivision (a)(9). (Id. at p. 575.)

Since Hughes Aircraft, a number of published decisions applying what is now subdivision (a)(9) have found that injuries suffered in recreational, social, or athletic settings were covered by workers' compensation.

In Smith v. Workers' Comp. Appeals Bd. (1987) 191 Cal. App. 3d 127 [236 Cal. Rptr. 248, 52 Cal. Comp. Cases 162] (hereafter Smith), a math teacher suffered fatal injuries while windsurfing at a math club picnic. (Id. at pp. 129–130.) The Court of Appeal considered the question "extremely close," but concluded that certain factors tipped the balance to compensability: (1) the teacher was classified as temporary and, thus, was vulnerable to pressure or suggestion that he participate to improve his chances of being rehired; (2) the club was an official school club, and the picnic was an annually scheduled event; (3) teachers were encouraged to participate in school club activities; (4) annual evaluations of teachers were based in part on their willingness to participate in club activities; (5) the event benefited the school by promoting better student–teacher relationships; (6) math club funds were used to provide food and refreshments; and (7) students were required to submit parental permission slips in order to participate. (Id. at 141.)

In Wilson v. Workers' Comp. Appeals Bd. (1987) 196 Cal. App. 3d 902 [239 Cal. Rptr. 719, 52 Cal. Comp. Cases 369] (hereafter Wilson), the claimant was a police officer who injured his ankle while running at a junior college track. As a member of the police department's special emergency response team (SERT), he had to pass physical tests four times a year in order to remain on the team. The tests included a requirement that officers over the age of 35 must be able to run two miles in 17 minutes. A SERT supervisor testified he told SERT officers that they would have to engage in off–duty exercise to pass the tests. (Id. at pp. 904, 908.) The Court of Appeal held the injury was compensable because "[i]t would be completely unrealistic to conclude that off–duty running was not expected" of a SERT member over 35 years old who wanted to pass the SERT tests. (Id. at p. 908.)

In Kidwell v. Workers' Comp. Appeals Bd. (1995) 33 Cal. App. 4th 1130 [39 Cal. Rptr. 2d 540, 60 Cal. Comp. Cases 296] (hereafter Kidwell), the Court of Appeal found compensable an injury suffered by a California Highway Patrol (CHP) officer while she was practicing a standing long jump at home. The standing long jump was a required protocol of the CHP's annual, mandatory fitness test. In past years, she had passed the fitness tests except for the standing long jump. Her failure to pass the standing long jump had significant consequences, including the loss of a $130 per month salary differential, loss of eligibility for certain assignments and overtime, issuance of a "fitness plan," and an entry in her performance evaluation. (Id. at pp. 1132, 1133 & fn. 4.) Under the circumstances, the court concluded that it would be "patently unreasonable" to find the CHP did not expect the claimant to practice for the standing long jump test. (Id. at p. 1139.)

On the other hand, a number of published decisions applying what is now subdivision (a)(9) have found that injuries suffered in recreational, social, or athletic settings were not covered by workers' compensation.

In Meyer v. Workers' Comp. Appeals Bd. (1984) 157 Cal. App. 3d 1036 [204 Cal. Rptr. 74, 49 Cal. Comp. Cases 459] (hereafter Meyer), a car salesman was injured while driving for a weekend visit to his supervisor's place near the Colorado River. (Id. at p. 1039.) The Court of Appeal concluded the injury was not compensable because (1) the employer did not subsidize or sponsor the event, and it was not regularly scheduled–it was just an informal invitation by a supervisor, (2) while the visit might foster improved morale, this is true of every social event and, therefore, it is not sufficient to impose compensability, and (3) there was insufficient evidence of pressure exerted to attend the outing. (Id. at p. 1043.) Simply stated, the "trip, although initiated by a supervisor, was not a reasonable expectancy of the employment." (Id. at p. 1044.)

In Todd v. Workers' Comp. Appeals Bd. (1988) 198 Cal. App. 3d 757 [243 Cal. Rptr. 925, 53 Cal. Comp. Cases 65] (hereafter Todd), the claimant suffered a knee injury while playing basketball on the employer's premises during a lunch break. The employer allowed employees to install a basketball hoop and backboard, and apparently condoned the games. (Id. at pp. 759, 760–761.) The Court of Appeal concluded the injury was not covered by workers' compensation because there was no substantial evidence the employee "reasonably believed he was expected to participate in basketball games during his lunch break, or that participation was expressly or impliedly required by the employment." (Id. at p. 760.)

In Taylor v. Workers' Comp. Appeals Bd. (1988) 199 Cal. App. 3d 211 [244 Cal. Rptr. 643, 53 Cal. Comp. Cases 115] (hereafter Taylor), the claimant was a police officer who was injured at a city–owned gymnasium while playing in a pickup game of basketball during his lunch hour. Although the police department expected officers to keep themselves in good physical condition, it provided no formal training sessions or guidelines, and there were no formal physical fitness tests. The department had issued a general order that athletic injuries would be considered to be suffered on duty if they were suffered in a pre–approved athletic event, but that workers' compensation benefits would not be awarded without advance approval of the event. (Id. at pp. 213, 214–215.) The Court of Appeal found that participation in the pickup game was voluntary, and it was not reasonably expected or required by the officer's employment. (Id. at p. 215.) The court added that it is reasonable to permit an employer to limit its liability for athletic injuries, as had the department. "To hold otherwise would in effect render the employer potentially liable for any injury sustained in any recreational or athletic activity if the activity contributed to the employee's physical fitness. Such broad potential liability would be contrary to the legislative intent of section 3600, subdivision (a)(9)." (Id. at p. 216.)

In Tensfeldt v. Workers' Comp. Appeals Bd. (1998) 66 Cal. App. 4th 116 [77 Cal. Rptr. 2d 691, 63 Cal. Comp. Cases 973], the claimant was a city water department employee who injured his knee while playing basketball with other department employees at a city gymnasium during the workday. The game was conducted during working hours because the employees had finished their job assignments early. (Id. at p. 119.) The Court of Appeal held the injury was not covered by workers' compensation. The fact the employee was not technically off duty at the time did not change the fact that participation was voluntary and was not reasonably expected or required by the employer. (Id. at p. 126–127.)

II.

The authorities discussed in part I, ante, illustrate the rule that when an employee is injured during voluntary, off–duty participation in a recreational, social, or athletic activity, the injury is not covered by workers' compensation, unless the activity was "a reasonable expectancy of, or [was] expressly or impliedly required by, the employment." (§ 3600, subd. (a)(9).)

In applying the reasonable expectancy test, we first consider whether the employee subjectively believed that participation in the activity was expected by the employer. (Ezzy, *supra*, 146 Cal. App. 3d at p. 260.) This issue is a question of fact, which we review under the substantial evidence rule. (Meyer, *supra*, 157 Cal. App. 3d at p. 1042.)

We then determine whether the employee's belief was objectively reasonable. (Ezzy, *supra*, 146 Cal. App. 3d at p. 260.) This issue is a question of law that we determine independently. (Meyer, *supra*, 157 Cal. App. 3d at p. 1042.)

In considering these issues, we must focus our attention on

the specific activity in which the employee was involved when the injury occurred. This is so because subdivision (a)(9) is not intended to replace the basic requirement that to be compensable, (1) an injury must occur while the employee is performing service growing out of and incidental to his or her employment and acting in the course of employment, and (2) the employment must be the proximate cause of the injury. (§ 3600, subd. (a)(2) & (3); Wilson, *supra*, 196 Cal. App. 3d at p. 905.) Subdivision (a)(9) was intended to limit, rather than to expand, the scope of liability that an excessively liberal application of the basic test might support. (Meyer, *supra*, 157 Cal. App. 3d at pp. 1040–1041; Hughes Aircraft Co., *supra*, 149 Cal. App. 3d at p. 575.)

Indeed, unless courts require a substantial nexus between an employer's expectations or requirements and the specific off–duty activity in which the employee was engaged, the scope of coverage becomes virtually limitless and contrary to the legislative intent of subdivision (a)(9). (Taylor, *supra*, 199 Cal. App. 3d at p. 216; see also Fireman's Fund, *supra*, 39 Cal. 2d at p. 534; City of Los Angeles, *supra*, 91 Cal. App. 3d at p. 764.)

Accordingly, general assertions that it would benefit the employer for, or even that the employer expects, an employee to stay in good physical condition are not sufficient to require workers' compensation for injuries suffered by the employee during any recreational or athletic activity in which the employee chooses to participate. (Taylor, *supra*, 199 Cal. App. 3d at p. 216; see also

Fireman's Fund, *supra*, 39 Cal. 2d at p. 534; City of Los Angeles, *supra*, 91 Cal. App. 3d at p. 764.)

The decisions that have allowed workers' compensation pursuant to subdivision (a)(9) have generally found the employer expected the employee to participate in the specific activity in which the employee was engaged at the time of injury. In Ezzy, the employer expected the employee to play on the law firm's softball team in a regularly scheduled game, and that is what she was doing when she was injured. (Ezzy, *supra*, 146 Cal. App. 3d at pp. 257–258, 263–264.) In Wilson, the employer expected the employee to engage in off–duty running in order to pass the running test to which he was subjected four times a year, and he was running when injured. Wilson, *supra*, 196 Cal. App. 3d at p. 908.) In Kidwell, the employer expected the employee to practice the standing long jump in order to meet its testing requirements, and that is what she was doing when injured. (Kidwell, *supra*, 33 Cal. App. 4th at p. 1139.)

We also must look for specific conduct of the employer that would reasonably convey to the employee that participation in a particular activity is expected. Again, general assertions of benefit to the employer, or that the employer condones or allows the activity, are insufficient. (Todd, *supra*, 198 Cal. App. 3d 760; Meyer, *supra*, 157 Cal. App. 3d at p. 1043; Hughes Aircraft, *supra*, 149 Cal. App. 3d at p. 575.)

Decisions that have found employee injuries compensable under subdivision (a)(9) have found specific conduct by the employer with respect to the activity at issue. In Ezzy, a partner of the law firm handed the employee a t–shirt and schedule and said the team would see her at the next game. While this was less than a direct order, it was not a mere invitation to play should she so desire. (Ezzy, *supra*, 146 Cal. App. 3d at pp. 257, 258.) In Smith, the teacher's annual evaluation was based in part on his willingness to participate in student club activities. (Smith, *supra*, 191 Cal. App. 3d at p. 141.) In Wilson, the employer required the employee to pass a specific running test four times a year. (Wilson, *supra*, 196 Cal. App. 3d at p. 908.) In Kidwell, a standing long jump was part of the employer's mandatory fitness testing program and there were significant adverse consequences for failure.

(Kidwell, *supra*, 33 Cal. App. 4th at p. 1139.)

III.

Turning to the facts of this case, we first conclude the evidence does not support a finding that Officer Jenneiahn subjectively believed that his employer expected him to engage in an occasional pickup game of basketball.

Officer Jenneiahn remembered that his employment application said an officer must be fit to do the job, some of his training officers advised him to stay in shape, and he believed that an officer should be in shape to do the job. However, he knew that he was not subject to any kind of physical fitness testing or examination, and he was not aware of any officer having been disciplined for not being physically fit.

Moreover, Officer Jenneiahn did not incorporate games of pickup basketball into a training regimen. He played only occasionally, maybe once a month. He believed that basketball was not necessary to maintain his physical fitness; he stayed in shape by running and through his officiating job at high school games. And he testified that he was in shape regardless of the occasional pickup basketball game.

In addition, the pickup game in which Officer Jenneiahn was playing when injured was wholly unconnected to his employer. It was in a private facility that was not owned or operated by the employer. The game was not part of a league or other scheduled event. There is nothing in the record to suggest the employer in any way sponsored, encouraged, condoned, or was even aware of the activity. In fact, the employer had issued a directive prohibiting any employee from using the private facility for any reason during the employee's work hours.

In sum, the evidence does not establish that Officer Jenneiahn believed that his employer expected him to participate in the game of pickup basketball. The record establishes only his belief that it was a good idea for a police officer to stay in good physical condition, and his leap to a conclusion that any physical activity in which an officer chooses to engage must be covered by workers' compensation. Such a belief is far too broad and inconsistent with the legislative intent of subdivision (a)(9).

We also conclude that even if there was evidence that Officer Jenneiahn subjectively believed his employer expected him to play in a pickup game of basketball, this belief would not have been objectively reasonable. The game had no connection whatsoever to the employer. It was conducted in a private facility over which the employer had no control. It was not a scheduled activity, and the employer did nothing to sponsor, encourage, or condone the activity. Although the employer expected its officers to maintain sufficient general physical fitness necessary to perform their duties, it did not subject officers to any form of physical fitness testing, let alone testing on the skills utilized in playing basketball. And Jenneiahn knew that playing basketball was unnecessary to his physical fitness for the job.

On this record, it is readily apparent that playing in the off–duty pickup game of basketball was a wholly voluntary choice by Officer Jenneiahn. His employer did not exert any form of pressure to make his choice less than voluntary. The general, and reasonable, expectation that a police officer will maintain sufficient physical fitness to perform his or her duties is not a sufficient basis to extend workers' compensation coverage to any and all off–duty recreational or athletic activities in which an officer voluntarily chooses to participate.

DISPOSITION

The award of workers' compensation benefits is annulled, and the matter is remanded to the Workers' Compensation Appeals Board with directions to enter an order denying such benefits. The parties shall bear their own costs in the proceedings before this court... .

Footnote 1. The provision that is now subdivision (a)(9) was added as subdivision (h) of section 3600. (Stats. 1978, ch. 1303, § 5, pp. 4262–4263.) Legislation in 1982 changed

the provision to subdivision (a)(8) of section 3600. (Stats. 1982, ch. 922, § 4, p. 3366.) It became subdivision (a)(9) in 1986 legislation. (Stats. 1986, ch. 755, § 1, p. 2474.)

Page 362, Column 1, delete fifth paragraph, beginning 'In Mason v. Lake Dolores Group...' through the end of the paragraph ending '...the following ruling' and insert the following:

In *Mason v. Lake Dolores Group, LLC* (2004) 69 Cal. Comp. Cases 353, the Court of Appeal, Fourth District, in a published decision finding that an employee's injury rendering him a paraplegic, after he rode a waterslide at his employer's place of business and crashed into a dam at the end of the slide, did not arise out of nor in the course of his employment, stated, in part:

Page 375, Column 2, fourth paragraph, insert following '...judge's decision.'

In *Zenith National Insurance Co., et al. v. WCAB (Ellis)* (2006) 71 Cal. Comp. Cases 658, an employee attended a co–worker's birthday celebration honoring a co–worker in the employer's breakroom. The employee (applicant) gave the co–worker a hug and a single spank on the top part of her buttocks. Five days later, the co–worker's fiancé assaulted and injured the applicant in the employer's parking lot after the co–worker pointed the applicant out to her fiancé.

The Appeals Board, in holding that the applicant's injuries arose out of his employment, stated in part:

(1) if the spank had led to an injury, the injury would have been compensable because it occurred on defendant's premises, (2) the spank led to the assault and the connection of the assault to Applicant's employment was not 'so remote that it [could not] be said to arise therefrom,' (3) the grievance leading to the assault was work–related, and (4) the encounter between Applicant and the co–worker's fiancé in the parking lot was a chance encounter... .

§ 6.10(JJ) Injured While Traveling to or From a Medical Facility for Treatment and/or Examination – Compensable Consequences

Page 453, Column 1, sixth paragraph, insert following '...Cases 107.'

In *Pleasant Valley School District, et al. v. WCAB (Padron)* (2005) 70 Cal. Comp. Cases 1043, the Board upheld a judge's finding that an injury to an applicant while in vocational rehabilitation was a compensable consequence of her prior industrial back injury.

§ 6.10(SS) Injured in a Nonindustrial Accident as a Result of a Prior Industrial Injury– Compensable Consequence

Page 461, Column 1, fifth paragraph, insert following '...industrial injury'

See also *Christian Salveson aka Merchant Refrigeration v. WCAB (Coble)* (2006) 71 Cal. Comp. Cases 1457, where the Board upheld a judge's decision finding that an applicant's liver disorder was a compensable consequence of the effects of medications he was taking for his industrial orthopedic injury.

§ 6.11(A) Cities, Counties, Districts, or Other Public Entities, Sheriff, Police, or Fire Depts.; Division of Forestry of the State Dept. of Natural Resources; Wildlife Protection Branch of the Dept. of Fish and Game; Employees of (Lab. Code Sec. 3212)

Page 467, Column 2, sixth paragraph, insert following '...otherwise stated.'

In an unpublished opinion holding that an employer's physician's report did not refute a correctional officer's heart trouble presumption because the report simply pointed out that there was nothing specific about the officer's job that caused his heart attack, the Court of Appeal, Third District, in *Jackson v. WCAB* (2005) 70 Cal. Comp. Cases 1085, stated, in part:

There is no dispute here that Davis, Sr., was an employee of the Department of Corrections with custodial duties who had heart trouble and therefore was entitled to the presumption contained in Labor Code section 3212.2. Thus, the question becomes whether there was substantial evidence to overcome that presumption that Davis, Sr.'s heart trouble arose out of and in the course of his employment.

The heart trouble presumption contained in Labor Code section 3212 et seq. (including Labor Code section 3212.2) "was adopted as a response to the ' "persisting cleavage in medical theory itself" . . . as to the relationship between stress, physical exertion and progressive heart disease.' [Citation.] Formerly, 'the fate of an individual worker's claim generally did not turn on the facts of his particular employment or heart attack, but rather was decided almost fortuitously on the basis of which of the two competing schools of medical thought [i.e., those who accept and those who reject the view that stress or exertion can contribute to the development of heart trouble] the lay referee or appeals board decided to endorse in the particular case.' [Citation.]

For 20 years the statute did not prevent proof of preexisting disease, and the Legislature found that in such form it 'failed to alleviate the gross inequities and unfairness which flowed from the inevitable and inconclusive "battle of the experts". . . . ' [Citation.] The preclusion was adopted as a solution." (Johnson v. Workers' Comp. Appeals Bd. (1985) 163 Cal. App. 3d 770, 775–776 [210 Cal. Rptr. 28, 50 Cal. Comp. Cases 71].)

The heart trouble presumption is a presumption affecting the burden of proof and is rebuttable. (Reeves v. Workers' Comp. Appeals Bd. (2000) 80 Cal. App. 4th 22, 30 [95 Cal. Rptr. 2d 74, 65 Cal. Comp. Cases 359].) It imposes the burden on the employer to prove that the applicant's heart trouble did not arise out of and in the course of his employment. (Ibid.)

The heart trouble presumption for some public safety workers contains what is called an "anti–attribution clause." For example, in section 3212.5 (which is applicable to police officers and highway patrol members), the anti–attribution clause further qualifies the heart trouble presumption: "Such heart trouble . . . so developing or manifesting itself in such cases shall in no case be attributed to any disease existing prior to such development or manifestation." Examining the effect of section 3212.5, the appellate court in Parish v. Workers' Comp. Appeals Bd. (1989) 210 Cal. App. 3d 92, 98 [258 Cal. Rptr. 287, 54 Cal. Comp. Cases 155], concluded it was the employer's burden to show "what '. . . contemporaneous nonwork–related event. . . . ,' if any, was the sole cause of applicant's heart trouble."

Stated another way, the presumption " 'does not guarantee [covered] employees that they will recover workers' compensation benefits for a heart attack which occurs during the course of their employment, but leaves the employer free to rebut the statutory presumption by proving that some contemporaneous nonwork–related event–for example, a victim's strenuous recreational exertion–was the sole cause of the heart attack.' [Citation.] That is, an employer may rebut the presumption, but only with proof of causation by a nonindustrial event occurring at the same time as the heart trouble developed or manifested itself." (Johnson v. Workers' Comp. Appeals Bd., *supra*, 163 Cal. App. 3d at p. 776.)

Thus, in Geoghegan v. Retirement Board (1990) 222 Cal. App. 3d 1525, 1528 [272 Cal. Rptr. 419, 55 Cal. Comp. Cases 301], the employer presented evidence that the employee's heart attack was caused by the cold and altitude he encountered on a skiing vacation to Vail, Colorado. The appellate court concluded this medical evidence was sufficient to overcome the presumption that the employee's heart trouble was job related. (Id. at pp. 1530–1531.)

The heart trouble presumption applicable to correctional officers contained in section 3212.2 does not contain an anti–attribution clause. " ' " 'The words of the statute must be construed in context, keeping in mind the statutory purpose, and statutes or statutory sections relating to the same subject must be harmonized, both internally and with each other, to the extent possible.' " ' " ' (Barajas v. Oren Realty & Development Co. (1997) 57 Cal. App. 4th 209, 216–217 [67 Cal. Rptr. 2d 62].) Because the correctional officers' statute (section 3212.2) does not prohibit the attribution of heart trouble to "any disease existing prior to such development or manifestation," the employer of a correctional officer may rebut the heart trouble presumption in a second way. It may present evidence that the heart trouble was attributable to pre–existing disease unrelated to the officer's employment.

Here, substantial evidence does not support the WCAB's finding that Davis, Sr.'s heart trouble was unrelated to his job. The only evidence on this subject was presented by Dr. Ogrod in his report. There, the doctor conclusively stated "there is nothing specific about the patient's occupation that would lead us to conclude that his viral infection and the secondary myocarditis was occupationally related." The doctor also stated, "[t]here would be nothing in this sequence of events that would be linked to a specific occupation or to suggest that his occupation placed him at greater risk for developing this set of problems." Simply pointing out that there is nothing specific about his job that caused his heart attack or put him at a greater risk for this condition does not satisfy the Department of Correction's burden to prove that a contemporaneous nonwork–related event was the sole cause of the heart attack in question. Moreover, this "evidence" does not demonstrate the heart trouble here was attributable to a pre–existing nonindustrial disease. Stated another way, there was no evidence in the record that Davis's respiratory illness was not related to his job as a correctional officer. The conclusion that there is "no medical basis that would justify linking this patient's acute medical problems to his occupation" further failed to establish that any nonwork–related event was the sole cause of this heart attack or that this heart disease was the result of a pre–existing disease unrelated to his job. Without any such evidence to controvert the presumption of Labor Code section 3212.2, that presumption controls. We, therefore, cannot uphold the WCAB's findings… .

§ 6.11(B)(1) Appeals Board May, Upon Request, Determine Disability of Public Employees' Retirement System Members As Well As City or County Employees

Page 475, Column 2, fourth paragraph, insert following '…disability retirement…'

See *Stephens v. County of Tulare, et al.* (2006) 71 Cal. Comp. Cases 571, for a California Supreme Court decision holding that a county employee was never "dismissed" from his employment because of disability within the meaning of Government Code section 31725. In explaining what the term "dismiss" means, the high Court stated, in part:

To "dismiss" means to "send or remove from employment." (Webster's 3d New Internat. Dict. (2002) p. 652.) As used in connection with section 31725,

"dismissed," "terminated," and "released" all share a common meaning. Those terms describe a circumstance in which the employment relationship, at the employer's election, has ended. Because the relationship has ended, (1) the employer no longer has an obligation to pay salary or other forms of compensation, and (2) the employee has no basis for expectation that a position exists, will be kept open, or will be made available upon the employee's offer to return to work. Because section 31725 is concerned only with the consequences of "[p]ermanent incapacity for the performance of duty," we can reasonably assume the statute addresses permanent, not merely temporary, absence from employment. An employee who is temporarily absent from the workplace due to illness or vacation, where both employer and employee understand the employee will return to work when the reason for the leave ceases, would have no need to pursue a disability retirement before the board of retirement… .

For a similar case where the Court of Appeal, Second District, relied on the above case, see *Kelly v. County of Los Angeles* (2006) 71 Cal. Comp. Cases 934.

§ 6.11(M) Peace officers, Definition of

Page 485, Column 2, second paragraph, insert following '…Cases 539.'

See also *Pettigrew v. WCAB* (2006) 71 Cal. Comp. Cases 1248.

§ 7.0   WHAT ARE THE BENEFITS?

§ 7.1   Transportation Expenses

Page 487, Column 1, delete last three lines in paragraph 4, commencing with 'of examination and back at the rate of 34 cents a mile...' and insert the following:

of examination and back at the rate of 48.5 cents a mile, as of time of publication of this book plus any bridge tolls. [See Section 8.0 of this book for detailed discussion of the benefits].

Intentionally blank

§ 8.0 MEDICAL BENEFITS

Page 493, Column 1, first paragraph, insert following '...Section 4600.'

Labor Code section 4601 provides:

(a) If the employee so requests, the employer shall tender the employee one change of physician. The employee at any time may request that the employer tender this one–time change of physician.

Upon request of the employee for a change of physician, the maximum amount of time permitted by law for the employer or insurance carrier to provide the employee an alternative physician or, if requested by the employee, a chiropractor, or an acupuncturist shall be five working days from the date of the request. Notwithstanding the 30–day time period specified in Section 4600, a request for a change of physician pursuant to this section may be made at any time. The employee is entitled, in any serious case, upon request, to the services of a consulting physician, chiropractor, or acupuncturist of his or her choice at the expense of the employer. The treatment shall be at the expense of the employer.

(b) If an employee requesting a change of physician pursuant to subdivision (a) has notified his or her employer in writing prior to the date of injury that he or she has a personal chiropractor, the alternative physician tendered by the employer to the employee, if the employee so requests, shall be the employee's personal chiropractor. For the purpose of this article, "personal chiropractor" means the employee's regular chiropractor licensed pursuant to Chapter 2 (commencing with Section 1000) of Division 2 of the Business and Professions Code, who has previously directed treatment of the employee, and who retains the employee's chiropractic treatment records, including his or her chiropractic history.

(c) If an employee requesting a change of physician pursuant to subdivision (a) has notified his or her employer in writing prior to the date of injury that he or she has a personal acupuncturist, the alternative physician tendered by the employer to the employee, if the employee so requests, shall be the employee's personal acupuncturist. For the purpose of this article,

"personal acupuncturist" means the employee's regular acupuncturist licensed pursuant to Chapter 12 (commencing with Section 4935) of Division 2 of the Business and Professions Code, who has previously directed treatment of the employee, and who retains the employee's acupuncture treatment records, including his or her acupuncture history.

In holding that Section 4601 is not applicable where an employer has established an MPN, the Board in *Laier v. WCAB* (2006) 71 Cal. Comp. Cases 856, stated, in part:

The applicant argues that Labor Code Section 4601(a) authorizes him to choose a treating physician outside the MPN. He argues that the legislature's failure to change Labor Code Section 4601 is an indication that it intended that injured workers should be able to select treating physicians outside their employer's MPN.

Medical Provider Networks are not mandatory. In the event that an employer does not establish an MPN, Labor Code Section 4600(c) allows the applicant to select a physician within a reasonable geographical area. The parties have agreed that this employer does have an MPN, and that physicians are available within that MPN to treat the applicant. Labor Code Section 4601 is not applicable. Even if it was, it provides that the employer shall provide an alternative physician. It does not provide for free choice… .

§ 8.6 Medical–Legal Expense – Laboratory, X–Ray and Medical Reports

Page 511, Column 2, delete fourth paragraph, beginning 'A nurse case manager...' through the end of the page ending '...then suggested a'

Page 511, Column 2, after 'Nurse Case Manager' heading insert the following:

A nurse case manager is included under the term "medical treatment" in Labor Code section 4600.

In *Lamin v. City of Los Angeles et. al.* (2004) 69 Cal.

Comp. Cases 1002, the Appeals Board set forth the preferred procedure for selecting a nurse case manager as follows:

(1) The employer or insurance carrier should initially designate a nurse case manager;

(2) If the applicant objects (at any time) to the person designated by the defendant, the parties should confer and *jointly* select a nurse case manager (i.e., an "agreed" nurse case manager); and

(3) If the parties are unable to agree on an appropriate nurse case manager within a reasonable period of time (which time period may vary depending on the particular circumstances of the case), a Workers' Compensation Judge should resolve the parties' dispute and appoint a nurse case manager.

The Board in this case stated, in part:

Preliminarily, contrary to defendant's assertion, we conclude that, where a nurse case manager is established to be reasonably required, this constitutes "medical treatment" within the meaning of Labor Code section 4600.

First, section 4600 specifically provides that "[m]edical . . . treatment, *including nursing*, . . . that is reasonably required to cure or relieve the injured worker from the effects of his or her injury shall be provided by the employer." (Lab. Code, § 4600 (emphasis added).) Thus, section 4600 covers the services of a nurse case manager. (*Castorena v. Liberty Mutual Insurance Co.* (2004) 32 Cal. Workers' Comp. Rptr. 74 (Appeals Board panel).) Indeed, "nursing" can even include services preformed [*sic*] by persons who are not licensed nurses, e.g., the services of a "practical nurse." (*Henson v. Workmen's Comp. Appeals Bd.* (1972) 27 Cal. App. 3d 452, 458 [103 Cal. Rptr. 785] [37 Cal. Comp. Cases 564]; *Pacific Electric Ry. Co. v. Industrial Acc. Com. (Patterson)* (1950) 96 Cal. App. 2d 651 [216 P.2d 135] [15 Cal. Comp. Cases 88]; Cal. *Casualty Indemnity Exchange v. Industrial Acc. Com. (Elliston)* (1948) 84 Cal. App. 2d 417 [190 P.2d 990] [13 Cal. Comp. Cases 50]; *Martinez v. Workers' Comp. Appeals Bd.* (1999) 64 Cal. Comp. Cases 1176 (writ den.).)

Second, even if we were to assume that the term "nursing" in section 4600 does not encompass a nurse case manager, section 4600 is inclusive and not exclusive; thus, its coverage extends to medically related services not specifically enumerated by it. (*Smyers v. Workers' Comp. Appeals Bd.* (1984) 157 Cal. App. 3d 36, 41 [203 Cal. Rptr. 521] [49 Cal. Comp. Cases 454].)

Accordingly, reasonably required medical treatment can include the services of a case manager, and this may occasionally be true even if the case manager is not a licensed professional, e.g., if he or she is not a licensed nurse or social worker. (See discussion below.)

Nevertheless, before a defendant may be held liable for a nurse case manager, several prerequisites must be met.

To begin with, a nurse case manager must be reasonably required to cure or relieve the effects of the injury. (Lab. Code, § 4600.)

Under the law presently in effect, "reasonably required" medical treatment "means treatment that is based upon . . .

the updated American College of Occupational and Environmental Medicine's Occupational Medicine Practice Guidelines [ACOEM guidelines]." (Lab. Code, § 4600(b).) These ACOEM guidelines are "presumptively correct on the issue of extent and scope of medical treatment, regardless of date of injury." (Lab. Code, § 4604.5(c).) This presumption of correctness "is rebuttable and may be controverted by a preponderance of the evidence establishing that a variance from the guidelines is reasonably required to cure and relieve the employee from the effects of his or her injury" (Lab. Code, § 4604.5(c)), however, it is a presumption affecting the burden of proof. (*Id.*; see also, Evid. Code, § § 605, 606.)

Thus, if the ACOEM guidelines cover applicant's type of injury, she must either: (1) show that the ACOEM guidelines call for a nurse case manager; (Footnote 3) or (2) prove by a preponderance of the evidence that a nurse case manager is reasonably required notwithstanding the ACOEM guidelines. (Lab. Code, § 4604.5(c).)

If the second situation applies, applicant's evidence in rebuttal to the presumption of correctness of the ACOEM guidelines might consist of the report(s) of a treating physician, an agreed medical evaluator ("AME"), or a qualified medical evaluator ("QME") (see Lab. Code, § § 4062(a), 4062.3, 5703(a)) or, perhaps, a medical treatment protocol published by another medical specialty society. (See Lab. Code, § 5703(h).) In order to rebut the presumption of correctness, however, any medical report(s) offered would have to specifically prescribe a nurse case manager *and* specifically explain why a nurse case manager is reasonably required in this case, even in the face of the ACOEM guidelines. A medical opinion with a conclusory statement that merely disagrees with the ACOEM guidelines will not be sufficient to rebut the presumption of correctness; rather, the medical opinion must provide specific facts and specific reasoning establishing that treatment other than that set forth in the ACOEM guidelines is reasonably required. (Lab. Code, § 4604.5(c); see also, *People v. Bassett* (1968) 69 Cal. 2d 122, 141, 144 [443 P.2d 777, 70 Cal. Rptr. 193] ["[t]he chief value of an expert's testimony . . . rests upon the [m]aterial from which his opinion is fashioned and the [r]easoning by which he progresses from his material to his conclusion; . . . it does not lie in his mere expression of conclusion" & "the opinion of an expert is no better than the reasons upon which it is based"]; *Hegglin v. Workmen's Comp. Appeals Bd.* (1971) 4 Cal. 3d 162, 169 [480 P.2d 967, 93 Cal. Rptr. 15] [36 Cal. Comp. Cases 93] ["[N]ot all expert medical opinion constitutes substantial evidence. . . . Medical reports and opinions are not substantial evidence if they are known to be erroneous, or if they are based on facts no longer germane, on inadequate medical histories and examinations, or on incorrect legal theories. Medical opinion also fails . . . if it is based on surmise, speculation, conjecture, or guess."]; *Owings v. Industrial Acc. Com.* (1948) 31 Cal. 2d 689, 692 [192 P.2d 1] [13 Cal. Comp. Cases 80] ["the value of an expert's opinion is dependent upon its factual basis"].) (Footnote 4)

Defendant, of course, can offer contrary evidence on this issue. (Footnote 5)

If the ACOEM guidelines do *not* cover her type of injury, applicant may come forward with evidence showing that the provision of a nurse case manager would be "in accordance with other evidence–based medical treatment guidelines generally recognized by the national medical community and that are scientifically based." (Lab. Code, § 4604.5(e); see also, § 5703(h).) Defendant may also present contrary evidence. Nevertheless, we observe (without deciding the issue) that other evidence in lieu of, in addition to, or in rebuttal to "evidence–based medical treatment guidelines" might also be admissible.

Even if applicant establishes that a nurse case manager is reasonably required, however, it still must be determined who that nurse case manager will be.

A nurse case manager has a singular role in a workers' compensation case. He or she must interact and coordinate with the injured employee, the employee's physician(s), the claims adjuster(s), the attorney(s), and/or others, who are all parties to the employee's need for medical care.

Because of the nurse case manager's unique role, we conclude that the preferred procedure for selecting a nurse case manager is as follows: (1) the employer or insurance carrier should initially designate a nurse case manager; (2) if the applicant objects (at any time) to the person designated by the defendant, the parties should confer and *jointly* select a nurse case manager (i.e., an "agreed" nurse case manager); and (3) if the parties are unable to agree on an appropriate nurse case manager within a reasonable period of time (which time period may vary depending on the particular circumstances of the case), the WCJ should resolve the parties' dispute and appoint a nurse case manager.

Regardless of which procedure is used, the nurse case manager should ordinarily be a registered nurse or other similarly qualified licensed medical professional, although occasionally there may be factual scenarios where someone other than a licensed medical professional might be a suitable case manager. In all events, however, the person selected should be *competent and appropriate* to act as a case manager. Therefore, in selecting a case manager, a number of factors should be considered, including (but not limited to): (1) the individual's training, experience, qualifications, skills, and effectiveness; (2) any potential conflicts of interest the individual may have (e.g., a close personal, familial, employment, financial, fiduciary, or other relationship with the applicant, the defendant, a lien claimant, or a physician involved in the case); and (3) the recommendation(s) of the applicant's treating physician and/or other physician reporting in the case.

We are aware that, in *Castorena v. Liberty Mutual Insurance Co., supra,* 32 Cal. Workers' Comp. Rptr. 74, an Appeals Board panel summarily affirmed a WCJ's decision to the effect that, because "the nurse case manager is intimately involved in [an] applicant's medical care," then "the applicant and his [or her] physician ought to have the right to choose [the] nurse case manager." (32 Cal. Workers' Comp. Rptr. at p. 76.)

We do not find *Castorena* to be inconsistent with our decision here. That is, in *Castorena,* the defendant initially selected the nurse case manager; the applicant's primary treating physician then suggested a different nurse case manager; thereafter, the parties apparently could not agree on the nurse case manager; and, therefore, the WCJ resolved the parties' dispute regarding the nurse case manager. We emphasize, however, that *Castorena* does *not* stand for the principle that an employee has a "free choice" in selecting a nurse case manager under Labor Code sections 4600(c) and 4601. A nurse case manager is not a "physician" within the meaning of Labor Code sections 4600(c) and 4601. (See Lab. Code, § 3209.3(a).) Therefore, the "free choice" provisions of those sections are not applicable in the context of a nurse case manager. (Footnote 6)

Here, there is no evidence in the record that would establish that a nurse case manager is reasonably required, under the ACOEM guidelines or otherwise, in accordance with the principles discussed above. Moreover, although there is some evidence in the record regarding Ms. Klinger's qualifications, training, experience, etc., to act as the case manager, we note she is not a licensed medical professional and that this factor (together with the others described above) should be reassessed by the WCJ, even if it is ultimately determined that a case manager is medically necessary.

Therefore, we will also rescind the findings regarding a nurse case manager.

In rescinding the provisions for a nurse case manager, we do not mean to imply any opinion (one way or the other) regarding the ultimate resolution of this issue... .

Footnote 3. Without deciding the issue, it appears that, under the "Managing Delayed Recovery" provisions of the ACOEM guidelines (specifically, the "Case Management in Delayed Recovery" and "Approach to the Patient" sections), a case manager is appropriate in at least some circumstances.

Footnote 4. Lay evidence regarding the applicant's ability or inability to manage his or her own medical care, such as that presented by Ms. Klinger at the December 3, 2003 trial, might also be admissible and relevant to the determination of whether a nurse case manager is reasonably required; however, lay evidence is not sufficient, by itself, to establish a need for a nurse case manager. (Cf., (*State Compensation Insurance Fund v. Industrial Acc. Com. (Willson)* (1924) 195 Cal. 174, 184 [231 P. 996] [11 IAC 277, 281]; *Ins. Co. of North America v. Workers' Comp. Appeals Bd. (Kemp)* (1981) 122 Cal. App. 3d 905, 911 [176 Cal. Rptr. 365] [46 Cal. Comp. Cases 913, 917]; *Bstandig v. Workers' Comp. Appeals Bd.* (1977) 68 Cal. App. 3d 988, 995, 996 [137 Cal. Rptr. 713] [42 Cal. Comp. Cases 114, 118, 119]; *Peter Kiewit & Sons v. Industrial Acc. Com. (McLaughlin)* (1965) 234 Cal. App. 2d 831, 838 [44 Cal. Rptr. 813] [30 Cal. Comp. Cases 188, 192].)

Footnote 5. Similarly, if the ACOEM guidelines indicate the need for a nurse case manager for applicant's type of injury, and defendant disputes the ACOEM guidelines, it can present evidence in rebuttal to be [*sic*] guidelines, consistent with a discussion above.

Footnote 6. We note in passing that *Castorena* issued at a time when former Labor Code section 4600 was in effect. Although the law now in effect gives employees a "free choice" of physicians in some circumstances (Lab. Code, §§ 4600(c), 4601), it does not give "free choice" in the context of medical provider networks. (See Lab. Code, §§ 4600(c), 4616.)

Page 512, Column 1, delete first paragraph, beginning 'different...' and ending 'nurse case manager. '

§ 8.7 Travel Expenses – Temporary Disability Indemnity While Submitting to an Evaluation

Page 512, Column 1, fourth paragraph, delete lines after '...599.631(a)' to '...per mile.' and insert the following:

Presently the mileage reimbursement rate is 48.5 cents per mile, effective January 1, 2007, regardless of the date of injury. Previously the rate was 44.5 cents per mile, effective July 1, 2006, and it was 34 cents per mile as of January 1, 2001.

Page 512, Column 1, fifth paragraph, delete beginning '...high Court stated, in part:...' through first paragraph on Column 2 ending '...in ruling otherwise.' and insert the following:

Lauher contends that "as a necessary means to the end of ensuring prompt medical treatment [pursuant to section 4600], [an] employee is entitled to temporary total disability indemnity for the time lost from work while attending necessary medical treatment." As we explain, because his industrial injury had become permanent and stationary, he was no longer entitled to receive TDI.

Two of the types of benefits available to the worker injured on the job are temporary disability indemnity, or TDI, and permanent disability indemnity, or PDI. Although both take the form of financial benefits, "[i]t must be remembered that temporary disability indemnity and permanent disability indemnity were intended by the Legislature to serve entirely different functions. Temporary disability indemnity serves as wage replacement during the injured worker's healing period for the industrial injury. [Citation.] In contrast, permanent disability indemnity compensates for the residual handicap and/or impairment of function after maximum recovery from the effects of the industrial injury have been attained. [Citation.] Permanent disability serves to assist the injured worker in his adjustment in returning to the labor market. [Citation.]" (*Maples v. Workers' Comp. Appeals Bd.* (1980) 111 Cal. App. 3d 827, 836 [168 Cal. Rptr. 884, 45 Cal. Comp. Cases 1106]; see also *Nickelsberg v. Workers' Comp. Appeals Bd.* (1991) 54 Cal. 3d 288, 294 [285 Cal. Rptr. 86, 814 P.2d 1328, 56 Cal. Comp. Cases 476].)

That TDI is intended as wage replacement is inferable from section 4653, which requires temporary total disability

be calculated as "two–thirds of the average weekly earnings during the period of such disability, consideration being given to the ability of the injured employee to compete in an open labor market." Because "[t]emporary disability indemnity is intended primarily to substitute for the worker's lost wages, in order to maintain a steady stream of income" (*J. T. Thorp, Inc. v. Workers' Comp. Appeals Bd.* (1984) 153 Cal. App. 3d 327, 333 [200 Cal. Rptr. 219, 49 Cal. Comp. Cases 224]; *Braewood Convalescent Hospital v. Workers' Comp. Appeals Bd., supra,* 34 Cal. 3d at p. 168), an employer's obligation to pay TDI to an injured worker ceases when such replacement income is no longer needed. Thus, the obligation to pay TDI ends when the injured employee either returns to work (*Huston v. Workers' Comp. Appeals Bd.* (1979) 95 Cal. App. 3d 856, 868 [157 Cal. Rptr. 355, 44 Cal. Comp. Cases 798]; see also § 4651.1) or is deemed able to return to work (*Bethlehem Steel Co. v. Ind. Acc. Com.* (1942) 54 Cal. App. 2d 585, 586–587 [129 P.2d 737, 7 Cal. Comp. Cases 250]), or when the employee's medical condition achieves permanent and stationary status (*Industrial Indem. Exch. v. Ind. Acc. Com.* (1949) 90 Cal. App. 2d 99 [202 P.2d 850, 14 Cal. Comp. Cases 25]; see generally *Kopitske v. Workers' Comp. Appeals Bd.* (1999) 74 Cal. App. 4th 623, 631 [88 Cal. Rptr. 2d 216, 64 Cal. Comp. Cases 972]; *Ritchie v. Workers' Comp. Appeals Bd.* (1994) 24 Cal. App. 4th 1174, 1179 [29 Cal. Rptr. 2d 722, 59 Cal. Comp. Cases 243]; 1 Hanna, Cal. Law of Employee Injuries and Workers' Compensation (rev. 2d ed., Peterson et al. edits., 2002) § 7.02[1], p. 7–7 (Hanna)).

By contrast, section 4650 provides that the first permanent disability payment must be made by the employer within "14 days after the date of the last payment of temporary disability indemnity." From this, we may infer the Legislature anticipates an employer has no legal obligation to pay PDI until the obligation to pay TDI has ceased. Accordingly, we held in *LeBoeuf v. Workers' Comp. Appeals Bd.* (1983) 34 Cal. 3d 234 [193 Cal. Rptr. 547, 666 P.2d 989, 48 Cal. Comp. Cases 587] that "[t]he right to permanent disability compensation does not arise until the injured worker's condition becomes 'permanent and stationary.' " (*Id.* at p. 238, fn. 2.) "A disability is considered permanent after the employee has reached maximum medical improvement or his or her condition has been stationary for a reasonable period of time." (Cal. Code Regs., tit. 8, § 10152; see *Gee v. Workers' Comp. Appeals Bd.* (2002) 96 Cal. App. 4th 1418, 1422, fn. 3 [118 Cal. Rptr. 2d 105, 67 Cal. Comp. Cases 236]; 1 Hanna, *supra,* § 8.03, pp. 8–16 to 8–17.)

That Lauher's industrial injury was permanent and stationary is undisputed. Lauher's physician, Dr. Houts, so reported, and Lauher entered into a stipulation with SCIF to that effect. That Lauher had returned to work is also undisputed. Under these circumstances, we conclude he was not entitled to any further TDI payments to compensate him for wages lost due to his attending medical appointments during the workday. "An injured employee cannot be temporarily and permanently disabled at the same time; thus, permanent disability payments do not begin until temporary disability payments cease." (*City of Martinez v.*

Workers' Comp. Appeals Bd. (2000) 85 Cal. App. 4th 601, 609 [102 Cal. Rptr. 2d 588, 65 Cal. Comp. Cases 1368]; see also *Ritchie v. Workers' Comp. Appeals Bd., supra,* 24 Cal. App. 4th at p. 1180 [same]; *New Amsterdam Cas. Co. v. Ind. Acc. Com.* (1951) 108 Cal. App. 2d 502, 507 [238 P.2d 1046, 16 Cal. Comp. Cases 312] [same]; 1 Hanna, *supra,* § 7.02[1], p. 7–8 [same].) Here, Lauher had passed out of the healing period (for which TDI serves as a wage replacement) and had agreed to a stipulation compensating him for his diminished ability in the workplace due to a permanent and stationary injury. Because Lauher had begun collecting PDI, he was no longer entitled to TDI.

Lauher's counterarguments are not persuasive. As did the WCJ, he first relies on section 4600, which relates generally to medical and hospital treatment for an injured worker. That section provides in pertinent part that "Medical, surgical, chiropractic, acupuncture, and hospital treatment, including nursing, medicines, medical and surgical supplies, crutches, and apparatus, including orthotic and prosthetic devices and services, that is reasonably required to cure or relieve from the effects of the injury shall be provided by the employer." He contends that section 4600 should be liberally construed to include replacement of lost wages occasioned by an employee's medical treatment. Although he is correct that "[t]he Legislature intended that section 4600 shall be liberally interpreted in favor of the employee's right to obtain reimbursement" (*McCoy v. Industrial Acc. Com.* (1966) 64 Cal. 2d 82, 86 [48 Cal. Rptr. 858, 410 P.2d 362, 31 Cal. Comp. Cases 93]; *Rodriguez v. Workers' Comp. Appeals Bd.* (1994) 21 Cal. App. 4th 1747, 1758 [27 Cal. Rptr. 2d 93, 59 Cal. Comp. Cases 14]), he is incorrect that even a liberal interpretation of section 4600 will extend so far as to authorize the payment of *temporary* disability indemnity to replace lost wages when an injury has become *permanent* and stationary.

Lauher apparently would have us analogize the right to reimbursement for sick and vacation leave used for seeking continuing treatment for a permanent and stationary industrial injury to the right to reimbursement for transportation costs. Citing *Avalon, supra,* 18 Cal. 4th 1165, *Hutchinson v. Workers' Comp. Appeals Bd.* (1989) 209 Cal. App. 3d 372 [257 Cal. Rptr. 240, 54 Cal. Comp. Cases 124], and *Bundock v. Herndon and Finnigan* (1923) 10 I.A.C. 32, Lauher contends that because section 4600 has been construed liberally to compensate an injured worker for transportation costs associated with obtaining medical treatment, we similarly should conclude he is entitled to TDI to compensate him for wages lost while seeking treatment with Dr. Houts. We disagree because the two situations are not comparable. In *Avalon,* we observed that although section 4600 "does not expressly refer to medical treatment transportation expenses as an aspect of medical treatment benefits, they have consistently been so regarded under the workers' compensation laws. [Citations.]" (*Avalon, supra,* at p. 1173.) "The board's practice . . . of awarding medical treatment transportation expenses," we observed, "is of long standing," noting that such benefits have been paid "[a]s early as 1923." (Id. at p. 1174.) No comparable precedent exists for compensating an injured

employee for his wage loss once his injury becomes permanent and stationary... .

§ 8.12 Medical Examinations

Page 517, Column 2, first paragraph, insert following '...its consideration.'

Further, Section 4050 examinations may not be used to circumvent the medical evaluation and reporting procedures of former Sections 4061 (unrepresented employees) and 4062 (represented employees) *Nunez v. WCAB* (2006) 71 Cal. Comp. Cases 161.

§ 8.13(D)(1) Utilization Review Process (UR)

Page 530, Column 1, sixth paragraph, ending 'Regs 9785...' insert the following:

See Appendix C of this supplement for the Administrative Director's Utilization Review Regulations.

Page 532, Column 2, delete fifth paragraph, beginning 'The Administrative...' and ending 'for the Regulations]' and insert the following:

The Administrative Director has adopted extensive Regulations to implement the new utilization review law. [See Appendix C for the Regulations].

Page 532, Column 2, eighth paragraph, beginning 'Further, strict...' and ending '...4610.' seventh line delete '...with...' and insert the following:

within

Page 533, Column 1, first paragraph, beginning 'Utilization Review...' and ending '...procedure' third line delete '...deadlines...' and insert the following:

timeframes

Page 533, Column 1, second paragraph, beginning 'If an employer...' and ending 'utilization review' fourth line delete '...AME...' and insert '...AMEs...'; fifth line delete '...QME...' and insert '...QMEs...'

Page 533, Column 1, delete third paragraph, beginning 'However...' and ending '...in part:' and insert the following:

However, an employer or insurance carrier who fails to meet the mandatory timeframes pursuant to Section

4610(g)(1) may use the procedures established pursuant to Section 4062(b) (for AME or QME reports), but in that event the employer becomes the "objecting party" and must meet the mandatory timeframes pursuant to Section 4062, unless the deadlines are extended for good cause or by mutual agreement. Commenting on this in *Sandhagen v. Cox and Cox Construction, Inc., SCIF* (2004) 69 Cal. Comp. Cases 1452, the Appeals Board, in an En Banc decision stated, in part:

Page 537, Column 2, third paragraph, insert following '...hereby, DISMISSED'

Both SCIF and Mr. Sandhagen petitioned for a Writ of Review. The Court of Appeal, Third District, in *SCIF v. WCAB* and *Sandhagen v. WCAB* (2006) 71 Cal. Comp. Cases 1541, in upholding the Board's decision and denying both SCIF's and Sandhagen's petitions for review, stated, in part:

The California Constitution directs the Legislature to create a system of workers' compensation that accomplishes "substantial justice in all cases expeditiously, inexpensively, and without incumbrance of any character." (Cal. Const., art. XIV, § 4.) A primary goal of the workers' compensation system is to secure prompt treatment for an injured worker to facilitate his or her return to the work force at the earliest possible time. (*Avalon Bay Foods v. Workers' Comp. Appeals Bd.* (1998) 18 Cal. 4th 1165, 1175–1176, 1178 [77 Cal. Rptr. 2d 552, 959 P.2d 1228].)

The employer of an injured worker is responsible for all medical treatment reasonably necessary to cure or relieve the worker from the effects of injury. (Lab. Code, § 4600, subd. (a).) (Footnote 1)

In order to protect the injured employee's right to prompt appropriate treatment and to reduce costs, in 2003 the Legislature directed the Administrative Director (Director) of the Division of Workers' Compensation to establish a medical treatment utilization schedule incorporating evidence–based, peer–reviewed, nationally recognized standards of care. (§ 5307.27.)

Under this statutory scheme, the treating physician submits a request for treatment to the employer or the employer's insurer. (Footnote 2)

"Utilization Review" (UR) is the process by which an employer reviews the recommendations of a treating physician and then decides whether to approve, modify, delay, or deny authorization for treatment based on medical necessity. In acting on treatment recommendations submitted under UR procedures, the employer is bound by section 4600, subdivision (b), which defines medical treatment that is reasonably required to cure or relieve the injured worker as treatment that is based upon guidelines adopted by the Director.

The UR process is subject to mandatory timeframes. Section 4610, subdivision (g)(1) requires an employer to timely approve, modify, delay, or deny treatment requests. UR decisions must be communicated within five working days from receipt of the information, and in no event more than 14 days from the date of the recommendation. (*Ibid.*)

In this review of a decision by the Workers' Compensation Appeals Board (WCAB), we consider the consequences that flow from an employer's failure to timely act on an injured worker's treatment request under the UR process. Brice Sandhagen, the injured employee, argues that by failing to timely respond to his treatment request, his employer forfeited its right to deny the request under the UR process. Sandhagen also insists that because the UR process is mandatory and the exclusive means by which an employer can modify, delay, or deny treatment, his treatment request must be granted by default.

The employer's insurer, State Compensation Insurance Fund (Fund), disagrees and asserts that only monetary penalties can be imposed for its tardiness; it retains the right to deny the treatment request under the UR process and may pursue remedies under the dispute resolution procedures set forth in section 4062.

The WCAB asserts, as a threshold matter, that its decision is not a final order and the petition for review is premature. On the merits, the WCAB argues it properly determined that as a result of Fund's failure to meet UR time deadlines, Fund is precluded from using UR procedures or medical reports to support the denial of Sandhagen's treatment request but retains the right to object to Sandhagen's treatment request under section 4062 based on other evidence. The practical consequences of Fund's untimeliness, under the WCAB's reasoning, would be to deprive Fund of any reliance on the UR report denying treatment and require it to bear the burden of proof and persuasion in proceedings under section 4062.

We shall deny Fund's and Sandhagen's petitions for writ of review...

DISCUSSION

I.

This case requires us to determine the meaning and effect of section 4610, which establishes the UR process, in relationship to section 4062, which provides for resolution of disputes between injured workers and their employers generally...

REMEDIES

Fund, Sandhagen, and the WCAB agree that section 4610 establishes mandatory timeframes for UR compliance. The parties disagree over the consequences of a failure to comply with the timeframes. The WCAB reasoned that because "section 4610(g)(1) imposes a mandatory duty on a defendant to comply with its deadlines, it would be incongruous to permit a defendant that fails to comply with the deadlines to nevertheless obtain a [UR] report and to then enter it into evidence."

Citing the penalty provisions of section 4610, Fund does not perceive an incongruity. Fund points out that the Legislature has recognized the need for speedy disposition of treatment requests, imposed tight time deadlines, and vested authority in the Director to impose administrative penalties for delay and to fashion other, unspecified relief. Because the statutory scheme vests remedial powers in the Director and does not mention the WCAB, or expressly provide that untimely UR reports shall be inadmissible, Fund questions the WCAB's authority to fashion its own evidence preclusion remedy. The WCAB's position is further weakened, according to Fund, by the fact that section 4610 is neither a discovery statute nor within the ambit of the WCAB's dispute resolution process.

The WCAB's responsive arguments are not entirely on point. There is little doubt, as the WCAB argues, that the Legislature in establishing the mandatory UR deadlines sought to ensure that an employer who seeks to undertake the UR process "does so expeditiously, so that any [UR] decision regarding what medical treatment is 'reasonably required' for the injured worker is not unduly delayed." There is also merit to the WCAB's assertion that the mandatory deadlines ensure both that (1) if an employer under the UR process authorizes treatment the employee will promptly receive such treatment, and (2) if, as a result of the UR process, the employer denies authorization for treatment, the injured employee can immediately begin the dispute resolution process and, if necessary, bring the issue before the WCAB through an expedited hearing or a nonexpedited mandatory settlement conference.

We are less persuaded by the WCAB's assertion that if administrative penalties are all an employer must fear, then it could indefinitely delay obtaining a UR report, notwithstanding the section 4610, subdivision (g)(1) deadlines, and, as a result, "the medical treatment dispute resolution process established by the Legislature would be thrown into utter chaos." (Footnote 8) An expression of the need for a rule, no matter how compelling, cannot fill a gap in legal authority. The WCAB's foreboding sheds no light on the source of its authority to exclude untimely UR reports.

Nevertheless, we conclude that the WCAB acted within its authority in prohibiting the use of a report generated by an untimely UR process in subsequent proceedings challenging the treatment decision.

Fund's assertion that the Director is vested with exclusive authority to impose remedies for violation of UR time deadlines misperceives the respective roles of the Director and the WCAB in relationship to the UR process. The UR process has two aspects. It provides a process for insuring the prompt review and disposition of treatment requests. In this aspect, it is not a vehicle for dispute resolution; indeed, one supposes that most requests for medical treatment are approved by employers without dispute or controversy. However, the UR process becomes part of the workers' compensation dispute resolution scheme when the employee is dissatisfied with the outcome, at which point the provisions of section 4062 and the full panoply of procedures before the WCAB come into play.

As a process for insuring the timely disposition of treatment requests, the UR process falls within the authority of the Director. Timeliness is a primary goal, and the power of the Director to impose monetary penalties and fashion other remedies serves to facilitate that goal. The tardy approval of a treatment request is no less a vice than a late disapproval. In either instance, the Director is empowered to act. In vesting authority in the Director to impose penalties and in providing that "[t]he administrative penalties shall

not be deemed to be an exclusive remedy for the [Director]" (§ 4610, subd. (i)), the Legislature was addressing the Director's role as overseer of the process established for the timely review and disposition of treatment requests.

However, the UR process becomes an integral part of the workers' compensation dispute resolution scheme when an employee or employer invokes the procedures set forth in section 4062. The procedural mechanism created by section 4062 implicates the authority of the WCAB, and the WCAB's authority is expressly acknowledged. While the UR process is a records review process, section 4062 is an evidence collection and evaluation process with one set of procedures that pertains when the employee is represented by counsel and another when the employee is unrepresented. Once the AME/QME process is completed, either party may bring the decision before a WCJ for review. (Footnote 9) The decision of the WCJ is then reviewable by the WCAB. Barring intervention by the Court of Appeal, the decision of the WCAB is final.

Section 133 grants the WCAB the power to "do all things necessary or convenient in the exercise of any power or jurisdiction conferred upon it." The WCAB's authority to develop and enforce rules of evidence cannot seriously be questioned. "[T]he WCAB is empowered to adopt reasonable rules of practice and procedure to regulate and prescribe the nature of proof and evidence in workers' compensation cases." (*Crawford v. Workers' Comp. Appeals Bd.* (1989) 213 Cal. App. 3d 156, 168 [259 Cal. Rptr. 414].) It may do so by formal rule making or may, as here, issue a precedent decision that interprets and applies the law in the course of a case–specific adjudication. (*Rea v. Workers' Comp. Appeals Bd.* (2005) 127 Cal. App. 4th 625, 648–649 [25 Cal. Rptr. 3d 828].)

The WCAB has previously considered the admissibility of UR reports in light of section 5703, subdivision (a), which states, in part: "The [WCAB] may receive as evidence either at or subsequent to a hearing, and use as proof of any fact in dispute, the following matters, in addition to sworn testimony presented in open hearing: [P] (a) Reports of attending or examining physicians." Section 5703, enacted prior to section 4610, would have made all UR reports inadmissible, since they are not reports of the attending or examining physicians but simply reflect a UR physician's opinion on the medical necessity of proposed treatment, formulated without examining the injured employee. (§ 4610, subds. (a)–(f).) In *Willette v. Au Electric Corp.* (2004) 69 Cal. Comp. Cases 1298 (*Willette*), the WCAB noted section 5703's exclusion of UR reports but attempted to harmonize the UR process with section 5703. The WCAB determined the statutorily created UR process yielded a UR report that was an essential part of the WCAB's record in any post–UR proceeding regarding a medical treatment dispute. Therefore, the WCAB held that section 4610 created a limited exception to section 5703's prohibition against admitting reports of nonattending, nonexamining physicians. The WCAB found this limited exception consistent with the overall statutory scheme. (*Willette, supra*, 69 Cal. Comp. Cases at pp. 1306–1307.)

In fashioning rules of evidence, the WCAB may properly take into account the purposes of the Workers'

Compensation Act and impose rules that advance those purposes. The *Willette* decision was an appropriate exercise of the WCAB's authority to interpret statutes in a manner consistent with their intended purpose and in harmony with the statutory framework as a whole.

One of the purposes of the Workers' Compensation Act is to guarantee prompt, limited compensation for an employee's work–related injuries. (*Land v. Workers' Comp. Appeals Bd.* (2002) 102 Cal. App. 4th 491, 496 [125 Cal. Rptr. 2d 432] (*Land*).) The Legislature intended the UR process to ensure quality, standardized medical care for workers. Mandatory deadlines facilitate the prompt, expeditious resolution of the employee's request for medical treatment. If, as a result of the UR process, the employer authorizes the treatment, then the employee will promptly receive such treatment. If the employer denies authorization, the employee can quickly begin the dispute resolution process. Untimely UR reports stymie the efficiency and efficacy of this process.

In light of this legislative purpose, the WCAB could properly determine that the limited exception to section 5703 created in the *Willette* decision should not be extended to UR reports prepared in violation of section 4610. To permit the consideration of untimely reports would be inimical to a core purpose of the Workers' Compensation Act, that of providing prompt compensation to injured workers and prompt resolution of disputes. Moreover, it would be anomalous to permit consideration of the reports in AME/QME proceedings while excluding them from consideration in proceedings before WCJ's and before the WCAB. We conclude the WCAB, which exercises exclusive original jurisdiction over all workers' compensation claims and any rights and responsibilities pertaining thereto, did not exceed its jurisdiction in deciding that untimely UR reports cannot be considered for any purpose.

V.

The WCAB argues that in order to harmonize the entire statutory scheme established by the Legislature for resolving medical treatment disputes, and to ensure the prompt provision of medical treatment to an injured employee, it correctly found an employer's failure to meet the UR mandatory deadlines renders any UR report inadmissible.

In addition, the WCAB contends the consequences of an employer's failure to comply with the mandatory timeframes are not limited, as Fund suggests, to civil penalties imposed by the Director or to section 5814 penalties imposed by the WCAB. The WCAB acknowledges that section 4610, subdivision (i) allows the Director to assess administrative penalties for failure to meet timeframes. However, section 4610, subdivision (i) also states: "The administrative penalties shall not be deemed to be an exclusive remedy for the [Director]." Therefore, the WCAB concludes, if penalties under section 4610, subdivision (i) are not the sole remedy available to the Director, who has no jurisdiction over workers' compensation proceedings, "then the availability of

administrative penalties certainly does not limit the remedies of the WCAB."

We find this reasoning persuasive. Section 133 grants the WCAB the power to "do all things necessary or convenient in the exercise of any power or jurisdiction conferred upon it." As noted earlier, among the purposes of the Workers' Compensation Act is the guarantee of prompt, limited compensation for an employee's work–related injuries. (*Land, supra*, 102 Cal. App. 4th at p. 496.) Requiring employers to comply with UR deadlines or forfeit the use of any UR reports squarely falls within the ambit of providing prompt treatment.

Fund also asserts the WCAB may impose penalties under section 5814 if an employer delays completion of the UR process. (Footnote 10) However, as discussed above, the availability of penalties under section 5814 does not automatically preclude the WCAB from excluding UR reports from evidence when untimely obtained. Courts have found section 5814 is not the exclusive remedy against a defendant whose actions are unreasonable. (See *Rhiner v. Workers' Comp. Appeals Bd.* (1993) 4 Cal. 4th 1213, 1227 [18 Cal. Rptr.2d 129, 848 P.2d 244] [section 4650 penalty does not duplicate or supersede section 5814; instead, section 4650 supplements the section 5814 penalty].)

VI.

The WCAB argues the admission of an untimely UR review is also precluded by section 5703, subdivision (a), which states, in part: "The [WCAB] may receive as evidence either at or subsequent to a hearing, and use as proof of any fact in dispute, the following matters, in addition to sworn testimony presented in open hearing: [P] (a) Reports of attending or examining physicians."

As the WCAB points out, under the UR process, a treating physician's report regarding proposed treatment is transmitted to a UR physician employed by, or under contract with, the defendant. The UR physician then renders an opinion on the medical necessity of proposed treatment, without examining the injured employee. (§ 4610, subds. (a)–(f).)

Section 5703 makes these UR reports inadmissible, since they are not reports of the attending or examining physicians. As discussed earlier, following the enactment of section 4610, the WCAB considered the admissibility of UR reports in *Willette, supra*, 69 Cal. Comp. Cases 1298.

From *Willette*, the WCAB extrapolates that an untimely UR report violates section 4610 and therefore does not come within the limited exception to section 5703. In other words, the *Willette* exception only applies to UR reports properly obtained under section 4610. Since Fund's UR report does not comply with section 4610's mandatory deadlines, it is inadmissible under section 5703.

Fund does not respond to this argument. We conclude the WCAB's interpretation of the effect of section 5703 on untimely UR reports provides additional support for its argument that such reports are inadmissible.

VII.

Sandhagen filed a separate writ of review, arguing a UR under section 4610 is required for every medical treatment request and only the employee may utilize section 4062 to dispute a medical treatment request. Fund disputes these interpretations of sections 4610 and 4062.

Sandhagen argues that section 4610 "clearly and unambiguously" requires employers to follow the UR procedure for *all* medical treatment requests. Section 4610, subdivision (g) states: "In determining whether to approve, modify, delay, or deny requests by physicians prior to, retrospectively, or concurrent with the provisions of medical treatment services to employees all of the following requirements must be met ... ." Sandhagen asserts this language places a mandatory duty on the employer to utilize the UR process for every treatment request.

Fund contends that although employers are required to establish a UR process, employers are not required to apply that process to every request for treatment. The WCAB's interpretation comports with Fund's interpretation: "[T]here is nothing in section 4610 that requires an employer to use the [UR] process in every case. To the contrary, section 4610 is silent on whether an employer must always use the utilization review procedure."

We agree with the analyses of both the WCAB and Fund. Section 4610, subdivision (b) states: "Every employer shall establish a utilization review process in compliance with this section, either directly or through its insurer or an entity with which an employer or insurer contracts for these services." Section 4610, subdivision (b) requires the establishment of a UR process; it does not mandate use of that process for each and every medical treatment request.

Section 4610, subdivision (g), quoted above, provides the requirements the employer's UR process must meet if the employer decides to utilize the UR process. Section 4610, subdivision (g) does not state that all medical treatment requests must be subject to these requirements.

The WCAB provided several rationales for not subjecting all requests to the UR process. For example, if an employer determines, without UR, that the recommended treatment is reasonably required, imposing the UR process would be both time consuming and expensive.

In addition, the WCAB noted the UR process by its nature does not involve either an interview with or a physical examination of the injured employee and ordinarily does not involve a thorough medical review. "Thus, in cases involving complex medical treatment issues–where either a physical or mental examination, a complete history of the injury, a complete medical history, or a complete medical record review could be called for–a utilization review may result in needless expense to the defendant, as well as needless to [sic] delay to the applicant." Instead, it may be more expeditious and economical for the employer to go directly to the QME/AME process.

We agree with the WCAB that the language of section 4610 does not impose the requirement that a UR must be used in every case. An employer has discretion to undertake or not undertake UR with respect to any particular proposed medical treatment.

Sandhagen also takes issue with the WCAB's finding that an employer may utilize section 4062. According to Sandhagen, only the employee may invoke section 4062.

Section 4062, subdivision (a) states: "If either the employee or employer objects to a medical determination made by the treating physician concerning any medical issues not covered by Section 4060 or 4061 and not subject to Section 4610, the objecting party shall notify the other party in writing of the objection ... ." Sandhagen argues that since UR under section 4610 must be used for every medical treatment request, there is no case in which section 4062 is available to employers in order to resolve a treatment dispute.

However, as previously noted, section 4610 does not require employers to utilize UR for each and every request. In addition, section 4062, subdivision (a) explicitly states, "If either the employee or employer objects ... ," making section 4610 available to both employers and employees. In construing a statute, we presume every word, phrase, and provision was intended to have some meaning, and a construction making some words surplusage is to be avoided. (*Hassan v. Mercy American River Hospital* (2003) 31 Cal. 4th 709, 715–716 [3 Cal. Rptr. 3d 623, 74 P.3d 726].)

Section 4610, subdivision (g)(3)(A) provides, in part: "If the request is not approved in full, disputes shall be resolved in accordance with Section 4062." However, as the WCAB noted: "This language means simply that, *if a defendant timely elects to follow the [UR] process* but does not fully authorize the proposed treatment after [UR] is completed, then any remaining disputes regarding the particular proposed treatment must be resolved using the procedure established by section 4062(a)."

Accordingly, the WCAB correctly found: "Any other interpretation of section 4062(a) would lead to absurd results, in violation of basic principles of statutory construction. [Citations.] As discussed above, the Legislature has not required a defendant to follow the [UR] process in every case. Yet, if a defendant elected to exercise its right not to undertake [UR], but then were entirely precluded from using the QME/AME process to resolve the medical treatment dispute, the defendant would be worse off than it would have been had section 4610 never been enacted."

DISPOSITION

Fund's petition for writ of review is denied. Sandhagen's petition for writ of review is denied. The parties shall bear their own costs in this writ proceeding... .

Footnote 1. All further statutory references are to the Labor Code.

Footnote 2. Referred to herein collectively as "employer."

Footnote 8. The WCAB insists that an employer's tardy UR report would force the employee to wait until the report was obtained to begin the QME or AME process under sections 4610, subdivisions (g)(3)(A), (g)(3)(B) and 4062, subdivision (a). The employer's initial tardiness, like a stalled car on a crowded freeway, slows down the entire process, including the employee's ability to request an expedited hearing.

Footnote 9. See Footnote 5, *ante*, at page 1062.

Footnote 10. Section 4610.1 states: "An employee shall not be entitled to an increase in compensation under Section

5814 for unreasonable delay in the provision of medical treatment for periods of time necessary to complete the [UR] process in compliance with Section 4610. A determination by the [WCAB] that medical treatment is appropriate shall not be conclusive evidence that medical treatment was unreasonably delayed or denied for purposes of penalties under Section 5814. In no case shall this section preclude an employee from entitlement to an increase in compensation under Section 5814 when an employer has unreasonably delayed or denied medical treatment due to an unreasonable delay in completion of the [UR] process set forth in Section 4610." **[Editor's Note:** At the time this book went to publication, the California State Supreme Court accepted this case for review].

Page 546, Column 2, insert following Footnote 9 following '...Board en banc).]'

In holding that an employer is not entitled to proceed under Section 4062 to dispute its *utilization review's doctor's finding of need for medical treatment* as there is no dispute under Section 4610, the Board is upholding a judge's decision in *City of Hayward et. al. v. WCAB (Rushworth–McKee)* (2007) 72 Cal. Comp. Cases 237, observed that in his decision the judge noted that Section 4062(a) provides that a medical–legal evaluation under this section may be obtained only if the employer or employee objects to a medical determination made by the treating physician concerning any medical issues not covered by Section 4060 and 4061 and not subject to Section 4610. The judge pointed out that, under Labor Code section 4062(a), if a defendant elects not to proceed with utilization review pursuant to Section 4610, that defendant may obtain a report through Section 4062. However, the question in the case was whether the employer's election to proceed with the utilization review process prevented it from seeking another medical evaluation under Section 4062, given applicant's request for an expedited hearing.

The Board quoted the judge as stating:

The language of the statutes cited above is clear and explicit as to results reached at trial. Labor Code Sections 4610 and 4062 provide that, if the request for medical care is *not* approved in full after Utilization Review, then any remaining disputes are to be resolved in accordance with § 4062. (See Labor Code § 4610(g)(3)(a).) However, § 4610 does not provide for further objection to medical treatment if the requested procedure *is* authorized under Utilization Review. While § 4062(b) says that an *employee* may object to a determination made under § 4610 and seek relief through Labor Code § 4062, there is no corresponding procedure within § 4062 for an employer to object to approval of treatment following Utilization Review. This is a logical conclusion, because following approval of treatment submitted to Utilization Review, there is no longer a *bona fide* dispute.

To permit an employer to repeatedly object to treatment and obtain a multitude of medical evaluations on the same issue is time consuming, will prove costly and is contrary to

Article XIV, sec. 4, of the *California Constitution*. As the Board knows, that provision requires "substantial justice in all cases expeditiously, inexpensively and without encumbrance of any character . . . (Art. XIV, sec. 4, California Constitution.)

Applicant's petition and Declaration of Readiness were filed on March 10, 2006. [T]he Expedited Hearing was set on April 10, 2006. The notice of hearing was sent on March 23, 2006. While defendant apparently filed an objection by the date of the hearing notice, it apparently did not schedule a QME evaluation before the date of hearing. At trial the applicant's counsel argued that the filing of an objection without scheduling an examination did not amount to due diligence. In denying defendant's continuance request, I was persuaded that the time constraints contained in § 5502(b) require an expeditious determination of the issue and negate a request for further discovery. In other words, good cause was not found. [*Emphases by WCJ*]... .

In *ICW Group/Explorer Ins. Co. v. WCAB (Ulloa)* (2005) 70 Cal. Comp. Cases 1176, the Appeals Board upheld a judge's finding that a defendant's utilization review reports relied upon by defendants to deny applicant further medical treatment requested by his treating physician were untimely and that ACOEM Guidelines did not apply because they were issued after the "90 day acute stage" following applicant's injury, citing *Willette, supra,* and *Hamilton v. Goodwill Industries,* 2004 Cal. Wrk. Comp. P.D. Lexis 87 (WCAB Panel Decision).

Page 547, Column 1, third paragraph, insert following, '...Section 4610.'

Complaint Form

Medical providers, injured workers, or others who find that utilization review is not being done according to the statutory law and regulations can file a complaint with the Administrative Director. The form set forth in Appendix C should be used to register a complaint regarding utilization review services connected with workers' compensation injuries and treatment.

Page 549, Column 1, fourth paragraph, change heading to read:

§ 8.14(A)(1) How Often Can an Injured Employee Change Treating Physicians?

Page 556, Column 1, second paragraph, insert following '…surgery exception.'

Spinal Surgery

The Board, in a *significant panel decision*, *Brasher v. Nationwide Studio Fund* (2006) 71 Cal. Comp. Cases 1282, held that a defendant, in responding to a treating physician's recommendation and request for authorization for spinal surgery, has essentially four options. They include:

(1) Authorize the surgery;
(2) Object to the surgery under Section 4062(b);
(3) Submit the request to utilization review; or
(4) Pursue options 2 and 3 either simultaneously or by filing an objection under Section 4062(b) after a utilization review denial, meeting the timelines for each process.

The Board stated, in part:

We previously granted applicant's petition for reconsideration to further study the factual and legal issues in this case. This is our Opinion and Decision After Reconsideration. (Footnote 1)

Applicant sought reconsideration of the April 18, 2006 Findings of Fact and Order, wherein the workers' compensation administrative law judge ("WCJ") found that defendant's initial objection to the treating physician's request for spinal surgery was timely; that the procedure instituted by the Division of Workers' Compensation ("DWC") Medical Unit, requiring utilization review and appeal from a denial of spinal surgery before the Administrative Director ("AD") selects a second opinion surgeon under Labor Code section 4062(b), (Footnote 2) was contemplated by sections 4062 and 4610; and that the Medical Unit's referral of the matter for a second opinion was, therefore, timely. The WCJ denied applicant's request for surgery, without prejudice, pending the second opinion.

Applicant contended the Medical Unit violated section 4062 when it rejected and failed to act on defendant's initial and timely objection to the treating physician's request for spinal surgery; that the Medical Unit lacked authority to require a second request in the form of an appeal from a utilization review denial, before acting on the objection; and that the remedy for the Medical Unit's failure to select a second opinion surgeon within 10 days after receipt of defendant's objection, and for the failure of the second opinion surgeon to issue a report with 45 days of the request for surgery, should be that defendant is required to authorize the surgery.

We have considered the Petition for Reconsideration and the WCJ's Report and Recommendation on Petition for Reconsideration, and we have reviewed the record in this matter. We have not received an Answer from defendant.

For the reasons discussed below, we will reverse the decision of the WCJ and hold that, in response to a treating physician's recommendation for spinal surgery, an employer has the following options: 1) authorize the surgery, 2) object to the surgery, pursuant to section 4062(b), by filing a DWC Form 233 within 10 days of receipt of the doctor's recommendation, 3) submit the recommendation to utilization review, or 4) pursue both options 2 and 3, either simultaneously or by filing an objection after a utilization review denial, meeting the timelines for each process. If the employer denies the surgery pursuant to its utilization review, the employee must object within 10 days of receipt by the employee of the employer's denial. The dispute will then be resolved under the second opinion procedures in section 4062(b).

In a case such as this, where the defendant has followed the statutory procedures and timelines, and the delay is due solely to the DWC's failure to comply with its obligation under section 4062(b), there is no reasonable basis for terminating the second opinion process. It should be completed, followed by a decision by the WCJ on the merits.

BACKGROUND

The parties stipulated that applicant sustained an industrial injury to her spine on April 22, 2002, while employed by defendant as a photographer. The issue of other body parts injured was deferred.

Having failed to control applicant's pain with other measures, treating physician Dr. Park requested approval for trial of spinal cord stimulation on February 10, 2006. Defendant referred this request for surgery to utilization review and, on February 17, 2006, denied Dr. Park's request, based on the utilization review report. Copies of the denial letter were sent to applicant and her attorney.

Additionally, on February 21, 2006, defendant filed a DWC Form 233 Objection To Treating Physician's Recommendation For Spinal Surgery with the Administrative Director. Applicant does not now dispute the timeliness of defendant's objection. (Footnote 3)

By letter, dated March 3, 2006, the DWC Medical Unit returned defendant's Form 233 objection for the following reason:

"Once the Utilization Review process has been completed and the UR has made a determination and does not certify the procedure, the injured worker has to send in their appeal by having his/her treating physician file an appeal if his/her treating physician still wishes to continue with the recommended procedure. You then have 10 days from receipt of the second request of treating physician's report containing the recommendation for spinal surgery . . . " (Joint Exhibit 6.) (Emphasis in original.) (Footnote 4)

A copy of this letter was sent to Dr. Park.

Dr. Park again requested a spinal cord stimulator trial by letter dated March 3, 2006. Declaring that the second request was received on March 15, 2006, defendant again objected on Form 233 on March 24, 2006, and requested assignment of a second opinion physician by the Administrative Director. On April 4, 2006, the Medical Unit designated Dr. Shortz for the spinal surgery second opinion.

Trial was held on April 18, 2006, on the following issues:

"1. Applicant's entitlement to a spinal cord stimulator trial;

"2 Whether defendant timely objected to the request for spinal surgery such as to trigger the requirement for a second opinion as set forth in Labor Code Section 4062(b);

"3. Whether the Division of Workers' Compensation Medical Unit appropriately followed procedures set forth in Labor Code Sections 4062(b) and 4610. What the proper remedy is if DWC fails to follow appropriate procedure. Specifically, applicant is objecting to the Medical Unit requiring a second opinion and extending the 45 days within which to obtain a second surgical opinion by requiring the treating physician to object to an appeal of the UR doctor's opinion." (Minutes of Hearing, p. 2.)"

The record does not indicate when or if Dr. Shortz issued his opinion on the requested spinal surgery.

DISCUSSION

This case presents novel issues regarding the interplay between section 4062, which concerns objections to treating physician recommendations, and the utilization review statute, section 4610, enacted in Senate Bill ("SB") 228, Stats 2003, ch.639. Section 4062, as amended by SB 228 and by SB 899, effective April 19, 2004, provides, in pertinent part,

"(a) If either the employee or employer objects to a medical determination made by the treating physician concerning any medical issues not covered by Section 4060 or 4061 and not subject to Section 4610, the objecting party shall notify the other party in writing of the objection within 20 days of receipt of the report if the employee is represented by an attorney or within 30 days of receipt of the report if the employee is not represented by an attorney. Employer objections to the treating physician's recommendation for spinal surgery shall be subject to subdivision (b), and after denial of the physician's recommendation, in accordance with Section 4610. If the employee objects to a decision made pursuant to Section 4610 to modify, delay, or deny a treatment recommendation, the employee shall notify the employer of the objection in writing within 20 days of receipt of that decision. These time limits may be extended for good cause or by mutual agreement. If the employee is represented by an attorney, a medical evaluation to determine the disputed medical issue shall be obtained as provided in Section 4062.2, and no other medical evaluation shall be obtained. If the employee is not represented by an attorney, the employer shall immediately provide the employee with a form prescribed by the medical director with which to request assignment of a panel of three qualified medical evaluators, the evaluation shall be obtained as provided in Section 4062.1, and no other medical evaluation shall be obtained.

"(b) The employer may object to a report of the treating physician recommending that spinal surgery be performed within 10 days of the receipt of the report. If the employee is represented by an attorney, the parties shall seek agreement with the other party on a California licensed board–certified or board–eligible orthopedic surgeon or neurosurgeon to prepare a second opinion report resolving the disputed surgical recommendation. If no agreement is reached within 10 days, or if the employee is not represented by an attorney, an orthopedic surgeon or neurosurgeon shall be randomly selected by the administrative director to prepare a second opinion report resolving the disputed surgical recommendation. Examinations shall be scheduled on an expedited basis. The second opinion report shall be served on the parties within 45 days of receipt of the treating physician's report. If the second opinion report recommends surgery, the employer shall authorize the surgery. If the second opinion report does not recommend surgery, the employer shall file a declaration of readiness to proceed. The employer shall not be liable for medical treatment costs for the disputed surgical procedure, whether through a lien filed with the appeals board or as a self–procured medical expense, or for periods of temporary disability resulting from the surgery, if the disputed surgical procedure is performed prior to the completion of the second opinion process required by this subdivision." (Emphasis added.)"

AD Rule 9788.1(a) (Cal. Code Regs., tit. 8, § 9788.1(a).) provides,

"An employer who objects to the treating physician's recommendation for spinal surgery shall serve the objection, by mail or other rapid means of delivery, on the Administrative Director, the employee, the employee's attorney, if any, and on the treating physician within 10 days of receipt of the treating physician's report containing the recommendation. The objection shall be written on the form prescribed by the Administrative Director in Section 9788.11 . . . "

Rule 9788.11 contains the Form for Employer's Objection To Report Of Treating Physician Recommending Spinal Surgery, DWC Form 233.

Section 4610(g)(3)(A), provides that, if, pursuant to utilization review, a physician's request for treatment "is not approved in full, disputes shall be resolved in accordance with Section 4062. If a request to perform spinal surgery is denied, disputes shall be resolved in accordance with subdivision (b) of Section 4062." (Emphasis added.) (Footnote 5)

Section 4062(a) addresses recommendations for spinal surgery in only one sentence: "Employer objections to the treating physician's recommendation for spinal surgery shall be subject to subdivision (b), and after denial of the physician's recommendation, in accordance with Section 4610." This sentence, in combination with the other provisions cited above, establishes two tracks, each leading to the spinal surgery second opinion process in section 4062(b).

The first track, the employer's objection, is simple and direct. The single sentence in section 4062(a) provides that employer objections shall be subject to section 4062(b). Section 4062(b) and AD Rule 9788.1 spell out the employer's and the AD's responsibilities in resolving spinal surgery disputes: The employer may object on DWC Form 233 within 10 days of receipt of the treating physician's recommendation. If no agreement is reached with a represented employee on a second opinion surgeon within 10 days, or if the employee is unrepresented, the AD shall randomly select an orthopedic surgeon or neurosurgeon to examine the employee and prepare a report resolving the dispute. In the present case, the employer did object within 10 days. The AD, however, did not follow up with the selection of a second opinion surgeon.

The second track, the employee's objection to a denial of the physician's recommendation, is more convoluted, and is explained in detail below. In brief, when an employer denies spinal surgery, based upon its utilization review, the employee has 10 days from receipt of that denial to file an objection with the AD. A second opinion surgeon must then be selected pursuant to section 4062(b).

The employee's track begins with section 4062(a)'s reference to section 4610 and the denial of the physician's recommendation, and with the language of section 4610(g)(3)(A). These provisions envision the possibility of utilization review of a recommendation for spinal surgery. If the employer conducts utilization review, and the requested surgery is denied, the employee is then obligated to object under section 4062(a), if he or she still desires the surgery. (See Willette v. Au Electric Corp. (2004) 69 Cal. Comp. Cases 1298, 1303 (Appeals Board en banc).) Ordinarily, an applicant would have 20 days to notify the employer of its objection to a utilization review denial, pursuant to section 4062(a); but section 4610(g)(3)(A) specifically provides that disputes regarding denials of spinal surgery be resolved under section 4062(b). Section 4062(b), however, refers only to employer objections, which must be made within 10 days. The 20–day period for objecting to a utilization review denial set forth in section 4062(a) is general; it does not refer specifically to spinal surgery requests. Indeed, the only reference to spinal surgery in section 4062(a) deals with employer objections and says that they shall be subject to subdivision (b). Thus, the only specific reference to employee objections to an employer's denial of spinal surgery is the requirement of section 4610(g)(3)(A) that the dispute be resolved under section 4062(b). Given the separate and expedited procedures for spinal surgery and the specific references to section 4062(b) in sections 4062(a) and 4610(g)(3)(A), we believe the time period, within which an applicant must object to a utilization review denial of a request for spinal surgery, is 10 days from receipt of the denial. This time period is parallel to the time for an employer to object and is not likely to pose a hardship, since the treating physician will already have issued the request. No specific format has yet been established for the applicant to object to the denial; but the employee's objection, like the employer's section 4062(b) objection, should be directed to the AD, and not be delayed by going to the employer first and then to the AD, as an attachment to an employer objection to the second request.

In this case, defendant pursued option 4, objecting under section 4062(b) and seeking utilization review. Both actions were timely. The Medical Unit failed to act on the initial section 4062(b) objection and waited until defendant, acting on its advice, objected a second time, after receiving a second request for surgery from Dr. Park.

Section 4062(b) requires that the second opinion report be served on the parties within 45 days of receipt of the treating physician's report. The Medical Unit's scheme delays the commencement of this 45 day period until after the treating physician appeals the utilization review denial to the employer. This delay cannot be justified by the statutory language and is an unwarranted obstacle for the employee seeking surgery.

Moreover, the procedure contemplated by the Medical Unit overlooks that an employer need not always conduct utilization review. (Sandhagen v. Cox & Cox Construction (2005) 70 Cal. Comp. Cases 208, 212. (Appeals Board en banc).) It is likely that an employer will bypass utilization review in many cases and simply object under section 4062(b). A reason why an employer might bypass utilization review is that, if an employer undertakes utilization review and the utilization review report concludes that surgery is justified, the dispute over surgery is over. There is no provision for an employer to dispute the utilization review recommendation. At that point, the defendant has lost its right to a second opinion by a "California licensed board–certified or board–eligible orthopedic surgeon or neurosurgeon" under section 4062(b). It must provide the surgery. Rather than be bound by a possible positive recommendation by a utilization review doctor who has not even examined the employee, an employer might well prefer to proceed directly to an examination of the employee by a second opinion surgeon, which is how the dispute will be resolved anyway, in the event of a utilization review denial and employee objection. In addition, utilization review may take up to 14 days from the date of the treatment recommendation. (Lab. Code § 4610(g)(1).) If the employer waits for the result of utilization review, and it is not completed within 10 days, the employer will have lost the opportunity to object under section 4062(b).

If a utilization review report recommends denying surgery, and the employee timely objects, thereby precipitating the second opinion process under section 4610(g)(3)(A), any second opinion process begun as a result of the employer's objection will also resolve the employee's objection to the utilization review denial. This situation will arise in cases such as the present one, where the employer both conducts utilization review and objects under section 4062(b).

The Medical Unit erred when it rejected and returned defendant's timely objection and directed defendant to pursue utilization review – a decision which was properly discretionary on defendant's part. The Medical Unit's responsibilities under section 4062(b) commenced with defendant's initial objection, and there was no legal basis for delaying the second opinion process until applicant appealed the utilization review denial.

Because defendant did everything the statute required, and even what it was misled to do by the Medical Unit, we will not deny defendant its right to a second opinion, for failure of the Medical Unit or the second opinion surgeon to meet the statutory timelines. We will allow the process to continue, completing the record for the WCJ's determination. As we said in Willette v. Au Electric Corp., *supra*, 69 Cal. Comp. Cases 1298, 1309, "in view of the relative newness of the statutory procedure, we will for purposes of this opinion forgive any failure to date to comply with the relevant statutory deadlines and we will not now address any potential consequences of failures to comply with the statutory timelines in the future." We likewise forgive, in this case, applicant's March 3, 2006 objection to the employer's February 17, 2006 denial of surgery – an objection that would otherwise be untimely, pursuant to our decision herein.

For the foregoing reasons,

IT IS ORDERED, as the Decision After Reconsideration of the Workers' Compensation Appeals Board, that the April 18, 2006 Findings of Fact and Order is RESCINDED, and the matter is RETURNED to the trial level for further proceedings and decision by the WCJ consistent with this opinion.

WORKERS' COMPENSATION APPEALS BOARD

Commissioner William K. O'Brien

I concur,

CONCUR BY:

Frank M. Brass

Commissioner Merle C. Rabine

Merle C. Rabine, Commissioner

CONCUR:

CONCURRING OPINION OF COMMISSIONER RABINE

I concur. I write separately to add the following comments.

The memorandum of the Medical Unit dated March 3, 2006, is a classic "underground regulation." It is a standard of general application adopted by the Administrative Director through her Medical Unit to interpret and make specific provisions of Labor Code sections 4062(a) and 4062(b) and to govern their procedure. Thus, it is a "regulation" pursuant to Government Code section 11342.600 and subject to the Administrative Procedure Act (Government Code sections 11340 et seq.). See Rea v. Workers' Comp. Appeals Bd. (Milbauer) (2005) 127 Cal. App. 4th 625 [25 Cal. Rptr. 3d 828] [70 Cal. Comp. Cases 312].

The Administrative Director has not complied with the requirements of the Administrative Procedure Act. Nor has she complied with the public hearing requirements of Labor Code sections 5307.3 and 5307.4. Therefore, the memorandum is void on its face, and the Medical Unit may not rely on it to refuse to select an orthopedic surgeon or neurosurgeon, as required by Labor Code section 4062(b).

Footnote 1. Commissioner Murray, who was on the panel that granted reconsideration, was unavailable for the decision in this matter. Commissioner Rabine was appointed to take her place.

Footnote 2. All further statutory references are to the Labor Code, unless otherwise indicated.

Footnote 3. Labor Code section 4062(b) requires that an employer's objection to a treating physician's recommendation of spinal surgery be filed within 10 days. At trial, applicant contended that defendant's February 21,

2006 objection to the February 10, 2006 recommendation was untimely, since it was filed on the 11th day. Because February 20, 2006, was a holiday, the period in which an objection could be filed was extended to February 21, 2006. (Gov. Code §§ 6707, 6700–6706; see also, Code Civ. Proc., §§ 10, 12–12b.)

Footnote 4. The Medical Unit's letter seems to imply that the employee is to object to a utilization review denial by resubmitting the request for surgery to the employer.

Footnote 5. Section 4062 refers to the treating physician's "recommendation" for spinal surgery. Section 4610(g)(3)(A) refers to a "request" to perform spinal surgery. We see no significant difference between the two terms and use them interchangeably. [**Editors Note:** The Court of Appeal, First District, denied applicant's Petition for Writ of Review on January 18, 2007. See *Brasher v. WCAB* (2007) 72 Cal. Comp. Cases 229, wherein applicant argued, to no avail, that the Appeals Board violated Labor Code section 4062(b) by creating a 10–day deadline for an injured employee, which does not exist in Labor Code section 4062(b) and which as a result of the Board's opinion shifts the burden of meeting the express deadline set forth in Section 4062(b) from the employer to the employee.]

See Appendix E for the Spinal Surgery Second Opinion Procedure Regulations.

If an employee in an employer's MPN desires to change physicians the change to an alternative position must be within the MPN. *Laier v. WCAB* (2006) 71 Cal. Comp. Cases 856.

See Appendix B for the Medical Provider Network (MPN) Regulations

In *Power Dodge of Valencia, et al. v. WCAB (Gonzalez)* (2006) 71 Cal. Comp. Cases 967, the Board ruled that the defendant was liable for the cost of medical treatment related to an applicant's spinal surgery performed on August 7, 2004 as well as for temporary total disability resulting from the surgery where the defendant failed to comply with the mandatory Administrative Director's Spinal Surgery Second Opinion Regulations, section 9788.1, adopted pursuant to Labor Code section 4062(d).

In the judge's decision, upheld by the Board, the judge stated, in part:

Petitioner argues that, under Labor Code section 4062(b), it is not liable for medical treatment costs or periods of temporary disability. Petitioner relies on the following provision in section 4062(b): "The employer shall not be liable for medical treatment costs for the disputed surgical procedure, whether through a lien filed with the appeals board or as a self–procured medical expense, or for periods of temporary disability resulting from the surgery, if the disputed surgical procedure is performed prior to the completion of the second opinion process required by this subdivision." (Emphasis added [by WCJ, Arthur Weinstein]).

On June 1, 2004, applicant's counsel served defense counsel with Dr. Obukhov's recommendation for spinal surgery. On June 7, 2004, defense counsel sent a letter to applicant's counsel, objecting to Dr. Obukhov's recommendation for spinal surgery and inquiring into the utilization of an AME for a second opinion consult with regard to the proposed back surgery.

On June 24, 2004, applicant's counsel sent a letter to defense counsel, acknowledging receipt of defendant's June 7, 2004, inquiry into the use of an AME, rejecting the offer to use an AME and advising defense counsel to obtain a QME "for purposes of objecting to the surgery." At this point, under Labor Code section 4062(b), because "no agreement [was] reached," the parties were under an obligation to request appointment of a physician "randomly selected by the administrative director to prepare a second opinion report." Only seven days later, on July 2, 2004, DWC's emergency spinal surgery regulations took effect, mandating the defendant to serve the Administrative Director with its objection.

Effective July 2, 2004, DWC's emergency spinal surgery second opinion procedure regulations took effect. WCAB Rule 9788.1 states in pertinent part: "An employer who objects to the treating physician's recommendation for spinal surgery shall serve the objection, by mail or other rapid means of delivery, on the Administrative Director, the employee, the employee's attorney, if any, and on the treating physician within 10 days of receipt of the treating physician's report containing the recommendation." (8 Cal. Code Reg. § 9788.1) (Emphasis added [by WCJ]). The work [sic] "shall" is mandatory. (Labor Code § 15). Rather than complying with the mandatory requirement of WCAB Rule 9788.1, which became effective on July 2, 2004, only seven days after a stalemate ensued in negotiations towards use of an AME, counsel for defendant bypassed Rule 9788.1 and Labor Code section 4062(b) by obtaining a defense QME medical opinion from Dr. Alan Roberts.

Labor Code section 4062(b) was not implemented in this case until the WCJ, in his Order Vacating Submission, dated May 6, 2005, ordered defendant to serve its objection to the treating physician's recommendation for spinal surgery on the Administrative Director, for random selection of a physician to prepare a second opinion report, in compliance with Labor Code section 4062(b) and 8 Cal. Code of Reg. Section 9788.1. Because defendant acted to implement Labor Code section 4062(b) under court order, almost one year after applicant's counsel served defendant with Dr. Obukhov's recommendation for spinal surgery, the circumstances in this case are distinguishable from "the run of cases" under section 4062(b). Therefore, it cannot be said that the Legislature intended for defendant in the instant case to possess immunity from liability for medical treatment costs or periods of temporary disability resulting from the surgery, where the surgery, as here, was performed nine months prior to the implementation of the second opinion process.

Defendant failed to comply with the mandatory requirements of WCAB Rule 9788.1. That rule took effect only seven days after the stalemate occurred in negotiations toward use of an AME. Rather than serve its objection on the Administrative Director, defendant chose to obtain a defense QME medical opinion. Because defendant failed to fulfill its mandatory duties under Labor Code section 4062(b) and Rule 9788.1, it should be held to have waived its right, under the same statute, to assert immunity from liability for medical treatment costs or periods of temporary disability resulting from the surgery. Moreover, if defendant believed that action by the WCJ was not in compliance with Labor Code section 4062(b), it should have filed a petition for reconsideration or a petition for removal to the May 6, 2005 Order Vacating Submission, which ordered defendant to serve its objection to the treating doctor's recommendation for spinal surgery on the Administrative Director, for random selection of a physician to prepare a second opinion report. No such petition was filed... .

If temporary disability exists, apart from the temporary disability resulting from spinal surgery, an applicant may be awarded such temporary disability even if he or she secured the spinal surgery prior to the completion of the requisite second opinion process. See *Travelers Property and Casualty Co. v. WCAB (Shuman)* (2005) 70 Cal. Comp. Cases 1049.

Page 557, Column 1, third paragraph insert following '...subdivision (c)(5).'

In *Gateway Chevrolet/GM Motors, et. al. v. WCAB (Welch)* (2006) 71 Cal. Comp. Cases 1864, the Board noted that Labor Code section 4062(b) does not mention whether an employer has a right to cross–examine a second opinion physician who recommends spinal surgery, but the Board upheld the judge's denial of right to cross–examine the second opinion surgeon who, in this case, recommended surgery.

§ 8.14(D) Payment of Employee–Selected Physician Bill as Well as Employer Designated Physician Bills

Filing Fee for Lien: $100.00

Page 565, Column 2, fourth paragraph delete words "Filing Fee for Liens: $100.00" and insert the following:

The Administrative Director has amended Sections of Regulation 10250 to delete the requirement of a lien claimant having to pay filing fees.

The Legislature has repealed Labor Code section 4903.05, effective July 12, 2006, thereby eliminating the $100.00 filing fee requirement for medical treatment and medical/legal liens.

However, it enacted Labor Code section 4903.6, also effective July 12, 2006, as noted below setting forth numerous time limits and procedures for medical providers to file liens against compensation or Applications for Adjudication. These time limits do not, however, apply to filing of liens filed by or on behalf of employees or employers.

Page 565, Column 2, fifth paragraph delete commencing "Labor Code section 4903.5 effective January 1, 2004, provides" and insert the following:

The Legislature, effective July 12, 2006, repealed Labor Code section 4903.5 and replaced it with Labor Code section 4903.6, which provides:

(a) Except as necessary to meet the requirements of Section 4903.5, no lien claim or application for adjudication shall be filed under subdivision (b) of Section 4903 until the expiration of one of the following:

   (1) Sixty days after the date of acceptance or rejection of liability for the claim, or expiration of the time provided for investigation of liability pursuant to subdivision (b) of Section 5402, whichever date is earlier.

   (2) The time provided for payment of medical treatment bills pursuant to Section 4603.2.

   (3) The time provided for payment of medical–legal expenses pursuant to Section 4622.

(b) No declaration of readiness to proceed shall be filed for a lien under subdivision (b) of Section 4903 until the underlying case has been resolved or where the applicant chooses not to proceed with his or her case.

(c) The appeals board shall adopt reasonable regulations to ensure compliance with this section, and shall take any further steps as may be necessary to enforce the regulations, including, but not limited to, impositions of sanctions pursuant to Section 5813.

(d) The prohibitions of this section shall not apply to lien claims, applications for adjudication, or declarations of readiness to proceed filed by or on behalf of the employee, or to the filings by or on behalf of the employer.

A medical provider's billing may constitute adequate proof of the reasonableness of the charges if the employer/insurer does not produce evidence to rebut the billing. *City of Los Angeles, PSI v. WCAB (Boney)* (2006) 71 Cal. Comp. Cases 520. See also *Cypress v. WCAB (Yturbe)* (2006) 71 Cal. Comp. Cases 655.

Page 565, Column 2, last paragraph insert after "Title 8, California Code of Regulations Section 10250 provides:" the following:

In light of the repeal of Labor Code section 4903.5, effective July 12, 2006, the Regulation is no longer relevant.

§ 8.16(D)   Expenses Incurred at Distant Locations

Page 592, Column 2, third paragraph, insert the following:

See also *City of Los Angeles, PSI v. WCAB (Boney)* (2006) 71 Cal. Comp. Cases 520, where the lien claimant was entitled to the full amount of its charges for surgery under principles set forth in *Kunz*.

In upholding the judge's award to the lien claimant, the Board stated, in part:

A lien for medical treatment in a compensable claim will be allowable only if the treatment rendered was reasonably required to cure or relieve the injured worker from the effects of the industrial injury. (Lab. Code § 4600 subd. (a)).

Furthermore, in our en banc decision in Kunz, *supra*, we held, in relevant part, that, although the Official Medical Fee Schedule generally does not apply to outpatient surgery facility fees, such fees must nevertheless be reasonable. In order to determine the reasonableness of an outpatient surgery facility fee, the Board may take into consideration a number of factors, including but not limited to the following: (1) the medical provider's usual fee and the usual fee of other medical providers in the same geographical area, which means the fee usually accepted, not the fee usually charged; (2) the fee the outpatient surgery center usually accepts for the same or similar services (both in a workers' compensation context and in a non–workers' compensation context, including contractually negotiated fees); and (3) the fee usually accepted by other providers in the same geographical area (including in–patient providers). (Kunz v. Patterson Floor Covering 67 Cal. Comp. Cas at 1590, *supra*.)

However, the defendant may rebut the evidence regarding the reasonableness of the lien claimant's billing by presenting (1) evidence that the facility fee billed by the outpatient surgery center is greater than the fee the outpatient surgery center usually accepts for the same or similar services, both in a workers' compensation context and a non–workers' compensation context, including contractually negotiated fees; or (2) evidence that the facility fee billed by the outpatient surgery center is greater than the fee usually accepted by other providers in the same geographical area, including in–patient providers. (Kunz v. Patterson Floor Covering 67 Cal. Comp. Cas at 1599, *supra*.)

Nevertheless, in the absence of persuasive rebuttal evidence from the defendant, the outpatient surgery center's billing, by itself, will normally constitute adequate proof that the fee being billed is what the outpatient surgery center usually accepts for the services rendered (and that the fee being billed is also consistent with what other medical providers in the same geographical area accept). (Kunz v. Patterson Floor Covering 67 Cal. Comp. Cas at 1598, *supra*.)

In this case, Dr. Sohn reported that applicant's second surgery was of questionable benefit to her and that her condition remained unchanged. Therefore, pursuant to Labor Code section 4600 subdivision (a), we find that

Bohm should take nothing on account of its June 17, 2003 lien.

Turning to Bohm's bill, dated April 23, 2002, for applicant's first surgery, we note that Dr. Sohn reported that the surgery was of some benefit to applicant providing some mild relief of pain. We further note that Bohm submitted its bill into evidence at trial. In order for defendant to have rebutted the reasonableness of Bohm's billing, defendant needed to present (1) evidence that the fees billed by Bohm were greater than the fee Bohm usually accepts for the same or similar services, both in a workers' compensation context and a non–workers' compensation context, including contractually negotiated fees; or (2) evidence that the fees billed by Bohm were greater than the fee usually accepted by other providers in the same geographical area, including in–patient providers. Defendant did not present any such evidence and the bill reviewer's testimony, even if admissible, does not respond to these issues. Therefore, in the absence of persuasive rebuttal evidence from the defendant, Bohm's billing, by itself, constitutes adequate proof that the fee billed is what Bohm usually accepts for the services rendered and is also consistent with what other medical providers in the same geographical area accept. As such, we find that defendant is liable to Bohm on its April 23, 2002 lien in the amount of $21,013.00 less $9,991.61 previously paid by defendant… .

A lien claimant may not be reimbursed for facility fees when it is *unlicensed* and *unaccredited* in violation of the Business and Professions Code and the Health and Safety Code. In so holding in *Zenith National Insurance Co. v. WCAB (Capi)* (2006) 71 Cal. Comp. Cases 374, the Court of Appeal, Fourth District stated, in part:

Our Legislature has recognized that many surgical procedures are performed in numerous types of outpatient settings and determined that, although the health professionals delivering the services are licensed, further quality assurance is needed to ensure that the services are safely and effectively performed. (Bus. & Prof. Code, § 2215.) To implement this intent, the Health and Safety Code contains regulatory and licensing provisions governing different types of outpatient settings. (Bus. & Prof. Code, § 2217.) Notably, it is illegal to operate an outpatient setting in California, including ambulatory surgical centers and surgical clinics, if the outpatient setting is not properly licensed or accredited. (Health & Saf. Code, §§ 1248, subd. (c), 1248.1, subd. (a), (d), (f) & (g), 1248.8.)

In workers' compensation matters, the burden of proof rests on the party or lien claimant "holding the affirmative of the issue." (Lab. Code, §§ 5705, 3202.5.) Where the injured employee does not prosecute his or her claim, the lien claimant bears the burden of establishing the injury, entitlement to benefits and the reasonable value of the services. (2 Cal. Workers' Comp. Practice (Cont.Ed.Bar 4th ed. 1998) § 15.82, p. 1108.) Although there is not a great deal of case law on this issue, a lien claimant must also prove that its services were properly provided, meaning it complied with applicable licensure or accreditation requirements. (PM & R Associates v. Workers' Comp. Appeals Bd. (2000) 80 Cal. App. 4th 357, 370 [94 Cal. Rptr.

2d 887, 65 Cal. Comp. Cas 347] [lien claimant had the burden to prove its liens were for properly provided services, including whether it had complied with the provisions of Business and Professions Code section 2069 and the attendant regulations governing medical assistants]; Hand Rehabilitation Center v. Workers' Comp. Appeals Bd. (1995) 34 Cal. App. 4th 1204, 1212–1213 [40 Cal. Rptr. 2d 734, 60 Cal. Comp. Cas 289] [lien claimant had the burden of proving lien was for properly provided services, including documentation that properly licensed personnel supervised the therapy as required by official medical fee schedule]; see Continental Medical Center etc. v. Workers Comp. Appeals Bd. (2000) 65 Cal. Comp. Cases 162, 164–165 [writ denied] [lien claimant medical center was not entitled to payment for medical treatment because it was not a professional corporation at the time of applicant's treatment]; 9 Witkin, Cal. Procedure (4th ed. 1996) Appeal, § 922, p. 960 [board decisions may be cited for their persuasive value].)

Accordingly, in order to establish their right to reimbursement, the lien claimants bore the burden of proving they were properly licensed or accredited. Although the Board stated that Zenith was attempting to shift the burden of proof to the lien claimants, the foregoing discussion establishes that the lien claimants bore the initial burden of proof on this issue and they failed to do so. Thus, the award was not supported by substantial evidence.

The Board also concluded that Zenith waived the issue by not raising it; however, this alleged failure did not obviate the lien claimants' burden of proof. (See Kunz v. Patterson Floor Coverings, Inc. (2002) 67 Cal. Comp. Cases 1588, 1591 [Appeals Board en banc opinion].) Based on these conclusions, we need not reach Zenith's alternative claim that the Board erred in denying reconsideration because the WCJ improperly barred it from presenting evidence that the lien claimants were operating illegally.

Therefore, we annul the Board's order and remand the matter to the Board for further proceedings, including, if necessary, further development of the record… .

See also *Universal Building Services, et al. v. WCAB* (2006) 71 Cal. Comp. Cases 655.

§ 8.17   Medical Legal Reports and Expenses

Page 600, Column 2, second paragraph, insert following '…oral testimony.'

A doctor's broad conclusion that a medical condition is work–related is not sufficient to establish work connectedness if no specific connection is made by the doctor between the medical condition and the work environment. *Georgia–Pacific Corp. v. WCAB* (1983) 48 Cal. Comp. Cases 443; *John Manville, et al. v. WCAB (Howell)* (2005) 70 Cal. Comp. Cases 986.

§ 8.19(B)   Medical–Legal Fee Schedule Regulations

Page 611, Column 1, sixth paragraph delete third line beginning 'However...' and insert the following:

However, the reader should note that Section 9795 has been amended to increase the multiplier in Labor Code section 9795(B) from $10.00 to $12.50, resulting in a 25% increase for Medical–Legal Expenses.

See Appendix G for the Medical–Legal Expenses and Comprehensive Medical–Legal Evaluation Regulations

.

Page 611, Column 2, second paragraph, second line, delete $10.00 and insert the following:

$12.50

§ 8.25   Liens

Page 621, Column 2, delete sixth through seventh paragraph and insert the following:

[**Editor's Note:** The Legislature has repealed Labor Code section 4903.05, effective July 12, 2006, thereby eliminating the $100.00 filing fee requirement for medical treatment and medical/legal liens].

Page 622, Column 1, delete paragraphs one and two.

§ 8A.0   MEDICAL BENEFITS PROVIDED TO ALL INDUSTRIALLY INJURED EMPLOYEES ON OR AFTER APRIL 19, 2004, REGARDLESS OF DATE OF INJURY

Page 623, Column 1, first paragraph, delete fourth and fifth lines beginning '...Labor Code section...' through the end of the page and insert the following:

as amended effective January 1, 2007, provides:

(a) Medical, surgical, chiropractic, acupuncture, and hospital treatment, including nursing, medicines, medical and surgical supplies, crutches, and apparatuses, including orthotic and prosthetic devices and services, that is reasonably required to cure or relieve the injured worker from the effects of his or her injury shall be provided by the employer. In the case of his or her neglect or refusal reasonably to do so, the employer is liable for the reasonable expense incurred by or on behalf of the employee in providing treatment.

(b) As used in this division and notwithstanding any other provision of law, medical treatment that is reasonably required to cure or relieve the injured worker from the effects of his or her injury means treatment that is based upon the guidelines adopted by the administrative director pursuant to Section 5307.27 or, prior to the adoption of those guidelines, the updated American College of Occupational and Environmental Medicine's Occupational Medicine Practice Guidelines.

(c) Unless the employer or the employer's insurer has established a medical provider network as provided for in Section 4616, after 30 days from the date the injury is reported, the employee may be treated by a physician of his or her own choice or at a facility of his or her own choice within a reasonable geographic area.

(d)

(1) If an employee has notified his or her employer in writing prior to the date of injury that he or she has a personal physician, the employee shall have the right to be treated by that physician from the date of injury if either of the following conditions exist:

(A) The employer provides nonoccupational group health coverage in a health care service plan, licensed pursuant to Chapter 2.2 (commencing with Section 1340) of Division 2 of the Health and Safety Code.

(B) The employer provides nonoccupational health coverage in a group health plan or a group health insurance policy as described in Section 4616.7.

(2) For purposes of paragraph (1), a personal physician shall meet all of the following conditions:

(A) The physician is the employee's regular physician and surgeon, licensed pursuant to Chapter 5 (commencing with Section 2000) of Division 2 of the Business and Professions Code.

(B) The physician is the employee's primary care physician and has previously directed the medical treatment of the employee, and who retains the employee's medical records, including his or her medical history. "Personal physician" includes a medical group, if the medical group is a single corporation or partnership composed of licensed doctors of medicine or osteopathy, which operates an integrated multispecialty medical group providing comprehensive medical services predominantly for nonoccupational illnesses and injuries. *"Personal physician" includes a medical group, if the medical group is a single corporation or partnership composed of licensed doctors of medicine or osteopathy, which operates an integrated multispecialty medical group providing comprehensive medical services predominantly for nonoccupational illnesses and injuries.*
[Editor's Note: The statute does not require the pre–designated personal physician to be within the employer's group health plan. Just that the above conditions be met. See Administrative Director's Newsline No. 06–07, January 26, 2007]

(C) The physician agrees to be predesignated.

(3) If the employer provides nonoccupational health care pursuant to Chapter 2.2 (commencing with Section 1340) of Division 2 of the Health and Safety Code, and the employer is notified pursuant to paragraph (1), all medical treatment, utilization review of medical treatment, access to medical treatment, and other medical treatment issues shall be governed by Chapter 2.2 (commencing with Section 1340) of Division 2 of the Health and Safety Code. Disputes regarding the provision of medical treatment shall be resolved pursuant to

Article 5.55 (commencing with Section 1374.30) of Chapter 2.2 of Division 2 of the Health and Safety Code.

(4) If the employer provides nonoccupational health care, as described in Section 4616.7, all medical treatment, utilization review of medical treatment, access to medical treatment, and other medical treatment issues shall be governed by the applicable provisions of the Insurance Code.

(5) The insurer may require prior authorization of any nonemergency treatment or diagnostic service and may conduct reasonably necessary utilization review pursuant to Section 4610.

(6) An employee shall be entitled to all medically appropriate referrals by the personal physician to other physicians or medical providers within the nonoccupational health care plan. An employee shall be entitled to treatment by physicians or other medical providers outside of the nonoccupational health care plan pursuant to standards established in Article 5 (commencing with Section 1367) of Chapter 2.2 of Division 2 of the Health and Safety Code..

(7) The division shall conduct an evaluation of this program and present its findings to the Governor and the Legislature on or before December 31, 2008.

(8) This subdivision shall remain in effect only until December 31, 2009, and as of that date is repealed, unless a later enacted statute that is enacted before *December 31, 2009,* deletes or extends that date.

(e)

(1) When at the request of the employer, the employer's insurer, the administrative director, the appeals board, or a workers' compensation administrative law judge, the employee submits to examination by a physician, he or she shall be entitled to receive, in addition to all other benefits herein provided, all reasonable expenses of transportation, meals, and lodging incident to reporting for the examination, together with one day of temporary disability indemnity for each day of wages lost in submitting to the examination.

(2) Regardless of the date of injury, "reasonable expenses of transportation" includes mileage fees from the employee's home to the place of the examination and back at the rate of twenty–one cents ($0.21) a mile or the mileage rate adopted by the Director of the Department of Personnel Administration pursuant to Section 19820 of the Government Code, whichever is higher, plus any bridge tolls. The mileage and tolls shall be paid to the employee at the time he or she is given notification of the time and place of the examination. **[Editor's Note:** At the time of publication of this book, the "reasonable expense of transportation" was 48.5 cents per mile, effective January 1, 2007, regardless of date of injury].

(f) When at the request of the employer, the employer's insurer, the administrative director, the appeals board, or a workers' compensation administrative law judge, an employee submits to examination by a physician and the employee does not proficiently speak or understand the English language, he or she shall be entitled to the services of a qualified interpreter in accordance with conditions and a fee schedule prescribed by the administrative director. These services shall be provided by the employer. For purposes of this section, "qualified interpreter" means a language interpreter certified, or deemed certified, pursuant to Article 8 (commencing with Section 11435.05) of Chapter 4.5 of Part 1 of Division 3 of Title 2 of, or Section 68566 of, the Government Code. **[Editor's Note:** The reader should note that the Legislature deleted the 7 percent limit on the maximum percent of employees in the state that may be predesignated.]

Page 624, delete Column 1, beginning '...duct reasonably...' and ending '...Labor Code section 4600(b)' and insert the following:

However, "medical treatment" now means treatment that is based upon the Guidelines adopted by the Administrative Director. The Administrative Director has adopted the medical treatment Guidelines set forth in the Guidelines recommended by the updated "American College of Occupational Medicine Practices Guidelines", commonly referred to as "ACOEM Guidelines". Labor Code section 4600 (b).

The Guidelines of the Director are designed to assist medical providers by offering an analytical framework for the evaluation and treatment of injured workers and must constitute medical care in accordance with Section 4600 for all injured workers diagnosed with industrial conditions. Labor Code section 4604.5(b).

Page 624, Column 1, eighth paragraph, insert following '...the Government Code.'

The Legislature has again amended Section 4600, effective January 1, 2007 to:

a. Eliminate a requirement that the right to predesignate a personal physician be limited to 7 percent of such predesignations in this state;

b. Permit employees eligible to predesignate personal physicians to include a medical group, if the medical group is a single corporation or partnership composed of licensed doctors of medicinal or osteopathy which operates an integrated multispecialty medical group providing comprehensive medical services predominantly for non–occupational illnesses and injuries;

c. Extend the right to predesignation of a personal physician to December 31, 2009 unless a later enacted statute that is enacted before December 31, 2009 deletes or extends that date; and

d. Define acupuncture treatment that is reasonably required to relieve an injured worker from the effects of his or her injury. It means:

"Treatment that is based upon the guidelines adopted by the administrative director pursuant to Section 5307.27 or, prior to the adoption of those guidelines, as set forth in the "Acupuncture and Electroacupuncture: Evidence–Based Treatment Guidelines–August 2004" published by the Council of Acupuncture and Oriental Medicine Associations and the Foundation for Acupuncture Research, and which shall include any subsequent updates of those Guidelines, or other Guidelines. Nothing in this section shall prohibit the administrative director from adopting treatment Guidelines for acupuncture if those guidelines are at least as comprehensive as the "Acupuncutre and Electroacupuncture: Evidence–Based Treatment Guidelines–August 2004"."

The newly enacted Section 4600, effective January 1, 2007, provides:

(a) Medical, surgical, chiropractic, acupuncture, and hospital treatment, including nursing, medicines, medical and surgical supplies, crutches, and apparatuses, including orthotic and prosthetic devices and services, that is reasonably required to cure or relieve the injured worker from the effects of his or her injury shall be provided by the employer. In the case of his or her neglect or refusal reasonably to do so, the employer is liable for the reasonable expense incurred by or on behalf of the employee in providing treatment.

(b) As used in this division and notwithstanding any other provision of law, medical treatment that is reasonably required to cure or relieve the injured worker from the effects of his or her injury means treatment that is based upon the guidelines adopted by the administrative director pursuant to Section 5307.27 or, prior to the adoption of those guidelines, the updated American College of Occupational and Environmental Medicine's Occupational Medicine Practice Guidelines.

(c) As used in this division and notwithstanding any other provisions of law, acupuncture treatment that is reasonably required to relieve the injured worker from the effects of his or her injury means treatment that is based upon the guidelines adopted by the administrative director pursuant to Section 5307.27 or, prior to the adoption of those guidelines, as set forth in the "Acupuncture and Electroacupuncture: Evidence–Based Treatment Guidelines–August 2004" published by the Council of Acupuncture and Oriental Medicine Associations and the Foundation for Acupuncture Research, and which shall include any subsequent updates of those guidelines, or other guidelines. Nothing in this section shall prohibit the administrative director from adopting treatment guidelines for acupuncture if those guidelines are at least as comprehensive as the "Acupuncutre and Electroacupuncture: Evidence–Based Treatment

Guidelines–August 2004.

(d) Unless the employer or the employer's insurer has established a medical provider network as provided for in Section 4616, after 30 days from the date the injury is reported, the employee may be treated by a physician of his or her own choice or at a facility of his or her own choice within a reasonable geographic area.

(e)
(1) If an employee has notified his or her employer in writing prior to the date of injury that he or she has a personal physician, the employee shall have the right to be treated by that physician from the date of injury if either of the following conditions exist:
(A) The employer provides nonoccupational group health coverage in a health care service plan, licensed pursuant to Chapter 2.2 (commencing with Section 1340) of Division 2 of the Health and Safety Code.
(B) The employer provides nonoccupational health coverage in a group health plan or a group health insurance policy as described in Section 4616.7.
(2) For purposes of paragraph (1), a personal physician shall meet all of the following conditions:
(A) The physician is the employee's regular physician and surgeon, licensed pursuant to Chapter 5 (commencing with Section 2000) of Division 2 of the Business and Professions Code.
(B) The physician is the employee's primary care physician and has previously directed the medical treatment of the employee, and who retains the employee's medical records, including his or her medical history. "Personal physician" includes a medical group, if the medical group is a single corporation or partnership composed of licensed doctors of medicine or osteopathy, which operates an integrated multispecialty medical group providing comprehensive medical services predominantly for nonoccupational illnesses and injuries.
(C) The physician agrees to be predesignated.
(3) If the employer provides nonoccupational health care pursuant to Chapter 2.2 (commencing with Section 1340) of Division 2 of the Health and Safety Code and the employer is notified pursuant to paragraph (1), all medical treatment, utilization review of medical treatment, access to medical treatment, and other medical treatment issues shall be governed by Chapter 2.2 (commencing with Section 1340) of Division 2 of the Health and Safety Code. Disputes regarding the provision of medical treatment shall be resolved pursuant to Article 5.55 (commencing with Section 1374.30) of Chapter 2.2 of Division 2 of the Health and Safety Code.
(4) If the employer provides nonoccupational health care, as described in Section 4616.7, all medical

treatment, utilization review of medical treatment, access to medical treatment, and other medical treatment issues shall be governed by the applicable provisions of the Insurance Code.

(5) The insurer may require prior authorization of any nonemergency treatment or diagnostic service and may conduct reasonably necessary utilization review pursuant to Section 4610.

(6) An employee shall be entitled to all medically appropriate referrals by the personal physician to other physicians or medical providers within the nonoccupational health care plan. An employee shall be entitled to treatment by physicians or other medical providers outside of the nonoccupational health care plan pursuant to standards established in Article 5 (commencing with Section 1367) of Chapter 2.2 of Division 2 of the Health and Safety Code.

(7) The division shall conduct an evaluation of this program and present its findings to the Governor and the Legislature on or before December 31, 2008.

(8) This subdivision shall remain in effect only until December 31, 2009, and as of that date is repealed, unless a later enacted statute that is enacted before December 31, 2009, deletes or extends that date.

(f)

(1) When at the request of the employer, the employer's insurer, the administrative director, the appeals board, or a workers' compensation administrative law judge, the employee submits to examination by a physician, he or she shall be entitled to receive, in addition to all other benefits herein provided, all reasonable expenses of transportation, meals, and lodging incident to reporting for the examination, together with one day of temporary disability indemnity for each day of wages lost in submitting to the examination.

(2) Regardless of the date of injury, "reasonable expenses of transportation" includes mileage fees from the employee's home to the place of the examination and back at the rate of twenty–one cents ($0.21) a mile or the mileage rate adopted by the Director of the Department of Personnel Administration pursuant to Section 19820 of the Government Code, whichever is higher, plus any bridge tolls. The mileage and tolls shall be paid to the employee at the time he or she is given notification of the time and place of the examination. **[Editor's Note:** The mileage reimbursement rate rose to 48.5 cents a mile, effective January 1, 2007, regardless of date of injury.]

(g) When at the request of the employer, the employer's insurer, the administrative director, the appeals board, or a workers' compensation administrative law judge, an employee submits to examination by a physician and the employee does not proficiently speak or understand the English language, he or she shall be entitled to the services of a qualified interpreter in accordance with

conditions and a fee schedule prescribed by the administrative director. These services shall be provided by the employer. For purposes of this section, "qualified interpreter" means a language interpreter certified, or deemed certified, pursuant to Article 8 (commencing with Section 11435.05) of Chapter 4.5 of Part 1 of Division 3 of Title 2 of, or Section 68566 of, the Government Code.

SEC. 3. Section 2.5 of this bill incorporates amendments to Section 4600 of the Labor Code proposed by both this bill and AB 2287. It shall only become operative if (1) both bills are enacted and become effective on or before January 1, 2007, (2) each bill amends Section 4600 of the Labor Code, and (3) this bill is enacted after AB 2287, in which case Section 2 of this bill shall not become operative. **[Editor's Note:** The Legislature in amending Section 4600 to allow for certain employees to predesignate their personal physician, stated: *The Legislature finds and declares, based on published research, that the results of medical treatment by physicians who have previously cared for the employee prior to the injury are comparable to the results of medical treatment by physicians chosen by employers of insurers, and that the right of an employee to designate a personal physician should not be permitted to expire on April 30, 2007.]*

Page 624, Column 2, second paragraph beginning 'The Guidelines...' delete lines one, two and three and insert the following:

The Guidelines the Director adopted are officially entitled "Medical Treatment Utilization Schedule" and the recommended Guidelines set forth in the Schedule are presumed "presumptively correct", as to the issue of extent and scope of medical treatment. **[Editor's Note:** See Appendix D of this book for Medical Treatment Utilization Schedule that became effective June 15, 2007.]

Page 624, Column 2, third paragraph beginning 'The ACOEM...' delete first lines and insert the following:

The ACOEM Guidelines, as of March 22, 2004, were presumptively

Page 624, Column 2, following third paragraph beginning 'The ACOEM...' insert the following:

See Appendix D for the Medical Treatment Utilization Schedule.

Page 626, Column 1, eighth paragraph, insert following '…§§4600(c), 4616.)'

In holding that the ACOEM Guidelines apply in determining disputes involving reasonableness of medical treatment, in all cases in which there is no order by the Appeals Board as of April 19, 2004, the Court of Appeal, Third District, in *Sierra Pacific Industries v. WCAB (Chatham)* (2006) 71 Cal. Comp. Cases 714, stated, in part:

> The usual rule is that the law in effect on the date of injury governs in workers' compensation cases because the industrial injury is the basis for the award. (Aetna Cas. & Surety Co. v. Ind. Acc. Com., *supra*, 30 Cal. 2d at p. 392.) Section 47 changes this usual rule by providing that SB 899 applies "regardless of the date of injury." Instead, the provisions of SB 899 apply "prospectively from the date of enactment," but are not grounds to reopen, rescind, alter or amend an existing order. Thus, we interpret section 47 to require application of the ACOEM guidelines to determine reasonable medical treatment to all cases in which there is not an order as of the date of enactment of SB 899… .

Page 628, Column 2, sixth paragraph insert following '…Section 4600(c).'

ACOEM

Commenting on what evidence may rebut the presumption of correctness of the ACOEM Guidelines, the Board in *Lake Tahoe Unified School District, et. al. v. WCAB (Kelly)* (2007) 72 Cal. Comp. Cases 138, stated, in part:

> We disagree with defendant's position that, "The crux of the dispute in this matter, therefore, is whether or not applicant has properly rebutted the presumption that the ACOEM Guidelines are correct." The issues, as stated in the Minutes of Hearing, are whether applicant is entitled to chiropractic treatment under the Award of June 9, 1998, and reimbursement for self–procured treatment, including the lien of Borges Chiropractic. There is no question that the ACOEM Guidelines are presumed correct. (Lab. Code § 4604.5(c).) The first issue that must be addressed, then, is whether the treatment at issue is justified under the ACOEM Guidelines. If the treatment falls within the Guidelines, then no rebuttal is necessary. Only if the Guidelines recommend against the treatment does the burden fall to applicant to show that a variance is necessary.
>
> In this case, applicant is long past the acute and sub–acute phases of her 1996 injury. The section of the ACOEM Guidelines that most directly addresses her situation is Chapter 6. Chapter 6 (Pain Suffering, and the Restoration of Function) deals with chronic pain and states, at page 107, "Successful pain management hinges on appreciating the dynamics of each patient's case and on proactively managing factors that might delay return to work or restoration of function." Similarly, at page 117, the Guidelines state, "Pain management focuses on functional restoration. Because return to function is essential to return to health, occupational health professionals are concerned with return to function." Chapter 6 does not include a specific recommendation regarding chiropractic care and certainly does not specify frequency of visits, but it does recommend multidisciplinary approaches.
>
> The stated goal of ACOEM is restoration of functional capacity, and the evidence shows that the treatment requested and previously provided contributes to that goal in applicant's case. Moreover, the evidence shows that applicant diligently performs a home exercise program and that, when she seeks chiropractic care for flare–ups, which she does judiciously, the treatment is time limited and goal oriented. The requested treatment in this case is justified under the ACOEM Guidelines.
>
> Even if applicant's treatment could not be justified under ACOEM, Dr. Kinney's report and applicant's testimony would be sufficient to constitute a rebuttal. To rebut ACOEM requires only that the preponderance of the evidence establish that a variance from the guidelines is reasonably required to cure and/or relieve the employee from the effects of his or her injury. (Lab. Code § 4604.5, subd. (c); *Grom v. Shasta Wood Products, supra,* 69 Cal. Comp. Cases 1567, 1570–1571.) It does not require reference to any guidelines, as described in § 4604.5(e), for injuries not covered by ACOEM. Nor does it require that the presumption be controverted by "a preponderance of the scientific medical evidence," as provided in subdivision (a), with regard to the utilization schedule to be adopted pursuant to Labor Code section 5307.27. " 'Preponderance of the evidence' means that evidence that, when weighed with that opposed to it, has more convincing force and the greater probability of truth." (Lab. Code § 3202.5.) Section 4604.5(c) does not specify the type of evidence that may constitute a preponderance of the evidence.
>
> Despite believing the treatment to be reasonable and necessary, the WCJ said in his Report that he was "constrained to recommend that defendant's Petition for Reconsideration be granted," because the "presumption of correctness of ACOEM Guidelines has not been rebutted by evidence–based medicine." As we have explained herein, no such constraint exists. We find the treatment in question to be justified by Chapter 6 of ACOEM and, even if the evidence were to be weighed, for purposes of rebutting ACOEM, the preponderance of the evidence would establish that a variance is reasonably required to cure and relieve from the effects of applicant's injury… .**[Editor's Note: The statement in this case that in establishing a variance from ACOEM the presumption need not be controverted by "a preponderance of the scientific medical evidence" is questionable in light of subsection (e) of 4604.5, which states:**
>
> > **For all injuries not covered by the American College of Occupational and Environmental Medicine's Occupational Medicine Practice Guidelines or official utilization schedule after adoption pursuant to Section 5307.27, authorized treatment shall be in accordance with other evidence based medical treatment guidelines generally recognized by the national medical community and that are scientifically based.]**

See Appendix A for Reporting Duties of Primary Treating Physician Regulations.

Page 629, Column 1, third paragraph beginning 'If any of the above...' delete third and fourth line and insert the following:

The designation of the personal physician or medical facility in writing prior to the date of injury.

Page 629, Column 1, delete seventh paragraph beginning 'The Legislature...' and ending '...Provider Network.'

Page 629, Column 1, seventh paragraph, insert following '...4604.5(d)(1).'

In *Regents of the University of California v. WCAB (Macari)* (2005) 70 Cal. Comp. Cases 1733, the Board upheld a judge's finding that an applicant who injured his low back on July 1, 1997, was entitled to 30 chiropractic visits per year, contrary to Chapter 12 of the ACOEM Guidelines where the judge and Board found that other studies, including the Glenevin (Canadian) Guidelines rebutted Chapter 12 of ACOEM. **[Editor's Note:** The date of this injury was prior to the limitation to twenty four chiropractic visits effective April 19, 2004.**]**

In *Zenith National Insurance Co., et al. v. WCAB (Moveira)* (2006) 71 Cal. Comp. Cases 661, applicant's neurosurgeon issued a medical report in which he diagnosed applicant with degenerative disc disease and foraminal stenosis at L4–5 and L5–S1, retrolisthesis at L5–S1, lumbar spinal stenosis at L4–5, and chronic pain syndrome. He recommended that the applicant undergo surgery to treat his symptoms and requested authorization for a lumbar discogram, a myelogram, CT scan and a pre–operative psychiatric evaluation.

Defendant obtained a utilization review report in which the treatment request was denied. Defendant also obtained a QME report in which it was found that surgery was not indicated.

Following an expedited hearing, the judge issued an award in which he found the applicant required further treatment to cure or relieve the effects of the industrial injury, including a discogram, myelogram, CT scan and a pre–operative psychiatric evaluation.

In his report on defendant's Petition for Reconsideration, the judge stated that he rejected the opinion of the QME because he was not a specialist in orthopedic surgery or neurosurgery and provided no rational for his opinion that surgery was not indicated. The judge stated, in part:

> The report of Dr. Baes [sic] does not state whether he meets the requirement of Labor Code section 4610 that he " . . . is competent to evaluate the specific clinical issues involved in the medical treatment services, and [that] . . . these services are within the scope of [his] practice." The opinion of Dr. Baes [sic] is not persuasive because he has

both misapplied the ACOEM Guidelines and has drawn an internally inconsistent conclusion as to the need for psychological testing. Dr. Baes [sic] stated that the testing requested should be denied in part because of the lack of a psychological evaluation, but at the same time recommends denying the request for a psychological evaluation.

Dr. Baes [sic] also recommended against discography. The ACOEM Guidelines do not preclude discography, however, where, as here, the criteria listed on page 305 of the Guidelines are met. Dr. Baes [sic] also recommended against myelography and a CT scan, but the Guidelines do not rule out such testing, particularly where, as here, applicant's symptomology [sic] has become chronic. The ACOEM Guidelines provide at page 287 that the clinical practice guidelines for treating low back conditions are for symptoms of less than three months duration. The Guidelines also provide at page 288 that if symptoms persist, further evaluation may be indicated. According to Dr. Jones, applicant's symptoms have persisted, and indeed have worsened, in the many months since his August 3, 2004 injury.

Moreover, insofar as the ACOEM Guidelines can be construed to discourage the testing requested by Dr. Jones, I concluded that the opinion of Dr. Jones, a respected neurosurgeon in San Francisco, constitutes "a preponderance of the scientific medical evidence establishing that a variance from the guidelines is reasonably required to cure or relieve" from the effects of the injury within the meaning of subdivision (a) of Labor Code section 4604.5... .

Page 630, Column 2, delete first paragraph beginning 'The medical treatment...' and ending '...2004, provides:' and insert the following:

The Medical Treatment Guidelines adopted by the Administrative Director are rebuttably presumed correct on the issue of extent and scope of medical treatment.

Labor Code section 4604.5 amended effectively April 19, 2004, provides:

Page 631, Column 1, delete third paragraph beginning 'However, pursuant...' and ending '...of the employer' and insert the following:

However, pursuant to the amendment to , *effective April 19, 2004,* an employer MUST, within one working day after an employee files a Claim Form, authorize ALL treatment (consistent with Guidelines adopted by the Administrative Director), for the alleged injury (as alleged on the Claim Form) and MUST continue to provide that medical treatment until the date of the claim is ACCEPTED or REJECTED.

However, liability for the medical treatment SHALL be limited to $10,000.00.

Such treatment does not give rise to a presumption of liability on the part of the employer.

Page 631, Column 1, fourth paragraph, insert below heading 'Pre–Designation of a Physician' the following:

Labor Code section 4600(d)

Page 631, Column 1, fifth paragraph after d. delete the Editor's Note

Page 631, Column 2, first paragraph ending '...unless reenacted.]' insert the following:

Effective January 1, 2007, the above Section has been amended to eliminate the 7 percent language and to allow pre–designation to a medical group. The change, as set forth in 4600 (d), in italics, provides:

(1) If an employee has notified his or her employer in writing prior to the date of injury that he or she has a personal physician, the employee shall have the right to be treated by that physician from the date of injury if either of the following conditions exist:

(A) The employer provides nonoccupational group health coverage in a health care service plan, licensed pursuant to Chapter 2.2 (commencing with Section 1340) of Division 2 of the Health and Safety Code.

(B) The employer provides nonoccupational health coverage in a group health plan or a group health insurance policy as described in Section 4616.7.

(2) For purposes of paragraph (1), a personal physician shall meet all of the following conditions:

(A) The physician is the employee's regular physician and surgeon, licensed pursuant to Chapter 5 (commencing with Section 2000) of Division 2 of the Business and Professions Code.

(B) The physician is the employee's primary care physician and has previously directed the medical treatment of the employee, and who retains the employee's medical records, including his or her medical history. *"Personal physician" includes a medical group, if the medical group is a single corporation or partnership composed of licensed doctors of medicine or osteopathy, which operates an integrated multispecialty medical group providing comprehensive medical services predominantly for nonoccupational illnesses and injuries.*

(C) The physician agrees to be predesignated.

(1) If the employer provides nonoccupational health care pursuant to Chapter 2.2 (commencing with Section 1340) of Division 2 of the Health and Safety Code, and the employer is notified pursuant to paragraph (1), all medical treatment, utilization review of medical treatment, access to medical treatment, and other medical treatment issues shall be governed by Chapter 2.2 (commencing with Section 1340) of Division

2 of the Health and Safety Code. Disputes regarding the provision of medical treatment shall be resolved pursuant to Article 5.55 (commencing with Section 1374.30) of Chapter 2.2 of Division 2 of the Health and Safety Code.

(2) If the employer provides nonoccupational health care, as described in Section 4616.7, all medical treatment, utilization review of medical treatment, access to medical treatment, and other medical treatment issues shall be governed by the applicable provisions of the Insurance Code.

(3) The insurer may require prior authorization of any nonemergency treatment or diagnostic service and may conduct reasonably necessary utilization review pursuant to Section 4610.

(4) An employee shall be entitled to all medically appropriate referrals by the personal physician to other physicians or medical providers within the nonoccupational health care plan. An employee shall be entitled to treatment by physicians or other medical providers outside of the nonoccupational health care plan pursuant to standards established in Article 5 (commencing with Section 1367) of Chapter 2.2 of Division 2 of the Health and Safety Code.

(5) The division shall conduct an evaluation of this program and present its findings to the Governor and the Legislature on or before December 31, 2008.

(6) This subdivision shall remain in effect only until December 31, 2009, and as of that date is repealed, unless a later enacted statute that is enacted before December 31, 2009, deletes or extends that date.

See Appendix A for the Pre–Designation of Personal Physician Regulations

Page 631, Column 2, seventh paragraph insert below heading 'Medical Provider Network (MPN)' the following:

(See Appendix B of this book for the Administrative Director's Medical Provider Network (MPN) Regulations).

Page 634, Column 2, second paragraph ending '...MPN statute.]' insert the following:

Employees that are covered by an employer's MPN must be given written notification of the plan in English and Spanish that informs the employee of information such as:

a. How to contact the *person designated* by the employer who is to be the contact person;

b. A description of the MPN services;

c. How to receive, review, or access the MPN's medical provider's directory;

d. How to access initial and subsequent care;

e. How to access treatment if on trips for the employer;

f. How to choose a physician in the MPN;

g. How to change a physician within the MPN;

h. What to do if he or she has trouble with an MPN provider;

i. How to obtain a referral to a specialist within the MPN, or outside if necessary;

j. How to use the second and third opinion process;

k. How to request an Independent Medical Review;

l. A description of the transfer of ongoing care process into the MPN; and

m. A description of the continuity of care policy, etc.

Failure to provide an injured employee with required notices about an MPN may make the employer liable for medical treatment self–procured by an applicant because of the employer's neglect. See *Knight v. United Parcel Service, Liberty Mutual Insurance Company* (2006) 71 Cal. Comp. Cases 1423, (En Banc decision) discussed hereafter.

The Medical Provider Network law may be applied retroactively to provide medical treatment by transferring injured workers into an MPN in conformity with applicable statutes and regulations regardless of the date of injury. Commenting on this in *Babbitt v. OW Jing dba National Market, et. al.* (2007) 72 Cal. Comp. Cases 70, the Appeals Board in an En Banc decision stated, in part:

Applicant petitioned for reconsideration of the October 18, 2006 Finding and Order wherein the workers' compensation administrative law judge (WCJ) found that "Defendant may require Applicant to obtain medical treatment within its Medical Provider Network" and ordered "that Applicant obtain medical treatment from physicians within Defendant's Medical Provider Network." Earlier, on April 8, 2003, applicant had obtained a stipulated award of further medical treatment for her admitted July 1, 1999 industrial injury. Applicant contends that she cannot be transferred into a medical provider network (MPN) because her date of injury and award predate the January 1, 2005 effective date of the MPN statutes enacted by the Legislature as part of Senate Bill 899 (SB 899) in April 2004. (Stats. 2004, ch. 34; Lab. Code, §§ 4600(c) and 4616 through 4616.7.) We granted reconsideration to study the legal issue presented. Because of its importance, and in order to secure uniformity of decision in the future, the Chairman of the Appeals Board, upon a majority vote of its members, assigned this case to the Appeals Board as a whole for an en banc decision. (Lab. Code, § 115.) (Footnote 1)

We hold that a defendant may satisfy its obligation under Labor Code section 4600 to provide reasonable medical treatment by transferring an injured worker into an MPN in conformity with applicable statutes and regulations regardless of the date of injury or the date of an award of future medical treatment. (Footnote 2)...

Applicant urges that the application of the MPN statutes in her case would violate section 47 of SB 899, which provides:

"The amendment, addition, or repeal of, any provision of law made by this act shall apply prospectively from the date of enactment of this act, regardless of the date of injury, *unless otherwise specified*, but shall not constitute good cause to reopen or rescind, alter, or amend any existing order, decision or award of the Workers' Compensation Appeals Board." (Stats. 2004, ch. 34, § 27, emphasis added.)"

However, nothing in the statute "specifies" that the MPN process is limited to injuries occurring after January 1, 2005. To the contrary, our decision is consistent with SB 899 by applying the MPN provisions prospectively from the date of enactment "regardless of the date of injury." (Stats. 2004, ch. 34, § 47.)

We also find that the section 5804 five–year limit on the rescission, alteration or amendment of an existing award does not preclude defendant from using the MPN to provide medical treatment. (Footnote 6)

Transferring medical treatment to an MPN does not rescind, alter or amend an award. To the contrary, applicant's substantive right to reasonable medical treatment is unchanged. Defendant continues to be liable under section 4600 and under the award to provide medical treatment reasonably required to cure or relieve applicant from the effects of her industrial injury. (*Knight, supra.*) The MPN statutes simply allow another method for providing that medical treatment.

3. An Injured Worker May Be Transferred To An Authorized MPN For Medical Treatment In Conformity With Applicable Statutes And Regulations.

Because of the unique aspects of the MPN statutes, we do not find that an employer or insurer must demonstrate that there has been a change of condition or defective or incomplete medical treatment before transferring an injured worker into an MPN. Unlike the statutes considered by the Supreme Court in *Voss*, *Zeeb* and *McCoy*, the MPN statutes do not give the employer complete control over the identity of a treating physician. To the contrary, injured workers under the MPN statutes have the right to select an MPN physician with recognized expertise or specialty in treating the particular injury or condition in question. (Lab. Code, § 4616.3(b); see also Cal. Code Regs., tit. 8, § 9767.12(a)(6).) They also have the right to change treating MPN physicians if they desire. (Lab. Code, § 4616.3(b); see also Cal. Code Regs., tit. 8, § 9767.12(a)(8).) In addition, the MPN statutes, unlike the employer controlled process under the earlier statutes, allows injured workers to obtain second and third opinions from other MPN physicians regarding diagnoses or treatment plans. (Lab. Code, §§ 4616(c) and 4616.4(b); see also Cal. Code Regs., tit. 8, § 9767.12(a)(10).) These MPN provisions address the concern expressed by the Supreme Court in *Zeeb* that "the purpose of securing proper medical care and speedy recovery" might be adversely affected by a change in treating physicians. These MPN provisions assure that injured workers continue to receive appropriate medical treatment even if a pre–existing physician–patient relationship is disturbed.

Moreover, the MPN statutes and regulations identify four specific situations where continued treatment is allowed for a period of time with the physician selected by the employee. (Lab. Code, § 4616.2(d)(3); see also Cal. Code Regs., tit. 8, § 9767.9.) These exceptions would be rendered null and void by an additional requirement that the employers or insurers prove there has been defective or incomplete medical treatment, or a change in condition, before transferring employees into an authorized MPN. It would be contrary to the intent of the MPN statutes to render meaningless the four exceptions described in those statutes. It also is not within our purview to impose limitations on the transfer of medical treatment to an MPN beyond those specified by the Legislature.

For the foregoing reasons,

IT IS ORDERED as the Decision After Reconsideration of the Appeals Board (En Banc) that the October 18, 2006 Finding and Order is AFFIRMED.

Footnote 1. En banc decisions of the Appeals Board are binding precedent on all Appeals Board panels and WCJs. (Cal. Code Regs., tit. 8, § 10341; *City of Long Beach v. Workers' Comp. Appeals Bd. (Garcia)* (2005) 126 Cal. App. 4th 298, 313, fn. 5 [23 Cal. Rptr. 3d 782] [70 Cal. Comp. Cases 109]; *Gee v. Workers' Comp. Appeals Bd.* (2002) 96 Cal. App. 4th 1418, 1425, fn. 6 [118 Cal. Rptr. 2d 105] [67 Cal. Comp. Cases 236]; see also Govt. Code, § 11425.60(b).)

Footnote 2. All further statutory references are to the Labor Code.

Footnote 6. Section 5804 provides in full: "No award of compensation shall be rescinded, altered, or amended after five years from the date of the injury except upon a petition by a party in interest filed within such five years and any counterpetition seeking other relief filed by the adverse party within 30 days of the original petition raising issues in addition to those raised by such original petition. Provided, however, that after an award has been made finding that there was employment and the time to petition for a rehearing or reconsideration or review has expired or such petition if made has been determined, the appeals board upon a petition to reopen shall not have the power to find that there was no employment."

In a concurring and dissenting opinion, Commissioner Brass stated, in part:

There may be cases when it is appropriate to transfer an injured worker into an authorized MPN for medical treatment. However, in the instant case, the evidence demonstrates that there is a lawfully established pre–existing physician–patient relationship between Frank Fine, M.D. and Sharron [sic] Babbitt and that she is satisfied with the relationship. There is no evidence of a change in her condition or that the medical treatment she is receiving is defective or incomplete. Consequently, I have chosen to be guided by the common sense of the Supreme Court, which has repeatedly held that a lawfully established physician–

patient relationship should be preserved unless there is a change of condition or the treatment provided is defective or incomplete. (*Voss v. Workmen's Comp. Appeals Bd.* (1974) 10 Cal. 3d 583 [516 P.2d 1377, 111 Cal. Rptr. 241] [39 Cal. Comp. Cases 56] (*Voss*); *Zeeb v. Workmen's Comp. Appeals Bd.* (1967) 67 Cal. 2d 496 [432 P.2d 361, 62 Cal. Rptr. 753] [32 Cal. Comp. Cases 441] (*Zeeb*); *McCoy v. Industrial Acc. Com.* (1966) 64 Cal. 2d 82 [410 P.2d 362, 48 Cal. Rptr. 858] [31 Cal. Comp. Cases 93] (*McCoy*).)

In my view, it is irrelevant if the physician–patient relationship was lawfully established following an award of medical treatment, or because 30 days passed from the date of injury as provided under section 4600(c), or because the employer neglected or refused to provide reasonable medical treatment as in *Knight v. United Parcel Service* (2006) 71 Cal. Comp. Cases 1423 (Appeals Board en banc), or in some other way. Furthermore, I agree with the Supreme Court that an efficacious physician–patient relationship is an ingredient aiding in the success of medical treatment because it inspires confidence in the patient. Thus, a lawfully established physician–patient relationship should be preserved in the absence of a change of condition or defective or incomplete medical treatment.

In *McCoy*, the Supreme Court addressed "the extent of the employer's privilege to control the course of the injured employee's medical care" under section 4600, which at that time was not limited to the first 30 days. The Court held that by refusing to provide reasonable medical care, the employer "voluntarily terminated his right to control the course of medical treatment." (*Id*, 64 Cal. 2d at 89.) For that reason, the injured worker was not obligated to inform the employer of the treating physician's diagnosis before he or she obtained the right to receive reimbursement for the cost of reasonable self–procured medical treatment. As Justice Mosk noted, an injured worker's right to obtain reasonable medical treatment takes precedence over an employer's interest in trying to control costs by controlling treatment.

In *Zeeb*, the injured worker self–procured treatment after the employer's physician asserted that a flare–up of the employee's condition was not work related. Thereafter, the employer conceded that there was a need for continued treatment and directed the employee to return to the employer's physician. The Supreme Court affirmed its conclusion in *McCoy* that medical considerations take precedence over cost control interests and found that the employer's failure to provide reasonable medical treatment terminated its right to control treatment and rendered it liable for the cost of reasonable medical treatment self–procured by the injured worker. Justice Peters explained:

"[W]here there is a conflict between the two purposes, *the purpose of securing proper medical care and speedy recovery must take precedence over the goal of minimization of cost . . .*

In other words, considerations of expense must be either disregarded or, at most, given limited weight where there is a substantial danger that they will interfere with the employee's right to secure necessary medical treatment of injuries due to the industrial accident and to achieve speedy recovery." (67 Cal. 2d at 501–502, emphasis added.)"

The Court further addressed the importance of the physician–patient relationship in providing successful medical treatment and the limited circumstances that would allow the interruption of such a relationship:

"Where, as in the present case, the employer has refused treatment causing the employee to procure his own medical treatment, medical considerations and adherence to the purposes of section 4600 would dictate that *a doctor–patient relationship which will inspire confidence in the patient is an ingredient aiding in the success of the treatment, and that, once such a relationship has been established, treatment should continue with the same doctor in the absence of a change of condition or evidence that the treatment is defective or additional treatment is necessary.* So far as appears from the record before us, petitioner is being treated by his private doctor whom he consulted after the employer's refusal to provide further necessary care, and *there is no evidence that there has been a change of condition or that the treatment provided is defective or incomplete. Accordingly, there is no substantial showing which would warrant an interruption of the existing treatment or commencement of new treatment.*" (67 Cal. 2d at 502, emphasis added.)"

As found in *Zeeb*, the relevant medical consideration is the preservation of the lawfully established physician–patient relationship. Under *Zeeb*, that relationship may be disrupted *only* when there is evidence of "a change of condition or that the treatment provided is defective or incomplete." (*Id*, 67 Cal. 2d at 502.)

In *Voss*, the Supreme Court reiterated that an employer may resume control of medical treatment "without the employee's consent only in limited situations." (*Id*, 10 Cal. 3d at 589.) The Court affirmed the principle that medical considerations must predominate. In *Voss*, the referee found that the employee's "apparent propensity to demand excessive medical attention was a 'change of circumstances . . . and justifies the order which establishes control of medical treatment in the defendant.' " (*Id*, 10 Cal. 3d at 589.) However, the Court disagreed, and Justice Sullivan wrote:

"[I]t is clear that a change in the *circumstances concerning cost of treatment is not the kind of 'change of condition' which would justify restoring control* over medical treatment to the carrier. It would appear that *'change of condition' refers to a change in the physical condition of the employee.* In the typical case the carrier loses the right to control medical treatment by refusing further treatment because the carrier deems such treatment unnecessary, when in fact the employee's condition requires it. *Once the employee has satisfactorily obtained adequate treatment for this condition, he is entitled to have that treatment continued, subject to the limitation that only reasonable expenses will be reimbursed.*

"However, if the employee's physical condition changes so that the condition which prompted the carrier to deny further treatment is not the employee's existing condition, it would seem proper for the carrier to resume control of the treatment of the condition as changed." (*Id*, 10 Cal. 3d at 590, emphasis added.)"...

Page 634, Column 2, ninth paragraph ending '...condition in question.' erase the Editor's Note ending '...have to approve.]'

Page 638, Column 2, sixth paragraph, insert new topic following '...5403(c).'

If the Employer has Established a Medical Provider Network, an Employee is Not Entitled to Designate a Physician Under Labor Code section 4601.

In holding that an applicant did not have the right under Labor Code section 4601 to designate a treating physician outside of his employer's Medical Provider Network where his employer had provided the applicant with a list of MPN providers and had notified the applicant that his treatment was being transferred to a physician within the MPN, the judge in *Laier v. WCAB* (2006) 71 Cal. Comp. Cases 856, stated, in part:

The applicant argues that LC § 4601(a) authorizes him to choose a treating physician outside the MPN. He argues that the legislature's failure to change LC § 4601 is an indication that it intended that injured workers should be able to select treating physicians outside their employer's MPN.

Medical Provider Networks are not mandatory. In the event that an employer does not establish an MPN, LC § 4600(c) allows the applicant to select a physician within a reasonable geographical area. The parties have agreed that this employer does have an MPN, and that physicians are available within that MPN to treat the applicant. LC § 4601 is not applicable. Even if it was, it provides that the employer shall provide an alternative physician. It does not provide for free choice…

Employees covered by an MPN are required to choose an alternative physician from with the MPN if a change is desired. Laier v. WCAB (2006) 71 Cal. Comp. Cases 856.

Page 638, Column 2, seventh paragraph, insert new topic following '...5403(c).'

Consequences of Failing to Comply with Medical Provider Regulations as to Notices.

An employee may be entitled to self–procure his or her own medical treatment and bypass his or her employer's Medical Provider Network if the employee is not provided the proper notices, as required by the Administrative Director. In *Knight v. United Parcel Service, Liberty Mutual Insurance Company* (2006) 71 Cal. Comp. Cases 1423, an En Banc decision, the Workers' Compensation Appeals Board held that the failure to provide required Medical Provider Network notices to the applicant subjected the employer, or its insurer, to liability for reasonable self–procured medical treatment obtained by the applicant. The Board stated, in part:

In 1973, applicant was first employed as a delivery person/driver with United Parcel Service (UPS), insured by Liberty Mutual Insurance Company (Liberty). On February 22, 2005, he was delivering a parcel in inclement weather when he slipped on a wet driveway and fell on his right side, injuring his right wrist, arm and shoulder. Industrial injury was acknowledged and he was referred by UPS to a U.S. HealthWorks clinic for examination and treatment. X–rays were taken and medication was dispensed. He was released to light duty for two days and was then returned to full duty. However, his elbow and shoulder symptoms worsened and he returned to U.S. HealthWorks. U.S. HealthWorks referred him to Anthony Zoppi, M.D. for a consultation. (Footnote 3)

In his April 26, 2005 report to Liberty, Dr. Zoppi provided a summary of his "examination, findings, diagnosis and treatment recommendations" following his "initial orthopedic evaluation" conducted that date "at the request of the treating physician" as authorized by Liberty. During his examination, Dr. Zoppi noted tenderness and restricted range of motion in the wrist, tenderness in the right elbow, and tenderness and "pain with impingement maneuver both Neer and Hawkins" in the right shoulder. He provided a diagnosis of "Right shoulder pain/strain" and "Right wrist scaphoid nonunion, old nonindustrial injury" and described his "consultation with the patient in which the diagnosis was explained in laymen's terms." He noted a need to "see the patient back following the completion of x–rays" of the shoulder to evaluate the potential for "underlying acromioclavicular joint degenerative joint disease" but concluded that applicant "can continue with his usual and customary work activities without the need for work restrictions." He wrote that "Treatment recommendations were discussed and/or communicated with the patient's treating physician."

It appears that copies of Dr. Zoppi's report were sent to "Treating Physician" and "U.S.HealthWorks Medical Group." However, there is no evidence that the report was ever sent to applicant. Nor is there any evidence that either U.S. HealthWorks or Dr. Zoppi was part of an MPN, or that applicant was being provided medical treatment through an MPN. There is no evidence that applicant was notified that an MPN physician had been designated as his primary treating physician. There is no evidence applicant was notified of his right to choose his primary treating physician within the MPN after the first visit. Nor is there evidence of any notice to him of his right to obtain second and third opinions regarding any MPN diagnosis or treatment plan.

Prior to attending his appointment with Dr. Zoppi, applicant had contacted an attorney regarding his claim. In an April 22, 2005 letter, the attorney advised Liberty that applicant was designating the Intercommunity Medical Group (Robert Hunt, M.D.) as his primary treating physician. It appears that at some point Dr. Hunt contacted Liberty to confirm insurance coverage, but was told he would not be paid for any services he provided because he was not in Liberty's MPN. (Footnote 4)

On May 11, 2005, Dr. Hunt contacted applicant's attorney and advised that he would not treat applicant unless Liberty changed its position and authorized coverage. This is the first evidence of any indication to applicant or his attorney that there was an MPN. That same date, the attorney contacted Liberty by telephone and requested a list of MPN providers.

On May 13, 2005, Liberty telephoned the attorney's office and offered to "go over [the MPN list] on the phone" or to send it by e–mail because it was "about 1,980 pages."

On May 16, 2005, Liberty was informed that the attorney did not have an e–mail address and his staff again asked that the list be sent by regular mail. Liberty responded that the list of MPN providers needed to be requested from the "California Division of Compensation."

On May 19, 2005, the attorney's staff sent a written request for the MPN list to the address provided by Liberty. A woman named Kathy "from California Division of Compensation" telephoned the attorney's staff on May 24, 2005, and told them to contact Liberty for the list of MPN providers. She also provided a telephone number for Liberty.

On May 25, 2005, the attorney's staff left a telephone message requesting a list of MPN providers at the telephone number provided by Kathy. Another message requesting a list of the MPN providers was left by the attorney on May 31, 2005.

On June 1, 2005, the attorney received a return telephone message that Liberty's adjuster was out on medical leave. The attorney that same date sent another written request for the list of MPN providers and left a voice message with another person at Liberty requesting the list. On June 6, 2005, applicant's attorney's staff again directed verbal and written request by facsimile to Chuck Allen at Liberty as follows:

"Please be advised we have requested a copy of the Medical Provider Network List (MPN) from the following, claims adjuster Mr. Frank Quesada on 5/11/05, who advised us we needed to request list from California Division of Compensation. Request was made on 5/19/05, Kathy advised our office to request it from Ann Taintor. Request once again was made on 6/1/05, per Ms. Taintor we now have to obtain it from you. Due to this delay our client is without medical care.

"Request is hereby made we be provided with copy of Medical Provider Network List (MPN) as soon as possible." (Emphasis added.)"

Not having received a list of MPN providers, the attorney on June 9, 2005, faxed a letter to Mr. Quesada at Liberty advising that "Pursuant to Labor Code, sections 4600 and 4603.3 (sic) and Section 9783 Of the Rules and Regulations" applicant was selecting his treating physician to be Norwalk Orthopedic Surgery (Jacob Rabinovich, M.D.). (Footnote 5)

Enclosed with that letter was a copy of the attorney's letter to applicant confirming that an appointment was scheduled with Dr. Rabinovich for June 16, 2005...

On June 14, 2005 a senior claims case manager with Liberty, sent a letter to applicant as follows:

"Recent changes in California workers' compensation law, specifically SB 899, now allow insurers and self–insured employers to direct injured employees to a medical provider network (MPN) for medical treatment. In response to these changes, your employer has implemented the Liberty Mutual UPS Medical Provider Network (MPN) effective, January 1, 2005, for any workers' compensation claims.

"This letter is acknowledgement that you have a workers' compensation injury or illness claim at implementation time of the Liberty Mutual UPS MPN. Our records indicate that your current treating provider, Dr. Robert Hunt is not part of the MPN.

"In order to confirm you continue to receive appropriate medical care please take a few moments to verify the information that best applies to your current treating physician by checking the appropriate box below and returning you response within 10 days . . .

" [] My current physician is part of the Liberty Mutual UPS MPN. You may continue to treat with this provider. If you need further treatment from another specialist, you and your physician must select a specialist from within the MPN. Contact your employer or the Claims Case Manager if you need assistance in locating an MPN specialist.

" [] My current physician is not part of the Liberty Mutual UPS MPN. You may qualify to continue treatment with your current provider under the Liberty Mutual UPS MPN Transfer of Treatment (TOC) Plan if your condition is acute, serious or chronic, if treatment is for remission, is to prevent deterioration, is a terminal illness or for a scheduled surgery or procedure that will occur within 180 days.

" [] My current physician is not part of the Liberty Mutual UPS MPN network. I do not have any of the conditions above; therefore, I will secure services from another MPN physician. If I need assistance in locating another physician, I will call my employer or Claims Case Manager.

"You must receive confirmation from the MPN to continue using a non–MPN provider. The MPN will contact your non–MPN physician to confirm his/her willingness to continue providing you with treatment under the MPN and the MPN will notify you as to your physician's decision. In the event the physician is not able to continue providing you with medical treatment and services the MPN will advise you to seek treatment from an MPN physician immediately." (Emphasis in original.)"

The letter concluded with a request that any questions be directed to the employer or the Claims Case Manager. A copy of the letter was sent to applicant's attorney.

The June 14, 2005 letter from Dana Previty is the first evidence of any written notice from Liberty to applicant or his attorney that refers to the existence of an MPN. However, the letter did not explain where and how applicant was to obtain medical treatment. The letter does not state whether treatment was initiated in the MPN by the employer's referral of applicant to U.S. HealthWorks or by its referral of applicant to Dr. Zoppi. It does not identify any MPN physician that had been designated as the primary treating physician. It does not notify applicant of his right to change the primary treating physician and choose a new primary treating physician within the MPN. It does not notify him of his right to obtain second and third medical opinions within the MPN or of his right to obtain review by an independent evaluator. It does not transmit a list of MPN

physicians notwithstanding the numerous requests for the list by applicant's attorney.

On a July 7, 2005, applicant's attorney wrote Frank Quesada at Liberty:

"Please be advised that we are referring our client for medical treatment pursuant to Labor Code section 4600. Our client reported the injury but referral for medical treatment by the employer has been refused and/or neglected.

"Be advised we shall seek penalties for each instance of refusal to authorize or any unreasonable delay in authorizing all medical treatment as indicated by our doctors(s)." "

Applicant was seen again by Dr. Rabinovich on July 28, 2005. Following an MRI and EMG and nerve conduction studies, Dr. Rabinovich in his report of July 28, 2005 diagnosed, "1) Tendinitis/impingement syndrome, right shoulder per MRI scan. 2) Bilateral carpal tunnel syndrome, per neurodiagnostic tests. 3) Bilateral ulnar nerve entrapment at the cubital fossae, clinically on the left and per neurodiagnostic tests on the right." Surgery was recommended.

On August 31, 2005, Dana Previty on behalf of Liberty sent a letter to applicant, with a copy to his attorney, as follows:

"This letter concerns the Liberty Mutual UPS Medical Provider Network (MPN). It is our understanding that Robert W. Hunt, MD (Intercommunity Medical Group) and Jacob Rabinovich (Norwalk Orthopedic Surgery) are not participating in the Liberty Mutual MPN.

"As you were aware the MPN was in place and decided to change to a NON UPS MPN physician, we are considering any and all treatment with these doctors self–procured. Therefore, you will be responsible for all medical treatment and service charges.

"It is also important to note that if you elect to continue treating with either of these doctors, you will be responsible for all medical treatment and service charges.

"Please direct any questions regarding this letter to your attorney. Thank you." "

Also on August 31, 2005, Dana Previty on behalf of Liberty sent the following letter to both Dr. Hunt and Dr. Rabinovich:

"This letter concerns the Liberty Mutual UPS Medical Provider Network (MPN). It is our understanding that you are not participating in the Liberty Mutual UPS MPN.

"As Mr. Knight was aware the MPN was in place and elected to treat with you anyway, we are considering any and all treatment with you self–procured. Therefore, Mr. Knight will be responsible for all medical treatment and service charges.

"Also be advised that if Mr. Knight elects to continue treatment with you, he will be responsible for all medical treatment and service charges." "

The physicians were requested to contact Liberty with any questions.

Also on August 31, 2005, Liberty wrote applicant's attorney:

"This letter concerns the Liberty Mutual UPS Medical Provider Network (MPN).

"I received your letter requesting a copy of the UPS MPN list. The file is very large, therefore I would like to email it to you. I spoke with Irene in your office today and she advised you would be out of the office until September 14, 2005. She was unable to give me your email address. Therefore I have enclosed a copy of all UPS MPN ortho's (sic) as of July 11, 2005.

"Please contact me with you email address so that I may supply you with a copy of the UPS MPN list, should you desire a copy." "

Any list of providers enclosed with that letter or otherwise sent by Liberty to applicant or his attorney is not in evidence.

In none of the correspondence described above did Liberty explain where or how applicant was to obtain medical treatment. He was never notified that treatment had or had not been initiated in the MPN. He was never notified that an MPN physician had or had not been designated as primary treating physician. He was never notified of his right to change any designated primary treating physician and his right to select a new primary treating physician of his choice within the MPN. He was never notified of his right to obtain second and third medical opinions within the MPN or of his right to obtain review by an independent evaluator. Instead, Liberty wrote only that the medical treatment he sought was unauthorized, without tendering any information about how he was to obtain treatment for the admitted injury.

On October 7, 2005, applicant filed a Declaration of Readiness to Proceed to Expedited Hearing on the issues of his entitlement to reasonable medical treatment and temporary disability indemnity. Defendant admitted specific injury to applicant's right shoulder, right elbow, right wrist and right upper extremity, and admitted a need for medical treatment. However, defendant denied liability for all treatment self–procured by applicant outside the MPN.

At the hearing on November 29, 2005, the above described materials were received into evidence along with applicant's testimony that he never received "any notice of his requirement to belong to an M.P.N. prior to his injury or after his injury." (Footnote 6)

On December 9, 2005, the WCJ issued his decision, finding that defendant had waived its right to require medical treatment through the MPN, and that it was estopped to deny coverage of medical treatment self–procured by applicant. (Footnote 7)

Applicant was awarded "surgery as recommended by Dr. Rabinovich."

Defendant petitioned for reconsideration of the WCJ's findings and award, contending that "all appropriate notices were sent to the applicant with regard to the Medical Provider Network" and requested that he be directed "to obtain treatment with a doctor on the Medical Provider Network list."

We find on this record that defendant is liable for medical treatment self–procured by applicant because it neglected or refused to provide reasonable medical treatment by failing to provide required notice to applicant of his rights under the MPN.

DISCUSSION

I. An Authorized MPN May Be Used To Satisfy The Obligation Of An Employer Or Insurer To Provide Reasonable Medical Treatment.

An employer or its insurer is obligated to provide all medical treatment "that is reasonably required to cure or relieve the injured worker from the effects of his or her injury." (Lab. Code, § 4600(a).) "In the case of his or her neglect or refusal reasonably to do so, the employer is liable for the reasonable expense incurred by or on behalf of the employee in providing treatment." (Lab. Code, § 4600(a).) An employer will not be relieved of the duty to furnish medical care absent good cause, and section 4600 has been liberally interpreted in favor of the employee's right to obtain reimbursement. (California Union Ins. Co. v. Industrial Acc. Com. (Mitchell) (1960) 183 Cal. App. 2d 644 [7 Cal. Rptr. 67] [25 Cal. Comp. Cases 172]; Simien v. Industrial Acc. Com. (1956) 138 Cal. App. 2d 397 [291 P.2d 951] [21 Cal. Comp. Cases 10].)

Before January 1, 1976, an employee could not choose a physician to treat an industrial injury if the employer made an unequivocal tender of medical treatment reasonably calculated to cure or relieve from the effects of the injury. However, if the employer had notice of the injury, it was obligated under section 4600 to promptly notify the employee about how and where to obtain medical treatment. The employer could not be passive; instead it had an affirmative duty to be active in offering treatment to the injured worker and in instructing the employee as to which physician to see. (United States Casualty Co. v. Industrial Acc. Com. (Moynahan) (1954) 122 Cal. App. 2d 427 [265 P.2d 35] [19 Cal. Comp. Cases 8]; Draney v. Industrial Acc. Com. (1949) 95 Cal. App. 2d 64 [212 P.2d 49] [14 Cal. Comp. Cases 256] (Draney).) The failure to provide that required notice of information was recognized to be neglect or refusal to provide reasonable medical treatment even if the employee did not ask for medical attention before self–procuring care. (Leadbettor v. Industrial Acc. Com. (1918) 179 Cal. 468 [177 P. 449] [5 I.A.C. 233]; Bethlehem Steel Co. v. Industrial Acc. Com. (Seaquist) (1945) 70 Cal. App. 2d 382 [161 P.2d 59] [10 Cal. Comp. Cases 171].) If the employer made an equivocal and inadequate offer of medical treatment, the employee could select his or her own physician and obtain reimbursement for the reasonable cost of reasonable self–procured medical treatment pursuant to section 4600. (Voss v. Workers' Comp. Appeals Bd. (1974) 10 Cal. 3d 583, 588 [516 P.2d 1377, 111 Cal. Rptr. 241] [39 Cal. Comp. Cases 56] (Voss); Zeeb v. Workers' Comp. Appeals Bd. (1967) 67 Cal. 2d 496, 501–503 [432 P.2d 361, 62 Cal. Rptr. 753] [32 Cal. Comp. Cases 441] (Zeeb); McCoy v. Industrial Acc. Com. (1966) 64 Cal. 2d 82, 86 [410 P.2d 362, 48 Cal. Rptr. 858] [31 Cal. Comp. Cases 93] (McCoy).)

Effective January 1, 1976, section 4600 was amended to provide that "after 30 days from the date the injury is reported, the employee may be treated by a physician of his own choice or at a facility of his own choice within a reasonable geographic area." (Lab. Code, § 4600(c).) In addition, an employee was allowed under certain circumstances to select his or her personal physician to provide treatment during the 30 day period following injury. (Lab. Code, § 4600(d).) An employee also had an essentially unlimited ability to change treating physicians. (Ralphs Grocery Company v. Workers' Comp. Appeals Bd. (Lara) (1995) 38 Cal. App. 4th 820 [45 Cal. Rptr. 2d 197] [60 Cal. Comp. Cases 840] (Lara).) Thus, the employee had the choice to select any treating physician, limited only by the employer's right to show good cause in a petition to the Administrative Director (AD) of the Division of Workers' Compensation that an order should issue directing the employee to select a new treating physician from a list of five selected by the employer. (Lab. Code, § 4603; Cal. Code Regs., tit. 8, § 9786.)

With the enactment of Senate Bill 899, section 4600(c) was again amended. It now provides: "Unless the employer or the employer's insurer has established a medical provider network as provided for in Section 4616, after 30 days from the date the injury is reported, the employee may be treated by a physician of his or her own choice or at a facility of his or her own choice within a reasonable geographic area." This amendment added another method by which an employer or insurer could meet its obligation to provide reasonable medical treatment by referring the employee to an MPN. (Lab. Code, §§ 4600(c) and 4616–4616.7; see also Cal. Code Regs., tit. 8, §§ 9767.1–9767.15.).)

An MPN is established by an employer or insurer subject to the approval of the AD. (Lab. Code, § 4616; Cal. Code Regs., tit. 8, § 9767.3.) Among other things, the regulations require that the employer or insurer's application for approval of an MPN include a statement of how the MPN will comply with the "employee notification process" and the "second and third opinion process." (Cal. Code Regs., tit. 8, §§ 9762.1 through 9762.3.) The statute and regulations also impose several other obligations upon both the insurer/employer and the injured worker.

In this case, we specifically address the provisions of section 4616.3 and California Code of Regulations, title 8, section 9767.12(a). Section 4616.3 provides in full:

" (a) When the injured employee notifies the employer of the injury or files a claim for workers' compensation with the employer, the employer shall arrange an initial medical evaluation and begin treatment as required by Section 4600.

"(b) The employer shall notify the employee of his or her right to be treated by a physician of his or her choice after the first visit from the medical provider network established pursuant to this article, and the method by which the list of participating providers may be accessed by the employee.

"(c) If an injured employee disputes either the diagnosis or the treatment prescribed by the treating physician, the employee may seek the opinion of another physician in the medical provider network. If the injured employee disputes the diagnosis or treatment prescribed by the second physician, the employee may seek the opinion of a third physician in the medical provider network."

(Emphasis added.)"

California Code of Regulations, title 8, section 9767.12(a) provides in full:

An employer or insurer that offers a Medical Provider Network Plan under this article shall notify each covered employee in writing about the use of the Medical Provider Network 30 days prior to the implementation of an approved MPN, at the time of hire, or when an existing employee transfers into the MPN, whichever is appropriate to ensure that the employee has received the initial notification. The notification shall also be sent to a covered employee at the time of injury. The notification(s) shall be written in English and Spanish. The initial written notification shall include the following information:

(1) How to contact the person designated by the employer or insurer to be the MPN contact for covered employees. The employer or insurer shall provide a toll free telephone number of the MPN geographical service area includes more than one area code;

(2) A description of MPN services;

(3) How to review, receive or access the MPN provider directory. Nothing precludes an employer or insurer from initially providing covered employees with a regional area listing of MPN providers in addition to maintaining and making available its complete provider listing in writing. If the provider directory is also accessible on a website, the URL address shall be listed;

(4) How to access initial care and subsequent care, and what the access standards are under section 9767.5;

(5) How to access treatment if (A) the employee is authorized by the employer to temporarily work or travel for work outside the MPN's geographical service area; (B) a former employee whose employer has ongoing workers' compensation obligations permanently resides outside the MPN geographical service area; and (C) an injured employee decides to temporarily reside outside the MPN geographical service area during recovery;

(6) How to choose a physician within the MPN;

(7) What to do if a covered employee has trouble getting an appointment with a provider within the MPN;

(8) How to change a physician within the MPN;

(9) How to obtain a referral to a specialist within the MPN or outside the MPN, if needed;

(10) How to use the second and third opinion process;

(11) How to request and receive an independent medical review;

(12) A description of the standards for transfer of ongoing care into the MPN and a notification that a copy of the policy shall be provided to an employee upon request; and

(13) A description of the continuity of care policy and a notification that a copy of the policy shall be provided to an employee upon request."

(Emphasis added.)"

Therefore, as relevant here, the employer is required to give the injured employee notice of information about use of the MPN, notice of the right to be treated by an MPN physician of choice after the first visit, notice of the method of accessing the list of MPN providers, and notice of the employee's right to use the second and third opinion process if he or she disputes either the diagnosis or the treatment prescribed by the MPN treating physician. (Footnote 8)

II. Failure To Provide Required Notice To An Employee Of Rights Under The MPN That Results In A Neglect Or Refusal To Provide Reasonable Medical Treatment Renders The Employer Or Insurer Liable For Reasonable Medical Treatment Self–Procured By The Employee.

Employers have long been obligated to provide notice of workers' compensation information to their employees as part of the obligation to provide reasonable medical treatment under section 4600. The duty to provide notice of workers' compensation information begins before the report of an injury. An employer is required to provide new employees with written notice of information about the workers' compensation process and about where and how to obtain medical treatment at the time of hire or before the end of the first pay period. (Lab. Code, § 3551; Cal. Code Regs., tit. 8, § 9880.) The employer is also obligated to post conspicuous notice in the workplace of information about the workers' compensation process and where and how to obtain medical treatment. (Lab. Code, § 3550; Cal. Code Regs., tit. 8, §§ 9881 and 9881.1.) The failure to properly post such notice "shall automatically permit the employee to be treated by his or her personal physician with respect to an injury occurring during that failure." (Lab. Code, § 3550(e).)

Additional notice obligations are triggered at the time of an industrial injury. Within one working day of receiving notice of injury, the employer must provide the employee with a claim form, information about benefits available to the employee and the workers' compensation process. (Lab. Code, §§ 5401 through 5402; Cal. Code Regs., tit. 8, §§ 9810 through 9812; see also Lab. Code, §§ 138.3 and 138.4.) The failure to properly provide such notice may toll the statute of limitations. (Reynolds v. Workers' Comp. Appeals Bd. (1974) 12 Cal. 3d 726 [572 P.2d 631, 117 Cal. Rptr. 79] [39 Cal. Comp. Cases 768]; Buena Ventura Gardens v. Workers' Comp. Appeals Bd. (Novak) (1975) 49 Cal. App. 3d 410 [122 Cal. Rptr. 714] [40 Cal. Comp. Cases 434].)

In the context of the provision of medical treatment, failure to provide other required notices may be a neglect or refusal to provide medical treatment that renders the employer or insurer liable for self–procured medical treatment. For example, failure to provide an injured worker with adequate notice that a designated alternative physician is the primary treating physician pursuant to section 4601 has been held to be such a neglect or refusal because the employee is not properly informed of where and how to obtain medical treatment. (Pinkerton, Inc. v. Workers' Comp. Appeals Bd. (Samuel) (2001) 89 Cal. App. 4th 1019 [107 Cal. Rptr. 2d 787] [66 Cal. Comp. Cases 695]; U.S. Flowers v. Workers' Comp. Appeals Bd. (Carranza) (1997) 62 Cal. Comp. Cases 244 (writ denied).)

Neglect or refusal to provide medical treatment in other situations has been held to render the employer or insurer liable for the reasonable cost of reasonable medical treatment self–procured by the employee. (Voss, *supra*; Zeeb, *supra*; McCoy, *supra*; Draney, *supra*; County of L. A. v. Industrial Acc. Com. (Allen) (1936) 13 Cal. App. 2d 69 [56 P.2d 577] [1 Cal. Comp. Cases 127]; see also Braewood

Convalescent Hospital v. Workers' Comp. Appeals Bd. (Bolton) (1983) 34 Cal. 3d 159 [666 P.2d 14, 193 Cal. Rptr. 157] [48 Cal. Comp. Cases 566].)

We hold that an employer or insurer's failure to provide required notice to an employee of rights under the MPN that results in a neglect or refusal to provide reasonable medical treatment renders the employer or insurer liable for reasonable medical treatment self–procured by the employee.

III. Defendant's Failure To Provide Applicant With Notice Of His Rights Under The MPN In This Case Resulted In A Neglect Or Refusal To Provide Reasonable Medical Treatment.

Defendant contends in its petition that applicant was required to use the MPN because he was provided "appropriate notice" of information. However, as discussed above, a significant part of an employer's obligation to provide reasonable medical treatment includes the responsibility to notify the injured worker about where and how to obtain that medical treatment.

The employee's right to change physicians within an MPN, and the right to be notified how to change physicians, is analogous to the right of an employee who is not being treated within an MPN to change physicians. (Lab. Code, § 4601; Lara, *supra*.) Moreover, the right of an employee to change physicians within an MPN – perhaps to a physician the employee trusts, or relates better to, or has better communication with, or in whom he or she has more confidence – is a crucial element of an employee's treatment rights under an MPN. The Supreme Court has stated that under section 4600, "a doctor–patient relationship which will inspire confidence in the patient is an ingredient aiding in the success of the treatment . . . " (Zeeb, *supra*, 67 Cal. 2d 496, 502; Voss, *supra*, 10 Cal. 3d 589.)

In regard to notice, the burden of proof rests on the party holding the affirmative of the issue. (Lab. Code, § 5705.) In the event of a dispute about whether the injured worker was provided notice of rights under an MPN, the employer carries the burden of proof. In this case, defendant not only failed to carry its burden of proving that it provided notice to applicant of his rights under the MPN, the evidence established that its failure to provide such notice was a neglect or refusal to provide reasonable medical treatment rendering it liable for applicant's self–procured treatment.

Applicant testified that he never received written notice about the MPN from defendant and there is no such written notice in evidence. This is contrary to the requirement that an employee be notified "in writing about the use" of the MPN prior to its implementation and at the time of injury. (Cal. Code Regs., tit. 8, § 9767.12(a).) Moreover, applicant was never notified if treatment had or had not been initiated in the MPN. He was never notified that an MPN physician had or had not been designated as primary treating physician. He was never provided notice of his right to be treated by an MPN physician of his choice after the first visit as required by section 4616.3(b). He was never notified of his right under section 4613(c) to dispute an MPN diagnosis and to obtain second and third opinions. The only evidence of notice regarding the "method" for accessing the list of MPN physicians as required by section 4613(b) are the uncertain and confusing references in the June 14, 2005 letter. Despite the June 6, 2005 letter from applicant's attorney notifying Liberty that applicant was without medical care, Liberty provided no guidance on how he was supposed to obtain medical treatment.

Information about how to access medical treatment, how to choose and change physicians, how to obtain independent medical review, and, thus, how to generally and specifically "use" the MPN, are all crucial to the provision of reasonable medical treatment. In this case, defendant failed to tender reasonable medical care through the MPN and failed to provide required notice to applicant of his rights under the MPN. Instead, defendant informed applicant, Dr. Hunt and Dr. Rabinovich that any medical treatment provided by those physicians would be deemed self–procured and applicant would be financially responsible for their charges.

In sum, the record in this case compels the conclusion that defendant neglected and refused to provide reasonable medical treatment by failing to provide applicant with required notice of his rights under the MPN. Because reasonable medical treatment was neglected or refused, applicant is entitled to self–procure reasonable treatment and defendant is liable under section 4600(a) for that treatment... .

Footnote 3. This opinion does not address the reasonableness of medical treatment provided during the first 30 days after the date of injury.

Footnote 4. Portions of the chronology of contacts between applicant's attorney, the physicians and Liberty are taken from Applicant's Exhibit 7, which was received into evidence without objection. The exhibit purports to be the notes of applicant's attorney's staff regarding their effort to obtain a list of MPN physicians from defendant. Quotations are taken from that exhibit unless otherwise stated.

Footnote 5. There was no section 4603.3 at that time.

Footnote 6. Defendant offered no evidence of any notices to applicant other than as described above. Although Applicant testified that he did not receive the June 14, 2005 letter from defendant because of a change of address, it appears a copy was sent to applicant's attorney. In all events, the letter does not include information required by section 4613.3 and California Code of Regulations, title 8, section 9767.12(a).

Footnote 7. Although both the WCJ's December 9, 2005 decision and defendant's petition for reconsideration reference Case No. AHM 129147, that case involves a denied claim of cumulative trauma injury to various body parts. It was agreed at trial that the only issues before the court were those presented in this Case No. AHM 127807 regarding the claim of specific injury. The parties stipulated that Case No. AHM 129147 "has no impact upon the issues presented." Accordingly, Case No. AHM 129147 is not addressed as part of this decision. Because we find that defendant neglected or refused to provide reasonable medical treatment, we do not reach the questions of waiver or estoppel.

Footnote 8. Also see section 4616.4(b) regarding the second and third opinion process.

§ 9.0 TEMPORARY DISABILITY BENEFITS

Page 640, Column 1, third paragraph, insert following '...114.'

Receipt of outside income, for example from investments, gifts, or other wealth, has no effect on an injured employee's right to receive temporary disability indemnity. *Orrego v. City of Emeryville* (1995) 23 CWCR 232.

Page 640, Column 1, fifth paragraph, insert following '...61.'

Generally, the period of an injured employee's temporary disability indemnity will continue for as long as the injured employee is off of work because of his or her injury, is in need of continuing medical treatment, his or her condition has not reached maximum medical improvement (permanent and stationary) and his or her disability reimbursement period does not exceed that allowed by law. *County of Los Angeles v. WCAB (King)* (1980) 45 Cal. Comp. Cases 248; *Maples v. WCAB* (1980) 45 Cal. Comp. Cases 1106.

The term "permanent and stationary" is now defined as *"the point when the employee's condition has reached maximum medical improvement, meaning his or her condition is well stabilized and unlikely to change substantially in the next year with or without medical treatment."* Title 8, Cal Code Reg. 9785(a)(8).

If an injured employee is back to full duty or in modified duty, he or she is not entitled to Labor Code section 4850 pay to attend examinations for medical treatment. *California Department of Rehabilitation v. WCAB (Lauher)* (2003), 68 Cal. Comp. Cases 831.

An employer may remain liable for temporary disability indemnity after terminating an employee from his or her modified work if good cause for the termination is not established by the employer. In such cases the temporary partial disability indemnity rate is determined based on the employee's modified work earnings.

Manpower Temporary Services v. WCAB (Rodriquez) (2006) 71 Cal. Comp. Cases 1614.

Page 641, Column 1, fifth paragraph, insert following '...injury.'

The waiting period is primarily designed to motivate an injured employee to return to work when his or her injury is minor.

Page 641, Column 2, sixth paragraph, insert following '...4652.'

In other words, where an employee was paid less than full wages on the day of his or her injury, this is, in effect, only a two–day waiting period for liability to provide temporary disability indemnity to the injured employee.

Page 642, Column 1, seventh paragraph, insert following '...time.'

More recently it is referred to as the point when the employee has reached maximum medical improvement, meaning his or her condition is well stabilized and unlikely to change *substantially* in the next year with or without medical treatment. Title 8, Cal Code Reg. section 9785(a)(8)

Page 642, Column 1, eighth paragraph, insert following '...9785(a)(8).'

In cases involving insidious, progressive diseases, "permanent and stationary" also means the employee's medical condition is not reasonably anticipated to change in the following year under usual medical standards. *Sweeney v. IAC* (1951) 16 Cal. Comp. Cases 264; *CIGA v. WCAB* (2006) 71 Cal. Comp. Cases 139;

City of Calexico, et al. v. WCAB (Valdez) (2006) 71 Cal. Comp. Cases 817.

Page 642, Column 2, sixth paragraph, insert following '…567.'

In *Meyers, supra,* the Court of Appeal, First District, discussed the distinction between an employee's ability to do "*light work*" and an employee who can only do "*odd jobs*". The Court stated, in part:

"Award is hereby made in favor of James D. Titsworth against U. S. Fidelity & Guaranty Company of the sum of $15.44 a week beginning July 29, 1939, until the termination of disability or further order of this Commission less the sum of $26.46 heretofore paid on account of compensation, and less $35.00 payable to Cleary and Zeff, as attorneys' fees."

James D. Titsworth while employed as a laborer in doing some carpenter work was injured. The injury occurred when he and others employed at the work were attempting to put the side of a cabin in place. The structure slipped and injured his left foot and ankle. Both at the time of the accident and prior thereto he had been engaged as a laborer doing any kind of labor in which he could find employment. The injury was such as to cause him to remain off of the foot at times, at other times to walk with crutches, and at still other times to walk with difficulty. There was evidence introduced that the disability was fifty per cent. No evidence was introduced that it was possible for a person so crippled to obtain any kind of employment nor was there any evidence that after the injury Titsworth was employed in any capacity whatsoever.

The petitioners contend that as a matter of law temporary partial disability carries with it legal inference that the employee is able to compete in an open labor market. They further contend that the finding of the commission infers that said employee is physically able to work and there is no finding or inference that work is not available to him of the type he can perform because of his injury. Finally the petitioners contend that the compensation law insures only against incapacity for work and not against lack of opportunity to work. That final contention is the gravamen of this application.

The respondents reply by stating that with the final contention of the petitioners they fully agree. Continuing they assert that the findings and award are not subject to the other attacks made by the petitioners and when read as a whole are unobjectionable.

We think the foregoing reply is entirely sufficient. The foregoing record does not show on its face that the petitioners have been held as on a contract tantamount to a policy of unemployment insurance.

There is a direct finding that ". . . work of a type which the employee could perform has not been available to him . . ." Bearing in mind that he is a common laborer, that under the facts he is practically one legged, that there is no evidence regarding vacant jobs for such employees, it may not be said that said finding is not sustained by the evidence. It further follows that it may not properly be said that there ". . . is no finding or inference that work is not available to him of the type he can perform because of his injury."

As recited above the petitioners contend that as a matter of law temporary partial disability carries with it legal inference that the employee is able to compete in an open labor market. That contention is too broad. As presented there is no such inference. Each case must rest upon its own facts. He who would rely on the inference as claimed should present a record supporting the inference. The record in the present case does not do so. As to what inference will arise depends on many factors including the specific injury, the extent thereof, and the tendency to heal or otherwise. For instance one can readily state a supposititious case in which a person suffers temporary partial disability which would not prevent him from doing his ordinary work. Again in another case temporary partial disability may be of such a nature as to render one a nondescript. Such, as we read the findings, the respondent commission found in the instant case. *The general rule we believe was stated and followed in White v. Tennessee Consolidated Coal Co., 162 Tenn. 380 [36 S.W.2d 902]. Commencing on page 904, the Supreme Court of Tennessee stated and quoted as follows: "The authorities draw a distinction between cases in which it appears that the injured employee can do light work of a general nature and where he is only fitted to do 'odd' jobs, or special work, not generally available. In the former, the burden is on the petitioner; the presumption being that his inability to obtain employment is due to the fluctuations in the labor market and not to the consequences of the accident. In the latter, the burden is on the employer to show that such special work is available to the petitioner. The rule is admirably stated by Judge Moulton in Cardiff Corp. v. Hall, (1911) 1 K. B. 1009, as follows: 'But, on the other hand, I am also of the opinion that there are cases in which the onus of showing that suitable work can in fact be obtained does fall upon the employer who claims that the incapacity of the workman is only partial. If the accident has left the workman so injured that he is incapable of becoming an ordinary workman of average capacity in any well-known branch of the labor market – if, in other words, the capacities for work left to him fit him only for special uses, and do not, so to speak, make his powers of labor a merchantable article in some of the well-known lines of the labor market, – I think it is incumbent on the employer to show that such special employment can, in fact, be obtained by him. If I might be allowed to use such an undignified phrase, I should say that if the accident leaves the workman's labor in the position of an "odd lot" in the labor market, the employer must show that a customer can be found who will take it.'" So in the instant case. If there were any "odd lots" of employment available to Titsworth the employer should have shown the facts.*

In the briefs the petitioners cite and rely on sections 4654 and 4657 of the Labor Code. After having carefully read the record we find no place in which the defendant commission failed to carefully follow the procedure delineated in those sections... .

The California Supreme Court in *Pacific Employers Insurance Company v. IAC* (1959) 24 Cal. Comp. Cases 144, in commenting on an employee's duty in cases of temporary partial disability to be willing to earn such wages as he or she is able considering his or her injury, and that if some cause other than the injury substantially contributes to his or her inability to earn wages, such separate cause must be separately evaluated and only the portion chargeable to the industrial injury allowed as compensation, stated, in part:

By this proceeding petitioner insurance carrier seeks an annulment of an award of maximum temporary partial disability benefits to respondent Tom L. Stroer.

The facts are not substantially in dispute. On July 29, 1957, Stroer, employed as a carpenter, sustained an admitted industrial injury to his back. The employer's insurance carrier, the petitioner, voluntarily furnished medical care, and paid compensation, until February 17, 1958. No challenge is made as to such payments and cost of such care.

On February 17, 1958, the temporary disability payments were terminated on the recommendation of the insurance carrier's doctor that Stroer was no longer totally disabled and should return to work. Stroer was unable to find appropriate work until July 7, 1958. The commission awarded Stroer maximum temporary partial disability payments for the period February 17, 1958, through July 6, 1958. The insurance carrier challenges that award.

Stroer testified before the commission that during the period in question he was unable to do "rough" carpentering, his regular job, but could have worked as a "finish" carpenter, which was work of a lighter nature; that on February 18, 1958, he registered at his union hiring hall for work as a finish carpenter; that he reported to the hall almost daily; that he would have accepted finish carpenter work had it been available; that no such work was offered to him because none was available. Stroer also produced the report of a doctor who had examined him on April 7, 1958. That report pointed out that, because of the industrial injury which had necessitated an operation, Stroer's back was still weak; that he recommended that Stroer wear a back support and should refrain from lifting any weight over 25 pounds, and that he should also avoid any work that required the employee to change his position frequently, or to crouch or stoop. Walking, according to the report, should be avoided.

The commission found that the industrial injury "caused temporary partial disability beginning February 17, 1958, to and including July 6, 1958, during which time work of a type which the applicant could perform was not available to him, entitling him to $40.00 per week during said time, based on maximum earnings."

In denying a petition for reconsideration a commission panel stated in its report and order that there was substantial evidence that until July 7, 1958, it was inadvisable for Stroer to engage in any of the activities that his doctor had recommended that he avoid, and that, for that reason there was no point in granting reconsideration "to either find that applicant, as a temporarily partially disabled person, was an odd lot on the labor market or to find that for all practical purposes he was totally disabled during the period in

question. In our opinion, the applicant was substantially disabled during this period, . . . and that he was without any significant earning capacity because of his disability during said time."

The insurance carrier does not complain of the finding that during the period in question the employee was temporarily partially disabled. Its major contention is that the commission, under section 4657 of the Labor Code, was required to make specific findings as to the "probable earnings" of the employee or as to "the proportionate loss of physical ability or earning power caused by the injury." It is contended that such express findings were not made, and that, for this reason, the award must be annulled.

Section 4657 provides: "In case of temporary partial disability the weekly loss in wages shall consist of the difference between the average weekly earnings of the injured employee and the weekly amount which the injured employee will probably be able to earn during the disability, to be determined in view of the nature and extent of the injury. In computing such probable earnings, due regard shall be given to the ability of the injured employee to compete in an open labor market. If evidence of exact loss of earnings is lacking, such weekly loss in wages may be computed from the proportionate loss of physical ability or earning power caused by the injury."

It is clear that this section does not require specific findings in all cases involving temporary partial disability. The section simply contains general instructions to the commission as to how "wage loss" shall be computed. Where the evidence, as here, reasonably supports the conclusion that the partial temporary disability accounts for a total wage loss, the finding as to the wages lost is the only ultimate fact that needs to be found. Specific findings relating to each factor set forth in the code section are not then required.

There *can be no doubt that section 4657 makes it quite clear that in cases of temporary partial disability the employee is expected to be willing to earn such wages as he is able considering his injury, and that if some other ascertainable cause other than the injury substantially contributes to his inability to earn wages, such separate cause must be separately evaluated, and only the proportion chargeable to the industrial injury allowed as compensation. In such a case specific findings are required. But where, as here, it appears that no other separate cause contributed to the employee's inability to earn wages during the period he was temporarily partially disabled, the wage loss is obviously 100 per cent, and that is the only ultimate fact that need be found. There can be no question but that, in such a case, keeping in mind the fact that the employee is entitled, of course, to full compensation, the award must be the same as would have been payable for total temporary disability. This is so because, in such a case, the entire wage loss is caused by the industrial injury. This was the holding in Meyers v. Industrial Acc. Com., 39 Cal. App. 2d 665, 667 [103 P.2d 1025]. (See also Transport Indem. Co. v. Industrial Acc. Com., 157 Cal. App. 2d 542 [321 P.2d 21].)* The panel's report, in denying reconsideration, referred to this last cited case, and stated that "for all practical purposes he was totally disabled during the period

§ 9.0

in question . . . the applicant . . . was without any significant earning capacity because of his disability during said time."

The insurance carrier contends, however, that the case of *California Comp. Ins. Co.* v. *Industrial Acc. Com.*, 128 Cal. App. 2d 797 [276 P.2d 148, 277 P.2d 442], held that specific findings on the criteria mentioned in section 4657 are required in all cases of temporary partial disability awards. In that case the court was primarily concerned with the legal effect to be given to the fact that a partially disabled employee had received unemployment compensation disability benefits for the identical period of disability for which he had received compensation. (Footnote 1) The commission had allowed the employee full compensation for this period. The award was annulled. After disposing of the main point involved, the court went on to discuss the form and sufficiency of the findings required by the section. The court stated (p. 813) that the evidence "was not such as to necessarily require a finding that Moore's disability was of a type which rendered him unable to compete in the open market," and then held (p. 813) that the "commission should have made appropriate findings of fact as to whether Moore was an 'odd–lot,' and if not, as to what earnings were reasonably to be anticipated by Moore in his then state of disability, taking into consideration the factors enumerated in section 4657." Whatever factors the court had in mind in that case are not involved in the instant one. Here, as is indicated by the report on reconsideration, the evidence shows that although the disability was only partial, the wage loss was total. For all practical purposes the disability was a temporary total one so far as wage loss is concerned. There was no evidence by the employer that any "light" work was available to Stroer; in fact, the evidence is the contrary. How a finding that Stroer was or was not an "odd lot" would help to clarify the situation does not appear. *The crucial questions were whether Stroer was disabled in an industrial accident; was that disability still existent; and, if so, what was the "wage loss" caused thereby?* These elements were covered in the commission's finding. If there is any language in the Moore case (128 Cal. App. 2d 797 [276 P.2d 148, 277 P.2d 442]) holding that in a case like the instant one more detailed findings are required as a matter of law, such language is wrong, and is disapproved.

While certainty and completeness in the findings of the commission are to be encouraged, and while the findings in the instant case could well have been in more detail, we cannot hold, as a matter of law, that they are insufficient. In interpreting such findings the basic rule "is to interpret them liberally in favor of sustaining the award, and even if a finding, by itself, is inadequate for uncertainty it will still be upheld if it can be made certain by reference to the record." (*Mercer–Fraser Co.* v. *Industrial Acc. Com.*, 40 Cal. 2d 102, 123 [251 P.2d 955].)

The award is affirmed... .

Footnote 1. The insurance carrier contends that this same issue is involved in the instant case. It is urged that, although Stroer did not in fact seek unemployment benefits, he was entitled to the same, and thus might have received double compensation. We are not concerned with what

might have happened. We are concerned only with what did happen. What did happen, according to the supported findings of the commission, is that Stroer, because of an industrial injury and although only partially disabled, suffered a total wage loss. He is entitled to compensation for that wage loss.

In *Butterball Turkey Company v. WCAB* (1999) (Esquivel) 65 Cal. Comp. Cases 61, an applicant sustained an admitted industrial injury on September 19, 1997, to his right upper extremity, including his shoulder. Defendant paid temporary total disability benefits for a short period until applicant returned to work on October 8, 1997, performing modified duties.

On November 21, 1997, a dispute arose. Applicant took a half–hour break without clocking out on his time card. Applicant considered it to be a "break" for which he was not required to clock out. Defendant considered it to be a "lunch break" for which he was required to clock out. As a result of the incident, applicant was terminated on December 3, 1997 for falsification of his time card.

On January 28, 1999, applicant underwent surgery to his shoulder which was necessary due to the industrial injury. Defendant paid temporary total disability. On March 22, 1999, applicant's treating physician medically released him to go back to modified work. Defendant stopped temporary total disability after March 24, 1999.

The judge held an expedited hearing on the temporary total disability issue. Defendant claimed that but for applicant's termination, applicant could have continued to perform his modified duties. Applicant disputed his termination. The judge awarded temporary total disability. The defendant appealed. The Board upheld the judge's award of temporary total disability. The Board quoted the judge, as stating:

"The parties stipulated that, in the absence of modified duty available at Defendant herein, Applicant would fit under the 'odd lot' doctrine and be entitled to temporary total disability indemnity payments."

Based upon the stipulation of defendant that applicant would be entitled to TTD under the "odd lot" theory if he did not self–disqualify himself from employment at defendant, essentially, defendant is seeking to avoid liability for TTD payments that are medically indicated, and that are secondary to a recent surgery that was industrially–related. Defendant simply did not meet their burden of proof on the issue at hand, per Labor Code § 5705[Deering's]. ...

Petitioner herein makes the bald–faced statement that there is some sort of a "burden" on applicant in this case, on this issue. Such is clearly incorrect. It is the burden on defendant to show that they do not have liability for the medically–indicated TTD payments, due to defendant having terminated applicant for misconduct on the part of applicant...

The issue simply is whether the applicant's own misconduct created the lack of ability to return to this modified work at Butterball. On this record, the Court cannot so state. ... [T]he record does not permit a finding that applicant was terminated because of his own misconduct. Defendant simply has not offered substantial evidence supporting such... .

The judge concluded that defendant failed to prove that applicant had engaged in misconduct causing his discharge, and that such "alleged misconduct of applicant rose to a level by which termination would have been proper under the company policies..." In this case, the finding of the judge was compelled by the evidence and by the simple application of Labor Code section 5705. See also *Calmar, Inc. v. WCAB (1974) (Noguera)* 39 Cal. Comp. Cases 422 and *Yates v. WCAB* (1974) 39 Cal. Comp. Cases 653. In *Yates, supra,* the fact that the employee was not permanent and stationary did not entitle him to temporary disability where the evidence showed he was a full–time student with part–time work activities.

If an employee unreasonably refuses medical treatment, including diagnostic testing requested by the treating doctor, he or she is not entitled to temporary disability indemnity during the refusal time. *Sisco v. WCAB* (1977) 42 Cal. Comp. Cases 973. However, an employee is permitted a reasonable period of time to decide whether to accept the treatment or tests. *Ford Motor Co. v. WCAB (Taylor)* (1975) 40 Cal. Comp. Cases 105.

Page 649, Column 1, second paragraph, add after 'January 1, 2005 to January 1, 2006........$840'

January 1, 2007 to January 1, 2008..........$881.66.
Beginning January 1, 2007, and every year thereafter, both the *maximum* and *minimum* will be increased by an amount equal to the percentage increase in the state average weekly wage during the prior year. Labor Code section 4453(a).

The weekly temporary disability rate is *two–thirds* of an employee's average weekly earnings, subject to *maximum* and *minimum* amounts that are determined by law. The *maximum* and *minimum* amounts that are in effect depend upon the date of injury, as shown on the following table:

TD Rates	2002	2003	2004	2005	2006	2007	2008
Minimum	Actual Wages	$126	$126	$126	$126	$132.25	$137.45
Maximum	$490		$602	$728	$840	$840	$881.66	$916.33

Temporary total disability payments made two or more years after the injury must be recalculated to reflect the rates in effect at the time of payment. *Lab. Code Sec. 4661.5*

The Legislature, in its 2002 reform of workers' compensation (AB 749 and AB 486) required that beginning with 2006 year work injuries, such rates must be adjusted annually to the greater of $840 or the State Average Weekly Wage (SAWW), which is defined as the average weekly wage paid to employees covered by employment insurance as reported by the US Department of Labor of California for the 12 month ending March 31 in the year preceding the injury. Labor Code section 4453(a)(10).

The SAWW for the 12 months ending March 31, 2005 was $838.42, so the maximum temporary disability rate and the maximum permanent total disability rate for 2006 injuries remained at $840. This was the same for 2005 year work injuries. However, the 4.96 percent increase in the SAWW for the 12 months ending March 31, 2006 increased the rate to $881.66 for injuries sustained on or after January 1, 2007. The Department wage figures ending March 31, 2007 will have to be consulted to determine the maximum and minimum 2008 year rate.

The minimum temporary total disability rate is also subject to SAWW so it increased from $126.00 to $132.25 for injuries sustained on or after January 1, 2007. See Section 45.3 of the main book for full discussion of minimum rates.

Page 652, Column 1, seventh paragraph, insert following '...petition.'

The Board is authorized, under Labor Code section 4651.3, to award an attorney fee reasonably incurred by an applicant in successfully refuting *"wholly"* a petition by a defendant to decrease or terminate a temporary disability award. Labor Code section 4651.3 provides:

Where a petition is filed with the appeals board pursuant to the provisions of Section 4651.1, and is subsequently denied wholly by the appeals board, the board may determine the amount of attorney's fees reasonably incurred by the applicant in resisting the petition and may assess such reasonable attorney's fees as a cost upon the party filing the petition to decrease or terminate the award of the appeals board... .

Page 656, Column 1, third paragraph, insert new topic following '...932.'

Temporary Disability Not Payable if A Person is Entirely Retired from the Labor Market

An injured employee who voluntarily retires from the labor market does not suffer a wage loss and is therefore not eligible for temporary disability indemnity benefits if he or she, at the time of retirement, has no intention of finding other employment. *Gonzales v. WCAB* (1998) 68 Cal. App. 4th 843, 81 Cal. Rptr. 2d 54. See also *Hopson v. WCAB* (2000) 65 Cal. Comp. Cases 258 (unpublished) where the Court of Appeal, Third District, held that it was improper for the Board to award temporary disability indemnity benefits to an applicant when the date of injury occurred after the date he retired on a service pension indicating that he was no longer interested in employment.

However, if an employee retires from work for health reasons that are subsequently determined to be work related, he or she may be entitled to temporary disability indemnity benefits. *Continental Cas. Ins. Co. v. WCAB*

(Barron) (1982) 47 Cal. Comp. Cases 687.

Whether or not an employee has retired from the labor market is a question of fact for the Board. *Argonaut Insurance v. WCAB (Palmer)* (2002) 4 WCAB Rptr. 10,075.

A seasonal employee who has no record of off–season earnings is not entitled to temporary disability indemnity during his or her off–season period. *Signature Fruit Company v. WCAB (Ochoa)* (2006) 71 Cal. Comp. Cases 1044.

§ 9.3 If Temporary Total Disability indemnity is Paid for Disability Two or More Years After the Date of Injury, Payment Must be Based on Current Rates (Also Applies to Benefits Paid for Rehabilitation and Death Benefits)

Page 663, Column 2, second paragraph, insert following '…1006.'

Overpayments

Overpayments of temporary disability indemnity commonly occur without negligence on the part of the claims administrator. In its observance of estoppel, equity favors allowing credit for the overpayment as against an applicant's permanent disability, if a permanent disability award is made.

In *Maples v. WCAB* (1980) 45 Cal. Comp. Cases 1106, the insurer was held to be estopped to claim credit because it had not only failed for several months to file and serve medical reports, but also failed to file a Petition to Terminate its continuing liability for temporary disability indemnity. However, in *Rogelio V. Connecticut Indem. Co.* 8F477795, April 20, 2006 (34 CWCR 188) the Appeals Board upheld a judge's order allowing an employer credit against its liability for permanent disability for an overpayment of temporary disability indemnity because the employer, out of *an abundance of caution*, decided to pay additional temporary disability indemnity benefits because of conflict in medical reports, not wanting to risk a penalty for unreasonable delay.

In response to applicant's argument that allowing defendant credit against permanent disability meant that she would be undercompensated for permanent disability, the judge explained she was actually compensated for the permanent disability sooner than she would have been in the absence of the overpayment. See also, *Reyerson Concrete Co. v. WCAB (Pena)* (1973) 38 Cal. Comp. Cases 649 and *McCabe v. SCIF* (1989) 72 CWCR 225 and *Cordes v. General Dynamics Astronomics* (1966) 31 Cal. Comp. Cases 429.

§ 9.4 Notices and Advice to Injured Employees

Page 671, Column 1, sixth paragraph, ending '…Initiation Document' insert the following:

See Appendix J for Notices for Injuries Involving Loss of Time From Work or Denial of Claim Regulations.

§ 9.9(B) Maximum Period of Temporary Disability Indemnity On or After January 1, 1979

Page 671, Column 2, fifth paragraph, ending '…Cases 476.' delete last line and insert the following:

period. This is so even if an applicant has received an award of further medical treatment. Commenting on this in *Nickelsberg v. WCAB* (1991) 56 Cal. Comp. Cases 476, the California Supreme Court, in a split decision, stated, in part:

We granted review to determine whether a workers' compensation judge had jurisdiction to award petitioner Dieter Nickelsberg (Nickelsberg) temporary total disability indemnity more than five years after the date of his original injury. We conclude, as did the Workers' Compensation Appeals Board (WCAB) and the Court of Appeal, that the workers' compensation judge lacked jurisdiction to award temporary total disability indemnity to Nickelsberg.

FACTS

Nickelsberg, a truck driver for the Los Angeles Unified School District, suffered industrial injuries to his back and legs in 1976 and again in 1979. Nickelsberg stipulated with the school district and with the State Compensation Insurance Fund that his injuries had resulted in temporary disability from January 6, 1979, through June 8, 1981, and in permanent disability of 663/4 percent. The parties also stipulated that Nickelsberg might need further medical treatment to cure or to relieve the injuries' effects. Pursuant to the stipulation, a workers' compensation judge awarded Nickelsberg indemnity for temporary and permanent disability and further medical treatment on February 2, 1983.

Nickelsberg underwent back surgery in July 1987. Pursuant to the original award, the school district paid for Nickelsberg's medical treatment. He was again temporarily, totally disabled from March 7, 1987, to November 25, 1987.

On February 8, 1988, more than nine years from the date of his 1979 injury, Nickelsberg filed a petition to reopen his original award. He claimed that he had suffered a "new and further disability" as defined in section 5410. He also claimed that, because the new period of disability was caused by medical treatment provided pursuant to his existing award, he was entitled to recover further temporary total disability indemnity under Labor Code section 4656 [Deering's] (Footnote 1) as amended in 1978 (see § 4656, as amended by Stats. 1978, ch. 937, § 1, p. 2913). In opposition to Nickelsberg's claim, the school district contended that an additional award would be barred by the time and jurisdictional limitations of sections 5804 and 5410.

Accepting Nickelsberg's argument, the workers' compensation judge awarded further temporary total disability indemnity on November 10, 1988, and the school district sought reconsideration by the WCAB. The WCAB determined that the school district's petition was untimely. However, because the WCAB determined that the workers' compensation judge erred in granting Nickelsberg further temporary total disability, it decided to grant reconsideration on its own motion. (§ 5900, subd. (b).)

The WCAB rescinded the award. The WCAB determined that "an award of further medical treatment does not implicitly carry with it a commensurate award of temporary total disability." On that basis, the WCAB concluded that Nickelsberg's petition to reopen was barred by section 5804 and that the workers' compensation judge therefore lacked jurisdiction to award further temporary total disability indemnity. The Court of Appeal affirmed.

DISCUSSION

(Footnote 2)

Former section 4656 provided that "[a]ggregate disability payments for a single injury causing temporary disability shall not extend for more than 240 compensable weeks within a period of five years from the date of the injury."

Section 4656 was amended in 1978. (Sen. Bill No. 1851 (1977–1978 Reg. Sess.) Stats. 1978, ch. 937, § 1, p. 2913.) The 1978 amendment removed the 240–week limitation on aggregate temporary total disability within a five–year post–injury period for injuries occurring on or after January 1, 1979. The statute now provides that "[a]ggregate disability payments for a single injury occurring prior to January 1, 1979, causing temporary disability shall not extend for more than 240 compensable weeks within a period of five years from the date of injury. [] Aggregate disability payments for a single injury occurring on or after January 1, 1979, causing temporary partial disability shall not extend for more than 240 compensable weeks within a period of five years from the date of the injury." (§ 4656, italics added.)

Relying on the current version of section 4656, Nickelsberg argues that the workers' compensation judge had jurisdiction to award further temporary total disability indemnity more than five years after the original injury. Nickelsberg assumes that an initial award of "future medical treatment" must reasonably be interpreted to include, as a "secondary consequence," an award of future temporary total disability indemnity resulting from such treatment and that section 4656, as amended, removes all limits on awards for temporary total disability. Based on that assumption, Nickelsberg argues that the workers' compensation judge simply enforced his original award under section 5803. (Footnote 3)

Implicit in Nickelsberg's argument is the understanding that the provisions in section 5804 for the amendment of an award (Footnote 4) and in 5410 for an award of "new and further disability" (Footnote 5) are inapplicable.

A. The Workers' Compensation Judge Was Not Merely Enforcing

Nickelsberg's Original Award Pursuant to Section 5803

As indicated, Nickelsberg argues that an award of future medical treatment implicitly includes, as a secondary consequence, an award of future temporary total disability indemnity. We disagree. Medical treatment and temporary total disability are two different classes of benefits. (Burton v. Workers' Comp. Appeals Bd. (1980) 112 Cal. App. 3d 85, 89 [169 Cal. Rptr. 72, 45 Cal. Comp. Cases 1122].) No reported opinion supports the conclusion that temporary total disability is merely a secondary consequence or benefit of a medical award.

Indeed, "[m]edical treatment and disability indemnity are separate and distinct elements of compensation which fulfill different, though complementary, legislative goals. Employer liability for medical and surgical services is provided in major part in order to facilitate the worker's speedy recovery and to maximize his [or her] productive employment. [Citation.] Temporary disability indemnity is intended primarily to substitute for the worker's lost wages, in order to maintain a steady stream of income. [Citation.] Permanent disability indemnity has a dual function: to compensate both for actual incapacity to work and for physical impairment of the worker's body, which may or may not be incapacitating. [Citation.]" (J. T. Thorp, Inc. v. Workers' Comp. Appeals Bd. (1984) 153 Cal. App. 3d 327, 333 [200 Cal. Rptr. 219, 49 Cal. Comp. Cases 224].) As the WCAB noted in the present case, "an award of further medical treatment does not implicitly carry with it a commensurate award of temporary total disability indemnity." Temporary total disability, which is paid as a result of missing work because of an injury, is a benefit separate and distinct from medical treatment.

Hence, Nickelsberg errs in assuming that temporary total disability indemnity is merely a secondary consequence of an award of further medical treatment. Based on this mistaken assumption, Nickelsberg further argues that when future medical treatment is included in an original award, section 4656, as amended, allows an applicant to recover temporary total disability benefits whenever, and for as long as, they are required. He is entitled to these benefits, he contends, as a mere enforcement of his original award under section 5803. We disagree.

The plain language of section 4656 does not support Nickelsberg's interpretation. "The fundamental purpose of statutory construction is to ascertain the intent of the lawmakers so as to effectuate the purpose of the law. [Citation.] In order to determine this intent, we begin by examining the language of the statute. [Citation.]" (People v. Pieters (1991) 52 Cal. 3d 894, 898 [276 Cal. Rptr. 918, 802 P.2d 420].) The 1978 amendment of section 4656 removed the 240–week limitation on aggregate temporary total disability indemnity within a five–year post–injury period. The removal of this limitation, however, does not imply that temporary total disability can now be awarded at any time and for any period as a result of an original award of future medical treatment. Such a broad interpretation of the amendment would abrogate the time and jurisdictional limitations of sections 5410 and 5804. (See, post, pp. 482–484 [typed maj. opn. at pp. 13–17].)

Nickelsberg bases his interpretation of the amendment to section 4656 on the preenactment comments of various participants in the legislative process. For example, the Department of Industrial Relations in its enrolled bill report stated that "[p]resent law provides that payment of temporary disability indemnity shall not be paid for more than 240 weeks within a period of 5 years from the date of injury. In most instances, temporary disability is concluded long before this point is reached. There are however cases which create a hardship situation where an industrial injury results in the need for surgery more than 5 years after the date of injury. Due to the arbitrary time limit, the employee is then only entitled to receive medical benefits and is precluded from receiving temporary disability indemnity resulting from the hospitalization and surgery. Although occurring rarely, these situations create an obvious hardship that is difficult to defend." (Agr. & Services Agency, Sen. Industrial Relations Com. Enrolled Bill Rep. and Recommendations to Governor on Sen. Bill No. 1851 (1977–1978 Reg. Sess.) as amended Aug. 14, 1978, p. 1.)

Nickelsberg also highlights a somewhat different interpretation of the amendment of section 4656 contained in an Assembly Ways and Means Committee staff analysis of Senate Bill No. 1851. The analysis states that the intent of the bill was "to provide disability benefits for temporary totally disabled persons beyond the existing week limit. Proponents contend that often surgery or other treatment is required years after an injury to remove sergically [sic] implanted devices (plates, pins, etc.)." (Assem. Ways and Means Com., Staff Analysis of Sen. Bill No. 1851 (1977–1978 Reg. Sess.) as amended Aug. 14, 1978, p. 1.)

However, other portions of the legislative history contradict Nickelsberg's interpretation of Senate Bill No. 1851. For example, an Assembly Finance, Insurance, and Commerce Committee analysis of the bill states that the removal of the limitation on temporary total disability indemnity "would provide for the payment of the workers' compensation temporary total disability benefits for as long as the temporary total disability continues ." (Assem. Finance, Insurance & Commerce Com., Analysis of Sen. Bill No. 1851 (1977–1978 Reg. Sess.) as amended May 10, 1978.)

This analysis of the bill indicates that, in amending section 4656, the Legislature intended to remove the cap of 240 weeks in a 5–year period for the payment of temporary total disability and to allow an applicant who is continuously temporarily totally disabled to continue to receive benefits without an arbitrary cutoff date. Such an interpretation is also supported by a consultant's report to the Senate Industrial Relations Committee. The report states that the proposed amendment to section 4656 "would eliminate the 240–week limitation on the payment of temporary disability benefits for a single injury, and instead provide that such benefits shall continue as long as the temporary disability continues ." (Rep. of Consultant Casey L. Young to the Sen. Industrial Relations Com. (Apr. 27, 1978) p. 1, italics added.)

Furthermore, the mandated cost estimate of the bill prepared by the Department of Finance states: "Although data is not available to predict the number of cases affected [by the amendment] and the additional losses per case, we believe that such cases will be quite rare. In most cases, either the disability becomes permanent and stationary and thus no longer temporary, or the worker recovers long before 240 weeks of temporary disability benefits are paid." (Dept. of Finance Mandated Cost Estimate (May 10, 1978) p. 2, italics added.)

As indicated, these statements, consistent with the language of the statute, suggest that the amendment to section 4656 was intended to permit an applicant to receive temporary total disability for as long as he or she is continuously disabled without an arbitrary cutoff date. These statements, however, do not suggest the Legislature intended to permit an applicant, based on an award of future medical benefits, to be able to invoke the WCAB's jurisdiction to award temporary total disability benefits whenever he or she requires medical treatment for a previous injury.

Moreover, the Department of Finance, in estimating the financial impact of the amendments to section 4656, indicated that the amendments would affect "very few cases" and that the costs of the amendment would be quite small. "Losses will increase less than 0.1 percent and thus no premium increase will be necessary. Thus insured local governmental entities will incur no additional costs." (Dept. of Finance, Man dated Cost Estimate (May 10, 1978) p. 1.) The mandated cost estimate of the amendment prepared by the Department of Finance further states: "We do not anticipate significant increases in loss–experience to result from this bill." (Id. , at p. 2.) These conservative cost estimates are inconsistent with an interpretation of section 4656 that would allow unlimited awards of temporary total disability indemnity in every case in which future medical benefits have been awarded. The cost estimates are consistent, however, with an interpretation of the amendment as only affecting applicants who are continuously disabled.

Although Nickelsberg contends his interpretation of the bill would effect only a limited number of cases, the implications of his proposed interpretation are broad. Settlements of workers' compensation claims often include an award of future medical care. Under Nickelsberg's interpretation, each of these cases would implicitly also include an award of future temporary total disability. As a result, employers would be liable for this further temporary total disability indemnity, although it was not contemplated in the original award.

As shown, temporary total disability indemnity and future medical benefits serve distinct and different roles in the workers' compensation system. The different roles of the two classes of benefits negate Nickelsberg's conclusion that an award of future medical treatment implicitly includes an award of future temporary total disability. Furthermore, the legislative history of Senate Bill No. 1851 does not conclusively support an interpretation of section 4656 as allowing a workers' compensation judge to award unlimited further temporary total disability as a secondary consequence of an award of further medical benefits. Hence, it is incorrect to characterize the award of further temporary total disability indemnity to Nickelsberg as a mere enforcement of his original award under section 5804.

Moreover, Nickelsberg's interpretation of Senate Bill No. 1851 would require us to conclude that the bill somehow amended or altered the time and jurisdictional limits of sections 5410 or 5804 to allow resumption of temporary total disability indemnity whenever an award of future medical benefits results in a period of further temporary total disability. We do not believe that the Legislature intended such a broad result. Nickelsberg's argument is contrary to both clear statutory construction and well–established judicial interpretation of sections 5410 and 5804. Moreover, it controverts the entire statutory scheme of workers' compensation judicial administration, which provides for time and jurisdictional limitations upon the commencement of proceedings and modifications of prior determinations.

The WCAB is vested with the authority and jurisdiction to conduct proceedings for the recovery of compensation. (§ 5300 et seq.) Concomitantly, it is empowered with continuing jurisdictional authority over all of its orders, decisions and awards. (§ 5803.) However, this power is not unlimited. The WCAB's authority under section 5803 to enforce its awards, including ancillary proceedings involving commutation, penalty assessment and the like, is not to be confused with its limited jurisdiction to IT+alter prior awards by benefit augmentation at a later date. The latter action is subject to the provisions of sections 5410 and 5804. (General Foundry Service v. Workers' Comp. Appeals Bd. (1986) 42 Cal. 3d 331 [228 Cal. Rptr. 243, 721 P.2d 124, 51 Cal. Comp. Cases 375] Broadway–Locust Co., Inc. v. Ind. Acc. Com. & Smith (1949) 92 Cal. App. 2d 287, 290–294 [206 P.2d 856, 14 Cal. Comp. Cases 111] Ruffin v. Olson Co. (1987) 52 Cal. Comp. Cases 335.)

It may not be inferred, as Nickelsberg suggests, that the 1979 amendment, removing the 240–week limitation on aggregate temporary total disability payments within a 5–year post–injury period, in any manner modified the time or jurisdictional limitations of either section 5410 or section 5804. Nickelsberg supports his conclusion, relying on the liberal construction mandate of section 3202. (Footnote 6)

However, the rule of liberal construction stated in section 3202 should not be used to defeat the overall statutory framework and fundamental rules of statutory construction. Furthermore, statutes should be interpreted in such a way as to make them consistent with each other, rather than obviate one another. (People v. Pieters (1991) 52 Cal. 3d 894, 899.) It is logical to presume that the Legislature was aware of the existence of all relevant statutes, including sections 5410 and 5804, when it considered the change in section 4656. Significantly, as observed by the Court of Appeal, the Legislature did not specifically amend sections 5410 and 5804 to accomplish the broad purpose Nickelsberg suggests motivated the change in section 4656.

Since the Legislature did not explicitly change the jurisdictional limitations of the WCAB or the time limitations of section 5410 (see Singh v. Workers' Comp. Appeals Bd. (1987) 52 Cal. Comp. Cases 15[writ denied]),

accepting Nickelsberg's contention would require us to conclude that the Legislature implicitly repealed sections 5804 and 5410. Repeals by implication are disfavored and are recognized only when potentially conflicting statutes cannot be harmonized. (Dew v. Appleberry (1979) 23 Cal. 3d 630, 636 [153 Cal. Rptr. 219, 591 P.2d 509].) Disharmony, however, between the provisions of section 4656 and those of sections 5410 and 5804 exists only if one takes – as does Nickelsberg – an overly broad view of when temporary total disability indemnity may be awarded. Such a view ignores both the statutory classification of these sections (Footnote 7) and the Legislature's presumed awareness, when it amended section 4656, of the long history of judicial interpretation of sections 5410 and 5804. (People v. Hallner , supra , 43 Cal. 2d at p. 719).

Furthermore, sound public policy supports the conclusion that the amendment to section 4656 does not serve to abrogate the time and jurisdictional limits of sections 5410 and 5804. Those sections do not express a mere concern for barring stale claims. The statutes express legislative concern for certainty and finality in the determination of compensation benefit obligations. The WCAB's own interpretation of its limited power to award temporary total disability more than five years after an original injury recognizes this need for certainty and finality. As was stated in Broadway Locust Co. v. Ind. Acc. Comm. & Smith , supra , 92 Cal. App. 2d at page 293: "This long continued interpretation by the commission of its own powers has necessarily led industry to recognize and adjust itself to liabilities and responsibilities consistent with well understood limitations as to time. ... It is important ... that the overall cost of workmen's [sic] compensation insurance should be ascertainable with reasonable certainty in order that business operations may be adjusted accordingly and state agencies ... may be enabled to operate with the greatest measure of efficiency and competency. Contingent liability unlimited as to time for which the commission now argues would result in great confusion. No employer or his insurance carrier would know what claims might emerge from cases long since settled and written off." (Footnote 8)

Finally, the WCAB's own determination that the workers' compensation judge lacked jurisdiction under section 4656, as amended, to award further temporary total disability is entitled to significant respect on judicial review. In the instant case, following the workers' compensation judge's award of further temporary total disability indemnity, the WCAB granted reconsideration on its own motion. (§ 5900, subd. (b).) The WCAB found that the original "award of further medical treatment does not implicitly carry with it a commensurate award of temporary total disability," and concluded that Nickelsberg's petition was time barred. The Court of Appeal agreed with the WCAB that "the workers' compensation judge lacked jurisdiction to award further temporary total disability indemnity." The WCAB's interpretation of its jurisdictional authority to grant new and further temporary disability, as expressed in its decision on reconsideration, is not only persuasive on this issue, its interpretation and application of these three statutes is entitled to significant respect upon judicial review. (Footnote 9)

Nipper v. California Auto. Assigned Risk Plan (1977) 19 Cal. 3d 35, 45 Cal. Rptr. 854, 560 P.2d 743]["We have generally accorded respect to administrative interpretations of a law and, unless clearly erroneous, have deemed them significant factors in ascertaining statutory meaning and purpose. [Citations.]"] Mudd v. McColgan (1947) 30 Cal. 2d 463, 470 [183 P.2d 10].) We conclude that the WCAB's interpretation and application of the relevant statutes was correct and adds further support to the conclusion that Nickelsberg's petition to recover temporary total disability is barred.

B. Nickelsberg Is Not Entitled to Receive Further

Temporary Total Disability Indemnity

Having rejected Nickelsberg's interpretation of the amendment of section 4656, we still must determine if the workers' compensation judge had jurisdiction under another section of the workers' compensation laws to award Nickelsberg further temporary total disability. Given our interpretation of section 4656, which precludes considering Nickelsberg's petition as merely an enforcement action under section 5803, Nickelsberg can only recover for temporary total disability at this point in time if: (1) the WCAB had authority to amend its original award under section 5804 or (2) he had suffered a "new and further disability" under section 5410 and had filed a timely claim for recovery. As will become evident, we conclude that Nickelsberg cannot bring his petition within either of these two avenues of possible recovery.

1. The WCAB Correctly Determined That the Workers' Compensation

Judge Lacked Jurisdiction Under Section 5804

The first theory under which Nickelsberg might be able to recover on his claim for temporary total disability is if the WCAB had jurisdiction to amend his original award. Section 5804 allows a party, in certain circumstances, to file a petition to rescind, alter, or amend an original award. However, such a petition must be filed within five years of the original injury. (§ 5804 see, ante , p. 479, fn. 4 [typed maj. opn., p. 5, fn. 4].) Nickelsberg's suffered his original injury on January 5, 1979, and filed his petition for further temporary total disability on February 8, 1988. Because Nickelsberg's petition to reopen his award was filed more than five years from the date of his original injury, the WCAB correctly determined that the workers' compensation judge lacked jurisdiction to alter or amend the original award under section 5804 to provide for further temporary total disability.

2. "New and Further Disability"

The second possible avenue of recovery is a petition for "new and further disability" under section 5410. An employee may institute proceedings, within five years from the date of the original injury, for the collection of compensation upon the ground that the original injury has caused new and further disability. (§ 5410 see, ante , p. 479, fn. 5 [typed maj. opn., pp. 5–6, fn. 5].) In the present case, Nickelsberg initially filed his petition to reopen his award claiming that he had suffered a new and further disability pursuant to section 5410. In his trial memorandum filed the

same day as the petition, however, Nickelsberg argued that he was seeking enforcement of his original award pursuant to section 4656.

The term "new and further disability" is not defined by statute and its meaning is not entirely clear. (Pizza Hut of San Diego, Inc. v. Workers' Comp. Appeals Bd . (1978) 76 Cal. App. 3d 818, 825 [143 Cal. Rptr. 131, 43 Cal. Comp. Cases 70].) However, one Court of Appeal has described a "new and further disability" as "a disability in addition to that for which the employer previously provided benefits as required by the statute." (Id. at p. 822.) "The phrase "further disability' presupposes that such disability is in addition to that disability for which proceedings were timely commenced or for which compensation already was paid (Kauffman v. Industrial Accident Com. (1918) 37 Cal. App. 500, 502–503 [174 P. 690, 5 I.A.C. 132]). It has also been recognized "[s]ome significance must be given to the word "new." (See Westvaco Chlorine Products Corp. v. Ind. Acc. Com. (1955) 136 Cal. App. 2d 60, 64–68 [228 P.2d 300, 20 Cal. Comp. Cases 248].)" (Id . at p. 825.)

The Court of Appeal in Pizza Hut further noted: "New and further disability can develop only after a cessation of temporary disability or an interruption of temporary disability by a period of nondisablement. A new period of temporary disability ... is a new and further disability. ... [] Historically, a change in physical condition necessitating further medical treatment had been considered new and further disability whether or not accompanied by time lost from work. [Citation.]' (Cal. Workmen's Compensation Practice (Cont.Ed.Bar 1973) § 4.21, pp. 108–109 see also 1 Hanna, Cal. LAW OF EMPLOYEE INJURIES AND WORKMEN'S COMPENSATION (2d ed.) § 9.03[2].) Thus, "[c]ommonly, new and further disability refers to a recurrence of temporary disability, a new need for medical treatment, or the change of a temporary disability into a permanent disability.' (Cal. Workmen's Compensation Practice (Cont.Ed.Bar 1973) § 12.12, p. 410.)" (Pizza Hut of San Diego, Inc. v. Workers' Comp. Appeals Bd. „supra , 76 Cal. App. 3d at p. 825.)

Nickelsberg's disability may indeed be a "new and further disability." After Nickelsberg's 1979 industrial injury, he received temporary total disability indemnity from January 6, 1979, through June 8, 1981. He received a permanent disability rating of 663/4 percent. After a period of nondisablement, Nickelsberg had back surgery in July 1987. As a result, he now seeks temporary total disability indemnity for the period of March 7, 1987, through November 25, 1987.

In the final analysis, however, we need not decide if Nickelsberg's disability qualifies as a new and further disability. If it does, his petition would be untimely under section 5410. If it does not, his action could only be brought as a petition to amend his award. However, as previously noted, such an action under section 5804 would also be untimely.

CONCLUSION

Nickelsberg seeks from this court an interpretation of section 4656 that would provide unlimited temporary total disability when an award of further medical treatment is made. Such an interpretation is not justified by either clear legislative intent or sound statutory construction. Hence, the workers' compensation judge lacked jurisdiction to award temporary total disability to Nickelsberg. The judgment of the Court of Appeal is affirmed. We concur... .

Footnote 1. All further statutory references are to the Labor Code unless otherwise indicated.

Footnote 2. The legislative history in support of Nickelsberg's position also expressly noted that the additional cost to the state, if Senate Bill No. 1851 were passed, would be negligible. This material refutes the majority's speculation that the cost of Senate Bill No. 1851, 1977–1978 Regular Session, if implemented as discussed in the legislative history, necessarily would be significant. (See maj. opn., ante, at pp. 481–482 [typed maj. opn. at pp. 11–12].)

Footnote 3. It is important to note that the majority never affirmatively reject the interpretation of the amendment to section 4656 proffered by Nickelsberg, but merely assert that "the legislative history of Senate Bill No. 1851 does not conclusively support [Nickelsberg's interpretation]" (maj. opn., ante , at p. 482 [typed maj. opn. at p. 12], italics added) in light of the "contradictory" history discussed in the majority opinion. Accordingly, a court interpreting section 4656 in the future (e.g. , to determine whether a workers' compensation judge may reserve jurisdiction to award temporary total disability) must consider how the legislative history presented by Nickelsberg, as well as that presented by the majority, affects the question presented to that court.

Footnote 4. The majority, in making a policy argument in favor of its position, grossly misstates the position that Nickelsberg advocates: "the implications of [Nickelsberg's] proposed interpretation are broad. Settlements of workers' compensation claims often include an award of future medical care. Under Nickelsberg's interpretation, each of these cases would implicitly also include an award of future temporary total disability. As a result, employers would be liable for this further temporary total disability indemnity, although it was not contemplated in the original award." (Maj. opn., ante , at p. 482 [typed maj. opn. at p. 12].)

Footnote 5. The majority opinion does not rule out the possibility that a worker's disability arising from medical treatment may in itself constitute a new, compensable injury for the purposes of the workers' compensation laws. (Cf. Rodgers v. Workers' Comp. Appeals Bd. (1985) 168 Cal. App. 3d 567, 571–574 [214 Cal. Rptr. 303, 50 Cal. Comp. Cases 299][injury incurred in the course of employer–provided rehabilitation constitutes a new, compensable injury].)

Footnote 6. There are, of course, circumstances in which a court is not justified in construing a statute in favor of the injured worker. A limiting construction may be required by the "unmistakable language of a statute" (Earl Ranch, Ltd. v. Industrial Acc. Com. (1935) 4 Cal. 2d 767, 769 [53 P.2d 154, 20 I.A.C. 399]), and the "Legislature's intent as expressed in the statute" cannot be ignored (Ruiz v. Industrial Acc. Com. (1955) 45 Cal. 2d 409, 413 [289 P.2d 229, 20 Cal. Comp. Cases 265] see Fuentes v. Workers' Comp. Appeals Bd. (1976) 16 Cal. 3d 1, 8 [128 Cal. Rptr. 673, 547 P.2d 449, 41 Cal. Comp. Cases 42]). Yet this is not such a case. There is no unmistakable language and no statutory expression of legislative intent to justify denying an injured employee in Nickelsberg's position temporary total disability indemnity. At best, the most the majority's argument does is put forward an alternative construction of section 4656, and, given two reasonable constructions of that statute, this court is required by law to adopt the construction which will permit recovery of benefits by the injured worker.

Footnote 7. The conclusion that the amendment of section 4656 does not alter other jurisdictional or time limitations is supported by analysis of the legislative placement and classification given sections 4656, 5410, 5803 and 5804. Section 4656 is found in chapter 2[Deering's], division 4, part 2 of the Labor Code. Part 2 is entitled "Computation of Compensation," and chapter 2 is designated "Compensation Schedules." Sections 5410, 5803 and 5804, in contrast, are placed in part 4, "Compensation Proceedings." Section 5410 is part of chapter 2, entitled "Limitations of Proceedings," and sections 5803 and 5804 are in chapter 6, entitled "Findings and Awards."

Footnote 8. Based on section 4656, as amended, and our decision in General Foundry Service v. Workers' Comp. Appeals Bd. (1986) 42 Cal. 3d 331, the Court of Appeal in this case indicated that it might be proper for the WCAB to reserve jurisdiction to award temporary total disability indemnity related to hospitalization or surgery occurring more than five years after the date of injury.

Footnote 9. See also, Ruffin v. Olson Glass Co. (1987) 52 Cal. Comp. Cases 335, 343[Appeals Board en banc decision] where the WCAB rejected the argument that the amendment to section 4656 permits an award of temporary total disability indemnity "upon the happening of some contingency, such as surgery." According to the WCAB in Ruffin , "[s]uch an award ... would be nothing more than a subterfuge to avoid the limitation of jurisdiction contained in Labor Code Sections 5410[Deering's] and 5804[Deering's]." (Ibid.)

Page 672, Column 2, after second paragraph, insert before word 'However...'

In *Sarabi v. WCAB* (2007) 72 Cal. Comp. Cases 778, the Court of Appeal, First District, annulled a Board decision that denied temporary total disability indemnity benefits to an applicant where a Petition to Reopen was filed within five years of the date of injury and the trial judge had awarded additional temporary total disability benefits because the new and *further disability had arisen* within the five–year period. The Court stated, in part:

Petitioner Mike Sarabi challenges an order of the Workers' Compensation Appeals Board (Board) holding it had no jurisdiction to award him additional temporary total disability (TTD) benefits for a period commencing more than five years after the date of his injury. The Board's holding was in error, and we therefore annul its order and remand the case for a new order consistent with this opinion.

I. FACTUAL AND PROCEDURAL BACKGROUND

Sarabi, a night manager at Narsi's Hofbrau, sustained an industrial injury to his right shoulder on *August 28, 1999*. In a findings and award dated December 15, 2000, the workers' compensation judge (WCJ) awarded Sarabi TTD benefits from August 29, 1999 through December 2, 1999, and found further medical treatment was necessary.

Sarabi underwent right shoulder surgery on *January 18, 2002, and filed a petition to reopen* on November 15, 2002, alleging that "a change in [his] condition [had] result[ed] in further periods of temporary disability." On May 26, 2004, orthopedic surgeon Dr. Gary P. McCarthy stated Sarabi was temporarily disabled and needed further right shoulder surgery in order to reach a permanent and stationary status. He stated he had "repeatedly requested" that this surgery take place. Sarabi was then evaluated by an agreed medical examiner (AME), Dr. Henry L. Edington, who reported on August 17, 2004, that Sarabi had a TTD and needed right shoulder surgery. According to Narsi's answer to Sarabi's petition for a writ of review, the surgery was postponed several times because Sarabi needed to be treated for a non–industrial condition before he could be medically cleared for surgery.

Also according to Narsi's answer, Dr. Edington issued a supplemental report on *October 7, 2005*, stating that *if* Sarabi could not be medically cleared for right shoulder surgery, he *could* be considered permanent and stationary as of August 17, 2005, one year to the day after Dr. Edington's initial report. (Footnote 1) (Italics added.) Prior to the supplemental report, Narsi had been voluntarily providing Sarabi with TTD benefits since December 26, 2000, but, after receiving the report, it informed Sarabi on *November 14, 2005*, that "[p]ayments are ending 11/03/05 because Dr. Edington has declared that you are permanent and stationary as of 08/17/05." "Benefits were paid to you as [TTD] from 12/26/2000 through 11/03/2005. Included in this amount is an overpayment totaling $3,516.45." (Footnote 2)

The case returned to the WCJ for a mandatory settlement conference on December 16, 2005. The parties agreed that the issue to be decided was whether Sarabi was entitled to additional TTD benefits beginning August 17, 2005, the date Narsi terminated its voluntary payment of TTD benefits based on Dr. Edington's supplemental report.

On June 28, 2006, the WCJ issued a Findings and Award granting Sarabi's request for additional TTD indemnity "from August 17, 2005 to date and continuing." The WCJ stated there was jurisdiction to issue the award even if the additional TTD arose on August 17, 2005, because Sarabi had filed a timely petition to reopen. He also noted that treatment for Sarabi's non–industrial condition was required before he could undergo surgery necessary to cure or relieve him of the effects of his industrial injury, citing to the "general rule . . . that liability to furnish medical treatment can include a duty to treat for non–industrial conditions

which may be interfering with the medical treatment necessary for the treatment of the industrially caused condition."

Narsi filed a petition for reconsideration, claiming there was no jurisdiction to award TTD benefits because Sarabi's petition to reopen was "skeletal" and because "jurisdiction was lost when the applicant was found to be permanent and stationary by the [AME]." Sarabi responded that TTD benefits should not have been terminated on August 17, 2005, and that Narsi was estopped from objecting to the petition to reopen, having voluntarily paid TTD benefits and having never questioned his TTD status before that date. In his report and recommendation, the WCJ recommended denying Narsi's petition for reconsideration, stating that "so long as the applicant's timely [p]etitions to [r]eopen remained pending, the [Board] continued to have jurisdiction to act upon those petitions and to award the applicant benefits caused by any 'new and further disability.' " He also noted there was no authority supporting Narsi's position that the Board loses jurisdiction to award temporary disability benefits when a medical examiner considers a worker's injuries to be " 'permanent and stationary.' " (Footnote 3)

The Board in a 2–1 decision granted Narsi's petition for reconsideration, holding it had no jurisdiction to award TTD benefits commencing August 17, 2005, and that Sarabi "shall take nothing on the petitions to reopen." The Board held that although an award of TTD benefits commencing August 17, 2004, may have been supported by Dr. Edington's initial report that surgery was necessary, there was no jurisdiction to award, as the WCJ did, TTD benefits beginning August 17, 2005, which was over five years after the date of injury. The dissent stated that because Dr. Edington found on August 17, 2004 that Sarabi was temporarily totally disabled and needed surgery, and there was no evidence that he stopped needing the surgery between then and August 17, 2005, there was continuing jurisdiction to award TTD benefits. Sarabi filed a timely petition for a writ of review, which this court granted.

II. DISCUSSION

A. The Board Had Jurisdiction to Order Additional TTD Benefits Because Sarabi Filed a Timely Petition to Reopen and His New and Further Disability Commenced within Five Years of the Date of His Injury.

1. Sarabi Filed a Timely Petition to Reopen.

Under Labor Code (Footnote 4) section 5410, an injured worker who has previously received workers' compensation benefits either voluntarily paid by the employer or pursuant to an award is entitled to claim benefits for "new and further disability" within five years of the date of injury. Section 5803 permits the reopening of a previously adjudicated case for "good cause" upon a petition filed by a party, also within five years from the date of injury. If a petition to reopen under either section is filed within the five–year period, the Board has jurisdiction to decide the matter beyond the five–year period. (§ 5804; *Bland v. Workers' Comp. Appeals Bd.* (1970) 3 Cal. 3d 324, 329, fn. 3; *see also General Foundry Service v. Workers' Comp. Appeals*

Bd. (1986) 42 Cal. 3d 331, 337 ["The Board clearly has the power to continue its jurisdiction beyond the five–year period when an application is made within that period"].)

Here, Sarabi filed the pertinent petition to reopen on November 15, 2002, less than five years from the date of his injury. Although Narsi argues the Board lacked jurisdiction to award TTD benefits because the petition was "skeletal," our Supreme Court has held that very broad or general petitions are sufficient. (*E.g., Bland v. Workers' Comp. Appeals Bd., supra,* 3 Cal. 3d at p. 329 [in light of the "strong policy" in favor of liberal treatment of disability claims, petition to reopen asking the Board to " 'take such steps as may be necessary to a redetermination of this matter' " is sufficient].) Indeed, an applicant has been excused from even filing a petition to reopen where the WCJ stated in a notice of hearing that the matter to be adjudicated was whether the applicant was entitled to additional benefits. (*Zurich Ins. Co. v. Workers' Comp. Appeals Bd.* (1973) 9 Cal. 3d 848, 852 [absence of petition could not have prejudiced employer and applicant could have been lulled by WCJ's notice into thinking there was no need to file petition].)

Sarabi's petition to reopen cited sections 5410 and 5803, alleged a "change in [his condition]" and requested further temporary disability benefits—the precise issue later adjudicated by the WCJ and the Board. Although the petition did not specify what the "change in . . . condition" was, it was sufficient to inform Narsi of the nature of the claim and to confer jurisdiction on the Board to determine whether he had suffered a new and further disability under section 5410, or whether there was good cause to reopen the prior award under section 5803. Moreover, Narsi can not persuasively claim it was prejudiced by the "skeletal" nature of the petition to reopen, as it was fully aware of Sarabi's condition throughout the years, making voluntary TTD payments and participating in various proceedings including having AMEs examine Sarabi to evaluate his disability. Because Sarabi filed a timely petition to reopen that was still pending at the time the matter returned to the WCJ for a hearing, the Board had continuing jurisdiction to render a decision in the matter after the five–year limitations period had expired.

2. Sarabi Suffered a New and Further Disability within Five Years of the Date of His Injury.

For an applicant to recover additional temporary disability benefits, he or she must not only have filed a petition to reopen within five years from the date of injury, but must also have suffered a "new and further disability" within that five–year period, unless there is otherwise "good cause" to reopen the prior award. (*Ruffin v. Olson Glass Co.* (1987) 52 Cal. Comp. Cases 335, 343 (*Ruffin* (Footnote 5)).) An injured worker therefore cannot confer jurisdiction on the Board by filing a petition to reopen an award before the five–year period has expired for anticipated new and further disability to occur thereafter. (*Ibid.*)

" ' "[N]ew and further disability" has been defined to mean disability . . . result[ing] from some demonstrable change in an employee's condition,' [citation]" including a " 'gradual increase in disability.' " (*Nicky Blair's*

Restaurant v. Workers' Comp. Appeals Bd. (1980) 109 Cal. App. 3d 941, 955.) " ' "Historically, a change in physical condition necessitating further medical treatment ha[s] been considered new and further disability . . . . [Citation.]" [Citations.] "Thus, [c]ommonly, new and further disability refers to a recurrence of temporary disability, a new need for medical treatment, or the change of a temporary disability into a permanent disability." [Citations.]' " (*Ibid.*) " 'Good cause' " includes a mistake of fact, a mistake of law disclosed by a subsequent appellate court ruling on the same point in another case, inadvertence, newly discovered evidence, or fraud. (*Id.* at p. 956.)

As the Board properly noted, Dr. Edington's opinion of August 17, 2004, that Sarabi had a TTD and required right shoulder surgery may have supported a finding of TTD beginning August 17, 2004. Dr. McCarthy had also been recommending surgery for some time before that date. Although this court held in *Hartsuiker, supra,* 12 Cal. App. 4th at page 213, that the Board cannot reserve jurisdiction to award additional benefits for *possible* surgery to take place after the five–year period, here, the need for surgery was clear as early as May 26, 2004, when Dr. McCarthy made his recommendation for right shoulder surgery, or at the latest by August 17, 2004, when Dr. Edington opined that Sarabi had a TTD and needed right shoulder surgery. Because Sarabi's disability worsened and further medical treatment in the form of right shoulder surgery became necessary within the five–year period, Sarabi suffered "new and further disability" within the meaning of section 5410 and the Board had jurisdiction to award him additional TTD benefits. (Footnote 6)

B. It Was Not Error for the WCJ to Award Benefits Commencing August 17, 2005, Because There Was No Need to Award Benefits Before That Date, As Narsi Was Making Voluntary TTD Payments Until Then.

The Board found the WCJ erred by awarding benefits commencing August 17, 2005, because this was more than five years after the date of Sarabi's injury. Although the Board was correct in holding that it has no jurisdiction to award benefits for a new and further disability arising more than five years from the date of injury, its conclusion that Sarabi was not entitled to additional benefits was in error.

The Board correctly held that the WCJ erred in stating there was jurisdiction to award additional benefits even if Sarabi's new and further disability arose after the five–year limitations period. However, the WCJ's conclusion that Sarabi was entitled to benefits commencing August 17, 2005, and continuing, was supported by the record, as the evidence showed that Sarabi's new and further disability arose within the five–year period, and that benefits were to begin on August 17, 2005, only because that was the date Narsi terminated its voluntary payments. In fact, the Board correctly acknowledged that Dr. Edington's report of August 17, 2004, may have supported an award of additional benefits because it was within the five–year limitations period. Because nothing prior to August 17, 2005, was at issue, there was no need for Sarabi to request, or for the WCJ to award, benefits commencing at any time before that date.

To deny TTD benefits on the facts of this case would permit an employer, knowing that an applicant has filed a timely petition to reopen and has suffered a new and further disability within the pertinent five–year period, to make voluntary payments until after the five–year period has elapsed, so that any award for additional benefits would be jurisdictionally barred as commencing more than five years after the date of injury. This would be an unjust result and would conflict with the longstanding rule that " ' "[l]imitations provisions in workmen's compensation law must be liberally construed in favor of the employee unless otherwise compelled by the language of the statute, and such enactment should not be interpreted in a manner which will result in" a loss of compensation.' " (*Martino v. Workers' Comp. Appeals Bd., supra*, 103 Cal. App. 4th at p. 489, quoting *Bland v. Workers' Comp. Appeals Bd., supra*, 3 Cal. 3d at pp. 330–331.)

III. DISPOSITION

The Board's order is hereby annulled. The case is remanded to the Board for a new order consistent with this opinion.

Footnote 1. The parties have not provided this court with a copy of Dr. Edington's supplemental report.

Footnote 2. It appears this "overpayment" is for payments Narsi made to Sarabi from August 17, 2005 (the date Narsi alleges Sarabi became permanent and stationary) and November 3, 2005 (the date Narsi terminated payments).

Footnote 3. Narsi does not dispute that Dr. Edington's opinion that Sarabi's condition could be considered permanent and stationary as of August 17, 2005, presupposed that he could not be medically cleared for right shoulder surgery. In fact, as Narsi acknowledges, Sarabi was later cleared for the surgery.

Footnote 4. All further statutory references are to the Labor Code unless otherwise stated.

Footnote 5. *Ruffin* is a writ–denied case and therefore has no stare decisis effect, but both our Supreme Court in *Nickelsberg v. Workers' Comp. Appeals Bd.* (1991) 54 Cal. 3d 288, 300 fn. 9, and the Court of Appeal in *Hartsuiker v. Workers' Comp. Appeals Bd.* (1993) 12 Cal. App. 4th 209, 218 fn. 5 quoted from it, agreeing that an award for additional benefits beyond the five–year period where the new and further disability did not arise within that period "would be nothing more than a subterfuge to avoid the limitation of jurisdiction contained in . . [s]ections 5410 and 5804." (*Ruffin, supra*, 52 Cal. Comp. Cases at p. 343.)

Footnote 6. Although Sarabi's new and further disability did not occur until after he filed his petition to reopen, an applicant is not required "to adhere to a strict chronological sequence when filing documents." (See *Martino v. Workers' Comp. Appeals Bd.* (2002) 103 Cal. App. 4th 485, 490 [applicant entitled to benefits even though incident supporting the claims made in her petition to reopen occurred after the filing of the petition].)

Page 673, Column 1, fourth paragraph, insert following '…award.'

In holding that it had jurisdiction to award temporary total disability to an applicant for a period beginning November 16, 2003 and continuing more than five years after the applicant's October 13, 1995 industrial injury, even though the applicant was not continuously temporarily totally disabled from the date of his injury, where the evidence disclosed that applicant had received a prior award of continuing temporary total disability and medical treatment that had never been legally terminated, and there had never been a findings and award of permanent disability, the Board, relied upon *Uniguard Ins. Co.*, above.

The Board, in *Denny's v. WCAB (Kakudo)* (2006) 71 Cal. Comp. Cases 831, agreed with the trial judge that *Nickelsberg* did not apply inasmuch as in that case there was a stipulated award of permanent disability, medical care and temporary total disability.

Page 673, Column 1, fifth paragraph, ending '…similar holdings.' insert the following

In *Gomez v. WCAB* (2006) 71 Cal. Comp. Cases 1721, the Court of Appeal, Fifth District, in an unpublished decision, noted that an applicant's right to temporary total disability is not indefinite under Section 4656 where he or she is claiming temporary total disability more than five years after the injury and where he or she has not been continually temporarily totally disabled within the five–year time limits. The Court stated, in part:

A. Standard of Review

The parties have not presented a factual dispute but rather disagree on whether the Labor Code authorizes continuing jurisdiction for the WCAB to award commencement of temporary disability more than five years following an injury. "Courts of review interpret governing statutes de novo, even though the WCAB's construction is entitled to great weight unless clearly erroneous." (*Green v. Workers' Comp. Appeals Bd.* (2005) 127 Cal. App. 4th 1426, 1435 [26 Cal. Rptr. 3d 527, 70 Cal. Comp. Cases 294].) Applying statutes of limitation to undisputed facts is a question of law subject to independent review. (*Martino v. Workers' Comp. Appeals Bd.* (2002) 103 Cal. App. 4th 485, 489 [126 Cal. Rptr. 2d 812, 67 Cal. Comp. Cases 1273] [statute of limitations for vocational rehabilitation benefits].)

B. Temporary Disability and Jurisdiction of the WCAB

"A temporary disability is an impairment reasonably expected to be cured or materially improved with proper medical treatment. [Citation.] Unlike permanent disability, which compensates an injured employee for diminished future earnings capacity or decreased ability to compete in the open labor market, temporary disability is intended as a substitute for lost wages during a period of transitory incapacity to work." (*Signature Fruit Co. v. Workers'*

Comp. Appeals Bd. (2006) 142 Cal. App. 4th 790, 795 [47 Cal. Rptr. 3d 878, 71 Cal. Comp. Cases 1044].)

Temporary disability may be either partial or total.

" 'Temporary partial disability exists during those periods in the convalescence of the employee when he is able to perform some work.' " (*Huston v. Workers' Comp. Appeals Bd.* (1979) 95 Cal. App. 3d 856, 866, fn. 14 [157 Cal. Rptr. 355, 44 Cal. Comp. Cases 798].) " 'Temporary disability, is "total" when it produces complete, or a substantially complete, cessation of earning power.' " (*Id.* at p. 866, fn. 15.)

Gomez contends Labor Code section 4656 supports an award of temporary total disability beyond five years from an industrial injury. (Lab. Code, (Footnote 1) § 4656.) This statute currently provides that aggregate temporary disability payments for an injury occurring between January 1, 1979, and April 19, 2004, causing temporary *partial* disability, shall not extend for more than 240 compensable weeks *within a period of five years* from the date of injury. (§ 4656, subd. (b).) Gomez asserts the five–year limitation does not apply to him because he is seeking temporary *total* disability rather than temporary *partial* disability. He essentially argues that absent an express time limit against temporary *total* disability, his entitlement to that benefit is indefinite under section 4656. We disagree for two reasons.

First, Gomez's evaluation of section 4656 contradicts the Supreme Court's interpretation in *Nickelsberg v. Workers' Comp. Appeals Bd.* (1991) 54 Cal. 3d 288 [814 P.2d 1328, 285 Cal. Rptr. 86, 56 Cal. Comp. Cases 476]. In *Nickelsberg*, the Supreme Court recognized the Legislature amended section 4656 in 1978 to remove the cap of 240 weeks in a five–year period for the payment of temporary *total* disability. (*Id.* at p. 295.) The Legislature's objective for this amendment, however, was not to facilitate potential inception of temporary total disability five years after an injury, but to allow an injured worker who is *continuously* temporarily totally disabled to continue to receive benefits without an arbitrary cutoff date. (*Id.* at p. 296.) In this case, Gomez was not continuously temporarily totally disabled within the five–year time limit. Despite Gomez's significant level of permanent partial disability, the WCJ found he did not first become temporarily totally disabled until June 22, 2005, more than five years following his injury. Section 4656 does not authorize initiation of temporary total disability benefits once five years have lapsed.

Secondly, statutory construction of section 4656 alone does not answer the question of whether it was error for the WCAB to rescind the temporary disability award. Concomitant with any limitations posed by section 4656, an award for temporary disability benefits must fall within the WCAB's jurisdiction. Although the WCAB has "continuing jurisdiction" over prior orders, decisions, and awards under section 5803, that jurisdiction is limited by sections 5410 and 5804.

Section 5410 states, "Nothing in this chapter shall bar the right of any injured worker to institute proceedings for the collection of compensation . . . within five years after the date of injury upon the ground that the original injury has *caused* new and further disability . . . . The jurisdiction of the appeals board in these cases shall be a continuing

jurisdiction within this period." (Italics added.) "The board may reopen under section 5410 of the Labor Code on the ground of new and further disability *occurring within the five–year period . . . .*" (*Argonaut Ins. Co. v. Workmen's Comp. App. Bd.* (1967) 247 Cal. App. 2d 669, 674 [55 Cal. Rptr. 810, 32 Cal. Comp. Cases 14], italics added.)

Section 5804 provides the WCAB with jurisdiction to rescind, alter, or amend an award for compensation so long as the interested party files a petition within five years of the date of injury. The parties do not contend Gomez filed a petition under section 5804. Absent a petition to rescind, alter or amend, and after expiration of the five year period, the WCAB can only act under section 5410. (*Argonaut Ins. Co. v. Workmen's Comp. App. Bd.*, *supra*, 247 Cal. App. 2d at p. 675.)

Gomez filed his Petition to Reopen within five years of his injury, but his new and further disability, as supported by medical evidence, did not occur until June 22, 2005, more than five years post–injury. In Gomez's August 4, 2004, Petition to Reopen, he claimed his knee condition worsened because injections are less effective in relieving his symptoms and his knees feel weaker and less stable. Despite these claims, according to the WCAB, the earliest medical report submitted into evidence on the Petition to Reopen is dated December 1, 2004, from Dr. Kucera, five years three months following the injury. The next report submitted into evidence was the February 10, 2005, report from Dr. Montoy. The WCJ wrote:

"Dr. Montoy does not give an explanation or provide any reason or justification for his opinion. Therefore, I find that Dr. Montoy's reports do not constitute substantial medical evidence to support a commencement date for temporary total disability." The WCJ held there was not substantial evidence of new and further disability, by way of temporary total disability, until June 22, 2005, the date of Dr. Dunklin's reporting. The WCJ concluded that Dr. Dunklin's reporting is well reasoned and persuasive. Thus, substantial evidence does not support Gomez's new and further disability until approximately 5 years 10 months following his August 27, 1999, injury.

In order to invoke the WCAB's continuing jurisdiction under section 5410, a timely petition to reopen must be filed and evidence of new and further disability must exist within the five–year period. Section 5410 does not provide the WCAB with continuing jurisdiction if an injured worker files a timely petition to reopen and essentially suggests he *will have* new and further disability.

In *Hartsuiker v. Workers' Comp. Appeals Bd.* (1993) 12 Cal. App. 4th 209, 211 [15 Cal. Rptr. 2d 719, 58 Cal. Comp. Cases 19], the appellate court held the WCAB cannot reserve jurisdiction to award future temporary total disability for an injured worker who anticipated needing benefits five years post–injury in conjunction with possible knee surgery. The court explained:

"We recognize the competing policy that workers should be compensated when they are required to forego work in order to obtain necessary treatment for their industrial injuries. The present statutory scheme, however, does not permit the reservation of jurisdiction to award temporary total disability in connection with future treatment occurring more than five years after the date of injury. Any change to accommodate this competing interest should be fashioned by the Legislature after receiving input from all interested parties." (*Hartsuiker v. Workers' Comp. Appeals Bd., supra,* 12 Cal. App. 4th at pp. 219–220.)"

Gomez argues that an injured worker can file a "skeletal" petition to reopen within five years of the injury and this is sufficient to preserve the WCAB's jurisdiction over any and all of its prior orders, decisions and awards. If this were true then any injured worker who received a finding and award within five years of the date of injury could simultaneously file a petition to reopen and enjoy a never–ending opportunity to seek permanent disability, temporary disability or vocational rehabilitation benefits. This goes against the policy of sections 5410 and 5804. The statutes "do not express a mere concern for barring stale claims. The statutes express legislative concern for certainty and finality in the determination of compensation benefit obligations." (*Nickelsberg v. Workers' Comp. Appeals Bd., supra,* 54 Cal. 3d at p. 299.)... .

Footnote 1. Further statutory references are to the Labor Code.

§ 9.10 Consequence of Intervening Events

Page 673, Column 2, fourth paragraph, insert following '...

Ongoing Award

A Petition to terminate temporary disability indemnity is expressly required when there is an ongoing award for such a benefit from the Board.

Receipt of State Disability Insurance Benefits

The fact that the Employment Development Department paid an applicant state disability insurance benefits during an alleged workers compensation temporary disability period may be considered on the issue of the extent of temporary disability but is not controlling. *Hydro Conduit Corp. v. WCAB (Reed)* 47 Cal. Comp. Cases 653.

§ 9.11(C) Special Payments to University of California Police Department Employees

Page 677, Column 1, sixth paragraph, ending '...Government Code' insert the following

In *City of Oakland, et. al. v. WCAB (Watson)* (2007) 72 Cal. Comp. Cases 249, the Board held that salary continuation benefits paid under Section 4850 are not subject to the two–year limitation period for temporary disability indemnity, under, Section 4656 as amended by Senate Bill 899. The Board, in upholding the judge's decision that so held stated, in part:

[A]t least two provisions of the Labor Code demonstrate that salary continuation benefits are intended to be distinct from temporary disability indemnity. Section 4853 provides that where an employee entitled to salary continuation benefits remains disabled beyond the one year section 4850 period, "such member shall thereafter be subject as to disability indemnity to the provisions of this division other than Section 4850 during the remainder of the period of said disability or until the effective date of his retirement under the Public Employee's Retirement Act, and the leave of absence shall continue." Thus, under the provision a public safety worker may become eligible to receive temporary disability benefits upon the termination of the one year leave of absence during the remainder of the period of his or her disability, subject to the limitations on payment of temporary disability benefits.

We note further that pursuant to section 4854, injured public safety workers who are receiving salary continuation benefits are specifically prohibited from receiving concurrent payment of temporary disability indemnity. This section provides that "[n]o disability indemnity shall be paid to any such officer or employee concurrently with wages or salary."

While salary continuation benefits paid pursuant to section 4850 may be considered compensation, they are clearly not temporary disability benefits and not interchangeable with temporary disability benefits... .

Inasmuch as Section 4661.5 addresses the payment of temporary disability benefits and not Labor Code section 4850 benefits, Section 4666.5 increases do not apply to salary or income benefits. *Nustad v. WCAB* (2007) 72 Cal. Comp. Cases 687.

§ 9.11(D) Special Payments to Policepersons, Firepersons, Sheriffs, Lifeguards, and Others (Labor Code section 4850 Benefits).

Page 677, Column 1, seventh paragraph, insert following '...Code.'

The entitlement to one year of full salary under Section 4850 is one year of full salary per injury. *City of Oakland, et al. v. WCAB (Harger)* (2006) 71 Cal. Comp. Cases 1319.

In *City of Oceanside v. WCAB (Gambino)* (2006) 71 Cal. Comp. Cases 524, the Board held that termination of benefits under Section 4850 was unreasonable where the police officer's medical condition was not permanent and stationary and he had not consented to his retirement.

In *City of Oceanside v. WCAB (Woodall)* (2006) 71. Cal Comp. Cases 255, the Board held that a police officer was entitled to Section 4850 benefits while participating in vocational rehabilitation.

See also *City of Martinez v. WCAB (Bonito)* (2000) 65 Cal. Comp. Cases 1368 and *City of Los Angeles, PSI v. WCAB (Boney)* (2006) 71 Cal. Comp. Cases 520.

§ 9.13 Procedure for Resolving Disputes Over the Compensability of Any Injury Sustained on or After January 1, 1994.

§ 9.13(B) Employee Represented

Page 688, Column 1, insert following fourth paragraph

Former Labor Code sections 4060, 4061, 4062 still apply for claims before January 1, 2005

In represented cases, medical evaluations and reporting procedures of former Labor Code section 4062 apply to cases with a date of injury before January 1, 2005. The Court of Appeal, Second District, in *Cortez v. WCAB* (2006) 71 Cal. Comp. Cases 155, in so holding, stated, in part:

Both this case and its companion case, Nunez v. Workers' Comp. Appeals Bd. (Feb. 7, 2006, B182381) – Cal. App. 4th – [38 Cal. Rptr. 3d 914, 71 Cal. Comp. Cases 161] (Nunez), concern the procedure to be applied for medical evaluation of a represented employee where the date of an industrial injury precedes January 1, 2005. In Nunez, we rejected the argument that the procedure enacted under Senate Bill No. 899 (Sen. Bill 899) applies to such cases. In this case, we reject the claim that neither the new nor the former procedure applies.

Manuel Cortez petitions this court to annul the order of the Workers' Compensation Appeals Board (Board), which compels a medical evaluation by his employer, respondent C.T. & F., Inc., under former section 4062. (Footnote 1)

Cortez contends that there is no applicable medical evaluation and reporting procedure since his industrial injury occurred in 1999 and he is represented by counsel. The procedure of former section 4062 was repealed and replaced by the procedure of section 4062.2 under Sen. Bill 899, which states under subdivision (a) that, "Whenever a comprehensive medical evaluation is required to resolve any dispute arising out of an injury or a claimed injury occurring on or after January 1, 2005, and the employee is represented by an attorney, the evaluation shall be obtained only as provided in this section."

For the reasons stated in Nunez, we conclude that the medical evaluation and reporting procedure of former section 4062 applies where the employee is represented and the date of the industrial injury is prior to January 1, 2005. We affirm the Board's decision… .

Footnote 1. Former Labor Code section 4062 was amended on April 19, 2004, as part of the comprehensive workers' compensation reform under Sen. Bill 899.

All further statutory references are to the Labor Code.

See also *Nunez v. WCAB* (2006) 71 Cal. Comp. Cases 161, where the Court of Appeal, Second District, affirmed a Board decision holding that pre–SB 899 version of Labor Code sections 4061 and 4062 apply when a medical evaluation in a represented case was required to resolve a permanent disability dispute arising out of an injury that occurred prior to January 1, 2005. The Court stated, in part:

In 2004, the Legislature enacted substantial changes in workers' compensation law. The legislative vehicle for these changes was Senate Bill No. 899 (2003–2004 Reg. Sess.) (Sen. Bill 899), enacted as an urgency measure on April 19, 2004. Most of the legislation was effective immediately, but the portion at issue in this case, relating to medical evaluation and reporting when the employee is represented by counsel, is only operative for injuries occurring on or after January 1, 2005.

Under the former version of Labor Code section 4060, (Footnote 1) a represented employee and his or her employer could each select a reporting medical evaluator when compensability of industrial injury was disputed. If liability was admitted by the employer and the dispute involved other issues, the parties were required to attempt selection of an agreed medical evaluator, and if unsuccessful, each side was entitled to select its own reporting medical evaluator under the former version of section 4061 or 4062.

Sen. Bill 899 imposed a new procedure to resolve these disputes, but with limitations in its application. Under this procedure, the represented employee and employer are required to attempt to reach agreement on a reporting medical evaluator. But if they are unsuccessful, either party may ask the Administrative Director of the Division of Workers' Compensation to assign the names of three possible reporting medical evaluators for the case. Each side is permitted to strike one, and the one remaining becomes the reporting medical evaluator. If a party does not timely choose to exercise the right to strike a name, the other party is entitled to choose the evaluator from among the three names.

There is a significant limitation to this new procedure, which is at the core of the present dispute. Section 4062.2, subdivision (a), provides: "Whenever a comprehensive medical evaluation is required to resolve any dispute arising out of an injury or a claimed injury occurring on or after January 1, 2005, and the employee is represented by an attorney, the evaluation shall be obtained only as provided in this section."

The issue before us is what procedure, if any, applies where the employee is represented and the injury occurred before January 1, 2005. The statute does not spell out the answer.

Lourdes Nunez, the petitioner and represented employee in this case, takes the position that the new medical evaluation and reporting procedure applies to her industrial injury of July 15, 2002, notwithstanding the provision limiting its application to cases where the date of injury is subsequent to 2004. Assoluto, Inc., her employer and the respondent in this case, argues that the former procedure applies in this situation. The workers' compensation administrative law judge (WCJ) in this case agreed with Assoluto and, more importantly, this also is the position taken by the Workers' Compensation Appeals Board (Board) in an earlier published decision, and implicitly in this case as shown by its decision not to remove this case to itself.

We believe the Board has the better of the argument. We are led to that position by the illogic of allowing a vacuum in which the employer would have no right to have a medical evaluation performed, the plain language of the new statute which confines its application in represented cases to injuries occurring after 2004, and by deference to the Board, a constitutional agency, which is charged with construction and application of workers' compensation law and administration of the workers' compensation system…

Footnote 1. All further statutory reference is to the Labor Code unless stated otherwise.

§ 9.13(C) Temporary Disability Indemnity Limits For Injuries Sustained On Or After April 19, 2004

Page 688, Column 2, second paragraph, ending '(l) Chronic lung disease.' insert the following

The Appeals Board in holding that the statutorily allowable period of temporary disability payments (104 compensable weeks of temporary disability within two years from date of injury) begins on the date when temporary disability is actually *paid* and not on the date when temporary disability indemnity is first *owed* stated in *Hawkins v. State Compensation Insurance Fund* (2007) 72 Cal. Comp. Cases 807:

INTRODUCTION

We granted defendant's petition for reconsideration of the September 5, 2006 Findings and Award to study the legal issue presented. It is admitted that applicant sustained a cumulative industrial injury to her spine while employed by Amberwood Products during a period ending July 16, 2004. In his decision, the workers' compensation administrative law judge (WCJ) found that defendant "commenced payment of temporary disability for the purposes of Labor Code section 4656(c)(1)" on May 3, 2005, and that defendant paid temporary disability benefits for the period from July 17, 2004 through July 14, 2006 (Footnote 1) The WCJ concluded that the "period of two years from the date of commencement of temporary disability payment" as provided in section 4656(c)(1) began on May 3, 2005, the date on which temporary disability indemnity was first *paid*, and not from July 17, 2004, the date for which temporary disability indemnity was first *owed*. Therefore, additional

temporary disability indemnity was awarded from July 15, 2006, to the date of the award and continuing because applicant continued to be temporarily disabled.

Defendant contends that the "the date of commencement of temporary disability payment" as used in section 4656(c)(1) is the date for which temporary disability indemnity is first *owed* instead of the date on which benefits are first *paid*.

Because of the importance of the legal issue presented, and in order to secure uniformity of decision in the future, the Chairman of the Appeals Board, upon a majority vote of its members, assigned this case to the Appeals Board as a whole for an en banc decision. (Lab. Code, § 115.) (Footnote 2)

We hold that "the date of commencement of temporary disability payment" as used in section 4656(c)(1) means the date on which temporary disability indemnity is first *paid*, and not the date for which temporary disability indemnity is first owed. The decision of the WCJ is affirmed.

FACTS

As shown by the minutes, the following facts were stipulated at the hearing on August 14, 2006:

"(1) Applicant, born 2/21/57, sustained injury on a cumulative trauma basis ending 7/16/04 to her cervical spine while working for Amberwood Products, then insured for workers' compensation by State Compensation Insurance Fund.

(2) EDD [Employment Development Department] paid benefits from 7/26/04 to 3/31/05 for which State Compensation Insurance Fund has reimbursed them.

(3) Applicant has received temporary disability benefits from the period 7/17/04 through 7/14/06.

(4) Applicant has not reached maximum medical improvement and is still unable to return to her usual and customary occupation.

(5) State Compensation Insurance Fund made its first payment of temporary disability on 5/03/05 (Covering the period 7/17/04 to 5/02/05) (Excess of EDD reimbursement)." (Parenthesis in original, bracketed material added.)

Based upon the stipulations that applicant was continuously temporarily disabled from the July 16, 2004 date of injury and that the first payment of temporary disability indemnity was not made until May 3, 2005, the WCJ entered the September 5, 2006 Findings and Award as described above.

The WCJ explained why he awarded additional temporary disability indemnity to applicant in his Report and Recommendation on Petition for Reconsideration (Report):

"The plain language [of section 4656(c)(1)] requires that the 2 year limitation starts when defendant commences payment. That must mean the date on which defendant made its first payment. That is the date on which payment commences. The Legislature could have said that the two years started 'On the date eligibility for benefits commences' or other language that would cause the result that defendant seeks. They could have left out the word 'payment' leaving the date as 'commencement of Temporary Disability'. They did not do so.

"They used the plain language that the 2 year limit begins on the date of commencement of payment. They included a word, payment, which must be given meaning. It cannot be other [than] that the limitation begins the date payment starts, not disability.

"In this case defendant did not make any payment of temporary disability until 5/3/05. That is the date that they commenced payment. They must pay up to 2 years from that date."

DISCUSSION

We agree with the WCJ that the limitation of 104 compensable weeks within two years described in section 4656(c)(1) begins on the date temporary disability indemnity is first paid.

Section 4656, as amended by the Legislature in April 2004 as part of Senate Bill 899 (SB 899) (Stats. 2004, ch. 34, § 29), now provides in full:

"(a) Aggregate disability payments for a single injury occurring prior to January 1, 1979, causing temporary disability shall not extend for more than 240 compensable weeks within a period of five years from the date of the injury.

"(b) Aggregate disability payments for a single injury occurring on or after January 1, 1979, and prior to the effective date of subdivision (c), causing temporary partial disability shall not extend for more than 240 compensable weeks within a period of five years from the date of the injury.

"(c)(1) Aggregate disability payments for a single injury occurring on or after the effective date of this subdivision, causing temporary disability shall not extend for more than 104 compensable weeks within a period of two years from the date of commencement of temporary disability payment.

(2) Notwithstanding paragraph (1), for an employee who suffers from the following injuries or conditions, aggregate disability payments for a single injury occurring on or after the effective date of this subdivision, causing temporary disability shall not extend for more than 240 compensable weeks within a period of five years from the date of the injury:

(A) Acute and chronic hepatitis B.
(B) Acute and chronic hepatitis C.
(C) Amputations.
(D) Severe burns.
(E) Human immunodeficiency virus (HIV).
(F) High-velocity eye injuries.
(G) Chemical burns to the eyes.
(H) Pulmonary fibrosis.
(I) Chronic lung disease." (Emphasis added.)

Subdivisions (a), (b) and (c)(2) of section 4656 all provide that temporary disability indemnity "shall not extend for more than 240 compensable weeks within a period of five years *from the date of the injury*." (Emphasis added.) The imposition of a time limit on temporary disability indemnity running from the employee's "date of injury" has been a component of section 4656 since its inception. (Footnote 3) Subdivision (c)(1), however, takes

an entirely different approach. It provides that "temporary disability shall not extend for more than 104 compensable weeks within a period of two years from the date of commencement of temporary disability payment." (Emphasis added.) Obviously, by using such distinctly different language in subdivision (c)(1), the Legislature intended this language to have a distinctly different legal effect. (People ex rel. Lockyer v. R.J. Reynolds Tobacco Co. (2005) 37 Cal.4th 707, 717 ("When the Legislature uses materially different language in statutory provisions addressing the same subject or related subjects, the normal inference is that the Legislature intended a difference in meaning"); American Airlines, Inc. v. County of San Mateo (1996) 12 Cal.4th 1110, 1137-1138 ("we generally do not construe different terms within a statute to embody the same meaning" [Court's emphasis]).) While section 4656(c)(1) plainly establishes a payment limit on temporary disability indemnity of 104 compensable weeks within a period of two years, the question is: When does the 104-week/two-year limitation period begin?

"Our task in interpreting a statute is to ascertain and effectuate legislative intent." (People v. Leal (2004) 33 Cal.4th 999, 1007 ("Leal") (internal quotations omitted); see also Nickelsberg v. Workers' Comp. Appeals Bd. (1991) 54 Cal.3d 288, 294 [56 Cal.Comp.Cases 476, 480].) In undertaking this task, "it is well-settled that we must look first to the words of the statute, because they generally provide the most reliable indicator of legislative intent." (Murphy v. Kenneth Cole Productions, Inc. (2007) 40 Cal.4th 1094, 1103 ("Murphy") (internal quotations omitted); see also Leal, supra, 33 Cal.4th at p. 1007.) We give a statute's words "their plain and commonsense meaning" (Murphy, supra, 40 Cal.4th at p. 1103; see also In re Jennings (2004) 34 Cal.4th 254, 263 ("Jennings")) and their "usual and ordinary meaning." (Smith v. Superior Court (2006) 39 Cal.4th 77, 83; Day v. City of Fontana (2001) 25 Cal.4th 268, 272 ("Day"); see also DuBois v. Workers' Comp. Appeals Bd. (1993) 5 Cal.4th 382, 388 [58 Cal.Comp.Cases 286, 289] ("DuBois") ("We are required to give effect to statutes according to the usual, ordinary import of the language employed …").) "If the statutory language is not ambiguous, then we presume the Legislature meant what it said, and the plain meaning of the language governs." (In re Young (2004) 32 Cal.4th 900, 906; accord: Day, supra, 25 Cal.4th at p. 272); see also Jennings, supra, 34 Cal.4th at p. 263 ("If the language of the statute is not ambiguous, the plain meaning controls and resort to extrinsic sources to determine the Legislature's intent is unnecessary." (internal quotations omitted)); Leal, supra, 33 Cal.4th at p. 1007 ("[w]hen the language of a statute is clear and unambiguous and thus not reasonably susceptible of more than one meaning, there is no need for construction, and courts should not indulge in it" and "[w]e may not, under the guise of construction, rewrite the law or give the words an effect different from the plain and direct import of the terms used" (internal quotations omitted)); DuBois, supra, 5 Cal.4th at pp. 387-388 [58 Cal.Comp.Cases at p. 289] ("[w]hen the language is clear and there is no uncertainty as to the legislative intent, we look no further and simply enforce the statute according to its terms");

Lennane v. Franchise Tax Bd. (1994) 9 Cal.4th 263, 268 ("[w]here the statute is clear, courts will not interpret away clear language in favor of an ambiguity that does not exist") (internal quotations omitted).)

Here, the language of section 4656(c)(1) is clear and unambiguous. It provides that "temporary disability shall not extend for more than 104 compensable weeks within a period of two years from the date of commencement of temporary disability payment." (Emphasis added.) The plain and commonsense meaning of "commencement" is "beginning." (The American Heritage® Dictionary of the English Language, Fourth Edition. Houghton Mifflin Company, 2004.) The usual and ordinary meaning of "payment" is "[t]he act of paying or the state of being paid." (Ibid.) Thus, by stating that "temporary disability shall not extend for more than 104 compensable weeks within a period of two years from the date of commencement of temporary disability payment," the Legislature clearly and specifically expressed its intention that the limitation of 104 weeks within two years begins on the date on which temporary disability indemnity is first paid, and not on the date for which it is first owed.

Because the statutory language is not ambiguous, we will presume the Legislature meant what it said and, therefore, the plain meaning will govern. We cannot and will not, under the guise of construction, rewrite section 4656(c)(1) or give its words an effect different from the plain and direct import of the terms used. Rather, we will enforce section 4656(c)(1) according to its actual terms.

Moreover, although not necessary to our decision, we observe that our construction of section 4656(c)(1) is in harmony with the workers' compensation statutory scheme. (Cf. Chevron U.S.A., Inc. v. Workers' Comp. Appeals Bd. (Steele) (1999) 19 Cal.4th 1182, 1194 [64 Cal.Comp.Cases 1, 22] ("Steele"); DuBois, supra, 5 Cal.4th at p. 388 [58 Cal.Comp.Cases at pp. 289-290].)

To qualify for workers' compensation benefits, a covered worker need only sustain a compensable injury. (Lab. Code, § 3600.) Liability is determined "irrespective of the fault of any party." (Cal. Const., art. XIV, § 4.) The system is intended to automatically provide an injured worker with medical treatment and temporary disability indemnity without delay.

Various provisions of the workers' compensation law create both economic incentives and disincentives to help ensure that an employer timely acts in good faith to provide benefits. Late payments of disability indemnity are automatically increased by 10 percent in most instances without regard to the reason for the delay. (Lab. Code, § 4650(d).) If an employer or insurer unreasonably delays or refuses to pay compensation, section 5814 provides for an increase in the award as a penalty. A claims administrator may also be penalized for any delayed payments discovered in an audit of its claims by the Division of Workers' Compensation. (Lab. Code, § 129.5.) By providing that the limitation in section 4656(c)(1) runs from the date payment of temporary disability indemnity commences, the Legislature created both an incentive for prompt payment and a disincentive for delay.

By encouraging timely action, section 4656(c)(1) advances the purpose of temporary disability indemnity, which is to promptly replace wages lost by the injured employee during the period of disability. (Lab. Code, §§ 4650-4657 and 4661-4661.5.) This purpose of temporary disability indemnity has been repeatedly emphasized by the appellate courts. In Nickelsberg v. Workers' Comp. Appeals Bd. (1991) 54 Cal.3d 288 [56 Cal. Comp. Cases 476], the Supreme Court said, "[t]emporary disability indemnity is intended primarily to substitute for the worker's lost wages, in order to maintain a steady stream of income." (54 Cal.3d at p. 294 [56 Cal. Comp. Cases at p. 479] (emphasis added, internal quotations omitted).) Similarly, in Granado v. Workmen's Comp. Appeals Bd. (1968) 69 Cal.2d 399 [33 Cal. Comp. Cases 647], the Supreme Court wrote that "[t]he primary element of temporary disability is wage loss," that "temporary disability payments [are] a substitute for lost wages," and that "[temporary disability] benefits are based … directly on lost wages." (69 Cal.2d at pp. 403, 404, 405 [33 Cal. Comp. Cases at pp. 650, 651] (emphasis added).) More recently, in Signature Fruit Co. v. Workers' Comp. Appeals Bd. (Ochoa) (2006) 142 Cal.App.4th 790, 801 [71 Cal. Comp. Cases 1044], the Court of Appeal observed that "[t]he essential purpose of temporary disability indemnity is to help replace the wages the employee would have earned, but for the injury, during his or her period(s) of temporary disability" and that "temporary disability is intended as a substitute for lost wages during a period of transitory incapacity to work." (142 Cal.App.4th at pp. 801, 795 [71 Cal. Comp. Cases at pp. 1052-1053, 1047] (emphasis added); see also, e.g., Gamble v. Workers' Comp. Appeals Bd. (2006) 143 Cal.App.4th 71, 79 [71 Cal. Comp. Cases 1015, 1017] ("The purpose of temporary disability indemnity is to provide interim wage replacement assistance to an injured worker during the period he or she is healing."); Western Growers Ins. Co. v. Workers' Comp. Appeals Bd. (Austin) (1993) 16 Cal.App.4th 227, 235 [58 Cal. Comp. Cases 323, 327] ("Temporary disability benefits are intended primarily to replace lost earnings.").)

Further, consistent with the declaration in the state constitution that a "complete system of workers' compensation includes adequate provisions for the comfort, health and safety and general welfare of any and all workers and those dependent upon them for support to the extent of relieving from the consequences of any injury … incurred or sustained by workers in the course of their employment" (Cal. Const., art. XIV, § 4 (formerly, art. XX, § 21) (emphasis added)), the Supreme Court long ago held:

"[T]he primary purpose of industrial compensation is to insure [sic] to the injured employee and those dependent upon him adequate means of subsistence while he is unable to work … By this means society as a whole is relieved of the burden of caring for the injured workman and his family, and the burden is placed upon the industry. That the injured workman and his dependents may be cared for, compensation in the form of disability benefits is provided for by the act approximating the wages earned by the employee." (Union Iron Works v. Industrial Acc. Com. (Henneberry) (1922) 190 Cal. 33, 39 [9 I.A.C. 223, 226] (emphasis added); see also: Moyer v. Workmen's Comp.

Appeals Bd. (1973) 10 Cal.3d 222, 233 [38 Cal. Comp. Cases 652, 659]; Zeeb v. Workmen's Comp. Appeals Bd. (1967) 67 Cal.2d 496, 500-501 [32 Cal. Comp. Cases 441, 443]; Aetna Casualty & Surety Co. v. Industrial Acc. Com. (Charlesworth) (1947) 30 Cal.2d 388, 407-408 [12 Cal. Comp. Cases 123, 134-135].)

Because section 4656(c)(1)'s limitation of 104 weeks within two years does not begin to run until "the date of commencement of temporary disability payment," there is a strong inducement to promptly start paying temporary disability indemnity. Prompt payment helps ensure that the injured employee and his or her dependents receive some replacement of the employee's lost wages and a means of subsistence during the period of temporary disability.

The balance struck by section 4656(c)(1) is also consistent with the Legislature's intent in enacting SB 899, as expressed in section 49 of that bill:

"This act is an urgency statute necessary for the immediate preservation of the public peace, health, or safety within the meaning of Article IV of the Constitution and shall go into immediate effect. The facts constituting the necessity are: [¶] In order to provide relief to the state from the effects of the current workers' compensation crisis at the earliest possible time, it is necessary for this act to take effect immediately." (Stats. 2004, ch. 34, § 49.)

As recognized by the Supreme Court, section 49 reflects that SB 899 was adopted as "an urgency measure designed to alleviate a perceived crisis in skyrocketing workers' compensation costs." (Brodie v. Workers' Comp. Appeals Bd. (2007) 40 Cal.4th 1313, 1329 [72 Cal.Comp.Cases __, __]; see also, Costco Wholesale Corp. v. Workers' Comp. Appeals Bd. (Chavez) (2007) __ Cal.App.4th __ [72 Cal.Comp.Cases __, 2007 WL 1492341, 2007 Cal.App. ("the workers' compensation ... reforms [of SB 899] were enacted as urgency legislation to drastically reduce the cost of workers' compensation insurance").)

By placing a limit of 104 weeks of temporary disability indemnity within two years from the date that payment commences, the Legislature has furthered the goal of SB 899 to "provide relief" from the workers' compensation "crisis" and to reduce workers' compensation costs. Immediately prior to SB 899, former section 4656 placed no limit whatsoever on temporary total disability indemnity payments. (See fn. 3, supra [discussing 1978 amendment to section 4656].) Also, although former section 4656 did place some limits on temporary partial disability indemnity, these limits were 240 weeks within five years of the date of injury. (Ibid.) Therefore, under new section 4656(c)(1), even an employer that significantly delays the "commencement of temporary disability payment" may have lesser liability – and, at least with temporary total disability indemnity, certainly will not have greater liability – than it would have had prior to section 4656(c)(1)'s adoption. Moreover, under section 4656(c)(1), the employer controls when the limitation on temporary disability benefits begins to run. Accordingly, the sooner the employer commences temporary disability indemnity payments, the sooner it obtains the benefit of the lower liability limits enacted by the Legislature as part of SB 899. And, of course, because section 4656(c)(1) encourages the prompt commencement of temporary disability indemnity payments, it also helps to ensure that an injured employee will seasonally receive some replacement for his or her lost wages, so that the employee – and his or her family – has a means of subsistence during the employee's period of temporary disability.

Our conclusion that the 104-week/two-year limitation of section 4656(c)(1) starts to run with the first actual payment of temporary disability indemnity is not affected by the provisions of section 4656(c)(2). Section 4656(c)(2) provides that temporary disability indemnity for certain injuries or conditions (e.g., hepatitis B and C, amputations, severe burns, HIV, pulmonary fibrosis, and chronic lung disease) may extend up "240 compensable weeks within a period of five years from the date of the injury." Thus, in enacting section 4656(c)(2), the Legislature exempted these specified injuries or conditions from the 104-week/two-year cap of section 4656(c)(1). Section 4656(c)(2)'s exemption of these specific injuries or conditions, however, does not mean that we can rewrite section 4656(c)(1) or give its words an effect different from their plain and ordinary meaning. As discussed above, the usual and commonsense meaning of the phrase "temporary disability shall not extend for more than 104 compensable weeks within a period of two years from the date of commencement of temporary disability payment" (emphasis added) is that the 104-week/two-year limitation starts on the date that temporary disability indemnity is first paid. While it is conceivable, as the dissent points out, that in some exceptional circumstances an injured employee could receive more temporary disability indemnity under section 4656(c)(1) than another employee could receive under section 4656(c)(2), the possible existence of such exceptional circumstances does not mean we can disregard the actual language used by the Legislature in section 4656(c)(1). (See, e.g., Gorham Co., Inc. v. First Financial Ins. Co. (2006) 139 Cal.App.4th 1532, 1543-1544 ("Although courts may disregard literal interpretation of a statute to avoid absurd results ..., they should do so rarely, and only in extreme cases – those in which, as a matter of law, the Legislature did not intend the statute to have its literal effect." (Internal citations and quotations omitted); accord: California Highway Patrol v. Superior Court (Quigley) (2007) 150 Cal.App.4th 207, __ [2007 WL 1447694, *4, 2007 Cal.App. LEXIS 764, *12].)

Finally, our conclusion that the section 4656(c)(1) limitation of 104 weeks within two years starts to run with the first actual payment of temporary disability indemnity is not affected by the fact that section 4656(c)(1) refers to "[a]ggregate disability payments." (Emphasis added.) Statutory phrases are not to be read in isolation; rather, they must be examined in the context of the entire statute so that its different parts may be harmonized. (State Farm Mut. Auto. Ins. Co. v. Garamendi (2004) 32 Cal.4th 1029, 1043; Steele, supra, 19 Cal.4th at p. 1194 [64 Cal.Comp.Cases at p. 22]; DuBois, supra, 5 Cal.4th at p. 388 [58 Cal.Comp.Cases at p. 289].) Here, section 4656(c)(1) reads, in total, "[a]ggregate disability payments for a single injury occurring on or after the effective date of this subdivision, causing temporary disability shall not extend for more than

104 compensable weeks within a period of two years from the date of commencement of temporary disability payment." (Emphasis added.) Therefore, for the reasons discussed above, the 104 weeks of temporary disability indemnity do not start to "aggregate" until payments actually commence.

In sum, because the language of section 4656(c)(1) is clear and unambiguous (i.e., that "temporary disability shall not extend for more than 104 compensable weeks within a period of two years from the date of commencement of temporary disability payment" (emphasis added)), we will enforce the statute in accordance with the plain and commonsense meaning of the words actually used by the Legislature, i.e., the 104-week/two-year limitation period begins (i.e., it "commence[s]") on the "date" on which temporary disability indemnity is first paid (i.e., the "payment"), and not on the date for which it is first owed.

DISPOSITION

In this case, temporary disability indemnity was first paid to applicant on May 3, 2005 and defendant made further payments through July 14, 2006. The first payment included retroactive temporary disability indemnity for the period of July 17, 2004 to May 2, 2005. However, none of that retroactive temporary disability indemnity was within the "104 compensable weeks within a period of two years from the date of commencement of temporary disability payment" limitation established by section 4656(c)(1). Instead, the 104-week/two-year limitation in this case began to run on May 3, 2005, the date temporary disability indemnity was first paid to applicant. Accordingly, the WCJ properly awarded temporary disability indemnity from the date defendant terminated its temporary disability indemnity payments (i.e., July 14, 2006) to the date of the award (i.e., September 5, 2006) and continuing thereafter.

We are aware that, in making a "continuing" award of temporary disability, the WCJ did not direct that payments were to be stopped on May 3, 2007. As the WCJ explained in his Report, however, it was appropriate to leave the award open-ended because temporary disability might terminate for some reason before the end of the two-year limitation period on May 3, 2007. (See Lab. Code, § 4651.1; Cal. Code Regs., tit. 8T, §§ 10462 and 10464.) Although our decision is issuing after May 3, 2007, we will not disturb the "continuing" award, for the reasons stated in the WCJ's Report.

Footnote 1. All further statutory references are to the Labor Code.

Footnote 2. En banc decisions of the Appeals Board are binding precedent on all Appeals Board panels and WCJs. (Cal. Code Regs., tit. 8, § 10341; City of Long Beach v. Workers' Comp. Appeals Bd. (Garcia) (2005) 126 Cal.App.4th 298, 313, fn. 5 [70 Cal.Comp.Cases 109, 120, fn. 5]; Gee v. Workers' Comp. Appeals Bd. (2002) 96 Cal.App.4th 1418, 1425, fn. 6 [67 Cal.Comp.Cases 236, 239, fn. 6]; see also Govt. Code, § 11425.60(b).)

Footnote 3. As enacted in 1937, section 4656 provided in full: "Aggregate disability payments for a single injury causing temporary disability shall not exceed three times the average annual earnings of the employee, nor shall the aggregate disability period for such temporary disability in any event extend beyond 240 weeks from the date of injury." (Stats. 1937, ch. 90, § 4656 (emphasis added).) Thus, in its original form, section 4656 limited both the maximum amount of temporary disability indemnity that could be paid to three times average annual earnings, and limited the number of weeks within which it could be paid to 240 weeks from the date of injury.

An amendment in 1947 increased the maximum amount that could be paid from "three times" average annual earnings to "four times" average annual earnings, but retained the time limit within which it could be paid as 240 weeks from the date of injury. (Stats. 1947, ch. 1033, § 4 (emphasis added).)

Following an amendment in 1955, section 4656 provided in full: "Aggregate disability payments for a single injury causing temporary disability shall not extend beyond 240 weeks from the date of injury." (Stats. 1955, ch. 956, § 5 (emphasis added).) The 1955 amendment removed the limit on the maximum amount of temporary disability indemnity that could be paid, but retained the time limit within which it could be paid as 240 weeks from the date of injury.

Section 4656 was amended again in 1959 to provide in full: "Aggregate disability payments for a single injury causing temporary disability shall not extend for more than 240 compensable weeks within a period of five years from the date of injury." (Stats. 1959, ch. 1189, § 12 (emphasis added).) With that amendment, the Legislature continued the 240-week time limit, but modified that time limit to provide that it could not extend beyond five years from the date of injury.

In 1978, section 4656 was amended again to state separate time limits for temporary total disability and temporary partial disability as follows:

"Aggregate disability payments for a single injury occurring prior to January 1, 1979, causing temporary disability shall not extend for more than 240 compensable weeks within a period of five years from the date of the injury.

"Aggregate disability payments for a single injury occurring on or after January 1, 1979, causing temporary partial disability shall not extend for more than 240 compensable weeks within a period of five years from the date of the injury." (Stats. 1978, ch. 937, § 1 (emphasis added).)

The earlier time limits on temporary disability indemnity were continued for all injuries occurring prior to January 1, 1979, but, for injuries occurring on or after that date, the amendment effectively eliminated the time limit for temporary total disability. However, for injuries on or after January 1, 1979, the amendment continued to provide that the time limits for temporary partial disability were 240 weeks within five years from the date of injury.**[Editor's Note:** Commissioner Brass dissented.]

In *Cruz v. Auto Dealers Compensation of California, Inc. v. WCAB* (2007) 72 Cal. Comp. Cases __ and Kirkpatrick v. Dominican Santa Cruz Hospital (2007)

72 Cal. Comp. Cases __ the Workers' Compensation Judge found that back surgery is an "amputation" for purposes of Labor Code section 4656(c)(2)(c), thereby allowing for temporary disability indemnity to be paid beyond the new 2–year limit.

The Appeals Board in an En Banc decision, *Cruz v. Mercedes Benz of San Francisco* (SFO 0501425) dated September 5, 2007 held that the common sense meaning of an amputation applies to loss of limb or part there of including digits. Consequently, the Board overrules the obsurd results in *Cruz* and *Kirpatrick* above.

The 104–week temporary disability indemnity is also applicable to industrial disability leaves. *Salmon v. State of California Dept. of Transp.* (34 CWCR 301).

Intentionally blank

§ 9A.0   DETERMINATION OF COMPENSABILITY, TEMPORARY DISABILITY, PERMANENT DISABILITY, NEED FOR MEDICAL CARE AND OTHER ISSUES

§ 9A.3   Labor Code section 4061 Procedure to Determine Permanent Disability Rating: Unrepresented Injured Worker (Effective April 19, 2004).

Page 698, Column 1, insert following fifth paragraph

See *Ward v. City of Desert Hot Springs, et al.* (2006) 71 Cal. Comp. Cases 1313, in Section 9A.7 of this book, for a significant panel decision, where the Board stated, in part:

A defendant cannot compel an applicant to attend a medical evaluation that would violate the provisions of Section 4060(c) and 4062.2 and that would generate an inadmissible medical report." The Board was referring to Labor Code Section 4064(d) reports... .

§ 9A.6   Procedure to Object to a Medical Determination Made by the Treating Physician Concerning Medical Issues Not Covered by Section 4060 or 4061 and Not Subject to Utilization Review Under Section 4610: Represented Employee (Effective January 1, 2005)

Page 703, Column 1, sixth paragraph, insert following '... additional evaluation'

If prior to being represented an applicant has requested and received a QME panel from the Administrative Director but becomes represented before the panel QME's evaluation is performed the applicant is not precluded from requesting a new QME panel pursuant to Section 4062.2.

Commenting on this in Romero v. Costco Wholesale (2007) 72 Cal. Comp. Cases 824, the Board stated:

Defendant seeks removal to the Appeals Board from the Order issued by the workers' compensation administrative law judge (WCJ) on October 2, 2006. In that order, the WCJ found that applicant sustained an admitted industrial injury to her neck and upper extremities while employed by defendant as a cashier during a period through September 4, 2005. In relevant part, the WCJ further found that the prior qualified medical evaluator (QME) panel, which consisted of three medical doctors and was issued by the Division of Workers' Compensation's Medical Unit (medical unit) while applicant was not represented by an attorney, has become inappropriate to resolve the parties' dispute over medical treatment recommended by applicant's treating physician because applicant, now represented by an attorney, wants to select from a new QME panel consisting of chiropractors. Accordingly, the WCJ ordered the medical unit to issue a new QME panel, comprised of three chiropractors.

Defendant contends that the WCJ erred in ordering a new panel to be issued and, instead, that applicant should be evaluated by the QME, Peter Salamon, M.D., an orthopedic surgeon, that defendant selected from the prior panel. Defendant argues that it properly followed the procedure set forth in Labor Code sections 4062 and 4062.1 for obtaining a panel QME while applicant was not represented by an attorney and that applicant is not entitled to a new QME panel now that she (Footnote 1) is represented by an attorney.

Applicant filed an answer to defendant's petition for removal.

I.

We have considered the allegations raised in defendant's petition and applicant's answer thereto, as well as the content of the WCJ's Report and Recommendation.

We hold, for purposes of sections 4062.1(e) and 4062.2(e), that an employee has "received" a comprehensive medical–legal evaluation when the employee attends and participates in the medical evaluator's examination. Here, although a QME panel issued while applicant was unrepresented, and defendant selected a physician from that panel, applicant never attended and participated in an examination by that physician. Accordingly, we will deny removal and, thereby, affirm the WCJ's order for a new QME panel.

II.

The relevant facts do not appear to be disputed.

Applicant sustained an admitted industrial injury to her neck and upper extremities while employed by defendant as a cashier during a period through September 4, 2005, as the cumulative result of her work duties.

While applicant was not represented by an attorney, her treating physician issued a report recommending physical therapy, including pool therapy. Defendant objected to the requested medical treatment, pursuant to section 4062, and advised applicant in writing of the applicable procedure to resolve the dispute. When defendant did not receive a response to its objection, it requested that the medical unit issue a QME panel comprised of three medical doctors. The medical unit, on May 22, 2006, issued the QME panel.

Meanwhile, on May 18, 2006, applicant became represented by an attorney. The parties attempted, unsuccessfully, to select an agreed medical evaluator and, when no agreement was reached, defendant subsequently scheduled an appointment for applicant's examination by Dr. Salamon, an orthopedic surgeon it selected from the QME panel.

Applicant, in the interim, selected a different treating physician, a chiropractor, and asserted that she is entitled to a new QME panel, compromised of chiropractors rather than orthopedic surgeons, to resolve the parties' medical treatment dispute. When the medical unit declined to issue a new panel as requested by applicant, she petitioned the Appeals Board for permission to obtain a new panel. The WCJ, subsequently, issued the disputed October 2, 2006, Order requiring the medical unit to issue a new QME panel, comprised of three chiropractors.

III.

Section 4062, subdivision (a), provides, in relevant part:

"If either the employee or employer objects to a medical determination made by the treating physician ... the objecting party shall notify the other party in writing of the objection within 20 days of receipt of the report if the employee is represented by an attorney or within 30 days of receipt of the report if the employee is not represented by an attorney. ... If the employee is represented by an attorney, a medical evaluation to determine the disputed medical issue shall be obtained as provided in Section 4062.2, and no other medical evaluation shall be obtained. If the employee is not represented by an attorney, the employer shall immediately provide the employee with a form prescribed by the medical director with which to request assignment of a panel of three qualified medical evaluators, the evaluation shall be obtained as provided in Section 4062.1 and no other medical evaluation shall be obtained."

In turn, section 4062.1 provides, in relevant part:

"(a) If an employee is not represented by an attorney, the employer shall not seek agreement with the employee on an agreed medical evaluator, nor shall an agreed medical evaluator prepare the formal medical evaluation on any issues in dispute.

"(b) If either party requests a medical evaluation pursuant to Section 4060, 4061, or 4062, either party may submit the form prescribed by the administrative director requesting the medical director to assign a panel of three qualified medical evaluators in accordance with Section 139.2. However, the employer may not submit the form unless the employee has not submitted the form within 10 days after the employer has furnished the form to the employee and requested the employee to submit the form. The party submitting the request form shall designate the specialty of the physicians that will be assigned to the panel.

"(c) Within 10 days of the issuance of a panel of qualified medical evaluators, the employee shall select a physician from the panel to prepare a medical evaluation, the employee shall schedule the appointment, and the employee shall inform the employer of the selection and the appointment. If the employee does not inform the employer of the selection within 10 days of the assignment of a panel of qualified medical evaluators, then the employer may select the physician from the panel to prepare a medical evaluation. ...

"(d) The evaluator shall give the employee, at the appointment, a brief opportunity to ask questions concerning the evaluation process and the evaluator's background. The unrepresented employee shall then participate in the evaluation as requested by the evaluator unless the employee has good cause to discontinue the evaluation. For purposes of this subdivision, "good cause" shall include evidence that the evaluator is biased against the employee because of his or her race, sex, national origin, religion, or sexual preference or evidence that the evaluator has requested the employee to submit to an unnecessary medical examination or procedure. If the unrepresented employee declines to proceed with the evaluation, he or she shall have the right to a new panel of three qualified medial evaluators from which to select one to prepare a comprehensive medical evaluation. If the appeals board subsequently determines that the employee did not have good cause to not proceed with the evaluation, the cost of the evaluation shall be deducted from any award the employee obtains.

"(e) If an employee has received a comprehensive medical–legal evaluation under this section, and he or she later becomes represented by an attorney, he or she shall not be entitled to an additional evaluation."

Furthermore, section 4062.2 provides, in relevant part:

"(a) Whenever a comprehensive medical evaluation is required to resolve any dispute arising out of an injury or a claimed injury occurring on or after January 1, 2005, and the employee is represented by an attorney, the evaluation shall be obtained only as provided in this section.

"(b) If either party requests a medical evaluation pursuant to Section 4060, 4061, or 4062, either party may commence the selection process for an agreed medical evaluator by making a written request naming at least one proposed physician to be the evaluator. The parties shall seek agreement with the other party on the physician, who need not be a qualified medical evaluator, to prepare a report resolving the disputed issue. If no agreement is reached within 10 days of the first written proposal that names a proposed agreed medical evaluator, or any additional time not to exceed 20 days agreed to by the parties, either party may request the assignment of a three–member panel of qualified medial evaluators to conduct a comprehensive medical evaluation. ...

[¶] ... [¶]

"(e) If an employee has received a comprehensive medical–legal evaluation under this section, and he or she later ceases to be represented, he or she shall not be entitled to an additional evaluation."

Therefore, section 4062.1 controls the procedure by which the parties may obtain a medical evaluation to address a disputed issue pursuant to sections 4060, 4061, or 4062 when the employee is not represented by an attorney, and section 4062.2 controls the procedure, for injuries and alleged injuries occurring on or after January 1, 2005, when the employee is represented by an attorney. Pursuant to subdivision (e) of those sections, an additional evaluation may not be obtained when the employee either changes from being unrepresented by an attorney to being represented or ceases being represented after previously having an attorney where the "employee has received a comprehensive medical–legal evaluation" under either 4062.1 or 4062.2. (Emphasis added.) We conclude that a comprehensive medical–legal evaluation is "received" when the employee attends and participates in the medical evaluator's examination.

Here, while applicant was unrepresented, defendant objected to her treating physician's recommendation for physical therapy and advised applicant in writing of the applicable procedure to resolve the dispute. When defendant did not receive a response to its objection from applicant, it requested and obtained from the administrative director a QME panel of medical doctors on May 22, 2006, pursuant to section 4062.1.

In the meantime, on May 18, 2006, applicant became represented by an attorney. The parties attempted, unsuccessfully, to select an agreed medical evaluator and, when no agreement was reached, defendant subsequently scheduled an appointment for applicant's examination by Dr. Salamon, an orthopedic surgeon it selected from the QME panel. However, because applicant had not attended and participated in the examination by the panel QME when she changed from being not represented by an attorney to being represented, she had not "received" a comprehensive medical–legal evaluation pursuant to section 4062.1 and is, therefore, not precluded from requesting a new QME panel pursuant to section 4062.2.

Therefore, the WCJ did not err in ordering the medical unit to issue a new QME panel consisting of chiropractors, the specialty designated by applicant as the party submitting the request for the panel, pursuant to section 4062.2. Accordingly, we will deny removal.

For the foregoing reasons,

IT IS ORDERED that removal from the Order of October 2, 2006, is DENIED.

———————

Footnote 1. All further statutory references are to the Labor Code.

§ 9A.7 Defendant is Not Entitled to Rebut an Opinion by a QME Selected From a Panel by Securing a Section 4050 Exam

Page 705, Column 1, insert following ninth paragraph

In a significant panel decision, *Ward v. City of Desert Hot Springs, et al.* (2006) 71 Cal. Comp. Cases 1313, the Board held that for industrial injuries allegedly occurring on or after January 1, 2005, in which an injured worker is represented by an attorney, disputes regarding compensability must be resolved pursuant to Labor Code section 4060(c) and the procedures provided in Labor Code section 4062.2. Further, the Board held evaluations regarding compensability may not be allowed pursuant to Labor Code section 4064(d) and if such a report is obtained it is not admissible at a hearing. The Board stated, in part:

On July 31, 2006, we granted defendant's petition for reconsideration or, in the alternative, petition for removal of the Findings and Order of May 5, 2006, wherein the workers' compensation administrative law judge (WCJ) found, in relevant part: (1) that applicant claims to have sustained industrial injury to her psyche and in the form of various internal conditions from June 8, 2000, through June 8, 2005, while employed by defendant as a development services manager; and(2) that medical reports regarding the compensability of applicant's psychiatric and internal injury claims must be obtained through the procedures established by Labor Code sections 4060 and 4062.2; therefore, defendant is not entitled to obtain a medical evaluation of applicant pursuant to Labor Code section 4064(d). (Footnote 1)

Defendant contends that it is entitled to a medical evaluation of applicant under section 4064(d), arguing that the amendments to section 4060, together with the enactment of section 4062.2, did not eliminate the right of either party to obtain at its own expense an admissible medical report from an evaluation obtained pursuant to section 4064(d). Applicant did not file an answer to defendant's petition, however, the WCJ prepared a Report and Recommendation (Report) suggesting that defendant's petition be dismissed, to the extent it seeks reconsideration, and that it be denied, to the extent it seeks removal.

For the reasons set forth in the WCJ's Report, which we adopt and incorporate by reference, and for the following reasons, we hold that for claimed industrial injuries occurring on or after January 1, 2005, in which the employee is represented by an attorney: (1) pursuant to section 4060(c), medical disputes regarding the compensability of the alleged industrial injury must be resolved solely by the procedure provided in section 4062.2; and (2) an evaluation regarding compensability may not be obtained pursuant to section 4064(d) – and, if obtained, it is not admissible.

Therefore, the Order of May 5, 2006, properly denied defendant's request to compel applicant's examination pursuant to section 4064(d). Accordingly, we will vacate our Order Granting Reconsideration of July 31, 2006, dismiss defendant's petition for reconsideration, as the disputed order is not a final order from which reconsideration may properly be sought, and deny removal.

BACKGROUND

Applicant claims to have sustained cumulative psychiatric and internal injury while employed as a development services manager by defendant from June 8, 2000, through June 8, 2005.

Defendant denied liability for the alleged industrial injury. On or about November 4, 2005, defendant arranged for applicant to be examined by Stuart Meisner, Ph.D. Applicant, through her counsel, refused to be examined by Dr. Meisner, asserting that the examination was impermissible pursuant to sections 4060 and 4062.2. Defendant sought to compel applicant's examination with Dr. Meisner and, on April 25, 2006, the parties proceeded to trial regarding the issue of whether defendant is entitled to obtain, and therefore compel, applicant's medical evaluation pursuant to section 4064(d).

On May 5, 2006, the WCJ issued the Findings and Order of which defendant sought reconsideration or, in the alternative, from which it seeks removal. In the Opinion on Decision, the WCJ explained, in relevant part, that, in cases in which the worker is represented, section 4060 allows an examination regarding the compensability of an alleged injury occurring on or after January 1, 2005, to be obtained only by the procedure set forth in section 4062.2 and that defendant "cannot circumvent" section 4060 and section 4062.2 by scheduling an examination pursuant to section 4064(d).

DISCUSSION

Section 4060 applies to "disputes over the compensability of any injury." Subsection (c) of section 4060, as amended pursuant to Senate Bill (SB) 899 (Stats. 2004, ch. 34, § 34), provides as follows:

"If a medical evaluation is required to determine compensability at any time after the filing of the claim form, and the employee is represented by an attorney, a medical evaluation to determine compensability shall be obtained only by the procedure provided in Section 4062.2." (Italics added.)"

In turn, section 4062.2(a), as adopted by SB 899 (Stats. 2004, ch. 34, § 18), provides as follows:

"Whenever a comprehensive medical evaluation is required to resolve any dispute arising out of an injury or a claimed injury occurring on or after January 1, 2005, and the employee is represented by an attorney, the evaluation shall be obtained only as provided in this section." (Italics added.)"

Section 4062.2 then goes on to provide that, in represented cases involving injuries on or after January 1, 2005, the parties shall either select an agreed medical examiner (AME) or select a qualified medical examiner (QME) from a three–member panel.

Accordingly, because sections 4060(c) and 4062.2(a) state that medical evaluations "shall be obtained only" by the procedure they specify, it appears the Legislature intended that this procedure be the exclusive method for obtaining medical evaluations on compensability. In this regard, we observe that "shall" is mandatory language. (Lab. Code, § 15; see also, Smith v. Rae–Venter Law Group (2003) 29 Cal. 4th 345, 357 [58 P.3d 367, 127 Cal. Rptr. 2d 516]; Jones v. Tracy School Dist. (1980) 27 Cal. 3d 99, 109 [611 P.2d 441, 165 Cal. Rptr. 100]; Morris v. County of Marin (1977) 18 Cal. 3d 901, 907 [559 P.2d 606, 136 Cal. Rptr. 251] [42 Cal. Comp. Cases 131].) Moreover, in the context of sections 4060(c) and 4062.2(a), the word "only" denotes a restriction or limitation. (See Funk & Wagnalls Standard College Dictionary (1974), p. 944 (defining "only" to mean "[i]n one manner" and "[s]olely; exclusively").)

Section 4064(d), provides in relevant part:

"[N]o party is prohibited from obtaining any medical evaluation or consultation at the party's own expense. In no event shall an employer or employee be liable for an evaluation obtained in violation of subdivision (b) of Section 4060. All comprehensive medical evaluations obtained by any party shall be admissible in any proceeding before the appeals board except as provided in subdivisions (d) and (m) of Section 4061 and subdivisions (b) and (e) of Section 4062." "

Prior to its amendment by SB 899, former section 4060(c) also allowed any party to "obtain additional reports at their own expense." However, that provision was deleted from section 4060(c) by SB 899 and was replaced with the current reference to the procedure requiring, in cases involving a represented employee, that "a medical evaluation to determine compensability shall be obtained only by the procedure provided in Section 4062.2."

However, section 4064 was not amended by SB 899. Thus, if there is an irreconcilable conflict between section 4064(d), on the one hand, and sections 4060 and 4062.2, on the other, then the latter statutes prevail as the more recently amended and enacted. (Cf. Collection Bureau of San Jose v. Rumsey (2000) 24 Cal. 4th 301, 310 [6 P.3d 713, 99 Cal. Rptr. 2d 792]; Fuentes v. Workers' Comp. Appeals Bd. (1976) 16 Cal. 3d 1, 7 [547 P.2d 449, 128 Cal. Rptr. 673] [41 Cal. Comp. Cases 42]; Graham v. Workers' Comp. Appeals Bd. (1989) 210 Cal. App. 3d 499, 505 [258 Cal. Rptr. 376] [54 Cal. Comp. Cases 160].) Here, the language of section 4064(d), allowing a party to obtain a medical evaluation or consultation at its own expense, cannot be harmonized either with SB 899's deletion of the language of former section 4060(c), which had permitted parties to obtain a additional examinations at their own expense, or with SB 899's inclusion of language in current sections 4060(c) and 4062.2(d) that medical evaluations "shall be obtained only" by the procedure they specify. Accordingly, sections 4060(c) and 4062.2(d), as the most recently enacted or amended statutes, control over section 4064(d).

Moreover, an interpretation that section 4064(d) cannot be used to circumvent the QME/AME procedures of sections 4060(c) and 4062.2(a) is consistent with recent

Court of Appeal decisions rejecting other attempts to circumvent the former QME/AME statutes. (Nunez v. Workers' Comp. Appeals Bd. (2006) 136 Cal. App. 4th 584, 594 [38 Cal. Rptr. 3d 914] [71 Cal. Comp. Cases 161] (section 4050 may not be used to circumvent former section 4060 et seq.); Cortez v. Workers' Comp. Appeals Bd. (2006) 136 Cal. App. 4th 596 [38 Cal. Rptr. 3d 922] [71 Cal. Comp. Cases 155] (neither section 4050 nor section 5701 may be used to circumvent former section 4060 et seq.); see also, Regents of the Univ. of Cal. v. Workers' Comp. Appeals Bd. (Ford) (1995) 60 Cal. Comp. Cases 1246 (writ den.).)

Therefore, for claimed industrial injuries occurring on or after January 1, 2005, in which the worker is represented by an attorney, we hold that disputes regarding the compensability of the alleged industrial injury must be resolved, pursuant to section 4060(c), by the procedure provided in section 4062.2 and that an evaluation regarding compensability may not be obtained pursuant to section 4064 – and, if a report is obtained, it is not admissible.

Consistent with this holding, we conclude that the WCJ's Order denying defendant's request to compel applicant to undergo a medical evaluation pursuant to section 4064(d) was proper. A defendant cannot compel an applicant to attend a medical evaluation that would violate the provisions of sections 4060(c) and 4062.2 and that would generate an inadmissible medical report. (Cf. Cortez v. Workers' Comp. Appeals Bd., *supra*, 136 Cal. App. 4th at p. 602 [71 Cal. Comp. Cases at p. 160].)

Accordingly, we will vacate our prior Order Granting Reconsideration and dismiss defendant's petition for reconsideration, as the Order of May 5, 2006, is not a final order. (Lab. Code, § 5900; Maranian v. Workers' Comp. Appeals Bd. (2000) 81 Cal. App. 4th 1068 [97 Cal. Rptr. 2d 418] [65 Cal. Comp. Cases 650]; Safeway Stores, Inc. v. Workers' Comp. Appeals Bd. (Pointer) (1980) 104 Cal. App. 3d 528 [163 Cal. Rptr. 750] [45 Cal. Comp. Cases 410]; Kaiser Foundation Hospitals v. Workers' Comp. Appeals Bd. (Kramer) (1978) 82 Cal. App. 3d 39 [147 Cal. Rptr. 30] [43 Cal. Comp. Cases 661].) Moreover, we will deny defendant's alternative request for removal, as the WCJ properly resolved the apparent conflict between sections 4060, 4062.2, and 4064... .

Footnote 1. All further statutory references are to the Labor Code.

Page 705, Column 2, first paragraph, following '...medical evaluation.' insert the following:

In *County of Santa Barbara, et. al. v. WCAB (Rucker)* (2006) 71 Cal. Comp. Cases 1449, the Board found defendant's QME report inadmissible where the defendant changed QMEs without showing that the original QME was unavailable and without showing good cause to change QMEs. The Board, in upholding the trial judge's finding that the QME's report was inadmissible, quoted the judge as follows:

In the case of *Ali vs. American Home Assurance Company* (2000) 28 CWCR 17, Writ denied [*sic*], the Appeals Board panel held that the same Qualified Medical Examiner is to be used throughout the entire process of the case to the extent possible. In *Ali* defendant had used one psychiatrist to examine the applicant on certain issues, and later had used a different psychiatrist as a QME to examine the applicant on other issues. The Appeals Board panel found that the intent of sections 4061 through 4067 reflected a legislative intent to limit the number of examinations and examining doctors, and that an up to date evaluation from the same doctor who had previously examined the applicant is required unless the original examining doctor is no longer available.

In this case defendant used Dr. Shlensky to examine the applicant as a QME on November 22, 2000. Subsequently in 2005 defendant had applicant reexamined as a QME in psychiatry by Dr. Stapen. Defendant has not made any showing that Dr. Shlensky was no longer available to conduct a reevaluation of the applicant, or other good cause why a change in examining doctors is reasonable. In fact, defendant did obtain a subsequent updated QME report from Dr. Shlensky, dated August 3, 2005... .

Intentionally blank

§ 10.0   PERMANENT DISABILITY BENEFITS

§ 10.4   Progressive Disease

Page 714, Column 1, second paragraph, insert following '...purposes....'

In a case involving hepatitis, the Board held it was not precluded by Labor Code section 5804 from reserving jurisdiction over the employee's issue of permanent disability where the firefighter (applicant) had contracted hepatitis in the course and scope of his employment. The Court of Appeal, Fourth District, in *City of Calexico v. WCAB (Valdez)* (2006) 71 Cal. Comp. Cases 817, in upholding the Board, stated, in part:

Rodolfo Valdez contracted Hepatitis C while working in the City of Calexico's fire department. He underwent various treatments for the disease, without success. Although his primary symptom at this time is fatigue his long–term prognosis is poor and he will most likely die from complications of the disease. In the meantime, he requires ongoing medical treatment, including new therapies as they become available and a possible liver transplant.

Because Valdez's symptoms of fatigue preclude him from performing heavy work, the parties stipulated to a 32–percent permanent disability rating. However, since Hepatitis C is a progressive disease, Valdez requested that the Workers' Compensation Administrative Law Judge (WCJ) reserve jurisdiction over permanent disability beyond the five–year statute of limitations in Labor Code section 5804. The request was first made at a pre–trial conference in 2002, but resolution of the issue was deferred until 2005 for further development of the medical evidence. Following a trial on this issue, the WCJ determined that reservation of jurisdiction was appropriate under General Foundry Service v. Workers' Comp. Appeals Bd. (Jackson) (1986) 42 Cal. 3d 331 [228 Cal. Rptr. 243, 721 P.2d 124, 51 Cal. Comp. Cases 375].

The City petitioned the Workers' Compensation Appeals Board (WCAB) for reconsideration. The WCAB denied reconsideration and the City filed this petition seeking review of the WCAB's decision. The City contends the

WCAB's decision is not supported by substantial evidence and the WCAB did not have the power to reserve jurisdiction in this instance. The City further contends that the WCAB may have violated Labor Code section 5908.5 because the WCAB's decision did not adequately respond to all of the issues raised by the City. We conclude review is not warranted in this case.

When an employee contracts an insidious, progressive occupational disease, the WCAB has the power to tentatively rate an employee's permanent disability and order advances based on the tentative ruling. The WCAB may then reserve jurisdiction for a final determination when the employee's condition is permanent and stationary or the employee becomes totally permanently disabled. (General Foundry Service, *supra*, 42 Cal. 3d at p. 333.) "Permanent and stationary" typically means the employee's condition has reached maximum medical improvement or the employee's condition has been stable for a reasonable period of time. (Id. At pp. 334–335.) For an employee with an insidious, progressive disease, "permanent and stationary" also means the employee's condition is not reasonably anticipated to change under usual medical standards. (Id. at p. 335; Sweeney v. Industrial Acc. Com. (1951) 107 Cal. App. 2d 155, 159 [236 P.2d 651, 16 Cal. Comp. Cases 264]; see also California Ins. Guarantee Ass'n v. Workers' Comp. Appeals Bd. (2006) 136 Cal. App. 4th 1528, 1539, fn.9 [39 Cal. Rptr. 3d 721, 71 Cal. Comp. Cases 139].)

In this case, the evidence indicates that Valdez's condition is permanent and stationary as that phrase is usually applied. He has exhausted his treatment options and his condition has remained stable for a period of time. However, the evidence also indicates his condition is not permanent and stationary as that phrase applies to an insidious, progressive disease. His disease has not responded to any of the available therapies and, consequently, his condition is expected to deteriorate further, eventually leading to his death. Accordingly, the WCAB properly applied the General Foundry Service case by tentatively rating Valdez's permanent disability and reserving jurisdiction for a final determination.

Nonetheless, the City argues that the WCAB is constrained by Valdez's doctor's determination that Valdez's condition is "permanent and stationary" and by Valdez's stipulation to the same effect. This argument ignores the fact that "permanent and stationary" has multiple meanings. This argument also ignores the context in which the doctor's determination and the stipulation occurred–after all treatment options had been exhausted, after Valdez's condition had been stable for a period of time, and while a request to reserve jurisdiction was pending. In this context, the most reasonable interpretation of the doctor's determination and the stipulation are that Valdez's condition was stable enough to be tentatively rated.

The City further argues that the WCAB had no power to reserve jurisdiction because the request to reserve jurisdiction occurred after the five–year statute of limitations had expired. However, the record indicates Valdez first requested reservation of jurisdiction in 2002, well within the five–year limitations period. Although the WCAB deferred the request until 2005, there is no evidence that the City objected to the deferral on procedural or other grounds. Moreover, as long as the request is first made within the limitations period, the WCAB has jurisdiction to decide the matter after the limitations period has expired. (See, e.g., Nicky Blair's Restaurant v. Workers' Comp. Appeals Bd. (1980) 109 Cal. App. 3d 941, 953–954 [167 Cal. Rptr. 516, 45 Cal. Comp. Cases 876].)

Finally, the City argues the WCAB may have violated Labor Code section 5908.5 because the WCAB's decision did not adequately respond to the City's statute of limitations argument. The record indicates otherwise. The WCAB's decision adopts and incorporates the WCJ's report and recommendation on reconsideration. The WCJ's reports [sic] concludes that, based on the legal principles articulated in the General Foundry Service case, the five–year limitations period does not preclude the reservation of jurisdiction under the facts presented in this case.

The petition is denied. Valdez's request to have the matter remanded to the WCAB for an award of supplemental attorney fees is also denied...

§ 10.11 Multiple Injuries Suffered Contemporaneously (Avoiding Overlap)

Page 724, Column 1, insert the following after heading

(Multiple Disability Rating Schedule)

Page 724, Column 1, fourth paragraph insert following '...100 percent.'

In holding that the multiple disability table was not repealed by SB 899, the Board in *Attia v. WCAB* (2006)

71 Cal. Comp. Cases 1825, stated, in part:

It is true that section 4664(c)(2) prevents a rating for a single injury from being more than 100% and that prevention of a rating higher than 100% is one of the rationales for use of the MDT. But it is not the only rationale. The introduction to the Scheduling for Rating Permanent Disabilities of April 1997, page 1–9, under the title "Pyramiding," instructs the disability rater to avoid pyramiding for multiple parts of the body by 1) rating each body part as if it stood alone before arriving at the final rating; and 2) avoid *pyramiding* by use of the MDT. Pyramiding of disability is "the unrealistic results achieved from simply adding factors together without consideration of the scheme of relative severity of disabilities established by the Schedule." (April 1997 Schedule, under "Pyramiding," page 1–9.) [*Emphasis by WCAB*]

Newly enacted section 4664 does not change the necessity of avoiding pyramiding as so defined. The MDT has been in the rating manual since at least 1966. We are not aware of any case law or other evidence holding that the MDT is manifestly unjust, and applicant has not presented such evidence in the instant case...

In addition, we disagree with applicant's interpretation of *Dykes, supra,* as being instructive on this issue. *Dykes* did not deal with the issue either explicitly or implicitly... .

Page 725, Column 2, change heading to read as follows:

§ 10.12 Determining Extent of Permanent Disability for Compensable Claims Arising on or After April 19, 2004

§ 10.18 How to Determine the Compensable Permanent Disability Award if the Overall Disability Is Composed of Industrial and Nonindustrial Factors, After April 1, 1972

Page 734, Column 2, third paragraph, insert following '...being rated.'

In *Welcher v. WCAB* (2006) 71 Cal. Comp. Cases 315, the Appeals Board held that *Fuentes, supra,* is still good law and that the appropriate method of apportioning permanent disability indemnity under SB 899 was first to determine the overall percentage of permanent disability and then to subtract the percentage of permanent disability caused by other factors. **[Editor's Note:** See Section 31A(10) for the California Supreme Court's reasoning in upholding this case]

Page 737, Column 1, second paragraph insert following '...own negligence.'

In *City of Santa Clara, PSI, et. al. v. WCAB (Navarette)* (2005) 70 Cal. Comp. Cases 1713, the Appeals Board held that Labor Code section 4664 (b), as enacted by SB 899, did not invalidate the holding in *Wilkinson* wherein it was held that permanent disability from successive injuries may be combined if the injuries became permanent and stationary at the same time, and quoted the trial judge as stating:

Nothing in SB 899 or Labor Code § 4664(b) reverses or renders inoperative the holding of the *Wilkinson* case. *Wilkinson* found an exception to the prohibitions of former Labor Code § 4750, which generally precluded combining permanent disabilities from a [*sic*] "prior" and "later" injuries. With the repeal of section 4750, Defendants argue, the Board may no longer combine permanent disabilities in any cases. In my view, Defendants have the argument backwards. Former section 4750 was a limiting section that prevented the combining of disabilities from multiple injuries, and *Wilkinson* was an exception to that limitation. If anything, the repeal of section 4750 gives more freedom to combine disabilities from multiple injuries. In this Applicant's cases, however, no extension of *Wilkinson* is required because the injuries would, of necessity, have become P&S at the same time for the reasons previously discussed.

Labor Code § 4664(b) only provides a conclusive presumption that Applicant retained *at least* the 29% level of permanent disability previously awarded. Nothing in that statute, or its legislative history, shows any intention to bar proof that the prior permanent disability has *increased*. In enacting section 4664(b) the Legislature was addressing claims that despite a prior adjudicated award of permanent disability, the worker had achieved medical rehabilitation from that disability and was now entitled to a new PD award, for a different injury, that apportioned out less or none of the prior permanent disability award. I made no finding in these cases that Applicant had achieved any reduction in his awarded permanent disability–on the contrary, I made the exact opposite finding, that his prior level of permanent disability still existed and has now substantially increased. Defendants will, of course, receive full credit against the current Findings and Award for permanent disability benefits they have already paid for Applicant's knee disability... .

§ 10.19 How to Determine the Permanent Disability Award if Two or More Injuries to the Same Part of the Body Become Permanent and Stationary at the Same Time, and Similar or Different Employers are Involved.

Permanent Disability: Minors Earnings

Page 743, Column 1, seventh paragraph, insert directly following heading 'Permanent Disability: Minors Earnings'

Minors, according to the Civil Code, are persons who have not reached the age of majority. The age of majority is 18 years of age. The earning capacity of minors is viewed differently by the Legislature when it comes to permanent disability benefits. Subject to the usual maximum and minimum limits for permanent disability benefits, the earnings are considered only "probable" per Labor Code section 4455.

The fact that someone is a minor, however, for the purpose of calculating earnings capacity for temporary disability, does not change the manner in which the calculation is done. It is the same calculation used for adults.

§ 10.20 Permanent Disability Indemnity Cannot be Paid Until the Right to All Temporary Disability Resulting From All Injuries Has Expired.

Page 743, Column 2, fifth paragraph, insert new topic following '...926.'

Credit for Overpayment of Temporary Disability Indemnity

The allowance of credit for overpayment of temporary disability indemnity against a permanent disability award is discretionary with the Board. See Section 9.3(A) of this book for full discussion of cases involving claims for credit.

§ 10.22   Aggregate Permanent Disability Indemnity Charts.

<u>Page 743, Column 2, seventh paragraph, insert following "with the Labor Code."</u>

Under workers' compensation law, a permanent disability rating involves the use of a specialized formula. The formula considers an employee's age and occupation at the time of injury or illness, diminished future earning capacity, plus any permanent impairments that the examining physician finds. The permanent disability rating produces a specific dollar amount. The exact amount depends on the date of injury, the percentage of disability and the employee's average weekly earnings at the time of injury. Once permanent disability payments begin, the employee receives payments every two weeks at his or her permanent disability rate. This rate is equal to two–thirds of employee's average weekly wages at the time of injury, subject to the established minimum and maximum rates. The following chart lists the maximum permanent disability payments for each percentage range.

Maximum Permanent Disability Payments					
Rating	07/1/96–12/31/02	2003	2004	2005	2006–2007
Up to 14.75%	$140	$185	$200	$220	$230
15% to 24.75%	$160	$185	$200	$220	$230
25% to 69.75%	$170	$185	$200	$220	$230
70% to 99.75%	$230	$230	$250	$270	$270
Minimum per week:	$ 70	$100	$105	$105	$130

If the permanent disability is total, the indemnity is based upon the average weekly earnings determined under Section 4453 and must be paid during the remainder of the injured employee's life. *Lab. C. Sec. 4659(b)*

See Appendix M for Defense Pro Inc., Permanent Disability Charts.

§ 10.24   Determining Percentage of Permanent Disability For Compensable Claims Arising on or After January 1, 2005 and Before, In Certain Circumstances

<u>Page 744, Column 1, fifth paragraph, insert following '...the years.'</u>

A new Schedule was adopted by the Administrative Director effective January 1, 2005.

<u>Page 745, Column 1, third paragraph, insert following '...for emphasis].'</u>

In *SCIF v. WCAB (Echeverria)* (2007) 72 Cal. Comp. Cases 33, the Court of Appeal, First District, held that a *single–sentence medical report* by a treating physician stating the physician's belief that permanent disability

was within a reasonable medical probability as a result of a July 21, 2004 industrial injury *did not* support the use of the 1997 Schedule. The Court stated, in part:

The State Compensation Insurance Fund (State Fund) petitions for review (Labor Code § 5952) (Footnote 1) of the decision after reconsideration of the Workers' Compensation Appeals Board (Board) affirming an award to respondent, Jose C. Echeverria. State Fund contends that the award was improperly calculated using the 1997 schedule for rating permanent disabilities (PD schedule) in effect prior to January 1, 2005, rather than the new PD schedule that went into effect on that date. As will be seen, we agree and annul the award.

Section 4660 governs the calculation of permanent disability awards. As amended effective April 19, 2004, the section requires regular revisions in the rating schedule and, as relevant here, provides generally that "[t]he schedule and any amendment thereto or revision thereof shall apply prospectively and shall apply to and govern only those permanent disabilities that result from compensable injuries received or occurring on and after the effective date of the adoption of the schedule . . . ." (§ 4660, subd. (d).) But the section also provides that for "compensable claims arising before January 1, 2005," the new schedule "shall apply to the determination of permanent disabilities when there has been either no comprehensive medical–legal report *or no report by a treating physician indicating the existence of permanent disability*." (§ 4660, subd. (d), emphasis ours.)

It is undisputed that Echeverria, employed as a logger, was injured on July 21, 2004. He sustained injury to his right ankle and low back, arising out of and in the course of his employment. State Fund is the insurer for Echeverria's employer, Hiatt Logging. His injuries became permanent and stationary on June 16, 2005.

On November 15, 2004, Echeverria's counsel faxed a letter to his treating physician, Dr. Morales. The letter read:

"Dear Dr. Morales:

"Changes have occurred in the California Workers' Compensation system. Elements of those changes may affect your patient's rights to permanent disability benefits.

"Please advise by merely signing and dating this letter if you believe permanent disability, as that term is now defined, is a reasonable medical probability as a result of your patient's industrial injury.

"This is very important so your immediate attention to this matter would be greatly appreciated.

"*I believe permanent disability is within reasonable medical probability emanating from this injury.*" Below this last sentence, spaces for date and signature appeared and contained the date of "12–15–04" written in and what appears to be the signature of Dr. Morales.

The Board agreed with the Workers' Compensation Judge (WCJ) that this last sentence, *read in light* of Dr. Morales's other reports, constituted a "report by a treating physician indicating the existence of permanent disability" within the meaning of section 4660, subdivision (d). The WCJ found, as well, that nothing in section 4660, subdivision (d) requires an opinion that the worker is permanent and stationary, and noted that the statute "does not require a medical determination of the amount of permanent disability. It only requires an indication of the existence of permanent disability."

Initially, State Fund argues that the WCJ could not consider Dr. Morales's statement because it did not meet the requirements for a physician's report specified in section 9785 of title 8 of the California Code of Regulations. (§ 4603.2, subd. (a).) We need not address the point, however, because State Fund made no objection to the introduction of the report at trial, thereby waiving the issue. (*Lumbermen's Mut. Cas. Co. v. Ind. Acc. Com.* (1946) 29 Cal. 2d 492, 499–500 [175 P.2d 823, 11 Cal. Comp. Cases 289]; § 5709.)

Nor do we need to address State Fund's contention that a [*sic*] "a report by a treating physician indicating the

existence of permanent disability" is necessarily contradicted and defeated by the fact that a worker is temporarily totally disabled and has not been declared permanent and stationary at the time the report is issued. As Echeverria acknowledges, in reviewing the Boards' decision, we must determine whether in view of the entire record substantial evidence supported the Board's findings. (*Braewood Convalescent Hospital v. Workers' Comp. Appeals Bd.* (1983) 34 Cal. 3d 159, 164 [666 P.2d 14, 193 Cal. Rptr. 157, 48 Cal. Comp. Cases 566]). On this record, assuming without deciding that the statute "only requires an indication of the existence of permanent disability," we conclude the Board's decision is not supported by substantial evidence.

" '[O]ur function . . . is to consider the weight or persuasiveness of all of the evidence, as contrasted with that tending to support the [B]oard's decision . . . .' [Citation.]" (*Rosas v. Workers' Comp. Appeals Bd.* (1993) 16 Cal. App. 4th 1692, 1702 [20 Cal. Rptr. 2d 778, 58 Cal. Comp. Cases 313].) A medical opinion is not substantial evidence if it is based on an inadequate history, speculation or guess. (*Escobedo v. Marshalls* (2005) 70 Cal. Comp. Cases 604, 620 [Appeals Board en ban opinion].) " '[W]hen the Board relies upon the opinion of a particular physician in making its determination, it may not isolate a fragmentary portion of his report... and disregard other portions that contradict or nullify the portion relied on; it must give fair consideration to all of his findings... .' [Citation.]" (*Rosas, supra,* at p. 1702.) And, to be substantial evidence, a medical report must indicate the reasoning behind the doctor's opinion. (*Granado v. Workmen's Comp. App. Bd.* (1968) 69 Cal. 2d 399, 407 [445 P.2d 294, 71 Cal. Rptr. 678, 33 Cal. Comp. Cases 647].)

In this case, the Board read Dr. Morales's December 14, 2004 single sentence statement in conjunction with all of his other reports, from September 20, 2004, through November 11, 2005. Dr. Morales's reports of September 20, 2004, and November 11, 2004, describe spinal range of motion problems which persist throughout his examinations of Echeverria. Nothing in the reports, however, appears to tie the range of motion and pain symptoms to Dr. Morales's December 15, 2004 prediction of permanent disability. To the contrary, the reports make no mention at all of prognosis, but instead simply declare that Echeverria remained temporarily totally disabled. None of the reports

provide any reasoning to support Dr. Morales's December 15, 2004 conclusion.

The Board's decision to apply the 1997 PD schedule is not supported by substantial evidence. It is therefore annulled and the matter is remanded to the Board for further proceedings consistent with this opinion... .

Footnote 1. Further statutory references are to this code.

In *Costco v. WCAB (Chavez)* (2007) 72 Cal. Comp. Cases 582, the Court of Appeal, First District, in a published decision, held that in order for the 1997 rating Schedule to apply to a given applicant's injuries, there must be an *indication of permanent disability* in a medical report prior to January 1, 2005.

The Court reasoned that the clear intent of the statute was to bring as many cases as possible under the new rating Schedule. In so holding, the Court declined to follow the applicant's interpretation of Labor Code section 4660(d) that any comprehensive medical report prior to January 1, 2005 was sufficient to preserve the 1997 rating Schedule. The Court looked first to the language of Labor Code section 4660(d) pertaining to the applicant's argument, then to the remaining circumstances in Labor Code section 4660 allowing for preservation of the 1997 Schedule and found that all of the other circumstances were consistent with the aim of bringing claims under the new Schedule based upon the American Medical Association Guidelines.

The Court further held that in order for the 1997 rating Schedule to apply based upon the notice requirement concurrent with the last payment of temporary disability, the last day of temporary disability must have occurred before January 1, 2005.

In so reasoning, the Court rejected the argument that the duty to issue the notice at a future date is triggered by the first payment of temporary disability. The Court again noted that this interpretation is inconsistent with the intent of the Legislature in enacting the provisions of Labor Code section 4660(d) and held that as the actual notice is not to be sent until the last payment of temporary disability, it is the date that the notice is actually to be sent that is to be considered for purposes of determining the correct rating Schedule to apply. The Court stated, in part:

Costco Wholesale Corporation and its third party claims administrator Sedgwick Claims Management Services (collectively, Costco) petitioned for review of the decision of the Workers' Compensation Appeals Board (Board) affirming an award to respondent Jorge Chavez (Chavez). Costco contends the award was improperly calculated using the 1997 schedule for rating permanent disabilities that was in effect before January 1, 2005, rather than the new schedule that went into effect on that date. We agree and annul the award.

I. BACKGROUND

Chavez was employed at a Costco warehouse in Novato. On June 5, 2004, he slipped and fell during the course of his employment, injuring his back, elbow and hip. Chavez was off work for two days and then placed on light duty work, which he continued to do until he was terminated in late 2004.

In September 2004, Chavez was evaluated by Vatche Cabayan, M.D., an orthopedic surgeon and qualified medical examiner. Dr. Cabayan issued a report on September 24, 2004, in which he recommended additional treatment and upgraded {Slip Opn. Page 2} Chavez's lifting restrictions. The report stated, "The patient is not permanent and stationary at this time," and opined that Chavez was "expected to be permanent and stationary hopefully in the next 90 days to 120 days." The report did not state whether any of Chavez's conditions would result in permanent disability. Moses Jacob, D.C., issued a report on October 25, 2005, diagnosing Chavez with back strain, joint disease, and elbow strain and declaring these conditions to be permanent and stationary.

A trial was held before a workers' compensation judge (WCJ). One of the issues presented was whether permanent disability should be rated using the 1997 schedule that was in effect at the time of Chavez's injury in 2004 or the schedule that went into effect on January 1, 2005. The WCJ issued an award that included permanent disability based on the 1997 schedule, a decision that was affirmed by the Board following a petition for reconsideration.

II. DISCUSSION

A. Introduction

Labor Code section 4660 (Footnote 1) governs the calculation of the percentage of permanent disability. Effective April 19, 2004, that statute was amended as part of Senate Bill 899 (2003–2004 Reg. Sess.), a comprehensive workers' compensation reform package, to require regular revisions of the permanent disability rating schedule. A new rating schedule incorporating the American Medical Association Guides to the Evaluation of Permanent Impairment (5th ed.) went into effect on January 1, 2005. This schedule superseded the 1997 rating schedule that was in effect when Chavez was injured in 2004. (See *State Comp. Ins. Fund v. Workers' Comp. Appeals Bd.* (2007) 146 Cal. App. 4th 1311, 1313.)

Section 4660, subdivision (d), provides in relevant part that "[t]he schedule and any amendments thereto or revision thereof shall apply prospectively and shall apply to and govern only those permanent disabilities that result from compensable injuries received or occurring on and after the effective date of the adoption of the schedule." {Slip Opn. Page 3} The statute then lists three exceptions to the rule that the date of injury governs the schedule to be applied. For compensable injuries occurring before 2005, the 2005 schedule will apply when, before January 1, 2005, "there has been either no comprehensive medical–legal report or no report by a treating physician indicating the existence of permanent disability, or when the employer is not required to provide the notice required by Section 4061 to the injured worker." (Section 4660, subd. (d).) In other words, when any of these three circumstances have occurred before January 1, 2005, the percentage of permanent disability will

be calculated using the earlier schedule that was in effect on the date of the injury. (Footnote 2)

The Board concluded that the 1997 schedule applied to Chavez's injury because the report issued by Dr. Cabayan on September 24, 2004, was a qualifying comprehensive medical–legal report. It adopted a finding by the WCJ that the report indicated "the existence of permanent disability," but concluded that such a finding was unnecessary. The Board reasoned, "The correct construction of the pertinent sentence, '*when there has been either no comprehensive medical–legal report or no report by a treating physician indicating the existence of permanent disability*,' requires a report by a treating physician to indicate the existence of permanent disability, while a comprehensive medical–legal report does not require an indication of permanent disability."

B. "Comprehensive Medical–Legal Report"

Costco asserts that the phrase "indicating the existence of permanent disability" applies both to a report by a treating physician and to a comprehensive medical–legal report. It contends the Board's decision must be annulled because the medical–legal report prepared by Dr. Cabayan on September 24, 2004, did not indicate the existence of permanent disability. We agree.

"The Board's conclusions on questions of law do not bind this court." (*Kuykendall v. Workers' Comp. Appeals Bd.* (2000) 79 Cal. App. 4th 396, 402 (*Kuykendall*).) The interpretation of section 4660, subdivision (d), and its phrase "no comprehensive medical–legal report or no report by a treating physician indicating the existence of permanent disability," is a legal issue subject to our de novo review (*Kuykendall, supra*, 79 Cal. App. 4th at p. 402; *California Insurance Guarantee Assn. v. Workers' Comp. Appeals Bd.* (2003) 112 Cal. App. 4th 358, 362.)

In construing section 4660, subdivision (d), the Board relied on the "last antecedent rule" of statutory construction, which generally provides that " 'qualifying words, phrases and clauses are to be applied to the words or phrases immediately preceding and are not to be construed as extending to or including others more remote.' " (*White v. County of Sacramento* (1982) 31 Cal. 3d 676, 680.) The Board reasoned that the lack of a comma after the word "physician" in the phrase, "no comprehensive medical–legal report or no report by a treating physician indicating the existence of permanent disability" (Section 4660, subd. (d)) signifies that the Legislature intended the words "indicating the existence of permanent disability" to apply only to the immediate antecedent–the report by a treating physician. "Evidence that a qualifying phrase is supposed to apply to all antecedents instead of only to the immediately preceding one may be found in the fact that it is separated from the antecedent by a comma." (*White v. County of Sacramento, supra,* 31 Cal. 3d at p. 680; see also *Garcetti v. Superior Court* (2000) 85 Cal. App. 4th 1113, 1120.)

Although grammatically sound, this interpretation of the statute is unpersuasive. "The rules of grammar and canons of construction are but tools, 'guides to help courts {Slip Opn. Page 5} determine likely legislative intent. [Citations.] And that intent is critical. Those who write statutes seek to solve human problems. Fidelity to their aims requires us to approach an interpretive problem not as if it were a purely logical game, like a Rubik's Cube, but as an effort to divine the human intent that underlies the statute.' " (*Burris v. Superior Court* (2005) 34 Cal. 4th 1012, 1017.)

The human problem to be solved by section 4660, subdivision (d), is the rating of permanent disability. That statute provides that the new rating schedule will apply to pre–2005 injuries unless one of three circumstances have occurred before 2005. One such circumstance is the preparation of a physician's report indicating the existence of permanent disability. Another (discussed more fully below) is the obligation of the employer to serve notice under section 4061, which advises the employee of the employer's position regarding the entitlement to permanent disability at the time the last payment of temporary disability is made. These two circumstances are clearly tied to a determination of permanent disability before January 1, 2005. We can conceive of no rational basis for the Legislature to include a third circumstance–the comprehensive medical–legal report at issue here–unless it was tethered to a similar requirement. A pre–2005 medical–legal report written about issues other than permanent disability, or a report that considered the issue but found no permanent disability, would supply no logical basis for applying the earlier rating schedule. It makes little sense to construe the statute as Chavez suggests, and hold that *any* medical–legal report could suffice, when the syntax of the statute is amenable to a construction that requires those reports to contain an indication of permanent disability. (See *Burris v. Superior Court, supra*, 34 Cal. 4th at p. 1018.)

The last antecedent rule does not trump these considerations. One exception to that rule exists when " " "several words are followed by a clause which is applicable as much to the first and other words as to the last, [and] the natural construction of the language demands that the clause be read as applicable to all." ' " (*Garcetti v. Superior Court, supra*, 85 Cal. App. 4th at p. 1121.) A second exception is made when " 'the sense of the entire act requires that a qualifying word or phrase apply to several preceding {Slip Opn. Page 6} [words]. . . .' " "This is, of course, but another way of stating the fundamental rule that a court is to construe a statute ' "so as to effectuate the purpose of the law." ' " (*White v. County of Sacramento, supra*, 31 Cal. 3d at p. 681.) Our reading of section 4660 as a whole is to require that the implementation of the new permanent disability rating schedule be tied to an actual indication of permanent disability prior to the statute's effective date. It follows that the requirement of an indication of permanent disability would apply to medical–legal reports as well as to reports prepared by a treating physician.

Chavez's proposed construction of section 4660, subdivision (d), to require no indication of permanent disability in a comprehensive medical–legal report, would be contrary to the spirit of the statute and the workers' compensation reform package as a whole. Those reforms were enacted as urgency legislation to drastically reduce the cost of workers' compensation insurance, and the Legislature intended that the majority of the changes go into

effect as soon as possible. (Stats. 2004, ch. 34, Section 49, p. 75; *Brodie v. Workers' Comp. Appeals Bd.* (May 3, 2007, S146979) ___ Cal. 4th ___ [2007 Cal. LEXIS 4334 at p. 34]; *Green v. Workers' Comp. Appeals Bd.* (2005) 127 Cal. App. 4th 1426, 1441.) The adoption of a new permanent disability rating scale was part of this scheme. The purpose of the reform package is not served by an interpretation of section 4660, subdivision (d), that delays the implementation of the new rating scale based on medical–legal reports that give no indication of permanent disability, and indeed, may have nothing to do with that subject.

Finally, we observe that section 4658, subdivision (d)(4), is a parallel provision that pertains to the computation of permanent disability payments and contains the necessary comma that Chavez claims is missing in section 4660, subdivision (d): "For compensable claims arising before April 30, 2004, the schedule provided in this subdivision shall not apply to the determination of permanent disabilities when there has been either *a comprehensive medical–legal report or a report by a treating physician, indicating the existence of a permanent disability*, or when the employer is required to provide the notice required by Section 4061 to the injured worker." (Italics added.) There would be no reason for the Legislature to have a different type of medical–legal report serve as the demarcation for permanent disability ratings and permanent disability compensation schedules.

We hold that under section 4660, subdivision (d), a medical–legal report, like a treating physician's report, must contain an indication of permanent disability to trigger use of the pre–2005 rating schedule. Although the WCJ and the Board both found that Dr. Cabayan's 2004 report indicated the existence of permanent disability, this finding is not supported by substantial evidence. (See *State Comp Ins. Fund v. Workers' Comp. Appeals Bd., supra*, 146 Cal. App. 4th at p. 1315.) The report stated that Chavez's condition was not permanent and stationary and it gave no opinion whatsoever about whether Chavez would suffer from permanent disability. Chavez has tacitly acknowledged as much by his failure to offer any argument regarding the evidence of permanent disability in opposition to Costco's writ. The Board's rating of permanent disability under the 1997 schedule cannot be upheld on the basis of a pre–2005 medical–legal report because there was no qualifying report indicating the existence of permanent disability. (Footnote 3)

C. Notice Under Section 4061

Chavez argues that the Board's decision should be upheld because a second circumstance listed in section 4660, subdivision (d), rendered the 1997 schedule applicable to his case. He contends that prior to January 1, 2005, Costco was required to {Slip Opn. Page 8} provide the notice required by section 4061 to the injured worker, thus triggering the earlier schedule. We disagree. (Footnote 4)

Section 4061 provides in relevant part, "(a) Together with the last payment of temporary disability indemnity, the employer shall, in a form prescribed by the administrative director pursuant to Section 138.4, provide the employee one of the following: (1) Notice either that no permanent disability indemnity will be paid because the employer alleges the employee has no permanent impairment or limitation resulting from the injury or notice of the amount of permanent disability indemnity determined by the employer to be payable. . . . (2) Notice that permanent disability indemnity may be or is payable, but that the amount cannot be determined because the employee's medical condition is not yet permanent and stationary. . . ."

Temporary disability benefits were paid to Chavez from October 20, 2004, until June 28, 2005. Costco was required to provide notice under section 4061, "together with the last payment of temporary disability indemnity" in June 2005. Because that notice was not required before January 1, 2005, the 2005 permanent disability rating schedule applies to Chavez's case.

Chavez argues that Costco was required to give notice under section 4061 before January 1, 2005, because the duty to provide such notice arises when temporary disability payments are commenced rather than when they are terminated. (Footnote 5) While the statute is not a model of linguistic clarity, its intent is clear. The intent is to apply the new rating schedule to injuries suffered prior to 2005 in three circumstances: (1) when a comprehensive medical–legal report issued prior to 2005 indicates permanent disability, {Slip Opn. Page 9} (2) when a report from a treating physician issued prior to 2005 indicates permanent disability, and (3) when an employer has been required to give notice under section 4061 prior to 2005 concerning its intentions regarding payment of permanent disability benefits. This interpretation supports the legislative goal of bringing as many cases as possible under the new workers' compensation law. (See Stats. 2004, ch. 34, Section 49, p. 75; *Green v. Workers' Comp. Appeals Bd., supra,* 127 Cal. App. 4th at p. 1441.) If, as Chavez argues, the commencement of any temporary disability payments before 2005 required application of the rating schedule in effect at the time of injury, this legislative goal would be defeated. It would be rare, indeed, for temporary disability payments not to be owed or paid prior to 2005 for an injury occurring in or before 2004. Such a limited exception would be pointless where the Legislature could more easily have drafted the statute to apply the schedule in effect on the date of injury in all cases.

Chavez's proposed interpretation of the section 4061 notice exception under section 4660, subdivision (d), would also render meaningless that portion of the statute that requires application of the 2005 schedule if, before 2005, there was "no comprehensive medical–legal report or no report by a treating physician indicating the existence of permanent disability . . . ." Temporary disability will have been paid or owed before January 1, 2005, in virtually every case where a qualified medical examiner or doctor prepared a pre–2005 medical report indicating permanent disability, meaning there would be no practical need for the other two exceptions. " '[A]n interpretation that renders statutory language a nullity is obviously to be avoided.' " (*Branciforte Heights, LLC v. City of Santa Cruz* (2006) 138 Cal. App. 4th 914, 937.)

Because it is uncontested that the last temporary disability payment to Chavez was made after January 1, 2005, and

because, as previously discussed, no pre–2005 medical legal report indicated the existence of permanent disability, Chavez's permanent disability must be rated under the 2005 schedule.

III. DISPOSITION

The petition for writ of review is granted. That portion of the award applying the 1997 permanent disability rating schedule is annulled, and the case is remanded for recalculation of Chavez's permanent disability rating under the schedule that went into effect on January 1, 2005. In all other respects, the award is affirmed. The parties shall bear their own costs herein... .

———

Footnote 1. Further statutory references are to the Labor Code.

Footnote 2. The full text of section 4660, subdivision (d), states: "The schedule shall promote consistency, uniformity, and objectivity. The schedule and any amendment thereto or revision thereof shall apply prospectively and shall apply to and govern only those permanent disabilities that result from compensable injuries received or occurring on and after the effective date of the adoption of the schedule, amendment or revision, as the fact may be. For compensable claims arising before January 1, 2005, the schedule as revised pursuant to changes made in legislation enacted during the 2003–04 Regular and Extraordinary Sessions shall apply to the determination of permanent disabilities when there has been either no comprehensive medical–legal report or no report by a treating physician indicating the existence of permanent disability, or when the employer is not required to provide the notice required by Section 4061 to the injured worker."

Footnote 3. Since issuing its opinion in the instant case, the Board has reversed its position and now construes the phrase "indicating the existence of permanent disability" to apply to comprehensive medical–legal reports as well as treating physicians' reports. (*Baglione v. AIG* (Apr. 6, 2007, SJO 0251644) __ Cal. Comp. Cases __ [2007 WL 1039088 (Cal. W.C.A.B.)].) The en banc decision in *Baglione* is not binding on this court, but we consider it for the limited purpose of pointing out the contemporaneous interpretation and application of the workers' compensation laws by the Board. (*Smith v. Workers' Comp. Appeals Bd.* (2000) 79 Cal. App. 4th 530, 537, fn. 2.)

Footnote 4. Although this was not the basis for the Board's decision, we consider the argument on the merits because the notice requirement was discussed by the parties in the trial briefs before the WCJ and because an administrative agency's erroneous reasoning is generally not prejudicial error where the result is correct. (See *Board of Administration v. Superior Court* (1975) 50 Cal. App. 3d 314, 319.)

Footnote 5. A similar argument was recently rejected by the Board in its en banc decision in *Pendergrass v. Duggan Plumbing and State Compensation Insurance Fund* (Apr. 6, 2007, SAL 0110868) __ Cal. Comp. Cases __ [2007 WL 1039089 (Cal. W.C.A.B.)]. **[Editor's Note:** The above is the first in what many expect to be several decisions that will issue from the Courts of Appeal on the application of the correct rating Schedule. Currently, multiple cases are pending before various District Courts of Appeal for determination of similar issues.]

In *Costa v. Hardy Diagnostics, SCIF* (2006) 71 Cal. Comp. Cases 1797, the Board stated, in part:

The New PDRS Applies To Injuries Before January 1, 2005, Unless One Of The Exceptions To Section 4660(d) Applies

Applicant also contends that the new PDRS does not apply to injuries prior to January 1, 2005, and therefore, his cumulative back injury ending in August 2004, should have been rated under the former PDRS. As set forth above, however, we determined en banc in *Aldi, supra,* 71 Cal. Comp. Cases 783, that contrary to applicant's argument, the PDRS adopted by the AD effective January 1, 2005, does apply to injuries which occurred before that date, pursuant to section 4660(d) "when there has been either no comprehensive medical–legal report or no report by a treating physician indicating the existence of permanent disability, or when the employer is not required to provide the notice required by section 4061 to the injured worker." Applicant has not alleged that any of these exceptions to section 4660(d) pertain here. Accordingly, we reject his contention, and find that his injury was properly rated under the new PDRS... .

Likewise, in *Pendergrass v. Duggar Plumbing, et. al.* (2007) 72 Cal. Comp. Cases 456, on April 6, 2007 the Board reviewed an earlier En Banc decision on the case (72 Cal. Comp. Cases 95, holding that defendant's duty to provide the notice required by Section 4061 arises when the first payment of temporary disability indemnity is made, which thereby triggers the 1997 Schedule) and in reversing its earlier decision, a majority of the Board stated:

Accordingly, we now reverse that prior en banc decision. Therefore, for the reasons discussed below, we will grant defendant's petition for reconsideration, rescind our prior decision, and affirm in its entirety the Findings and Order issued by the WCJ on December 11, 2006, applying the 2005 Schedule.

II.

Subsection (d) of section 4660 provides as follows:

"The [2005] schedule shall promote consistency, uniformity, and objectivity. The schedule and any amendment thereto or revision thereof shall apply prospectively and shall apply to and govern only those permanent disabilities that result from compensable injuries received or occurring on and after the effective date of the adoption of the schedule, amendment or revision, as the fact may be. For compensable claims arising before January 1, 2005, the [2005] schedule as revised pursuant to changes made in legislation enacted during the 2003–04 Regular and Extraordinary Sessions shall apply to the determination of permanent disabilities when there has been either no comprehensive medical–legal report or no report by a treating physician indicating the existence of permanent

disability, or when the employer is not required to provide the notice required by Section 4061 to the injured worker."

In turn, subsection (a) of section 4061 provides as follows:

"Together with the last payment of temporary disability indemnity, the employer shall, in a form prescribed by the administrative director pursuant to Section 138.4, provide the employee one of the following:

"(1) Notice either that no permanent disability indemnity will be paid because the employer alleges the employee has no permanent impairment or limitations resulting from the injury or notice of the amount of permanent disability indemnity determined by the employer to be payable. The notice shall include information concerning how the employee may obtain a formal medical evaluation pursuant to subdivision (c) or (d) if he or she disagrees with the position taken by the employer. The notice shall be accompanied by the form prescribed by the administrative director for requesting assignment of a panel of qualified medical evaluators, unless the employee is represented by an attorney. If the employer determines permanent disability indemnity is payable, the employer shall advise the employee of the amount determined payable and the basis on which the determination was made and whether there is need for continuing medical care.

"(2) Notice that permanent disability indemnity may be or is payable, but that the amount cannot be determined because the employee's medical condition is not yet permanent and stationary. The notice shall advise the employee that his or her medical condition will be monitored until it is permanent and stationary, at which time the necessary evaluation will be performed to determine the existence and extent of permanent impairment and limitations for the purpose of rating permanent disability and to determine the need for continuing medical care, or at which time the employer will advise the employee of the amount of permanent disability indemnity the employer has determined to be payable. If an employee is provided notice pursuant to this paragraph and the employer later takes the position that the employee has no permanent impairment or limitations resulting from the injury, or later determines permanent disability indemnity is payable, the employer shall in either event, within 14 days of the determination to take either position, provide the employee with the notice specified in paragraph (1)." "

In *Aldi v. Carr, McClellan, Ingersoll, Thompson & Horn* (2006) 71 Cal. Comp. Cases 783, 785 (Appeals Board en banc), writ den. sub nom. *Aldi v. Workers' Comp. Appeals Bd.* (2006) 71 Cal. Comp. Cases 1822, we specifically held that, " . . . the revised permanent disability rating schedule, adopted by the Administrative Director of the Division of Workers' Compensation, effective January 1, 2005, applies to injuries occurring on or after that date, and that in cases of injury occurring prior to January 1, 2005, the revised permanent disability rating schedule applies, unless one of the exceptions delineated in the third sentence of section 4660 (d) is present."

Section 4660(d) states that the new schedule will apply if, before January 1, 2005, the "employer is not required to provide the notice required by Section 4061 to the injured worker." Section 4061(a) requires that notice be provided "[t]ogether with the last payment of temporary disability indemnity . . . ." Here, temporary disability indemnity was paid continuously from June 30, 2004, through July 19, 2005. Pursuant to the plain language of sections 4660(d) and 4061, defendant's obligation to provide notice did not arise until the actual last payment of temporary disability indemnity in July 2005. Contrary to the dissenting opinion, the fact that this quoted portion of section 4660(d) uses the present tense rather than the past tense does not alter the plain meaning of section 4660(d).

Additionally, the language of section 4660(d) must be viewed in light of the entire statutory scheme of which it is a part. (See *Chevron U.S.A., Inc. v. Workers' Comp. Appeals Bd.* (*Steele*) (1999) 19 Cal. 4th 1182 [969 P.2d 613, 81 Cal. Rptr. 2d 521] [64 Cal. Comp. Cases 1].) In this regard, we note that the first sentence of section 4660(d) clearly expresses the legislative intent to "promote consistency, uniformity, and objectivity" by adopting the revised rating schedule. Section 4660(d) was adopted as part of a comprehensive reform of the workers' compensation statutes (Senate Bill 899). Section 49 of Senate Bill 899 provides a clear expression of the legislative intent:

"This act is an urgency statute necessary for the immediate preservation of the public peace, health, or safety within the meaning of Article IV of the Constitution *and shall go into immediate effect*. The facts constituting the necessities are: In order to provide relief to the State from the effects of the current workers' compensation crisis *at the earliest possible time, it is necessary for this act to take effect immediately.*"

(Emphasis added.)"

Thus, the Legislature intended that the changes in the law take effect "immediately" so as to provide relief "*at the earliest possible* time." In *Aldi, supra*, 71 Cal. Comp. Cases at p. 793, fn. 6, we noted the Court of Appeal's observation in *Green v. Workers' Comp. Appeals Bd.* (2005) 127 Cal. App. 4th 1426, 1441 [26 Cal. Rptr. 3d 527] [70 Cal. Comp. Cases 294] that section 49 reflects " 'the Legislature's intent to solve the [workers' compensation crisis] as quickly as possible by bringing as many cases as possible under the umbrella of the new law.' " (See also *Kleemann v. Workers' Comp. Appeals Bd.* (2005) 127 Cal. App. 4th 274 [25 Cal. Rptr. 3d 448] [70 Cal. Comp. Cases 133]; *Rio Linda Union School District v. Workers' Comp. Appeals Bd.* (*Sheftner*) (2005) 131 Cal. App. 4th 517 [31 Cal. Rptr. 3d 789] [70 Cal. Comp. Cases 999].)

Consequently, if section 4660(d) is to be construed so as to effectuate the Legislature's intent to provide relief "*at the earliest possible time*", it must be construed in the manner that ensures that the revised rating schedule applies "*at the earliest possible time*." We believe that interpreting section 4660(d) so that the triggering of the employer's obligation to provide section 4061 notice attaches with the last payment of temporary disability accomplishes this Legislative intent.

The dissent's analysis would render an entire subdivision meaningless, in violation of the basic rule that interpretations are to be avoided that render some words surplusage, defy common sense, or lead to mischief or absurdity. (*Fields v. Eu* (1976) 18 Cal. 3d 322, 328 [556 P.2d 729, 134 Cal. Rptr. 367]; Cal. *Insurance Guarantee Assn. v. Workers' Comp. Appeals Bd. (White/Torres)* (2006) 136 Cal. App. 4th 1528, 1534 [39 Cal. Rptr. 3d 721] [71 Cal. Comp. Cases 139, 141–142].)

Accordingly, we will grant reconsideration, rescind the Opinion and Order Granting Reconsideration and Decision After Reconsideration of January 24, 2007, and affirm the initial Findings and Order of December 11, 2006, in its entirety... .

Three members of the Board dissented, stating:

We dissent. We would deny reconsideration and affirm our prior en banc decision.

We first observe that the Appeals Board, as a judicial body, should not respond to hastily drafted legislation with the goal of affording relief to businesses "at the earliest possible time," as a catch–all for every situation. Nowhere does SB 899 state that such relief must come at the expense of injured workers, or that the express words of statutes are to be recrafted to suit this goal. Words are the tools of lawyers, courts, and legislators. We must assume that the words used were the words the Legislature intended to use. In construing the effect those words may have in everyday practice, we must look at the plain language before us and not presume that the Legislature meant something other than it stated in the statutes.

Therefore, as explained in our prior en banc decision in this case, we conclude, for purposes of determining the applicable permanent disability rating schedule pursuant to Labor Code section 4660, that an employer's duty "to provide the notice required by" section 4061 arises with the first payment of temporary disability indemnity. Therefore, if the first date of compensable temporary disability occurred prior to January 1, 2005, then the 1997 Schedule applies to determine the extent of permanent disability.

The new permanent disability rating schedule mandated by section 4660 was adopted by the Administrative Director in Rule 9805 (Cal. Code Regs., tit. 8, § 9805), and became effective on January 1, 2005.

We conclude for purposes of section 4660 that an employer's duty "to provide the notice required by" section 4061 arises with the first payment of temporary disability indemnity. There is no obligation to provide any section 4061 notice unless temporary disability indemnity has been paid or should have been paid. Thus, as soon as the first date of compensable temporary disability occurs, the duty to give section 4061 notice comes into existence. This is an absolute duty, and there is no circumstance under which an employer may avoid that duty.

We distinguish here between when the duty arises and when the duty is required to be executed. The duty arises when the first payment of temporary disability indemnity is made. The execution of that duty occurs when the last payment of temporary disability indemnity is made. If there is no temporary disability, no duty to give notice under section 4061 arises.

We also note that the first two exceptions to the general provision of section 4660(d), applying the 2005 Schedule to pre–2005 injuries are phrased in the past perfect tense (i.e. "when there has been"), but that the third exception is phrased in the present tense (i.e. "is not required"). Thus, the most persuasive interpretation of that phrase is that the employer "is required" to provide the notice required by section 4061 once the first payment of temporary disability indemnity is made, although the timing of the notice is contingent on the duration of temporary disability indemnity and the content of the notice is contingent on the employee's medical condition at the time of "the last payment" of temporary disability indemnity.

Thus, here, defendant's duty to provide the notice required by section 4061 arose on June 30, 2004, when the first payment of temporary disability indemnity was made. Accordingly, the 1997 Schedule applies to calculate applicant's permanent disability. Therefore, we would deny reconsideration of the Opinion and Order Granting Reconsideration and Decision After Reconsideration of January 24, 2007.

See also *Owens v. WCAB* (2007) 72 Cal. Comp. Cases 148.

Likewise, In *Baglione v. Hertz Car Sales, et. al.* (2007) 72 Cal. Comp. Cases 444 the Appeals Board in an En Banc decision issued on April 6, 2007 reversed its earlier En Banc decision (72 Cal. Comp. Cases 86, holding that a medical report from a treating physician need only be a compensable medical–legal report in order for the former PDRS to be applied) and held that for the 1997 Schedule to apply under Section 4660(d), the existence of permanent disability must have been indicated in either a pre–2005 comprehensive medical–legal report or a pre–2005 report from a treating physician and not simply a comprehensive medical–legal report issued prior to January 1, 2005. A majority on the Board stated, in part:

Accordingly, we now reverse our prior en banc decision. Therefore, for the reasons discussed below, we will grant defendant's petition for reconsideration, rescind our prior decision, and affirm in its entirety the Findings and Award issued by the WCJ on October 23, 2006, applying the 2005 Schedule.

II.

Section 4660(d) provides as follows:

"The schedule shall promote consistency, uniformity and objectivity. The schedule and any amendment thereto or revision thereof shall apply prospectively and shall apply to and govern only those permanent disabilities that result from compensable injuries received or occurring on and after the effective date of the adoption of the schedule, amendment or revision, as the fact may be. *For compensable claims arising before January 1, 2005, the schedule as revised pursuant to changes made in legislation enacted during the 2003–04 Regular and Extraordinary Sessions shall apply to the determination of permanent disabilities when there has been either no comprehensive medical–legal report or no report by a treating physician indicating the existence of permanent disability, or when the employer is not required to provide the notice required by Section 4061 to the injured worker.*" (Emphasis added.)"

We read the exceptions under section 4660(d) for applying the 1997 Schedule to require that a "comprehensive medical–legal report," as well as a report from a treating physician, must indicate "the existence of permanent disability." We must consider the language in light of the entire statutory scheme of which it is a part. (*Chevron U.S.A., Inc. v. Workers' Comp. Appeals Bd. (Steele)* (1999) 19 Cal. 4th 1182, 1194 [969 P.2d 613, 81 Cal. Rptr. 2d 521] [64 Cal. Comp. Cases 1, 8–9].) In this regard we note that the first sentence of section 4660(d) expresses the legislative intent to "promote consistency, uniformity, and objectivity" by adopting a new schedule. We also note that section 4660(d) was adopted as part of a comprehensive reform of the workers' compensation statutes (SB 899). Section 49 of SB 899 states the legislative intent and reasons for the enactment of SB 899 as follows:

"This act is an urgency statute necessary for the immediate preservation of the public peace, health, or safety within the meaning of Article IV of the Constitution *and shall go into immediate effect.* The facts constituting the necessities are: In order to provide relief to the State from the effects of the current workers' compensation crisis *at the earliest possible time, it is necessary for this act to take effect immediately.*" (Emphasis added.)"

Thus, the Legislature intended the changes in the law it adopted as part of SB 899 to take effect at the earliest possible time. In *Aldi v. Carr, McClellan, Ingersoll, Thompson & Horn* (2006) 71 Cal. Comp. Cases 783, 793, fn. 6 (Appeals Board en banc), writ den. sub nom. *Aldi v. Workers' Comp. Appeals Bd.* (2006) 71 Cal. Comp. Cases 1822, the Appeals Board noted the observation of the Court in *Green v. Workers' Comp. Appeals Bd.* (2005) 127 Cal. App. 4th 1426, 1441 [26 Cal. Rptr. 3d 527] [70 Cal. Comp. Cases 294, 306] that section 49 reflects "the Legislature's intent to solve the [workers' compensation] crisis as quickly as possible by bringing as many cases as possible under the umbrella of the new law." (See also *Kleemann v. Workers' Comp. Appeals Bd.* (2005) 127 Cal. App. 4th 274, 282 [25 Cal. Rptr. 3d 448] [70 Cal. Comp. Cases 133, 137]; *Rio Linda Union School District v. Workers' Comp. Appeals Bd. (Scheftner)* (2005) 131 Cal. App. 4th 517, 529 [31 Cal. Rptr. 3d 789] [70 Cal. Comp. Cases 999, 1007].)

Against this background, we must decide if the Legislature intended that the 2005 Schedule not be used in *all* pre–2005 cases where a comprehensive medical–legal report issued before January 1, 2005, or only in cases where such a report has issued that indicates the existence of permanent disability.

In light of the legislative goal of promoting consistency, uniformity, and objectivity at the earliest possible time, we perceive no rationale for delaying use of the 2005 Schedule merely because a comprehensive medical–legal report has issued. Delaying use of the 2005 Schedule in those cases interferes with this legislative goal and delays the full implementation of section 4660(d). However, we can understand why the Legislature would intend that the rating schedule in effect at the time permanent disability is first indicated should apply to rate that permanent disability.

This exception might facilitate the informal resolution of claims and provide certainty for the parties in concluding a case.

Based on the above, we conclude that the 2005 Schedule should apply in all cases, except those where either a pre–2005 treating physician report indicates the existence of permanent disability or a pre–2005 comprehensive medical–legal report indicates the existence of permanent disability. This conclusion is consistent with the legislative intent expressed in adopting section 4660(d) and the language of the statute. (Footnote 3)

Furthermore, although the reference to a "comprehensive medical–legal report" is not directly antecedent to the phrase "indicating the existence of permanent disability" in section 4660(d), we do not find the mere order of the words to be determinative of the substantive issue presented in light of the overall legislative goal as discussed above. The language and the need to consider the obvious purpose of section 4660(d) requires that we look beyond the mere order of the words to the underlying intent of the statute. In addressing the order of words in a statute, the Supreme Court further noted in *Renee J. v. Superior Court* (2001) 26 Cal. 4th 735, 743–744 [28 P.3d 876, 110 Cal. Rptr. 2d 828] (*Renee J.*):

"A longstanding rule of statutory construction–the 'last antecedent rule'–provides that qualifying words, phrases and clauses are to be applied to the words or phrases immediately preceding and are not to be construed as extending to or including others more remote. Exceptions to the rule, however, have been identified. *One provides that when several words are followed by a clause that applies as much to the first and other words as to the last . . . Another provides that when the sense of the entire act requires that a qualifying word or phrase apply to several preceding words, its application will not be restricted to the last.* This is, of course, but another way of stating the fundamental rule that a court is to construe a statute so as to effectuate the purpose of the law. *Where a statute is theoretically capable of more than one construction [a court must] choose that which most comports with the intent of the Legislature.* Principles of statutory construction are not rules of independent force, but merely tools to assist courts in discerning legislative intent." (Citations and quotations omitted, emphasis added).) (Footnote 4)

Moreover, it has long been held that:

"A fundamental rule of statutory construction is that a court should *ascertain the intent of the Legislature so as to effectuate the purpose of the law*. In construing a statute, our first task is to look to the language of the statute itself. When the language is clear and there is no uncertainty as to the legislative intent, we look no further and simply enforce the statute according to its terms. Additionally, however, *we must consider the [statutory language] in the context of the entire statute and the statutory scheme of which it is a part*. We are required to give effect to statutes according to the usual, ordinary import of the language employed in framing them. If possible, significance should be given to every word, phrase, sentence and part of an act in pursuance of the legislative purpose. *When used in a statute [words] must be construed in context, keeping in mind the nature and*

obvious purpose of the statute where they appear. Moreover, the various parts of a statutory enactment must be harmonized by considering the particular clause or section in the context of the statutory framework as a whole." (*Renee J.*, *supra*, 26 Cal. 4th at p. 743 (citations omitted, emphasis added); cf. *Phelps v. Stostad* (1997) 16 Cal. 4th 23, 32 [939 P.2d 760, 65 Cal. Rptr. 2d 360] [62 Cal. Comp. Cases 863, 868].)"

Thus, our holding that either a comprehensive medical–legal report or a treating physician's report must "indicate the existence of permanent disability . . . " for the exception to apply most comports with the legislative intent and construes that language in the context of the entire statute and statutory scheme of which it is a part.

Finally, we recognize that section 4658(d)(4) provides that the amended schedule of weeks of compensable permanent disability set forth by that subdivision "shall not apply to the determination of permanent disabilities when there has been either a comprehensive medical–legal report or a report by a treating physician, indicating the existence of permanent disability . . . ." We disagree, however, with the dissent's assertion that this section further supports its position (i.e., that the comma after the word "physician" evidences a different legislative intent). On the contrary, given the legislative intent and purpose of the statutes enacted by SB 899, including section 4660(d), as set forth above, the fact that section 4658(d)(4) requires that both the comprehensive medical–legal report and the report by a treating physician indicate the existence of permanent disability for the amended schedule of weeks not to apply, supports our analysis of section 4660(d). In other words, we disagree that the implementation of the 2005 Schedule may be defeated by the omission of a comma.

Therefore, we conclude that the overall purpose of the law requires that section 4660(d) be read to require that the existence of permanent disability exception allowing use of the 1997 Schedule only applies in cases where there has issued either a pre–2005 treating physician report indicating the existence of permanent disability or a pre–2005 comprehensive medical–legal report indicating the existence of permanent disability. (Footnote 5)

Accordingly, we affirm in its entirety the WCJ's decision of October 23, 2006, applying the 2005 Schedule... .

Three members of the Board dissented, stating:

We dissent. We would deny reconsideration and affirm our prior en banc decision.

We first observe that the Appeals Board, as a judicial body, should not respond to hastily drafted legislation with the goal of affording relief to businesses "at the earliest possible time," as a catch–all for every situation. Nowhere does SB 899 state that such relief must come at the expense of injured workers, or that the express words of statutes are to be recrafted to suit this goal. Words are the tools of lawyers, courts, and legislators. We must assume that the words used were the words the Legislature intended to use. In construing the effect those words may have in everyday practice, we must look at the plain language before us and not presume that the Legislature meant something other than it stated in the statutes.

In *Aldi v. Carr, McClellan, Ingersoll, Thompson & Horn* (2006) 71 Cal. Comp. Cases 783, 793 (Appeals Board en banc), writ den. sub nom. *Aldi v. Workers' Comp. Appeals Bd.* (2006) 71 Cal. Comp. Cases 1822, the Appeals Board concluded that the 2005 Schedule mandated by section 4660 is applicable to pending cases where the injury occurred before January 1, 2005, unless one of the exceptions set forth in section 4660(d) applied.

Section 4660(d) can be properly construed in accordance with accepted principles of statutory construction. In this regard, it is important to consider the entire part of the sentence in issue. After stating that the new rating schedule applies prospectively, the Legislature specifically stated that there is an exception for claims arising before January 1, 2005, "when there has been either no comprehensive medical–legal report or no report by a treating physician indicating the existence of permanent disability . . . ."

To properly construe this provision, it is only necessary to apply a longstanding rule of statutory construction: the last antecedent rule. Simply stated, the last antecedent rule means that "qualifying words, phrases and clauses are to be applied to the words of phrases immediately preceding and are not to be construed as extending to or including others more remote." (*Bd. of Port Commrs. v. Williams* (1937) 9 Cal. 2d 381, 389 [70 P.2d 918]; *People v. Corey* (1978) 21 Cal. 3d 738, 742 [581 P.2d 644, 147 Cal. Rptr. 639]; *White v. County of Sacramento* (1982) 31 Cal. 3d 676, 680 [646 P.2d 191, 183 Cal. Rptr. 520] (*White*); *Garcetti v. Superior Court* (Blake) (2000) 85 Cal. App. 4th 1113, 1120 [102 Cal. Rptr. 2d 703].) Evidence that a qualifying phrase is supposed to apply to all antecedents instead of only to the immediately preceding one may be found in the fact that it is separated from the antecedents by a comma. (*White, supra,* 31 Cal. 3d at p. 680; *Blake, supra,* 85 Cal. App. 4th at p. 1120.)

In section 4660(d), the reference to a "report by the treating physician" is the immediately preceding antecedent to the qualifying phrase "indicating the existence of permanent disability," and that qualifying phrase is not separated from "no comprehensive medical–legal report or no report by a treating physician" by a comma. For that reason, the plain language of section 4660(d), as construed by the last antecedent rule, provides that an indication of the existence of permanent disability is only required if the report is by a treating physician. If the report is a "comprehensive medical–legal report," no such qualification applies.

The legislative intent is further shown by the use of the word "or" between "comprehensive medical–legal report *or* report by a treating physician." (Emphasis added.) Use of the disjunctive word "or" in a statute indicates a legislative intent to designate alternative or separate categories. (*White, supra,* 31 Cal. 3d at p. 680; *People v. Smith* (1955) 44 Cal. 2d 77, 78–79 [279 P.2d 33].) Moreover, the two kinds of reports are further distinguished as separate categories by the use of the introductory word "either." The section describes two distinct categories of reports: *either* a "comprehensive medical–legal report" *or* a "report by a treating physician indicating the existence of permanent disability." As to the rationale of the Legislature for drawing this distinction, we note that concerns of predictability and fairness, as discussed in the dissent, would apply equally in cases where either a comprehensive medical–legal report has been prepared or a treating physician has prepared a report indicating the existence of permanent disability.

We also note that section 4658(d)(4) provides that the schedule of weeks of compensable permanent disability set forth by that subdivision "shall not apply to the determination of permanent disabilities when there has been *either a comprehensive medical–legal report or a report by a treating physician, indicating the existence of permanent disability* . . . " As construed by the last antecedent rule, this statute requires that both the comprehensive medical–legal report and the report by a treating physician indicate the existence of permanent disability for the amended schedule of weeks not to apply. Because the language of section 4658(d)(4) is different from the language of section 4660(d), we must assume that this difference is intended. (*American Airlines, Inc. v. County of San Mateo* (1996) 12 Cal. 4th 1110, 1137–1138 [912 P.2d 1198, 51 Cal. Rptr. 2d 251]; *People v. Shabazz* (2004) 125 Cal. App. 4th 130, 149 [22 Cal. Rptr. 3d 472]; *People v. Stewart* (2004) 119 Cal. App. 4th 163, 171 [14 Cal. Rptr. 3d 353]; *Kray Cabling Co. v. County of Contra Costa* (1995) 39 Cal. App. 4th 1588, 1593 [46 Cal. Rptr. 2d 674]; *Campbell v. Zolin* (1995) 33 Cal. App. 4th 489, 497 [39 Cal. Rptr. 2d 348].)

As the issue here is simply addressed by construing the plain language of the statute in accordance with accepted principles of statutory construction, it is not necessary to consider whether the comprehensive medical–legal report indicates the existence of permanent disability. Therefore, we would affirm the prior en banc decision of January 24, 2007, in which we determined that the permanent disability rating schedule that was in effect at the time of Dr. Messinger's June 18, 2004 comprehensive medical–legal report is applicable, and which returned this matter to the trial level to rate applicant's permanent disability under the 1997 Schedule.

Footnote 3. See fn. 2, *supra.*

Footnote 4. See also *In re Marriage of Walker* (2006) 138 Cal. App. 4th 1408, 1421 [42 Cal. Rptr. 3d 325] [construing the phrase "upon request" in Family Code section 1100(e) to apply to the entire last sentence, not just to duties articulated immediately before that phrase]; *Anthony J. v. Superior Court* (2005) 132 Cal. App. 4th 419, 425–426 [33 Cal. Rptr. 3d 677] [citing to *Renee J.* for the proposition that when several words are followed by a clause that applies as much to the first and other words as to the last, the natural construction of the language demands that the clause be read as applicable to all]; Cal. *School Employees Assn v. Governing Bd. of South Orange County Community College Dist.* (2004) 124 Cal. App. 4th 574, 584 [21 Cal. Rptr. 3d 451].

Footnote 5. See fn. 2, *supra.*

Page 745, Column 2, second paragraph, insert following '...this subdivision.'

In *Costa v. Hardy Diagnostics, SCIF* (2006) 71 Cal. Comp. Cases 1797, the Appeals Board, in an En Banc decision held that the Administrative Director's adopting of the new Permanent Disability Rating Schedule was not improper and was valid. The Board stated, in part:

A. To Invalidate The New PDRS, Petitioner Has The Burden Of Showing That The Actions Of The AD Were Arbitrary, Capricious Or Inconsistent With Section 4660

Section 4660 gave the AD some specific directions for adopting the new PDRS. Concerning "the nature of the [employee's] physical injury or disfigurement" under section 4660(a), the new PDRS adopted by the AD was to first incorporate the 5th Edition of the AMA Guides to the Evaluation of Permanent Impairment (subdivision (b)(1)). With respect to an employee's DFEC under section 4660(a), the AD was then required under subdivision (b)(2) to "formulate the adjusted rating schedule based on empirical data and findings from the Evaluation of California's Permanent Disability Rating Schedule, Interim Report (December 2003), prepared by the RAND Institute for Civil Justice [the RAND 2003 Interim Report], and upon data from additional empirical studies." The DFEC was described in subdivision (b)(2) as a "numeric formula based on empirical data and findings that aggregate the average percentage of long–term loss of income resulting from each type of injury for similarly situated employees." The AD was also required under subdivision (c) to "amend the schedule for the determination of the percentage of permanent disability in accordance with this section at least once every five years," and under subdivision (e) "[o]n or before January 1, 2005 . . . [to] adopt regulations to implement the changes made to this section by the act that added this subdivision." (Footnote 13)

B. On This Record Petitioner Has Not Met His Burden Of Proving The New PDRS Invalid

Applicant contends, in essence, that the PDRS adopted by the AD is invalid because (1) the legislative goal established by the RAND 2003 Interim Report adopted in section 4660(b)(2) was to increase permanent partial disability, not decrease it; and (2) the adjustment factor or DFEC is not based on empirical data and findings and on additional empirical studies as required by section 4660(b)(2). (Footnote 14)

We reject applicant's contention that the new PDRS is invalid because it fails to increase permanent partial disability benefits and the RAND 2003 Interim Report adopted in section 4660 by SB 899 established a legislative goal to do so.

We first note that section 4660 is devoid of any language stating that the new PDRS should increase benefits. Moreover, the RAND 2003 Interim Report, in its Preface at page v lists the issues addressed in the report as follows:

"We address several questions: Does the system ensure that the highest compensation goes to the most severely disabled individuals? Do injured workers with impairments to different parts of the body but similar employment outcomes receive similar compensation? Will different physicians evaluating the same injury produce similar ratings? And finally, how can the rating system be changed to improve outcomes for injured workers and employers in California?" "

Thus, the RAND 2003 Interim Report is a study of benefit "equity" and the variability of ratings based on the identity of the evaluating physician, not a study of benefit "adequacy." In this regard, it devotes less than two of its forty–nine pages to reference *previous* work on wage loss replacement rates. We therefore find unpersuasive petitioner's assertion that the Legislature's directive to adopt the RAND 2003 Interim Report is indicative of their intent that the new PDRS should increase benefits, (Footnote 15) and accordingly, we reject this basis for invalidating the new PDRS.

We now address applicant's contention that the new PDRS is invalid because it is not based on empirical data and findings and on additional empirical studies as required by section 4660(b)(2).

Applicant asserts that all of the empirical data and findings from the RAND 2003 Interim Report were "based on ratings assigned under the pre–SB 899 PDRS." Yet section 4660(b)(2) expressly required the AD to formulate the adjusted rating schedule based on those specific data and findings. Also, as set forth by the WCJ in both his opinion on decision and his report and recommendation, the AD who adopted the new PDRS, Andrea Hoch, testified repeatedly at the Senate Labor and Industrial Relations hearing of December 7, 2004 (applicant's exhibit 3), that in arriving at the mathematical formula for the adjusted schedule's DFEC factor, she did in fact use the empirical data and findings from the RAND 2003 Interim Report. Moreover, as further noted by the WCJ, Ms. Hoch's testimony in this regard was corroborated by that of Robert Reville, Ph.D., one of the authors of the RAND 2003 Interim Report. (The WCJ cites to at least twenty different pages where such testimony is given by Ms. Hoch and five pages by Dr. Reville.)

For example, the former AD first testified that the DFEC adjustment was a positive multiplier or an upward adjustment applied to the AMA whole person impairment rating. (Transcript, p. 16, ll. 16–23.) On page 18, line 5 to page 19, line 7 of the transcript from the December 7, 2004 Senate Labor and Industrial Relations hearing, the former AD testified that 22 body injury categories were developed from the empirical data contained in the RAND 2003 Interim Report, and that an adjustment factor of 1.1 to 1.4 was developed to rank the injury categories in terms of proportional wage loss based on the RAND data, those having higher proportional wage loss being at the higher (1.4) end of the scale. (Footnote 16)

The former AD further testified that the DFEC was "based on empirical data and findings that aggregate the average percentage of long term loss of income resulting from each type of injury." (Transcript, p. 57, ll. 14–17.) Dr. Reville testified that he understood the logic of the AD's use of ratios of .45 through 1.81 and adjustment factors of 1.1 to 1.4, and that they were based on numbers RAND provided (transcript, p. 61, ll. 21–23), more specifically, "upon the ratio of ratings to wage loss where ratings were based on the old permanent disability rating system." (Transcript, p. 61, l. 25 to p. 62, l. 3.)

Section 4660(b)(2) further provides, however, that the adjusted rating schedule also is to be based "upon data from additional empirical studies." Dr. Reville testified that RAND did a full search for all potential data and that to his knowledge no other empirical data existed which could have been collected. (Transcript, p. 82, l. 21 to p. 83, l. 11.) (Footnote 17)

Dr. Reville also testified that a proposed "crosswalk" study between the old PDRS and the AMA Guidelines, which was ultimately rejected by the AD, would have provided greater validity, but could not have been completed by the January 1, 2005 statutory deadline. (Transcript, p. 87, ll. 20–23.) A crosswalk or dual rating study would correlate the disability ratings assigned under the former PDRS to those assigned under the new PDRS.

With respect to her determination not to pursue the crosswalk study, the former AD testified as to the lack of time to collect sufficient data (transcript, p. 104, l. 17 to p. 105, l. 5), and her concerns with the validity and usefulness of such a study, i.e., because of the wide range of PD ratings that can result from different physicians and raters looking at the same information (transcript, p. 105, ll. 6–13) and as to correlating the range of ratings under the old system with the AMA whole person impairment rating under the new PDRS. (Transcript, p. 106, ll. 10–15.) In addition to time constraints and these other concerns, the former AD also testified that because the PDRS was an ongoing process, (Footnote 18) she determined that once data was collected under the new PDRS, "you don't need the crosswalk anymore because you use the information you have on the current system to evaluate whether the PD ratings in the current system–the current system meaning the post 1/1/05 system–and the wage loss and whether there need to be adjustments based on that." (Transcript, p. 107, l. 22 to p. 108, l. 12.)

The RAND 2004 Data Paper details the analysis performed by RAND that enabled the AD to utilize the empirical data and findings from the RAND 2003 Interim Report, which was based on the old PDRS, to calculate the DFEC required by the new PDRS. Consistent with the testimony of the former AD and Dr. Reville, the results of the empirical data analysis, as shown in Table 5, page 13, list 22 impairment categories and set forth the ratio of ratings over losses for each category that was determined under the old PDRS, ranging from .45 to 1.81. These impairment categories and ratios were utilized by the AD in formulating the DFEC in the new PDRS.

The record therefore establishes that the AD incorporated the empirical data and findings from the RAND 2003 Interim Report in formulating the adjusted rating schedule (the DFEC) as mandated by section 4660(b)(2), and that in doing so she used the analysis contained in the RAND 2004 Data Paper. The record further reflects that there were no additional empirical studies available from which to formulate the adjusted schedule by the statutory deadline of January 1, 2005, and that the AD, in her discretion, decided that a crosswalk study should not be undertaken. According

to the AD's testimony, this determination was made because of time constraints, her concerns with correlating the ratings under the old and new PDRS, and because of the ongoing review process included in the new PDRS.

Under the totality of these circumstances, applicant has not met his burden of proving that the AD's actions were arbitrary or capricious or inconsistent with section 4660.

We reiterate, as stated in *Tomlinson v. Qualcomm, supra,* 97 Cal. App. 4th at page 940, citing *Ford Dealers Assn. v. Department of Motor Vehicles, supra,* 32 Cal. 3d at page 355: "An administrative regulation is presumptively valid, and if there is a reasonable basis for it, a reviewing court will not substitute its judgment for that of the administrative body; the role of the reviewing court is limited to the legality rather than the wisdom of the challenged regulation." In addition, in the absence of an arbitrary and capricious decision, a reviewing court will defer to an administrative agency's expertise and will not superimpose its own policy judgment upon the agency. (*Pitts v. Perluss, supra,* 58 Cal. 2d at p. 832; *Agricultural Labor Relations Bd., supra,* 16 Cal. 3d at p. 411.)

Here, the evidence demonstrates that the former AD complied with section 4660 by adopting a new PDRS which incorporated the specified AMA Guides and which was adjusted based on empirical data and findings from the RAND 2003 Interim Report. One, of course, may argue that the former AD could have ignored the statutory deadline of January 1, 2005 (see *Plastic Pipe & Fittings Assn. v. California Building Standards Com.* (2004) 134 Cal. App. 4th 1390, 1411) to conduct further studies, including the crosswalk study noted above, because data from additional empirical studies were not available. Nevertheless, the AD's decision to comply with the January 1, 2005 deadline was not arbitrary or capricious, or inconsistent with the authorizing statute, as that deadline was expressly imposed by subdivision (e) of section 4660. Similarly, one may disagree with the former AD's interpretation of the findings and data contained in the RAND 2003 Interim Report and the RAND 2004 Data Paper in computing the adjustment factor for the DFEC. However, nothing in the record before us, including the additional evidence admitted, indicates that at the time the former AD made these determinations, she acted in an arbitrary or capricious manner, or that her adoption of the new PDRS under the circumstances here was inconsistent with section 4660.

With respect to the additional evidence, applicant's Exhibit 6, The Dual Rating Study by Christopher Brigham of the WCIRB, and applicant's Exhibit 7, "Differences in Workers' Compensation Disability and Impairment Ratings under Old and New California Law," by Paul Leigh, Ph.D, we first note that the only mention of these documents in any of the pleadings filed by applicant occurs at page 20 of his petition for reconsideration: " . . . [T]he release of two crosswalk studies by Dr. Paul Leigh and Mr. Christopher Brigham, clearly demonstrate that the AD could have complied with the statutory requirement to link ratings to lost wages within the time limit set in statute." Not only does applicant's statement conflict with the testimony cited above of both Dr. Reville and the former AD, but both studies are dated *after* the January 1, 2005 statutory deadline (May 19, 2005 and March 10, 2005, respectively), and even assuming their validity, there has been no showing that either study is substantially similar in methodology and scope to what would be required for purposes of adjusting the PDRS. In fact, the study by Mr. Brigham, which was done for the purposes of estimating workers' compensation costs in consideration of setting the pure premium rate, was based on a relatively small sample of 250 cases, some of which were not ratable, while the study by Dr. Leigh was not based on a random sample and only one disability evaluator was used to determine ratings under the former PDRS.

With respect to WCAB Exhibit Y, the CHSWC report of February 23, 2006, although it is arguably more relevant than the two studies just cited, and contains thoughtful public policy considerations and analysis, we are not persuaded that its proposed *future* revisions to the PDRS (Footnote 19) successfully challenge the validity of the PDRS at the time it was adopted by the former AD on January 1, 2005. That is, it fails to demonstrate that the actions of the former AD when she adopted the PDRS were arbitrary or capricious or inconsistent with section 4660. As noted above, we must defer to the administrative agency's expertise and are precluded from superimposing our own policy judgment on the former AD's actions or from reviewing the wisdom of those actions... .

Footnote 13. AD Rule 9805 (Cal. Code Regs., tit. 8, § 9805) provides: "The method for the determination of percentages of permanent disability is set forth in the Schedule for Rating Permanent Disabilities, which has been adopted by the Administrative Director effective January 1, 2005, and which is hereby incorporated by reference in its entirety as though it were set forth below. The schedule adopts and incorporates the American Medical Association (AMA) Guides to the Evaluation of Permanent Impairment 5th Edition. The schedule shall be effective for dates of injury on or after January 1, 2005 and for dates of injury prior to January 1, 2005, in accordance with subdivision (d) of Labor Code section 4660, and it shall be amended at least once every five years . . . "

Footnote 14. There is no dispute under section 4660(b)(1) that the appropriate AMA Guides, which comprise the component of a rating before its adjustment by the DFEC under the new PDRS, were timely incorporated by the former AD.

Footnote 15. The Legislature did, however, express its intent to increase PD benefits for more severely injured workers by increasing the number of weeks for each percent of PD over 70% (section 4658(d)(1)). While PD benefits were also increased for workers where an employer (with 50 or more employees) does not offer them regular, modified or alternate work within 60 days of becoming permanent and stationary (section 4658(d)(2)), PD benefits were concurrently decreased by 15% for those employees who were offered such work (section 4658(d)(3)(A)).

Footnote 16. The adjustment factor when applied to the AMA rating will increase the rating by 10% (the 1.1 adjustment) to 40% (the 1.4 adjustment).

Footnote 17. As requested by the acting AD and for the reasons set forth previously, we have taken judicial notice of an excerpt from the AD's PDRS Rulemaking File, The RAND 2004 Data Paper. While we are not necessarily persuaded that this document constitutes "data from additional empirical studies," as has been contended, in that it indicates at page two that "[the] data we use here are the same as used previously by . . . Reville, Seabury and Neuhauser (2003)," which is the December 2003 RAND Interim Report, it is additional evidence at least as to how the DFEC was formulated.

Footnote 18. In addition to the provision in section 4660(c) that the AD "shall amend the schedule for the determination of the percentage of permanent disability in accordance with this section at least once every five years," AD Rule 9805.1(Cal. Code Regs., tit. 8, § 9805.1) provides that the AD shall "(1) collect for 18 months permanent disability ratings under the 2005 Permanent Disability Rating Schedule (PDRS) . . . (2) evaluate the data to determine the aggregate effect of the diminished future earning capacity adjustment on the permanent partial disability ratings under the 2005 PDRS; and (3) revise, if necessary, the diminished future earning capacity adjustment to reflect consideration of an employee's diminished future earning capacity for injuries based on the data collected. If the Administrative Director determines that there is not a sufficient amount of data to perform a statistically valid evaluation, the Administrative Director shall continue to collect data until a valid statistical sample is obtained. If there is a statistically valid sample of data that the Administrative Director determines supports a revision to the diminished future earning capacity adjustment, the Administrative Director shall revise the PDRS before the mandatory five year statutory revision contained in Labor Code section 4660(c)."

Footnote 19. Indeed, as envisioned by AD Rule 9805.1 (Cal. Code Regs., tit. 8, § 9805.1), cited above, the CHSWC report indicates in its conclusion at page 20 that revision of the PDRS is an ongoing process: "Additional data acquired since the adoption of the 2005 schedule can be used to revise the schedule to more nearly accomplish the State's policy goals. Data that will become available in the future can be used to regularly update the schedule to accomplish these goals. Recognizing that any solution is provisional and any solution may be revised and improved as more complete data become available, CHSWC recommends that a process be established to regularly update the schedule using the latest available research to implement the State's policy goals."

The parties may present rebuttal evidence from experts such as vocational rehabilitation consultants to establish a rating under the Permanent Disability Rating Schedule inasmuch as the Schedule is only *prima facie evidence of the percentage of permanent disability to be attributed to each injury covered by the Schedule"*. Commenting on this in *Costa v. Hardy Diagnostics, SCIF*

(2006) 71 Cal. Comp. Cases 1797, the Board, in an En Banc decision stated, in part:

Although SB 899 Made Sweeping Changes To Section 4660, It Did Not Alter The Provision Which Allows The Parties To Present Rebuttal Evidence To A Rating Under The PDRS

As is readily apparent, SB 899 made sweeping changes to section 4660, including, of course, as previously discussed, a wholly new permanent disability rating schedule. The only language remaining from former section 4660, as highlighted above, was that which required taking into account "the nature of the physical injury or disfigurement, the occupation of the injured employee, and his or her age at the time of the injury" (subdivision (a)), and that the PDRS "shall be available for public inspection and, without formal introduction in evidence, shall be prima facie evidence of the percentage of permanent disability to be attributed to each injury covered by the schedule." (Former subdivision (b), now subdivision (c).)

This last provision, that the PDRS "shall be prima facie evidence of the percentage of permanent disability to be attributed to each injury covered by the schedule," has allowed the introduction of rebuttal evidence to ratings under the PDRS. (Footnote 20)

As stated, for example, in *Universal Studios, Inc. v. Workers' Comp. Appeals Bd.* (*Lewis*) (1979) 99 Cal. App. 3d 647, 662–663 [160 Cal. Rptr. 597] [44 Cal. Comp. Cases 1133, 1143]:

"The percentage of disability determined by use of the rating schedule is only prima facie evidence of the percentage of permanent disability to be attributed to each injury. Thus it is not absolute, binding and final. (Lab. Code, § 4660; *Liberty Mut. Ins. Co. v. Industrial Acc. Com* [*Serafin*] [1948], *supra,* 33 Cal. 2d 89 [13 Cal. Comp. Cases 267, 270].) It is therefore not to be considered all of the evidence on the degree or percentage of disability. Being prima facie it establishes only presumptive evidence. Presumptive evidence is rebuttable, may be controverted and overcome." "

In *Glass v. Workers' Comp. Appeals Bd.* (1980) 105 Cal. App. 3d 297, 307 [164 Cal. Rptr. 312] [45 Cal. Comp. Cases 441, 449], the Court cited *Lewis,* among other cases, to conclude that "[t]he Board may not rely upon alleged limitations in the Rating Schedule to deny the injured worker a permanent disability award which accurately reflects his true disability." Thus, in *Nielsen v. Workmen's Comp. Appeals Bd.* (1974) 36 Cal. App. 3d 756, 758 [111 Cal. Rptr. 796] [39 Cal. Comp. Cases 83, 84], the Court found that the customary 13% permanent disability rating applied to skin sensitivity cases was arbitrary, unreasonable and not supported by the evidence in the case of a bank vault teller's sensitivity to nickel and copper. This was because the 13% rating was apparently premised on the erroneous assumption of rehabilitation and of finding employment within one year which did not involve exposure to the sensitive substance, when there were few, if any, occupations on the open labor market which did not involve contact with nickel and copper.

Another factor considered in rebutting and/or determining a permanent disability rating under the former PDRS was evidence, testimony and reports of vocational rehabilitation counselors, of an injured worker's inability to participate in vocational rehabilitation because he or she could not be retrained for any suitable gainful employment. (*LeBoeuf v. Workers' Comp. Appeals Bd.* (1983) 34 Cal. 3d 234, 242–243 [666 P.2d 989, 193 Cal. Rptr. 547] [48 Cal. Comp. Cases 587, 594]; *Gill v. Workers' Comp. Appeals Bd.* (1985) 167 Cal. App. 3d 306, 307 [213 Cal. Rptr. 140] [50 Cal. Comp. Cases 258, 260].) Conversely, completion of vocational rehabilitation might increase an injured worker's ability to compete in the open labor market, and thus, could conceivably reduce his or her permanent disability. (*LeBoeuf, supra,* 34 Cal. 3d 234, at p. 243 [48 Cal. Comp. Cases at p. 594]; *Gill, supra,* 167 Cal. App. 3d at p. 308 [50 Cal. Comp. Cases at p. 261].)

It appears that in choosing to retain the language that the PDRS "shall be prima facie evidence of the percentage of permanent disability to be attributed to each injury covered by the schedule" in section 4660 (while changing almost everything else in that section), the Legislature intended to continue to allow the parties the opportunity to present rebuttal evidence to ratings under the new PDRS. The effect, if any, of the changes to section 4660 as to what evidence may actually rebut a rating under the new PDRS will be decided, at least initially, on a case by case basis.

Here, we agree with the WCJ's determination that the testimony of Ms. Wallace did not rebut the PD rating in this case. As stated in the WCJ's opinion on decision, Ms. Wallace, among other things: (1) apparently based her assumptions on an incorrect disability factor, a restriction to light work, and not the restriction from heavy lifting, repeated bending and stooping given by the agreed medical examiner (AME), Dr. Scheinberg, in his April 7, 2005 report; (2) inappropriately considered non–industrial factors; and (3) incorrectly calculated the applicant's pre–injury earnings capacity.

As to the costs for Ms. Wallace's testimony and report, however, we will rescind the WCJ's determination, and allow the parties to adjust such costs, with jurisdiction reserved at the trial level in event of dispute. We believe that Ms. Wallace, who as stated previously, was listed as a witness on applicant's DOR and testified without objection, is entitled to be reimbursed by SCIF for the reasonable costs associated with her testimony under section 5811. (Footnote 21)

In addition, although her report has been excluded from evidence, some of her work in preparing that report may have provided a foundation for her testimony... .

Footnote 20. Also see section 5704, which was not amended by SB 899. That section provides: "Transcripts of all testimony taken without notice and copies of all reports and other matters added to the record, otherwise than during the course of an open hearing, shall be served upon the parties to the proceeding, and an opportunity shall be given to produce evidence in explanation or rebuttal thereof before decision is rendered."

Footnote 21. Section 5811(a) provides in pertinent part: "In all proceedings under this division before the appeals board, costs as between the parties may be allowed by the appeals board."

=Page 745, Column 2, second paragraph, following '...this subdivision.' delete Editor's Note beginning '...A question...' and ending '...be allowed.]' and insert the following:

Return to Work

Page 746, Column 1, second paragraph, insert following '...in this area].'

See Appendix H for Return to Work Regulations.

Page 747, Column 2, third paragraph, insert following '...worker.'

In *Aldi v. Carr, McClellan, Ingersoll, Thompson & Horn* (2006) 71 Cal. Comp. Cases 783, the Board, in an En Banc decision stated, in part:

We hold that section 4660(d) requires that the revised permanent disability rating schedule be applied to injuries arising on or after the January 1, 2005 effective date of the rating schedule, subject to the specified exceptions for "compensable claims arising before January 1, 2005 . . . " The prior rating schedule may only be used to rate permanent disabilities arising from compensable injuries that occurred prior to January 1, 2005, where one of the exceptions described in the third sentence of section 4660(d) has been established. If none of the specified exceptions is established, the revised permanent disability rating schedule applies to injuries occurring before its January 1, 2005 effective date (Footnote 4)... .

_____

Footnote 4. The right to workers' compensation benefits is wholly statutory and, therefore, a legislative amendment or repeal of a statutory right may be applied to matters that were pending prior to the amendment or repeal. (*McCarthy v. Workers' Comp. Appeals Bd.* (2006) 135 Cal. App. 4th.1230, 1236–1237 [37 Cal. Rptr. 3d 909] [71 Cal. Comp. Cases 16]; *Rio Linda Union School Dist. V. Workers' Comp. Appeals Bd. (Scheftener)* (2005) 131 Cal. App. 4th 571, 527–528 [31 Cal. Rptr. 3d 789] [70 Cal. Comp. Cases 999]; *Kleemann v. Workers' Comp. Appeals Bd.* (2005) 127 Cal. App. 4th 274, 283 & fns. 17–21 [25 Cal. Rptr. 3d 448] [70 Cal. Comp. Cases 133]; *Abney v. Aera Energy* (2004) 69 Cal. Comp. Cases 1552, 1558–1559 (Appeals Board en banc).)

In *Biller v. WCAB* (2006) 71 Cal. Comp. Cases 513, the Board held that the post SB–899 permanent disability rating Schedule applied to an applicant where the facts disclosed that he was injured on July 29, 2003, was evaluated by his physician for permanent and stationary status and disability on December 22, 2004, but the examining physician did not sign the permanent and stationary report indicating permanent disability until

January 20, 2005.

The Board observed that the new Schedule applied to claims occurring before January 1, 2005 where there has been no comprehensive medical–legal report or no report by a treating physician indicating the existence of permanent disability, or when the employer is not required to provide notice pursuant to Section 4061.

In a dissenting opinion, Commissioner Caplane stated, in part:

It has long been the custom in workers' compensation cases that the injured worker is deemed permanent and stationary on the date he or she was examined by the reporting doctor, not on the date the medical report was written or received. The date of the exam marks the end of an applicant's entitlement to temporary disability indemnity and the beginning of permanent disability benefits. This custom benefits defendants by relieving them of the ongoing and open–ended obligation to pay temporary disability indemnity. In fact, had the defendant been ordered to pay temporary disability indemnity after the date of the permanent and stationary exam, it would have been entitled to be relieved of that order and/or to obtain credit against permanent disability for any payments made.

For all intents and purposes, an applicant's permanent disability begins when he or she is permanent and stationary, and the permanent disability schedule in effect on that date should apply. To find otherwise not only flies in the face of decades of workers' compensation practice, but is illogical... .

Page 749, Column 2, second paragraph, insert following '...subdivision.'

§ 10.24(A) Permanent Partial Disability Credit Against Permanent Total Disability

Inasmuch as *permanent partial disability* is a different benefit than *permanent total disability*, a defendant is not entitled to a credit of earlier permanent partial disability indemnity against a subsequent award of permanent total disability that clearly follows a formal Petition to Reopen by an applicant. Such was the case in *City of San Buenaventura, et al. v. WCAB (Schulte)* (2006) 71 Cal. Comp. Cases 823, where defendant was found *not* entitled to credit a prior stipulated permanent partial disability award of 30½ percent permanent disability against a subsequent total permanent disability award of 100 percent following her successful Petition to Reopen because permanent partial disability and permanent total disability are distinctly different benefits and the applicant was held to be entitled to the full benefit of each award.

Permanent Disability (PD) Apportionment

In a significant panel decision in *Erickson v. Southern California Permanente Medical Group, et. al.* (2007) 72 Cal. Comp. Cases 103, the Board held that where the issue of calculation of amount of permanent disability due to an applicant that was pending before the California Supreme Court decision in *Brodie,* and other cases, a defendant should withhold sufficient sums for attorney's fees if possible. The Board stated, in part:

For the reasons that follow, we grant reconsideration and amend the WCJ's decision to defer the issue of the *calculation of the amount of the permanent disability indemnity due* to applicant, pending issuance of the Supreme Court's decision(s) in *Brodie v. Workers' Comp. Appeals Bd.*, review granted November 15, 2006, S146979 (2006 Cal. LEXIS 13527), in *Welcher v. Workers' Comp. Appeals Bd.*, review granted November 15, 2006, S147030 (2006 Cal. LEXIS 13523), or in any other case in which the Supreme Court issues an opinion that resolves this issue. We also defer the related issue of attorney's fees. Defendant should pay, or continue to pay, applicant any uncontested permanent disability indemnity, but it should withhold sufficient sums for attorney's fees, if possible. Upon request by applicant's counsel, an interim attorney's fee may be allowed by the WCJ – either from accrued sums, from sums withheld for fee purposes, or by way of commutation if deemed appropriate – after allowing a reasonable time for, and considering, any objections thereto... .

See Section 31A.2 of this book for a full discussion of *Brodie, Welcher* and other cases on point. [**Editor's Note:** The California Supreme Court has resolved the issue and applies Fuentes. See Section 31A.2 for the full discussion of the high Court's decision, filed on May 3, 2007.]

Intentionally blank

California Workers' Compensation Claims and Benefits, 12th Ed. Supplement (2007)

§ 11.0   OFFSETS

Page 751, Column 2, third paragraph, correct CMS website to read:

http://www.cms.hhs.gov/WorkersCompAgencyServices/
04_wcsetaside.asp

Intentionally blank

§ 13.0   DEATH BENEFITS

Page 755, Column 1, delete first paragraph, beginning with "Dependents of an..." and insert the following:

Dependents of an industrially injured employee who dies as a result of an industrial injury are entitled to death benefits, including a burial expense. [**Editor's Note:** Formerly, the deceased employees' estate was also entitled to death benefits but the Court of Appeal, Second District, in *Six Flags, Inc., et. al. v. WCAB (Bunyanunda)* (2006) 71 Cal. Comp. Cases 1759, as discussed hereafter, declared unconstitutional awarding of death benefits to a deceased employee's estate.]

The Legislature has amended Labor Code section 4702, to clarify that the survivors of deceased employees are entitled to receive the full statutory death benefit, notwithstanding any amount of accrued or unpaid compensation to which the survivor is entitled.

§13.2(B)   Death Benefits Changes

Page 757, Column 2, end of seventh paragraph after words "...and the decedent." Insert the following:

The total death benefit is contingent on the number of surviving dependents at the time of injury or illness resulting in death. Once dependency is determined, the employer must pay the death benefit in installments at the decedent's temporary disability rate. However, the rate must not be less than $224 per week until the employer pays the total death benefit, or, if dependency involves a minor child, until the minor child is 18 years old. For injuries on or after January 1, 2003, benefits must be paid to a dependent child for life when physically or mentally incapacitated from earning. The following table shows the distribution of maximum death benefits.

Death Benefit Maximums For Date of Injury on or After January 1, 2007	
One total dependent and no partial dependents	$250,000
Two total dependents (No increase for partial dependents)	$290,000
Three or more total dependents (No increase for partial dependents)	$320,000
One total dependent and one or more partial dependents (**$250,000** + 4 times support of partial dependents but not more than)	$290,000
No total dependents and one or more partial dependents (8 times support of partial dependents but not more than)	$250,000
No total dependents and no partial dependents (Employee does not leave any person entitled to a dependency, benefit payment to Department of Industrial Relations)	$250,000

Special Note:

Death benefits are paid in payments at the same rate as temporary total disability unless otherwise ordered by a judge. The minimum payment is $224.00 per week. Two years from the date of the employee's death payments must be increased to the temporary total disability rate currently in effect at the date of payment.

- The following dependents are conclusively presumed wholly dependent on a deceased employee:
  - (a) minor child or a child of any age found to be physically or mentally incapacitated from earning who was either living with the deceased parent or the deceased parent is legally liable at the time of injury;
  - (b) spouse earning less than $30,000 in the preceding 12 months at time of the deceased employee's death.
- Where there is one or more totally dependent minor children, payments must continue after the maximum is paid until the youngest child attains the age of 18 or until the death of a child physically or mentally incapacitated from earnings.
- Where there are two or more total dependents, there is no increase for partial dependents.
- If there are no total dependents and one or more partial dependents, the partial dependents share in accordance with their relative extent of dependency.
- The death payment to an employee's estate has been declared unconstitutional.
- Temporary or permanent disability payments, if any, cease at an employee's death. All accrued and unpaid compensation must be paid to the dependents. All

accrued disability compensation is in addition to death benefits.

§13.2(E)   Who Qualifies as a Dependent?

Page 760, Column 2, delete fifth and sixth paragraph, beginning with "In Finnerty..." and ending '...decedents household' and insert the following:

In *Finnerty v. W.C.A.B.* (1982) 47 Cal. Comp. Cases 1411, a male live–in alleged that he was dependent upon a male deputy district attorney who committed suicide. The Court of Appeal, in commenting on this type of a relationship, stated:

> Merely because two persons of the same sex occupy a single residential structure does not indicate either the sexual influences or dependency of this relationship within the meaning of the code....See also S.C.I.F. v. W.C.A.B. (Donovan) (1984) 49 Cal. Comp. Cases 577, where the Board found that decedent employee's 20–year–old male lover was a good faith member of decedent's household and entitled to death benefits even though the homosexual relationship was not a recognized marriage and the *dependent* allegedly had homosexual relations with other people during the time he was a member of the decedent's household

§ 13.2(H)(3) For Deaths Resulting From Injuries Sustained on or After January 1, 1981

Page 772, Column 1, first paragraph, insert following '...4558.'

and notwithstanding any amount of compensation paid or otherwise owing to the surviving dependent, personal representative, heir, or other person entitled to a deceased employee's accrued and unpaid compensation, the death benefit in cases of total dependency shall be as follows:

Page 772, Column 2, second paragraph, insert following '...January 1, 2006.'

(6) (A) in the case of a police officer who has no total dependents and no partial dependents, for injuries occurring on or after January 1, 2003, and prior to January 1, 2004, two hundred fifty thousand dollars ($250,000) to the estate of the deceased police officer. (B) For injuries occurring on or after January 1, 2004, in the case of no total dependents and no partial dependents, two hundred fifty thousand dollars ($250,000) to the estate of the deceased employee... .

Page 773, Column 1, first paragraph, insert following '...dependency.'

Constitutionality of Death Benefits to an Estate

The awarding of death benefits to a deceased employee's estate was held unconstitutional in *Six Flags, Inc., et. al. v. WCAB (Bunyanunda)* (2006) 71 Cal. Comp. Cases 1759, by the Court of Appeal, Second District, relating to Labor Code section 4702, subdivision (a)(6)(B), providing for a death benefit to heirs, where the employee leaves no dependents.

In this case, Bantita Rackchamroon, an operator hostess for Six Flags, Inc., sustained industrial injury and death on April 9, 2004. Rackchamroon died with no dependents.

On June 1, 2004, the administrator of the Estate of Bantita Rackchamroon (the estate) filed an Application for Adjudication of a worker's compensation death benefit claim. The administrator alleged that an amusement park ride struck Rackchamroon, who suffered fatal injury in the course and scope of her employment.

In the workers' compensation proceedings, Six Flags' insurer, petitioner Pacific Employers Insurance, administered by ESIS, Inc. (Pacific), asserted that section 4702, subdivision (a)(6)(B), was unconstitutional. The workers' compensation judge, however, awarded $250,000.00 to the estate, payable by Pacific. Pursuant to Section 4706.5, the Workers' Compensation Judge also awarded $125,000.00 to the Department of Industrial Relations, Death Without Dependents Unit.

Pacific filed a Petition for Reconsideration. The Workers' Compensation Judge issued a report recommending that the Workers' Compensation Appeals Board (the Board) deny the Petition for Reconsideration. *The judge explained that Workers' Compensation Judges do not have authority to rule on the constitutionality of statutes because article III, Section 3.5 of the California Constitution prohibits an administrative agency from declaring a statute unconstitutional.* (See also *Greener v. Workers' Comp. Appeals Bd.* (1993) 6 Cal. 4th 1028, 1038 [863 P.2d 784, 25 Cal. Rptr. 2d 539, 58 Cal. Comp. Cases 793].)

Subsequently, the Board issued an order denying Pacific's Petition for Reconsideration. Pacific filed a Petition for Writ of Review to contest the award to the estate.

In declaring Section 4702(a)(6)(B) *unconstitutional*, the Court stated, in part:

> As approved by the voters in 1918, the predecessor to article XIV, section 4, identified two classes of beneficiaries of workers' compensation benefits: (1) workers and (2) dependents. The California Supreme Court has twice declared statutes unconstitutional when the Legislature attempted to expand the class of beneficiaries of workers' compensation benefits beyond the two classes identified in the Constitution. (See Yosemite, *supra*, 187 Cal. 774 & Commercial Cas., *supra*, 211 Cal. 210.)

The first case, Yosemite, invalidated a workers' compensation statute, enacted in 1919, which created the state as a third beneficiary of workers' compensation death benefits. The statute required employers to pay $350 to the state when a worker suffered fatal injury in the course and scope of employment and the worker left no dependents to whom a death benefit could be paid. The money was to be used for the vocational rehabilitation of workers in general. (Yosemite, *supra*, 187 Cal. at pp. 775–776.)

In 1922, the Yosemite court declared this statute unconstitutional. Because the predecessor to article XIV, section 4, did not identify the state as a beneficiary of workers' compensation benefits, the court held that the Legislature did not have constitutional authority to impose upon employers an obligation to contribute funds to a state fund to benefit workers in general. (Yosemite, *supra*, 187 Cal. at p. 780.)

The Yosemite court analyzed the statements in the pamphlet distributed to the voters when the Legislature placed the predecessor to article XIV, section 4, on the ballot. As to consideration of voter pamphlets, the Yosemite court explained: "It is to be assumed that the arguments prepared by the author of the amendment state fairly and with reasonable fullness the meaning of the amendment and the effect it is expected to produce." (Yosemite, *supra*, 187 Cal. at pp. 781–782.) Based upon review of the pamphlet, the court concluded that the authors of the predecessor to article XIV, section 4, did not intend to impose upon employers an obligation to contribute funds to the state for the benefit of disabled workers in general. (Yosemite, at p. 782.)

The second case, Commercial Cas., invalidated another workers' compensation statute, enacted in 1929, which again declared the state to be a beneficiary of workers' compensation death benefits. (Commercial Cas., *supra*, 211 Cal. at p. 217.) The statute required employers to pay into a " 'subsequent injuries fund' " when an employee died in the course and scope of employment and left no dependents to whom a death benefit could be paid. (Id. at pp. 211–212.)

The Commercial Cas. court declared the 1929 statute unconstitutional. Like the 1919 statute, the 1929 statute attempted to expand the class of beneficiaries of workers' compensation benefits to include the state. As discussed above, however, the constitutional enabling provision, the predecessor to article XIV, section 4, did not identify the state as a beneficiary entitled to workers' compensation death benefits. (Commercial Cas., *supra*, 211 Cal. at pp. 211–212.)

After summarizing the Yosemite case, the Commercial Cas. court explained: "We can see no escape from the logic of [the Yosemite] decision. That case is identical in principle with the proceeding before us. In each case the liability sought to be imposed upon the employer is not one in favor of his employee nor the dependents of any deceased employee. In each case the jurisdiction to determine this liability is attempted to be conferred upon the Industrial Accident Commission. We feel bound by this authority not only by reason of the rule of stare decisis, but on account of the manifest soundness of the decision." (Commercial Cas., *supra*, 211 Cal. at p. 215, italics in original.)…

6. Under Present Law, Estates Are Not Dependents

At present, sections 3501 through 3503 define "dependents." Generally, there are two types of dependents: (1) presumed dependents (minors, incapacitated adults and spouses earning $30,000 or less in the year prior to the employee's death); (Footnote 10) and (2) those persons who must establish dependency based upon the facts existing at the time of death. (Footnote 11)

In addition, to qualify as a dependent, an individual must stand in a specified relationship to the deceased. (Footnote 12)

An estate is defined in Probate Code section 353: " 'Estate' means a trust estate, a decedent's estate, a guardianship or conservatorship estate, or other property that is the subject of a donative transfer." In Tanner v. Best (1940) 40 Cal. App. 2d 442 [104 P.2d 1084], the court explained: "The 'estate' of a decedent is not an entity known to the law. It is neither a natural nor an artificial person. It is merely a name to indicate the sum total of the assets and liabilities of a decedent, or of an incompetent, or of a bankrupt." (Id. at p. 445.)

In addition, a plain reading of the statute at issue in this case supports the conclusion that the Legislature knew that an estate is not a dependent. Section 4702, subdivision (a)(6)(B), only grants the estate (i.e., heirs or devisees) a worker's compensation death benefit "in the case of no total dependents and no partial dependents."

Therefore, by definition, pursuant to section 4702, payment of a death benefit to an estate does not constitute payment of a death benefit to a dependent. This further supports the conclusion that as used in article XIV, section 4, the term "dependents" does not include a deceased employee's estate… .

DISPOSITION

The petition for writ of review is granted in part and denied in part. We annul the award of $250,000 to the estate of Rackchamroon. We affirm the award of $125,000 to the state…

Footnote 10. Section 3501 provides: "(a) A child under the age of 18 years, or a child of any age found by any trier of fact, whether contractual, administrative, regulatory, or judicial, to be physically or mentally incapacitated from earning, shall be conclusively presumed to be wholly dependent for support upon a deceased employee–parent with whom that child is living at the time of injury resulting in death of the parent or for whose maintenance the parent was legally liable at the time of injury resulting in death of the parent, there being no surviving totally dependent parent. [P] (b) A spouse to whom a deceased employee is married at the time of death shall be conclusively presumed to be wholly dependent for support upon the deceased employee if the surviving spouse earned thirty thousand dollars ($30,000) or less in the twelve months immediately preceding the death."

Footnote 11. Section 3502 provides: "In all other cases, questions of entire or partial dependency and questions as to who are dependents and the extent of their dependency shall be determined in accordance with the facts as they exist at the time of the injury of the employee."

Footnote 12. Section 3503 provides: "No person is a dependent of any deceased employee unless in good faith a member of the family or household of the employee, or unless the person bears to the employee the relation of husband or wife, child, posthumous child, adopted child or stepchild, grandchild, father or mother, father–in–law or mother–in–law, grandfather or grandmother, brother or sister, uncle or aunt, brother–in–law or sister–in–law, nephew or niece."

§ 13.2(L)   Deceased Employee Leaves No Dependents or Leaves Dependents That Are Not Entitled to the Full Amount of the Total Death Benefits That Would be Payable to a Surviving Spouse With No Dependent Children

The Legislature has amended Labor Code section 4706.5 to specify that the request to pay the death benefit to the Department of Industrial Relations when a deceased employee has no surviving dependents does not apply if the death benefit or accrued and unpaid compensation is paid to the deceased employee's estate. However, as previously noted in this supplement, Section 4702(a)(6)(B) providing for death benefits to a deceased employee's estate has been declared unconstitutional.

Page 775, Column 1, third paragraph, insert following '…loss.'

(h) This section does not apply where there is no surviving person entitled to a dependency death benefit or accrued and unpaid compensation if a death benefit is paid to any person under paragraph (6) of subdivision (a) of Section 4702. **[Editor's Note:** The Legislature corrected the inconsistency that previously existed between Section 4702 and Section 4706.5 by amending Section 4706.5 and by adding (h) above.]

If an employee dies under circumstances that would entitle the employee to compensation benefits the employer must notify the Administrative Director of the death except where the employer has actual knowledge or notice that the deceased employee left a surviving dependent. Lab. C. Sec. 4706.5(f). Failure to give such notice prevents the running of the one year statute of limitations to file a death claim. *City of Los Angeles v. WCAB (Barrett)* (2006) 71 Cal. Comp. Cases 61.

Page 783, Column 2, end of paragraph reading "…mission to the Administrative Director", insert the following:

§ 13.2(T)   Department of Transportation Employees

The Legislature has amended Government Code section 21537.5, effective September 6, 2006, to allow the survivor of a State miscellaneous member in State Bargaining Unit 12, employed by the Department of Transportation, to collect a *special death benefit* if the member's death was a direct result of injury arising out of and in the course of his or her official duties performing highway maintenance on the California highway system.

§ 14.0   SUPPLEMENTAL JOB DISPLACEMENT BENEFITS

Page 785, Column 2, sixth paragraph, insert following '...time of injury.'

See Appendix I for the Supplemental Job Displacement Regulations.

Intentionally blank

§ 15.0   SERIOUS AND WILLFUL MISCONDUCT BENEFITS

Page 803, Column 2, following second paragraph, after words "...problems for her..." insert the following:

§ 15.2   Misconduct By Employer

Threats and Assault by Student on Teacher

[**Editor's Note:** The Court of Appeal, Third District, in *Elk Grove Unified School District v. WCAB (Stroth)* (2007) 72 Cal. Comp. Cases 399, in an unpublished decision, annulled a Board decision awarding Serious and Willful Misconduct benefits to a school teacher who was injured by a student who charged into her and knocked her down on a school bus, when the Court found that the school district had not deliberately or consciously failed to act for the teacher's safety or failed to take corrective action.

The Court noted that the school had notice of the student's bad behavior of pushing students and making sexual innuendoes to girls but had been stymied by a lack of consent or a waffling of consent of the students' parents to put him in a special behavior–based program. Consequently they did not deliberately fail to take corrective action.]

§ 15.2(B)   The Following Circumstances Have Been Held to Have Constituted Serious and Willful Misconduct on the Part of the Employer Which Proximately Caused Injury to the Employee, Thereby Justifying an Award of Such Benefits Against the Employer

Page 810, Column 2, seventh paragraph, insert immediately following section heading.

Permitting a massage therapist to work on a slippery and oily floor where evidence showed that the employer knew that the slippery floor presented a dangerous condition because the applicant and other employees had informed management about the condition on several occasions (the employer had been notified that five employees had fallen on the floor in the month preceding applicant's fall). *Meadowood Residential Hotel v. WCAB (Wallace)* (2005) 70 Cal. Comp. Cases 1730.

§ 15.2(E)   What is the Additional Compensation Based Upon?

Page 816, Column 2, third paragraph, insert following '...60 Cal. Comp. Cases 275.'

See *Tillery (Son) et. al v. WCAB* (2007) 72 Cal. Comp. Cases 727, where the Board concluded that increases in compensation provided in Section 4553 is to be calculated on the entire award, provided it does not exceed the amount necessary to fully compensate the employee.

Intentionally blank

§ 16.0   SUBSEQUENT INJURIES FUND BENEFITS

§ 16.6   When Claim Must Be Filed

Page 827, Column 2, second paragraph, insert immediately following '…Fund.'

In this case, the California Supreme Court stated, in part:

We should, in the absence of statutory direction and to avoid an injustice, prevent the barring of an applicant's claim against the Fund before it arises. Therefore, we hold that where, prior to the expiration of five years from the date of injury, an applicant does not know and could not reasonably be deemed to know that there will be substantial likelihood he will become entitled to subsequent injuries benefits, his application against the Fund will not be barred – even if he had applied for normal benefits against his employer – if he files a proceeding against the Fund within a reasonable time after he learns from the Board's findings on the issue of permanent disability that the fund has probable liability… .

Page 827, Column 2, second paragraph, insert following '…96.'

In *Grob v. SIF Oak* 27 3127, December 2, 2005, the Board found that a claim against the Subsequent Injuries Fund was not barred because the injured employee did not know, before the expiration of the five–year period, that a substantial likelihood existed that he would become entitled to the benefit. The Board relied upon the California Supreme Court case of *SIF v. WCAB (Talcott)* (1970) 35 Cal. Comp. Cases 80.

Intentionally blank

California Workers' Compensation Claims and Benefits, 12th Ed. Supplement (2007)

§ 17.0   DISCRIMINATION BECAUSE OF SUSTAINING AN INDUSTRIAL INJURY

Page 829, Column 2, first paragraph, insert following '...1484.'

A higher degree of proof requirement to establish a prima facie case of discrimination was set forth by the California State Supreme Court in *Department of Rehabilitation/State of California v. WCAB (Lauher)* (2003) 68 Cal. Comp. Cases 831. Prior to that decision, an employee could establish a prima facie case of discrimination by merely showing that as a result of an industrial injury, the employer engaged in conduct detrimental to him or her.

The high Court, in setting forth the higher standard, stated, in part:

Lauher next claims that his employer discriminated against him within the meaning of section 132a because he had suffered an industrial injury. This discrimination, he claims, took the form of his employer's insistence that he use his accumulated sick and vacation leave for the time he was out of the office seeing Dr. Houts for treatment of his injury. Lauher claims he was thus "treated differently than other employees who had not sustained a work–related injury . . . ." (Footnote 6)

Section 132a provides: "It is the declared policy of this state that there should not be discrimination against workers who are injured in the course and scope of their employment. [P] (1) Any employer who discharges, or threatens to discharge, *or in any manner discriminates* against any employee because he or she has filed or made known his or her intention to file a claim for compensation with his or her employer or an application for adjudication, or because the employee has received a rating, award, or settlement, is guilty of a misdemeanor and the employee's compensation shall be increased by one–half, but in no event more than ten thousand dollars ($10,000), together with costs and expenses not in excess of two hundred fifty dollars ($250). Any such employee shall also be entitled to reinstatement and *reimbursement* for lost wages and *work benefits* caused by the acts of the employer." (Italics added.) No criminal penalty is at issue in this case; we address only the Board's imposition of a $10,000 administrative penalty on Lauher's employer.

"[T]o warrant an award [pursuant to section 132a] the employee must establish at least a prima facie case of lost wages and benefits caused by the discriminatory acts of the employer." (*Dyer v. Workers' Comp. Appeals Bd.* (1994) 22 Cal. App. 4th 1376, 1386 [28 Cal. Rptr. 2d 30, 59 Cal. Comp. Cases 96].) The employee must establish discrimination by a preponderance of the evidence (*Western Electric Co. v. Workers' Comp. Appeals Bd.* (1979) 99 Cal. App. 3d 629, 640 [160 Cal. Rptr. 436, 44 Cal. Comp. Cases 1145]), at which point the burden shifts to the employer to establish an affirmative defense (*Barns v. Workers' Comp.*

Appeals Bd. (1989) 216 Cal. App. 3d 524, 531 [266 Cal. Rptr. 503, 54 Cal. Comp. Cases 433]). Although we defer to the Board's determination of facts if supported by substantial evidence, we review the Board's legal decisions de novo, for "[i]t is for the court to decide whether the facts found by the Board constitute a violation of section 132a." (*Id.* at pp. 530–531.)

To decide the merits of Lauher's claim, we must decide what section 132a means when it refers to "discrimination." As one appellate court has noted, "[n]either the Legislature nor the courts have fashioned a clear rule for distinguishing those forms of discrimination which are actionable under section 132a and those forms which are not." (*Smith v. Workers' Comp. Appeals Bd.* (1984) 152 Cal. App. 3d 1104, 1108 [199 Cal. Rptr. 881, 49 Cal. Comp. Cases 212] (*Smith*).) Nevertheless, some boundary markers have been delineated. Under its express terms, an employer may not "discharge[], or threaten[] to discharge" an employee because, like Lauher, he has filed a claim for compensation. Moreover, citing the prefatory statement that "[i]t is the declared policy of this state that there should not be discrimination against workers who are injured in the course and scope of their employment" (§ 132a), we have explained that the type of discriminatory actions subject to penalty under section 132a is not limited to those enumerated in the statute. Instead, we have interpreted section 132a liberally to achieve the goal of preventing discrimination against workers injured on the job. (*Judson Steel Corp. v. Workers' Comp. Appeals Bd.* (1978) 22 Cal. 3d 658, 666–669 [150 Cal. Rptr. 250, 586 P.2d 564, 43 Cal. Comp. Cases 1205].) We immediately cautioned, however, that "[s]ection 132a does not compel an employer to ignore the realities of doing business by 'reemploying' unqualified employees or employees for whom positions are no longer available." (*Id.* at p. 667.)

Noting this last passage, the court in *Smith, supra,* 152 Cal. App. 3d 1104, held that "save for the two exceptions just described [i.e., reemploying employees who are unqualified or for whom no position is available], action *which works to the detriment of the employee* because of an injury is unlawful under section 132a." (*Id.* at p. 1109, italics added.) This test of "detriment" to the employee was accepted as the applicable standard in *Barns v. Workers' Comp. Appeals Bd., supra,* 216 Cal. App. 3d at page 531 ("a worker proves a violation of section 132a by showing that as the result of an industrial injury, the employer engaged in conduct detrimental to the worker") as well as by at least one commentator (1 Hanna, *supra,* § 10.11[1], p. 10–20 ["[t]he critical question is whether the employer's action caused detriment to an industrially–injured employee"]).

The Court of Appeal in this case, however, found the *Smith* formulation "analytically incomplete." The court explained that, although Lauher had clearly suffered a detriment by having to use his accumulated sick leave and vacation time for his visits to see Dr. Houts, he never established he "had a legal *right* to receive TDI and retain his accrued sick leave and vacation time, and that [his employer] had a corresponding legal *duty* to pay TDI and refrain from docking the sick leave and vacation time." (Footnote 7)

Thus, said the court, "[t]o meet the burden of presenting a prima facie claim of unlawful discrimination in violation of section 132a, it is insufficient that the industrially injured worker show only that . . . he or she suffered some adverse result as a consequence of some action or inaction by the employer that was triggered by the industrial injury. The claimant must also show that he or she had a legal right to receive or retain the deprived benefit or status, and the employer had a corresponding legal duty to provide or refrain from taking away that benefit or status."

We agree that for Lauher merely to show he suffered an industrial injury and that he suffered some detrimental consequences as a result is insufficient to establish a prima facie case of discrimination within the meaning of section 132a. As we explained, *ante,* our system of workers' compensation does not provide a make–whole remedy. "The Workers' Compensation Law is intended to award compensation for *disability* incurred in employment. 'The purpose of the award is not to make the employee whole for the loss which he has suffered but to prevent him and his dependents from becoming public charges during the period of his disability.' " (*Universal City Studios, Inc. v. Worker's Comp. Appeals Bd., supra,* 99 Cal. App. 3d at pp. 659–660.) "The purpose of workmen's compensation is to rehabilitate, not to indemnify, and its intent is limited to assuring the injured workman subsistence while he is unable to work and to effectuate his speedy rehabilitation and reentry into the labor market." (*Solari v. Atlas–Universal Service, Inc.* (1963) 215 Cal. App. 2d 587, 600 [30 Cal. Rptr. 407, 28 Cal. Comp. Cases 277].) Consistent with this view, for example, section 4653 provides that payment for temporary total disability is only "two–thirds of the average weekly earnings during the period of such disability."

An employer thus does not necessarily engage in "discrimination" prohibited by section 132a merely because it requires an employee to shoulder some of the disadvantages of his industrial injury. By prohibiting "discrimination" in section 132a, we assume the Legislature meant to prohibit treating injured employees differently, making them suffer disadvantages not visited on other employees because the employee was injured or had made a claim.

Lauher claims he was subjected to discrimination within the meaning of section 132a because he "was treated differently than other employees who had not sustained a work–related injury and were not under the mandates of the Labor Code."

He claims "[t]he employer's actions were directly related to the work injury and the resultant time the injured employee had to miss from work because of the medical appointments to cure or relieve the effects of the work injury." Lauher's argument fails to appreciate that, although his injury was industrial, nothing suggests his employer

singled him out for disadvantageous treatment because of the industrial nature of his injury. We assume that employees with nonindustrial injuries must follow the same rule and use their sick leave when away from the office attending medical treatment. Certainly nothing Lauher alleges suggests otherwise. For example, he does not allege he alone is being singled out for the requirement that he use his sick leave, or that other employees are permitted to leave the office for medical appointments related to nonindustrial injuries and are not required to use their sick leave.

Because Lauher does not allege that other employees are permitted to be away from their workplace for medical care yet need not use their sick leave if they wish to be paid their full salaries, we conclude Lauher fails to demonstrate he was the victim of discrimination within the meaning of section 132a. To hold otherwise would elevate those who had suffered industrial injuries to a point where they enjoyed rights superior to those of their coworkers. Nothing in the history or meaning of section 132a's antidiscrimination rule supports such an interpretation. (Footnote 8)... .

Footnote 6. Although Lauher argued in the Court of Appeal that this discrimination also took the form of failure to pay him TDI for his time away from work seeing Dr. Houts, it does not appear he has renewed that claim in this court. In any event, as we find he was not entitled to TDI once his industrial injury became permanent and stationary, SCIF cannot be found to have discriminated against him by failing to pay TDI in this circumstance.

Footnote 7. As noted, *ante,* Lauher no longer claims he is entitled to a penalty under section 132a due to his employer's failure to pay TDI.

Footnote 8. Because we find Lauher failed to establish a prima facie case of discrimination within the meaning of section 132a, we need not address SCIF's contention that employer had a legitimate business reason for requiring Lauher to use his sick leave and vacation time when away from the office seeing Dr. Houts for treatment. For the same reason, we also decline to address the argument by amicus curiae California Employment Law Council that we should reexamine and discard the holding of *Judson Steel Corp. v. Workers' Comp. Appeals Bd., supra,* 22 Cal. 3d 658, that section 132a should be liberally construed in favor of injured workers. We also decline to address the invitation to reinterpret section 132a to require proof of discriminatory intent. These arguments are not necessary to resolve the present matter and, in any event, were not raised by any party or amicus curiae before the WCJ, the WCAB, or the Court of Appeal.

Page 832, Column 2, eighth paragraph, insert following '...support.'

In *Abratte v. WCAB* (2003), 68 Cal. Comp. Cases 451, the Board stated, in part:

"...in the context of a governmental entity, allocating finite financial resources not for profit but for the general welfare of the public, the 'realities of doing business' defense will be met where the employer reasonably believes that business realities compelled it to take the action it did."...

"Here, the evidence of record indicated that although the County has a budget of over $15 billion, there is little flexibility in spending that revenue. After allowing for "fixed" and "non–flexible" costs, 7.1% of the overall budget remains to pay for those programs in "flexible" costs, which the Board of Supervisors has divided into two categories: public protection and all other costs. The amount allocated for all other costs in the County's 2000–2001 budget was $683.7 million."

"The evidence at trial, however, indicated that even with this $683.7 million, the County has unmet needs of approximately $500 million each year. (Statement of Decision of the Commission on State Mandates, defendant's exhibit F; testimony of Sharon Bunn, Chief Deputy, Chief Administrative Office.) Some examples of these unmet needs include updating voting machinery, reopening certain sheriff's substations closed in prior financial crises, purchasing parking lot lights for the Registrar–Recorder, and funding for a juvenile drug court. In addition, the recently enacted Proposition 36 mandates drug treatment for certain offenders, which will have to be funded by the County; the federal bailout of the County's health care crisis in the amount of $900 million will expire in less than four years, creating a shortfall in the health care system; and the State's current massive budget deficit will almost certainly mean less revenue available to the County. (As set forth at trial, for the fiscal year 2000–2001, $3.634 billion was received from the State, or 23% of the County's overall budget.)"

"The reality is that the County, unlike a business, does not have the ability to generate additional revenue by increasing prices to offset rising costs. Also, unlike a business, the County is not motivated by economic incentive, but exists to provide essential services to its residents, which it must do through the confines of a limited budget."

"In this case, we find no evidence that the allocation of funds at issue here, made by an elected representative body through a formal budget process, in which input is received not only from the public at large, but also from unions representing employees, was either unreasonable, not made in good faith, or a pretext for unlawful discrimination. Accordingly, it is our decision that defendant County has met its burden of proving the defense of "business realities," and that therefore, it did not violate Labor Code section 132a. [WCAB's Footnote omitted]"... .

In *Andersen v. WCAB* (2007) 72 Cal. Comp. Cases 389, the Court of Appeal, Second District, annulled a Board decision and held that the City of Santa Barbara discriminated against applicant, a finance supervisor, by requiring him to use earned vacation time rather than sick leave to attend medical appointments necessitated by his industrial injury, following his return to work while permitting employees with non–industrial injuries to use their sick leave for medical appointments. The Court, in finding discrimination, stated, in part:

John Andersen sustained industrial injuries while working for respondent City of Santa Barbara (City). Andersen filed a workers' compensation claim contending that City discriminated against him by forcing him to use vacation time rather than sick leave to obtain medical care for those injuries. (Lab. Code, (Footnote 1) §132a.) He also argued that the Workers' Compensation Appeals Board (Board) improperly applied the apportionment provisions of Senate Bill No. 899 (2003–2004 Reg. Sess.) (SB 899) retroactively, and no substantial evidence supports the opinion of the agreed medical examiner (AME) regarding apportionment. On April 6, 2006, Board concluded that City did not violate the anti–discrimination provisions of section 132a, and therefore, Andersen is not entitled to restoration of the vacation time he used for such medical appointments.

Andersen petitioned this court for a writ of review. We summarily denied this petition and Andersen sought review in our Supreme Court. His petition to the Supreme Court raised only the issue of whether City violated section 132a. The Supreme Court granted the petition, and transferred the matter back to this court with directions to vacate our summary denial and issue a writ of review to be heard on calendar. We have done so.

We now conclude that City violated section 132a by requiring Andersen to use his earned vacation time rather than sick leave to attend medical appointments to care for his industrial injuries. We also conclude that Board properly applied SB 899, and substantial evidence supports the apportionment opinion of the AME...

Local Laws and Contract Provisions

City's municipal code provides that "[w]here sickness or injury is sustained in the course of employment with the City, such officer or employee shall be compensated under the provisions of the Workers' Compensation Insurance and Safety Act of the State and not under the provisions of this chapter . . . ." (Santa Barbara Mun. Code, § 3.08.220.)

City's MOU states that "a. The parties agree that Municipal Code Section 3.08.220 shall be amended to provide that general employees who sustain illness or injury arising out of and in the course of their City employment shall receive benefits equal to those mandated by the State of California . . . ." (At § 59.) The MOU also provides that "[a]n employee may use sick leave for a medical appointment when it is not possible to arrange such appointment on non–work time subject to . . . [r]easonable advance notice . . . [and] supervisory approval . . . ." (At § 45; and see Santa Barbara Mun. Code, § 3.08.140 [on accrual of sick leave].) Section 59 of the MOU proclaims, however, "[t]his section shall not be construed to grant employees the use of sick leave benefits in lieu of or to supplement workers' compensation benefits provided herein or by State law."

City has construed the above provisions to require industrially injured workers to charge vacation time rather than sick leave when such workers need to attend medical appointments for their work–related injuries. But, City permits its workers to use sick leave to attend medical appointments for non–industrial injuries. (MOU, § 45, subd.

(c); and see Santa Barbara Mun. Code, § 3.08.140 [on accrual of sick leave].)

Andersen contends City violated section 132a by forcing him to use vacation time rather than sick leave for this purpose, and he is entitled to an award pursuant to section 132a. We independently construe these statutory and contractual provisions according to the rules stated above. (Civ. Code, §§ 1636, 1639, 1641, 1642, 1644, 1647; Code Civ. Proc., §§ 1856–1862; *Pellandini v. Valadao* (2003) 113 Cal. App. 4th 1315, 1319 [7 Cal. Rptr. 3d 413].)

Application of Section 132a

The antidiscrimination provisions of section 132a are not limited to protecting only its enumerated rights, such as workers' compensation ratings or awards. (See *Judson Steel Corp. v. Workers' Comp. Appeals Bd., supra,* 22 Cal. 3d at p. 667; *Stemler v. Workers' Comp. Appeals Bd.* (1988) 204 Cal. App. 3d 577, 580 [251 Cal. Rptr. 364, 53 Cal. Comp. Cases 390].) An employer action that " 'in any manner . . . discriminat[es]' " against an industrially injured employee to the detriment of his or her receipt or exercise of employment rights is compensable under section 132a. (*Judson, supra,* at p. 667 [loss of seniority]; accord, *Lauher, supra,* 30 Cal. 4th at pp. 1299–1300; § 132a.) Section 132a precludes discrimination that detrimentally affects industrially injured workers in any significant way. (See *County of Santa Barbara v. Workers' Comp. Appeals Bd.* (1980) 109 Cal. App. 3d 211, 215–216 [167 Cal. Rptr. 65, 45 Cal. Comp. Cases 872] [reduction in status or pay].) Discriminatory and detrimental actions taken by local government entities pursuant to a collective bargaining agreement are also protected under section 132a. (*Judson, supra,* at pp. 665, fn. 5, 667; *Stemler, supra,* at p. 580.)

Courts evaluate section 132a cases using the preponderance of the evidence standard. (*Lauher, supra,* 30 Cal. 4th at p. 1298.) If the employee carries this burden, the burden shifts to the employer to establish an affirmative defense of a reasonable and legitimate business reason for such practice. (*Ibid.*)

Both sides rely on *Lauher* to support their positions. *Lauher* concerned a workers' compensation petition to recover penalties under section 132a because applicant was charged vacation time and sick leave for attending medical appointments related to his disability. Crucial facts in *Lauher* are distinguishable from the instant case.

Even after Lauher had become permanent and stationary (P&S), he sought temporary disability indemnity (TDI). In addition, he sought nearly 200 hours of vacation time and sick leave for treatment of his injury, after the parties had stipulated he had become P&S with a permanent disability (PD). He asked for penalties pursuant to section 132a, arguing that his employer discriminated against him by not reimbursing him for the leave time.

Board granted Lauher's application and denied reconsideration. The Court of Appeal disagreed with Board and annulled the Board's decision. Our Supreme Court affirmed the decision of the Court of Appeal, denying Lauher the reimbursement he sought. Our high court explained that Lauher's employer did not single him out for disadvantageous treatment in the use of sick leave and

vacation time based on the industrial nature of his injury. All workers with injuries or sickness had to use sick leave or vacation time to leave the office for medical treatment. (*Lauher, supra,* 30 Cal. 4th at pp. 1300–1301.) (Footnote 2)

Moreover, he was not entitled to receive PD and temporary disability (TD) simultaneously.

Andersen established that City has a written, discriminatory policy which requires only industrially injured workers to use earned vacation time for attending medical appointments, while non–industrially injured workers could use sick leave for such appointments. (See MOU, §§ 45, 59; Santa Barbara Mun. Code, §§ 3.08.140, 3.08.220.) City admitted this, and did not establish a reasonable, legitimate business purpose for this discriminatory policy.

City claims that because sick leave is a creature of local law and regulation, section 132a, which is a state law concerning workers' compensation, does not apply to it. City contends it may preclude its employees from using sick leave for medical appointments related to industrial injuries, forcing them to use it only for non–industrial injuries and sickness. (See Gov. Code, § 21163, formerly § 21025.2 [permitting local entities to pass ordinances for sick leave].) (Footnote 3)

We disagree. Local government entities and unions may not create policies that discriminate against their industrially injured employees to their detriment, even if they have plenary power to provide sick leave. The creation and use of such policies contravene the mandate of section 132a. (See generally *Healy v. Industrial Acc. Commission, supra,* 41 Cal. 2d at pp. 121–122; *Judson Steel Corp. v. Workers' Comp. Appeals Bd., supra,* 22 Cal. 3d at p. 665, fn. 5; also see *County of Santa Barbara v. Workers' Comp. Appeals Bd., supra,* 109 Cal. App. 3d at pp. 215–216 [demotion of industrially injured deputy sheriff based on expectation that return to work was unlikely].)

City points to various Court of Appeal cases to support its position, but they are distinguishable. (*Patton v. Governing Board* (1978) 77 Cal. App. 3d 495 [143 Cal. Rptr. 593] [no payment to local government employee for accumulated sick leave prior to commencement of disability retirement]; accord, *Campbell v. City of Monrovia* (1978) 84 Cal. App. 3d 341 [148 Cal. Rptr. 679]; cf. *Marsille v. City of Santa Ana* (1976) 64 Cal. App. 3d 764 [134 Cal. Rptr. 743] [similar but concerning statutory leave of absence prior to disability retirement under PERS]; see also *Robertson v. City of Inglewood* (1978) 84 Cal. App. 3d 400 [148 Cal. Rptr. 560, 43 Cal. Comp. Cases 1499] [fireman received leave of absence with full pay under § 4850 but not accumulated sick leave before disability retirement]; *Willis v. City of Garden Grove* (1979) 93 Cal. App. 3d 208, 212–213 [155 Cal. Rptr. 493] [sick employee limited to specified option for receipt of accumulated sick leave before disability retirement]; accord, *Batters v. City of Santa Monica* (1980) 101 Cal. App. 3d 595, 605–607 [161 Cal. Rptr. 728] [fireman receiving disability leave of absence pursuant to § 4850 not entitled to accumulate sick leave as well before disability retirement].)

The case before us does not concern payment for accumulated sick leave prior to disability retirement, statutory leave of absence with pay in lieu of sick leave, or payment of TD. This case concerns the use of ordinary sick leave by active, industrially injured employees for medical appointments. City has made the use of sick leave dependent solely on whether or not the worker is industrially or non–industrially injured. Such disparate and detrimental treatment constitutes illegal discrimination in contravention of section 132a. (See *Healy v. Industrial Acc. Commission, supra,* 41 Cal. 2d at pp. 121–122; *Judson Steel Corp. v. Workers' Comp. Appeals Bd., supra,* 22 Cal. 3d at p. 665, fn. 5.)

City could choose not to provide sick leave to any of its employees. But, if City provides sick leave to its employees, it cannot refuse to permit its use for industrially–related medical appointments when non–industrially injured workers are not so restricted. Here, City permits non–industrially injured persons to use sick leave for medical appointments but requires industrially injured persons to use earned vacation time.

In conclusion, City may not discriminate against active, industrially–injured workers in the use of sick leave for medical appointments, as compared to non–industrially injured workers. Such a policy contravenes section 132a... .

Footnote 1. All statutory references are to the Labor Code unless otherwise stated.

Footnote 2. Our Supreme Court first explained that Lauher was not entitled to receive both TDI and PD after he had become P&S and returned to work. (See *Lauher, supra,* at pp. 1291–1292.) The employer's obligation to pay TDI ceases when the injured employee returns to work, is able to return to work, or achieves P&S status. (*Id.,* at pp. 1292–1293, 1297, 1300.) Lauher did not establish he had a legal right to receive TDI from his employer and retain his vacation time and sick leave. (*Id.,* at pp. 1299–1300.) We are not presented with this issue here.

Footnote 3. Former Government Code section 21025.2 provides, in pertinent part, that "[T]he retirement of a member [of PERS] who has been granted or is entitled to sick leave . . . shall not become effective until the expiration of such sick leave with compensation . . . unless the member applies for or consents to his retirement as of an earlier date. Sick leave shall be subject to the regular requirements of law and rules governing the use of sick leave."

Page 834, Column 1, sixth paragraph, insert following '…employment.'

In observing that prior to 2003 an employee could establish a prima facia case of discrimination by merely showing that as a result of an industrial injury the employer engaged in conduct detrimental to the applicant but, following *Lauher (supra),* above, an employee *must not only show detriment, but must also show that he or she was singled out for disadvantageous treatment because of his or her injury*; the Court of Appeal, Second District, in *County of San Louis Obispo v. WCAB (Martinez)* (2005) 70 Cal. Comp. Cases 1247, in so holding, stated, in part:

The County of San Luis Obispo (County) petitions for a writ of review to determine the lawfulness of a decision of the Workers' Compensation Appeals Board (WCAB) finding the County discriminated against its employee, Art Martinez, for sustaining a work–related injury. (Lab. Code, § 132a.) (Footnote 1)

The County contends it permissibly took Martinez off work because his medical restrictions were inconsistent with the requirements of his job. We agree that Martinez failed to establish a prima facie case of discrimination and that the County met its burden of showing reasonable business necessity…

Prior to 2003, an employee could establish a prima facie case of discrimination merely by showing that, as the result of an industrial injury, the employer engaged in conduct detrimental to him. (Barns v. Workers' Comp. Appeals Bd., *supra,* 216 Cal. App. 3d at p. 531.) If the employee made this showing, the burden shifted to the employer to show that its conduct was necessitated by the realities of doing business. (Ibid.)

However, an employee's burden of showing a prima facie case of discrimination was made heavier by the Supreme Court in Department of Rehabilitation v. Workers' Comp. Appeals Bd. (2003) 30 Cal. 4th 1281, 1298 [70 P.3d 1076, 135 Cal. Rptr. 2d 665, 68 Cal. Comp. Cases 831] (Lauher). "[F]or [an employee] merely to show he suffered an industrial injury and that he suffered some detrimental consequences as a result is insufficient to establish a prima facie case of discrimination within the meaning of section 132a." (Id. at p. 1300.) Lauher requires an employee not only to show detriment but also show that he was singled out for disadvantageous treatment because of his injury. (Id. at p. 1301.)

The parties argued and the WCAB decided this case under the Barns standard. Because the WCAB and the parties did not proceed under the correct legal standard, the record before the court contains no evidence that Martinez was singled out for disadvantageous treatment. Without such evidence, we cannot determine whether Martinez met his burden of proof. *It is unnecessary, however, to remand for the taking of evidence on this issue because the County has met its burden of showing it terminated Martinez because of a good faith belief that he could not perform the duties of his employment without risk of reinjuring himself.*

Reasonable Business Necessity

"Section 132a does not compel an employer to ignore the realities of doing business by 'reemploying' unqualified employees or employees for whom positions are no longer available." (Judson Steel Corp. v. Workers' Comp. Appeals Bd., *supra,* 22 Cal. 3d at p. 667.) An employer is not guilty of retaliatory discrimination when the employee cannot perform the customary work without risk of either reinjury or further injury. (Barns v. Workers' Comp. Appeals Bd., *supra,* 216 Cal. App. 3d at p. 534; Bennett v. Workers' Comp. Appeals Bd. (1997) 62 Cal. Comp. Cases 171 (writ den.); Carlock v. Workers' Comp. Appeals Bd. (1995) 60 Cal. Comp. Cases 1227 (writ den.).) (Footnote 2)

The WCAB's conclusion that the County did not meet its burden of showing reasonable business necessity is based on several errors of fact and law. The WCAB found the County did not meet its burden of showing business necessity because it was aware when it returned Martinez to work in February 2003 that he had work restrictions precluding him from subduing combative students. This finding is not supported by the evidence. The record shows that the County returned Martinez to work in February 2003 based on Dr. Kissel's opinion that Martinez was capable of handling altercations. It was not until after Martinez returned to work that Dr. Hutchinson and Dr. Ruda issued opinions contrary to that of Dr. Kissel and imposed work restrictions precluding Martinez from engaging in altercations.

The WCAB also erred by focusing on what the County knew at the time it returned Martinez to work. It is the employer's knowledge at the time it terminates an employee, not its knowledge at the time it returns him to work, that is relevant in determining whether an employer established reasonable business necessity. (Leamon v. Workers' Comp. Appeals Bd. (1987) 190 Cal. App. 3d 1409, 1414–1415 [235 Cal. Rptr. 912, 52 Cal. Comp. Cases 146].) *An employer may be justified in terminating an employee if at the time of termination the employer reasonably believes that returning the employee to his position would endanger the employee or others.* (Kirkman v. Workers' Comp. Appeals Bd. (1983) 48 Cal. Comp. Cases 805 (writ den.).)

The WCAB also found discrimination because the County did not obtain an additional medical opinion before it terminated Martinez. Again, this finding is not supported by the record or the law. Dr. Kissel's opinion that Martinez was able to handle aggressive students was contradicted by the later opinions of Martinez's own qualified medical examiner and treating physician. Under these circumstances, an additional medical opinion was not required. (See, e.g., Rossi v. Workers' Comp. Appeals Bd. (2001) 66 Cal. Comp. Cases 538 (writ den.) [no discrimination where employee's primary treating physician opined employee could return to work without restrictions, but later the employee's QME imposed significant restrictions]; Rosas v. Workers' Comp. Appeals Bd. (1998) 63 Cal. Comp. Cases 781 (writ den.) [no discrimination where employee's primary treating physician and QME opined employee could not perform usual and customary duties without modification]; see also Smith v. Workers' Comp. Appeals. Bd. (1996) 61 Cal. Comp. Cases 137, 139 (writ den.) [employer's decision to terminate is not discriminatory when the medical evidence is unclear or ambiguous]; Bergman v. Workers' Comp. Appeals Bd. (1989) 54 Cal. Comp. Cases 103 (writ den.) [no discrimination where medical reports as to an employee's ability to return to work are conflicting].)

The WCAB found the County acted in "bad faith" because it "manipulated the job analysis" by changing the maximum weight of students at Vicente School from 150 pounds to 300 pounds. Again, this finding could only have been reached by ignoring critical evidence. The record contains undisputed testimony from Martinez's department head, his supervisor, and Martinez himself, that students at Vicente sometimes weighed 300–350 pounds. This evidence demonstrates that the County corrected the job description to reflect the actual conditions at the school, not as a pretext for discrimination.

Substantial evidence supports the County's defense of reasonable business necessity. The order of the WCAB is annulled… .

Footnote 1. All statutory references are to the Labor Code.

Footnote 2. Although lacking precedential value, WCAB decisions reported in the California Compensation Cases reporter are of great weight in revealing the WCAB's contemporaneous interpretation and application of the workers' compensation laws. (Smith v. Workers' Comp. Appeals Bd. (2000) 79 Cal. App. 4th 530, 537, fn. 2 [94 Cal. Rptr. 2d 186, 65 Cal. Comp. Cases 277].)

In upholding the Board's finding that the employer discriminated against an employee by refusing to return her to her driving position after she was released to return to work by her treating physician, as well as by the AME, and there was no contrary medical evidence recommending she stay off of work, the Court of Appeal, Fourth District, in *San Diego Transit, et al. v. WCAB (Calloway)* (2006) 71 Cal. Comp. Cases 445, stated, in part:

Norma Calloway has been a bus driver for San Diego Transit (employer) since 1977. She sustained industrial injuries to her right upper body, shoulder, neck and back in 1996 and to her knees in 1998. Calloway was placed on temporary total disability for both injuries for two months, and resumed her usual duties as a driver in 1999. The agreed medical examiner issued a permanent and stationary report in June 2000 imposing restrictions on Calloway precluding her from engaging in certain activities and recommending a patella stabilizing brace for the right knee.

Calloway was on temporary total disability for two months in 2001 and again for 11 days in mid–2003. When she was cleared to work on these occasions, she provided her employer a release to return to work from her doctor, just as she had in the past, and resumed work as a driver. At the end of August 2003, Calloway experienced swelling in her right knee and her doctor (Dr. Towne) took her off work and referred her to another doctor (Dr. Close), who prescribed a different kind of brace (a neoprene knee sleeve). On September 8, 2003, Dr. Close gave Calloway a release to return to work.

On September 8 Calloway presented her employer with the release singed by Dr. Close, but her employer refused to honor it because it was not from her primary doctor. Calloway made an appointment to see Dr. Towne, obtained a release from him on September 12, and presented it to her employer the same day. The employer indicated Calloway would have to obtain a full examination report from Dr. Towne.

On September 29 Dr. Towne performed a full examination, wrote a narrative report and authorized Calloway to return to work; Calloway took the release to her employer that same day and was advised that someone would get in touch with her. After several days without a response, Calloway called the employer's human resources manager, who promised to call her back. Several more days passed before the human resources manager informed her that he still did not know what was happening. After waiting several more days, Calloway went to the human resources office to inquire about her return to work. The human resources manager called the employer's adjuster and then told Calloway he could not answer her questions and she should call her attorney. At the risk manager's direction, Calloway later scheduled an examination with the agreed medical examiner.

On October 20 Calloway told the agreed medical examiner she was desperate to return to work. The agreed medical examiner examined Calloway, and gave her a written report and a return to work release, which Calloway presented to her employer. Despite continued calls to her employer, Calloway was not given a date to return to work. In November the employer scheduled her for a fitness–for–duty exam with Dr. Torres. Dr. Torres issued a report dated November 28, finding Calloway could safely return to work as a bus driver. Calloway returned to work in December 2003.

Calloway filed a petition for Labor Code section 132a (Footnote 1) discrimination penalties based on the employer's delay in allowing her return to work as a driver. The workers' compensation judge found the employer had violated section 132a and awarded Calloway $10,000. The employer filed a petition for reconsideration. The Workers' Compensation Appeals Board (Board) denied reconsideration. The employer followed with this petition.

Review of a Board decision is limited to whether the Board acted without or in excess of its powers, and whether the order, decision or award was unreasonable, not supported by substantial evidence, or procured by fraud (§ 5952.)

The employer asserts the releases are not substantial evidence of discrimination because Calloway admitted making material misrepresentations to obtain them. Although Calloway conceded she minimized her pain to the agreed medical examiner, she testified she was completely truthful with Dr. Close, who cleared her for return, and completely truthful with Dr. Towne, who gave her a full examination, confirmed she could return to her customary duties as a bus driver and provided a full written report and return–to–work slips. In addition, the agreed medical examiner noted in his report that, although Calloway had no subjective complaints, he fully examined her and found her neck, back, upper body, and left knee objectively normal, "[t]he only residual . . . [being] her right knee, where she continues to exhibit tenderness and have a positive apprehension maneuver." The agreed medical examiner also reviewed her job description, concluded Calloway could return to her usual and customary duties, and determined the neoprene knee sleeve recommended by Dr. Close appropriate. The releases constitute substantial evidence.

Next, the employer argues the Board improperly denied its defense of business necessity despite its risk manager's testimony that the releases raised "red flags" because they purported to return Calloway to work without restrictions when she was wearing a brace, and the risk manager

thought the new brace looked more restrictive than the old brace and had concerns for public safety. The employer also asserts the law entitles it to assess each medical report for itself, unilaterally decide if a doctor's report constitutes substantial evidence, and make a business decision on the employee's ability to return to work.

The credibility determinations of the workers' compensation judge are entitled to great weight and should not be disturbed when they are supported by substantial evidence because the judge has the opportunity to observe the demeanor of witnesses and weigh their statements with their manner in testifying. (Garza v. Workers' Comp. Appeals Bd. (1970) 3 Cal. 3d 312, 318–319 [90 Cal. Rptr. 355, 475 P.2d 451, 35 Cal. Comp. Cas 500].) Here, the workers' compensation judge found the employer's representative was not "totally credible" and that her so–called concerns about Calloway's ability to return to work were "an attempt at an after–the–fact rationalization for the employer's actions." The workers' compensation judge explained her doubts about credibility were amplified by the risk manager's testimony that the new brace seemed more restrictive than the old one although the old brace was a Don Joy Legend knee brace with hinges that restricted knee motion. The new brace is by contrast a neoprene knee sleeve that stabilizes the patella, does not restrict motion and does not have hinges. The judge also noted none of the risk manager's purported questions were shared with the doctors, and any expression of concern for public safety came "almost as an afterthought" to the risk manager's testimony. We add, despite the risk manager's apparent confusion about the releases authorizing Calloway to return to work without restrictions when she was attempting to return wearing a brace, review of the reports should have made it clear that Dr. Towne and the agreed medical examiner wanted Calloway to wear the neoprene sleeve while she worked.

We also reject the employer's argument that the law allows it to decide unilaterally a doctor's report does not constitute substantial evidence and disregard it. None of the authorities cited by the employer stand for that proposition. Moreover, it is difficult to perceive that we would approve an employer's unilateral determination that there was no substantial evidence where, as here, the employer had releases from three doctors, narrative reports from two doctors that cleared the employee to resume her customary duties and were consistent with one another, and there was no other medical opinion.

Finally, we reject the argument that the Board applied an incorrect legal standard under Department of Rehabilitation v. Workers' Comp. Appeals Bd. (2003) 30 Cal. 4th 1281 [135 Cal. Rptr. 2d 665, 70 P.3d 1076, 68 Cal. Comp. Cas 831]. During the period between September and November 2003 when she was not allowed to return to work, Calloway received less than 75 percent of her salary. Calloway also testified other drivers who had industrial injuries were allowed to return to work; other drivers worked wearing a brace; Calloway was off of work for medical reasons 20 to 30 times in the past and was always able to return to her usual and customary work; and September 2003 was the only time the employer ever second–guessed her doctor's release or conducted an investigation before allowing her to return to work... .

Footnote 1. All statutory references are to the Labor Code.

Page 834, Column 1, sixth paragraph insert following '...of employment.'

In holding that an employer did not discriminate against an applicant where the employer used applicant's sick leave and vacation time when applicant, who had become permanent and stationary, returned to work following an industrial injury and took time off work to attend medical appointments for the injury, the California Supreme Court in *Department of Rehabilitation/State of California v. WCAB (Lauher)* (2003) 68 Cal. Comp. Cases 831 stated, in part:

Lauher next claims that his employer discriminated against him within the meaning of section 132a because he had suffered an industrial injury. This discrimination, he claims, took the form of his employer's insistence that he use his accumulated sick and vacation leave for the time he was out of the office seeing Dr. Houts for treatment of his injury. Lauher claims he was thus "treated differently than other employees who had not sustained a work–related injury . . . ." (Footnote 6)

Section 132a provides: "It is the declared policy of this state that there should not be discrimination against workers who are injured in the course and scope of their employment. [P] (1) Any employer who discharges, or threatens to discharge, *or in any manner discriminates* against any employee because he or she has filed or made known his or her intention to file a claim for compensation with his or her employer or an application for adjudication, or because the employee has received a rating, award, or settlement, is guilty of a misdemeanor and the employee's compensation shall be increased by one–half, but in no event more than ten thousand dollars ($10,000), together with costs and expenses not in excess of two hundred fifty dollars ($250). Any such employee shall also be entitled to reinstatement and *reimbursement* for lost wages and *work benefits* caused by the acts of the employer." (Italics added.) No criminal penalty is at issue in this case; we address only the Board's imposition of a $10,000 administrative penalty on Lauher's employer.

"[T]o warrant an award [pursuant to section 132a] the employee must establish at least a prima facie case of lost wages and benefits caused by the discriminatory acts of the employer." (*Dyer v. Workers' Comp. Appeals Bd.* (1994) 22 Cal. App. 4th 1376, 1386 [28 Cal. Rptr. 2d 30, 59 Cal. Comp. Cases 96].) The employee must establish discrimination by a preponderance of the evidence (*Western Electric Co. v. Workers' Comp. Appeals Bd.* (1979) 99 Cal. App. 3d 629, 640 [160 Cal. Rptr. 436, 44 Cal. Comp. Cases 1145]), at which point the burden shifts to the employer to establish an affirmative defense (*Barns v. Workers' Comp. Appeals Bd.* (1989) 216 Cal. App. 3d 524, 531 [266 Cal. Rptr. 503, 54 Cal. Comp. Cases 433]). Although we defer to the Board's determination of facts if supported by substantial evidence, we review the Board's legal decisions de novo, for "[i]t is for the court to decide whether the facts found by the Board constitute a violation of section 132a." (*Id.* at pp. 530–531.)

To decide the merits of Lauher's claim, we must decide what section 132a means when it refers to "discrimination." As one appellate court has noted, "[n]either the Legislature nor the courts have fashioned a clear rule for distinguishing those forms of discrimination which are actionable under section 132a and those forms which are not." (*Smith v. Workers' Comp. Appeals Bd.* (1984) 152 Cal. App. 3d 1104, 1108 [199 Cal. Rptr. 881, 49 Cal. Comp. Cases 212] (*Smith*).) Nevertheless, some boundary markers have been delineated. Under its express terms, an employer may not "discharge[], or threaten[] to discharge" an employee because, like Lauher, he has filed a claim for compensation. Moreover, citing the prefatory statement that "[i]t is the declared policy of this state that there should not be discrimination against workers who are injured in the course and scope of their employment" (§ 132a), we have explained that the type of discriminatory actions subject to penalty under section 132a is not limited to those enumerated in the statute. Instead, we have interpreted section 132a liberally to achieve the goal of preventing discrimination against workers injured on the job. (*Judson Steel Corp. v. Workers' Comp. Appeals Bd.* (1978) 22 Cal. 3d 658, 666–669 [150 Cal. Rptr. 250, 586 P.2d 564, 43 Cal. Comp. Cases 1205].) We immediately cautioned, however, that "[s]ection 132a does not compel an employer to ignore the realities of doing business by 'reemploying' unqualified employees or employees for whom positions are no longer available." (*Id.* at p. 667.)

Noting this last passage, the court in *Smith, supra,* 152 Cal. App. 3d 1104, held that "save for the two exceptions just described [i.e., reemploying employees who are unqualified or for whom no position is available], action *which works to the detriment of the employee* because of an injury is unlawful under section 132a." (*Id.* at p. 1109, italics added.) This test of "detriment" to the employee was accepted as the applicable standard in *Barns v. Workers' Comp. Appeals Bd., supra,* 216 Cal. App. 3d at page 531 ("a worker proves a violation of section 132a by showing that as the result of an industrial injury, the employer engaged in conduct detrimental to the worker") as well as by at least one commentator (1 Hanna, *supra,* § 10.11[1], p. 10–20 ["[t]he critical question is whether the employer's action caused detriment to an industrially–injured employee"]).

The Court of Appeal in this case, however, found the *Smith* formulation "analytically incomplete." The court explained that, although Lauher had clearly suffered a detriment by having to use his accumulated sick leave and vacation time for his visits to see Dr. Houts, he never established he "had a legal *right* to receive TDI and retain his accrued sick leave and vacation time, and that [his employer] had a corresponding legal *duty* to pay TDI and refrain from docking the sick leave and vacation time." (Footnote 7)

Thus, said the court, "[t]o meet the burden of presenting a prima facie claim of unlawful discrimination in violation of section 132a, it is insufficient that the industrially injured worker show only that . . . he or she suffered some adverse result as a consequence of some action or inaction by the employer that was triggered by the industrial injury. The claimant must also show that he or she had a legal right to receive or retain the deprived benefit or status, and the employer had a corresponding legal duty to provide or refrain from taking away that benefit or status."

We agree that for Lauher merely to show he suffered an industrial injury and that he suffered some detrimental consequences as a result is insufficient to establish a prima facie case of discrimination within the meaning of section 132a. As we explained, *ante,* our system of workers' compensation does not provide a make–whole remedy. "The Workers' Compensation Law is intended to award compensation for *disability* incurred in employment. 'The purpose of the award is not to make the employee whole for the loss which he has suffered but to prevent him and his dependents from becoming public charges during the period of his disability.' " (*Universal City Studios, Inc. v. Worker's Comp. Appeals Bd., supra,* 99 Cal. App. 3d at pp. 659–660.) "The purpose of workmen's compensation is to rehabilitate, not to indemnify, and its intent is limited to assuring the injured workman subsistence while he is unable to work and to effectuate his speedy rehabilitation and reentry into the labor market." (*Solari v. Atlas–Universal Service, Inc.* (1963) 215 Cal. App. 2d 587, 600 [30 Cal. Rptr. 407, 28 Cal. Comp. Cases 277].) Consistent with this view, for example, section 4653 provides that payment for temporary total disability is only "two–thirds of the average weekly earnings during the period of such disability."

An employer thus does not necessarily engage in "discrimination" prohibited by section 132a merely because it requires an employee to shoulder some of the disadvantages of his industrial injury. By prohibiting "discrimination" in section 132a, we assume the Legislature meant to prohibit treating injured employees differently, making them suffer disadvantages not visited on other employees because the employee was injured or had made a claim.

Lauher claims he was subjected to discrimination within the meaning of section 132a because he "was treated differently than other employees who had not sustained a work–related injury and were not under the mandates of the Labor Code."

He claims "[t]he employer's actions were directly related to the work injury and the resultant time the injured employee had to miss from work because of the medical appointments to cure or relieve the effects of the work injury." Lauher's argument fails to appreciate that, although his injury was industrial, nothing suggests his employer *singled him out for disadvantageous treatment because of the industrial nature of his injury.* We assume that employees with nonindustrial injuries must follow the same rule and use their sick leave when away from the office attending medical treatment. Certainly nothing Lauher alleges suggests otherwise. For example, he does not allege he alone is being singled out for the requirement that he use his sick leave, or that other employees are permitted to leave the office for medical appointments related to nonindustrial injuries and are not required to use their sick leave.

Because Lauher does not allege that other employees are permitted to be away from their workplace for medical care yet need not use their sick leave if they wish to be paid their full salaries, we conclude Lauher fails to demonstrate he was the victim of discrimination within the meaning of section 132a. To hold otherwise would elevate those who had suffered industrial injuries to a point where they enjoyed rights superior to those of their coworkers. Nothing in the history or meaning of section 132a's antidiscrimination rule supports such an interpretation. (Footnote 8)... .

Footnote 6. Although Lauher argued in the Court of Appeal that this discrimination also took the form of failure to pay him TDI for his time away from work seeing Dr. Houts, it does not appear he has renewed that claim in this court. In any event, as we find he was not entitled to TDI once his industrial injury became permanent and stationary, SCIF cannot be found to have discriminated against him by failing to pay TDI in this circumstance.

Footnote 7. As noted, *ante,* Lauher no longer claims he is entitled to a penalty under section 132a due to his employer's failure to pay TDI.

Footnote 8. Because we find Lauher failed to establish a prima facie case of discrimination within the meaning of section 132a, we need not address SCIF's contention that employer had a legitimate business reason for requiring Lauher to use his sick leave and vacation time when away from the office seeing Dr. Houts for treatment. For the same reason, we also decline to address the argument by amicus curiae California Employment Law Council that we should reexamine and discard the holding of *Judson Steel Corp. v. Workers' Comp. Appeals Bd., supra*, 22 Cal. 3d 658, that section 132a should be liberally construed in favor of injured workers. We also decline to address the invitation to reinterpret section 132a to require proof of discriminatory intent. These arguments are not necessary to resolve the present matter and, in any event, were not raised by any party or amicus curiae before the WCJ, the WCAB, or the Court of Appeal.

§ 17.0.1 Appeals Board May Not Interpret Collective Bargaining Agreement to Rule on Discrimination

Page 874, Column 1, fourth paragraph, insert immediately following '...67.)'

See also *Roadway Express, Inc. v. WCAB (McCormick)* (2006) 71 Cal. Comp. Cases 864, where the judge stated, in part:

In an analysis of anti–discrimination rights under California's Fair Employment and Housing Act (FEHA), a District Court found no preemption of FEHA under the LMRA. The Court explained that the right to be free from discrimination exist [sic] independently of private agreements and cannot be altered or waived. FEHA creates non–negotiable state rights independent of rights under a collective bargaining agreement. Perez v. Proctor & Gamble Manufacturing Co., 161 F.Supp.2d 1110 (E.D.Ca. 2001).

Another District Court rejected an employer's claim that the LMRA preempted the New Jersey Law Against Discrimination (NJLAD). Kube v. New Penn Motor Express, Inc., 865 F.Supp. 221, 228, 229 (D.N.J. 1994) explained that the state law right to be free from discrimination because of physical handicap or medical condition was defined and enforced under state law without reference to the terms of any collective bargaining agreement, even where the collective bargaining agreement itself allowed discrimination. In language especially relevant to the argument in this case, where Roadway justifies its actions based on the modified work program established in the parties' collective bargaining agreement, the District Court in Kube cautioned that "even if the collective bargaining agreement had incorporated some sort of modified work program, defendant still could not escape the obligations established by the NJLAD." [Emphasis by WCJ]

The Court of Appeal in Dechene v. Pinole Point Steel Co., 76 Cal. App. 4th 33, 90 Cal. Rptr.2d 15 (1999) declined to find preemption by the LMRA of the employee's claims for wrongful termination in violation of public policy and for discrimination in retaliation for giving deposition testimony, explaining that the LMRA cannot be read broadly to preempt non–negotiable rights conferred on individual employees under state law.

Finally, the Workers' Compensation Appeals Board itself has expressly declined to find LMRA preemption of the individual worker's rights under Labor Code section 132a. Bellflower Unified School District v. WCAB (Reynolds), [(2002) 68 Cal. Comp. Cases 55 (writ denied)]; The Vons Companies v. WCAB (McVea), [(1999) 64 Cal. Comp. Cases 930 (writ denied)]; Albertson's, Inc. v. WCAB (Gordon), [(1994) 59 Cal. Comp. Cases 430 (writ denied)]; see General Telephone v. WCAB (Gomez), [(1994) 59 Cal. Comp. Cases 490 (writ denied)]... .

Page 874, Column 1, eighth paragraph, insert following '...1109.)'

In *McFadden v. WCAB* (2005) 70 Cal. Comp. Cases 1180, the Board upheld a judge's ruling that the Board lacked subject matter jurisdiction over applicant's Labor Code §132a claim, under which applicant alleged that he was wrongfully denied his seniority rights to return to work after his industrial injury, when determination of the applicant's seniority rights was dependent on interpretation of collective bargaining agreement between applicant's employer and the union. The Board found that interpretation of the collective bargaining agreement was preempted by the Federal Railway Labor Act.

The judge noted that once applicant's seniority rights were determined pursuant to the collective bargaining agreement, the 132a claim could be heard by the Board.

§ 18.0   TIME LIMITATIONS

§ 18.1   Normal Injury Benefits

Issue Must Be Raised at Mandatory Settlement Conference

Page 896, Column 2, sixth paragraph, insert immediately following heading: Issue Must Be Raised at Mandatory Settlement Conference

If a defendant has a statute of limitations defense, but does not raise that defense as an issue at a mandatory settlement conference, the issue will be deemed waived at trial.

§ 18.11   Estoppel to Raise Defense of Statute of Limitations

Page 918, Column 1, third paragraph, insert following '...of limitations.'

See *Davenport v. WCAB* (2005) 70 Cal. Comp. Cases 1566, where failure to give an employee a claim form tolled the statute of limitations.

Page 919, Column 2, thirteenth paragraph, insert following '...attachment.'

When an employer has knowledge that an employee has suffered an occupational injury and fails to give the employee notice about workers' compensation benefits, the employer may be precluded from relying on the defense of the statute of limitations. See *Kaiser Foundation Hospitals v. Workers' Compensation Appeals Board (Martin)* (1985) 39 Cal. 3d 57. See also *Ocean View School District v. WCAB (Angelique Estrada)* (2006) 8 WCAB Rptr. 10,085, where the employee immediately informed her employer of her injury and the employer gave her a workers' compensation claim form, but there was no evidence in the record that the employer complied with Regulation 9880 [written notice to new employees about their rights to workers' compensation] and Regulation 9881 [posting of notice to the employer's employees about rights to workers' compensation]. Both Regulations include a requirement that the employee be informed of the time limits for filing compensation claims.

§ 18.11(A)   Employee Notices

Page 932, Column 2, first paragraph, insert following '...in this case.'

The Court of Appeal, Second District, in *Arciga v. WCAB* (2007) 72 Cal. Comp. Cases 1, an unpublished but well reasoned opinion, in describing whether a farm worker should have been aware her aching hands were caused by a cumulative trauma injury, stated, in part:

Maria Arciga petitioned this court for writ of review after the Workers' Compensation Appeals Board (Board) denied her claim for workers' compensation (WC) benefits. We denied her petition. Our Supreme Court transferred the matter back to this court with directions to vacate our order and issue a writ of review.

We have done so. For the reasons we shall explain, we remand the matter to the Board to reconsider whether, under Labor Code section 5402, (Footnote 1) Kendall Jackson Wine Estates, Ltd. (KJ) had inquiry notice of possible industrial injury to Arciga's hands while she was pruning vines for it. The Board shall also determine whether Arciga knew she had sustained cumulative trauma (CT) before KJ terminated her from work under section 5412. The Board in its discretion may send the matter back to the WCJ to take additional evidence if it deems it necessary to do so.

FACTS AND PROCEDURAL HISTORY

KJ repeatedly hired Arciga as a seasonal farm worker between May 1999 and January 12, 2004. Before January 2004, her tasks included tying and "training" vines, removing buds, and picking grapes. She had never pruned vines before. In January 2004, KJ permitted Arciga and some other women to prune vines for the first time.

On January 5, 2004, Arciga and about 120 other farm workers began pruning KJ's vines six days per week, under supervision. After two days of training, the workers were required to meet daily production quotas. The quotas required workers to make roughly 14,000 pruning cuts per day. They were told that if they failed to meet the quotas, they would be laid off.

On the third day of pruning, Arciga's hands began to hurt. The next day, Arciga complained to the foreman, Celestino Torres, that her hands were blistered and hurt. Torres provided Arciga with tape to wrap her hands. She also told the vineyard manager, Monica Thompson, she could not sleep because of pain in her hands. Thompson told Arciga it was her decision whether or not to continue working.

Arciga did not quit. Instead, KJ terminated her for cause on January 12, 2004, several days after she complained of injuries, for failing to meet its production quotas. Of the 120 workers, only about a third met the production quotas. Of those, KJ considered only about 20 workers sufficiently productive not to be terminated. As in the past, KJ gave Arciga a layoff notice which she signed but did not read. Arciga is poorly educated, and believed the notice was just a prerequisite for obtaining unemployment insurance. Above her signature, however, the layoff notice declared that Arciga had suffered no work–related injuries.

Two days later, on January 14, 2004, Arciga saw her family physician, Dr. Zuckerbraun, and complained of pain in both her hands and forearms. After examining her, Dr. Zuckerbraun reported that she may have "early carpal tunnel syndrome from working with grapes," and "strained wrists." He prescribed medication for her injuries.

On January 21, 2004, Arciga went to California Rural Legal Assistance (CRLA). They gave her a WC application which she provided to Arthur Montelongo, the human resources manager at KJ. Montelongo filled out an accident report and referred her to the Industrial Medical Group (IMG). Arciga saw Doctors Paul Christensen and Simon Boughey at IMG. They diagnosed and treated her for bilateral hand tendonitis. Doctor Christensen released Arciga for limited work, but precluded pruning. Her own orthopedist, Doctor Richard D. Scheinberg, recommended similar work restrictions, precluding work involving gripping and grasping.

Arciga filed this WC claim on April 21, 2004, after the 30–day limit set forth in section 5400. The WCJ found her claim was barred because she filed it after she was terminated. (§ 3600, subd. (a)(10).) The WCJ explained that Arciga knew she had to report industrial injuries immediately and failed to do so.

In her petition for reconsideration, Arciga asserted she did not know she had suffered from a cumulative trauma (CT) injury at work, but KJ was on notice of her work injuries. She argued that KJ should be equitably estopped to assert the post–termination rule because she had complained that her hands hurt and she could not sleep while she was still working for KJ.

In recommending denial of her petition for reconsideration, the WCJ said he could not accept "the leap" that complaints about aches and pains from "hard and heavy work" constitute actual, suggested or implied knowledge (notice) of industrial injury to KJ, which would trigger the duty to provide WC. The Board adopted the WCJ's recommendation and denied reconsideration.

DISCUSSION

Thirty–Day Notice

In general, a written claim for WC must be served upon the employer within 30 days after an industrial injury occurs and before one is terminated. (§ 5400; *Honeywell v. Workers' Comp. Appeals Bd.* (2005) 35 Cal. 4th 24, 32 [105 P.3d 544, 24 Cal. Rptr. 3d 179, 70 Cal. Comp. Cases 97].) Section 5402 provides, however, that "[k]nowledge of an injury, obtained from any source, on the part of an employer, his or her managing agent, ... foreman, or other person in authority, or knowledge of the assertion of a claim of injury sufficient to afford opportunity to the employer to make an investigation into the facts, is equivalent to service

under Section 5400." Such inquiry notice supersedes the 30–day limitation to file claims which is set forth in section 5400.

Section 3600, subdivision (a)(10)(A), also provides an exception to the 30–day post–termination rule. When a claim for WC is filed after notice of termination or layoff, and it is for injury occurring prior to the termination notice, no compensation shall be paid "unless the employee demonstrates by a preponderance of the evidence that one or more of the following conditions apply: [P] (A) The employer has notice of the injury, . . . prior to the notice of termination or layoff." (*Ibid.*)

Arciga testified at the WC hearing that on the third and fourth days she pruned the vines, she informed both Torres and Thompson that her hands hurt. She told Thompson she could not sleep because of the pain in her hands. She contends that these complaints are tantamount to notice of industrial injury; therefore, her complaints triggered KJ's duty to provide WC. Torres testified that she might have complained at that time, and he remembered giving tape to one of the workers to cover her blisters. When Montelongo filled out the accident report, he listed the date of injury as January 7, 2004, sent her to a doctor, but concluded the claim was untimely.

The short, 30–day limitations provision should be narrowly construed so as to favor the employee and provide WC coverage. (*Bland v. Workmen's Comp. App. Bd.* (1970) 3 Cal. 3d 324, 329 [475 P.2d 663, 90 Cal. Rptr. 431, 35 Cal. Comp. Cases 513]; and see *City of Fresno v. Workers' Comp. Appeals Bd.* (1985) 163 Cal. App. 3d 467, 473 [209 Cal. Rptr. 463, 50 Cal. Comp. Cases 53] [statute of limitations should not begin to run until employee receives medical advice].) Indeed, rigid formalism about such procedural matters has been deemed an "ironic anachronism." (*Bland, supra,* at p. 334.) Furthermore, although the employee bears the burden of timely notifying the employer of an injury, express notice that one has sustained a "work–related injury" is unnecessary if the employer is already aware of the injury or finds out about it from other sources. (*Honeywell v. Workers' Comp. Appeals Bd., supra,* 35 Cal. 4th at p. 33.) The facts suggest that by January 7, 2004, KJ was on inquiry notice that Arciga had sustained an industrial injury.

The WCJ and Board concluded that this claim was foreclosed because it was filed after Arciga was terminated, and concerned aches and pains that are a normal part of hard work that do not constitute industrial injury. Therefore they dismissed Arciga's complaints, concluding that she must have known that work caused her injury. The WCJ and Board found that Arciga's complaints "about hard and heavy work" is not the equivalent of actual, suggested or implied knowledge of an injury. But, Arciga told supervisors that her hands were so painful and blistered she could not sleep. It thus appears she reported her injuries while working, even though she did not articulate her injury as "work–related" or "disabling."

Despite these painful injuries, Arciga continued to work. As Thompson testified, Arciga was "a loyal . . . employee" who had "a good work ethic." Indeed, KJ had hired her each season for the past five years. Arciga had never filed a WC claim before against KJ, despite being laid off several times. It is clear that Arciga did not want to create trouble.

Arciga's reports of pain in her hands, and her supervisor's reactions to her comments, appear to establish that KJ was on inquiry notice that she was injured and would be entitled to WC. Nonetheless, they did not provide her with immediate medical care or give her appropriate WC forms to file a claim.

Our Supreme Court has said that "[t]he law does not award compensation for mere pain or physical impairment, unless it is of such character as to raise a presumption of incapacity to earn." (*Marsh v. Industrial Acc. Com.* (1933) 217 Cal. 338, 344 [18 P.2d 933, 19 I.A.C. 159].) When work causes pain so severe that one cannot sleep, it should be deemed disabling for purposes of WC.

All of the foregoing suggest the Board may have taken too narrow a view of WC coverage in this case.

Cumulative Trauma

Section 3208.1 defines the "cumulative injury" exception to the 30–day rule. It states that "cumulative injury" occurs from "repetitive . . . physically traumatic activities extending over a period of time, the combined effect of which causes any disability or need for medical treatment." (*Ibid.*) The date of such injury "is that date upon which the employee first suffered disability therefrom and either knew, or in the exercise of reasonable diligence should have known, that such disability was caused by his present or prior employment." (§ 5412.)

"Disability" for this purpose means an impairment of some bodily function that results in incapacity to perform some tasks usually encountered at work, and a concomitant loss of earning capacity. (See *Chavira v. Workers' Comp. Appeals Bd.* (1991) 235 Cal. App. 3d 463, 474 [286 Cal. Rptr. 600, 56 Cal. Comp. Cases 631]; *Permanente Medical Group v. Workers' Comp. Appeals Bd.* (1985) 171 Cal. App. 3d 1171, 1179–1180 [217 Cal. Rptr. 873, 50 Cal. Comp. Cases 491]; *J.T. Thorp, Inc. v. Workers' Comp. Appeals Bd.* (1984) 153 Cal. App. 3d 327, 336 [200 Cal. Rptr. 219, 49 Cal. Comp. Cases 224]; § 5412.) Thus, CT concerns work injuries that develop over time due to repetitive trauma, and cause earning capacity to be impaired. One may still be able to work while suffering from such an injury.

In general, workers are not deemed to know that cumulative trauma injuries are work related. In assessing the worker's knowledge, courts should consider the intelligence, training and qualifications of the worker as well as the nature of the disability. (*City of Fresno v. Workers' Comp. Appeals Bd., supra,* 163 Cal. App. 3d at p. 473.) Any doubts as to compensability of injuries, for purposes of WC, must be resolved in favor of the worker. (*E & J Gallo Winery v. Workers' Comp. Appeals Bd.* (2005) 134 Cal. App. 4th 1536, 1552–1553 [37 Cal. Rptr. 3d 208, 70 Cal. Comp. Cases 1644]; *Fresno, supra,* at p. 474; § 3202.)

That Arciga's hands hurt over the course of several days of pruning does not necessarily lead to the conclusion that she was aware of or should have known she was suffering from CT.

Usually employees are not aware they are suffering from CT because the injury or disease takes time to become apparent. Here, there was no sudden, specific injury, and Arciga could work despite her pain. Furthermore, CT concerns not only incremental injury but disability, or the loss of earning capacity. Because Arciga did not quit, she did not suffer loss of income at the time. It is likely she did not know she would suffer the loss of earning capacity. Both of her supervisors, Thompson and Torres, testified they did not know what cumulative trauma was. It would be unreasonable to expect a farm worker like Arciga, with limited education, to understand the concept of cumulative trauma.

When an employer is on inquiry notice that a worker may have sustained CT on the job, it is estopped to assert the 30–day limitations period. (See *Pacific Employers Ins. Co. v. Industrial Accident Commission* (1949) 92 Cal. App. 2d 124, 126 [206 P.2d 372, 14 Cal. Comp. Cases 82] [employer on inquiry notice when worker tells supervisor his shoulder hurt from lifting boxes of peaches]; also see *Buena Ventura Gardens v. Workers' Comp. Appeals Bd.* (1975) 49 Cal. App. 3d 410, 416 [122 Cal. Rptr. 714, 40 Cal. Comp. Cases 434].) In this case, Arciga told her field foreman that her hands hurt and he brought tape to wrap her hands. She then told Thompson, the vineyard manager, that her hands hurt so badly she could not sleep.

Arciga's ability to understand and articulate her condition and circumstances, before she was provided medical and legal assistance, appears quite limited. (See *Fruehauf Corp. v. Workmen's Compensation Appeals Bd.* (1968) 68 Cal. 2d 569, 577 [440 P.2d 236, 68 Cal. Rptr. 164, 33 Cal. Comp. Cases 300] [unreasonable to hold that employee suffering several minor traumas should be deemed injured for purposes of statute of limitations until injury ripens into disability and worker knows its etiology was work]; see also *Chambers v. Workmen's Compensation Appeals Bd.* (1968) 69 Cal. 2d 556, 559 [446 P.2d 531, 72 Cal. Rptr. 651, 33 Cal. Comp. Cases 722]; *Paula Insurance Co. v. Workers' Comp. Appeals Board* (1998) 63 Cal. Comp. Cases 1300 (writ denied) [Spanish speaking farm laborer should not be charged with responsibility for knowledge of medical/legal causation].)

The conclusions reached by the Board do not appear to comport with case law concerning cumulative injuries and the solicitude to be accorded workers like Arciga. Where there is doubt about whether a worker has sustained industrial injury, the determination whether a worker is entitled to WC must favor the worker. (§ 3202.)

It appears that the Board has construed the post–termination rules concerning employer knowledge and CT too narrowly. Accordingly, we remand this matter with directions that the Board annul its decision and conduct further proceedings to determine whether Arciga sustained CT and whether KJ was on inquiry notice while she was working that she was suffering from work–related injuries... .

Footnote 1. All statutory references are to the Labor Code unless otherwise stated.

Intentionally blank

§ 19.0 HOW TO APPLY FOR NORMAL BENEFITS

§ 19.1 Claim Form

Page 944, Column 1, second paragraph, insert following '…5402.'

However, the California State Supreme Court in *Honeywell, supra,* stated that the Appeals Board's "reasonably certain" standard which looks to negligence in assessing whether an industrial injury has occurred or is being asserted, is inequitable. Further, the high Court stated, "the Board's standard, moreover, ignores the detrimental reliance element of equitable estoppel…" See section 19.1.1 of this book for a full discussion of the *Honeywell* case.

§ 19.1.1 Presumption of Compensability – Labor Code section 5402

Page 958, Column 2, third paragraph, insert following '…792.'

A presumption is an assumption of fact that the law requires to be made from another fact or group of facts or otherwise established in an action and may be considered at anytime, is mandatory on the Board and not dependent upon whether a party timely raises the presumption as an issue at a Mandatory Settlement Conference.

A judge may raise the issue of a presumption of compensability as provided for in Labor Code section 5402 sua sponte (at his or her own will) at trial. *Leprino Foods v. WCAB (Owens)* (2007) 72 Cal. Comp. Cases 605.

See *Fleetwood Enterprises, Inc. v. WCAB (Moody)* (2005) 70 Cal. Comp. Cases 1659, where the Court of Appeal, Fourth District, explained that although an employer's knowledge of an industrial injury makes it unnecessary for the employee to provide prompt notice, it does trigger the employer's duty to provide workers' compensation information to the employee, but an employer has no duty to reject a claim until an employee actually files a claim form with the employer. The Court stated, in pertinent part:

However, shortly after the petition was filed, the Supreme Court decided *Honeywell v. Workers' Comp. Appeals Bd.* (2005) 35 Cal. 4th 24, 29 [105 P.3d 544, 24 Cal. Rptr. 3d 179, 70 Cal. Comp. Cas 97] (*Honeywell*), in which it held

that the employer's duty to notify the employee that his or her claim is rejected *only* arises when the employee actually files a formal claim. The court explained that although the employer's knowledge of an industrial injury makes it unnecessary for the employee to provide prompt notice (§§ 5400, 5402, subd. (a)), and *does* trigger the employer's duty to provide information, the plain language of section 5402 compels the conclusion that the employer has no duty to reject a claim until it is actually filed.

Applicant attempts belatedly to fit this case under the sole exception recognized in *Honeywell*–estoppel. The Supreme Court stated that if the employer is aware of an industrial injury (see fn. 5), and either refuses to provide a claim form or leads the employee to believe no claim is necessary, the 90–day period may begin before the claim is actually filed *if* the employee "suffered some loss of benefits or setback as to the claim." (*Honeywell, supra,* 35 Cal. 4th at p. 37.) However, on the record before us we reject the contention… .

§ 19.2 Administrative Assistance

Page 972, Column 2, sixth paragraph, delete chart, insert the following:

DIVISION OF WORKERS COMPENSATION INFORMATION AND ASSISTANCE OFFICERS DISTRICT OFFICES

Bureau Headquarters
Bob C. Wong, Manager

1515 Clay Street
17th Floor
Oakland, CA 94612
Tel: (510) 286–7100
Fax: (510) 286–7155
Recorded information: (800) 736–7401
Website: www.dir.ca.gov/dwc
Email: dwc@dir.ca.gov

Anaheim
1661 No. Raymond Avenue, Suite 200
Anaheim, CA 92801
Tel: (714) 738–4038

Bakersfield
1800 30th Street, Suite 100
Bakersfield, CA 93301
Tel: (661) 395–2514

Eureka
100 "H" Street, Room 201
Eureka, CA 95501–0421
Tel: (707) 441–5723

Fresno
2550 Mariposa Street, Room 2035
Fresno, CA 93721–2280
Tel: (559) 445–5355

Goleta
6755 Hollister Avenue, Room 100
Goleta, CA 93117
Tel: (805) 968–4158

Grover Beach
1562 W. Grand Avenue
Grover Beach, CA 93433–2261
Tel: (805) 481–3296

Long Beach
300 Oceangate Street, 3rd floor
Long Beach, CA 90802–4460
Tel: (562) 590–5240

Los Angeles
320 W. 4th Street, 9th floor
Los Angeles, CA 90013
Tel: (213) 576–7389

Marina del Rey
4720 Lincoln Blvd
Marina del Rey, CA 90292
Tel: (310) 482–3820

Oakland
1515 Clay Street, 6th floor
Oakland, CA 94612
Tel: (510) 622–2861

Oxnard
2220 E. Gonzales Road, Suite 100
Oxnard, CA 93030
Tel: (805) 485–3528

Pomona
732 Corporate Center Drive
Pomona, CA 91768
Tel: (909) 623–8568

Redding
2115 Akard, Room 21
Redding, CA 96001–2796
Tel: (530) 225–2047

Riverside
3737 Main Street, Room 300
Riverside, CA 92501
Tel: (951) 782–4347

San Bernardino
464 W. Fourth Street, Suite 239
San Bernardino, CA 92401
Tel: (909) 383–4522

San Diego
7575 Metropolitan Drive, Suite 202
San Diego, CA 92102–4402
Tel: (619) 767–2082

San Francisco
455 Golden Gate Avenue, 2nd floor
San Francisco, CA 94102
Tel: (415) 703–5020

San Jose
100 Paseo de San Antonio, Room 240
San Jose, CA 95113
Tel: (408) 277–1292

Santa Ana
28 Civic Center Plaza, Room 451
Santa Ana, CA 92701–4701
Tel: (714) 558–4597

Sacramento
2424 Arden Way, Suite 230
Sacramento, CA 95825
Tel: (916) 263–2741

Salinas
1880 North Main Street, Suite 100
Salinas, CA 93906–2204
Tel: (831) 443–3058

Santa Rosa
50 "D" Street, Room 430
Santa Rosa, CA 95404
Tel: (707) 576–2452

Stockton
31 East Channel Street, Room 450
Stockton, CA 95202
Tel: (209) 948–7980

Van Nuys
6150 Van Nuys Blvd., Room 105
Van Nuys, CA 91401–3373
Tel: (818) 901–5367

The Division of Workers' Compensation provides detailed information and forms at its website:
www.dir.ca.gov/dwc

§ 19.3 Rights of Employer to Notification of Claim From Insurance Carrier and Right to Objection to Claims/Settlements – Employer's Bill of Rights

Page 983, Column 1, first paragraph, insert following '...3759.'

In *Leegin Creative Leather Products, Inc. v. WCAB (Diaz)* (2005) 70 Cal. Comp. Cases 1108, an employer brought a fraud action against one of its employees alleging the employee had knowingly filed a fraudulent workers' compensation claim. The employer's alleged damages [were] the increased insurance premiums it will be required to pay as a result of the claim. The employee filed a special motion to strike the employer's complaint under Code of Civil Procedure section 425.16, the so–called "anti–SLAPP statute."

The lower Court granted the employee's motion and awarded attorney fees and costs. The employer appealed and, in affirming the lower Court's decision because there was no probability the employer would prevail on the fraud claim, the Court stated, in part:

Leegin contends: "As a matter of law, [its] fraud claim is not encompassed under the exclusivity provision of the [Workers' Compensation Act]." (Underscoring omitted.) Leegin reviews at length case law discussing the doctrine of workers' compensation exclusivity. However, Leegin's contention and analysis misframe the issue. With limited exceptions, the exclusivity provisions (Lab. Code, §§ 3601 and 3602) bar actions by an employee against an employer seeking redress for injury to an employee. The provisions do not address an employer's right to sue an employee. (See Charles J. Vacanti, M.D., Inc. v. State Comp. Ins. Fund (2001) 24 Cal. 4th 800, 810–812 [14 P.3d 234, 102 Cal. Rptr. 2d 562, 65 Cal. Comp. Cases 1402].)

Given the procedural posture of this case – dismissal of the complaint pursuant to an anti–SLAPP motion – the real issue is whether Leegin has demonstrated a probability it will prevail upon the merits of its fraud claim. (Footnote 4)

It did not and cannot do so.

"Under California law, a cause of action for fraud requires the plaintiff to prove (a) a knowingly false misrepresentation by the defendant, (b) made with the intent to deceive or to induce reliance by the plaintiff, (c) justifiable reliance by the plaintiff, and (d) resulting damages. [Citation.]" (Wilkins v. National Broadcasting Co. (1999) 71 Cal. App. 4th 1066, 1081 [84 Cal. Rptr. 2d 329].) In this case, Leegin can not establish the elements either of justifiable reliance or resulting damage.

Leegin's complaint alleged that it reasonably relied upon Santiaguin's misrepresentations by forwarding her claim to its insurer SCIF. However, as a matter of law, Leegin's forwarding of the claim to its insurer does not constitute detrimental reliance. To the contrary, as we now explain, controlling law, as well as the SCIF policy, establish that Leegin was required to forward the claim to SCIF. Because Leegin had no choice but to send SCIF the claim, it could not have "relied" upon any misrepresentations made by Santiaguin.

Labor Code section 5401, subdivision (a), requires an employer to provide an employee with a workers' compensation claim form and a notice of potential eligibility for benefits within one working day after it receives notice or knowledge of an injury. The employee completes and files the claim form with the employer. (Lab. Code, § 5401, subd. (c).) The employer is then required to provide a copy of the completed form to its workers' compensation insurer. (Lab. Code, § 5401, subd. (c); see also 8 Cal. Code Regs., § 10119.) Once the insurer receives the claim, "the insurer assumes responsibility for adjusting the claim . . . . [P] The [insurer] must accept or reject the claim within 90 days after the claim form is filed; otherwise, the injury will be presumed compensable . . . . [P] If [the insurer] decides to reject the claim, it must send a notice denying liability for all compensation benefits within 14 days after the decision to deny, stating the reasons for the denial, and stating the claimant's remedies." (Cal. Workers' Compensation Practice (Cont.Ed.Bar 4th ed. 2004) §§ 1.21, 1.22, p. 18.)

Leegin's workers' compensation policy with SCIF tracks these statutory obligations. Part Four of the policy is entitled: "Your Duties If Injury Occurs." (Footnote 5)

It recites: "Tell us at once if an injury occurs that may be covered by this policy." (Italics added.) The policy requires Leegin to furnish SCIF with all information related to the workers' compensation claim, to promptly give SCIF "all notices, demands and legal papers related to the injury, claim, proceeding or suit[,]" and to cooperate and assist in SCIF's investigation and defense of the claim.

Given this framework, Leegin's claim of reasonable reliance fails as a matter of law. Simply stated, Leegin had no choice but to forward the claim to SCIF. It was required to do so both by law and by the insurance policy provisions. Leegin was nothing more than a conduit in passing the claim onto its insurer. Leegin therefore errs, as a matter of law, in alleging that it sent the claim to SCIF in reliance upon Santiaguin's misrepresentations. (Footnote 6)

Hence, Leegin's claim of fraud cannot be sustained.

Furthermore, we note that if an employer such as Leegin believes a claim is fraudulent, it has a statutory remedy within the workers' compensation framework. Labor Code section 3761 provides that if, while the claim is pending, the employer has actual knowledge of facts that would tend to disprove any aspect of the employee's claim, it must promptly notify its insurer in writing. (Lab. Code, § 3761, subd. (b).) This provision is consistent with the general principle that it is the insurer who investigates a claim and decides whether or not to contest or settle it.

In addition to failing to establish the element of reliance, Leegin failed to establish damages. "In order to recover for fraud, as in any other tort, the plaintiff must plead and prove the 'detriment proximately caused' by the defendant's tortious conduct. (Civ. Code, § 3333.) Deception without resulting loss is not actionable fraud. [Citation.]" (Service by Medallion, Inc. v. Clorox Co. (1996) 44 Cal. App. 4th 1807, 1818 [52 Cal. Rptr. 2d 650].)

Leegin's complaint alleged damages in the form of increased premiums. This claim is premature because Santiaguin's claim has not yet been adjudicated. If it is determined that Santiaguin's claim is false, Leegin will not suffer any damages. (Footnote 7)When an employer properly notifies its insurer of any facts suggesting a fraudulent claim (Lab. Code, § 3761, subd. (b)) and the Appeals Board thereafter determines that the employee is *not* entitled to compensation, (Footnote 8) "the insurer shall reimburse the employer for any premium paid solely due to the inclusion of the successfully challenged payments in the calculation of the employer's experience modification." (Footnote 9)

(Lab. Code, § 3761, subd. (d).) (Footnote 10)

In its letter brief to this court (see fn. 3, *supra*), Leegin amplified its claim of damages. Because Santiaguin was no longer working, Leegin claimed it either had to pay other employees overtime to cover her job or had to spend money to hire and train a new employee. However, these expenses have nothing to do with whether or not Santiaguin's claim is false. As Leegin itself notes, "the loss of any employee to a company for an extended period of time, whether because of injury, sickness, leave, or dismissal, creates the need to either replace that employee with an existing company employee or to hire a new employee to perform the same tasks as the former employee." In other words, the genuineness of Santiaguin's workers' compensation claim has no relationship to any costs occasioned by her absence. There is simply no causal connection between the veracity of her claim and whatever expenses Leegin incurs because she is now absent from the workplace. Lastly, there is no merit to Leegin's argument that it has "suffered actual damages in the form of lost productivity and work from its existing employees due to low worker moral[e] created by [Santiaguin's] fraud[.]" That claim of damages is simply too speculative to support its fraud cause of action.

In sum, Leegin failed to demonstrate that its complaint presents a legally sufficient claim supported by a prima facie showing of facts sufficient to sustain a judgment in its favor. (See, e.g., Zamos v. Stroud (2004) 32 Cal. 4th 958, 965 [87 P.3d 802, 12 Cal. Rptr. 3d 54].) The trial court properly struck the complaint.

Finally, we observe that sound policy considerations support this conclusion. Permitting an employer to bring a civil action for fraud against an employee while the workers' compensation proceeding is pending could have a chilling effect on an employee's exercise of the right to file a workers' compensation claim. In addition, the workers' compensation system already provides the proper vehicle for an employer to raise a claim of fraud (Footnote 11) and to protect itself from the damages (higher premiums) caused by a fraudulent claim. (Lab. Code, § 3761, subds. (b) and (d).)…

Footnote 4. Pursuant to Government Code section 68081, we requested and received letter briefs from the parties on this issue.

Footnote 5. Leegin included a copy of its policy as an exhibit to its brief that answered the four questions posed by the trial court.

Footnote 6. In its letter brief to this court (see fn. 3, *supra*), Leegin wrote: "Leegin concedes for purposes of this appeal only, that its insurance policy with State Compensation Insurance Fund ('SCIF') requires the company to notify its carrier of any claims made for benefits."

Footnote 7. To support its argument that it should be able to sue Santiaguin for fraud, Leegin notes that "the WCAB is not constitutionally or statutorily empowered to make specific determinations regarding the existence or non–existence of fraud by an applicant. Nor is fraud listed among

any of the extensively enumerated list of conditions essential to an award of compensation and benefits for a compensable injury, pursuant to Labor Code Section 3600." The argument misses the mark. The WCAB "does have the power to find that an applicant has committed fraud and, on that basis, to determine either that there is no industrial injury or that disability and the need for medical treatment is not so extensive as the applicant claims. [Citation.]" (Herlick, Cal. Workers' Compensation Handbook (24th ed. 2005) § 9.18, pp. 9–32 to 9.33)

Footnote 8. Labor Code section 3761, subdivision (b) provides that if the employer provides the insurer with written notice questioning the validity of the claim, the appeals board may not approve a compromise and release agreement or stipulation that provides compensation to the employee unless the insurer notifies the employer of the hearing at which the compromise and release agreement or stipulation is to be approved.

Footnote 9. Labor Code section 3762, subdivision (a) requires an insurer to discuss "all elements of the claim file that affect the employer's premium with the employer, and shall supply copies of the documents that affect the premium at the employer's expense during reasonable business hours."

Footnote 10. The employee is not required to refund the challenged payment. (Lab. Code, § 3761, subd. (d).)

Footnote 11. Presenting a fraudulent workers' compensation claim can also result in civil and criminal sanctions. It is unlawful to present any knowingly false or fraudulent statement in support of a workers' compensation claim. (Lab. Code, § 3820, subd. (b).) Violation of the provision results, in addition to any other penalties prescribed by law, in the imposition of civil penalties to be recovered in a civil action by the district attorney. (Lab. Code, § 3820, subds. (d), (e) and (f).) If the insurer learns of a fraudulent claim, the insurer is obligated to notify the local district attorney and the Bureau of Fraudulent Claims of the Department of Insurance. (Ins. Code, § 1877.3 , subd. (b)(1); Mosby v. Liberty Mutual Ins. Co. (2003) 110 Cal. App. 4th 995, 1004 [2 Cal. Rptr. 3d 286, 68 Cal. Comp. Cases 1126].) Insurance Code section 1871.4 defines the crime of presenting a false workers' compensation claim and sets forth its punishment range. A conviction of workers' compensation fraud "that materially affects the basis of any order, decision, or award of the appeals board shall be sufficient grounds for a reconsideration of that order, decision, or award." (Lab. Code, § 5803.5.)

§ 20.0   FILING AN APPLICATION

Page 987, Column 1, third paragraph, insert following '...required....'

An employer who has been named in an application may file an application joining other employers an applicant has been employed by, even if the applicant does not want the new application againt other employers to be filed.

In *Knight Transportation, et al. v. WCAB* (2005) 70 Cal. Comp. Cases 1036, the Board held that applicant's first employer and its insurance company had standing to file an Application for Adjudication of claim against applicant's second employer, alleging that the applicant sustained a cumulative trauma injury while in the employ of the subsequent employer, even where the applicant did not want the new application to be filed.

§ 20.12.1(D) Addresses

Page 987, Column 1, third paragraph, insert following '...required....'

WORKERS' COMPENSATION APPEALS BOARD
455 Golden Gate Avenue, 9th floor
San Francisco, CA 94102
Tel: (415) 703–4554
Fax: (415) 703–4549
Website: www.dir.ca.gov/wcab

Mail Address:
P. O Box 429459
San Francisco, CA 94142–9459

COMMISSIONERS
Hon. Joseph M. Miller, **Chairperson**
Hon. Frank M. Brass
Hon. Ronnie Caplane
Hon. James C. Cuneo
Hon. Alfonso J. Moresi
Hon. Janice Murray
Hon. William K. O'Brien

DEPUTY COMMISSIONERS
Hon. Dennis J. Hannigan, Secretary
Hon. Rick Dietrich, Assistant Secretary
Hon. Neil P. Sullivan, Assistant Secretary

DIVISION OF WORKERS' COMPENSATION

ADMINISTRATIVE DIRECTOR
Hon. Carrie Nevans
1515 Clay Street, 17th Floor
Oakland, CA 94612
Tel: (510) 286–7100
Fax: (510) 286–7144
Website: www.dir.ca.gov/dwc

Email: dwc@dir.ca.gov
Recorded information: (800) 736–7401

COURT ADMINISTRATOR
Hon. Keven Star
1515 Clay Street
17th Floor
Oakland, CA 94612
Tel: (510) 286–7121
Website: www.dir.ca.gov

ASSOCIATE CHIEF JUDGES
Hon. Mark Kahn (Southern Region: Van Nuys)
Hon. Joel K. Harter (Northern Region: Sacramento)

MEDICAL DIRECTOR
Anne Searcy, M.D.

CHIEF LEGAL COUNSEL
Destie Overpeck

PROGRAMMATIC SERVICES
Angela Michael, Chief

LEGISLATION AND POLICY
Susan Gard, Chief

AUDIT UNIT
Bob Walensa, Manager

MANAGER–COMMUNICATIONS
Richard Stephens

DISABILITY EVALUATION UNIT
Blair Megowan, Manager

INFORMATION & ASSISTANCE UNIT
Bob C. Wong, Manager

INFORMATION OFFICER
Susan Gard

REHABILITATION UNIT
Otis Byrd, Manager

RESEARCH UNIT
Bill Kahley, Manager

UEBTF/SIBTF CLAIMS UNIT
Shirley H. James, Manager

WORKERS' COMPENSATION APPEALS BOARD DISTRICT OFFICES WITH PRESIDING JUDGES

Anaheim
1661 N. Raymond Avenue, Room 200
Anaheim, CA 92801–1162
Tel: (714) 738–4000
Hon. Ellen L. Flynn

Bakersfield
1800 30th Street, Suite 100
Bakersfield, CA 93301–1929
Tel: (661) 395–2723
Hon. Robert Norton

Eureka
100 "H" Street, Suite 202
Eureka, CA 95501–0481
Tel: (707) 445–6518
Hon. Robert Kutz

Fresno
2550 Mariposa Street, Suite 4078
Fresno, CA 93721–2280
Tel: (559) 445–5051
Hon. Abel Shapiro

Goleta
6755 Holister Ave, Suite 100
Goleta, CA 93117–3018
Tel: (805) 968–0258
Hon. Robert Ebenstein

Grover Beach
1562 Grand Avenue
Grover Beach, CA 93433–2261
Tel: (805) 481–4912
Hon. Michael LeCover

Long Beach
300 Oceangate Drive, Suite 200
Long Beach, CA 90802–4339
Tel: (562) 590–5001
Hon. Joseph Rebeck

Los Angeles
320 West 4th Street, 9th Floor
Los Angeles, CA 90013–1105
(213) 576–7335
Hon. David Marcus

Marina del Rey
4720 Lincoln Blvd, 2nd Floor
Marina del Rey, CA 90292
Tel: (310) 482–3820
Hon. Robert Hjelle

Oakland
1515 Clay Street, 6th Floor
Oakland, CA 94612–1402
Tel: (510) 622–2866
Hon. Kenneth Peterson

Oxnard
2220 East Gonzales Road, Suite 100
Oxnard, CA 93036–8293
Tel: (805) 485–2533
Hon. David Brotman

Pomona
732 Corporate Center Drive
Pomona, CA 91768–1601
Tel: (909) 623–4301
Hon. J. Michael Morgan

Redding
2115 Civic Center Drive, Suite 15
Redding, CA 96001–2796
Tel: (530) 225–2845
Hon. Kathleen Ortega

Riverside
3737 Main Street, Suite 300
Riverside, CA 92501–3337
Tel: (951) 782–4269
Hon. Elena Jackson

Sacramento
2424 Arden Way, Suite 230
Sacramento, CA 95825–2403
Tel: (916) 263–2735
Hon. Joel Harter

Salinas
1880 North Main Street, Suite 100 & 200
Salinas, CA 93906–2016
Tel: (831) 443–3060
Hon. Thomas Clarke

San Bernardino
464 W. Fourth St., Suite 239
San Bernardino, CA 92401–1411
Tel: (909) 383–4341
Hon. Charles Regnell

San Diego
7575 Metropolitan Road, Suite 202
San Diego, CA 92108–4402
Tel: (619) 767–2083
Hon. Cliff Levy

San Francisco
455 Golden Gate Avenue, 2nd Floor
San Francisco, CA 94102–3660
Tel: (415) 703–5011
Hon. Susan Hamilton

San Jose
100 Paseo de San Antonio, Room 241
San Jose, CA 95113–1482
Tel: (408) 277–1246
Hon. Oliver Boyer

Santa Ana
28 Civic Center Plaza, Suite 451
Santa Ana, CA 92701–4070
Tel: (415) 558–4121
Hon. William Whiteley

Santa Rosa
50 "D" Street, Suite 420
Santa Rosa, CA 95404–4760
Tel: (707) 576–2391
Hon. James Johnson

Stockton
31 East Channel Street, Room 344
Stockton, CA 95202–2393
Tel: (209) 948–7759
Hon. David Bovett

Van Nuys
6150 Van Nuys Blvd. Suite 105
Van Nuys, CA 91401–3373
Tel: (818) 901–5367
Hon. Linda Morgan

§ 21.0   DECLARATION OF READINESS

Page 1009, Column 1, ninth paragraph, insert following '...own motion.'

Prior to filing a Declaration of Readiness to Proceed, a party must attempt to resolve the issue(s) raised in its Declaration of Readiness to Proceed, otherwise sanctions may be imposed. *Holland, et. al. v. WCAB (2005) 70 Cal. Comp. Cases 1515.*

Intentionally blank

§ 22.0   ARBITRATION

Page 1015, Column 1, third paragraph, insert immediately following '...submission.'

But see *Faeth v. WCAB (Gault)* (2006) 71 Cal. Comp. Cases 355, where the Court of Appeals, Fifth District, in an unpublished opinion, upheld an arbitrator's untimely decision because of applicant's failure to timely raise the issue. The Court stated, in part:

I. Timeliness of Arbitrator's Decision

Addressing matters submitted for arbitration, section 5277, subdivision (a) requires "[t]he arbitrator's findings and award shall be served on all parties within 30 days of submission of the case for decision." Under section 5277, subdivision (b), the arbitrator must also comply with section 5313, which similarly requires:

"The appeals board or the workers' compensation judge shall, within 30 days after the case is submitted, make and file findings upon all facts involved in the controversy and an award, order, or decision stating the determination as to the rights of the parties. Together with the findings, decision, order or award there shall be served upon all the parties to the proceedings a summary of the evidence received and relied upon and the reasons or grounds upon which the determination was made."

The 30–day period in section 5313 runs "from the date of the submission of the application for decision and the provisions requiring the decision within such 30–day period shall be deemed mandatory and not merely directive." (§ 5800.5.) Specifically, applicable to arbitrations, "Unless all parties agree to a longer period of time, the failure of the arbitrator to submit the decision within 30 days shall result in forfeiture of the arbitrator's fee and shall vacate the submission order and all stipulations." (§ 5277, subd. (e).) WCAB regulations require the Minutes of Hearing and Summary of Evidence to be prepared "at the conclusion of each hearing." (Calif. Code of Regs., tit.8, § 10566.)

The arbitrator's Minutes of Hearing stated the parties would submit additional briefing and the arbitrator would prepare the Minutes of Hearing, at which time the matter would stand submitted. However, the arbitrator issued the Minutes of Hearing, Summary of Evidence, Finding of Fact and Order, and Opinion on Decision all on January 31, 2005. Faeth contends the arbitrator circumvented the 30–day time period to issue an opinion by issuing the Minutes of Hearing at the same time he rendered his decision, over six months after the parties submitted their final arguments. Farmers contends the arbitrator's opinion was timely because the Minutes of Hearing expressly delayed submission of the case until that document was prepared.

We agree with Faeth the logic of the arbitrator and Farmers bypasses the 30–day statutory mandate to issue a decision after a matter is submitted. We nevertheless also agree with Farmers that Faeth waived the error by failing to raise it before the arbitrator while she waited six months for the Minutes of Hearing. "Under the doctrine of waiver, a party loses the right to appeal an issue caused by affirmative conduct or by failing to take the proper steps at trial to avoid or correct the error." (*Telles Transport, Inc. v. Workers' Comp. Appeals Bd.* (2001) 92 Cal. App. 4th 1159, 1167 [112 Cal. Rptr. 2d 540, 66 Cal. Comp. Cases 1290].) Moreover, Faeth has not shown the result might have been different had the arbitrator timely issued the decision or that the delay alone prejudiced her in any way... .

Intentionally blank

§ 23.0   JUDGES AND MANDATORY SETTLEMENT CONFERENCES

Page 1019, Column 1, ninth paragraph, insert following '…discussions.'

In holding that the testimony of a vocational rehabilitation counselor on the issue of whether the applicant was vocationally feasible and permanently totally disabled under *LeBoeuf,* where the name of the counselor was listed on the MSC statement but the substance of his testimony was not disclosed, was properly allowed by the trial judge the Court of Appeal, Third District, in *Grupe Company et al. v. WCAB (Ridgeway)* (2005) 70 Cal. Comp. Cases 1232, stated, in part:

Petitioners contend the WCAB's decision to admit the testimony of Sidhu runs afoul of section 5502, former subdivision (d)(3), which states: "If the claim is not resolved at the mandatory settlement conference, the parties shall file a pretrial conference statement noting the specific issues in dispute, each party's proposed permanent disability rating, and listing the exhibits, and disclosing witnesses. Discovery shall close on the date of the mandatory settlement conference. Evidence not disclosed or obtained thereafter shall not be admissible unless the proponent of the evidence can demonstrate that it was not available or could not have been discovered by the exercise of due diligence prior to the settlement conference." (Italics added.)

The purpose of the disclosure requirement in section 5502 is self–evident: " 'to guarantee a productive dialogue leading, if not to expeditious resolution of the whole dispute, to thorough and accurate framing of the stipulations and issues for hearing.' [Citation.]" (State Compensation Ins. Fund v. Workers' Comp. Appeals Bd. (1995) 37 Cal. App. 4th 675, 684–685 [43 Cal. Rptr. 2d 660, 60 Cal. Comp. Cases 717].)

In the present case, the parties filed a mandatory settlement conference statement (statement) at the mandatory settlement conference on July 10, 2001. The statement listed "Dan Sidhu re Le Beauf [sic]." The statement contains no reference to any report or exhibit relating to Sidhu, nor is there any reference to the substance of Sidhu's proposed testimony. The WCJ closed discovery on July 10, 2001, with the exception of allowing the parties to send film to the respective doctors for comment.

At trial, Sidhu testified he received the referral requesting his services on July 11, 2001. Sidhu met with Ridgeway thrice, and all meetings took place after the close of discovery on July 10, 2001. He testified he made his determination as to Ridgeway's vocational prospects after August 17, 2001. Sidhu did not prepare a report prior to trial, nor did Ridgeway request such a report. Sidhu described the evaluation process as on a "rush basis."

Ridgeway claims expert testimony opinion is not "further discovery" governed by section 5502. According to Ridgeway, "Respondent's expert was disclosed at the [mandatory settlement conference], which is all that is required . . . . Moreover, Respondent could not have acted with more diligence in regard to this witness, as the respondent made clear her intention to present expert opinion regarding LeBoeuf factors as early as January 11, 2001 in writing to the defendant." Ridgeway also asserts "It was improper for the WCJ to view expert opinion testimony as 'discovery'. It is not expert opinion until it is given. It can change at the time of trial."

The amicus curiae echoes Ridgeway's characterization of expert testimony as outside the scope of section 5502: "Preparation of trial testimony by a witness for the party intending to offer that testimony is not an identified discovery activity except where that witness is a medical expert. While the act of an adverse party to ascertain the likely testimony of such an individual by deposition clearly falls within discovery within a workers' compensation claim. The preparation for such testimony is not discovery."

"In construing a statute, our role is limited to ascertaining the Legislature's intent so as to effectuate the purpose of the law. [Citations.] We look first to the words of the statute because they are the most reliable indicator of legislative intent. [Citation.] If the statutory language on its face answers the question, that answer is binding unless we conclude the language is ambiguous or it does not accurately reflect the Legislature's intent. [Citations.]" (Palmer v. GTE California, Inc. (2003) 30 Cal. 4th 1265, 1271 [70 P.3d 1067, 135 Cal. Rptr. 2d 654].)

Here, if the mandatory settlement conference does not settle the dispute between the parties, section 5502 requires the filing of a pretrial conference statement identifying the specific issues in dispute, each party's proposed permanent disability rating, the exhibits, and the witnesses. Nothing in the plain language of section 5502 requires the disclosure of the content or substance of the witness's testimony. (Footnote 5)

The standardized pretrial conference statement forms filled out by the parties in this case provide no space for descriptions of the witnesses' proposed testimony, only space to identify witnesses.

However, as petitioners point out, section 5502, former subdivision (d)(3) also provides that "[d]iscovery shall close on the date of the mandatory settlement conference" and that "[e]vidence not disclosed or obtained thereafter shall not be admissible unless the proponent of the evidence can demonstrate that it was not available or could not have been discovered by the exercise of due diligence prior to the settlement conference." In our view, "discovery" as used in section 5502 is a reference to pretrial processes undertaken to obtain information about an opposing party's case in preparation for trial. It consists of actions calculated to discover information about an adversary's case, not the collection and organization of information about one's own case. Therefore, the discovery restriction in section 5502 is not implicated in the present dispute.

Section 5502 also provides that evidence not disclosed or obtained after the mandatory settlement conference will not be admissible. Disclosure refers to the disclosure of exhibits and witnesses in the pretrial conference statement. Therefore, evidence not disclosed on the statement or obtained after the conference is not admissible. The question becomes, what constitutes evidence in this case? Is the substance of the expert's testimony "evidence" that is obtained after the conference?

Since section 5502 requires only disclosure of exhibits and witnesses, evidence not disclosed on the pretrial conference statement or obtained subsequent to the conference can only refer to the identity of witnesses and specification of exhibits. As noted, the language of section 5502 does not require disclosure of the substance or content of a witness's testimony. Since disclosure of content is not required, failure to disclose or later development of such testimony does not run afoul of section 5502.

If a party fails to disclose the identity of a witness or an exhibit in the pretrial conference statement, such evidence is inadmissible under section 5502. If a party subsequently locates an exhibit or obtains a witness following the filing of the pretrial conference statement, again, such evidence is inadmissible under section 5502, unless the party can show the witness was unavailable or could not have been discovered through due diligence. (Footnote 6)

The content of a witness's testimony suffers no such infirmity. Here, Ridgeway disclosed Sidhu as a witness in the pretrial conference statement. In addition, although not required to do so, Ridgeway further disclosed Sidhu would testify regarding LeBoeuf. Clearly, Ridgeway obtained Sidhu as a witness and disclosed his identity in conformity with section 5502.

Nor does Sidhu's subsequent development of his testimony run afoul of section 5502. Section 5502 does not require that a witness disclosed in the pretrial conference statement formulate his or her testimony prior to the filing of the statement.

We do not fear this interpretation of section 5502 will lead to abuse by parties seeking to conceal testimony from their opponents. The WCJ possesses the power to order depositions and at the mandatory settlement conference may make orders and rulings regarding the admission of evidence, including admission of offers of proof and stipulations of testimony where appropriate and necessary. (§ 5710; Cal. Code Regs., tit. 8, § 10353(a).) Faced with a party's "sandbagging" an opposing party by failing to develop expert testimony prior to the settlement conference, a WCJ may allow the deposition of the expert after the mandatory settlement conference or even exclude the witness's testimony as antithetical to the aim of fruitful settlement discussions… .

Footnote 5. The disclosure requirements under Labor Code section 5502 are less rigorous than those required under Code of Civil Procedure section 2034. Section 2034 requires, under some circumstances, that parties include as part of expert witness disclosure a brief narrative statement of the general substance of the expert's proposed testimony. (Code Civ. Proc., § 2034, subd. (f)(2)(B).)

Footnote 6. However, under certain circumstances, such evidence may be admitted by the WCJ. (See Cal. Code Regs., tit. 8, § 10353(a), giving WCJ's the power to make orders and rulings regarding admission of evidence and discovery matters.)

Page 1028, Column 1, sixth paragraph, insert following '...with this opinion.'

In *Savemart Stores, Inc. v. WCAB (Oneto)* (2006) 71 Cal. Comp. Cases 1727, the defendant attempted to offer into evidence a video tape taken of the applicant after an MSC. In upholding the Board's exclusion of the tape, because there was no showing why similar film could not have been discovered by the exercise of due diligence prior to the MSC, the Court of Appeal, Fifth District, in an unpublished decision, stated, in part:

B. Admissibility of Additional Surveillance Film

SaveMart contends the WCAB exceeded its authority in not admitting the 2006 surveillance films into evidence. SaveMart argues the WCAB was required to develop the record by including the films, and its failure to admit them denied SaveMart due process. Based on the limited facts before us, we disagree.

Section 5502, subdivision (e)(3) provides a deadline for disclosure of evidence. This statute establishes that if a workers' compensation claim is not resolved at the MSC, discovery closes on the date of the conference. "Evidence not disclosed or obtained thereafter *shall not* be admissible unless the proponent of the evidence can demonstrate that it was not available or could not have been discovered by the exercise of due diligence prior to the settlement conference." (*Ibid.*, italics added.) When a party requests "introduction of evidence which was not disclosed at the time of the MSC, the party must explain either why the evidence was not earlier available or why it could not have been discovered in the exercise of due diligence." (*San Bernardino Community Hospital v. Workers' Comp. Appeals Bd.* (1999) 74 Cal. App. 4th 928, 936 [88 Cal. Rptr. 2d 516, 64 Cal. Comp. Cases 986].)

Policy objectives for closing discovery at the MSC include facilitating effective preparation for trial and minimizing delays. (*Telles Transport, Inc. v. Workers' Comp. Appeals Bd.*, *supra*, 92 Cal. App. 4th at p. 1164.) Equally, if not more important, the discovery rule encourages both parties to fully prepare their case in anticipation of the MSC, with complete disclosure of relevant evidence so that realistic and intelligent settlement negotiations can occur. (*Ibid.*)

The surveillance film at issue was obtained not only subsequent to the August 3, 2005, MSC, but also following the December 6, 2005, trial. SaveMart's petition for writ of review is devoid of any argument or explanation as to why similar film could not have been discovered by the exercise of due diligence prior to the MSC. On reconsideration, SaveMart suggested it chose not to resume surveillance investigation until after the January 6, 2006, permanent disability rating "[a]s this was the first indication that there existed a potential finding of 100% disability . . . ." However, the first indication of potential permanent total disability arose when Dr. Adelberg's August 4, 2003, report was served, not when the recommended rating was issued or when the Rater was cross–examined. The WCJ's rating instructions, which triggered the 100 percent permanent disability rating, replicated the permanent restrictions Dr. Adelberg provided in his August 4, 2003, report. In order for SaveMart to appreciate its potential exposure and decide whether additional surveillance would be worthwhile, it merely needed to evaluate the report and calculate a permanent disability rating before the August 3, 2005, MSC. SaveMart's failure to act should not be confused with an inability to obtain or unavailability of evidence, which section 5502, subdivision (e)(3) identifies as the only exceptions to the discovery cutoff.

The WCAB abuses its discretion if it allows the receipt of additional evidence without a showing of statutory good cause. (*San Bernardino Community Hospital v. Workers' Comp. Appeals Bd., supra*, 74 Cal. App. 4th at p. 938.) Because SaveMart has not made such a showing, section 5502, subdivision (e)(3) bars reopening of discovery for admission of the films.

SaveMart cites *Weishaar v. Workers' Comp. Appeals Bd.* (2004) 69 Cal. Comp. Cases 151, writ denied, as support for the proposition the WCAB should admit contradictory surveillance film after issuing a finding for permanent total disability. However, the WCAB did not address section 5502, subdivision (e)(3) in that case as the parties settled rather than set the case for hearing, forgoing implementation of pretrial discovery cutoff procedures.

Irrespective of the express requirements of section 5502, subdivision (e)(3), SaveMart argues the WCAB should have accepted the films as part of its duty to develop the evidentiary record. (*Tyler v. Workers' Comp. Appeals Bd.* (1997) 56 Cal. App. 4th 389, 394 [65 Cal. Rptr. 2d 431, 62 Cal. Comp. Cases 924].) The WCAB has a duty to adequately develop the record based on the constitutional mandate, under article XIV, section 4 of the California Constitution, to accomplish substantial justice. (*Telles Transport, Inc. v. Workers' Comp. Appeals Bd., supra*, 92 Cal. App. 4th at p. 1164.) Section 5701 provides the WCAB with discretion to develop the record, allowing it to effectuate additional evidence including testimony, inspection of the injury site, and medical evaluations. (Footnote 2)

Section 5906 permits the WCAB to grant reconsideration and direct the taking of additional evidence. Regardless, "[t]he [WCAB]'s power to develop the record cannot be used to circumvent the clear intent and language of section 5502, subdivision [(e)(3)]." (*San Bernardino Community Hospital v. Workers' Comp. Appeals Bd., supra*, 74 Cal. App. 4th at p. 935.)

SaveMart contends rejection of the additional surveillance evidence violates due process under the 14th Amendment of the United States Constitution. Enforcing the terms of section 5502, subdivision (e)(3), however, does not equate to denial of due process.

"The essence of due process is simply notice and the opportunity to be heard . . . . [P] The constitutional right to due process does not prohibit the enactment of reasonable rules of procedure or restrictions on evidence. [Citations.] It is also well established that restrictions on the introduction of evidence which arise, for example, from a party's failure to comply with discovery rules are not inherently repugnant to the Constitution. [Citation.] Furthermore, it is often said that the paramount concern of the due process clause is simply *fairness*. [Citation.] There is nothing fundamentally inequitable in requiring a party to comply with established procedural rules which are designed to improve the overall fairness and efficiency of an adjudicatory procedure." (*San Bernardino Community Hospital v. Workers' Comp. Appeals Bd., supra*, 74 Cal. App. 4th at pp. 936–937.)"

SaveMart does not contend it did not receive notice of the December 6, 2005, trial. SaveMart's attorney was present at the hearing, presented numerous exhibits, and even engaged in cross–examination of Oneto. Section 5502, subdivision (e)(3) is an established procedural rule and does not operate as an absolute bar against admission of surveillance film or other evidence following a MSC. Absent SaveMart demonstrating good cause for not seeking the films before the MSC, the WCAB properly denied admission under section 5502, subdivision (e)(3)... .

Footnote 2. Surveillance film is absent from the enumerated types of evidence provided in section 5701.

Intentionally blank

California Workers' Compensation Claims and Benefits, 12th Ed. Supplement (2007)

§ 24.0   HEARING

§ 24.1(A)   Petition to Disqualify a Judge

Page 1043, Column 2, fifth paragraph, insert following '…(B).]'

In a significant panel decision, *Robbins v. Sharp Healthcare, et al.* (2006) 71 Cal. Comp. Cases 1291, the Board, in addressing the issue of a judge's appearance of bias against an attorney or his or her law firm, stated, in part:

1. Bias or the appearance of bias solely against an attorney or law firm, as opposed to the party that the attorney or law firm represents, may be a ground for disqualification of a WCJ.

We first examine whether bias or the appearance of bias by a WCJ solely against an attorney or law firm, as opposed to the party that the attorney or law firm represents, may be a ground for disqualification.

Labor Code section 5311 provides that a WCJ may be disqualified per CCP section 641. (Footnote 9)

CCP section 641 lists seven grounds for disqualification. (Footnote 10)

Bias or prejudice against a party is listed as one ground, but not listed is bias or prejudice toward an attorney or law firm. Thus, under CCP section 641(g), the bias or prejudice that must be shown is against a party, not the party's attorney. (Hustedt v. Workers' Comp. Appeals Bd. (1981) 30 Cal. 3d 329, 334, fn. 1 [636 P.2d 1139] [46 Cal. Comp. Cases 1284].)

CCP sections 170.1(a)(6)(B) and 170.6(a)(1) do provide that bias or prejudice against a party's attorney is a ground for disqualification. Nevertheless, as noted by the Court Administrator in his email of December 13, 2005, CCP sections 170.1 and 170.6 directly apply only to judicial officers of the Superior Court, not WCJs. (CCP, §§ 170.5(a) (defining "Judge," for the purposes of sections 170 to 170.5, to mean "judges of the superior courts, and court commissioners and referees" (emphasis added)); 170.6(a)(1) (providing that "[n]o judge, court commissioner, or referee of any superior court . . . shall try . . . nor hear any matter . . . when it [is] established . . . that the judge or court commissioner is prejudiced against any party or attorney or the interest of any party or attorney . . . " (emphasis added));

Gai v. City of Selma (1998) 68 Cal. App. 4th 213, 230–233 [79 Cal. Rptr. 2d 910] (the disqualification standards for judges set forth in CCP sections 170 et seq. do not apply to administrative hearings).)

However, this does not dispose of the issue of whether a WCJ may be disqualified based upon bias or the appearance of bias against a party's attorney. There are other grounds – established by case law, statute, and regulation – upon which a WCJ may be disqualified.

Preliminarily, due process requires a fair hearing before a neutral, unbiased decision maker, including in administrative proceedings. (Haas v. County of San Bernardino (2002) 27 Cal. 4th 1017, 1024–1027 [45 P.3d 280, 119 Cal. Rptr. 2d 341]; e.g. Withrow v. Larkin (1975) 421 U.S. 35, 41–47 [95 S.Ct. 1456, 43 L.Ed.2d 712].) Due process is violated where there is even an appearance of bias or unfairness in administrative hearings. (Haas v. County of San Bernardino, *supra*, 27 Cal. 4th at p. 1034; Quintero v. City of Santa Ana (2003) 114 Cal. App. 4th 810, 812 [7 Cal. Rptr. 3d 896]; Nightlife Partners v. City of Beverly Hills (2003) 108 Cal. App. 4th 81, 90 [133 Cal. Rptr. 2d 234]; see also, Yaqub v. Salinas Valley Memorial Healthcare System (2004) 122 Cal. App. 4th 474, 483–486 [18 Cal. Rptr. 3d 780].)

Of more direct relevance here, however, is that Labor Code section 123.6(a) requires WCJs to abide by both the Code of Judicial Ethics and the commentary to that Code:

"All workers' compensation administrative law judges employed by the administrative director and supervised by the court administrator shall subscribe to the Code of Judicial Ethics adopted by the Supreme Court pursuant to subdivision (m) of Section 18 of Article VI of the California constitution for the conduct of judges and shall not otherwise, directly or indirectly, engage in conduct contrary to that code or to the commentary to the Code of Judicial Ethics." (Footnote 11)

Canon 1 of the Code of Judicial Ethics provides, in pertinent part:

"An independent and honorable judiciary is indispensable to justice in our society. A judge should participate in establishing, maintaining, and enforcing high standards of conduct, and shall personally observe those standards so that the integrity and independence of the judiciary will be preserved. The provisions of this Code are to be construed and applied to further that objective." "

Canon 2 is entitled: "A judge shall avoid impropriety and the appearance of impropriety in all of the Judges' activities." Canon 2(A) requires, in pertinent part, that a judge shall "act at all times in a manner that promotes public confidence in the integrity and impartiality of the judiciary." The Advisory Committee Commentary under Canon 2(A) states, in relevant part:

"A judge must avoid all impropriety and appearance of impropriety. . . . The test for the appearance of impropriety is whether a person aware of the facts might reasonably entertain a doubt that the judge would be able to act with integrity, impartiality, and competence." "

Thus, the "appearance of impropriety" test, as set forth in Canon 2 and in the Commentary to Canon 2(A), is an objective one, i.e., would a reasonable person with knowledge of the facts entertain doubts concerning the WCJ's impartiality. (Yaqub v. Salinas Valley Memorial Healthcare System, supra, 122 Cal. App. 4th at p. 486; Hall v. Harker (1999) 69 Cal. App. 4th 836, 841 [82 Cal. Rptr. 2d 44], disapproved on another ground in Casa Herrera, Inc. v. Beydoun (2004) 32 Cal. 4th 336, 346, 349 [83 P.3d 497, 9 Cal. Rptr. 3d 97].) This is essentially the same test as that under CCP sections 170.1 and 170.6. (Christie v. City of El Centro (2006) 135 Cal. App. 4th 767, 776 [37 Cal. Rptr. 3d 718]; Briggs v. Superior Court (2001) 87 Cal. App. 4th 312, 319 [104 Cal. Rptr. 2d 445].)

Canon 3 is entitled: "A judge shall perform the duties of judicial office impartially and diligently." Moreover, Canon 3(E)(1) provides that "[a] judge shall disqualify himself or herself in any proceeding in which disqualification is required by law." The Commentary to this Canon states:

"Canon 3(E)(1) sets forth the general duty to disqualify applicable to a judge of any court. Sources for determining when recusal or disqualification is appropriate may include the applicable provisions of the Code of Civil Procedure, other provisions of the Code of Judicial Ethics, the Code of Conduct for United States Judges, the American Bar Association's Model Code of Judicial Conduct, and related case law." "

We do not believe that the provision of Labor Code section 123.6 – mandating that WCJs "shall not . . . engage in conduct contrary to the [Code of Judicial Ethics] or the commentary to [that] Code" (emphasis added) – means that, via the commentary to Canon 3(E)(1), all disqualification requirements of the CCP, of the Code of Judicial Ethics, and of federal law are to be imported wholesale and applied to the disqualification of WCJs. In this regard, we point out that Canon 3(E)(1) refers to the "applicable provisions" of the CCP. As discussed above, it is only CCP section 641 which is specifically "applicable" to WCJs (Lab. Code, § 5311), while CCP sections 170.1 and 170.6 are specifically applicable only to judicial officers of the Superior Court (see CCP §§ 170.5(a), 170.6(a)(1)) and they are not applicable to judicial officers presiding over administrative proceedings. (Gai v. City of Selma, supra, 68 Cal. App. 4th at pp. 230–233.) Moreover, WCJs obviously are not "United States Judges."

Nevertheless, because WCJs must abide even with the commentary to the Code of Judicial Ethics, then the reference in the commentary to Canon 3(E)(1) to the disqualification provisions of the CCP, the Code of Judicial Ethics, and the Code of Conduct for United States Judges indicates that these provisions may be looked to for guidance, even if they are not directly applicable to WCJs.

As discussed above, CCP sections 170.1(a)(6)(B) and 170.6(a)(1) provide that bias or prejudice against a party's attorney is a basis for disqualification of a Superior Court judge. Moreover, CCP section 170.1(a)(6)(A)(ii) and (iii) require disqualification of a Superior Court judge if "[t]he judge believes there is a substantial doubt as to his or her capacity to be impartial" or if "[a] person aware of the facts might reasonably entertain a doubt that the judge would be able to be impartial."

Similarly, Code of Judicial Ethics, Canon 3(E)(5)(f)(iii), provides that "[d]isqualification of an appellate justice is . . . required" if the justice "has a personal bias or prejudice concerning a party or a party's lawyer." (Emphasis added.) Additionally, Canon 3(E)(4)(b) and (c) require disqualification of an appellate justice if "the justice substantially doubts his or her capacity to be impartial" or if "the circumstances are such that a reasonable person aware of the facts would doubt the justice's ability to be impartial."

Accordingly, although these provisions relating to Superior Court judges and appellate justices are not directly applicable to WCJs, they suggest that disqualification of a WCJ based on bias against an attorney – or the appearance of bias against an attorney – may be appropriate in some circumstances.

The Code of Conduct for United States Judges, referred to in the commentary to Canon 3(E)(1), provides further support for this conclusion.

Like CCP section 641, the federal statutes regarding disqualification of federal judges require bias or prejudice against a party. (28 U.S.C. §§ 144, 455(b)(1).) (Footnote 12)

Therefore, most federal courts addressing the issue have concluded that bias against the attorney for a party ordinarily is not a sufficient basis for disqualification. (E.g., Baldwin Hardware Corp. v. Franksu Enterprise Corp. (Fed. Cir. 1996) 78 F.3d 550, 557–558; Standing Committee on Discipline v. Yagman (9th Cir. 1995) 55 F.3d 1430, 1444; Souder v. Owens–Corning Fiberglas Corp. (8th Cir. 1991) 939 F.2d 647, 653; Henderson v. Dept. of Public Safety and Corrections (5th Cir. 1990) 901 F.2d 1288, 1296; Panzardi–Alvarez v. United States (1st Cir. 1989) 879 F.2d 975, 984; In re Beard (4th Cir. 1987) 811 F.2d 818, 830; Hinman v. Rogers (10th Cir. 1987) 831 F.2d 937, 939.)

Nevertheless, the federal courts occasionally do find a basis for disqualification where the judge is actually or apparently biased against the attorney for a party. This is because a federal judge is also subject to disqualification "in any proceeding in which his [or her] impartiality might reasonably be questioned." (28 U.S.C. § 455(a) (emphasis added).) As stated by the United States Supreme Court, the question of bias or prejudice is "to be evaluated on an objective basis, so that what matters is not the reality of bias or prejudice but its appearance. Quite simply and quite universally, [disqualification] is required whenever 'impartiality might reasonably be questioned.'" (Liteky v. United States (1994) 510 U.S. 540, 548 [114 S.Ct. 1147, 127 L.Ed.2d 474].) "The judge does not have to be subjectively biased or prejudiced, so long as he appears to be so." (Liteky v. United States, *supra*, 510 U.S. at p. 553, fn. 2.)

The Fifth Circuit has held that, "[s]ince the goal of section 455(a) is to avoid even the appearance of impropriety, [disqualification] may well be required even where no actual partiality exists." (United States v. Bremers (5th Cir. 1999) 195 F.3d 221, 226.) Accordingly, in a series of cases, the Fifth Circuit has concluded that there is an appearance of impropriety if a judge presides over a case where one of the parties is represented by an attorney who had recently testified against the judge in Judicial Council disciplinary proceedings, i.e., a reasonable person, advised of all the circumstances of the case, would harbor doubts about the judge's impartiality under these circumstances. (United States v. Bremers, *supra*, 195 F.3d at pp. 226–227; United States v. Avilez–Reyes (5th Cir. 1998) 160 F.3d 258, 259; United States v. Anderson (5th Cir. 1998) 160 F.3d 231, 233; see also, United States v. Ritter (10th Cir. 1976) 540 F.2d 459, 462 (stating that "if a judge is biased in favor of an attorney, his impartiality might reasonably be questioned in relationship to the party").) Thus, under federal law, bias against an attorney may be grounds for disqualification.

Therefore, to summarize the discussion above, due process requires disqualification of a WCJ where there is even an appearance of bias. Moreover, the Code of Judicial Ethics, by which WCJs are bound, requires a WCJ to avoid even the appearance of impropriety – which is an objective test, i.e., would a person aware of the facts reasonably entertain a doubt that the WCJ would be able to act with impartiality. Further, the commentary to the Code of Judicial Ethics, by which WCJs also are bound, requires WCJs – and the Appeals Board – to consider other sources that may not be directly applicable to WCJs (such as the CCP provisions for Superior Court judges, the Canons applicable to appellate justices, and the federal provisions applicable to United States judges) in determining whether disqualification is appropriate. These other sources suggest that actual bias against an attorney, or even the appearance of bias against an attorney, may necessitate disqualification.

In accordance with the principles of due process and the provisions of the Code of Judicial Ethics and its commentary – as made applicable to WCJs by Labor Code section 123.6(a) – we conclude that a WCJ's actual bias and/or the "appearance of bias" solely against an attorney or law firm may be grounds for disqualification. We further conclude that there is an "appearance of bias" if a person with knowledge of the facts might reasonably entertain doubts concerning the WCJ's impartiality.

We next turn to whether there is actual bias or the appearance of bias that would justify disqualification of Judge Ordas in this case.

2. While there is no actual bias on the part of Judge Ordas, there is an appearance of bias sufficient to justify granting the petition for disqualification.

TIPD has filed a petition for disqualification of Judge Ordas which must be determined by the Appeals Board based upon principles described above.

Is there actual bias? Judge Ordas has stated unequivocally in his Report and Recommendation that he is not presently biased against TIPD or any of its attorneys. There is a presumption that those serving as judges do so with honesty and integrity. (People v. Chatman (2006) 38 Cal. 4th 344, 364 [133 P.3d 534, 42 Cal. Rptr. 3d 621]; e.g. also, Withrow v. Larkin, *supra*, 421 U.S. at p. 47.) Here, we have no reason to doubt the honesty or integrity of Judge Ordas in his representation that he is no longer biased against TIPD or its attorneys. The representation is accepted. There is nothing in the record which would justify a contrary conclusion. Despite being given the opportunity by our March 24, 2006 notice of intention, TIPD has not come forward with any verified declarations of present actual bias.

Nevertheless, our inquiry cannot end there because actual bias is not the only ground for disqualification. The appearance of bias may be sufficient to require disqualification. As to the appearance of bias, the objective test to be applied is whether a person aware of the facts might reasonably entertain a doubt that the judge would be able to act with impartiality.

Here, Judge Ordas commenced recusing himself in about 2001 whenever attorneys from the law firm of TIPD represented a party in a case assigned to him. These recusals occurred because Judge Ordas indicated he was actually biased – or he recognized the appearance of bias – due to the testimony by certain TIPD attorneys against him in ethics proceedings. (Footnote 13)

Subsequently, DWC established a definite policy that participation in any kind of proceeding by any WCJ who had expressed bias was inadvisable and contrary to the mandate of the Canons for Judicial Ethics. Thus, cases involving TIPD were no longer assigned to Judge Ordas. That policy remained in effect until the Court Administrator's email of December 8, 2005, when blanket recusals were eliminated. In that email, the Court Administrator also stated that the ability to "perform judicial duties without bias or prejudice . . . is a minimum qualification for the position which you hold" and that "[if] any of you feel that you are unable to meet that minimum qualification for the position you hold, please let me know and I will see what other opportunities exist . . . within [DWC]." Even then, however, Judge Ordas was reluctant to follow the new policy and instead concluded that he was still obligated to follow the older policy set by DWC in December 2001. But, in a second email of December 13, 2005, that was specifically directed to Judge Ordas (with a copy to Judge Udkovich, among others), the Court Administrator reiterated that there was no automatic recusal policy. In that second email, the Court Administrator stated, "[a]gain, . . . impartiality and lack of bias are minimum qualifications for the position which you hold." Thus, the

Court Administrator's email stated that, if Judge Ordas could not comply the policy of no blanket recusals, "there are other options which I would prefer to refrain from, but among them are transfers to different offices." Shortly thereafter, Judge Ordas stopped recusing himself. He maintained that "the passage of time" had helped to "remove the bias once held," enabling him "to put the past aside" and to be "fair and impartial." He further stated his belief that he was now "unencumbered by past bias" and that "now [he] can act with integrity and impartiality." Because Judge Ordas is no longer recusing himself in matters involving TIPD, this has led to multiple petitions for disqualification, including in this case.

Using the objective test for the appearance of bias discussed above, we conclude that a reasonable person with knowledge of the facts might reasonably entertain a doubt about Judge Ordas's impartiality.

In 2001, Judge Ordas began recusing himself from proceedings involving TIPD attorneys because of actual bias – or, at least, the appearance of bias. Shortly thereafter, the administration of DWC established a policy that cases involving TIPD would not be assigned to Judge Ordas. Then, in December 2005, the Court Administrator rescinded this policy of blanket refusals. At the same time, the Court Administrator stated that he would "see what other opportunities exist for [Judge Ordas] within [DWC]" and that he would consider options of "transfers to other offices" if Judge Ordas felt that he could not perform duties at the San Diego District Office without bias. Thereafter, Judge Ordas declared that he had "put . . . aside" and was now "unencumbered" by his former bias against TIPD and its attorneys, such that he could be "fair and impartial" in cases involving them.

In light of the warnings from the Court Administrator about "other opportunities" within DWC and about "transfers to other offices", a reasonable person might conclude that the representation of no current bias or prejudice by Judge Ordas could have been motivated, consciously or unconsciously, by a desire to protect his position with DWC as a WCJ at the San Diego District Office. Accordingly, there is the appearance of bias. Therefore, we will grant the petition for disqualification herein and disqualify Judge Ordas in this case.

But, our conclusion in this regard should not be construed as implying that a petition for disqualification will be automatically granted whenever TIPD or one of its attorneys represents a party in a future case assigned to Judge Ordas.

As discussed above, Judge Ordas's Report denies any actual bias against either TIPD or any of its attorneys at the present time. TIPD has not come forward with any evidence of current actual bias. Moreover, there is a presumption that a judicial officer is acting without bias. (People v. Chatman, supra, 38 Cal. 4th at p. 364; e.g. also, Withrow v. Larkin, supra, 421 U.S. at p. 47.) Therefore, we are not granting the current petition for disqualification on the basis of actual bias. Instead, we are granting because there is an appearance of bias. The appearance of bias exists because a reasonable person aware of the facts might conclude that Judge Ordas's declaration of no current bias arises from a wish to keep his

job – in the face of the Court Administrator's admonitions – and not because he in fact no longer harbors any bias against TIPD or its attorneys.

This appearance of bias will not necessarily exist indefinitely or exist at all times. For example, the appearance of bias might pass after a time. (Cf. United States v. Avilez–Reyes, supra, 160 F.3d at p. 259 (finding an appearance of impropriety where a federal judge continued to preside over cases involving attorneys who had recently testified against him, but endorsing a Judicial Council Order precluding the judge's participation in such cases for a period of only three years).) Similarly, after the passage of time, the appearance of bias might not extend to all TIPD attorneys. (Cf. United States v. Vadner (5th Cir. 1998) 160 F.3d 263, 264 (Fifth Circuit held that disqualification is not warranted merely because one of the parties is represented by an attorney working in the same office with lawyers who had testified against the judge in disciplinary proceedings, i.e., there is no "inherent and pervasive specter of impartiality . . . any time a lawyer from the same office appears in [the judge's] court"); Trevino v. Johnson (5th Cir. 1999) 168 F.3d 173, 178–179 (Fifth Circuit held that disqualification is not warranted where one of the parties is represented by an attorney who merely had been subpoenaed to testify at the judge's disciplinary proceedings, but never actually testified).)

Accordingly, in the future, TIPD may elect to file petitions for disqualification against Judge Ordas, but disqualification will not be automatic. TIPD will either have to establish actual bias or it will have to establish the appearance of bias, i.e., circumstances that might lead a reasonable person to doubt his impartiality. In either event, TIPD will have to support any petition(s) with affidavits or declarations, under penalty of perjury, specifying in detail the basis for the alleged bias or appearance of bias. (Lab. Code, § 5311; Cal. Code Regs., tit. 8, § 10452; see People v. Ladd (1982) 129 Cal. App. 3d 257, 261 [181 Cal. Rptr. 29] (an unverified statement of disqualification is formally defective and may be disregarded); Mackie v. Dyer (1957) 154 Cal. App. 2d 395, 399 [316 P.2d 366] (allegations in a statement charging bias and prejudice of a judge must set forth specifically the facts on which the charge is predicated; a statement containing nothing but conclusions and setting forth no facts constituting a ground of disqualification may be ignored.) (Footnote 14)

Based on the above, we will grant the petition for disqualification of Judge Ordas in the present case, and as our Decision After Disqualification, order Judge Ordas disqualified from hearing this case, and return the matter to the Presiding Judge for reassignment of the case to a new WCJ other than Judge Ordas.

We observe that, if this matter happens to be reassigned to Judge Udkovich, then defendant may elect, but may choose not, to file a new petition for disqualification, including on the basis of the Budar decision, discussed above. As noted above, in Budar, an Appeals Board panel concluded that, if two married WCJs work at the same District Office of the WCAB, and if one spouse has been disqualified under Labor Code section 5311 and WCAB Rule 10452 – or has been automatically challenged under

WCAB Rule 10453 – then CCP section 641(b) provides a valid basis to petition for disqualification of the other spouse. If such a petition for disqualification is filed, it will be determined on its merits.

3. Although a judge's actual or appearance of bias toward an attorney may be grounds for disqualification, not every adverse interaction between a judge and an attorney is sufficient to warrant disqualification.

We emphasize that although a judge's actual bias or appearance of bias toward a party's attorney may be a ground for a petition for disqualification, not every adverse interaction between a judge and an attorney will be sufficient to establish bias or the appearance of bias.

A judge's disagreement with an attorney's legal arguments, and even erroneous rulings by a judge, ordinarily are not sufficient to establish bias or prejudice against the attorney. (E.g., People v. Guerra (2006) 37 Cal. 4th 1067, 1112 [129 P.3d 321, 40 Cal. Rptr. 3d 118]; People v. Samuels (2005) 36 Cal. 4th 96, 115 [113 P.3d 1125, 30 Cal. Rptr. 3d 105]; Andrews v. Agricultural Labor Relations Bd. (1981) 28 Cal. 3d 781, 795 [623 P.2d 151, 171 Cal. Rptr. 590]; McEwen v. Occidental Life Insurance Co. (1916) 172 Cal. 6, 11 [155 P. 86].) Similarly, a judge's disagreement with an attorney's interpretation of the evidence or assessment of the credibility of witnesses generally does not establish bias. (Kreling v. Superior Court (1944) 25 Cal. 2d 305, 312 [153 P.2d 734]; Moulton Niguel Water Dist. v. Colombo (2003) 111 Cal. App. 4th 1210, 1219–1220 [4 Cal. Rptr. 3d 519].) Further, a judge's mere frustration or irritation with an attorney does not suggest bias or prejudice. (Hernandez v. Superior Court (2003) 112 Cal. App. 4th 285, 303 [4 Cal. Rptr. 3d 883]; Scott v. Family Ministries (1976) 65 Cal. App. 3d 492, 502 & 509 [135 Cal. Rptr. 430]; see also, Offutt v. United States (1954) 348 U.S. 11, 17 [75 S.Ct. 11, 99 L.Ed. 11] ("a modicum of quick temper . . . must be allowed even judges").) Even a judge's critical remarks to an attorney usually do not establish bias. (People v. Brown (1993) 6 Cal. 4th 322, 336 [862 P.2d 710, 24 Cal. Rptr. 2d 710].)

On the other hand, bias or prejudice may be established where a judge is so personally embroiled with an attorney as to call into question the judge's capacity for impartiality. (See In re Buckley (1973) 10 Cal. 3d 237, 256 & fn. 24 [514 P.2d 1201, 110 Cal. Rptr. 121]; Offutt v. United States, *supra*, 348 U.S. at pp. 16–17.) Other standards may also apply. (See Charron v. United States (Fed.Cir. 1999) 200 F.3d 785, 788 (disqualification warranted where a judge's bias or prejudice against a party's attorney becomes so pervasive that "the client's rights are likely to be affected"); Baldwin Hardware Corp. v. Franksu Enterprise Corp. (9th Cir. 1996) 78 F.3d 550, 557–558 (disqualification warranted where a judge's bias or prejudice against a party's attorney results "in material and identifiable harm to that party's case"); In re Betts (Bkrtcy.N.D.Ill. 1994) 165 B.R. 233, 238 (in order to warrant disqualification, any "apparent antagonism or animosity towards counsel must be of such character and intensity as to warrant a reasonable belief that the judge might not be able to impartially consider arguments in the case before the court").)

Under no circumstances, however, can a party's unilateral and subjective perception of an appearance of bias afford a basis for disqualification. (Haas, *supra*, 27 Cal. 4th at p. 1034; Andrews, *supra*, 28 Cal. 3d at p. 792 (questioned on other grounds by Hass, *supra*, 27 Cal. 4th at pp. 1032–1034.) (Footnote 15)

Otherwise, we would have "a system in which disgruntled or dilatory litigants can wreak havoc with the orderly administration of dispute resolving tribunals." (Haas, *supra*, 27 Cal. 4th at p. 1034, quoting from Andrews, *supra*, 28 Cal. 3d at p. 792; see also, Standing Committee on Discipline v. Yagman, *supra*, 55 F.3d at 1443–1444 (attorney cannot force recusal or disqualification of a judge by engaging in harsh and intemperate criticism of or personal attacks on the judge).)

We also observe that, if there is a basis to disqualify a WCJ, there also may be a basis for recusal. We emphasize, however, that a WCJ should never recuse himself or herself lightly. As our appellate courts have repeatedly stated:

"Judicial responsibility does not require shrinking every time an advocate asserts the object and fair judge appears to be biased. The duty of a judge to sit where not disqualified is equally as strong as the duty not to sit when disqualified. (United Farm Workers of America v. Superior Court (1985) 170 Cal. App. 3d 97, 100 [216 Cal. Rptr. 4] (italics in original; underscoring added); accord: People v. Carter (2005) 36 Cal. 4th 1215, 1243 [117 P.3d 544, 32 Cal. Rptr. 3d 838]; Briggs v. Superior Court (2001) 87 Cal. App. 4th 312, 319 [104 Cal. Rptr. 2d 445]; Flier v. Superior Court (1994) 23 Cal. App. 4th 165, 170 [28 Cal. Rptr. 2d 383].)"

And:

"[A] . . . judge has certain powers and duties to perform. Upon assuming his office he takes and subscribes to an oath that he will support the State and Federal Constitutions and that he will faithfully discharge the duties of his office as a judge . . . to the best of his ability. . . . One of those duties is to hear and determine causes presented to him unless in a particular cause he is disqualified or unable to act. He may not evade or avoid that duty. In proceedings too numerous to need citation of authority a . . . judge has been required to discharge that duty when no good cause appeared to justify a refusal to act." (Austin v. Lambert (1938) 11 Cal. 2d 73, 75 [77 P.2d 849].)"

For the foregoing reasons,

IT IS ORDERED that the petition for disqualification filed by Trovillion, Inveiss, Ponticello & Demarkis is hereby GRANTED.

IT IS FURTHER ORDERED that as the Appeals Board's Decision After Disqualification, Workers' Compensation Administrative Law Judge Ordas is hereby DISQUALIFIED from hearing the case identified as SDO 0335934, and this case is RETURNED to the Presiding Workers' Compensation Administrative Law Judge for reassignment to a new Workers' Compensation Administrative Law Judge, other than Judge Ordas... .

Footnote 9. Lab. Code § 5311 provides: "Any party to the proceeding may object to the reference of the proceeding to a particular workers' compensation judge upon any one or more of the grounds specified in Section 641 of the Code of Civil Procedure and the objection shall be heard and disposed of by the appeals board. Affidavits may be read and witnesses examined as to the objection."

Footnote 10. CCP § 641 provides: "A party may object to the appointment of any person as referee, on one or more of the following grounds: (a) A want of any of the qualifications prescribed by statute to render a person competent as a juror, except a requirement of residence within a particular county in the state. (b) Consanguinity or affinity, within the third degree, to either party, or to an officer of a corporation which is a party, or to any judge of the court in which the appointment shall be made. (c) Standing in the relation of guardian and ward, conservator and conservatee, master and servant, employer and clerk, or principal and agent, to either party; or being a member of the family of either party; or a partner in business with either party; or security on any bond or obligation for either party. (d) Having served as a juror or been a witness on any trial between the same parties. (e) Interest on the part of the person in the event of the action, or in the main question involved in the action. (f) Having formed or expressed an unqualified opinion or belief as to the merits of the action. (g) The existence of a state of mind in the potential referee evincing enmity against or bias toward either party."

Footnote 11. See also, Fremont Indemnity Co. v. Workers' Comp. Appeals Bd. (Zepeda) (1984) 153 Cal. App. 3d 965, 974 [200 Cal. Rptr. 762] [49 Cal. Comp. Cases 288] ("[WCJs] are officers of a judicial system performing judicial functions and are 'judges' for the purposes of the Code of Judicial Conduct. As such they are subject to the same rules and constraints in the performance of the duties of their office, and in their adjudicative responsibilities, as are the judges of the other courts of this state.")

Footnote 12. Section 144 applies only to judges conducting proceedings "in a district court," while section 455(b)(1) applies to all federal judges, including appellate judges.

Footnote 13. The June 12, 2001 joint memo of Judges Ordas and Udkovich said that they needed to recuse themselves from cases involving certain "attorneys and their law firms" because "bias now exists involving either, or both, Judge Ordas and Judge Udkovich." In his June 27, 2001 Recusal Order, Judge Ordas clearly stated that he "is biased" against the attorneys that testified against him, as well as a law firms of those attorneys. Moreover, in his January 27, 2006 Report, Judge Ordas refers to "bias once held" and "past bias" against TIPD. These statements indicate that, at least at one time, there was more than the mere appearance of bias. There was actual bias.

Footnote 14. Where disqualification is sought, due process does not mandate that the judge submit to cross-examination regarding his judicial role, actions, and demeanor. (Garcia v. Superior Court (1984) 156 Cal. App. 3d 670, 681–682 [203 Cal. Rptr. 290].)

Footnote 15. See also, In re Betts, *supra*, 165 B.R. at p. 238 ("A judge is not disqualified . . . merely because a litigant has transformed his fear of an adverse decision into a fear that the judge will not be impartial.").)

§ 24.12 Agreed Medical Examiners (AMEs)

Page 1061, Column 2, third paragraph, insert following '...one time examination...'

See also *Washington Mutual Card Services, et. al. v. WCAB (Gaines–Hills)* (2007) 72 Cal. Comp. Cases 278, where the Board upheld a judge's decision where he gave more weight to applicant's treating physician than the AME in finding applicant's injury to be industrial observing that the AME saw the applicant on only one occasion for an hour and ten minutes; that the treating doctor's reports were comprehensive, that the treating doctor was more familiar with applicant's condition; and had a thorough understanding of applicant's injury, history, symptoms and limitations.

In contrast, the judge found the AME's report to be conclusionary and inconsistent with the injury without offering any further explanation other than that the applicant's presentation of the facts of injury to the AME was inconsistent with the industrial injury. Under the circumstances, the judge concluded that the great weight to be given to AME's opinion was overcome.

§ 24.14 Rules of Evidence

Page 1071, Column 1, first paragraph, insert following '...Comp. Cases 99.'

A judge has the duty to develop the record where failing to do so would result in an injustice. *West v. IAC (Best)* (1947) 12 Cal. Comp. Cases 86.

§ 24.14(A) Binding Authority of En Banc Decisions and Significant Panel Decisions

Page 1071, Column 1, third paragraph, insert following '...judge.'

Significant panel decisions are published to augment the body of published Appeals Board En Banc decisions and Appellate Court opinions on *novel* or *recurring issues about which there is little available case law.* Such decisions are published only when each member of the Appeals Board believes the issue(s) in the cases to be of general interest to the public and agrees that the decisions in the cases are significant and merit general dissemination. *They are not binding on the judges.*

§ 24.14(B) Liberal Construction

<u>Page 1071, Column 1, fifth paragraph, insert following '...221.'</u>

If the facts so support, an employee is entitled to *inferences* that support the providing of a benefit, but only inferences that *reasonably can be drawn* from the evidence presented. *Abreu v. Svenhard's Swedish Bakery* 208 Cal. App. 3d 1446, 1456 (1989).

§ 24.14(B)(1) Providing of Benefits Not Due Is Not an Admission of Liability

<u>Page 1075, Column 1, sixth paragraph, erase first line beginning 'In Fairmont...' and insert the following:</u>

In *Fairmont Insurance Co. v. WCAB (Romano)* (1991) 56 Cal.

<u>Page 1075, Column 1, sixth paragraph, erase last line beginning 'surgery, stated:' and insert the following:</u>

surgery, in an unpublished case with a strong dissent, stated:

OPINION:

I.

On March 8, 1985, respondent Pasquale Romano sustained a fracture of his right fifth toe when a hammer was dropped on it. The injury arose out of and in the course of his employment as a laborer by Dubois Building Services, insured for workers' compensation by petitioner Fairmont Insurance Company (Fairmont). Romano saw Dr. Fackrell for treatment of this injury. Dr. Fackrell noted the presence of a heel spur and referred Romano to Dr. James Boccio, a podiatrist. Romano had been experiencing heel pain for several weeks before the toe injury. Dr. Boccio received permission from Fairmont to perform surgery to remove the spur. Surgery was performed on June 12, 1985, and was paid for by Fairmont.

Fairmont exercised its right to have an independent evaluation of Romano in October 1985, when he was examined by Dr. John Lang. Dr. Lang reported that Romano's toe injury caused him to change his customary method of shovelling, and "[t]his apparently brought on pain in and about the plantar aspect of his right heel." Dr. Lang did not question industrial responsibility for the heel pain, but did express reservations about further surgery. Nevertheless, Fairmont authorized and paid for additional surgical treatment, and Dr. Boccio performed two more surgeries in connection with the heel spur on January 29, 1986, and September 17, 1986. It is undisputed that Romano's toe fracture healed with no residual problems. He became permanently disabled, however, as a result of the heel condition, apparently due largely to the surgical treatments. (Footnote 1)

Subsequent evaluations of Romano in 1987 and 1988 by Dr. Henry Edington and Dr. Roger Mann, a foot specialist, indicated that Romano's heel condition was unrelated to the toe fracture. A hearing was held before the workers' compensation judge (WCJ) on December 11, 1989, and February 8, 1990. On April 11, 1990, the WCJ filed his findings of fact, award and order, holding in pertinent part: "Applicant did not sustain injury to his right heel arising out of or occurring in the course of his employment." (Footnote 2)

The WCJ's opinion on decision stated, in relevant part: "The applicant had been experiencing right heel pain for several weeks before the incident in which his toe was fractured. X–rays of his foot revealed the presence of a heel spur. The applicant was referred to a podiatrist for treatment of the spur. Three surgical procedures later, the applicant is now quite seriously disabled, largely as a result of the treatment itself, which was authorized and paid for by the defendant. [] All the medical evaluators agree that the development of heel spur symptomatology was not related to work activities... . Despite the applicant's sincere testimony that his work activities caused the increasing symptoms in his heel, there is no substantial medical evidence to support a cause–and–effect relationship. [] This case presents a truly tragic situation for the applicant, who simply followed the advice of his treating doctor. While the heel spur was discovered in the course of treatment for the applicant's industrial toe injury [which resolved without residuals after several months], the heel condition itself was not proximately caused by, or related to, the applicant's employment. The insurance carrier acted properly in authorizing medical treatment which, at the time, seemed to be an industrial responsibility. It would not be good public policy to find the carrier liable for the resulting permanent disability, simply because the apparently ill–advised treatment had such unexpectedly bad consequences."

In a petition for reconsideration, Romano argued that the treatment provided after his toe injury had been to the entire right foot and that the employer should be liable for the disabling consequences of that treatment. In his report on reconsideration, the WCJ reaffirmed his findings "that the applicant's heel spur pre–existed his toe fracture and that there was initially no industrial injury to the heel." He recommended, however, that the petition for reconsideration be granted and Fairmont held liable for the permanent disability on estoppel principles: "At the time that the applicant's heel spur was first surgically treated, both parties had a reasonable expectation that the carrier would be legally responsible for all disability resulting from the treatment. It is well settled that the employer is liable for any disability arising out of frank [sic] malpractice or poor results of surgery in the treatment of industrial injuries. Here, the applicant justifiably relied upon the protection of his employer's workers' compensation coverage in undergoing surgical treatment. The defendant, which is deemed to have expertise in questions of industrial causation, failed, for whatever reason, to recognize the possibility that the heel condition was not an industrial responsibility. The carrier could have referred the applicant to a foot specialist for an evaluation before authorizing

surgery. Instead, the defendant accepted liability. []
Although the medical issues have now been clarified, the
damage has already been done. The defendant must be
estopped from denying liability under these circumstances.
If the carrier, with all the expertise and resources at its
disposal, did not have reason to question its liability at the
time of surgery, the unsophisticated applicant should not
now have to bear the responsibility for the defendant's
failure to get a more expert opinion." The WCJ
recommended that the case be remanded for further
proceedings on the issue of permanent disability and
apportionment. The WCJ noted that apportionment could be
a significant issue on remand as Fairmont might be able to
establish that Romano's heel condition would have
progressed to cause some permanent disability even in the
absence of the surgical procedures.

The Board granted reconsideration, adopted the WCJ's
report on reconsideration, rescinded its decision of April 11,
1990, and, on October 24, 1990, remanded the matter for
further proceedings. This timely petition for writ of review
followed.

II.

In this unique case, respondent sustained an industrial
injury to one part of the foot, and a second injury to another
part of the foot was discovered in the course of treatment.
The second injury was reasonably believed to be related to
the industrial injury by both the worker's doctor (Fackrell)
and the carrier's doctor (Lang). Accordingly, the carrier
agreed to pay for surgery to correct the second injury. That
surgery was detrimental to the worker, who is now
permanently disabled as a result.

Subsequent medical evaluations revealed that the second
injury was unrelated to the first. The WCJ so found, but
ruled that the carrier "acted properly" in authorizing
payment for the surgery because it appeared industrially
related at the time. The WCJ initially concluded, however,
that the carrier should not be liable "simply because the
apparently ill–advised treatment had such unexpectedly bad
consequences," because this "would not be good public
policy." The WCJ's decision does not cite section 4909.

Section 4909 provides, in pertinent part: "Any payment,
allowance, or benefit received by the injured employee
during the period of his incapacity ... which by the terms of
this division was not then due and payable or when there is
any dispute or question concerning the right to
compensation, shall not, in the absence of any agreement,
be an admission of liability for compensation on the part of
the employer ... ."

On reconsideration, the WCJ reversed himself invoking
"estoppel," but again without citation to the statute. The
WCJ found that at the time of surgery "both parties had a
reasonable expectation that the carrier would be legally
responsible for all disability resulting from the treatment. It
is well settled that the employer is liable for any disability
arising out of frank [sic] malpractice or poor results of
surgery in the treatment of industrial injuries." The WCJ
noted that the worker here merely relied on medical advice
and his expectation of workers' compensation coverage.
The WCJ seemed to have invoked estoppel to preclude the

carrier from denying liability not because of section 4909,
but because the carrier, "which is deemed to have expertise
in questions of industrial causation," failed to investigate
and adequately evaluate the true medical cause of the
second injury. "The defendant must be estopped from
denying liability under these circumstances. If the carrier,
with all the expertise and resources at its disposal, did not
have reason to question its liability at the time of surgery,
the unsophisticated applicant should not now have to bear
the responsibility for the defendant's failure to get a more
expert opinion."

The purpose of section 4909 is to encourage the voluntary
and prompt payment of workers' compensation benefits to
injured employees. "In paying compensation and furnishing
medical treatment, the employer does not thereby admit
being under any legal obligation to pay or continue to pay.
This provision is designed to protect the employer who
might make such payments by mistake for a nonindustrial
condition and to encourage prompt payment of benefits." (1
Herlick, Cal. Workers' Compensation Law (4th ed. 1990)
§ 6.16, p. 6–19.) "It is generally true that in voluntarily
paying compensation, the employer and/or his carrier do not
thereby admit that he is under any legal obligation to pay or
continue to pay benefits. (§ 4909 see Herrera v. Workmen's
Comp. App. Bd. (1969) 71 Cal. 2d 254, 258 [78 Cal. Rptr.
497, 455 P.2d 425, 34 Cal. Comp. Cases 382] Reiman v.
Workers' Comp. Appeals Bd. (1977) 66 Cal. App. 3d 732,
742 [136 Cal. Rptr. 218, 42 Cal. Comp. Cases 106].)"
(Huston v. Workers' Comp. Appeals Bd. (1979) 95 Cal.
App. 3d 856, 866 [157 Cal. Rptr. 355, 44 Cal. Comp. Cases
798], fn. omitted [benefits paid pursuant to a stipulation not
voluntary].)

A number of courts have held that generally a workers'
compensation insurance carrier "may, notwithstanding
voluntary payment of compensation or the furnishing of
hospital or medical care, urge the defense that the case was
not within the coverage of the policy." (Annot., Voluntary
Payment or Other Relief by Insurance Carrier Under
Workmen's Compensation Act as Estoppel to Deny
Issuance of Policy or That Case is Within Coverage (1934)
91 A.L.R. 1530.) This case is not determined by the
provisions of section 4909. The WCJ's equity–oriented
approach is consistent with the general tenet that
compensation laws be construed liberally to the maximum
benefit of the injured worker.

Section 4909 is not the best focus for the resolution of the
petition for review. The case should not be styled around the
seemingly "either–or" issue of whether section 4909 affixes
liability or exonerates the carrier. Section 4909, however,
merely provides that a voluntary payment by the carrier is
not an admission of liability. The statute has the laudable
purpose of encouraging carriers to promptly pay for medical
treatment which appears necessary at the time, without
worry that the act of payment will be admissible against
them on the ultimate question of liability down the road.
Thus, the statute appears evidentiary, like the statute which
renders repairs to dangerous conditions inadmissible in tort
cases. The statute does not say that payment will preclude
liability if it later turns out the injury was not industrially
related.

We do not focus on who paid for the disabling treatment, but whether the treatment is sufficiently related to the treatment for the industrial injury that it falls within the general principle stated by the WCJ: "both parties had a reasonable expectation that the carrier would be legally responsible for all disability resulting from the treatment. It is well settled that the employer is liable for any disability arising out of frank [sic] malpractice or poor results of surgery in the treatment of industrial injuries." If the treating doctors – including the carrier's – think at the time that injury B is part of industrial injury A, and recommend treatment for B which disables respondent, the carrier should still be liable because the treatment was administered as part of the treatment for the industrial injury. The belated revelation that B was independent of A does not relieve the carrier of liability for events which transpired within the context of treatment for an industrial injury. The issue of who paid for the treatment can be set to one side: the factual issue is whether at the time of treatment it was reasonably believed that the treatment was medically necessary. Otherwise, the worker is ultimately responsible merely because he follows doctor's advice which turns out to be wrong. On this factual issue, the WCJ made factual findings sufficient to support an award to the worker.

Furthermore, the carrier induced the worker to accept the treatment without proper investigation of the injury's cause. Had that investigation been done, the surgery would not have been authorized and the worker would not have been victimized by the apparent malpractice.

The petition is denied. I Concur...

The majority decision, which holds petitioner liable for a disability arising from treatment for a heel spur which was not industrial in origin, runs counter to the very purpose of our worker's compensation system – to compensate employees for injuries suffered in the course of and arising out of their employment without regard to fault – and does violence to Labor Code section 4909, (Footnote 1) which provides that voluntary payment shall not be an admission of liability on the part of the employer. (Footnote 2)

"At common law, when an employee was injured in the course of his employment and sued his employer, the latter would escape liability in three situations: (a) Where the employee was guilty of contributory negligence (b) where the employee had assumed the risk of the employment and (c) where the injury was due to the negligence of another employee. [] Workmen's compensation laws (now called workers' compensation laws in California) abolish these defenses of contributory negligence, assumption of risk, and fellow–servant rule, and establish an absolute liability on the part of the employer, irrespective of the negligence of either party. The statutes "rest on the underlying notion that the common–law remedy by action, with the requirements of proof incident to that remedy, involves intolerable delay and great economic waste, gives inadequate relief for loss and suffering, operates unequally as between different individuals in like circumstances, and that, whether viewed from the standpoint of the employer or that of the employee, it is inequitable and unsuited to the conditions of modern industry.'[Citations.]" (2 Witkin, Summary of Cal. Law (9th ed. 1987) Workers' Compensation, § 1, pp. 560–561.)

"From an economic standpoint the basic philosophy of workers' compensation is generally as follows: (1) employers and employees in industry are engaged in a common venture for the furnishing of goods or services to society, anticipating profits or wages, as the case may be, as a reward (2) their relationship is not solely one created by simple contract with each other, but amounts to a kind of industrial status (3) the risk of injury and financial burden resulting therefrom should be borne by industry as a whole rather than fall solely upon the employee involved and (4) the burden of the wearing out and destruction of human, as well as inanimate, machinery should be borne by industry just as other costs of production are assumed by the employer and ultimately passed on to the public. It is in effect a special tax and a part of the operating expense, just as truly as any other cost of repair or operation. The industry as a whole is subject to the same hazard, and no unequal burden is placed upon a particular employer's establishment. Furthermore, placing such a responsibility upon industry, through a system which provides financial reward to the individual employer for a lowered accident rate, tends by the spur of competition to reduce accidents, thus furthering the general social policy." (2 Hanna, Cal. LAW OF EMPLOYEE INJURIES AND WORKMEN'S COMPENSATION (2d ed. 1990), § 1.05[2], pp. 1–26 to 1–27, fns. omitted.)

Article XIV, section 4, of the State Constitution provides that all persons have a liability to compensate their workers for injury or disability sustained "in the course of their employment, irrespective of the fault of any party ... ." (Emphasis added.) Pursuant to the plenary power granted by the Constitution, the Legislature has enacted a comprehensive system of workers' compensation in Division 4 of the Labor Code. (§§ 3200–6002.)

Two conditions essential to the strict liability for compensation on the part of an employer are (1) that, at the time of injury, the employee is performing services growing out of and incidental to employment and is acting within the course of employment (§ 3600, subd. (a)(2)), and (2) that the injury is proximately caused by the employment, either with or without negligence (§ 3600, subd. (a)(3)). (2 Witkin, op . cit . supra , § 184, p. 748.) The employer is required to promptly provide medical treatment required for industrial injuries: "Medical, surgical ... and hospital treatment ... which is reasonably required to cure or relieve from the effects of the injury shall be provided by the employer. In the case of his or her neglect or refusal seasonably to do so, the employer is liable for the reasonable expense incurred by or on behalf of the employee in providing treatment... ." (§ 4600.)

The majority decision here is both contrary to the law as expressed in the workers' compensation statutes of this state, and in no way commensurate with the philosophy underlying the workers' compensation system.

The surgeries involved here were performed on respondent's heel spur, a condition the WCJ expressly found not to be industrial in origin: "Applicant did not sustain injury to his right heel arising out of or occurring in the course of his employment." In his report on the petition for reconsideration, the WCJ reaffirmed this finding, which is fully supported by the medical evidence. Despite this finding, the Board accepted the following recommendation of the WCJ that petitioner be held liable on estoppel principles: "The defendant, which is deemed to have expertise in questions of industrial causation, failed, for whatever reason, to recognize the possibility that the heel condition was not an industrial responsibility. The carrier could have referred the applicant to a foot specialist for an evaluation before authorizing surgery. Instead the defendant accepted liability. [] Although the medical issues have now been clarified, the damage has already been done. The defendant must be estopped from denying liability under these circumstances ... ." (Emphasis added.)

The Board's decision rests upon two factors: (1) petitioner accepted liability and paid for the treatment and (2) petitioner did not obtain a further evaluation from a foot specialist before authorizing surgery. Section 4909, however, precludes holding petitioner liable for disability based upon the first factor. (Footnote 3)

As the majority opinion recognizes, "[i]n paying compensation and furnishing medical treatment, the employer does not thereby admit being under any legal obligation to pay or continue to pay. [Section 4909] is designed to protect the employer who might make such payments by mistake for a nonindustrial condition and to encourage prompt payment of benefits. [Citation.]" (1 Herlick, Cal. Workers' Compensation Law (4th ed. 1990) § 6.16, p. 6–19.) That is exactly what occurred here – petitioner paid for the surgery in the mistaken belief that it was treatment required for an industrial injury.

I cannot comprehend the majority's novel assertion that section 4909 "appears evidentiary" and "merely provides" that evidence of voluntary payment is not admissible on the question of liability. Section 4909 is clearly substantive – it provides that voluntary payment cannot be the basis of a holding of further or continuing compensation liability. In effect, section 4909 is an "anti–estoppel" statute it permits the assertion of the defense that a claim is noncompensable because it does not arise out of the course of employment. This factor is fundamental to the workers' compensation scheme. Even so, terming section 4909 "evidentiary" does not lessen its effect in this case – it still precludes a finding of liability based upon the fact that petitioner previously "accepted liability."

The policy behind statutes such as section 4909 and court decisions holding that an employer or insurer is not estopped by voluntary payment to later deny compensation liability was expressed long ago by the Utah Supreme Court: "It would be unjust to both the employee and the insurance carrier if the law were that when the insurance carrier once undertakes to provide medical or other care for an injured workman it has lost all right to afterwards defend against what it believes to be an unjust or illegal claim. The insurance carrier cannot and ought not wait until full investigation has been made before providing necessary care and treatment for injured men." (Harding v. Industrial Commission of Utah (Utah 1934) 28 P.2d 182, 184.) Adopting a contrary position "would encourage employers to contest all employment related injuries to avoid later being estopped from raising their claims [of noncoverage]." (Olsen v. Industrial Com'n of Utah (Utah App. 1989) 776 P.2d 937, 941, aff'd. (Utah 1990) 797 P.2d 1098.)

These principles are equally applicable under the California Workers' Compensation Act, which seeks to encourage prompt payment of compensation benefits. "It is the policy of the state law that compensation injuries be swiftly recognized and payments commenced and that medical care and hospitalization be speedily furnished ... ." (City etc. of San Francisco v. Workmen's Comp. App. Bd. (1970) 2 Cal. 3d 1001, 1010 [88 Cal. Rptr. 371, 472 P.2d 459, 35 Cal. Comp. Cases 390].) To encourage prompt payment, penalties are assessed when compensation is unreasonably delayed or refused. (§ 5814.) "[Section 5814] was intended to encourage employers and carriers to make voluntary, timely compensation payments by making delay or refusal to pay more costly, and to place the burden of nonpayment on the employer." (Jardine v. Workers' Comp. Appeals Bd. (1984) 163 Cal. App. 3d 1, 8 [209 Cal. Rptr. 139, 49 Cal. Comp. Cases 787].) If employers and insurers were estopped to deny coverage in circumstances such as those presented in this case, the risk of penalties for refusal to pay might often seem more attractive than the risk of being estopped to later deny continuing liability, thus frustrating the state policy to encourage prompt payment of claims.

The second factor upon which the Board's decision is based is petitioner's failure to obtain a further evaluation from a foot specialist before authorizing surgery. First, it does not appear from the facts of this case that there was any reason for petitioner to do this. Dr. Boccio, as a podiatrist, was a foot specialist. In any event, the facts in this case fail to give rise to an estoppel as a matter of law. (Footnote 4)

Equitable estoppel entails "... (a) a representation or concealment of material facts (b) made with knowledge, actual or virtual, of the facts (c) to a party ignorant, actually and permissibly, of the truth (d) with the intention, actual or virtual, that the latter act upon it and (e) the party must have been induced to act upon it . [Citations.] ... [] There can be no estoppel where one of these elements is missing. [Citations.]" (11 Witkin, Summary of Cal. Law (9th ed. 1990) Equity, § 177, p. 859.) The majority states that "the carrier induced the worker to accept the treatment without proper investigation of the injury's cause. Had that investigation been done, the surgery would not have been authorized and the worker would not have been victimized by the apparent malpractice." (Emphasis added.) To the contrary, there is no evidence whatsoever that petitioner induced respondent to have the surgeries, and the majority opinion, not surprisingly, cites none. Petitioner merely agreed to pay for the surgeries recommended by the podiatrist to whom respondent had been referred by his original physician. There is also no evidence of lack of proper investigation. The surgeries were recommended by a podiatrist, and Dr. Lang, the carrier's physician, did not question industrial causation.

The majority's holding flies in the face of the basic principle that employers should be held responsible for workers' compensation, without regard to fault, only for industrial injuries, and completely undermines what it acknowledges as section 4909's "laudable purpose of encouraging carriers to promptly pay for medical treatment which appears necessary at the time." Unlike the majority, I do not see this as a "unique" case and believe it presents precisely the type of situation to which section 4909 was intended to apply. Petitioner here did just what it was supposed to do under the statutory scheme. If there was malpractice in the performance of the surgeries, that is very unfortunate. However, the compensation carrier which merely fulfilled its obligation to pay for what appeared to be medical care required for an industrial injury, but was not, should not be held responsible for any malfeasance arising out of treatment for a nonindustrial injury.

In upholding what it terms an "equity–oriented" approach of the WCJ, the majority runs roughshod over the law, and imposes liability on the employer and its compensation carrier for an injury that is indisputably nonindustrial. I fear the ramifications of this decision will be that compensation carriers will be slow to authorize treatment until they have eliminated any possibility that the condition for which treatment is sought is nonindustrial in nature. This will not only frustrate public policy by delaying what should be the prompt delivery of medical care, but will also increase the ultimate costs.

I would annul the decision of the Workers' Compensation Appeals Board.

All further statutory references are to the Labor Code unless otherwise indicated.

Footnote 1. All further statutory references are to the Labor Code.

Footnote 2. Section 4909 provides, in pertinent part: "Any payment, allowance, or benefit received by the injured employee during the period of his incapacity ... which by the terms of this division was not then due and payable or when there is any dispute or question concerning the right to compensation, shall not, in the absence of any agreement, be an admission of liability for compensation on the part of the employer ... .

Footnote 3. The majority asserts that "[t]his case is not determined by the provisions of section 4909." To the contrary, the question of the propriety of the Board's reliance upon petitioner having "accepted liability" is expressly governed by the provisions of that statute.

Footnote 4. Contrary to the suggestion in the majority opinion, it is not my view that section 4909 precludes liability whenever voluntary compensation payments have been made on the basis of an injury which later turns out to be nonindustrial. Section 4909 simply precludes premising liability on such payment. When other factors exist which do give rise to estoppel under appropriate legal principles, liability may exist.

§ 24.14(C)   Presumptions

Page 1076, Column 1, sixth paragraph, insert following '…32A. 902'

A presumption is an assumption of fact that the law requires to be made from another fact or group of facts or otherwise established in an action and may be considered at anytime, is mandatory on the Board and not dependent upon whether a party timely raises the presumption as an issue at a Mandatory Settlement Conference.

A judge may raise the issue of a presumption of compensability as provided for in Labor Code section 5402 sua sponte (his or her own will) at trial. *Leprino Foods v. WCAB (Owens)* (2007) 72 Cal. Comp. Cases 605.

§ 24.15   Collateral Estoppel

Page 1081, Column 2, third paragraph, insert following '…claim.'

In *Spectra F/X, Inc., et al. v. WCAB (Avalos)* (2005) 70 Cal. Comp. Cases 1609, the Board held that a judge's finding of employer negligence in applicant's third party case was binding on the applicant's employer's workers' compensation insurer for purposes of determining eligibility for a credit against applicant's workers' compensation case and that the insurer was collaterally estopped from relitigating the issue of applicant's employer's negligence at the Appeals Board when the insurer was a party to the civil suit as plaintiff in intervention but elected to settle its lien prior to trial in exchange for dismissal from the civil action, and chose, therefore, not to participate in the civil trial, and the Board found the insurer was in privity with the applicant for purposes of applying the doctrine of collateral estoppel.

The trial judge found support for his position in the case of *Serrano v. WCAB* (1971) 36 Cal. Comp. Cases 233, wherein the Court stated, in part:

> We perceive, moreover, that whether the trial court did or did not reduce the amount of petitioner's judgment by the amount of compensation received by him is not determinative of the issue before us. The key to deciding the issue whether the employer or his carrier are entitled to a credit against an employee's net recovery in a third party action under the Labor Code credit provisions (§§ 3858, 3861) is the determination that the employer was concurrently negligent. In Nelsen v. Workmen's Comp. App. Bd. [(1970)] 11 Cal. App. 3d 472, 478–479 [35 Cal. Comp. Cases 442, 89 Cal. Rptr. 638], n1 it was held that the Board cannot allow a credit where the employer's negligence has been previously determined in a third party action. Accordingly, an employee may "assert the employer's adjudicated negligence 'defensively' against the employer's claim of credit, and the employer is collaterally estopped by the determination made against him on that

issue in the third party action. [Citations.]" (At p. 479.) The rationale in Nelsen is that, in the absence of express statutory terms to the contrary, the provisions of Civil Code section 3517 which provide that "No one can take advantage of his own wrong," a principle embraced in Witt (57 Cal. 2d at p. 72), require the conclusion that "If the court cannot allow a lien where the employer was concurrently negligent, logic dictates that the Board cannot allow a credit where the employer's negligence has been previously determined in the employee's third party action." (11 Cal. App. 3d at p. 479.) In sum, where the employer has been determined to be concurrently negligent, the employer or his carrier must bear the entire compensation burden. (Nelsen v. Workmen's Comp. App. Bd., *supra*; see Smith v. Trapp [(1967)] 249 Cal. App. 2d 929, 939 [32 Cal. Comp. Cases 191, 58 Cal. Rptr. 229].).... .

Page 1081, Column 2, fourth paragraph, insert following '...doctrine.'

In *Atlantic Mutual Insurance Company v. WCAB (Brewer)* (2006) 71 Cal. Comp. Cases 244, the Board held it did not have jurisdiction to set aside a finding by a judge regarding insurance coverage under Labor Code section 5804, when the judge's finding became final more than five years after the date of injury and the fact that the insurance carrier did not request that the findings of coverage be set aside until more than five years after the injury.

In the opinion upheld by the Board, the judge stated, in part:

Estoppel: Atlantic Mutual Insurance Company made several appearances before this Board and stipulated that it had coverage for the San Francisco Chronicle on May 22, 1998. The Stipulations were set forth in the November 10, 2003 mandatory settlement conference statement and were recorded in to the minutes by the WCJ on April 1, 2004. As a result of those stipulations, this court issued a Finding of Fact concerning coverage and issued an award against Atlantic Mutual Insurance Company on June 28, 2004. Said Finding of Fact and Award became final (and the law of this case) on July 23, 2004, the day the reconsideration period ended.

In this court's opinion, Atlantic Mutual Insurance Company is estopped to deny coverage for the San Francisco Chronicle on the date of applicant's injury. This court as well as the applicant relied on the stipulations made by the attorney for Atlantic Mutual Insurance Company concerning coverage. Had there been no stipulation concerning coverage, there never would have been an award issued against Atlantic Mutual Insurance Company.

Jurisdiction: Labor Code Section 5804 states that no award of compensation shall be rescinded, altered, or amended after five years from the date of injury except upon a petition by a party in interest filed within such five years. As is stated above, the Findings of Fact concerning coverage and the award based thereon became final on July 23, 2004. Obviously, this date is more than five years from the date of injury. On November 23, 2004, Atlantic Mutual Insurance Company advised this board of the mistake it had

made concerning coverage. It is respectfully submitted that Atlantic Mutual Insurance Company was too late. By the terms of Labor Code Section 5804, this Board no longer has jurisdiction to set aside Findings of Fact (and Awards) as the five year period has expired...

Concerning the estoppel issue, the California Supreme Court held in Granco Steel, Inc. v WCAB (Robinson) [(1968) 68 Cal. 2d 191, 65 Cal. Rptr. 287, 436 P.2d 287, 33 Cal. Comp. Cases 50] that an insurance carrier was estopped to deny coverage when the representation of coverage was relied on by the applicant and the WCAB trial court in rendering its decision. Granco Steel involved representations made by a broker concerning coverage. In the instant case, reliance was made upon representations by Atlantic Mutual's attorney representing that his client had coverage. All of the elements concerning estoppel set forth by the California Supreme Court, at page 59, are present in the instant case: (1) the party to be estopped must be apprised of the facts (Atlantic Mutual was well aware that it was not the carrier despite Mr. Willens' stipulation that it was); (2) the party must intend that his conduct be acted upon or must so act that the parties asserting the estoppel had a right to believe that it was so intended (both applicant and this court relied on the representation concerning coverage in this courts' [sic] decisions were based on said representation); (3) the other party must be ignorant of the true state of facts (Mr. Brewer only knew that his checks were being sent by Atlantic Mutual; he had no idea concerning any adjustment contract between Atlantic Mutual's subsidiary and Reliance Insurance Company); (4) he must rely upon the conduct to his injury (Mr. Brewer is currently not receiving the benefit of his award and obviously, has relied on the representations concerning coverage to his injury). [Emphasis by WCJ]... .

§ 24.16   The Hearing Procedure

Page 1093, Column 1, sixth paragraph, insert following '...thereafter.'

Although workers' compensation proceedings are not governed by the Evidence Code, parties are entitled to constitutional due process such as the right to cross–examine a witness and the presentation of rebuttal evidence. Labor Code section 5708 and 5709; *Hegglin v. WCAB* (1971) 36 Cal. Comp. Cases 93; *Pence v. IAC* (1965) 30 Cal. Comp. Cases 207.

§ 24.17   Lien Claimant

Page 1105, Column 1, fourth paragraph, insert following '...42.7.'

A lien claimant is not denied due process if it chooses not to take advantage of the right to be heard on its lien and does not appear at a lien hearing after which a judge denies the lien. *Rubio v. National Legion Fire Co.*; STK 174055, Feb. 3, 2006,. 34 CWCR 53.

**Page 1106, Column 2, second paragraph, insert
following 'p. 695...)'**

If a lien claimant proceeds to trial on its lien after an applicant has settled his or her claim by means of a Compromise and Release which contains a *Thomas* finding, the lien claimant stands in the applicant's shoes and to prevail is required to meet the same evidentiary burden of proof as the applicant if applicant had been attempting to establish his or her claim. *Amini v. WCAB (Portillo)* (2006) 71 Cal. Comp. Cases 510.

§ 24.20 Sanctions and Fines for Bad Faith Actions or Tactics

**Page 1110, Column 2, seventh paragraph,
insert following '...issues.'**

See also *Ira D. Johns v. WCAB* (2006) 71 Cal. Comp. Cases 1327.

**Page 1113, Column 2, second paragraph,
insert following '...Appeals Board.'**

In *Blanpea v. WCAB* (2006) 71 Cal. Comp. Cases 1441, sanctions in the amount of $2,250.00 were imposed against an applicant for filing two Petitions for Reconsideration objecting to defendant's right to credit for permanent disability advances in a Compromise and Release following a first denial of her Petition for Reconsideration. The judge, in justifying the sanctions, observed that applicant litigated the same issue three times and the dispute should have been resolved when the Board previously denied reconsideration.

Filing of a penalty petition based on failure of defendant to pay $2.50 of interest due on a settlement was deemed frivolous and a bad faith action in *Holland, et. al. v. WCAB* (2005) 70 Cal. Comp. Cases 1515, justifying an order requiring applicant attorney to pay defense counsel a fee of $1,520.00.

Intentionally blank

§ 25.0   RIGHT TO APPEAL THE JUDGE'S DECISION

§ 25.2   The Petition for Reconsideration

Page 1119, Column 2, ninth paragraph, delete chart and insert the following:

Workers' Compensation Appeals Board
455 Golden Gate Avenue, 9th floor
San Francisco, CA 94102

Page 1119, Column 2, eleventh paragraph, delete chart and insert the following:

Mail Address
P.O. Box 429459
San Francisco, CA 94142–9459
Attn: Reconsideration Unit

Page 1126, Column 2, eleventh paragraph, insert following '…Board.'

Failure of a party to follow technical rules of procedure adopted by the Appeals Board does not deprive the Board of jurisdiction where there is no showing of *prejudice* to the complaining party.

Commenting on this in *Enoch v. WCAB* (2006) 71 Cal. Comp. Cases 904, the Court of Appeal, Fifth District, in an unpublished opinion stated, in part:

We concur with the WCAB that neither the failure to serve a copy of a petition on the Rehabilitation Unit nor reference to a wrong WCAB case number divests the WCAB with jurisdiction over an otherwise timely filed appeal. Under section 5300, workers' compensation proceedings "are instituted before the appeals board, and not elsewhere," unless expressly provided by the statute. Given the Legislature's plenary authority to create and enforce a compete system of workers' compensation, we disagree with Enoch that a state regulation enacted by the WCAB necessarily confers or deprives the WCAB with jurisdiction over a particular matter…

We similarly conclude Summit's listing of the wrong case number on the appeal petition did not deprive the WCAB of jurisdiction. As the WCAB explained, the procedural error is "trivial." Moreover, not only did Summit use the wrong case number, but subsequently so did Enoch, the hearing reporter, and the WCJ. Most significantly, there is no showing of prejudice to any party or the WCAB. (Rubio v. Workers' Comp. Appeals Bd. (1985) 165 Cal. App. 3d 196, 200 [211 Cal. Rptr. 461, 50 Cal. Comp. Cases 160] ["The Board's procedural rules 'serve the convenience of the tribunal and litigant[s] and facilitate the proceedings. They do not deprive the tribunal of power to dispense with compliance when the purpose of justice requirement it, particularly when the violation is formal and does not prejudice the other party' "].) Accordingly, we refuse to strictly apply technical rules of procedure to deprive the WCAB the ability to issue a decision on the merits… .

Page 1127, Column 1, fourth paragraph, insert following '…petition.'

In an unpublished opinion in *McAuliffe v. WCAB* (2006) 71 Cal. Comp. Cases 696, the Court of Appeal, Third District, in noting that a failure to serve documents in a Board proceeding is an omission of substance, which denies a party that has a right to service of the documents of a fundamental right, stated, in part:

Here, Century, through Katz, sent a letter to the WCAB dated July 1, 2005, formally requesting reconsideration of the WCAB's June 21, 2005, ruling in McAuliffe's favor. Century failed to serve McAuliffe with a copy of the request. McAuliffe did not receive a copy of the letter until the WCJ issued its recommendation, served on July 19, 2005, with the letter enclosed.

McAuliffe's ignorance of the petition prevented her from responding to Century's claims. Nor did McAuliffe have any opportunity to respond to the claims prior to or after the granting of the petition: the WCAB granted the petition and rescinded the WCJ's decision in one fell swoop. A failure to serve documents in a WCAB proceeding in the manner required by statute is not a "mere irregularity" but, rather, an omission of substance which denies a fundamental right. (Hartford Accident & Indem. Co. v. Workers' Comp. Appeals Bd. (1978) 86 Cal. App. 3d 1, 3 [149 Cal. Rptr. 878, 43 Cal. Comp. Cases 1193].) Century's lack of service of the petition on McAuliffe deprived her of any opportunity to state her case or present any evidence prior to the WCAB's ruling against her.

McAuliffe also points to Century's failure to verify its petition, a failure noted by the WCJ. Section 5902 provides, in part: "The petition for reconsideration [before the WCAB]… shall be verified upon oath in the manner required for verified pleadings in courts of record… ." However, verification of a petition for reconsideration is not a jurisdictional requirement that mandates dismissal. (Wings West Airlines v. Workers' Comp. Appeals Bd. (1986) 187 Cal. App. 3d 1047, 1055 [232 Cal. Rptr. 343, 51 Cal. Comp. Cases 609].)

In Lucena v. Diablo Auto Body (2000) 65 Cal. Comp.

Cases 1425 [Appeals Board significant panel decision] (Lucena), the WCAB dismissed a petition for reconsideration that the respondent 'failed to verify. The WCJ noted the petition was unverified and recommended the petition be dismissed unless within a reasonable period the defendant submitted verification. The defendant failed to do so.

In dismissing the petition, the WCAB observed: "The statutory requirement for verification is clear on its face, assuring accuracy and responsibility in the pleadings, and compliance with this statutory requirement should be expected and required." (Lucena, *supra*, 65 Cal. Comp. Cases at p. 1427.) However, in a Footnote the WCAB also acknowledged it possessed the discretion not to dismiss an unverified petition: "Therefore, under some circumstances (e.g., where the petitioner is a pro per applicant or a pro per defendant, where the failure to verify is not pointed out by the WCJ's report or the respondent's answer, and/or where we believe no prejudice results from the failure to verify), we may elect not to dismiss an unverified petition. In the usual case, however, we will dismiss, so the prudent practitioner will verify, as required by statute." (Id. at p. 1427, fn. 4.)… .

Page 1128, Column 1, third paragraph, insert immediately following '…reconsideration.'

See *Los Angeles County Metropolitan Transit Authority v. WCAB (Hicks)* (2006) 71 Cal. Comp. Cases 641, where the failure to attach a verification to a Petition for Reconsideration was excusable and not grounds for dismissal where applicant was not represented by counsel and defendant was not prejudiced by the lack of verification.

Petitions to Remove

Page 1128, Column 2, first paragraph, insert immediately following heading 'Petitions to Remove'

Any party has the right to petition the Appeals Board to review an Order / Decision or other action of a trial judge because of the parties belief that:
1. The order, decision or action will result in significant prejudice, or
2. The order decision or action will result in irreparable harm.

Page 1128, Column 2, ninth paragraph, insert at end of page following '…Regs 10390.'

Amended Awards

When an award is amended by the judge before a Petition for Reconsideration is filed, the time for seeking reconsideration runs from the date of the original order when the amendment is *clerical* in nature. However, when the amendment affects a *substantial or material change* in the award or involves the exercise of a judicial

function or judicial discretion, the time runs instead from the date of the amended order.

Commenting on this in *Nestle Ice Cream Co. v. WCAB (Ryerson)* (2007) 72 Cal. Comp. Cases 13, the Court of Appeal, Fifth District stated, in part:

A Workers' Compensation judge (WCJ) awarded disability and vocational rehabilitation benefits to respondent Ken Ryerson (Ryerson). At Ryerson's request, the WCJ amended the award to correctly state the names of the parties and to increase the amount awarded. Employer Nestle Ice Cream Company (Nestle) filed a petition for reconsideration before the Workers' Compensation Appeals Board (Board) that was timely as to the amended award, but untimely as to the original award. The Board dismissed the petition as untimely.

When an award is amended by the WCJ before a petition for reconsideration is filed, the time for seeking reconsideration runs from the date of the original order when the amendment is clerical in nature. When the amendment effects a substantial or material change in the award or involves the exercise of a judicial function or judicial discretion, the time runs instead from the date of the amended order. In this case, the WCJ's amendment effected a substantial and material change in the award and amounted to a judicial act, rather than the mere correction of a clerical error. We annul the Board's order dismissing the petition for reconsideration as untimely and remand the matter for resolution on the merits.

FACTS AND PROCEDURAL HISTORY

Ryerson worked as a financial analyst for Nestle, which is self–insured for purposes of the workers' compensation law. He developed back, neck and wrist problems and filed a worker's compensation claim for cumulative trauma during a period ending on November 1, 2001. Ryerson was placed on leave and was diagnosed with chronic cervical and thoracic strain, bilateral cervicobrachial syndrome and repetitive strain injury. These conditions were exacerbated when Ryerson used a computer keyboard, which his job required him to do almost continuously.

Ryerson's primary treating physician was Dr. Brendan Morley, who declared on March 2, 2004 that Ryerson could return to work with the restriction that he could work no more than eight hours a day or 40 hours a week. Dr. Morley released Ryerson to resume his full duties without restriction on April 27, 2004, and pronounced his condition permanent and stationary as of July 15, 2004. On November 8, 2004, Dr. Morley wrote a report clarifying that he had fully released Ryerson in April because Nestle would not allow him to return with any restrictions and Ryerson wanted to resume his duties. Meanwhile, a rehabilitation plan was developed to enable Ryerson to become a real estate broker, which would require less desk time and less work on a computer.

The case went to trial before the WCJ, who found that Ryerson had become permanent and stationary on July 15, 2004, and was 28 percent disabled, entitling him to a total of $19,337.50 in permanent disability benefits. (Lab. Code, § 4658.) (Footnote 1)

She awarded additional temporary disability benefits at $728 per week from March 22, 2004 (the date temporary disability payments had ceased), through July 15, 2004 (the date Ryerson was declared permanent and stationary). (§§ 4650, subd. (a), 4653.) She determined that Ryerson was entitled to a vocational rehabilitation maintenance allowance at the temporary disability rate with no cap, and set a split rate of $728 per week through December 31, 2004, and $840 per week thereafter. (§ 139.5, former § 4642.) The WCJ further found that Nestle had unreasonably delayed in providing vocational rehabilitation services and in making permanent disability advances, warranting a 25–percent penalty as to each. (§ 5814, subd. (a).)

The WCJ's findings and award was filed and served on April 3, 2006. Ryerson's counsel sent a letter to the WCJ on April 10, asking her to correct the names of the parties in the text of the award, which erroneously stated "AWARD IS MADE in favor of Marsha Hattem and against Safeway Inc., et al . . . ." Counsel also asked that the court increase the rate of temporary disability and the vocational rehabilitation maintenance allowance to $840 per week for the entire period rather than $728 per week for portions thereof, because retroactive temporary disability must be calculated at the current rate, rather than the rate applicable to the period of disability, when payment is made more than two years after the date of injury. The WCJ issued an order amending the findings and award, which made the changes requested and was filed and served on April 14, 2006.

Nestle filed a petition for reconsideration on May 4, 2006, 20 days after the amended award was filed and served. In that petition, Nestle alleged: (1) temporary disability should not have been awarded for the period after March 2, 2004, when Ryerson was released for work with the only restriction being an eight–hour work day and 40–hour work week; (2) Ryerson was not entitled to vocational rehabilitation benefits when he had been released to return to work and even if he was, the amount awarded was excessive when the statute authorizing payment at the rate of temporary disability without a cap (former § 4642) had been repealed; and (3) the Board exceeded its powers when it awarded penalties based on unreasonable delay in providing rehabilitation benefits and advances for permanent disability. Ryerson argued in opposition that the petition for reconsideration was late because such petitions must be filed within 20 days of the date an award is served (§ 5903), and Nestle's was not filed within 20 days of the date of service of the original award. Nestle responded that the petition should not be dismissed when it was filed and served within 20 days of service of the amended award.

The Board dismissed the petition for reconsideration as untimely without a discussion of the merits, although it remanded the case to the WCJ to correct the award in two unrelated respects: (1) temporary disability was awarded through April 27, 2004, the date Ryerson was released to return to work with no restrictions, rather than July 15, 2004, the date his condition became permanent and stationary; and (2) the amount of penalties for the delay in providing benefits was capped at $10,000, as required by statute. Nestle seeks a writ of review, arguing that its

petition for reconsideration was timely and raising the same challenges to the award as were raised in that petition.

DISCUSSION

A petition for reconsideration must be filed within 20 days of service of the WCJ's award. (§ 5903.) The Board is without jurisdiction to grant an untimely petition. (*Scott v. Workers' Comp. Appeals Bd.* (1981) 122 Cal. App. 3d 979, 984 [176 Cal. Rptr. 267, 46 Cal. Comp. Cases 1008].) Nestle's petition for reconsideration was filed and served more than 20 days from the date of service of the WCJ's original award on April 3, 2006, but within 20 days of service of the amended award on April 14, 2006. Ryerson and the Board argue that the 20–day period ran from the date of the original award and that the reconsideration petition was properly dismissed.

Title 8, section 10858, of the California Code of Regulations allows the WCJ to correct a mathematical, clerical or procedural error in the award or to modify it for good cause before a petition for reconsideration is filed. (Footnote 2)

Title 8, section 10859, allows a WCJ to amend or modify the award within 15 days after the date a timely petition for reconsideration is filed and specifies that the time for filing a (second) petition for reconsideration runs from the date of the amended order. (Footnote 3)

No petition for reconsideration had been filed when the WCJ issued her amended order in this case, so title 8, section 10858 applies.

Section 10858 of title 8 of the California Code of Regulations, unlike section 10859, does not specify whether an amendment to the award triggers a new 20–day period for filing a petition for reconsideration. No published appellate decision is on point, but Board panels faced with amendments made by a WCJ before a petition for reconsideration is filed have calculated the 20–day period to run from the date of the original order when the amendment is merely "cleriCal. " (*Los Angeles County–U.S.C. Medical Center, PSI, c/o Presidium, Inc. v. Workers' Comp. Appeals Bd. (Jamarillo)* (1999) 64 Cal. Comp. Cases 565 [writ den.]; *City of Concord v. Workers' Comp. Appeals Bd. (Bullock)* (1998) 63 Cal. Comp. Cases 1522 [writ den.]; *Rockwell International Corporation v. Worker's Comp. Appeals Bd. (Carlisle)* (1988) 53 Cal. Comp. Cases 92 [writ den.].) By contrast, an amendment correcting a judicial error triggers a new 20–day period for a petition for reconsideration. (*Johns–Manville Corporation v. Workers' Comp. Appeals Bd. (Pease)* (1990) 55 Cal. Comp. Cases 315 [writ den.].)

In the case of a civil judgment, the period for filing a notice of appeal is not extended by an amendment that corrects a clerical error, but it is extended by an amendment that effects a substantial or material change or involves the exercise of a judicial function or judicial discretion. (*Stone v. Regents of University of California* (1999) 77 Cal. App. 4th 736, 743–744 [92 Cal. Rptr. 2d 94]; *CC–California Plaza Associates v. Paller & Goldstein* (1996) 51 Cal. App. 4th 1042, 1048 [59 Cal. Rptr. 2d 382].) " 'The effect of an amended judgment on the appeal time period depends on whether the amendment substantially changes the judgment or, instead, simply corrects a clerical error: . . . When the trial court amends a nonfinal judgment in a manner amounting to a *substantial modification* of the judgment (e.g., on motion for new trial or motion to vacate and enter different judgment), the amended judgment supersedes the original and becomes the appealable judgment (there can be only one "final judgment" in an action [citation].) Therefore, a new appeal period starts to run from notice of entry or entry of the *amended* judgment . . . . On the other hand, if the amendment merely corrects a *clerical error* and does not involve the exercise of judicial discretion, the original judgment remains effective as the only appealable final judgment; the amendment does *not* operate as a new judgment from which an appeal may be taken.' " (*CC–California Plaza Associates, supra,* at p. 1048, quoting Eisenberg et al., Cal. Practice Guide: Civil Appeals & Writs (The Rutter Group 1995) P P 3:56 to 3:56.2, pp. 3–19 to 3–20; [citation].)

A challenge to a WCJ's award via a petition for reconsideration is analogous to an appeal from a civil judgment, and the distinction between clerical and judicial acts is a sound one when determining whether the time for seeking reconsideration runs from the date of the original or amended award. The timeliness of Nestle's petition thus depends on the nature of the amendment. If it was merely clerical, the petition was filed too late. If, on the other hand, it effected a substantial or material change, or involved a judicial act, the petition was timely and should have been considered on its merits. In determining whether an amendment to a judgment is clerical in nature, the question is " 'whether the error [corrected] was made in rendering the judgment, or in recording the judgment rendered.' " (*In re Candelario* (1970) 3 Cal. 3d 702, 705 [477 P.2d 729, 91 Cal. Rptr. 497].)

The amendment in this case had two components: the correction of the parties' names in the award and the increase in the weekly rate of benefits. To the extent the amendment changed the names of the parties in the award, the situation is similar to that presented in *CC–California Plaza Associates v. Paller & Goldstein, supra,* 51 Cal. App. 4th 1042, in which a judgment of nonsuit incorrectly stated which party had lost the motion. We concluded that an amendment correcting the name of the losing party was not merely cleriCal. "To us the issue is relatively easy; we cannot imagine a more substantial or material change in the form of a judgment than in the identity of the losing party . . . . [I]t was hardly a mere 'clerical' correction when . . . the trial court changed the judgment to reflect the correct name of the losing party on the nonsuit motion." (*Id.* at pp. 1048–1049.)

Nestle argues that the use of the wrong names in the original award was clerical error because it is clear the WCJ did not deliberate on the issue and decide to use the names of two parties who have no involvement in these proceedings. Even if we were to conclude that that the use of the wrong names was, under these specific circumstances, the equivalent of an error in the recording of the judgment (*In re Candelario, supra,* 3 Cal. 3d at p. 705), the other aspect of the amendment, which increased the amount of the award, cannot be characterized as such.

In addition to changing the parties' names, the WCJ amended the award to increase the amount of retroactive temporary disability payments and the vocational rehabilitation maintenance allowance so that all were made at the higher weekly rate of $840 that was in effect at the time of the award. A portion of the original award had been calculated by using the lower temporary disability rate in effect until December 31, 2004, but Ryerson's counsel argued in a letter to the WCJ after the award issued that the more generous rate was required by section 4661.5, which provides: "[W]hen any temporary total disability indemnity payment is made two years or more from the date of injury, the amount of this payment shall be computed in accordance with the temporary disability indemnity average weekly earnings amount specified in Section 4453 in effect on the date each temporary total disability payment is made . . . ." Counsel also cited *Hofmeister v. Workers' Comp. Appeals Bd.* (1984) 156 Cal. App. 3d 848 [203 Cal. Rptr. 100, 49 Cal. Comp. Cases 438], a decision that construed the statute to require payment at the current, higher rate when temporary disability has extended more than two years from the date of the injury.

Payment of benefits at a higher rate constituted a substantial and material change in the award. Amending the award to comport with section 4661.5 and the case law applying it was a judicial function, not merely a clerical one. It is of no moment that Nestle is not currently challenging the aspects of the award that were changed by the amendment. The issue is whether the amendment was of sufficient import that it superseded the original award. In this case it did, and the time for filing a petition for reconsideration ran from the time of the amended award.

When reviewing the Board's dismissal of the petition, we consider whether it acted without or in excess of its powers, and whether its order was unreasonable, not supported by substantial evidence, or procured by fraud. (§ 5952.) Even if we accord "great weight" to the Board's application of the statutes governing the timing of a petition for reconsideration (see *Rea v. Workers' Comp. Appeals Bd.* (2005) 127 Cal. App. 4th 625 [25 Cal. Rptr. 3d 828, 70 Cal. Comp. Cases 312]), the order dismissing Nestle's petition as untimely was unreasonable when reconsideration was sought within 20 days of service of an amended order that effected a substantial and material change in the award and involved a judicial act.

DISPOSITION

The Board's order dismissing the petition for reconsideration as untimely is annulled. The case is remanded to the Board for consideration of the issues raised in that petition on their merits. The parties shall bear their own costs herein... .

Footnote 1. All further statutory references are to the Labor Code unless otherwise indicated.

Footnote 2. "Before a petition for reconsideration is filed, a workers' compensation judge may correct the decision for clerical, mathematical or procedural error or amend the decision for good cause under the authority and subject to the limitations set out in [sections 5803 and 5804.]" (Cal. Code Regs., tit. 8, § 10858.)

Footnote 3. "After a petition for reconsideration has been timely filed, a workers' compensation judge may, within the period of fifteen (15) days following the date of filing of that petition for reconsideration, amend or modify the order, decision or award or rescind the order, decision or award and conduct further proceedings . . . . The time for filing a petition for reconsideration pursuant to Labor Code section 5903 will run from the filing date of the new, amended or modified [order] . . . ." (Cal. Code Regs., tit. 8, § 10859.)

§ 25.5   Petition for Removal of Case from Judge to Appeals Board

Page 1132, Column 2, first paragraph, insert at end of page following '...be granted...'

In *Gallagher v. Fireman's Fund Ins. Co.* SR 96641, October 26, 2000, a Board panel not only denied a Petition for Removal, but also issued a notice of intention to sanction petitioner for filing such a Petition without merit. See *Costa v. Hardy Diagnostics, SCIF* (2006) 71 Cal. Comp. Cases 1797, where the Board found no basis to grant a removal.

Intentionally blank

§ 27.0   RIGHT TO APPEAL THE APPEALS BOARD'S DECISION

Page 1146, Column 1, second paragraph, insert following '...article.'

Although an Appellate Court will not disturb a Board's award merely because it is susceptible to opposing inferences, it may not accept factual findings that are *illogical, improbable, or inequitable* considering the entire record. *Judson Steel Corporation v. WCAB (Maese)* (1978) 43 Cal. Comp. Cases 1205, *Western Growers Insurance Company v. WCAB (Austin)* (1993) 58 Cal Comp. Cases 323. However, an Appellate Court is precluded from substituting its choice of the most convincing evidence or re–weighing the evidence to decide disputed questions of *fact*.

Intentionally blank

§ 28.0   PETITION FOR REVIEW – DISTRICT COURT OF APPEAL

Page 1151, Column 1, second paragraph, insert following 'reconsideration.'

The fact that a Petition for Writ of Review has been filed, standing alone, does not affect the operation of an En Banc decision of the Appeals Board and its decision remains binding precedent during the review on all Appeals Board panels as well as all its judges.

Commenting on this in *Diggle v. Sierra Sands Unified School District, et al.* (2005) 70 Cal. Comp. Cases 1480, the Board, in an En Banc decision stated, in part:

> Of course, if an appellate court "stay[s] or suspend[s] the operation" of an en banc decision under section 5956 (see also, Lab. Code, 6000), (Footnote 6) then the binding effect of the en banc decision on Appeals Board panels and WCJs is also stayed or suspended – at least until the suspension or stay order is lifted.
>
> Also, if an appellate court issues an opinion that explicitly or implicitly overrules an en banc decision of the Appeals Board, then, under the principle of stare decisis, the Court's decision is controlling and the en banc decision no longer can be followed by the Appeals Board or any WCJ. (Auto Equity Sales v. Superior Court (1962) 57 Cal. 2d 450, 455 [369 P.2d 937, 20 Cal. Rptr. 321]; Escobedo v. Marshalls (2005) 70 Cal. Comp. Cases 604, 609, fn. 4 (Appeals Board en banc).) There may be some exceptions to this standard principle (e.g., when an en banc decision is only partially overruled, or where it is indirectly overruled in a non–published appellate opinion), however, we need not and will not address any such scenarios here... .

Footnote 6. Section 6000 states:

"The operation of any order, decision, or award of the appeals board under the provisions of this division or any judgment entered thereon, shall not at any time be stayed by the court to which petition is made for a writ of review, unless an undertaking is executed on the part of the petitioner."

§ 28.1   When Does Statutory Time to File Commence to Run?

Page 1152, Column 1, second paragraph, insert following '...served.'

In *Halladay v. WCAB* (2006) 71 Cal. Comp. Cases 693, in an unpublished opinion, the Court of Appeal, Fifth District, in observing that unlike the filing of a Petition for Reconsideration with the Appeals Board, the 45–day window to file a Petition for Writ of Review in an Appellate Court is not extended for mailing under the Code of Civil Procedure section 1013, stated, in part:

Like the WCAB, this court also has a jurisdictional time limit to review a workers' compensation claim. "The application for a writ of review must be made within 45 days after the petition for reconsideration is denied. . . . " (Lab. Code, § 5950.) "It has been repeatedly held that the statutorily prescribed time limitation set forth in section 5950 is jurisdictional. [Citations.] Where the petition is not presented within the time specified in section 5950, the appellate court has 'no jurisdiction of the attempted proceeding' and the petition must therefore be denied. [Citation.]" (Southwest Airlines v. Workers' Comp. Appeals Bd. (1991) 234 Cal. App. 3d 1421, 1424 [286 Cal. Rptr. 347, 56 Cal. Comp. Cases 616].) Moreover, unlike filing a petition for reconsideration before the WCAB, the 45–day window to file petition for writ of review in an appellate court is not extended for mailing under Code of Civil Procedure section 1013. (Camper v. Workers' Comp. Appeals Bd. (1992) 3 Cal. 4th 679, 688 [836 P.2d 888, 12 Cal. Rptr. 2d 101, 57 Cal. Comp. Cases 644]; Southwest Airlines, *supra*, at p. 1431.)

Notwithstanding the earlier date stated on Halladay's letter, his deemed Petition for Writ of Review was received by this court 49 days after the WCAB denied reconsideration. (Footnote 2)

Moreover, he violated California Rules of Court, rule 57(a), by not supplying a copy of the WCAB's decision, the WCJ's minutes and summary of evidence, the WCJ's findings and decision, and any relevant evidence to support his substantial evidence claim. Without legal authority to review Halladay's contentions, we must deny his claim. Moreover, even had his Petition for Writ of Review been timely filed, Halladay fails to demonstrate legal error within this court's scope of appellate review. (Lab. Code, § 5952.)... .

Footnote 2. Technically, the letter was received by this court on June 8, 2006, and was not filed by the clerk until June 13, 2006. We nevertheless treat the Petition for Writ of Review as though it were filed on the earlier date of June 8, 2006.

§ 28.4   Must Be Verified

Page 1156, Column 2, third paragraph, delete chart and insert the following

California Supreme Court: Main Office
Earl Warren Building
Mailing Address:
Supreme Court of California
350 McAllister Street, Room 1295

San Francisco, CA 94102
Tel: (415) 865–7000
Office Hours: 9:00 a.m. to 5:00 p.m.

Supreme Court Clerk/Administrator
Frederick K. Ohlrich

California Supreme Court: Los Angeles Office
Ronald Reagan Building
Mailing Address:
300 South Spring Street
Los Angeles, CA 90013
Tel: (213) 830–7570

California Supreme Court: Sacramento
Stanley Mosk Library and Courts Building
Mailing Address:
914 Capitol Mall
Sacramento, CA 95814

Page 1156, Column 2, eighth paragraph, delete chart and insert the following:

FIRST DISTRICT, COURT OF APPEAL
350 McAllister Street
San Francisco, CA 94102
Tel: (415) 865–7300
Fax: (415) 865–7309
E–mail: First.District@jud.ca.gov
Office Hours: 8:00 a.m. to 5:00 p.m.

SECOND DISTRICT, COURT OF APPEAL
Divisions 1 – 5, 7 & 8
Ronald Reagan State Building
300 So. Spring St. 2nd Floor
Los Angeles, CA 90013
Tel: (213) 830–7000
Office Hours: 9:00 a.m. to 4:30 p.m.

DIVISION 6
Court Place
200 East Santa Clara Street
Ventura, CA 93001
Tel: (805) 641–4700
Office Hours: 9:00 a.m. to 4:30 p.m.
* All documents to be filed in division 6 should be mailed to
the address above.

THIRD DISTRICT, COURT OF APPEAL
900 N Street, Room 400
Sacramento, CA 95814–4869
Tel: (916) 654–0209
Office Hours: 8:30 a.m. to 5:00 p.m.

FOURTH DISTRICT, COURT OF APPEAL

Division 1
Symphony Towers
750 B Street, Suite 300
San Diego, California 92101
Tel: (619) 645–2760
Fax: (619) 645–2495
Office Hours: 9:00 a.m. to 5:00 p.m.

Division 2
3389 Twelfth Street
Riverside, CA 92501
Tel: (951) 248–0200
Office Hours: 9:00 a.m. to 4:30 p.m.

Division 3
925 N. Spurgeon Street
Santa Ana, California 92701
Tel: (714) 558–4312
Fax: (714) 543–1318
Office Hours: 8:00 a.m. to 4:00 p.m.

FIFTH DISTRICT, COURT OF APPEAL
2525 Capitol Street
Fresno, California, 93721
Tel: (559) 445–5491
Fax: (559) 445–5769
Office Hours: 8:30 a.m. to 5:00 p.m.

SIXTH DISTRICT, COURT OF APPEAL
333 W. Santa Clara Street, Suite 1060
San Jose, CA 95113
Tel: (408) 277–1004
Office Hours: 9:00 a.m. to 5:00 p.m.

§ 30.0   PETITION TO REOPEN SUBSEQUENT TO A FINDINGS AND AWARD OR ORDER

Page 1171, Column 1, second paragraph, insert following '...Cases 876.'

A party does not have an absolute right to Petition to Reopen an award upon the discovery of new evidence. Some good grounds not previously known which render the award inequitable must be shown. Commenting on this in *Wal–Mart Stores, Inc. v. WCAB (Collier)* (2007) 72 Cal. Comp. Cases 210, the Court of Appeal, Fifth District, in an unpublished decision stated, in part:

DISCUSSION

Wal–Mart asks this court to find the WCAB erred in not reopening Collier's stipulated disability rating, that it issued an award based on insubstantial evidence, and that Collier failed to follow the proper procedures to dispute Wal–Mart's denial of medical care. We find Wal–Mart's contentions nothing more than a transparent third attempt to retract from its stipulated award and relitigate Collier's level of disability and need for further medical care. Wal–Mart apparently does not understand the effect of a stipulated award, the grounds for reopening a WCAB determination, or the role of the appellate courts.

I. Good Cause to Open a Prior Award

As a constitutional court, the WCAB issues final decisions with res judicata effect, prohibiting the relitigation of an issue after a fair trial. (*Azadigian v. Workers' Comp. Appeals Bd.* (1992) 7 Cal. App. 4th 372, 376, 380 [8 Cal. Rptr. 2d 643, 57 Cal. Comp. Cases 391].) Unlike judicial determinations, however, the WCAB maintains continuing jurisdiction over a disability claim for five years from the date of injury if the employee suffers a "new and further disability" or upon a showing of "good cause." (§§ 5410, 5803, 5804; see 2 Hanna, Cal. Law of Employee Injuries and Workers' Compensation (rev. 2d ed. 2007) §§ 28.03[1], 31.02, 31.04.) Wal–Mart did not mention either a new or further disability, good cause, or any statutory legal authority in its December 14, 2004, petition to reopen. Instead, it alleged almost entirely:

" "Defendants are seeking to reopen the Stipulations with Request for Award and Award that was entered into on April 19, 2004, at 100%. [P] Furthermore, as indicated in the body of the Stipulations, the 100% was not based on work restrictions, but on evidence presented, that Applicant could not return to the work force. However, since that time, technology has advanced and, per the enclosed correspondence from Ms. Cheryl Chandler, dated November 8, 2004, there is a possibility that Applicant could return to the work force at this time. [Exhibit citation.] [P] Furthermore, since Applicant's injury occurred on January 7, 2000, Defendants are still within their Statute of Limitations." "

Because Wal–Mart did not present evidence of a change in Collier's medical condition, the WCAB's authority to modify its award approving the stipulated agreement was dependent upon a showing of "good cause" under section 5803. (*Azadigian, supra,* 7 Cal. App. 4th at p. 378.) "Without such proof, the board has no power to disturb its prior ruling." (*Ibid.*)

A party does not have an absolute right to reopen a claim upon the discovery of new evidence, and the WCAB should exercise the power to reopen with great caution. (*Nicky Blair's Restaurant v., Workers' Comp. Appeals Bd.* (1980) 109 Cal. App. 3d 941, 957 [167 Cal. Rptr. 516, 45 Cal. Comp. Cases 876].) "The principle of reopening for 'good cause' does not permit an attempt to simply relitigate the original award." (*Id.* at p. 956.) Thus, a party may not submit "medical evidence obtained subsequent to the original decision which merely disagrees with the medical opinion relied upon by the Board at the time of the original decision." (*Id.* at p. 956.) To demonstrate good cause to reopen a workers' compensation claim, the new evidence:

" '(a) must present some good ground, not previously known to the Appeals Board, which renders the original award inequitable, (b) must be more than merely cumulative or a restatement of the original evidence or contentions, and (c) must be accompanied by a showing that such evidence could not with reasonable diligence have been discovered and produced at the original hearing.' " (*Ibid.*)"

The only evidence Wal–Mart offered the WCAB at the time of the hearing was a report from vocational counselor Chandler suggesting Collier might be able to perform some limited amount of work with voice activation software and a job announcement with a signed checkmark from Dr. McHenry expressing his opinion Collier could perform the specified duties. Wal–Mart did not, however, make any legitimate attempt to convince the WCAB that this information constituted good cause to reopen the award. Significantly, Wal–Mart failed to explain why such evidence was unavailable prior to entering into the stipulated award. While Wal–Mart referred to recent "technological advances" that made the original award inappropriate, the stipulated award issued only months earlier and Chandler's second report even noted she previously advised Collier of the possibility of using voice activated software at the time of her original evaluation. Wal–Mart's claim of good cause to reopen the award lacks any semblance of credibility.

II. Substantial Evidence of Collier's Total Permanent Disability

Wal–Mart argues the WCAB disregarded "substantial evidence" that Collier is no longer 100 percent permanently disabled. Wal–Mart contends Chandler's report and Dr. McHenry's box-checking is more substantial than the original medical reports leading the parties and WCAB to all agree Collier was 100 percent disabled. Even assuming Collier may perform certain job duties, Collier's physical ailments have not changed and Wal–Mart does not present any authority that the existence of a new job prospect warrants a change in an employee's level of permanent disability once an award has issued.

Regardless, even if this court agreed Collier is not 100 percent disabled simply because she can perform some type of work, the issue is not properly before this court. As set forth above, Wal–Mart failed to demonstrate good cause to reopen Collier's award. Accordingly, the WCAB did not amend Collier's April 19, 2004, stipulated award and did not issue a new finding of permanent disability... .

Page 1173, Column 1, first paragraph, insert following '...Reopen.'

In *CMIS/Springfield Ins. Co. v. WCAB (Guillen)* (2006) 71 Cal. Comp. Cases 274, the Board, in upholding a judge's finding that applicant's Petition to Reopen, filed more than five years after her injury, was not barred by the statute of limitations because a medical report from applicant's psychologist detailing all of applicant's new complaints was served on all parties within the five–year period, coupled with other medical reports served *within the five–year period* provided the defendant with full knowledge of applicant's potential claim for injury to additional body parts, quoted the judge as stating:

Labor Code Section 5804 indicates an award of compensation shall not be rescinded, altered or amended after five years from the date of injury except with a petition by a party in interest filed within five years. By reference to the statute defendant argues that the WCAB has lost jurisdiction under Labor Code Sections 5804 and 5410. However, the Court has considered the totality of evidence in the record to find that the medical report of Dr. Konstat dated 4/12/99 and date stamped at the Santa Monica Board 4/28/99 can be construed as a Petition to Reopen. The board has liberally construed the requirements for a Petition to Reopen for New and Further Disability. Dr. Konstat describes psychiatric disability that resulted from applicant's industrial injury. The psychiatric report also details the applicant's post–traumatic cephalgia and dizziness, status post lumbar surgery, cervical radiculopathy, right, C6 mainly, recurrent lumbar radiculopathy with reference to a recommendation in Dr. Alban's AME report for psychological treatment in order for the applicant to reach maximum orthopedic improvement. Dr. Konstat also made reference to the 9/10/98 medical report of Dr. Chodakiewicz in which it was recommended that the applicant undergo a trial of epidural or facets blocks for the applicant's pain complaints and surgical treatment to decompress the applicant's right–sided nerve.

Defendant asserts the defense of laches. This requires unreasonable delay with consequent prejudice. There was delay, but clearly defendant was not prejudiced. Defendant secured defense medical reports from Dr. Nathan and Dr. Paul Grodin, and consented to the AME examination with Dr. Alban. This defendant was not prejudiced.

In Beaida v. WCAB [(1968) 263 Cal. App. 2d 204, 69 Cal. Rptr. 516, 33 Cal. Comp. Cases 345,] the Court recognized the letter by applicant's physician as a Petition to Reopen. A doctor's letter to the Appeals Board was held to be a Petition to Reopen by a party in interest since the letter was written on the applicant's behalf claiming that the original award was inadequate compensation for existing pain and disability, and was delivered to be [sic] Appeals Board within five years of the date of injury. Defendant complains that the facts in the instant case are distinguishable since Dr. Konstat's report did not claim any inadequacy as to the Stipulations with Request for Award. However, the inference can easily be drawn that the applicant's new psychiatric complaints result from the prior industrial injury. Dr. Konstat states on page 12 of the 4/12/99 medical report, "As a result of the industrial injury, subsequent level of disability, and non–resolution of pain, the patient suffered severe anxiety and depression. Thus, apart from the fact that this patient has also sustained industrial injuries, she has also sustained a psychological emotional injury as a consequence of her industrial physical injuries."...

In County of San Diego v. WCAB [(2005) 70 Cal. Comp. Cases 126 (court of appeal opinion not published in official reports),] the Court of Appeal stated, "The County contends Rojas–Melzer's request for an increased award was untimely and the WCAB therefore acted without jurisdiction in granting the request. . . . " We reject the County's contentions and affirm the WCAB's decision. Although Rojas–Melzer made no formal request for an increased award within five years of her injury, the County had notice of her claim well before the expiration of the five–year statute of limitations and was not prejudiced by her pursuit of additional benefits." [sic] In this case the County of San Diego was served with medical reporting that indicated increased disability, and its own physician also examined the applicant. Prior to the expiration of five years, the applicant filed a DOR with the medical report. Applicant did not file a Petition to Reopen within five years. However, the Court found that the defendant was not prejudiced in any manner by applicant's failure to file a formal Petition to Reopen.

Similarly, in the case at bar defendant had full knowledge of the body parts alleged by the applicant. All body parts specified in Dr. Konstat's report should be considered as alleged in the Petition to Reopen. Like the doctor's note in Beaida, the referee's letter in Zurich Insurance Company, and the medical report with DOR in County of San Diego, the defendant herein was given notice of applicant's alleged disability. Defendant had even obtained medical evaluations from Dr. Nathan for the psychiatric issue, Dr. Paul Grodin on internal issues, and the AME Dr. Alban in regard to orthopedic issues.

Dr. Konstat's 4/12/99 psychiatric report details the applicant's psychiatric, internal, and orthopedic complaints, and it should be treated as a Petition to Reopen for New and Further Disability for all body parts described therein. This will be consistent with the findings of the above–cited Court of Appeal and Supreme Court cases....

Page 1180, Column 2, second paragraph, insert following '...of this case].'

Petition to Terminate a Medical Award

Labor Code section 4607 provides:

Where a party to a proceeding institutes proceedings to terminate an award made by the appeals board to an applicant for continuing medical treatment and is unsuccessful in such proceedings, the appeals board may determine the amount of attorney's fees reasonably incurred by the applicant in resisting the proceeding to terminate the medical treatment, and may assess such reasonable attorney's fees as a cost upon the party instituting the proceedings to terminate the award of the appeals board.

In holding that an applicant's attorney was entitled to attorney fees for successfully enforcing an award for future medical care, the Court of Appeal, Second District, in *Smith–Amar v. WCAB* (2007) 72 Cal. Comp. Cases 27, stated, in part:

An employee receives a workers' compensation award which includes future medical care. The insurance carrier refuses to furnish some of the treatment but does not institute proceedings to terminate care pursuant to Labor Code section 4607. (Footnote 1)

Here we hold the employee's attorney who succeeds in enforcing the award may receive attorney fees. (Footnote 2)

In *Smith*, the worker had been awarded partial permanent disability (PPD), including future medical treatment. Later, his insurance carrier informally denied treatment for Smith's back, but did not file a petition to terminate medical care. (§ 4607.) Counsel for Smith, William A. Herreras, successfully challenged the carrier's denial of that medical care. The Workers' Compensation Appeals Board (Board) denied counsel's request for attorney fees.

In *Amar*, the parties previously stipulated to an award of future medical care for a foot injury. That care included a weight loss program and treatment for nonindustrial diabetes. The carrier denied both aspects of medical care without filing a petition to terminate care. Amar's attorneys sought reinstatement of this medical care. The Board deemed the weight loss program to be medically necessary treatment, and ordered it reinstated, but it denied attorney fees to Amar's counsel, Russell Ghitterman of Ghitterman, Ghitterman, and Feld (Ghitterman).

Facts and Procedural History

Smith

Smith sustained industrial injuries from cumulative trauma to his right shoulder, neck and psyche while working for the California Youth Authority (CYA). He was awarded PPD, including future medical treatment.

Eight years later, the carrier for CYA, State Compensation Insurance Fund (SCIF), refused to authorize epidural injections to Smith's back. Smith called Herreras, the attorney who originally filed his petition for workers' compensation. Herreras sought utilization review (UR). Pursuant to court order, Smith was examined by an agreed medical examiner (AME) (§§ 4067, 4610), who concluded that Smith needed the injections to relieve his back pain,

which was precipitated by work–related injuries. SCIF then authorized the injections without a formal hearing.

The Workers' Compensation Judge (WCJ) denied Smith's request for attorney fees of $1,485, incurred in challenging the carrier's informal denial of medical treatment. The WCJ stated that because the denial of care was not the result of a formal petition to terminate medical treatment, Smith did not establish the right to attorney fees pursuant to section 4607. In a split decision, the Board denied Smith's petition for reconsideration.

The Board majority acknowledged that attorney fees would be available to an applicant who is forced to challenge an insurer's complete refusal to authorize future treatment covered by an award. But, because SCIF refused to provide only part of Smith's care, the Board did not allow attorney fees.

Amar

In *Amar*, the parties stipulated to an award of future medical care after he sustained an industrial injury to his right foot. That care included treatment for a weight loss program and nonindustrial diabetes, both of which were related to his industrial foot injury. The award provided that "medical–legal expenses" would be paid by defendant, Mel Clayton Ford. Amar's counsel, Ghitterman, received a fee from that initial award.

Based on further UR, SCIF unilaterally denied both aspects of Amar's medical care without petitioning for termination of that care pursuant to section 4607. SCIF refused to pay for further medical care for his diabetes or weight loss program. The Board found that the weight loss program remained medically necessary to relieve the effects of his industrial foot injury, but that continued treatment for diabetes was unnecessary for that purpose. The Board ordered the weight loss program reinstated.

The WCJ ruled that section 4607 does not apply to the *Amar* case, and denied attorney fees to Ghitterman. On reconsideration, the WCJ opined that SCIF made a good faith denial of medical care. The WCJ did not find that SCIF refused to provide necessary medical care or engaged in unreasonable delay in providing care. Furthermore, the WCJ did not find that SCIF improperly denied previously awarded medical treatment. The Board recommended that section 4607 fees be denied. The Board adopted the WCJ's report, and denied reconsideration.

These petitions for review ensued to challenge the Board's denial of Smith's and Amar's requests for reasonable attorney fees. We granted these petitions to consider whether Herreras and Ghitterman are entitled to such fees.

Discussion

Smith and Amar contend they are entitled to attorney fees within the meaning and spirit of section 4607. Section 4607 provides, in pertinent part, "[w]here a party to a proceeding institutes proceedings to terminate an award made by the appeals board to an applicant for continuing medical treatment and is unsuccessful in such proceedings, the appeals board may determine the amount of attorney's fees reasonably incurred by the applicant in resisting the proceeding . . . and may assess . . . reasonable attorney's fees as a cost . . . ."

We independently review the meaning and application of WC statutes. (*Honeywell v. Workers' Comp. Appeals Bd.* (2005) 35 Cal. 4th 24, 34 [105 P.3d 544, 24 Cal. Rptr. 3d 179, 70 Cal. Comp. Cases 97].) "Although contemporaneous administrative construction of a statute by the Board, as the agency charged with its enforcement and interpretation, is of great weight, it is not necessarily controlling; and courts will depart from the Board's construction where it is clearly erroneous or unauthorized. [Citations.]" (*Hutchinson v. Workers' Comp. Appeals Bd.* (1989) 209 Cal. App. 3d 372, 375 [257 Cal. Rptr. 240, 54 Cal. Comp. Cases 124].)

To ascertain the Legislature's intent, we read the words of the statute as a whole, keeping in mind its nature and obvious purpose. (*Hutchinson v. Workers' Comp. Appeals Bd., supra,* 209 Cal. App. 3d at p. 375.) Courts consider the consequences that flow from an interpretation of a statute to prevent mischief or absurdity in its application. (*Dyna–Med, Inc. v. Fair Employment & Housing Com.* (1987) 43 Cal. 3d 1379, 1392 [743 P.2d 1323, 241 Cal. Rptr. 67].) We must liberally construe WC statutes for the purpose of "extending their benefits for the protection of persons injured in the course of their employment." (§ 3202; and see *Claxton v. Waters* (2004) 34 Cal. 4th 367, 373 [96 P.3d 496, 18 Cal. Rptr. 3d 246, 69 Cal. Comp. Cases 895].)

SCIF contends we should not construe section 4607 to authorize attorney fees to Smith or Amar because the statute, read literally, does not provide for them unless their attorney is opposing a formal petition to terminate care. But, a literal reading under these facts defeats the statute's purpose. The Board acknowledges that when a carrier informally denies all care, applicant is entitled to attorney fees to enforce the award. We see no difference when a carrier informally denies some of the treatment that is a necessary part of medical care previously awarded. This is tantamount to a petition to deny medical care even though the carrier continues to provide treatment for some of applicant's medical care. (See generally *County of Sonoma v. W.C.A.B. (Callahan)* (1997) 62 Cal. Comp. Cases 973 (writ denied); *United Airlines, RSKCo. v. W.C.A.B. (Dickerson)* (1999) 64 Cal. Comp. Cases 1511 (writ denied).) The carrier may not control the awarding of fees to applicant's counsel by choosing not to file a formal petition under section 4607.

Because counsel was required to enforce part of their awards, Smith and Amar are entitled to attorney fees. Providing such fees comports with the cardinal rule of workers' compensation law that it "shall be liberally construed by the courts with the purpose of extending their benefits for the protection of persons injured in the course of their employment." (§ 3202.)

Smith and Amar cite two persuasive cases. In *United Airlines, RSKCo. v. W.C.A.B. (Dickerson), supra,* 64 Cal. Comp. Cases 1511, the applicant's initial claim for a groin injury was settled by a stipulated award which included future medical care. Later, applicant sought authorization for left hip replacement surgery. Defendant denied authorization for the surgery, contending that the need for it did not arise from the industrial injury. Defendant did not petition to terminate medical care, and continued to provide other care. Applicant successfully petitioned for coverage of the hip surgery, which the WCJ deemed was necessary due to the industrial groin injury.

Applicant filed for both section 5814 penalties for delay in providing care, and for attorney fees pursuant to section 4607. Applicant argued that defendant constructively filed a petition to terminate care by refusing to authorize the hip surgery related to his industrial injury. Although the WCJ denied penalties under section 5814, because there was genuine doubt whether the hip surgery was reasonably related to the groin injury, the WCJ concluded that applicant was entitled to attorney fees under section 4607 because he was forced to institute proceedings to enforce the award of future medical treatment. Defendant's petition for reconsideration was denied.

In *County of Sonoma v. W.C.A.B. (Callahan), supra,* 62 Cal. Comp. Cases 973, the worker sustained an industrial back injury and was awarded permanent disability (PD) with future medical benefits. Later, defendant terminated payments for medical care without filing a petition to do so under section 4607. Applicant sought penalties under section 5814. The WCJ found that the treatment requested was reasonable and necessary, and awarded penalties for delay under section 5814, and attorney fees under section 4607. The WCJ concluded that defendant's denial of care was tantamount to filing a petition to terminate care, thus forcing applicant to institute proceedings to enforce the prior award. The Board denied reconsideration and defendant's petition for review was denied.

As we have stated above, our task is to determine the purpose and intent of the statute, reading it as a whole and in context with the statutory scheme. The meaning of a statute is not limited to a literal reading of its words, especially if such an interpretation leads to mischief or absurdity. In *Hutchinson v. Workers' Comp. Appeals Bd., supra,* 209 Cal. App. 3d at page 375, for example, we annulled a decision of the Board that denied payment for transportation costs incurred in obtaining needed prescription medications even though the literal terms of section 4600 did not provide for such transportation costs. The right to obtain necessary prescription medicines would be hollow unless the means to obtain them were also provided.

Similarly, it would be absurd to deny attorney fees to industrially injured workers simply because the carrier withdrew care without bothering to file a formal petition to do so. If attorney fees are available to counsel who oppose formal petitions, they should be available to counsel who must initiate proceedings to challenge the informal denial of medical care.

California's workers' compensation law functions in large part through the expertise, dedication and professionalism of the attorneys who represent the parties involved in individual cases. Attorneys representing insurance carriers are not expected to work for free. Neither are applicants' attorneys. Insurance carriers who fail to provide previously awarded medical care may not avoid attorney fees to successful applicants' attorneys through the expedient of an informal denial, even when they do so in good faith.

Accordingly, the Board is directed to annul its decisions denying Smith and Amar reasonable attorney fees, and to enter new and different decisions awarding such fees... .[**Editor's Note:** This case, at the time this book went to publication, was under review by the California Supreme Court.]

Intentionally blank

§ 31.0   ADDITIONAL ACTIONS AGAINST EMPLOYER, CO–EMPLOYEE, OR OTHERS

Page 1189, Column 2, second paragraph, insert following '...Cal. 4ᵗʰ 679.'

See unpublished opinion in *Squaglia v. Mascitto* (2007) 72 Cal. Comp. Cases 623, where the Court of Appeal, First District, affirmed a trial court's dismissal of a civil cause of action for alleged intentional infliction of emotional distress where the facts disclosed an alleged assault occurred when a co-worker yelled at plaintiff, but made attempt or threat to touch her. In upholding the summary judgment the Court, stated, in part:

Respondent clearly met his initial burden of producing evidence sufficient to make a prima facie showing that he did nothing on February 22, 2003, or thereafter for that matter, that would constitute intentional infliction of emotional distress upon appellant. Most specifically, in support of his motion he presented a substantial portion of appellant's September 2004 deposition. There, appellant testified that, on the day of the major confrontation with respondent, February 22, the latter entered the back room where appellant was working, "kicked all my [empty cardboard] boxes and knocked my stuff off my dolly," "stepped over the dolly and [got] right in my face," i.e., "one inch" away, and "started screaming, '[w]hat the hell you been doing out there? What the hell you doing for the last four hours?' Appellant testified he could remember "[n]othing more" that respondent said to him at that time and place. He testified that he did not say a "single word to" respondent afterwards, and described his reaction to the encounter in these terms: "I remember being shocked. I couldn't understand why he would come at me. I remember being shocked. I walked out. I went to lunch." After lunch, appellant went back to work.

In answer to a follow-up question from respondent's counsel, appellant reiterated that he had said nothing in response to respondent's angry words to him, again testifying: "I was just in shock. My mouth was open."

In its order granting summary judgment, the trial court found that appellant had not produced sufficient evidence to establish that there were triable issues of material fact regarding either (1) respondent's exercise of "extreme and outra-geous conduct" towards appellant on February 22 or (2) the impact of that conduct on appellant. We agree with both conclusions.

On the first point, the trial court's order granting summary judgment states: "[T]he undisputed material facts establish as a matter of law that Defendant's alleged conduct was not extreme or outrageous... ." This holding is consistent with the applicable law, which is clear that a workplace argument of the sort involved here, no matter how inappropriate, loud or unfair it or its origins might have been, simply does not qualify as a basis for a claim of intentional infliction of emotional distress.

The leading case summarizing the requirements of this tort is Cervantez v. J.C. Penney Co. (1979) 24 Cal.3d 579, 593 [595 P.2d 975, 156 Cal. Rptr. 198], where a unanimous California Supreme Court held: "The elements of a prima facie case for the tort of intentional infliction of emotional distress are: (1) extreme and outrageous conduct by the defendant with the intention of causing, or reckless disregard of the probability of causing, emotional distress; (2) the plaintiff's suffering severe or extreme emotional distress; and (3) and actual and proximate causation of the emo-tional distress by the defendant's outrageous conduct. [Citations.] 'Whether treated as an element of the prima facie case or as a matter of defense, it must also appear that the defendants' conduct was unprivileged.' [Citations.] Conduct to be outrageous must be so extreme as to exceed all bounds of that usually tolerated in a civilized community. [Citations.]" (Id. at p. 593.)

Several appellate decisions apply these principles to claims of the intentional infliction of the employment context. These include two subsequent Supreme Court decisions, as well as a decision of the federal Court of Appeals for the Ninth Circuit. (See Cole, supra, 43 Cal.3d at p. 155, fn. 7; Shoemaker, supra, 52 Cal.3d at p. 25; and Schneid-er v. TRW (9th Cir. 1991) 938 F.2d 986, 992-993 (Schneider).)... .

Page 1189, Column 2, eighth paragraph, insert following '...subdivision (a).'

In *The People, ex rel. Monterey Mushrooms, Inc. v. Thompson, et al.* (2006) 71 Cal. Comp. Cases 35, the Court of Appeal, Sixth District, in an unpublished opinion affirming a trial Court's judgment held that a civil action for violation of Insurance Code section 1871.7(e) arising from fraudulent acts made unlawful by Penal Code section 550(a)(10) did not violate the exclusive remedy provision of workers' compensation under Labor Code section 3820. The Court stated, in part:

After a court trial, defendants Steven Thompson, Aster Kifle–Thompson, and the corporations they had formed were found to have violated Insurance Code section 1871.7, subdivision (b), by submitting fraudulent claims for compensation proscribed by Penal Code section 550. On appeal, defendants contend that the case should have been dismissed because (1) it belonged exclusively in a workers' compensation forum, (2) the People failed to meet the statutory prerequisites for bringing the lawsuit, and (3) defendants' conduct was not unlawful. Defendants further contend that the trial court should have applied a "clear and convincing evidence" standard of proof, that joint and several liability was inappropriate on the facts of the case, and that the damages imposed were unauthorized and excessive. We find no error and affirm the judgment…

The application of Insurance Code section 1871.7, subdivision (b), was clearly authorized in this case. As the trial court recognized, this statute was intended to encompass fraudulent claims for workers' compensation benefits. It specifically provides for civil penalties for claims for compensation under Labor Code section 3207, which is part of the WCA. (Footnote 7)

Indeed, in enacting the Insurance Frauds Prevention Act, the Legislature clearly expressed its intent to promote the investigation and prosecution of insurance fraud, including workers' compensation fraud, which "harms employers by contributing to the increasingly high cost of workers' compensation insurance and self–insurance and harms employees by undermining the perceived legitimacy of all workers' compensation claims." (Ins. Code, § 1871, subd. (d).) "Prevention of workers' compensation insurance fraud may reduce the number of workers' compensation claims and claim payments thereby producing a commensurate reduction in workers' compensation costs. Prevention of workers' compensation insurance fraud will assist in restoring confidence and faith in the workers' compensation system, and will facilitate expedient and full compensation for employees injured at the workplace." (Id., subd. (e).) Lest there be any residual confusion over the authority to proceed, Insurance Code section 1871.7, subdivision (k), makes it clear that the remedies it provides are "in addition to any other remedies provided by existing law."

Furthermore, Penal Code section 550, on which the Insurance Code section 1871.7 allegations were predicated in this case, prohibits the knowing submission of false or fraudulent claims for payment of health care benefits. The statute specifically defines "a claim for payment of a health care benefit" to include a "claim for payment submitted by or on the behalf of a provider of any workers' compensation health benefits under the Labor Code." (Pen. Code, § 550, subd. (a)(10).)

The express inclusion of workers' compensation claims thus demonstrates the Legislature's intention to allow civil actions under Insurance Code section 1871.7 arising from fraudulent acts made unlawful by Penal Code section 550, notwithstanding applicability of the WCA. None of the cases cited by defendants compels or suggests a different conclusion. We therefore agree with the trial court's conclusion that the exclusivity provisions of the WCA did not bar this action… .

Footnote 7. Labor Code section 3207 defines "compensation" as "compensation under this division [including] every benefit or payment conferred by this division upon an injured employee, or in the event of his or her death, upon his or her dependents, without regard to negligence."

§ 31.1(B)   Employer

Page 1209, Column 1, ninth paragraph, insert following '…161.)'

In holding that a teacher's civil tort action alleging such acts as harassment and intimidation were barred by the exclusive remedy provisions of workers' compensation, the Court of Appeal, First District, in a unpublished opinion in *Holford v. West Contra Costa Unified School District* (2006) 71 Cal. Cal. Cases 752, stated, in part:

When a plaintiff alleges injury sustained and arising out of the course of employment, the exclusive remedy provisions of the Workers' Compensation Act (Lab. Code, §§ 3600 et seq.) apply, "notwithstanding that the injury resulted from the intentional conduct of the employer, and even though the employer's conduct might be characterized as egregious." (Shoemaker v. Myers (1990) 52 Cal. 3d 1, 15 [801 P.2d 1054, 276 Cal. Rptr. 303, 55 Cal. Comp. Cases 494] (Shoemaker).) (Footnote 2)

"[W]hen the misconduct attributed to the employer is actions which are a normal part of the employment relationship, such as demotions, promotions, criticism of work practices, and frictions in negotiations as to grievances, an employee suffering emotional distress causing disability may not avoid the exclusive remedy provisions of the Labor Code by characterizing the employer's decisions as manifestly unfair, outrageous, harassment, or intended to cause emotional disturbance resulting in disability." (Cole v. Fair Oaks Fire Protection Dist. (1987) 43 Cal. 3d 148, 160 [729 P.2d 743, 233 Cal. Rptr. 308, 52 Cal. Comp. Cases 27] (Cole).)

Plaintiff contends workers' compensation is not her exclusive remedy because her tort causes of action alleged intentional harassment. Allegations of intentional employer misconduct, however, are not sufficient to avoid the exclusivity provisions of the workers' compensation system. (Cole, *supra*, 43 Cal. 3d at pp. 159–161 [noting that "[a]n employer's supervisory conduct is inherently 'intentional' "].) Moreover, the cases on which plaintiff relies involve general liability insurance coverage, not workers' compensation. (See Coit Drapery Cleaners, Inc. v. Sequoia Ins. Co. (1993) 14 Cal. App. 4th 1595, 1601 [18 Cal. Rptr. 2d 692]; Bank of the West v. Superior Court (1992) 2 Cal. 4th 1254, 1258 [833 P.2d 545, 10 Cal. Rptr. 2d 538].) Those cases are "irrelevant, because the proper subjects of private insurance do not bear on the proper scope of exceptions to the exclusive coverage of workers' compensation." (Soares v. City of Oakland (1992) 9 Cal. App. 4th 1822, 1830, 1831 [12 Cal. Rptr. 2d 405, 57 Cal. Comp. Cases 711] [exceptions to the exclusive coverage of workers' compensation are to be narrowly construed, and the court "must avoid the 'fallacy of importing tort concepts into workers' compensation law' "].) (Footnote 3)

Plaintiff's third amended complaint is based on alleged employer conduct that was a normal part of the employment relationship as described in Cole, and her claims were therefore barred by the exclusivity provisions of the Workers' Compensation Act. (See Cole, *supra*, 43 Cal. 3d at p. 160.) Even plaintiff's cause of action for emotional distress is within the ambit of the employment relationship and therefore flawed. The cases plaintiff cites do not support her argument that allegations of "defendant's failure to provide a hostile free environment," which "caused plaintiff to suffer subjective emotional distress," are sufficient to remove her claims from within the scope of workers' compensation, without allegations of conduct that would violate a fundamental public policy. (Cf. Soares v. City of Oakland, *supra*, 9 Cal. App. 4th at p. 1831 [sexual harassment "not viewed as a risk of employment"], citing Hart v. National Mortgage & Land Co. (1987) 189 Cal. App. 3d 1420, 1424, 1430 [235 Cal. Rptr. 68] coworker's alleged acts of grabbing plaintiff's genitals and making sexually suggestive remarks and gestures were not a normal part of employment]; Lopez v. Sikkema (1991) 229 Cal. App. 3d 31, 34, 39–40, 44 [280 Cal. Rptr. 7, 56 Cal. Comp. Cases 272] [wrongful death and civil rights claims not precluded when death of employee was caused by shooting intended to break a strike, with weapons provided by employer]; Renteria v. County of Orange (1978) 82 Cal. App. 3d 833, 841 [147 Cal. Rptr. 447, 43 Cal. Comp. Cases 899] [exception to exclusivity applied in absence of compensable disability, where employer misconduct was allegedly motivated by racial discrimination].) (Footnote 4)

She makes no such allegations. Plaintiff's cause of action for intentional infliction of emotional distress is barred by the exclusive remedy provisions of the workers' compensation law. (*Shoemaker, supra*, 52 Cal. 3d at p. 25; *Cole, supra*, 43 Cal. 3d at pp. 159–161; *Valenzuela v. State of California* (1987) 194 Cal. App. 3d 916, 923–924 [240 Cal. Rptr. 45].) Judgment on the pleadings was properly granted… .

Footnote 2. "The function of the exclusive remedy provisions is to give efficacy to the theoretical 'compensation bargain,'" pursuant to which "[t]he employee is afforded relatively swift and certain payment of benefits to cure or relieve the effects of industrial injury without having to prove fault but, in exchange, gives up the wider range of damages potentially available in tort. [Citations.]" (Shoemaker, *supra*, 52 Cal. 3d at p. 16.)

Footnote 3. The cases cited by plaintiff are also factually distinguishable. In Coit, the court considered whether a general liability insurance policy covered sexual harassment in deciding the issue of the insurance company's duty to defend. (Coit Drapery Cleaners, Inc. v. Sequoia Ins. Co., *supra*, 14 Cal. App. 4th at pp. 1599, 1601–1602, 1607, 1613.) In Bank of the West, the court determined that a comprehensive general liability insurance policy did not cover claims for advertising injury that arose under the Unfair Business Practices Act. (Bank of the West v. Superior Court, *supra*, 2 Cal. 4th at p. 1258.) None of those circumstances are presented here.

Footnote 4. The *Renteria* decision was criticized by our Supreme Court in *Livitsanos v. Superior Court* (1992) 2 Cal. 4th 744 [828 P.2d 1195, 7 Cal. Rptr. 2d 808, 57 Cal. Comp. Cases 355], which held that "claims for intentional or negligent infliction of emotional distress are preempted by the exclusivity provisions of the workers' compensation

law, notwithstanding the absence of any compensable physical disability." (*Id.* at p. 747.) The Supreme Court described the analysis in *Renteria* as "fatally flawed," rejecting both "the proposition that intentional or egregious employer conduct is necessarily outside the scope of the workers' compensation scheme" and the *Renteria* court's distinction between physical and emotional injury. (*Livitsanos, supra*, at p. 752.) The Supreme Court further noted that "racial discrimination appears to have been the motivating force behind the employer's misconduct" in *Renteria* for which other remedies would be available. (*Livitsanos, supra*, at p. 755, fn. 7.) Subsequent authority has also discounted "the *Renteria* 'exception' to the exclusivity of the workers' compensation remedy," concluding it "should no longer be followed." (*Horn v. Bradco Internat., Ltd.* (1991) 232 Cal. App. 3d 653, 661, 665–670 [283 Cal. Rptr. 721]; see also *Operating Engineers Local 3 v. Johnson* (2003) 110 Cal. App. 4th 180, 188–189, fn. 5 [1 Cal. Rptr. 3d 552, 68 Cal. Comp. Cases 1135].)

§ 31.1(B)(1) False Imprisonment

Page 1244, Column 2, third paragraph, insert following '…fees.'

See also unpublished case of *Moylen, et al. v. Tosco Operating Company* (2005) 70 Cal. Comp. Cases 1584, where the Court of Appeal, First District, affirmed a trial Court's holding that plaintiffs' civil action against their employer for infliction of emotional distress was barred and workers' compensation was their exclusive remedy, when plaintiffs claimed emotional distress from witnessing suffering and death of co–workers in an explosion and fire at defendant's refinery.

§ 31.1(B)(3) Disability Discrimination (FEHA) and (ADA)

Page 1259, Column 2, second paragraph, insert following '…disability.'

Duty to engage in informal interaction process to explore reasonable accommodation with employees or applicants whom it regards as disabled.

In holding that an employer must engage in an *informal interactive process* and provide a necessary and *reasonable accommodation* to an applicant or an employee whom it regards as physically disabled, the Court of Appeal, Second District, in *Gelfo v. Lockheed Martin Corporation* (2006) 71 Cal. Comp. Cases 726, stated, in part:

An employer must explore reasonable accommodations for and engage in an interactive dialogue with applicants or employees whom it regards as disabled.

In addition to a general prohibition against unlawful employment discrimination based on disability, FEHA provides an independent cause of action for an employer's failure to provide a reasonable accommodation for an applicant's or employee's known disability. (§ 12940, subd. (a), (m).) "Under the express provisions of the FEHA, the employer's failure to reasonably accommodate a disabled individual is a violation of the statute in and of itself." (Jensen, *supra*, 85 Cal. App. 4th at p. 256; Bagatti v. Department of Rehabilitation (2002) 97 Cal. App. 4th 344, 357 [118 Cal. Rptr. 2d 443, 67 Cal. Comp. Cases 528] [same] (Bagatti).) Similar reasoning applies to violations of Government Code section 12940, subdivision (n), for an employer's failure to engage in a good faith interactive process to determine an effective accommodation, once one is requested. (§ 12940, subd. (n); Claudio v. Regents of University of California (2005) 134 Cal. App. 4th 224, 243 [35 Cal. Rptr. 3d 837].)

Two principles underlie a cause of action for failure to provide a reasonable accommodation. First, the employee must request an accommodation. (Prilliman v. United Air Lines, Inc. (1997) 53 Cal. App. 4th 935, 954 [62 Cal. Rptr. 2d 142].) Second, the parties must engage in an interactive process regarding the requested accommodation and, if the process fails, responsibility for the failure rests with the party who failed to participate in good faith. (See Jensen, *supra*, 85 Cal. App. 4th at p. 266.) While a claim of failure to accommodate is independent of a cause of action for failure to engage in an interactive dialogue, each necessarily implicates the other.

Relying on federal authorities interpreting the ADA, Lockheed maintains the right to reasonable accommodation flows only to an applicant or employee who is "actually" disabled. Lockheed also asserts that requiring an employer to participate in an interactive process with an individual "regarded as" disabled promotes form over function. Such a requirement, in its view, compels employers to engage in an expensive but futile process, because employees merely "regarded as" disabled do not qualify for a reasonable accommodation. (See Gilday v. Mecosta County (6th Cir. 1997) 124 F.3d. 760, 764 [a person without an actual disability needs no accommodation].) The trial court agreed and directed verdicts against Gelfo on his causes of action for "failure to accommodate" and "failure to engage in the interactive process." The directed verdicts were a mistake.

On these issues, which are novel to California and on which the federal courts are divided, we conclude that employers must reasonably accommodate individuals falling within any of FEHA's statutorily defined "disabilities," including those "regarded as" disabled, and must engage in an informal, interactive process to determine any effective accommodations.

a. An employer must reasonably accommodate an applicant or employee whom it regards as disabled.

So far, only federal courts have considered the issues before us, and only under federal law. Those decisions provide substantial guidance. Like FEHA, the ADA requires an employer "to make reasonable accommodation for the known physical or mental" condition of an employee or applicant. (42 U.S.C. § 12112(b)(5)(A).) In interpreting the ADA, the Eighth Circuit held employees who are regarded as disabled by their employers have no right to a reasonable accommodation. (Weber v. Strippit, Inc. (8th Cir. 1999) 186 F.3d 907, 915–917 (Weber).) In Weber, the court found that

application of the reasonable accommodation requirement in cases of perceived disability under the ADA "would lead to bizarre results" by entitling non–disabled employees to an accommodation denied to similarly situated employees based on their employers' misperceptions. (Weber, *supra*, 186 F.3d at pp. 916–917.)

The Ninth Circuit followed suit in Kaplan v. City of North Las Vegas (9th Cir. 2003) 323 F.3d 1226, 1232–1233 (Kaplan). (Footnote 16)

In Kaplan, a police officer, unable to hold a gun or grasp objects with one hand, was misdiagnosed with rheumatoid arthritis. Based on the misdiagnosis, the employer believed the injury was permanent, concluded he would not be able to hold or use a gun effectively or perform other essential job functions, and fired him. While the court found Kaplan was not "actually disabled," it determined he was "regarded as" disabled because his employer believed he was permanently disabled by arthritis. Relying primarily on Weber, the court held "regarded as" plaintiffs are not entitled to a reasonable accommodation under the ADA. (Kaplan, *supra*, 323 F.3d at pp. 1232–1233.) The court acknowledged the ADA's definition of a "qualified individual with a disability" (i.e., those to whom reasonable accommodation is owed under the ADA) does not differentiate among the three disjunctive prongs of the "disability" definition. (Id. at p. 1232.) Nonetheless, it concluded "[t]he absence of a stated distinction . . . [was] not tantamount to an explicit instruction by Congress that 'regarded as' individuals are entitled to reasonable accommodations." (Ibid.) Because a formalistic reading of the plain language of the statute would lead to "bizarre results," courts must look beyond the literal language of the ADA.

Kaplan reasoned that, if "regarded as" plaintiffs are entitled to reasonable accommodations, "impaired employees would be better off under the statute if their employers treated them as disabled even if they were not." Such a result would be "perverse and troubling" under a statute aimed at dispelling stereotypes. (Kaplan, *supra*, 323 F.3d at p. 1232.) An entitlement to a reasonable accommodation to "regarded as" plaintiffs would not motivate individuals to educate their employers about their true abilities or encourage employers to see their employees' true talents. Rather, it would confer on non–disabled employees a "windfall" by perpetuating employers' erroneous misperceptions about their limitations, and compel employers to squander resources better devoted to employees with actual disabilities who genuinely needed an accommodation. (Ibid.)

Weber and Kaplan were decided under the ADA. No published California case has considered whether an employer has a duty under FEHA to provide a reasonable accommodation to an applicant or employee who is not "actually" disabled, but is "regarded as" having a disability. (Footnote 17)

Because the ADA and FEHA share the goal of eliminating discrimination, we often look to federal case authority to guide the construction and application of FEHA, particularly where parallel statutory language is involved. However, because FEHA "provides protections independent from those in the [ADA]" and "afford[s] additional protections than the [ADA]" (§ 12926.1, subd. (a)), state law will part ways with federal law in order to advance the legislative goal of providing greater protection to employees than the ADA. (See Diaz v. Federal Express Corp. (C.D.Cal. 2005) 373 F.Supp.2d 1034, 1053–1054.) To that end, we are unpersuaded by the reasoning of Weber and Kaplan, whose shortcomings are explored in the better–reasoned decision of Williams, *supra*, 380 F.3d 751, and its progeny.

In Williams, a police officer developed severe depression after 24 years on the police department and, as a result, was unable to carry a gun. As an accommodation, the officer requested a radio room assignment. The department refused the officer's request on the ground that if the officer were assigned to the radio room, he would have access to firearms and would work in close proximity to others who carried guns. (Williams, *supra*, 380 F.3d at p. 766.) The officer was denied the radio room assignment because his employer erroneously perceived that, not only could he not carry a gun, he could not be around others who did or have access to firearms due to his mental condition. (Id. at pp. 766, 776.) The officer was terminated. Suing under the ADA, the officer argued his employer regarded him as having limitations (the inability to have access to firearms or be around others carrying guns) in excess of his actual limitation (the inability to personally carry a gun) that resulted from his condition. (Id. at pp. 766–767.)

The court held employees who are "regarded as" disabled are entitled to accommodation under the ADA. Turning first to a point acknowledged in passing in Kaplan and Weber, the court said: "[T]he statutory text of the ADA does not in any way 'distinguish between [actually] disabled and 'regarded as' individuals in requiring accommodation.' [Citation.]" (Williams, *supra*, 380 F.3d at p. 774.)

Williams acknowledged the possibility, noted in Kaplan and Weber, that applying the reasonable accommodation requirement in favor of "regarded as" disabled employees could produce a "bizarre result." (Williams, *supra*, 380 F.3d at p. 774.) Nonetheless, that remote possibility provided "no basis for an across–the–board refusal to apply the ADA in accordance with the plain meaning of its text." (Footnote 18)

(Ibid.) Moreover, legislative history and Supreme Court authority, which Congress specifically endorsed in crafting the "regarded as" prong of ADA's definition of "disability," reflect a congressional intent to protect "one who is 'disabled' by virtue of being 'regarded as' disabled in the same way as one who is 'disabled' by virtue of being 'actually disabled,' because being perceived as disabled 'may prove just as disabling.' " (Williams, *supra*, 380 F.3d at p. 774; quoting legislative history of the ADA.[H.R.Rep. No. 101–485 (III), 1990 U.S.C.C.A.N. 445, 453]; see also School Bd. of Nassau County v. Arline (1987) 480 U.S. 273 [107 S. Ct. 1123, 94 L. Ed. 2d 307].)

Williams also rejected the "windfall" theory posited in Kaplan and Weber. On the facts, the court noted that, had the employer not misperceived William's inability to be around guns due to his emotional condition, the radio room assignment would have been available to him just as it would have been to another similarly situated officer. Thus, "[t]he employee whose limitations are perceived accurately gets to work, while Williams is sent home unpaid. This is precisely the type of discrimination the 'regarded as' prong literally protects from . . . ." (Id. at pp. 775–776.)

Arguments advanced in Kaplan and Weber also were examined and rejected in Kelly. After Kelly's discharge from the hospital for a pulmonary embolism, her employer refused to permit her to use oxygen at work; "he did not want the responsibility because she might 'fall over dead.' " (Kelly, *supra*, 410 F.3d at pp. 672–673.) Kelly was fired. It was undisputed that, with supplemental oxygen, Kelly could have performed the essential functions of her job. (Id. at p. 672.) Kelly sued on the theory she was "regarded as" disabled, and was denied reasonable accommodation on that basis. A jury agreed and awarded her $50,000. (Id. at p. 674.)

On appeal, the court rejected Weber's concern that a literal application of the ADA would create a "bizarre result" affording more favorable treatment to employees regarded as disabled by their employers, than to those not similarly regarded. (Kelly, *supra*, 410 F.3d at pp. 675–676.) The court noted it is "in the nature of any 'regarded as disabled' claim that an employee who seeks protections accorded to one who is impaired but not regarded as disabled does so because of the additional component – 'regarded as' disabled." (Id. at p. 676.) Thus, that "rationale provides no basis for denying validity to a reasonable accommodation claim." (Ibid.) The court also rejected the argument that accommodating perceived disabilities would " 'do nothing to encourage . . . employees to educate employers of their capabilities' or to 'encourage the employers to see their employees' talents clearly.' [citing Weber, *supra*, 186 F.3d at p. 917]" (Id. at p. 676.) "The ADA is concerned with safeguarding the employees' livelihood from adverse actions taken on the basis of 'stereotypic assumptions not truly indicative of individual ability' of the employee . . . . [T]he real danger is not that the employee will fail to educate an employer concerning her abilities, but that '[t]he employee whose limitations are perceived accurately gets to work, while [the employee perceived as disabled] is sent home unpaid.' " (Ibid., quoting Williams, *supra*, at p. 775.) Stated differently, the ADA's educational function is actually advanced by providing accommodations to "regarded as" disabled employees because "an employer who is unable or unwilling to shed his or her stereotypic assumptions based on a faulty or prejudiced perception of an employee's abilities must be prepared to accommodate the artificial limitations created by his or her faulty perceptions. In this sense, the ADA encourages employers to become more enlightened about their employees' capabilities, while protecting employees from employers whose attitudes remain mired in prejudice." (Id. at p. 676.) Finally, Kelly noted that, by failing to make any definitional distinction between an employee who was actually disabled and one who was merely regarded as disabled, Congress did not consider it inherently unreasonable to provide an accommodation for an employee whom an employer only regarded as disabled. (Ibid.; 42 U.S.C. § 12111(9).)

Based on similar reasoning, numerous other courts rejected the argument that courts are free to ignore a statute's plain language and conclude an employer has no duty under the ADA to provide an accommodation unless an employee is actually disabled. In D'Angelo, *supra*, 422 F.3d 1220, the court held, "an individual falling within the 'regarded as' category of disability under the ADA is entitled to a reasonable accommodation no less than an individual satisfying the actual–impairment definition of disability." (Id. at p. 1239.) D'Angelo also questioned whether a plain reading of the ADA would yield the "bizarre result" envisioned by Weber and Kaplan. First, it pointed out that Weber's conclusion that providing an accommodation would produce a disparity "among impaired but non–disabled employees'" failed "to appreciate that the ADA defines individuals with impairments that do not substantially limit their ability to perform a major life activity, but that are nonetheless treated by the individual's employer as constituting such a limitation, as disabled." (Ibid., original emphasis.) In other words, "'regarded as' plaintiffs are not 'impaired but non–disabled' individuals, but rather are disabled within the meaning of the statute." (Ibid., original emphasis.) Moreover, when two employees have the same impairment (which does not rise to the level of an actual disability), but one employee is entitled to an accommodation to which the other is not, it is because the two are not similarly situated. The employee who receives statutory protection has suffered an adverse employment action; the other has not. (Ibid.) (Footnote 19)

The legal analysis in Williams, Kelly, D'Angelo and Jacques is equally applicable in this case. For the reasons stated in those cases, we conclude the trial court erred in concluding an employer has no duty, as a matter of law, to provide a reasonable accommodation to an applicant or employee who is "regarded as" disabled under FEHA. As with its federal counterpart, FEHA's disjunctive definition of "physical disability" offers no statutory basis for differentiating among the three types of plaintiffs in determining which individuals are entitled to a reasonable accommodation. Moreover, the protections provided employees by FEHA are broader than those provided by the ADA. (§ 12926.1, subds. (a), (d)(1).) To further the societal goal of eliminating discrimination, the statute must be liberally construed to accomplish its purposes and provide individuals with disabilities the greatest protection. (See § 12993, subd. (a); see also Richards v. CH2M Hill, Inc. (2001) 26 Cal. 4th 798, 819 [29 P.3d 175, 111 Cal. Rptr. 2d 87]; Colmenares v. Braemar Country Club, Inc., *supra*, 29 Cal. 4th at p. 1026.)

In sum, we hold the trial court erred in directing a verdict for Lockheed on the cause of action for failure to provide reasonable accommodation on the ground FEHA imposes on an employer no duty to accommodate an applicant or employee who is not actually disabled. (Footnote 20)

b. An employer must engage in an informal dialogue to determine effective reasonable accommodations with an applicant or employee regarded as disabled.

Under section 12940, subdivision (n), it is an unlawful employment practice "[f]or an employer . . . to fail to engage in a timely, good faith, interactive process with the employee or applicant to determine effective reasonable accommodations, if any, in response to a request for reasonable accommodation by an employee or applicant with a known physical . . . disability . . . ." The statute provides an independent basis for liability. (Claudio v. Regents of University of California, *supra*, 134 Cal. App. 4th at p. 243.) Nonetheless, an employer's duty to accommodate is inextricably linked to its obligation to engage in a timely, good faith discussion with an applicant or employee whom it knows (Footnote 21) is disabled, and who has requested an accommodation, to determine the extent of the individual's limitations, before an individual may be deemed unable to work.

Lockheed argues an employer owes no duty to engage in a "futile" discussion with an applicant or employee who is merely "regarded as" disabled and to whom no duty of reasonable accommodation is or will be owed. This argument is rejected for the same reasons we rejected the argument an employer need not accommodate an employee who is "regarded as" disabled. Indeed, the argument for enforcing a duty to engage in a discussion may be more compelling in the context of the interactive process.

As the court stated in Jensen, in words equally apt here, "[t]he interactive process is at the heart of the [FEHA's] process and essential to accomplishing its goals. It is the primary vehicle for identifying and achieving effective adjustments which allow disabled employees to continue working without placing an 'undue burden' on employers." (Jensen, *supra*, 85 Cal. App. 4th at pp. 261–262.) "In a practical sense," as another court observed in the ADA context, "the interactive process is more of a labor tool than a legal tool, and is a prophylactic means to guard against capable employees losing their jobs even if they are not actually disabled. It is clearly a mechanism to allow for early intervention by an employer, outside of the legal forum, for exploring reasonable accommodations for employees who are perceived to be disabled . . . ." (Jacques, *supra*, 200 F.Supp.2d at p. 170.) Realistically, when an employer is aware of an employee's disability, the employer's interest is not in assessing whether the individual's impairment may legally be considered an "actual disability." (Footnote 22)

Rather, "[t]he focus of the interactive process centers on employee–employer relationships so that capable employees can remain employed if their medical problems can be accommodated, rather than sounding a clarion call to legal troops to opine on whether the employee's impairment is an actual disability within the legal nuances of the [Statute]." (Id. at p. 169.)

In sum, when an employer needs to fill a position and an applicant or employee desires the position, the interactive process is designed to bring the two parties together to speak freely and to determine whether a reasonable, mutually satisfactory accommodation is possible to meet their respective needs. (See Prilliman v. United Air Lines, Inc. (1997) 53 Cal. App. 4th 935, 950 [62 Cal. Rptr. 2d 142] [Noting that a reasonable accommodation envisions a cooperative exchange of information "'between employer and employee where each seeks and shares information to achieve the best match between the employee's capabilities and available positions' "].)

We conclude the trial court erred in directing a verdict for Lockheed on the cause of action for failure to engage timely and in good faith in the interactive process to determine effective reasonable accommodations. The determination of error is based on the ground FEHA does not impose on an employer a duty to engage in discussions with an applicant or employee who is not actually disabled. (Footnote 23)

6. Gelfo failed to establish an entitlement to punitive damages.

Section 3294 permits punitive damages against a corporate employer if the employee is sufficiently high in the corporation's decision–making hierarchy to be an "officer, director or managing agent." (Civ. Code, § 3294, subds. (a), (b); White v. Ultramar, Inc. (1999) 21 Cal. 4th 563, 572 [981 P.2d 944, 88 Cal. Rptr. 2d 19] (White); see also Cruz v. HomeBase (2000) 83 Cal. App. 4th 160, 167 [99 Cal. Rptr. 2d 435] [" 'Managing agents' are employees who 'exercise[] substantial discretionary authority over decisions that ultimately determine corporate policy.' [Citation.]" (italics omitted)].)

The trial court granted Lockheed's motion for directed verdict on the ground Gelfo failed to present sufficiently clear and convincing evidence to permit the jury to find a corporate decision–maker was involved in rescinding his job offer.

The only Lockheed employee who potentially falls into such a category is Harbeson's supervisor, Bob MacPherson, whom Harbeson testified was a Lockheed vice–president. MacPherson did not testify at trial, and Gelfo did not introduce any evidence to establish his position in Lockheed's corporate hierarchy. No evidence was presented regarding MacPherson's duties or authority, let alone substantial evidence, that MacPherson "exercise[d] substantial discretionary authority over decisions that ultimately determine corporate policy." (White, supra, 21 Cal. 4th at p. 573.)

Gelfo contends the issue of managing agent is a factual question for the jury, and the trial court invaded the jury's province by granting the motion for a directed verdict. Whether an employee is a managing agent must be made on a case–by–case basis. (White, supra, 21 Cal. 4th at p. 567). However, where insufficient evidence supports a verdict in the plaintiff's favor, no factual issue remains for the jury to decide. Were this not the case, motions for directed verdict and nonsuit would not exist. Viewing the evidence in the light most favorable to Gelfo, we similarly conclude no substantial evidence showed MacPherson was a managing agent. "[O]n this record[,] the jury could not have made the finding that [MacPherson] was a managing agent, which finding is essential for the imposition of punitive damages against [Lockheed]." (Kelly–Zurian v. Wohl Shoe Co. (1994) 22 Cal. App. 4th 397, 421 [27 Cal. Rptr. 2d 457], fn. omitted.)… .

Footnote 16. The Fifth and Sixth Circuits have reached similar conclusions, but the cases contain virtually no legal analysis on the issue. (See Newberry v. East Texas State University (5th Cir. 1998) 161 F.3d 276, 280; Workman v. Frito–Lay, Inc. (6th Cir. 1999) 165 F.3d 460, 467.)

We adopt the opposite view, as have the First, Third, Tenth, Eleventh and, to a limited extent, the Second Circuits. (See Katz v. City Metal Co., Inc. (1st Cir. 1996) 87 F.3d 26, 33; Williams v. Philadelphia Housing (3d Cir. 2004) 380 F.3d 751, 772–776, cert. denied (2005) 544 U.S. 961 [125 S. Ct. 1725, 161 L. Ed. 2d 602, 2005 U.S. LEXIS 2974, 73 U.S.L.W. 3593] (Williams); Kelly v. Metallics West. Inc. (10th Cir. 2005) 410 F.3d 670, 675–676 (Kelly); D'Angelo v. Conagra Foods, Inc. (11th Cir. 2005) 422 F.3d 1220, 1235–1239 (D'Angelo); Jacques v. DiMarzio, Inc. (E.D.N.Y. 2002) 200 F.Supp.2d 151, 163–169, affirmed in pertinent part, 386 F.3d 192, 204 (Jacques).) The Fourth and Seventh Circuits have not yet taken a position. (See e.g., Cigan v. Chippewa Falls School Dist. (7th Cir. 2004) 388 F.3d 331, 335.

Footnote 17. Lockheed points to two California cases, Jensen, supra, 85 Cal. App. 4th 245 and Brundage v. Hahn (1997) 57 Cal. App. 4th 228 [66 Cal. Rptr. 2d 830] (Brundage), to support its contention that FEHA requires an "actual," not merely a "perceived," disability to support a cause of action for failure to accommodate. Neither case advances its cause. Jensen never reached the issue after finding the plaintiff failed to establish a "regarded as" claim under either the ADA or FEHA. (Jensen, supra, 85 Cal. App. 4th at pp. 259–260.) While Brundage involved claims brought under both the ADA and FEHA, not only was the legal analysis in Brundage premised entirely on federal law, the court found the plaintiff was not "regarded as" disabled at the time she was fired. (Brundage, supra, 57 Cal. App. 4th at pp. 235–236.)

Footnote 18. In FEHA, the Legislature specifically addressed and eliminated the potentially "bizarre result" posited by Weber and Kaplan. The statute requires an employee and employer to engage in the interactive process in good faith. The purpose of the informal exchange of information is to determine effective reasonable accommodations, "if any," that might be made for an employee. (§ 12940, subd. (n).) Thus, as a result of discussions, if the employer determines an accommodation is unnecessary, none need be provided. This inquiry is different than whether a particular accommodation is "unreasonable" or poses an undue hardship. (§ 12940, subd. (m); Cal. Code Regs., tit.2, §§ 7293.8, 7293.9.)

Footnote 19. The latter is point is well–illustrated by a case in which an employee was fired because her employer regarded her as disabled based on the belief that her bipolar disorder impeded her workplace interactions. (Jacques, supra, 200 F.Supp.2d at p. 170.) The court noted: "[A]n employee who is simply impaired and an employee who is impaired and 'regarded as' disabled are not similarly situated since [only] the 'regarded as' disabled employee is subject to the stigma of the disabling and discriminatory attitudes of others." (Id. at p. 170.) "Categorically denying reasonable accommodations to 'regarded as' plaintiffs would allow the prejudices and biases of others to impermissibly deny an impaired employee his or her job because of the mistaken perception that the employee suffers from an actual disability. This is the concern addressed by Congress [in the ADA], but ignored by Weber." (Id. at p. 168; see also Jewell v. Reid's Confectionary Co. (D.C. Me. 2001) 172 F.Supp.2d 212, 218–219 [Concluding it is hardly a "bizarre result" to hold accountable – indeed the ADA was intended, in part, to punish – an employer who wrongly regards an employee as disabled, but fails to explore that employee's need for accommodations, choosing instead to take adverse action based on assumptions not truly indicative of an employee's ability].)

Footnote 20. Lockheed maintains it did everything within its power to accommodate Gelfo's medical restrictions, but was unable to accommodate the restrictions against prolonged sitting and standing. Gelfo insists that, had Lockheed discussed the matter with him, it would have learned his restrictions – to the extent they required any accommodation at all – could easily have been accommodated by permitting him an additional break or two, or allowing him to occasionally sit on a stool. These are factual questions properly decided on remand in the first instance.

Footnote 21. FEHA's reference to a "known" disability is read to mean a disability of which the employer has become aware, whether because it is obvious, the employee has brought it to the employer's attention, it is based on the employer's own perception – mistaken or not – of the existence of a disabling condition or, perhaps as here, the employer has come upon information indicating the presence of a disability.

Footnote 22. Typically, an applicant or employee triggers the employer's obligation to participate in the interactive process by requesting an accommodation. (§ 12940, subd. (n).) Although it is the employee's burden to initiate the process, no magic words are necessary, and the obligation arises once the employer becomes aware of the need to consider an accommodation. Each party must participate in good faith, undertake reasonable efforts to communicate its concerns, and make available to the other information which is available, or more accessible, to one party. Liability hinges on the objective circumstances surrounding the parties' breakdown in communication, and responsibility for the breakdown lies with the party who fails to participate in good faith. (See Jensen, *supra*, 85 Cal. App. 4th at p. 266; see also Allen v. Pacific Bell (9th Cir. 2003) 348 F.3d 1113, 1115 [ADA].)

Footnote 23. Lockheed asserts that, if it had a duty to engage in the interactive process, the duty was discharged. "If anything," it argues, "it was Gelfo who failed to engage in a good faith interactive process." Gelfo counters Lockheed made up its mind before July 2002 that it would not accommodate Gelfo's limitations, and nothing could cause it reconsider that decision. Because the evidence is conflicting and the issue of the parties' efforts and good faith is factual, the claim is properly left for the jury's consideration.

In upholding a lower Court's finding that an employer reasonably accommodated an employee, the Court of Appeal, Second District in *Daidone v. City of Glendale* (2006) 71 Cal. Comp. Cases 910, (unpublished) stated, in part:

A. Scope of the City's Duty to Accommodate

Daidone's principal contention is that the City owed a continuing duty to interact with him and give him priority to open positions until some undesignated time, presumably until the accommodation satisfied all of his desires and/or resulted in no loss of income to him. Daidone's theory of a perpetual duty is contrary to the law. "Any reasonable accommodation is sufficient to meet an employer's obligations . . . . the employer need not adopt the most reasonable accommodation nor must the employer accept the remedy preferred by the employee. [Citation.] . . . . [P] . . . '[W]here the employer has already reasonably accommodated the employee's . . . needs, the . . . inquiry [ends].' [Citation.]" (Soldinger v. Northwest Airlines, Inc. (1996) 51 Cal. App. 4th 345, 370 [58 Cal. Rptr. 2d 747] (Soldinger).) (Footnote 6)

Daidone relies on Humphrey v. Memorial Hospitals Association (9th Cir. 2001) 239 F.3d 1128 (Humphrey) but that case does not support his version of a perpetual duty to accommodate. Rather, the court in Humphrey stated that an employer must engage in an interactive process and continue to attempt accommodation until a successful accommodation is reached. (Id. at p. 1139.) Humphrey does not stand for the proposition advanced by Daidone that a successful accommodation is one that completely satisfies the employee's desires. Once a reasonable accommodation had been reached, the City owed no further duty to apprise Daidone of open positions within his restrictions or to grant him priority in obtaining any such position.

Daidone also criticizes the City for a failure to keep a list of employees entitled to disability transfers and for otherwise not matching precisely the interactive processes reviewed in the pertinent cases. This attempt to impose formulaic requirements on the interactive process is contrary to the law. (Hanson, *supra*, 74 Cal. App. 4th at p. 228.) The reasonableness of an accommodation and the adequacy of the interactive process are determined on a case–by–case basis and are not dependent upon rigid formulas of behavior. (Soldinger, *supra*, 51 Cal. App. 4th at p. 370.)

Therefore, with respect to Daidone's failure to accommodate and interact claim, the relevant question is whether substantial evidence supports the trial court's determination that the City interacted with Daidone in good faith and reasonably accommodated his disability. We are satisfied that the City did so.

B. The Interactive Process and Reasonable Accommodations

After his promotion to electrical line mechanic, Daidone suffered two injuries, an incident in which his arm nearly failed while holding a span of wire, and discomfort in his neck and shoulders while pulling cable and working overhead. The City temporarily placed him in light duty positions to accommodate the resulting work restrictions imposed by his treating physician. By all accounts, those temporary positions were within his work restrictions. There is no evidence that those positions constituted anything other than reasonable temporary accommodations.

Similarly, the record supports the conclusion that both the interactive process leading to and the permanent accommodation eventually reached fulfilled the City's legal obligations. While it is true that Daidone expressed a preference for a Howard center dispatch job in his discussions with the City about a permanent accommodation, no such position was available at that time. Once Daidone was declared permanent and stable, the City employed a reasonable procedure for locating a suitable job. According to that procedure, the City first looked for vacancies in the electrical section where Daidone was already employed because that section generally had higher–paying jobs than other departments. The City found a vacant senior construction inspector position in the electrical section. Because Daidone was already performing that position on a temporary basis and was doing well, that job seemed a good fit. He was offered and he accepted a permanent position there. Daidone later told Doyle and Hall that he was satisfied with the position. At that point, the City reasonably believed that the accommodation process was successfully concluded. Understandably, the City did not continue to keep Daidone apprised of openings, nor did it consider Daidone entitled to priority for any of those positions.

The City also acted reasonably and in good faith in November 2000, when Daidone complained for the first time of the incident with Wolf and Hernandez that had occurred over a year earlier. The City responded by undertaking an investigation and concluded that until Daidone was deemed permanent and stationary in March 2000, the City owed no duty to specially accommodate him by transfer to a Howard center position. Acknowledging the impropriety of the comments made by Wolf and Hernandez, the City disciplined them. Even though the senior inspector job qualified as a reasonable accommodation, the City nevertheless created a new position to accommodate employees like Daidone who could no longer perform their electric line mechanic duties. Daidone was medically transferred into that position, which raised his salary closer to what it had been prior to his disability.

This evidence supports the finding that the City generally met its obligation to interact with Daidone and accommodate his disability. Once the City learned Daidone's disability was permanent, it transferred him into a new position within his restrictions and "y–rated" his salary so that he would not lose compensation. While his rating precluded him from receiving the same cost of living increases that the line mechanics received, he was paid at a level higher than other senior inspectors until such time as their pay, through cost of living increases, caught up with his. A net decrease in compensation does not dictate that an accommodation must be found unreasonable. (Hanson, *supra*, 74 Cal. App. 4th at p. 228) Furthermore, when Daidone complained about his accommodated position, the City undertook to create a new position at a higher pay rate and gave Daidone preference in transferring into that job.

(See Raine v. City of Burbank (2006) 135 Cal. App. 4th 1215, 1226 [37 Cal. Rptr. 3d 899] [employer not required to create position to accommodate disabled worker].)…

Daidone also complains that the City failed to move him into supervisory positions. But the City owned no duty to accommodate Daidone by promoting him. *(Hastings v. Department of Corrections* (2003) 110 Cal. App. 4th 963, 972–973 [2 Cal. Rptr. 3d 329].) Nor did the City owe a continuing duty to accommodate Daidone by giving him preferential treatment after he was placed in the senior inspector position. Furthermore, with respect to the station electrician/operator supervisor I position, Daidone placed eighth on the hiring list after testing, and his name was not reached before the position was filed. Finally, with respect to the supervisor II position, Daidone lacked the minimum required supervisory experience.

Substantial evidence thus supports the trial court's conclusion that the City interacted with Daidone in good faith and reasonably accommodated his disability… .(Footnote 8)

Footnote 6. While Soldinger is a religious discrimination case, it has been relied upon by this court in previous disability discrimination cases. (Hanson, *supra*, 74 Cal. App. 4th at p. 228.)

Footnote 8. Because we find the judgment supported by substantial evidence, it is not necessary to address the City's statue of limitations defense.

Page 1263, Column 2, sixth paragraph, insert following '…Moreno, J'.

See *Albertson's, Inc. v. FEHC* (2006) 71 Cal. Comp. Cases 178, for an unpublished decision of the Court of Appeal, Second District, holding a settlement approved by the Appeals Board resolving applicant's workers' compensation claims between applicant and employer that included applicant's release of known and unknown civil actions against employer did not apply to a Department of Fair Employer and Housing (DFEH) claim because: (1) DFEH was not a party to the settlement between applicant and employer and was not bound by that agreement, and (2) in the FEHA action DFEH was prosecuting state's interests in issuing prosecutions and accusations related to disability discrimination claims and not representing applicant's private interests and distinguished the *Jefferson* case.

§ 31.8(A) Action Against An Independent Claims Administrator of a Self–Insured Employer

Page 1311, Column 1, fourth paragraph, following '…(1989)' delete 56 and insert 54.

Page 1314, Column 1, fifth paragraph, insert following '...289.'

In upholding a lower Court's dismissal of an action against a self–insured employer and its third party administrator for breach of contract and bad faith due to defendant's refusal to pay plaintiff's continuing medical award, the Court of Appeal, Second District, in *Garcia v. Helmsman Management Services, Inc.* (2007) 72 Cal. Comp. Cases 53, (unpublished) stated, in part:

Plaintiff and appellant Luis Manuel Garcia appeals from a judgment of dismissal entered after the Superior Court sustained without leave to amend the demurrer of defendant and respondent Helmsman Management Services, Inc. (Helmsman). We conclude that Labor Code, section 5300 (Footnote 1) vests exclusive jurisdiction over Garcia's complaint in the Workers' Compensation Appeals Board (WCAB). We therefore affirm...

C. WCAB Has Exclusive Jurisdiction Over Garcia's Complaint

The existence of the WCAB award is subject to judicial notice. (Evid. Code, § 452; *Rangel v. Interinsurance Exchange* (1992) 4 Cal. 4th 1, 6 fn. 3 [842 P.2d 82, 14 Cal. Rptr. 2d 783, 57 Cal. Comp. Cases 780].) Garcia did not object to the trial court taking judicial notice of the WCAB award, nor does he claim on appeal that the trial court erred in doing so. In fact, Garcia submitted and relied upon the award himself in his opposition to Helmsman's demurrer. Although Garcia consistently characterizes the award as a "settlement" or "agreement," we are not required to accept that characterization, and Garcia has pleaded no facts establishing an independent agreement between himself and either SBC or Helmsman regarding compensation for his work–related injuries. To the contrary, Garcia conceded both below and in this court that his claim to compensation from Helmsman is based upon the WCAB award. Accordingly, the sole question before us is whether Garcia may sue in Superior Court to enforce his right to receive workers' compensation benefits under the WCAB award.

The Workers' Compensation Act (Act), codified at section 3201 et seq., governs all claims for work–related injuries by California employees against their employers and their employers' insurance carriers. Section 3602 provides that the right to recover workers' compensation benefits is the "sole and exclusive remedy" available to an injured employee against his or her employer. (§ 3602, subd. (a); *Marsh & McLennan, Inc. v. Superior Court* (1989) 49 Cal. 3d 1, 5 [774 P.2d 762, 259 Cal. Rptr. 733, 54 Cal. Comp. Cases 265] (*Marsh*).) Because the Act defines "employer" to include "insurer" (§ 3850, subd. (b)), the Act also preempts nearly all claims by an injured employee against the employer's insurance carrier, independent claims administrator and/or adjuster. (*Marsh, supra,* 49 Cal. 3d at pp. 6 & 9–10.) Consistent with this, section 5300 confers exclusive jurisdiction to the WCAB to adjudicate, among other things, proceedings "for the recovery of compensation" and to enforce "against the employer or an insurer . . . any liability for compensation imposed upon the employer by [WCAB] in favor of the injured employee[.]"

(Footnote 6) (§ 5300, subds. (a) & (b); *Marsh, supra,* 49 Cal. 3d at p. 5.)

The California Supreme Court has held specifically that the Act preempts "private causes of action by injured employees against the independent insurance claims administrators and adjusters hired by their self–insured employers that unreasonably delay or refuse to pay compensation benefits." (*Marsh, supra,* 49 Cal. 3d at p. 10.) Because the denial or delay of benefits is "a normal part of the claims process, misconduct stemming from the delay or 'discontinuance of payments . . . is properly addressed by the WCAB.' [Citation.] Indeed, California courts have invariably barred statutory and tort claims alleging that [a workers' compensation] insurer unreasonably avoided or delayed payment of benefits even though the insurer committed fraud and other misdeeds in the course of doing so." (*Charles J. Vacanti, M.D., Inc. v. State Comp. Ins. Fund* (2001) 24 Cal. 4th 800, 821 & fn. 8 [14 P.3d 234, 102 Cal. Rptr. 2d 562, 65 Cal. Comp. Cases 1402] [citing cases] (*Vacanti*), quoting *Marsh, supra,* 49 Cal. 3d at p. 11.) The aggrieved employee's exclusive remedy in such cases is set forth in section 5814, subdivision (a): "When payment of compensation has been unreasonably delayed or refused, either prior to or subsequent to the issuance of an award, the amount of the payment unreasonably delayed or refused shall be increased up to 25 percent or up to ten thousand dollars ($10,000), whichever is less." (§ 5814, subd. (a); see *Vacanti, supra,* 24 Cal. 4th at p. 818 [quoting prior version of § 5814].)

The only wrongful conduct that Garcia alleges is that Helmsman and SBC "refused to pay the bills" for his treatment, that the bills "remain unpaid," and that Helmsman and SBC "refused and continue to refuse to pay Plaintiff's legitimate claims." This is precisely the sort of conduct that the Supreme Court held in *Marsh, supra,* 49 Cal. 3d 1, and *Vacanti, supra,* 24 Cal. 4th 800, to be within the exclusive jurisdiction of the WCAB. As the court in *Vacanti* stated, "[t]he mere fact that an individual insurer has a pattern or practice of bad faith delays or denials of payment is not enough to insulate a cause of action from preemption where, as here, each wrongful act is closely connected to a normal insurer activity – the processing of medical lien claims. Indeed, such misconduct is indistinguishable from the insurer misconduct alleged in the claims barred by *Marsh, supra,* 49 Cal. 3d at pages 9–11." (*Vacanti, supra,* 24 Cal. 4th at p. 828.) Whatever Helmsman's alleged motivation for doing so, the "delay or refusal to pay benefits, even if done intentionally and with full knowledge of the hardship to the injured claimant, is insufficient to avoid exclusive [WCAB] jurisdiction." (*Mitchell v. Scott Wetzel Services, Inc.* (1991) 227 Cal. App. 3d 1474, 1479 [278 Cal. Rptr. 474, 56 Cal. Comp. Cases 120].)

Garcia cites numerous cases to establish that Garcia is entitled to workers' compensation benefits, that he has standing to sue Helmsman as a third–party beneficiary to Helmsman's claims–administration contract with SBC, or to support the general proposition that an insured may sue his or her insurer in tort for insurance bad faith. None of these cases is relevant. In his reply brief, Garcia contends, in a single sentence, that "[w]orkers' compensation law does not prevent the filing of an action for damages at common law against a [d]efendant who commits bad faith by failing to pay a disability claim." Garcia does not, however, distinguish, discuss, or even cite *Marsh, supra,* 49 Cal. 3d 1, *Vacanti, supra,* 24 Cal. 4th 800, or their progeny. The cases Garcia relies upon do not support his contention. (Footnote 7) We therefore hold that the WCAB has exclusive jurisdiction over Garcia's complaint.

Garcia did not request leave to amend in the trial court, and he does not do so on appeal. We have nevertheless reviewed the record, and conclude that Garcia has failed to establish a reasonable possibility that he could cure the defect in his complaint by amendment. (See *Scott v. City of Indian Wells* (1972) 6 Cal. 3d 541, 549 [492 P.2d 1137, 99 Cal. Rptr. 745].) To do so, he would have to allege that Helmsman engaged in "wrongful acts that are independent of its role as insurer of workers' compensation benefits." (*Hughes v. Argonaut Ins. Co.* (2001) 88 Cal. App. 4th 517, 530 [105 Cal. Rptr. 2d 877, 66 Cal. Comp. Cases 454], citing *Vacanti, supra,* 24 Cal. 4th at p. 822.) Garcia has identified no such acts, and none appears in the record... .

Footnote 1. All further statutory references are to the Labor Code, unless otherwise stated.

Footnote 6. Section 5300 provides, in relevant part: "All the following proceedings shall be instituted before the appeals board and not elsewhere, except as otherwise provided in Division 4:

"(a) For the recovery of compensation, or concerning any right or liability arising out of or incidental thereto.

"(b) For the enforcement against the employer or an insurer of any liability for compensation imposed upon the employer by this division in favor of the injured employee, his or her dependents, or any third person."

Footnote 7. *Mariscal v. Old Republic Life Ins. Co.* (1996) 42 Cal. App. 4th 1617 [50 Cal. Rptr. 2d 224], is not a workers' compensation case, but concerns a bad faith action under an accidental death and dismemberment policy. *Tarsio v. Provident Ins. Co.* (D. N.J. 2000) 108 F.Supp.2d 397, concerns a bad faith action under New Jersey law against a private disability insurer. *Unruh v. Truck Insurance Exchange* (1972) 7 Cal. 3d 616 [498 P.2d 1063, 102 Cal. Rptr. 815, 37 Cal. Comp. Cases 590] (*Unruh*), permitted a tort action against a worker's compensa- tion insurer for extreme and outrageous conduct, but both *Marsh, supra,* 49 Cal. 3d at pp. 6–7, and *Vacanti, supra,* 24 Cal. 4th at pp. 819–23, explicitly hold that *Unruh* does not permit claims like Garcia's. *Hernandez v. General Adjustment Bureau* (1988) 199 Cal. App. 3d 999 [245 Cal. Rptr. 288, 53 Cal. Comp. Cases 128], which predates *Marsh,* permitted a claim for emotional distress against an independent adjuster hired by a workers' compensation insurer, reasoning that the adjuster was *not* the insurer, and therefore fell outside the scope of workers' compensation exclusivity. To the extent *Hernandez* might survive the Supreme Court's holding in *Marsh,* it is inapposite. (See

Mitchell v. Scott Wetzel Services, Inc., supra, 227 Cal. App. 3d at p. 1481.)

§ 31.12   Altercations – Initial Physical Aggressor

Page 1329, Column 1, eighth paragraph, insert following '...laws...'.

The facts in *Mathews* were as follows:

Page 1329, Column 1, ninth paragraph, insert following '...1288'.

The Court of Appeal, Second District, in *Six Flags, Inc., et. al. v. WCAB (Bunyanunda)* (2006) 71 Cal. Comp. Cases 1759, in discussing the widow's argument stated, in part:

In *Mathews v. Workmen's Comp. Appeals Bd.* (1972) 6 Cal. 3d 719 [493 P.2d 1165, 100 Cal. Rptr. 301, 37 Cal. Comp. Cases 124] (*Mathews*), the Supreme Court reviewed the history of the workers' compensation constitutional enabling provision and corresponding statutes to determine whether former section 3600, subdivision (g), violated the Constitution. (*Mathews,* at pp. 728–735.) Former section 3600, subdivision (g), denied death benefits when an injury resulted from an altercation in which the injured employee was the aggressor. (*Mathews,* at pp. 725–726.) In *Mathews,* an employee's widow argued that former section 3600, subdivision (g), was unconstitutional because article XX, section 21 (the predecessor to art. XIV, § 4) gave the Legislature the power to create a system of workers' compensation to provide benefits " 'irrespective of the fault of any party.' " The widow argued the word "fault" included intentional as well as negligent acts. (*Mathews, supra,* 6 Cal. 3d at p. 728.)

The Supreme Court explained that the constitutional provision at issue, article XX, section 21 (now art. XIV, § 4) "was added to the Constitution . . . for the sole purpose of removing all doubts as to the constitutionality of the then existing workmen's compensation statutes." (*Mathews, supra,* 6 Cal. 3d at pp. 734–735.) The *Mathews* court concluded that the constitutional provision could not "be read as invalidating basic features of those laws as they [had] existed since 1911." (*Id.* at p. 735.) Thus, to ascertain the meaning of the phrase " 'irrespective of the fault of any party,' " the *Mathews* court examined the workers' compensation statutes pre–dating the 1918 constitutional enabling provision, then numbered as article XX, section 21.

Specifically, the court examined (1) the Roseberry Act of 1911 (Stats. 1911, ch. 399, p. 796), (Footnote 5) (2) the Boynton Act of 1913 (Stats. 1913, ch. 176, p. 279), (Footnote 6) and (3) Workmen's Compensation, Insurance and Safety Act of 1917 (Stats. 1917, ch. 586, p. 832). (*Mathews, supra,* 6 Cal. 3d at pp. 729–734.) Based upon a review of these statutes, the *Mathews* court found that the phrase " 'irrespective of the fault of any party' " was "intended only to give the Legislature power to grant benefits unhampered by common law tort concepts of negligence." (*Id.* at p. 728, italics omitted.) The phrase was not included in article XX, section 21, to prohibit the Legislature from preventing an award of workers' compensation benefits based upon intentional wrongdoing. (*Mathews*, at p. 728.)... .

Footnote 5. As explained by the *Mathews* court, the Roseberry Act of 1911 "established a voluntary system of [workers'] compensation." (*Matthews* [*sic*], *supra*, 6 Cal. 3d at p. 729.) One month after the Roseberry Act became effective, the voters approved article XX, section 21, which, in its original 1911 form, provided: " 'The legislature may by appropriate legislation create and enforce a liability on the part of all employers to compensate their employees for any injury incurred by said employees in the course of their employment irrespective of the fault of either party.' " (*Mathews*, at p. 730, italics omitted.)…

Footnote 6. Because few employers voluntarily provided workers' compensation coverage under the voluntary Roseberry Act, the Legislature exercised its powers pursuant to article XX, section 21, to create compulsory workers' compensation legislation, entitled the Boynton Act. (*Mathews*, *supra*, 6 Cal. 3d at p. 730.)

Then in 1917, the Legislature substantially revised the Boynton Act and promulgated the Workmen's Compensation, Insurance and Safety Act of 1917. (*Mathews*, *supra*, 6 Cal. 3d at p. 731.) The same month that the Legislature enacted the Workmen's Compensation, Insurance and Safety Act of 1917, the Legislature also recommended to the voters an amendment to article XX, section 21, which they approved in 1918. (*Mathews*, at p. 733.) The 1918 version of article XX, section 21, is the predecessor constitutional provision to article XIV, section 4.

§ 31A.0   APPORTIONMENT

**Page 1333, Column 1, second paragraph, following
'…new law in…' change §31A.10 to §31A.12**

§ 31A.2   Medical Treatment

**Page 1341, Column 1, fourth paragraph,
insert following '…64.)'**

In *County of Stanislaus v. WCAB (Credille)* (2006) 71 Cal. Comp. Cases 1381, the Court of Appeal, Fifth District, in an unpublished decision denied defendant's Petition for Writ of Review and in holding that substantial evidence existed, consisting of a 1997 award for future medical treatment and two physician's opinions that applicant was entitled to leg braces on an industrial basis [even though applicant received only a 1 percent permanent disability award because she had substantial pre–existing permanent disability because of polio] stated, in part:

Credille was diagnosed with polio in 1956 and began wearing leg braces at the age of four. She worked for the County as a social worker from 1976 through February 11, 1993, when she suffered a cumulative trauma injury to her back, lower extremities, and left shoulder. (Footnote 2)

Credille attributed her leg symptoms to standing and walking while working for the County.

On March 31, 1997, a Workers' Compensation Administrative Law Judge (WCJ) awarded Credille permanent partial disability of one percent, amounting to $420 in payment, after apportioning out the vast majority of her disability to her preexisting disease based on medical reporting from Dr. Bryan Barber. The award also required the County to provide Credille "further medical treatment as may be reasonably required to cure or relieve from the effects of said injury."

The County provided periodic adjustments to Credille's leg braces for nine years after the award was issued. In June 2005, Credille's treating physician, Dr. Patrick Rhoades, recommended that her braces be refitted and replaced. The County disagreed based on medical reporting of Dr. James Stark.

After submitting the dispute to the WCAB, the WCJ concluded in March 2006 that Credille was entitled to leg braces on an industrial basis per the 1997 award for future medical treatment and based on the reporting of Drs. Rhoades and Barber. The County filed a petition for

reconsideration, which the WCAB denied by adopting the report and recommendation of the WCJ…

"Apportionment is the process employed by the Board to segregate the residuals of an industrial injury from those attributable to other industrial injuries, or to nonindustrial factors, in order to fairly allocate the legal responsibility." (*Ashley v. Workers' Comp. Appeals Bd.* (1995) 37 Cal. App. 4th 320, 326 [43 Cal. Rptr. 2d 589, 60 Cal. Comp. Cases 683].) Unlike permanent disability, medical treatment cannot be apportioned to nonindustrial factors. (*Granado v. Workmen's Comp. App. Bd.* (1968) 69 Cal. 2d 399, 405–406 [445 P.2d 294, 71 Cal. Rptr. 678, 33 Cal. Comp. Cases 647].) "[T]he right of an injured employee to recover medical expense reasonably necessary to relieve from the effects of the injury is independent of the right to recover for disability and the issue of apportionment." (*Cedillo v. Workrmen's Comp. App. Bd.* (1971) 5 Cal. 3d 450, 454 [487 P.2d 1039, 96 Cal. Rptr. 471, 36 Cal. Comp. Cases 497].) Once it has been established that an industrial injury contributed to the need for medical treatment, section 4600 requires the employer to provide the treatment. (*Rouseyrol v. Workers' Comp. Appeals Bd.* (1991) 234 Cal. App. 3d 1476, 1485 [286 Cal. Rptr. 250, 56 Cal. Comp. Cases 624].) Medical treatment specifically includes "crutches, and apparatus, including orthotic and prosthetic devices and services, that is reasonably required to cure or relieve the injured worker from his or her injury. . . . " (§ 4600, subd. (a).)…

We conclude the medical evidence, combined with the 1997 award, "is more than a mere scintilla" to support the findings of the WCAB. (*Braewood Convalescent Hospital v. Workers' Comp. Appeals Bd.*, *supra*, 34 Cal. 3d at p. 164.) The WCAB previously concluded that Credille's employment with the County aggravated her preexisting polio–related disease, resulting in an award for medical treatment. As the WCJ advised in his report and recommendation, the WCAB lacked jurisdiction to address the prior award. Dr. Rhoades unequivocally recommended new braces. Dr. Barber agrees that Credille's continuing problems with her lower extremities are partially industrial and that she continues to require treatment for her injury. Even Dr. Stark admitted treatment needed to be provided on an industrial basis based on the prior award. Accordingly, substantial evidence supports the WCAB's determination… .

Footnote 2. "A cumulative injury is one which results from repetitive events, occurring during each days work, which in combination cause any disability or need for medical treatment." (*Western Growers Ins. Co. v. Workers' Comp. Appeals Bd.* (1993) 16 Cal. App. 4th 227, 234 [20 Cal. Rptr. 2d 26, 58 Cal. Comp. Cases 323].)

Page 1341, Column 2, first paragraph, insert following '…injury.'

The Court stated, in part:

"Although the workers' compensation statutes are primarily procedural in nature, "they make it possible for the third party to be held liable "for all the wrong his tortfeasance brought about' [citation.] regardless of whether it is the employee or the employer who brings suit." (County of San Diego v. Sanfax Corp., *supra*, 19 Cal. 3d at p. 873.) Thus, to the extent that the damages which the employee recovers from a third party simply duplicate benefits which the employee has already received from the employer, the employee's own recovery provides a fund from which the employer may draw. (Id. At pp. 872–873.)

One commentator has noted that the reimbursement of benefits paid out when the employee recovers a personal injury judgment or settlement against the third–party tortfeasor is a necessary part of the underlying workers' compensation scheme. "Subrogation in workers' compensation insurance involves California employers because it affects the rates they pay for insurance it also has a relationship to the level of workers' compensation benefits paid and in this regard affects the interest of all employees, not merely those with third–party actions. The connection of such subrogation policies with industrial safety practices is also a matter of concern to the public generally as well as to employers and their employees." (Lasky, Subrogation Under the California Workmen's Compensation Laws – Rules, Remedies and Side Effects (1972) 12 Santa Clara L. Rev. 1, 4. See also Burrow v. Pike (1987) 190 Cal. App. 3d 384, 399 [235 Cal. Rptr. 408].)

Based upon the foregoing, we discern a clear legislative policy militating in favor of reimbursement whenever possible. The employer who assumes the burden of paying benefits for all damages proximately related to an industrial accident, including those caused by a subsequent third party tortfeasor, surely is entitled to seek reimbursement from the party only to the extent the tort injury exacerbated the employee's condition, i.e., only to the extent compensation was increased by the tort injury. (See Breese v. Price, *supra*, 29 Cal. 3d at pp. 928–931, Hodge v. Workers' Comp. Appeals Bd. (1981) 123 Cal. App. 3d 501, 512, 515 [176 Cal. Rptr. 675, 46 Cal. Comp. Cases 1034], Rhode v. National Medical Hosp. (1979) 93 Cal. App. 3d 528, 535 [155 Cal. Rptr. 797, 44 Cal. Comp. Cases 706.])

As we see it, such a construction of section 3852 renders the statutory procedures fully consistent with common law principles of equitable subrogation… .

§ 31A.10 Apportionment of Permanent Disability on or After April 19, 2004

Page 1375, Column 1, fifth paragraph, delete the Editor's Note following '…injury'

Page 1375, Column 2, second paragraph, insert following '…injury'

Meaning of an Order Approving a Compromise and Release Within Meaning of Section 4664(b)

The Appeals Board, in an en banc decision, *Pasquotto v. Hayward Lumber* (2006) 71 Cal. Comp. Cases 223, held that an approved *Compromise and Release*, without more, does not constitute an "award of permanent disability" under Section 4664(b).

However, the Board noted that such a *Compromise and Release* may be relevant in determining whether any of the permanent disability found after a subsequent industrial injury was caused by "other factors" under Sections 4663.

Further, the Board held that Section 4663 does not preclude an applicant from the showing that prior to the injury or injuries, for which he or she is now claiming permanent disability, that he or she had medically rehabilitated from the disabling effects of an earlier industrial or non–industrial injury. *This situation must be distinguished from an actual prior award under Section 4664(b) from which there can be no rehabilitation for apportionment purposes under SB 899. The Board stated, in part:*

A. An Order Approving A Compromise And Release Agreement, Without More, Is Not A "Prior Award of Permanent Disability" Within The Meaning Of Section 4664(b).

Section 4664(b) provides: "If the applicant has received a prior *award of permanent disability*, it shall be conclusively presumed that the prior permanent disability exists at the time of any subsequent industrial injury." (Emphasis added.)

For the reasons that follow, we conclude that an approved compromise and release agreement, without more, does not constitute an "award of permanent disability" under section 4664(b).

A compromise and release agreement approved by the WCAB generally constitutes an "award." The Labor Code permits the parties to a workers' compensation case to reach a compromise regarding the amount of compensation payable to the injured employee and to release the defendant(s) from further potential liability for compensation. (Lab. Code, § 5000 et seq.) Such a compromise and release agreement, once approved by the WCAB (Lab. Code, § 5001), is an "award" that has the same force and effect as any other workers' compensation award. (Lab. Code, § 5002; *Smith v. Workers' Comp. Appeals Bd.* (1985) 168 Cal. App. 3d 1160, 1169–1170 [214

Cal. Rptr. 765] [50 Cal. Comp. Cases 311]; *City of Anaheim v. Workers' Comp. Appeals Bd. (Davis)* (1982) 128 Cal. App. 3d 200, 206 [180 Cal. Rptr. 132] [47 Cal. Comp. Cases 52]; *Raischell & Cottrell, Inc. v. Workmen's Comp. Appeals Bd. (Adamson)* (1967) 249 Cal. App. 2d 991, 997 [58 Cal. Rptr. 159] [32 Cal. Comp. Cases 135]; *Jones v. Fremont Ins. Co.* (1986) 14 Cal. Workers' Comp. Rptr. 79 (Appeals Board panel); see also *Kaiser Foundation Hospitals v. Workmen's Comp. Appeals Bd. (Keifer)* (1974) 13 Cal. 3d 20, 25 [528 P.2d 766, 117 Cal. Rptr. 678] [39 Cal. Comp. Cases 857]; *Ogdon v. Workmen's Comp. Appeals Bd.* (1974) 11 Cal. 3d 192, 196 [520 P.2d 1022, 113 Cal. Rptr. 206] [39 Cal. Comp. Cases 297]; *Johnson v. Workmen's Comp. Appeals Bd.* (1970) 2 Cal. 3d 964, 973 [471 P.2d 1002, 88 Cal. Rptr. 202] [35 Cal. Comp. Cases 362.)

Nevertheless, the fact that an approved compromise and release agreement generally constitutes an "award" does not mean that it is an "award of permanent disability" under section 4664(b), even if the compromise and release agreement resolved the issue of permanent disability.

This is illustrated by the facts of the case before us. The 1999 compromise and release agreement did not stipulate to or otherwise specify the percentage of permanent disability – or the factors of disability – attributable to applicant's May 9, 1998 back injury. In paragraph 6 of the agreement, in which "[t]he parties represent that the following facts are true," there is no representation regarding the percentage of factors of permanent disability. There also are no such representations in paragraph 10 of the agreement, which contained "additional information" regarding the compromise and release. To the contrary, paragraph 10 incorporated an addendum, which expressly stated that "the nature and extent of permanent disability" was "in issue."

We are cognizant of defendant's assertion that the 1999 compromise and release necessarily contemplated that applicant's May 9, 1998 back injury had resulted in a preclusion from heavy work and in a preclusion from lifting more than 30 pounds, as found by Dr. Kahmann's May 10, 1999 report – which was the only permanent and stationary report in evidence as to the back.

However, such a conclusion would be entirely speculative. The compromise and release agreement contained neither any stipulation regarding applicant's percentage of permanent disability nor any language specifying the nature of his back disability. Moreover, while it might be fair to assume that some of the $35,000 in settlement money was for applicant's back, there is no way to determine – at least on this record – how much of this consideration was for his back *permanent disability* – particularly given: (1) the compromise and release specified there was an "issue" regarding the "nature and extent of permanent disability," which implies there was a dispute regarding applicant's back permanent disability; (2) we do not know whether, absent the settlement, either party would have obtained supplemental medical reports on the issue of applicant's back permanent disability; and (3) we cannot determine how much of the settlement money was in consideration for releasing issues other than applicant's back permanent disability. This last point is of no small

significance, given that applicant had a post–surgical back; yet, he settled his right to any further medical treatment. Moreover, in addition to appli– cant's back, there apparently also were issues regarding pulmonary disability and/or treatment.

Further, in this case – and in other cases – there is no reliable way to determine how much of the settlement monies paid under an approved compromise and release agreement represent compensation for permanent disability, at least where the compromise and release agreement does not contain any specific stipulation or representation regarding the applicant's percentage of or factors of permanent disability. There are many factors that may motivate parties to settle by way of a compromise and release agreement, some of which might not be disclosed in the compromise and release agreement and might have no relation to the percentage of or the nature of the applicant's permanent disability. These factors can include, but certainly are not limited to: undisclosed issues regarding injury, employment, the statute of limitations, insurance coverage, or fraud; an applicant's desire to extricate him or herself from the workers' compensation system; an applicant's wish to avoid the delays inherent in obtaining a decision or the risks inherent in litigation; an applicant's non–industrial health factors; an applicant's immediate financial needs or desire for a lump sum; an undisclosed agreement that the applicant will resign his or her employment in conjunction with the compromise and release; a defendant's wish to avoid the risks and costs of litigation; a defendant's desire to close its file – thereby eliminating its need to maintain reserves for possible future benefits (if the case were to be reopened), eliminating its costs of maintaining the file for the lifetime of the employee (in the event of an award of further medical treatment), and reducing its risks of penalties; a defendant's desire to keep its costs down in multiple party cases or cases likely to entail multiple or extended proceedings; a defendant's desire to settle around liens; and third–party recovery issues.

We are aware that, in any given case, evidence outside the four corners of an approved compromise and release agreement conceivably might be presented in an attempt to show that some discrete portion of the settlement was for permanent disability. We conclude that such extrinsic evidence should not be allowed.

In this regard, an analogous situation was presented in *Claxton v. Waters* (2004) 34 Cal. 4th 367 [96 P.3d 496, 18 Cal. Rptr. 3d 246, 69 Cal. Comp. Cases 895].

In *Claxton,* an employee had sued her employer and other defendants for civil damages, alleging workplace sexual harassment. Previously, however, the employee had filed workers' compensation claims, including one for injury to the "psyche due to sexual harassment." The employee then settled her workers' compensation claims through a standard pre–printed compromise and release agreement, approved by the WCAB, which made no reference to the pending civil lawsuit. Thereafter, the civil defendants moved for summary judgment on the ground that the compromise and release agreement had settled the employee's civil sexual harassment claim. In opposition, the employee filed a declaration stating her belief that the compromise and release agreement "did not include" her civil damages claim and stating she had not authorized her workers' compensation attorney to settle her civil action. Her workers' compensation attorney filed a similar declaration.

The Supreme Court concluded that, to show that the standard pre–printed workers' compensation compromise and release agreement released the employee's civil claims, the civil defendants would have to produce a separate agreement expressly so stating. That is, the civil defendants cannot rely on extrinsic evidence to show that the compromise and release intended to settle claims outside the workers' compensation scheme. Among other things, the Court said:

"We are . . . convinced that extrinsic evidence should not be admissible to show that the standard preprinted workers' compensation release form also applies to claims *outside* the workers' compensation system. To allow such evidence would unduly burden our courts. Illustrative of this point are [various] Court of Appeal decisions [citations omitted]. In those cases, as here, the employer relied on standard language in the preprinted workers' compensation release form as an affirmative defense in the worker's civil lawsuit and later as the basis for a motion for summary judgment in that action. In each case, the appellate court determined that there were triable issues of fact as to whether the parties intended the workers' compensation settlement to also apply to claims outside the workers' compensation system, thus requiring further proceedings. This necessitated the presentation of evidence on that issue, and ultimately required resolution of disputed issues of fact as to what occurred in negotiations at the workers' compensation proceedings. Thus, allowing such extrinsic evidence would require our trial courts, which currently are under severe budgetary restraints, to expend their already scarce resources to divine and reconcile the parties' intentions in signing a standard preprinted workers' compensation release form. And parties too would have to spend time and money in presenting this evidence." (*Claxton v. Waters, supra,* 34 Cal. 4th at p. 377.)"

The same or similar problems would occur if extrinsic evidence were allowed to establish what permanent disability, if any, was "awarded" under an approved compromise and release. As discussed above, the reasons are many and varied why parties agree to settle a workers' compensation claim by compromise and release, and the amount of the settlement may have no clear relation to the nature and extent of the employee's permanent disability. To permit extrinsic evidence to be developed through discovery and then introduced at trial – so that the WCAB could attempt to "divine and reconcile" the parties' intention on the issue of permanent disability, if they had a common intention or, indeed, any intention at all – would result in delays and expenses that would be inconsistent with the constitutional mandate that the California workers' compensation system "shall accomplish substantial justice in all cases expeditiously, inexpensively, and without incumbrance [sic] of any character." (Cal. Const., art. XIV, § 4.) Moreover, if a party to a subsequent case attempted to develop and present evidence from outside the four corners

of an earlier compromise and release, regarding what was discussed or agreed to during settlement negotiations leading to that compromise and release, there could be significant potential legal problems. For example, attorney–client privilege issues could arise, even with respect to information that counsel for one party to the compromise and release disclosed to counsel for the other party – at least if those disclosures were reasonably necessary to further the interests of both parties in finalizing negotiations. (*Oxy Resources Calif. LLC v. Superior Court* (2004) 115 Cal. App. 4th 874, 898 [9 Cal. Rptr. 3d 621]; *STI Outdoor LLC v. Superior Court* (2001) 91 Cal. App. 4th 334, 339–341 [109 Cal. Rptr. 2d 865].)

Accordingly, for all of the reasons above, an approved compromise and release agreement, without more, does not constitute "an award of permanent disability," within the meaning of section 4664(b

B. Where There Is No "Prior Award of Permanent Disability" Within The Meaning Of Section 4664(b), The Medical Reports And Other Evidence Relating To A Prior Industrial Injury Settled By A Compromise and Release May Be Relevant In Determining Whether Any Of The Permanent Disability Found After A Subsequent Industrial Injury Was Caused By "Other Factors" Under Section 4663.

At trial, defendant raised the issue of "apportionment." Under SB 899, there are two statutory avenues for apportionment: section 4663 and section 4664. Thus, although we have concluded there is no basis for apportionment under section 4664(b) because the October 15, 1999 OACR was not a "prior award of permanent disability," there may still be a basis for apportionment under section 4663. (Footnote 9)

Under section 4663, apportionment is based on the causation of the permanent disability and the WCAB must determine what approximate percentage of the permanent disability was caused by the direct result of the injury and what approximate percentage of the permanent disability was caused by "other factors . . . , including prior industrial injuries." (Lab. Code, § 4663(a), (b), & (c); *Escobedo v. Marshalls* (2005) 70 Cal. Comp. Cases 604 [2005 Cal. Wrk. Comp. LEXIS 71, 2005 WL 910490] (Appeals Board en banc), writ den. sub nom. *Escobedo v. Workers' Comp. Appeals Bd.* (2005) 70 Cal. Comp. Cases 1506 [2005 Cal. Wrk. Comp. LEXIS 272], review den. 2005 Cal. LEXIS 13096 [Nov. 16, 2005, S137275].) Accordingly, if a prior injury was settled by an approved compromise and release agreement, then the medical reports and other evidence relating to that prior injury may be relevant in determining whether any of the current overall permanent disability was caused by "other factors" under section 4663.

In this case, however, the WCJ has not yet addressed the issue of apportionment under section 4663. Moreover, Dr. Ovadia's report issued on September 15, 2003 – before the enactment of SB 899 – and Dr. Kahmann's May 17, 2004 report do not discuss apportionment under section 4663 in accordance with the standards set out in *Escobedo.* Therefore, we will remand the matter to the WCJ to address section 4663 apportionment in the first instance. On remand, the WCJ shall redetermine the issues of permanent disability and apportionment under section 4663, without applying section 4664(b).

C. The Concept of Medical Rehabilitation From A Prior Industrial Disability Remains Viable Under Section 4663; However, Even If An Injured Employee Has Medically Rehabilitated From A Prior Industrial Disability, This Does Not Necessarily Preclude A Prior Industrial Injury From Being An "Other Factor" Causing The Employee's Present Disability.

The facts of this matter may raise questions of whether applicant had medically rehabilitated from the effects of his May 9, 1998 injury before he sustained his December 2001 and August 2, 2002 injuries and, if so, whether any such medical rehabilitation would affect the determination of apportionment under section 4663 in this case.

In our en banc decisions in *Sanchez v. County of Los Angeles* (2005) 70 Cal. Comp. Cases 1440 and *Strong v. City and County of San Francisco* (2005) 70 Cal. Comp. Cases 1460, we construed the language of section 4664(b), which states, in relevant part: "If the applicant has received a prior award of permanent disability, it shall be conclusively presumed that the prior permanent disability exists at the time of any subsequent industrial injury." We held that if there has been a "prior award of permanent disability" within the meaning of section 4664(b), then the permanent disability underlying that award is "conclusively presumed" to still exist; therefore, the applicant is not permitted to show medical rehabilitation from the disabling effects of the earlier industrial injury or injuries. (*Sanchez v. County of Los Angeles, supra,* 70 Cal. Comp. Cases at p. 1452; *Strong v. City and County of San Francisco, supra,* 70 Cal. Comp. Cases at p. 1472.) Thus, we concluded that where there has been a prior permanent disability award, section 4664(b) abrogates the line of cases that had allowed an injured employee to show he or she had medically rehabilitated from the effects of an earlier injury at the time of a subsequent injury. (See *Mercier v. Workers' Comp. Appeals Bd.* (1976) 16 Cal. 3d 711, 716, fn. 2 [548 P.2d 361, 129 Cal. Rptr. 161] [41 Cal. Comp. Cases 205]; *State Comp. Ins. Fund v. Industrial Acc. Com. (Hutchinson)* (1963) 59 Cal. 2d 45, 56 [377 P.2d 902, 27 Cal. Rptr. 702] [28 Cal. Comp. Cases 20]; *Robinson v. Workers' Comp. Appeals Bd.* (1981) 114 Cal. App. 3d 593, 602–603 [171 Cal. Rptr. 48] [46 Cal. Comp. Cases 78]; *Bookout v. Workers' Comp. Appeals Bd.* (1976) 62 Cal. App. 3d 214, 223–224 [132 Cal. Rptr. 864] [41 Cal. Comp. Cases 595]; *Amico v. Workmen's Comp. Appeals Bd.* (1974) 43 Cal. App. 3d 592, 607–608 [117 Cal. Rptr. 831] [39 Cal. Comp. Cases 845].)

Nevertheless, in both *Sanchez* and *Strong,* we expressly did not address the issue of whether an injured employee may still show medical rehabilitation from a prior industrial or non–industrial condition to avoid apportionment *under section 4663.* (*Sanchez v. County of Los Angeles, supra,* 70 Cal. Comp. Cases at p. 1452, fn. 14; *Strong v. City and County of San Francisco, supra,* 70 Cal. Comp. Cases at p. 1472, fn. 15.)

When construing a statute, the Appeals Board's fundamental purpose is to determine and effectuate the Legislature's intent. (*DuBois v. Workers' Comp. Appeals Bd.* (1993) 5 Cal. 4th 382, 387 [853 P.2d 978, 20 Cal. Rptr. 2d 523] [58 Cal. Comp. Cases 286, 289]; *Nickelsberg v. Workers' Comp. Appeals Bd.* (1991) 54 Cal. 3d 288, 294 [814 P.2d 1328, 285 Cal. Rptr. 86] [56 Cal. Comp. Cases 476, 480]; *Moyer v. Workmen's Comp. Appeals Bd.* (1973) 10 Cal. 3d 222, 230 [514 P.2d 1224, 110 Cal. Rptr. 144] [38 Cal. Comp. Cases 652, 657].) Because the statutory language generally provides the most reliable indicator of that intent, the Appeals Board's first task is to look to at [*sic*] the language of the statute itself. (*Ibid.*; e.g., also, *People v. Smith* (2004) 32 Cal. 4th 792, 797 [86 P.3d 348, 11 Cal. Rptr. 3d 290].)

If the statutory language is clear and unambiguous, the Appeals Board must enforce the statute according to its plain terms. (*DuBois v. Workers' Comp. Appeals Bd., supra,* 5 Cal. 4th at pp. 387–388 [58 Cal. Comp. Cases at p. 289]; *Atlantic Richfield Co. v. Workers' Comp. Appeals Bd. (Arvizu)* (1982) 31 Cal. 3d 715, 726 [644 P.2d 1257, 182 Cal. Rptr. 778] [47 Cal. Comp. Cases 500, 508].)

If, however, the statutory language is ambiguous and susceptible of more than one reasonable interpretation, then the Appeals Board may look beyond the statutory language to other evidence of the Legislature's intent. (*In re Reeves* (2005) 35 Cal. 4th 765, 771 [110 P.3d 1218, 28 Cal. Rptr. 3d 4]; *Estate of Griswold* (2001) 25 Cal. 4th 904, 911 [24 P.3d 1191, 108 Cal. Rptr. 2d 165].) For example, where a statute relating to a particular subject contains a critical word or phrase, then the omission of that word or phrase from another statute on the same subject generally shows a different legislative intent. (*People v. Valentine* (1946) 28 Cal. 2d 121, 142 [169 P.2d 1]; *Reeves v. Workers' Comp. Appeals Bd.* (2000) 80 Cal. App. 4th 22, 28 [95 Cal. Rptr. 2d 74] [65 Cal. Comp. Cases 359]; see also *Ferguson v. Workers' Comp. Appeals Bd.* (1995) 33 Cal. App. 4th 1613, 1621 [39 Cal. Rptr. 2d 806] [60 Cal. Comp. Cases 275]; *Clark v. Workers' Comp. Appeals Bd.* (1991) 230 Cal. App. 3d 684, 696 [281 Cal. Rptr. 485] [56 Cal. Comp. Cases 331].) This principle applies with particular force when the two statutes relating to the same subject matter were enacted by the same bill and chaptered at the same time. (See *International Business Machines v. State Bd. of Equalization* (1980) 26 Cal. 3d 923, 932 [609 P.2d 1, 163 Cal. Rptr. 782]; *Krumme v. Mercury Ins. Co.* (2004) 123 Cal. App. 4th 924, 943, fn.6 [20 Cal. Rptr. 3d 485]; *People v. Hitchings* (1997) 59 Cal. App. 4th 915, 922 [69 Cal. Rptr. 2d 484]; *Conservatorship of Bryant* (1996) 45 Cal. App. 4th 117, 122 [52 Cal. Rptr. 2d 755].)

Sections 4663 and 4664 are both apportionment statutes that were enacted and chaptered at the same time. (Stats. 2004, ch. 34, §§ 34 & 35.) Section 4664(b) specifically states that, in "prior award" situations, "it shall be *conclusively presumed* that the prior permanent disability exists at the time of any subsequent industrial injury." (Emphasis added.) Section 4663, however, contains no such language – notwithstanding the fact that it also applies in cases of "prior industrial injuries." (Lab. Code, § 4663(c).) Because the Legislature omitted the conclusive presumption terminology from a concurrently adopted statute concerning the same subject, we conclude the Legislature did *not* intend, under section 4663, to bar an applicant from demonstrating that he or she had medically rehabilitated from the disabling effects of earlier industrial injuries. Accordingly, the line of medical rehabilitation cases – referred to above – remain valid, to that extent. (Footnote 10)

Nevertheless, section 4663 ultimately is concerned with the *causation* of permanent disability. (Lab. Code, § 4663(a), (b), & (c); *Escobedo v. Marshalls, supra,* 70 Cal. Comp. Cases at p. 611.) The WCAB must determine what percentage of the permanent disability was directly *caused* by the industrial injury and what percentage was *caused* by other factors, including prior industrial injuries. (Lab. Code, § 4663(c); *Escobedo v. Marshalls, supra,* 70 Cal. Comp. Cases at pp. 607, 611–612.)

Even if an injured employee establishes medical rehabilitation from his or her prior industrial injury, this does not necessarily mean that the prior industrial injury cannot be an "other factor" that is "causing" some of the employee's present disability under section 4663. This, however, is an issue of proof requiring substantial medical evidence. (*Escobedo v. Marshalls, supra,* 70 Cal. Comp. Cases 604.)

Here, as discussed above (see Section II–B, *supra*), neither Dr. Ovadia's September 15, 2003 report nor Dr. Kahmann's May 17, 2004 report discuss apportionment under section 4663 – including any potential medical rehabilitation issue – in accordance with the principles set out in *Escobedo.* Moreover, the WCJ has had the opportunity to observe the demeanor of applicant and to weigh his statements in connection with his manner on the stand. *(Garza v. Workmen's Comp. Appeals Bd.* (1970) 3 Cal. 3d 312, 318–319 [475 P.2d 451, 90 Cal. Rptr. 355] [35 Cal. Comp. Cases 500]; see also, *Gay v. Workers' Comp. Appeals Bd.* (1979) 96 Cal. App. 3d 555, 564–565 [158 Cal. Rptr. 137] [44 Cal. Comp. Cases 817].)

Therefore, in addition to remanding the general issue of section 4663 apportionment to the WCJ to address (see Section II–B, above), we will also remand this matter to the WCJ so that he may determine, in the first instance, whether applicant's claims of medical rehabilitation from his May 9, 1998 injury are credible and, even if so, whether his May 9, 1998 injury nevertheless may be an "other factor" that is "causing" his current disability pursuant to section 4663… .

Footnote 8. At this time, we need not and will not address the universe of circumstances, if any, under which an OACR might constitute a "prior award of permanent disability" under section 4664(b).

Footnote 9. We do not mean to imply an opinion that sections 4663 and 4664 are mutually exclusive. In some cases, it may be that both sections 4663 and 4664 will apply.

Footnote 10. This is true even though former section 4750, upon which the medical rehabilitation cases were predicated, was repealed by SB 899. (Stats. 2004, ch. 34, § 37). Like former section 4750, which addressed cases

involving pre–existing disability, current section 4663 also addresses cases where "disability was caused by other factors . . . before . . . the industrial injury, including prior industrial injuries." (Lab. Code, § 4663(c).)

In holding that an applicant was not entitled to prove that he was *medically rehabilitated* from a prior permanent disability *award* when he sustained a subsequent industrial injury, the Court of Appeal, Third District, in *Kopping v. WCAB* (2006) 71 Cal. Comp. Cases 1229, stated, in part:

The question here is whether the presumption established by subdivision (b) of Labor Code (Footnote 1) section 4664 (section 4664(b)) is conclusive or rebuttable. That statute, which is one of the workers' compensation statutes enacted in 2004 to govern apportionment of permanent disability (Stats. 2004, ch. 34, § 35), (Footnote 2) provides that "[i]f the applicant has received a prior award of permanent disability, it shall be conclusively presumed that the prior permanent disability exists at the time of any subsequent industrial injury. This presumption is a presumption affecting the burden of proof."

Petitioner Ed Kopping contends this statute is internally inconsistent, because the second sentence means the section 4664(b) presumption is actually rebuttable, not conclusive as the first sentence says it is. Kopping contends the statute must be construed liberally in his favor and thus interpreted to create a rebuttable presumption of the continued existence of a prior permanent disability that can be rebutted by proof of medical rehabilitation prior to the subsequent industrial injury.

For reasons we will explain, we conclude the Legislature intended the section 4664(b) presumption to be conclusive, not rebuttable, notwithstanding the second sentence of the statute. That means the Workers' Compensation Appeal Board (Board) correctly determined that Kopping is not entitled to prove he was medically rehabilitated from his prior permanent disability when he sustained a subsequent industrial injury. However, the Board incorrectly determined that Kopping has the burden of disproving overlap between his current permanent disability and his previous disability in order to establish his claim to permanent disability benefits. Instead, we conclude State Compensation Insurance Fund (State Fund), the adjusting agency for Kopping's employer, has the burden of proving overlap between the current disability and the previous disability in order to establish its right to apportionment of Kopping's permanent disability. Accordingly, we will annul the Board's decision and remand the matter for further proceedings.

FACTUAL AND PROCEDURAL BACKGROUND

In 1996, Kopping injured his spine while working as a traffic officer for the California Highway Patrol (CHP). The parties stipulated that the injury caused permanent disability of 29 percent, and Kopping was awarded $20,357.50 in permanent disability benefits. At the time, the agreed medical examiner described Kopping's factors of disability as restrictions in spinal motion and subjective complaints of intermittent to frequent slight to moderate pain.

In December 2002, Kopping sustained another back injury while working for the CHP. The parties stipulated that Kopping's level of permanent disability is now 27 percent, based on factors of disability described by another agreed medical examiner (Dr. Barber) as "approximating halfway between a disability precluding repetitive motions of the back and a disability precluding heavy lifting." In his report, Dr. Barber concluded there should be no apportionment of Kopping's permanent disability to the 1996 injury "based on Mr. Kopping's remarks that he completely recovered from this prior low back industrial injury with no ongoing physical limitations."

State Fund, the adjusting agency for the CHP, argued that notwithstanding Kopping's claim of rehabilitation from the prior injury, the permanent disability resulting from that injury had to be treated as still existing because of the conclusive presumption of section 4664(b). The workers' compensation administrative law judge (WCJ) agreed and concluded that Kopping was not entitled to any permanent disability benefits for his 2002 injury because the level of disability (29 percent) resulting from the 1996 injury exceeded the level of disability (27 percent) resulting from the 2002 injury. (Footnote 3)

Kopping filed a petition for reconsideration with the Board challenging the WCJ's construction of section 4664(b). Kopping also argued that even if the presumption of section 4664(b) is conclusive, the WCJ still erred in deducting the prior percentage of permanent disability from the current percentage of disability to the extent the factors of disability did not overlap.

The Board granted reconsideration. In its decision after reconsideration, the Board rescinded the WCJ's decision and returned the matter to the trial level to allow the parties to further develop the record, if necessary, and for the WCJ to reconsider the matter in light of two recent en banc decisions by the Board on the issue of apportionment: *Sanchez v. County of Los Angeles* (2005) 70 Cal. Comp. Cases 1440 [Appeals Board en banc opinion] (*Sanchez*) and *Strong v. City & County of San Francisco* (2005) 70 Cal. Comp. Cases 1460 [Appeals Board en banc opinion] (*Strong*).

In *Sanchez* and *Strong*, the Board held that "[w]hen the [employer (Footnote 4)] has established the existence of any prior permanent disability award(s) . . . , the permanent disability underlying any such award(s) is conclusively presumed to still exist, i.e., the applicant is not permitted to show medical rehabilitation from the disabling effects of the earlier industrial injury or injuries." (*Sanchez*, *supra*, 70 Cal. Comp. Cases at p. 1442; *Strong*, *supra*, 70 Cal. Comp. Cases at p. 1462.) The Board further held that in such cases, "the percentage of permanent disability from the prior award(s) will be subtracted from the current overall percentage of permanent disability, unless the applicant *disproves* overlap, i.e., the applicant demonstrates that the prior permanent disability and the current permanent disability affect different abilities to compete and earn, either in whole or in part." (Footnote 5)

(*Sanchez*, *supra*, 70 Cal. Comp. Cases at p. 1442.) Thus, the Board returned this case to the WCJ to determine whether Kopping had disproved (or *could* disprove)

overlap, *not* to allow Kopping to prove medical rehabilitation from the disabling effects of his earlier injury.

Kopping petitioned this court for a writ of review of the Board's decision after reconsideration, which we granted to consider the intended meaning of section 4664(b). (Footnote 6)

DISCUSSION

"The fundamental rule of statutory construction is to ascertain and effectuate the intent of the Legislature in enacting the statute. [Citation.] We construe the workers' compensation scheme as a whole and consider the words used in their usual, commonsense meaning. [Citation.] We liberally construe all aspects of workers' compensation law in favor of the injured worker." (*Henry v. Workers' Comp. Appeals Bd.* (1998) 68 Cal. App. 4th 981, 984 [80 Cal. Rptr. 2d 631, 63 Cal. Comp. Cases 1481].) [T]he "so–called 'liberality rule,' " however, (which is found in section 3202) "cannot supplant the intent of the Legislature as expressed in a particular statute." (*Fuentes v. Workers' Comp. Appeals Bd.* (1976) 16 Cal. 3d 1, 8 [547 P.2d 449, 128 Cal. Rptr. 673, 41 Cal. Comp. Cases 42].) If the Legislature's intent appears from the language and context of the relevant statutory provisions, then we must effectuate that intent, "even though the particular statutory language 'is contrary to the basic policy of the [workers' compensation law].' " (*Ibid.*, quoting *Earl Ranch, Ltd. v. Industrial Acc. Com.* (1935) 4 Cal. 2d 767, 769 [53 P.2d 154].)

Read in isolation, the first sentence of section 4664(b) is clear: "If the applicant has received a prior award of permanent disability, it shall be *conclusively* presumed that the prior permanent disability exists at the time of any subsequent industrial injury." (Italics added.) "Where the law makes a certain fact a 'conclusive presumption' evidence cannot be received to the contrary." (*Estate of Mills* (1902) 137 Cal. 298, 303.) Thus, if section 4664(b) creates a conclusive presumption of the continued existence of a prior permanent disability, then upon proof that the applicant received a prior award of permanent disability, evidence cannot be received that the prior permanent disability associated with that award did *not* exist at the time of any subsequent industrial injury. Here, that would mean Kopping would be forbidden from proving he was medically rehabilitated from the permanently disabling effects of his 1996 back injury when he injured his back again in 2002. (Footnote 7)

Had the Legislature stopped with the first sentence of section 4664(b), this case would not be here. The Legislature, however, did not stop there; instead, it saw fit to add a second sentence to the statute, explaining that "[t]his presumption is a presumption affecting the burden of proof."

Without reference to the Evidence Code, this provision can be readily explained. Under workers' compensation law before the enactment of section 4664(b), the burden of proving apportionment fell on the employer, because "[i]t is the employer who benefits from a finding of apportionment." (*Pullman Kellogg v. Workers' Comp. Appeals Bd.* (1980) 26 Cal. 3d 450, 456 [605 P.2d 422, 161 Cal. Rptr. 783, 45 Cal. Comp. Cases 170].) Thus, the employer had the burden of proving the applicant had a prior industrial injury and that the present level of permanent disability was apportionable, in whole or in part, to that injury, for which the employer was not responsible. This would have included proving an overlap between the prior disability and the current disability, since overlap is part of apportionment. (See *Mercier v. Workers' Comp. Appeals Bd.* (1976) 16 Cal. 3d 711, 715–716 [548 P.2d 361, 129 Cal. Rptr. 161, 41 Cal. Comp. Cases 205].) Accordingly, without reference to the Evidence Code, the two sentences of section 4664(b) can be reconciled as follows: The conclusive presumption of section 4664(b) is a presumption affecting the burden of proof because it affects the employer's burden of proving apportionment by conclusively establishing that the permanent disability resulting from a previous industrial injury still existed at the time of the subsequent injury. Of course, under this reading of the statute, the employer would still have to prove that the previous disability, which was conclusively presumed to still exist, overlapped with the current disability.

If we turn to the Evidence Code, however, we can see a potential conflict in the two sentences of section 4664(b). This is so because Evidence Code section 601 provides that "[a] presumption is either conclusive or rebuttable. Every rebuttable presumption is either (a) a presumption affecting the burden of producing evidence or (b) a presumption affecting the burden of proof." Further, Evidence Code section 606 provides that "[t]he effect of a presumption affecting the burden of proof is to impose upon the party against whom it operates the burden of proof as to the nonexistence of the presumed fact."

Thus, the Evidence Code gives the phrase "presumption affecting the burden of proof" a technical meaning, using it to describe a type of rebuttable presumption that imposes on the party against whom it operates the burden of proving the nonexistence of the presumed fact. Read in light of these provisions, the second sentence of section 4664(b) can be understood to say that the presumption of that statute is rebuttable. Under this reading of the statute, upon proof of a prior permanent disability award it would be presumed that the permanent disability on which that award was based still existed at the time of the subsequent injury, unless and until the applicant carried his or her burden of proving that it did not, e.g., by proving medical rehabilitation from the earlier injury.

The problem with reading the second sentence of section 4664(b) in light of Evidence Code sections 601 and 606 is that this reading of the statute appears to utterly negate that aspect of the first sentence which plainly identifies the presumption as "conclusive" in nature. As Evidence Code 601 explains, "[a] presumption is *either* conclusive *or* rebuttable" (italics added) – it cannot be both. Under this reading of the statute, either the first sentence is what the Legislature intended (the presumption is conclusive), and the second sentence is meaningless, or the second sentence (read in light of the Evidence Code) is what the Legislature intended (the presumption is rebuttable), and the word "conclusively" in the first sentence is meaningless.

In *Sanchez*, *supra*, 70 Cal. Comp. Cases at pages 1453 to 1455, the Board purported to harmonize the two sentences

to avoid this dilemma. The Board's analysis on this point, which we set out at length, is as follows: "[W]e conclude that, once [an employer] has established the existence of a prior award of permanent disability relating to the same region of the body, then the percentage of permanent disability found under the prior award will be subtracted from the current overall percentage of disability, *unless* the applicant *disproves* overlap by establishing that the prior permanent disability does not overlap the current permanent disability, either in whole or in part.

"This interpretation of section 4664(b) harmonizes its first sentence . . . with its second sentence . . . . That is, consistent with the first sentence, the prior permanent disability still will be conclusively presumed to 'exist,' and the applicant cannot show that he or she has medically rehabilitated from it. Nevertheless, consistent with the second sentence, the applicant will have the opportunity to disprove or negate apportionment, in whole or in part, by showing that his or her most recent injury caused some *new* permanent disability that did *not* previously 'exist,' i.e., that the new injury has produced separate and independent permanent disability that does not overlap the pre–existing permanent disability because the new disability affects *different* abilities to compete and earn. If, however, the applicant fails to disprove overlap, then the applicant cannot avoid the application of the conclusive presumption that the prior permanent disability still 'exists' and, therefore, the prior percentage permanent disability rating will be deducted from the current overall percentage permanent disability rating where the disabilities are in the same region as described in section 4664(c).

"Further, the phrase 'prior permanent disability' in section 4664(b) does *not* mean the *factors of disability* upon which the prior permanent disability award was based. To so interpret section 4664(b) would mean that, before the conclusive presumption could attach, the [employer] would have both the burden of proving the existence of a prior permanent disability award *and* the burden of proving the nature of the permanent disability upon which that award was based. As noted earlier, the trigger for the conclusive presumption is the existence of a prior award of permanent disability, not the factors of permanent disability underline [*sic*] such an award.

"Additionally, if [an employer] were required to establish the prior factors of permanent disability as well as the existence of the prior permanent disability award, this effectively would cause the *second* sentence of section 4664(b) to be read out of the statute . . . . Once more, the second sentence of section 4664(b) provides, in essence, that the conclusive presumption that the prior permanent disability exists 'is a presumption affecting the burden of proof.' [A] 'presumption affecting the burden of proof' requires the party *against* whom the presumption operates to establish the *nonexistence* of the presumed fact. [Citation.] Reading the first and second sentences of section 4664(b) together, as we must, the conclusive presumption of the existence of prior permanent disability in the first sentence of section 4664(b) operates *in favor* of [the employer]. Therefore, any interpretation of the second sentence must require applicant to *disprove* something, while at the same time not nullifying whatever has been conclusively established.

"Both of these aspects of section 4664(b) are fulfilled by requiring the applicant to *disprove* the existence of overlap by establishing the nature of the permanent disability upon which the prior permanent disability award was based, rather than by requiring [the employer] to *prove* the existence of overlap by establishing the nature of that permanent disability. This is because, once the character of the permanent disability underlying the prior permanent disability award is established, the determination of apportionment is essentially a mechanical process – not a burden of proof issue – i.e., . . . it is determined using substantially the same overlap principles that have been historically applied . . . . Thus, if [an employer] had to prove not only the existence of a prior permanent disability award, but also the character of the permanent disability upon which the prior award was predicated, there would be nothing left for the applicant to *disprove*, in contravention to the second sentence of section 4664(b).

"Moreover, . . . a conclusive presumption is a substantive rule of law adopted to further some particular public policy or purpose. [Citations.] Similarly, a presumption affecting the burden of proof is intended to 'implement some public policy other than to facilitate the determination of the particular action in which the presumption is applied.' [Citation.] It appears that the public policies behind the twofold conclusive and rebuttable presumptions of section 4664(b) are that apportionment of pre–existing disability will occur (i.e., the pre–existing disability will be deducted), unless some showing is made (other than medical rehabilitation) why apportionment should not occur. To interpret section 4664(b) to mean that, once a prior permanent disability award has been established, the prior permanent disability percentage will be deducted *unless* applicant shows that the present and pre–existing disabilities do *not* overlap, in whole or in part, is consistent with these policies." (*Sanchez, supra,* 70 Cal. Comp. Cases at pp. 1454–1456, fn. omitted.)

Understandably, Kopping rejects the Board's interpretation of section 4664(b) because it precludes him from rebutting the continued existence of the prior disability through evidence of medical rehabilitation. In contrast to the Board, Kopping contends that "the only reasonable interpretation of the meaning of this statute, applying established rules of statutory construction, is that where the [employer] proves the existence of a prior permanent disability award, [section] 4664(b) operates to shift the burden of proof to the injured worker to demonstrate that the prior disability no longer exists or has diminished. To interpret this statute any other way would render useless the second sentence of [the statute]."

The primary flaw in this argument is that Kopping's interpretation of section 4664(b) contravenes the very principle he urges us to follow – that "[i]nterpretive constructions which render some words surplusage . . . are to be avoided." (*California Mfrs. Assn. v. Public Utilities Com.* (1979) 24 Cal. 3d 836, 844 [598 P.2d 836, 157 Cal. Rptr. 676].) If Kopping is correct, and section 4664(b) simply operates to shift the burden of proof to the claimant

to prove the prior disability no longer exists or has diminished, then there is nothing at all "conclusive" about the presumption that the prior disability continues to exist, and that word in the first sentence of the statute is rendered meaningless.

In any event, the rule that Kopping urges us to follow – and which the Board attempted to follow in *Sanchez* – has been described elsewhere as the "cardinal rule of statutory construction that in attempting to ascertain the legislative intention effect should be given, *whenever possible*, to the statute as a whole and to every word and clause thereof, leaving no part or provision useless or deprived of meaning." (*Weber v. County of Santa Barbara* (1940) 15 Cal. 2d 82, 86 [98 P.2d 492], italics added.) Thus, while every reasonable attempt should be made to give meaning to every part of a statute, this rule recognizes that sometimes it is impossible to achieve this goal. The question for us is whether this is one of those times.

Turning back to the Board's interpretation of the statute, Kopping complains that the Board's interpretation – which he characterizes as creating a single, " 'quasi–rebuttable presumption' " – "find[s] no support in any of the actual statutory language." We tend to agree. As we have noted, a presumption is either conclusive or rebuttable; it cannot be both. Moreover, to the extent *Sanchez* can be read as finding *two* presumptions in section 4664(b) – one conclusive (regarding the continued existence of the prior disability) and one rebuttable (regarding whether the prior disability and the new disability overlap) – that approach is not supported by the language of the statute. The reference in the second sentence of the statute to "[t]his presumption" is clearly a reference to the conclusive presumption set out in the first sentence of the statute. While we laud the Board's attempt to give meaning to both sentences in the statute, we do not believe the statute can be *reasonably* interpreted as creating two different, but related, presumptions that apply in apportionment cases. Section 4664(b) creates only a single presumption, which is either conclusive or rebuttable. The question is, which is it?

Kopping contends that construing section 4664(b) as creating a rebuttable presumption would "harmonize [the statute] with the remainder of the apportionment statutes created by SB 899" – the bill that modified the workers' compensation law in 2004. (Footnote 8)

He first points to subdivision (a) of section 4664 (section 4664(a)), which provides that "[t]he employer shall only be liable for the percentage of permanent disability directly caused by the injury arising out of and occurring in the course of employment." According to Kopping, "[t]o interpret [section 4664(b)] as a conclusive presumption resulting in deduction of prior disability awards by operation of law is inconsistent with the mandate of [section] 4664(a) that the employer *shall be* liable for the percentage of disability caused by the injury."

We disagree. If *permanent* disability is understood as "the *irreversible* residual of an injury" (1 Cal. Workers' Compensation Practice (Cont.Ed.Bar 4th ed. 2005) § 5.1, p. 276, italics added) (as contrasted with *temporary* disability), then it is anomalous that an injured worker who was determined to have a *permanent* disability could prove, at a later date, that he actually recovered from that disability. If section 4664(b) is understood as representing the Legislature's common sense recognition that there *can be* no recovery from a *permanent* disability, then there is no inconsistency between that statute and section 4664(a). This is so because a new industrial injury cannot be the cause (direct or otherwise) of a preexisting permanent disability. Thus, the presumption that a permanent disability continues to exist throughout the claimant's lifetime is perfectly consistent with the provision in section 4664(a) that limits an employer's liability to the percentage of permanent disability directly caused by the new injury. The employer should not be liable for a preexisting disability because the injury for which the employer is liable cannot be the cause of that disability.

Kopping next points to subdivision (c) of section 4663 (section 4663(c)), which provides as follows: "In order for a physician's report to be considered complete on the issue of permanent disability, it must include an apportionment determination. A physician shall make an apportionment determination by finding what approximate percentage of the permanent disability was caused by the direct result of injury arising out of and occurring in the course of employment and what approximate percentage of the permanent disability was caused by other factors both before and subsequent to the industrial injury, including prior industrial injuries. If the physician is unable to include an apportionment determination in his or her report, the physician shall state the specific reasons why the physician could not make a determination of the effect of that prior condition on the permanent disability arising from the injury. The physician shall then consult with other physicians or refer the employee to another physician from whom the employee is authorized to seek treatment or evaluation in accordance with this division in order to make the final determination."

Kopping asks, "[i]f the Legislature intended [section 4664(b)] to create a conclusive presumption requiring deduction of prior awards by operation of law, what would be the purpose of requiring physicians to calculate the percentage of current permanent disability caused by prior industrial injuries?" One answer to that question is that section 4664(b) creates a presumption arising from "a prior award of permanent disability," not from a prior industrial injury. It is possible that an applicant may have had a prior industrial injury, but never applied for or received an award of permanent disability resulting from that injury. In such a case, in the event of a subsequent industrial injury, the presumption of section 4664(b) would have no effect, but a physician could still determine, as a matter of fact, that the applicant's present level of permanent disability was partially caused by the previous industrial injury.

Kopping next contends that his interpretation of section 4664(b) benefits employers, compared to the prior law, because under his interpretation of the statute the claimant bears the burden of proving medical rehabilitation from the prior disability. Kopping cites no authority for the proposition he implies – that under prior law it was the employer's burden to *disprove* rehabilitation. In any event, even if we assume that deeming the presumption in section

4664(b) to be rebuttable would have *some* benefit for employers, that does not compel us to read the word "conclusively" out of the statute, as Kopping would have us do. We can do that only if we are left with no other reasonable choice, which, as we will explain, we are not.

This brings us to Kopping's reliance on the rule of liberality. In essence, he suggests that because section 4664(b) must be "liberally construed by the courts with the purpose of extending [its] benefits for the protection of persons injured in the course of their employment" (§ 3202), we should interpret section 4664(b) as creating a rebuttable presumption, rather than a conclusive one, because the rebuttable presumption is more favorable to claimants. If the apparent conflict in the statute could not be resolved any other way, Kopping's argument might carry the day. But that is not the case. Here, we need not read the word "conclusive" out of the statute under the guise of liberally construing it in favor of claimants because we conclude the apparent conflict in the statute can be resolved another way.

It is important to keep in mind that while section 4664(b) expressly uses the word "conclusive" to describe the presumption it creates, the statute does *not* use the word "rebuttable." The only reason the inconsistent concept of a rebuttable presumption arises is because the phrase "presumption affecting the burden of proof," which appears in the second sentence of section 4664(b), is used in the Evidence Code to identify a type of rebuttable presumption. But if the Legislature did not mean to use that phrase in section 4664(b) in the technical sense in which that phrase is used in the Evidence Code, then the problem vanishes.

We are given no particular reason to believe the Legislature intended the phrase "presumption affecting the burden of proof" in section 4664(b) to have the same meaning it has under the Evidence Code, other than it must be so. Having examined the legislative history of the statute, we have found nothing there to support that assumption. The first sentence of section 4664(b) can be traced to a bill introduced in the Assembly in February 2003, which addressed the apportionment of permanent disability. (Assem. Bill No. 1481 (2003–2004 Reg. Sess.) as introduced Feb. 21, 2003.) Section 2 of Assembly Bill No. 1481 proposed to add a statute to the workers' compensation law confirming that the burden of proving apportionment rests on the employer and setting out, in identical language, the conclusive presumption that now appears in the first sentence of section 4664(b). (Assem. Bill No. 1481, *supra*, § 2.) That language stood by itself, with nothing like the second sentence in section 4664(b) attached to it.

Although Assembly Bill No. 1481 went nowhere, its provisions – including the conclusive presumption that now appears in section 4664(b) – reappeared in July 2003 in a Senate amendment to a different Assembly bill on workers' compensation. (Assem. Bill No. 1579 (2003–2004 Reg. Sess.) § 38, as amended July 2, 2003.) Assembly Bill No. 1579 was one of 20 workers' compensation bills that were submitted to conference committee in July 2003 "for the purpose of ensuring a cohesive and carefully crafted package of workers' compensation reform measures." (Sen.

Comm. on Labor & Industrial Relations, Analysis of Assem. Bill 1579 (2003–2004 Reg. Sess.) July 8, 2003, p. 7.)

The result of the conference committee's work was Senate Bill No. 899. (See Sen. Rules Com., Off. of Sen. Floor Analyses, Analysis of Sen. Bill No. 899 (2003–2004 Reg. Sess.) Apr. 15, 2004, p. 1.) The apportionment provisions of Assembly Bill No. 1579 formed part of the basis for Senate Bill No. 899, and the conclusive presumption language that now appears in the first sentence of section 4664(b) transitioned between the two bills unscathed. (See Sen. Bill No. 899 (2003–2004 Reg. Sess.) § 35, as proposed Apr. 15, 2004.) By the time Senate Bill No. 899 emerged from the conference committee, however, the second sentence of what is now section 4664(b) had been added. (See Sen. Bill No. 899 (2003–2004 Reg. Sess.) § 35, as proposed Apr. 15, 2004.) Unfortunately, however, there is no explanation in the legislative history of the purpose of this provision. More importantly, there is nothing in the legislative history to indicate the Legislature intended the phrase "presumption affecting the burden of proof" in this provision to have the same meaning as the Evidence Code assigns to that phrase.

While we have found no particular reason to believe the Legislature intended the phrase "presumption affecting the burden of proof" in section 4664(b) to have the same meaning it has under the Evidence Code, we have one very good reason for believing otherwise – doing so avoids the internal inconsistency that otherwise arises between a conclusive presumption on one hand and a rebuttable presumption on the other. As we explained earlier, if section 4664(b) is read without reference to the Evidence Code, then the two sentences of the statute can be reconciled by understanding that the conclusive presumption of section 4664(b) *is* a presumption affecting the burden of proof because it affects the employer's burden of proving apportionment by conclusively establishing that the permanent disability resulting from a previous industrial injury still existed at the time of the subsequent injury. Although the conclusive presumption thus *affects* the employer's burden of proving apportionment by conclusively establishing the continued existence of a prior disability, it does not completely carry that burden, because the employer still has to prove the overlap, if any, between the previous disability and the current disability in order to establish that apportionment is appropriate.

This construction of section 4664(b) has the significant virtue of giving meaning to every word in the statute. It also avoids the Board's well–meaning but anomalous solution of reading the statute as creating either one quasi–rebuttable presumption or two different presumptions, one conclusive and one rebuttable.

Because, under this construction of section 4664(b), the burden of proving overlap remains on the employer, it could be argued that there is, in effect, a rebuttable presumption in favor of the claimant that the two disabilities do *not* overlap, and that therefore this interpretation of the statute, like that of the Board, construes the statute as creating two different presumptions. That is not the case. True, the conclusive presumption that a prior permanent disability continues to

exist at the time of a subsequent injury arises from section 4664(b). But the rebuttable presumption that the two disabilities do not overlap does *not* arise from the statute. Instead, that presumption arises from the long–standing principle – which remains valid – that the burden of proving apportionment falls on the employer because it is the employer that benefits from apportionment.

Under our construction of the statute, what section 4664(b) does is simply prevent a claimant from defeating an employer's showing of apportionment by proving medical rehabilitation from a prior permanent disability for which he or she received permanent disability benefits. In such a case, the employer otherwise continues to bear the burden of proof on the issue of apportionment. First, the employer must prove the existence of the prior permanent disability award. Then, having established by this proof that the permanent disability on which that award was based still exists, the employer must prove the extent of the overlap, if any, between the prior disability and the current disability. Under these circumstances, the employer is entitled to avoid liability for the claimant's current permanent disability *only* to the extent the employer carries its burden of proving that some or all of that disability overlaps with the prior disability and is therefore attributable to the prior industrial injury, for which the employer is not liable.

Thus, we conclude the Board did not err in determining that section 4664(b) creates a conclusive presumption of the continued existence of a prior permanent disability when the claimant received an award of permanent disability benefits based on that disability, thereby precluding the claimant from proving medical rehabilitation from the prior disability. The Board did err, however, in imposing on the claimant the burden of disproving overlap between the prior disability and the current disability. The burden of proving overlap is part of the employer's overall burden of proving apportionment, which was not altered by section 4664(b), except to create the conclusive presumption that flows from proving the existence of a prior permanent disability award. Accordingly, we will remand this matter to the Board, so that the Board can send the case back to the trial level to apply the principles set forth in this opinion.

DISPOSITION

The Board's decision after reconsideration is annulled. The matter is remanded for further proceedings consistent with the views expressed herein. The parties shall bear their own costs in the proceedings before this court. (Cal. Rules of Court, rule 56(l)(2).)... .

Footnote 1. All further statutory references are to the Labor Code unless otherwise indicated.

Footnote 2. "Apportionment is the process employed . . . to segregate the residuals of an industrial injury from those attributable to other industrial injuries, or to nonindustrial factors, in order to fairly allocate the legal responsibility." (*Ashley v. Workers' Comp. Appeals Bd.* (1995) 37 Cal. App. 4th 320, 326 [43 Cal. Rptr. 2d 589, 60 Cal. Comp. Cases 683].)

Footnote 3. The WCJ did award further medical treatment to cure or relieve the effects of the injury.

Footnote 4. The Board uses the term "defendant," rather than "employer" – presumably to encompass the workers' compensation insurers who are often the named party on the other side in a workers' compensation case. We use the term "employer" to avoid confusion, but obviously intend that term to include an insurer who stands in the employer's shoes.

Footnote 5. This exact sentence appears only in *Sanchez* because, for a reason we cannot discern, the Board used slightly different wording in *Strong*. The difference is not significant. (Compare *Sanchez, supra,* 70 Cal. Comp. Cases at p. 1442 and *Strong, supra,* 70 Cal. Comp. Cases at p. 1462.) Nevertheless, we quote from *Sanchez* in preference to *Strong* because *Sanchez*, like this case, involved successive injuries to the same region of the body, while *Strong* involved successive injuries to different regions of the body.

Footnote 6. State Fund contends Kopping's petition for a writ of review was premature because: (1) "there is no longer any decision or award to challenge because the WCAB *rescinded* it"; and (2) "the WCAB's decision did not . . . determine any substantial right or liability of those involved in the case" or "conclusively determine a substantial issue basic to Kopping's entitlement to benefits." We disagree.

In relevant part, section 5950 provides that "[a]ny person affected by [a] decision . . . of the appeals board may . . . apply . . . for a writ of review, for the purpose of inquiring into and determining the lawfulness of the . . . decision . . . following reconsideration." Here, Kopping has asked us to review the Board's decision after reconsideration, which adversely affects him by precluding him from arguing on remand that he was medically rehabilitated from his prior disability when he was injured in 2002.

"[A] petition for review of an order by the WCAB lies when the order conclusively determines, for purposes of the compensation proceeding, a substantial issue basic to the employee's entitlement to benefits." (*Maranian v. Workers' Comp. Appeals Bd.* (2000) 81 Cal. App. 4th 1068, 1078 [97 Cal. Rptr. 2d 418, 65 Cal. Comp. Cases 650].) Here, in remanding the case to the WCJ for reconsideration in light of *Sanchez* and *Strong*, the Board conclusively determined that Kopping was *not* entitled to prove medical rehabilitation from his prior injury. We deem this a substantial issue basic to Kopping's entitlement to benefits and therefore deem the Board's decision after reconsideration reviewable under *Maranian*.

Footnote 7. Under the law prior to the enactment of section 4664(b), apportionment to a prior injury was not proper if the applicant was rehabilitated from the disabling effects of that injury at the time of the subsequent injury. (See, e.g., *County of Los Angeles v. Workers' Compensation Appeals Board* (1997) 62 Cal. Comp. Cases 504 [writ denied]; *State Compensation Ins. Fund v. Industrial Acc. Com.* (1963) 59 Cal. 2d 45, 56 [377 P.2d 902, 27 Cal. Rptr. 702, 28 Cal. Comp. Cases 20].)

Footnote 8. "On April 19, 2004, Governor Schwarzenegger signed into law Senate Bill No. 899 (2003–2004 Reg. Sess.), a package of reforms to the workers' compensation laws. (Stats. 2004, ch. 34.) (Bill No. 899.) The legislation took effect immediately as urgency legislation. [Citation.] Bill No. 899 changed, among other things, the law with regard to apportionment of permanent disability. (Stats. 2004, ch. 34, §§ 33 [repealed Lab. Code, § 4663 (former § 4663)], 34 [added new Lab. Code, § 4663 (§ 4663)], 35 [added Lab. Code, § 4664 (§ 4664)], 37 [repealed Lab. Code, § 4750 (former § 4750)], 38 [repealed Lab. Code, § 4750.5 (former § 4750.5)]).)" (*Rio Linda Union School Dist. v. Workers' Comp. Appeals Bd.* (2005) 131 Cal. App. 4th 517, 521, fn. omitted [31 Cal. Rptr. 3d 789, 70 Cal. Comp. Cases 999].)

In *Kaiser Foundation Hospitals, PSI, v. WCAB (Dragomir–Tremoureux)* (2006) 71 Cal. Comp. Cases 538, the Appeals Board held that where an applicant is conclusively presumed to be 100% permanently totally disabled under Section 4662(b), the total disability cannot be apportioned under Section 4664(b) to a prior award. The Board stated, in part:

In interpreting the method by which awards of permanent disability are calculated after apportionment to permanent disability caused by other factors under section 4663(c) or previously awarded under section 4664(b), in *Nabors v. Piedmont Lumber & Mill Company* (2005) 70 Cal. Comp. Cases 856 (hereafter "*Nabors*"), the Appeals Board en banc held that "the amount of indemnity due applicant is calculated by determining the overall percentage of permanent disability and then subtracting the percentage of permanent disability" caused by other factors or previously awarded. However, in *Nabors, supra,* the Appeals Board did not address, because it was not at issue in that case, when apportionment to "previously awarded" permanent disability under section 4664(b) applies to reduce an injured worker's entitlement to permanent disability indemnity for a subsequent industrial injury.

Here, we conclude that, although section 4664(b) applies and, therefore, it is conclusively presumed that applicant's 18.75% permanent partial wrist disability existed at the time of the subsequent injuries at issue herein, the conclusive presumption of permanent total disability pursuant to section 4662(b) also applies and precludes apportionment of any kind, including apportionment to a prior award under section 4664(b)... .

Further, the Board concluded that evidence of applicant's prior award, which existed at the time of her subsequent injuries, could not rebut the Labor Code section 4662(b) conclusive presumption. In this regard, the Board noted, in pertinent part, as follows:

Moreover, our conclusion that the evidence of prior disability under section 4664(b) cannot rebut the conclusive presumption of permanent total disability pursuant to section 4662(b) is supported by the plain language of section 4664(c)(1), which precludes the "accumulation of all permanent disability awards issued with respect to any one region of the body" from exceeding 100% over the injured employee's lifetime *"unless the employee's injury or illness is conclusively presumed to be total"* pursuant to section 4662. (Italics added [by WCAB].) Therefore, as applicant's permanent disability for her loss of use of both hands is conclusively presumed to be total pursuant to section 4662(b), her lifetime accumulation of awards for her upper extremity "region of the body" properly, under section 4664(c)(1), may exceed 100%... .

Page 1376, Column 1, ninth paragraph, insert following '...repealed.'

The Legislature, in its 2006 session, amended Section 4663 to exempt specified public safety members and employees, such as peace officers and firefighters, with specific medical conditions such as hernias, heart trouble and pneumonia from the new requirements pertaining to apportionment of permanent disability, to provide:

Labor Code Section 4663.

(a) Apportionment of permanent disability shall be based on causation.

(b) Any physician who prepares a report addressing the issue of permanent disability due to a claimed industrial injury shall in that report address the issue of causation of the permanent disability.

(c) In order for a physician's report to be considered complete on the issue of permanent disability, the report must include an apportionment determination. A physician shall make an apportionment determination by finding what proximate percentage of the permanent disability was caused by the direct result of injury arising out of and in the course of employment and what proximate percentage of the permanent disability was caused by other factors both before and subsequent to the industrial injury, including prior industrial injuries. If the physician is unable to include an apportionment determination in his or her report, the physician shall state the specific reasons why the physician could not make a determination of the affect of that prior condition on the permanent disability arising from the injury. The physician shall then consult with other physicians or refer the employee to another physician from whom the employee is authorized to seek treatment or evaluation in accordance with this division in order to make the final determination.

(d) An employee who claims an industrial injury shall, upon request, disclose all previous permanent disabilities or physical impairments.

(e) *Subdivisions (a), (b), and (c) shall not apply to injuries or illnesses covered under sections 3212, 3212.1, 3212.2, 3212.3, 3212.4, 3212.5, 3212.6, 3212.7, 3212.8, 3212.85, 3212.9, 3212.10, 3212.11, 3212.12, 3213, and 3213.2.*

SEC. 2. It is the intent of the Legislature that this act be construed as declaratory of existing law.

Therefore, apportionment of permanent disability may not be based on causation as to injury to any of the following special groups:

a. Firefighters incurring *cancer*, including *leukemia* (See Labor Code section 3212.1);

b. Employees of Department of Corrections having custodial duties, each employee of the Department of Youth Authority having group supervisory duties and each security officer employed at the Atascadero State Hospital incurring *heart trouble*. (See Labor Code section 3212.2);

c. Peace officer employed by the Department of Highway Patrol incurring *heart trouble* or *pneumonia*. (See Labor Code section 3212.3);

d. Employee of the University of California Fire Department incurring *heart trouble, hernia, or pneumonia*. (See Labor Code section 3214.4);

e. Employees of a police department of a city or municipality, or a member of the State Highway Patrol incurring *heart trouble* or *pneumonia*. (See Labor Code section 3212.5);

f. Members of a police department of a city or county or a member of the sheriff's office of a county, or a member of the California Highway Patrol or an inspector or an investigator in a district attorney's office of any county where their duties consist of active law enforcement service, or a prior or jail guard or correctional officer, or members of a fire department of any city, county or district who incurs *tuberculosis*. (See Labor Code section 3212.6);

g. Employees in the Department of Justice falling within the "state safety" class incurring *heart trouble, hernia, pneumonia or tuberculosis*. (See Labor Code section 3212.7);

h. Employees of a sheriff's office, police or fire department of cities, counties, districts, or other public or municipal corporations or political subdivisions or a member of the Department of Forestry and Fire prohibits of any county forestry or firefighting department incurring *tuberculosis*. (See Labor Code section 3218.8);

i. Peace officers and members of fire department incurring *illness* or *death* due to exposure to *biochemical substances*. (See Labor Code section 3212.85);

j. Employees of police departments of a city, county, or city and county, or member of its sheriff's department of a county or a member of the California Highway Patrol or county probation officer or investigator or inspector in the district attorney's office incurring *meningitis*. (See Labor Code section 3212.9);

k. Employees of the Department of Corrections or a peace officer of the Department of Youth Authority incurring heart *trouble, pneumonia, tuberculosis, and meningitis*. (See Labor Code section 3212.10);

l. Lifeguards employed by a city, county, city and county, district or other public or municipal corporation or public subdivision and employed by the Department of Parks and Recreation incurring *skin cancer*. (See Labor Code section 3212.11);

m. Peace officers and employees of California Conservation Corps incurring *lime disease*.

n. Member of the University of California Police Department incurring *heart trouble* and *pneumonia*. (See Labor Code section 3213);

o. Member of a police department of a city, county or city or a member of the sheriff's office or a peace officer employed by the Department of California Highway Patrol or the University of California who is required to wear a duty belt, incurring *lower back impairment*. (See Labor Code section 3213.2). [**Editor's Note:** The reader should refer to the specific code section if an issue of apportionment arises as to any of the group listed above as there are other unique requirements as to each group. Further, the Legislature makes it clear that the amendment is declaratory of existing law.]

Page 1376, Column 1, eighth paragraph, following '…is repealed' delete the rest of the page, delete next page (page 1377), delete column 1 of page 1378 and Footnote 4 on page 1378 and insert in its place:

The New Law Applies to All Cases Regardless of Date of Injury, Except Those Cases That Are Finally Concluded Subject Only to the Appeals Board Continuing Jurisdiction under Sections 5803 and 5804.

The change in the laws as to apportionment is so sweeping that it applies to all cases, regardless of date of injury, that are not subject to further appeal rights, subject only to the jurisdictions of the Appeals Board under Labor Code sections 5803 and 5804.

In *Scheftner v. Rio Linda School District, PSI,* (2004) 69 Cal. Comp. Cases 1281 the Appeals Board in an En Banc decision held that "submission orders" and "orders closing discovery" issued prior to the enactment of SB 899 on April 19, 2004 are "existing orders" that cannot be reopened due to the prohibition in Section 47 of SB 899. However, the Court of Appeal, Third District, in *Rio Linda Union School District, PSI v. WCAB (Scheftner)* (2005) 70 Cal. Comp. Cases 999, in *reversing* the Board stated, in part:

On April 19, 2004, Governor Schwarzenegger signed into law Senate Bill No. 899 (2003–2004 Reg. Sess.), a package of reforms to the workers' compensation laws. (Footnote 1) (Stats. 2004, ch. 34.) (SB 899.) The legislation took effect immediately as urgency legislation. (Stats. 2004, ch. 34, § 49.) SB 899 changed, among other things, the law with regard to apportionment of permanent disability. (Stats. 2004, ch. 34, § 33 [repealed Lab. Code, § 4663 (former § 4663)], § 34 [added new Lab. Code, § 4663 (§ 4663)], § 35 [added Lab. Code, § 4664 (§ 4664)], § 37 [repealed Lab. Code, § 4750 (former § 4750)], § 38 [repealed Lab. Code, § 4750.5 (former § 4750.5)]].)

In this case we consider whether the new laws enacted by SB 899 requiring apportionment based on causation (§§ 4663, 4664) apply to a workers' compensation case submitted to a workers' compensation judge (WCJ) for decision prior to the April 19, 2004 effective date of SB 899, but on which an award and findings was not issued until April 23, 2004, four days after the effective date of SB 899. We conclude the new laws, Labor Code sections 4663 and 4664 should have been applied and annul the decision of the Workers' Compensation Appeals Board (WCAB) finding to the contrary. We need not reach the other issues raised. We shall remand for further proceedings consistent with this opinion...

A. Contentions Asserted by Parties and Amicus

Petitioner District contends on review the WCAB was incorrect in holding the apportionment provisions of SB 899 do not apply to pending cases where there has been an order of submission or an order closing discovery. (Footnote 2)

District claims the Legislature intended the new apportionment laws to take immediate effect on April 19, 2004, the effective date of SB 899, and to apply to all pending cases except those in which there is an existing order, decision or award of the WCAB that affects substantive rights of the parties and that is not subject to further appeal rights, i.e., cases that have been concluded subject to the continuing jurisdiction of the WCAB under Labor Code sections 5803 and 5804. According to the District, this application of the new apportionment laws is consistent with the rule that workers' compensation benefits are a statutory right and do not vest until a final award is entered.

Scheftner contends the WCAB correctly ruled SB 899 is inapplicable to her case because discovery had been mainly closed and the issues submitted for decision prior to the effective date of SB 899.

Amicus curiae California Workers' Compensation Defense Attorneys' Association (CWCDAA) and California Workers' Compensation Institute (CWCI) support District's interpretation of the applicability of the new apportionment laws. They contend such interpretation best fits the Legislature's interest in addressing the workers' compensation system crisis by reducing costs in the key area of apportionment. CWCI claims such an interpretation is actually a "prospective" application of SB 899...

In section 47, the Legislature stated: "The amendment, addition, or repeal of, any provision of law made by this act shall apply prospectively from the date of enactment of this act, regardless of the date of injury, unless otherwise specified, but shall not constitute good cause to reopen or rescind, alter, or amend any existing order, decision, or award of the Workers' Compensation Appeals Board." (Stats. 2004, ch. 34, § 47, italics added; hereafter section 4)...

We believe the question of the appropriate application of the new apportionment requirements is answered by a consideration of the nature of the workers' compensation system, the nature of the Legislature's action regarding apportionment in SB 899, and the language of section 47.

The nature of the workers' compensation system was well described in *Graczyk v. Workers' Comp. Appeals Bd.* (1986) 184 Cal. App. 3d 997 [229 Cal. Rptr. 494, 51 Cal. Comp. Cases 408] (*Graczyk*). "California workers' compensation law ([Lab. Code,] § 3200 et seq.) is a statutory system enacted pursuant to constitutional grant of plenary power to the Legislature to establish a complete and exclusive system of workers' compensation. [Citations.] It is 'an expression of the police power' ([Lab. Code,] § 3201) and has been upheld as a valid exercise of the police power. [Citations.] [P] The right to workers' compensation benefits is 'wholly statutory' [citations], and is not derived from common law. [Citations.] [P] This statutory right is exclusive of all other statutory and common law remedies, and substitutes a new system of rights and obligations for the common law rules governing liability of employers for injuries to their employees. [Citations.] Rights, remedies and obligations rest on the status of the employer–employee relationship, rather than on contract or tort. [Citations.]" (*Graczyk, supra*, at pp. 1002–1003; see *DuBois v. Workers' Comp. Appeals Bd.* (1993) 5 Cal. 4th 382, 388 [853 P.2d 978, 20 Cal. Rptr. 2d 523, 58 Cal. Comp. Cases 286]; see *Northstar at Tahoe v. Workers' Comp. Appeals Bd.* (1996) 42 Cal. App. 4th 1481, 1484 [50 Cal. Rptr. 2d 475, 61 Cal. Comp. Cases 174].)

Given the complete statutory nature of the workers' compensation system, it is apparent the specific right to compensation under such system for any industrial injury resulting in permanent disability because of "the acceleration, aggravation, or 'lighting up' of a prior nondisabling disease" (*Pullman Kellogg v. Workers' Comp. Appeals Bd., supra*, 26 Cal. 3d at p. 454; former § 4663) was a purely statutory right. SB 899 did not purport to "amend" this right. SB 899 "repealed" former section 4663. (Stats. 2004, ch. 34, § 33.) In its place, the Legislature substituted a new statutory right to compensation for the percentage of permanent disability directly caused by an industrial injury. (§§ 4663, 4664.)

"It is an established canon of interpretation that statutes are not to be given a retrospective operation unless it is clearly made to appear that such was the legislative intent." (*Aetna Casualty & Surety Co. v. Industrial Acc. Com.* (1947) 30 Cal. 2d 388, 393 [182 P.2d 159, 12 Cal. Comp. Cases 123]; see *Evangelatos v. Superior Court* (1988) 44 Cal. 3d 1188, 1207 [753 P.2d 585, 246 Cal. Rptr. 629].) "A statute has retrospective effect when it substantially changes the legal consequences of past events. [Citation.]" (*Western Security Bank v. Superior Court* (1997) 15 Cal. 4th 232, 243 [933 P.2d 507, 62 Cal. Rptr. 2d 243].) The theory against retroactive application of a statute is that the parties affected have no notice of the new law affecting past conduct. (*Hughes v. Board of Architectural Examiners* (1998) 17 Cal. 4th 763, 793 [952 P.2d 641, 72 Cal. Rptr. 2d 624].)

However, the repeal of a statutory right or remedy triggers the application of rules distinct from the traditional law regarding the prospective or retroactive application of a statute. "A well–established line of authority holds: ' " 'The unconditional repeal of a special remedial statute without a saving clause stops all pending actions where the repeal finds them. If final relief has not been granted before the repeal goes into effect it cannot be granted afterwards, even if a judgment has been entered and the cause is pending on appeal. The reviewing court must dispose of the case under the law in force when its decision is rendered.' " [Citations.]' [Citations.]" (*Physicians Com. for Responsible Medicine v. Tyson Foods, Inc.* (2004) 119 Cal. App. 4th 120, 125 [13 Cal. Rptr. 3d 926], italics omitted; see *Younger v. Superior Court* (1978) 21 Cal. 3d 102, 109 [577 P.2d 1014, 145 Cal. Rptr. 674]; see *Governing Board v. Mann* (1977) 18 Cal. 3d 819, 831 [558 P.2d 1, 135 Cal. Rptr. 526]; see *Callet v. Alioto* (1930) 210 Cal. 65, 67 [290 P. 438].) "The justification for this rule is that all statutory remedies are pursued with full realization that the [L]egislature may abolish the right to recover at any time." (*Callet v. Alioto, supra*, at pp. 67–68.)

This rule is applicable here since the Legislature by SB 899 repealed the purely statutory right to workers' compensation for any industrial injury resulting in permanent disability because of the aggravation of a prior nondisabling disease as may reasonably be attributed to the injury. The repeal of such statutory right applies to *all* pending cases, at whatever stage the repeal finds them, unless the Legislature has expressed a contrary intent by an express saving clause or by implication from contemporaneous legislation. (*Younger v. Superior Court, supra*, 21 Cal. 3d at p. 110.)

In the uncodified portion of SB 899, section 47, the Legislature did express its intent to save a limited number of pending cases from the ordinary effect of repeal. Section 47 states: "The . . . repeal of, any provision of law made by this act shall apply prospectively from the date of enactment of this act, (Footnote 6) regardless of the date of injury, unless otherwise specified, (Footnote 7) but shall not constitute good cause to reopen or rescind, alter, or amend any existing order, decision, or award of the Workers' Compensation Appeals Board."

The language "regardless of the date of injury" clearly reflects the understanding and intent of the Legislature that SB 899 would be applicable to pending workers' compensation cases and not just to new compensable injuries occurring after April 19, 2004, the effective date of SB 899. Indeed, this immediate effect of the new law is the usual result, as we have explained, when a prior statutory right is repealed. However, the Legislature goes on to exclude some pending cases from the effect of the new law, by stating SB 899 "shall not constitute good cause to reopen or rescind, alter, or amend any existing order, decision, or award." (Stats. 2004, ch. 34, § 47.) This language essentially tracks the continuing jurisdiction language of Labor Code section 5803 (Footnote 8) (section 5803) and 5804 (section 5804). (Footnote 9)

Under sections 5803 and 5804, the WCAB has continuing jurisdiction over all of its orders, decisions, and awards for a period of five years from the date of injury. During this period of time, the WCAB "may rescind, alter or amend any order, decision, or award, good cause appearing therefor." (§ 5803.) This authority is also referred to as the continuing jurisdiction of the board to "reopen" an award or other decision. (See, e.g., 2 Witkin, Summary of Cal. Law (9th ed. 1987) Workers' Compensation, "Continuing Jurisdiction of Board. 1. Reopening Case for Good Cause.," § 428, p. 978; Herlick, Cal. Workers' Compensation Law (6th ed. 2003) Notice, Statute of Limitations, and Continuing Jurisdiction, § 14.08 [1] Good Cause to Reopen, p. 14–33; O'Brien & O'Brien, Cal. Workers' Compensation Claims & Benefits (10th ed. 2000) § 30 Petition to Reopen Subsequent to a Findings and Award, p. 707.) Such continuing jurisdiction to reopen a case is different from the WCAB's reconsideration of a "final" order of the WCAB or a WCJ pursuant to Labor Code section 5900. (Footnote 10)

(*Argonaut Ins. Co. v. Workmen's Compensation Appeals Bd.* (1967) 247 Cal. App. 2d 669, 673 [55 Cal. Rptr. 810, 32 Cal. Comp. Cases 14]; *Maranian v. Workers' Comp. Appeals Bd.* (2000) 81 Cal. App. 4th 1068, 1074–1075 [97 Cal. Rptr. 2d 418, 65 Cal. Comp. Cases 650] [defines "final" orders subject to reconsideration].) Among other things, reconsideration under section 5900 is not conditioned upon a showing of good cause; reopening is. (*Argonaut Ins. Exchange v. Industrial Acc. Com.* (1958) 49 Cal. 2d 706, 711 [321 P.2d 460, 23 Cal. Comp. Cases 34].)

"[T]he Legislature is deemed to be aware of existing law." (*American Financial Services Ass'n v. City of Oakland* (2005) 34 Cal. 4th 1239, 1261 [104 P.3d 813, 23 Cal. Rptr. 3d 453].) A substantive change in the applicable law has been held to be "good cause" for reopening a workers' compensation case under section 5803. (*Knowles v. Workmen's Comp. App. Bd.* (1970) 10 Cal. App. 3d 1027, 1030, 1033 [89 Cal. Rptr. 356, 35 Cal. Comp. Cases 411].) And so we can presume the Legislature in using the entire phrase "shall not constitute good cause to reopen or rescind, alter, or amend any existing order, decision, or award of the Workers' Compensation Appeals Board" was intentionally referring to the continuing jurisdiction authority of the WCAB under sections 5803 and 5804. The majority decision of the WCAB fails to recognize this. Instead the majority decision incorrectly focuses on the Legislature's choice of the word "existing" in section 47 to conclude significant interlocutory orders, including orders of submission and orders closing discovery cannot be "reopened" by SB 899. Such orders are not, however, the type of orders, decisions or awards to which the entire phrase in section 47 refers. The language chosen by the Legislature, read as a complete phrase, indicates the Legislature did not want the changes of law made by SB 899 to be the basis for reopening cases otherwise concluded under the workers' compensation procedures for decision (Lab. Code, § 5313), reconsideration (Lab. Code, § 5900), and judicial review (Lab. Code, § 5950).

Thus, we hold the repeal of former section 4663 was effective immediately on enactment of SB 899 on April 19, 2004, and new section 4663 and section 4664 are applicable to any case still pending, except those cases that are finally concluded subject only to the WCAB's continuing jurisdiction under sections 5803 and 5804.

The Legislature's use of the word "prospectively" in section 47 does not change this conclusion. In context with the other language of the section, (Footnote 11) it appears the Legislature was only trying to clarify and or emphasize that the changes of law contained in SB 899 would apply to pending cases from the date of enactment forward.

Amicus CAAA argues against the conclusion we have reached, contending the word "prospectively" in section 47 must at least mean something different than the clearly retroactive intent expressed in section 46 of SB 899 regarding the repeal of the personal physician's or chiropractor's presumption of correctness. (Stats. 2004, ch. 34, § 46 (section 46).) Section 46 provides: "The repeal of the personal physician's or chiropractor's presumption of correctness . . . shall *apply to all cases,* regardless of the date of injury, but shall not constitute good cause to reopen or rescind, alter, or amend any existing order, decision, or award of the Workers' Compensation Appeals Board." (Italics added.)

The application of section 46 is not before us, but we can discern a possible purpose for the Legislature to use different language in section 46 from that used in section 47. Consider the hypothetical situation of a workers' compensation case that has been concluded subject only to the continuing jurisdiction of the WCAB. Both sections 46 and 47 make it clear the Legislature does not intend the provisions of SB 899 to be used as the basis for reopening such a case. However, if the case is properly reopened for other "good cause," the Legislature may have intended from its use of the phrase "shall apply to all cases" in section 46 that the repeal of the physician's or chiropractor's presumption of correctness apply to the reopened case. However, it may not intend in such situation to backtrack and require reassessment of causation of the permanent disability to apply the new apportionment law. The new apportionment law applies only "prospectively," i.e., from April 19, 2004 forward, to cases which were not concluded as of April 19, 2004. Whether this suggestion is correct or not, we at least do not find the difference in language between sections 46 and 47 precludes our conclusion regarding the cases to which the new apportionment law applies.

CAAA asserts alternate interpretations from that provided by the WCAB's decision may render the application of SB 899 unconstitutional because article XIV, section 4 of the California Constitution guarantees that injured workers will be adequately compensated for their injuries, and requires that the workers' compensation system "accomplish substantial justice in all cases expeditiously, inexpensively, and without incumbrance of any character . . . ." We are not prepared to say the change in apportionment law denies workers "adequate" compensation or fails to "accomplish substantial justice" when the new law still requires the employer to pay compensation "for the percentage of permanent disability directly caused by the injury arising out of and occurring in the course of employment." (§ 4664, subd. (a).) The California Constitution does not make a workers' right to benefits absolute. (*Wal–Mart Stores, Inc. v. Workers' Comp. Appeals Bd., supra,* 112 Cal. App. 4th at pp. 1442–1443.)

Nor are we allowed to second–guess the apparent policy decision of the Legislature, in addressing the workers' compensation crisis (Stats. 2004, ch. 34, § 49), that it was necessary to change the apportionment law and that the cost–savings of immediately applying the new apportionment law to most pending cases offsets the concomitant cost burden and delay in those cases. (*Neighbours v. Buzz Oates Enterprises* (1990) 217 Cal. App. 3d 325, 334 [265 Cal. Rptr. 788, 55 Cal. Comp. Cases 44] ["It is for the Legislature, not the courts, to pass upon the social wisdom of such an enactment"].)

We conclude the WCAB was incorrect in holding the apportionment provisions of SB 899 did not apply to this case. We shall annul the WCAB decision and remand for further proceedings consistent with this opinion. (Lab. Code, § 5953.) We do not reach the other issues raised by District in its petition for writ of review.

DISPOSITION

The decision of the WCAB is annulled and the matter is remanded for further proceedings consistent with this opinion. Costs are awarded to petitioner. (Cal. Rules of Court, rule 27(a).)... .

_____

Footnote 1. Undesignated statutory references are to the Labor Code.

Footnote 2. District also disputes there were such orders in this case.

Footnote 6. SB 899 became effective on April 19, 2004, as urgency legislation. Section 49 of SB 899 states the facts constituting the necessity for making the legislation an urgency statute as follows: "In order to provide relief to the state from the effects of the current workers' compensation crisis at the earliest possible time, it is necessary for this act to take effect immediately." (Stats. 2004, ch. 34, § 49.)

Footnote 7. There is no otherwise specified date of applicability for the new apportionment laws.

Footnote 8. Labor Code section 5803 provides: "The appeals board has continuing jurisdiction over all its orders, decisions, and awards made and entered under the provisions of this division, and the decisions and orders of the rehabilitation unit established under Section 139.5. At any time, upon notice and after an opportunity to be heard is given to the parties in interest, the appeals board may rescind, alter, or amend any order, decision, or award, good cause appearing therefor.

"This power includes the right to review, grant or regrant, diminish, increase, or terminate, within the limits prescribed by this division, any compensation awarded, upon the grounds that the disability of the person in whose favor the award was made has either recurred, increased, diminished, or terminated."

Footnote 9. Labor Code section 5804 provides: "No award of compensation shall be rescinded, altered, or amended after five years from the date of the injury except upon a petition by a party in interest filed within such five years and any counterpetition seeking other relief filed by the adverse party within 30 days of the original petition raising issues in addition to those raised by such original petition. Provided, however, that after an award has been made finding that there was employment and the time to petition for a rehearing or reconsideration or review has expired or such petition if made has been determined, the appeals board upon a petition to reopen shall not have the power to find that there was no employment."

Footnote 10. Labor Code section 5900 provides: "(a) Any person aggrieved directly or indirectly by any final order, decision, or award made and filed by the appeals board or a workers' compensation judge under any provision contained in this division, may petition the appeals board for reconsideration in respect to any matters determined or covered by the final order, decision, or award, and specified in the petition for reconsideration. The petition shall be made only within the time and in the manner specified in this chapter.

"(b) At any time within 60 days after the filing of an order, decision, or award made by a workers' compensation judge and the accompanying report, the appeals board may, on its own motion, grant reconsideration."

Footnote 11. "A reviewing court's 'first task in construing a statute is to ascertain the intent of the Legislature so as to effectuate the purpose of the law. In determining such intent, a court must look first to the words of the statute themselves, giving to the language its usual, ordinary import and according significance . . . to every word, phrase and sentence in pursuance of the legislative purpose.' (*Dyna-Med, Inc. v. Fair Employment & Housing Com.* (1987) 43 Cal. 3d 1379, 1386–1387 [743 P.2d 1323, 241 Cal. Rptr. 67].)" (*Pacific Gas & Electric Co. v. Workers' Comp. Appeals Bd., supra,* 114 Cal. App. 4th at p. 1180.)

In *Hill v. WCAB* (2005) 70 Cal. Comp. Cases 1028, the Board upheld a judge's finding that under the *doctrine of res judicata* applicant's earlier stipulation as to the amount of permanent disability was binding on the parties and not subject to Sections 4664(b) under SB 899 as the stipulation was not timely appealed.

Page 1379, Column 2, seventh paragraph, following '…1006–1007)' delete the Editor's Note.

Page 1384, Column 2, fourth paragraph, insert following '…p 630.)'

This case reappears in *Escobedo v. WCAB* (2005) 70 Cal. Comp. Cases 1506, wherein the Appeals Board found, amongst other things, that apportionment caused by "other factors both before and subsequent to the industrial injury including prior industrial injuries", pursuant to Labor Code section 4663(c), may include disability that *could have been* apportioned prior to SB 899 as well as disability that *could not have been apportioned* such as *"pathology"*, provided there was *substantial evidence* supporting a finding that these *other factors* caused permanent disability.

Further, even when a medical report does address the issue of permanent disability apportionment, the report may not be relied upon unless it also constitutes *"substantial evidence"*.

Page 1400, Colum 2, second paragraph, add following Footnote 21:

Although a doctor expressed confusion over the new apportionment law, nevertheless, the Court of Appeal, Fifth District, in *Marsh v. WCAB* (2007) 72 Cal. Comp. Cases 336, (unpublished) upheld a Board's decision finding apportionment based on the doctor's opinion and stated, in part:

We have reviewed the deposition transcript of Dr. Holmboe, as well as the medical records previously filed with this court by the WCAB in the original proceedings, and conclude they reasonably support the WCAB's determination. Although Dr. Holmboe expressed his understandable confusion with the evolving law of apportionment and was therefore reluctant to make any apportionment conclusion with 100 percent accuracy, he was unwavering that in his medical opinion, Marsh suffered from preexisting osteopenia which attributed 50 percent to Marsh's current level of disability. When asked if Marsh would suffer a work restriction from preexisting pathology even absent the industrially related compression fractures, Dr. Holmboe explained:

" "A. Well, if he had never had a compression fracture and showed that he had significant osteopenia, I would be giving him prophylactic preclusions as I would any patient that had this condition. Basically tell him I don't want you to do any heavy lifting. I don't want you to slip and fall on your butt at the ice rink or roller rink or getting the paper on a frosty morning. I don't want you to do anything jolting your back because you're likely to have a compression fracture. And that's what most any physician would tell their patient with this condition.

"Q. Now, keeping in mind, taking Mr. Marsh, who has both compression fractures that we're assuming happened at work and the underlying osteopenia that you've indicated there would be restrictions even without the compression fractures, would it be fair, then, to go back to your opinion from March of 2003 and say that, you know, 50 percent of these work restrictions I've given are due to the fact that he has osteopenia and I would give to anybody who has osteopenia of this severity, and the other 50 percent is due to the fact he actually has compression fractures that we're saying happened at work because of the osteopenia?

"A. Yes...

"Q. Again, just to clarify, then, you feel that 50 percent of the work restrictions you've given at this point or 50 percent of the permanent disability you've given at this point is due to the osteopenia, and basically, prophylactic restrictions because of that osteopenia, and the other 50 percent is due to the actual compression fractures that occurred at work?

"A. Yes, sir, that's what I intended to say."

Although Marsh points to specific instances of inconsistencies in Dr. Holmboe's statements after being repeatedly questioned on his apportionment findings, his ultimate conclusion that 50 percent of Marsh's disability was caused by preexisting pathology, based on his medical opinion and objective medical evidence, remained consistent with his original reporting. We therefore conclude substantial evidence supports the WCAB's determination... .

Page 1400, Column 2, 13 lines from the bottom, commencing with Section 47.50 should read:

The Supreme Court in *Fuentes v. WCAB* (1976), 41 Cal. Comp. Cases 42 stated, in part:

Page 1403, Column 2, sixth paragraph, beginning 'The WCAB and the Appellate Courts...' and ending with the words '...very near future.' delete it and insert the following:

Just as this book was about to go to the print, the California Supreme Court (on May 3, 2007) issued its decisions in *Brodie v. WCAB, Welcher v. WCAB, Strong v. WCAB, Lopez v. WCAB* and *Williams v. WCAB (2007) 72 Cal. Comp. Cases 565,* and held that *Fuentes* is *still good law* as to the apportionment formula (formula A) concerning how compensation should be computed in apportionment cases.

The high Court, in a unanimous decision, held that SB 899 did not change the apportionment formula set forth in *Fuentes, supra,* and that formula A was still the formula to use.

The Court did not find a legislative intent to overthrow long established principles when it enacted SB 899. The Court reviewed the Senate Rules Committee bill summary and found only silence on any change of apportionment of prior industrial or non–industrial disability. Because the first argument in support of SB 899 was the need to reduce the highest state compensation costs in the nation, it is unlikely, said the high Court, the Legislature intended to adopt a new formula giving rise to significant increases in awards without saying so. In *Dykes, Nabors II* and *Brodie* the lower Courts had reached the opposite conclusion by assuming the repeal of Section 4750 demonstrated a legislative intent to change the law and argued that Sections 4663 and 4664 do not dictate any particular approach. Since the lower Court perceived uncertainty, and Labor Code section 3202 resolves uncertainty in favor of the applicant, they held for *formula C.* The high Court explained why Section 4750 was deleted. Finally, the Court stated, given the apparent absence of any legislative intent to change the law on apportionment of a previous disability, "we have, on occasion, to resort to reliance on the statutory rule of liberality of Section 3202".

For historical purposes, we are leaving the Courts of Appeals cases that follow involving all of the cases the high Court considered, and because of its critical importance to the workers' compensation community, we set forth the entire high Court decision, *Brodie v. WCAB* (2007) 72 Cal. Comp. Cases 565. The high Court states:

These consolidated cases present the following question: When a worker suffers an industrial injury that results in permanent disability, how should the compensation owed based on the current level of permanent disability be discounted for either previous industrial injury or nonindustrial disabilities? The issue was originally settled by this court in *Fuentes v. Workers' Comp. Appeals Bd.* (1976) 16 Cal. 3d 1 (*Fuentes*), but the 2004 omnibus reform of California's workers' compensation scheme created doubt as to whether the apportionment formula we adopted in *Fuentes* had been superseded and a different formula should now be employed. We conclude it has not been superseded and the *Fuentes* formula remains the correct one to apply in apportioning compensation between causes of disability.

FACTUAL AND PROCEDURAL BACKGROUND

These cases arise from five workers' compensation proceedings with widely differing facts but two unifying aspects. First, in each the injured worker's current permanent disability level could be attributed in part to one or more previous industrial injuries or to nonindustrial causes. Second, in each the workers' compensation judge (WCJ) applied the *Fuentes* apportionment method, under compulsion of the Workers' Compensation Appeals Board's (Board) divided en banc decision holding that notwithstanding the 2004 legislation, the *Fuentes* method of calculating apportionment was still correct. (See *Nabors v. Piedmont Lumber & Mill Co.* (2005) 70 Cal. Comp. Cases 856, 862 (en banc) (*Nabors I*).)

Stan Brodie, a firefighter for the Contra Costa County Fire Protection District, sustained an industrial injury to his back, spine, and right knee in December 2000 and subsequent cumulative trauma to his back and spine that resulted in 74 percent permanent disability. Over the previous 30 years of his career as a firefighter, Brodie had sustained several industrial injuries to the same body parts for which he was awarded compensation based on a 44.5 percent permanent disability rating. (Footnote 1) The WCJ awarded him $20,867.50 in compensation based on the difference between these ratings, 29.5 percent, and the Board denied reconsideration.

Kenneth Dee Welcher sustained an industrial injury in July 1990 when his right arm and leg were caught in a conveyor belt. His permanent disability level was stipulated at 62.5 percent. His current claim arose from cumulative injury to his right leg sustained as a laborer for Hat Creek Construction, Inc. Welcher had his right leg amputated below the knee, and the parties stipulated to a 71 percent permanent disability rating. The WCJ awarded Welcher $3,360 in compensation based on the difference between these ratings, 8 percent (rounding down), and the Board denied reconsideration.

Jack Strong, a City and County of San Francisco engineer, suffered a 1995 industrial left knee injury and received a 34.5 percent permanent disability rating. In 1999, he sustained additional industrial injuries to his left shoulder, left knee, left ankle, and right wrist, resulting in permanent disability of 42 percent. In 2002, he sustained a third industrial injury while working for the city, this time to his back. The parties stipulated that Strong's overall level of permanent disability was now 70 percent. Based on

evidence from a disability evaluation specialist, the WCJ determined the current injury caused permanent disability of 10 percent, with the remaining 60 percent attributable to the previous injuries, and awarded $4,235. The Board granted reconsideration but thereafter affirmed the award. (*Strong v. City & County of San Francisco* (2005) 70 Cal. Comp. Cases 1460 (en banc).)

Aurora Lopez, a Department of Social Services employee, injured her back and lower extremities; the parties stipulated she was 100 percent permanently disabled and stipulated further that 79 percent of this was attributable to the industrial injury and 21 percent to nonindustrial causes. The WCJ awarded Lopez permanent disability benefits of $80,910.73, plus a small life pension based on disability in excess of 70 percent, and the Board denied reconsideration.

Henry L. Williams, Jr., a United Airlines mechanic, injured his lumbar spine and received a 28 percent permanent disability rating. Thereafter, in 2003 Williams injured his spine again, and the parties stipulated to a 43 percent permanent disability rating. The WCJ awarded $9,296.25 in permanent disability benefits based on the difference, 15 percent, and the Board denied reconsideration.

In *Brodie v. Workers' Comp. Appeals Bd.*, the First District Court of Appeal, Division Three, granted writ review and annulled the Board's decision. It agreed with earlier Court of Appeal decisions from the Fifth District and First District, Division Two, insofar as they held that the 2004 legislation superseded *Fuentes*. (*E & J Gallo Winery v. Workers' Comp. Appeals Bd.* (2005) 134 Cal. App. 4th 1536, 1548–1550 (*Dykes*); (Footnote 2) *Nabors v. Workers' Comp. Appeals Bd.* (2006) 140 Cal. App. 4th 217, 228 (*Nabors II*).) As we shall discuss, it disagreed in other respects, concluding that the correct method for calculating an award was a third approach different from that adopted either in *Fuentes* or in *Dykes* and *Nabors II*.

In *Welcher v. Workers' Comp. Appeals Bd.*, the Third District consolidated the cases of Welcher, Strong, Lopez, and Williams and affirmed, expressly disagreeing with *Dykes* and *Nabors II* and holding, in agreement with the Board majority in *Nabors I*, *supra*, 70 Cal. Comp. Cases at page 862, that the *Fuentes* formula was still correct.

We granted review to resolve the split of authority.

DISCUSSION

We take as a given that each injured worker in these cases has a level of permanent disability and that some but not all of that current level of permanent disability is properly apportioned to the most recent industrial injury. The common question we must answer is: How should compensation for that portion be computed?

I. The Apportionment Problem

California's workers' compensation system was established to provide for the health, safety, and welfare of workers in the event of industrial injury by " 'relieving [them] from the consequences of any injury incurred by employees in the course of their employment.' " (*Mathews v. Workmen's Comp. Appeals Bd.* (1972) 6 Cal. 3d 719, 731, fn. 8, quoting Stats. 1917, ch. 586, § 1, p. 832; see also

Claxton v. Waters (2004) 34 Cal. 4th 367, 372.)

The panoply of benefits the system provides includes compensation for permanent disability. "[P]ermanent disability is understood as 'the irreversible residual of an injury.' " (*Kopping v. Workers' Comp. Appeals Bd.* (2006) 142 Cal. App. 4th 1099, 1111, quoting 1 Cal. Workers' Compensation Practice (Cont.Ed.Bar 4th ed. 2005) § 5.1, p. 276, italics omitted.) "A permanent disability is one '. . . which causes impairment of earning capacity, impairment of the normal use of a member, or a competitive handicap in the open labor market.' " (*State Compensation Ins. Fund v. Industrial Acc. Com.* (1963) 59 Cal. 2d 45, 52.) Thus, permanent disability payments are intended to compensate workers for both physical loss and the loss of some or all of their future earning capacity. (Lab. Code, § 4660, subd. (a); (Footnote 3) *Livitsanos v. Superior Court* (1993) 2 Cal. 4th 744, 753.)

Permanent disability payments are calculated by first expressing the degree of permanent disability as a percentage (Footnote 4) and then converting that percentage into an award based on a table. (§ 4658.) *Until April 1972, the table was straightforward: an injured worker received four weeks of benefits for each percentage point of disability.* (Former § 4658, added by Stats. 1959, ch. 1189, § 13, p. 3280; *Fuentes, supra,* 16 Cal. 3d at p. 4.) *Thus, for example, a worker determined to have suffered 10 percent permanent disability would receive 40 weeks of benefits, while one with a 90 percent disability would receive 360 weeks of benefits.*

Employers must compensate injured workers only for that portion of their permanent disability attributable to a current industrial injury, not for that portion attributable to previous injuries or to nonindustrial factors. "Apportionment is the process employed by the Board to segregate the residuals of an industrial injury from those attributable to other industrial injuries, or to nonindustrial factors, in order to fairly allocate the legal responsibility." (*Ashley v. Workers' Comp. Appeals Bd.* (1995) 37 Cal. App. 4th 320, 326.) Under the pre–1972 table, apportionment to previous injuries was relatively straightforward. Because the additional compensation for each additional percentage point of disability was linear, it mattered not whether one focused on the difference in percent between the current level of disability and the previous level of disability, or the difference in dollars between the payout at the current level of disability and the payout at the previous level of disability; either method of subtraction would lead to the same current award.

However, in 1971 the Legislature amended the table to create a sliding scale of benefits and more generously compensate for more severe disabilities. Under the new table, benefits rose not linearly but exponentially. Thus, for example, under the revised table a worker with a 10 percent disability would receive approximately three weeks of benefits for each percent of disability (for an award of 30.25 weeks), while a worker with a 90 percent disability would receive approximately six weeks of benefits for each percent of disability (for an award of 541.25 weeks). (Former § 4658, Stats. 1971, ch. 1750, § 5, p. 3776; *Fuentes, supra,* 16 Cal. 3d at p. 4.)

This amendment created a new apportionment problem in situations where a previously disabled worker suffered a new injury. Consider again the worker who was already 10 percent disabled, but after the new injury was 90 percent disabled. Under the new tables, the difference between the award for a 90 percent disability and the award for a 10 percent disability was no longer equal to the award for an 80 percent disability, the difference between these two disability levels. (Footnote 5) *Thus, it mattered whether one either (1) calculated the percentage of disability attributable to the new injury by subtracting the old rating from the new rating, then consulted the table for the award due this difference (an approach dubbed "formula A" (Fuentes, supra, 16 Cal. 3d at p. 5)), or (2) consulted the table for the award due at the new disability rating, then subtracted from that the amount that would have been awarded under the old disability rating (an approach dubbed "formula C" (ibid.)).* (Footnote 6)

II. Fuentes v. Workers' Compensation Appeals Board

This court resolved the apportionment problem in Fuentes, concluding based on statutory interpretation that the formula A approach was correct. Fuentes, the injured worker, was 58 percent permanently disabled, with 33.75 percent of this due to industrial causes and the rest attributable to a nonindustrial disability. In deciding how to determine compensation, we interpreted former section 4750, which provided: "An employee who is suffering from a previous permanent disability or physical impairment and sustains permanent injury thereafter *shall not receive from the employer compensation for the later injury in excess of the compensation allowed for such injury when considered by itself and not in conjunction with or in relation to the previous disability.* The employer shall not be liable for compensation to such an employee for the combined disability, but only for that portion due to the later injury *as though no prior disability or impairment had existed.*" (Former § 4750, added by Stats. 1945, ch. 1161, § 1, p. 2209, italics added.) This language, we reasoned, required the current industrial portion of the disability to be considered in isolation, wholly independent of any nonindustrial or previous industrial disability. (*Fuentes, supra,* 16 Cal. 3d at pp. 5–6.) Thus, a worker with a 60 percent industrial disability, 30 percent current and 30 percent preexisting, and a worker with a 60 percent current disability, 30 percent industrial and 30 percent nonindustrial, should each be treated the same as a worker with a 30 percent industrial disability. We described the policy behind this section and rule as "encourag[ing] employers to hire the handicapped" (*id.* at p. 5), (Footnote 7) because an employer who did so would not have to fear greater compensation costs if a worker with a preexisting disability were to be injured. Accordingly, we adopted formula A, which alone among the proposed formulas apportioned to every current industrial disability of a given level the same compensation, irrespective of previous or nonindustrial disabilities. (*Fuentes,* at p. 6.)

Fuentes argued that this rule was inconsistent with the revised section 4658's adoption of progressive sliding–scale payments. We disagreed, explaining that section 4658 should be read as "a general provision establishing the amount of compensation benefits for a permanent disability, and section 4750 . . . as a specific rule limiting the benefits available in those cases where the employee has a preexisting permanent disability and thereafter sustains a further permanent injury." (*Fuentes, supra*, 16 Cal. 3d at p. 7.) We also rejected the argument that section 3202, which requires that the workers' compensation statutes be read liberally in favor of extending benefits to injured workers (see *Claxton v. Waters, supra*, 34 Cal. 4th at p. 373), required a different result; where the Legislature's intent in enacting a particular statute is clear, section 3202's general rule of liberal construction will not compel a contrary result. (*Fuentes*, at p. 8.)

Fuentes involved apportionment between industrial and nonindustrial disabilities, but nothing in the majority opinion suggested former section 4750 might be read differently when apportioning between a current industrial disability and a previous one. Thereafter, the courts and the Board routinely applied formula A in apportioning between industrial disabilities as well. (E.g., *Department of Education v. Workers' Comp. Appeals Bd.* (1993) 14 Cal. App. 4th 1348, 1353; *Ramirez v. Workers' Comp. Appeals Bd.* (2001) 66 Cal. Comp. Cases 1128, 1129–1131.)

III. Senate Bill No. 899 and Its Application to the Apportionment Problem

So the law stood, settled, for 28 years. Then in 2004, the Legislature enacted omnibus reform of the workers' compensation system. Of significance here, Senate Bill No. 899 (2003–2004 Reg. Sess.) overhauled the statutes governing apportionment, repealing both section 4663 and section 4750—the statute we relied on in Fuentes, supra, 16 Cal. 3d 1, as compelling adoption of formula A—and enacting a revised section 4663 and new section 4664. (Stats. 2004, ch. 34, §§ 33 [repealing former § 4663], 34 [revising § 4663], 35 [adding new § 4664], 37 [repealing former § 4750].) These changes raised the question: Is the Fuentes formula A approach still valid?

The Board and various Courts of Appeal have reached three different conclusions. Some, like the Court of Appeal in *Welcher* and the Board majority, hold that formula A is still correct. (*Nabors I, supra*, 70 Cal. Comp. Cases at p. 862 (en banc).) Others reason that by repealing section 4750, Senate Bill No. 899 (2003–2004 Reg. Sess.) effectively superseded *Fuentes*, and formula C is now correct. (*Dykes, supra*, 134 Cal. App. 4th at p. 1553; *Nabors II, supra*, 140 Cal. App. 4th at p. 228 [following *Dykes*]; *Nabors I, supra*, at p. 864 (dis. opn. of Comr. Caplane).) The Court of Appeal in *Brodie* adopted a third approach, holding that while *Fuentes* has been superseded, the correct formula is a modification of formula C in which one subtracts not the actual award previously paid out in old dollars, but the award for that previous percentage disability that would be due today in current dollars. (Footnote 8)

Having reviewed both the language of Senate Bill No. 899 (2003–2004 Reg. Sess.) and its legislative history, we conclude formula A, the formula approved by *Fuentes*, remains the law.

In interpreting the new provisions enacted by Senate Bill No. 899 (2003–2004 Reg. Sess.), our goal is to divine and give effect to the Legislature's intent. (*Elsner v. Uveges* (2004) 34 Cal. 4th 915, 927.) We begin with a comparison and analysis of the language of the old and new statutes. (See *DuBois v. Workers' Comp. Appeals Bd.* (1993) 5 Cal. 4th 382, 387.) Former section 4663 provided only limited apportionment where an industrial injury aggravated a preexisting disease or condition: "In case of aggravation of any disease existing prior to a compensable injury, compensation shall be allowed only for the proportion of the disability due to the aggravation of such prior disease which is reasonably attributed to the injury." (Former § 4663, added by Stats. 1937, ch. 90, § 4663, p. 284 and repealed by Stats. 2004, ch. 34, § 33.) In contrast, revised section 4663, subdivision (a) provides: "Apportionment of permanent disability shall be based on causation." Subdivision (b) requires physicians preparing permanent disability reports to address causation. Subdivision (c) requires in relevant part that permanent disability reports "include an apportionment determination. A physician shall make an apportionment determination by finding what approximate percentage of the permanent disability was caused by the direct result of injury arising out of and occurring in the course of employment and what approximate percentage of the permanent disability was caused by other factors both before and subsequent to the industrial injury, including prior industrial injuries." (§ 4663, subd. (c).)

Building on this principle of apportionment according to cause, section 4664, subdivision (a) provides: "The employer shall only be liable for the percentage of permanent disability directly caused by the injury arising out of and occurring in the course of employment." Further, "[i]f the applicant has received a prior award of permanent disability, it shall be conclusively presumed that the prior permanent disability exists at the time of any subsequent industrial industry. This presumption is a presumption affecting the burden of proof." (*Id.*, subd. (b).) The remainder of section 4664 sets limits on cumulative permanent disability awards.

While section 4663, subdivision (a) authorizes apportionment by causation, and section 4664, subdivision (a) confines an employer's liability to the percentage of disability directly caused by the current industrial injury, neither provision specifies how they are to be used in conjunction with section 4658, the table that converts a disability percentage into an actual award. Certainly nothing in current section 4663 or section 4664 expressly requires formula A, B, C, modified C, or any other approach to calculating compensation. Nor does anything in the language implicitly do so. We thus agree with the Courts of Appeal in *Brodie* and *Dykes* insofar as they recognized that "[i]n adopting Sen[ate] Bill 899, the Legislature did not outline any particular method for apportioning either a permanent disability award or a life pension." (*Dykes, supra*, 134 Cal. App. 4th at p. 1552.) Contrary to the arguments of both sides, the plain language of these provisions considered in isolation does not resolve the problem. However, as we shall explain, neither does the repeal of section 4750 (which *did* implicitly compel application of formula A) now require rejection of that formula.

The answer to the problem is more readily apparent when we reframe the question and ask: By adopting new and different language governing apportionment, did the Legislature intend to adopt a new and different formula? *As we have explained, "[w]e do not presume that the Legislature intends, when it enacts a statute, to overthrow long–established principles of law unless such intention is clearly expressed or necessarily implied." (People v. Superior Court (Zamudio)* (2000) 23 Cal. 4th 183, 199; accord, *Regency Outdoor Advertising, Inc. v. City of Los Angeles* (2006) 39 Cal. 4th 507, 526.) *We conclude the answer is no and the formula we approved in Fuentes still applies. To explain why this is so, we explore the nature of apportionment and the problem the Legislature was trying to solve.*

Until 2004, former section 4663 and case law interpreting the workers' compensation scheme closely circumscribed the bases for apportionment. Apportionment based on causation was prohibited. (*Pullman Kellogg v. Workers' Comp. Appeals Bd.* (1980) 26 Cal. 3d 450, 454 ["It is disability resulting from, rather than a cause of, a disease which is the proper subject of apportionment; 'pathology' may not be apportioned"].) Instead, a disability resulting from industrial and nonindustrial causes was apportionable "only if the [B]oard finds that part of the disability would have resulted from the normal progress of the underlying nonindustrial disease." (*Ibid.*) This rule left employers liable for any portion of a disability that would not have occurred but for the current industrial cause; if the disability arose in part from an interaction between an industrial cause and a nonindustrial cause, but the nonindustrial cause would not alone have given rise to a disability, no apportionment was to be allowed. (*Ballard v. Workmen's Comp. App. Bd.* (1971) 3 Cal. 3d 832, 837 [where an industrial injury "lights up or aggravates a previously existing [nonindustrial] condition resulting in disability, liability for the full disability without proration is imposed upon the employer"]; *Gay v. Workers' Comp. Appeals Bd.* (1979) 96 Cal. App. 3d 555, 562 ["In apportioning under [former] Labor Code section 4663 it must be shown that the apportioned percentage of nonindustrial permanent disability would have resulted . . . even in [the] absence of the industrial injury"].)

Under these rules, in case after case courts properly rejected apportionment of a single disability with multiple causes. (See, e.g., *Pullman Kellogg v. Workers' Comp. Appeals Bd., supra,* 26 Cal. 3d at pp. 454–455 [no apportionment of lung injury between industrial inhalation of toxic fumes and nonindustrial pack–a–day smoking habit]; *Zemke v. Workmen's Comp. App. Bd.* (1968) 68 Cal. 2d 794, 796–799 [no apportionment of back disability between industrial back injury and nonindustrial arthritis]; *Berry v. Workmen's Comp. App. Bd.* (1968) 68 Cal. 2d 786, 788–790 [no apportionment of knee disability where industrial knee injury triggered "advancement" of previously dormant nonindustrial fungal disease]; *Idaho Maryland etc. Corp. v. Ind. Acc. Com.* (1951) 104 Cal. App. 2d 567 [no apportionment between industrial exposure to

mine gas and nonindustrial latent heart disease].) In short, so long as the industrial cause was a but–for proximate cause of the disability, the employer would be liable for the entire disability, without apportionment.

While former section 4663 was interpreted as constraining employers in their ability to show apportionment based on nonindustrial causes, former section 4750 was interpreted as granting employees wide latitude to disprove apportionment based on prior permanent disability awards by demonstrating that they had substantially rehabilitated the injury. (See, e.g., *National Auto. & Cas. Ins. Co. v. Industrial Acc. Com.* (1963) 216 Cal. App. 2d 204.) In *National Auto.,* the employee sustained a back injury and was rated 65 percent permanently disabled. He later sustained a second back injury and was rated 78 percent permanently disabled, but introduced medical testimony, accepted by the Board's predecessor, the Industrial Accident Commission, that he had rehabilitated his injury to the point that he was only 39 percent disabled immediately before the second injury. The Court of Appeal affirmed an award of 78 – 39 = 39 percent disability, not the 78 – 65 = 13 percent the insurer argued for, concluding that former section 4750 permitted proof of rehabilitation. (*National Auto.,* at pp. 207–212; see also *Mercier v. Workers' Comp. Appeals Bd.* (1976) 16 Cal. 3d 711, 716, fn. 2 [approving rehabilitation principle in dicta]; *Robinson v. Workers' Comp. Appeals Bd.* (1981) 114 Cal. App. 3d 593 [rejecting any apportionment under former § 4750, despite prior permanent disability award, where evidence showed full rehabilitation between first and second injury].)

The plain language of new sections 4663 and 4664 demonstrates they were intended to reverse these features of former sections 4663 and 4750. (*Kleeman v. Workers' Comp. Appeals Bd.* (2005) 127 Cal. App. 4th 274, 284–285 & fns. 25–27.) Thus, new sections 4663, subdivision (a) and 4664, subdivision (a) eliminate the bar against apportionment based on pathology and asymptomatic causes (*E.L. Yeager Construction v. Workers' Comp. Appeals Bd.* (2006) 145 Cal. App. 4th 922, 926–927; *Escobedo v. Marshalls* (2005) 70 Cal. Comp. Cases 604, 617 (en banc)), while section 4664, subdivision (b) was intended to reverse the rule based on former section 4750 that permitted an injured employee to show rehabilitation of an injury for which a permanent disability award had already been issued (*Kopping v. Workers' Comp. Appeals Bd., supra,* 142 Cal. App. 4th at p. 1115; *Sanchez v. County of Los Angeles* (2005) 70 Cal. Comp. Cases 1440, 1452 (en banc)).

This explains the Legislature's purpose in adopting a revised section 4663 and a new section 4664. Further, one can see why it was necessary to repeal former sections 4663 and 4750. These provisions, as interpreted by the courts, were inconsistent with the new regime of apportionment based on causation, as well as the conclusive presumption that previous permanent disability still existed for apportionment purposes. (Footnote 9) (§§ 4663, subd. (a), 4664, subds. (a), (b).) Former section 4750 required consideration of the new injury "by itself and not in conjunction with or in relation to the previous disability or impairment" and further called for compensation for the later injury to be determined "as though no prior disability or impairment had existed." But under Senate Bill No. 899 (2003–2004 Reg. Sess.), the new approach to apportionment is to look at the current disability and parcel out its causative sources—nonindustrial, prior industrial, current industrial—and decide the amount directly caused by the current industrial source. This approach requires thorough consideration of past injuries, not disregard of them. Thus, repeal of section 4750 was necessary to effect the Legislature's purposes in adopting a causation regime.

Given that repeal of section 4750 was necessary to carry out the Legislature's intended switch to apportionment by causation, and that intended switch alone provides a sufficient explanation for the repeal, it is unnecessary to impute to the Legislature a further intent to also change the long–settled method for computing compensation awards in order to explain its actions. Occam's razor—avoid hypothesizing complicated explanations when a simpler one is available—applies here. (Footnote 10)

However, because the plain language of the current sections 4663 and 4664 and the repeal of section 4750 do not alone conclusively repudiate any intent to change how disability percentages are converted to compensation awards, we consider as well the legislative history. If the Legislature had intended a departure from formula A, one would expect to find some trace of this intent in the legislative history, just as the legislative history explicitly identifies more than two dozen other intended reforms enacted by Senate Bill No. 899 (2003–2004 Reg. Sess.), including numerous intended changes to the apportionment scheme. As the facts of these five consolidated cases demonstrate, a change from formula A to formula B or either version of formula C would have dramatic fiscal consequences for employers and insurers (as well as, of course, for employees). (Footnote 11) Such a change, if intended, would likely have been remarked upon.

Instead, one hears only silence. The Senate Rules Committee's bill summary exhaustively catalogues the changes wrought by Senate Bill No. 899 (2003–2004 Reg. Sess.) and highlights a series of intended changes in the apportionment rules, the very changes we have already discussed: the bill would "(24) replace present law on apportionment with [a] statement that apportionment of permanent disability is based on causation; (25) require physicians evaluating permanent disability to assess percentage of disability due to work; (26) make[] employer liable only for portion of disability directly caused by injury, [and] restrict[] accumulated percentage of disability for any body region to 100% over lifetime." (Sen. Rules Com., Off. of Sen. Floor Analyses, Conf. Rep. No. 1 on Sen. Bill No. 899 (2003–2004 Reg. Sess.) as amended Apr. 15, 2004, p. 3.) The summary highlights the Legislature's intent to change how one *arrives* at the percentage disability for which an employer or insurer is liable, but makes no mention of any intent to change how that percentage, once arrived at, is to be converted to an award. The same is true of the analyses of the bills that fed into Senate Bill No. 899; we find in our review of them no mention of any intent to alter the approach to calculating awards based on the

percentage attributable to a current industrial injury. (Footnote 12) This silence offers no reason to believe the Legislature intended to abandon the settled application of formula A.

Several additional considerations buttress this conclusion. First, as Justice Sims noted in his concurring opinion in *Welcher*, Senate Bill No. 899 (2003–2004 Reg. Sess.) was an urgency measure designed to alleviate a perceived crisis in skyrocketing workers' compensation costs. (See Stats. 2004, ch. 34, § 49 [bill urgency measure needed "to provide relief to the state from the effects of the current workers' compensation crisis at the earliest possible time"]; Assem. Republican Caucus, Analysis of Sen. Bill No. 899 (2003–2004 Reg. Sess.) as amended Apr. 15, 2004, p. 6 [listing as first argument in support of the bill the need to reduce the highest state workers' compensation costs in the nation]; Assem. Com. on Insurance, Analysis of Sen. Bill No. 899 (2003–2004 Reg. Sess.) as proposed to be amended July 9, 2003, p. 4 [identifying "crisis" linked to "skyrocketing costs"].) This makes it especially unlikely the Legislature would intend to adopt a new formula giving rise to significant increases in awards without saying so much as a word in either the text of the statutes or the analyses of the proposed changes. (Footnote 13)

We note as well that in the post–2004 world of apportionment by causation, formula C, the formula advocated by the injured workers and adopted in modified form by the Court of Appeal in *Brodie*, can no longer logically be applied to all cases.

The intuitive appeal of formula C is clearest in a case of two sequential industrial injuries. Assume a first injury that results in 30 percent permanent disability, followed by a second overlapping injury that results in a combined 60 percent permanent disability. Under formula C, though the employer is still only liable for the 30 percent increase in disability, the award is computed based on the compensation for the range of 30 percent disability to 60 percent disability, rather than the range of 0 percent to 30 percent. This has the salutary consequence of ensuring that a 60 percent permanently disabled employee always receives the full compensation indicated by section 4658 for 60 percent permanent disability, irrespective of whether that disability arises from one injury, two injuries, or many. (Footnote 14)

In cases of apportionment for causation, however, the notion of a "first" 30 percent and a "second" 30 percent will frequently not apply. Where an industrial cause and nonindustrial cause simultaneously interact and are equally responsible for a 60 percent injury, there is no first 30 percent or second 30 percent. There are two possible resolutions to this conundrum, each problematic. Either (1) the original or *Brodie*-modified formula C applies here as well, despite there being no logic or equity to making the employer liable for the more expensive second 30 percent, the range from 30 to 60 percent; or (2) formula C does not apply, in which case either formula B applies, or perhaps formula A still applies, despite the fact that nothing in the statutes suggests the Legislature intended a complicated partial override of the old rule and adoption of a new formula only for a certain subset of apportionment cases.

Finally, the Board has extensive expertise in interpreting and applying the workers' compensation scheme. Consequently, we give weight to its interpretations of workers' compensation statutes unless they are clearly erroneous or unauthorized. (Honeywell v. Workers' Comp. Appeals Bd. (2005) 35 Cal. 4th 24, 34; Judson Steel Corp. v. Workers' Comp. Appeals Bd. (1978) 22 Cal. 3d 658, 668– 669.) The Board concluded in Nabors I, supra, 70 Cal. Comp. Cases at page 862, that Senate Bill No. 899 (2003– 2004 Reg. Sess.) did not overrule use of formula A and that that formula should continue to be employed. The Board's conclusion was not clearly erroneous and is entitled to deference.

Those Courts of Appeal reaching the opposite conclusion—the Fifth District in *Dykes*; the First District, Division Two, in *Nabors II*; and the First District, Division Three, in *Brodie*—reached that conclusion through a common line of reasoning. First, the repeal of section 4750 demonstrated a legislative intent to change the law of apportionment. Second, the new language of sections 4663 and 4664 does not dictate any particular approach. Third, section 3202, the statutory rule of liberality, requires that uncertainties be resolved in favor of an extension of fully compensatory benefits. Because the new statutory language is ambiguous and grants some measure of latitude, these courts reason, each settles on an original or modified version of formula C, the formula most generous to injured workers. (*Dykes, supra,* 134 Cal. App. 4th at pp. 1550– 1553; *Nabors II, supra,* 140 Cal. App. 4th at pp. 223–225, 228.)

The problem with these analyses is in the very first step. It is true that wholesale changes in language generally signify an intent to change existing law. (See *People v. Mendoza* (2000) 23 Cal. 4th 896, 916.) As we have discussed, the Legislature *did* intend to significantly alter the law of apportionment—just not *this* aspect of the law of apportionment, the formula for computing an apportioned award after the employer/insurer's percentage liability has been determined.

Given the apparent absence of any legislative intent to change the law in this regard, we have no occasion to resort to reliance on the statutory rule of liberality as the Courts of Appeal did. Section 3202 is a tool for resolving statutory ambiguity where it is not possible through other means to discern the Legislature's actual intent. It is of little or no use here, where other tools permit us to divine that the Legislature did not intend to amend settled law and alter the status quo concerning the appropriate formula. (See *Fuentes, supra,* 16 Cal. 3d at p. 8.)

In the end, the relevant portions of Senate Bill No. 899 (2003–2004 Reg. Sess.) and the history behind them reflect a clear intent to charge employers only with that percentage of permanent disability directly caused by the current industrial injury. The tables in section 4658 are for compensating the current injury only, not the totality of an injured worker's disabilities; a 30 percent disability is a 30 percent disability, not a 90 minus 60 percent disability or a 60 minus 30 percent disability. The changes wrought by Senate Bill No. 899 affect how one goes about identifying the percentage of permanent disability an employer is

responsible for, but not how one calculates the compensation due for that disability once a percentage is determined. We disapprove *E & J Gallo Winery v. Workers' Comp. Appeals Bd., supra,* 134 Cal. App. 4th 1536 [*Dykes*], and *Nabors v. Workers' Comp. Appeals Bd., supra,* 140 Cal. App. 4th 217, to the extent they are inconsistent with this opinion.

DISPOSITION

For the foregoing reasons, the Court of Appeal's judgment in *Welcher* is affirmed and the Court of Appeal's judgment in *Brodie* is reversed and remanded for further proceedings consistent with this opinion... .

Footnote 1. The WCJ disregarded additional industrial injuries to other body parts, as they did not overlap with the current injuries and thus provided no basis for apportionment.

Footnote 2. Workers' compensation decisions are often referred to by the name of the injured worker. *E & J Gallo Winery v. Workers' Comp. Appeals Bd., supra,* 134 Cal. App. 4th 1536, generally has been referred to as the *Dykes* decision by courts, commentators, and practitioners.

Footnote 3. All further unlabeled statutory references are to the Labor Code.

Footnote 4. Notably, however, "[t]he percentage level of permanent disability represents only a point on a relative scale." (1 Hanna, Cal. Law of Employee Injuries and Workers' Compensation (rev. 2d ed. 2007), § 8.02[2], p. 8– 6.) Thus, a rating of 50 percent has no real world significance, other than to indicate that the injured worker is more disabled than someone with a 45 percent rating and less disabled than someone with a 55 percent rating.

Footnote 5. Subsequent amendments have created even starker differences in the compensation for different disability levels. Injured workers now receive three weeks of payments for each disability percent below 10 percent, but 16 weeks for each percent above 70 percent (§ 4658, subd. (d)(1)); the amount of the weekly payments rises once various threshold percentages (15, 25, and 70) are reached (§ 4453, subd. (b)); and a life pension is required for permanent disabilities of 70 percent or greater (§ 4659).

Footnote 6. Under formula B, discussed in *Fuentes, supra,* 16 Cal. 3d at page 5, one consults the table for the number of weeks of statutory benefits due at the new disability rating (say, the weeks of benefits for a 90 percent disability in our 90/10 hypothetical) and then multiplies this figure by the portion of current disability attributable to the new injury (in the hypothetical, (90–10)/90 = 88.9 percent). Justice Mosk, the lone dissenter in *Fuentes,* advocated formula B's adoption. (*Id.* at p. 9 (dis. opn. of Mosk, J.).) No party in these cases prefers formula B; instead, as in *Fuentes,* the employers and insurers argue for formula A, while the workers argue for one version or another of formula C.

Footnote 7. As an earlier court once put it, former section 4750 was intended to remove any employer excuse for "refus[ing] to hire one–armed, one–legged, or one–eyed men." (*Wolski v. Industrial Accident Com.* (1945) 70 Cal. App. 2d 427, 432.)

Footnote 8. In dissent in *Nabors I*, then Board Chairman Rabine advocated a fourth approach, the formula B approach described in *Fuentes, supra,* 16 Cal. 3d at page 5. (*Nabors I, supra,* 70 Cal. Comp. Cases at p. 864 (dis. opn. of Chairman Rabine).)

Footnote 9. As previously noted, former section 4750 had been interpreted as allowing workers' compensation judges to disregard a previous disability or impairment in making apportionment decisions where the applicant proved rehabilitation, a rule squarely at odds with new section 4664, subdivision (b).

Footnote 10. "[T]he principle of Occam's razor—that the simplest of competing theories should be preferred over more complex and subtle ones—is as valid juridically as it is scientifically." (*Swann v. Olivier* (1994) 22 Cal. App. 4th 1324, 1329, fn. omitted, disapproved on another ground in *Alcaraz v. Vece* (1997) 14 Cal. 4th 1149, 1166.)

Footnote 11. For example, under formula A, Kenneth Dee Welcher received $3,360, but he would be entitled to nearly $38,000 plus a life pension under modified formula C or nearly $68,000 plus a life pension under the original formula C. Under formula A, Stan Brodie was awarded just over $20,000, while under modified formula C he would receive $67,700 plus a life pension, or more than $114,000 over his remaining life expectancy. Under formula A, Jack Strong received $4,325, while under the two versions of formula C he would receive between $35,000 and $40,000 plus a life pension, or roughly $59,000 over his life expectancy.

Footnote 12. Senate Bill No. 899 (2003–2004 Reg. Sess.) started out as a minor bill designed to change one aspect of workers' compensation wholly unrelated to apportionment. (See Sen. Com. on Labor and Industrial Relations, Analysis of Senate Bill No. 899 (2003–2004 Reg. Sess.) as amended Apr. 21, 2003.) It was but one of 20 different bills to reform workers' compensation passed out of the Senate or Assembly in 2003. (Sen. Rules Com., Off. of Sen. Floor Analyses, Rep. on Sen. Bill No. 899 (2003–2004 Reg. Sess.) as amended July 14, 2003, pp. 2–3.) Senate and Assembly leaders responded to this plethora of overlapping measures by submitting them to a joint conference to digest the bills and incorporate their provisions into a single omnibus reform measure. (Assem. Com. on Insurance, Analysis of Sen. Bill No. 899 (2003–2004 Reg. Sess.) as proposed to be amended July 9, 2003, p. 6.)

Reform of the apportionment process was originally proposed as part of Assembly Bill No. 1481 (2003–2004 Reg. Sess.), Assembly Bill No. 1579 (2003–2004 Reg. Sess.), and Senate Bill No. 714 (2003–2004 Reg. Sess.). Even in the text and committee analyses of these other measures, however, one finds no reflection of an intent to override the settled formula A approach and substitute a different method. (See, e.g., Assem. Com. on Insurance, Analysis of Assem. Bill No. 1481 (2003–2004 Reg. Sess.) as introduced Feb. 22, 2003, pp. 1–2; Sen. Com. on Labor and Industrial Relations, Analysis of Assem. Bill No. 1579

(2003–2004 Reg. Sess.) as proposed to be amended July 9, 2003, p. 4; Sen. Com. on Labor and Industrial Relations, Analysis of Sen. Bill No. 714 (2003–2004 Reg. Sess.) as amended Apr. 21, 2003, pp. 1–2.)

Footnote 13. While it is true, as the injured workers argue, that some aspects of Senate Bill No. 899 (2003–2004 Reg. Sess.) had the effect of expanding worker benefits (see §§ 139.48 [funding small employer worksite accommodations of disabled workers], 4658, subd. (d)(1) [increasing benefits for workers with 70 percent or greater disability], 4658, subd. (d)(2) [increasing benefits for disabled workers denied prompt return to work], 5402, subd. (c) [providing additional medical benefits]), the modifications to apportionment did not. These included a requirement that doctors include apportionment discussions in their reports (§ 4663, subds. (b), (c)), a prohibition against avoiding apportionment by proving that a prior injury had been rehabilitated (§ 4664, subd. (b)), a cap on awards based on injuries to any one body part (§ 4664, subd. (c)(1)), and a reversal of the case–law–imposed prohibition against apportionment based on cause and corresponding expansion of the range of bases that would trigger apportionment (§ 4663, subd. (a)).

Moreover, the benefit–expanding modifications the injured workers highlight *were* mentioned in Senate Bill No. 899's legislative history. (Sen. Rules Com., Off. of Sen. Floor Analyses, Conf. Rep. No. 1 on Sen. Bill No. 899 (2003–2004 Reg. Sess.) as amended Apr. 15, 2004, pp. 2 [item 16: § 5402 medical benefits; item 21: increased benefits for those with 70 percent or greater disability], 3 [item 3: § 139.48 accommodation funding], 6 [item 14: § 5402 medical benefits], 7 [items 17–18: additional benefits under § 4658]; Assem. Republican Caucus, Analysis of Sen. Bill No. 899 (2003–2004 Reg. Sess.) as amended Apr. 15, 2004, p. 7 [§ 4658, subd. (d)(2) return–to–work incentives, § 5402 medical benefits].) They provide no support for the notion that the Legislature would, sub silentio, change another part of the compensation scheme with potential fiscal consequences dramatically larger than many of the changes highlighted in the bill analyses.

Footnote 14. While formula C ensures that all employees with a certain level of permanent disability receive the same compensation, formula A ensures that all employers responsible for a certain level of permanent disability pay the same compensation. Thus, each formula ensures equality—just equality from a different perspective, one employee–based and the other employer–based. Formula B ensures neither equality, but does arrive at a rough compromise between the two perspectives.

In *Nabors,* the Appeals Board, in an En Banc decision stated, in part:

Page 1407, Column 1, second paragraph, insert following '...Therefore I dissent'

In reversing the Appeals Board and holding that *formula C* is the correct method for calculating Nabors' permanent disability benefits, the Court of Appeal, Fifth District, in *Nabors v. WCAB* (2006) 71 Cal. Comp. Cases 704, stated, in part:

INTRODUCTION

Danny Nabors petitions for review of the opinion and decision after reconsideration of the Workers' Compensation Appeals Board (Board), which affirmed the award of a Workers' Compensation Judge (WCJ). Nabors challenges the Board's permanent disability apportionment formula.

BACKGROUND

In May 1996, Nabors sustained industrial injury to his low back and lower extremities while employed by Piedmont Lumber as a foreman, lumber stacker and forklift driver, resulting in an August 2001 stipulated award of $42,476 based on 49 percent permanent disability. Thereafter, while working for Piedmont as a mill supervisor, he sustained injury to the same body parts cumulative to August 19, 2002. After a hearing, the WCJ found the cumulative injury caused 31 percent of Nabors's permanent disability and awarded him $22,610. The Board granted Nabors's petition for reconsideration, and affirmed the award in an en banc opinion and decision. This timely writ petition followed.

DISCUSSION

In his opinion on decision, the WCJ explained that in apportioning disability between Nabors's two industrial injuries, he followed the rationale of *Fuentes v. Workers' Comp. Appeals Bd.* (1976) 16 Cal. 3d 1 [547 P.2d 449, 128 Cal. Rptr. 673, 41 Cal. Comp. Cases 42] (*Fuentes*), and the plain meaning of Labor Code section 4664. (Footnote 1)

In *Fuentes*, our Supreme Court considered the extent of an employer's liability for a worker's permanent disability that was attributable to both an industrial and a preexisting injury, under then–recent amendments to section 4658 (the permanent disability schedule), which changed the method for calculating compensation from four weeks of benefits for each percentage point of permanent disability to a formula in which the number of weekly benefits increases exponentially in proportion to the percentage of disability. (*Fuentes, supra,* 16 Cal. 3d at pp. 3–4.) The court set out three computational formulas and concluded the Board had properly applied formula A, subtracting from the total percentage of disability the portion that was nonindustrial. The court believed that although that approach deprived the injured worker of amended section 4658's exponential increase in benefits, (Footnote 2) it was required by section 4750. (Footnote 3) (*Id.* at p. 6.) Since that time, section 4750 has been repealed and section 4664 has been added. (Stats. 2004, ch. 34 (Sen. Bill No. 899), §§ 35 & 37, pp. 151, 152.) Section 4664 provides, in pertinent part, "(a) The employer shall only be liable [*sic*] for the *percentage of permanent disability directly caused* by the injury arising out of and occurring in the course of employment. [P] (b) If the applicant has received a prior award of permanent disability, it shall be conclusively presumed that the prior permanent disability exists at the time of any subsequent

industrial injury. This presumption is a presumption affecting the burden of proof." (Italics added.) (Footnote 4)

The majority of the Board agreed with the WCJ that absent clear indication the Legislature had abandoned its intention to encourage employment of the disabled, repeal of section 4750 did not entirely undermine *Fuentes*'s rationale, especially in light of new section 4664 and amended section 4663, subdivision (c) (Stats. 2004, ch. 34, § 34, pp. 150–151 [physician apportioning permanent disability must determine "approximate percentage" caused by industrial injury and "approximate percentage" caused by other factors]), both of which speak in terms of "percentage of permanent disability," and the public policy underlying the new statutes: "to provide relief to the state from the effects of the current workers' compensation crisis" (Stats. 2004, ch. 34, § 49, p. 157).

Then–Board chairman Rabine dissented on the grounds that repeal of former section 4750 removed the underpinnings of *Fuentes*, and the express language of section 4663 requires application of formula B (*Fuentes, supra,* 16 Cal. 3d at p. 5): number of weekly benefits authorized by section 4658 for total permanent disability (80 percent) multiplied by percentage of total permanent disability attributable to current injury (31/80). Rabine noted the absence of evidence that application of formula A for almost 30 years has, in fact, encouraged employment of the handicapped. In his analysis, "percentage of permanent disability" refers not to the degree to which a particular injury diminishes a worker's capacity to compete for employment in the open market (here, 31 percent), but to the ratio of the disability caused by the current injury to the total disability (31/80).

While agreeing with Rabine that repeal of section 4750 undercut the continuing validity of the *Fuentes* court's holding, dissenting Commissioner Caplane disagreed about the effect of the new statutes, believing the express language of sections 4663 and 4664 require application of formula C (*Fuentes, supra,* 16 Cal. 3d at p. 5): dollar value of previous award ($42,476) subtracted from dollar value of total current permanent disability ($118,795) (see *ante,* fn. 2), because unlike repealed section 4750, the new statutes do not include the limiting language italicized in Footnote 3, *ante,* and formula C furthers the purpose of section 4658's exponential increases. Not surprisingly, Nabors asks us to reject the Board's majority opinion, and adopt that of Commissioner Caplane.

While this petition was pending before us, the Fifth District Court of Appeal issued an opinion in *E & J Gallo Winery v. Workers' Comp. Appeals Bd.* (2005) 134 Cal. App. 4th 1536 [37 Cal. Rptr. 3d 208, 70 Cal. Comp. Cases 1644] (*Dykes*) (review den. Mar. 1, 2006, S140645) in which, after an exhaustive analysis (see *post,* pt. A), the court held that "where an employee sustains multiple disabling injuries while working for the same self–insured employer, the employee is entitled to compensation for the total disability above any percentage of permanent disability previously awarded." (*Id.* at p. 1540.) In other words, it adopted the formula C method of computing benefits. (*Id.* at p. 1553.) We requested letter briefs from the parties (including amicus curiae California Applicants' Attorneys

Association) on the issue of *Dykes*'s effect on this case. In addition to their responses, we received amicus briefs from the California Workers' Compensation Institute (CWCI) and the California Chamber of Commerce (CCC), to which the parties had an opportunity to respond (Cal. Rules of Court, rule 13(c)). For the reasons set out below, nothing in this additional briefing persuades us to diverge from the reasoning and result in *Dykes*.

A. The *Dykes* Opinion (Footnote 5)

Winery worker David Dykes sustained an industrial back injury in 1996, resulting in an award based on 20.5 percent permanent disability. In 2002, he became 73 percent permanently disabled after a second industrial back injury. The WCJ awarded Dykes benefits based on 73 percent permanent disability, less the amount of compensation previously awarded for the earlier injury. In other words, the WCJ computed the amount of the award using *Fuentes*'s formula C. Gallo, Dykes's self–insured employer, petitioned for reconsideration, which was summarily denied. (*Dykes, supra,* 134 Cal. App. 4th at p. 1541.) Gallo petitioned for review, urging the application of formula A. (*Id.* at pp. 1543, 1554.)

After surveying the applicable statutes (*Dykes, supra,* 134 Cal. App. 4th at pp. 1541–1543), the *Fuentes* opinion (*id.* at pp. 1544–1547), and the en banc decision in *Nabors* (*id.* at pp. 1547–1548; see *ante,* fn. 5), the court concluded *Fuentes* was no longer controlling after Senate Bill No. 899 (*id.* at p. 1548). First, the court noted that the *Fuentes* court repeatedly stated its holding was required by the express and unequivocal language of section 4750, going so far as to suggest that repeal of that section would create the opportunity to apply another apportionment formula, and a year later, in *Wilkinson v. Workers' Comp. Appeals Bd.* (1977) 19 Cal. 3d 491, 500 [564 P.2d 848, 138 Cal. Rptr. 696, 42 Cal. Comp. Cases 406] (*Wilkinson*), confirmed that its adoption of formula A rested exclusively on section 4750. (*Dykes,* at pp. 1548–1549.) Next, the court pointed out the "significantly different approaches" to apportionment between former section 4750 (current injury considered by itself as if no prior disability existed) and new section 4664 (conclusive presumption that prior disability still exists). (*Id.* at p. 1549.) Finally, the court rejected the *Nabors* en banc majority's conclusion that the policy of encouraging employers to hire the disabled dictates the use of formula A, noting the new legislation's presumption that prior disability exists, the lack of evidence that any apportionment formula promotes hiring the disabled better than another, and the numerous anti–discrimination statutes enacted since *Fuentes*. (*Id.* at p. 1550.) In sum, the court concluded that "the Legislature contemplated a variation in determining apportionment by repealing section 4750 and replacing it with different language in section 4664 for apportioning liability among multiple injuries." (*Ibid.*)

Turning its attention to the meaning of the new apportionment provision, the court concluded the plain language of section 4664, subdivision (a) (*ante,* pp. 2–3) means that "[a]n employer is liable for the direct consequences of a work–related injury, nothing more and nothing less." (*Dykes, supra,* 134 Cal. App. 4th at p. 1551.)

Furthermore, "section 4664 contemplates accumulating multiple disability awards rather than subtracting percentage levels of disability." (*Ibid.*) (Footnote 6)

But the court noted that while the new statutes, in conjunction with the permanent disability schedule (see *ante,* p. 2) and the life pension provision, (Footnote 7) may be interpreted to permit several different approaches to apportioning liability, yielding quite disparate results, the Legislature did not specify any particular method of calculating an award. (*Id.* at pp. 1551–1552.)

Guided by the specific legislative mandate of section 4664, subdivision (a), as well as the overriding principle of liberal construction of workers' compensation laws for the benefit of injured workers (§ 3202), and mindful of the exponentially progressive nature of the permanent disability tables, which serve to compensate employees with higher levels of permanent disability "in greater proportion" to those with lower levels, the court concluded that only formula C ensures both that an employee is adequately compensated and that an employer is liable only for the percentage of disability directly caused by the current injury. In other words, an employer is liable for that part of a worker's overall disability that exceeds his prior disability level. (*Dykes, supra,* 134 Cal. App. 4th at pp. 1552–1553.)

The *Dykes* court could "ascertain no legislative intent to compensate an employee who has sustained two or more disabling injuries while employed by the same self–insured employer less than a similarly situated employee who has sustained a single industrial injury resulting in the same level of permanent disability. By not recognizing the injured employee's total disability[,] and artificially shifting compensation down on the permanent disability tables, all of the other formulas shortchange an employee by treating him or her as though no prior injury or disability existed, which is . . . no longer permitted under Sen[ate] Bill [No.] 899." (*Dykes, supra,* 134 Cal. App. 4th at p. 1553.) Moreover, any other formula for apportionment among multiple injuries "creates a windfall to the employer and places an unreasonable burden on the injured employee who must compete in the open labor market with a permanent disability." (*Ibid.*) Finally, the court pointed out that under the old law, evidence that Dykes had been rehabilitated from his prior injury would have defeated any apportionment at all, rendering Gallo liable for an award based on 73 percent permanent disability, in addition to the benefits already paid for the earlier injury. (*Id.* at p. 1554.) Under present law, taking his prior level of disability into account, as required by section 4664, subdivision (a), the "percentage of permanent disability directly caused by" the current industrial injury is the additional percentage of disability that takes him from 20.5 percent to 73 percent disabled. Dykes was therefore entitled to an award reflecting the difference between a 20.5 percent disability and a 73 percent disability on the permanent disability table applicable to the subsequent injury. (*Ibid.*)

B. A Distinction Without a Difference

The *Dykes* court expressly limited its analysis to the "narrow context" (*Dykes, supra,* 134 Cal. App. 4th at p. 1540) in which "the injured employee received a prior disability award while working for the same self–insured employer." (*Id.* at pp. 1550–1551.) In this case, the employer was not self–insured, but had a different carrier for each of Nabors's injuries. While every party pointed out this factual distinction, only the employer's current carrier, respondent State Compensation Insurance Fund (SCIF), suggested that the distinction is sufficient to render *Dykes* inapplicable to this case. But even SCIF did not actually *argue* for that position. It simply noted, "A critical question that arises in the multiple carrier situation that is absent in the *Dykes* situation is whether the current carrier should be saddled with having to pay increased indemnity due to the earlier injury by operation of the graduated permanent disability scale." SCIF does not answer this "critical question," nor point to any other context in which this distinction affects the amount of benefits to which an injured worker is entitled.

In our view, the *Dykes* court's limiting language merely expresses its adherence to the principle of judicial restraint. The practice of distinguishing one case from another is based, after all, on the assumption that the holding of an appellate court is limited to the facts of the case before it. The *Dykes* court did not say that its holding does not or should not apply to a case in which the employer is not self–insured. In fact, it "express[ed] no opinion whether formula C should also be applied where an employee received a prior disability award with another employer, where the employer was separately insured at the time of the injuries, or where the medical evidence reveals that a portion of the injured employee's disability is not compensable." (*Dykes, supra*, 134 Cal. App. 4th at p. 1553.)

We are not persuaded that *Dykes* is inapplicable to this case simply because the employer here was insured by two different carriers rather than being self–insured.

C. The Dykes Rationale

In addition to the requested briefing on the issue of *Dykes*'s applicability to the instant case, we received and have considered various arguments that *Dykes* itself was wrongly decided. "We acknowledge we are not bound by an opinion of another District Court of Appeal, however persuasive it might be. [Citation.] We respect stare decisis, however, which serves the important goal of stability in the law and predictability of decision. Thus we ordinarily follow the decisions of other districts without good reason to disagree. [Citation.]" (*Greyhound Lines, Inc. v. County of Santa Clara* (1986) 187 Cal. App. 3d 480, 485 [231 Cal. Rptr. 702].) Although the *Dykes* case is the only reported decision to date on this issue, no compelling reason has been advanced, on the facts of this case, to disagree with it.

Both respondents and amici curiae CWCI and CCC have asked us to reject the reasoning of *Dykes*. Much of their briefing consists of an historical overview of workers' compensation apportionment law, as they see it. They all include reference to the Subsequent Injuries Benefits Trust Fund (§§ 4751–4755), which provides additional compensation to injured employees with prior disabilities under certain specific circumstances. Since none of those circumstances is present in this case, the issue of whether there might ever be any inconsistency between formula C and the subsequent injuries fund is not before us.

Much of the argument against *Dykes* is based on section 4664's use of the term "percentage of permanent disability," language CWCI claims "codifies" the formula chosen by the *Fuentes* court, and prohibits the formula chosen by the *Dykes* court. The issue is not, however, whether to employ what CWCI calls "the percentage principle," but rather what the Legislature *meant* by "percentage of permanent disability"–how to calculate benefits on this basis– especially in light of section 4658's exponentially progressive benefits schedule. For that reason, the verbal sleight of hand by which CCC labels formula A "the percentage method" and formula C "the dollar value method" is of no avail. Formula A and formula C are alternate methods of calculating benefits based on the *percentage* of total disability caused by each of two successive injuries. (See *Dykes, supra*, 134 Cal. App. 4th at p. 1554.) The *Dykes* court focused its inquiry on which formula best reflects the Legislature's intent, not, as CCC suggests, on its own notion of "fairness," a word that does not even appear on the cited page of the opinion (*id.* at p. 1553).

CWCI also asserts that to the extent the 2004 workers' compensation reform changed the apportionment rules, it was intended to overturn not *Fuentes*, but *Wilkinson, supra*, 19 Cal. 3d 491, in which the court held that its decision in *Fuentes* had not impliedly overruled the doctrine established in *Bauer v. County of Los Angeles* (1969) 34 Cal. Comp. Cases 594 [Appeals Board significant panel decision], that "whenever a worker, while working for the same employer, sustains successive injuries to the same part of his body and these injuries become permanent at the same time, the worker is entitled to an award based on the combined disability" (*Wilkinson, supra*, 19 Cal. 3d at p. 494). The court reasoned that in such a case, *Fuentes* did not apply because there was no "previous permanent disability" within the meaning of former section 4750. (*Id.* at pp. 497, 500.) Neither *Dykes* nor this case concerns injuries that became permanent and stationary at the same time, but CWCI argues that in the past 30 years, courts have expanded what it calls the *Wilkinson* exception until it has swallowed the rule of *Fuentes*, requiring reform of the apportionment statutes to overrule *Wilkinson* and reinstate *Fuentes*. Without going into the details of its tortured argument, suffice it to say that CWCI has failed to demonstrate either the truth of its premise–that *Wilkinson* and its progeny "swallowed" *Fuentes*– or the logic of its conclusion–that the Legislature repealed section 4750 in order to "purge" cases that did not rely upon it, and "reinforce" the one that did.

CWCI further contends that any compensation calculation other than formula A violates the anti–merger laws, i.e., sections 3208.1 (distinguishing between specific and cumulative injuries), 3208.2 (when disability results from combined effect of two or more injuries, questions of fact and law are separately determined) and 5303 (one cause of action for each injury). But as CWCI acknowledges, the anti–merger statutes were enacted to prevent the defeat of statutes of limitation by the merger of specific into cumulative injuries. (*Western Growers Ins. Co. v. Workers' Comp. Appeals Bd.* (1993) 16 Cal. App. 4th 227, 236–237 [20 Cal. Rptr. 2d 26, 58 Cal. Comp. Cases 323].) Those statutes have no application to the apportionment of disability at issue in the present case. (See *Wilkinson, supra*, 19 Cal. 3d at pp. 501–502, fn. 5.)

Amici also assert that the policy of encouraging employers to hire and retain disabled employees survived repeal of section 4750, but the *Dykes* court did not imply otherwise. On the contrary, as previously indicated (*ante*, p. 6), it expressly considered and rejected the notion that under current law that policy mandates the use of formula A.

Both respondents and CCC advance arguments based on hypotheticals. Respondents posit a case in which "formula C [is] taken to its logical extreme" (worker hired with 99 percent disability becomes 100 percent disabled by injury not statutorily presumed totally disabling (§ 4662)), while CCC sets out a "scenario" (50 percent disability in 1991 followed by 2006 injury resulting in a total of 99 percent disability) in which application of formula C would cost the employer's carrier considerably more than formula A. Even assuming the calculations to be correct and based on all relevant facts and realistic probabilities (a premise disputed by the California Applicants' Attorneys Association), anomalies at the extremes do not undermine the rationale of *Dykes* to the extent that they result not from the use of formula C, but from section 4658's exponentially progressive permanent disability schedule. In any event, we express no opinion about whether formula C should be applied in such cases, but like the *Dykes* court, exercise appropriate restraint by limiting our inquiry to the proper formula for calculating the benefits due under the facts of that case (having been asked to reject its reasoning) and this one.

Finally, CWCI points out that en banc Board decisions are generally entitled to great weight (*Judson Steel Corp. v. Workers' Comp. Appeals Bd.* (1978) 22 Cal. 3d 658, 668 [586 P.2d 564, 150 Cal. Rptr. 250, 43 Cal. Comp. Cases 1205]). In this case, however, the majority view in a seriously splintered Board decision has been expressly rejected in a well–reasoned published appellate court opinion. (See *Hoechst Celanese Corp. v. Franchise Tax Bd.* (2001) 25 Cal. 4th 508, 524 [22 P.3d 324, 106 Cal. Rptr. 2d 548] [amount of deference owed to administrative construction depends on several factors including validity of reasoning and consistency with later pronouncements].)

D. Conclusion

Since none of the parties or their amici have shown either that the *Dykes* analysis is inapplicable to this case, or that *Dykes* itself was wrongly decided, we hold that formula C is the correct method of calculating Nabors's permanent disability benefits. Furthermore, since Nabors's subsequent injury directly caused him to become 80 percent permanently disabled, a life pension was imposed as a matter of law under section 4659, subdivision (a). (*Dykes, supra*, 134 Cal. App. 4th at p. 1555.)

DISPOSITION

The Board's opinion and decision after reconsideration is annulled, and the matter returned to the Board with directions to reverse the WCJ's order and recalculate the amount of Nabors's permanent disability benefits in accordance with this opinion... .

Footnote 1. Unless otherwise indicated, all further statutory references are to the Labor Code.

Footnote 2. In this case, for example, the benefits for 49 percent permanent disability ($42,476) plus the benefits for 31 percent permanent disability ($22,610) (see *ante*, p. 1) add up to appreciably less than the benefits for Nabors's total current permanent disability of 80 percent ($118,795).

Footnote 3. Section 4750, whose purpose was "to encourage employers to hire physically handicapped persons" (*Fuentes, supra*, 16 Cal. 3d at p. 6), then provided in its entirety, "An employee who is suffering from a previous permanent disability or physical impairment and sustains permanent injury thereafter shall not receive from the employer compensation for the later injury in excess of the compensation allowed for such injury *when considered by itself* and not in conjunction with or in relation to the previous disability or impairment. [P] The employer shall not be liable for compensation to such an employee for the combined disability, but only for that portion due to the later injury *as though no prior disability or impairment had existed*. (Italics added.)

Footnote 4. Although it does not directly affect this case, we note an apparent logical inconsistency in this subdivision. "A presumption is either conclusive or rebuttable. Every rebuttable presumption is either (a) a presumption affecting the burden of producing evidence or (b) a presumption affecting the burden of proof." (Evid. Code, § 601; see also Evid. Code, §§ 605 & 606.) It is hard to see, therefore, how a conclusive presumption could affect the burden of proof.

Footnote 5. In order to understand the analysis in *Dykes* and its relationship to this case, it is helpful to keep in mind the intertwined procedural histories of the two cases. Dykes obtained his original award in November 2004 (*Dykes, supra*, 134 Cal. App. 3d at p. 1541); Nabors obtained his the following month. In January 2005, a Board panel denied Gallo's petition for reconsideration in *Dykes* (*ibid.*), and Gallo petitioned for writ of review. While that petition was pending in the Fifth District Court of Appeal, the Board granted Nabors's petition for reconsideration (March 2005) and issued its en banc decision after reconsideration (June 2005). Nabors petitioned this court for writ of review in July 2005, which we granted in October. In December, while this petition was pending, the Fifth District filed its opinion in *Dykes*.

Footnote 6. "The accumulation of all permanent disability awards issued with respect to any one region of the body in favor of one individual employee shall not exceed 100 percent over the employee's lifetime" except under certain enumerated circumstances. (§ 4664, subd. (c)(1).)

Footnote 7. "If the permanent disability is at least 70 percent, but less than 100 percent, 1.5 percent of the average weekly earnings for each 1 percent of disability in excess of 60 percent is to be paid during the remainder of life, after payment for the maximum number of weeks specified in Section 4658 has been made." (§ 4659, subd. (a).)

Page 1407, Column 1, delete second paragraph, beginning 'In E & J Gallo...' which ends with the words "...of Appeal stated' and insert:

In *E & J Gallo Winery v. WCAB (Dykes)* (2006) 70 Cal. Comp. Cases 1644, the Fifth District Court of Appeal stated, in part:

Page 1411, Column 2, fourth paragraph, insert following '...for the petition.'

The Fifth District in *Brodie v. WCAB* (2006) 71 Cal. Comp. Cases 1007, while agreeing with the apportionment formula applied in *Nabors* and *E & J Gallo Winery*, applied the formula in a slightly different way. The Court stated, in part:

INTRODUCTION

California's Workers' Compensation law was extensively amended in 2004 by an urgency statute that took immediate effect and was intended to address a "crisis" in the availability and affordability of workers' compensation insurance. (Stats. 2004, ch. 34, § 49.) This case involves the application of certain parts of the new law that require apportionment where a claimant's permanent disability is due, in part, to a prior injury. The issue discussed here has been addressed in two published decisions of the Court of Appeal: *E & J Gallo Winery v. Workers' Comp. Appeals Bd.* (2005) 134 Cal. App. 4th 1536 [37 Cal. Rptr. 3d 208] (*Dykes*) (review den. Mar. 1, 2006, S140645), and *Nabors v. Workers' Comp. Appeals Bd.* (2006) 140 Cal. App. 4th 217 [44 Cal. Rptr. 3d 312] (review den. Aug. 23, 20006, S145097). While we agree with the apportionment formula applied in those cases, we apply it in a slightly different way.

In this case, Contra Costa County Firefighter Stan Brodie petitions for review of an order of the Workers' Compensation Appeals Board (Board) denying reconsideration of the permanent disability award of a workers' compensation judge (WCJ). He seeks the use of a different apportionment formula from that applied by the WCJ and the Board. We will annul the decision of the Board and remand the matter with directions to recompute Brodie's permanent disability award according to the formula described in our decision.

FACTS AND PROCEDURAL HISTORY

Brodie sustained an industrial injury to his back, spine and right knee on December 4, 2000, and injury to his back and spine cumulative to September 2002, that resulted in 74 percent permanent disability. Over the previous 30 years of his career as a firefighter, Brodie had sustained several industrial injuries to the same body parts for which he was

awarded compensation based on a 44.5 percent permanent disability rating. So, in calculating the award in this case, the WCJ was required to apportion Brodie's disability between his prior injuries and the injuries that underlie his current claim, and in so doing applied new Labor Code sections 4663 and 4664 (Stats. 2004, ch. 34, §§ 34 & 35; see *post*, p. 690). (Footnote 1)

In her decision, the WCJ declared herself bound to follow the Board's en banc decision in *Nabors v. Piedmont Lumber & Mill Company* (2005) 70 Cal. Comp. Cases 856, 857–858 (*Nabors*), which was then pending in Division Two of this court on a petition for review. In *Nabors*, a four–to–two majority of the Board concluded that when apportioning permanent disability benefits, the amount of indemnity is calculated by determining the overall percentage of permanent disability and subtracting therefrom the percentage of disability caused by factors other than the current industrial injury. This formula ("formula A") was determined to be an appropriate method of apportionment under former section 4750 (Footnote 2) in *Fuentes v. Workers' Comp. Appeals Bd.* (1976) 16 Cal. 3d 1, 5–6 [128 Cal. Rptr. 673, 547 P.2d 449] (*Fuentes*). The WCJ thus subtracted 44.5 from 74 and awarded Brodie benefits totaling $20,867.50 based on a 29.5 percent permanent disability rating. But she did so reluctantly, and considered the dissenting view in *Nabors*–in repealing section 4750 and enacting section 4664, the Legislature contemplated a new apportionment formula–to be a more compelling argument. (See *Nabors, supra,* 70 Cal. Comp. Cases at pp. 864–865, dis. opn. of Caplane, Comr.)

In her report and recommendation on Brodie's petition for reconsideration, the WCJ again expressed her disagreement with the *Nabors* majority, and her belief that under section 4664, an employer is liable for that portion of a worker's overall disability that exceeds his prior level of disability. But she was bound by *Nabors*, and urged the Board to grant reconsideration and revisit its *Nabors* analysis. (By this time, Division Two of this court had granted review in *Nabors*.) (Footnote 3) The Board denied reconsideration, and adopted and incorporated that part of the WCJ's report that acknowledged her duty to follow the Board's en banc decisions (Cal. Code Regs., tit. 8, § 10341), which also binds the Board until such decisions are stayed or overruled by an appellate court (*Diggle v. Sierra Sands Unified School District* (2005) 70 Cal. Comp. Cases 1480, 1481 ["significant" Board panel decision]).

This timely writ petition followed.

DISCUSSION

The issue here is: When making an award for permanent disability under the 2004 amendments to the workers' compensation law, how does a prior permanent disability affect the measure of indemnity due to a claimant? Two sections of the new law address the apportionment of employer responsibility for such injuries. Section 4663, subdivision (a) provides that "[a]pportionment of permanent disability shall be based on causation." Section 4664, subdivision (a) provides, "The employer shall only be liable for the percentage of permanent disability directly caused by the injury arising out of and occurring in the course of employment." So, any award of permanent disability must take causation into account, and an employer is responsible for the percentage of disability caused by a work–related injury.

But fulfilling the legislative mandate to apportion employer responsibility on the basis of causation is not so easy, because "[i]n adopting Sen[ate] Bill 899, the Legislature did not outline any particular method for apportioning either a permanent disability award or a life pension." (*Dykes, supra*, 134 Cal. App. 4th at p. 1552.) In choosing the appropriate formula, we will follow the statutory mandate that an "employer shall only be liable for the percentage of permanent disability directly cased by the injury" (§ 4664, subd. (a)) with several precepts of statutory construction in mind: The workers' compensation laws are to be liberally construed to extend benefits to people injured while working. (§ 3202.) To the extent the words of the statute can lead us to the result, we will follow them, giving words their ordinary and proper meaning. (*People v. Mel Mack Co.* (1975) 53 Cal. App. 3d 621, 626 [126 Cal. Rptr. 505].) But we are also aware of the historical background that led to the passage of Senate Bill No. 899 (2003–2004 Reg. Sess.), and to the extent the statutory language does not suffice, we will consider this historical context. (*People v. Mel Mack Co., supra*, 53 Cal. App. 3d 621.)

In *Dykes* and *Nabors*, two different districts of the Court of Appeal considered the issue presented here. "We acknowledge we are not bound by an opinion of another District Court of Appeal, however persuasive it might be. [Citation.] We respect stare decisis, however, which serves the important goals of stability in the law and predictability of decision. Thus, we ordinarily follow the decisions of other districts without good reason to disagree. [Citation.]" (*Greyhound Lines, Inc. v. County of Santa Clara* (1986) 187 Cal. App. 3d 480, 485 [231 Cal. Rptr. 702].) So we largely follow the decisions in *Dykes* and *Nabors*.

The *Dykes* and *Nabors* courts discussed and applied an apportionment formula first articulated but rejected by our Supreme Court in *Fuentes, supra*, 16 Cal. 3d 1. There, the court announced the appropriate method to determine an employer's liability for a permanent disability in cases where the overall disability is due in part to a preexisting injury. (*Id.* at pp. 3–4.) The issue arose because 1971 amendments changed the schedule of permanent disability benefits (§ 4658) from a linear one that awarded four weeks of compensation for each one percent of permanent disability, to one in which the number of weekly benefits increases *exponentially* in proportion to increasing percentages of disability. (*Fuentes, supra*, at p. 4.) Thus, for example, the benefits for 44.5 percent permanent disability plus the benefits for 29.5 percent permanent disability add up to appreciably less than the benefits for 74 percent permanent disability.

The *Fuentes* court's analysis was informed by and turned upon the interplay between section 4658 and former section 4750 (see *ante*, fn. 2), which was repealed by the 2004 amendments to the workers' compensation law. (*Fuentes, supra*, 16 Cal. 3d at p. 6; Stats. 2004, ch. 34, § 37.) The court considered three possible formulas that could be used to apportion liability. Under "formula A" the percentage of

non–industrial disability is subtracted from the claimant's overall disability to determine the compensable percentage. Under "formula B" the number of weeks of compensation allowable for a claimant's total disability is multiplied by the percentage of the injury that was industrially related to arrive at the compensable portion of disability. Under "formula C" the percentage of overall current disability is converted to its monetary equivalent, from which is subtracted the dollar value of the percentage of prior disability. (*Fuentes, supra*, at p. 5.)

The *Fuentes* court applied formula A because it was the method of apportionment that best gave effect to former section 4750 (*Fuentes, supra*, 16 Cal. 3d at p. 8), but the *Dykes* court concluded the *Fuentes* decision is no longer controlling in light of the repeal of section 4750 (*Dykes, supra*, 134 Cal. App. 4th at pp. 1548–1549). We agree. Amendment of a statute that has received judicial construction is an indication of legislative intent to change the law. (*O'Brien v. Dudenhoeffer* (1993) 16 Cal. App. 4th 327, 335 [19 Cal. Rptr. 2d 826].)

"[T]he Legislature contemplated a variation in determining apportionment by repealing section 4750 and replacing it with different language in section 4664 for apportioning liability among multiple injuries." (*Dykes, supra*, 134 Cal. App. 4th at p. 1550; *Nabors, supra*, 140 Cal. App. 4th at pp. 223–224.) While the new law can be interpreted to permit several different approaches to apportionment that would yield disparate results, the plain language of section 4664, subdivision (a) means that "[a]n employer is liable for the direct consequences of a work–related injury, nothing more and nothing less." (*Dykes, supra*, at p. 1551.) Like the *Dykes* and *Nabors* courts, we find formula C to be the method that best effectuates the directive of section 4664, subdivision (a) when apportioning responsibility between a current and prior disabling injury. (Footnote 4)

Although Senate Bill No. 899 repealed section 4750, the exponentially progressive permanent disability tables embodied in section 4658, which most clearly justify the use of formula C, survive. The other formulas considered in *Fuentes* treat the employee as though no prior permanent disability existed, and in light of the exponentially progressive permanent disability tables, create a windfall to the employer at the employee's expense. They do not seem to fix responsibility for an award in a way that takes both causation and the progressive nature of disability into account. Before Senate Bill No. 899, a claimant could defeat apportionment by showing that he or she was completely rehabilitated from the prior injury; this is no longer possible (§ 4664, subd. (b)). (Footnote 5) Section 4664, subdivision (a) requires that an award take into account the prior disability by ensuring that benefits are awarded only for the "percentage of permanent disability directly caused by" the recent injury. Formula C compensates for the additional percentage of disability caused by the most recent compensable injury. Finally, by taking prior disability into account and fixing employer responsibility for only that portion of a disability caused by the current injury, section 4664 fulfills the purpose of former section 4750 "to encourage employers to hire physically handicapped persons" (*Fuentes, supra,* 16 Cal. 3d at p. 6; see also *Dykes, supra,* 134 Cal. App. 4th at p. 1550). Application of formula C does not undermine that objective. All these reasons lead us to conclude that formula C is the proper means to apportion employer responsibility between prior and current permanently disabling injuries.

But in applying formula C, we respectfully elaborate upon and clarify the approach taken in *Dykes.* To arrive at the amount of compensation due the claimant, the *Dykes* court applied a dollar credit equal to the amount of a previous disability award against the scheduled benefits for the current overall disability level. (*Dykes, supra,* 134 Cal. App. 4th at p. 1555.) This is one way to interpret the statement in the very same paragraph that Dykes was "entitled to the difference between a 20.5 percent disability and a 73 percent disability on the permanent disability table applicable for the subsequent injury." (*Dykes, supra,* at p. 1554.) (Footnote 6) Interpreting that language somewhat differently, we calculate the dollar value of a prior award in such a way that the measure of compensation reflects "the direct consequences of a work–related injury, nothing more and nothing less" (*id.* at p. 1551).

In cases like these, a prior permanent disability award might be many years old. Thus, simply crediting the *amount* of the prior award against the benefits due for current overall disability seems to work a disadvantage to the employer. It fails to take into account the relative worth of the prior award over time, as well as possible changes in benefit schedules or an employee's average weekly earnings, which are factors in the permanent disability computation (§ 4658). A simple dollar–for–dollar credit is also unworkable when the prior disability was caused by a nonindustrial injury, in which case there would be no prior award at all.

Instead, we favor the literal application of formula C as articulated in *Fuentes:* the overall current disability "is converted into its monetary equivalent" and "[f]rom this figure is subtracted the [current] dollar value ... of the ... percent of [prior] disability." (*Fuentes, supra,* 16 Cal. 3d at p. 5.) This formulation does not apply a credit for or subtract the amount of a previous *award.* Instead, the *Fuentes* court calculated the value of the noncompensable portion of the award (attributable in that case to a prior *non*industrial injury) and subtracted that value from the value of the current overall disability. (*Ibid.*) This application of formula C ensures that irrespective of the passage of time since a prior award, its size, or whether the prior injury was even compensable, an employer will be responsible only for the additional portion of disability caused by the current compensable injury, "nothing more and nothing less."

Applying formula C in this way to Brodie's case illustrates the point. Brodie injured his back, spine and right knee in 2000, and had an injury to his back and spine cumulative to September 2002. Following these injuries, he received a permanent disability rating of 74 percent, which would entitle him to an award of $106,375. (Footnote 7) Prior injuries to these same body parts had left Brodie with a preexisting permanent disability rating of 44.5 percent, for which he had received awards totaling $27,167.50.

The *Dykes* decision would permit us to subtract from the total benefits payable for a 74 percent disability the amount of Brodie's prior award. Therefore, Brodie's total award for the most recent 29.5 percent of his disability would be $79,207.50. But this amount of benefits exceeds the currently scheduled amount for that portion of a 74 percent disability that occurs after a rating of 44.5 percent. Moreover, it does not reflect a reduction for the relative value today of the $27,167.50 that Brodie was awarded in 1987 and 1999. (Footnote 8) Nor does subtraction of the prior award reflect any possible changes in benefit schedules or Brodie's employment status that might affect the calculation of a current award.

We think the better approach is to subtract from the amount of benefits currently scheduled for a 74 percent permanent disability rating, the current dollar value of the percentage of preexisting disability. (Footnote 9) Brodie's prior 44.5 percent disability is now valued at $38,675. When this is subtracted from the $106,375 scheduled for a 74 percent disability, Brodie's permanent disability award is $67,700 for the last 29.5 percent of his disability. This amount reflects the scheduled amount due Brodie for the final percentage of his disability caused by the most recent compensable injuries, nothing more and nothing less.

Finally, just as in *Dykes* and *Nabors,* since Brodie's total disability exceeds 70 percent due to his most recent injuries, a life pension was imposed as a matter of law under section 4659, subdivision (a). (*Dykes, supra,* 134 Cal. App. 4th at p. 1555; *Nabors, supra,* 140 Cal. App. 4th at p. 228.)

DISPOSITION

The Board's order denying reconsideration is annulled, and the matter is returned to the Board with directions to grant reconsideration, reverse the WCJ's order, and recalculate the amount of permanent disability benefits due Brodie in accordance with the method described in this opinion... .

Footnote 1. All further statutory references are to the Labor Code.

Footnote 2. Former section 4750 provided in its entirety, "An employee who is suffering from a previous permanent disability or physical impairment and sustains permanent injury thereafter shall not receive from the employer compensation for the later injury in excess of the compensation allowed for such injury *when considered by itself* and not in conjunction with or in relation to the previous disability or impairment. [P] The employer shall not be liable for compensation to such an employee for the combined disability, but only for that portion due to the later injury *as though no prior disability or impairment had existed.* (Italics added.)

Footnote 3. Hereafter, "*Nabors*" will refer to the appellate opinion in that case (see *ante,* p. 688).

Footnote 4. The *Dykes* court limited its holding to the situation in which an employee received the prior disability award while working for the same self–insured employer. (*Dykes, supra,* 134 Cal. App. 4th at p. 1540.) The *Nabors* court did not consider that limitation to be an obstacle to applying the *Dykes* rationale in a broader context (*Nabors, supra,* 140 Cal. App. 4th at pp. 225–226), and neither do we.

Footnote 5. This subdivision provides in pertinent part, "If the applicant has received a prior award of permanent disability, it shall be conclusively presumed that the prior permanent disability exists at the time of any subsequent industrial injury."

Footnote 6. The *Nabors* court ended its summary of the *Dykes* opinion with this language (*Nabors, supra,* 140 Cal. App. 4th at p. 225), but held only that formula C was the correct method of calculating Nabors's permanent disability benefits (*id.* at p. 228), without, as it were, doing the math.

Footnote 7. In calculating Brodie's benefits, we note that it appears uncontested that his salary entitled him to maximum weekly benefits. Based on his dates of injury, we apply the values for disability found in 2 O'Brien, California Workers' Compensation Claims and Benefits (11th ed. 2004) Appendix 7–Permanent Disability Indemnity Chart.

Footnote 8. Under various methods of computing the relative value of money, Brodie's 1987 award of $2,835 and his 1999 award of $24,332.50 can range from $32,234.94 to $40,251.95 in 2006 dollars. The range of relative value results from the growth index that is used to make a comparative value calculation. Application of changes in gross domestic product, the consumer price index or unskilled wage rates all yield different results. (See generally Williamson, *What Is the Relative Value?* (Economic History Services, June 2006) <http://eh.net/hmit/compare/> [as of August 30, 2006].)

Footnote 9. At oral argument, counsel for Brodie acknowledged the conceptual preferability of this approach. This approach would have no practical effect in *Dykes,* where it appears the claimant was entitled to maximum benefits and the same benefit schedule applied to his preexisting and current injuries. (See *Dykes, supra,* 134 Cal. App. 4th at p. 1541, and *ante,* fn. 7.) In *Nabors,* though the claimant appears to be entitled to maximum benefits, the method we describe yields a different result than would a credit for the dollar amount of the previous award, because of an intervening change in the benefits schedule. (See *Nabors, supra,* 140 Cal. App. 4th at p. 220, and *ante,* fn. 7.)

In a decision affirming the Board's decision in *Nabors* but declining to follow the apportionment formula applied in *E & J Gallo Winery*, the Court of Appeal, Third District, in *Welcher et al v. WCAB* (2006) 71 Cal. Comp. Cases 1087 stated, in part:

These four consolidated cases raise the issue of how to properly apportion permanent disability in light of the 2004 amendments to the workers' compensation law. (Stats. 2004, ch. 34.) We conclude that in repealing Labor Code (Footnote 1) section 4750 and in enacting new sections 4663 and 4664 to govern apportionment, the Legislature did not intend to alter the apportionment method adopted by the California Supreme Court 30 years ago in *Fuentes v. Workers' Comp. Appeals Bd.* (1976) 16 Cal. 3d 1 [128 Cal.

Rptr. 673, 547 P.2d 449] (*Fuentes*). In so concluding, we agree with the decision of the Workers' Compensation Appeals Board (WCAB) in *Nabors v. Piedmont Lumber & Mill Company* (2005) 70 Cal. Comp. Cases 856 (*Nabors*) and disagree with our colleagues in the Fifth Appellate District, who reached the opposite conclusion in *E & J Gallo Winery v. Workers' Comp. Appeals Bd.* (2005) 134 Cal. App. 4th 1536 [37 Cal. Rptr. 3d 208] (*Gallo*), as well as our colleagues in Division Two of the First Appellate District, who followed *Gallo* in *Nabors v. Workers' Comp. Appeals Bd.* (2006) 140 Cal. App. 4th 217 [44 Cal. Rptr. 3d 312]. Accordingly, we will affirm the decisions of the WCAB in these cases.

FACTUAL AND PROCEDURAL BACKGROUND

We begin by briefly summarizing the factual and procedural background of each case now before us.

A.

Kenneth Dee Welcher

Welcher sustained an industrial injury in July 1990 when his right arm and leg were caught in a conveyor belt. A stipulated award determined that this injury resulted in a permanent disability of 62.5 percent, and Welcher received $32,193 in permanent disability benefits.

Later work as a laborer for Hat Creek Construction, Inc., through March 2001 resulted in cumulative injury to Welcher's right leg that led to amputation below the knee. The parties stipulated that Welcher's level of permanent disability is now 71 percent.

The workers' compensation judge (WCJ) determined that "[a]pportionment is decided by subtracting percentage from percentage" and awarded Welcher $3,360 in permanent disability benefits from State Compensation Insurance Fund (SCIF) (Hat Creek's workers' compensation carrier). Apparently, the WCJ reached this figure by subtracting Welcher's previous level of permanent disability (62.5) from his current level of permanent disability (71) and rounding the result down (8.5 down to 8). Thus, by the WCJ's calculation, SCIF was liable for 8 percent of Welcher's permanent disability, which corresponds to 24 weeks of payments at $140 per week (24 x $140 = $3,360). (See §§ 4453, subd. (b)(2), 4658, subd. (b)(1) & (2).)

Welcher filed a petition for reconsideration with the WCAB, arguing that his benefits should be determined not by subtracting his previous level of permanent disability from his current level of permanent disability, but by subtracting the monetary value of his previous award ($32,193) from the monetary value of a current award of 71 percent disability ($100,165). Relying on its own en banc decision in *Nabors, supra,* 70 Cal. Comp. Cases at page 856, (Footnote 2) the WCAB disagreed and denied Welcher's petition.

B.

Jack Strong

In November 1995, while employed by the City and County of San Francisco (the City), Strong sustained an industrial injury to his left knee which resulted in permanent disability of 34.5 percent. He received permanent disability benefits of $25,830.

In February 1999, Strong sustained another industrial injury while employed by the City, this time to his left shoulder, left knee and ankle, and right wrist, resulting in permanent disability of 42 percent (after apportionment for the prior injury) and permanent disability benefits of $35,700.

In May 2002, Strong sustained a third industrial injury while working for the City, this time to his back. The parties stipulated that Strong's overall level of permanent disability is now 70 percent. A disability evaluation specialist determined that 60 percent of Strong's permanent disability was due to his prior injuries to his shoulder, knee, ankle, and wrist, while 10 percent was due to his current injury to his back. Based on this apportionment, the WCJ determined the current injury caused permanent disability of 10 percent, and thus the WCJ awarded Strong permanent disability benefits of $4,235 (30.25 weeks of payments at $140 per week).

Strong filed a petition for reconsideration with the WCAB, arguing that "there cannot be apportionment to disability occurring to other regions of the body" and that, even if there can be, "apportionment should be determined by subtracting the monetary equivalent of the pre–existing disability from the current monetary equivalent of the overall disability."

The WCAB granted Strong's petition and in an en banc decision determined that section 4664 "requires the apportionment of overlapping permanent disabilities," even when those disabilities involve different regions of the body. Based on its decision in *Nabors*, the WCAB also concluded that the WCJ had properly apportioned Strong's permanent disability between the prior and current injuries. Accordingly, the WCAB affirmed the WCJ's award.

C.

Aurora Lopez

Lopez sustained an industrial injury to her back and lower extremities in September 1998. The parties stipulated that she has an overall permanent disability of 100 percent: 79 percent caused by her industrial injury and 21 percent caused by other factors. Applying the WCAB's decision in *Nabors*, the WCJ awarded Lopez permanent disability benefits of $80,910.73 for a 79 percent permanent disability.

Lopez filed a petition for reconsideration with the WCAB, arguing that *Nabors* was wrongly decided and that she "should receive the benefit of [a] 100 percent disability rating, which, in [her] case, is $172.20 per week for life," minus the amount of benefits that would be payable for 21 percent permanent disability ("$ 12,080.00 payable in 75.50 weeks at $159.43 per week"). The WCAB denied her petition.

D.

Henry L. Williams, Jr.

While employed by United Airlines, Williams sustained a cumulative industrial injury to his lumbar spine ending in August 2003. The parties stipulated that Williams's overall level of permanent disability is 43 percent. Williams had previously received $17,972.50 in permanent disability

benefits for a 28 percent permanent disability based on an earlier injury to his lumbar spine while working for the same employer. The WCJ apportioned Williams's permanent disability pursuant to *Nabors*, concluding that the current injury resulted in 15 percent permanent disability, for an award of $9,296.25 in permanent disability benefits.

Williams filed a petition for reconsideration with the WCAB, arguing that *Nabors* was wrongly decided and that "the proper way to apportion is to convert [his] present overall percentage of permanent disability into its current monetary equivalent and then subtract the dollar value of [his] prior permanent disability award." The WCAB denied his petition.

DISCUSSION

I.

Apportioning Permanent Disability

The primary question in these four cases is how permanent disability is to be apportioned in light of the Legislature's recent overhaul of the workers' compensation laws. Under *Nabors*, the WCAB apportions permanent disability by subtracting the percentage of permanent disability caused by factors other than the current industrial injury from the overall percentage of permanent disability, thus determining the percentage of permanent disability caused by the current injury. The WCAB then determines the monetary value of permanent disability benefits payable for this percentage of permanent disability. The four claimants contend this is incorrect and that the WCAB should instead subtract the monetary value of the percentage of permanent disability caused by other factors from the monetary value of the overall percentage of permanent disability.

For reasons we will explain, we conclude the WCAB's approach is the correct one.

We begin with a discussion of permanent disability, followed by tracing how permanent disability has been apportioned in California. We will then turn to the WCAB's position on apportionment under the current law, and a recent appellate court opinion on the subject, before turning to our own analysis of the law.

A.

Fuentes and Former Section 4750

"Permanent disability is the disability that remains after the healing period. An injured worker is entitled to payments for a permanent disability that affects the worker's ability to compete in the open labor market." (1 Cal. Workers' Compensation Practice (Cont. Ed. Bar 4th ed. 2005) § 5.1, p. 276.)

"Permanent disability is expressed in percentages. If the disability is less than 100 percent, it is permanent partial disability. A worker who suffers permanent partial disability is entitled to a certain number of weeks of indemnity payments for each percent of the rating." (1 Cal. Workers' Compensation Practice, *supra*, § 5.7, at p. 280.)

Section 4658 provides generally that if an industrial injury causes permanent disability, then "the percentage of disability to total disability shall be determined, and the disability payment computed" as described in that statute. (§ 4658, subds. (a), (b), (c), & (d).) "Section 4658, as it read prior to April 1, 1972, provided that, for each percentage point of permanent disability which was of industrial origin, an injured worker was entitled to four weeks of compensation." (*Fuentes*, *supra*, 16 Cal. 3d at p. 4.) Thus, a worker who was 10 percent permanently disabled was entitled to 40 weeks of payments, while a worker who was 90 percent permanently disabled was entitled to 360 weeks of payments. (Footnote 3) (See *ibid.*)

"However, in 1971 the Legislature amended section 4658, establishing a different method for computing the number of weekly benefits to be awarded. Under the new statute, ... the number of weekly benefits increase[d] exponentially in proportion to the percentage of the disability." (*Fuentes*, *supra*, 16 Cal. 3d at p. 4.) As an illustration of this change, under the new statute a worker who was 10 percent permanently disabled (who was formerly entitled to 40 weeks of payments) was now entitled to 30.25 weeks of payments, while a worker who was 90 percent permanently disabled (who was formerly entitled to 360 weeks of payments) was now entitled to 541.25 weeks of payments. (See *ibid.*)

This change in the law gave rise to conflicts over the proper method for apportioning an employee's permanent disability. "Apportionment is the process employed ... to segregate the residuals of an industrial injury from those attributable to other industrial injuries, or to nonindustrial factors, in order to fairly allocate the legal responsibility." (*Ashley v. Workers' Comp. Appeals Bd.* (1995) 37 Cal. App. 4th 320, 326 [43 Cal. Rptr. 2d 589].) "Generally, an employer is held responsible in the workers' compensation system only for the disability of an injured employee arising from the particular employment with that employer, but not for disability fairly attributable to periods of employment elsewhere or to nonindustrial conditions." (*Ibid.*)

The conflicts over the proper method for apportioning permanent disability in light of the 1971 amendment to section 4658 reached the Supreme Court five years later in *Fuentes*. In that case, the worker suffered from "cumulative injury to his lungs resulting in an over–all permanent disability rating of 58 percent. One–half of this disability was found by the referee to be industrially related, one–quarter (25 percent) was the result of cigarette smoking, and the final one–quarter (25 percent) due to nonindustrial causes. Of the 25 percent attributable to cigarette smoking, one–third (8.33 percent of over–all disability) was found to have been incurred in the course of 'on–the–job' smoking and [wa]s accordingly compensable. Thus, of the total 58 percent disability, approximately 33.75 percent (58 percent x 58.33 percent) was industrially related. The remaining 24.25 percent was attributable to other factors, and being nonindustrial in origin [wa]s not compensable." (*Fuentes*, *supra*, 16 Cal. 3d at pp. 3–4.)

The parties in *Fuentes* "suggested that in computing the number of weekly benefits to which [the worker wa]s entitled under the new section 4658 there [we]re three possible methods which m[ight] be utilized, described for the sake of convenience, as formulas A, B, and C. Under former section 4658 the compensation was the same regardless of which formula was applied. However, as a result of the 1971 amendments substantial differences ensue[d] in the amount awarded a claimant depending on which formula [wa]s utilized.

"Under formula A, ... there [wa]s subtracted from the total disability that portion which [wa]s nonindustrial, the remainder being the amount of compensable disability. Thus in the matter before [the Supreme Court] 24.25 percent, representing nonindustrial origin, [wa]s deducted from the 58 percent total disability with a net compensable disability of 33.75 percent. Under the schedule established by section 4658, subdivision (a), this entitled [the worker] to 143.25 weekly benefits which [could] be converted in terms of dollars to an award of $10,027.50.

"Formula B contemplate[d], first, determination of the number of statutory weekly benefits authorized under section 4658 for a 58 percent disability, namely, 297. This figure [wa]s then multiplied by the percentage of industrially related disability (58.33). The product [wa]s 173.25 weeks, which result[ed] in a total monetary award of $12,127.50.

"[Under] formula C, ... the 58 percent permanent disability [wa]s converted into its monetary equivalent of $20,790. From this figure [wa]s subtracted the dollar value ($ 6,422.50) of the 24.25 percent of the noncompensable, nonindustrial disability. The result [wa]s an award of $14,367.50, or the equivalent of 205.25 weekly benefits." (*Fuentes*, *supra*, 16 Cal. 3d at p. 5.)

Based on "the express and unequivocal language of [former] section 4750," the Supreme Court concluded that formula A was "the proper one." (*Fuentes*, *supra*, 16 Cal. 3d at p. 6.) At that time, former section 4750 provided as follows: " 'An employee who is suffering from a previous permanent disability or physical impairment and sustains permanent injury thereafter shall not receive from the employer compensation for the later injury in excess of the compensation allowed for such injury when considered by itself and not in conjunction with or in relation to the previous disability or impairment. [P] The employer shall not be liable for compensation to such an employee for the combined disability, but only for that portion due to the later injury as though no prior disability or impairment had existed.' " (*Fuentes*, *supra*, 16 Cal. 3d at p. 5.)

According to the Supreme Court, "In enacting section 4750, the Legislature ... expressed a clear intent that the liability of one who employs a previously disabled worker shall, in the event of a subsequent injury, be limited to that percentage of the over–all disability resulting from the later harm considered alone and as if it were the original injury. The principle has been expressed that '... [I]ndustry is to be charged only for those injuries arising out of and in the course of employment and only for the result of that particular injury when considered by itself and not in conjunction with or in relation to a previous injury.' " (*Fuentes*, *supra*, 16 Cal. 3d at p. 6, quoting *Gardner v. Industrial Acc. Com.* (1938) 28 Cal. App. 2d 682, 684 [83 P.2d 295].)

The court explained that "only formula A results in an award complying with the provisions of section 4750. [The worker] has suffered a compensable disability of 33.75

percent. Under formula B, however, he would receive an award which, under the rates provided for in section 4658, subdivision (a), is equivalent to the amount given for a disability carrying a rating of approximately 39 percent. Application of formula C results in a recovery which is the same as that authorized by section 4658, subdivision (a), for a rating of 44 percent. This arithmetic leads to the inevitable conclusion that neither method B nor C can be reconciled with the mandate of section 4750 that the compensation for a subsequent injury be computed 'as though no prior disability or impairment had existed.' On the contrary, B and C result in an enhancement of the benefits due to the existence of a preexisting physical impairment." (*Fuentes, supra*, 16 Cal. 3d at p. 6.)

The court disagreed with an argument that there was "an irreconcilable conflict between the legislative intent to increase workers' compensation benefits as manifested by section 4658, on the one hand, and the limiting effect of section 4750 on the other" and stated the following: "Section 4658 may be considered as a general provision establishing the amount of compensation benefits for a permanent disability, and section 4750 may be viewed as a specific rule limiting the benefits available in those cases where the employee has a preexisting permanent disability and thereafter sustains a further permanent injury. When so construed the statutes in question are complementary, not contradictory, and function together quite harmoniously, thus, serving the twin goals of providing proportionately greater benefits for more serious injuries while at the same time protecting employers from bearing a disproportionate share of a financial burden resulting from cumulative injuries." (*Fuentes, supra*, 16 Cal. 3d at p. 7.)

The court recognized that "under formula A ... a worker who suffers a single injury resulting in, for example, a disability rating of 50 percent, will receive greater benefits than one who sustains two successive injuries each of which causes a permanent disability of 25 percent when considered alone. This result, however, is neither unjust nor unfair ... . Rather, it is a consequence of the recent amendments to section 4658 and is consistent with the ... policy of encouraging employers to hire the disabled. There being no evidence to the contrary, this court must assume that such a result was contemplated by the Legislature." (Footnote 4) (*Fuentes, supra*, 16 Cal. 3d at p. 8.)

B.

Senate Bill No. 899 and Sections 4663 and 4664

"On April 19, 2004, Governor Schwarzenegger signed into law Senate Bill No. 899 (2003–2004 Reg. Sess.), a package of reforms to the workers' compensation laws. (Stats. 2004, ch. 34.) (Bill No. 899.) The legislation took effect immediately as urgency legislation. [Citation.] Bill No. 899 changed, among other things, the law with regard to apportionment of permanent disability. (Stats. 2004, ch. 34, §§ 33 [repealed Lab. Code, § 4663 (former § 4663)], 34 [added new Lab. Code, § 4663 (§ 4663)], 35 [added Lab. Code, § 4664 (§ 4664)], 37 [repealed Lab. Code, § 4750 [former § 4750]], 38 [repealed Lab. Code, § 4750.5 [former § 4750.5]].)" (*Rio Linda Union School Dist. v. Workers' Comp. Appeals Bd.* (2005) 131 Cal. App. 4th 517, 521 [31

Cal. Rptr. 3d 789], fn. omitted.)

Under Senate Bill No. 899 (2003–2004 Reg. Sess.) (Sen. Bill No. 899), two new statutes govern apportionment: sections 4663 and 4664. Section 4663 provides as follows:

"(a) Apportionment of permanent disability shall be based on causation.

"(b) Any physician who prepares a report addressing the issue of permanent disability due to a claimed industrial injury shall in that report address the issue of causation of the permanent disability.

"(c) In order for a physician's report to be considered complete on the issue of permanent disability, it must include an apportionment determination. A physician shall make an apportionment determination by finding what approximate percentage of the permanent disability was caused by the direct result of injury arising out of and occurring in the course of employment and what approximate percentage of the permanent disability was caused by other factors both before and subsequent to the industrial injury, including prior industrial injuries. If the physician is unable to include an apportionment determination in his or her report, the physician shall state the specific reasons why the physician could not make a determination of the effect of that prior condition on the permanent disability arising from the injury. The physician shall then consult with other physicians or refer the employee to another physician from whom the employee is authorized to seek treatment or evaluation in accordance with this division in order to make the final determination.

"(d) An employee who claims an industrial injury shall, upon request, disclose all previous permanent disabilities or physical impairments."

Second, section 4664 provides as follows:

"(a) The employer shall only be liable for the percentage of permanent disability directly caused by the injury arising out of and occurring in the course of employment.

"(b) If the applicant has received a prior award of permanent disability, it shall be conclusively presumed that the prior permanent disability exists at the time of any subsequent industrial injury. This presumption is a presumption affecting the burden of proof.

"(c)(1) The accumulation of all permanent disability awards issued with respect to any one region of the body in favor of one individual employee shall not exceed 100 percent over the employee's lifetime unless the employee's injury or illness is conclusively presumed to be total in character pursuant to Section 4662. As used in this section, the regions of the body are the following:

"(A) Hearing.

"(B) Vision.

"(C) Mental and behavioral disorders.

"(D) The spine.

"(E) The upper extremities, including the shoulders.

"(F) The lower extremities, including the hip joints.

"(G) The head, face, cardiovascular system, respiratory system, and all other systems or regions of the body not listed in subparagraphs (A) to (F), inclusive.

"(2) Nothing in this section shall be construed to permit the permanent disability rating for each individual injury sustained by an employee arising from the same industrial accident, when added together, from exceeding 100 percent."

In *Rio Linda Union School Dist. v. Workers' Comp. Appeals Bd.*, *supra*, 131 Cal. App. 4th at page 531, this court held that "new section 4663 and section 4664 are applicable to any case still pending [on enactment of Senate Bill No. 899 on April 19, 2004], except those cases that are finally concluded subject only to the WCAB's continuing jurisdiction under sections 5803 and 5804." (See also *Kleemann v. Workers' Comp. Appeals Bd.* (2005) 127 Cal. App. 4th 274 [25 Cal. Rptr. 3d 448]; *Marsh v. Workers' Comp. Appeals Bd.* (2005) 130 Cal. App. 4th 906 [30 Cal. Rptr. 3d 598].)

C.

Nabors

In *Nabors*, *supra*, 70 Cal. Comp. Cases at page 856, the WCAB considered, en banc, the proper method for apportioning permanent disability in light of Senate Bill No. 899. In *Nabors*, a four–member majority of the WCAB (Commissioners O'Brien, Cuneo, Murray, and Brass) decided that when the WCAB "awards permanent disability after apportionment, the amount of indemnity due [the] applicant is calculated by determining the overall percentage of permanent disability and then subtracting the percentage of permanent disability caused by other factors under section 4663(c) or previously awarded under section 4664(b); the remainder is [the] applicant's final percentage of permanent disability for which indemnity is calculated pursuant to section[s] 4453 and 4658." (*Nabors*, *supra*, 70 Cal. Comp. Cases at pp. 857–858.) The majority based its decision on "[t]he plain terms of sections 4663(c) and 4664(a)," which "mandate that the percentage of non–industrial or previously awarded permanent disability be subtracted from the overall percentage of permanent disability in the same manner as formula A adopted by the Supreme Court in *Fuentes*." (*Nabors*, *supra*, 70 Cal. Comp. Cases at p. 861.)

One dissenting member of the WCAB believed "that the express language of section 4663 as amended by SB 899 requires that application of formula B discussed in *Fuentes*." (*Nabors*, *supra*, 70 Cal. Comp. Cases at p. 862 (dis. opn. of Rabine, Chairman).) The other dissenting member believed "that the express language of sections 4663 and 4664 as amended by SB 899 requires the application of formula C discussed in *Fuentes*." (*Nabors*, *supra*, 70 Cal. Comp. Cases at p. 864 (dis. opn. of Caplane, Comr.).)

D.

Gallo

In *Gallo*, *supra*, 134 Cal. App. 4th at page 1536, the claimant was rendered 73 percent disabled following an industrial injury to his back in October 2002. (*Id.* at p. 1541.) He had previously received a permanent partial disability award for an earlier industrial injury to his back in September 1996 while working for the same employer. (*Ibid.*) By stipulation, that earlier award (amounting to $11,680) was based on a determination that he was 20.5 percent permanently disabled. (*Ibid.*)

Following a hearing in November 2004, the WCJ apportioned the claimant's permanent disability by determining the monetary value of a 73 percent disability award ($ 104,305) and subtracting the $11,680 the claimant previously received for his earlier injury. (*Gallo*, *supra*, 134 Cal. App. 4th at p. 1541.) Essentially, this was the equivalent of applying formula C from *Fuentes* (except that in *Fuentes* formula C involved subtracting "the dollar value ... of the [percentage of] noncompensable, nonindustrial disability"). (*Fuentes*, *supra*, 16 Cal. 3d at p. 5.)

The employer petitioned the WCAB for reconsideration, "contending that the Labor Code mandated subtracting the percentage, not dollar amount, of the prior award." (*Gallo*, *supra*, 134 Cal. App. 4th at p. 1541.) Five months before the WCAB's en banc decision in *Nabors*, a three–member panel of the WCAB denied reconsideration. (Footnote 5) (*Gallo*, at p. 1541.) The employer sought appellate court review, and the Fifth Appellate District affirmed the denial of reconsideration, approving the use of formula C to apportion permanent disability under new sections 4663 and 4664. (*Gallo*, *supra*, 134 Cal. App. 4th at pp. 1553–1555.) The *Gallo* court, however, expressly "limit[ed its] analysis to the [situation] where the injured employee received a prior disability award while working for the same self–insured employer." (Footnote 6) (*Id.* at pp. 1550–1551.) Recently, Division Two of the First Appellate District followed *Gallo* because the court found "no compelling reason ha[d] been advanced ... to disagree with it." (*Nabors v. Workers' Comp. Appeals Bd.*, *supra*, 140 Cal. App. 4th at p. 226.)

E.

Apportionment Under Sections 4663 and 4664

In each of the four cases before us, the primary question is whether the WCAB properly apportioned permanent disability by subtracting the percentage of permanent disability caused by factors other than the current industrial injury from the overall percentage of permanent disability to determine the percentage of permanent disability for which the employer or its insurer is liable, before determining the compensation payable for that percentage of disability under section 4658. To answer this question, we must construe the new apportionment statutes, sections 4663 and 4664.

"The fundamental rule of statutory construction is to ascertain and effectuate the intent of the Legislature in enacting the statute. [Citation.] We construe the workers' compensation scheme as a whole and consider the words used in their usual, commonsense meaning. [Citation.] We liberally construe all aspects of workers' compensation law in favor of the injured worker." (*Henry v. Workers' Comp. Appeals Bd.* (1998) 68 Cal. App. 4th 981, 984 [80 Cal. Rptr. 2d 631].) The "so–called 'liberality rule,' " however, (which is found in § 3202) "cannot supplant the intent of the Legislature as expressed in a particular statute." (*Fuentes*, *supra*, 16 Cal. 3d at p. 8.) If the Legislature's intent appears from the language and context of the relevant statutory provisions, then we must effectuate that intent, "even though the particular statutory language 'is contrary to the basic policy of the [workers' compensation law].' " (*Ibid.*, quoting *Earl Ranch, Ltd. v. Industrial Acc. Com.* (1935) 4

Cal. 2d 767, 769 [53 P.2d 154].)

In interpreting sections 4663 and 4664, we are further guided by " 'the policy that it should not "be presumed that the Legislature in the enactment of statutes intends to overthrow long–established principles of law unless such intention is made clearly to appear either by express declaration or by necessary implication." ' " (*Fuentes*, *supra*, 16 Cal. 3d at p. 7, quoting *Theodor v. Superior Court* (1972) 8 Cal. 3d 77, 92 [104 Cal. Rptr. 226, 501 P.2d 234].)

Here, it was established law under *Fuentes* for almost 30 years that permanent disability is apportioned by subtracting the percentage of the disability attributable to factors other than the current industrial injury from the overall percentage of disability to determine the percentage of the disability that is compensable, then determining the amount of permanent disability benefits payable under section 4658 by reference to the compensable percentage of disability. Thus, we begin with the question of whether, by repealing the former law (including former § 4750) and enacting new sections 4663 and 4664, the Legislature clearly expressed or necessarily implied an intent to abandon this approach and adopt instead the approach advocated by the claimants here (and the appellate court in *Gallo*)–namely, converting the percentages of disability into their monetary equivalents under section 4658 *before* performing the necessary subtraction.

In our view, no such intent appears in the new apportionment provisions. Section 4663 expresses the principle that apportionment of permanent disability is to "be based on causation" "of the permanent disability." (§ 4663, subds. (a), (b).) Moreover, a physician addressing the issue of permanent disability must "make an apportionment determination by finding what approximate percentage of the permanent disability was caused by the direct result of injury arising out of and occurring in the course of employment and what approximate percentage of the permanent disability was caused by other factors both before and subsequent to the industrial injury, including prior industrial injuries." (§ 4663, subd. (c).)

Thus, section 4663 speaks of apportioning permanent disability based on causation by determining the percentage of the permanent disability directly caused by the current industrial injury as distinguished from the percentage of the permanent disability caused by other factors. Subdivision (a) of section 4664 then expressly provides that the employer is liable *only* for the former percentage–that is, "the percentage of permanent disability directly caused by the injury arising out of and occurring in the course of employment." (§ 4664, subd. (a).)

In our view, these provisions neither clearly express nor necessarily imply an intent to abandon formula A from *Fuentes* for apportioning permanent disability. On the contrary, we conclude these provisions compel the continued application of that formula. By its plain terms, section 4664 limits an employer's liability for a claimant's overall permanent disability to "the percentage of permanent disability directly caused by" the present industrial injury. Thus, the employer is *not* liable for "the percentage of permanent disability" caused by any other factors–including both nonindustrial factors and previous

industrial injuries. In this context, the phrase "percentage of permanent disability" is easily referable to the phraseology used in section 4658 to express the extent of permanent disability caused by an injury, which in turn is used to determine the amount of permanent disability benefits payable to a claimant for that injury. That statute provides that where an industrial injury "causes permanent disability, the percentage of disability to total disability shall be determined, and the disability payment computed" by awarding the claimant a certain amount of money for a certain number of weeks "for each 1 percent of disability." (§ 4658, subds. (a), (b), (c), (d).)

We are given no reason to believe that the Legislature intended the term "percentage of permanent disability," as used in sections 4663 and 4664, to have a different meaning than the term "percentage of disability," as used in section 4658. In his dissenting opinion in *Nabors*, Chairman Rabine concluded that a different meaning *was* intended, which compelled him to conclude that formula B from *Fuentes* is now the proper way to apportion permanent disability. (*Nabors*, *supra*, 70 Cal. Comp. Cases at pp. 862–864.) None of the claimants in these four cases, however, proposes we adopt Chairman Rabine's approach. Moreover, we are unpersuaded by his reasoning. He asserts in his opinion that "percentage," as used in sections 4663 and 4664, "is the ratio of the disability caused by the industrial injury to the [claimant's] overall disability." (*Nabors*, *supra*, 70 Cal. Comp. Cases at p. 863.) Thus, where the claimant had an overall permanent disability of 80 percent, with a prior permanent disability award of 49 percent, Chairman Rabine concluded that "the percentage of his disability that was directly caused by his present injury is 31/80ths" (*ibid.*)–that is to say, 38.75 percent–rather than the 31 percent that is obtained by subtracting 49 from 80 under formula A from *Fuentes*.

In our view, there is no sound explanation for why the Legislature would have intended "percentage," as used in sections 4663 and 4664, to mean the ratio of a claimant's partial disability to his overall disability, when that same word is used in section 4658 to mean the ratio of a claimant's disability to *total* disability.

"The words of [a] statute must be construed in context, keeping in mind the statutory purpose, and statutes or statutory sections relating to the same subject must be harmonized, both internally and with each other, to the extent possible." (*Dyna–Med, Inc. v. Fair Employment & Housing Com.* (1987) 43 Cal. 3d 1379, 1387 [241 Cal. Rptr. 67, 743 P.2d 1323].) Here, we conclude that sections 4663 and 4664 can best be harmonized with section 4658 by construing the word "percentage" as having the same meaning in both contexts. Thus, "percentage of permanent disability," as that term is used in sections 4663 and 4664, means the percentage of permanent disability *to total disability*. Indeed, the primary definition of "percentage" is "a part of *a whole* expressed in hundredths." (Merriam–Webster's Collegiate Dict. (10th ed. 2000) p. 859, col. 1, italics added.) In this context, the "whole" is total (i.e., 100 percent) permanent disability, and a "percentage of permanent disability" is any part of *that whole* expressed in hundredths.

What this means is that under section 4663, permanent disability must be apportioned based on causation by determining the percentage of the permanent disability *to total disability* that was directly caused by the current industrial injury as distinguished from the percentage of the permanent disability *to total disability* that was caused by other factors. Then, under subdivision (a) of section 4664, the employer is liable only for the percentage of the permanent disability *to total disability* that was directly caused by the current industrial injury. Having thus complied with the requirement of section 4658 to determine "the percentage of [permanent] disability to total disability" that is compensable for the current industrial injury, the amount of permanent disability benefits payable to the claimant for that injury is computed by awarding the claimant the requisite number of weeks of payments for each percent of permanent disability directly caused by that injury. Thus, the approach to apportionment adopted by the majority in *Nabors* is correct.

Having reached this conclusion, we turn back to the Fifth Appellate District's opinion in *Gallo*, upon which the claimants in this case primarily rely to support their claim that formula C is now the proper method for apportioning permanent disability. As we will explain, we cannot agree with the *Gallo* court's analysis or its conclusion that the Legislature intended formula C to supplant formula A.

" '[I]t should not "be presumed that the Legislature in the enactment of statutes intends to overthrow long–established principles of law unless such intention is made clearly to appear either by express declaration or by necessary implication." ' " (*Fuentes, supra,* 16 Cal. 3d at p. 7.) However, the *Gallo* court did not discuss whether the Legislature expressly declared or necessarily implied in Senate Bill No. 899 that it intended to overthrow the use of formula A from *Fuentes* to apportion permanent disability. The *Gallo* court also did not attempt to construe the term "percentage of permanent disability" in sections 4663 and 4664 consistently with the term "percentage of disability" in section 4658.

The *Gallo* court concluded "the Legislature contemplated a variation in determining apportionment by repealing section 4750 and replacing it with different language in section 4664." (*Gallo, supra,* 134 Cal. App. 4th at p. 1550.) Of particular importance to the *Gallo* court was its conclusion that "[t]he Supreme Court's holding in *Fuentes* expressly rested on ... language in section 4750 that the level of permanent disability caused by a subsequent injury was to be determined without reference to or consideration of the employee's prior condition." (*Gallo, supra,* 134 Cal. App. 4th at p. 1549.) According to the *Gallo* court, Senate Bill No. 899 "reversed that policy. Now, a prior award is conclusively presumed to exist as a means of establishing the level of permanent disability directly caused by the subsequent injury. (§ 4663, subd. (b).) Evaluating physicians must also make similar apportionment percentage determinations. (§ 4664, subd. (c).) The WCAB may no longer apportion liability without considering a prior or other noncompensable disability." (Footnote 7) (*Gallo,* at p. 1549.)

We cannot agree with the *Gallo* court's conclusion that in

apportioning permanent disability under former section 4750, "*the level of permanent disability* caused by a subsequent injury was to be determined without reference to or consideration of the employee's prior condition," while under new sections 4663 and 4664, the employee's prior condition must (for the first time) be taken into account in performing that task. (*Gallo, supra,* 134 Cal. App. 4th at p. 1549, italics added.) The limiting language in former section 4750 to which the *Gallo* court was referring was not directed at *the determination of* the *level of permanent disability* caused by the current industrial injury, but rather at *the payment of compensation* based on that injury. Thus, former section 4750 provided that an employee who sustained a subsequent industrial injury was not entitled to "*compensation for the later injury* in excess of the compensation allowed for such injury when considered by itself and not in conjunction with or in relation to the previous disability or impairment," and the employer was liable "only for that portion [of the compensation] due to the later injury as though no prior disability or impairment had existed." (Italics added.) The purpose of this language in former section 4750 was to ensure that the employer was not "required to compensate the employee for an aggregate disability which included a previous injury" (*Fuentes, supra,* 16 Cal. 3d at p. 6), but instead was required to compensate the employee only for the permanent disability stemming from the current industrial injury.

Of course, to accomplish this result, it was *always* necessary to compare the claimant's present overall level of permanent disability to his or her previous level of disability in order to identify the portion of the overall permanent disability that stemmed from the current industrial injury. This is what formula A from *Fuentes* did. Under that formula (for the claimant in that case), "24.25 percent, representing [the portion of the claimant's permanent disability of] nonindustrial origin, [wa]s deducted from the 58 percent total [or overall] disability with a net compensable disability of 33.75 percent." (*Fuentes, supra,* 16 Cal. 3d at p. 5.) Thus, contrary to the *Gallo* court's conclusion, even under former section 4750 as the Supreme Court applied that statute in *Fuentes*, "the level of permanent disability caused by a subsequent injury" could not be determined *except by* "reference to ... the employee's prior condition." (*Gallo, supra,* 134 Cal. App. 4th at p. 1549.)

Accordingly, the enactment of sections 4663 and 4664 did *not* represent a reversal of policy on this point. Now, as then, the level of permanent disability caused by the current industrial injury can be determined only by reference to the level of disability attributable to other factors–including the claimant's prior condition. Once the level of permanent disability caused by the current industrial injury has been isolated from the level of disability attributable to other factors, then compensation can be awarded for the portion of the disability attributable to the current injury. It is in the awarding of compensation, once the level of disability attributable to the current injury has been isolated, that the claimant's prior condition is necessarily ignored.

Because Senate Bill No. 899 did not evidence any change of policy on this point, we cannot agree with the *Gallo* court's conclusion "the Legislature contemplated a variation in determining apportionment by repealing section 4750 and replacing it with different language in section 4664." (*Gallo, supra,* 134 Cal. App. 4th at p. 1550.)

We acknowledge that "[i]t is ordinarily to be presumed that the Legislature by deleting an express provision of a statute intended a substantial change in the law." (*People v. Valentine* (1946) 28 Cal. 2d 121, 142 [169 P.2d 1]; see *Gallo, supra,* 134 Cal. App. 4th at p. 1550, quoting *Lockheed Martin Corp. v. Workers' Comp. Appeals Bd.* (2002) 96 Cal. App. 4th 1237, 1246 [117 Cal. Rptr. 2d 865].) That presumption, however, is rebutted here with respect to the Legislature's repeal of former section 4750 by replacement of that section with a new section covering the same subject. Where former section 4750 limited an employer's liability for compensation to "that portion [of the claimant's combined disability] due to the later injury as though no prior disability or impairment had existed," subdivision (a) of section 4664 now limits the employer's liability for compensation to "the percentage of permanent disability directly caused by the [current industrial] injury." We perceive no intended change in meaning between these two provisions; thus, the presumption on which the *Gallo* court relied is not controlling here. The remaining portions of former section 4750, which the Legislature did not reenact in the new law, were likely omitted because they were simply superfluous.

Unable to discern in Senate Bill No. 899 "any particular method for apportioning ... a permanent disability award," the *Gallo* court relied on the liberality rule of section 3202, "keep[ing] firmly in mind the exponentially progressive nature of the workers' compensation disability tables, the increasing maximum weekly benefit rates, and the lifetime pension for disabilities over 70 percent—all of which serve to compensate employees with higher levels of permanent disability in greater proportion to those with lower levels of permanent disability." (*Gallo, supra,* 134 Cal. App. 4th at pp. 1552–1553.) Based on these factors, the *Gallo* court concluded that "only formula C ensures both that an employee is adequately compensated and that an employer is directly liable for the percentage of disability directly caused by the injury arising out of employment." (*Id.* at p. 1553.) According to the court, "By not recognizing the injured employee's total disability and artificially shifting compensation down on the permanent disability tables, all of the other formulas shortchange an employee by treating him or her as though no prior injury or disability existed, which is now no longer permitted." (*Ibid.*)

We cannot agree with this reasoning. First, the language of sections 4663 and 4664 shows the legislative intent to continue applying formula A from *Fuentes* to apportion permanent disability. Only the continued application of formula A ensures that an employer is liable only for "the percentage of permanent disability directly caused by the [current industrial] injury," as section 4664 requires, and harmonizes the use of the word "percentage" in sections 4663 and 4664 with the use of that word in section 4658.

Second, as to the liberality rule of section 3202, we are guided by the admonition in *Fuentes* that that rule "cannot supplant the intent of the Legislature as expressed in a particular statute." (*Fuentes, supra,* 16 Cal. 3d at p. 8.) Here, we have discerned the legislative intent to continue applying formula A and therefore the rule of liberal construction is of no moment.

Third, to the extent the *Gallo* court's analysis was driven by what it perceived to be the unfairness of applying formula A—because under that formula a claimant who sustains a given level of permanent disability as a result of a single industrial injury will receive more compensation than a claimant who sustains the same level of disability as a result of multiple industrial injuries—the Supreme Court rejected the same claim of unfairness in *Fuentes*. (*Fuentes, supra,* 16 Cal. 3d at p. 8.) Moreover, for nearly 30 years following *Fuentes*, the Legislature left section 4750 in place, thus allowing formula A to govern apportionment of permanent disability for a substantial period of time. The Legislature then enacted sections 4663 and 4664, which, in our view, compel the continued application of that formula. It is not for us to question the wisdom or fairness of that decision. (See *Schnyder v. State Bd. of Equalization* (2002) 101 Cal. App. 4th 538, 549 [124 Cal. Rptr. 2d 571].)

In any event, as section 4658 and former section 4750 did when *Fuentes* was decided, we conclude that sections 4658, 4663, and 4664 "function together quite harmoniously, ... serving the twin goals of providing proportionately greater benefits for more serious injuries while at the same time protecting employers from bearing a disproportionate share of a financial burden resulting from cumulative injuries." (*Fuentes, supra,* 16 Cal. 3d at p. 7.) Any unfairness to injured workers in this system is balanced against the unfairness to employers that would result if formula C were applied. (Footnote 8)

In closing our comments on *Gallo*, we note that the court there attempted to limit the reach of its decision by restricting that decision to situations where "an employee sustains multiple industrial injuries working for the same self–insured employer." (*Gallo, supra,* 134 Cal. App. 4th at p. 1553.) It may well be that, in such a situation, the policy of "protecting employers [and their insurers] from bearing a disproportionate share of a financial burden resulting from cumulative injuries" has little or no weight, since the same employer is liable for the compensation stemming from all of the claimant's industrial injuries in any event. Be that as it may, we find no basis in the law (nor did the *Gallo* court offer one) for construing the operative statutes one way when multiple employers and/or insurers are involved, and another way when only a single, self–insured employer is involved. Absent any such basis, the law must be consistently applied, even if its application to claimants like Strong and Williams—who sustained all of their industrial injuries while working for the same, self–insured employers—appears unfair when compared to other, hypothetical claimants who sustained similar levels of permanent disability from a single industrial injury.

We have examined the arguments presented by the four claimants on this issue and found nothing in them to which we have not already responded in the analysis set forth above. Accordingly, we conclude the WCAB applied the proper method for apportioning permanent liability in each of their cases. (Footnote 9)

II. Apportioning Permanent Disability Between Parts of the Body

Our conclusion on the previous issue disposes of three of the four cases before us. In the fourth case, however, the claimant (Strong) asserts two additional arguments, to which we now turn our attention.

As we previously explained, Strong sustained three industrial injuries while working for the same employer: (1) an injury to his left knee in 1995 which resulted in permanent disability of 34.5 percent; (2) an injury to his left shoulder, left knee and ankle, and right wrist in 1999, resulting in permanent disability of 42 percent (after apportionment for the prior injury); and (3) an injury to his back in 2002 which resulted in an overall permanent disability of 70 percent (before apportionment). A disability evaluation specialist determined that 60 percent of Strong's permanent disability was due to his prior injuries to his shoulder, knee, ankle, and wrist, while 10 percent was due to his current injury to his back. Based on this apportionment, the WCJ determined the current injury caused permanent disability of 10 percent.

Strong filed a petition for reconsideration with the WCAB, arguing that "there cannot be apportionment to disability occurring to other regions of the body." The WCAB granted Strong's petition and in an en banc decision determined that section 4664 "requires the apportionment of overlapping permanent disabilities," even when those disabilities involve different regions of the body. (*Strong v. City & County of San Francisco* (2005) 70 Cal. Comp. Cases 1460, 1461–1462 (*Strong*).) In reaching this conclusion, the WCAB undertook a thorough analysis of the apportionment of overlapping permanent disabilities prior to the enactment of Senate Bill No. 899. In part, the WCAB explained as follows:

"In applying former section 4750 [to apportion permanent disability], when the permanent disability resulting from a new injury included factors of disability that were the same as ones that already existed as the result of a prior injury or condition, the disabilities were said to 'overlap.' [Citations.] If all of the factors of permanent disability attributable to the subsequent industrial injury already existed as a result of the prior injury or condition, then there was 'total' overlap, and the employee was not entitled to any additional permanent disability indemnity; if, however, the subsequent industrial injury caused some new factors of permanent disability that were not pre–existing, then there was 'partial' overlap, and the employee was entitled to permanent disability indemnity to the extent the subsequent industrial injury further restricted his or her earning capacity or ability to compete." (*Strong, supra*, 70 Cal. Comp. Cases at pp. 1465–1466; see also *Mercier v. Workers' Comp. Appeals Bd.* (1976) 16 Cal. 3d 711 [129 Cal. Rptr. 161, 548 P.2d 361].)

Under this preexisting law, "it was not the part of the body involved in the subsequent industrial injury that was important; rather, it was the nature of the disability resulting from the new injury in relation to the pre–existing disability that was determinative." (*Strong, supra*, 70 Cal. Comp. Cases at pp. 1466–1467.)

Turning to the new apportionment statutes enacted in 2004, the WCAB concluded "there is nothing in new section 4664 that evinces a clear expression of legislative intent to abandon the long–standing policy of encouraging employers to hire workers with disabilities by assuring that such employers are not made liable for pre–existing disabilities if those workers subsequently sustain an industrial injury. ... [P] Thus, we conclude that, as was true before the repeal of former section 4750 and continuing with the enactment of new section 4664, an employee is not entitled to be compensated for permanent disability resulting from a new industrial injury to the extent that this permanent disability is overlapped by prior permanent disability, even where the prior permanent disability involves and/or includes different regions of the body." (*Strong, supra*, 70 Cal. Comp. Cases at pp. 1469–1470.)

Strong contends the WCAB's decision on this point is incorrect, but he makes no real effort to refute the WCAB's reasoning. He does suggest that because subdivision (c)(1) of section 4664 generally provides that "[t]he accumulation of all permanent disability awards issued with respect *to any one region of the body* in favor of one individual employee shall not exceed 100 percent over the employee's lifetime" (italics added), this implies there is no such limitation "to the whole body or to all regions of the body combined." That may be true, but it has no bearing on the WCAB's conclusion here. If a claimant with a preexisting permanent disability of 60 percent based on an industrial injury to his leg sustains a subsequent injury to his back that results in a permanent disability of 60 percent, *and* the permanent disability resulting from the subsequent back injury is based entirely on *new* factors of permanent disability that are *different* from the factors of permanent disability caused by the prior leg injury, then in that instance *there would be no overlap*, and two awards of 60 percent permanent disability would be permitted. There is nothing in section 4664, however, that indicates the Legislature intended to repudiate the long–standing legal principles applied to apportioning permanent disability where there *is* overlap in the factors of disability.

Here, the WCAB explained that Strong "succeeded in disproving total overlap ... between his current disability [caused by his back injury] and the disability upon which his prior permanent disability awards were based [caused by the previous injuries to other parts of his body]," but there remained a partial overlap. (*Strong, supra*, 70 Cal. Comp. Cases at p. 1478.) According to the board, the evidence established that at the time of his back injury, Strong "had pre–existing overall disability consisting of a limitation to light work." (*Ibid.*) The evidence also established that the 70 percent permanent disability that resulted from his back injury was "based on an *overall* limitation to semi–sedentary work." (*Ibid.*) Finally, the evidence established that "the *increase* in disability from a limitation to light work to a limitation to semi–sedentary work [wa]s the result of [his] back injury." (*Ibid.*)

A disability evaluation specialist concluded that Strong's "pre–existing light work limitation rated 60%, after adjustment for his current occupation," and neither party raised any issue with respect to that adjustment. (*Strong, supra*, 70 Cal. Comp. Cases at pp. 1463, 1478, fn. 19.) Accordingly, it was a matter of simple mathematics to "deduct[] the pre–existing 60% disability ... from the stipulated 70% of overall disability" to determine that Strong's back injury had caused 10 percent permanent disability. (*Id.* at p. 1478.)

Strong has shown no rational basis why, under the new statutes governing apportionment, having been fully compensated for a disability consisting of limitation to light work, he should also receive the *full* value of a disability consisting of a limitation to semi–sedentary work, which overlaps his preexisting disability. In the absence of such a showing, we conclude the WCAB properly apportioned Strong's permanent disability based on the overlap between his prior and current disabilities.

III. The Presumption of a Prior Disability

Strong purports to raise one further issue regarding subdivision (b) of section 4664, which relates to the apportionment of permanent disability when the claimant received a prior award of permanent disability. That statute provides that "[i]f the applicant has received a prior award of permanent disability, it shall be conclusively presumed that the prior permanent disability exists at the time of any subsequent industrial injury. This presumption is a presumption affecting the burden of proof."

Strong contends the statute is contradictory because "if an award of permanent disability is 'conclusively presumed', then it cannot be rebutted by any evidence. However, the next sentence in the same subsection (b) indicates that 'this is a presumption affecting the burden of proof.' He contends this apparent contradiction can be reconciled by holding that "the conclusive presumption applies to what level of disability existed at the time of the prior stipulation or award, which then goes to the burden of proof of whether that level of disability remained immediately prior to or at the same time of any subsequent injury ... from which rehabilitation can be demonstrated."

We need not attempt to decipher the meaning or purpose of this argument, because ultimately Strong fails to show how the WCAB's application of this statute to his case operated to his detriment, or how the application of his approach to the statute would operate to his benefit. Strong does not contend that he wanted to, but was prohibited from, trying to prove before the WCJ that his prior permanent disability no longer existed at the time of his back injury. Accordingly, we will leave for another day how this apparently contradictory statute is to be interpreted.

DISPOSITION

In the Welcher and Lopez cases (cases Nos. C051263 and C051790), the WCAB's opinions and orders denying reconsideration are affirmed.

In the Strong case (case No. C051409), the WCAB's opinion and decision after reconsideration is affirmed.

In the Williams case (case No. C051894), the WCAB's order denying reconsideration is affirmed.

The parties shall bear their own costs on appeal. (Cal. Rules of Court, rule 56 (l)(2).)

Butz, J., concurred.

CONCUR BY: Sims

CONCUR: SIMS, Acting P. J., Concurring.–I concur in Justice Robie's fine opinion.

I write separately to add another reason why, with respect, I think *E & J Gallo Winery v. Workers' Comp. Appeals Bd.* (2005) 134 Cal. App. 4th 1536 [37 Cal. Rptr. 3d 208] was wrongly decided.

New Labor Code sections 4663 and 4664 were enacted by the sweeping overhaul of the workers' compensation laws effected in 2004 by Senate Bill No. 899 (2003–2004 Reg. Sess.). (Stats. 2004, ch. 34, § 49.)

Section 49 of that enactment provides:

"This act is an urgency statute necessary for the immediate preservation of the public peace, health, or safety within the meaning of Article IV of the Constitution and shall go into immediate effect. The facts constituting the necessity are:

"*In order to provide relief to the state from the effects of the current workers' compensation crisis* at the earliest possible time, it is necessary for this act to take effect immediately." (Stats. 2004, ch. 34, § 49, italics added.)

The "workers' compensation crisis" referred to in section 49 of the enactment is described in a report prepared by the RAND Institute for Civil Justice at the request of the California Commission on Health and Safety and Workers' Compensation as follows: "By 2004, the state's workers' compensation system was associated with the highest employer costs in the nation despite evidence indicating that the state's injured workers were not being adequately compensated." (RAND Institute for Civil Justice, "An Evaluation of California's Permanent Disability Rating System" (2005) ch. one, p. 1.)

The "workers' compensation crisis" was therefore, in the main, a crisis of high costs imposed on private sector employers. It was reported that employers were leaving the state as a consequence. (See, e.g., Garcia & Cohen, "Learning from California: The Macroeconomic Consequences of Structural Changes" (1993) Berkeley Roundtable on the International Economy, § 4.2.) It is inconceivable to me that the Legislature intended to fix this "crisis" in workers' compensation costs by abandoning the long–established formula of apportionment of permanent disability announced in *Fuentes v. Workers' Comp. Appeals Bd.* (1976) 16 Cal. 3d 1 [128 Cal. Rptr. 673, 547 P.2d 449], and by adopting a new formula that would dramatically increase awards to employees and therefore *increase* employers' costs...

Footnote 1. All further statutory references are to the Labor Code unless otherwise indicated.

Footnote 2. Division Two of the First Appellate District reversed the WCAB's decision in *Nabors v. Workers' Comp. Appeals Bd.*, *supra*, 140 Cal. App. 4th at page 217.

Footnote 3. Payments are generally made at two–thirds of the claimant's average weekly earnings, subject to certain minimum and maximum rates. (See §§ 4453, 4658, subds. (a)(2) & (b)(2).)

Footnote 4. "Since the Supreme Court decided *Fuentes*, ... the workers' compensation system has become even more progressive. [Citation.] Now, in addition to permanent disability tables providing for exponentially progressive higher number of weeks of payments, the maximum weekly benefit payments also increase at specific levels of permanent disability." (*Gallo, supra,* 134 Cal. App. 4th at p. 1551.)

Footnote 5. As the appellate court in *Gallo* pointed out, the three members of the WCAB who denied reconsideration in that case, thereby approving the use of formula C from *Fuentes* to apportion permanent disability, were, five months later, three of the four–member majority in *Nabors* who decided that formula A from *Fuentes* is the proper method for apportionment under new sections 4663 and 4664. (See *Gallo, supra,* 134 Cal. App. 4th at pp. 1541, 1548, fn. 4.)

Footnote 6. Thus, by its own terms, *Gallo* does not apply "where an employee received a prior disability award with another employer, where the employer was separately insured at the time of the injuries, or where the medical evidence reveals that a portion of the injured employee's disability is not compensable." (*Gallo, supra,* 134 Cal. App. 4th at p. 1553.) This limitation renders the *Gallo* court's holding directly applicable only to Strong's case and Williams's case here.

Footnote 7. The language of former section 4750 to which the *Gallo* court was apparently referring is italicized in the following quotation of the statute: "An employee who is suffering from a previous permanent disability or physical impairment and sustains permanent injury thereafter shall not receive from the employer compensation for the later injury in excess of the compensation allowed for such injury when considered by itself *and not in conjunction with or in relation to the previous disability or impairment.* [P] The employer shall not be liable for compensation to such an employee for the combined disability, but only for that portion due to the later injury *as though no prior disability or impairment had existed.*"

Footnote 8. For example, if an employer that hired a worker with a preexisting permanent disability of 20 percent (sustained in earlier employment for another employer) had to pay compensation for a new injury that took the employee's overall level of disability to 40 percent, under formula C that employer would have to pay substantially more compensation than the first employer, even though the percentage of permanent disability directly caused by each injury was the same–20 percent.

Footnote 9. Amici curiae County of Los Angeles and California Workers' Compensation Institute have each filed a request for judicial notice along with their amicus curiae briefs. Because we find the materials of which they ask us to take judicial notice unnecessary to our decision, we deny those requests.

In *Davis–Torres v. WCAB* (2006) 71 Cal. Comp. Cases 1669, the Court of Appeal, Sixth District, applied *formula A* in calculating permanent disability compensation in cases where current disability is subject to apportionment to a preexisting disability. The Court stated, in part:

I. INTRODUCTION

The question in these workers' compensation cases is whether the Legislature's 2004 overhaul of the workers' compensation statutes (Stats. 2004, ch. 34.) was intended to alter the formula used to calculate a permanent disability award when the employee's overall disability is subject to apportionment. We conclude that, notwithstanding the recent changes to the law, the calculation adopted by *Fuentes v. Workers' Comp. Appeals Bd.* (1976) 16 Cal. 3d 1 [128 Cal. Rptr. 673, 547 P.2d 449] (*Fuentes*) continues to be appropriate. In so concluding we disagree with *E & J Gallo Winery v. Workers' Comp. Appeals Bd.* (2005) 134 Cal. App. 4th 1536 [37 Cal. Rptr. 3d 208] (*Dykes*) (Fifth Dist.) and *Nabors v. Workers' Comp. Appeals Bd.* (2006) 140 Cal. App. 4th 217 [44 Cal. Rptr. 3d 312] (*Nabors*) (First Dist., Div. Two). (Footnote 1)

II. FACTUAL AND PROCEDURAL BACKGROUND

The facts may be briefly stated. In the first case (case No. H029544), petitioner Fortunata Mary Davis suffered a work–related back injury that left her 100 percent permanently disabled. Davis had suffered a prior work–related injury for which she received an award for permanent partial disability of 35 percent. Using the formula prescribed by the Supreme Court in *Fuentes*, the Workers' Compensation Administrative Law Judge (WCJ) deducted the 35 percent disability from the overall disability of 100 percent and awarded Davis compensation for permanent partial disability of 65 percent, which was $65,662.50. Davis petitioned the Workers' Compensation Appeals Board (WCAB) for reconsideration arguing that the WCJ should have used the formula later approved by the appellate court in *Dykes, supra,* 134 Cal. App. 4th 1536. The *Dykes* formula would have given her the full benefit allowed for 100 percent disability less credit to her employer for the dollar value of the prior award. This calculation would have resulted in payments of approximately $420,649.21 over Davis's remaining life expectancy.

In the second case (case No. H029834), petitioner Moises Torres injured his back and his knees while working for respondent Williams Tank Lines, leaving him with an overall disability rating of 52 percent. He had previously received an award for permanent partial disability of 24 percent as the result of a spinal injury. The WCJ applied the *Fuentes* calculation, which gave Torres a permanent partial disability award of $16,277.50. (Footnote 2) Torres also petitioned the WCAB for reconsideration, urging it to use the alternative calculation, which would have resulted in an award of $31,360.

In denying the petitions the WCAB followed the en banc decision in *Nabors v. Piedmont Lumber & Mill Co.* (2005) 70 Cal. Comp. Cases 856, which held that the *Fuentes* formula had not been affected by the 2004 changes to the apportionment statutes. *Dykes, supra,* 134 Cal. App. 4th 1536 later overruled *Nabors v. Piedmont* and shortly thereafter *Nabors v. Piedmont* was reversed by *Nabors, supra*, 140 Cal. App. 4th 217. We issued writs of review in the present cases and ordered the two cases considered together for purposes of oral argument and decision.

III. ISSUE

Thirty years ago, *Fuentes* set forth the formula to use when calculating permanent disability compensation in cases where the current disability is subject to apportionment for a preexisting disability. (*Fuentes, supra,* 16 Cal. 3d 1.) Under *Auto Equity Sales, Inc. v. Superior Court* (1962) 57 Cal. 2d 450, 455 [20 Cal. Rptr. 321, 369 P.2d 937], we are bound to follow the decisions of the Supreme Court unless they are overruled, altered by statute, or can be validly distinguished. We cannot rely upon cases decided under prior law to interpret a quite different code section. (*People v. Valentine* (1946) 28 Cal. 2d 121, 144 [169 P.2d 1].) On the other hand, when the Legislature enacts a statute, we presume that the Legislature did not intend to overthrow long–established principles of law unless such an intention is clearly expressed or necessarily implied. (*People v. Superior Court* (*Zamudio*) (2000) 23 Cal. 4th 183, 199 [96 Cal. Rptr. 2d 463, 999 P.2d 686]; see also *Fuentes, supra,* 16 Cal. 3d at p. 7; *Theodor v. Superior Court* (1972) 8 Cal. 3d 77, 92 [104 Cal. Rptr. 226, 501 P.2d 234].) Unless the Legislature plainly intends to change a judicial result based upon an earlier version of a statute we are bound by the prior judicial result. (*People v. Eastman* (1993) 13 Cal. App. 4th 668, 676 [16 Cal. Rptr. 2d 608].)

The statutory basis for the *Fuentes* holding was former Labor Code section 4750. (Footnote 3) Although the Legislature repealed former section 4750 in 2004, it also repealed two related sections pertaining to apportionment and "recast" the substance of all three provisions in new sections 4663 and 4664. (Stats. 2004, ch. 34.) The question before us, therefore, is whether these changes demonstrate that the Legislature clearly intended to alter the *Fuentes* rule. We begin by comparing the former law with the new sections pertaining to apportionment...

F. CONCLUSION

In sum, we find no clear legislative intent to abandon the use of formula A as adopted by *Fuentes* 30 years ago. The plain language of section 4664 implies that when an employee's overall permanent disability is subject to apportionment for a preexisting disability the calculation of compensation is to be made by subtracting the preexisting percentage of permanent disability from the overall percentage of permanent disability, i.e., by applying formula A. Furthermore, the policy underlying *Fuentes*'s selection of formula A continues to be an important public policy in this state and the effect of adopting any calculation other than formula A would be contrary to the overall intent of Senate Bill No. 899. We are not convinced, therefore, that simply by enacting Senate Bill No. 899 the Legislature intended to reject the reasoning and result of the *Fuentes* decision. Even assuming that *Fuentes* is no longer directly controlling, we conclude in light of all the foregoing that it is appropriate to continue to apply the *Fuentes* rule... .

Footnote 1. The issue is presently before the Supreme Court in *Brodie v. Workers' Comp. Appeals Bd.*, review granted Nov. 15, 2006, S146979 and *Welcher v. Workers' Comp. Appeals Bd.,* review granted Nov. 15, 2006, S17030.

Footnote 2. The WCJ first subtracted the percentage of disability attributable to the preexisting disability and then reduced the number to reflect the portion of Torres's knee disability that was due to nonindustrial factors. The parties do not discuss the WCJ's method of accounting for the nonindustrial portion of the knee disability. Accordingly, we do not consider that aspect of the apportionment problem.

Footnote 3. Hereafter, all unspecified code references are to the Labor Code

Substantial Evidence Must Support Apportionment

To support apportioning a percentage of permanent disability, a medical opinion must be based on *substantial evidence and disclose the doctor's familiarities with the concepts of apportionment* under SB 899.

Commenting on this in *E.L. Yeager Construction v. WCAB (Gatten)* (2006) 71 Cal. Comp. Cases 1687, the Court of Appeal, Fourth District, stated, in part:

E.L. Yeager Construction and its workers' compensation insurer (collectively referred to as "petitioner") petition for a writ of review to determine the lawfulness of an award and an order denying reconsideration in a proceeding before the Workers' Compensation Appeals Board (Board). They contend that the Board erred by not correctly applying the newly enacted apportionment statutes and in rejecting the independent medical examiner's (IME) opinion on apportionment. We agree and, accordingly, annul the order.

FACTUAL AND PROCEDURAL BACKGROUND

Applicant sustained an admitted injury to his lower back in 1996 while working for petitioner. The injury occurred when he fell from a five–and–one–half–foot wall, landing on his buttocks. At the time of the injury, he was diagnosed with a lumbar strain/sprain with a compression facture at L2.

Prior to this injury, applicant had occasional back pain and had received two to three chiropractic adjustments for the pain in the preceding 10–year period.

Following his injury, applicant saw various physicians and eventually the workers' compensation administrative law judge (WCJ) appointed Dr. Akmakjian as the IME.

Dr. Akmakjian apportioned 20 percent of applicant's present disability to chronic degenerative disease of his lumbar spine. He testified that applicant's magnetic resonance imaging (MRI) taken in 1997 showed dehydration, indicating early degenerative change at almost every disc in his back. The doctor explained that this is a "wear–and–tear phenomenon" where the fine structure of the disc begins to change and wear out, loses its blood supply, and slowly starts to degenerate. He noted that this is a naturally occurring process that everyone gets, but it bothers some people and others it does not.

Although Dr. Akmakjian could not tell when this process started, he opined that the MRI taken within a year of the injury date showed the degenerative changes had already begun. "If you go back to your MRI from 1997, it says you have disc dehydration, indicating early degenerative change at almost every disc in your back, and that was within a year of your injury date, so, you know, all that stuff was there, it's bottom line. The arthritic changes, beginning degeneration, it was there."

When he was asked if he could find it, "medically probable that [applicant] had some back problems that you can apportion to prior to his injury of 1996," Dr. Akmakjian replied, "That, plus the MRI findings, yes."

The WCJ found applicant's industrial back injury caused a 74 percent permanent disability with no basis for apportionment. The WCJ rejected Dr. Akmakjian's opinion regarding apportionment as not supported by substantial evidence. Petitioner now seeks review of this finding of no apportionment.

DISCUSSION

In 2004, the Legislature made a diametrical change in the law with respect to apportionment to an employee's preexisting injury by enacting Senate Bill No. 899 (2003–2004 Reg. Sess.) (SB 899). Prior to their repeal by this bill, apportionment under former Labor Code section 4663 (Footnote 1) <,> (Footnote 2) was limited to circumstances where the apportioned disability was the result of the natural progression of a preexisting, nonindustrial condition and such nonindustrial disability would have occurred in the absence of the industrial injury. Apportionment based on causation was prohibited. Thus, "[p]rior to 2004, apportionment could never be made on the basis of pathology, either in a case of preexisting disability or in a case of an aggravation of an existing condition; it had to be made on the basis of causation of permanent disability. Many times the reporting physician might find preexisting pathology, such as old x–rays showing asymptomatic spinal changes or heart disease that could not have happened overnight, but these were insufficient, absent actual disability, for apportionment." (1 Hanna, Cal. Law of Employee Injuries and Workers' Compensation (rev. 2d ed. 2006) Apportionment–Specific Applications, § 8.06, p. 8–36.1, fns. omitted.)

"The rule under the law prior to [SB] 899 was 'an employer takes the employee as he finds him at the time of the employment. Accordingly, when a subsequent injury lights up or aggravates a previously existing condition resulting in disability, liability for the full disability without proration is imposed upon the employer, and the appeals board may apportion the disability under [former section 4663] "only in those cases in which part of the disability would have resulted, in the absence of the industrial injury, from the 'normal progress' " of the preexisting disease. [Citations.]' [Citation.] That is, the [Board] was required to 'allow compensation not only for the disability resulting solely from the employment, but also for that which results from the acceleration, aggravation, or "lighting up" of a prior nondisabling disease.' [Citation.] Apportionment was allowed in limited situations, but could not be based on the cause of the disease; 'pathology' could not be apportioned. [Citations.]" (Rio Linda Union School Dist. v. Workers'

Comp. Appeals Bd. (2005) 131 Cal. App. 4th 517, 525–526 [31 Cal. Rptr. 3d 789, 70 Cal. Comp. Cases 999] (Rio Linda).)

"[SB] 899 repealed former section 4663. [SB] 899 added a new section 4663 (Footnote 3) and section 4664 (Footnote 4) affirmatively requiring, among other things, apportionment of permanent disability based on causation and limiting the employer's liability under certain circumstances. [Citations.]" (Rio Linda, supra, 131 Cal. App. 4th at p. 526.) The new section 4663 also requires that a reporting physician address the apportionment issue in a specific manner.

SB 899 became effective April 19, 2004, and applies to all cases that were not yet final at the time of its effective date. (*Rio Linda, supra*, 131 Cal. App. 4th at p. 523; *Kleemann v. Workers' Comp. Appeals Bd.* (2005) 127 Cal. App. 4th 274 [25 Cal. Rptr. 3d 448, 70 Cal. Comp. Cases 133].)

The WCJ and the Board, in its answer to this petition, acknowledge that the new law governing apportionment applies to this case, and that, consequently, apportionment may be based on pathology and asymptomatic prior conditions. The Board asserts, however, that petitioner has not carried its burden of proof in establishing the percentage of disability caused by nonindustrial factors. More specifically, it contends that Dr. Akmakjian's opinion attributing 20 percent of applicant's disability to nonindustrial factors does not constitute substantial evidence on this issue.

It is certain the mere fact that a report addresses the issue of causation of the permanent disability, and makes an apportionment determination by finding the approximate relative percentages of industrial and nonindustrial causation does not necessarily render the report one upon which the Board may rely. This is because it is well established that any decision of the Board must be supported by substantial evidence. (§ 5952, subd. (d); Garza v. Workmen's Comp. App. Bd. (1970) 3 Cal. 3d 312, 317 [475 P.2d 451, 90 Cal. Rptr. 355, 35 Cal. Comp. Cases 500].)

In order to constitute substantial evidence, a medical opinion must be predicated on reasonable medical probability. (McAllister v. Workmen's Comp. App. Bd. (1968) 69 Cal. 2d 408, 413, 416–417, 419 [445 P.2d 313, 71 Cal. Rptr. 697, 33 Cal. Comp. Cases 660].) Also, a medical opinion is not substantial evidence if it is based on facts no longer germane, on inadequate medical histories or examinations, on incorrect legal theories, or on surmise, speculation, conjecture, or guess. (Hegglin v. Workmen's Comp. App. Bd. (1971) 4 Cal. 3d 162, 169 [480 P.2d 967, 93 Cal. Rptr. 15, 36 Cal. Comp. Cases 93].) Further, a medical report is not substantial evidence unless it sets forth the reasoning behind the physician's opinion, not merely his or her conclusions. (Granado v. Workmen's Comp. App. Bd. (1968) 69 Cal. 2d 399, 407 [445 P.2d 294, 71 Cal. Rptr. 678, 33 Cal. Comp. Cases 647].)

The medical opinion must disclose familiarity with the concepts of apportionment, describe in detail the exact nature of the apportionable disability, and set forth the basis for the opinion, so that the Board can determine whether the physician is properly apportioning under correct legal principles.

The Board has taken the position "to be substantial evidence on the issue of the approximate percentages of permanent disability due to the direct results of the injury and the approximate percentage of permanent disability due to other factors, a medical opinion must be framed in terms of reasonable medical probability, it must not be speculative, it must be based on pertinent facts and on an adequate examination and history, and it must set forth reasoning in support of its conclusions. [P] For example, if a physician opines that approximately 50% of an employee's back disability is directly caused by the industrial injury, the physician must explain how and why the disability is causally related to the industrial injury (e.g., the industrial injury resulted in surgery which caused vulnerability that necessitates certain restrictions) and how and why the injury is responsible for approximately 50% of the disability. And, if a physician opines that 50% of an employee's back disability is caused by degenerative disc disease, the physician must explain the nature of the degenerative disc disease, how and why it is causing permanent disability at the time of the evaluation, and how and why it is responsible for approximately 50% of the disability." (*Escobedo v. Marshalls* (2005) 70 Cal. Comp. Cases 604, 621, fn. omitted [Appeals Board en banc opinion].) In *Escobedo*, the Board concluded that substantial evidence supported a doctor's apportionment of 50 percent to the work injury and 50 percent to applicant's arthritis because (1) the doctor based his opinion on the "trivial nature" of the applicant's left knee injury; (2) because of the almost immediate onset of right knee symptoms after that injury; and (3) because of the "obvious, significant degenerative arthritis in both knees" reflected in a presurgical MRI of the applicant's left knee taken shortly after the injury and reflected in postsurgical X–rays. In addition, the doctor had expressed his apportionment opinion in terms of reasonable medical probability.

Here, Dr. Akmakjian based his opinion of apportionment on the MRI, which clearly showed degenerative disc disease at almost every level of his lower spine and the fact that applicant was occasionally having minor back problems prior to the injury. Although the doctor does not state in his report that the apportionment is based on reasonable medical probability, he does do so in the deposition. This constitutes a sufficient basis for the apportionment.

The WCJ criticized the doctor's opinion, pointing out "[a]lthough a 'history of chronic degenerative disease' is cited by Dr. Akmakjian he acknowledged that the condition had not resulted in a period of disability or evidence of any modified work performance and had only been involved with limited chiropractic care over the applicant's 30 year working history." But, prior disability or evidence of modified work performance is no longer a prerequisite to apportionment. If the presence of these factors is necessary to constitute substantial evidence, there would have been no purpose in changing the law.

The WCJ also found insufficient support in the testimony for the conclusion the degenerative disease was chronic in terms of ongoing pathology, treatment, or disability. But again, degenerative disease can be asymptomatic and still apportionable under the new law.

The WCJ also refers to two doctors who examined applicant and states neither identified a progressive disease as a factor in disability, but these reports were compiled prior to the change in the law on apportionment. Dr. Akmakjian is the only doctor who addressed apportionment after the law change–besides being the court appointed IME.

The WCJ also criticizes the apportionment on the ground that it was based on age alone. However, the doctor indicated that the MRI and X–rays showed degenerative disc disease and this condition only gets worse because of age, i.e., wear and tear on the body.

Even though Dr. Akmakjian does make assumptions, his conclusion is based on specific evidence of applicant's condition. In contrast, the Board's rejection of his opinion on apportionment is based on an analysis of the facts that would have been appropriate under the prior law, rather than the current one. While paying lip service to the new standard that apportionment can be warranted if there is a preinjury asymptomatic condition, the doctor's report is criticized in large part because of the absence of significant preinjury medical treatment or disability. It points out, for instance, that applicant suffered from minor episodic back pain prior to his injury, but notes that such pain is not a ratable disability. This is, of course, true, but this fact is not significant under the new law. An asymptomatic prior condition would not involve a ratable disability, so that the fact that applicant here did not have a history of medical treatment or lost time due to his degenerative back condition is not significant under the new apportionment standards and does not serve as a basis to disregard Dr. Akmakjian's opinion. If the Board's analysis were the norm, apportionment under the new standard could rarely, if ever, be found.

Moreover, the Board too readily dismisses the facts upon which Dr. Akmakjian bases his conclusion, characterizing his reliance on applicant's MRI as "questionable" given the latter's insignificant history of back pain. We find nothing questionable about a medical expert's reliance on an accepted diagnostic tool. A medical expert may well view a person's history of minor back problems as being more significant in light of the evidence of substantial degeneration of the back shown by an MRI. Dr. Akmakjian did so here. His conclusion cannot be disregarded as being speculative when it was based on his expertise in evaluating the significance of these facts. This was a matter of scientific medical knowledge and the Board impermissibly substituted its judgment for that of the medical expert.

Finally, the 20 percent figure that Dr. Akmakjian used is based on his subjective evaluation, but we cannot conclude that it is merely a random number that he settled upon. He himself noted that apportionment would have been greater if applicant had had more extensive treatment for his back. On the other hand, the doctor may have given applicant a higher disability rating because he appeared to be in more pain than other patients with similar injuries because of the preexisting pathology. In Dr. Akmakjian's words, applicant just did not have a normal back. The doctor made a determination based on his medical expertise of the approximate percentage of permanent disability caused by degenerative condition of applicant's back. Section 4663, subdivision (c), requires no more.

DISPOSITION

The order is annulled and the matter is remanded to the Board with directions to order the WCJ to make an award consistent with this opinion... .

Footnote 1. All further statutory references will be to the Labor Code unless otherwise indicated.

Footnote 2. Former section 4663, repealed effective April 19, 2004 by SB 899 (Stats. 2004, ch. 34, § 33), provided as follows: "In case of aggravation of any disease existing prior to a compensable injury, compensation shall be allowed only for the proportion of the disability due to the aggravation of such prior disease which is reasonably attributed to the injury."

Footnote 3. Section 4663 now reads: "(a) Apportionment of permanent disability shall be based on causation. [P] (b) Any physician who prepares a report addressing the issue of permanent disability due to a claimed industrial injury shall in that report address the issue of causation of the permanent disability. [P] (c) In order for a physician's report to be considered complete on the issue of permanent disability, it must include an apportionment determination. A physician shall make an apportionment determination by finding what approximate percentage of the permanent disability was caused by the direct result of injury arising out of and occurring in the course of employment and what approximate percentage of the permanent disability was caused by other factors both before and subsequent to the industrial injury, including prior industrial injuries. If the physician is unable to include an apportionment determination in his or her report, the physician shall state the specific reasons why the physician could not make a determination of the effect of that prior condition on the permanent disability arising from the injury. The physician shall then consult with other physicians or refer the employee to another physician from whom the employee is authorized to seek treatment or evaluation in accordance with this division in order to make the final determination. [P] (d) An employee who claims an industrial injury shall, upon request, disclose all previous permanent disabilities or physical impairments."

Footnote 4. Section 4664 now provides in part: "(a) The employer shall only be liable for the percentage of permanent disability directly caused by the injury arising out of and occurring in the course of employment."

Wilkinson Doctrine Not Invalidated by SB 899

In *City of Santa Clara, PSI, et. al. v. WCAB (Navarette)* (2005) 70 Cal. Comp. Cases 1713, the Appeals Board held that Labor Code section 4664(b), as enacted by SB 899, did not invalidate the holding in *Wilkinson v. WCAB* (1977) 42 Cal. Comp. Cases 406, wherein it was held that permanent disability from

successive injuries may be combined if the injuries became permanent and stationary at the same time and quoted the trial judge as stating:

Nothing in SB 899 or Labor Code § 4664(b) reverses or renders inoperative the holding of the *Wilkinson* case. *Wilkinson* found an exception to the prohibitions of former Labor Code § 4750, which generally precluded combining permanent disabilities from a [*sic*] "prior" and "later" injuries. With the repeal of section 4750, Defendants argue, the Board may no longer combine permanent disabilities in any cases. In my view, Defendants have the argument backwards. Former section 4750 was a limiting section that prevented the combining of disabilities from multiple injuries, and *Wilkinson* was an exception to that limitation. If anything, the repeal of section 4750 gives more freedom to combine disabilities from multiple injuries. In this Applicant's cases, however, no extension of *Wilkinson* is required because the injuries would, of necessity, have become P&S at the same time for the reasons previously discussed.

Labor Code § 4664(b) only provides a conclusive presumption that Applicant retained *at least* the 29% level of permanent disability previously awarded. Nothing in that statute, or its legislative history, shows any intention to bar proof that the prior permanent disability has *increased*. In enacting section 4664(b) the Legislature was addressing claims that despite a prior adjudicated award of permanent disability, the worker had achieved medical rehabilitation from that disability and was now entitled to a new PD award, for a different injury, that apportioned out less or none of the prior permanent disability award. I made no finding in these cases that Applicant had achieved any reduction in his awarded permanent disability–on the contrary, I made the exact opposite finding, that his prior level of permanent disability still existed and has now substantially increased. Defendants will, of course, receive full credit against the current Findings and Award for permanent disability benefits they have already paid for Applicant's knee disability... .

Effect of New Apportionment Law on Petition to Reopen

The Appeals Board has held that SB 899 apportionment statutes apply to an issue of increased permanent disability alleged in a Petition to Reopen, *that was pending* on April 19, 2004, but that in applying the new statutes to issues of increased permanent disability, the issue of apportionment must be determined without reference to *how, or if,* apportionment was determined in the original award. In making this finding in *Vargas v. Atascadero State Hospital et al* (2006) 71 Cal. Comp. Cases 500, the Board, in an En Banc decision, stated:

OPINION AND ORDER DENYING PETITION FOR REMOVAL (EN BANC)

Applicant has filed a Petition for Removal (Footnote 1) challenging the Workers' Compensation Administrative Law Judge's (WCJ's) order at a hearing on applicant's petition to reopen, authorizing defendant to obtain supplemental medical reports to address the new apportionment provisions of Senate Bill (SB) 899. (Footnote 2)

Because of the important legal issues presented, and in order to secure uniformity of decision in the future, the Chairman of the Appeals Board, upon a majority vote of its members, assigned this case to the Appeals Board as a whole for an en banc decision. (Section 115.) (Footnote 3)

We conclude that the WCJ's order is correct, and therefore we will deny applicant's petition for removal. In so doing, we hold that:

(1) The new apportionment provisions of SB 899 apply to the issue of *increased* permanent disability alleged in any petition to reopen (see sections 5803, 5804, 5410) that was pending at the time of the legislative enactment on April 19, 2004, regardless of date of injury;

(2) Consistent with Section 47 of SB 899, the new apportionment statutes cannot be used to revisit or recalculate the level of permanent disability, or the presence or absence of apportionment, determined under a final order, decision, or award issued before April 19, 2004; and

(3) In applying the new apportionment provisions to the issue of *increased* permanent disability, the issue must be determined without reference to how, or if, apportionment was determined in the original award.

BACKGROUND

On March 22, 1995, applicant sustained an admitted injury to her left upper extremity and neck. Subsequently she underwent cervical spine surgery by Dr. Kissel, a neurosurgeon. By Findings and Award (F&A) dated January 21, 1998, the WCJ found that applicant also sustained injury to her left ear, and that the 1995 injury resulted in permanent disability of 67%. The permanent disability was determined by "baseball arbitration" under former Section 4065. (Footnote 4)

That is, applicant had submitted a proposed standard rating of 80% for the neck, 20% for the left upper extremity, and 5% for the left ear, which, after adjustment for age and occupation, and application of the Multiple Disabilities Table (MDT), produced a permanent disability rating of 97%. Defendant had submitted a proposed standard rating of 60% for the neck and 1% for the left ear, which adjusted to 67%. (Defendant's proposed rating did not include a rating for the left upper extremity.) The WCJ chose defendant's proposed rating because it was closest to a recommended rating obtained by the WCJ, which rated the disability at 65% standard, adjusting to 71%. The recommended rating was based on the work restrictions and objective and subjective factors of disability for the neck and left upper extremity set forth in Dr. Kissel's May 8, 1996 report, as well as the factors of disability set forth in the June 30, 1997 defense QME report of Dr. Di Bartolomeo with regard to the left ear.

As to the neck and left upper extremity, the objective factors included minimal limitation in range of motion of the cervical spine. The subjective factors included moderate and intermittent neck pain which occurs with any type of activity for greater than one hour length of time, and applicant having some days with moderate to severe pain on an occasional basis. The work restriction was a limitation to semi–sedentary work, with an inability to perform work reaching above head or with repetitive bending and twisting of the cervical spine and difficulty with computer work activity, which would exacerbate applicant's symptoms.

As to the left ear, the factors of disability included an "audiometric demonstration of a sloping high frequency auditory deficit" as well as "mild left tinnitus and/or myoclonus, and generalized left ear pain."

According to the Disability Evaluator ("rater"), the left ear factors rated 0%. Thus, the recommended rating of 71% was based on the neck and left upper extremity disability. (Footnote 5)

In his Opinion on Decision, the WCJ stated that the permanent disability award was based on "the finding of the factors of disability, the recommended rating of those factors of disability, and [because] the defendant's proposed rating was closer to the true disability than the applicant's proposed rating."

There was no apportionment in the F&A of January 21, 1998.

Applicant filed a timely Petition to Reopen under sections 5803, 5804 and 5410, alleging that her condition had worsened, resulting in new and further temporary (Footnote 6) and permanent disability, and that she had seen Dr. Kissel again. Later the petition was amended to include an allegation of psyche injury, and the parties eventually stipulated to compensable consequence injuries to the psyche and TMJ syndrome (jaw injury). They also agreed to Dr. Di Bartolomeo as the AME for the left ear injury and Dr. Wells as the AME for the psyche injury.

Applicant filed a Declaration of Readiness to Proceed (DOR), and the petition to reopen proceeded to hearing on March 2, 2004. The DOR included reference to a medical report from Dr. Gabriel, a dentist. Defendant raised the issue of apportionment, and the WCJ delayed submission to allow defendant to file a medical report from Dr. Adler, the defense QME on the TMJ claim.

On April 8, 2004, the WCJ served rating instructions and a recommended rating of 91:2%. (Footnote 7)

With respect to the neck and left upper extremity, the instructions were identical to the 1998 instructions, but the rating was done by a different rater, who now rated the neck and left upper extremity disability using a standard rating of 60%, adjusting to 67%, as compared with the 1998 recommended rating of 65% standard, adjusting to 71%.

For the left ear, the instructions referred to the March 7, 2002 report of Dr. Di Bartolomeo, which included as a factor of disability an average 19 decibel reduction of hearing of the right ear and 2% loss of hearing of the left ear.

For the psyche injury, the instructions were based on the August 2, 2002 report of Dr. Wells, which described impairment in the eight work function categories ranging from none, to very slight to slight.

For the TMJ injury, the instructions relied on the objective factors of disability and restrictions described in the October 6, 2003 report of Dr. Gabriel. The restrictions included "no cradling the phone between the facial, neck, shoulder musculature; avoidance of excessive talking of twenty minutes straight, without a ten minute rest; improper posture due to a non–ergonomically designed environment; restricted from pushing, pulling, and lifting objects more than ten pounds; avoidance of cold environment, which will cause increased myofacial pain; avoidance of emotional stress that would \give rise to nervousness, irritability and tension such as working close deadlines, dealing with contentious, unreasonable or otherwise exasperating members of the public and work that requires precision and attention to detail under distracting conditions."

On April 12, 2004, applicant filed a DOR, requesting cross–examination of the rater. (Footnote 8)

On April 15, the District Office served notice of hearing for cross–examination of the rater set for May 20, 2004. On April 19, 2004, SB 899 was enacted. On April 23, 2004, the WCJ informed the parties that he would apply the new law of apportionment under SB 899, and that further development of the record would be addressed at the May 20 hearing. At that hearing, the WCJ issued the following ruling:

"Defendant's request to leave the record open to obtain supplemental reports from Dr. Wells and Dr. Di Bartolomeo regarding the 4–19–04 change in the law regarding apportionment is granted. Defendant is allowed 30 days to submit the additional reports or show good cause for an extension of time to do so. Applicant has the right to obtain rebuttal to these reports.

"Applicant informs WCAB that if the record is left open she is informally indicating depositions of Dr. Kissel on 6–30–04, of Dr. Wells on 7–21–04, Dr. DeBartolomeo [sic] on 7–2–04, and Dr. Gabriel on 6–25–04." "

Applicant filed a timely Petition for Removal, contending, in substance, that the new law of apportionment cannot be applied retroactively where the medical reports were prepared (Footnote 9) before the enactment of SB 899, and that when the WCJ vacated submission and allowed further development of the record, he violated applicant's right to an expeditious and unencumbered hearing under the California Constitution, as well as her statutory right, under section 5313, to a prompt determination of the merits.

The Appeals Board invited briefs from the workers' compensation community to address the issues raised by the petition. Defendant, State Compensation Insurance Fund (SCIF), then filed a response. The Board also received and considered briefs from the California Workers' Compensation Institute, the California Self–Insurers Association, and the Law Office of Ernest A. Canning.

DISCUSSION

(1) The New Apportionment Provisions Of SB 899 Apply To The Issue Of Increased Permanent Disability Alleged In Any Petition To Reopen (See Sections 5803, 5804, 5410) That Was Pending At The Time Of The Legislative Enactment On April 19, 2004, Regardless Of Date Of Injury.

In *Marsh v. Workers' Comp. Appeals Bd.* (2005) 130 Cal. App. 4th 906 [30 Cal. Rptr. 3d 598] [70 Cal. Comp. Cases 787], wherein a petition to reopen was pending on the date of SB 899's enactment, the Court held that the apportionment provisions of SB 899 must be applied to all cases not yet final at the time of the legislative enactment on

April 19, 2004, regardless of the earlier dates of injury and any interim decision. (See also, *Kleemann v. Workers' Comp. Appeals Bd.* (2005) 127 Cal. App. 4th 274 [25 Cal. Rptr. 3d 448] [70 Cal. Comp. Cases 133] (in which the Court reached a similar conclusion wherein a petition to reopen was pending on the date of SB 899's enactment); cf., *Rio Linda Union School Dist. v. Workers' Comp. Appeals Bd.* (*Scheftner*) (2005) 131 Cal. App. 4th 517 [31 Cal. Rptr. 3d 789] [70 Cal. Comp. Cases 999].)

Accordingly, and consistent with the principles stated in *Marsh,* we conclude that the new apportionment provisions of SB 899 apply to the issue of *increased* permanent disability alleged in any petition to reopen (see sections 5803, 5804, 5410) that was pending at the time of the legislative enactment on April 19, 2004, regardless of date of injury.

In this case, applicant's petition to reopen was pending on April 19, 2004, so the new apportionment provisions apply, and the WCJ correctly granted defendant's request to obtain supplemental reports from its medical evaluators to address apportionment under the new law.

(2) Consistent With Section 47 Of SB 899, The New Apportionment Statutes Cannot Be Used To Revisit Or Recalculate The Level Of Permanent Disability, Or The Presence Or Absence Of Apportionment, Determined Under A Final Order, Decision, Or Award Issued Before April 19, 2004.

Marsh, Kleemann and *Scheftner* make it clear that the apportionment provisions of SB 899 may not be used to reopen an award of permanent disability that was final as of April 19, 2004. Section 47 of SB 899 states:

"The amendment, addition, or repeal of, any provision of law made by this act shall apply prospectively from the date of enactment of this act, regardless of the date of injury, unless otherwise specified, *but shall not constitute good cause to reopen or rescind, alter, or amend any existing order, decision, or award of the Workers' Compensation Appeals Board.*" (Italics added.)"

The second clause of Section 47 precludes using the new statutes to establish a basis to reopen the original existing award.

In *Marsh*, it was noted that the Court in *Kleemann* examined the phrase, "shall not constitute good cause to reopen or rescind, alter, or amend any existing order, decision or award," and explained that this "language resembled that generally applied when the WCAB exercises its continuing jurisdiction to readdress a prior WCAB determination within five years from the date of injury for good cause or new and further disability" under Sections 5410, 5803 and 5804. (*Marsh, supra,* 130 Cal. App. 4th at p. 914 [70 Cal. Comp. Cases at pp. 792–793].)

In *Kleemann*, the Court also commented that "applying apportionment under new sections 4663 and 4664 does not in this case reopen, rescind, alter or amend a previous 'existing order, decision, or award' of permanent disability. *There is no reimbursement of previously awarded compensation under the new statutes . . .* " (127 Cal. App. 4th at pp. 287–288 [70 Cal. Comp. Cases at pp. 143–144], italics added.) Thus, if Kleemann's case had involved 'reimbursement of previously awarded compensation,' the

Court may have precluded application of new sections 4663 and 4664. The Court's negative reference to 'reimbursement of previously awarded compensation' supports the conclusion that the new apportionment sections cannot be used to reach back and reduce the original award, or revisit the basis for that award.

In *Scheftner*, the Court said in a similar vein:

" . . . And so we can presume the Legislature in using the entire phrase 'shall not constitute good cause to reopen or rescind, alter, or amend any existing order, decision, or award of the Workers' Compensation Appeals Board' was intentionally referring to the continuing jurisdiction authority of the WCAB under sections 5803 and 5804 . . . The language chosen by the Legislature, read as a complete phrase, indicates the Legislature did not want the changes of law made by Bill No. 899 to be the basis for reopening cases otherwise concluded under the workers' compensation procedures for decision (§ 5313), reconsideration (§ 5900), and judicial review (§ 5950)." (131 Cal. App. 4th at pp. 530–531 [70 Cal. Comp. Cases at p. 1009].)"

Further, in considering the scenario of a concluded workers' compensation case subject only to the continuing jurisdiction of the WCAB, but with the case properly reopened for good cause, the Court stated that the Legislature "may not intend in such situation to backtrack and require reassessment of causation of the permanent disability to apply the new apportionment law." (*Scheftner*, *supra*, 131 Cal. App. 4th at p. 532 [70 Cal. Comp. Cases at p. 1010].) (Footnote 10)

Accordingly, we conclude, consistent with Section 47 of SB 899, that the new apportionment statutes cannot be used to revisit or recalculate the level of permanent disability, or the presence or absence of apportionment, determined under a final order, decision, or award issued before April 19, 2004.

(3) In Applying The New Apportionment Provisions To The Issue Of Increased Permanent Disability, The Issue Must Be Determined Without Reference To How, Or If, Apportionment Was Determined In The Original Award.

The WCJ has not issued a final order on applicant's petition to reopen. We observe, however, that apportionment of the *increased* permanent disability alleged in applicant's petition to reopen may include not only disability that could have been apportioned prior to SB 899, but may also include disability that formerly could not have been apportioned (e.g., pathology, asymptomatic prior conditions, and retroactive prophylactic work preclusions). (See *Escobedo v. Marshalls* (2005) 70 Cal. Comp. Cases 604 [Appeals Board en banc].)

In this case, to the extent that applicant's neck and upper extremity injury may have resulted in *increased* permanent disability, any such *increased* disability will be subject to apportionment under the new law, provided there is substantial medical evidence establishing that these other factors have caused *increased* permanent disability. Consistent with part (2) of this opinion, however, the new apportionment statutes cannot be used to revisit or recalculate the level of permanent disability, or the presence or absence of apportionment, determined under a final order, decision, or award issued before April 19, 2004.

(4) Application Of These Principles To the Present Case.

The WCJ was correct in authorizing further development of the record, because the issue of applicant's *increased* permanent disability, if any, must be determined using the new apportionment provisions, and the reporting physicians have yet to address the issue.

In this regard, after applicant filed her petition to reopen, the parties stipulated to compensable consequence injuries to the psyche and TMJ syndrome (jaw injury). There is no existing order, decision, or award of permanent disability concerning the compensable consequence injuries, and the WCJ has not issued a final order on them in connection with applicant's petition to reopen. Moreover, there are no medical reports in the WCAB's present record that address the issue of apportionment of the psyche or TMJ disability, if any, in accordance with the new apportionment statutes and in accordance with the standards set out in *Escobedo*.

Finally, we deny applicant's contention that application of SB 899 in the reopening proceedings will result in a denial of her constitutional and statutory rights to expeditious proceedings and a prompt determination. Similar contentions were rejected in *Kleemann*, *Marsh* and *Scheftner*.

For the foregoing reasons,

IT IS ORDERED, as the Appeals Board's decision en banc, that applicant's Petition for Removal be, and the same hereby is, DENIED... .

CONCURRING OPINION OF COMMISSIONER RABINE

I reluctantly concur under compulsion of *Marsh*. Even though the parties did not raise the issue of the applicability of the apportionment statutes of SB 899 to petitions to reopen, and even though the Court does not address that issue specifically in its opinion, there is no doubt that the Court held that "the apportionment provisions of SB 899 must be applied to all cases such as Marsh's [that is, cases where a petition to reopen is pending] not yet final at the time of the legislative enactment . . . " (130 Cal. App. 4th at p. 909 [70 Cal. Comp. Cases at p. 788].) We are an "inferior court," and we are "jurisdictionally required to adhere to and follow the decisions of the Court of Appeal." (*Brannen v. Workers' Comp. Appeals Bd.* (1996) 46 Cal. App. 4th 377, 384, fn. 5 [53 Cal. Rptr. 2d 768] [61 Cal. Comp. Cases 554].)

But if I were writing on a clean slate, I would read the plain language of Section 47 of SB 899 to forbid application of the apportionment provisions to petitions to reopen awards that issued prior to April 19, 2004.

The history of workers' compensation reform from 1989 to 2004 is a history of increasing, sometimes bewildering complexity. Nonetheless, where there is more than one possible reading of a legislative provision, I would apply Occam's razor ("Entities should not be multiplied unnecessarily") (Footnote 11) and prefer the simpler to the more complicated. Here, Section 47 provides that the apportionment provisions "shall not constitute good cause to reopen or rescind, alter, or amend any existing order, decision, or award . . . " The issue of good cause to reopen is precisely the issue that is pending in this case, and the simplest reading of Section 47 is that the new apportionment statutes do not apply.

As it happens, the new and further disability, if any, in this case appears to be attributable to compensable consequences (TMJ, psyche). Therefore, the application of the apportionment statutes to these disabilities would be no more complicated than to disabilities subject to initial determination (that is to say, very complicated). But in the garden–variety petition to reopen, where there is, for example, a back injury with a pre–existing disease process not subject to apportionment at the time of the original award, the evaluating physicians will have to determine not only whether there is any new and further disability, but also whether any of that disability is attributable to the natural progression of the underlying disease process from the date of the original award through the date of the subsequent evaluation. It is conceivable that physicians will be able to make these determinations, but the difficulty is extraordinary.

As the Court in *Marsh* stated, there is a "finite number of cases blind–sided by SB 899's adoption[.]" (130 Cal. App. 4th at p. 916 [70 Cal. Comp. Cases at p. 795]). The number of cases that involve petitions to reopen awards that issued prior to April 19, 2004 is a mere subset of that finite number. I do not believe that the level of complexity required by this decision, with which I agree, is required by a plain reading of Section 47. But that train has already left the station... .

Footnote 1. See Labor Code section 5310. Unless otherwise specified, all further statutory references are to the Labor Code.

Footnote 2. Stats. 2004, ch. 34, § 35, enacted April 19, 2004.

Footnote 3. The Appeals Board's en banc decisions are binding precedent on all Appeals Board panels and WCJs. (Cal. Code Regs., tit. 8, § 10341; *City of Long Beach v. Workers' Comp. Appeals Bd. (Garcia)* (2005) 126 Cal. App. 4th 298, 313, fn. 5 [23 Cal. Rptr. 3d 782] [70 Cal. Comp. Cases 109]; *Gee v. Workers' Comp. Appeals Bd.* (2002) 96 Cal. App. 4th 1418, 1425, fn. 6 [118 Cal. Rptr. 2d 105] [67 Cal. Comp. Cases 236]; see also Govt. Code, § 11425.60(b).)

Footnote 4. Enacted 1993 and repealed 2002, the statute provided, in relevant part, that "(a) [. . .] where either the employer or the employee have obtained evaluations of the employee's permanent impairment and limitations from a [QME] under Section 4061 and either party contests the . . . medical evaluation of the other party, the [WCJ] or the appeals board shall be limited to choosing between either party's proposed permanent disability rating. [P] "(b) The employee's permanent disability benefit awarded under paragraph (a) shall be adjusted based on the disability rating selected by the appeals board. [. . .]" (See *Britt v. Workers' Comp. Appeals. Bd.* (2001) 66 Cal. Comp. Cases 1182 [writ denied].)

Footnote 5. The formula used by the rater was as follows:

```
7.-65%-35F-
65-71:0
18.1-65%-35F- 71:0
65-71:0
1/2              0:0
(0:0)
                           71:0
3.1-0%-35J-0                        0:0
                                          71:0
```

MULTIPLE
DISABILITIES
TABLE

Footnote 6. The claim for temporary disability was resolved by interim litigation that is now final, so that only the claim for increased permanent disability remains outstanding.

Footnote 7. The formula used by the rater was as follows:

```
1.4 --          17:2
8% -35J-
14-
2% (3.          0:2
111-15%-
25J-23-
28:0)
4.5-30%-        47:2
35J-41-
                7.-60%-
                35F-60-
                67:0
                18.1-60%-    67:0
                35F-60-
                67:0
                             0:0
                1/2 (0:0)
                             67:0
```

MULTIPLE
DISABILITY
TABLE:
91:2

Footnote 8. The basis for applicant's objection to the instructions/rating was not specified. However, there may be an issue as to how the neck/upper extremity disability can be less now than what it was in 1998, based on the same factors of disability.

Footnote 9. Subdivision (b) of section 4663 states, "[a]ny physician who prepares a report addressing the issue of permanent impairment due to a claimed industrial injury shall in that report address the issue of causation of the permanent disability."

Footnote 10. See also *Draper v. Workers' Comp. Appeals Bd.* (1983) 147 Cal. App. 3d 502, 508 [195 Cal. Rptr. 248] [48 Cal. Comp. Cases 748, 753], wherein the Court stated that the Appeals Board "cannot . . . go behind [a prior] award and speculate as to what other determination might have been made at that time."

Footnote 11. See Eco, *Il nome della rosa* (1980).

Intentionally blank

§ 34.0   ATTORNEYS

Page 1425, Column 2, seventh paragraph, insert following '…1263.'

In a significant panel decision *In The Matter of John H. Hoffman, Jr.* (2006) 71 Cal. Comp. Cases 609, in explaining why a former attorney, who had been *disbarred* or *suspended* from *the practice of law* by the State Bar, cannot represent parties including lien claimants before the Board, but *may engage in legal work such as legal research, assembling data, or assisting in the drafting of pleadings and briefs and other similar documents involving workers' compensation matters*, the Board stated, in part:

John H. Hoffman, Jr. (Hoffman), has filed a petition seeking reconsideration of the Findings and Order issued by the workers' compensation administrative law judge (WCJ) on August 9, 2005. In that decision, the WCJ found that Hoffman has violated the provisions of Workers' Compensation Appeals Board (WCAB) Rule 10779. (Cal. Code Regs., tit. 8, § 10779.) Rule 10779 provides, in essence, that a former attorney who has been disbarred or suspended, who has been placed on involuntary inactive status, or who has resigned while disciplinary action is pending, shall be deemed unfit to appear as a representative of any party before the WCAB, unless he or she petitions the Appeals Board and receives prior permission to appear. The WCJ ordered that Hoffman be barred from any further appearances before the WCAB unless: (1) he complies with the provisions of Rule 10779 by petitioning the Appeals Board for permission to appear; and (2) he is given permission to appear by the Appeals Board.

In his petition for reconsideration, Hoffman contends, in substance that: (1) Rule 10779 only precludes disbarred and other attorneys who fall within its scope from appearing as a representative of a "party" before the WCAB, and that the lien claimants he represents are not "parties" as contemplated by Rule 10779; and (2) even if lien claimants can be "parties" under Rule 10779 in some circumstances, Rule 10301(l) (Cal. Code Regs., tit. 8, § 10301(l)) makes lien claimants "parties" only when either the applicant's case has been settled by way of a compromise and release agreement or the applicant has chosen not to proceed with his or her case.

On October 26, 2005, we granted reconsideration in order to further study this matter. As our Decision After Reconsideration, we conclude that: (1) both Rule 10779 and the State Bar Act preclude any non–reinstated former attorney who has been disbarred or suspended by the Supreme Court (for reasons other than nonpayment of State Bar fees), who has been placed on involuntary inactive status by the State Bar, or who has resigned with disciplinary proceedings pending against him or her from

appearing as a representative of any party before the WCAB (at least if they have not received permission under Rule 10779); (Footnote 1) (2) this preclusion against appearing as a representative of any "party" extends to appearing on the behalf of any litigant, including but not limited to lien claimants; and (3) this preclusion against "appearing as a representative" in WCAB proceedings extends to any activity that would constitute the practice of law. Accordingly, we affirm the WCJ's August 9, 2005 Findings and Order.

This case involves the question of whether Hoffman has violated WCAB Rule 10779 (Cal. Code Regs., tit. 8, § 10779), which provides:

"An attorney who has been disbarred or suspended by the Supreme Court for reasons other than nonpayment of State Bar fees, or who has been placed on involuntary inactive enrollment status by the State Bar, or who has resigned while disciplinary action is pending shall be deemed unfit to appear as a representative of any party before the Workers' Compensation Appeals Board during the time that the attorney is precluded from practicing law in this state. Any attorney claiming to be qualified to appear as a representative before the Workers' Compensation Appeals Board despite disbarment, suspension or resignation may file a petition for permission to appear. The petition shall set forth in detail:

(1) "the facts leading to the disbarment, suspension or resignation; and

(2) "the facts and circumstances alleged by the attorney to establish competency, qualification and moral character to appear as a representative before the Workers' Compensation Appeals Board.

"The petition shall be verified, shall be filed in the San Francisco office of the Appeals Board and a copy thereof served on the State Bar of California." "

In relation to this question, the following facts are established by the evidence and/or by admissions in Hoffman's pleadings.

Hoffman was admitted to the State Bar of California in December 1972.

In 1985, Hoffman pled guilty to two courts of grand theft (Pen. Code, § 487(1)) and one court of forgery (Pen. Code, § 470), which are all felonies. At the time he entered his guilty pleas to the three felonies, he admitted in writing that, "with the intent to defraud and to use the money and property of others for my own personal uses," he took $60,000.00 from two people on February 23, 1981, he took another $8,500.00 from those two people on June 6, 1981, and he then forged an assignment of a deed of trust on December 6, 1982. (Footnote 2)

On April 19, 1985, Hoffman voluntarily became an inactive member of the State Bar.

On June 27, 1986, Hoffman formally resigned from the State Bar, with disciplinary proceedings pending against him.

The Appeals Board has no record of any petition from Hoffman seeking permission to appear before the WCAB pursuant to Rule 10779, filed on or after June 27, 1986.

Nevertheless, in 1989, Hoffman began representing medical lien claimants before the WCAB. From 1989 to 1990, he worked for Fisher–Hoffman Resolution Services, Inc. Then, from 1990 to 1995, he worked for Hoffman, Hoffman & Associates, Inc. Since 1995, he has been employed by Integrated Healthcare Recovery Services, a California corporation, dba Hoffman, Hoffman & Associates.

On June 11, 2004, a notice was prepared stating that Hoffman, Hoffman & Associates had become the "attorney/lien representative of record" and the "attorney of record" for lien claimants – LAGS Spine Treatment Center; and Sportcare and Spine Treatment Center – in Case No. GOL 0089767. This notice of representation indicated it was signed by Hoffman. At trial, Hoffman denied the signature was his, but he acknowledged having authorized various staff members of Hoffman, Hoffman & Associates to sign his name for him. The notice of representation was filed with the WCAB on June 14, 2004, which was after a WCJ had issued a November 12, 2002 order approving a compromise and release agreement settling the applicant's underlying claim in the matter.

On January 20, 2005, Hoffman appeared as the representative of lien claimant – Cypress Surgery Center – at a lien trial in Case No. GOL 0097353 before a WCJ at the WCAB's Goleta district office. No one else from Hoffman, Hoffman & Associates appeared at that hearing. This appearance occurred after a WCJ's August 20, 2004 order approving a compromise and release resolved the applicant's underlying claim in the matter.

On January 26, 2005, Hoffman appeared as the representative for lien claimants – Galileo Surgery Center; and Cypress Surgery Center – at a lien trial in Case No. GOL 0026960 before a WCJ at the WCAB's Goleta District Office. No one else from Hoffman, Hoffman & Associates appeared at that hearing. This appearance occurred after a WCJ's February 21, 2003 order approving a compromise and release that had settled the applicant's claim in the matter.

On March 8, 2005, a notice was prepared stating that Hoffman, Hoffman & Associates had become the "attorney of record" for lien claimant – Bay Surgery Center – in Case No. OAK 0277268. The notice of representation indicated it had been signed by Hoffman, but he denied this at trial. Again, however, he acknowledged there were staff people who he had authorized to sign his name for him. This notice of representation was filed with the WCAB on March 11, 2005.

On May 2, 2005, a notice was prepared stating that Hoffman, Hoffman & Associates had become the "attorney/lien representative of record" and the "attorney of record" for lien claimant – Bay Surgery Center – in Case No. OAK 0289010. Although the notice of representation purported to bear Hoffman's signature, he asserted at trial that the signature was not his. We reiterate, however, he acknowledged that several staff members had the authority to sign for him. This notice of representation was filed with the WCAB on May 5, 2005.

On June 13, 2005, a trial occurred on the issue of why Hoffman should not be barred from further appearances before the WCAB on the basis of alleged violations of Rule 10779.

On August 9, 2005, the WCJ issued her Findings and Order. She found that Hoffman has violated the provisions of Rule 10779 because he had resigned from the State Bar with disciplinary proceedings pending, but then had appeared in WCAB proceedings without having petitioned the Appeals Board for permission to do so. She then ordered that Hoffman be barred from further appearances before the WCAB unless he both complies with Rule 10779 and receives permission to appear from the Appeals Board.

Hoffman then filed the petition for reconsideration now pending before us.

II. DISCUSSION

A. Any Non–Reinstated Former Attorney Who Was Disbarred Or Suspended, Who Was Placed On Involuntary Inactive Status, Or Who Resigned With Disciplinary Proceedings Pending Is Precluded From Appearing As A Representative Of Any Party Before The WCAB.

As a general rule, a person who is not licensed to practice law is allowed to practice before the WCAB. (Lab. Code, §§ 5501, 5700; see also, Eagle Indemnity Co. v. Industrial Acc. Com. (Hernandez) (1933) 217 Cal. 244, 248 [18 P.2d 341] [19 I.A.C. 150]; 99 Cents Only Stores v. Workers' Comp. Appeals Bd. (Arriaga) (2000) 80 Cal. App. 4th 644, 648 [95 Cal. Rptr. 2d 569] [65 Cal. Comp. Cases 456]; Longval v. Workers' Comp. Appeals Bd. (1996) 51 Cal. App. 4th 792, 798 [59 Cal. Rptr. 2d 463] [61 Cal. Comp. Cases 1396].) (Footnote 3)

Under both the WCAB's Rules and the State Bar Act, however, there is an exception to this general rule when the person had once been licensed to practice law in California, but lost that license.

WCAB Rule 10779 provides, in essence, that any former attorney who was disbarred or suspended by the Supreme Court (for reasons other than nonpayment of State Bar fees), who was placed on involuntary inactive status by the State Bar, or who resigned with disciplinary proceedings pending cannot appear as a representative of any party before the WCAB unless either: (1) the former attorney petitions the Appeals Board for permission to appear and that permission is granted in advance; or (2) the former attorney's right to practice law is reinstated. (Cal. Code Regs., tit. 8, § 10779.) Rule 10779 is predicated on Labor Code section 4907, which provides that the privilege of any person (other than a licensed attorney) to appear as a representative of any party before the WCAB may be "removed, denied, or suspended by the Appeals Board." (Footnote 4)

Rule 10779 was adopted by the Appeals Board pursuant both to its rulemaking power (Lab. Code, § 5307) and its broad authority "to do all things necessary or convenient in the exercise of any power or jurisdiction conferred upon it." (Lab. Code, § 133.)

Rule 10779 – which precludes disbarred, suspended and other specified former attorneys from appearing before the WCAB without prior Appeals Board approval, even though Labor Code sections 5501 and 5700 generally allow non–attorneys to appear – is consistent with the provisions of the State Bar Act and the case law construing that Act.

In Benninghoff v. Superior Court (2006) 136 Cal. App. 4th 61 [38 Cal. Rptr. 3d 759] (rehg. den., 2006 Cal. App. LEXIS 198; rev. den., 2006 Cal. LEXIS 4780), the Court of Appeal considered the case of a former lawyer (Benninghoff), who had resigned from the State Bar with disciplinary charges pending after he had been convicted of four federal felonies (including conspiracy to defraud the United States and making various false statements). This resignation with disciplinary proceedings pending meant he could not practice law. (Bus. & Prof. Code, § 6126.) After his resignation, however, Benninghoff began representing parties before state administrative boards and commissions as a "lay representative." He asserted he could do so, arguing that because laypeople may represent parties in state administrative hearings, this kind of representation must not constitute the practice of law. The Court flatly rejected this assertion, stating: "Representing parties in state administrative hearings constitutes the practice of law [even] [a]s a 'lay representative. . . . ' By representing parties in state administrative hearings, Benninghoff practiced law in California–something he has lost the right to do by reason of his resignation from the State Bar with disciplinary charges pending." (Benninghoff, supra, 136 Cal. App. 4th at p. 65.)

In reaching this determination, the Court declared that the State Bar Act differentiates between a true layperson and a "defrocked" attorney: (Footnote 5)

"Benninghoff is not the typical layperson–he used to be a lawyer. The statute prohibiting the unauthorized practice of law treats true laypeople differently than lawyers who have lost their bar membership. [Business and Professions Code] [s]ection 6126, subdivision (a) addresses true laypeople. It provides that '[A]ny person . . . practicing law who is not an active member of the State Bar, or otherwise authorized pursuant to statute or court rule to practice law in this state at the time of doing so, is guilty of a misdemeanor.' (Italics added.) Section 6126, subdivision (b) addresses lawyers like Benninghoff. It provides that '[a]ny person who . . . has resigned from the State Bar with charges pending, and thereafter practices or attempts to practice law . . . is guilty of a crime punishable by imprisonment in the state prison or county jail.'[(Footnote 6)] Thus, a true layperson may practice law when 'authorized pursuant to statute or court rule'; a defrocked lawyer like Benninghoff may not practice law at all. (§ 6126, subds. (a) & (b).)" (Benninghoff, supra, 136 Cal. App. 4th at pp. 67–68 (italics in original; Court's Footnote omitted).)"

After concluding that "defrocked" attorneys cannot practice law under any circumstances, the Court next addressed the question of "whether the representation of parties in state administrative hearings constitutes practicing law." (Benninghoff, supra, 136 Cal. App. 4th at p. 68.) The Court held that it does, stating:

"The California Supreme Court addressed what it means to 'practice law' in Baron v. City of Los Angeles (1970) 2 Cal. 3d 535 . . . (Baron). There, . . . our Supreme Court had no difficulty resolving the . . . question of 'whether participation on behalf of another in hearings and proceedings before a board or commission constitutes the practice of law.' (Baron, supra, 2 Cal. 3d at p. 543 . . .) 'The cases uniformly hold that the character of the act, and not the place where it is performed, is the decisive element, and if the application of legal knowledge and technique is required, the activity constitutes the practice of law, even if conducted before an administrative board or commission.' (Ibid.)" (Benninghoff, supra, 136 Cal. App. 4th at p. 68 (Footnote and parallel citations omitted).)"

And:

"We reject Benninghoff's suggestion that representing parties in state administrative hearings cannot constitute practicing law because laypeople (arguably) are allowed to do so. As we explained ante, the law differentiates between laypeople and defrocked lawyers. Lawyers who resign with disciplinary charges pending may not practice law, without exception. (§ 6126, subd. (b).) In contrast, laypeople may practice law when 'authorized pursuant to statute or court rule.' (§ 6126, subd. (a).) If the various APA sections and regulations that Benninghoff cites do in fact allow laypeople to represent parties in administrative hearings, they constitute the statutory authorization contemplated by section 6126, subdivision (a)." (Benninghoff, supra, 136 Cal. App. 4th at p. 69.) (Footnote 7)

"In support of its determination that appearing before administrative boards and commissions constitutes the practice of law, Benninghoff also cited to the Supreme Court's 1933 decision in Eagle Indemnity Co. v. Industrial Acc. Com. (Hernandez), supra, 217 Cal. 244, which held that a layperson who appeared before the Industrial Accident Commission (the predecessor to the WCAB) was practicing law without a license, albeit permissibly. Benninghoff observed:

"In Eagle Indem. Co. v. Industrial Acc. Com. [(Hernandez)] (1933) 217 Cal. 244 . . . the Supreme Court allowed a layperson to recover attorney fees for his successful representation of an injured employee before the Industrial Accident Commission.[(Footnote 8)] (Id. at pp. 248–249.) The parties did not dispute that 'the services performed by [the layperson] in the prosecution of the claim before the Commission were legal services.' (Id. at p. 247.) And the court noted that 'as a general rule, no one may practice law without a license.' (Ibid.) But it also noted that '[e]xceptions to this general rule have been established and long recognized.' (Ibid.) It then reviewed the Workmen's Compensation Act, and concluded that 'the [L]egislature has [therein] provided a further exception to the general rule, as to practice before the Industrial Accident Commission.' (Id. at p. 248.) If the APA allows lay representation, presumably it does so as another exception to the general rule against laypeople practicing law. It does not remove that representation from the practice of law, or invalidate the absolute bar against defrocked lawyers practicing law." (Benninghoff, supra, 136 Cal. App. 4th at p. 70 (Footnote and parallel citations omitted).) (Footnote 9)

"The Court then pronounced: "Thus, Benninghoff, whom

the State Bar Act prohibits from practicing law, may not represent parties in state administrative hearings. This representation constitutes the practice of law, from which defrocked lawyers are categorically barred." (Benninghoff, *supra*, 136 Cal. App. 4th at p. 70.)

Therefore, under both Rule 10779 and the State Bar Act (as interpreted in Benninghoff, which is binding upon us (Auto Equity Sales v. Superior Court (1962) 57 Cal. 2d 450, 455 [369 P.2d 937, 20 Cal. Rptr. 321])), former attorneys who have lost their licenses cannot represent any party before the WCAB, at least if they have not received permission under Rule 10779. Indeed, Benninghoff specifically pointed out: "Today, the Workers['] Compensation Appeals Board expressly prohibits disbarred lawyers from representing parties before it. (Cal. Code Regs., tit. 8, § 10779.)" (Benninghoff, *supra*, 136 Cal. App. 4th at p. 70, fn. 7.)

B. The Preclusion Against Attorneys Who Have Lost Their Licenses From Appearing As A Representative Of Any "Party" Bars Their Appearances On Behalf Of Any Litigant, Including But Not Limited To Lien Claimants.

Labor Code section 4907 provides that the Appeals Board may remove, deny, or suspend the privilege of any non–attorney admitted "to appear in any proceeding as a representative of any party before the appeals board." (Lab. Code, § 4907 (emphasis added).)

Similarly, WCAB Rule 10779 provides that a former attorney who lost his or license "shall be deemed unfit to appear as a representative of any party before the [WCAB] during the time that the attorney is precluded from practicing law in this state." (Cal. Code Regs., tit. 8, § 10779 (emphasis added).)

Hoffman argues, in substance that: (1) a lien claimant is never a "party," as contemplated by section 4907 and Rule 10779; or (2) even if a lien claimant can be a "party" under some circumstances, Rule 10301(l) (Cal. Code Regs., tit. 8, § 10301(l)) makes a lien claimant a "party" only where the applicant's case has been settled by way of a compromise and release or where the applicant chooses not to proceed with his or her case. (Footnote 10)

Hoffman misapprehends the scope and intent of section 4907 and Rule 10779.

As just discussed, section 4907 gives the Appeals Board the power to remove, deny, or suspend the privilege of non–attorneys "to appear in any proceeding as a representative of any party." (Emphasis added.) The term "party" is not defined or limited by section 4907, nor is it otherwise defined or limited by any provision of Division 4 of Labor Code. Moreover, a statute should be construed to promote, rather than defeat, its general purpose and to avoid absurd consequences. (Torres v. Parkhouse Tire Service, Inc. (2001) 26 Cal. 4th 995, 1003 [30 P.3d 57, 111 Cal. Rptr. 2d 564, 66 Cal. Comp. Cas 1036]; Estate of Griswold (2001) 25 Cal. 4th 904, 911 [24 P.3d 1191, 108 Cal. Rptr. 2d 165]; Wilcox v. Birtwhistle (1999) 21 Cal. 4th 973, 977–978 [987 P.2d 727, 90 Cal. Rptr. 2d 260].) The obvious purpose of section 4907 is to give the Appeals Board the power to preclude non–attorneys who are not fit to practice from appearing in WCAB proceedings. It would be absurd to construe the term "party" in section 4907 to mean that the

Appeals Board can bar non–attorneys who are representing applicants or defendants from appearing before the WCAB, but that it cannot bar non–attorneys who are representing lien claimants from appearing, even if they are equally unfit, particularly given that case law clearly establishes that a lien claimant is a "party in interest" (Charles J. Vacanti, M.D., Inc. v. State Comp. Ins. Fund (2001) 24 Cal. 4th 800, 811 [14 P.3d 234, 102 Cal. Rptr. 2d 562] [65 Cal. Comp. Cases 1402]), (Footnote 11) even in circumstances where the applicant is still actively pursuing his or her case. (E.g., Beverly Hills Multispecialty Group, Inc. (Pinkney), *supra*, 26 Cal. App. 4th 789 (holding that, at least where there is a threshold issue fundamental to a lien claimant's claim, the lien claimant has the "right to participate in the worker's case–in–chief," and annulling the WCAB's decision because the lien claimant was not served with the employer's medical reports, was not served with mandatory settlement conference and trial notices; and was not allowed to cross–examine a witness); Cedeno v. American National Ins. Co. (1997) 62 Cal. Comp. Cases 939 (Appeals Board panel decision) (lien claimant denied due process where WCAB required it to conduct its cross–examination of witnesses by submitting questions to applicant's attorney).) (Footnote 12)

The same reasoning, of course, holds true with respect to Rule 10779. If an attorney who has lost his or her license is "unfit to appear as a representative" before the WCAB (Cal. Code Regs., tit. 8, § 10779), then he or she is unfit to appear for all purposes – not just unfit to represent applicants and defendants.

We recognize that Rule 10301(l) defines "party" to mean "an Applicant or Defendant, or a lien claimant where the applicant's case has been settled by way of a compromise and release, or where the applicant chooses not to proceed with his or her case." (Cal. Code Regs., tit. 8, § 10301(l).) However, even if we were to construe this definition to apply to Rule 10779, notwithstanding the discussion above, the evidence establishes that Hoffman was representing lien claimants in proceedings after the injured employees had settled their cases by compromise and release. Therefore, he was violating Rule 10779 in any event.

Beyond Rule 10779, however, Benninghoff makes it emphatically clear that a "defrocked" attorney cannot represent anyone – a party or a non–party – under any circumstances, in judicial or quasi–judicial administrative proceedings. Benninghoff flatly states that a defrocked attorney: "has lost the right" to practice law (Benninghoff, *supra*, 136 Cal. App. 4th at p. 65), is "strip[ped] [of] the privilege of practicing law" (id., at p. 67, fn. 5), "may not practice law at all" (id., at p. 68), "may not practice law, without exception" (id., at p. 69), and is "categorically barred" from practicing law. (Id., at p. 70.) This is true even for "state administrative hearings." (Id., at pp. 65, 68–69, 70.)

In this regard, we observe that, in addition to the statutory reasons discussed above, Benninghoff also cited policy reasons for its conclusion that the former attorney before it could not practice as a lay representative, even before state administrative boards and commissions:

"Our conclusion is bolstered by public policy

considerations. Benninghoff was convicted of four federal felonies, including conspiracy to defraud the United States and making false statements. Disbarment was an inevitable formality, as 'the Supreme Court shall summarily disbar' an attorney convicted of any felony requiring the specific intent to defraud or make false statements. (§ 6102, subd. (c).) In addition, his offenses were crimes of moral turpitude, which is an independent basis for summary disbarment. (Ibid.; see also In re Lesansky (2001) 25 Cal. 4th 11, 16 . . . [offense reveals moral turpitude if it 'shows a deficiency in any character trait necessary for the practice of law (such as trustworthiness, honesty, [or] candor)'].) 'Moral turpitude has been defined by many authorities as an act of baseness, vileness or depravity in the private and social duties which a man owes to his fellowmen, or to society in general.' (In re Craig (1938) 12 Cal. 2d 93, 97. . . .) Benninghoff avoided the indignity of actual disbarment only by resigning from the State Bar with disciplinary charges pending. Nonetheless, he suffers the same disqualifications as a bar member who has been tried on disciplinary charges and found wanting. (§ 6126, subd. (b).) He is unfit to practice law; he has forfeited the privilege of speaking for others under the law." (Benninghoff, *supra*, 136 Cal. App. 4th at pp. 70–71(emphasis added; parallel citations omitted).)"

Accordingly, an attorney who has lost his or her license is barred from appearing before the WCAB on behalf of any litigant, including lien claimants, at least if they have not received permission under Rule 10779.

C. The Preclusion Against "Appearing As A Representative" Of Any Party Before The WCAB Extends To Any Activity That Would Constitute The Practice Of Law.

Rule 10779 generally precludes a former attorney who has been disbarred or suspended, who has been placed on involuntary inactive status, or who has resigned with disciplinary proceedings pending from "appearing as a representative" before the WCAB.

The phrase "appearing as representative" means more than just physical appearances in a hearing room before the WCJ, although it obviously includes that. (See Rules Prof. Conduct, rule 1–311(B)(2).) Legal services outside the hearing room have a significant impact on WCAB proceedings and they are as central to them as are appearances before a WCJ. Accordingly, Rule 10779's preclusion against "appearing as representative" means that an attorney who has lost his or her license cannot perform any legal services that would constitute the practice of law.

Moreover, as discussed above, Benninghoff patently establishes that a "defrocked" attorney cannot "practice law" under any circumstances, including in judicial or quasi–judicial administrative proceedings, such as proceedings before the WCAB.

The term "practice of law" is not defined by statute, "but the cases on illegal practice have given it a most comprehensive meaning." (1 Witkin, Cal. Procedure (4th ed. 1996) Attorneys, § 408, p. 499.) As early as 1922, before the passage of the modern State Bar Act, the Supreme Court adopted the definition of "practice of law" used in an Indiana case:

"[A]s the term is generally understood, the practice of the law is the doing or performing services in a court of justice in any matter depending therein, throughout its various stages, and in conformity to the adopted rules of procedure. But in a larger sense it includes legal advice and counsel and the preparation of legal instruments and contracts by which legal rights are secured although such matter may or may not be []pending in a court." (People v. Merchants' Protective Corp. (1922) 189 Cal. 531, 535 [209 P. 363] (quoting Eley v. Miller (1893) 7 Ind.App. 529, 34 N.E. 836, 837); accord: Birbrower, Montalbano, Condon & Frank v. Superior Court (1998) 17 Cal. 4th 119, 127 [949 P.2d 1, 70 Cal. Rptr. 2d 304]; In re Utz (1989) 48 Cal. 3d 468, 483, fn. 11 [769 P.2d 417, 256 Cal. Rptr. 561]; Baron, *supra*, 2 Cal. 3d at p. 542; Benninghoff, *supra*, 136 Cal. App. 4th at p. 68.)"

Thus, the "practice of law" clearly precludes giving any legal advice and preparing any legal documents, whether or not a claim has been filed or is being adjudicated. (See also, Rules Prof. Conduct, rule 1–311(B)(1).) Of course, the "practice of law" is broader than this. Although it is not feasible to set out an all–encompassing definition of what constitutes the practice of law (People v. Landlords Professional Services (1989) 215 Cal. App. 3d 1599, 1609 [264 Cal. Rptr. 548]), we will highlight some of the activities that Hoffman and other similarly situated defrocked former attorneys cannot perform, including in the context of workers' compensation cases:

(1) filing pleadings reflecting that the defrocked attorney is "appearing" on behalf of another (Gentis v. Safeguard Business Systems, Inc. (1998) 60 Cal. App. 4th 1294, 1308 [71 Cal. Rptr. 2d 122]);

(2) negotiating and settling claims on behalf of a client with third parties (Birbrower, *supra*, 17 Cal. 4th at p. 131; Morgan v. State Bar (1990) 51 Cal. 3d 598, 603 [797 P.2d 1186, 274 Cal. Rptr. 8]; Benninghoff, *supra*, 136 Cal. App. 4th at p. 69; see also, Rules Prof. Conduct, rule 1–311(B)(4));

(3) preparing stipulations and other documents for mandatory settlement conferences and trials (Morgan, *supra*, 51 Cal. 3d at p. 603; Arm v. State Bar (1990) 50 Cal. 3d 763, 773–774, 778 [789 P.2d 922, 268 Cal. Rptr. 741]);

(4) appearing at depositions on behalf of another (Ex Parte McCue (1930) 211 Cal. 57, 68 [293 P. 47]; see also, Rules Prof. Conduct, rule 1–311(B)(3)); and

(5) engaging in discovery or responding to discovery requests (Benninghoff, *supra*, 136 Cal. App. 4th at p. 69).

There are, however, some legal–related activities that may be performed by former attorneys who have been disbarred or suspended, who are involuntarily inactive, or who have resigned with disciplinary proceedings pending may perform. For example, they may engage in: (1) legal work of a preparatory nature, such as legal research, assembling data and other necessary information, or assisting in the drafting of pleadings, briefs, and other similar documents (Rules Prof. Conduct, rule 1–311(C)(1)); (2) direct communication with the client or third parties regarding matters such as scheduling, billing, updates, confirmation of receipt or sending of correspondence and messages (Rules Prof. Conduct, rule 1–311(C)(2)); or (3) accompanying an active member in attending a deposition or other discovery matter for the limited purpose of providing clerical assistance to the active member who will appear as the representative of the client (Rules Prof. Conduct, rule 1–311(C)(3)).

As a final point, we observe that Hoffman has not petitioned the Appeals Board for permission to appear under Rule 10779. Accordingly, we need not and will not now express an opinion regarding whether, in light of Benninghoff's interpretation of the State Bar Act, the portion of Rule 10779 that allows former attorneys who have lost their licenses to petition the Appeals Board for permission to appear continues to be valid. If, however, Hoffman chooses to file a petition for permission to appear, he should address whether Benninghoff has any effect on the continuing validity of that portion of Rule 10779.

For the foregoing reasons,

IT IS ORDERED that the Findings and Order issued by the workers' compensation administrative law judge on August 9, 2005, be, and it is hereby, AFFIRMED…

Footnote 1. There is no petition requesting permission to appear under Rule 10779 now pending before us. Therefore, we presently need not and will not address the effect of the State Bar Act on the portion of Rule 10779 that allows former attorneys who have lost their licenses to petition the Appeals Board for permission to appear.

Footnote 2. The WCJ never ruled on Hoffman's objection to the admission in evidence of the records of the Supreme Court regarding his State Bar disciplinary proceedings, which included his guilty plea in Superior Court to the two counts of grant theft and one count of forgery.

On reconsideration, however, the Appeals Board may address all issues that were presented for determination to the WCJ, even if those issues were not raised in the petition for reconsideration. (Great Western Power Co. v. Industrial Acc. Com. (Savercool) (1923) 191 Cal. 724, 729 [218 P. 1009] [10 I.A.C. 322]); State Comp. Ins. Fund v. Industrial Acc. Com. (George) (1954) 125 Cal. App. 2d 201, 203 [270 P.2d 55] [19 Cal. Comp. Cases 98]; Tate v. Industrial Acc. Com. (1953) 120 Cal. App. 2d 657, 663 [261 P.2d 759] [18 Cal. Comp. Cases 246]; Pacific Employers Ins. Co. v. Industrial Acc. Com. (Sowell) (1943) 58 Cal. App. 2d 262, 266–267 [136 P.2d 633] [8 Cal. Comp. Cases 79].)

Here, for the reasons that follow, we will admit in evidence Hoffman's "Guilty Plea in Superior Court," which contains his admission of facts that furnished the basis for his guilty plea, and which was filed in Superior Court on July 10, 1985.

First, Hoffman testified at trial to having been convicted of grand theft and forgery, which sufficiently authenticates the guilty plea. (Evid. Code, §§ 1400, 1414; see, StreetScenes v. ITC Entertainment Group, Inc. (2002) 103 Cal. App. 4th 233, 244 [126 Cal. Rptr. 2d 754]; Cal. Metal Enameling Co. v. Waddington (1977) 74 Cal. App. 3d 391, 395, fn. 6 [141 Cal. Rptr. 443].)

Second, judicial notice may be taken of the records of any state court. (Evid. Code, § 452 (d).) Because Hoffman's guilty plea here is a record of both the Superior Court and the Supreme Court, it is properly the subject of judicial notice. (E.g., Duggal v. G.E. Capital Communication Services, Inc. (2000) 81 Cal. App. 4th 739, 745 [sic; the intended citation is to 81 Cal. App. 4th 81, 86].) Moreover, we may accept the truth of a guilty plea entered into court records. (Cote v. Henderson (1990) 218 Cal. App. 3d 796, 801–803 [267 Cal. Rptr. 274]; accord: Sosinsky v. Grant (1992) 6 Cal. App. 4th 1548, 1567 [8 Cal. Rptr. 2d 552].)

Third, Hoffman's guilty plea to three felonies is an admission against interest that is admissible in a subsequent civil proceeding. (Evid. Code, § 1220; Interinsurance Exchange v. Flores (1996) 45 Cal. App. 4th 661, 672–673 [53 Cal. Rptr. 2d 18].)

Footnote 3. Labor Code section 5501 provides, in relevant part: "[An] application may be filed with the appeals board by any party in interest, his attorney, or other representative authorized in writing. A representative who is not an attorney licensed by the State Bar of this state shall notify the appeals board in writing that he or she is not an attorney licensed by the State Bar of this state." (Emphasis added.)

Labor Code section 5700 provides, in relevant part: "Either party may be present at any hearing, in person, by attorney, or by any other agent, and may present testimony pertinent under the pleadings." (Emphasis added.)

Footnote 4. Although section 4907 purports to give the Appeals Board the authority to remove or deny the privilege of "any person" to appear in any WCAB proceedings, the Supreme Court has held that only it – and not the WCAB – has the power to discipline licensed attorneys. (Hustedt v. Workers' Comp. Appeals Bd. (1981) 30 Cal. 3d 329 [636 P.2d 1139, 178 Cal. Rptr. 801] [46 Cal. Comp. Cases 1284].)

Footnote 5. The Court used the term "defrocked" lawyer to refer to disbarred lawyers, suspended lawyers, lawyers involuntarily enrolled as inactive State Bar members, and lawyers who resign from the State Bar with disciplinary charges pending. (Benninghoff, *supra*, 136 Cal. App. 4th at p. 68, fn. 5.)

Footnote 6. Benninghoff excerpts only a partial quote from Business and Professions Code section 6126(b). Therefore, we will emphasize that section 6126(b) does not criminalize the practice of law only by former attorneys who "resigned from the State Bar with charges pending." Instead, it criminalizes the practice of law by "[a]ny person who has been involuntarily enrolled as an inactive member of the State Bar, or has been suspended from membership from the State Bar, or has been disbarred, or has resigned from the State Bar with charges pending." (Bus. & Prof. Code, § 6126(b).)

Footnote 7. We will briefly explain the Court's statement that laypeople "arguably" can appear in state administrative hearings and its comment that "[i]f the various APA sections and regulations that Benninghoff cites do in fact allow laypeople to represent parties in administrative hearings."

Benninghoff had argued, based on various provisions of

the APA (Administrative Proce– dure Act), as well as various regulations, that laypeople may represent parties in state administrative hearings. (Benninghoff, *supra*, 136 Cal. App. 4th at pp. 66–67 & fns. 2&3.) The Court, however, merely assumed, without actually deciding, that laypeople may represent parties before state administrative agencies. (Id., 136 Cal. App. 4th at p. 67.)

We observe that, in addition to the WCAB, other judicial or quasi–judicial administrative agencies do allow non–attorneys to appear before them. (E.g., Welfare Rights Org. v. Crisan (1993) 33 Cal. 3d 766, 770 [661 P.2d 1073, 190 Cal. Rptr. 919] [welfare hearings]; Consumers Lobby Against Monopolies v. Public Utilities Com. (1979) 25 Cal. 3d 891, 913–914 [603 P.2d 41, 160 Cal. Rptr. 124] [Public Utilities Commission]; Unemp. Ins. Code, § 1957 [Unemployment Insurance Appeals Board].)

Footnote 8. In 1991, Labor Code sections 4903(a) and 5710(b)(4) were amended to allow fee awards for representing injured employees only to licensed attorneys, and not to non–attorney representatives. (Longval v. Workers' Comp. Appeals Bd., *supra*, 51 Cal. App. 4th 792.)

Footnote 9. Although not cited by Benninghoff, the Supreme Court's opinion in Hustedt also supports the conclusion that appearances before the WCAB constitute the practice of law. There, in discussing WCAB proceedings, the Court said:

"It is well established that 'participation on behalf of another in hearings and proceedings before a board or commission constitutes the practice of law. The cases uniformly hold that the character of the act, and not the place where it is performed, is the decisive element, and if the application of legal knowledge and technique is required, the activity constitutes the practice of law, even if conducted before an administrative board or commission.' (Baron v. City of Los Angeles (1970) 2 Cal. 3d 535, 543 . . .)" (Hustedt v. Workers' Comp. Appeals Bd., *supra*, 30 Cal. 3d at pp. 335–336 (internal parallel citations omitted).)

Footnote 10. Rule 10301(l) provides: "As used in this chapter: . . . (l) 'Party' means an Applicant or Defendant, or a lien claimant where the applicant's case has been settled by way of a compromise and release, or where the applicant chooses not to proceed with his or her case." (Cal. Code Regs., tit. 8, § 10301(l).)

Footnote 11. E.g., also, Premier Medical Management Systems, Inc. v. Cal. Ins. Guarantee Assn. (2006) 136 Cal. App. 4th 464, 468 [39 Cal. Rptr. 3d 43] [71 Cal. Comp. Cases 210]; Boehm & Associates v. Workers' Comp. Appeals Bd. (Brower) (2003) 108 Cal. App. 4th 137, 149–150 [133 Cal. Rptr. 2d 396] [68 Cal. Comp. Cases 548]; Hand Rehabilitation Center v. Workers' Comp. Appeals Bd. (Obernier) (1995) 34 Cal. App. 4th 1204, 1210 [40 Cal. Rptr. 2d 734] [60 Cal. Comp. Cases 289]; Beverly Hills Multispecialty Group, Inc. v. Workers' Comp. Appeals Bd. (Pinkney) (1994) 26 Cal. App. 4th 789, 803 [32 Cal. Rptr. 2d 293] [59 Cal. Comp. Cases 461].

Footnote 12. See also, Civ. Code, § 3511, which states that "[w]here the reason is the same, the rule should be the same." If Labor Code section 4907 were construed to

provide that the Appeals Board may bar only non–attorneys who are representing applicants or defendants from appearing before the WCAB, then the Appeals Board would be powerless to remove, deny, or suspend the privilege of defrocked attorneys and other non–attorneys representing lien claimants – even ones, for example, who do not respect or obey the laws of the state, who do not respect the judicial process, who do not respect the rights of others, or who are dishonest, deceitful or outright fraudulent, and the like.

§ 34.1 Fees

Page 1432, Column 1, ninth paragraph, insert following '…evaluation.'

Enforcing an Award

An attorney may be awarded reasonable attorney fees for services rendered in enforcing an award. Labor Code section 5814.5 provides:

Reasonable attorneys' fees awarded when payment of compensation delayed or refused.

When the payment of compensation has been unreasonably delayed or refused subsequent to the issuance of an award by an employer that has secured the payment of compensation pursuant to Section 3700, the appeals board shall, in addition to increasing the order, decision, or award pursuant to Section 5814, award reasonable attorneys' fees incurred in enforcing the payment of compensation awarded… **[Editor's Note: Please see Section 30.0 of this book for the recent Court of Appeal, Second District, decision in *Smith–Amar v. WCAB* (2007) 72 Cal. Comp. Cases 27.]**

In *Meek v. John Muir Hospital, STK 166711, March 29, 2006 (34 CWCR 106)*, the Board held that an attorney fee to enforce an award under Section 5814.5 for a defendant's failure to timely pay the award should be based on the time reasonably incurred *at a reasonable hourly rate* in the same manner as with fees for services performed in connection with vocational rehabilitation and frivolous appeals.

Intentionally blank

Intentionally blank

292   California Workers' Compensation Claims and Benefits, 12 Ed. Supplement (2007)

§ 35.0   BAD FAITH

§ 35.12   Settlement of a Subrogation Claim in a Third–Party Suit for Less Than the Workers' Compensation Insurance Benefits Paid, Where the Settlement Will Result in a Loss to the Insured, May Not Constitute "Bad Faith"

Page 1481, Column 2, fifth paragraph, insert following '…rights.'

In affirming the trial Court's judgment dismissing insured's action after sustaining workers' compensation insurer's demurrer without leave to amend and holding that the insurer's alleged failure to *properly investigate third party responsibility for an accident suffered by insured's employee* was not actionable, the Court of Appeal, Third District, in *Tilbury Constructors, Inc. v. SCIF* (2006) 71 Cal. Comp. Cases 393, stated, in part:

Plaintiff Tilbury Constructors, Inc., sued its workers compensation insurance carrier, State Compensation Insurance Fund (State Fund), asserting causes of action for breach of contract, breach of the implied covenant of good faith and fair dealing, and three other claims. Tilbury's complaint is primarily based on the contention that State Fund "performed an incompetent investigation into the responsibility for an accident suffered by one of Tilbury's employees, and, as a result, [State Fund] unreasonably settled a third–party claim for less than one–fiftieth of the value of the employee's claim. Because [State Fund] obtained almost no setoff from the responsible party, Tilbury's premiums skyrocketed." We shall conclude State Fund's conduct does not give rise to a cause of action for breach of the insurance contract or a cause of action for the tortious breach of the covenant of good faith and fair dealing. We shall affirm the judgment dismissing the action after the trial court sustained State Fund's demurrer without leave to amend. n1…

Tilbury Has Not Alleged An Actionable Breach Of The Covenant Of Good Faith And Fair Dealing

Tilbury argues the trial court erred in dismissing its cause of action for tortious breach of the covenant of good faith and fair dealing. Tilbury contends this tort "is available to prevent the insurer from taking unreasonable actions that will increase future premiums." While this rule holds true in some circumstances, it does not apply here.

"Every contract imposes on each party an implied duty of good faith and fair dealing. [Citation.] Simply stated, the burden imposed is ' "that neither party will do anything which will injure the right of the other to receive the benefits of the agreement." ' [Citations.] Or, to put it another way, the 'implied covenant imposes upon each party the obligation to do everything that the contract presupposes they will do to accomplish its purpose.' [Citations.] A ' "breach of the implied covenant of good faith and fair dealing involves something beyond breach of the contractual duty itself," and it has been held that " '[b]ad faith implies unfair dealing rather than mistaken judgment . . . .' [Citation.]" [Citation.]' [Citation.] For example, in the context of the insurance contract, it has been held that the insurer's responsibility to act fairly and in good faith with respect to the handling of the insured's claim ' "is not the requirement mandated by the terms of the policy itself–to defend, settle, or pay. It is the obligation . . . under which the insurer must act fairly and in good faith in discharging its contractual responsibilities." [Citation.]' [Citation.]" (Chateau Chamberay Homeowners Assn. v. Associated Internat. Ins. Co. (2001) 90 Cal. App. 4th 335, 345–346 [108 Cal. Rptr. 2d 776].)

"Insurance contracts are unique in nature and purpose. [Citation.] An insured does not enter an insurance contract seeking profit, but instead seeks security and peace of mind through protection against calamity. [Citation.] The bargained–for peace of mind comes from the assurance that the insured will receive prompt payment of money in times of need. [Citation.] Because peace of mind and security are the principal benefits for the insured, the courts have imposed special obligations, consonant with these special purposes, seeking to encourage insurers promptly to process and pay claims. *Thus, an insurer must investigate claims thoroughly [citation]; it may not deny coverage based on either unduly restrictive policy interpretations [citation] or standards known to be improper [citation]; it may not unreasonably delay in processing or paying claims [citation]."* (Love v. Fire Ins. Exchange (1990) 221 Cal. App. 3d 1136, 1148 [271 Cal. Rptr. 246].) "These special duties, at least to the extent breaches thereof give rise to tort liability, find no counterpart in the obligations owed by parties to ordinary commercial contracts. The rationale for the difference in obligations is apparent. If an insurer were free of such special duties and could deny or delay payment of clearly owed debts with impunity, the insured would be deprived of the precise benefit the contract was designed to secure (i.e., peace of mind) and would suffer the precise harm (i.e., lack of funds in times of crisis) the contract was designed to prevent. [Citation.] To avoid or discourage conduct which would thus frustrate realization of the contract's principal benefit (i.e., peace of mind), special and heightened implied duties of good faith are imposed on insurers and made enforceable in tort. While these 'special' duties are akin to, and often resemble, duties which are also owed by fiduciaries, the fiduciary–like duties arise because of the unique nature of the insurance contract, not because an insurer is a fiduciary." (Ibid.)

In Love, the insureds sought to estop the insurance company from asserting the statute of limitations because the insurance company had an obligation to disclose that an excluded loss was a covered loss under certain circumstances. (Love v. Fire Ins. Exchange, supra, 221 Cal. App. 3d at p. 1144.) The insureds claimed this duty arose out of the fact that the insurance company owed the insureds a fiduciary duty to disclose this legal argument that would provide them with coverage. (Ibid.) In rejecting this argument, the Love court noted, "because of the 'special relationship' inherent in the unique nature of an insurance contract, the insurer's obligations attendant to its duty of good faith are heightened. Such obligations have been characterized as akin to fiduciary–type responsibilities. [Citation.] Because of this unique 'special relationship,' a breach of the obligation of good faith may give rise to tort (rather than mere contractual) remedies. [Citation.]" (Id. at p. 1147.) The court continued, "However, the California Supreme Court has never squarely held that an insurer is a true fiduciary to its insured." (Ibid.) The court pointed out that "[u]nique obligations are imposed upon true fiduciaries which are not found in the insurance relationship. For example, a true fiduciary must first consider and always act in the best interests of its trust and not allow self–interest to overpower its duty to act in the trust's best interests. [Citation.] An insurer, however, may give its own interests consideration equal to that it gives the interests of its insured [citation]; it is not required to disregard the interests of its shareholders and other policyholders when evaluating claims [citation]; and it is not required to pay noncovered claims, even though payment would be in the best interests of its insured [citation]." (Id. at pp. 1148–1149.) In discussing the covenant of good faith and fair dealing, the Love court held, "there are at least two separate requirements to establish breach of the implied covenant: (1) benefits due under the policy must have been withheld; and (2) the reason for withholding benefits must have been unreasonable or without proper cause." (Id. at p. 1151.)

State Fund relies on New Plumbing Contractors, Inc. v. Nationwide Mutual Ins. Co. (1992) 7 Cal. App. 4th 1088 [9 Cal. Rptr. 2d 469, 57 Cal. Comp. Cas 515]. There, the court was called upon to decide "whether an employer who has assigned its subrogation rights to its workers' compensation insurance carrier has a cause of action against the carrier for negligence or breach of the implied covenant of good faith and fair dealing when the carrier does not actively pursue those subrogation rights." (Id. at p. 1091.) The court concluded the insured employer had no cause of action. (Ibid.) *In New Plumbing, the employer alleged that its workers' compensation carrier failed to properly investigate or pursue its subrogation rights and as a result the employer lost the opportunity to have its experience modification reduced and receive a refund of premiums for several years. (Id. at p. 1092.) The court first examined the insured employer's causes of action for negligence and the breach of the covenant of good faith and fair dealing. (Id. at p. 1093.) In that examination, the court concluded that the insurance carrier had no duty to diligently pursue its*

subrogation rights. (Ibid.) The court explained that under the workers' compensation statutes, an insurance carrier has three statutory options to assert its right to subrogation. (Ibid.) First, it can file suit against the third party in its own name. (Lab. Code, §§ 3850, 3852.) Second, it may intervene in an action filed by the employee against the third party. (Lab. Code, § 3853.) Third, the insurer can take no action, but instead claim a lien against any judgment recovered by the employee. (Lab. Code, § 3856, subd. (b).) The New Plumbing court concluded that requiring the carrier to chose the method that was most favorable to its insured would vitiate the choices presented by the statutory scheme because the carrier would always have to file an action on its own behalf. (New Plumbing Contractors, at p. 1094.) The court stated, "Rather than impose a duty on the carrier to proceed in a specific manner, the statutory scheme gives the carrier its choice of proceeding in any manner. Furthermore, because subrogation is a right, not an obligation, the insurer presumably has the option of not pursuing subrogation recovery at all. Likely, this is often the case when the amount of benefits are relatively small and it would be economically unreasonable to pursue subrogation." (Id. at p. 1095.)

The New Plumbing court also separately examined the insured employer's cause of action for breach of the covenant of good faith and fair dealing. The court stated, "neither the duty nor the covenant of good faith and fair dealing extends beyond the terms of the insurance contract in force between the parties." (New Plumbing Contractors, Inc. v. Nationwide Mutual Ins. Co., supra, 7 Cal. App. 4th at p. 1096.) The insurance contract between Nationwide and New Plumbing provided that " 'We [Nationwide] have your rights, and the rights of persons entitled to the benefits of this insurance to recover our payments from anyone liable for the injury. You [New Plumbing] will do everything necessary to protect those rights for us and to help us enforce them.' " (Id. at pp. 1091–1092.) Thus, the "carrier's decision regarding pursuing its subrogation rights after it has properly paid claims under the insurance policy does not affect the insured's receiving the benefits of the insurance agreement." (Id. at p. 1096.) The court concluded that because the insurance carrier had paid the claim for which the employer was insured and there were no allegations of impropriety in the carrier's claims handling, the subsequent increase in premiums did not deny the employer of any benefits under the policy. (Ibid.) Rather, this act implicated the marketplace aspect of the relationship between the insured and its insurance carrier. (Id. at p. 1097.)

Here, the insurance contract provides, "We may enforce your rights, and the rights of persons entitled to the benefits of this insurance, to recover our payments from anyone liable for the injury. You will do everything necessary to protect those rights for us and to help us enforce them." As demonstrated by New Plumbing, State Fund's right to obtain subrogation under this provision, and under the relevant Labor Code provisions is just that, a right. Tilbury has alleged no defalcations in the manner in which State Fund handled the claim, paid out the benefits, or dealt with the claims handling portion of the case. The right of subrogation is not a duty under the contract, nor can it be transformed into a duty by virtue of tort law. Thus, because the decision of how and when it shall pursue subrogation, including the decision not to pursue subrogation at all, is State Fund's right. Tilbury cannot state a cause of action for tortious breach of the covenant of good faith and fair dealing based on State Fund's alleged failure to diligently and properly pursue its own right.

Tilbury further argues the insured employer has an interest in third party recoveries because Insurance Code section 11751.8 provides, in relevant part: "An insurer shall report to its rating organization as corrections or revisions of losses, pursuant to the unit statistical plan and uniform experience rating plans approved by the commissioner, if any of the following is applicable: [P] . . . [P] (c) The carrier has recovered in an action against a third party." This provision, however, does not require the carrier to pursue its subrogation rights, nor does it impose any duty on the carrier that runs contrary to the four separate options it is entitled to chose from when deciding whether and how to exercise its own subrogation rights.

Our conclusion is further buttressed by Jonathan Neil & Assoc., Inc. v. Jones (2004) 33 Cal. 4th 917 [94 P.3d 1055, 16 Cal. Rptr. 3d 849]. There, our Supreme Court declined to extend the tort remedies for the breach of the covenant of good faith and fair dealing to claims the insurance company retroactively and in bad faith billed its insured for increased premiums. (Id. at pp. 938, 941.) In Jonathan Neil, the insureds defended a collection action against them for the failure to pay insurance premiums and filed a cross–complaint against the insurance company for breach of the covenant of good faith and fair dealing when the insurance company "retroactively and knowingly charged [them] a substantially higher premium than was actually owed." (Id. at p. 923.) The Supreme Court explained that it had previously declined to extend the tort of the breach of the covenant of good faith and fair dealing to the employer–employee relationship for three major reasons. (Id. at p. 938.) First, when an insurance company fails to settle or pay a claim, the insured cannot turn to the marketplace to find another insurance company willing to pay that claim, while an employer can always find a new employee. (Ibid.) Second, the role of an employer is different from the "quasi public" role of the insurance company with whom policyholders specifically contract to obtain protection from specific economic harm. (Ibid.) Third, in the insurance context, the insurer and insured's interests are financially at odds, while in the employment context, the employer and the employee are presumably looking toward the same goal. (Ibid.) The court concluded that an insurance company's ability to charge excessive premiums will be disciplined by the marketplace by competition among insurers. (Id. at p. 939.) In addition, the court concluded three other factors counseled against the extension of tort liability to this postclaim practice. (Ibid.) First, the billing dispute, by itself, did not "deny the insured the benefits of the insurance policy the security against losses and third party liability." (Ibid.) Second, the "dispute [did] not require the insured to prosecute the insurer in order to enforce its rights, as is the case of bad faith claims and settlement practices." (Ibid.)

And, third, "traditional tort remedies may be available to the insured who is wrongfully billed a retroactive premium," such as a malicious prosecution action, or a defamation action, or intentional interference with contract action. (Ibid.)

Similarly, here, most of the factors Jonathan Neil relies upon persuade us that Tilbury has not stated a claim. (Footnote 2)

First, and most importantly, State Fund has not denied Tilbury any benefits due to Tilbury under the insurance policy. None of its actions arise out of its conduct in fulfilling its obligations of defending, investigating, reserving, and settling claims. There are no allegations in the complaint that State Fund improperly handled the underlying claim in any manner. There are no allegations that State Fund failed to investigate the claim, delayed payment of the claim, or failed to defend and indemnify Tilbury. Thus, the subrogation failures did not deny Tilbury any benefits under the policy.

Second, State Fund's alleged failures did not require Tilbury to sue to enforce its rights to benefits under the policy.

Third, to the extent that Tilbury is dissatisfied with State Fund's subrogation record, they can go out into the market and purchase workers' compensation insurance from a separate carrier in future years. While its premiums may be higher in the first years after obtaining a new carrier, Tilbury will be able to reap the benefit of an insurer who pursues subrogation in a manner closer to Tilbury's liking in the market.

Fourth, State Fund's and Tilbury's interests are not at odds in the context of subrogation, but rather are closely aligned. Both insurer and insured desire to recover as much as possible: State Fund to reduce its losses and Tilbury to reduce its premiums. Thus, it is not within State Fund's interests to do a poor job of investigating and pursuing subrogation claims.

Tilbury also argues that a series of cases starting with Security Officers Service, Inc. v. State Compensation Ins. Fund (1993) 17 Cal. App. 4th 887 [21 Cal. Rptr. 2d 653, 58 Cal. Comp. Cas 561] (Security Officers), (Footnote 3) stand for the proposition that when an insurance carrier discharges a discretionary function in bad faith and in a manner that impacts the premiums paid by the insured, then the tort of breach of the implied covenant of good faith and fair dealing will lie. This is true when the conduct arises out of claims handling practices. It does not apply to the carrier's right of subrogation.

In Security Officers, the plaintiff insured sued State Fund for its systematic failure to process claims diligently and its unreasonable inflation of the reserves assigned to those claims. (Security Officers, supra, 17 Cal. App. 4th at pp. 889–890.) State Fund's bad faith delaying the resolution of claims and inflating its reserves operated to inflate the experience rating factor of its insured and permitted State Fund to charge excess premiums and pay less in dividends. (Id. at pp. 891–892.) The appellate court explained that this conduct, if true, established a breach of the implied covenant of good faith and fair dealing that gave rise to tort and contract damages. (Id. at pp. 894, 899.) Specifically,

Security Officers held, "[w]e therefore conclude, in light of all of the authorities heretofore discussed, that the policy's implied covenant of good faith and fair dealing required [State Fund] to conduct its functions of defending, investigating, reserving, and settling claims with good faith regard for their effect upon plaintiff's premiums, as determined under the policy and governing regulations." (Id. at p. 898.)

We reject Tilbury's proffer of these cases for the same reasons that Jonathan Neil rejected their application to the postclaim billing of premiums. (Jonathan Neil & Assoc. v. Jones, *supra*, 33 Cal. 4th at pp. 940–941.) As the court noted, in each of those cases, "the overcharging of premiums was inextricably linked to the mishandling of claims–precisely the kind of bad faith behavior that goes to the heart of the special insurance relationship and gives rise to tort remedies. The premium overbilling alleged in this case is separate from any allegations of claims mishandling." (Id. at p. 940, fn. omitted.) The same holds true here. It is not simply the increase in premium that gives rise to the tortious breach of the covenant of good faith and fair dealing. Rather, it is the underlying conduct that arises out of the insurance company's duties to defend, investigate, reserve, and settle claims that gives rise to the tort. State Fund's subrogation rights are independent and separate from those duties under the policy. Thus, the cases addressing the obligations of an insurer in the execution of its duties under the policy do not apply to its subrogation right.

The trial court, thus, properly sustained the demurrer without leave to amend as to this cause of action.

II.

Tilbury Has Not Alleged An Actionable Breach Of Contract

In addressing its cause of action for breach of contract, Tilbury argues, "the Courts of Appeal have repeatedly and consistently recognized that an employer has a remedy at law when its workers' compensation insurance carrier takes an unreasonable discretionary action that increases the employer's future premiums." In support of this position, Tilbury cites Lance Camper Manufacturing Corp. v. Republic Indemnity Co. (2001) 90 Cal. App. 4th 1151 [109 Cal. Rptr. 2d 515, 66 Cal. Comp. Cas 852] (Lance Camper II); Notrica v. State Comp. Ins. Fund, *supra*, 70 Cal. App. 4th 911; MacGregor Yacht Corp. v. State Comp. Ins. Fund, *supra*, 63 Cal. App. 4th 448; Tricor California, Inc. v. State Compensation Ins. Fund, *supra*, 30 Cal. App. 4th 230; Security Officers, *supra*, 17 Cal. App. 4th 887. We reject this argument.

A closer examination of these cases reveals that it is not the discretionary nature of the actions of the insurance company that gives rise to liability, but rather the fact that these actions take place in the context of the primary duties of the insurance company under the policy. In each of the cases mentioned above, the insured employer's claim of breach of contract related to how the insurance company handled claims asserted against its insured. In Lance Camper II, 90 Cal. App. 4th at pages 1155–1156, the insured claimed the insurance company inflated the reserves

in bad faith. In Notrica v. State Comp. Ins. Fund, *supra*, 70 Cal. App. 4th at page 918, the insured based its claims against State Fund on its reserve and claims handling policies and practices. In Tricor California, Inc. v. State Compensation Ins. Fund, *supra*, 30 Cal. App. 4th at page 238, the insured claimed the insurer failed to adequately and promptly investigate claims, failed to pay only legitimate claims, failed to permit the insured to review claims files, and failed to accurately set premiums and dividend rates. In MacGregor Yacht Corp. v. State Comp. Ins. Fund, *supra*, 63 Cal. App. 4th at page 455, the insured asserted that the insurer failed to investigate, defend, or settle claims properly. Finally, in Security Officers, *supra*, 17 Cal. App. 4th at page 891, the insured alleged that State Fund failed to pay benefits promptly, failed to set reserves at reasonable levels, and that its sloth in resolving claims constituted a breach of State Fund's duty to defend and resolve claims in a diligent fashion.

Against this backdrop, where the core duties of the insurance company under its insurance contract are at issue, these courts have concluded, "an insurer's pattern of failing to pay claims promptly, defend them diligently, or assign them reasonable reserves, followed by improperly failing to pay dividends to the insured, may constitute breach of the express and implied contractual terms in a workers' compensation insurance policy." (Lance Camper II, 90 Cal. App. 4th at p. 1155.) Thus, a " 'failure to reasonably evaluate claims prior to setting reserves, inadequate monitoring of claims by the insurer, failure to minimize claims, failure to communicate with the insured, hiring of inadequate and incompetent legal and medical counsel, [and] unnecessary delays in closing claims' constitute claims handling practices that are actionable." (Ibid.) Each of these cases expressly focuses on the claims handling actions of the insurer. This is not surprising because this is the obligation of the insurer under the express language of the policy.

Here, for example, State Fund's policy obligates it to "promptly pay when due to those eligible under this policy the benefits required of [Tilbury] by the workers' compensation law." The policy also provides that State Fund has the "duty to defend at our expense any claims or proceedings against [Tilbury] . . . ." It is precisely because these paragraphs of the policy impose affirmative duties on State Fund for the benefit of the insured that the contract and the contractual implied covenant of good faith and fair dealing require State Fund to undertake and perform these actions in good faith. It is for this same reason that State Fund is liable for contractual damages when it fails to meet this standard of good faith in the execution of these duties. The complaint before us does not allege any improprieties in these actions.

By contrast, in the context of subrogation, the policy provides that State Fund "may enforce [Tilbury's] rights, and the rights of persons entitled to the benefits of this insurance, to recover [State Fund's] payments from anyone liable for the injury." This subrogation right inures to the benefit of State Fund. It is written with the word "may" indicating of the permissive nature of the right State Fund enjoys under the policy, and under the Labor Code. (See

New Plumbing Contractors, Inc. v. Nationwide Mutual Ins. Co., *supra*, 7 Cal. App. 4th at p. 1093 [the insured may choose from four options, including not pursuing subrogation at all].) Thus, State Fund's determination to exercise its right of subrogation in either good or bad faith is not actionable as a breach of the insurance contract's express terms or the covenant of good faith and fair dealing. The trial court did not err in concluding otherwise and properly sustained the demurrer without leave to amend... .

Footnote 2. Obviously, State Fund is acting in a quasi–public role in providing insurance, and it appears that no other traditional tort remedies exist to redress the impact of increased premiums.

Footnote 3. See also Notrica v. State Comp. Ins. Fund (1999) 70 Cal. App. 4th 911 [83 Cal. Rptr. 2d 89, 64 Cal. Comp. Cas 378]; MacGregor Yacht Corp. v. State Comp. Ins. Fund (1998) 63 Cal. App. 4th 448 [74 Cal. Rptr. 2d 473, 63 Cal. Comp. Cas 398]; Lance Camper Manufacturing Corp. v. Republic Indemnity Co. (1996) 44 Cal. App. 4th 194 [51 Cal. Rptr. 2d 622, 61 Cal. Comp. Cas 371]; Tricor California, Inc. v. State Compensation Ins. Fund (1994) 30 Cal. App. 4th 230 [35 Cal. Rptr. 2d 550, 59 Cal. Comp. Cas 916].

Intentionally blank

§ 37.0   CONFIDENTIAL INFORMATION

§ 37.1   Medical Confidentiality Act of 1982

§ 37.2   Providers of Health Care

Page 1500, Column 2, after fourth paragraph, ending with '…information disclosed.' insert the following

The Legislature, effective January 1, 2007, amended Section 56.10 of the Civil Code authorizing health care providers to disclose medical information regarding patients to local health departments, under specific circumstances for the purpose of preventing and/or controlling disease, injury or disability. The Section now provides:

56.10.

(a) No provider of health care, health care service plan, or contractor shall disclose medical information regarding a patient of the provider of health care or an enrollee or subscriber of a health care service plan without first obtaining an authorization, except as provided in subdivision (b) or (c).

(b) A provider of health care, a health care service plan, or a contractor shall disclose medical information if the disclosure is compelled by any of the following:

(1) By a court pursuant to an order of that court.

(2) By a board, commission, or administrative agency for purposes of adjudication pursuant to its lawful authority.

(3) By a party to a proceeding before a court or administrative agency pursuant to a subpoena, subpoena duces tecum, notice to appear served pursuant to Section 1987 of the Code of Civil Procedure, or any provision authorizing discovery in a proceeding before a court or administrative agency.

(4) By a board, commission, or administrative agency pursuant to an investigative subpoena issued under Article 2 (commencing with Section 11180) of Chapter 2 of Part 1 of Division 3 of Title 2 of the Government Code.

(5) By an arbitrator or arbitration panel, when arbitration is lawfully requested by either party, pursuant to a subpoena duces tecum issued under Section 1282.6 of the Code of Civil Procedure, or any other provision authorizing discovery in a proceeding before an arbitrator or arbitration panel.

(6) By a search warrant lawfully issued to a governmental law enforcement agency.

(7) By the patient or the patient's representative pursuant to Chapter 1 (commencing with Section 123100) of Part 1 of Division 106 of the Health and Safety Code.

(8) By a coroner, when requested in the course of an investigation by the coroner's office for the purpose of identifying the decedent or locating next of kin, or when investigating deaths that may involve public health concerns, organ or tissue donation, child abuse, elder abuse, suicides, poisonings, accidents, sudden infant deaths, suspicious deaths, unknown deaths, or criminal deaths, or when otherwise authorized by the decedent's representative. Medical information requested by the coroner under this paragraph shall be limited to information regarding the patient who is the decedent and who is the subject of the investigation and shall be disclosed to the coroner without delay upon request.

(9) When otherwise specifically required by law.

(c) A provider of health care or a health care service plan may disclose medical information as follows:

(1) The information may be disclosed to providers of health care, health care service plans, contractors, or other health care professionals or facilities for purposes of diagnosis or treatment of the patient. This includes, in an emergency situation, the communication of patient information by radio transmission or other means between emergency medical personnel at the scene of an emergency, or in an emergency medical transport vehicle, and emergency medical personnel at a health facility licensed pursuant to Chapter 2 (commencing with Section 1250) of Division 2 of the Health and Safety Code.

(2) The information may be disclosed to an insurer, employer, health care service plan, hospital service plan, employee benefit plan, governmental authority, contractor, or any other person or entity responsible for paying for health care services rendered to the patient, to the extent necessary to allow responsibility for payment to be determined and payment to be made. If (A) the patient is, by reason of a comatose or other disabling medical condition, unable to consent to the disclosure of medical information and (B) no other arrangements have been made to pay for the health care services being rendered to the patient, the information may be disclosed to a governmental authority to the extent necessary to determine the patient's eligibility for, and to obtain, payment under a governmental program for health care services provided to the patient. The information may also be disclosed to another provider of health care or health care service plan as necessary to assist the other provider or health care service plan

in obtaining payment for health care services rendered by that provider of health care or health care service plan to the patient.

(3) The information may be disclosed to any person or entity that provides billing, claims management, medical data processing, or other administrative services for providers of health care or health care service plans or for any of the persons or entities specified in paragraph (2). However, no information so disclosed shall be further disclosed by the recipient in any way that would be violative of this part.

(4) The information may be disclosed to organized committees and agents of professional societies or of medical staffs of licensed hospitals, licensed health care service plans, professional standards review organizations, independent medical review organizations and their selected reviewers, utilization and quality control peer review organizations as established by Congress in Public Law 97–248 in 1982, contractors, or persons or organizations insuring, responsible for, or defending professional liability that a provider may incur, if the committees, agents, health care service plans, organizations, reviewers, contractors, or persons are engaged in reviewing the competence or qualifications of health care professionals or in reviewing health care services with respect to medical necessity, level of care, quality of care, or justification of charges.

(5) The information in the possession of any provider of health care or health care service plan may be reviewed by any private or public body responsible for licensing or accrediting the provider of health care or health care service plan. However, no patient–identifying medical information may be removed from the premises except as expressly permitted or required elsewhere by law, nor shall that information be further disclosed by the recipient in any way that would violate this part.

(6) The information may be disclosed to the county coroner in the course of an investigation by the coroner's office when requested for all purposes not included in paragraph (8) of subdivision (b).

(7) The information may be disclosed to public agencies, clinical investigators, including investigators conducting epidemiologic studies, health care research organizations, and accredited public or private nonprofit educational or health care institutions for bona fide research purposes. However, no information so disclosed shall be further disclosed by the recipient in any way that would disclose the identity of any patient or be violative of this part.

(8) A provider of health care or health care service plan that has created medical information as a result of employment–related health care services to an employee conducted at the specific prior written request and expense of the employer may disclose to the employee's employer that part of the information that:

(A) Is relevant in a lawsuit, arbitration, grievance, or other claim or challenge to which the employer and the employee are parties and in which the patient has placed in issue his or her medical history, mental or physical condition, or treatment, provided that information may only be used or disclosed in connection with that proceeding.

(B) Describes functional limitations of the patient that may entitle the patient to leave from work for medical reasons or limit the patient's fitness to perform his or her present employment, provided that no statement of medical cause is included in the information disclosed.

(9) Unless the provider of health care or health care service plan is notified in writing of an agreement by the sponsor, insurer, or administrator to the contrary, the information may be disclosed to a sponsor, insurer, or administrator of a group or individual insured or uninsured plan or policy that the patient seeks coverage by or benefits from, if the information was created by the provider of health care or health care service plan as the result of services conducted at the specific prior written request and expense of the sponsor, insurer, or administrator for the purpose of evaluating the application for coverage or benefits.

(10) The information may be disclosed to a health care service plan by providers of health care that contract with the health care service plan and may be transferred among providers of health care that contract with the health care service plan, for the purpose of administering the health care service plan. Medical information may not otherwise be disclosed by a health care service plan except in accordance with the provisions of this part.

(11) Nothing in this part shall prevent the disclosure by a provider of health care or a health care service plan to an insurance institution, agent, or support organization, subject to Article 6.6 (commencing with Section 791) of Part 2 of Division 1 of the Insurance Code, of medical information if the insurance institution, agent, or support organization has complied with all requirements for obtaining the information pursuant to Article 6.6 (commencing with Section 791) of Part 2 of Division 1 of the Insurance Code.

(12) The information relevant to the patient's condition and care and treatment provided may be disclosed to a probate court investigator engaged in determining the need for an initial conservatorship or continuation of an existent conservatorship, if the patient is unable to give informed consent, or to a probate court investigator, probation officer, or domestic relations investigator engaged in determining the need for an initial guardianship or continuation of an existent guardianship.

(13) The information may be disclosed to an organ procurement organization or a tissue bank processing the tissue of a decedent for transplantation into the body of another person, but only with respect to the donating decedent, for the purpose of aiding the transplant. For the purpose of this paragraph, the terms "tissue bank" and "tissue" have the same meaning as defined in Section 1635 of the Health and Safety Code.

(14) The information may be disclosed when the disclosure is otherwise specifically authorized by law, such as the voluntary reporting, either directly or indirectly, to the federal Food and Drug Administration of adverse events related to drug products or medical device problems.

(15) Basic information, including the patient's name, city of residence, age, sex, and general condition, may be disclosed to a state or federally recognized disaster relief organization for the purpose of responding to disaster welfare inquiries.

(16) The information may be disclosed to a third party for purposes of encoding, encrypting, or otherwise anonymizing data. However, no information so disclosed shall be further disclosed by the recipient in any way that would be violative of this part, including the unauthorized manipulation of coded or encrypted medical information that reveals individually identifiable medical information.

(17) For purposes of disease management programs and services as defined in Section 1399.901 of the Health and Safety Code, information may be disclosed as follows: (A) to any entity contracting with a health care service plan or the health care service plan's contractors to monitor or administer care of enrollees for a covered benefit, provided that the disease management services and care are authorized by a treating physician, or (B) to any disease management organization, as defined in Section 1399.900 of the Health and Safety Code, that complies fully with the physician authorization requirements of Section 1399.902 of the Health and Safety Code, provided that the health care service plan or its contractor provides or has provided a description of the disease management services to a treating physician or to the health care service plan's or contractor's network of physicians. Nothing in this paragraph shall be construed to require physician authorization for the care or treatment of the adherents of any well–recognized church or religious denomination who depend solely upon prayer or spiritual means for healing in the practice of the religion of that church or denomination.

(18) The information may be disclosed, as permitted by state and federal law or regulation, to a local health department for the purpose of preventing or controlling disease, injury, or disability, including, but not limited to, the reporting of disease, injury, vital events such as birth or death, and the conduct of public health surveillance, public health investigations, and public health interventions, as authorized or required by state or federal law or regulation.

(d) Except to the extent expressly authorized by the patient or enrollee or subscriber or as provided by subdivisions (b) and (c), no provider of health care, health care service plan, contractor, or corporation and its subsidiaries and affiliates shall intentionally share, sell, use for marketing, or otherwise use any medical information for any purpose not necessary to provide health care services to the patient.

(e) Except to the extent expressly authorized by the patient or enrollee or subscriber or as provided by subdivisions (b) and (c), no contractor or corporation and its subsidiaries and affiliates shall further disclose medical information regarding a patient of the provider of health care or an enrollee or subscriber of a health care service plan or insurer or self–insured employer received under this section to any person or entity that is not engaged in providing direct health care services to the patient or his or her provider of health care or health care service plan or insurer or self–insured employer.

The Legislature, effective January 1, 2007, amended Section 56.10 of the Civil Code pertaining to the disclosure requirements of medical information to family members and relatives. That Section now provides:

For disclosures not addressed by Section 56.1007, unless there is a specific written request by the patient to the contrary, nothing in this part shall be construed to prevent a general cute care hospital, as defined in subdivision (a) of Section 1250 of the Health and Safety Code, upon an inquiry concerning a specific patient, from releasing at its discretion any of the following information: the patient's name, address, age, and sex; a general description of the reason for treatment (whether an injury, a burn, poisoning, or some unrelated condition); the general nature of the injury, burn, poisoning, or other condition; the general condition of the patient; and any information that is not medical information as defined in subdivision (c) of Section 56.05.

The Legislature also, effective January 1, 2007, added section 56.1007 to the Civil Code, pertaining to the disclosure requirements of medical information to family and relatives of a patient. Section 56.1007 of the Civil Code provides:

(a) A provider of health care, health care service plan, or contractor may, in accordance with subdivision (c) or (d), disclose to a family member, other relative, domestic partner, or a close personal friend of the patient, or any other person identified by the patient, the medical information directly relevant to that person's involvement with the patient's care or payment related to the patient's health care.

(b) A provider of health care, health care service plan, or contractor may use or disclose medical information to notify, or assist in the notification of, including identifying or locating, a family member, a personal representative of the patient, a domestic partner, or another person responsible for the care of the patient of the patient's location, general condition, or death. Any use or disclosure of medical information for those notification purposes shall be in accordance with the provisions of subdivision (c), (d), or (e), as applicable.

(c) (1) Except as provided in paragraph (2), if the patient is present for, or otherwise available prior to, a use or disclosure permitted by subdivision (a) or (b) and has the capacity to make health care decisions, the provider of health care, health care service plan, or contractor may use or disclose the medical information if it does any of the following:

(A) Obtains the patient's agreement.

(B) Provides the patient with the opportunity to object to the disclosure, and the patient does not express an objection.

(C) Reasonably infers from the circumstances, based on the exercise of professional judgment, that the patient does not object to the disclosure. (2) A provider of health care who is a psychotherapist, as defined in Section 1010 of the Evidence Code, may use or disclose medical information pursuant to this subdivision only if the psychotherapist complies with subparagraph (A) or (B) of paragraph (1).

(d) If the patient is not present, or the opportunity to agree or object to the use or disclosure cannot practicably be provided because of the patient's incapacity or an emergency circumstance, the provider of health care, health care service plan, or contractor may, in the exercise of professional judgment, determine whether the disclosure is in the best interests of the patient and, if so, disclose only the medical information that is directly relevant to the person's involvement with the patient's health care. A provider of health care, health care service plan, or contractor may use professional judgment and its experience with common practice to make reasonable inferences of the patient's best interest in allowing a person to act on behalf of the patient to pick up filled prescriptions, medical supplies, X–rays, or other similar forms of medical information.

(e) A provider of health care, health care service plan, or contractor may use or disclose medical information to a public or private entity authorized by law or by its charter to assist in disaster relief efforts, for the purpose of coordinating with those entities the uses or disclosures permitted by subdivision (b). The requirements in subdivisions (c) and (d) apply to those uses and disclosures to the extent that the provider of health care, health care service plan, or contractor, in the exercise of professional judgment, determines that the requirements do not interfere with the ability to respond to the emergency circumstances.

(f) Nothing in this section shall be construed to interfere with or limit the access authority of Protection and Advocacy, Inc., the Office of Patients' Rights, or any county patients' rights advocates to access medical information pursuant to any state or federal law.

§ 40.0   COMPROMISE AND RELEASE

§ 40.3   Rehabilitation Cases – Thomas Finding

Page 1527, Column 1, sixth paragraph, insert following '...309.'

If a lien claimant proceeds to trial on its after an applicant has settled his or her claim by means of a Compromise and Release which contains a *Thomas* finding, the lien claimant stands in the applicant's shoes and to prevail is required to meet the same evidentiary burden of proof as the applicant would, as if the applicant had been attempting to establish his or her own claim. *Amini v. WCAB (Portillo)* (2006) 71 Cal. Comp. Cases 510.

§ 40.4   Effect of an Earlier Compromise and Release on a Subsequent Claim of Injury to the Same Part of an Employee's Body

Page 1528, Column 2, third paragraph, insert following '...annulled.'

In *Fire Craft Technology, et al. v. WCAB (Escalante)* (2005) 70 Cal. Comp. Case 1024, the Board held that applicant's *cumulative trauma* claim was not barred under the doctrine of res judicata by a prior Compromise and Release agreement that settled her *specific injury* claim for injury to the same body parts. In upholding the trial judge's decision allowing the cumulative trauma claim to proceed, the Board stated, in part:

The Legislature has recognized two distinct classifications of injury in workers' compensation proceedings; "specific" injuries, and "cumulative" injuries. (Labor Code § 3208.1.) Following this classification, the Legislature has provided that these separate forms of injury constitute separate causes of action. "There is but one cause of action for each injury coming within the provisions of the division . . . no injury, whether specific or cumulative, shall, for any purpose whatsoever, merge into or form a part of another injury" (Labor Code § 5303.)

The release approved in Case No. LAO 784994 involved a claim of "specific" injury arising on a certain date, December 2, 1999. I this case, a "cumulative" injury is claimed as a result of events occurring over several years. The medical evidence supports this distinction. In his September 26, 2002 report, Dr. Larsen notes, "This patient presents today for orthopedic attention with respect to a continuous trauma injury she was involved in while working for Fire Craft Technology. This patient has been previously seen by myself in the office regarding a specific injury which possibly may well overlap this continuous trauma injury. I would like to have further information regarding the specific injury which she was involved in previously."

The mere fact the two claims happen to involve the same body parts does not, in and of itself, cause the settlement in the earlier case to be res judicata. If this were so, no employee could never [sic] claim injury to the same body part after obtaining an award based on an earlier injury to that body part.

Because the cause of action released in Case No. LAO 081353 is different than the cause of action alleged in this case, the release approved in the earlier action is not res judicata and does not bar applicant's right to proceed.

Finally, we note that the express terms of the release in Case No. LAO 0813534 is [sic] limited to the specific injury on December 2, 1999, and does not release any claim for cumulative injury. The intent of the parties to limit the release in Case No. LAO 0813534 to the specific injury on December 2, 1999, is clearly evidenced by the striking out of contrary language on the first page of the release agreement. Had the parties intended to compromise a claim for cumulative injury, the phrase "and any other period of employment" would not have been stricken. We consider the striking out of language on the first page to be probative of the intent of the parties. Moreover, paragraphs 2 and 3 of the settlement document describe the settlement and release only in terms of "said" injury. The same is true of the "boilerplate" language included in the Addendum 'A' concerning "all aspects of the applicant's alleged injury." It is self evident that the alleged injury being referenced is the specific injury of December 2, 1999, which is referenced in paragraph 1 on the first page.

Because the compromise and release in Case No. LAO 0813534 does not cover the cumulative trauma injury alleged in this case and is not res judicata, we will deny defendant's Petition for Reconsideration... .

§ 40.6 Approval and Setting Aside of a Compromise and Release

Page 1533, Column 2, sixth paragraph, insert following '...WCI.'

See *World Mark Resorts, et al. v. WCAB (Ramsey)* (2005) 70 Cal. Comp. Cases 1616, where the Board found no good cause to rescind a Compromise and Release agreement based on mutual mistake of fact where the agreement provided defendant with credit in the amount of $4,060 for permanent disability advances made when, in actuality, defendant had advanced $20,471.00 in permanent disability indemnity when defendant made no offer of proof as to how the mistake was made in the settlement agreement or that it was misled by the applicant.

If the parties settle a case with actual or constructive knowledge that the issue(s) settled is pending in the Appellate Court(s), a subsequent Appellate Court decision may not justify a grant of reconsideration of the settlement. *Mackill v. WCAB* (2006) 71 Cal. Comp. Cases 1336.

§ 40.7 Offset of Social Security or Pension Plan Benefits

Page 1537, Column 1, erase fourth paragraph beginning 'If you have...' and ending '...Compensation Coordinator.

Page 1539, Column 2, after second paragraph insert the following:

§ 40.11 Structured Settlements

As an alternative to an all cash settlement, as occurs with a general Compromise and Release, a procedure has evolved commonly referred to as a structured settlement whereby an injured employee may obtain immediate cash as well as receive future periodic payments to provide for medical and financial needs funded by a workers' compensation insurance carrier, or a self–insured, purchase of a re–insurance policy or an annuity policy from a life insurance company.

To create a structured settlement, the general Compromise and Release agreement is utilized.

The general Compromise and Release agreement is modified to create a structured settlement by adding a separate addendum to provide for the tax free nature of the periodic payments from the re–insurance or annuity policy. It is important that the workers' compensation defendant (employer/insurer) purchase the annuity or re–insurance policy to insure that the periodic payments will be tax free under Internal Revenue Code Section 104(a)(1).

Whereas under the terms of an Award, benefits cease upon the death of the deceased injured employee (other than accrued amounts owed), a structured settlement may provide for guarantee payments for a specified number of years to an employee's estate in the event of the employee's untimely death.

In determining the amount of the settlement often a Life Care Plan is needed to estimate the value of the employee's lifetime medical needs as well as to address issues with Medicare for purposes of obtaining a Medicare Set Aside.

In addition, some form of a trust or custodial account must be established if Medicare is or may become involved in the employee's future medical care.

Potential Social Security Disability benefits as well as other possible disability policy benefits that may be available to the injured employee must be considered to maximize the employee's financial future. This can be accomplished in a structured settlement by consideration of the amounts and timing of the periodic payments in relation to other retirement benefits.

The injured employer's attorney fee may also be paid at the time he or she receives the up–front cash, prior to commencement of the periodic payments.

Because of the complexity of establishing a structured settlement agreement, a workers' compensation attorney should consult with a structured settlement expert in preparing such a settlement agreement.

Cost incurred for the expert as well as for the Life Care Plan may be recovered under Labor Code section 5811.

§ 42.0   COSTS

Page 1543, Column 1, sixth paragraph, insert following '...English.'

In *Doughty v. Sacramento County Sheriff's Department,* SAC 341890, October 31, 2005, 34 CWCR 76, the Board held that it was appropriate to find that an applicant (who was not a minor) was entitled to the cost of a medical–legal report on the issue of his physical or mental learning incapacity in order to determine the extent of his dependency on his father who sustained a fatal injury while employed by the Sheriff's Department in the course of his employment. The applicant alleged he had been a special education student most of his school years, had been diagnosed with defects in language and visual motor skills and had a spotty work history. The Board noted costs could not be allowed for medical–legal reports under Section 4060 as this section refers only to disputes over compensability and refers to "the employee" and that historically costs have not been addressed under Section 5811 because to do so could result in costs being awarded against employees in cases where an employer prevails.

See *Sellars v. WCAB (Gibson)* (1977) 42 CCC 904 where costs were denied for an accident reconstruction expert; see also *Holzer–Reyes v. WCAB* (1999) 63 CCC 84 and *Zarate v. WCAB* (1979) 44 CCC 1180, *Los Angeles Unified School District v. WCAB (Kilgore)* (1984) 49 CCC 631, *Santa Cruz County Office of Education v. WCAB (Clarke)* (2000) 65 CCC 1188, *Digiovanni v. Vons Co., Inc.* (1995) 23 CWCR 110 for cases where costs were allowed for such matters as charges for a retired disability evaluators testimony, copy of a deposition, costs incurred for answering a Petition for Writ of Review that was denied and costs for printing an Answer to a Petition for Writ of Review.

In *Lussier v. Southern California Rapid Transit Department*, VNO 218576, (1993) and (*Lussier v. WCAB* (1994) 60 Cal. Comp. Cases 1), costs were assessed against an applicant for failure to appear at a medical examination.

In *Rodriguez v. SIF*, SJ 221796, 225511, April 5, 2006 (34 CWCR 166) the Appeals Board upheld a judge's decision awarding costs for a vocational rehabilitation evaluator under Section 5811.

See also *Zenith National Insurance Co. v. WCAB* (1978) 43 CCC 254 and *Caddele v. Compaq Computer Corporation*, 55 233802, February 21, 2006.

§ 42.1   Answering Petition for Writ of Review

Page 1544, Column 2, second paragraph, insert following '...323].)'

In an unpublished decision, *County of Stanislaus v. WCAB (Credille)* (2006) 71 Cal. Comp. Cases 1381, the Court of Appeal, Fifth District, in awarding attorney fees to applicant's counsel because it found no reasonable basis for defendant's petition for Writ of Review stated, in part:

Reasonable Basis for Petition for Writ of Review

Credille asks this court to award her attorney fees because the County's Petition for Writ of Review lacks a reasonable basis. Section 5801 provides that if the employee "prevails in any petition by the employer for a writ of review from an award of the appeals board and the reviewing court finds that there is *no reasonable basis* for the petition, it shall remand the cause to the appeals board for the purpose of making a supplemental award awarding . . . a reasonable attorney's fee for services rendered in connection with the petition for writ of review." (§ 5801, emphasis added.) "Attorneys' fees are not, however, automatically awarded simply because an appellate court affirms the WCAB's decision." (*Crown Appliance v. Workers' Comp. Appeals Bd.* (2004) 115 Cal. App. 4th 620, 627 [9 Cal. Rptr. 3d 415, 69 Cal. Comp. Cases 55].) An appellate court may conclude that a Petition for Writ of Review lacks a reasonable basis " 'when an employer contends that an award is not supported by substantial evidence and a review of the evidence shows that the award is supported by the competent opinion of one physician, although inconsistent with other medical opinions. . . . ' " (*Ibid.*)

The County did not present to this court a question of law and only argued that the WCAB's decision was unsupported by substantial evidence in light of the entire record. The 1997 award and medical reporting from Drs. Rhoades and Barber support the WCAB's determination that new braces are reasonably required to cure or relieve from the effects of her industrial injury. Moreover, the reasonableness of the 1997 award in which the County stipulated it would provide Credille with future related medical care is beyond the jurisdiction of this court. The County ignores the weight of the evidence in favor of the WCAB's decision and instead asks this court to consider evidence deemed unpersuasive to the WCAB.

DISPOSITION

The Petition for Writ of Review is denied. Respondent Judy B. Credille's request for attorney fees under section 5801 is granted. The matter is remanded to the WCAB to issue a supplemental award of attorney fees for the services rendered in connection with the petition for writ of review. This opinion is final forthwith as to this court... .

Enforcing an Award

An attorney may be awarded reasonable attorney fees for services rendered in enforcing an award.

Labor Code section 5814.5 provides:

Reasonable attorneys' fees awarded when payment of compensation delayed or refused.

When the payment of compensation has been unreasonably delayed or refused subsequent to the issuance of an award by an employer that has secured the payment of compensation pursuant to Section 3700, the appeals board shall, in addition to increasing the order, decision, or award pursuant to Section 5814, award reasonable attorneys' fees incurred in enforcing the payment of compensation awarded.

In *Meek v. John Muir Hospital*, STK 166711, March 29, 2006 (34 CWCR 106), the Board held that attorney fees to enforce an award under Section 5814.5 for a defendant's failure to pay interest should be based on the time reasonably incurred at a reasonable hourly rate in the same manner as with fees for services performed in connection with vocational rehabilitation and frivolous appeals.

Page 1546, Column 1, fourth paragraph, insert following '...378]'

In *Smith v. WCAB* (2007) 72 Cal. Comp. Cases and *Amar v. WCAB* (2007) 72 Cal. Comp. Cases 27, the Court of Appeal, Second District, held that an applicant's attorney was entitled to a fee when an insurance carrier refused to furnish *some medical treatment* pursuant to an award for further medical but did not institute proceedings to terminate under Section 4667 thereby causing applicant to petition the Board to enforce the award. The Court stated, in part:

In *Smith*, the worker had been awarded partial permanent disability (PPD), including future medical treatment. Later, his insurance carrier informally denied treatment for Smith's back, but did not file a petition to terminate medical care. (§ 4607.) Counsel for Smith, William A. Herreras, successfully challenged the carrier's denial of that medical care. The Workers' Compensation Appeals Board (Board) denied counsel's request for attorney fees.

In *Amar*, the parties previously stipulated to an award of future medical care for a foot injury. That care included a weight loss program and treatment for nonindustrial diabetes. The carrier denied both aspects of medical care without filing a petition to terminate care. Amar's attorneys sought reinstatement of this medical care. The Board deemed the weight loss program to be medically necessary treatment, and ordered it reinstated, but it denied attorney fees to Amar's counsel, Russell Ghitterman of Ghitterman, Ghitterman, and Feld (Ghitterman)...

Amar

In *Amar*, the parties stipulated to an award of future medical care after he sustained an industrial injury to his right foot. That care included treatment for a weight loss program and nonindustrial diabetes, both of which were related to his industrial foot injury. The award provided that "medical–legal expenses" would be paid by defendant, Mel Clayton Ford. Amar's counsel, Ghitterman, received a fee from that initial award.

Based on further UR, SCIF unilaterally denied both aspects of Amar's medical care without petitioning for termination of that care pursuant to section 4607. SCIF refused to pay for further medical care for his diabetes or weight loss program. The Board found that the weight loss program remained medically necessary to relieve the effects of his industrial foot injury, but that continued treatment for diabetes was unnecessary for that purpose. The Board ordered the weight loss program reinstated.

The WCJ ruled that section 4607 does not apply to the *Amar* case, and denied attorney fees to Ghitterman. On reconsideration, the WCJ opined that SCIF made a good faith denial of medical care. The WCJ did not find that SCIF refused to provide necessary medical care or engaged in unreasonable delay in providing care. Furthermore, the WCJ did not find that SCIF improperly denied previously awarded medical treatment. The Board recommended that section 4607 fees be denied. The Board adopted the WCJ's report, and denied reconsideration.

These petitions for review ensued to challenge the Board's denial of Smith's and Amar's requests for reasonable attorney fees. We granted these petitions to consider whether Herreras and Ghitterman are entitled to such fees.

DISCUSSION

Smith and Amar contend they are entitled to attorney fees within the meaning and spirit of section 4607. Section 4607 provides, in pertinent part, "[w]here a party to a proceeding institutes proceedings to terminate an award made by the appeals board to an applicant for continuing medical treatment and is unsuccessful in such proceedings, the appeals board may determine the amount of attorney's fees reasonably incurred by the applicant in resisting the proceeding . . . and may assess . . . reasonable attorney's fees as a cost . . . ."

We independently review the meaning and application of WC statutes. (*Honeywell v. Workers' Comp. Appeals Bd.* (2005) 35 Cal. 4th 24, 34 [105 P.3d 544, 24 Cal. Rptr. 3d 179, 70 Cal. Comp. Cases 97].) "Although contemporaneous administrative construction of a statute by the Board, as the agency charged with its enforcement and interpretation, is of great weight, it is not necessarily controlling; and courts will depart from the Board's construction where it is clearly erroneous or unauthorized. [Citations.]" (*Hutchinson v. Workers' Comp. Appeals Bd.*

(1989) 209 Cal. App. 3d 372, 375 [257 Cal. Rptr. 240, 54 Cal. Comp. Cases 124].)

To ascertain the Legislature's intent, we read the words of the statute as a whole, keeping in mind its nature and obvious purpose. (*Hutchinson v. Workers' Comp. Appeals Bd., supra,* 209 Cal. 3d at p. 375.) Courts consider the consequences that flow from an interpretation of a statute to prevent mischief or absurdity in its application. (*Dyna–Med, Inc. v. Fair Employment & Housing Com.* (1987) 43 Cal. 3d 1379, 1392 [743 P.2d 1323, 241 Cal. Rptr. 67].) We must liberally construe WC statutes for the purpose of "extending their benefits for the protection of persons injured in the course of their employment." (§ 3202; and see *Claxton v. Waters* (2004) 34 Cal. 4th 367, 373 [96 P.3d 496, 18 Cal. Rptr. 3d 246, 69 Cal. Comp. Cases 895].)

SCIF contends we should not construe section 4607 to authorize attorney fees to Smith or Amar because the statute, read literally, does not provide for them unless their attorney is opposing a formal petition to terminate care. But, a literal reading under these facts defeats the statute's purpose. The Board acknowledges that when a carrier informally denies all care, applicant is entitled to attorney fees to enforce the award. We see no difference when a carrier informally denies some of the treatment that is a necessary part of medical care previously awarded. This is tantamount to a petition to deny medical care even though the carrier continues to provide treatment for some of applicant's medical care. (See generally *County of Sonoma v. W.C.A.B. (Callahan)* (1997) 62 Cal. Comp. Cases 973 (writ denied); *United Airlines, RSKCo. v. W.C.A.B. (Dickerson)* (1999) 64 Cal. Comp. Cases 1511 (writ denied).) The carrier may not control the awarding of fees to applicant's counsel by choosing not to file a formal petition under section 4607.

Because counsel was required to enforce part of their awards, Smith and Amar are entitled to attorney fees. Providing such fees comports with the cardinal rule of workers' compensation law that it "shall be liberally construed by the courts with the purpose of extending their benefits for the protection of persons injured in the course of their employment." (§ 3202.)

Smith and Amar cite two persuasive cases. In *United Airlines, RSKCo. v. W.C.A.B. (Dickerson), supra,* 64 Cal. Comp. Cases 1511, the applicant's initial claim for a groin injury was settled by a stipulated award which included future medical care. Later, applicant sought authorization for left hip replacement surgery. Defendant denied authorization for the surgery, contending that the need for it did not arise from the industrial injury. Defendant did not petition to terminate medical care, and continued to provide other care. Applicant successfully petitioned for coverage of the hip surgery, which the WCJ deemed was necessary due to the industrial groin injury.

Applicant filed for both section 5814 penalties for delay in providing care, and for attorney fees pursuant to section 4607. Applicant argued that defendant constructively filed a petition to terminate care by refusing to authorize the hip surgery related to his industrial injury. Although the WCJ denied penalties under section 5814, because there was genuine doubt whether the hip surgery was reasonably related to the groin injury, the WCJ concluded that applicant was entitled to attorney fees under section 4607 because he was forced to institute proceedings to enforce the award of future medical treatment. Defendant's petition for reconsideration was denied.

In *County of Sonoma v. W.C.A.B. (Callahan), supra,* 62 Cal. Comp. Cases 973, the worker sustained an industrial back injury and was awarded permanent disability (PD) with future medical benefits. Later, defendant terminated payments for medical care without filing a petition to do so under section 4607. Applicant sought penalties under section 5814. The WCJ found that the treatment requested was reasonable and necessary, and awarded penalties for delay under section 5814, and attorney fees under section 4607. The WCJ concluded that defendant's denial of care was tantamount to filing a petition to terminate care, thus forcing applicant to institute proceedings to enforce the prior award. The Board denied reconsideration and defendant's petition for review was denied.

As we have stated above, our task is to determine the purpose and intent of the statute, reading it as a whole and in context with the statutory scheme. The meaning of a statute is not limited to a literal reading of its words, especially if such an interpretation leads to mischief or absurdity. In *Hutchinson v. Workers' Comp. Appeals Bd., supra,* 209 Cal. App. 3d at page 375, for example, we annulled a decision of the Board that denied payment for transportation costs incurred in obtaining needed prescription medications even though the literal terms of section 4600 did not provide for such transportation costs. The right to obtain necessary prescription medicines would be hollow unless the means to obtain them were also provided.

Similarly, it would be absurd to deny attorney fees to industrially injured workers simply because the carrier withdrew care without bothering to file a formal petition to do so. If attorney fees are available to counsel who oppose formal petitions, they should be available to counsel who must initiate proceedings to challenge the informal denial of medical care.

California's workers' compensation law functions in large part through the expertise, dedication and professionalism of the attorneys who represent the parties involved in individual cases. Attorneys representing insurance carriers are not expected to work for free. Neither are applicants' attorneys. Insurance carriers who fail to provide previously awarded medical care may not avoid attorney fees to successful applicants' attorneys through the expedient of an informal denial, even when they do so in good faith.

Accordingly, the Board is directed to annul its decisions denying Smith and Amar reasonable attorney fees, and to enter new and different decisions awarding such fees.... .
[Editor's Note: The Supreme Court has accepted these two cases for review].

Page 1546, Column 2, fifth paragraph, starting 'Even if the...' and ending '...stated, in part:' following '...4064' erase (b) and insert (c)

§ 42.5 Disability Evaluation Testimony

Page 1553, Column 2, sixth paragraph, insert following '...5811'

In allowing costs for the testimony of a vocational rehabilitation consultant, the Board in *Costa v. Hardy Diagnostics, SCIF* (2006) 71 Cal. Comp. Cases 1797, stated, in part:

It appears that in choosing to retain the language that the PDRS "shall be prima facie evidence of the percentage of permanent disability to be attributed to each injury covered by the schedule" in section 4660 (while changing almost everything else in that section), the Legislature intended to continue to allow the parties the opportunity to present rebuttal evidence to ratings under the new PDRS. The effect, if any, of the changes to section 4660 as to what evidence may actually rebut a rating under the new PDRS will be decided, at least initially, on a case by case basis.

Here, we agree with the WCJ's determination that the testimony of Ms. Wallace did not rebut the PD rating in this case. As stated in the WCJ's opinion on decision, Ms. Wallace, among other things: (1) apparently based her assumptions on an incorrect disability factor, a restriction to light work, and not the restriction from heavy lifting, repeated bending and stooping given by the agreed medical examiner (AME), Dr. Scheinberg, in his April 7, 2005 report; (2) inappropriately considered non–industrial factors; and (3) incorrectly calculated the applicant's pre–injury earnings capacity.

As to the costs for Ms. Wallace's testimony and report, however, we will rescind the WCJ's determination, and allow the parties to adjust such costs, with jurisdiction reserved at the trial level in event of dispute. We believe that Ms. Wallace, who as stated previously, was listed as a witness on applicant's DOR and testified without objection, is entitled to be reimbursed by SCIF for the reasonable costs associated with her testimony under section 5811. (Footnote 21)

In addition, although her report has been excluded from evidence, some of her work in preparing that report may have provided a foundation for her testimony... .

Footnote 21. Section 5811(a) provides in pertinent part: "In all proceedings under this division before the appeals board, costs as between the parties may be allowed by the appeals board."

In *Rea et. al. v. WCAB (Dabanian)* (2007) 72 Cal. Comp. Cases 497, the Appeals Board, in upholding an award of a fee in the amount of $1,260 for the testimony of a vocational expert, quoted with approval the judge as stating:

Defendant has cited two cases for the proposition that the WCAB does not construe costs to include expert witness fees. These cases are *Sellars v. WCAB*, 42 CCC 904 (1977, *writ denied*), and *Barrett v. WCAB*, 47 CCC 122 (1982, *writ denied*). Neither case properly stands for the proposition for which it is cited by Defendant. In *Sellars*, the WCAB denied reimbursement for the cost of an accident reconstruction specialist and a toxicologist on the ground that there was "no compelling reason" to allow the costs. This is a far cry from the blanket prohibition claimed by Defendant; in fact, *Sellars* stands for the principle that allowance of such costs is permissible and discretionary. Similarly, the *Barrett* case contains a holding quite different from that cited by defendant. In *Barrett*, the Applicant sought to submit vocational rehabilitation evidence in the form of a report, instead of live testimony from the expert. Since the report was held inadmissible, the costs were denied. *Barrett* is clearly distinguishable from the instant case, since here, the expense was incurred in order to prepare and obtain live expert testimony, explicitly held admissible by the *Le Boeuf* case. The *Barrett* case has nothing whatever to say about the propriety of allowing the cost of procuring *admissible* evidence.

Defendant has also cited the case of *Davis v. KGO–TV*, 17 Cal. 4th 436 (1998) in support of this contention. Since *Davis* concerned the construction of a different code section outside the Worker's Compensation system, and made no mention whatever of the Labor Code in general, or Section 5811 in particular, I was unable to understand the significance of this citation...

Once again, SIF cites several cases with no direct bearing on the issue at hand. First, Defendant SIF cites *Brown v. WCAB*, 36 CCC 627 (1971) for the proposition that a determination of PD must be solely based upon medical evidence and the opinion of the rater. This case pre–dates *Le Boeuf* by some ten years, had nothing to do with the SIF, and to the extent it holds vocational rehabilitation irrelevant to determining PD, was overruled by *Le Boeuf* 24 years ago. Defendant next cites the case of *Hansen v. WCAB*, 53 CCC 420 (1988, *writ denied*) for the proposition that VR testimony is not allowed on a case where only permanent disability is at issue. This is not an accurate summary of the holding in *Hansen*. First, the vocational testimony proffered in *Hansen* was allowed into evidence by the trial judge, and this determination was not disturbed by the Board. The case held that the WCJ had discretion to refuse to follow the vocational evidence where he found it unconvincing, and not that it was irrelevant, a holding which would have been squarely at odds with the Supreme Court's holding in *Le Boeuf*.

As pointed out by Applicant in his verified Answer, these two contentions have been raised with great regularity by the SIF. At present there is no binding precedent at the Board level for the guidance of WCJs on this issue. Any actions the Board could take to remedy this lack and resolve this issue would be very helpful when next this issue is raised, as surely it will be... .

§ 42.7   Medical–Legal Costs

<u>Page 1562, Column 1, second paragraph,
insert following '…claimant….'</u>

In *Doughty v. Sacramento County Sheriff's
Department, SAC 341890, October 31, 2005, 34 CWCR
76*, the Board found that an applicant (who was not a
minor) was entitled to the cost of a medical–legal report
on the issue of his physical or mental learning incapacity
in order to determine the extent of his dependency on
his father who sustained a fatal injury while employed by
the Sheriff's Department in the course of his
employment. The applicant alleged he had been a
special education student most of his school years, had
been diagnosed with defects in language and visual
motor skills and had a spotty work history. The Board
noted the costs could not be allowed for medical–legal
reports under Section 4060, as this section refers only to
disputes over compensability and refers to "the
employee".

§ 42.7(B)   Right of Lien Claimants to Due Process

<u>Page 1572, Column 2, fifth paragraph, insert
immediately following '…opinion.'</u>

See Section 24.17 of this book for full discussion of
lien claimant's rights.

Intentionally blank

§ 44.0   DISCOVERY

Page 1596, Column 1, eighth paragraph, insert following '...relationship".'

The right to privacy is guaranteed by the California Constitution Article 1, which provides:

"Any invasion of the right must be justified by substantial countervailing interests and lack of an effective alternative with a lower impact on privacy."

This is true even though a party has waived a statutory privilege. *San Diego Trolley, Inc., et. al. v. Superior Court (Kinder)* (2001) 66 Cal. Comp. Cases 352. A prudent defense attorney should be prepared, in the above situation, to make an offer of proof to demonstrate the existence of relevant prior medical history, its relevance, and that no less intrusive means exist to obtain it.

Page 1596, Column 1, tenth paragraph, insert following '...2032.'

Filing a claim for an industrial injury does not result in an unlimited waiver of the physician–patient privilege. Although an applicant waives his or her physician–patient privilege as to all information concerning the medical conditions that he or she puts in issue by filing a claim for workers' compensation benefits, that waiver extends only to information relating to the medical conditions in issue and does not automatically open up a person's past medical history to scrutiny. *Morales v. Travelers Insurance Company* STK 192122, July 31, 2006 (34 CWCR 230).

See also *In re Lifschutz* (1970) 2 Cal. 3d 415, for a California Supreme Court decision where the high Court stated that an expansive construction of the patient–litigant exception "might effectively deter many patients from instituting legitimate lawsuits out of fear of opening up all past communications to discovery".

Page 1601, Column 2, eighth paragraph, insert following '...deposition.'

Social Security Records

Applicant's Social Security psychiatric records were held discoverable in *Jackson v. WCAB* (2006) 71 Cal. Comp. Cases 638, even though applicant did not file a psychiatric claim, where the Agreed Medical Evaluator indicated in a report that applicant's psychiatric condition was relevant to determining the extent of the permanent disability and the apportionment to other factors under Labor Code section 4063.

Intentionally blank

§ 45.0   EARNINGS

§ 45.2   Section 4453 Amended Effective January 1, 2003

Page 1611, Column 2, insert addition to second paragraph, immediately following '...employments.'

[Editor's Note: The purpose of these different methods of computing earning capacity has been explained by the California Supreme Court in *Argonaut Ins. Co. v. IAC (Montana)* (1962) 27 Cal. Comp. Cases 130, as:

When an employee is steadily employed at a full–time job his earning capacity is determined by an appropriate formula [citation]. When the employment is for less than 30 hours a week or when a formula 'cannot reasonably and fairly be applied' the [Board] must make its own estimate of weekly earning capacity at the time of the injury. [LC Section 4453(c)(4) . . .] The purpose of this provision is to equalize for compensation purpose the position of the full–time, regularly employed worker whose earning capacity is merely a multiple of his daily wage and that of the worker whose wage at the time of injury may be aberrant or otherwise a distorted basis for estimating true earning power. It would hardly be consistent with that purpose to foreclose a worker from a maximum temporary or permanent award simply because a brief recession had forced him to work sporadically or at a low wage....]

Page 1617, Column 2, third paragraph, insert following '...per week'

In holding that an attorney's average weekly earnings should be based on his regular wages while employed by the State Compensation Insurance Fund, rather than the $5.00 a day he earned as a juror where he was injured, the Court of Appeal, Third District, in *Court of San Joaquin v. WCAB* (2007) 72 Cal. Comp. Cases 187, stated, in part:

The County of San Joaquin (County) petitions this court for a writ of review of the Workers' Compensation Appeals Board's (Board) decision that James Davis (Davis) is a maximum wage earner for purposes of calculating his temporary and permanent disability indemnity benefits.

Davis was employed by the State Compensation Insurance Fund (State Fund) as an attorney and paid a monthly salary of $7,299. While employed there, he was called for jury duty by the County, which paid jurors $5.00 a day for jury service. On his first and only day of jury duty,

Davis sustained an admitted industrial injury to his lower back. He returned to work at State Fund and continued to work there, suffering ongoing back pain. Upon his application for temporary and permanent disability benefits, the Board calculated his "average weekly earnings" based upon his salary at State Fund, which entitled him to receive compensation at the maximum rate of pay.

The County contends the Board erred in concluding Davis is entitled to maximum rate benefits, arguing that the rate of pay is governed by Labor Code section 4453, subdivision (c)(2). (Footnote 1)

That provision limits the injured worker's "average weekly earnings" to the hourly rate received from the employer where the injury occurred. If that provision is applicable, Davis's indemnity benefits would be calculated at the minimum rate based upon the nominal juror fee paid by the County.

We find that provision is inapplicable however and conclude the Board properly determined that section 4453, subdivision (c)(4) (hereafter subdivision (c)(4)) sets forth the proper method for determining Davis's average weekly earnings. Subdivision (c)(4) provides that "[w]here the employment is for less than 30 hours per week, or where for any reason the foregoing methods of arriving at the average weekly earnings cannot reasonably and fairly be applied, the average weekly earnings shall be taken at 100 percent of the sum which reasonably represents the average weekly earning capacity of the injured employee at the time of his or her injury, due consideration being given to his or her actual earnings from all sources and employments."

This case is a prime example of one calling for application of section 4453, subdivision (c)(4). We shall therefore affirm the Board's decision, order, and award. (Footnote 2)

FACTUAL AND PROCEDURAL BACKGROUND

The facts are undisputed. Fifty–five year–old Davis was employed as an attorney at State Fund and paid a monthly salary of $7,299. While employed there, he was called for jury duty by the County. He reported for duty at 8:30 a.m. on November 15, 2000, where he sustained an admitted industrial injury to his lower back. He remained on duty until 11:30 a.m. and returned to work at the State Fund later that day. The County paid its jurors $5 per day for jury service and sent Davis a check for that amount, which he turned over to the State Fund as required. (Code Civ. Proc., § 215.) Davis continued to have back problems, underwent back surgery in early 2001, and returned to work at State Fund while continuing to receive treatment for back pain.

Davis filed a claim against the County (STK 164337) for the injury to his lower back on November 15, 2000, and a claim against State Fund (STK 164334) for cumulative trauma to his lower back through April 2, 2002.

The matter went to trial and after several hearings and reconsideration, the Workers' Compensation Judge (WCJ) issued amended findings, award and order, determining that Davis was temporarily totally disabled from January 16, 2001, to March 17, 2001, that at the time of injury, he earned $5.00 a day for jury service and $7,299 a month for his work at State Fund, which produced a maximum temporary disability rate of $490.00 per week and a maximum permanent disability rate of $170.00 per week. (See Lab. Code, §§ 4453, subd. (a)(7) and 4653.) (Footnote 3)

In the Opinion on Decision, the WCJ concluded that Davis should be paid the maximum wage under section 4453, subdivision (c)(4).

Both parties filed petitions for reconsideration. The County claimed, inter alia, that the Board erred by finding Davis was a maximum wage earner for purposes of calculating his benefits because on the day he was injured, he worked for the County which paid him $5.00 per day. As to that claim, the Board denied the County's petition, adopting and incorporating the WCJ's report and recommendation, in which she reaffirmed her decision that Davis was a maximum wage earner at the time of his injury. In so doing, the WCJ stated as follows, "I can't think of anything more unreasonable and more unfair and more inconsistent with the reasoning of all relevant case law on this issue than to ignore Mr. Davis' earnings capacity as an attorney for [State Fund] and limit him to the nominal $5 daily stipend for calculation of his [average weekly earnings]."

On June 30, 2006, the County filed a petition for writ of review in this court (Cal. Const., art. XIV, § 4; §§ 5950, 5955) challenging the Board's determination that Davis is entitled to be paid at the maximum disability rate. (Footnote 4)

DISCUSSION

I.

Standard of Review

Our review of the Board's decision upon a petition for writ of review is governed by section 5952. In conducting that review, we may consider whether the Board acted without or in excess of its powers, whether its order, decision, or award was unreasonable or unsupported by substantial evidence, and whether the findings of fact support the order, decision, or award. (§ 5952.) In reviewing questions of fact, we determine whether there is substantial evidence to support the Board's action unless its findings are unreasonable, illogical, improbable or inequitable in light of the overall statutory scheme. In reviewing questions of law, we review the Board's determination de novo. (*Smith v. Workers' Comp. Appeals Bd.* (2000) 79 Cal. App. 4th 530, 535–536 [94 Cal. Rptr. 2d 186, 65 Cal. Comp. Cases 277].)

The question raised by the County, whether section 4453, subdivision (c)(2) rather than subdivision (c)(4) is the applicable method in determining Davis' "average weekly earnings," is a question of law. The County does not claim the Board's order is unsupported by substantial evidence or that the evidence is insufficient to support the Board's findings of fact.

II.

Maximum Rate of Pay

Disability payments for temporary total disability and for permanent partial disability are computed at two–thirds of the worker's "average weekly earnings." (§§ 4453, subd. (b), 4653, 4658; *Gonzales v. Workers' Comp. Appeals Bd.* (1998) 68 Cal. App. 4th 843, 846 [81 Cal. Rptr. 2d 54, 63 Cal. Comp. Cases 1477]; S. Herlick, Cal. Workers' Compensation Law (6th ed.) § 5.01.) "Average weekly earnings" are determined under the provisions of section 4453, (Footnote 5) which provides four methods for making that calculation. (*Pham v. Workers' Comp. Appeals Bd.* (2000) 78 Cal. App. 4th 626, 633 (*Pham*) [93 Cal. Rptr. 2d 115, 65 Cal. Comp. Cases 139]; *Gonzales v. Workers' Comp. Appeals Bd., supra,* 68 Cal. App. 4th at p. 846.)

Although the statute uses the legal term "average weekly earnings," it is well established that "earning capacity" remains the benchmark for determining "average weekly earnings" regardless of which statutory method is applicable. (*Gonzales v. Workers' Comp. Appeals Bd., supra,* 68 Cal. App. 4th at p. 846; *West v. Industrial Acc. Com.* (1947) 79 Cal. App. 2d 711, 722 [180 P.2d 972, 12 Cal. Comp. Cases 86][earning capacity is the "touchstone" in determining average earnings].)

Moreover, "[e]arning capacity is not locked into a straitjacket of the actual earnings of the worker at the date of injury; the term contemplates his general over–all capability and productivity; the term envisages a dynamic, not a static, test and cannot be compressed into earnings at a given moment of time. The term does not cut 'capacity' to the procrustean bed of the earnings at the date of injury." (*Goytia v. Workers' Comp. Appeals Bd.* (1970) 1 Cal. 3d 889, 894 [464 P.2d 47, 83 Cal. Rptr. 591, 35 Cal. Comp. Cases 27] (*Goytia*).)

Nevertheless, with respect to permanent employees, application of the first three statutory methods will generally result in a determination of earning capacity that is equivalent to the worker's actual earnings. (*Pham, supra,* 78 Cal. App. 4th at p. 633; *Argonaut Ins. Co. v. Industrial Acc. Com.* (1962) 57 Cal. 2d 589, 594 [371 P.2d 281, 21 Cal. Rptr. 545, 27 Cal. Comp. Cases 130] (*Montana*).) As the Supreme Court explained in *Goytia, supra,* "the Legislature deliberately established earning capacity as the test for the fourth subdivision as distinguished from the actual earnings for the other three subdivisions. Section 4453 provides for the computation of both temporary and permanent disability indemnity. Subdivisions (a), (b), and (c) relate to full–time employees, employees working for two or more employers, and employment at an irregular rate, such as piecework or work on a commission basis. Each of those subdivisions provide for computation of 'average annual earnings for purposes of permanent disability indemnity' based upon earnings prior to the injury." (1 Cal. 3d at p. 894, fn. omitted.)

By contrast, the fourth method, formerly subdivision (d) of section 4453 (Stats. 1939, ch. 308, § 2, p. 1581), now codified in subdivision (c)(4), provides that when "employment is for less than 30 hours per week, or where for any reason the foregoing methods of arriving at the average weekly earnings cannot reasonably and fairly be applied, the average weekly earnings shall be taken at 100 percent of the sum which reasonably represents the average weekly earning capacity of the injured employee at the time of his or her injury, due consideration being given to his or her actual earnings from all sources and employments."

The purpose of this fourth method "is to equalize for compensation purposes the position of the full–time, regularly employed worker whose earning capacity is merely a multiple of his daily wage and that of the worker whose wage at the time of injury may be aberrant or otherwise a distorted basis for estimating true earning power." (*Montana, supra,* 57 Cal. 2d at p. 594 [construing former subd. (d)].)

In light of these purposes, the courts have applied the fourth method to allow consideration of post and pre–injury earnings for applicants meeting the statutory requirements in cases involving temporary workers such as Davis (*Goytia, supra,* 1 Cal. 3d at pp. 897–898 [seasonal worker entitled to benefits based upon post injury permanent full–time employment]; *Westside Produce Co. v. Workers' Comp. Appeals Bd.* (1978) 81 Cal. App. 3d 546, 552 [146 Cal. Rptr. 498, 43 Cal. Comp. Cases 653] [seasonal worker entitled to benefits based on past and future earnings had she not been injured]) and part–time or full–time employees involved in educational self–improvement activities that greatly increased their earning capacity. (*Jeffares v. Workmen's Comp. App. Bd.* (1970) 6 Cal. App. 3d 547 [*sic*], 553 [6 Cal. App. 3d 548, 86 Cal. Rptr. 288, 35 Cal. Comp. Cases 201]) [teaching credential]; *Pascoe v. Workmen's Comp. App. Bd.* (1975) 46 Cal. App. 3d 146, 153 [120 Cal. Rptr. 199, 40 Cal. Comp. Cases 191] [registered nursing license].)

We find the Board properly used subdivision (c)(4) in determining Davis's average weekly earnings. As stated, that provision is applicable when "the employment is for less than 30 hours per week, or where for any reason the foregoing methods . . . cannot reasonably and fairly be applied . . . ." Davis satisfies both predicates. First, he worked for the County for less than 30 hours, three hours to be exact. Second, as the Board found, it would be unreasonable, unfair, and inconsistent with relevant case law to ignore Mr. Davis's earnings capacity as an attorney for State Fund and limit him to the nominal $5 daily stipend paid for short–term temporary work. Clearly, Davis's earning capacity is better reflected by his work as an attorney at State Fund before and after his injury than by the nominal payment made by the County for his three hours of jury service. Indeed, the nominal daily fee paid to jurors is an aberrant, distorted, and inequitable basis for estimating Davis's true earning power. (*Montana, supra,* 57 Cal. 2d at p. 594.)

While acknowledging that subdivision (c)(2) is not applicable for determining temporary disability because Davis was disabled from both jobs during his recovery, the County nevertheless maintains it is the proper method for calculating Davis's permanent disability. We disagree.

Subdivision (c)(2) contemplates an hourly rate of pay and neither the County nor State Fund paid Davis an hourly rate. Moreover, this method directs that "the average weekly earnings shall be taken as the aggregate of these earnings . . . ." Here, there were no "aggregate earnings" because as a state worker, (Footnote 6) Davis did not earn wages from the County. Code of Civil Procedure section 215 provides that a juror who is employed by a state government entity and who receives regular compensation and benefits while performing jury service, may not be paid a jury fee. Similarly, California Code of Regulations, title 2, section 599.672 provides that "[n]o deductions shall be made from the salary of an employee while on jury duty if the fee for jury duty is remitted to the State." Since Davis testified that he gave the County check to State Fund, he did not receive aggregate earnings.

The County's claim rests solely on *Leeth v. Workers' Comp. Appeals Bd.* (1986) 186 Cal. App. 3d 1550 [231 Cal. Rptr. 468, 51 Cal. Comp. Cases 540], which it asserts was improperly ignored by the Board. We find *Leeth* is inapposite because it involved dual permanent employment while the present case involves temporary employment.

In *Leeth*, the court upheld the Board's decision that subdivision (c)(2) rather than subdivision (c)(4) was applicable in determining the applicant's average weekly earnings. The applicant was injured while working at his permanent part–time job where he was paid $75 for two weekends a month. He also had permanent full–time employment during the regular work week where he was paid an hourly rate of pay. The court gave great weight to the Board's construction of the statute and found subdivision (c)(4) did not apply to dual or multiple employment situations simply because determination of the average weekly earnings under subdivision (c)(2) would reduce the benefits to a minimum rate of disability. (186 Cal. App. 3d at p. 1557.) The court further found the applicant had failed to meet his burden of proving that subdivision (c)(2) could not fairly and reasonably be applied. (*Ibid.*)

Nevertheless, the court in *Leeth* noted that "there will be situations in which subdivision (c)(4) should be applied when a worker with two or more jobs is injured in lesser–paying part–time employment." (186 Cal. App. 3d at p. 1557.) In so stating, the court cited several single employment cases (see *Pascoe v. Workmen's Comp. Appeals Bd., supra,* 46 Cal. App. 3d 146, *Goytia, supra,* 1 Cal. 3d 889), as illustrative of situations where subdivision (c)(4) was properly used because the applicant had received or was likely to receive a higher salary after the date of injury. (*Leeth, supra,* 186 Cal. App. 3d at p. 1557.)

However, there is nothing in subdivision (c)(4), which limits its application to single employment cases and we see no reason for such a limitation. The benchmark for determining a worker's "average weekly earnings" is the worker's "earning capacity" (*Gonzales v. Workers' Comp.*

Appeals Bd., supra, 68 Cal. App. 4th at p. 846) and as the court in *Montana, supra,* explained, it would hardly be consistent with the purpose of subdivision (c)(4) "to foreclose a worker from a maximum . . . permanent award simply because a *brief recession* had forced him to work sporadically or at a low wage." (57 Cal. 2d at p. 594, italics added.) Davis was compelled to work for the County for a brief period of time and at a very low wage, an amount that clearly does not reflect his earning capacity before or after his injury. Accordingly, we hold that subdivision (c)(4) is the proper method for determining Davis's earning capacity and conclude the Board properly determined he is entitled to benefits computed at the maximum rate of pay... .

Footnote 1. All further section references are to the Labor Code unless otherwise specified.

Footnote 2. Pursuant to Davis's concession at oral argument, we deny his request to remand the cause to the Board for an award of attorney's fees pursuant to section 5801.

Footnote 3. Davis was awarded a total benefit of $44,030 for permanent disability less credits and specified attorney fees and reimbursement for items not here relevant. The County was ordered to pay 90 percent of the award and State Fund was ordered to pay 10 percent.

Footnote 4. State Fund does not seek review of the WCAB's decision.

Footnote 5. Section 4453, subdivision (c) states: "(c) Between the limits specified in subdivisions (a) and (b), the average weekly earnings, except as provided in Sections 4456 to 4459, shall be arrived at as follows:

"(1) Where the employment is for 30 or more hours a week and for five or more working days a week, the average weekly earnings shall be the number of working days a week times the daily earnings at the time of the injury.

"(2) Where the employee is working for two or more employers at or about the time of the injury, the average weekly earnings shall be taken as the aggregate of these earnings from all employments computed in terms of one week; but the earnings from employments other than the employment in which the injury occurred shall not be taken at a higher rate than the hourly rate paid at the time of the injury.

"(3) If the earnings are at an irregular rate, such as piecework, or on a commission basis, or are specified to be by week, month, or other period, then the average weekly earnings mentioned in subdivision (a) shall be taken as the actual weekly earnings averaged for this period of time, not exceeding one year, as may conveniently be taken to determine an average weekly rate of pay.

"(4) Where the employment is for less than 30 hours per week, or where for any reason the foregoing methods of arriving at the average weekly earnings cannot reasonably and fairly be applied, the average weekly earnings shall be taken at 100 percent of the sum which reasonably represents the average weekly earning capacity of the injured employee at the time of his or her injury, due consideration being given to his or her actual earnings from all sources and employments." "

Footnote 6. State Fund is a state public agency created by statute. (Ins. Code, § 11773; *Burum v. State Compensation Ins. Fund* (1947) 30 Cal. 2d 575, 585 [184 P.2d 505, 12 Cal. Comp. Cases 210]; *State Compensation Ins. Fund v. Riley* (1937) 9 Cal. 2d 126, 131 [69 P.2d 985].)

Page 1634, Column 1, eighth paragraph, insert following '...999.'

Seasonal employment is common in the agricultural industry and usually refers to workers that pick from job to job or from field to field and then stop. They are laid off until another seasonal crop comes in for picking or until the next season begins on that same crop.

Page 1636, Column 2, second paragraph, insert following '...omitted.]'

In holding that it would be illogical to award a seasonal employee temporary disability indemnity as wage replacement where it is was undisputed that there otherwise would be no wage to replace, the Court of Appeal, Fifth District, in *Signature Fruit Company v. WCAB (Ochoa)* (2006) 71 Cal. Comp. Cases 1044, stated, in part:

Signature Fruit Company petitions this court to review a decision of the Workers' Compensation Appeals Board awarding one of its seasonal employees, Eva Ochoa, temporary disability benefits. We recognize that, effective January 1, 2003, an amendment to the workers' compensation laws established a minimum level of average weekly earnings. This case presents a unique twist to what otherwise might be a fairly simple calculation. The parties stipulated that Ochoa would be employed only during the season, from July 29 through September 9, 2003. The record supports the stipulation by revealing that Ochoa could only recall working as a seasonal employee with Signature Fruit Company in recent years. Under these unique circumstances, we conclude that Ochoa is not entitled to receive temporary disability payments for a time when there is no question that she would not have been working and earning income–whether injured or not.

To illustrate the point, we will assume Ochoa remained temporarily disabled throughout all of 2004. If she did, the WCAB's award would result in her receiving well over 200 percent of her regular annual income for a time when there is no question that she would not have been working. In enacting workers' compensation reform, we do not believe the Legislature intended this result. That said, our decision is a narrow one. We express no opinion on calculating a seasonal employee's off–season temporary disability where the employee maintains off–season earnings below the minimum average weekly earnings rate.

PROCEDURAL AND FACTUAL HISTORIES

Eva Ochoa worked as a seasonal sanitation worker for Signature Fruit Company (Signature) since 1998. The parties stipulated that (1) Ochoa's 2003 employment "in–season" ran from July 29 though September 9 with average weekly earnings of $548.38; and (2) she did not have any earnings or engage in any employment during her "off–season" throughout the remainder of the year.

On September 1, 2003, Ochoa was washing a floor at a Signature worksite in Modesto when a passing forklift jerked a water hose out of her hand. Signature admitted Ochoa suffered an industrial injury but disputed the nature and extent of the injury. She continued working for several days until she sought medical treatment at Signature's expense on September 4, 2003, with Bradley Tourtlotte, M.D. Dr. Tourtlotte restricted Ochoa to limited use of her right hand for up to eight hours per day and instructed her to return to check her condition on September 8, 2003.

Signature was unable to accommodate Ochoa's work restrictions and paid her temporary disability from September 4 through September 8, 2003, at a rate of $365.59 per week based on two–thirds of her in–season average weekly earnings. There is no indication in the record that Ochoa returned for follow–up with Dr. Tourtlotte on September 8, 2003, as directed. Signature laid off Ochoa at the end of her annual employment season on September 9, 2003, and stopped providing her with temporary disability payments. On October 6, 2003, Ochoa commenced treatment with a chiropractor, Pedram Vaezi, D.C., who certified that she was totally temporarily disabled. The chiropractor referred Ochoa to a physician, Bal Rajagopalan, M.D., at an orthopedic and sports medicine clinic who described Ochoa on February 26, 2004, as "having subacromial tendonitis and frozen shoulder," but also noted that her muscle activity electromyogram results were negative and her MRI was "essentially normal."

Ochoa believed she should have been awarded temporary disability payments during her off–season in addition to the four days of temporary disability Signature provided. She brought that limited issue before the Workers' Compensation Appeals Board (WCAB) for an expedited hearing on April 13, 2004. Relying on a January 1, 2003, amendment to the workers' compensation law recasting an employee's minimum average weekly earnings at $189, the workers' compensation administrative law judge (WCJ) agreed with Ochoa and concluded she was entitled to temporary disability payments at two–thirds that minimum average weekly earnings rate, or $126 per week, during her off–season of regular unemployment. (Lab. Code, (Footnote 1) § 4453, subd. (a)(8).)

Signature petitioned the WCAB for reconsideration, claiming the medical evidence failed to demonstrate that Ochoa was temporarily totally disabled beyond September 8, 2003, and that even if such evidence existed, Ochoa was not entitled to temporary disability payments after her seasonal employment term ended. The WCJ who issued the decision resigned from state service and did not prepare a report and recommendation to the WCAB. The WCAB granted Signature's petition and subsequently issued its own Opinion and Decision After Reconsideration. The WCAB concluded that the substantial–evidence claim was not properly before it since it was not raised at the expedited hearing and concurred with the WCJ that Ochoa was

entitled to temporary disability payments of $126 per week during her off–season...

In response to Signature's petition for reconsideration, the WCAB affirmed its holding in Jimenez that temporary disability may be awarded at distinct in–season and off–season rates. The WCAB also concluded that section 4453, subdivision (a), no longer permits an employee's off–season average weekly earnings to fall below the statutory minimum of $189:

"[W]e conclude that the same analysis set forth in Jimenez is still a valid analysis, and that in seasonal worker cases, temporary disability indemnity may be awarded at two different rates, i.e., an in–season rate based upon actual earnings and an off–season rate based upon the employee's off–season earning capacity taking into consideration such factors . . . as the employee's earning history, his/her ability to work, age, and health, education, and skill as well as other employment opportunities and the general condition of the labor market. Thus, in a situation where there is no earnings history or other factors to indicate that the applicant has an earnings capacity above zero to $189, the applicant is simply entitled to the minimum rate. The amendment to Labor Code section 4453, re–establishing a floor for the temporary disability indemnity rate, does not require a different analysis, but simply re–inserts a minimum average weekly earning capacity rather than an earnings capacity that may fall to zero.

"Since the WCJ found that applicant is entitled to the minimum rate of $126.00 per week in the off–season, that finding is consistent with the foregoing analysis of temporary disability indemnity being awarded at two different rates, with the floor of $126.00 per week where the injured employee has no off–season earning capacity. Accordingly, we will affirm the WCJ's decision." "

The WCAB's statement that the "amendment to Labor Code section 4453, re–establishing a floor for the temporary disability indemnity rate" references the former method of determining minimum average weekly earnings before 1990 when section 4453, subdivision (a)(1)–(2), as well as prior versions of the statute, did not contain the alternate method of multiplying the employee's actual earnings by 1.5. (Pham v. Workers' Comp. Appeals Bd., *supra*, 78 Cal. App. 4th at p. 632, fn. 6.) While the WCAB acknowledged that Assembly Bill No. 749 resurrected the former method of establishing an injured employee's average weekly earnings for purposes of setting temporary disability, it did not address in its opinion how average weekly earnings would have been determined for seasonal employees under the prior scheme.

Arguing that the law before 1990 would not have permitted a seasonal employee's off–season earnings to fall below the statutory minimum, Signature relies on Westside Produce Co. v. Workers' Comp. Appeals Bd. (1978) 81 Cal. App. 3d 546 [146 Cal. Rptr. 498, Cal. Comp. Cases 653] (Avila), where the employer alleged that an injured seasonal worker's regular employment period would have ended a week after she sustained an industrial injury to her wrist. (Id. at p. 549.) Former section 4453, similar to current section 4453, subdivision (c), mandated that the employee's average weekly earnings for purposes of temporary disability were to fall between $52.50 and $231. (Avila, *supra*, 81 Cal. App. 3d at pp. 550–551.) The Avila court reasoned that, "[i]n determining the earnings for purposes of temporary disability, the question is whether the injured would have continued working at a given wage for the duration of the disability." (Id. at p. 551.) The court concluded that, because the employee "was hired as a seasonal worker, temporary disability is payable based upon earnings at the time of injury only for that period the employment would have continued." (Id. at p. 552.) "After the employment would have terminated, [the employee] is entitled to temporary disability considering her past earnings history and her anticipated future earnings had she not been injured." (Ibid.)

While Avila supports the WCAB's application of separate in–season and off–season average weekly earnings rates for employees with distinct employment seasons, it does not answer the more specific question whether an employee's off–season temporary disability could fall below two–thirds of the statutory minimum average weekly earnings before 1990. Avila simply did not address whether the former versions of section 4453, without the alternative method of calculating average weekly earnings, established some sort of entitlement for a seasonal employee to receive off–season permanent disability. We nevertheless find the legislative amendments to calculating average weekly earnings under section 4453 over the years not controlling in the determination of off–season temporary disability.

We concur with the WCAB's conclusion in Jimenez, although for a different reason, that a seasonal employee is not entitled to temporary disability during her off–season where the parties stipulated she did not have any off–season earnings. Interpreting Assembly Bill No. 749's amendments to section 4453, subdivision (a), in isolation, we agree with the WCAB and Ochoa that the Legislature effectively established a minimum average weekly earnings that, per subdivision (c), may not fall below $189. Section 4453, however, does not set the level of temporary disability payments an injured employee is entitled to receive; by its own terms, section 4453 only establishes the employee's average weekly earnings used in calculating the employee's temporary disability. Section 4653 establishes the method of setting the permanent disability payments. That section provides: "If the injury causes temporary total disability, the disability payment is two–thirds of the average weekly earnings during the period of such disability, consideration being given to the ability of the injured employee to compete in an open labor market." (Italics added.) This second phrase of section 4653 is particularly applicable here.

Accepting as true, as we must, Ochoa's stipulation that she was routinely unemployed during her off season, she lacked the ability–whether the capacity, the opportunity, or the willingness–to compete in the open labor market beyond her seasonal employment with Signature. Ochoa therefore never intended to work past September 9, 2003, until her next employment season. Interpreting the statute in its entirety, section 4653 requires the WCAB to take an injured worker's particular employment history and prospects into account before mechanically multiplying her average

weekly earnings by two–thirds to determine the temporary disability payment. In the vast majority of situations, we presume that the two–thirds average weekly earnings mathematical calculation alone results in the appropriate level of permanent disability contemplated by the Legislature that must be awarded. In the case of a seasonal employee with no off–season earnings, however, the mathematical calculation is irrational. By simply multiplying the $189 nominal average weekly earnings minimum by two–thirds to award Ochoa weekly temporary disability payments of $126 when she otherwise would not be working, the WCAB failed to issue a temporary disability award with "consideration being given to [her] ability . . . to compete in an open labor market." (§ 4653.) Because section 4653 requires the WCAB to consider employment marketability in awarding temporary disability, we conclude that a seasonal employee who voluntarily or by necessity makes herself unavailable for employment during part of the year may not receive temporary disability payments during her regular off–season of unemployment. Since the issue is not before us, we do not address the situation where a seasonal employee has a history or potential for some minimal level of off–season earnings below the minimum average weekly earnings rate set forth in section 4453. (Nabors v. Workers' Comp. Appeals Bd. (2006) 140 Cal. App. 4th 217, 225 [44 Cal. Rptr. 3d 312, 71 Cal. Comp. Cases 704] ["The practice of distinguishing one case from another is based, after all, on the assumption that the holding of an appellate court is limited to the facts of the case before it"].)

Our reading of section 4653 conforms not only with the plain reading of the statute, but also with the state's long–standing policy for providing injured employees with temporary disability. It is well settled that temporary disability is intended as a substitute for an injured worker's lost wages. (Lauher, *supra*, 30 Cal. 4th at p. 1291; Nickelsberg v. Workers' Comp. Appeals Bd. (1991) 54 Cal. 3d 288, 294 [814 P.2d 1328, 285 Cal. Rptr. 86, 56 Cal. Comp. Cases 476]; Braewood Convalescent Hospital v. Workers' Comp. Appeals Bd. (1983) 34 Cal. 3d 159, 168 [666 P.2d 14, 193 Cal. Rptr. 157, 48 Cal. Comp. Cases 566]; Granado v. Workmen's Comp. App. Bd. (1968) 69 Cal. 2d 399, 403 [666 P.2d 14, 193 Cal. Rptr. 157, Cal. Comp. Cases 566].) "[T]he case law makes clear that the essential purpose of temporary disability indemnity is to help replace the wages the employee would have earned, but for the injury, during his or her period(s) of temporary disability." (Jimenez, *supra*, 67 Cal. Comp. Cases at p. 78.) "In contrast, permanent disability indemnity compensates for the residual handicap and/or impairment of function after maximum recovery from the effects of the industrial injury have been attained." (Lauher, *supra*, 30 Cal. 4th at p. 1291.) We do not address here the question of Ochoa's ability to obtain a permanent disability rating and, if so, the appropriate amount.

The Supreme Court has explained that, because temporary disability serves to replace lost wages, "an employer's obligation to pay [temporary disability insurance] to an injured worker ceases when such replacement income is no longer needed." (Lauher, *supra*,

30 Cal. 4th at pp. 1291–1292.) Temporary disability payments end when the employee returns to work, is deemed able to return to work, or achieves permanent and stationary status and therefore becomes eligible for permanent disability. (Ibid.) Under the same reasoning, it would be illogical to award an employee temporary disability as a wage replacement where it is undisputed that there otherwise would not be a wage to replace.

Ochoa's situation exemplifies the absurdity of awarding her off–season temporary disability based solely on section 4453's minimum average weekly earnings rate. Ochoa's regular employment season ran almost exactly six weeks between July 29 and September 9, 2003. According to her stipulated earnings of $548.38 per week, she would have earned a total of $3,290.28 in 2003 had she not been injured. ($548.38 x 6 weeks = $3,290.28.) Yet here, Ochoa became temporarily disabled on September 4, 2003, and Signature replaced four days of her regular daily earnings with temporary disability at the rate of $365.59 per week, leaving her with $3,185.83 in combined in–season earnings and temporary disability–a reduction of only $104.45 as a result of her industrial injury. (($548.38 x 4/7) – ($365.59 x 4/7) = $104.45 loss in earnings.) Considering first the remainder of 2003, the WCAB effectively awarded Ochoa approximately 16 weeks of off–season temporary disability from September 10 though December 31, 2003, at $126 per week amounting to $2,016 in temporary disability. (16 weeks x $126 = $2,016.) Under the WCAB's award, Ochoa's 2003 income would increase to $5,201.83–158 percent of the $3,290.28 she would have otherwise earned had she not been injured. If Ochoa remained temporarily disabled throughout all of 2004, the WCAB's award would grant her an annual income of $7,989.54. ((46 weeks x $126) + (6 weeks x $365.59) = $7,989.54.) She would therefore earn nearly 243 percent of her regular $3,290.28 annual income. A system that rewards a seasonal employee for sustaining an industrial injury likely would create an economic incentive for employees to exaggerate their level of disability and encourage them to malinger on temporary disability. We cannot condone this type of windfall to an injured employee where the Legislature has specifically mandated that an employee's ability to compete in the open labor market must be considered in calculating temporary disability.

Ochoa's counsel waited until oral argument to advise us about a similar workers' compensation case, Magana v. Nat'l Union Fire Ins. Co. (2005) 33 Cal. Workers' Comp. Rptr. 190 [2005 Cal. Wrk. Comp. P.D. LEXIS 26] (Magana), summarized in the California Workers' Compensation Reporter monthly newsletter. This delay is difficult to understand because Ochoa's appellate counsel argued Magana on behalf of another employee against the same employer, Signature, addressing an identical question. The WCAB denied reconsideration of Magana on April 26, 2005. In doing so, the WCAB summarily adopted the WCJ's rejection of the en banc Jimenez decision to award a seasonal employee "with no significant earnings" during the off–season temporary disability of $126 per week. Without distinguishing between employment seasons, the WCAB annualized the employee's actual weekly earnings and

awarded a consistent level of temporary disability throughout the year based on the revised $189 minimum average weekly earnings rate. (Magana, *supra*, at p. 191.) Ochoa's counsel apparently brought Magana to our attention at this late point in the appeal as authority to award Ochoa minimum temporary disability payments during her off–season in light of the recent amendment to section 4453. Unlike Magana, however, Ochoa seeks not only the minimum rate during her off–season, but also the higher temporary disability rate based on her stipulated earnings during her in–season.

It is well settled that WCAB decisions and denials of reconsideration reported in the California Compensation Cases and California Workers' Compensation Reporter are properly citable authority to the extent they point out the WCAB's "contemporaneous interpretation and application of the workers' compensation laws. . . . " (Smith v. Workers' Comp. Appeals Bd. (2000) 79 Cal. App. 4th 530, 537, fn. 2 [94 Cal. Rptr. 2d 186, 65 Cal. Comp. Cases 277].) Magana, however, does not take us toward that goal with respect to the treatment of seasonal employees. On May 10, 2005, two of the three WCAB commissioners who denied reconsideration in Magana just two weeks earlier reconsidered the same question in Ochoa's case and issued a written Opinion and Decision After Reconsideration reaching a very different conclusion. Further, no party in Ochoa's case, including the WCAB, advocates abandoning Jimenez's application of distinct in–season and off–season rates. We therefore find Magana unpersuasive in expressing the WCAB's interpretation of the effects of Assembly Bill No. 749 on seasonal employees and disagree with its reasoning.

Consistent with the legislative intent of section 4653, we conclude that temporary disability during a seasonal employee's in–season period of regular employment is payable based upon two–thirds of the employee's in–season average weekly earnings, subject to the minimum and maximum levels established under section 4453. Where, however, an employee does not have any off–season earnings and does not compete in the open labor market during a portion of the year, the employee is not entitled to temporary disability payments during that season. We do not express any opinion in calculating a seasonal employee's off–season temporary disability where the employee maintains some level of off–season earnings below the minimum average weekly earnings rate.

DISPOSITION

The WCAB's Opinion and Decision After Reconsideration is annulled. The matter is remanded to the Workers' Compensation Appeals Board to recalculate Ochoa's temporary disability award. Ochoa's request for attorney fees under section 5801 is denied. The parties shall bear their own costs on appeal... .

Footnote 1. Further statutory references are to the Labor Code.

See also, *Gamble v. WCAB* (2006) 71 Cal. Comp. Cases 1015 (unpublished decision) where the Court of Appeal, Fourth District, stated, in part:

However, the payment made to a temporarily partially disabled worker must take into account wages earned (or expected to be earned) by the worker in an alternative lower–paying job. Such benefits are "often called the 'wage–loss' benefit, because it pays a portion of the earnings that the injured worker loses" during the period of healing (or until their condition become permanent or stationary). (1 Cal. Workers' Compensation Practice, *supra.* Section 4.2, at p. 228.) Stated another way, employers of these workers are given a credit for any wages earned by the employee able to work less hours or at a lower–paying position.

Section 4657 delineates the formula to calculate the "loss in wages" for the temporarily partially disabled worker. The payment equates to the difference "between the [AWE] of the injured employee and the weekly amount which the injured employee will probably be able to earn during the disability, to be determined in view of the nature and extent of the injury... .(Footnote 6)

Footnote 6. If a totally disabled employee collecting temporary disability indemnity obtains new employment, he or she must immediately notify the employer who is making the payment. (See Section 3820.) If the work is for fewer hours or at a lower–paying job, the indemnity payment will be recalculated using the "weekly loss in wages" formula described above: The payment is two–thirds of his or her "weekly loss in wages," which consists of the difference between the worker's AWE and the weekly amount the employee can earn during the disability. (See Section 4657.)

Page 1636, Column 2, second paragraph, insert following '...labor market [Footnote omitted]'

The Board, in a Footnote in *Jimenez, supra,* noted that its holding was limited to *"true seasonal employees"* whom the Board defined as workers like agricultural workers who work *"reasonably identifiable and defined seasons of reasonably identifiable and defined duration".*

The holding in the case did not apply to *intermittent employees* like temporary agency and construction workers who work periodically throughout the entire year. *Beltran v. Kelly Services,* MON 331881, December 4, 2006, 35 CWCR 62. See also *Signature Fruit Company v. WCAB (Ochoa)* (2006) 71 Cal. Comp. Cases 1044.

Page 1638, Column 2, third paragraph, insert following '...§53.1.'

Concurrent Employment

Concurrent employment means employment that is contemporaneous to other employment. It needs to be simultaneous to or co–exist with the other employment being claimed in order for the Appeals Board to consider it in calculations of average weekly earnings.

It is often referred to as *multiple employment* and falls under Labor Code section 4453(c)(2), "Where the employee is working for two or more employers at or about the time of the injury... "

Concurrent employment is distinguished from *joint employment* situations where, for example, two employers may be held jointly and severally liable for benefits.

A *concurrent employment* situation holds one employer solely liable for the benefits, but permits earnings at multiple employments to be used to calculate average weekly earnings to arrive at a correct earnings capacity.

This is done by taking the aggregate of all the earnings from all employments computed in terms of one week. The earnings, however, from employments other than the one where the injury took place, may not be taken at a higher rate than the hourly rate in effect paid to the worker at the employer where the injury took place at the time of injury.

In *Gamble v. WCAB* (2006) 71 Cal. Comp. Cases 1015, a defendant was denied credit for applicant's earnings in a concurrent situation against defendant's liability for vocational maintenance allowance benefits relating to an industrial injury that was from separate employment.

The Time of Injury

The "time of injury" is used as the commencement date, as the date when benefit calculations take place and not "the date of injury". This is the starting point called for in Labor Code section 4453.5. As a general rule, the date of injury and time of injury will coincide, but not always. When there is a specific injury, the date of injury will coincide with the time of injury. The benefit level is therefore fixed as of the date under Labor Code section 5411. Calculations for cumulative traumas and occupational diseases may present other problems because the definition of date of injury depends on Labor Code section 5412, where knowledge of industrial causation and disability are present.

Page 1639, Column 2, at end of first paragraph delete "week while temporarily disabled." and add

week for injuries sustained between January 1, 2003 and January 1, 2005. However, the minimum temporary disability rate is now subject to the State Average Weekly Wage (SAWW) so the minimum weekly rate increases to $132.25 for injuries sustained on or after January 1, 2007.

§ 45.4   Effects of State and Federal Income Taxes on Benefits

Page 1639, Column 2, insert at end of second paragraph

Odd Lot Doctrine

If an employee remains disabled following an injury and is not permanent and stationary to the extent that he or she can only find marginal sporadic employment, so that he or she occupies a position of an "*odd–lot*" on the open labor market, the burden shifts to the employer to show that employment is available to such a partially disabled employee. See Section 9.0 of this book for a discussion of cases involving such a doctrine.

§ 45.5   Undocumented Workers

Often undocumented injured employees have difficulty in establishing their true earnings record. In such situations an earnings expert may be necessary to establish an estimation of the undocumented employee's earnings as records to support such earnings may not exist. This is especially true when determining the diminished future earning capacity (by first determining the injured employee's pre–injury earnings base) of the injured employee under SB 899. Cost of experts to establish future earning capacity may be awarded to an employee under Section 5811.

Intentionally blank

§ 45A.0   FRAUD

Page 1643, Column 2, sixth paragraph, insert following '…2004.'

Types of Workers' Compensation Fraud

The following are a some common types of workers' compensation fraud that may be committed by medical providers. There are many others. Whether a specific act constitutes *fraud* or *abuse* is determined on a case by case basis.

Medical Provider Fraud

This may include:

- Performing unnecessary medical treatment;
- Unnecessary diagnostic testing for type of injury;
- Allowing unlicensed or unqualified medical personnel to take patient history and/or provide medical care;
- Charging for unnecessary translation services;
- Charging for translation services by an unqualified provider;
- Treatment or testing provided by untrained or unlicensed persons and then billing for medical care as though treatment was provided by a physician or qualified personnel;
- Durable medical equipment (DME) delivered/mailed to patient's residence that was never prescribed;
- Having an employee sign sign–in sheet multiple times at first visit and then billing for services never provided;
- Medical cost shifting by billing the higher paying venue rather than the correct venue (group health v. workers' compensation);
- Medical provider billing both the workers' compensation payer, a third–party carrier for the original or subsequent injury carrier, and the group health payer (and not reimbursing the duplicate payment);
- Medical services provided without proper utilization review authorization, unless emergency;
- Accepting payments for medical treatment from injured workers or employer when the claim has been accepted and is also being paid by the claims administrator;
- Providing services outside the scope and authority of the physician's medical license such as Manipulation Under Anesthesia by chiropractors, without an Anesthesiologist in attendance;
- Providing treatment based on financial incentive rather than the patient's need (in–house physical therapy, pharmacy or radiology and surgical centers);
- Providing treatment without a license or while the professional license is suspended; or
- Billing for services, medical tests and treatment that was never performed.

Employee (Claimant) Fraud

This may include:

- Making a knowingly false claim;
- Claiming a non–industrial injury as industrial;
- Claiming non–existing symptoms or disability following a valid claim;
- Lying about work status while receiving temporary disability benefits;
- Failing to disclose prior medical records or accidents to a physician, or during a deposition, for the purpose of receiving workers' compensation benefits;
- Lying about pre–existing symptoms for the purpose of receiving workers' compensation benefits;
- Accepting prescription drugs for injury prescribed by treating physician not using the drugs but telling the physician he or she is using the drugs;
- Failing to advise the Employment Development Department or workers' compensation insurance carrier of receipt of benefits from each other during the same time period; or

- Lying to a Workers' Compensation Judge for the purpose of receiving workers' compensation benefits.

Employer Fraud

This may include:

- Lying to deny benefits to an injured employee;
- Lying to reduce level of benefits due (i.e., underreporting wages so temporary disability Indemnity and/or permanent disability rates are fraudulently low);
- Paying claim(s) costs (beyond first aid) to prevent an injured employee from reporting his/her injury;
- Threatening an employee to prevent filing of claim;
- Giving an employee misleading information to discourage the filing of a claim;
- Fraudulently verifying claims for non–employees or employees not injured in the course of employment (usually done as a substitute for health insurance);
- Assuming a false identity to file a claim for workers' compensation benefits (i.e., the "employer" and the "claimant" are one and the same person); or
- Lying to a Workers' Compensation Judge for the purpose of denying benefits to a injured employee.

Employer Premium / Policy Fraud

This may include:

- Underreporting wages;
- Misclassifying payroll;
- Misrepresenting the nature of the company business; or
- Conspiring with others to use fake or altered certificates of insurance to avoid paying premium for the employees of subcontractors.

Broker / Agent Fraud

This may include:

- Providing false information when applying for coverage for a client. (This may be done with, or without, the knowledge of the client.);
- Conspiring with a client or medical providers to fraudulently discourage or deny claims; or
- Embezzling money from a client by fraudulently reducing the premium paid to the insurer, but continuing to collect an inflated amount of money from the client.

Page 1646, Column 1, fourth paragraph, insert following '...Eagle.'

In holding that an employee's fraudulent use of a Social Security card and green card to obtain employment and thus putting a false Social Security number on his workers' compensation claim *did not* constitute a violation of Section 1871.4, the Court of Appeal, Second District, in *Farmer Brothers Coffee v. WCAB (Ruiz)* (2005) 70 Cal. Comp. Cases 1399, stated, in part:

Petitioner contends that Ruiz's use of a fraudulent Social Security card and fraudulent green card to obtain employment, and then putting a false Social Security number on his workers' compensation claim form, violated Insurance Code, section 1871.4, which makes it a criminal offense to make a knowingly false or fraudulent material representation for the purpose of obtaining workers' compensation benefits. (Footnote 9)

A claimant who has been convicted of a violation of section 1871.4 is barred from receiving or retaining any compensation obtained as a direct result of the fraudulent misrepresentation. (Tensfeldt v. Workers' Comp. Appeals Bd. (1998) 66 Cal. App. 4th 116, 123–124 [77 Cal. Rptr. 2d 691, 63 Cal. Comp. Cases 973]; Ins. Code, § 1871.5.) There is no evidence of a conviction in this record. Further, Ruiz was not required to be a lawfully documented alien to be an employee entitled to workers' compensation benefits. (See §§ 3351, 3357.) It was employment, not the compensable injury, that Ruiz obtained as a direct result of the use of fraudulent documents...

Footnote 9. Petitioner has attached as an exhibit to its petition, a copy of a newspaper article that was not before the Board, and petitioner discusses the article without asking that we take judicial notice of it or explaining its relevance. We disregard the article and petitioner's discussion of it.

See Section 5.9 (w) of this book for full decision of this case.

In *The People, ex rel. Monterey Mushrooms, Inc. v. Thompson, et al.* (2006) 71 Cal. Comp. Cases 35, the Court of Appeal, Sixth District, in an unpublished opinion, upheld a trial Court's judgment holding that a civil action for violation of Insurance Code section 1871.7(b) arising from fraudulent acts made unlawful by Penal Code section 550(a)(10) did not violate the exclusive remedy provision of workers' compensation under Labor Code section 3820 stating, in part:

After a court trial, defendants Steven Thompson, Aster Kifle–Thompson, and the corporations they had formed were found to have violated Insurance Code section 1871.7, subdivision (b), by submitting fraudulent claims for compensation proscribed by Penal Code section 550. On appeal, defendants contend that the case should have been dismissed because (1) it belonged exclusively in a workers' compensation forum, (2) the People failed to meet the statutory prerequisites for bringing the lawsuit, and (3) defendants' conduct was not unlawful. Defendants further contend that the trial court should have applied a "clear and convincing evidence" standard of proof, that joint and several liability was inappropriate on the facts of the case, and that the damages imposed were unauthorized and excessive. We find no error and affirm the judgment…

The application of Insurance Code section 1871.7, subdivision (b), was clearly authorized in this case. As the trial court recognized, this statute was intended to encompass fraudulent claims for workers' compensation benefits. It specifically provides for civil penalties for claims for compensation under Labor Code section 3207, which is part of the WCA. (Footnote 7)

Indeed, in enacting the Insurance Frauds Prevention Act, the Legislature clearly expressed its intent to promote the investigation and prosecution of insurance fraud, including workers' compensation fraud, which "harms employers by contributing to the increasingly high cost of workers' compensation insurance and self–insurance and harms employees by undermining the perceived legitimacy of all workers' compensation claims." (Ins. Code, § 1871, subd. (d).) "Prevention of workers' compensation insurance fraud may reduce the number of workers' compensation claims and claim payments thereby producing a commensurate reduction in workers' compensation costs. Prevention of workers' compensation insurance fraud will assist in restoring confidence and faith in the workers' compensation system, and will facilitate expedient and full compensation for employees injured at the workplace." (Id., subd. (e).) Lest there be any residual confusion over the authority to proceed, Insurance Code section 1871.7, subdivision (k), makes it clear that the remedies it provides are "in addition to any other remedies provided by existing law."

Furthermore, Penal Code section 550, on which the Insurance Code section 1871.7 allegations were predicated in this case, prohibits the knowing submission of false or fraudulent claims for payment of health care benefits. The statute specifically defines "a claim for payment of a health care benefit" to include a "claim for payment submitted by or on the behalf of a provider of any workers' compensation health benefits under the Labor Code." (Pen. Code, § 550, subd. (a)(10).)

The express inclusion of workers' compensation claims thus demonstrates the Legislature's intention to allow civil actions under Insurance Code section 1871.7 arising from fraudulent acts made unlawful by Penal Code section 550, notwithstanding applicability of the WCA. None of the cases cited by defendants compels or suggests a different conclusion. We therefore agree with the trial court's conclusion that the exclusivity provisions of the WCA did not bar this action… .

Footnote 7. Labor Code section 3207 defines "compensation" as "compensation under this division [including] every benefit or payment conferred by this division upon an injured employee, or in the event of his or her death, upon his or her dependents, without regard to negligence."

Chiropractic Fraud

Suspected chiropractic fraud must be reported by the Fraud Division to the appropriate disciplinary body. Insurance Code section 1872.84 provides:

The commissioner shall ensure that the Fraud Division forwards to the appropriate disciplinary body, in addition to the names and supporting evidence of individuals described in subdivision (a) of Section 1872.83, the names, along with all supporting evidence, of any individuals licensed under the Chiropractic Initiative Act who are suspected of actively engaging in fraudulent activity…

Page 1647, Column 2, twelfth paragraph, insert following '…employees.'

In reviewing a lower Court's decision and holding that plaintiff/applicant's malicious prosecution claim against an employer's workers' compensation insurer was not an anti–SLAPP suit because the insurer *acted with malice by withholding medical and videotape evidence* when forwarding the claim to the District Attorney that related to applicant's alleged exaggeration of his injury, the Court of Appeal, Fourth District, in *Mosby v. Liberty Mutual Insurance Company* (2006) 71 Cal. Comp. Cases 487, stated, in part:

Freddie Curtis Mosby, Jr., a former employee of Best Buy Company, sued Liberty Mutual Insurance Company, Best Buy's workers' compensation insurer, for malicious prosecution when an insurance fraud case against him was dismissed by the District Attorney's office. The insurance fraud case was based on the evidence Liberty Mutual provided to the District Attorney's office in support of its claim that Mosby had exaggerated an on–the–job injury. (An air conditioning unit fell on him while he was operating a fork lift.) Mosby's complaint was initially dismissed on demurrer based on the theory that Mosby's exclusive remedies were in workers' compensation. This court, however, reversed the dismissal, holding that Liberty Mutual had stepped out of its shoes as a workers' compensation insurer, and in any event the applicable statute, section 1877.5 of the Insurance Code, expressly contemplates no civil immunity for malicious reporting of workers' compensation fraud. (See Mosby v. Liberty Mutual Insurance Company (2003) 110 Cal. App. 4th 995 [2 Cal. Rptr. 3d 286, 68 Cal. Comp. Case 1126].)

On remand, Liberty Mutual tried and succeeded again to dismiss the case, this time on the theory that Mosby's malicious prosecution action was a "SLAPP" suit. (See Code Civ. Proc., § 425.16.) Since there is no question that a malicious prosecution action meets the "threshold" prong for an anti–SLAPP motion (see Dickens v. Provident Life and Accident Insurance Co (2004) 117 Cal. App. 4th. 705 [11 Cal. Rptr. 3d 877]), the case turns on the "probability" prong of the anti–SLAPP statute. (See Commonwealth Energy Corp. v. Investor Data Exchange, Inc. (2003) 110 Cal. App. 4th 26, 31–32 [1 Cal. Rptr. 3d 390].) As this court has recently pointed out, the probability prong is analyzed this way: "The plaintiff must demonstrate the complaint is both legally sufficient and is supported by a prima facie showing of facts sufficient to sustain a favorable judgment if the evidence submitted by the plaintiff is given credit." (Ruiz v. Harbor View Community Association (2005) 134 Cal. App. 4th 1456, 1466 [37 Cal. Rptr. 3d 133].)

There is substantial evidence that Mosby might have been faking or exaggerating his workers' compensation claim deriving from an air conditioning unit which fell and struck him. Indeed, in some ways the case seems like a parody of the movie, The Fortune Cookie, in which Jack Lemmon spends much of the movie wearing a neck brace in order to fake a personal injury claim against a football team (Lemmon plays a TV cameraman accidentally hit in the stands by a thrown football, and is convinced by his ambulance–chaser lawyer brother–in–law played by Walter Matthau to play up the claim for big bucks). Thus, Mosby was videotaped coming out of a doctor's office wearing a cervical collar and using a crutch under one arm, but, once home, appeared to walk up a set of stairs without difficulty. (Footnote 1)

But, as this court recognized in Ruiz, the probability prong for an anti–SLAPP suit is not tested on the overall weight of the evidence, or whether the moving party has substantial evidence to win its case, but on whether, if the evidence of the responding plaintiff is credited, the plaintiff has made a prima facie showing of facts sufficient to sustain a favorable judgment. So we now turn to the hard evidence that Mosby presented in his opposition to the anti–SLAPP suit dismissal motion that Liberty Mutual might have known he had a valid claim, and acted maliciously in turning the case over to the District Attorney's office. (Footnote 2)

Liberty Mutual secretly made five surveillance videos of Mosby going about his daily activities. Liberty Mutual turned over four of the tapes to the District Attorney. But it didn't turn over a videotape made on July 2, 1998. One of Liberty Mutual's investigators, John Waterson, admitted at a deposition that this particular videotape showed "Mr. Mosby acting in a way that was consistent with his claimed injuries." This videotape showed Mosby, among other things, supporting himself as he descended some stairs, wearing a neck brace and moving slowly and deliberately. (Italics added.) (To be fair to Liberty Mutual, this tape was mentioned in the timeline prepared for the District Attorney.)

The beginning of another tape, made on April 28, 1998, which was turned over the District Attorney's office, initially shows an apparently healthy person driving a car. This person was described by Liberty Mutual in a timeline presented to the District Attorney as "claimant." In point of fact, this healthy person was not Mosby at all, but Liberty Mutual did not bring that fact to the District Attorney's attention in turning over the case.

Liberty Mutual showed only two of the five videotapes to Dr. Stuart Green, an agreed–upon medical examiner. (This medical examiner would later claim that Mosby "did not give [him] an honest examination.") In particular, Liberty Mutual did not show Dr. Green the tape of Mosby acting consistently with his claimed injuries.

Dr. Alan Cohen conducted a nerve conduction examination on Mosby. Dr. Cohen's report said: "Needle electrode examination showed evidence of both active denervation and some evidence of chronic reinnervation bilaterally involving nerve roots C5, C6 and C7. Of these, the right seems slightly more involved than the left and C6 seems slightly more abnormal than C5 and C7." Liberty Mutual knew about Dr. Cohen's report because the file had a letter from Dr. Hooshang Pak to Dr. Tyrone Reece (Mosby's treating doctor) on September 15, 1997, noting that nerve conduction studies had been recommended, and had already been performed by Dr. Cohen. However, Liberty Mutual did not include the Cohen report in the exhibits it turned over to the District Attorney.

Dr. Reid Thompson conducted a neurosurgical consultation with Mosby. According to Dr. Stuart Green's review of the chart prepared by Dr. Thompson: "Significant degenerative changes were noted and findings of autofusion at numerous levels. Doctor Thompson felt that continued conservative measures including physical therapy were indicated. Doctor Thompson felt that an anterior cervical fusion of C2–3 and C3–4 would unlikely provide him with significant relief and would in fact ultimately exacerbate the problem in the cervical spine." While Dr. Green's second hand [sic] review of Dr. Thompson's chart was given to the District Attorney, a letter from Dr. Thompson to Dr. Reece contained even stronger information corroborating real injuries to Mosby, and that letter was not included in the material turned over to the District Attorney. That letter said, in part: "His MRI and plain x–rays show the presence of severe cervical spondylosis. There is evidence of autofusion at numerous levels and there is, in fact, fusion apparent at the C2–3 level present." (Spondylosis is forward displacement of vertebrae producing pain by compression of the nerve roots.)

The question arises: Is this evidence – particularly the withheld videotape and diagnosis of spondylosis based on MRIs and x–rays – enough to show that Liberty Mutual acted maliciously in turning Mosby's case over to the District Attorney?

Yes. The deliberate withholding of exculpatory evidence can itself support an inference of malice. (Laible v. Superior Court (1984) 157 Cal. App. 3d 44 [203 Cal. Rptr. 513]; Jacques Interiors v. Petrak (1987) 188 Cal. App. 3d 1363 [234 Cal. Rptr. 44].) Let us explain:

In Laible, as here, the plaintiff had been accused of a crime. He had been arrested for participating in a robbery, but discharged at the preliminary hearing for lack of evidence. He then sued the city for false arrest and false imprisonment. The trial court granted the city a partial summary judgment, implicitly finding that there was insufficient evidence the city acted with malice. However, the arresting officer had learned that bills with which the plaintiff had used on a clothing shopping spree did not match the bills taken in the robbery; even so, the arresting officer did not give this bit of exculpatory information to the magistrate who issued the arrest warrant. Also, the officer did not inform the magistrate that he used a three–year old photo in a photospread that led to the plaintiff's identification, and finally, that a certain witness was unable to identify the plaintiff in a lineup.

In reversing, the appellate court first noted the obvious point that presenting affirmatively false evidence presents a stronger case of malice than merely withholding exculpatory evidence. (Laible v. Superior Court, *supra*, 157 Cal. App. 3d at p. 53.) Even so, withholding of "significant" exculpatory evidence can support an inference of malice. (Ibid. ["But where, as asserted here, significant exculpatory evidence has been withheld, an inference of malice may be reasonably drawn. It is for the trier of fact, not the law and motion court, to weigh the available inferences against Inspector Ryan's profession of pure motives."].)

In Jacques Interiors, an independent claims adjuster withheld certain photographs (and a cover letter from an independent fire investigator) from his client insurer that tended to exonerate a tenant from having caused the fire. The insurer ultimately sued the tenant in subrogation (by way of cross–complaint, because the fire got out of hand), but, after the claims adjuster's withholding of information came to light, dismissed its subrogation suit against the tenant. The tenant then sued the claims adjuster, the jury awarded a large damage award against the adjuster (including punitive damages) and the appellate court affirmed the judgment as against a lack of substantial evidence argument. In particular, the appellate court noted that the withholding of the exculpatory photographs meant that the adjuster was acting for "an improper purpose, with an awareness that the action would not be resolved in [the insurer's] favor unless the fact–finder was misled." (See Jacques Interiors, *supra*, 188 Cal. App. 3d at p. 1371.)

The case before us presents a similar situation. Possibly, the withheld videotape might not be enough by itself to show anything – Jack Lemmon managed to wear the neck brace in The Fortune Cookie for much of the movie, so acting "consistently" with injuries doesn't mean they still aren't being faked. Even so, the fact that the insurer here did not turn over the fact that there were x–rays and an MRI which had shown hard evidence of cervical spondylosis and various fusions of vertebrae is very troubling. The fact is susceptible of the inference that, to parallel Jacques Interiors, the insurer realized that the District Attorney might not have filed the action against Mosby unless the District Attorney's office was misled by the absence of exculpatory evidence. And, as in Laible, it is for the trier of fact and not the law and motion court to weigh the evidence as to whether Mosby really has been exaggerating. Whether Liberty Mutual's withholding of the hard evidence of the x–rays and the MRI, in combination with the withheld videotape, was an innocent judgment call (or forgetfulness) or, on the other hand, the product of a recognition by Liberty Mutual employees that the District Attorney's office might not have proceeded at all if the office had been in possession of that exculpatory evidence is for the trier of fact to decide.

We need only add that the equation made by Laible and Jacques Interiors between the deliberate withholding of exculpatory evidence and an inference of malice and a weak case is a sound one. It disposes of the idea that just because Liberty Mutual had some evidence, indeed much evidence,

that Mosby was faking his claim, that the insurer ipso facto had probable cause to send the case to the District Attorney and therefore could not be liable for malicious prosecution.

Sometimes, "probable cause" to bring an action must be gauged by the totality of known facts, rather than just a selective portion of them. For example, in Zamos v. Stroud (2004) 32 Cal. 4th 958, 960 [87 P.3d 802, 12 Cal. Rptr. 3d 54] attorneys who originally did have probable cause to instigate a fraud action but who later received information exonerating the defendant could be held liable for malicious prosecution. (Footnote 3)

Of course, the archetypical example of how the selective presentation of evidence is Shakespeare's Iago, who is consumed with hatred for Othello. When Iago tells Othello that he saw a potential lover of Othello's wife Desdemona wiping his brow with a particular pattern handkerchief that Othello had given Desdemona, he isn't lying – he is just not telling the whole truth, namely, that he planted the handkerchief among the potential lover's personal belongings where it might be found and used to mop a brow. The ultimate result of the fact that Iago doesn't tell Othello the whole truth and excludes the evidence that would exonerate Desdemona is malicious prosecution with a vengeance.

Now, of course, the evidence at this point hardly shows that Liberty Mutual has or had anything like an Iago–like animus toward Mosby. And we are perfectly willing to agree with the trial judge that the totality of the evidence could readily exonerate the company. Indeed, we are aware of the irony wrought by the stringent standard of review in SLAPP motions as it applies to this case: This court is required to look selectively at Mosby's evidence, and determine whether, assuming that evidence were credited by the trier of fact, Mosby has merely made a prima facie showing of facts sufficient to sustain a favorable judgment. We therefore cannot weigh the totality of evidence on whether he is faking his injuries or whether Liberty Mutual sent his case to the District Attorney maliciously; the irony is that Mosby's evidence itself centers on Liberty Mutual being selective in what it presented to the District Attorney. In that light, it may also be true, as Liberty Mutual points out, that the District Attorney may not have wanted "everything." Even so, the fact that Liberty Mutual didn't turn over to the District Attorney the fact that certain hard evidence in the form of x–rays and MRIs corroborated Mosby's claim precludes us – in the procedural posture of this case – from determining that Liberty Mutual necessarily did not act without probable cause and without malice. Soft tissue subjectivity is one thing. X–rays and MRIs are something else.

Accordingly, the judgment is reversed. Since today's disposition is, once again, interlocutory in nature, we will not award appellate costs in this proceeding. Rather, the trial court will have the discretion to award the costs of this trip to the Court of Appeal to the ultimately prevailing party… .

Footnote 1. Or pump gas, as Mosby was also shown doing on a tape. Mosby's explanation was that while he might have the hand strength to put a gasoline pump nozzle in his car, he is not strong enough to hold the nozzle to complete filling the tank.

Footnote 2. In our previous opinion, we noted that assertions of racial animus in the complaint could support Mosby's malice claim. In the SLAPP motion, Mosby did not make use of any assertions of racial animus. However, logically, that doesn't prove that Liberty Mutual could not have acted maliciously in reporting Mosby for workers' compensation fraud – at most it proves is that if it did act maliciously, race was not a motive for that maliciousness.

Footnote 3. The fraud action was against a former attorney, based on the claim of his former client, that he had made false representations to the client to induce her to settle a foreclosure suit. The former attorney (the defendant in the fraud action) later sent transcripts of certain hearings in the foreclosure suit that undercut the client's claims of misrepresentation. Even so, the attorneys in the fraud action continued to prosecute. (Zamos, *supra*, 32 Cal. 4th at pp. 961–962.) [**Editor's Note:** A Strategic Lawsuit Against Public Participation (SLAPP) is a form of litigation filed by a large organization or in some cases an individual plaintiff, to intimidate and silence less powerful critics by so severely burdening them with the cost of a legal defense that they abandon their criticism.]

In *Premiere Medical Management Systems, Inc., et al., v. CIGA, et al.,* (2006) 71 Cal. Comp. Cases 210, the Court of Appeal, Second District, held that a civil action by plaintiff representatives of treating physicians against defendants (CIGA and workers' compensation insurers) was an anti–SLAPP action that is prohibited under Code of Civil Procedure 425.16.

In this case defendants, and others, petitioned the Appeals Board to consolidate pending cases involving claims filed by a medical group in litigated cases covered by CIGA based on allegations that premiere and its affiliates were engaging in illegal fee–sharing in violation of Business and Professions Code section 650. Premiere opposed the consolidation petitions, arguing that they were brought for the improper purpose of delay. The Board ordered consolidation and stayed all liens on the ground that the business practice of Premiere and its affiliates were common issues in each of the cases for which consolidation was sought. Premiere and five affiliated physicians filed a complaint against CIGA and other defendants under the Racketeer Influenced and Corrupt Organizations Act 18 United States Code section 1961 et seq. (RICO), contending that after Premier submitted the affiliates physician's bills to defendants for payment, defendants collectively conspired to contest, delay, and avoid payment of these bills and liens. Alleging that the defendants acted with malice Premier sought $15,000,000.00 in compensatory damages and restitution, as well as punitive damages, injunctive relief costs and fees.

CIGA and some of the other defendants argued that the complaint was an anti–SLAPP lawsuit because it was based entirely on the defendants' constitutional right to petition the board. The trial court denied defendant's special motion to strike on the ground that the

requirements of the anti–SLAPP statute had not been met and that plaintiffs had shown a probability of success on the merits. Defendants appealed.

The court in reversing the trial court's denial of defendant's motion to strike plaintiff's complaint stated in part:

DISCUSSION

I.

An anti–SLAPP motion "requires the court to engage in a two–step process. First, the court decides whether the defendant has made a threshold showing that the challenged cause of action is one arising from protected activity . . . . If the court finds that such a showing has been made, it then determines whether the plaintiff has demonstrated a probability of prevailing on the claim." (*Equilon Enterprises v. Consumer Cause, Inc. (2002) 29 Cal.4th 53, 67 [52 P.3d 685, 124 Cal. Rptr. 2d 507] (Equilon*).) "Under section 425.16, subdivision (b)(2), the trial court in making these determinations considers 'the pleadings, and supporting and opposing affidavits stating the facts upon which the liability or defense is based.' " (*Ibid.*) On appeal, its determination of each step is subject to de novo review. (*Governor Gray Davis Com. v. American Taxpayers Alliance (2002) 102 Cal.App.4th 449, 456 [125 Cal. Rptr. 2d 534].)*

The moving defendant must demonstrate that the conduct on which the plaintiff's complaint is based falls within one of the four categories described in section 425.16, subdivision (e), which defines acts "in furtherance of a person's right of petition or free speech under the United States or California Constitution . . . ." (*Equilon, supra, 29 Cal.4th at p. 66.*) "In the anti–SLAPP context, the critical point is whether the plaintiff's cause of action itself was based on an act in furtherance of the defendant's right of petition or free speech. (*Equilon, supra, 29 Cal.4th at pp. 67–68;* see also *Briggs* [*v. Eden Council for Hope & Opportunity* (1999)] *19 Cal.4th [1106,] 1114' " (City of Cotati v. Cashman (2002) 29 Cal.4th 69, 78 [52 P.3d 695, 124 Cal. Rptr. 2d 519],* italics omitted.) The principal thrust or gravamen of the claim determines whether section 425.16 applies. (*Mann v. Quality Old Time Service, Inc. (2004) 120 Cal.App.4th 90, 102–103 [15 Cal. Rptr. 3d 215] (Mann*).)

Subdivision (e) of section 425.16 provides in relevant part that, as used in that statute, " 'act in furtherance of a person's right of petition or free speech under the United States or California Constitution in connection with a public issue' includes: (1) any written or oral statement . . . made before a legislative [or] executive . . . proceeding . . . ; (2) any written or oral statement . . . made in connection with an issue under consideration or review by a legislative [or] executive . . . body . . . ; (3) any written or oral statement . . . made in a place open to the public or a public forum in connection with an issue of public interest; (4) or any other conduct in furtherance of the exercise of the constitutional right of . . . free speech in connection with a public issue or an issue of public interest."

The moving defendants argue that the entire complaint is an anti–SLAPP suit, subject to a special motion to strike. This is so because the complaint "wholly arises from, and is predicated upon, [defendants'] acts and communications in connection with or in proceedings before the [Board]." Defendants argue that the entire process of submitting bills and lien claims for medical services in pending WCAB cases is inherently part of the WCAB litigation process.

In support of that proposition, they rely on *Vacanti, supra, 24 Cal.4th 800,* which held that claims by workers' compensation medical providers for damages arising out of insurers' failure to make full and timely payment on their lien claims came within the exclusive remedy provisions of the WCA. The court concluded that "the alleged injury underlying all of plaintiffs' causes of action is collateral to or derivative of a compensable workplace injury and falls within the scope of the exclusivity provisions." (*Vacanti, supra, 24 Cal.4th at p. 815.*)

The moving defendants reason that they were sued because they exercised their statutory right to object to plaintiffs' bills and liens claims. They also observe that plaintiffs pursued payment in workers' compensation litigation. The moving defendants invoke the rule that communications preparatory to litigation are included within the ambit of the anti–SLAPP law.

The Premier plaintiffs argue that the entire complaint does not come within section 425.16, citing allegations that the defendants conspired to delay, avoid, and obstruct payment on bills and lien claims. These activities, they contend, had nothing to do with petitioning the WCAB. Plaintiffs cite paragraph 40 of their complaint, which alleges that defendants combined to "contest, object to, litigate, delay payment on and/or not pay at all on Plaintiffs' valid and proper bills and lien claims for medical treatment and/or services provided to Employers' Applicants."

Paragraph 40 further alleges defendants conspired to:

" "(b) limit or reduce the amount Defendants would pay on valid and proper bills and lien claims for Employers' Applicants who Physicians had provided medical services to;

" . . .

" (e) agree to only pay a certain price, unilaterally agreed upon by Defendants, on Plaintiffs' valid and proper bills and lien claims for Employers' Applicants who Physicians had provided medical services to;

"(f) establish or settle, between each Defendant, the payment for valid and proper bills and lien claims for Employers' Applicants who Physicians had provided medical services to, so as to directly or indirectly affect free and unrestricted competition between Plaintiffs and, among others, those medical treatment and service providers, other than Physicians, which Defendants preferred treat and provide medical services to Employers' Applicants." "

Plaintiffs argue that none of these allegations refers to petitioning the WCAB, but instead address delay and avoidance of payment to Premier, activity which is not protected and therefore does not fall within the ambit of section 425.16.

The moving defendants have the better argument. In the context of determining whether a case comes within section 425.16, the Supreme Court has held that the constitutional right to petition includes the basic act of seeking administrative action. (*Briggs v. Eden Council for Hope &*

Opportunity, supra, 19 Cal.4th at p. 1115.) We applied this principle in *Dove Audio, Inc. v. Rosenfeld, Meyer & Susman (1996) 47 Cal.App.4th 777 [54 Cal. Rptr. 2d 830].* In that case, the plaintiff sued for libel and interference with economic relationship in a dispute which arose because the defendant intended to file a complaint with the California Attorney General seeking an investigation of whether the plaintiff had honored its contractual obligation to pay the proceeds of a celebrity recording to charity. The factual predicate of the lawsuit was a letter the defendant had sent to various celebrities who had participated in the recording that sought support for a complaint defendant initiated to the Attorney General. (*Dove*, at p. 780.)

We held the action fell within the ambit of the anti–SLAPP statute because the defendant's communication "raised a question of public interest: whether money designated for charities was being received by those charities. The communication was made in connection with an official proceeding authorized by law, a proposed complaint   to the Attorney General seeking an investigation. 'The constitutional right to petition . . . includes the basic act of filing litigation or otherwise seeking administrative action.' [Citation.] Just as communications preparatory to or in anticipation of the bringing of an action or other official proceeding are within the protection of the litigation privilege[,] we hold that such statements are equally entitled to the benefits of section 425.16. [Citation.]" (*Dove Audio, Inc. v. Rosenfeld, Meyer & Susman, supra, 47 Cal.App.4th at p. 784.*)

In *Dickens v. Provident Life & Accident Ins. Co. (2004) 117 Cal.App.4th 705, 714 [11 Cal. Rptr. 3d 877],* we held that contact with the executive branch of government and its investigators about a potential violation of law was preparatory to commencing an official proceeding authorized by law–a criminal prosecution for mail fraud–and thus came within the ambit of the anti–SLAPP law. A similar result was reached in *ComputerXpress, Inc. v. Jackson (2001) 93 Cal.App.4th 993 [113 Cal. Rptr. 2d 625],* which concerned a lawsuit based on the defendants' filing of a complaint with the Securities and Exchange Commission. The issue was whether the complaint fell within the ambit of section 425.16. Finding that the purpose of the complaint was to solicit an investigation by that agency, the *ComputerXpress* court had "little difficulty in concluding that the filing of the complaint qualified at least as a statement before an official proceeding" under section 425.16, subdivision (e). (*Id. at p. 1009.*) Communications to an administrative agency designed to prompt action by that agency come within the definition of an official proceeding, even though they "*may precede the initiation of formal proceedings.*" (*ComputerXpress, Inc. v. Jackson, supra, 93 Cal.App.4th at p. 1009,* citing *Slaughter v. Friedman (1982) 32 Cal.3d 149, 156 [649 P.2d 886, 185 Cal. Rptr. 244]* [in context of *Civil Code section 47* privilege], and *Edwards v. Centex Real Estate Corp. (1997) 53 Cal.App.4th 15, 30 [61 Cal. Rptr. 2d 518]* [*Civil Code section 47* privilege applied to communications or complaints by citizens to public officials or authorities charged with investigating, prosecuting or remedying alleged wrongdoing].)

In their brief and at oral argument, plaintiffs argued that the complaint was not based on defendants' handling of liens and claims through the workers' compensation system. Instead, they contended it is based on anticompetitive activity that occurred outside the normal claims handling process. Plaintiffs cited declarations to the effect that Lynn Devine, who represented defendants CIGA, ICW, and Elite Personnel Services before the WCAB, encouraged third parties to refuse to honor settlements reached with plaintiffs in cases not covered by the stay.

The problem with this contention is that there is no allegation in the complaint that defendants conspired to stop third parties from honoring settlements of plaintiffs' liens and claims. For example, paragraph 36 alleges that in an effort to gain an economic advantage over plaintiffs, and to impede their business, "Defendants, in a concerted conspiracy with each other, banded together to contest, object to, litigate, delay payment on and/or not pay at all on valid, proper and lawful billings and lien claims. Said conspiratorial acts by Defendants were perpetrated with the knowledge that such concerted activity would result in an overwhelmingly negative effect on Plaintiffs' ability to collect on services rendered to Employers' Applicants, thereby resulting in extreme pressure on Plaintiffs to concede to Defendants wrongful and unlawful attempts to lower Plaintiffs' billings and lien claims for Employers' Applicants."

Paragraph 40 alleges that defendants acted in combination to "object to, litigate, delay payment on and/or not pay at all on Plaintiffs' valid and proper bills and lien claims." Seven subparagraphs detail defendants' allegedly improper behavior, but do not allege that defendants improperly persuaded third parties to refuse to pay settlements which had previously been agreed upon.

If we were reviewing a ruling on a demurrer, the rules of liberal construction might suggest that plaintiffs be allowed to amend their complaint to allege the claims regarding the impact of defendants' conspiracy on third–party settlement payments. On review of an anti–SLAPP motion to strike however, the standard is akin to that for summary judgment or judgment on the pleadings. We must take the complaint as it is.

"In order to establish a probability of prevailing on the claim (§ 425.16, subd. (b)(1)), a plaintiff responding to an anti–SLAPP motion must ' "*state*[] and substantiate[] a legally sufficient claim.' " (*Briggs v. Eden Council for Hope & Opportunity*[,*supra,*] *19 Cal.4th 1106, 1123 [81 Cal.Rptr.2d 471, 969 P.2d 564],* quoting *Rosenthal v. Great Western Fin. Securities Corp. (1996) 14 Cal.4th 394, 412 [58 Cal.Rptr.2d 875, 926 P.2d 1061].*) Put another way, the plaintiff 'must demonstrate that the *complaint is both legally sufficient* and supported by a sufficient prima facie showing of facts to sustain a favorable judgment if the evidence submitted by the plaintiff is credited.' (*Matson v. Dvorak (1995) 40 Cal.App.4th 539, 548 [46 Cal.Rptr.2d 880];* accord, *Rosenaur v. Scherer (2001) 88 Cal.App.4th 260, 274 [105 Cal.Rptr.2d 674].*) In deciding the question of potential merit, the trial court considers the pleadings and

evidentiary submissions of both the plaintiff and the defendant (§ 425.16, subd. (b)(2)); though the court does not weigh the credibility or comparative probative strength of competing evidence, it should grant the motion if, as a matter of law, the defendant's evidence supporting the motion defeats the plaintiff's attempt to establish evidentiary support for the claim. (*Paul for Council v. Hanyecz (2001) 85 Cal.App.4th 1356, 1365 [102 Cal.Rptr.2d 864].)*" (*Wilson v. Parker, Covert & Chidester (2002) 28 Cal.4th 811, 821 [50 P.3d 733, 123 Cal. Rptr. 2d 19],* italics added.)

Applying these principles and confining our review to the conduct alleged in the complaint, we are satisfied that the gravamen of plaintiffs' action arises from the activity of defendants in litigating lien claims through the workers' compensation process. This includes communications preceding the filing of the petitions for consolidation. The entire complaint falls within the scope of section 425.16. Section 425.16, subdivision (e) states that " 'an act in furtherance of a person's right of petition or free speech under the United States or California Constitution in connection with a public issue' includes: (1) . . . (2) any written or oral statement or writing *made in connection with an issue under consideration or review by [an] executive . . . body, or any other official proceeding authorized by law.*" (Italics added.) All of the acts alleged fall within this category. The moving defendants satisfied their initial burden under section 425.16, taking us to the second step of the analysis.

II.

The second step usually requires that plaintiffs "demonstrate that the complaint is both legally sufficient and supported by a sufficient prima facie showing of facts to sustain a favorable judgment if the evidence submitted by the plaintiff is credited.' " [Citations.]" (*Navellier v. Sletten (2002) 29 Cal.4th 82, 88–89 [52 P.3d 703, 124 Cal. Rptr. 2d 530].*) Here the focus of the special motion to strike was on affirmative defenses raised by the moving defendants. If defendants have an affirmative defense to a cause of action, they may assert it in the special motion to strike. "[A]lthough section 425.16 places on the plaintiff the burden of substantiating its claims, a defendant that advances an affirmative defense to such claims properly bears the burden of proof on the defense. (See, e.g., *Mann*[,*supra,*] *120 Cal.App.4th at p. 109* [noting, in the context of a section 425.16 analysis, that defendants had failed to carry their burden of establishing their allegedly defamatory statements were protected under the conditional privilege of *Civil Code section 47, subd. c*].)" (*Peregrine Funding, Inc. v. Sheppard Mullin Richter & Hampton LLP (2005) 133 Cal.App.4th 658, 676 [35 Cal. Rptr. 3d 31].*)

Plaintiffs argue that because their complaint is not directed at protected activity, defendants cannot demonstrate a probability of prevailing on the merits of their affirmative defenses. They rely on *Mann, supra, 120 Cal.App.4th at page 106,* which held that a plaintiff need only show a probability of prevailing on any part of its claim, the plaintiff need not substantiate all theories presented within a single cause of action. The *Mann* court concluded that reviewing courts need not engage in the time–consuming task of determining whether the plaintiff can substantiate all theories presented within a single cause of action and need not parse the cause of action so as to leave only those portions it has determined have merit. (*Ibid.*)

Here, however, defendants invoke affirmative defenses which apply to all of plaintiffs' claims. Defendants bear the burden of establishing a probability of prevailing on those defenses. We turn to an examination of the affirmative defenses.

III.

Moving defendants argue that all of plaintiffs' causes of action are barred either by the absolute litigation privilege of *Civil Code section 47*, subdivision (b), or by the broader *Noerr–Pennington* (Footnote 5) doctrine. Because we conclude that the *Noerr–Pennington* issue is dispositive, we do not reach the *Civil Code section 47* issue.

The *Noerr–Pennington* doctrine, which arose in the context of antitrust law, holds that "[t]hose who petition government for redress are generally immune from antitrust liability." (*Professional Real Estate Investors, Inc. v. Columbia Pictures Industries, Inc. (1993) 508 U.S. 49, 56 [113 S. Ct. 1920, 123 L. Ed. 2d 611] (Real Estate Investors*).) In *Noerr, supra, 365 U.S. at page 137,* the Supreme Court concluded that the Sherman Act does not punish political activity through which the people "freely inform the government of their wishes."

The *Noerr–Pennington* doctrine was extended by the Supreme Court in *California Transport v. Trucking Unlimited (1972) 404 U.S. 508, 510 [92 S. Ct. 609, 30 L. Ed. 2d 642]* to "the approach of citizens . . . to administrative agencies . . . and to courts." It has been applied to commercial speech and competitive activity, as well as to anticompetitive activity. (*Ludwig v. Superior Court (1995) 37 Cal.App.4th 8, 21–22 [43 Cal. Rptr. 2d 350] (Ludwig).*) The immunity applies to "virtually any tort, including unfair competition and interference with contract." (*Id. at p. 21, fn. 17.) Noerr–Pennington* immunity also has been applied to Cartwright Act (*Blank v. Kirwan (1985) 39 Cal.3d 311 [703 P.2d 58, 216 Cal. Rptr. 718]*) and RICO claims. (*International Broth. of Teamsters v. Phillip Morris (7th Cir. 1999) 196 F.3d 818, 826.*) In *Ludwig,* the court explained: "Obviously, ' "the principle of constitutional law that bars litigation arising from injuries received as a consequence of First Amendment petitioning activity [should be applied], regardless of the underlying cause of action asserted by the plaintiffs." [Citation.] "[T]o hold otherwise would effectively chill the defendants' First Amendment rights." [Citation.]' " (*Ludwig, supra, 37 Cal.App.4th at p. 21, fn. 17,* quoting *Hi–Top Steel Corp. v. Lehrer (1994) 24 Cal.App.4th 570, 577–578 [29 Cal. Rptr. 2d 646].*)

Defendants argue the *Noerr–Pennington* doctrine applies to their alleged conduct before the WCAB. They point out that this action was filed after they objected to and successfully petitioned for consolidation of the plaintiffs' lien claims before the WCAB. All of the actions which form the basis for the complaint took place in anticipation of, or

during, proceedings before the WCAB. Each of plaintiffs' causes of action incorporates the allegations of the previous causes of action. As we have discussed, these allegations are based on the moving defendants' exercise of their right to petition the WCAB to stay all claims involving plaintiffs in order to obtain an adjudication of the defendants' claims against plaintiffs. We conclude that the defendants have demonstrated that the *Noerr–Pennington* immunity applies to each cause of action.

There is an exception to *Noerr–Pennington* immunity; it does not apply to sham activities. (*Wilson v. Parker, Covert & Chidester, supra, 28 Cal.4th 811, 820.*) But plaintiffs do not rely on that exception here and present no evidence establishing its applicability. In their reply brief, plaintiffs address related arguments made by defendants under the litigation privilege, *Civil Code section 47*. But they fail to address *Noerr–Pennington* and the cases cited by defendants in support of their argument that this doctrine bars the complaint. They provide a broad statement that the litigation privilege (*Civ. Code, § 47*) applies only to communications and not to actions or other noncommunicative conduct. But unlike *Civil Code section 47*, the *Noerr–Pennington* doctrine extends to conduct in exercise of the right to petition, as well as to communications.

As we have discussed, the gravamen of the complaint is defendants' successful activity in petitioning the WCAB to stay processing of workers' compensation bills and lien claims by plaintiffs. Defendants have established that these activities were taken in the exercise of their First Amendment right to petition and so fall within the *Noerr–Pennington* doctrine. Plaintiffs have not addressed this defense and have not invoked the sham activity exception. We conclude the moving defendants established a probability of prevailing on this defense and that the trial court erred in denying the moving defendants' special motion to strike under section 425.16. Moving defendants are entitled to their reasonable attorney fees on appeal. (*Dove Audio, Inc. v. Rosenfeld, Meyer & Susman, supra, 47 Cal.App.4th 777, 785.*)

DISPOSITION

The order of the trial court denying the special motion to strike is reversed. Moving defendants are to have their costs and fees on appeal.

Footnote 5. Eastern R. Conf. v. Noerr Motors (1961) 365 U.S. 127 [81 S. Ct. 523, 5 L. Ed. 2d 464] (Noerr); Mine Workers v. Pennington (1965) 381 U.S. 657 [85 S. Ct. 1585, 14 L. Ed. 2d 626].

Page 1648, Column 1, insert as first paragraph.

Civil Monetary Penalties for Fraud

In addition to the criminal penalties previously discussed in this book, the Legislature has enacted legislation to impose civil monetary penalties for unlawful conduct involving the workers' compensation program. Labor Code section 3820, effective January 1, 2004, provides:

(a) In enacting this section, the Legislature declares that there exists a compelling interest in eliminating fraud in the workers' compensation system. The Legislature recognizes that the conduct prohibited by this section is, for the most part, already subject to criminal penalties pursuant to other provisions of law.

However, the Legislature finds and declares that the addition of civil money penalties will provide necessary enforcement flexibility.

Legislature, in exercising its plenary authority related to workers' compensation, declares that these sections are both necessary and carefully tailored to combat the fraud and abuse thatis rampant in the workers' compensation system.

(b) It is unlawful to do any of the following:

(1) Willfully misrepresent any fact in order to obtain workers' compensation insurance at less than the proper rate.

(2) Present or cause to be presented any knowingly false or fraudulent written or oral material statement in support of, or in opposition to, any claim for compensation for the purpose of obtaining or denying any compensation, as defined in Section 3207.

(3) Knowingly solicit, receive, offer, pay, or accept any rebate, refund, commission, preference, patronage, dividend, discount, or other consideration, whether in the form of money or otherwise, as compensation or inducement for soliciting or referring clients or patients to obtain services or benefits pursuant to Division 4 (commencing with Section 3200) unless the payment or receipt of consideration for services other than the referral of clients or patients is lawful pursuant to Section 650 of the Business and Professions Code or expressly permitted by the Rules of Professional Conduct of the State Bar.

(4) Knowingly operate or participate in a service that, for profit, refers or recommends clients or patients to obtain medical or medical–legal services or benefits pursuant to Division 4 (commencing with Section 3200).

(5) Knowingly assist, abet, solicit, or conspire with any person who engages in an unlawful act under this section.

(c) For the purposes of this section, "statement" includes, but is not limited to, any notice, proof of injury, bill for services, payment for services, hospital or doctor records, X–ray, test results, medical–legal expenses as defined in Section 4620, or other evidence of loss, expense, or payment.

(d) Any person who violates any provision of this section shall be subject, in addition to any other penalties that may be prescribed by law, to a civil penalty of not less than four thousand dollars ($4,000) nor more than ten thousand dollars ($10,000), plus an assessment of not more than three times the amount of the medical treatment expenses paid pursuant to Article 2 (commencing with Section 4600) and medical–legal expenses paid pursuant to Article 2.5 (commencing with Section 4620) for each claim for compensation submitted in violation of this section.

(e) Any person who violates subdivision (b) and who has a prior felony conviction of an offense set forth in Section 1871.1 or 1871.4 of the Insurance Code, or in Section 549 of the Penal Code, shall be subject, in addition to the penalties set forth in subdivision (d), to a civil penalty of four thousand dollars ($4,000) for each item or service with respect to which a violation of subdivision (b) occurred.

(f) The penalties provided for in subdivisions (d) and (e) shall be assessed and recovered in a civil action brought in the name of the people of the State of California by any district attorney.

(g) In assessing the amount of the civil penalty the court shall consider any one or more of the relevant circumstances presented by any of the parties to the case, including, but not limited to, the following: the nature and seriousness of the misconduct, the number of violations, the persistence of the misconduct, the length of time over which the misconduct occurred, the willfulness of the defendant's misconduct, and the defendant's assets, liabilities, and net worth.

(h) All penalties collected pursuant to this section shall be paid to the Workers' Compensation Fraud Account in the Insurance Fund pursuant to Section 1872.83 of the Insurance Code. All costs incurred by district attorneys in carrying out this article shall be funded from the Workers' Compensation Fraud Account. It is the intent of the Legislature that the program instituted by this article be supported entirely from funds produced by moneys deposited into the Workers' Compensation Fraud Account from the imposition of civil money penalties for workers' compensation fraud collected pursuant to this section. All moneys claimed by district attorneys as costs of carrying out this article shall be paid pursuant to a determination by the Fraud Assessment Commission established by Section 1872.83 of the Insurance Code and on appropriation by the Legislature.

Page 1669, Column 1, third paragraph insert following '…award…'

See *The People v. Todd Owen Balcom (2006)* 71 Cal. Comp. Cases 494, for an unpublished decision by the Second District, where the Court in discussing restitution stated, in part:

Victim Restitution

Balcom was convicted of violating both Penal Code section 550, subdivision (b)(3) (Footnote 1) and Insurance Code section 1871.4, subdivision (a)(1). (Footnote 2)

Both statutes relate to insurance fraud. Penal Code section 550 is a general statute prohibiting all types of insurance fraud. Insurance Code section 1871.4 specifically targets workers' compensation fraud.

Balcom was ordered to pay a restitution fine under Penal Code section 1202.4, subdivisions (b) and (m) (Footnote 3);

a restitution fine under Insurance Code section 1871.4, subdivision (b) (Footnote 4); and victim restitution under Penal Code section 1202.4, subdivision (f). (Footnote 5)

The trial court's restitution order included the total amount of workers' compensation benefits received by Balcom. A trial court has discretion in imposing a restitution fine under Penal Code section 1202.4. (*People v. Smith, supra,* 24 Cal. 4th at pp. 852–853.) Here, however, victim restitution is in the form of workers' compensation benefits, and special rules apply.

Insurance Code section 1871.5 (Footnote 6) expressly limits victim restitution to workers' compensation benefits that were obtained as a direct result of the fraud for which the defendant was convicted. In *Tensfeldt v. Workers' Comp. Appeals Bd.* (1998) 66 Cal. App. 4th 116, 123 [77 Cal. Rptr. 2d 691, 63 Cal. Comp. Cases 973], the court interpreted Insurance Code section 1871.5 as follows: "[S]ection 1871.5 clearly states that 'Any person convicted of workers' compensation fraud . . . shall be ineligible to receive or retain any compensation . . . where that compensation was owed or received *as a result of a violation . . . for which the recipient of the compensation was convicted.*' . . . Giving the language its ordinary meaning, section 1871.5 unambiguously provides that an injured worker must return only 'that compensation' obtained by fraud, and may not receive further compensation stemming from the fraud." (See also *Farmers Ins. Group of Companies v. Workers' Comp. Appeals Bd.* (2002) 104 Cal. App. 4th 684, 688, fn. 2 [128 Cal. Rptr. 2d 353, 67 Cal. Comp. Cases 1545] [benefits that were not fraudulently obtained may be retained]; and see *People v. O'Casey* (2001) 88 Cal. App. 4th 967, 973 [106 Cal. Rptr. 2d 263, 66 Cal. Comp. Cases 464] [workers' compensation insurer was direct victim of fraud and entitled to victim restitution "for losses occasioned by [the] fraudulent claim"].)

Majestic does not dispute the fact that a compensable injury occurred or that Balcom was entitled to benefits. Under Insurance Code section 1871.5 and *Tensfeldt v. Workers' Comp. Appeals Bd., supra,* 66 Cal. App. 4th 116, restitution is limited to the amount of earnings Balcom received while he was receiving temporary disability payments and investigative expenses and attorney's fees that Majestic incurred as a result of the fraud. (Pen. Code, § 1202.4, subd. (f)(3)(H) [requiring restitution for "[a]ctual and reasonable attorney's fees and other costs of collection"]; *People v. Maheshwari* (2003) 107 Cal. App. 4th 1406, 1409–1410 [132 Cal. Rptr. 2d 903] [investigatory expenses attributable to defendant's criminal conduct recoverable under Pen. Code, § 1202.4, subd. (f)(3)(H)].) Balcolm was entitled to retain workers' compensation benefits that were not obtained by fraud.

We reverse the judgment only as it pertains to the amount of victim restitution and remand for recalculation of that amount. The sum to be ordered is the amount Balcom received from working while on temporary disability, Majestic's attorney's fees and investigative costs.... .

Footnote 1. Penal Code section 550, subdivision (b)(3) states: "It is unlawful to do, or to knowingly assist or conspire with any person to do, any of the following: [P] . . . [P] (3) Conceal, or knowingly fail to disclose the occurrence of, an event that affects any person's initial or continued right or entitlement to any insurance benefit or payment, or the amount of any benefit or payment to which the person is entitled."

Footnote 2. Insurance Code section 1871.4, subdivision (a)(1) states: "It is unlawful to do any of the following: [P] (1) Make or cause to be made a knowingly false or fraudulent material statement or material representation for the purpose of obtaining or denying any compensation, as defined in Section 3207 of the Labor Code."

Footnote 3. Penal Code section 1202.4 states in pertinent part: "(b) In every case where a person is convicted of a crime, the court shall impose a separate and additional restitution fine, unless it finds compelling and extraordinary reasons for not doing so, and states those reasons on the record. [P] . . . [P] (m) In every case in which the defendant is granted probation, the court shall make the payment of restitution fines and orders imposed pursuant to this section a condition of probation . . . ."

Footnote 4. Insurance Code section 1871.4, subdivision (b) states in part: "Every person who violates subdivision (a) shall be punished by . . . a fine not exceeding one hundred fifty thousand dollars ($150,000) or double the value of the fraud, whichever is greater . . . . Restitution shall be ordered, including restitution for any medical evaluation or treatment services obtained or provided. The court shall determine the amount of restitution and the person or persons to whom the restitution shall be paid. A person convicted under this section may be charged the costs of investigation at the discretion of the court."

Footnote 5. Penal Code section 1202.4, subdivision (f) states in part: "[I]n every case in which a victim has suffered economic loss as a result of the defendant's conduct, the court shall require that the defendant make restitution to the victim or victims in an amount established by court order . . . . The court shall order full restitution unless it finds compelling and extraordinary reasons for not doing so, and states them on the record."

Footnote 6. Insurance Code section 1871.5 states: "Any person convicted of workers' compensation fraud pursuant to Section 1871.4 or Section 550 of the Penal Code shall be ineligible to receive or retain any compensation, as defined in Section 3207 of the Labor Code, where that compensation was owed or received as a result of a violation of Section 1871.4 or Section 550 of the Penal Code for which the recipient of the compensation was convicted." The parties failed to raise section 1871.5 in their briefs. Prior to oral argument, we requested the parties file letter briefs discussing the applicability of this statute.

Page 1683, Column 2, add at end of fifth paragraph

Judge's Duty to Report Fraud

If, in the course of adjudicating a claim for workers' compensation benefits, a Workers' Compensation Judge discovers conduct that appears to constitute workers' compensation fraud, Administrative Director Rule 9721.32 provides that:

> When circumstances warrant, a referee [WCJ] shall take or initiate appropriate disciplinary measures against a referee [WCJ], lawyer, party, witness, or other persion who participates in the workers' compensation process for unprofessional, fraudulent or other improper conduct of which the referee becomes aware.

For guidance in this area, the Appeals Board's Policy and Procedure Manual provides that if a judge becomes aware of possible workers' compensation fraud during proceedings, the judge should be sensitive to his or her obligations under the Code of Judicial Ethics as the case progresses.

The obligation imposed by Administrative Director Rule 9721.32 to report misconduct and fraud must be balanced against a recognition that the Code of Judicial Ethics, out of concern that a judge's actions not diminish the appearance of fairness and objectivity in judicial proceedings, places limits on a judge's communications involving pending cases.

Under Canon 3A(7), a judge is prohibited from discussion a pending or impending case outside the presence of the parties.

Canon 3A(7) prevents a judge from making a nonpublic comment that might substantially interfere with a fair trial or hearing.

If a judge determines that he or she is aware of reportable misconduct, the judge may report that misconduct to the appropriate authorities once the case in which that misconduct occurred is no longer pending before the judge.

In view of the ethical demands required of judges by the Code of Judicial Ethics, the Division would prefer that judges not directly refer cases involving suspected fraud to outside authorities.

A judge who desires to report misconduct should refer the matter, with as much specificity and documentary evidence as is available to him or her, to the chief judge.

This course of action would be consistent with Canon 3B(7)(b), which allows judges to consult with court personnel whose function it is to advise the judge in carrying out the judge's responsibilities.

§ 49.0   INTEREST ON AWARD

Page 1695, Column 1, sixth paragraph, insert following '…rate of 7%.'

However, under Labor Code section 4603.2, a medical provider is entitled to interest, retroactively, within 45 days of the date the employer or insurer receives each separate itemization bill for medical services with any required reports for reasonable and necessary medical services. Labor Code section 4603.2 provides, in part:

(1) Except as provided in subdivision (d) of Section 4603.4, or under contracts authorized under Section 5307.11, payment for medical treatment provided or authorized by the treating physician selected by the employee or designated by the employer shall be made at reasonable maximum amounts in the official medical fee schedule, pursuant to Section 5307.1, in effect on the date of service. Payments shall be made by the employer within 45 working days after receipt of each separate, itemization of medical services provided, together with any required reports and any written authorization for services that may have been received by the physician. If the itemization or a portion thereof is contested, denied, or considered incomplete, the physician shall be notified, in writing, that the itemization is contested, denied, or considered incomplete, within 30 working days after receipt of the itemization by the employer. A notice that an itemization is incomplete shall state all additional information required to make a decision. Any properly documented list of services provided not paid at the rates then in effect under Section 5307.1 within the 45–working–day period shall be increased by 15 percent, together with interest at the same rate as judgments in civil actions retroactive to the date of receipt of the itemization, unless the employer does both of the following:

   (A) Pays the provider at the rates in effect within the 45–working–day period.
   (B) Advises, in the manner prescribed by the administrative director, the physician, or another provider of the items being contested, the reasons for contesting these items, and the remedies available to the physician or the other provider if he or she disagrees. In the case of an itemization that includes services provided by a hospital, outpatient surgery center, or independent diagnostic facility, advice that a request has been made for an audit of the itemization shall satisfy the requirements of this paragraph.

   An employer's liability to a physician or another provider under this section for delayed payments shall not affect its liability to an employee under

Section 5814 or any other provision of this division.

(2) Notwithstanding paragraph (1), if the employer is a governmental entity, payment for medical treatment provided or authorized by the treating physician selected by the employee or designated by the employer shall be made within 60 working days after receipt of each separate itemization, together with any required reports and any written authorization for services that may have been received by the physician… .

Page 1695, Column 1, sixth paragraph, insert following '…interest rate.'

In *Currie v. WCAB* (2001) 66 Cal. Comp. Cases 208, the California Supreme Court held that under Labor Code section 132a, a $200,000 award applicant received was subject to *prejudgment interest* as being consistent with the statutory goal of making victims of wrongful discrimination whole.

Compound

Although there are no workers' compensation cases relating to *compound interest* known to this writer, it is generally accepted in civil cases that *prejudgment interest* may be compounded "upon the theory that in the absence of evidence to the contrary, [a trustee] will be presumed to have received such profits from their use." (Guardianship of O'Connor (1938) 28 Cal. App. 2d 527, 530 [83 P.2d 65], quoting *Wheeler v. Bolton* (1891) 92 Cal. 159, 172.)

However, as to *postjudgment interest*, the Court of Appeal, Fourth District, in *Westbrook v. Fairchild* (1992) 7 Cal. App. 4th 889, 9 Cal. Rptr. 2d 277, held that compounding of interest in postjudgment awards is *not permissible*. The Court stated, in part:

> [1c] The only exception to the rule that interest on interest (i.e. compound interest) may not be recovered is in situations in which interest is included in a judgment which then bears interest at the legal rate. (45 [7 Cal. App. 4th 895] Am.Jur.2d, Interest and Usury, § 78, p. 71.) One common situation occurs when a judgment is renewed. At that time, accrued interest is included in the new judgment, and the new judgment bears interest at the legal rate.
>
> The renewal sections were also added in 1982 as a result of Law Revision Commission recommendations. (Recommendation Relating to Enforcement of Judgments Law, 16 Cal. Law Revision Com. Rep. 1001 (1982) pp. 1032–1034.) Specifically, Code of Civil Procedure section 683.110 was enacted to provide for renewal, but to prevent renewal more often than every five years.

The commission explained its recommendation as follows: "By preventing the renewal of a judgment more often than once every five years, subdivision (b) of Section 683.110 prevents the judgment creditor from renewing a judgment more frequently merely to compound the interest on the judgment. Renewal has the effect of compounding the interest on the judgment, since interest accrues on the total amount of the judgment as renewed [citations] and the judgment as renewed includes accrued interest on the date of filing the application for renewal." (Cal. Law Revision Com. com., Deering's Ann. Code Civ. Proc., § 683.110 (1982) p. 161.)

By adopting this section, the Legislature apparently considered it desirable to limit the compounding effect of interest on a judgment to once every five years. By allowing compounding over some unspecified lesser period, which could be as often as daily, the trial court has interpreted Code of Civil Procedure section 685.010 in such a way as to nullify the legislative purpose behind Code of Civil Procedure section 683.110.

This is improper. In Big Bear Properties, Inc. v. Gherman (1979) 95 Cal. App. 3d 908 [157 Cal. Rptr. 443], the debtor argued that allowing interest on the portion of the judgment which contained interest was an impermissible compounding of interest. The court stated: " 'Although compound interest generally is not allowable on a judgment, it is established that a judgment bears interest on the whole amount from its date even though the amount is in part made up of interest. ... As a consequence, compound interest may in effect be recovered on a judgment whereby the aggregate amount of principal and interest is turned into a new principal. ...' " (Id., at p. 913, italics added.)

Another common situation in which interest on interest is allowed is when prejudgment interest is incorporated in a judgment which then bears interest. (Cal. Rules of Court, rule 875.) Here, there is already a significant compounding effect because two years of prejudgment interest was incorporated [7 Cal. App. 4th 896] into the judgment. Mr. Westbrook seeks to obtain additional compound interest by having the interest on the judgment also compounded. There is no constitutional or statutory authorization for the award he seeks. Since we are modifying the October 30, 1989, amended judgment, the new amount of that judgment bears postjudgment simple interest of 10 percent from that date (Snapp v. State Farm Fire & Cas. Co. (1964) 60 Cal. 2d 816, 818–819 [36 Cal. Rptr. 612, 388 P.2d 884].)... .

The dissenting Justice stated, in part:

The majority opinion cites 47 Corpus Juris Secundum, Interest, section 21, for the proposition that "[As] a general rule, judgments do not bear interest as a matter of legal right, or under the common law; and, in the absence of statute, courts of chancery [i.e., equity courts] could not grant interest subsequent to the date of the decree on debts of simple contract, not bearing interest in terms." (Maj. opn., ante, at p. 897, italics added.) Here, of course, the plaintiff's claim was based in part not on simple contract, but on constructive fraud. The relevant inquiry, then, should be whether courts of chancery had the power to grant

interest in constructive fraud cases. They did have such power and could "compound interest annually, or at longer or shorter periods, according to the delinquency of the trustee." (90 C.J.S., Trusts, § 342, at p. 599, fn. omitted; Bogert, Trusts & Trustees (2d ed. rev. 1982) § 863 at p. 51: " 'Independent of contract or statute, a court of equity in its sound discretion may require one who has converted to his own use the funds of another to pay damages equal to the legal rate of interest, as compensation to the complainant for the loss of the use of his fund.' " (Fn. omitted, quoting Cree v. Lewis (1911) 49 Colo. 186 [112 P. 326, 328].) This power included the power to compound interest. (Bogert, supra, § 863 at pp. 55–56.) [7 Cal. App. 4th 900]

There do not seem to be any California cases explicitly, as opposed to implicitly, on point as to whether the power to compound interest applied to both pre– and postjudgment interest, because generally the cases make no distinction between pre– and postjudgment interest. However, in Estate of William Stott (1877) 52 Cal. 403, an executor who commingled funds of the estate with his own business funds was found liable for the presumed profits on the commingled sums. On appeal, the executor contended that he should not have been charged with compound interest, contending, among other things, that compound interest "is expressly forbidden in all judgments by the Civil Code ... [section 1920]." (Id. at p. 405.) Held, any trustee who uses trust property for any purpose unconnected with the trust shall be charged with "legal interest with annual rests," i.e., with interest compounded annually. (Id. at p. 406.) Although the court did not specifically refer to whether its holding applied to postjudgment, as well as prejudgment, interest, the fact that the executor argued that compound interest was forbidden by then Civil Code section 1920, which prohibited compounding the interest on judgments, indicates that the holding applied to postjudgment interest.

In Jeanes v. Hamby (Tex.Ct.App. 1984) 685 S.W.2d 695, 700, the Texas Court of Appeals recognized that postjudgment interest could be compounded annually if equity so required, but that the trial judge who had rendered the judgment had not so concluded.

In Bobb v. Bobb (1887) 89 Mo. 411 [4 S.W. 511], a seminal case relied upon by the authorities cited in Palmer v. Palmer (Mo.App. 1991) 805 S.W.2d 326, it was held that a trustee could be charged, in lieu of profits, with interest compounded annually on "balances in his hands" (id. at p. 515, italics added), the implication being that postjudgment interest on all sums not paid over to the wronged beneficiary could be compounded.

In addition to the treatises and cases noted above which indicate that at common law courts had the equitable power to compound postjudgment interest, the history of the statutes and constitutional provisions related to the compounding of interest and the award of postjudgment interest indicate that this equitable power still exists... .

Page 1695, Column 1, eighth paragraph,
insert following '…interest rate.'

    The first date that interest is payable occurs 24 hours after the award issues. *Holston–Harris v. WCAB* (1998) 63 Cal. Comp. Cases 639.

Intentionally blank

§ 50.0   JURISDICTION OF THE APPEALS BOARD

Page 1698, Column 1, delete sixth paragraph beginning 'Inasmuch as it is...' through paragraph twelfth which ends with the words '...or federal regulations.' and insert the following:

However, the Board does have jurisdiction to rule on the constitutionality of a Regulation promulgated by the Administrator Director. *Medina v. Golden Eagle Insurance Company* (1997) 25 CWCR 305.

Page 1701, Column 1, fourteenth paragraph, insert following '...future.'

In *Atlantic Mutual Insurance Company v. WCAB (Brewer)* (2006) 71 Cal. Comp. Cases 244, the Board held it did not have jurisdiction to set aside a finding by a judge regarding insurance coverage under Labor Code section 5804, where the judge's finding became final more than five years after the date of injury and the fact that the insurance carrier did not request that the finding of coverage be set aside until more than five years after the injury. In the opinion, upheld by the Board, the judge stated, in part:

Estoppel: Atlantic Mutual Insurance Company made several appearances before this Board and stipulated that it had coverage for the San Francisco Chronicle on May 22, 1998. The Stipulations were set forth in the November 10, 2003 mandatory settlement conference statement and were recorded in to the minutes by the WCJ on April 1, 2004. As a result of those stipulations, this court issued a Finding of Fact concerning coverage and issued an award against Atlantic Mutual Insurance Company on June 28, 2004. Said Finding of Fact and Award became final (and the law of this case) on July 23, 2004, the day the reconsideration period ended.

In this court's opinion, Atlantic Mutual Insurance Company is estopped to deny coverage for the San Francisco Chronicle on the date of applicant's injury. This court as well as the applicant relied on the stipulations made by the attorney for Atlantic Mutual Insurance Company concerning coverage. Had there been no stipulation concerning coverage, there never would have been an award issued against Atlantic Mutual Insurance Company.

Jurisdiction: Labor Code Section 5804 states that no award of compensation shall be rescinded, altered, or amended after five years from the date of injury except upon a petition by a party in interest filed within such five years. As is stated above, the Findings of Fact concerning coverage and the award based thereon became final on July 23, 2004. Obviously, this date is more than five years from the date of injury. On November 23, 2004, Atlantic Mutual Insurance Company advised this board of the mistake it had made concerning coverage. It is respectfully submitted that Atlantic Mutual Insurance Company was too late. By the terms of Labor Code Section 5804, this Board no longer has jurisdiction to set aside Findings of Fact (and Awards) as the five year period has expired...

Concerning the estoppel issue, the California Supreme Court held in Granco Steel, Inc. v WCAB (Robinson) [(1968) 68 Cal. 2d 191, 65 Cal. Rptr. 287, 436 P.2d 287, 33 Cal. Comp. Cases 50] that an insurance carrier was estopped to deny coverage when the representation of coverage was relied on by the applicant and the WCAB trial court in rendering its decision. Granco Steel involved representations made by a broker concerning coverage. In the instant case, reliance was made upon representations by Atlantic Mutual's attorney representing that his client had coverage. All of the elements concerning estoppel set forth by the California Supreme Court, at page 59, are present in the instant case: (1) the party to be estopped must be apprised of the facts (Atlantic Mutual was well aware that it was not the carrier despite Mr. Willens' stipulation that it was); (2) the party must intend that his conduct be acted upon or must so act that the parties asserting the estoppel had a right to believe that it was so intended (both applicant and this court relied on the representation concerning coverage in this courts' [sic] decisions were based on said representation); (3) the other party must be ignorant of the true state of facts (Mr. Brewer only knew that his checks were being sent by Atlantic Mutual; he had no idea concerning any adjustment contract between Atlantic Mutual's subsidiary and Reliance Insurance Company); (4) he must rely upon the conduct to his injury (Mr. Brewer is currently not receiving the benefit of his award and obviously, has relied on the representations concerning coverage to his injury)... .

Page 1703, Column 2, insert as first paragraph

En Banc Decision

The Appeals Board has the power to issue En Banc decisions. Such decisions are voted on by the entire Board and a *majority vote* makes them binding precedent authority on all Board Panels and all Workers' Compensation Judges.

Labor Code section 115 provides:

Actions of the appeals board shall be taken by decision of a majority of the appeals board except as otherwise expressly provided.

The chairman shall assign pending cases in which reconsideration is sought to any three members thereof for hearing, consideration and decision. Assignments by the chairman of members to such cases shall be rotated on a case–by–case basis with the composition of the members so assigned being varied and changed to assure that there shall never be a fixed and continued composition of members. Any such case assigned to any three members in which the finding, order, decision or award is made and filed by any two or more of such members shall be the action of the appeals board unless reconsideration is had in accordance with the provisions of Article 1 (commencing with Section 5900), Chapter 7, Part 4, Division 4 of this code. Any case assigned to three members shall be heard and decided only by them, unless the matter has been reassigned by the chairman on a majority vote of the appeals board to the appeals board as a whole in order to achieve uniformity of decision, or in cases presenting novel issues.

California Code of Regulations section 10341 provides:

En banc decisions of the Appeals Board are binding on panels of the Appeals Board and Workers' Compensation Judges as legal precedent under the principle of stare decisis.

The fact that a Petition for Writ of Review has been filed, standing alone, does not affect the operation of an En Banc decision of the Appeals Board and its decision remains binding precedent on all Appeals Board panels as well as all its judges pending the outcome of the review. Commenting on this in *Diggle v. Sierra Sands Unified School District, et al.* (2005) 70 Cal. Comp. Cases 1480, the Board, in an En Banc opinion stated, in part:

Of course, if an appellate court "stay[s] or suspend[s] the operation" of an en banc decision under section 5956 (see also, Lab. Code, 6000), (Footnote 6) then the binding effect of the en banc decision on Appeals Board panels and WCJs is also stayed or suspended – at least until the suspension or stay order is lifted.

Also, if an appellate court issues an opinion that explicitly or implicitly overrules an en banc decision of the Appeals Board, then, under the principle of stare decisis, the Court's decision is controlling and the en banc decision no longer can be followed by the Appeals Board or any WCJ. (Auto Equity Sales v. Superior Court (1962) 57 Cal. 2d 450, 455 [369 P.2d 937, 20 Cal. Rptr. 321]; Escobedo v. Marshalls (2005) 70 Cal. Comp. Cases 604, 609, fn. 4 (Appeals Board en banc).) There may be some exceptions to this standard principle (e.g., when an en banc decision is only partially overruled, or where it is indirectly overruled in a non–published appellate opinion), however, we need not and will not address any such scenarios here... .

Footnote 6. Section 6000 states:
"The operation of any order, decision, or award of the appeals board under the provisions of this division or any judgment entered thereon, shall not at any time be stayed by the court to which petition is made for a writ of review, unless an undertaking is executed on the part of the petitioner."

§ 50.5 Concurrent Jurisdiction With Superior Court

Page 1721, Column 2, paragraph 3, insert following '...omitted]'

See *Sullivan v. WCAB* (2006) 71 Cal. Comp. Cases 1065, where the Court of Appeal, Fifth District, in an unpublished decision, held that the Appeals Board had no jurisdiction over a Labor Code section 132a claim filed against an Indian Tribe, stating, in part:

Indian tribes possess common–law immunity from suit traditionally enjoyed by sovereign powers. (Santa Clara Pueblo v. Martinez (1978) 436 U.S. 49, 58 [98 S. Ct. 1670, 56 L. Ed. 2d 106].) "Thus, suits against Indian tribes are barred 'absent a clear waiver by the tribe or congressional abrogation.' " (Sac and Fox Nation v. Hanson (10th Cir. 1995) 47 F.3d 1061, 1063.) "[W]hile Congress can authorize suits against Indian Nations, a waiver of sovereign immunity cannot be implied but must be unequivocally expressed." (People ex rel. Dept. of Transportation v. Naegele Outdoor Advertising Co. (1985) 38 Cal. 3d 509, 519 [698 P.2d 150, 213 Cal. Rptr. 247].)

"[A] tribe may consent to suit and thus waive its tribal sovereign immunity. However, such consent cannot be implied and, while no talismanic words are required, it must nonetheless be 'clear.' [Citations.] If the tribe has consented to suit, any conditional limitation imposed on its consent must be strictly construed and applied. [Citation.]" (Campo Band of Mission Indians v. Superior Court (2006) 137 Cal. App. 4th 175, 182–183 [39 Cal. Rptr. 3d 875] (Campo Band.)"

"Generally speaking, the issue of whether a court has subject matter jurisdiction over an action against an Indian tribe is a question of law subject to de novo review." (Warburton/Buttner v. Superior Court (2002) 103 Cal. App. 4th 1170, 1180 [127 Cal. Rptr. 2d 706].) However, where the resolution of the issue turns upon the credibility of properly admitted conflicting extrinsic evidence, an appellate court must uphold the decision if supported by substantial evidence. (Ibid.) An injured worker of an Indian tribe "seeking relief afforded under the state workers' compensation laws has the burden of proving the requisite jurisdictional facts." (Middletown Rancheria of Pomo Indians v. Workers' Comp. Appeals Bd. (1998) 60 Cal. App. 4th 1340, 1353 [71 Cal. Rptr. 2d 105, 63 Cal. Comp. Cases 15].)

Table Mountain is a federally–recognized sovereign Indian tribe under the Indian Gaming Regulatory Act of 1988 (IGRA). (18 U.S. C. § 1166 et seq.; 25 U.S.C. § 2701 et seq.) Preempting state law, the IGRA authorizes tribal gaming while allowing the state to play a role in its regulation. (Campo Band, *supra*, 137 Cal. App. 4th at p. 182.) A tribe may operate class III gaming, which includes casino and slot machine gambling, on the land of federally–recognized tribes only in conformity with a gaming compact entered into between the Indian tribe and the state. (25 U.S.C. §§ 2703, subds. (6)–(8), 2710, subd. (d).)

The September 10, 1999, gaming compact offered by

Table Mountain was signed by California Governor Gray Davis and Table Mountain Chairperson Leanne Walker–Grant, as witnessed by California Secretary of State Bill Jones. Sullivan argues sections 8.1.11 and 10.3(a) of the compact compel a finding that Table Mountain waived its sovereign immunity as to Sullivan. Section 8.1.11 requires Table Mountain to maintain a closed circuit television surveillance system as a condition of operating class III gaming. Because Sullivan's job duties as a security surveillance agent were required under the compact, he argues he fell within Table Mountain's waiver of sovereign immunity under section 10.3(a). Section 10.3(a) mandates participation in either the state workers' compensation program or a comparable tribal workers' compensation system, and there is no evidence Table Mountain maintained an alternative system.

Table Mountain disagrees, contending the compact only mandates providing state or tribal workers' compensation benefits to employees of its Gaming Operation. Table Mountain refers to the language of section 10.3(a), which provides that "In lieu of permitting the Gaming Operation to participate in the state statutory workers' compensation system, the Tribe may create and maintain a system that provides for redress for employee work–related injuries . . . ." Table Mountain submitted testimony at trial from its benefits and insurance manager, gaming commissioner, and legal counsel explaining the organization and governance of Table Mountain. They differentiated the Gaming Operation's casino from Table Mountain's government and explained that an employee worked for one or the other, but not both, and the regulatory need for the separation. Even Sullivan admitted at the hearing he worked for the Table Mountain government and not the Gaming Operation casino, and that he was not permitted to socialize with casino employees so as not to jeopardize security operations.

Conducting our own independent review of the compact, we agree with Sullivan the compact arguably suggests Table Mountain waived its sovereign immunity with regard to his position as a surveillance agent. We may not, however, interpret an ambiguous and poorly–written gaming compact as waiving an Indian tribe's immunity. A waiver of sovereign immunity subjecting an Indian tribe to state proceedings must be clear, express, and unequivoCal. (People ex rel. Dept. of Transportation v. Naegele Outdoor Advertising Co., *supra*, 38 Cal. 3d 509 at p. 519; Campo Band, *supra*, 137 Cal. App. 4th at pp. 182–183.) Accordingly, we must deny Sullivan's petition for writ of review.

DISPOSITION

The petition for writ of review, filed December 5, 2005, is denied. This opinion is final forthwith as to this court…

Page 1721, Column 2, paragraph 6,
insert following '…case'

An argument that a court lacks jurisdiction can be raised at any time, including on appeal. In *McKinny v. Board of Trustees of the Oxnard Union High School District*, 31 Cal. 3d 79, 90 (1982), the Court stated, in part:

Defendants contend that plaintiffs do not have standing to maintain this action. Although this argument was not raised in the trial court, it is properly before us. It is elementary that a plaintiff who lacks standing cannot state a valid cause of action; therefore, a contention based on a plaintiff's lack of standing cannot be waived under Code of Civil Procedure section 430.80 and may be raised at any time in the proceeding. (Horn v. County of Ventura (1979) 24 Cal. 3d 605, 619 [156 Cal. Rptr. 718, 596 P.2d 1134]; Parker v. Bowron (1953) 40 Cal. 2d 344, 351 [254 P.2d 6].) [31 Cal. 3d 91]… .

Intentionally blank

§ 52.0   LIENS

§ 52.12(B)   First Lien of Medi–Cal

**Page 1758, Column 1, sixth paragraph,
insert following '...to Medi–Cal. '**

For a similar holding, see *Rancho Los Amigos County Medical Rehabilitation Center v. WCAB (Wilkerson)* (2007) 72 Cal. Comp. Cases 270, where the Board stated, in part:

In the instant case, County asserts that (1) it already reimbursed Medi–Cal and therefore is not bound by *Brower*; (2) the lien in this case was filed under the Labor Code and not Welfare & Institutions Code 14124.791.

First of all, as to the issue of reimbursement, County is simply wrong. It has not reimbursed Medi–Cal. It intends to do so, once it has been reimbursed by another payer. It is unable to point to any evidence of any transfer of funds, electronic or otherwise, from County to Medi–Cal. Indeed, Medi–Cal has a lien in the WCAB file.

As to the issue of preemption, County essentially asserts that existence of the Medical/Medicaid federal statutes should be disregarded, because Applicant received medical services arising out of workers' compensation injury. While, it is true that the employer is liable for medical treatment pursuant to Labor Code Section 4600, it is clear that County participates in the Medi–Cal system and is thus subject to federal statutes which control the entire Medical scheme. In *Olszewski*, our Supreme Court held that the plaintiff and the third party beneficiary were not liable to the lien provider because the lien provider accepted Medi–Cal payments. It would make no sense to require UEF to pay County, when UEF stands in shoes of the third party defendant... .

Intentionally blank

§ 54.0   NOTICE BY EMPLOYEE TO EMPLOYER OF INJURY

Page 1765, Column 1, delete commencing with fourth paragraph, beginning 'However, effective...' to Page 1766, Column 2, and ending '...Sec. 5705.' and add the following:

Labor Code section 5400 provides:

Except as provided by sections 5402 and 5403, no claim to recover compensation under this division shall be maintained unless within thirty days after the occurrence of the injury which is claimed to have caused the disability or death, there is served upon the employer notice in writing, signed by the person injured or someone in his behalf, or in case of the death of the person injured, by a dependent or someone in the dependent's behalf.

Labor Code section 5401 provides:

(a) Within one working day of receiving notice or knowledge of injury under Section 5400 or 5402, which injury results in lost time beyond the employee's work shift at the time of injury or which results in medical treatment beyond first aid, the employer shall provide, personally or by first-class mail, a claim form and a notice of potential eligibility for benefits under this division to the injured employee, or in the case of death, to his or her dependents. As used in this subdivision, "first aid" means any one-time treatment, and any followup visit for the purpose of observation of minor scratches, cuts, burns, splinters, or other minor industrial injury, which do not ordinarily require medical care. This one-time treatment, and followup visit for the purpose of observation, is considered first aid even though provided by a physician or registered professional personnel. "Minor industrial injury" shall not include serious exposure to a hazardous substance as defined in subdivision (i) of Section 6302. The claim form shall request the injured employee's name and address, social security number, the time and address where the injury occurred, and the nature of and part of the body affected by the injury. Claim forms shall be available at district offices of the Employment Development Department and the division. Claim forms may be made available to the employee from anyother source.

(b) Insofar as practicable, the notice of potential eligibility for benefits required by this section and the claim form shall be a single document and shall instruct the injured employee to fully read the notice of potential eligibility. The form and content of the notice and claim form shall be prescribed by the administrative director after consultation with the Commission on Health and Safety and Workers' Compensation. The notice shall be easily understandable and available in both English and Spanish. The content shall include, but not be limited to, the following:

(1) The procedure to be used to commence proceedings for the collection of compensation for the purposes of this chapter.

(2) A description of the different types of workers' compensation benefits.

(3) What happens to the claim form after it is filed.

(4) From whom the employee can obtain medical care for the injury.

(5) The role and function of the primary treating physician.

(6) The rights of an employee to select and change the treating physician pursuant to subdivision (e) of Section 3550 and Section 4600.

(7) How to get medical care while the claim is pending.

(8) The protections against discrimination provided pursuant to Section 132a.

(9) The following written statements:

(A) You have a right to disagree with decisions affecting your claim.

(B) You can obtain free information from an information and assistance officer of the state Division of Workers' Compensation, or you can hear recorded information and a list of local offices by calling (applicable information and assistance telephone number(s)).

(C) You can consult an attorney. Most attorneys offer one free consultation. If you decide to hire an attorney, his or her fee will be taken out of some of your benefits. For names of workers' compensation attorneys, call the State Bar of California at (telephone number of the State Bar of California's legal specialization program, or its equivalent).

(c) The completed claim form shall be filed with the employer by the injured employee, or, in the case of death, by a dependent of the injured employee, or by an agent of the employee or dependent. Except as provided in subdivision (d), a claim form is deemed filed when it is personally delivered to the employer or received by the employer by first-class or certified mail. A dated copy of the completed form shall be provided by the employer to the employer's insurer and to the employee, dependent, or agent who filed the claim form.

(d) The claim form shall be filed with the employer prior to the injured employee's entitlement to late payment supplements under subdivision (d) of Section 4650, or prior to the injured employee's request for a medical evaluation under Section 4060, 4061, or 4062.

Filing of the claim form with the employer shall toll, for injuries occurring on or after January 1, 1994, the time limitations set forth in Sections 5405 and 5406 until the claim is denied by the employer or the injury becomes presumptively compensable pursuant to

Section 5402. For purposes of this subdivision, a claim form is deemed filed when it is personally delivered to the employer or mailed to the employer by first-class or certified mail.

Labor Code section 5401.7 provides:

The claim form shall contain, prominently stated, the following statement:

"Any person who makes or causes to be made any knowingly false or fraudulent material statement or material representation for the purpose of obtaining or denying workers' compensation benefits or payments is guilty of a felony." The statements required to be printed or displayed pursuant to Sections 1871.2 and 1879.2 of the Insurance Code may, but are not required to, appear on the claim form.

Labor Code section 5402 provides:

(a) Knowledge of an injury, obtained from any source, on the part of an employer, his or her managing agent, superintendent, foreman, or other person in authority, or knowledge of the assertion of a claim of injury sufficient to afford opportunity to the employer to make an investigation into the facts, is equivalent to service under Section 5400.

(b) If liability is not rejected within 90 days after the date the claim form is filed under Section 5401, the injury shall be presumed compensable under this division. The presumption of this subdivision is rebuttable only by evidence discovered subsequent to the 90–day period.

(c) Within one working day after an employee files a claim form under Section 5401, the employer shall authorize the provision of all treatment, consistent with Section 5307.27 or the American College of Occupational and Environmental Medicine's Occupational Medicine Practice Guidelines, for the alleged injury and shall continue to provide the treatment until the date that liability for the claim is accepted or rejected. Until the date the claim is accepted or rejected, liability for medical treatment shall be limited to ten thousand dollars ($10,000).

(d) Treatment provided under subdivision (c) shall not give rise to a presumption of liability on the part of the employer.

Labor Code section 5705 provides:

(a) The appeals board, at any time after an application is filed and prior to the expiration of its jurisdiction may, upon the agreement of a party to pay the cost, direct an unrepresented employee to be examined by a qualified medical evaluator selected by the appeals board, within the scope of the qualified medical evaluator's professional training, upon any clinical question then at issue before the appeals board.

(b) The administrative director or his or her designees, upon the submission of a matter to an information and assistance officer, may, upon the agreement of a party to pay the cost, and with the consent of an unrepresented employee direct the injured employee to be examined by a qualified medical evaluator selected by the medical director, within the scope of the qualified medical evaluator's professional training, upon any clinical question, other than those issues specified in Section 4061, then pertinent to the investigation of the information and assistance officer.

(c) The 1989 and 1990 amendments to this section shall become operative for injuries occurring on and after January 1, 1991.

§ 55.0 NOTICE BY EMPLOYER TO EMPLOYEE OF POSSIBLE BENEFITS

Page 1767, Column 1, delete first paragraph, and the insert the following:

Employers must advice employees of their rights to workers' compensation benefits by posting a special notice and giving them written information.

Posted Notice

Page 1767, Column 1, seventh paragraph, insert following '…this notice.'

An employer may be assessed a civil penalty of up to $7,000.00 for failure to post this notice. Lab. C. Sec. 6431.

Employee Information

Page 1767, Column 1, Column 2, and Page 1768 first paragraph, delete Regulations sections 9880, 9881 and 9882 and insert the following:

Regulation section 9880,
Written Notice to New Employees
(a) Every employer shall provide to every new employee, either at the time of hire or by the end of the first pay period, the Written Notice to New Employees concerning the rights, benefits and obligations under worker's compensation law. The content of the notice must be approved by the Administrative Director.
(b) The notice shall be easily understandable. It shall be available in both English and Spanish where there are Spanish–speaking employees.
(c) The notice provided shall be in writing, in non–technical terms and shall include the following information:
    (1) The name of the current compensation insurance carrier of the employer at the time of distribution, or when such is the fact, that the employer is self–insured, and who is responsible for claims adjustment;
    (2) How to get emergency medical treatment, if needed;
    (3) The kind of events, injuries and illnesses covered by workers' compensation;
    (4) The injured employee's right to receive medical care;
    (5) How to obtain appropriate medical care for a job injury;
    (6) The role and function of the primary treating physician;
    (7) The rights of the employee to select and change the treating physician pursuant to the provisions of Labor Code Sections 4600 to 4601;
    (8) A form that the employee may use as an optional method for notifying the employer of the name of the employee's "personal physician," as defined by Labor Code Section 4600, or "personal chiropractor," as defined by Labor Code Section 4601;
    (9) The rights of the employee to receive temporary disability indemnity, permanent disability indemnity, vocational rehabilitation services, supplemental job displacement benefits, and death benefits, as appropriate;
    (10) To whom the injuries should be reported;
    (11) The existence of time limits for the employer to be notified of an occupational injury;
    (12) The protections against discrimination provided pursuant to Section 132a; and
    (13) The location and telephone number of the nearest information and assistance officer, including an explanation of services available.

NOTE: Authority cited: Sections 133, 138.3, 138.4, 3550, 3551 and 5307.3, Labor Code. Reference: Sections 139.5, 139.6, 3550, 3551, 3600, 4600, 4601, 4603, 4650, 4651, 4658.5, 4658.6, 4700, 4702 and 4703, Labor Code.

HISTORY
1. New Article 8.5 (Sections 9880–9882) filed 1–28–76 as an emergency; effective upon filing (Register 76, No. 5).
2. Certificate of Compliance filed 1–29–76 (Register 76, No. 5).
3. Repealer and new section filed 11–9–77; effective thirtieth day thereafter (Register 77, No. 46).
4. Amendment filed 10–16–81; effective thirtieth day thereafter (Register 81, No. 42).
5. Editorial correction restoring Article 8.5 (Sections 9880–9883), which was inadvertently repealed by a 7–15–83 order (Register 83, No. 33).
6. Repealer and new section filed 7–11–89; operative 10–1–89 (Register 89, No. 28).
7. Amendment of section and Note filed 7–7–2004; operative 8–1–2004 pursuant to Government Code section 11343.4 (Register 2004, No. 28).

Regulation section 9881,
Posting of Notice to Employees
(a) Every employer shall post and keep posted in a conspicuous location frequented by employees during the hours of the workday a Notice to Employees.
(b) The Notice to Employees poster shall be easily understandable. It shall be posted in both English and Spanish where there are Spanish–speaking employees.

§ 55.0

(c) The Notice to Employees poster shall include the following information:

(1) The name of the current compensation insurance carrier of the employer, or when such is the fact, that the employer is self–insured, and who is responsible for claims adjustment.

(2) How to get emergency medical treatment, if needed.

(3) Emergency telephone numbers for physician, hospital, ambulance, police and firefighting services.

(4) The kinds of events, injuries and illnesses covered by workers' compensation.

(5) Advice that the employer may not be responsible for compensation because of an injury due to the employee's voluntary participation in any off–duty recreational, social, or athletic activity that is not a part of the employee's work–related duties.

(6) The injured employee's right to receive medical care.

(7) The rights of the employee to select and change the treating physician pursuant to the provisions of Labor Code Section 4600.

(8) The rights of the employee to receive temporary disability indemnity, permanent disability indemnity, vocational rehabilitation services, supplemental job displacement benefits, and death benefits, as appropriate.

(9) To whom the injuries should be reported.

(10) The existence of time limits for the employer to be notified of an occupational injury.

(11) The protections against discrimination provided pursuant to Labor Code Section 132a.

(12) The location and telephone number of the nearest information and assistance officer/

(c) The employer may post the Administrative Director's approved Notice to Employee Poster provided in Section 9881.1. If the employer chooses not to use the Notice to Employee Poster provided in Section 9881.1, the employer may use a poster which meets the posting requirements of Labor Code Section 3550, includes the information required by this regulation, and has been approved by the Administrative Director.

NOTE: Authority cited: Sections 133, 138.3, 139.6, 3550 and 5307.3, Labor Code. Reference: Sections 139.5, 3550, 3600, 4600, 4601, 4603, 4658.5 and 4658.6, Labor Code.

HISTORY
1. Repealer and new section filed 7–11–89; operative 10–1–89 (Register 89, No. 28).
2. Amendment of section heading, section and Note filed 7–7–2004; operative 8–1–2004 pursuant to Government Code section 11343.4 (Register 2004, No. 28).

Regulation section 9882,
Written Notice to Injured Employees; Pamphlet Contents
NOTE: Authority cited: Sections 133, 138.3, 138.4, 139.6, and 5402, Labor Code. Reference: Sections 132a, 139.5,

3600, 4600, 4601, 4650, 4658, 4700, 4701, 4702, 4703, 4401–4411 and 5400–5412, Labor Code.

HISTORY
1. Repealer and new section filed 7–11–89; operative 10–1–89 (Register 89, No. 28).
2. Repealer filed 7–7–2004; operative 8–1–2004 pursuant to Government Code section 11343.4 (Register 2004, No. 28).

Page 1768, Column 1, second paragraph, add new heading following '...filed 7–11–89.'

Publication of Employee Information

Page 1768, Column 1, third paragraph, delete Regulation section 9883 and insert the following:

Regulation section 9883,
Publication of Information, Approval, Spanish Translation

(a) Insurers, employers or private enterprises may prepare and publish for their use or sale the Notice to Employees poster and/or the Written Notice to New Employees required by this Article upon prior approval of the form and content by the Administrative Director. The Notice to Employees poster and/or Written Notice to New Employees may include a logotype. The addition only of a logotype to a previously approved Notice to Employees poster or Written Notice to New Employees does not require additional approval.

(1) Any published Written Notice to New Employees shall be available in English and Spanish and shall include the information specified in Section 9880.

(2) Any published Notice to Employees poster shall be available in English and Spanish, where there are Spanish-speaking employees, and shall include the information specified in Section 9881.

(b) All matter published subsequent to the effective date of this regulation shall indicate that the written informational material has been approved by the Administrative Director.

(c) Publications other than those of the Administrative Director or the Workers' Compensation Appeals Board may reflect the employer, private publisher or insurance carrier identifier or logotype.

NOTE: Authority cited: Sections 133, 139.6, 3550, 3551 and 5307, Labor Code. Reference: Sections 139.6, 3550 and 3551, Labor Code.

HISTORY
1. New section filed 7-27-79; effective thirtieth day thereafter (Register 79, No. 30).
2. Change without regulatory effect of NOTE filed 7-11-86; effective upon filing (Register 86, No. 28).
3. Repealer and new section filed 7-11-89; operative 10-1-89 (Register 89, No. 28).
4. Amendment of section and Note filed 7-7-2004; operative 8-1-2004 pursuant to Government Code section 11343.4 (Register 2004, No. 28).

Page 1770, Column 2, second paragraph, insert following '...jury.'

In *Davenport v. WCAB* (2005) 70 Cal. Comp. Cases 1566, the Court of Appeal, Third District, in an unpublished decision, held that an applicant's claim for workers' compensation benefits was not barred by the one–year statute of limitations in Section 5405, even though the applicant did not file his claim until approximately *six (6) years* after his injury, when the Court found that the employer never provided the employee with the notice required by Section 5401. The Court stated, in part:

To conclude the statute of limitations barred Thomas Davenport's claim for benefits, the Workers' Compensation Appeals Board (WCAB) jumped from evidence that the petitioner Thomas Davenport spoke with a lawyer to the conclusion that Davenport was "aware that he might have a workers' compensation claim." Because it is undisputed Davenport's employer did not provide him with the statutorily required notice concerning his workers' compensation rights, and the State Compensation Insurance Fund (SCIF) failed to meet its burden of proving Davenport knew he might be entitled to benefits under the workers' compensation system, we shall annul the WCAB's order.

FACTUAL AND PROCEDURAL BACKGROUND

Davenport worked for Michael Faeth Cleaners in 1997. Faeth had a contract with Camp Pendleton to dry–clean military clothing. During his employment, Davenport lived in a hotel on the base and Faeth paid for Davenport's room and board. Davenport worked for Faeth until the business closed in August or September 1997.

On April 1, 1997, Davenport burned himself while in his hotel room. He was cooking in the kitchen area when a grease fire started. He tried to carry the flaming pan of grease out of his room, but slipped during the attempt. As a result, he burned his arms, hand, and face. A member of the hotel staff called an ambulance that picked Davenport up at the hotel and transported him to the hospital.

The next day, Davenport told Faeth about the circumstances of his injury. Someone from Faeth took him back to Tri–City Hospital because he needed more medical care. When he was admitted to the hospital, he explained the circumstances of his injuries and the hospital admitted him under Medi–Cal. Medi–Cal later denied payment of these bills. Davenport believed that Faeth paid the Tri–City bill.

During his stay at the hospital, Davenport spoke with an attorney who told him he did not have a case. For that reason, Davenport did not pursue a workers' compensation claim nor did he ask the employer to pay his bills.

Faeth also took Davenport to a hand specialist to treat his burnt hand. The hand specialist who treated Davenport referred him to the Grossman Burn Center. A Faeth representative claimed Faeth would pay that bill too. After six to nine days of treatment at the Grossman Burn Center, Davenport was released and returned to work at Faeth. Davenport received a bill for $69,000 from the Grossman Burn Center while he was still working for Faeth.

Faeth did not offer to pay any other bills and did not provide Davenport with any workers' compensation forms.

In 2003, Davenport discovered that his medical bills still appeared as derogatory information on his credit reports. He had previously believed that this information would fall off his credit report.

Davenport claimed he discovered he might have a workers' compensation claim in 2003. He filed this claim on June 5, 2003.

The administrative law judge (ALJ) concluded that Davenport's claim was barred by the one–year statute of limitations contained in Labor Code section 5405. The ALJ found that Davenport was "aware that he might have a workers' compensation claim as he consulted an attorney by telephone in 1997 or 1998 to see if he had a viable case." The ALJ also concluded that the SCIF was prejudiced by the lapse of time because the records of Davenport's treatment had been lost and SCIF was unable to contact the employer which had gone out of business.

In her report and recommendation to the WCAB on Davenport's petition for reconsideration, the ALJ reiterated her finding that Davenport testified "he did not file a workers' compensation claim because he had discussed it with an attorney who told him he did not have a case." She recommended denial of the petition. The WCAB denied Davenport's petition.

DISCUSSION

Under Labor Code (Footnote 1) section 5405, "The period within which proceedings may be commenced for the collection of the benefits provided by Article 2 (commencing with Section 4600) or Article 3 (commencing with Section 4650), or both, of Chapter 2 of Part 2 is one year from any of the following: [P] (a) The date of injury. [P] (b) The expiration of any period covered by payment under Article 3 (commencing with Section 4650) of Chapter 2 of Part 2. [P] (c) The last date on which any benefits provided for in Article 2 (commencing with Section 4600) of Chapter 2 of Part 2 were furnished."

Under section 5401, subdivision (a), within one day of receiving notice of knowledge of a qualifying injury, an employer is required to provide an injured worker with a claim form that provides the worker with information about his workers' compensation rights. That notice must include information about how to commence proceedings for workers' compensation and what happens after a worker files a claim. The notice must also inform the worker that the worker has the right to disagree with decisions about the claim, a description of available benefits, how the worker may obtain treatment, the worker's rights concerning the physician and treatment, that a worker can obtain information from the division of workers' compensation, and the prohibition against discrimination from the employer for seeking benefits. (§ 5401, subd. (b).) (Footnote 2)

In analyzing the substantially similar notice requirements contained in the regulations that predated section 5401, our supreme court stated, "The clear purpose of these rules is to protect and preserve the rights of an injured employee who may be ignorant of the procedures or, indeed, the very existence of the workmen's compensation law. Since the employer is generally in a better position to be aware of the employee's rights, it is proper that he should be charged with the responsibility of notifying the employee, under circumstances such as those existing here, that there is a possibility he may have a claim for workmen's compensation benefits." (Reynolds v. Workmen's Comp. Appeals Bd. (1974) 12 Cal. 3d 726, 729 [527 P.2d 631, 117 Cal. Rptr. 79, 39 Cal. Comp. Cases 768].) Thus, the court concluded because the employer "was obligated to give the notices prescribed by the administrative rules and failed to do so, it may not raise the technical defense of the statute of limitations to defeat petitioner's claim." (Id. at p. 730.)

In Kaiser Foundation Hospitals v. Workers' Comp. Appeals Bd. (1985) 39 Cal. 3d 57 [702 P.2d 197, 216 Cal. Rptr. 115, 50 Cal. Comp. Cases 411], the court concluded that "Reynolds stands for the proposition that when an employer fails to perform its statutory duty to notify an injured employee of his workers' compensation rights, and the injured employee is unaware of those rights from the date of injury through the date of the employer's breach, then the statute of limitations will be tolled until the employee receives actual knowledge that he may be entitled to benefits under the workers' compensation system." (Kaiser, at p. 63.) The court held that the remedy for the "breach of an employer's duty to notify [of the employee's workers' compensation rights] is a tolling of the statute of limitations if the employee, without that tolling, is prejudiced by that breach." (Id. at p. 64.) "If between the date of injury and the date the employer breaches, an employee gains the requisite actual knowledge of his [or her] workers' compensation rights, he [or she] will not be prejudiced by failure of [the] employer to notify him [or her] of those rights, and there is no reason to toll the statute of limitations even if [the] employer never advises him [or her] of his [or her] workers' compensation rights. If the employee remains ignorant of his [or her] rights past the time the employer breaches its duty to notify, the employee will be prejudiced from the date of breach until the employee gains actual knowledge that he [or she] may be entitled to benefits under the workers' compensation system." (Id. at pp. 64–65.) Moreover, the court held the burden of establishing the affirmative defense of statute of limitations is on the proponent of that defense. (Id. at p. 67, fn. 8.)

In Gonzalez v. Workers' Comp. Appeals Bd. (1986) 186 Cal. App. 3d 514, 517 [230 Cal. Rptr. 649, 51 Cal. Comp. Cases 485], the injured employee admitted that he consulted with an attorney the day he entered the hospital for his injury. The attorney "mentioned a claim, and the [injured employee] told the attorney he would contact the attorney later if he wanted to pursue the claim." (Ibid.) The court adopted the applicant's concession that the statute of limitations was not tolled in these circumstances because the injured employee admitted he became aware of his rights through discussions with his attorney while he was in the hospital. (Id. at pp. 521–522.)

By contrast, in Galloway v. Workers' Comp. Appeals Bd. (1998) 63 Cal. App. 4th 880, 887 [74 Cal. Rptr. 2d 374, 63 Cal. Comp. Cases 532], the court concluded that an employer was estopped from asserting the statute of limitations against its injured employee when it failed to provide him with the statutorily required notice. While the employee may have known he was required to file a claim, there was no evidence in the record that established that the employee knew the appropriate time limitations for filing a claim. (Ibid.) Because the burden was on the employer to demonstrate that knowledge and there was no evidence to support that inference, the defense of the statute of limitations failed. (Id. at pp. 887–888.)

Here, the undisputed evidence is that Faeth never provided Davenport with the statutorily required notice that would have provided him with information about his ability to file a claim. That notice would have also provided him with the other information required by section 5401, subdivision (b). Our review of the record discloses no evidence from which it can be inferred that Davenport had actual knowledge that he might be entitled to benefits under the workers' compensation system. The closest the evidence comes on this point is Davenport's admission that he spoke to an attorney and the attorney advised him he had no case. This admission, however, does not constitute evidence that Davenport gained actual knowledge that he might be entitled to benefits under the workers' compensation system. To the contrary, this evidence negates the inference that Davenport had the requisite actual knowledge. Having been told by an attorney that he had no case, Davenport had no reason to know he might actually be entitled to benefits. Without any other evidence of Davenport's knowledge, the statute of limitations defense fails. (Footnote 3)... .

Footnote 1. All further statutory references are to the Labor Code unless otherwise indicated.

Footnote 2. "Insofar as practicable, the notice of potential eligibility for benefits required by this section and the claim form shall be a single document and shall instruct the injured employee to fully read the notice of potential eligibility. The form and content of the notice and claim form shall be prescribed by the administrative director after consultation with the Commission on Health and Safety and Workers' Compensation. The notice shall be easily understandable and available in both English and Spanish. The content shall include, but not be limited to, the following: [P] (1) The procedure to be used to commence proceedings for the collection of compensation for the purposes of this chapter. [P] (2) A description of the different types of workers' compensation benefits. [P] (3) What happens to the claim form after it is filed. [P] (4) From whom the employee can obtain medical care for the injury. [P] (5) The role and function of the primary treating physician. [P] (6) The rights of an employee to select and change the treating physician pursuant to subdivision (e) of Section 3550 and Section 4600. [P] (7) How to get medical care while the claim is pending. [P] (8) The protections against discrimination provided pursuant to Section 132a. [P] (9) The following written statements: [P] (A) You have a right to disagree with decisions affecting your claim. [P] (B) You can obtain free information from an information and assistance officer of the state Division of Workers'

Compensation, or you can hear recorded information and a list of local offices by calling [applicable information and assistance telephone number(s)]. [P] (C) You can consult an attorney. Most attorneys offer one free consultation. If you decide to hire an attorney, his or her fee will be taken out of some of your benefits. For names of workers' compensation attorneys, call the State Bar of California at [telephone number of the State Bar of California's legal specialization program, or its equivalent]." (§ 5401, subd. (b).)

Footnote 3. Given our disposition, we decline to address the question of whether section 5402's presumption of compensation was waived. The WCAB made no finding on this issue as it rejected the claim solely on statute of limitation grounds.

[**Editor's Note:** The Court obviously had the *Honeywell* case in mind.]

Failure to give employees statutorily required notices, including pamphlets, advising them of their rights and responsibilities, can have serious consequences for employers. In *Davenport v. WCAB (2005) 70 Cal. Comp. Cases 1566*, the statute of limitations was held not to bar a claim filed *six years* after an injury, where the employer failed to give an employee the statutorily required notice following knowledge by the employer that the employee suffered an industrial injury.

Intentionally blank

California Workers' Compensation Claims and Benefits, 12th Ed. Supplement (2007)

§ 57.0   INCREASED COMPENSATION FOR DELAY IN PROVIDING BENEFITS ("PENALTY")

§ 57.3   What Constitutes Reasonable Delay? – Genuine Doubt from Legal or Medical Point of View as to Liability

Page 1798, Column 2, fourth paragraph, insert following '...the vehicle.'

In *Creel v. WCAB* (2005) 70 Cal. Comp. Cases 1154, the Board held defendant did not unreasonably delay payment of medical benefits, in the form of housekeeping services, when the Board found a genuine legal and medical doubt for those services, because defendants timely denied the request based upon a report from a utilization review physician. The Board stated, in part:

Here, following applicant's low back discectomy and fusion, Dr. Conner recommended that she receive a firm orthopedic mattress. He explained in deposition the medical necessity of an appropriate mattress in the immediate post–operative period to help relieve applicant's pain associated with sleeping and in the long–term to help maintain her pain and prevent flare–ups. He also testified in his deposition that applicant informed him that the mattress she was using was not comfortable. Moreover, applicant testified at trial that she had difficulty sleeping and, therefore, needed an orthopedic mattress.

In contrast, defendants presented no evidence to contradict Dr. Conner's recommendations for a firm orthopedic mattress or to contradict applicant's testimony. In light of the entire record, we conclude that substantial evidence supports the WCJ's determination of applicant's entitlement to an orthopedic mattress pursuant to Labor Code section 4600 to treat her admitted industrial injuries. (See *LeVesque v. Workmen's Comp. Appeals Bd.* (1970) 1 Cal. 3d 627 [83 Cal. Rptr. 208, 463 P.2d 432] [35 Cal. Comp. Cases 16]; *Fremont Comp. Ins. Co. v. Workers' Comp. Appeals Bd. (Hamilton), supra,* 66 Cal. Comp. Cases 756.)

As for the housekeeping services recommended by Dr. Conner, he testified in deposition that applicant's need for that treatment ended by May 13, 2004, because she stopped taking "additional" pain medicine. Therefore, there is no current medical necessity for housekeeping assistance.

Moreover, applicant testified at trial that she self–procured housekeeping assistance following her February 2004 industrial back surgery from her sister and from a friend. However, applicant neither claimed nor presented any evidence that she paid for the housekeeping. Applicant did not seek reimbursement for housekeeping expenses, which might have been compensable if medically reasonable and necessary. See *Smyers v. Workers' Comp. Appeals Bd.* (1984) 157 Cal. App. 3d 36 [203 Cal. Rptr. 521] [49 Cal. Comp. Cases 454]; *Kaiser Foundation Hospital v. Workers' Comp. Appeals Bd. (Yturralde)* (1996) 61 Cal. Comp. Cases 876 [writ denied]; *County of Los Angeles v. Workers' Comp. Appeals Board (Brown)* (1999) 64 Cal. Comp. Cases 1282 [writ denied].) Therefore, we conclude that there is not [*sic*] substantial evidence supporting applicant's present need for housekeeping services and, accordingly, we will reverse the finding of the WCJ entitling applicant to housekeeping.

As for the penalties imposed against defendants, we conclude that there were genuine legal and medical doubts as to applicant's entitlement to an orthopedic mattress and to housekeeping assistance such that the imposition of penalties is not supported.

Regarding the penalty for housekeeping, defendants' utilization review physician's report of March 10, 2004, provided that there was no medical necessity shown for housekeeping. In the caption of the report, it is asserted that Dr. Conner's recommendations for home care were received on March 8, 2004. Applicant provided no evidence that defendants received the report earlier than March 8, 2004. The utilization review denial of March 10, 2004, was within 14 days of defendants' receipt of the recommendations on March 8, 2004, and was, therefore, timely pursuant to Labor Code section 4610. As such, defendants had a genuine legal and medical doubt as to applicant's entitlement to housekeeping. Accordingly, defendants did not unreasonably refuse to provide that benefit and a penalty is not warranted. [See *Ralphs Grocery Co. v. Workers' Comp. Appeals Bd. (Lara)* (1995) 38 Cal. App. 4th 820 [45 Cal. Rptr. 2d 197] [60 Cal. Comp. Cases 840].)

Regarding the penalty for the orthopedic bed, we also conclude that defendants had a genuine legal and medical doubt as to applicant's entitlement such that imposition of a penalty is not warranted. Dr. Conner's initial recommendations for the orthopedic bed in January and February 2004 were made on a prescription pad without explanation as to the medical necessity of the bed and without explanation as to the connection between the need for the bed and applicant's admitted industrial injury. Dr.

Conner did not address these issues until his deposition on June 3, 2004.

While we conclude that Dr. Conner addressed the medical necessity for the recommended orthopedic bed and the connection between the need for the bed and applicant's admitted industrial injuries sufficiently in his deposition testimony to support applicant's entitlement to the bed, defendants still had a genuine legal doubt as to applicant's entitlement such that their refusal to provide the bed was not unreasonable. Dr. Conner testified in his deposition that he did not personally inspect applicant's mattress, although he also testified that applicant told him that it was uncomfortable. At trial, applicant confirmed that she had sleeping problems with her current mattress. Until then, defendants' uncertainty about the medical necessity of the bed was, in light of the entire record, not unreasonable.

Therefore, we will grant reconsideration to find that applicant is not entitled to housekeeping at this time and to find that defendants are not liable for penalties for their refusal to provide applicant with an orthopedic mattress and with housekeeping services. We will affirm the finding of applicant's entitlement to the orthopedic mattress... .

§ 57.10   Interest Delay

Page 1846, Column 2, fifth paragraph,
insert following '...the omission.'

Failure to pay one day of interest ($2.50) was not deemed unreasonable where the delay was inadvertent and the amount was promptly paid by defendant upon learning of the error. *Holland, et al. v. WCAB* (2005) 70 Cal. Comp. Cases 1515.

§ 57.21   Temporary Disability or Permanent Disability Checks Not Issued on Time

Page 1866, Column 2, second paragraph,
insert following '...Cases 755.'

Where injury, disability or indemnity rate is disputed, no Section 4650(d) penalty arises if the disputed disability indemnity payments are made within 14 days of a final order, decision or award imposing liability for those benefits or within 14 days of a defendant's acceptance of liability for the injury and disability payments. Further, an order, decision or award becomes final for purposes of Section 4650(d) when a defendant has exhausted all of its appellate rights or has not pursued them.

Commenting on this in *Leinon v. Fisherman's Grotto, et. al* (2004) 69 Cal. Comp. Cases 995, the Appeals Board in an En Banc decision stated:

On April 3, 2003, the Appeals Board granted reconsideration of the Supplemental Findings and Award issued by the workers' compensation administrative law judge ("WCJ") on January 13, 2003. In that decision, the WCJ found defendant Mid–Century Insurance Company liable for a penalty under Labor Code section 4650(d) (Footnote 1) on all temporary disability indemnity ("TDI"), where it paid the TDI within fourteen (14) days after finality of a prior Findings and Award that had determined the disputed issues of injury and temporary disability.

In its petition for reconsideration, defendant contended that it avoided a section 4650(d) penalty by sending applicant a delay letter, that there is no obligation to pay benefits until adjudication of industrial injury, that there is no penalty in this case because TDI was timely paid, that the imposition of a section 4650(d) penalty is a denial of due process and equal protection, that section 4650 does not apply in a post–award situation, and that the WCJ's decision is not supported by the legislative record and scheme relating to penalties.

Applicant filed an answer.

In order to secure uniformity of decision in the future, and because of important legal issues raised by the Court of Appeal in Rivera v. Workers' Comp. Appeals Bd. (2003) 112 Cal. App. 4th 1124 [6 Cal. Rptr. 3d 16] [68 Cal. Comp. Cas 1460], the Chairman of the Appeals Board, upon a majority vote of its members, assigned this case to the Appeals Board as a whole for an en banc decision. (Lab. Code, § 115.) (Footnote 2)

Based on our review of the relevant statutory and case law, we hold that where injury, disability or indemnity rate is disputed, no section 4650(d) penalty arises if the disputed disability indemnity payments are made within 14 days of a final order, decision or award imposing liability for those benefits or within 14 days of a defendant's acceptance of liability for the injury and disability benefits. We also hold that an order, decision or award becomes final for purposes of section 4650(d) when a defendant has exhausted all of its appellate rights or has not pursued them.

BACKGROUND

Applicant claimed a cumulative trauma (CT) injury to his spine, left hip, and right knee for the period ending November 1, 1998. Defendant disputed injury from the outset by sending applicant a timely delay letter; later it timely denied the claim. (Footnote 3)

In a Findings and Award issued May 30, 2001, the WCJ found that applicant sustained the CT injury as alleged, and that the injury caused temporary total disability from November 2, 1998 to March 6, 2001 and continuing. The Appeals Board denied defendant's petition for reconsideration, followed by the Court of Appeal's denial of defendant's petition for writ of review, followed by the Supreme Court's denial of review on January 3, 2002. Thereafter, applicant claimed that defendant failed to pay a section 4650(d) penalty when it paid the TDI required by the May 30, 2001 Findings and Award. The WCJ heard the penalty claim based on the parties' stipulation that on January 9, 2002 (i.e., within 14 days of the Supreme Court's denial of review), defendant paid the correct amount of TDI but did not include any section 4650(d) penalty. In the decision reconsidered here, the WCJ found defendant liable for a section 4650(d) penalty on the TDI due under the May 30, 2001 Findings and Award.

DISCUSSION

Section 4650 provides in relevant part:

""(a) If an injury causes temporary disability, the first payment of temporary disability indemnity shall be made not later than 14 days after knowledge of the injury and disability, on which date all indemnity then due shall be paid, unless liability for the injury is earlier denied."

""(b) If the injury causes permanent disability, the first payment shall be made within 14 days after the date of last payment of temporary disability indemnity. When the last payment of temporary disability indemnity has been made pursuant to subdivision (c) of Section 4656, and regardless of whether the ex–tent of permanent disability can be determined at that date, the employer nevertheless shall commence the timely payment required by this subdivision and shall continue to make these payments until the employer's reasonable estimate of permanent disability indemnity due has been paid, and if the amount of permanent disability indemnity due has been determined, until that amount has been paid."

""(c) Payment of temporary or permanent disability indemnity subsequent to the first payment shall be made as due every two weeks on the day designated with the first payment."

""(d) If any indemnity payment is not made timely as required by this section, the amount of the late payment shall be increased 10 percent and shall be paid, without application, to the employee, unless the employer continues the employee's wages under a salary continuation plan, as defined in subdivision (g). No increase shall apply to any payment due prior to or within 14 days after the date the claim form was submitted to the employer under Section 5401. No increase shall apply when, within the 14–day period specified under subdivision (a), the employer is unable to determine whether temporary disability indemnity payments are owed and advises the employee, in the manner prescribed in rules and regulations adopted pursuant to Section 138.4, why payments cannot be made within the 14–day period, what additional information is required to make the decision whether temporary disability indemnity payments are owed, and when the employer expects to have the information required to make the decision.""

In Gangwish v. Workers' Comp. Appeals Bd. (2001) 89 Cal. App. 4th 1284, 1293 [108 Cal. Rptr. 2d 1] [66 Cal. Comp. Cas 584, 590–591], the Court stated that "[t]he legislative history indicates that the purpose of enacting the [1989] changes to section 4650 was to promote prompt payment of benefits and certainty of timing . . . The new legislation also included increased compensation for late payments as an incentive, apart from the increased compensation for unreasonable refusal or delay under section 5814." (Citations omitted.) (Footnote 4)

Thus, the language of section 4650 includes multiple references to the words "injury" and "disability," and the statute's purpose is to promote the prompt payment of benefits and certainty of timing. We conclude that it is consistent with the language and purpose of the statute to construe the section 4650(d) penalty as being applicable only where liability for injury and disability benefits is not in dispute.

In Rivera v. Workers' Comp. Appeals Bd. (2003) 112 Cal. App. 4th 1124 [6 Cal. Rptr. 3d 16] [68 Cal. Comp. Cas 1460], liability for injury and disability benefits was not in dispute, and the injured worker claimed penalties under sections 4650(d) and 5814 for late payment of an approved Stipulations and Award. The Award included accrued and continuing periodic indemnity payments, and was accompanied by a simultaneous order of commutation of the future indemnity payments into a lump sum. The Court affirmed the Appeals Board's en banc decision in Rivera v. Tower Staffing Solutions (2002) 67 Cal. Comp. Cas 1473 [Appeals Board en banc decision], holding that section 4650 does not apply to lump sums that are commuted future periodic indemnity payments. (See 112 Cal. App. 4th at 1136 [68 Cal. Comp. Cas at 1468].) The Court also addressed the issue of whether the section 4650(d) penalty applies to accrued indemnity payments. The Court concluded that application of section 4650(d) to accrued TDI and PDI is consistent with the statute's "broader" purpose of not only providing for scheduled indemnity payments, but "also a procedure for ensuring financial support to injured workers during the recovery period following an industrial injury." (112 Cal. App. 4th at 1135 [68 Cal. Comp. Cas at 1468], citation omitted.) The section 4650(d) penalty applies to accrued disability indemnity because "the needs addressed by section 4650 are even greater where periodic disability indemnity has accrued during the recovery period and has not been paid." (Id.) As noted above, Rivera involved an approved Stipulations and Award, i.e. liability for injury and indemnity payments was not in dispute. Thus, the Court concluded that section 4650(d) applies to accrued indemnity in a case where liability had been accepted. However, the Court did not define when accrued benefits are "due" for purposes of section 4650(d).

The question of when accrued benefits are "due" was addressed by the Appeals Board in Mike v. Workers' Comp. Appeals Bd. (2003) 68 Cal. Comp. Cas 266 [writ denied], which involved section 4650(d) and 5814 penalties for failure to pay TDI at the correct rate during a good–faith earnings dispute. After the WCJ issued an award resolving the dispute, defendant paid the correct TDI within 14 days. The Appeals Board quoted subdivisions (a) and (d) of section 4650 and stated, "[o]n its face, the language of the statute refers to periodic payments. Defendants have an incentive to make periodic payments, i.e., if a defendant misses a periodic payment it has the option of immediately picking up payments and 'self–imposing' a 10% penalty on the missed payment, instead of risking a section 5814 penalty on the entire species of temporary (or permanent) disability indemnity. Therefore, the statute should be applied only to periodic payments where liability is accepted." (68 Cal. Comp. Cas at 273.) The Appeals Board denied both the section 4650(d) penalty and the section 5814 penalty, noting that defendant's liability for the higher TDI rate was not certain until the WCJ issued an award, after which the differential was paid within 14 days. Quoting subdivision (a) again, the Appeals Board stated that "the difference in the temporary disability rate from that paid and that ultimately found by the WCJ only became 'then due' within the meaning of the statute at the time the WCJ made the decision on the disputed issues of earnings and [TDI] rate . . . " (Id.) The Appeals Board concluded, "in a case where there is a bona fide dispute over the correct indemnity rate, the increased payment is not 'due' until the WCJ decides that it is due . . . the parties stipulated that payment on the Award . . . was made within 14 days. Therefore, defendant's payment of the award was 'timely' under section 4650(d)." (Id.)

Thus, section 4650 is phrased in terms of an accepted injury, and benefits which are not in dispute are payable for this accepted injury. Therefore, the section 4650(d) penalty will not apply under the conditions described in subdivisions (a) and (d) (further discussed below), and the increase will not apply when injury or indemnity benefits are disputed, thus taking the matter outside of section 4650, until that dispute is finally resolved. Accordingly, based on the language and purpose of section 4650 as discussed in Gangwish and Rivera, and consistent with the Appeals Board's analysis in Mike, we hold that the penalty under section 4650(d) applies only to periodic payments, including accrued periodic payments, where liability is accepted or where liability is ultimately imposed and the determination becomes final. An award becomes final for purposes of section 4650(d) when a defendant has exhausted all of its appellate rights or has not pursued them. Thus, an award becomes final after a WCJ issues an award and reconsideration is not sought, or after the Appeals Board makes a determination on reconsideration and review is not sought in the Court of Appeal, or after appellate review of the Appeals Board's decision is denied (or the decision is affirmed). In the instant case, the award of disputed benefits did not become final until the Supreme Court's ultimate denial of review.

However, there is no "grace period" for delay in payment provided by the statutory right to reconsideration or ap-pellate review. (See Jensen v. Workers' Comp. Appeals Bd. (1985) 170 Cal. App. 3d 244, 247 [216 Cal. Rptr. 33] [50 Cal. Comp. Cas 369, 371]; California Highway Patrol v. Workers' Comp. Appeals Bd. (Erebia) (2003) 68 Cal. Comp. Cas 227, 232 [writ denied].) Thus, if a defendant does not file a petition for reconsideration from an award of disputed benefits but does not pay within 14 days of the award, it must include a section 4650(d) penalty. Likewise, if a defen-dant does not file a petition for writ of review from an adverse decision after reconsideration but does not pay within 14 days of that decision, it must include a section 4650(d) penalty.

By reference to the 14-day period for timely payment set forth in section 4650, and consistent with Mike, supra, we also hold that in a disputed case, the defendant has 14 days to pay the disputed benefits after a final determination of the dispute, without risk of incurring the section 4650(d) penalty. This conclusion is consistent with the Supreme Court's approach to penalties on medical mileage in Avalon Bay Foods v. Workers' Comp. Appeals Bd. (Moore) (1998) 18 Cal.4th 1165 [959 P.2d 1228, 77 Cal. Rptr. 2d 552] [63 Cal. Comp. Cas 902]. In that case, the Court adopted from

section 4603.2(b) the 60-day time limit for timely payment of medical treatment bills; the Court allowed employers 60 days to pay medical treatment mileage bills without risk of incurring a penalty under section 5814. (See 18 Cal.4th at pp. 1179-1180 [63 Cal.Comp.Cases at pp. 912-913].)

Finally, we observe that section 4650 describes several situations in which the penalty will be avoided. Under subdivision (a), no increase on TDI will apply where liability for the injury is denied within 14 days after knowledge of the injury and disability. Under subdivision (b), no increase on PDI will apply where the first payment is made within 14 days after the date of last payment of TDI and the employer continues the payments until the employer's reasonable estimate of PDI due has been paid, and if the amount of PDI has been determined, until that amount has been paid. Under subdivision (d), the penalty will not apply where the employer continues the employee's wages under a defined salary continuation plan, and no increase shall apply to any payment due prior to or within 14 days after the date the claim form was submitted to the employer under Section 5401.

And there is no penalty when, within the 14-day period specified under subdivision (a), the employer is unable to determine whether TDI payments are owed and advises the employee, in a specified manner, why payments cannot be made within the 14-day period.

In this case, it was stipulated that defendant paid TDI within 14 days of the final determination rendering the TDI due for purposes of section 4650 (i.e., the Supreme Court's denial of review of the May 30, 2001 Findings and Award). Accordingly, there is no basis for applying the penalty under section 4650(d), and we will reverse the WCJ's decision.

For the foregoing reasons,

IT IS ORDERED, as the Decision After Reconsideration of the Appeals Board (En Banc), that the Supplemental Findings and Award of January 13, 2003 is RESCINDED, and the following Findings are SUBSTITUTED in its place:

FINDINGS

"1. When it paid the May 30, 2001 Findings and Award, defendant paid the correct amount of retroactive temporary disability payments calculated on a weekly rate of $ 485.06, plus post-award interest, by check to applicant dated January 9, 2002."

"2. As injury and disability was in dispute, defendant was not obligated to include the 10% increase under Labor Code section 4650(d)."

"3. Applicant's demand for penalty under section 4650(d) is denied."

Footnote 1. All statutory references are to the Labor Code, unless otherwise indicated.

Footnote 2. The Appeals Board's en banc decisions are binding precedent on all Appeals Board panels and WCJs. (Cal. Code Regs., tit. 8, § 10341; Gee v. Workers' Comp. Appeals Board (2002) 96 Cal.App.4th 1418, 1425, fn. 6 [118 Cal. Rptr. 2d 105] [67 Cal.Comp.Cases 236, 239, fn. 6].)

Footnote 3. Section 5402(b) provides in part that "[i]f liability is not rejected within 90 days after the date the claim form is filed under Section 5401, the injury shall be presumed compensable . . . rebuttable only by evidence discovered subsequent to the 90–day period."

Footnote 4. Before 1989, section 4650 provided in relevant part, "[i]f an injury causes temporary disability, a disability payment shall be made for one week in advance as wages on the fourth day after the injured employee leaves work as a result of the injury... If the injury causes permanent disability, a disability payment shall be made for one week in advance as wages on the fourth day after the injury becomes permanent or the date of the last payment of temporary disability, whichever date first occurs." Section 4651 provided in relevant part, "[s]uch permanent or temporary disability payments shall thereafter be made not less frequently than twice in each calendar month, unless otherwise ordered by the appeals board." Thus, the statutes had no penalty provisions and no clear timing of periodic payments.

Footnote 5. Based on the language of section 5401, no section 4650(d) penalty will apply to any payment due prior to or within 14 days after a claim form is personally delivered to the employer or mailed to the employer by first–class or certified mail.

See also Zimarik v. WCAB (2006) 71 Cal. Comp. Cases 1111.

§ 57.31 Penalty for Failure to Promptly Pay Expenses Necessary to Prove a Contested Claim to Medical Provider

Page 1878, Column 2, eighth paragraph, insert following '...72.0 of this book.'

In an unpublished decision holding that CIGA was not liable for Section 5814 penalties assessed against an insolvent insurer's pre–liquidation delays, when the Court found that the amendment to Insurance Code section 1063.1(c)(8), effective January 1, 2004, in which the Legislature excluded Labor Code section 5814 penalties from the definition of "Covered claim:definition" for which CIGA was liable, the Court of Appeal, Fifth District, in *Hernandez v. WCAB* (2006) 71 Cal. Comp. Cases 369, stated, in part:

The widow and minor of a fatally injured worker petition for a writ of review contending the Workers' Compensation Appeals Board (WCAB) erred by reversing previously imposed penalties against the California Insurance Guarantee Association (CIGA). We will deny the petition in light of the Legislature's amendment to the Insurance Code eliminating the penalties from the CIGA's liability.

BACKGROUND

Twenty–one–year–old Jose Alatorre (Alatorre) fell and drowned on February 22, 2001, while repairing a sump–hole pump valve for Aguiar–Faria & Sons Dairy (Dairy) in Merced County. Alatorre was survived by his totally dependent widow and infant son (Petitioners).

The Dairy admitted Alatorre's death was industrially related and paid Petitioners death benefits at the rate of $255 per week based on two–thirds of Alatorre's $382.50 weekly earnings. In February 2002, a workers' compensation administrative law judge (WCJ) determined Petitioners were entitled to the maximum statutory death benefits of $490 per week based on Alatorre's potential earnings. The WCAB summarily denied the Dairy's petition for reconsideration in April 2002. The Dairy petitioned the Court of Appeal, Third Appellate District for a writ of review; that court also summarily denied the petition and awarded supplemental attorney fees to Alatorre's family in July 2002. (Footnote 1)

(*Aguiar–Faria & Sons Dairy v. Workers' Comp. Appeals Bd.* (2002) 67 Cal. Comp. Cases 927 [writ denied]; Lab. Code, § 5801.)

The Dairy's workers' compensation insurer, Legion Insurance Company (Legion), became insolvent and the CIGA assumed responsibility for the Alatorre family's workers' compensation claim in April 2003. (See Ins. Code, § 119.5 et seq.)

In August 2003, the matter again came before a WCJ to address Petitioners' increased benefit and penalty claims. On October 29, 2003, the WCJ determined that, pursuant to newly enacted statutory rates, the Petitioners were entitled to weekly death benefits of $490 before 2003, $602 during 2003, and $666.67 after 2003. The WCJ also found the Dairy, while insured by Legion, engaged in seven acts of unreasonably delaying or failing to issue death benefit payments and attorney fees, warranting separate 10 percent penalties under Labor Code section 5814 (section 5814). (Footnote 2)

The CIGA petitioned the WCAB for reconsideration in November 2003, raising various abuse of discretion and insufficient evidence claims. In December 2003, the WCJ reported to the WCAB that the Dairy engaged in "a lengthy history and pattern of failure to properly and timely pay benefits both due under the undisputed evidence and then later ordered pursuant to findings and award."

In January 2004, the WCAB granted reconsideration "in order to allow opportunity to further study the factual and legal issues in this case." Nearly a year later, in January 2005, the WCAB issued a Notice of Intention to Submit inviting supplemental briefing to address the relevance of the WCAB's recent en banc decision, *Martinez v. Jack Neal & Sons* (2004) 69 Cal. Comp. Cases 775 [Appeals Board en banc opinion] (*Martinez*), regarding CIGA's liability for penalties under section 5814. (Footnote 3)

On June 28, 2005, the WCAB issued an Opinion and Decision after Reconsideration. Following *Martinez,* the WCAB concluded that pursuant to the amendment to Insurance Code section 1063.1, subdivision (c)(8) (section 1063.1(c)(8)), the CIGA is not liable for penalties under section 5814 issued after January 1, 2004, based on an insolvent insurer's pre–liquidation delay. The WCAB rescinded the penalties awarded by the WCJ because the amendment "applies prospectively to any section 5814 awards issued on or after the effective date."

DISCUSSION

The CIGA was created in 1969 under the Guarantee Act (Ins. Code, Art. 14.2) to provide "insolvency insurance" against the loss arising from insolvent insurers. (*Denny's v. Workers' Comp. Appeals Bd.* (2003) 104 Cal. App. 4th 1433, 1438 [129 Cal. Rptr. 2d 53, 68 Cal. Comp. Cases 1].) " 'It is a statutory entity that depends on the Guarantee Act for its existence and for a definition of the scope of its powers, duties, and protections.' " (*Ibid.*) It is only authorized to pay the statutorily defined "covered claims" of an insolvent insurer. (*Ibid.*)

" 'Workers' Compensation insurance is a class of insurance covered by the provisions of the CIGA statutes.' " (*Denny's v. Workers' Comp. Appeals Bd., supra,* 104 Cal. App. 4th at p. 1439.) Effective January 1, 2004, however, the Legislature expressly excluded from the definition of covered claims in section 1063.1(c)(8) "any amount awarded by the Workers' Compensation Appeals Board pursuant to Section 5814 or 5814.5 because payment of compensation was unreasonably delayed or refused by the insolvent insurer." (Stats. 2003, ch. 635, § 6 (Assem. Bill No. 227).) In *Martinez,* the WCAB concluded "the clear and unambiguous import of this statutory language is that section 1063.1(c)(8) applies prospectively to any section 5814 (or section 5814.5) awards issued on or after its effective date, i.e., awards issued on or after January 1, 2004." (*Martinez, supra,* 69 Cal. Comp. Cases 775, 779.)

Petitioners' contend the WCAB acted without or in excess of its powers by determining the CIGA is not liable for Legion's pre–liquidation unreasonable delay because the WCJ issued the section 5814 penalties on October 29, 2003, before the penalties were eliminated from the CIGA's coverage as of January 1, 2004. Petitioners agree with the WCAB's en banc decision in *Martinez* that the section 1063.1(c)(8) amendment applies "prospectively," but disagree with the WCAB's application of the amendment rescinding the penalties previously levied against the CIGA. Given Petitioners' concession, we do not address the propriety of the *Martinez* decision.

This court recently addressed a similar issue regarding the effective date of newly enacted apportionment provisions under Senate Bill No. 899 (Sen. Bill 899) in *Marsh v. Workers' Comp. Appeals Bd.* (2005) 130 Cal. App. 4th 906 [30 Cal. Rptr. 3d 598, 70 Cal. Comp. Cases 787]. Noting the express legislative intent of Sen. Bill 899 that its provisions apply "prospectively from the date of enactment," we concluded the WCJ's determination was not final for purposes of applying the new legislation while the matter was pending before the WCAB on reconsideration. (*Id.* at pp. 915–916.) We found the new apportionment provisions must be applied to all cases not yet final at the time of enactment, regardless of any interim WCJ decisions. (*Ibid.*; see also *Rio Linda Union School Dist. v. Workers' Comp. Appeals Bd.* (2005) 131 Cal. App. 4th 517 [31 Cal. Rptr. 3d 789, 70 Cal. Comp. Cases 999]; *Kleemann v. Workers' Comp. Appeals Bd.* (2005) 127 Cal. App. 4th 274 [25 Cal. Rptr. 3d 448, 70 Cal. Comp. Cases 133].) As the Second Appellate District, Division Eight explained in the context of whether a subsequent amendmenft to section 5814 applied retroactively:

" "When new legislation repeals statutory rights, the rights normally end with repeal unless vested pursuant to contract or common law. In workers' compensation, where rights are purely statutory and not based on common law, repeal ends the right, absent a savings clause. Rights end during litigation if statutory repeal occurs before final judgment; by definition there is no final judgment if an appeal is pending. There is no injustice if statutory rights end before final judgment because parties act and litigate in contemplation of possible repeal." (*Green v. Workers' Comp. Appeals Bd.* (2005) 127 Cal. App. 4th 1426, 1436 [26 Cal. Rptr. 3d 527, 70 Cal. Comp. Cases 294], fns. omitted.)" In light of the Legislature's amendment to section 1063.1(c)(8) removing from the definition of a covered claim section 5814 penalties incurred by an insolvent insurer, we agree with the WCAB's decision to rescind the penalties previously awarded by the WCJ. Accordingly, we deny the petition for writ of review.

DISPOSITION

The petition for writ of review is denied. This opinion is final forthwith as to this court... .

Footnote 1. The current petition was properly filed in this appellate district because Petitioners reside in Merced County. (Lab. Code, § 5950; Gov. Code, § 69100, subd. (e).)

Footnote 2. In 2003, section 5814 provided: "When payment of compensation has been unreasonably delayed or refused, either prior to or subsequent to the issuance of an award, the full amount of the order, decision, or award shall be increased by 10 percent. Multiple increases shall not be awarded for repeated delays in making a series of payments due for the same type or specie of benefit unless there has been a legally significant event between the delay and the subsequent delay in payments of the same type or specie of benefits. The question of delay and the reasonableness of the cause therefore shall be determined by the appeals board in accordance with the facts. This delay or refusal shall constitute good cause under Section 5803 to rescind, alter, or amend the order, decision, or award for the purpose of making the increase provided for herein."

Footnote 3. While not relevant here, the WCAB also invited further arguments related to another recent en banc WCAB decision, *Leinon v. Fisherman's Grotto* (2004) 69 Cal. Comp. Cases 995 [Appeals Board en banc opinion], addressing a self–imposed 10 percent penalty under section 4650, subdivision (d).

§ 57.36(A) Penalty Under Labor Code section 5814 as Amended Effective July 1, 2004

Page 1888, Column 2, eighth paragraph, insert following '…between the parties.'

(In *All Tune and Lube, et al v. WCAB (Derboghossian)* (2006) 71 Cal. Comp. Cases 795, the Board upheld a judge's award of multiple penalties in excess of $10,000 under Section 5814, where there was evidence of numerous unreasonable separate and distinct acts of delays   such as delayed home health care, nursing services, transportation, cost of a computer, physical therapy costs, costs of a seeing–eye dog, etc.)

Page 1889, Column 1, third paragraph, insert following '…compensation was due.'

See *Pacific Steel & Engineering, et al v. WCAB (Finley)* (2005) 70 Cal. Comp. Cases 1365, where a timely petition was found under this new law.

Page 1889, Column 1, fifth paragraph, insert following '…June 1, 2004.'

In interpreting this new penalty law, the Court of Appeal, First District, in *New United Motors Manufacturing v. WCAB (Gallegos)* (2006) 71 Cal. Comp. Cases 1037, reversed a Board decision awarding a Labor Code section 5814 penalty, where defendant paid a self–imposed 10 percent penalty within 47 days of being informed by applicant's counsel that permanent disability benefits were being unreasonably withheld. *The Court noted that it does not matter how a defendant became aware of an unreasonably delayed benefit if it pays within 90 days of such notice and pays the 10 percent additional benefit before an "employee claims a penalty".* The Court stated, in part:

New United Motors Manufacturing, Inc. (NUMMI) challenges the Workers' Compensation Appeals Board's (WCAB) refusal to reconsider an order to pay a penalty and attorney fees for delaying payment of workers' compensation benefits to respondent John Gallegos (applicant). The WCAB concluded NUMMI unreasonably delayed providing the benefits, and penalized the company an amount equal to 25 percent of the amount of the benefits delayed. The WCAB further awarded applicant the attorney fees he incurred in enforcing payment of the delayed benefits and penalty.

NUMMI contends the WCAB exceeded its authority because it ordered the penalty based on a misinterpretation of the relevant statute, recently enacted Labor Code section 5814. (Footnote 1)

It further contends no proper basis exists for the WCAB's award of – attorney fees under section 5814.5. We agree, and thus vacate the WCAB's order denying reconsideration.

FACTUAL AND PROCEDURAL BACKGROUND

In June 2001, by a stipulated settlement, applicant was awarded $31,535 in benefits for a work–related injury. Great American Insurance (GAI), a third party administrator (TPA) acting on NUMMI's behalf, made timely payments on the award until September 2002. At that time, GAI transferred responsibility for the case to TPA Gallagher Basset, incorrectly noting in applicant's file that all permanent disability had been paid. Accordingly, payments to applicant ceased.

Applicant thereafter advised his attorney that payments had ceased, and his attorney, on August 12, 2003, sent a letter to NUMMI requesting a benefit printout regarding applicant's award. The letter did not advise NUMMI of the interruption in applicant's payments. NUMMI provided applicant the benefit printout on September 10, 2003.

On November 12, 2003, applicant's attorney sent a letter to NUMMI requesting an explanation why only $17,490 of applicant's $31,535 award had been paid. Forty–seven days later, on December 28, NUMMI issued two checks to applicant, one in the amount of $13,381.43 representing the amount owed for unpaid benefits, and the other in the amount of $1304.14 representing a self–imposed 10 percent late–payment penalty. On February 11, 2004, applicant filed a claim for penalty under section 5814.

The matter proceeded to trial February 14, 2005. Applying section 5814, subdivision (a), operative July 2004, the Workers' Compensation Judge (WCJ) found NUMMI had unreasonably delayed payment of applicant's benefits for 47 days – from the date applicant advised the company of the payment interruption to the date the company paid applicant the delayed benefits plus the 10 percent self–imposed penalty. The WCJ thus imposed a 25 percent penalty on NUMMI, less the $1304.14 NUMMI previously paid, and awarded applicant attorney fees. In so ruling, the WCJ rejected NUMMI's argument that, under subdivision (b) of the new statute, NUMMI's 10 percent self–imposed penalty – paid within 90 days of the date the company discovered the delay and before applicant claimed a penalty under subdivision (a) – precluded the additional penalty.

On October 11, 2005, NUMMI filed a request for reconsideration, which the WCAB denied on December 5 in accordance with the WCJ's recommendation. NUMMI's timely petition for writ of review followed. We thereafter granted the petition and requested supplemental briefing from the parties, which they provided.

DISCUSSION

A. Standard of Review

This case requires us to interpret and apply sections 5814 and 5814.5, enacted in 2004 by Senate Bill 899. Reviewing courts interpret statutes de novo, although the WCAB's interpretation is entitled to great weight unless clearly erroneous. (*Green v. Workers' Comp. Appeals Bd.* (2005) 127 Cal. App. 4th 1426, 1435 [26 Cal. Rptr. 3d 527, 70 Cal. Comp. Cases 294].) While reviewing courts need not accept factual findings that are erroneous, unreasonable, illogical, improbable, or inequitable; they must affirm where those findings are supported by substantial evidence when viewed in light of the entire record and the statutory scheme. (*Ibid.*)

B. Labor Code Section 5814

In interpreting a statute, courts generally look first to the plain or ordinary meaning of the statute's language to determine the Legislature's intent. (*Green, supra,* 127 Cal. App. 4th at p. 1435, citing *DuBois v. Workers' Comp. Appeals Bd.* (1993) 5 Cal. 4th 382, 387–88 [853 P.2d 978, 20 Cal. Rptr. 2d 523, 58 Cal. Comp. Cases 286].) "Every word and clause is given effect so that no part or provision is useless, deprived of meaning, or contradictory." (*Ibid.*)

Moreover, if "more than one interpretation is reasonable, the language is interpreted consistent with the purpose of the statute and the statutory framework as a whole, using rules of construction or legislative history in determining legislative intent." (*Ibid.*)

Section 5814, provides in relevant part:

"(a) When payment of compensation has been unreasonably delayed or refused, either prior to or subsequent to the issuance of an award, the amount of the payment unreasonably delayed or refused shall be increased up to 25 percent or up to ten thousand dollars ($10,000), whichever is less. In any proceeding under this section, the appeals board shall use its discretion to accomplish a fair balance and substantial justice between the parties.

"(b) If a potential violation of this section is discovered by the employer prior to an employee claiming a penalty under this section, the employer, within 90 days of the date of the discovery, may pay a self–imposed penalty in the amount of 10 percent of the amount of the payment unreasonably delayed or refused, along with the amount of the payment delayed or refused. This self–imposed penalty shall be in lieu of the penalty in subdivision (a)." "

The WCAB imposed a 25 percent penalty on NUMMI under subdivision (a) of the statute, adopting the WCJ's finding that NUMMI had unreasonably delayed payment of applicant's benefits for 47 days – from November 12, 2003 when applicant's letter provided notice of the delay until December 28 when the company paid the delayed benefits plus a 10 percent self–imposed penalty. In so ruling, the WCAB rejected applicant's claim that NUMMI unreasonably delayed payment for 15 months – from September 2002 when NUMMI's TPA erroneously stopped payments until December 28, 2003 when NUMMI paid the delayed benefits and self–imposed penalty: "It was not the fifteen (15) month delay that I found to be unreasonable. It was the six week (47 day) delay in payment to applicant, after [NUMMI] had notice of the delay, that I found to be unreasonable."

The WCAB declined to apply section 5814, subdivision (b) to excuse the 25 percent penalty, despite NUMMI's payment of a 10 percent self–imposed penalty before applicant claimed any penalty and less than 90 days after the company discovered the delay. Adopting the WCJ's reasoning, it concluded subdivision (b) was inapplicable because applicant, not NUMMI, first discovered the "potential violation" of section 5814, after examining a benefit printout in September 2003.

We reject the WCAB's conclusion. Section 5814, subdivision (b), in plain and unambiguous terms, permits employers to pay a 10 percent self–imposed penalty "in lieu of the penalty in subdivision (a)" if: (1) "a potential violation of [section 5814] is discovered by the employer prior to an employee claiming a penalty under this section," and (2) the penalty is paid "within 90 days of the date of the [employer's] discovery." By its terms, the statute thus does not limit its application to the event where the employer discovers a potential violation before the employee. (Footnote 2)

Rather, the statute limits its application to the event where, as here, the employer discovers a potential violation *before the employee claims a penalty.* Had the Legislature intended another limitation to apply, it could have drafted it into the statute. It did not.

We also reject the WCAB's suggestion that proper interpretation of the statute's language "is discovered" requires that its application be limited to the event where the employer learns of the potential violation through its own investigation rather than through an employee's or third person's investigation. As respondents point out, such interpretation would encourage employers to carefully monitor administration of workers' compensation benefits to promptly discover and cure delays.

While that certainly is a laudable policy objective, we find nothing in the case law or section 5814's legislative history to support it. Moreover, the legal definition of the term "discovery" is "[t]he act or process of finding or learning something that was previously unknown." (Black's Law Dict. (Pocket Edition 1996) p. 193.) The definition thus focuses on the fact that the discoverer becomes aware of new information. It does not focus on, or even refer to, how or through what source the discoverer becomes aware of it. (Accord *Debro v. Los Angeles Raiders* (2001) 92 Cal. App. 4th 940, 951 [112 Cal. Rptr. 2d 329] [in the context of the limitations period for common law fraud, defining the term "discovery" as a person's awareness of facts sufficient to make a reasonable prudent person suspicious of fraud].) We must conclude that, had the Legislature intended to vary common usage of the term "discovery," it would have made its intention manifest. (*Green, supra,* 127 Cal. App. 4th at p. 1435 [courts generally look first to the plain or ordinary meaning of the statute's language to determine the Legislature's intent], citing *DuBois v. Workers' Comp. Appeals Bd., supra,* 5 Cal. 4th 382, 387–88.)

In summary, the WCAB reads into section 5814, subdivision (b) limitations not provided for by the statute's plain and unambiguous language. The law forbids that: "When the statutory language is clear and unambiguous, there is no room for interpretation and the WCAB must simply enforce the statute according to its plain terms." (*Abney v. Workers' Comp. Appeals Bd.* (2004) 69 Cal. Comp. Cases 1552, 1556–1557 [en banc]; see also *DuBois v. Workers' Comp. Appeals Bd., supra,* 5 Cal. 4th at pp. 387–88.)

In reaching our conclusion, we acknowledge applicant's concern that rejecting the WCAB's interpretation could encourage employers to improperly delay providing employees wage–replacement benefits for 90 days, at a cost increase of just 10 percent. It appears the WCJ may have had that concern in mind in ruling as she did.

But while this concern may be well–founded, we still cannot square the WCAB's interpretation with section 5814's statutory language for at least two reasons. First, the Legislature itself drafted the 90–day safe harbor into the statute. If employers' dilatory tactics are a concern under that safe harbor, it is for the Legislature to amend or delete it. Second, the Legislature included provisions elsewhere in the new law to protect against employers' dilatory tactics, and in turn to discourage abuse of section 5814's safe harbor. Section 5814.6, for example, provides that an employer or insurer that "knowingly violates section 5814 with a frequency that indicates a general business practice is liable for administrative penalties not to exceed $400,000." (Footnote 3)

We found nothing in respondents' briefing that requires the alternative interpretation. Rather, their primary argument appears to be to "den[y] that the imposition [of the 25 percent penalty] was solely due to a 47–day delay in the payment of the permanent disability." They suggest instead that NUMMI's "termination of benefits . . . appears to have been a deliberate and calculated act" that occurred in September 2002 when TPA Gallagher Basset took the case from TPA Great American Insurance. They also suggest a duty to investigate applicant's file arose when TPA Gallagher Basset took the case in September 2002 or, at a minimum, when his attorney requested a benefit printout in August 2003. Because NUMMI failed that duty, they reason, a decision to vacate the WCAB's order would reward NUMMI's "dilatory behavior."

Respondents' argument is unsupported by the WCJ's and WCAB's findings below. In particular, the WCJ found no "deliberate and calculated act" to deprive applicant of benefits, nor any duty to investigate his file in September 2002 or August 2003. Rather, the WCJ found that NUMMI first received notice of an interruption in applicant's benefits on November 12, 2003, and then unreasonably delayed payment for 47 days, until December 28. Respondents did not challenge those factual findings below, so we do not permit them to do so here. (Footnote 4) (*Griffith v. Workers' Comp. Appeals Bd.* (1989) 209 Cal. App. 3d 1260, 1265 [257 Cal. Rptr. 813, 54 Cal. Comp. Cases 145] [issue not raised at trial level waived on appeal].)

C. Labor Code Section 5814.5

NUMMI challenges the WCAB's award of attorney fees to applicant under section 5814.5. That statute provides in relevant part:

"When the payment of compensation has been unreasonably delayed or refused subsequent to the issuance of an award by an employer . . . , the appeals board shall, in addition to increasing the order, decision, or award pursuant to Section 5814, award reasonable attorneys' fees incurred in enforcing the payment of compensation awarded." "

Here, the record does not reveal the amount of attorney fees, if any, applicant incurred in enforcing payment of the unreasonably delayed benefits. It reveals only that, after receiving notice of the delayed benefits from applicant's

attorney, NUMMI paid the benefits and a 10 percent penalty on its own initiative and in accordance with section 5814, subdivision (b). Given the undeveloped state of the record, we are unwilling to decide here whether the WCAB's award of attorney fees was proper. Accordingly, we remand to the WCAB to reconsider the issue after further proceedings.

D. Applicant's Request for Attorney Fees

Applicant requests an award of the attorney fees he incurred in responding to this petition under section 5801 on the ground the petition "has no reasonable basis." For the reasons stated above, we disagree. Accordingly, we deny his request.

DISPOSITION

The order denying reconsideration is vacated, and the matter is returned to the WCAB with directions to grant reconsideration, to reverse its order imposing a 25 percent penalty against NUMMI, and to reconsider its award of attorney fees after further proceedings... .

Footnote 1. All statutory references herein are to the Labor Code unless otherwise indicated.

Footnote 2. As NUMMI notes, employees often will discover potential violations before their employers. While the employee likely manages only one workers' compensation check per month – the one he expects to receive from the employer – the employer or its administrator may manage hundreds or even thousands of them.

Footnote 3. In any event, we do not believe this result is likely to encourage employers to improperly delay payments for 90 days because the employer will lose the benefit provided under section 5814, subdivision (b) if the employee claims a penalty under the statute within the 90–day period. Employers are not likely to take that risk.

Footnote 4. We also decline to address applicant's argument, raised here for the first time, that the WCAB improperly applied the new version of section 5814, operative July 2004, rather than the earlier version. (*Griffith, supra*, 209 Cal. App. 3d at p. 1265; see also *Abney, supra*, 69 Cal. Comp. Cases at p. 1560.)

The extension of reasonable attorney fees for unreasonable delay or refusal to pay compensation subsequent to an award only applies to private employers for injuries sustained on or after January 1, 2003. See *Khan, supra.*

Page 1892, Column 2, ninth paragraph, insert following '…953–957.'

For a concurring opinion by the First District Court, see *United Airlines, et al v. WCAB* (2005) 70 Cal. Comp. Cases 804, an unpublished decision.

Stipulations and orders approved and finalized by a Workers' Compensation Judge are not subject to retroactive application of the new Section 5814. *The Earthgrains Company et al v. WCAB (Adams)* (2005) 70 Cal. Comp. Cases 1348.

In *Khan v. WCAB* (2006) 71 Cal. Comp. Cases 1168, the Board amended a judge's award of a maximum penalty for defendant's failure to pay applicant's attorney fee in a timely manner because the payment check was sent to the wrong address, and awarded 10 percent of the payment and ordered it *paid to the applicant* where his counsel's check was delayed. The Board stated, in part:

> By providing for the imposition of a penalty, "up to 25 percent or up to ten thousand dollars ($10,000), whichever is less," the statute plainly contemplates that the degree of penalty imposed will be adjusted depending upon the circumstances of the delay. Thus, the maximum penalty should apply in those cases where the conduct was most egregious, such as intentional bad faith refusal to pay.

> This case does not present the type of concern that justifies imposition of the maximum penalty. Although defendant offers no good excuse to explain how they sent the check to the wrong address, it was stipulated that the error was promptly corrected when the check was returned by the postal service. The evidence does not show a willful disregard of the defendant' [*sic*] legal duties or the rights of the applicant or his attorneys. Nevertheless, there was a delay and absent any evidence of a good excuse, the delay is deserving of a penalty. In our view, an appropriate penalty in this case is 10% of the delayed amount, and we will amend the award to provide for that penalty, payable to the applicant. (See *Winters v. Workers' Comp. Appeals Bd.* (2000) 65 Cal. Comp. Cases 1354 (writ den.); *Mintzer v. Workers' Comp. Appeals Bd.* (1996) 61 Cal. Comp. Cases 1491 (writ den.).).... .

The extension of reasonable attorney's fees for unreasonable delay to pay compensation subsequent to an award only applies to private employers for injuries sustained on or after January 1, 2003. See *Kahn, supra.*

Page 1892, Column 2, tenth paragraph, insert following '...holdings.'

Multiple Penalties

Multiple penalties for separate unreasonable delays totaling in excess of $10,000 was held not to violate the $10,000 cap of penalties under the SB 899 amendment to Section 5814 in *All Tune and Lube, et al v. WCAB (Derboghossian)* (2006) 71 Cal. Comp. Cases 795.

§ 58.0   REOPENING A CASE AFTER AN ORDER OR FINDINGS AND AWARD HAS BEEN ISSUED BY THE APPEALS BOARD

§ 58.1   On Grounds That the Disability Has Recurred, Increased, Diminished, or Terminated

Page 1901, Column 1, second paragraph, insert following '…332.'

In *Sarabi v. WCAB* (2007) 72 Cal. Comp. Cases 778, the Court of Appeal, First District, annulled a Board decision denying an applicant temporary disability indemnity benefits where the Board concluded it did not have jurisdiction to award temporary disability indemnity more than five years after the date of injury even though the applicant had filed a Petition to Reopen for new and further disability within the five–year period. The Court stated, in part:

Petitioner Mike Sarabi challenges an order of the Workers' Compensation Appeals Board (Board) holding it had no jurisdiction to award him additional temporary total disability (TTD) benefits for a period commencing more than five years after the date of his injury. The Board's holding was in error, and we therefore annul its order and remand the case for a new order consistent with this opinion.

I. Factual and Procedural Background

Sarabi, a night manager at Narsi's Hofbrau, sustained an industrial injury to his right shoulder on *August 28, 1999.* In a findings and award dated December 15, 2000, the workers' compensation judge (WCJ) awarded Sarabi TTD benefits from August 29, 1999 through December 2, 1999, and found further medical treatment was necessary.

Sarabi underwent right shoulder surgery on *January 18, 2002, and filed a petition to reopen* on November 15, 2002, alleging that "a change in [his] condition [had] result[ed] in further periods of temporary disability." On May 26, 2004, orthopedic surgeon Dr. Gary P. McCarthy stated Sarabi was temporarily disabled and needed further right shoulder surgery in order to reach a permanent and stationary status. He stated he had "repeatedly requested" that this surgery take place. Sarabi was then evaluated by an agreed medical examiner (AME), Dr. Henry L. Edington, who reported on August 17, 2004, that Sarabi had a TTD and needed right shoulder surgery. According to Narsi's answer to Sarabi's petition for a writ of review, the surgery was postponed several times because Sarabi needed to be treated for a non–industrial condition before he could be medically cleared for surgery.

Also according to Narsi's answer, Dr. Edington issued a supplemental report on *October 7, 2005,* stating that *if* Sarabi could not be medically cleared for right shoulder surgery, he *could* be considered permanent and stationary as of August 17, 2005, one year to the day after Dr. Edington's initial report. (Footnote 1) (Italics added.) Prior to the supplemental report, Narsi had been voluntarily providing Sarabi with TTD benefits since December 26, 2000, but, after receiving the report, it informed Sarabi on *November 14, 2005,* that "[p]ayments are ending 11/03/05 because Dr. Edington has declared that you are permanent and stationary as of 08/17/05." "Benefits were paid to you as [TTD] from 12/26/2000 through 11/03/2005. Included in this amount is an overpayment totaling $3,516.45." (Footnote 2)

The case returned to the WCJ for a mandatory settlement conference on December 16, 2005. The parties agreed that the issue to be decided was whether Sarabi was entitled to additional TTD benefits beginning August 17, 2005, the date Narsi terminated its voluntary payment of TTD benefits based on Dr. Edington's supplemental report.

On June 28, 2006, the WCJ issued a Findings and Award granting Sarabi's request for additional TTD indemnity "from August 17, 2005 to date and continuing." The WCJ stated there was jurisdiction to issue the award even if the additional TTD arose on August 17, 2005, because Sarabi had filed a timely petition to reopen. He also noted that treatment for Sarabi's non–industrial condition was required before he could undergo surgery necessary to cure or relieve him of the effects of his industrial injury, citing to the "general rule . . . that liability to furnish medical treatment can include a duty to treat for non–industrial conditions which may be interfering with the medical treatment necessary for the treatment of the industrially caused condition."

Narsi filed a petition for reconsideration, claiming there was no jurisdiction to award TTD benefits because Sarabi's petition to reopen was "skeletal" and because "jurisdiction was lost when the applicant was found to be permanent and stationary by the [AME]." Sarabi responded that TTD benefits should not have been terminated on August 17, 2005, and that Narsi was estopped from objecting to the petition to reopen, having voluntarily paid TTD benefits and having never questioned his TTD status before that date. In his report and recommendation, the WCJ recommended denying Narsi's petition for reconsideration, stating that "so long as the applicant's timely [p]etitions to [r]eopen remained pending, the [Board] continued to have jurisdiction to act upon those petitions and to award the applicant benefits caused by any 'new and further disability.' " He also noted there was no authority supporting Narsi's position that the Board loses jurisdiction to award temporary disability benefits when a medical examiner considers a worker's injuries to be " 'permanent and stationary.' " (Footnote 3)

The Board in a 2–1 decision granted Narsi's petition for reconsideration, holding it had no jurisdiction to award TTD benefits commencing August 17, 2005, and that Sarabi "shall take nothing on the petitions to reopen." The Board held that although an award of TTD benefits commencing August 17, 2004, may have been supported by Dr. Edington's initial report that surgery was necessary, there was no jurisdiction to award, as the WCJ did, TTD benefits beginning August 17, 2005, which was over five years after the date of injury. The dissent stated that because Dr. Edington found on August 17, 2004 that Sarabi was temporarily totally disabled and needed surgery, and there was no evidence that he stopped needing the surgery between then and August 17, 2005, there was continuing jurisdiction to award TTD benefits. Sarabi filed a timely petition for a writ of review, which this court granted.

II. DISCUSSION

A. The Board Had Jurisdiction to Order Additional TTD Benefits Because Sarabi Filed a Timely Petition to Reopen and His New and Further Disability Commenced within Five Years of the Date of His Injury.

1. Sarabi Filed a Timely Petition to Reopen.

Under Labor Code (Footnote 4) section 5410, an injured worker who has previously received workers' compensation benefits either voluntarily paid by the employer or pursuant to an award is entitled to claim benefits for "new and further disability" within five years of the date of injury. Section 5803 permits the reopening of a previously adjudicated case for "good cause" upon a petition filed by a party, also within five years from the date of injury. If a petition to reopen under either section is filed within the five–year period, the Board has jurisdiction to decide the matter beyond the five–year period. (§ 5804; *Bland v. Workers' Comp. Appeals Bd.* (1970) 3 Cal. 3d 324, 329, fn. 3; *see also General Foundry Service v. Workers' Comp. Appeals Bd.* (1986) 42 Cal. 3d 331, 337 ["The Board clearly has the power to continue its jurisdiction beyond the five–year period when an application is made within that period"].)

Here, Sarabi filed the pertinent petition to reopen on November 15, 2002, less than five years from the date of his injury. Although Narsi argues the Board lacked jurisdiction to award TTD benefits because the petition was "skeletal," our Supreme Court has held that very broad or general petitions are sufficient. (*E.g., Bland v. Workers' Comp. Appeals Bd., supra,* 3 Cal. 3d at p. 329 [in light of the "strong policy" in favor of liberal treatment of disability claims, petition to reopen asking the Board to " 'take such steps as may be necessary to a redetermination of this matter' " is sufficient].) Indeed, an applicant has been excused from even filing a petition to reopen where the WCJ stated in a notice of hearing that the matter to be adjudicated was whether the applicant was entitled to additional benefits. (*Zurich Ins. Co. v. Workers' Comp. Appeals Bd.* (1973) 9 Cal. 3d 848, 852 [absence of petition could not have prejudiced employer and applicant could have been lulled by WCJ's notice into thinking there was no need to file petition].)

Sarabi's petition to reopen cited sections 5410 and 5803, alleged a "change in [his condition]" and requested further temporary disability benefits—the precise issue later adjudicated by the WCJ and the Board. Although the petition did not specify what the "change in . . . condition" was, it was sufficient to inform Narsi of the nature of the claim and to confer jurisdiction on the Board to determine whether he had suffered a new and further disability under section 5410, or whether there was good cause to reopen the prior award under section 5803. Moreover, Narsi can not persuasively claim it was prejudiced by the "skeletal" nature of the petition to reopen, as it was fully aware of Sarabi's condition throughout the years, making voluntary TTD payments and participating in various proceedings including having AMEs examine Sarabi to evaluate his disability. Because Sarabi filed a timely petition to reopen that was still pending at the time the matter returned to the WCJ for a hearing, the Board had continuing jurisdiction to render a decision in the matter after the five–year limitations period had expired.

2. Sarabi Suffered a New and Further Disability within Five Years of the Date of His Injury.

For an applicant to recover additional temporary disability benefits, he or she must not only have filed a petition to reopen within five years from the date of injury, but must also have suffered a "new and further disability" within that five–year period, unless there is otherwise "good cause" to reopen the prior award. (*Ruffin v. Olson Glass Co.* (1987) 52 Cal. Comp. Cases 335, 343 (*Ruffin* (Footnote 5)).) An injured worker therefore cannot confer jurisdiction on the Board by filing a petition to reopen an award before the five–year period has expired for anticipated new and further disability to occur thereafter. (*Ibid.*)

" ' "[N]ew and further disability" has been defined to mean disability . . . result[ing] from some demonstrable change in an employee's condition,' [citation]" including a " 'gradual increase in disability.' " (*Nicky Blair's Restaurant v. Workers' Comp. Appeals Bd.* (1980) 109 Cal. App. 3d 941, 955.) " ' "Historically, a change in physical condition necessitating further medical treatment ha[s] been considered new and further disability . . . . [Citation.]" [Citations.] "Thus, [c]ommonly, new and further disability refers to a recurrence of temporary disability, a new need for medical treatment, or the change of a temporary disability into a permanent disability." [Citations.]' " (*Ibid.*) " 'Good cause' " includes a mistake of fact, a mistake of law disclosed by a subsequent appellate court ruling on the same point in another case, inadvertence, newly discovered evidence, or fraud. (*Id.* at p. 956.)

As the Board properly noted, Dr. Edington's opinion of August 17, 2004, that Sarabi had a TTD and required right shoulder surgery may have supported a finding of TTD beginning August 17, 2004. Dr. McCarthy had also been recommending surgery for some time before that date. Although this court held in *Hartsuiker, supra,* 12 Cal. App. 4th at page 213, that the Board cannot reserve jurisdiction to award additional benefits for *possible* surgery to take place after the five–year period, here, the need for surgery was clear as early as May 26, 2004, when Dr. McCarthy made his recommendation for right shoulder surgery, or at the latest by August 17, 2004, when Dr. Edington opined that Sarabi had a TTD and needed right shoulder surgery. Because Sarabi's disability worsened and further medical treatment in the form of right shoulder surgery became necessary within the five–year period, Sarabi suffered "new and further disability" within the meaning of section 5410 and the Board had jurisdiction to award him additional TTD benefits. (Footnote 6)

B. It Was Not Error for the WCJ to Award Benefits Commencing August 17, 2005, Because There Was No Need to Award Benefits Before That Date, As Narsi Was Making Voluntary TTD Payments Until Then.

The Board found the WCJ erred by awarding benefits commencing August 17, 2005, because this was more than five years after the date of Sarabi's injury. Although the Board was correct in holding that it has no jurisdiction to award benefits for a new and further disability arising more than five years from the date of injury, its conclusion that Sarabi was not entitled to additional benefits was in error.

The Board correctly held that the WCJ erred in stating there was jurisdiction to award additional benefits even if Sarabi's new and further disability arose after the five–year limitations period. However, the WCJ's conclusion that Sarabi was entitled to benefits commencing August 17, 2005, and continuing, was supported by the record, as the evidence showed that Sarabi's new and further disability arose within the five–year period, and that benefits were to begin on August 17, 2005, only because that was the date Narsi terminated its voluntary payments. In fact, the Board correctly acknowledged that Dr. Edington's report of August 17, 2004, may have supported an award of additional benefits because it was within the five–year limitations period. Because nothing prior to August 17, 2005, was at issue, there was no need for Sarabi to request, or for the WCJ to award, benefits commencing at any time before that date.

To deny TTD benefits on the facts of this case would permit an employer, knowing that an applicant has filed a timely petition to reopen and has suffered a new and further disability within the pertinent five–year period, to make voluntary payments until after the five–year period has elapsed, so that any award for additional benefits would be jurisdictionally barred as commencing more than five years after the date of injury. This would be an unjust result and would conflict with the longstanding rule that " ' "[l]imitations provisions in workmen's compensation law must be liberally construed in favor of the employee unless otherwise compelled by the language of the statute, and such enactment should not be interpreted in a manner which will result in" a loss of compensation.' " (*Martino v. Workers' Comp. Appeals Bd., supra*, 103 Cal. App. 4th at p. 489, quoting *Bland v. Workers' Comp. Appeals Bd., supra*, 3 Cal. 3d at pp. 330–331.)

III. Disposition

The Board's order is hereby annulled. The case is remanded to the Board for a new order consistent with this opinion... .

Footnote 1. The parties have not provided this court with a copy of Dr. Edington's supplemental report.

Footnote 2. It appears this "overpayment" is for payments Narsi made to Sarabi from August 17, 2005 (the date Narsi alleges Sarabi became permanent and stationary) and November 3, 2005 (the date Narsi terminated payments).

Footnote 3. Narsi does not dispute that Dr. Edington's opinion that Sarabi's condition could be considered permanent and stationary as of August 17, 2005, presupposed that he could not be medically cleared for right shoulder surgery. In fact, as Narsi acknowledges, Sarabi was later cleared for the surgery.

Footnote 4. All further statutory references are to the Labor Code unless otherwise stated.

Footnote 5. *Ruffin* is a writ–denied case and therefore has no stare decisis effect, but both our Supreme Court in *Nickelsberg v. Workers' Comp. Appeals Bd.* (1991) 54 Cal. 3d 288, 300 fn. 9, and the Court of Appeal in *Hartsuiker v. Workers' Comp. Appeals Bd.* (1993) 12 Cal. App. 4th 209, 218 fn. 5 quoted from it, agreeing that an award for additional benefits beyond the five–year period where the new and further disability did not arise within that period "would be nothing more than a subterfuge to avoid the limitation of jurisdiction contained in . . [s]ections 5410 and 5804." (*Ruffin, supra*, 52 Cal. Comp. Cases at p. 343.)

Footnote 6. Although Sarabi's new and further disability did not occur until after he filed his petition to reopen, an applicant is not required "to adhere to a strict chronological sequence when filing documents." (See *Martino v. Workers' Comp. Appeals Bd.* (2002) 103 Cal. App. 4th 485, 490 [applicant entitled to benefits even though incident supporting the claims made in her petition to reopen occurred after the filing of the petition].)

In *Atlantic Mutual Insurance Company v. WCAB (Brewer)* (2006) 71 Cal. Comp. Cases 244, the Board held it did not have jurisdiction to set aside a finding by a judge regarding insurance coverage under Labor Code section 5804, where the judge's finding became final more than five years after the date of injury and the fact that the insurance carrier did not request the finding of coverage be set aside until more than five years after the injury. In his opinion, the judge stated, in part:

Estoppel: Atlantic Mutual Insurance Company made several appearances before this Board and stipulated that it had coverage for the San Francisco Chronicle on May 22, 1998. The Stipulations were set forth in the November 10, 2003 mandatory settlement conference statement and were recorded in to the minutes by the WCJ on April 1, 2004. As a result of those stipulations, this court issued a Finding of Fact concerning coverage and issued an award against Atlantic Mutual Insurance Company on June 28, 2004. Said Finding of Fact and Award became final (and the law of this case) on July 23, 2004, the day the reconsideration period ended.

In this court's opinion, Atlantic Mutual Insurance Company is estopped to deny coverage for the San Francisco Chronicle on the date of applicant's injury. This court as well as the applicant relied on the stipulations made by the attorney for Atlantic Mutual Insurance Company concerning coverage. Had there been no stipulation concerning coverage, there never would have been an award issued against Atlantic Mutual Insurance Company.

Jurisdiction: Labor Code Section 5804 states that no award of compensation shall be rescinded, altered, or amended after five years from the date of injury except upon a petition by a party in interest filed within such five years. As is stated above, the Findings of Fact concerning coverage and the award based thereon became final on July 23, 2004. Obviously, this date is more than five years from the date of injury. On November 23, 2004, Atlantic Mutual Insurance Company advised this board of the mistake it had made concerning coverage. It is respectfully submitted that Atlantic Mutual Insurance Company was too late. By the terms of Labor Code Section 5804, this Board no longer has jurisdiction to set aside Findings of Fact (and Awards) as the five year period has expired…

Concerning the estoppel issue, the California Supreme Court held in Granco Steel, Inc. v WCAB (Robinson) [(1968) 68 Cal. 2d 191, 65 Cal. Rptr. 287, 436 P.2d 287, 33 Cal. Comp. Cases 50] that an insurance carrier was estopped to deny coverage when the representation of coverage was relied on by the applicant and the WCAB trial court in rendering its decision. Granco Steel involved representations made by a broker concerning coverage. In the instant case, reliance was made upon representations by Atlantic Mutual's attorney representing that his client had coverage. All of the elements concerning estoppel set forth by the California Supreme Court, at page 59, are present in the instant case: (1) the party to be estopped must be apprised of the facts (Atlantic Mutual was well aware that it was not the carrier despite Mr. Willens' stipulation that it was); (2) the party must intend that his conduct be acted upon or must so act that the parties asserting the estoppel had a right to believe that it was so intended (both applicant and this court relied on the representation concerning coverage in this courts' [sic] decisions were based on said representation); (3) the other party must be ignorant of the true state of facts (Mr. Brewer only knew that his checks were being sent by Atlantic Mutual; he had no idea concerning any adjustment contract between Atlantic Mutual's subsidiary and Reliance Insurance Company); (4) he must rely upon the conduct to his injury (Mr. Brewer is currently not receiving the benefit of his award and obviously, has relied on the representations concerning coverage to his injury). [Emphasis by WCJ]"… .

Page 1905, Column 1, tenth paragraph, insert following '…process.'

Although causation of an employee's condition at the time of the original decision cannot be re–litigated as "new and further disability" under Labor Code section 5410, such an issue may be re–opened if "good cause" is established under Section 5803. *Aliano v. WCAB* (1979) 44 Cal. Comp. Cases 1156. See also *Walker v. WCAB* (2006) 71 Cal. Comp. Cases 1077.

§ 59.0   RECOUPMENT OF OVERPAYMENT –RESTITUTION

Page 1910, Column 2, after first paragraph insert

In *Act I Personnel Services, et. al. v. WCAB (Denny)* (2007) 72 Cal. Comp. Cases 469, the Board allowed defendant a credit for overpayment of permanent disability against any future permanent disability indemnity payments but denied credit against future medical care. The Board noted that credit against future medical treatment, while not inequitable per se, is not strongly favored since a denial may undermine the purpose and policy behind Labor Code section 4600 entitling the applicant to all reasonable and necessary medical expenses. Allowing credit, said the Board, would discourage applicant from undergoing necessary medical care.

Intentionally blank

§ 64.0   SUBROGATION

Page 1926, Column 1, following last paragraph that ends '...Lab. Code Sec. 3853' insert the following:

In *McKinnon v. Otis Elevator Company* (2007) 72 Cal. Comp. Cases 427, the Court of Appeal, Third District, in holding that an employee's claim against an alleged tortfeasor was not precluded when the employer settled with the alleged tortfeasor but failed to adequately notify its employee of its subrogation lawsuit (with knowledge of this failure by the tortfeasor, stated, in part:

In this matter involving workers' compensation and an employer's subrogation action against an alleged third–party tortfeasor, we construe the employer/employee notice and consent obligations of Labor Code sections 3853, 3859 and 3860, subdivision (a). (Footnote 1)

We conclude that when an employer fails to adequately notify its employee of its subrogation lawsuit and proposed settlement involving the alleged third–party tortfeasor and fails to obtain the employee's consent to the settlement of that suit, and when the settling alleged third–party tortfeasor, prior to settlement, was or reasonably should have been aware of the possibility of the employee's claim for damages against the tortfeasor, the alleged tortfeasor cannot use the mere settlement and dismissal of the employer's subrogation action to bar the employee from maintaining her own action for damages against the alleged tortfeasor. (§§ 3853, 3859, 3860, subd. (a).) The employee's action for damages against the alleged tortfeasor, however, must account for any workers' compensation benefits paid to the employee, or to be paid, so as to preclude double recovery for the employee and double liability for the tortfeasor.

Accordingly, we reverse the summary judgment in favor of the alleged third–party tortfeasor here...

DISCUSSION

The issue in this appeal is whether the trial court erroneously granted summary judgment against Employee in favor of the alleged third–party tortfeasor, Otis. This issue requires us to construe the notice and consent provisions of sections 3853, 3859 and 3860, subdivision (a). This presents a question of law based on undisputed facts that we determine independently. (*Reader's Digest Assn. v. Franchise Tax Bd.* (2001) 94 Cal. App. 4th 1240, 1245 [115 Cal. Rptr. 2d 53].) We conclude the trial court erroneously granted summary judgment to Otis.

First, some background.

The basic bargain underlying the workers' compensation system is that an injured worker forgoes the pursuit of tort damages against her employer in return for an expeditious financial resolution of her workplace injury. (*Shoemaker v. Myers* (1990) 52 Cal. 3d 1, 15–16 [801 P.2d 1054, 276 Cal. Rptr. 303, 55 Cal. Comp. Cases 494].)

"The California workers['] compensation scheme not only fixes the right of an employee who suffers a job–related injury to recover compensation from his or her employer . . . [,] but also significantly defines the rights of action of both an employee and an employer in the event that a third party is responsible for the employee's injury [§ 3850 et seq.]. These statutory provisions [i.e., § 3850 et seq.] are 'primarily procedural.' (*Roe v. Workmen's Comp. Appeals Bd.* (1974) 12 Cal. 3d 884, 889 [528 P.2d 771, 117 Cal. Rptr. 683, 39 Cal. Comp. Cases 791].) They seek to insure, first, that, regardless of whether it is the employee or the employer who sues the third party, both the employee and the employer recover their due, and, second, that, as far as possible, the third party need defend only one lawsuit.

"To these ends, the workers['] compensation statutes set up procedures which guarantee an employee and an employer notice of each other's action, authorize the employee and the employer to intervene in each other's lawsuit, provide for mandatory consolidation of separate employee and employer actions, and grant the employee and the employer the right to share in each other's judgment or settlement." (*County of San Diego v. Sanfax Corp.* (1977) 19 Cal. 3d 862, 872 [568 P.2d 363, 140 Cal. Rptr. 638, 42 Cal. Comp. Cases 866] (*Sanfax*).) In this way, "*employer and employee third–party actions are interchangeable*" under the workers' compensation scheme. (*Ibid.*)

The statutory scheme of section 3850 et seq. is designed to prevent double recovery by an employee or an employer, and to preclude double liability being imposed on a third–party tortfeasor. (*O'Dell v. Freightliner Corp.* (1992) 10 Cal. App. 4th 645, 653 [12 Cal. Rptr. 2d 774, 57 Cal. Comp. Cases 689] (*O'Dell*); *Sanfax, supra,* 19 Cal. 3d at p. 873; *Board of Administration v. Glover* (1983) 34 Cal. 3d 906, 911–912, 917 [671 P.2d 834, 196 Cal. Rptr. 330, 49 Cal. Comp. Cases 807] (*Glover*).) This statutory scheme is designed to hold the third party liable, "as far as possible" (*Sanfax, supra,* at p. 872) in " 'one total action,' " " 'for all the wrong his tortfeasance brought about' [citation] regardless of whether it is the employee or the employer who brings suit." (*Sanfax, supra,* at p. 873, italics omitted; *Glover, supra,* at p. 912.)

As we have noted, at issue here are sections 3853, 3859, and 3860, subdivision (a) of the statutory scheme codified in section 3850 et seq.

To set the stage, though, we must begin with section 3852, which provides in relevant part:

" "The claim of an employee . . . for [workers'] compensation does not affect his or her claim or right of action for all damages proximately resulting from the injury or death against any person other than the employer. Any employer who pays, or becomes obligated to pay [workers'] compensation . . . may likewise make a claim or bring an action against the third person." "

Section 3853 pertains to notice regarding employee or employer third–party lawsuits and specifies:

" "If either the employee or the employer brings an action against such third person, he shall forthwith give to the other a copy of the complaint by personal service or certified mail. Proof of such service shall be filed in such action. If the action is brought by either the employer or employee, the other may, at any time before trial on the facts, join as party plaintiff or shall consolidate his action, if brought independently." "

Here, Employer did not serve Employee with a copy of its subrogation complaint for negligence against Otis, but merely provided a letter to Employee, dated June 10, 2003, from the attorney for its workers' compensation insurer. This letter stated:

" "I represent American Commercial Claims Administrators [ACCA] in its subrogation against Otis Elevator. We are representing ACCA in an attempt to recover the benefits paid to you or on your behalf as a result of the incident on Otis Elevator which occurred on May 24, 2002.

'I am interested to know whether or not you are pursuing a third[–]party action against the elevator company and whether or not you have filed a lawsuit. If you could please provide me with the information to that cnd I would appreciate it. You can contact me by telephone or by mail at the above address." "

About a week later, Employee responded to this letter, stating:

" "In response to you [sic] request I am undecided at this time if I plan to pursue a third part [sic] action. It depends on the outcome of my foot and toes." "

Indisputably, Employer did not satisfy the notice requirements of section 3853. It did not serve, either personally or by certified mail, its subrogation complaint on Employee. It did not even mention in its June 10, 2003, letter that there was a subrogation *complaint or lawsuit*. It suggested that Employee could pursue an independent third–party action, and it said nothing about the mandatory consolidation of such an action required by section 3853. (See *Carden v. Otto* (1974) 37 Cal. App. 3d 887 [112 Cal. Rptr. 749, 39 Cal. Comp. Cases 318] (*Carden*) [to satisfy section 3853 requires *"proper notice"* (*id.* at p. 896); "Since the right to intervene exists up to the time of trial on the facts, proper notice of the trial date is essential. Proper and orderly procedure dictates that the notice be a formal one and not be left to informal communication between counsel" (*id.* at p. 897)].)...

We also observe that because third–party actions under the section 3850 et seq. statutory scheme always involve either a fully knowledgeable employer or employee (§ 3852), sections 3853, 3859 and 3860, subdivision (a), specifically impose their notice and consent obligations upon employers and employees. Section 3860, subdivision (a), however, adds that a release or settlement is invalid "as to *any party thereto*" if the nonsettling employer or employee has not received notice that provides an opportunity for full recovery. (Italics added.)

Consequently, what we distill from sections 3853, 3859 and 3860, subdivision (a), and from *Glover, Pope, INA,* and *O'Dell*–as applied to the situation before us in which an employer, who settles with a "knowing" alleged third–party tortfeasor, fails to provide notice and obtain consent as to its employee–is the following. Under section 3853, the employer must provide the employee with a copy of the subrogation complaint by personal service or certified mail, and must file proof of such service in that action. Under section 3859, a settling employer has a duty to obtain the employee's consent to the settlement. Under section 3860, subdivision (a), a settling employer has a duty to provide notice to the employee in a way that provides the employee with the opportunity to recover all damages the employee has suffered. The sued and/or settling alleged third–party tortfeasor does not directly have notice and consent duties under these statutes. But if that alleged tortfeasor, prior to settlement, is or reasonably should be aware of the possibility of the employee's claim for damages, such a "knowing" tortfeasor settles with the employer at the peril of being sued by the employee if the employer has failed to carry out its statutory notice and consent duties to the employee.

Here, there is no question that Employer failed to adequately notify Employee of its subrogation complaint against Otis. (§ 3853.) There is also no question that Employer failed to obtain Employee's consent to a settlement of that lawsuit and failed to notify Employee of that settlement in a way that would allow Employee the opportunity to recover all damages she had suffered. (§§ 3859, 3860, subd. (a), respectively.) And there is no question that Otis, prior to settlement, was or reasonably should have been aware of the possibility of Employee's claim for damages, given that the Employer's negligence–based subrogation complaint against Otis specified all of the identifying and factual details of Employee's accident and injury involving the Otis elevator. (*Glover, supra,* 34 Cal. 3d at p. 919.) Consequently, the settlement and dismissal of Employer's subrogation lawsuit against Otis does not bar Employee's lawsuit against Otis. (See *Roski, supra,* 17 Cal. App. 3d at pp. 846–847.) As to Employee's lawsuit against Otis, Employee will not be allowed double recovery and Otis will not be subjected to double liability. (See *American Home, supra,* 48 Cal. App. 4th at pp. 1903, 1908–1909.)

Our conclusion comports with the following two bedrock principles underlying the section 3850 et seq. statutory scheme:

One, this scheme "seek[s] *to insure, first,* that, regardless of whether it is the employee or the employer who sues the third party, both the employee and the employer recover their due, *and, second, that, as far as possible,* the third party need defend only one lawsuit." (*Sanfax, supra,* 19 Cal. 3d at p. 872, italics added.)

And two, the "fair implementation of subrogation rights within th[is] statutory scheme, as well as general principles of equity, compel [the] result here" that forecloses the Employer/Otis settlement and dismissal from barring Employee's action against Otis. (*Glover, supra,* 34 Cal. 3d at p. 916; see also, *American Home, supra,* 48 Cal. App. 4th at pp. 1908–1909.) It is unfair to allow Otis, a "knowing" alleged tortfeasor, to rely on section 3853 to argue that Employee's action against Otis is time–barred on the basis that Employee failed to join in or consolidate with Employer's subrogation action, when there was no compliance with section 3853's notice requirement to Employee.

DISPOSITION

The judgment in favor of Otis is reversed. Employee (McKinnon) shall recover her costs on appeal... .

Footnote 1. Hereafter, undesignated section references are to the Labor Code.

Page 1927, Column 1, delete third paragraph, beginning 'The action...' and ending '...cases 866.' and insert:

The action, whether by the injured employee or the employer or its workers' compensation insurance carrier, must be brought within the statutory time limitation commencing from the date of injury. *County of San Diego v. Sanfax Corp.* (1971) 42 Cal. Comp. Cases 866.

Page 1931, Column 1, sixth paragraph, delete beginning 'There is a...' through ...following year' and insert:

There is a *two–year statute of limitations* for filing a claim of personal injury or wrongful death against a third–party in California. Code of Civil Procedure section 335.1 (former Section 340(3)). The two–year statute of limitations accrues on the date of the injury of the following second year.

Page 1933, Column 2, second paragraph, insert following '...are denominated.':

However, under Code of Civil Procedure section 338(a), an action may be brought within *three years* if it is an action upon a "liability" created by statute other than penalty forfeiture.

Further, the civil statute of limitations may be tolled while a plaintiff is pursuing a workers' compensation claim where the employer does not carry workers' compensation insurance inasmuch as under Labor Code section 3706 an action under that section differs markedly from a common law negligence action. Commenting on this is *Valdez v. Himmelfarb* (2006) 71 Cal. Comp. Cases 1574, the Court of Appeal, Second District, stated, in part:

An employer who failed to carry workers' compensation insurance as required by law is being sued by a former employee for personal injury, unfair competition and declaratory relief. Plaintiff Elias Valdez claims he was injured in the course of his employment as a cook, janitor, dishwasher and gardener at defendants' Malibu restaurant. Defendants' motion for summary judgment did not dispute

Valdez's allegation they failed to carry workers' compensation insurance for their employees. Rather, defendants contended Valdez's causes of action for negligence and declaratory relief were barred by the one–year statute of limitations in effect at the time of his injury and his unfair competition cause of action failed to include a prayer for relief within the trial court's jurisdiction. The trial court granted defendants' summary judgment motion and sanctioned Valdez and his attorneys jointly in the sum of $54,601 for bringing the action in bad faith.

Valdez filed a timely appeal from the judgment for defendants but no appeal was filed on behalf of Valdez or his attorneys from the sanction order.

As we shall explain, the trial court committed prejudicial error in its analysis of the applicable statutes of limitations. This error not only requires reversal of the judgment for defendants but undermines the basis for the court's sanction order. Although we have no jurisdiction to reverse that order, (Footnote 1) it would be an abuse of discretion for the trial court, after remand, not to reconsider its order under Code of Civil Procedure section 1008, subdivision (c).

FACTS AND PROCEEDINGS BELOW

The principal facts are undisputed.

In 2001 Valdez filed a timely workers' compensation claim with the Workers' Compensation Appeals Board (WCAB) alleging he injured his lower back while removing a tree stump at the direction of his employer and in the course of his employment at the Mission Club where he worked as an "assistant cook, laborer, janitor, dishwasher and gardener."

In May 2003 Valdez filed the present action for personal injury, unfair competition and declaratory relief alleging the Mission Club was a business operated by defendant Himmelfarb and others who "intentionally and without good cause . . . failed and refused to maintain workers' compensation coverage for the benefit of their employees all as required by law." (Footnote 2)

In his unverified complaint Valdez alleged he discovered defendants' lack of workers' compensation insurance in August 2002.

Defendants answered with a general denial and moved for summary judgment and sanctions against Valdez and his attorneys.

As to the personal injury cause of action defendants based their motion on evidence "plaintiff discovered defendants did not maintain workers' compensation insurance prior to December 31, 2001 and as early as August 2001." (Footnote 3)

Defendants argued, and the trial court agreed, a personal injury action against an employer who does not have workers' compensation insurance must be filed within one year from the date the plaintiff discovers the employer is uninsured. The court found there was undisputed evidence showing Valdez had actual or constructive knowledge the defendants were uninsured at least by December 20, 2001 and therefore his personal injury action filed in May 2003 was time barred. (Footnote 4)

This ruling also disposed of the declaratory relief claim because that cause of action is inextricably tied to the personal injury claim. (Footnote 5)

Treating the motion for summary judgment as to the unfair competition cause of action as a motion for judgment on the pleadings the trial court granted the motion on the ground the prayer of the complaint did not ask for an injunction or restitution, the only remedies available to a private party under the unfair competition law.

The trial court also granted defendants' motion for sanctions under Code of Civil Procedure section 128.7 against Valdez and his attorneys in this action. (Footnote 6)

The court reasoned defendants "conclusively established" Valdez knew no later than December 2001 defendants did not have workers' compensation insurance. Therefore: "If the complaint had at all times so reflected the truth, defendants could have successfully demurred and saved themselves the time and expense of this lawsuit." The court sanctioned Valdez and his attorneys $54,601 for their "bad faith."

DISCUSSION

I. DEFENDANTS FAILED TO PRODUCE UNDISPUTED EVIDENCE SHOWING THE STATUTE OF LIMITATIONS HAD RUN ON VALDEZ'S PERSONAL INJURY CAUSE OF ACTION.

The strong public policy for employers to compensate their injured employees is reflected in our state constitution which vests the Legislature with "plenary power . . . to create and enforce a complete system of workers' compensation . . . and in that behalf to create and enforce liability on the part of any or all persons to compensate any or all of their workers for injury or disability . . . sustained by the said workers in the course of their employment, irrespective of the fault of any party . . . [and to] accomplish substantial justice in all cases expeditiously, inexpensively, and without incumbrance [sic] of any character; all of which matters are expressly declared to be the social public policy of this State[.]" (Footnote 7)

In carrying out this public policy the Legislature has directed the workers' compensation laws "shall be liberally construed by the courts with the purpose of extending their benefits for the protection of persons injured in the course of their employment."
(Footnote 8)

Normally this liberal construction operates in favor of awarding workers' compensation, not in permitting civil litigation. (Footnote 9)

As we discuss below, however, the Legislature has made an exception to the rule favoring workers' compensation over civil litigation when the employer is illegally uninsured.

An employer's failure to carry workers' compensation insurance for its employees can result in criminal punishment, including a fine or imprisonment or both, (Footnote 10) administrative penalties (Footnote 11) and a civil suit for damages by an injured employee. (Footnote 12)

As relevant to this case Labor Code section 3700 requires "[e]very employer" to "secure the payment of compensation

in one or more of the following ways: (a) By being insured against liability to pay compensation by one or more insurers . . . [or] (b) By securing from the Director of Industrial Relations, a certificate of consent to self–insure[.]" Absent compliance with one of these alternatives an employee is not subject to the exclusive remedy of workers' compensation but may bring a claim before the WCAB and a tort action against the uninsured employer. (Footnote 13)

This is what Valdez chose to do. He first filed a workers' compensation claim with the WCAB under Labor Code section 3715 and later filed a personal injury action in the superior court under Labor Code section 3706.

As we discuss below, in an action brought under Labor Code section 3706 an employer's liability is determined under rules of pleading and proof which differ significantly from those of a common law personal injury action. For that reason we conclude section 3706 creates a statutory cause of action for personal injuries subject to the three year statute of limitations. (Footnote 14)

As an independently sufficient reason for reversing the judgment we conclude even if the former one year statute of limitations for negligence actions applies to this case the statute was tolled while Valdez pursued his workers' compensation remedy. (Footnote 15)

Under either alternative holding it is irrelevant whether Valdez discovered defendants' lack of workers' compensation insurance in December 2001 or March 2002. Thus there is no basis for the trial court's sanction order which was premised on the theory if Valdez had alleged the "true" date of discovery defendants could have prevailed on a demurrer to the complaint and saved the time and expense of a summary judgment motion.

A. A Suit Based On Labor Code Section 3706 Is Governed By The Three Year Limitation Period Because The Employer's Liability Is Created By Statute.

Under Code of Civil Procedure section 338, subdivision (a) an action may be brought within three years if it is "[a]n action upon a liability created by statute, other than a penalty or forfeiture."

As a general rule, an action brought under Labor Code section 3706 differs markedly from a common law negligence action. In describing these differences in *Rideaux v. Torgrimson* our Supreme Court explained: "If an employer fails to secure the payment of compensation, either an injured employee or his dependents may sue the employer . . . for damages. In such an action the plaintiff may attach the property of the employer and is given the benefit of a presumption that the employer was negligent. The employer may not defend upon the ground that the employee was contributorily negligent, or assumed the risk of the hazards attending his employment, or that he was injured through the negligence of a fellow servant." (Footnote 16)

After considering the dissimilarities between the two actions the court concluded the Legislature, by enacting the predecessor to Labor Code section 3706, "provided a statutory cause of action for personal injuries quite different from that of the common law." (Footnote 17)

In *Hall v. Copco Pacific Ltd.* the Ninth Circuit, relying on *Rideaux's* construction of section 3706 as creating "a statutory cause of action," held an action brought under that section was subject to the three year limitations period for "an action upon a liability created by statute." (Footnote 18)

The Court of Appeal concurred with *Hall* in *Lewis v. Hinman–Ball & Bonner* observing: "The statute of limitations upon an action under Labor Code section 3706 appears to be no more than three years. (Footnote 19)

In the present case the undisputed facts show Valdez was injured in July 2001 and commenced his section 3706 action in May 2003, less than three years from the date of his injury. Thus, regardless of when Valdez discovered defendants were uninsured he brought this action well within the three year limitations period of Code of Civil Procedure section 338, subdivision (a). (Footnote 20)

B. Valdez's Personal Injury Action Is Not Barred By The One Year Statute Of Limitations Because The Statute Was Equitably Tolled While He Pursued His Workers' Compensation Claim.

As a separate and independently sufficient reason for reversing the summary judgment as to the personal injury cause of action we hold, under our Supreme Court's decision in *Elkins v. Derby*, (Footnote 21) even if the former one year statute of limitations for a negligence action applied to this case the statute was tolled until Valdez obtained a final determination of his workers' compensation claim.

In arguing the one year statute of limitations bars Valdez's personal injury cause of action defendants rely on the provision of Labor Code section 3706 which states an employee of an uninsured employer may bring an action for damages "as if [the workers' compensation law] did not apply." If the workers' compensation law "does not apply," defendants reason, then an action authorized by Labor Code section 3706 must be governed by the laws governing negligence actions generally including the statute of limitations for an action based on negligence. (Footnote 22)

The limitations period begins to run, defendants maintain, when the employee discovers the employer is uninsured.

Defendants' argument overlooks our high court's decision in *Elkins v. Derby* which held the one year period for bringing a personal injury action was tolled while the plaintiff, acting in good faith, pursued his workers' compensation remedy against his employer. (Footnote 23)

Although Elkins' personal injury action did not arise under Labor Code section 3706 we conclude the court's reasoning is applicable to such cases.

In *Elkins* the plaintiff first pursued a workers' compensation claim against defendants whom he believed were his employers. Several months later the workers' compensation referee determined plaintiff had not been an employee of defendants at the time of his injury and dismissed his claim. Approximately one month after the referee's decision became final the plaintiff filed a personal injury action against the same defendants for the same injury which had served as the basis for his workers' compensation claim. The trial court sustained the defendants' demurrer on the ground the action was barred

by the one year statute of limitations because it was filed more than a year from the date of plaintiff's injury. (Footnote 24)

The Supreme Court reversed holding plaintiff's action was not barred by the one year statute of limitations because the limitations period was equitably tolled while he pursued his workers' compensation claim. (Footnote 25)

The court gave several reasons for tolling the statute of limitations on Elkins' personal injury cause of action.

Principally, the court concluded tolling would not interfere with the primary purpose of the statute of limitations to " '[prevent] surprises through the revival of claims that have been allowed to slumber until evidence has been lost, memories have faded and witnesses have disappeared.' " (Footnote 26)

Loss of evidence is not a concern because the "[d]efendants' interest in being promptly apprised of claims against them in order that they may gather and preserve evidence is fully satisfied when prospective tort plaintiffs file compensation claims within one year of their injuries." (Footnote 27)

The court also pointed out a civil action, even if filed while the compensation claim was pending, would normally not move forward until the compensation claim was resolved. (Footnote 28)

Finally, the court noted *requiring* an injured employee to maintain duplicate actions against the employer before the WCAB and a civil court might work an inequity upon an injured employee, would be "inefficient, awkward and laborious" and lead to the assertion of "mutually inconsistent" allegations before different tribunals. (Footnote 29)

In sum, *Elkins* stands for the proposition that when an injured person has two legal remedies and reasonably and in good faith pursues one, the statute of limitations should not bar pursuit of the second unless doing so would unfairly prejudice the defendant. (Footnote 30)

Defendants have not shown prejudice in the present case. They make a perfunctory argument "evidence has been lost, memories have faded, and witnesses may have disappeared" but they produced no evidence to back up these contentions. Furthermore, in *Elkins* the Supreme Court held as a matter of law the likelihood "the employer will suffer prejudice if the compensation claimant files a tort action more than a year after the date of injury is minimal." (Footnote 31)

The court reasoned filing the workers' compensation claim is enough to put an employer on notice it needs to identify and locate witnesses with knowledge of the events causing the injury and the nature and extent of the injury. (Footnote 32)

"The likelihood, however, that the employer will suffer prejudice if the compensation claimant files a tort action more than a year after the date of injury is minimal. After the filing of a compensation claim, the employer can identify and locate persons with knowledge of the events or circumstances causing the injury. By doing so, he takes the critical steps necessary to preserve evidence respecting fault. Although he may choose not to gather evidence bearing on fault from these parties when faced only with a compensation claim, he will be able in most instances to

recontact these people, particularly if they are continuing employees, for further evidentiary contributions should a controversy as to fault later arise in a tort action."
(Footnote 33)

In a case such as the one before us, where the employer knows it is uninsured, it has an even greater incentive to initially gather evidence of fault because it can anticipate having to rebut the presumption of negligence in a civil action under section 3706.
(Footnote 34)

As the court explained in *Elkins*, an employer who even suspects the claimant may seek tort remedies "may well choose to obtain evidence of fault immediately upon the filing of a compensation application even though no court action has yet been initiated." (Footnote 35)

The employer cannot assume the claimant will *not* file a tort action. "He thus may elect to gather evidence of fault immediately in order to save himself the trouble later."
(Footnote 36)

Defendants attempt to distinguish *Elkins* on the ground the plaintiff in that case filed his civil complaint within a month after learning he was not eligible for workers' compensation and only a year and three months from his date of injury. In contrast Valdez did not file his civil complaint until more than a year after learning defendants were uninsured and almost two years after his date of injury. We find this argument unpersuasive. Even if Valdez had filed his civil action the same day he learned defendants were uninsured the action would have been held in abeyance pending a determination of his workers' compensation claim. (Footnote 37)

As previously noted, Labor Code section 3715 explicitly permits an employee of an uninsured employer to proceed simultaneously on a workers' compensation claim and a civil action for negligence. (Footnote 38)

Furthermore an interval of less than two years between Valdez's injury in July 2001 and the filing of his civil suit in May 2003 is not unreasonable considering that effective January 1, 2003 the limitations period for bringing a negligence action increased from one year to two. (Footnote 39)

If Valdez had suffered his injury a year later this case would not even be before us.

Nor is there any merit in defendants' argument Valdez cannot rely on equitable tolling to defeat their motion for summary judgment because he did not plead facts to support that theory in his complaint. (Footnote 40)

Valdez pled all the facts necessary to raise the issue of equitable tolling under the alternative remedies rule of *Elkins*. His complaint alleged he was employed by defendants, he was injured in the course and scope of his employment, he filed a workers' compensation claim against defendants, he subsequently learned defendants did not carry workers' compensation insurance and he was bringing this action under Labor Code section 3706.

In addressing the issue of when the tolling period ends, *Elkins* stated: "There can be little doubt that a tolling rule must suspend the running of the limitations period through the date on which the final compensation decision becomes

final rather than the date on which the first compensation decision is filed." (Footnote 41)

It is not clear what the high court meant by "the date on which the final compensation decision becomes final." In the workers' compensation system a "final compensation decision" may not occur for ten years or more after the claim is filed if by "final compensation decision" the court meant a final adjudication of issues regarding the claimant's permanent disability.

We do not believe the *Elkins* court meant the tolling period could extend for the length of time it takes to adjudicate the claimant–plaintiff's permanent disability. This would make no sense in the context of the *Elkins* case because the plaintiff in *Elkins* was denied workers' compensation benefits on the ground he was not an employee of the alleged employer. There would never have been an adjudication of the plaintiff's permanent disability because he was not entitled to any workers' compensation benefits. Furthermore, none of the cases the court cited on the tolling issue involved the extent of a workers' compensation claimant's disability. In fact, none of the cases the court cited involved workers' compensation. (Footnote 42)

The only similarity between *Elkins* and the cases it cited is that they all could be loosely described as involving "coverage" or "eligibility" issues. We believe, therefore, when the *Elkins* court used the term "final compensation decision" it was referring to a threshold determination such as the claimant's lack of eligibility or the employer's lack of insurance which would trigger the claimant's right to seek a tort remedy in a civil action.

Assuming an action under Labor Code section 3706 is subject to the limitations period for an ordinary negligence action we hold the time for bringing such an action is equitably tolled until there has been a final determination in the workers' compensation proceeding the employer is uninsured. This tolling, of course, is subject to the rule a person who seeks equity must do equity. (Footnote 43)

Thus tolling may end if the employer can show the plaintiff has unreasonably delayed a final determination as to whether the employer is insured. (Footnote 44)

II. IT WOULD BE AN ABUSE OF DISCRETION FOR THE TRIAL COURT NOT TO RECONSIDER ITS SANCTION ORDER UPON REMAND.

Under Code of Civil Procedure section 1008, subdivision (c), "If a court at any time determines that there has been a change of law that warrants it to reconsider a prior order it entered, it may do so on its own motion and enter a different order." This provision applies to all orders, interim and final. (Footnote 45)

Our decision on the statute of limitations issue in this case constitutes a "change of law" for purposes of Code of Civil Procedure section 1008, subdivision (c). (Footnote 46)

Although our decision is not without precedent, no previous California appellate court decision specifically held actions under Labor Code section 3706 are covered by the three year statute of limitations in Code of Civil Procedure section 338, subdivision (a) or that a section 3706 action is subject to equitable tolling under the rule announced in *Elkins v. Derby*. Our decision is certainly a change in the law from what the trial court believed the law to be. The trial court ruled Code of Civil Procedure section 338, subdivision (a) "does not apply because Labor Code section 3706 does not create a cause of action." We have held to the contrary. (Footnote 47)

The trial court also ruled Valdez's arguments based on *Elkins v. Derby*, equitable tolling and Labor Code section 3706 were not "relevant to this motion." We have held to the contrary on this point as well. (Footnote 48)

The change of law represented by our decision cuts the ground from under the trial court's $54,000 sanction order which was based on the premise there would have been no need for defendants to litigate a summary judgment motion if Valdez's complaint had "reflected the truth" about when Valdez discovered defendants were uninsured (which the trial court determined was no later than December 2001). If Valdez's complaint had alleged the correct date, the court reasoned, "defendants could have successfully demurred and saved themselves the time and expense of this lawsuit." As we have held, however, the date on which Valdez discovered his employer was uninsured is irrelevant to the question whether his action is time–barred. Furthermore, prior to defendants' filing their motion for summary judgment, counsel for Valdez wrote to counsel for defendants explaining why he believed the statute of limitations was tolled under the holding in *Elkins v. Derby*. Defendants chose to ignore this letter and litigate the issue. This of course was their right but it would be logically indefensible to allow defendants to collect $54,000 from Valdez for making legal arguments an appellate court has rejected.

III. VALDEZ'S FAILURE TO PRAY FOR RELIEF WITHIN THE COURT'S JURISDICTION IS NOT FATAL TO HIS CAUSE OF ACTION FOR UNFAIR COMPETITION.

Treating defendants' motion for summary judgment on the unfair competition cause of action as a motion for judgment on the pleadings, (Footnote 49) the court granted the motion on the ground the complaint failed to pray for injunctive or restitutionary relief, the only two remedies available to a private party under the unfair competition law. (Footnote 50)

Failure to pray for the proper form of relief is not fatal to a complaint. (Footnote 51)

On remand the trial court should allow Valdez to amend his complaint to request the appropriate relief. (Footnote 52)... .

Footnote 1. An order imposing sanctions in excess of $5,000 is an appealable order. (Code Civ. Proc., § 904.1, subd. (a)(12).) If an order is appealable, an aggrieved party must file a timely appeal from the order to obtain appellate review; a notice of appeal from the judgment alone is insufficient. (*Sole Energy Co. v. Petrominerals Corp.* (2005) 128 Cal. App. 4th 212, 239 [26 Cal. Rptr. 3d 798].)

Footnote 2. The purpose of the declaratory relief cause of action is to obtain a prejudgment attachment of defendants'

property to secure the payment of any judgment ultimately obtained from an uninsured employer. (Lab. Code, § 3707.)

Footnote 3. Defendants Ruth and Ella Hirshfield moved for summary judgment on the separate ground they were not Valdez's employers. The trial court did not address that issue and the parties have not briefed it on appeal. Therefore we will not consider that issue in this opinion.

Footnote 4. We note, however, the first WCAB document naming Himmelfarb as Valdez's employer was dated March 15, 2002. But even if this was the date on which Valdez first discovered Himmelfarb was his uninsured employer the complaint was filed more than a year after this discovery.

Footnote 5. *Embarcadero Municipal Improvement District v. County of Santa Barbara* (2001) 88 Cal. App. 4th 781, 793 [107 Cal. Rptr. 2d 6].

Footnote 6. Valdez is represented in this action by a different law firm than handled his workers' compensation claim.

Footnote 7. California Constitution, article 14, section 4.

Footnote 8. Labor Code section 3202.

Footnote 9. *Arriaga v. County of Alameda* (1995) 9 Cal. 4th 1055, 1065 [892 P.2d 150, 40 Cal. Rptr. 2d 116, 60 Cal. Comp. Cases 316].

Footnote 10. Labor Code section 3700.5

Footnote 11. Labor Code section 3711.

Footnote 12. Labor Code section 3706.

Footnote 13. *DuBois v. Workers' Comp. Appeals Bd.* (1993) 5 Cal. 4th 382, 392 [853 P.2d 978, 20 Cal. Rptr. 2d 523, 58 Cal. Comp. Cases 286]. Labor Code section 3706 states: "If any employer fails to secure the payment of compensation, any injured employee or his dependents may bring an action at law against such employer for damages, as if this division did not apply." Labor Code section 3715, subdivision (a) provides in relevant part: "Any employee . . . whose employer has failed to secure the payment of compensation as required by this division, . . . may, in addition to proceedings against his or her employer by civil action in the courts as provided by Section 3706, file his or her application with the appeals board for compensation in like manner as in other claims . . . ."

Footnote 14. Code of Civil Procedure section 338, subdivision (a).

Footnote 15. *Elkins v. Derby* (1974) 12 Cal. 3d 410 [525 P.2d 81, 115 Cal. Rptr. 641].

Footnote 16. *Rideaux v. Torgrimson* (1939) 12 Cal. 2d 633, 636 [86 P.2d 826, 4 Cal. Comp. Cases 37].

Footnote 17. *Rideaux v. Torgimson, supra,* 12 Cal. 2d at page 636 (construing section 29b of the Workmen's Compensation Insurance and Safety Act of 1917, the predecessor of Labor Code sections 3706 and 3708). We acknowledge there is dictum in *Rideaux* describing Labor Code section 3706 as "having somewhat the nature of a penalty." *Rideaux, supra,* 12 Cal. 2d at page 637. An action on a statutory "penalty" is expressly excluded from the three year limitations period of Code of Civil Procedure section 338, subdivision (a) and falls within the one year limitations period of Code of Civil Procedure section 340, subdivision (a) if the action is given to an individual. An action on a penalty, however, is generally considered one in which the plaintiff is allowed to recover from a wrongdoer without regard to the actual damages sustained. (*Low v. Lan* (2002) 96 Cal. App. 4th 1371, 1381 [118 Cal. Rptr. 2d 60].) In this context, Labor Code section 3706 is clearly remedial in nature, not penal.

Footnote 18. *Hall v. Copco Pacific Ltd.* (9th Cir. 1955) 224 F.2d 884, 886 [20 Cal. Comp. Cases 321] (construing former Code Civ. Proc., § 338(1), now § 338, subd. (a).)

Footnote 19. *Lewis v. Hinman–Ball & Bonner* (1957) 154 Cal. App. 2d 710, 714–715 [316 P.2d 673], citing *Hall, supra,* 224 F.2d at page 886. See also 1 Hanna, California Law of Employee Injuries and Workers' Compensation (Rev. 2d Ed. 2006) § 11.02[4][m], page 11–35: "[I]f the suit is based on Labor Code section 3706, it is covered by the three–year statutory period of Code of Civil Procedure section 338(a), because the employer's liability is created by statute." [Citing *Hall v. Copco Pacific Ltd., supra,* 224 F.2d at page 886.]

Footnote 20. Because Valdez filed his civil action within three years from the date of his injury we need not decide whether a cause of action under Labor Code section 3706 accrues at a later date, e.g., the date the employee discovers his employer is uninsured, or whether the limitations period is tolled while the employee pursues his workers' compensation remedy against the uninsured employer under Labor Code section 3715. But see discussion in subpart B, below.

Footnote 21. *Elkins v. Derby, supra,* 12 Cal. 3d at pages 414–420.

Footnote 22. At all times relevant to this action former Code of Civil Procedure section 340(3) required an action for any injury "caused by the wrongful act or neglect of another" to be brought "within one year."

Footnote 23. *Elkins v. Derby, supra,* 12 Cal. 3d at pages 414–420.

Footnote 24. *Elkins v. Derby, supra,* 12 Cal. 3d at page 413.

Footnote 25. *Elkins v. Derby, supra,* 12 Cal. 3d at page 412.

Footnote 26. *Elkins v. Derby, supra,* 12 Cal. 3d at page 417, Footnote and citations omitted.

Footnote 27. *Elkins v. Derby, supra,* 12 Cal. 3d at pages 417–418.

Footnote 28. *Elkins v. Derby, supra,* 12 Cal. 3d at page 417, Footnote 4.

Footnote 29. *Elkins v. Derby, supra,* 12 Cal. 3d at pages 419–420.

Footnote 30. See our discussion of *Elkins* in *Collier v. City of Pasadena* (1983) 142 Cal. App. 3d 917, 923 [191 Cal. Rptr. 681] [statute of limitations for disability pension claim tolled while pursuing workers' compensation claim].

Footnote 31. *Elkins v. Derby, supra,* 12 Cal. 3d at page 418.

Footnote 32. *Elkins v. Derby, supra,* 12 Cal. 3d at page 418. In the present case Valdez filed his workers' compensation claim within a month from the date of his injury giving defendants early warning they needed to gather evidence regarding the claim.

Footnote 33. *Elkins v. Derby, supra,* 12 Cal. 3d at page 418[.]

Footnote 34. See Labor Code section 3706 discussed at page 7, above [71 Cal. Comp. Cases 1579].

Footnote 35. *Elkins v. Derby, supra,* 12 Cal. 3d at page 418.

Footnote 36. *Elkins v. Derby, supra,* 12 Cal. 3d at page 418.

Footnote 37. *Elkins v. Derby, supra,* 12 Cal. 3d at page 417, Footnote 4.

Footnote 38. See *Aetna Casualty & Surety Co. v. Aceves* (1991) 233 Cal. App. 3d 544, 558–559 [284 Cal. Rptr. 477, 56 Cal. Comp. Cases 495].

Footnote 39. Code of Civil Procedure section 335.1 providing a two year limitations period replaced Code of Civil Procedure section 340(3) effective January 1, 2003. (Stats. 2002, ch. 448, § 2.)

Footnote 40. See *Mills v. Forestex Co.* (2003) 108 Cal. App. 4th 625, 641 [134 Cal. Rptr. 2d 273].

Footnote 41. *Elkins v. Derby, supra,* 12 Cal. 3d at page 413, Footnote 1.

Footnote 42. *Elkins v. Derby, supra,* 12 Cal. 3d at page 413, Footnote 1, citing *Myers v. County of Orange* (1970) 6 Cal. App. 3d 626, 634–635 [86 Cal. Rptr. 198], *Lee C. Hess Co. v. City of Susanville* (1959) 176 Cal. App. 2d 594, 598 [1 Cal. Rptr. 586], *County of Santa Clara v. Hayes Co.* (1954) 43 Cal. 2d 615, 619 [275 P.2d 456], *Record Machine & Tool Co. v. Pageman Holding Corp.* (1959) 172 Cal. App. 2d 164, 175 [342 P.2d 402].

Footnote 43. See *Cortez v. Purolator Air Filtration Products Co.* (2000) 23 Cal. 4th 163, 180 [999 P.2d 706, 96 Cal. Rptr. 2d 518].

Footnote 44. See *Prudential–LMI Com. Insurance v. Superior Court* (1990) 51 Cal. 3d 674, 700 [798 P.2d 1230, 274 Cal. Rptr. 387].

Footnote 45. Code of Civil Procedure section 1008, subdivision (d).

Footnote 46. See *International Ins. Co. v. Superior Court* (1998) 62 Cal. App. 4th 784, 786–787 [72 Cal. Rptr. 2d 849] [an appellate decision may constitute a "change of law" for purposes of Code of Civil Procedure section 1008, subdivision (c)].

Footnote 47. See discussion at pages 7–8, above [71 Cal. Comp. Cases 1579–1580].

Footnote 48. See discussion at pages 9–14, above [71 Cal. Comp. Cases 1580–1584].

Footnote 49. See *Cordova v. 21st Century Ins. Co.* (2005) 129 Cal. App. 4th 89, 109 [28 Cal. Rptr. 3d 170].

Footnote 50. *Korea Supply Co. v. Lockheed Martin Corp.* (2003) 29 Cal. 4th 1134, 1144 [63 P.3d 937, 131 Cal. Rptr. 2d 29].

Footnote 51. Code of Civil Procedure section 580, subdivision (a) states in relevant part: "[T]he court may grant the plaintiff any relief consistent with the case made by the complaint and embraced within the issue[.]" Defendants do not contend the complaint fails to state facts sufficient to support injunctive or restitutionary relief.

Footnote 52. Compare *Mills v. Forestex Co., supra,* 108 Cal. App. 4th at page 641.

[**Special Note:** Inasmuch as failure to timely file an action may be fatal to a plaintiff's cause because of the statute of limitations and because some different causes of action have different time limitations within which a cause of action must be filed to be timely, the reader is cautioned to review the Code of Civil Procedure and seek appropriate legal advice if unsure as to the correct statute of limitations]

§ 64.7 Credit to Employer Against an Employee's Third–Party Recovery

Page 1944, Column 2, eighth paragraph, insert following '…benefits.'

In *Spectra F/X, Inc., et al. v. WCAB (Avalos)* (2005) 70 Cal. Comp. Cases 1609, the Board held that a judge's finding of employer negligence in applicant's third party case was binding on the applicant's employer's workers' compensation insurer for purposes of obtaining credit in applicant's workers' compensation case and that the insurer was collaterally estopped from re–litigating the issue of applicant's employer's negligence at the Appeals Board when the insurer was party to the civil lawsuit as plaintiff–in–intervention but nevertheless elected to settle its lien prior to trial in exchange for dismissal from the civil action and chose, therefore, not to participate in the civil action. The Board found the insurer was in privity with the applicant for purposes of applying the doctrine of collateral estoppel. See Sections 18.12 and 24.15 of this book for discussions of collateral estoppel.

Page 1962, Column 2, seventh paragraph, insert following '…360.'

The Board is not bound by the terms adopted by an injured worker and the settling third party, rather, the Board has the power to grant the employer credit, or to increase the amount of the credit, by adopting its own allocation of settlement proceeds. *Reid v. WCAB* (1995) 60 Cal. Comp. Cases 360.

In *Kaiser Foundation Hospitals v. WCAB (Needles)* (2006) 71 Cal. Comp. Cases 850 the defendant employer was not entitled to a credit against an injured employee's future workers' compensation benefits from applicant's third party medical malpractice settlement where the evidence showed that, in arriving at the third party settlement the parties had taken collateral sources into account. See also Bernstein v. WCAB (1996) 61 Cal. Comp. Cases 484; Monarrez v. WCAB (1991) 56 Cal. Comp. Cases 453 and Graham v. WCAB (1989) 54 Cal. Comp. Cases 160.

§ 64.7(A)(1) Loss of Consortium

Page 1966, Column 1, add to end of sixth paragraph, immediately following '…discussion'

and *CNA Casualty of California v. WCAB (Kirkeby)* (2006) 71 Cal. Comp. Cases 149, where the Court of Appeal, First District, in an unpublished case, held that the Appeals Board had the equitable power to reallocate proceeds of a third–party settlement when the facts disclosed that the injured employee and spouse colluded in a civil case to make a bad faith or fraudulent allocation of settlement proceeds in order to defeat the employer's third–party credit rights.

Page 1971, Column 2, add to end of last paragraph, following '…Labor Code.]'

§ 64.8(B)(1) Permanent Partial Disability Against Permanent Total Disability.

Inasmuch as permanent partial disability is a different benefit than permanent total disability, a defendant is not entitled to a credit of earlier permanent partial disability against a subsequent award of permanent total disability following a formal Petition to Reopen by an applicant. Such was the case in *City of San Buenaventura, et al. v. WCAB (Schulte)* (2006) 71 Cal. Comp. Cases 823, where defendant was found *not* entitled to credit a prior stipulated permanent partial disability award of 30½ percent permanent disability against a subsequent total permanent disability award (100 percent) following her successful Petition to Reopen because permanent partial disability and permanent total disability are distinctly different benefits and the applicant was held to be entitled to the full benefit of each award.

Intentionally blank

§ 68.0   INSURANCE

§ 68.2(A)   Restrictions on Power of Insurance Carrier to Cancel an Insurance Policy

Page 2017, Column 1, following fourth paragraph, ending with words '…one year.' insert

The Legislature amended Insurance Code Section 677, effective January 1, 2007, to require insurers to provide policy holders with specific information supporting a reason(s) for cancellation and the information that supports those reasons. Section 677 now provides:

677.

  (a) All notices of cancellation shall be in writing, mailed to the named insured at the address shown in the policy, or to his or her last known address, and shall state, with respect to policies in effect after the time limits specified in Section 676, (1) which of the grounds set forth in Section 676 is relied upon, and, in accordance with the requirements of subdivisions (a) and (e) of Section 791.10, and (2) the specific information supporting the cancellation, the specific items of personal and privileged information that support those reasons, if applicable, and corresponding summary of rights.

  (b) For purposes of this section, a lienholder's copy of those notices shall be deemed mailed if, with the lienholder's consent, it is delivered by electronic transmittal, facsimile, or personal delivery.

677.2.

  (a) This section applies only to policies covered by Section 675.5.

  (b) A notice of cancellation shall be in writing and shall be delivered or mailed to the producer of record, provided that the producer of record is not an employee of the insurer, and to the named insured at the mailing address shown on the policy. Subdivision (a) of Section 1013 of the Code of Civil Procedure is applicable if the notice is mailed. The notice of cancellation shall include the effective date of the cancellation and the reasons for the cancellation.

  (c) The notice of cancellation shall be given at least 30 days prior to the effective date of the cancellation, except that in the case of cancellation for nonpayment of premiums or for fraud the notice shall be given no less than 10 days prior to the effective date of the cancellation. Notice of a proposed cancellation pursuant to subdivision (d) of Section 676.2 given prior to a finding of the commissioner shall satisfy the requirements of this section if it is given no less than 30 days prior to the effective date of the cancellation and if it states that cancellation will be effective only upon the approval of the commissioner.

  (d) This section applies only to cancellations pursuant to Section 676.2.

677.4.

  A notice of cancellation with respect to a policy covered under Section 675 shall be delivered at least 20 calendar days prior to the effective date of the cancellation, except that in the case of a cancellation for nonpayment of premiums, or for fraud, the notice shall be given at least 10 calendar days prior to the effective date of the cancellation. Subdivision (a) of Section 1013 of the Code of Civil Procedure is applicable if the notice is mailed.

§ 68.8   Coverage for Owners of a Business

Page 2021, Column 2, add to end of third paragraph, immediately following '…reconsideration.'

See *Barka v. WCAB* (2006) 71 Cal. Comp. Cases 800, where coverage was denied to the owner/president of a service station where he had reported wages on himself as a mechanic without informing his broker or the workers' compensation insurance company. At the time the business procured the workers' compensation policy, the owner/president functioned solely as an excecutive. In upholding the Board's finding of no coverage for an injury sustained by the owner/president while working as a mechanic, the Court of Appeal, Fourth District, in denying a writ, stated:

Petitioner Frank Barka is president of Barka NF, Inc., which owns and operates a Unocal Station in Point Loma. The business's workers' compensation insurance policy, which is provided by Safeco Insurance Company, specifically excludes coverage for officers and directors. At the time the business procured the policy, Barka functioned solely as an executive and did not receive any compensation from the business.

Circumstances changed and, in October 2003, Barka began working as a mechanic for the business in addition to performing his executive duties. Consequently, he added himself to the business's payroll and paid himself on the same basis as the other mechanics.

Generally, when the business adds a new employee to the payroll, the employee is automatically covered by the workers' compensation policy. The business reports the employee's wages to Safeco through an audit process at the end of the policy period and Safeco adjusts the premium as necessary. Based on this process and notwithstanding the exclusion, Barka believed he could obtain coverage for himself as a mechanic by simply adding himself to the payroll. He did not contact his insurance broker or Safeco to confirm this belief.

Approximately six weeks after he began working as a mechanic, Barka suffered a severe on–the–job injury. He immediately filed a workers' compensation claim, which Safeco denied based on the officers and directors exclusion. Barka and Safeco submitted the coverage issue to mandatory arbitration. The arbitrator found in favor of Safeco. Barka petitioned the Workers' Compensation Appeals Board (WCAB) for reconsideration and the WCAB denied his petition. Barka filed this petition to obtain review of the WCAB's decision.

We conclude review is not warranted in this case because the record indicates the WCAB acted within its powers, its decision was reasonable, and its decision was supported by appropriate findings and substantial evidence. (Lab. Code, § 5952.) The plain language of the policy excludes coverage for Barka, Barka identifies no policy provision that would negate the exclusion under the circumstances presented, and Barka did not attempt to contact his broker or Safeco to determine how to remove the exclusion.

The petition is denied.

Page 2021, Column 2, add after § 68.9

§ 68.10   Self–Insurance

Many large employers with substantial financial assets choose to establish what is commonly called a self–insured employers' program whereby the employers self–insure their workers' compensation liabilities themselves. Labor Code section 3700.

To self–insure, an employer must secure a certificate of consent to self–insure either as an individual employer, or as one employer in a group of employers, from the Department of Industrial Relations.

Self–insured employers must make a security deposit of no less than $220,000 with the Director. Surety requirements are set forth in Labor Code section 3701.

The Director may revoke a certificate of consent to self–insure for good cause, after a hearing. Good cause includes, among other things, the impairment of the solvency of the employer to the extent that there is a marked reduction of the employer's financial strength, failure to maintain a security deposit as required by Section 3701, failure to pay assessments of the Self–Insurers' Security Fund, frequent or flagrant violations of state safety and health orders, the failure or inability of the employer to fulfill his or her obligations, or any of the following practices by the employer or his or her agent in charge of the administration of obligations under this division:

(1) Habitually and as a matter of practice and custom inducing claimants for compensation to accept less than the compensation due or making it necessary for them to resort to proceedings against the employer to secure compensation due;

(2) Where liability for temporary disability indemnity is not in dispute, intentionally failing to pay temporary disability indemnity without good cause in order to influence the amount of permanent disability benefits due;

(3) Intentionally refusing to comply with known and legally indisputable compensation obligations;

(4) Discharging or administering his or her compensation obligations in a dishonest manner; or

(5) Discharging or administering his or her compensation obligations in such a manner as to cause injury to the public or those dealing with the employer. Labor Code Section 3702.

Reinsurance Insurance / Excess Insurance Coverage

As part of its self–insurance, a self–insured employer will secure reinsurance, to protect its solvency in the event of huge losses, from an insurer, commonly called an excess insurance carrier providing for coverage above a specified agreed amount, commonly called a Self–Insured Retention (SIR) or simply Retention. Such Retentions are commonly for $250,000, $500,000, $1,000.000 or more. The reinsurance absorbs the loss when a claim penetrates the Retention.

The typical reinsurance policy provides that the self–insured employer (called the Insured) will give immediate notice to the Reinsurer upon learning of certain events in the management of a claim. Typically, the policy between the self–insured and the Reinsurer will provide:

The insured (Self–Insured) shall be responsible for the investigation, settlement, defense or appeal of any claim made or suit brought, or proceeding instituted against the Insured and shall give *immediate notice* to the Reinsurer upon learning of any of the following:

(a) *Any claim, suit or proceeding that appears to involve indemnity by the Reinsurer;*

(b) *Any occurrence, claim, award or proceeding judgment which exceeds 50% of the Retention stated in the Declarations;*

(c) Any occurrence which causes serious injury to two or more employees;

(d) Any case involving:

(1) Amputation of a major extremity;

(2) *Brain or spinal cord injury;*

(3) Death;

(4) *Disability for a period of nine months or more;*

(5) *Permanent total disability, as defined in the Workers' Compensation Act of the applicable state named in Item 3 of the Declarations;*

(6) Any second or third degree burn of 25% or more of the body; or

(e) The reopening of any case in which further award might involve liability of the Reinsurer.

The Insured shall make no voluntary settlement involving loss to the Reinsurer except with written consent of the Reinsurer.

The Insured shall forward promptly to the Reinsurer any information it may request on the individual occurrences, claims or cases. The Insured shall render to the Reinsurer, within 45 days of the end of the contract period, an experience report, upon a form satisfactory to the Reinsurer showing in detail the amounts disbursed during the contract period in settling claims and the estimated future payments on, or reserves for, outstanding claims.

The Reinsurer, at its own election and expense and in addition to any indemnity for claim expenses provided by this policy, shall have the right, but not the duty, to participate with the Insured in, or to assume in the name of the Insured, control over the investigation, settlement, defense or appeal of any claim, suit or proceeding which might involve liability of the company.

Reinsurers (Excess Carriers) have often argued that failure of the self–insured to comply with the immediate notice provisions provides a basis for disclaiming coverage. Courts have not interpreted these provisions uniformly, so inconsistent decisions have been handed down across the country regarding when notice must be given and the effect of late notice. In many states, the question of whether notice was untimely is intertwined with the question of prejudice to the reinsurer resulting from the late notice. Disputes also arise as to what constitutes efficient immediate notice. Claims adjusters must be alert as to the requirements of notice set forth in the Excess Carrier's policy to avoid a dispute with the Excess Carrier over coverage.

§ 68.11 Claim File Maintenance

Every claims administrator must maintain a claim file for each work–injury, including all claims denied.

Title 8, California Code of Regulations, Section 10101 provides:

This section applies to maintenance of claims files for injuries occurring before January 1, 1994.

Every claims administrator shall maintain a claim file of each work–injury claim including claims which were denied. All open claim files shall be kept at the adjusting location for the file. The file shall contain but not be limited to:

(a) An employer date stamped copy of the Employee's Claim for Workers' Compensation Benefits, DWC Form 1, or documentation of reasonable attempts to obtain the form.

(b) Employers Report of Occupational Injury or Illness, DLSR Form 5020, or documentation of reasonable attempts to obtain it.

(c) Every notice or report sent to the Division of Workers' Compensation.

(d) A copy of every Doctor's First Report of Occupational Injury or Illness, DLSR Form 5021, or documentation of reasonable attempts to obtain them.

(e) The original or a copy of every medical report pertaining to the claim, or documentation of reasonable attempts to obtain them.

(f) All orders or awards of the Workers' Compensation Appeals Board pertaining to the claim.

(g) A record of payment of compensation.

(h) A copy of the application(s) for adjudication of claim filed with the Workers' Compensation Appeals Board, if any.

(i) Copies of all notices sent to the employee pursuant to the requirements of the Benefit Notice Program established by Labor Code Section 138.4 and the notices required by Article 2.6 of Chapter 2 of Part 2 of the Labor Code, commencing with Section 4635.

Section 10101.1 provides:

This section applies to maintenance of claim files for injuries occurring on or after January 1, 1994.

Every claims administrator shall maintain a claim file of each work–injury claim including claims which were denied. All open claim files shall be kept at the adjusting location for the file. The file shall contain but not be limited to:

(a) Either (1) a copy of the Employee's Claim for Workers' Compensation Benefits, DWC Form 1, showing the employer's date of knowledge of injury, the date the employer provided the form to the employee and the date the employer received the completed form from the employee; or (2) if the employee did not return the claim form, documentation of the date the employer provided a claim form to the employee. If the administrator cannot obtain the form or determine that the form was provided to the employee by the employer, the file shall contain documentation that the administrator has provided the claim form to the employee as required by Title 8, California Code of Regulations Section 10119.

(b) A copy of the Employer's Report of Occupational Injury or Illness, DLSR Form 5020, or documentation of reasonable attempts to obtain it;

(c) A copy of every notice or report sent to the Division of Workers' Compensation.

(d) A copy of every Doctor's First Report of Occupational Injury or Illness, DLSR Form 5021, or documentation of reasonable attempts to obtain them.

(e) The original or a copy of every medical report pertaining to the claim, or documentation of reasonable attempts to obtain them.

(f) All orders or awards of the Workers' Compensation Appeals Board or the Rehabilitation Unit pertaining to the claim.

(g) A record of payment of compensation.

(h) A copy of the application(s) for adjudication of claim filed with the Workers' Compensation Appeals Board, if any.

(i) Copies of the following notices sent to the employee:

(1) Benefit notices, including vocational rehabilitation notices, required by Title 8, California Code of Regulations, Division 1, Chapter 4.5, Subchapter 1, Article 8, beginning with Section 9810, or by Title 8, California Code of Regulations, Division 1, Chapter 4.5, Subchapter 1.5, Article 7, beginning with Section 10122;

(2) Notices related to the Qualified Medical Evaluation process required by Labor Code Section 4061;

(j) Documentation sufficient to determine the injured worker's average weekly earnings in accordance with Labor Code Sections 4453 through 4459. Unless the claims administrator accepts liability to pay the maximum temporary disability rate, including any increased maximum due under Labor Code §4661.5, the information shall include:

(1) Documentation whether the employee received the following earnings, and if so, the amount or fair market value of each: tips, commissions, bonuses, overtime, and the market value of board, lodging, fuel, or other advantages as part of the worker's remuneration, which can be estimated in money, said documentation to include the period of time, not exceeding one year, as may conveniently be taken to determine an average weekly rate of pay;

(2) Documentation of concurrent earnings from employment other than that in which the injury occurred, or that there were no concurrent earnings, or of reasonable attempts to determine this information;

(3) If earnings at the time of injury were irregular, documentation of earnings from all sources of employment for one year prior to the injury, or of reasonable attempts to determine this information.

(4) If the foregoing information results in less than maximum earnings, documentation of the worker's earning capacity, including documentation of any increase in earnings likely to have occurred but for the injury (such as periodic salary increases or increased earnings upon completion of training status), or of reasonable attempts to determine this information.

(k) Notes and documentation related to the provision, delay, or denial of benefits, including any electronically stored documentation.

(l) Notes and documentation evidencing the legal, factual, or medical basis for non–payment or delay in payment of compensation benefits or expenses.

(m) Notes describing telephone conversations relating to the claim which are of significance to claims handling, including the dates of calls, substance of calls, and identification of parties to the calls.

Section 10102 provides:

(a) All claim files shall be maintained at least until the latest of the following dates:

(1) five years from the date of injury;

(2) one year from the date compensation was last provided;

(3) all compensation due or which may be due has been paid;

(4) if an audit has been conducted within the time specified in (a)(1), until the findings of an audit of the file have become final.

(b) Open and closed claim files may be maintained in whole or in part in an electronic or other non–paper storage medium.

Section 10103.2 provides:

This section shall govern claim log maintenance on or after January 1, 2003.

(a) The claims administrator shall maintain annual claim logs listing all work–injury claims, open and closed. Each year's log shall be maintained for at least five years from the end of the year covered. Separate claim logs shall be maintained for each self–insured employer and each insurer for each adjusting location.

(b) Each entry in the claim log shall contain at least the following information:

(1) Name of injured worker.

(2) Claims administrator's claim number.

(3) Date of injury.

(4) An indication whether the claim is an indemnity or medical–only claim.

(5) An entry if all liability for a claim has been denied at any time. All liability is considered to have been denied even if the administrator accepted liability for medical–legal expense.

(6) If the claim log is for a self–insured employer and a Certificate of Consent to Self–Insure has been issued, the name of the corporation employing the injured worker. If the claim log consists of claims for two or more members of an insurer group, the log shall identify the insurer for each claim.

(7) If the claim has been transferred from one adjusting location to another, the address of the new location shall be identified on the initial adjusting location's log. Claims that are transferred from one adjusting location to another shall be listed on the claim log of the new adjusting location for the year in which the claim was initially reported, not for the year in which the claim was transferred.

(c) The entries on a log provided to the Administrative Director shall reflect current information, to show at least any changes in status of a claim which occurred 45 days or more before the claim log was provided. However, once all liability for a claim has been denied the log shall designate the claim as a denial, even if the claim was later accepted.

(d) The claim log of each former self–insured employer and each self–insured employer that changes or terminates the use of a third–party administrator shall be maintained by that self–insured employer as required by subsection (a).

(e) A claims administrator shall provide a copy of a claim log within 14 days of receiving a written request from the Administrative Director.

Section 15400 provides:

(a) Every self–insurer or its administrative agency shall keep a claim file of each indemnity and medical–only work–injury occurring on or after January 1, 1990, in accordance with Title 8, Section 10101 and Section 10101.1.

(b) For work injuries occurring prior to January 1, 1990, every self insurer shall keep a claim file including those claims which were denied. Said claim file shall contain, but not be limited to, a copy of:

(1) Employers Report of Occupational Injury or Illness, Form No. 5020;

(2) Every report made to the Administrative Director of the Division of Industrial Accidents; including but not limited to the letter of denial to the employee;

(3) Doctor's First Report of Occupational Injury or Illness, Form No. 5021;

(4) Every subsequent relevant medical report;

(5) All applicable orders of the Workers' Compensation Appeals Board and reports relating thereto;

(6) A record of payment of compensation benefits as compensation is defined in Section 3207 of the Labor Code, together with a record of the periods covered by disability payments, including a copy of DIA Form 500, Notice of Termination of Benefits;

(c) For injuries reported on or after January 1, 2006, each self administering self insurer and claims administrative agency shall maintain a claim file for each indemnity and medical–only claim, including denied claims, and shall ensure that each file is complete and current for each claim. Contents of claim files may be in hard copy, in electronic form, or some combination of hard copy and electronic form. Files maintained in hard copy shall be in chronological order with the most recently dated documents on top, or subdivided into sections such as medical reports, benefit notices, correspondence, claim notes, and vocational rehabilitation. In addition to the contents specified in Title 8, California Code of Regulations, Section 10101.1, each indemnity file shall contain itemized written documentation showing the basis for the calculation of estimated future liability and for each change in estimated future liability for the claim. Files or portions of files maintained in electronic form shall be easily retrievable.

Section 15400.1 provides:

(a) After January 1, 1993, every self–insurer or its administrative agency shall maintain:

(1) a manually prepared log of all work injury claims for each self–insurer at each adjusting location in accordance with Title 8, Section 10103 and 10103.1; or

(2) a computerized log of claims for each self–insurer at each adjusting location in accordance with Title 8, Section 10103 and 10103.1.

(b) The claim log shall be maintained at each of the self–insurer's or its administrative agency's claims adjusting locations. The claim log at each location shall be kept current and shall include all claims reported to the adjusting location.

(c) A claim log shall be found to be materially deficient if it fails to contain the elements of Title 8, Section 10103 and 10103.1; or fails to include all reported claims; or is not provided to the Manager or any subsequent administrator in readable form.

Section 15400.2 provides:

(a) All claim files shall be kept and maintained for a period of five years from the date of injury or from the date on which the last provision of compensation benefits occurred as defined in Labor Code Section 3207, whichever is later. Claim files with awards for future benefits shall not be destroyed, but two years after the date of the last provision of workers' compensation benefits as defined in Labor Code Section 3207, they may be converted to an inactive or closed status by the administrator, but only if there is no reasonable expectation that future benefits will be claimed or provided.

(b) Inactive and closed claim files may be microfilmed for storage, however, the original paper files shall be maintained for at least two years after the claim has been closed or become inactive. Such microfilmed files must be readily reproducible into legible paper form if requested by the Manager for audit.

(c) All claim files and the claim logs shall be kept and maintained in California unless the Manager has given written approval to a self insurer or former self insurer to administer its workers' compensation self–insurance plan from a location outside of California.

(d) All claim files and claim logs, together with records of all compensation benefit payments, shall be readily available for inspection by the Manager or his representative.

Estimating Reserves

The Administrative Director has established very specific requirements for self–insurers insofar as establishing reserves of estimated future liability for each indemnity claim as well as medical–only claims. Title 8, California Code of Regulations, Section 15300 provides:

(a) A list of open indemnity claims shall be submitted with each self insurer's annual report as required by Section 15251(b)(5)(A)–(B) and (c)(7).

(b) The administrator shall set a realistic estimate of future liability for each indemnity claim listed on the self insurer's annual report based on computations which reflect the probable total future cost of compensation and medical benefits due or that can reasonably expected to be due over the life of the claim. Each estimate listed on the self insurer's annual report shall be based on information in possession of the administrator at the–ending date of the period of time covered by the annual report. Estimated future liabilities listed on the annual report must represent the probable total future cost of compensation for the injury or disease based on information documented as in possession of the administrator at the ending date of the period of time covered by the annual report. In setting estimates of future liability, the administrator shall adhere to the following principles:

(1) Each estimate of future liability shall separately reflect an indemnity component and a medical component. The indemnity component shall include the estimated future cost of all temporary disability, permanent disability, death benefits including burial costs, and vocational rehabilitation including vendor costs. The medical component shall include the estimated future cost of all medical treatment, including costs of medical cost containment programs if those costs are allocated to the particular claim, and the estimated future cost of medical evaluations. Estimates of future liability shall include any increases in compensation in either component reasonably expected to be payable pursuant to Labor Code Sections 132a, 4553, and/or 5814.

(2) In estimating future permanent disability costs, where there are conflicting permanent disability ratings, the estimate shall be based on the higher rating unless there is sufficient evidence in the claim file to support a lower estimate.

(3) In estimating future medical costs where the injured worker's injury has not reached maximum medical improvement or permanent and stationary status, the estimate shall be based on projected costs for the total anticipated period of treatment throughout the life of the claim.

(4) In estimating future medical costs where the injured worker's injury has reached maximum medical improvement or permanent and stationary status, the estimate shall be based on average annual costs over the past three years since the injury reached maximum medical improvement or permanent and stationary status, or a lesser period if three years have not passed since the injury reached maximum medical improvement or permanent and stationary status, projected over the life expectancy of the injured worker. Estimates shall include any additional costs such as medical procedures or surgeries that can reasonably be expected over the life of the claim.

(5) Estimates based on average past costs shall be increased to include any costs that can reasonably be expected to occur that are not included within the averages. Estimates based on average past costs may be reduced to account for any treatment not reasonably expected to occur in the future based on medical documentation in possession of the administrator.

(6) Estimates of future medical costs based on average past costs shall not be reduced based on undocumented anticipated reductions in frequency of treatment or to reflect the substitution of treatments with a lower cost than utilized by the injured worker that may be available but that the injured worker is not utilizing. Estimates based on average past costs may be reduced based on reductions in the approved medical fee schedule and based on utilization review, except that reductions in estimates based on utilization review may not be reduced if the reductions are reasonably disputed. Estimates of future liability may be reduced based on the expectation of a third party recovery only in instances where an Order allowing credit has been issued pursuant to Labor Code Section 3861.

(7) Estimates of lifetime medical care and life pension benefits shall be determined based on the injured worker's life expectancy according to the most recent U.S. Life Expectancy Tables as reported by the U.S. Department of Health and Human Services, Centers for Disease Control and Prevention. Note: the most recent life expectancy tables can be found at http://www.cdc.gov/nchs/datawh/nchsdefs/lifeexpe ctancy.htm .

(8) Estimates of permanent disability shall not be reduced based on apportionment unless the claim file includes documentation supporting apportionment.

(9) Estimates shall not be reduced to reflect present value of future benefits.

(c) All medical–only claims reported on the self insurer's annual report shall be estimated on the basis of computations which will develop the total future cost of medical benefits due or that can reasonably expected to be due based on information documented as in possession of the administrator at the ending date of the period of time covered by the annual report.

(d) Estimates of future liability shall not be decreased based on projected third party recoveries or projected reimbursements from aggregate excess insurance, nor shall reported paid costs be decreased based on third party recoveries or aggregate excess insurance reimbursements.

(e) The incurred liability estimate on known claims may be capped at the retention level of any specific excess workers' compensation insurance policy to the extent that each claim has not been denied in writing by the carrier. The self insurer's claims administrator shall list each claim covered by a specific excess insurance policy on Part VI–B of the Self Insurer's Annual Report. An adjustment to the total deposit required to be posted shall be made for claims covered by specific excess insurance policy on the annual report to the extent that they meet the requirements in Section 15251(b)(5)(B) of these regulations.

(f) Estimates of incurred liability, payments–made–to–date and estimated future liability of all compensation benefits shall be made immediately available at the time of audit if not already documented in the claim file, or when requested by the Manager.

(g) The administrator shall adjust the estimate immediately upon receipt of medical reports, orders of the Appeals

Board, or other relevant information that affects the valuation of the claim. Each estimate shall be reviewed no less than annually. Estimates set by a prior administrator shall be reviewed by the current administrator before filing the Self Insurer's Annual Report.

Intentionally blank

California Workers' Compensation Claims and Benefits, 12th Ed. Supplement (2007)

§ 69.0   UNINSURED EMPLOYERS' BENEFITS TRUST FUND

§ 69.1   Uninsured Employers' Benefits Trust Fund

Page 2040, Column 2, delete chart and add the following:

Eureka, Redding, Sacramento, Stockton:
UEF Claims Unit
2424 Arden Way, Suite 355
Sacramento, CA 95825
Tel: (916) 263–2774

Bakersfield, Fresno, Oakland, Salinas, San Francisco, San Jose, Santa Rosa, Walnut Creek:
UEF Claims Unit
1515 Clay Street, 17th floor
Oakland, CA 94612
Tel: (510) 286–7067

Grover Beach, Long Beach, Los Angeles, Norwalk, Pasadena, Santa Barbara, Santa Monica, Oxnard, Ventura, Van Nuys:
UEF Claims Unit
320 W. 4th Street, Suite 690
Los Angeles, CA 90013
Tel: (213) 576–7300

Further, a copy of an application to the Uninsured Employers Fund should now be send to Labor Standards Enforcement at the following address:

Labor Standards Enforcement Special Programs Section

San Francisco–Headquarters
455 Golden Gate Avenue, 9th Floor
San Francisco, CA 94102
(415) 703–4810

Bakersfield
5555 California Avenue, Suite 200
Bakersfield, CA 93309
Tel: (661) 395–2710
Fax: (661) 859–2462

Redding
2115 Civic Center Drive, Room 17
Redding, CA 96001
Tel: (530) 225–2655
Fax: (530) 229–0565

San Jose
100 Paseo de San Antonio, Room 120
San Jose, CA 95113
Tel: (408) 277–1266
Fax: (408) 277–3711

El Centro
1550 W. Main St.
El Centro, CA 92243
Tel: (760) 353–0607
Fax: (760) 353–2544

Sacramento
2031 Howe Avenue, Suite 100
Sacramento, CA 95825
Tel: (916) 263–1811
Fax: (916) 263–5378

Santa Ana
28 Civic Center Plaza, Room 625
Santa Ana, CA 92701
Tel: (714) 558–4910
Fax: (714) 558–4574

Eureka
619 Second Street, Room 109
Eureka, CA 95501
Tel: (707) 445–6613
Fax: (707) 441–4604

Salinas
1870 N. Main St., Suite 150
Salinas, CA 93906
Tel: (831) 443–3041
Fax: (831) 443–3029

Santa Barbara
411 E. Canon Perdido, Room 3
Santa Barbara, CA 93101
Tel: (805) 568–1222
Fax: (805) 965–7214

Fresno
770 E. Shaw Avenue, Room 315
Fresno, CA 93710
Tel: (559) 244–5340
Fax: (559) 248–8398

San Bernardino
464 W. Fourth Street, Room 348
San Bernardino, CA 92401
Tel: (909) 383–4334
Fax: (909) 889–8120

Santa Rosa
50 "D" Street, Suite 360
Santa Rosa, CA 95404
Tel: (707) 576–2362
Fax: (707) 576–2459

Long Beach
300 Oceangate, Suite 302
Long Beach, CA 90802
Tel: (562) 590–5048
Fax: (562) 491–0160

San Diego
7575 Metropolitan Dr., Room 210
San Diego, CA 92108
Tel: (619) 220–5451
Fax: (619) 682–7221

Stockton
31 E. Channel Street, Room 317
Stockton, CA 95202
Tel: (209) 948–7771
Fax: (209) 941–1906

Los Angeles
320 W. Fourth Street, Suite 450
Los Angeles, CA 90013
Tel: (213) 620–6330
Fax: (213) 576–6227

San Francisco
455 Golden Gate Ave., 10th Floor
San Francisco, CA 94102
Tel: (415) 703–5300
Fax: (415) 703–5444

Van Nuys
6150 Van Nuys Blvd., Room 206
Van Nuys, CA 91401
Tel: (818) 901–5315
Fax: (818) 908–4556

Oakland
1515 Clay Street, Suite 801
Oakland, CA 94612
Tel: (510) 622–3273
Fax: (510) 622–2660

Page 2046, Column 2, fourth paragraph, insert following '…§ 57.34."

The Uninsured Employers' Benefit Trust Fund may be liable to reimburse an insurance carrier that has paid benefits on the mistaken belief that it insured an employer when in fact the employer was uninsured for the period of injury that thus the Fund was liable for benefits paid. *UEBTF v. WCAB (Fisher)* (2006) 71 Cal. Comp. Cases 1193.

§ 70.0   MEANS OF SECURING PAYMENT OF COMPENSATION

Page 2054, Column 1, first paragraph, insert following ' (916) 483–3392.'

Self–insured employers must file annual reports with the Director and the Director must make aggregated summaries of reports available to the public. *Labor Code* section 3702.2 provides:

(a) All self–insured employers shall file a self–insurer's annual report in a form prescribed by the director.

(b) To enable the director to determine the amount of the security deposit required by subdivision (c) of Section 3701, the annual report of a self–insured employer who has self–insured both state and federal workers' compensation liability shall also set forth (1) the amount of all compensation liability incurred, paid–to–date, and estimated future liability under both this chapter and under the federal Longshore and Harbor Workers' Compensation Act (33 U.S.C. Sec. 901 et seq.) and (2) the identity and the amount of the security deposit securing the employer's liability under state and federal self–insured programs.

(c) The director shall annually prepare an aggregated summary of all self–insurer employer liability to pay compensation reported on the self–insurers' employers annual reports, including a separate summary for public and private employer self–insurers. The summaries shall be in the same format as the individual self–insured employers are required to report that liability on the employer self–insured's annual report forms prescribed by the director. The aggregated summaries shall be made available to the public on the self–insurance section of the department's Internet Web site. Nothing in this subdivision shall authorize the director to release or make available information that is aggregated by industry or business type, that identifies individual self–insured filers, or that includes any individually identifiable claimant information.

(d) The director may release a copy, or make available an electronic version, of the data contained in any public sector employer self–insurer's annual reports received from an individual public entity self–insurer or from a joint powers authority employer and its membership. However, the release of any annual report information by the director shall not include any portion of any listing of open indemnity claims that contains individually identifiable claimant information, or any portion of excess insurance coverage information that contains any individually identifiable claimant information.

Intentionally blank

§ 72.0 CALIFORNIA INSURANCE GUARANTEE ASSOCIATION

Page 2059, Column 2, first paragraph, insert the following:

Insurance Code section 1063.1 in defining the terms "member insurer" and "insolvent insurer" provides:

"Member insurer" means an insurer required to be a member of the association in accordance with subdivision (a) of Section 1063, except and to the extent that the insurer is participating in an insolvency program adopted by the United States government.

"Insolvent insurer" means an insurer that was a member insurer of the association, consistent with paragraph (11) of subdivision (c), either at the time the policy was issued or when the insured event occurred, and against which an order of liquidation or receivership within a finding of insolvency has been entered by a court of competent jurisdiction, or, in the case of the State Compensation Insurance Fund, if a finding of insolvency is made by a duly enacted legislative measure... .

Effective July 20, 2007 Insurance Code section 11691 was amended to provide that if an insurance carrier is liquidated any money owing the carrier is to be paid to CIGA and not the estate whether the carrier is in or out of the state of California.

§ 72.2 California Insurance Guarantee Association's Liability For Cumulative Trauma Injuries

Page 2063, Column 2, second paragraph, insert following '...proceedings.'

In *County of Riverside v. WCAB (Cannell)* (2006) 71 Cal. Comp. Cases 530, the Board held that CIGA, on behalf of applicant's general employer, was relieved of liability and entitled to reimbursement for compensation paid to an applicant while working for a permissibly self–insured special employer when it found that Insurance Code section 1163 did not apply and that *the special employer's self–insurance constituted "other insurance" under* Insurance Code section 1063.1(c)(9) and Labor Code section 3211 and *Denny's, Inc. v. WCAB (Bachman)* (2003) 68 Cal. Comp. Cases 1. The Board stated, in part:

In the instant case, there is no dispute that on the date of injury, County was the permissibly self–insured special employer of applicant. Insurance Code section 11663 does not apply because CIGA is not an "insurer" within the meaning of the statute. Absent section 11663, County has joint and several liability for applicant's benefits. Pursuant to *Denny's* and Labor Code section 3211, the County of Riverside, as an employer self–insured for workers' compensation purposes, provides "other insurance of a class covered by" the Guarantee Act within the meaning of Insurance Code section 1063.1(c)(9). Accordingly, we will affirm the WCJ's decision.

With regard to petitioner's argument that it is inequitable to make the taxpayers of Riverside County pay for CIGA's supposed obligation, we note that, while the argument may carry some theoretical or rhetorical interest, it is not supported by any statutory or case law. In *Denny's*, moreover, the Court rejected a similar contention. In this case, the County's invocation of its taxpayers does not persuade us to overturn the WCJ's decision... .

In *Blue Cross of California v. WCAB (Gorge)* (2006) 71 Cal. Comp. Cases 1587, the Appeals Board held that a group health insurance provided to an applicant constituted "insurance" and that the lien claimant (Blue Cross) was a "health care service provider" and "insurer" and that the lien of Blue Cross was not a "Covered claim" within the meaning of Insurance Code section 1063.1(c)(5) for which CIGA was liable.

In *CIGA v. WCAB (Gutierrez)* (2006), 71 Cal. Comp. Cases 1661, the Court of Appeal, Second District, in an unpublished decision, held that a lien from the University of California, Davis Medical Center, is an obligation of the State pursuant to Insurance Code section 1063.1(c)(4) because the University of California is an agency of the State, so CIGA is not obligated to pay the lien.

§ 72.3(A)   Multiple and Successive Specific Injuries

<u>Page 2066, Column 1, first paragraph, commencing 'Recently,...' delete first two lines and insert:</u>

Recently, the Court of Appeal, Second District, in *CIGA v. WCAB (Weitzman)* (2005), 70 Cal. Comp.

<u>Page 2069, Column 1, eighth paragraph, insert following '...lien claim.'</u>

See *SCIF v. WCAB (Martinez)* (2006) 71 Cal. Comp. Cases 973, where the Board followed *Weitzman*. The Board quoted, with approval the judge, in part:

Weitzman is the law that controls this case. *CIGA v. WCAB* (Weitzman) [(2005) 128 Cal. App. 4th 307, 26 Cal. Rptr. 3d 845, 70 Cal. Comp. Cases 556], expressly stated that *Gomez* was incorrectly decided. While it did indicate it did not have to decide that particular case on the issues raised in Gomez, it decided it was important to instruct the legal community regarding its interpretation of the Insurance Code Section 1063.1 Subdivision (c)(9)(i). The court concluded that the responsibility for medical treatment caused by successive industrial injures [*sic*] was joint and several, subject only to the rights of contribution between employers. S.C.I.F. has no right of reimbursement from CIGA for its portion of payment of joint/several benefits [California Ins. Guarantee Assn. v. W.C.A.B. (Hooten) [(2005) 128 Cal. App. 4th 569, 27 Cal. Rptr. 3d 205, 70 Cal. Comp. Cases 551]. Yet under Ins. Code Sec. 1063.2(b), CIGA has ["] the same rights as the insolvent insurer would have had if not in liquidation." This WCJ concluded that CIGA per *Weitzman* and 1063.2(b) is entitled to reimbursement of the joint/several benefits it paid for these injuries without apportionment from the solvent carrier. An award so finding was issued... .

In explaining why SCIF, rather than CIGA, should administer future benefits, the judge stated:

. . . This WCJ is concerned that if CIGA is appointed as administrator of future benefits, including medical treatment, temporary disability and VR that it will not pay as there is [*sic*] no penalty rights against CIGA and it has a defense that it is not responsible to pay as S.C.I.F. has the covered claim and there is "other insurance" to pay for the future benefits. It follows that S.C.I.F. must administer applicant's future benefits... .

The judge further concluded that, if there is "other insurance" available in cases of successive injuries, that other insurance provides coverage when there is joint and several liability with CIGA. Further, the judge found that, under Insurance Code § 1063.1(b), CIGA

has a right of reimbursement, without apportionment, of benefits it paid that were covered by the "other insurance," and that the solvent carrier is the appropriate administrator, rather than CIGA, of future benefits.

See also *Allianz Insurance Company v. WCAB (Hernandez)* (2006) 71 Cal. Comp. Cases 1437, for a somewhat similar holding where the judge stated, in part:

I found nothing in the case of Frank Hernandez which warranted a departure from what appears to be the relatively clear mandate of the statute, especially when considering the court decisions, that another insurer may not obtain reimbursement or contribution from the California Insurance Guarantee Association by way of contribution or subrogation. Admittedly, as noted by Allianz in its Petition for Reconsideration, there are facts in the case of Frank Hernandez which differ to some degree from the facts in the cases cited. I fail, however, to see that any of the factual distinctions are such as to warrant a departure from what appears to be a general rule barring contribution or reimbursement from California Insurance Guarantee Association by another insurer such as Allianz... .

If joint and several liability does not exist between CIGA and a solvent carrier, CIGA is only entitled to reimbursement from a solvent insurer for the sum equal to the solvent insurer's proportionate share of benefits for an applicant's successive injury. Commenting on this in *CIGA et al v. WCAB (Hernandez)* (2006) 71 Cal. Comp. Cases 1832, the Board stated, in part:

In both *Garcia* and *Weitzman*, it was determined that the "other insurance" exception to CIGA liability was applicable when there existed joint and several liability between CIGA and the carrier. Here, however, there is no overlap in insurance coverage between the two claims. CIGA is wholly responsible for the earlier specific injury, and SCIF was the only carrier on the risk, and thus wholly responsible, for the subsequent cumulative trauma. In other words, because SCIF insured against only the later injury, any claims payable as a result of the earlier specific injury were not covered by "other insurance"... .

§ 72.3(C)   General–Special Employment Relationship

<u>Page 2069, Column 2, first paragraph, delete line nine commencing 'The opinions of...' and ending '...litigation.' and insert:</u>

The opinions of the Appeals Board, the Court of Appeal, Second District and the California Supreme Court in *Miceli et. al. v. Jacuzzi, Inc., CIGA* (2003) 68 Cal. Comp. Cases 434, below are provided in their entirety to assist the reader in obtaining insight as to the positions of the parties involved in this litigation.

Page 2072, Column 2, sixth paragraph, delete line six commencing 'After review...' and ending '...as follows.' and insert the following:

After review of information and comment provided by the Workers' Compensation Insurance Rating Bureau and Department of Insurance, the Court of Appeal, Second District, in *General Casualty Insurance et. al. v. WCAB* 70 Cal. Comp. Cases 953 stated, as follows:

Page 2080, Column 1, eighth paragraph, insert following '...for publication.'

Thereafter, the Appeals Board in *Miceli v. Jacuzzi, Inc., Remedy Temp, Inc. et. al.* (2006) 71 Cal. Comp. Cases 599, following a return of the case by the Court of Appeal, rescinded its earlier decision and stated, in part:

OPINION AND DECISION AFTER REMITTITUR
(EN BANC)

INTRODUCTION

In an opinion ordered by the Supreme Court not to be published, the Court of Appeal found that the special employer's insurance in this case is not "other insurance" available to applicant within the meaning of Insurance Code section 1063.1(c)(9). Based on that finding, the Court of Appeal reversed our earlier en banc decision, set aside the dismissal of the California Insurance Guarantee Association (CIGA) as a defendant, and returned the matter to the Appeals Board for further proceedings. The remittitur included no award of costs. In reaching its decision, the Court of Appeal took judicial notice of additional documents and considered responses submitted by the Workers' Compensation Insurance Rating Bureau (WCIRB) and the California Commissioner of Insurance (Insurance Commissioner) to questions asked by the Court.

Following remittitur, RemedyTemp, Inc. (RemedyTemp) and CIGA jointly filed a letter with the Appeals Board requesting that the May 14, 2002 order consolidating and staying all cases involving RemedyTemp, with dates of injury between July 22, 1997 and April 1, 2001, continue in effect pending a decision on RemedyTemp's request to be dismissed from each of the consolidated cases. CIGA and RemedyTemp also jointly requested that the Appeals Board provide guidance to parties and the workers' compensation administrative law judges on how they should proceed pending resolution of RemedyTemp's request for dismissal from the consolidated cases. In addition, American Home Assurance Co. (Assurance) filed a petition with the Appeals Board requesting an award of costs it claimed to have incurred on appeal. We now address the effect of the Court of Appeal decision, the letter jointly filed by RemedyTemp and CIGA, and Assurance's petition to recover costs on appeal. (Footnote 1)

We conclude:

1. Our en banc decision in this case was reversed by the Court of Appeal and for that reason it is not legal precedent. In addition, the unpublished Court of Appeal decision in this case may not be generally cited or relied upon in any other action, except when relevant under the doctrines of law of the case, res judicata or collateral estoppel;

2. The May 14, 2002 consolidation and stay order was only intended to apply during the pendency of the appellate proceedings in this case and it is now rescinded so that each case covered by that order may be individually resolved on its own particular facts;

3. The request by RemedyTemp to be dismissed from each of the consolidated cases is denied because the consolidation order no longer applies and there is no authority to support dismissal because the Court of Appeal decision was decertified for publication by the Supreme Court.

4. The joint request by RemedyTemp and CIGA for a new consolidation and/or stay order is denied because each case must be evaluated on its own facts, including consideration of the intent of the parties and the effect of the various insurance policies involved;

5. The petition filed by Assurance for reimbursement of costs it claims to have incurred in the Court of Appeal proceeding is dismissed.

We will return this case to the trial level for further proceedings in accordance with this decision and the decision of the Court of Appeal.

FACTUAL AND PROCEDURAL BACKGROUND

Applicant injured his left ring finger on March 1, 2000, while working as a shipper/receiver on the property of defendant and special employer Jacuzzi, Inc. (Jacuzzi). (Footnote 2)

Applicant's general employer at that time was the staffing company, RemedyTemp. RemedyTemp was insured for workers' compensation purposes by Reliance National Indemnity Co. (Reliance), and Jacuzzi was insured by both Reliance for its special employees and by Assurance for its own employees. Under a written agreement between RemedyTemp and Jacuzzi, RemedyTemp was to provide workers' compensation insurance coverage for applicant and to hold Jacuzzi harmless from any workers' compensation claims involving employees of Reliance.

Reliance, for RemedyTemp, admitted the industrial injury to applicant and began to provide workers' compensation benefits. Thereafter, Reliance was declared insolvent and CIGA became responsible for Reliance's covered claims. CIGA petitioned for dismissal from the action on the ground that Jacuzzi's insurer, Assurance, was "other insurance" available to applicant pursuant to Insurance Code section 1063.1(c)(9), which provides in pertinent part, " 'Covered claims' does not include (i) any claim to the extent it is covered by any other insurance of a class covered by this article available to the claimant or insured . . . "

On May 14, 2002, Associate Chief Judge Kahn, Regional Manager of the Division of Workers' Compensation, issued an Amended Order of Consolidation and Stay of Proceedings for all cases involving RemedyTemp with dates of injury between July 22, 1997 and April 1, 2001. The consolidation and stay order affected more than 500 cases. This case was allowed to proceed so that the legal issue of insurance coverage believed to be common to the consolidated cases could be addressed.

On October 31, 2002, the workers' compensation administrative law judge (WCJ) issued the Findings and Order in this case. The WCJ found that Assurance's policy was "other insurance" available to applicant within the meaning of Insurance Code section 1063.1(c)(9), and ordered CIGA's dismissal from the case. In December 2002, defendants Jacuzzi, RemedyTemp and Assurance all petitioned for reconsideration of the October 31, 2002 Findings and Order. On January 6, 2003, reconsideration was granted by the Appeals Board in order to allow further study of the factual and legal issues.

On March 28, 2003, the Appeals Board issued an en banc decision affirming the WCJ's finding that the Assurance policy was other insurance available to applicant within the meaning of Insurance Code section 1063.1(c)(9), and affirming the dismissal of CIGA as a defendant in this case. RemedyTemp, Jacuzzi and Assurance petitioned the Court of Appeal for a writ of review. A writ of review was issued and on October 20, 2004, the Court of Appeal filed a decision affirming the Appeal Board's March 28, 2003 en banc decision that CIGA was properly dismissed as a defendant. However, Assurance, RemedyTemp and Jacuzzi timely petitioned for rehearing and those petitions were granted by the Court of Appeal.

Upon rehearing, the Court of Appeal took judicial notice of additional documents attached to Assurance's petition and requested responses from the WCIRB and the Insurance Commissioner to questions posed by the Court. (Footnote 3)

After considering the additional documents and responses, the Court of Appeal vacated its earlier decision and issued a new decision on July 25, 2005. The new decision, which was initially certified for publication by the Court of Appeal, reversed the Appeals Board's March 28, 2003 en banc decision, and held that CIGA should not have been dismissed as a defendant because "other insurance" within the meaning of Insurance Code section 1063.1(c)(9) was *not* available to applicant.

CIGA petitioned for Supreme Court review of the July 25, 2005 decision by the Court of Appeal. On October 12, 2005, the Supreme Court denied CIGA's petition for review. However, the Supreme Court ordered that the Court of Appeal decision *not* be published in the official reports.

On October 2, 2005, RemedyTemp filed a request with the Appeals Board for an order dismissing it from every case covered by the May 14, 2002 consolidation and stay

order. CIGA filed an objection to that request. On November 3, 2005, this case was remitted to the Appeals Board by the Court of Appeal for further proceedings consistent with its unpublished decision. No award of costs was included in the remittitur. Following remittitur, Assurance filed a petition with the Appeals Board requesting reimbursement of costs it claimed to have incurred in the appeal process before the Court of Appeal. (Footnote 4)

On February 17, 2006, RemedyTemp and CIGA jointly filed a letter with the Appeals Board asking that we "address the considerable uncertainty that exists among the applicants, insurers and employers and their respective counsel as to the status of the consolidated *Miceli* cases following the Court of Appeal's decision." In requesting action, CIGA and RemedyTemp note that "the status of the more than 500 claims that were consolidated for purposes of resolving the common legal issue relating to CIGA's responsibilities has become a source of confusion and dispute . . . some parties continue to seek discovery or to conduct other proceedings in some individual cases." Noting RemedyTemp's earlier October 2, 2005 petition to be dismissed from the consolidated proceedings, CIGA and RemedyTemp specificallyrequested that the Appeals Board:

"[O]rder that all proceedings in all of the consolidated actions be stayed pending a final ruling on [RemedyTemp's] pending request for dismissal, with the exception of (1) matters relating to the rights or obligations of a party or parties pertaining to medical issues under Labor Code Section 4060, 4061, 4600, 4600.4, 4601 and 4603, or to discovery rights or obligations under those sections,, (sic) and (2) any proceeding in which the alleged special employer was separately insured pursuant to Labor Code Section 3700 solely by an insolvent insurer. In the alternative, the parties respectfully request that the [Appeals] Board issue further guidance on how the parties and judges are to proceed pending a resolution of the request for dismissal." "

I.

THE EFFECT OF THE JULY 25, 2005 COURT OF APPEAL OPINION

California Rules of Court, rule 976(b) provides that an opinion of the Court of Appeal is to be "published in the Official Reports if a majority of the rendering court certifies the opinion for publication before the decision is final in that court." In this case, the Court of Appeal initially certified its July 25, 2005 opinion for publication. However, California Rules of Court, rule 976(d)(2) further provides that, "The Supreme Court may order that an opinion certified for publication is not to be published . . . " In this case, the Supreme Court ordered on October 12, 2005, that the Court of Appeal decision not be published in the official reports.

California Rules of Court, rule 977 addresses the citation and use of unpublished opinions as follows:

"(a) Unpublished opinion

Except as provided in (b), an opinion of a California Court of Appeal or superior court appellate division that is not certified for publication or ordered published must not be cited or relied on by a court or a party in any other action.

(b) Exceptions

An unpublished opinion may be cited or relied on:

(1) when the opinion is relevant under the doctrines of law of the case, res judicata, or collateral estoppel . . . ""

Because the July 25, 2005 Court of Appeal opinion in this case was decertified for publication by the Supreme Court, it may not be relied upon or cited as authority in any other case, including all the other cases covered by the May 14, 2002 Amended Order of Consolidation and Stay of Proceedings, unless an exception of res judicata or collateral estoppel is found to apply. It appears that collateral estoppel may apply in some cases, but its application would be limited to cases involving the same parties and the same issue litigated to finality in this case. All other cases must be addressed on their own facts in light of citeable precedent and legal authority.

II.

THE STATUS OF THE MAY 14, 2002 AMENDED ORDER OF CONSOLIDATION AND STAY OF PROCEEDINGS

As we stated in our March 28, 2003 en banc decision, the consolidation and stay order issued by Associate Chief Judge Kahn on May 15, 2002, was to remain in effect "pending finality" of our March 28, 2003 en banc decision. The condition of "finality" anticipated that the stay would continue in place through the course of any appellate proceedings involving our en banc decision. It was anticipated that the Court of Appeal or Supreme Court would either affirm our en banc decision, or replace it with a published decision that would provide precedent to assist in resolving the issue of CIGA's liability in the consolidated cases.

However, our en banc decision in this case was reversed, but was not superseded by a published decision of the Court of Appeal or the Supreme Court. Nevertheless, the reason for consolidating and staying the other cases "pending finality" of our March 28, 2003 en banc decision no longer applies because the decision in this case is final. Because our March 28, 2003 en banc decision was reversed by the Court of Appeal, it no longer is binding precedent on all Appeals Board panels and WCJs. (Cal. Code Regs., tit.8, § 10341; *City of Long Beach v. Workers' Comp. Appeals Bd.* (*Garcia*) (2005) 126 Cal. App. 4th 298, 313, fn. 5 [23 Cal. Rptr. 3d 782] [70 Cal. Comp. Cases 109]; *Gee v. Workers' Comp. Appeals Bd.* (2002) 96 Cal. App. 4th 1418, 1425, fn. 6 [118 Cal. Rptr. 2d 105] [67 Cal. Comp. Cases 236]. *Diggle v. Sierra Sands Unified School District* (2005) [70 Cal. Comp. Cases1480] (significant panel decision).) Because the May 15, 2002 Amended Order of Consolidation and Stay of Proceedings has no further purpose, it is rescinded and is of no further force and effect.

Because the consolidation and stay order is rescinded, each case previously covered by that order must now be individually addressed on its own particular facts. With regard to the issue of the application of Insurance Code section 1063.1(c)(9), individual consideration of each case may require consideration of the particular insurance policies and endorsements in effect in each case. If it is found in a case that "other insurance" within the meaning of Insurance Code section 1063.1(c)(9) is available to an applicant, an order dismissing CIGA may be appropriate. If it is found that "other insurance" within the meaning of Insurance Code section 1063.1(c)(9) is not available to an applicant, an order dismissing CIGA would not be appropriate, but an order dismissing the general employer may be appropriate. Each case must be addressed on its own facts.

III.

REMEDYTEMP'S REQUESTS FOR DISMISSAL

In light of our decision that each consolidated case must be addressed on its own particular facts, it would not be appropriate to dismiss RemedyTemp from any of those cases at this time. As discussed above, the July 25, 2005 Court of Appeal opinion is not binding or citeable precedent in any of the other cases covered by the May 15, 2002 consolidation and stay order, absent some proper application of the doctrines of law of the case, res judicata, or collateral estoppel. Instead, each of those other cases must be individually addressed on its own facts, and RemedyTemp's liability must be individually addressed in each of those cases.

As to RemedyTemp's request to be dismissed from this case, that issue is not before us as part of the remittitur but it may be addressed in the first instance by the WCJ upon return of this case to the trial level.

IV.

THE JOINT REQUEST BY CIGA AND REMEDYTEMP FOR A NEW ORDER STAYING AND CONSOLIDATING CASES

We recognize the difficulties now faced by the parties in the cases covered by the earlier May 15, 2002 consolidation and stay order. However, we find that a new consolidation and stay order is not appropriate. A stay order will not assist in resolving issues that that must be addressed by consideration of the particular facts in each case. Instead, each case must proceed on its own, with supplementation of the record to include the various insurance policies and endorsements as may be necessary and appropriate. This will assure that the record in each individual case is properly developed and that a decision is reached in each based upon its own particular facts.

V.

ASSURANCE'S PETITION FOR REIMBURSEMENT OF COSTS ON APPEAL

Assurance filed a petition with the Appeals Board for reimbursement of costs it claimed to have incurred as part of the litigation in the Court of Appeal. Assurance's petition is not properly directed to the Appeals Board and will be dismissed.

The Appeals Board has authority to award costs incurred by a party in responding to a petition for writ of review when the petition is summarily denied, or if the Court of Appeal otherwise allows costs. (*Johnson v. Workers' Comp. Appeals Bd.* (1984) 37 Cal. 3d 235 [689 P.2d 1127, 207 Cal. Rptr. 857] [49 Cal. Comp. Cases 716] (*Johnson*).) However, after a writ of review is granted, the issue of appellate costs must be addressed by the Court of Appeal in accordance with the California Rules of Court, which are "applicable to costs in proceedings for review of WCAB decisions." (*Johnson*, *supra*; Lab. Code, § 5954; Code Civ. Proc., §§ 1027, 1109.) Under the California Rules of Court, the clerk of the Court of Appeal is to insert a judgment awarding costs to the prevailing party in the remittitur unless the costs are otherwise awarded or denied by the Court in the interests of justice. (Cal. Rules of Court, rule 27(a)(4) and rule 27(b)(1).) If the court clerk "fails to enter judgment for costs, the court may recall the remittitur for correction on its own motion, or on a party's motion made not later than 30 days after the remittitur issues." (Cal. Rules of Court, rule 27(b)(2).)

In this case, the remittitur issued on November 3, 2005, but it contains no judgment for costs. To our knowledge, the clerk's failure to enter judgment for costs was not addressed within 30 days after the remittitur issued by a party bringing a motion to correct the omission or by the Court of Appeal on its own motion. In short, Assurance's petition for costs incurred on appeal is directed to the wrong court. Because the petitions for writ of review were granted, not summarily denied, the Appeals Board is without authority in this case to award costs on appeal to any party. (*Johnson*, *supra*; Cal. Rules of Court, rule 27.)

For the foregoing reasons,

IT IS ORDERED as the decision after remittitur of the Appeals Board (en banc) that the Appeals Board's March 28, 2003 en banc decision, and the October 31, 2002 Findings and Order of the workers' compensation administrative law judge are RESCINDED and the following is SUBSTITUTED in its place:

FINDINGS

1. At the time of applicant's injury, defendant, RemedyTemp, Inc., was applicant's general employer, insured by Reliance National Indemnity Co., now in liquidation, and defendant Jacuzzi, Inc., was applicant's special employer, insured by American Home Assurance Co.

2. Jacuzzi, Inc.'s policy of insurance with American Home Assurance Co. is not available to applicant following the insolvency of Reliance National Indemnity Co.

3. The policy of American Home Assurance Co. is not "other insurance" within the meaning of Insurance Code section 1063.1(c)(9).

ORDERS

IT IS ORDERED that the petition of the California Insurance Guarantee Association to be dismissed as a defendant is DENIED and petitioner remains a party in this case.

IT IS FURTHER ORDERED that the request by RemedyTemp, Inc., for dismissal from all cases covered by the May 14, 2002 Amended Order of Consolidation and Stay of Proceedings is DENIED.

IT IS FURTHER ORDERED that the May 14, 2002 Amended Order of Consolidation and Stay of Proceedings issued by Associate Chief Judge Kahn, Regional Manager of the Division of Workers' Compensation, for all cases involving RemedyTemp, Inc., with dates of injury between July 22, 1997 and April 1, 2001, is RESCINDED, and is of no further force or effect.

IT IS FURTHER ORDERED that the Joint Request by RemedyTemp, Inc. and the California Insurance Guarantee Association for a new order consolidating and staying cases is DENIED.

IT IS FURTHER ORDERED that the Petition for Reimbursement of Costs and Disbursements on Appeal on Behalf of Defendant American Home Assurance Company filed herein on December 15, 2005, is DISMISSED.

IT IS FURTHER ORDERED that this matter be RETURNED to the trial level for further proceedings and decision by the workers' compensation administrative law judge in accordance with this decision and the decision of the Court of Appeal... .

Footnote 1. Chairman Miller and Commissioner Caplane recused themselves from participation in this decision.

Footnote 2. A complete statement of the facts is included in our earlier en banc decision and in the decision of the Court of Appeal and will not be repeated herein.

Footnote 3. The documents include Exhibits A–D. Exhibit A is a California Endorsement Approved Form No. 11. submitted to the Workers' Compensation Insurance Rating Bureau (WCIRB) in another matter by Assurance. Exhibit B is an August 10, 2004 letter from the WCIRB to Assurance requesting an explanation of the purpose for Form No. 11 (Exh. A). Exhibit C is Assurance's August 25, 2004 response to the WCIRB's request for information about Form 11. Exhibit D is a September 13, 2004 fax from the WCIRB to Assurance advising that Form No. 11 (Exh. A) would not be appropriate for the purpose described by Assurance in its response (Exh. C). Also received by the Court of Appeal at its request was a December 16, 2004 letter from Gary Cohen, General Counsel for the Department of Insurance, that provides an opinion in response to the questions posed by the Court of Appeal, and a December 16, 2004 response by the WCIRB to the questions posed by the Court of Appeal, with an attached September 15, 1967 Ruling No. 157 of the Insurance Commissioner.

Footnote 4. Jacuzzi also petitioned for sanctions and penalties against CIGA pursuant to Labor Code section 5813. However, that petition will not be further addressed in this decision because it is not properly before us as part of the remittitur. Instead, Jacuzzi may direct its petition for sanctions and penalties to the WCJ for consideration in the first instance upon return of the case to the trial level.

§ 72.3(D)   Other Forms of Insurance Available to The Injured Worker

Page 2081, Column 1, eighth paragraph, insert following '...the proceeding.'

In observing that CIGA was established *"to provide a limited form of protection for the public and not a fund for the protection of the insurance companies from the insolvencies of fellow members"*, the Court of Appeal, First District, in reversing a trial Court's decision in *Parkwoods Community Association v. CIGA* (2006) 71 Cal. Comp. Cases 1275, held CIGA liable in a case where the general contractor and developer's excess insurance policies had not been exhausted, stated, in part:

This action was brought by plaintiff Parkwoods Community Association (Parkwoods) following the settlement of its earlier construction defect action arising out of the construction of the Parkwoods condominium development in Oakland. Five of the subcontractor defendants in the earlier action (the Reliance Insureds) were insured by Reliance Insurance Company (Reliance), a Pennsylvania insurance company that was placed into liquidation, causing defendant California Insurance Guarantee Association (CIGA) to assume their defense. The prior action was resolved by a settlement in which the developer and general contractor paid Parkwoods an amount that exhausted their primary commercial general liability (CGL) coverage and included a contribution from their excess insurance carrier that did not exhaust the excess insurance limits. Parkwoods and CIGA agreed upon the amount that CIGA would pay Parkwoods if CIGA is required to pay the obligations of Reliance and the Reliance Insureds, and agreed that this declaratory relief action would be brought to resolve their dispute as to whether Parkwoods' claim is a "covered claim" within the meaning of Insurance Code section 1063.1, subdivision (c) (Footnote 1) that CIGA is obligated to pay. CIGA contends that it is not a "covered claim" because there was other insurance that did cover the claim, namely the excess policy of the developer and the general contractor. Parkwoods argues, and the trial court held, that the excess policy covering the liability of these other parties does not constitute "other insurance" for this purpose, so that judgment was entered requiring CIGA to pay the disputed amount. We disagree and shall reverse the judgment.

RELEVANT FACTS

This matter was resolved below on the basis of a stipulated statement of facts and cross motions for summary judgment. It was agreed that the Reliance Insureds and the developer and general contractor were jointly and severally liable to Parkwoods "as to those aspects of the defective construction that the Reliance Insureds were responsible for," and that under their subcontract agreements each of the Reliance Insureds agreed to fully indemnify the developer and general contractor under "Type I" indemnity agreements (Footnote 2) "to the fullest extent allowed under California law."

Prior to the entry of the settlement agreement between Parkwoods and the developer and the general contractor, CIGA advised Parkwoods of its position that it was not obligated to, and would not, contribute to any settlement, for the reasons that it continues to assert in the present litigation. Parkwoods proceeded to enter the settlement agreement in which the payments on behalf of the developer and general contractor exhausted their CGL coverage for this loss. "In addition," it was stipulated, "while the general contractor and developer's excess insurance policy paid out settlement monies to resolve this loss, . . . such excess insurance limits were not exhausted as a result of the settlements reached with" the other parties, and the unexhausted excess policy limits exceeded $925,000, which is the amount the parties agreed CIGA is responsible to pay on behalf of the Reliance Insureds if the claim is a "covered claim." The settlement agreement between Parkwoods and the other parties was approved as a good faith settlement under Code of Civil Procedure section 877.6 in an order that provided that "any further claims by any other joint tortfeasor or co–obligor against Settling Parties for contribution and/or equitable comparative indemnity, based upon comparative negligence or comparative fault, in conjunction with any past, present or future claims or damages arising out of the facts in the above–entitled case shall be forever barred."

ANALYSIS

"CIGA was created by the Legislature to establish a fund from which insureds could obtain financial and legal assistance if their insurers became insolvent. [Citation.] CIGA ' "was created to provide a limited form of protection for insureds and the public, not to provide a fund to protect insurance carriers." . . . " 'CIGA is not, and was not created to act as, an ordinary insurance company . . . . It is a statutory entity that depends on the Guarantee Act for its existence and for a definition of the scope of its powers, duties and protections.' . . . 'CIGA issues no policies, collects no premiums, makes no profits, and assumes no contractual obligations to the insureds.' . . . 'CIGA's duties are not co–extensive with the duties owed by the insolvent insurer under its policy.' " ' [Citation.] [P] CIGA's authority and liability are limited to paying ' "covered claims." ' " (*California Ins. Guarantee Assn. v. Workers' Comp. Appeals Bd.* (2005) 128 Cal. App. 4th 307, 312–313 [26 Cal. Rptr. 3d 845, 70 Cal. Comp. Cases 556] (*WCAB*).)

The governing statute defines "covered claims" to mean "the obligations of an insolvent insurer . . . (i) imposed by law and within the coverage of an insurance policy of the insolvent insurer; (ii) which were unpaid by the insolvent insurer; (iii) which are presented as a claim to the liquidator in this state or to [CIGA] . . . ; . . . . (v) for which the assets of the insolvent insurer are insufficient to discharge in full" and which satisfy certain other requirements. (§ 1063.1, subd. (c)(1).) However, the statute also specifies numerous types of claims that are not "covered claims." (§ 1063.1, subd. (c)(3–12).) CIGA relies on one such provision, section 1063.1, subdivision (c)(9), which provides in relevant part, " 'Covered claims' does not include (i) any claim to the extent it is covered by any other insurance of a class covered by this article available to the claimant or insured..."

CIGA contends that the excess insurance policy of the developer and the contractor provided other insurance that was available to Parkwoods, so that its claim against CIGA is not covered. While it is true, as the trial court noted in rejecting CIGA's contention, that "the Reliance Insureds did not purchase the excess insurance, have no contractual right to coverage under the developer's policy, and were not additional insureds under that policy," those facts are not dispositive. The issue under subdivision (c)(9)(i) is whether there is any other insurance (Footnote 3) that is *available to the claimant or insured.*" The excess coverage may not have been available to the Reliance Insureds (the "insured") for the reasons noted by the trial court, but it was available to Parkwoods (the "claimant"). Since the parties stipulated that the developer and contractor were jointly and severally liable to Parkwoods for all construction defects for which the Reliance Insureds were responsible, the coverage provided by the unexhausted excess coverage policy was available to satisfy Parkwoods' claim.

While the trial court felt there was no "California case holding that the insurance policy of a *third party* is other insurance within the ambit of Section 1063 (c)(9)(i) [*sic*]," the decision in *WCAB, supra,* 128 Cal. App. 4th 307 is directly on point. In *WCAB,* a worker suffered three successive back injuries while employed by two different employers, resulting in identical compensation awards for each of the injuries. The workers' compensation insurer of the first employer paid the full benefits awarded to the worker and sought reimbursement from CIGA of the proportionate amount for which insolvent insurers of the second employer were responsible. The Court of Appeal held that the first insurer's claim was not a covered claim under subdivisions (c)(5) and (9)(ii) of section 1063.1, which exclude obligations to other insurers and assignees and claims for contribution and indemnity (*WCAB, supra,* at pp. 313–316), and that it also was not a covered claim by reason of subdivision (c)(9)(i). The *WCAB* court relied on the decision in *Industrial Indemnity Co. v. Workers' Comp. Appeals Bd.* (1997) 60 Cal. App. 4th 548 [70 Cal. Rptr. 2d 295, 62 Cal. Comp. Cases 1661] (*Garcia*), in which the court "held that CIGA was not liable [to pay an injured worker's claim on behalf of an insolvent insurer where there were two other successive insurers that were solvent] since all insurance carriers during the period of

exposure were jointly and severally liable for benefits to an employee for cumulative trauma." (*WCAB, supra,* at p. 318.)

The court in *WCAB* quoted at length from *Garcia*: " 'Reasonably read, the statute indicates that a claim does not rise to the level of a "covered claim" where other insurance providing the required coverage is available to either the claimant or the insured. Here, solvent insurers . . . provided coverage to Garcia's employer during the period for cumulative injury . . . . Garcia proved his cumulative injury against his employer, [and the solvent insurers]. Hence, even though Garcia's employer's three workers' compensation policies did not overlap chronologically, [the solvent insurers] were jointly and severally liable to Garcia for his entire disability during the statutory liability period . . . . Since such "other insurance" provided by [the solvent insurers] was thus available to cover Garcia's benefit award, CIGA was statutorily prohibited from making any payment toward his award . . . . [P] 'In sum, the Legislature did not intend CIGA to defray or diminish the responsibility of other carriers. Instead, the Legislature intended CIGA to benefit claimants otherwise unable to obtain insurance in payment of their claims. Here, insurance other than insolvent [insurer's] policy was available to satisfy the employer's liability to Garcia, to wit, the policies of solvent carriers . . . . Garcia had the substantive right to collect his entire benefit award from [the solvent insurers] since each was jointly and severally liable. Since Garcia's benefits claim was fully protected by solvent insurers . . . , both Garcia and his employer had "other insurance" available within the meaning of Insurance Code section 1063.1, subdivision (c) . . . .' (*Garcia, supra,* 60 Cal. App. 4th at pp. 558–559, citations omitted.)" (*WCAB, supra,* 128 Cal. App. 4th at p. 319.) Hence, the court concluded in *WCAB* that, since the first employer was jointly and severally liable for the successive injuries for which the second employer was responsible, the first employer's policy provided "other insurance" that was available to the claimant within the meaning of section 1063.1, subdivision (c)(9)(i), even though the solvent insurer provided coverage for only the first employer. (*WCAB, supra,* at p. 320.)

The trial court in the present case was also influenced by the fact that under the terms of the good faith settlement, if CIGA is not obligated to pay the $925,000 owed by the Reliance Insureds, Parkwoods will be unable to recover that amount from anyone. The trial court considered this to be outside the purpose of subdivision (c)(9)(i) – "to prevent a person from twice receiving benefits for the same loss" (*CD Investment Co. v. California Ins. Guarantee Assn.* (2000) 84 Cal. App. 4th 1410, 1427 [101 Cal. Rptr. 2d 806])–since "there is no threat of a double recovery from the developer's excess insurance policy." But Parkwoods brought this predicament upon itself by settling with the developer and contractor, who were jointly and severally liable for all damages caused by the Reliance Insureds, with full knowledge of CIGA's position. Parkwoods cannot bootstrap its claim against CIGA by releasing its right to recover under an available policy and claiming that as a result there is no other coverage.

Since there was joint and several liability and the Reliance Insureds agreed to indemnify the developer and contractor for all losses sustained by Parkwoods, Parkwoods could have sued only the developer and contractor, leaving them to obtain indemnity from the Reliance Insureds and Reliance. However, upon Reliance's insolvency, neither the developer and contractor nor their insurers were entitled to obtain indemnity or contribution from CIGA. (§ 1063.1, subds. (c)(5), (c)(9)(ii).) As the court noted in *Garcia*, "if Garcia had elected to proceed only against [one of the solvent insurers] and succeeded in proving his cumulative injury, he would have received an award for all his benefits and [the solvent insurers] would have been obligated to pay the entire award. Although [the solvent insurer] would have had the right to institute supplemental proceedings against other carriers for contribution [citation], such proceedings would not lie against CIGA due to Insurance Code section 1063.1, subdivision [now (c)(5)]." (*Garcia, supra,* 60 Cal. App. 4th at p. 559, fn. 8; *WCAB, supra,* 128 Cal. App. 4th at pp. 319–320.) Permitting Parkwoods to recover from CIGA in the present case would, in effect, sanction an indirect recovery that could not be obtained directly. Such avoidance of the statutory limitations is not permissible. (*Collins–Pine Co. v. Tubbs Cordage Co.* (1990) 221 Cal. App. 3d 882, 886–888 [271 Cal. Rptr. 20]; *E. L.White, Inc. v. City of Huntington Beach* (1982) 138 Cal. App. 3d 366, 371 [187 Cal. Rptr. 879].) The fact that as part of its settlement with the developer and contractor Parkwoods chose to accept the risk of pursuing the claim against CIGA cannot increase the extent of CIGA's statutory liability.

In defending the decision below, Parkwoods puts heavy reliance on the absence from the record of numerous categories of evidence which it asserts are necessary to establish that the excess policy of the developer and the contractor "drops down" to cover their liability over and above the exhausted coverage of their primary insurers. The record does not contain the terms of the excess insurance policy or even the name of the excess insurer, nor does it reflect the precise construction defects for which the Reliance Insureds were responsible. Nor has there been a prior adjudication, Parkwoods argues, "as to whether the Developer/General Contractor and the Reliance Insureds were jointly and severally liable with respect to anything." Even if these omissions were critical, it would not follow, as Parkwoods assumes, that the judgment below establishing CIGA's liability should stand. It would follow only that there are additional facts that need to be established before summary judgment can be granted for either party.

However, the missing facts are not essential in view of the facts to which the parties expressly stipulated. To permit the court to decide the legal issue over which they disagreed on cross motions for summary judgment, the parties stipulated that "the Reliance Insureds and the developer and general contractor . . . were jointly and severally liable to [Parkwoods] as to those aspects of the defective construction that the Reliance Insureds were responsible for." Further, "Reliance Insureds, CIGA, and [Parkwoods] agree . . . that as a result of the settlements completed in the action, the general contractor and developer . . . exhausted all of their primary Commercial General Liability ('CGL') coverage which responded to this loss. In addition, while the general contractor and developer's excess insurance policy paid out settlement monies to resolve this loss, Reliance Insureds, CIGA, and [Parkwoods] agree that such excess insurance limits were not exhausted as a result of the settlements reached with other parties in this action. The unexhausted excess policy limits exceeded $925,000.00." Thus, it is not necessary to know the specifics of the construction defect claims because, whatever they were, the developer, contractor and Reliance Insureds were jointly and severally liable for them. It is not necessary to establish whether Parkwoods would have prevailed at trial because the parties agreed to pay the amounts in question in settlement of its claims. And it is not necessary to know the precise language of the excess policy to determine whether its coverage "dropped down" because it was stipulated that the excess insurer did in fact assume liability for the uncovered amount of the claim against the developer and the contractor, and that there was sufficient additional coverage under that policy to cover the amount for which the parties agreed the Reliance Insureds were liable.

Hence, it is clear from these stipulated facts that other insurance was available to satisfy Parkwoods' claim.

Because other insurance was available to Parkwoods, under section 1063.1, subdivision (c)(9)(i) its claim is not a "covered claim." The fact that CIGA is not obligated to satisfy that claim is entirely consonant with the legislative determination in establishing CIGA "to provide a limited form of protection for the public, not a fund for the protection of other insurance companies from the insolvencies of fellow members." (*California Union Ins. Co. v. Central National Ins. Co.* (1981) 117 Cal. App. 3d 729, 734 [173 Cal. Rptr. 35].)

DISPOSITION

The judgment is reversed. The matter is remanded with instructions to vacate the judgment entered in favor of Parkwoods and to enter judgment in favor of CIGA... .

Footnote 1. All statutory references are to the Insurance Code unless otherwise indicated.

Footnote 2. A "Type I" agreement "provides 'expressly and unequivocally' that the indemnitor is to indemnify the indemnitee for, among other things, the negligence of the indemnitee. Under this type of provision, the indemnitee is indemnified whether his liability has arisen as the result of his negligence alone [citation], or whether his liability has arisen as the result of his co–negligence with the indemnitor [citation]." (*MacDonald & Kruse, Inc. v. San Jose Steel Co.* (1972) 29 Cal. App. 3d 413, 419 [105 Cal. Rptr. 725].)

Footnote 3. There is no dispute that the excess coverage policy of the developer and contractor is of the same class as the Reliance policy.

§ 72.3(E) CIGA and Liens of Employment Development Department (EDD)

Page 2082, Column 2, first paragraph, insert following '...to pay.'

In going beyond *Karaiskos, supra* and holding that it makes no difference when the EDD lien is litigated (i.e. with all the other issues or separately after the applicant settled other issues with the employer/insurer, CIGA is not required to pay an EDD lien), the Court of Appeal, Second District in *CIGA v. WCAB (White) (Torres)* (2006) 71 Cal. Comp. Cases 139, stated, in part:

INTRODUCTION

After the State Employment Development Department (EDD) paid temporary unemployment compensation disability (UCD) benefits to disabled workers, Harry White and Francisco Torres, EDD filed lien claims for reimbursement with the Workers' Compensation Appeals Board (Board). (Footnote 1)

The insurers for White's and Torres's employers were insolvent. Under applicable California law (Ins. Code, § 1063 et seq.), California Insurance Guarantee Association (CIGA) had assumed the insolvent carriers' obligations, but refused to satisfy EDD's liens. CIGA argued it was only required to pay a "covered claim" and EDD's liens are excluded from the definition of "covered claims" as they are obligations to the State of California. (Ins. Code, § 1063.1, subd. (c)(4).) (Footnote 2)

CIGA also relied on the decision in *California Ins. Guarantee Assn. v. Workers' Comp. Appeals Bd.* (*Karaiskos*) (2004) 117 Cal. App. 4th 350 [12 Cal. Rptr. 3d 12, 69 Cal. Comp. Cases 183].) In both the Torres and White cases, the Board ruled against CIGA. The Board relied on *Viveros v. North Ranch Country Club* (2002) 67 Cal. Comp. Cases 900 (en banc) and reasoned that *Karaiskos, supra*, applied only to EDD liens litigated separately after the injured worker and the employer's insurance carrier had entered into a settlement agreement on all other issues. The Board found the fact that the liens here were not litigated separately to be significant. (Footnote 3)

CIGA petitioned this court for a writ of review. (Lab. Code, § 5950.)

We hold an EDD lien is an obligation to a state because the EDD is a department of the State of California. Therefore, its lien claim is not a "covered claim" that CIGA is required to pay. (Ins. Code, § 1063.1, subd. (c)(4).) We also hold that it makes no difference when the lien is litigated, with all other issues or separately after the claimant has settled other issues with the employer and insurer. Therefore the reasoning of *Karaiskos* applies equally here. Accordingly, we annul the Board's decisions. (Footnote 4)

DISCUSSION

1. The standard of review and rules of statutory interpretation.

Construction of a statute is question of law which appellate courts review de novo. (*California Ins. Guarantee Assn. v. Liemsakul* (1987) 193 Cal. App. 3d 433, 438 [238 Cal. Rptr. 346].)

"[W]e apply the usual rules of statutory interpretation. 'The fundamental rule . . . is to ascertain the intent of the Legislature in order to effectuate the purpose of the law . . . . In doing so, we first look to the words of the statute and try to give effect to the usual, ordinary import of the language, at the same time not rendering any language mere surplusage. The words must be construed in context and in light of the nature and obvious purpose of the statute where they appear... the statute " 'must be given a reasonable and commonsense interpretation consistent with the apparent purpose and intention of the Legislature, practical rather than technical in nature, and which, when applied, will result in wise policy rather than mischief or absurdity...' " ' [Citation.]" (*Klajic v. Castaic Lake Water Agency* (2001) 90 Cal. App. 4th 987, 997 [109 Cal. Rptr. 2d 454].) When statutory language is "clear and unambiguous there is no need for construction, and courts should not indulge in it." (*California Ins. Guarantee Assn. v. Liemsakul* (1987) 193 Cal. App. 3d 433, 439 [238 Cal. Rptr. 346].)

2. CIGA is not obligated to pay EDD's lien.

a. Principles governing CIGA.

CIGA was created by legislation to establish a fund from which insureds could obtain financial and legal assistance in the event their insurers became insolvent. " 'Although funded by a compulsory membership of insurance companies doing business in California, CIGA "was created to provide a *limited* form of protection for insureds and the public, not to provide a fund to protect insurance carriers." [Citations.] CIGA's role in guaranteeing workers' compensation claims is therefore *limited*: [P] " ' " 'CIGA is not, and was *not created to act as, an ordinary insurance company*. [Citation.] It is a statutory entity that depends on the Guarantee Act for its existence and for a definition of the scope of its powers, duties, and protections.' [Citation.] 'CIGA issues no policies, collects no premiums, makes no profits, and assumes no contractual obligations to the insureds.' [Citation.] 'CIGA's duties are not co–extensive with the duties owed by the insolvent insurer under its policy.' [Citation.]" ' " (*California Insurance Guarantee Assn. v. Workers' Comp. Appeals Bd.* (2003) 112 Cal. App. 4th 358, 363 [Cal. Rptr. 3d 127, 68 Cal. Comp. Cases 1444], italics added, quoting *Denny's Inc. v. Workers' Comp. Appeals Bd.* (2003) 104 Cal. App. 4th 1433, 1438 [129 Cal. Rptr. 2d 53, 68 Cal. Comp. Cases 1].) We consider CIGA's responsibility in the present case in light of the fact it is strictly a creation of statute.

b. CIGA is not authorized to pay obligations to a state.

"CIGA's authority and liability in discharging 'its statutorily circumscribed duties' are limited to paying the amount of 'covered claims.' [Citations.]" (*California Insurance Guarantee Assn. v. Workers' Comp. Appeals Bd., supra,* 112 Cal. App. 4th at p. 363.) With certain exceptions, "covered claims" are "the obligations of an insolvent insurer' " (Ins. Code, § 1063.1, subd. (c)(1)), including the obligation "to provide workers compensation benefits under the workers' compensation law of this state." (Ins. Code, § 1063.1, subd. (c)(1)(vi).) Specifically *excluded* from the definition of "covered claims" is among others, "*any obligations to any state or to the federal government.*" (Ins. Code, § 1063.1, subd. (c)(4), italics added.)

There is no dispute about what the governmental exclusion of Insurance Code section 1063.1, subdivision (c)(4) says: Claims requiring the payment of any obligation *to any state* are *not* "covered claims" for which CIGA is liable. "The logical and natural reading of the statute, then, is that covered claims do not include obligations to 'any state.' Period." (*County of Orange v. FST Sand & Gravel, Inc.* (1998) 63 Cal. App. 4th 353, 357 [73 Cal. Rptr. 2d 633].) In *Karaiskos,* the Court reasoned that EDD's lien claim for reimbursement of UCD benefits mistakenly paid to a disabled worker constitutes an obligation to a state because, "(1) EDD is a department of an agency of the State of California, and (2) the Unemployment Insurance Code contemplates reimbursement be made to the EDD's Unemployment Compensation Disability Fund in general, rather than to a particular disabled workers' account." (*Karaiskos, supra,* 117 Cal. App. 4th at p. 357.)

3. EDD's right to reimbursement from solvent insurers and employers does not supersede CIGA's release from obligations to the state.

In its answer and at oral argument, EDD contended that CIGA is required to provide workers' compensation benefits and, therefore, it is bound to reimburse EDD. EDD argues that the Legislature has provided a variety of programs to provide benefits to unemployed workers and UCD benefits are only for situations in which the disability sustained by the worker is not work related. (Unemp. Ins. Code, § 2601 et seq.) EDD argues that Unemployment Insurance Code section 2629.1 requires it to advance disability benefits when the character of the disability is in dispute, and the recovery provisions provided in section 2629.1 along with those provided for in Labor Code sections 4903 and 4904 require mandatory recoupment of EDD funds when there has been an adjudication, finding of industrial disability and award. If EDD is not reimbursed for its advanced funds in situations in which the unemployment is based on work related injury, EDD is, in effect, acting much like a workers' compensation insurer.

Undisputedly, EDD is entitled to reimbursement pursuant to those statutes and conditions when the employer's insurance company is solvent. However, the Legislature has concluded that not all workers' compensation laws should apply to CIGA. Thus, CIGA's obligations are not coextensive with those of solvent insurers. As relevant here, the Legislature has declared by statute that CIGA is not liable for obligations owed to the state or federal government. UCD liens are not the only obligations from which CIGA has been excused by law. For example, in cases where both an insolvent and a solvent insurer would be liable for a portion of a cumulative trauma injury, CIGA is excused from contributing its percentage and the solvent insurer must absorb the entire cost. (Ins. Code, § 1063.1, subd. (c)(9); *Denny's Inc. v. Workers' Comp. Appeals Bd., supra,* 104 Cal. App. 4th 1433; *Industrial Indemnity Co. v. Workers' Comp. Appeals Bd.* (*Garcia*) (1997) 60 Cal. App. 4th 548 [70 Cal. Rptr. 2d 295, 62 Cal. Comp. Cases 1661].) CIGA is not liable for penalties for unreasonable delay in payment of workers' compensation benefits by the insolvent insurer for which a solvent insurer would be liable under Labor Code sections 5814 and 5814.5. (Ins. Code, § 1063.1, subd. (c)(8).) (Footnote 5)

And even when CIGA's obligations were expanded to include obligations of insolvent self–insured employers, section 1063.1, subdivision (c)(13) limited that obligation to $500,000 per claim. (Footnote 6)

EDD argues that requiring it to pay workers' compensation benefits compromises the integrity of two separate and distinct programs. It cites *Department of Employment Dev. v. Workers' Comp. Appeals Bd.* (*Garcia*) (1976) 61 Cal. App. 3d 470 [131 Cal. Rptr. 204, 41 Cal. Comp. Cases 489] which quotes *California Comp. Ins. Co. v. Ind. Acc. Com.* (1954) 128 Cal. App. 2d 797 [277 P.2d 442, 19 Cal. Comp. Cases 287] as follows: "The statutes here under examination are part of a comprehensive, integrated program of social insurance which, operating in their respective spheres, are calculated to alleviate the burden of a loss of wages by a protected employee during a particular period of time . . . . [The statutes] are interrelated by the common principle implicit therein of *permitting only a single recovery of benefits* by an employee in a case involving temporary . . . disability." (*Garcia, supra,* 61 Cal. App. 3d at p. 474.) (Footnote 7)

We appreciate the understandable legislative policy that ensures that a worker who is unemployed, for whatever reason, is able to obtain immediate financial assistance and avoids the possibility of the worker obtaining duplicate benefits from different sources. (*California Comp. Ins. Co. v. Ind. Acc. Com.* (1954) 128 Cal. App. 2d 797, 806 [277 P.2d 442, 19 Cal. Comp. Cases 287].) Double recovery is not at issue here, but more to the point the Legislature has also made a policy decision that CIGA is to have limited liability. Whether CIGA's exclusions negatively impact the UCD fund involves a legislative choice with which we are not free to tinker.

The Legislature is presumed to have in mind existing law when it passes a statute. (*Cumero v. Public Employment Relations Bd.* (1989) 49 Cal. 3d 575, 596 [778 P.2d 174, 262 Cal. Rptr. 46].) The Legislature revisited Insurance Code section 1063.1 in 2003 when subdivision (c)(8) was amended and again in 2005 to add subdivision (c)(13). We also assume the Legislature properly considers existing judicial decisions at the time legislation is enacted. (*People v. Overstreet* (1986) 42 Cal. 3d 891, 897 [726 P.2d 1288, 231 Cal. Rptr. 213].) To the extent our colleagues in Division Three did not correctly assess the Legislature's intent when it issued the *Karaiskos'* opinion in 2004, the Legislature has had opportunities to rectify any error. It has not acted. We conclude, therefore, that the statutory arrangement for providing benefits to disabled unemployed workers does not supersede the statutes governing CIGA's obligations. (Footnote 8)

4. The principle enunciated in Karaiskos, that EDD's lien is an obligation of the state applies on these facts as well.

The Board held, and EDD argues, that *Karaiskos* is distinguishable because there the EDD lien was litigated after a settlement agreement and here the lien was litigated along with the injured worker's other claims. EDD has offered no persuasive policy or practical reason to support such a distinction, and we conceive of no reason why EDD's lien should be considered differently when it is litigated with other issues as opposed to following settlement. There is nothing in the language of section 1063.1, subdivision (c)(4) that would suggest such a dichotomy.

EDD is required to compensate a worker who is unemployed due to a disability (Ins. Code, § 2600 et. seq.) Typically, an EDD lien claim is created against an injured worker's potential compensation recovery when the employer disputes that the alleged injury is work related and has denied liability for the worker's claim, or disputes the injured worker's entitlement to temporary disability or vocational rehabilitation maintenance allowance. (*Park Inn International v. Workers' Comp. Appeals Bd.* (1998) 63 Cal. Comp. Cases 776 [writ denied].) (Footnote 9)

When EDD's payment period corresponds to an injured worker's temporary disability period or vocational rehabilitation maintenance allowance period, EDD is entitled to file a lien for reimbursement if it is determined by the Workers' Compensation Appeals Board that the injured worker is entitled to temporary disability or vocational rehabilitation maintenance allowance during that period. (Lab. Code, §§ 4903, subds. (f) & (g); 4904 subds. (b)(1) & (b)(2), *EDD v. Workers' Comp. Appeals Bd. (Garcia), supra,* 61 Cal. App. 3d at p. 473; Cal. Workers' Compensation Practice, (Cont.Ed.Bar 2004 Update) § 1549, p. 1085.) (Footnote 10)

When parties settle their rights, the approved and preferred form of compromise and release document is a preprinted form by the Workers' Compensation Appeals Board. (Cal. Workers' Compensation Practice (Cont.Ed.Bar 4th ed. 2004 Update) § 1624, pp. 1150–1152.) The Board's Form 15 requires an entry denoting the actual dates of the periods of temporary disability, permanent disability and vocational rehabilitation entitlement that are disputed. The compromise and release

must be approved by the workers' compensation judge. (Lab. Code, § 5001, Cal. Code Regs., tit. 8, § 10882.)

If EDD does not join the settlement agreement, its right to establish its lien in full in subsequent proceedings remains intact. EDD has the burden of proving the injury was work related and the worker was entitled to temporary disability indemnification, vocational rehabilitation maintenance allowance, or permanent disability indemnification and, during a period corresponding to the worker's receipt of UCD, the worker was entitled to temporary disability indemnity or vocational rehabilitation maintenance allowance. (Lab. Code, §§ 3202.5, 5705; Cal. Workers' Compensation Practice (Cont.Ed.Bar 4th ed. 2004 Update) § 1642, p. 1168.) Whichever procedure is followed, whether EDD's lien is litigated along with the injured worker or after the employer and employee have settled, the results will be the same.

In any event, there is nothing in the procedural setting that changes the legal nature of EDD's lien: it is still an obligation to the state. That is the foundation of the decision in *Karaiskos* and that remains so here. The chronology of the lien claim in the litigation process was of no significance to the decision in *Karaiskos* and has no root in section 1063.1. *Karaiskos* effectively overruled the Board's en banc decision in *Viveros v. North Ranch Country Club* (*Viveros*) the companion to *Karaiskos* at the workers' compensation proceeding, and the facts of *Viveros* were similar to those here. (Footnote 11)

"It defies logic and produces a ludicrous result to conclude that a payment to a department of the State is not a payment to a state. [Fn. omitted.]" (*Karaiskos, supra,* 117 Cal. App. 4th at p. 362.)

5. CIGA is not estopped from relying on Karaiskos.

EDD also contends that CIGA should be estopped from now arguing that *Viveros* was effectively overruled by *Karaiskos* because essentially CIGA took a contrary position in its petition for review in *Karaiskos*. Judicial estoppel precludes a party from asserting a position in a judicial proceeding that is inconsistent with a position previously successfully asserted, to obtain an unfair advantage. (*Drain v. Betz Laboratories, Inc.* (1999) 69 Cal. App. 4th 950, 956 [81 Cal. Rptr. 2d 864, 64 Cal. Comp. Cases 55].) (Footnote 12)

We find the rule has no application. First, the prior position was not successful; CIGA lost in *Viveros*. Second, the precise arguments CIGA made in *Karaiskos* are not germane here as CIGA did not argue that *Karaiskos* should be decided in its favor because it was different than *Viveros*. Third, we conclude nothing CIGA did gave it an unfair advantage. CIGA appears to have merely chosen to appeal one case (*Karaiskos*) which it perceived at the time to be stronger than the other (*Viveros*). Now CIGA has found a case that it believes is the proper extension of *Karaiskos*. (Footnote 13)

DISPOSITION

We annul the Board's orders after consideration... .

Footnote 1. When the employer disputes that the worker's absence is due to a work–related disability, the injured worker is entitled to receive unemployment compensation–disability from EDD during the period he or she is unable to work pending a final decision regarding the workers' compensation claim. (Unemp. Ins. Code, § 2629.1; Lab. Code, § 4903, subds. (f) & (g).) EDD may file a lien for reimbursement of the UCD with the Workers' Compensation Appeals Board. (Lab. Code, § 4903, subds. (f) & (g); § 4904, subds. (a) & (b).)

UCD is familiarly known as State Disability Insurance. (Cal. Workers' Compensation Practice (Cont.Ed.Bar 4th ed. June 2004 Update) § 1638, p. 1163.)

Footnote 2. Insurance Code section 1063.1, subdivision (c)(4) states: " 'Covered claims' does not include any obligations of the insolvent insurer arising out of any reinsurance contracts, nor any obligations incurred after the expiration date of the insurance policy or after the insurance policy has been replaced by the insured or canceled at the insured's request, or after the insurance policy has been canceled by the association as provided in this chapter, or after the insurance policy has been canceled by the liquidator, *nor any obligations to any state or to the federal government.*" (Italics added.)

Footnote 3. The settlement of "other issues" may include whether the injury is work–related and whether the injured worker is entitled to benefits such as, temporary disability indemnity, medical treatment, permanent disability indemnity, and future medical treatment. (Cal. Workers' Compensation Practice (Cont. Ed. Bar 4th ed. June 2004 update) § 1.7, pp. 7–8.)

Footnote 4. The Torres and White petitions filed by CIGA have been consolidated for the purpose of this opinion. Each concerns a lien filed by EDD to recover UCD paid to the injured worker. In both cases the issue of reimbursement of EDD's lien was litigated along with all other issues and not considered in a separate trial after the parties had entered into a settlement agreement on the other issues.

Footnote 5. Previously, (c)(8) stated: " 'Covered claims' does not include any amount awarded as punitive or exemplary damages . . . ." As amended, (c)(8) now states: " 'Covered claims' does not include any amount awarded as punitive or exemplary damages, *nor any amount awarded by the Workers' Compensation Appeals Board pursuant to section 5814 or 5814.5 because payment of compensation was unreasonably delayed or refused by the insolvent insurer.* (Italics added.)" (Stats. 2003, ch. 635.)

Footnote 6. The amendment reads, in relevant part, "(13) 'Covered claims' shall also include obligations arising under an insurance policy written to indemnify a permissibly self–insured employer pursuant to subdivision (b) or (c) of section 3700 of the Labor Code for its liability to pay workers' compensation benefits in excess of a specific or aggregate retention, provided, however, that for purposes of this article, those claims shall not be considered workers' compensation claims and therefore are subject to the per claim limit in paragraph (7) and any payments and expenses related thereto shall be allocated to category (c) for claims other than workers' compensation, homeowners, and automobile, as provided in section 1063.5."

Section 1063.1(c)(7) states, "Covered claims" does not include that portion of any claim, other than a claim for workers' compensation benefits, that is in excess of five hundred thousand dollars ($500,000).

Footnote 7. EDD also contends that "these inter–related provisions are designed to help insure that the workers' own wages which fund non–industrial disability benefits are not being used to fund the workers' compensation program." The court in *Karaiskos* rejected EDD's contention that the disability from which payments were made were "the workers' own wages" being used to fund the workers' compensation programs. EDD had argued, unconvincingly, that it was merely a conduit for compensation that inured to the benefit of the specific injured worker's account in the Unemployment Compensation Disability Fund. The Court found that EDD's particular bookkeeping methodology had no actual effect on an employee's eligibility for future benefits, because the employee has no right to any additional UCD benefits related to that specific injury after adjudication and, if the employee suffered a new disability covered by UCD benefits, a new disability benefit period would start, regardless of whether EDD's lien for the prior injury had been satisfied. The Court further noted: "[A] lien claim for a UCD reimbursement is asserted by the EDD on its own behalf . . . . [And] an employee's receipt of UCD benefits does not relieve his or her employer or the employer's insurance carrier of liability to pay workers' compensation insurance. (Lab. Code, § 3752.)" (*Id.* at pp. 357–358.)

Footnote 8. At oral argument, the parties were unable to suggest any other obligation to the state that the Legislature might have had in mind when it drafted subdivision (c)(4). In its brief, EDD posed the following tautology for the Court's consideration – if a rich uncle loaned the money to the injured worker rather than EDD advancing UCD benefits, CIGA would have been liable for the entire amount. Even if true, an obligation to a rich uncle is not an obligation to the state.

Footnote 9. Vocational rehabilitation maintenance allowance is a benefit due to a worker engaged in job retraining after the worker has become medically permanent and stationary. (Cal. Workers' Compensation Practice (Cont. Ed. Bar 4th ed. 2004 update) Vol. 1, § 4.20, p. 238; §§ 6.110–6.111, pp. 440–441.) A disability is permanent and stationary when the condition has reached maximum improvement or when changes are not reasonably anticipated under usual medical standards.

(*Sweeney v. Industrial Acc. Com.* (1951) 107 Cal. App. 2d 155 [236 P.2d 651, 16 Cal. Comp. Cases 264].) Before the worker is medically permanent and stationary, he or she continues to receive temporary disability indemnity.

Footnote 10. For injuries after January 1, 1994, permanent disability compensation awarded is also available for reimbursement of EDD's lien if EDD's payments were for the same injury (sometimes UCD is paid for a combination of nonindustrial and industrial injuries). (Cal. Workers' Compensation Practice (Cont. Ed. Bar 4th ed. 2004 update) Vol. 2, § 15.49, p. 1085.)

Footnote 11. *Viveros* and *Karaiskos v. Metagenics, Inc.* were consolidated in 2002 by the Board for the purpose of issuing an en banc decision. (See 67 Cal. Comp. Cases 900.) Without making any factual distinctions, the Board held EDD's liens were not obligations of the state. CIGA petitioned for review of the Board's decision only in *Karaiskos v. Metagenics, Inc.* In the Court of Appeal opinion in *Karaiskos*, the court held EDD's lien was an obligation of the State and CIGA was not obliged to reimburse EDD.

Footnote 12. We grant EDD's motion for judicial notice of the Board's en banc decisions in *Karaiskos* and *Viveros*. (Evid Code, § 459.)

Footnote 13. We address one issue applicable to only one of the two consolidated cases before us. In respondent White's case, the Board adopted the WCJ's decision as its own. The WCJ concluded that *Cole v. California Ins. Guarantee Assn.* (2004) 122 Cal. App. 4th 552 [18 Cal. Rptr. 3d 801] conflicted with *Karaiskos,* and *Cole* governed. *Cole* considered whether CIGA should be liable for injuries claimed under an uninsured motorist policy. CIGA claimed there was "other insurance," covering the injury, that is, federal Social Security disability insurance and state unemployment compensation insurance. *Cole* held these types of insurance covered losses different than uninsured motorist insurance. Therefore, CIGA was obligated to reimburse those agencies. *Cole* is inapplicable here because in this context unemployment disability compensation and workers' disability compensation generally compensate for the same type of loss.

Page 2083, Column 2, last paragraph, insert following '…claim.'

§ 72.3(G)   Contribution

CIGA has a right to pursue contribution against other insurance on behalf of the insurer(s) in liquidation for any pre–insolvency and past insolvency benefits paid. In such an event, the recovery of benefits paid for pre–insolvency benefits would be placed in assets of the liquidated insurer's estate and past insolvency benefits paid by CIGA would be retained by CIGA. See *Marin, supra.*

§ 72.3(H)   Credit

In *Lake v. WCAB* (2005) 70 Cal. Comp. Cases 1722, the Board held that CIGA was entitled to a credit against applicant's future workers' compensation costs when applicant settled his third party action from which he received a net recovery of $100,000.00 even though the liability carrier was Washington's State Insurance Guarantee Association (WIGA), a state agency. The judge noted that CIGA was merely exercising a right to take a third party's credit for a civil settlement, as it would have a right to do in any other case including any other defendant who might be liable for damages in a civil case and there was no distinction between WIGA as a guarantor agency and any private insurance carrier paying damages.

§ 72.3(I)   Assigned Liens Not Covered Claims

Assignment of a medical lien is not a "covered claim".

Insurance Code section 1063.1(c)(9) states covered claims do not include:

...(ii) any claim by any person other than the original claimant under the insurance policy in his or her own name, his or her assignee as the person entitled thereto under a premium finance agreement as defined in Section 673 and entered into prior to insolvency, his or her executor, administrator, guardian or other personal representative or trustee in bankruptcy and does not include any claim asserted by an assignee or one claiming by right of subrogation, except as otherwise provided in this chapter... .

Insurance Code section 19 and Labor Code section 18 give the definition of "person" as follows:

"Person means any person, association, organization, partnership, business trust, limited liability company, or corporation."

There is no known Court of Appeal decision directly on point on the issue of whether assignment of a medical lien is excluded from the definition of a "covered claim".

The Board held, in *Mendez v. CIGA*, ANA 0339697, that an assigned medical lien is not a covered claim. See also civil cases *Baxter Healthcare Corp. v. CIGA* (2000) 85 Cal. App. 4th 306 and *CIGA v. WCAB, American Motorists (Weitzman)* 70 Cal. Comp. Cases 556.

§ 72.3(J)   Time Limitations to Seek Reimbursement/Contribution

In *Majestic Insurance Company, et. al. v. WCAB (Marin)* (2005) 70 Cal. Comp. Cases 1519, the Board held that CIGA's claim for reimbursement/contribution against solvent insurance carriers for all benefits paid by itself and previously paid by insolvent insurance carrier was timely under Section 5500.5 where the claim by CIGA was filed *within one year* of a judge's approval of a settlement between the applicant and the solvent carrier.

Further, the Board held that CIGA had a right to reimbursement from solvent insurance carriers for pre–insolvency payments made by the insolvent insurance carrier. The Board stated, in part:

> Although Majestic argues that CIGA's lien was untimely filed on January 22, 2003, we are persuaded that CIGA's proceedings are in the nature of contribution/reimbursement, and not in the nature of lien claims. However, CIGA filed its petition for contribution/reimbursement within one year of the approved compromise and release of September 24, 2002 and this would satisfy the one year time requirement under Labor Code section 5500.5(e).

> Therefore, turning to the merits of CIGA's petition, we agree that it is entitled to reimbursement for that which it paid and to the payments made solely by the insolvent carrier HIH. In *Liberty Mutual Fire Ins. Co. v. Workers' Comp. Appeals Bd. (Barineau)* (2001) [66 Cal. Comp. Cases 1108] (writ denied), the Board found that Insurance Code section 1063.2(b) allowed CIGA to be a party in interest in proceedings involving a covered claim and gives them the same rights as the insolvent insurer would have had, had it not been in liquidation. This includes the right to adjust, compromise, settle and pay a covered claim. The recovery from an insolvent insurance carrier fits within this language. Thus, the fact that CIGA has the same rights as the insolvent insurer would have had, if it had not been in liquidation, means that CIGA has the right to pursue subrogation from third parties to the same extent the insurer could have pursued subrogation, if it were not in liquidation. In *Barineau, supra,* the Board ruled, "since the proceeding for contribution is in the nature of a subrogation proceeding, if CIGA is authorized to institute subrogation proceedings, they are also authorized to institute contribution proceedings." (*Id.*, p. 1110.) We specifically note that the Court of Appeal allowed to stand the assertion that CIGA could collect through subrogation proceedings and once having done that, they could keep the funds if they have made the payments, but had to turn the funds over to the insurance commissioner if they had not. Under either circumstance, CIGA would have the right to institute subrogation proceedings and we are persuaded that the disbursement of those assets is irrelevant to the right to collect them.

> Further, in *Lewis v. California Insurance Guarantee Association* (2004) 69 Cal. Comp. Cases 490, a recent Board panel decision, the Appeals Board found, based on a letter brief submitted by California Department of Insurance (citing Insurance Code §§ 1063.2(b) and 1037(b)), that CIGA was a proper party to pursue contributions on behalf of the insurer in liquidation for any pre–insolvency and post–insolvency benefits paid; that CIGA would be entitled to recover benefits paid by the insurer in liquidation prior to its insolvency, which would be placed in assets of liquidated insurer's estate;

and that the benefits paid by CIGA and recovered by it could be retained by it.

> On this basis, we will amend the WCJ's decision to reflect that CIGA does have standing to seek reimbursement for that portion of its lien based on pre–insolvency payments made by HIH... .

§ 72.3(K)   Penalties

See Section 57.33 of this book for detailed discussion of liability of CIGA for penalties prior to January 1, 2004.

In an unpublished decision holding that CIGA was not liable for Labor Code section 5814 penalties assessed against an insolvent insurer's pre–liquidation delays, where the Court found that the amendment to Insurance Code section 1063.1(c)(8), effective January 1, 2004, in which the Legislature excluded Section 5814 penalties from the definition of covered claims for which CIGA was liable, the Court of Appeals, Fifth District, in *Hernandez v. WCAB* (2006) 71 Cal. Comp. Cases 369 stated, in part:

> The widow and minor of a fatally injured worker petition for a writ of review contending the Workers' Compensation Appeals Board (WCAB) erred by reversing previously imposed penalties against the California Insurance Guarantee Association (CIGA). We will deny the petition in light of the Legislature's amendment to the Insurance Code eliminating the penalties from the CIGA's liability.

> *BACKGROUND*

> Twenty–one–year–old Jose Alatorre (Alatorre) fell and drowned on February 22, 2001, while repairing a sump–hole pump valve for Aguiar–Faria & Sons Dairy (Dairy) in Merced County. Alatorre was survived by his totally dependent widow and infant son (Petitioners).

> The Dairy admitted Alatorre's death was industrially related and paid Petitioners death benefits at the rate of $255 per week based on two–thirds of Alatorre's $382.50 weekly earnings. In February 2002, a workers' compensation administrative law judge (WCJ) determined Petitioners were entitled to the maximum statutory death benefits of $490 per week based on Alatorre's potential earnings. The WCAB summarily denied the Dairy's petition for reconsideration in April 2002. The Dairy petitioned the Court of Appeal, Third Appellate District for a writ of review; that court also summarily denied the petition and awarded supplemental attorney fees to Alatorre's family in July 2002. (Footnote 1)

> (*Aguiar–Faria & Sons Dairy v. Workers' Comp. Appeals Bd.* (2002) 67 Cal. Comp. Cases 927 [writ denied]; Lab. Code, § 5801.)

> The Dairy's workers' compensation insurer, Legion Insurance Company (Legion), became insolvent and the CIGA assumed responsibility for the Alatorre family's workers' compensation claim in April 2003. (See Ins. Code, § 119.5 et seq.)

In August 2003, the matter again came before a WCJ to address Petitioners' increased benefit and penalty claims. On October 29, 2003, the WCJ determined that, pursuant to newly enacted statutory rates, the Petitioners were entitled to weekly death benefits of $490 before 2003, $602 during 2003, and $666.67 after 2003. The WCJ also found the Dairy, while insured by Legion, engaged in seven acts of unreasonably delaying or failing to issue death benefit payments and attorney fees, warranting separate 10 percent penalties under Labor Code section 5814 (section 5814). (Footnote 2)

The CIGA petitioned the WCAB for reconsideration in November 2003, raising various abuse of discretion and insufficient evidence claims. In December 2003, the WCJ reported to the WCAB that the Dairy engaged in "a lengthy history and pattern of failure to properly and timely pay benefits both due under the undisputed evidence and then later ordered pursuant to findings and award."

In January 2004, the WCAB granted reconsideration "in order to allow opportunity to further study the factual and legal issues in this case." Nearly a year later, in January 2005, the WCAB issued a Notice of Intention to Submit inviting supplemental briefing to address the relevance of the WCAB's recent en banc decision, *Martinez v. Jack Neal & Sons* (2004) 69 Cal. Comp. Cases 775 [Appeals Board en banc opinion] (*Martinez*), regarding CIGA's liability for penalties under section 5814. (Footnote 3)

On June 28, 2005, the WCAB issued an Opinion and Decision after Reconsideration. Following *Martinez,* the WCAB concluded that pursuant to the amendment to Insurance Code section 1063.1, subdivision (c)(8) (section 1063.1(c)(8)), the CIGA is not liable for penalties under section 5814 issued after January 1, 2004, based on an insolvent insurer's pre–liquidation delay. The WCAB rescinded the penalties awarded by the WCJ because the amendment "applies prospectively to any section 5814 awards issued on or after the effective date."

DISCUSSION

The CIGA was created in 1969 under the Guarantee Act (Ins. Code, Art. 14.2) to provide "insolvency insurance" against the loss arising from insolvent insurers. (*Denny's v. Workers' Comp. Appeals Bd.* (2003) 104 Cal. App. 4th 1433, 1438 [129 Cal. Rptr. 2d 53, 68 Cal. Comp. Cases 1].)

" 'It is a statutory entity that depends on the Guarantee Act for its existence and for a definition of the scope of its powers, duties, and protections.' " (*Ibid.*) It is only authorized to pay the statutorily defined "covered claims" of an insolvent insurer. (*Ibid.*)

" 'Workers' Compensation insurance is a class of insurance covered by the provisions of the CIGA statutes.' " (*Denny's v. Workers' Comp. Appeals Bd., supra,* 104 Cal. App. 4th at p. 1439.) Effective January 1, 2004, however, the Legislature expressly excluded from the definition of covered claims in section 1063.1(c)(8) "any amount awarded by the Workers' Compensation Appeals Board pursuant to Section 5814 or 5814.5

because payment of compensation was unreasonably delayed or refused by the insolvent insurer." (Stats. 2003, ch. 635, § 6 (Assem. Bill No. 227).) In *Martinez,* the WCAB concluded "the clear and unambiguous import of this statutory language is that section 1063.1(c)(8) applies prospectively to any section 5814 (or section 5814.5) awards issued on or after its effective date, i.e., awards issued on or after January 1, 2004." (*Martinez, supra,* 69 Cal. Comp. Cases 775, 779.)

Petitioners' contend the WCAB acted without or in excess of its powers by determining the CIGA is not liable for Legion's pre–liquidation unreasonable delay because the WCJ issued the section 5814 penalties on October 29, 2003, before the penalties were eliminated from the CIGA's coverage as of January 1, 2004. Petitioners agree with the WCAB's en banc decision in *Martinez* that the section 1063.1(c)(8) amendment applies "prospectively," but disagree with the WCAB's application of the amendment rescinding the penalties previously levied against the CIGA. Given Petitioners' concession, we do not address the propriety of the *Martinez* decision.

This court recently addressed a similar issue regarding the effective date of newly enacted apportionment provisions under Senate Bill No. 899 (Sen. Bill 899) in *Marsh v. Workers' Comp. Appeals Bd.* (2005) 130 Cal. App. 4th 906 [30 Cal. Rptr. 3d 598, 70 Cal. Comp. Cases 787]. Noting the express legislative intent of Sen. Bill 899 that its provisions apply "prospectively from the date of enactment," we concluded the WCJ's determination was not final for purposes of applying the new legislation while the matter was pending before the WCAB on reconsideration. (*Id.* at pp. 915–916.) We found the new apportionment provisions must be applied to all cases not yet final at the time of enactment, regardless of any interim WCJ decisions. (*Ibid.*; see also *Rio Linda Union School Dist. v. Workers' Comp. Appeals Bd.* (2005) 131 Cal. App. 4th 517 [31 Cal. Rptr. 3d 789, 70 Cal. Comp. Cases 999]; *Kleemann v. Workers' Comp. Appeals Bd.* (2005) 127 Cal. App. 4th 274 [25 Cal. Rptr. 3d 448, 70 Cal. Comp. Cases 133].) As the Second Appellate District, Division Eight explained in the context of whether a subsequent amendment to section 5814 applied retroactively:

" "When new legislation repeals statutory rights, the rights normally end with repeal unless vested pursuant to contract or common law. In workers' compensation, where rights are purely statutory and not based on common law, repeal ends the right, absent a savings clause. Rights end during litigation if statutory repeal occurs before final judgment; by definition there is no final judgment if an appeal is pending. There is no injustice if statutory rights end before final judgment because parties act and litigate in contemplation of possible repeal." (*Green v. Workers' Comp. Appeals Bd.* (2005) 127 Cal. App. 4th 1426, 1436 [26 Cal. Rptr. 3d 527, 70 Cal. Comp. Cases 294], fns. omitted.)"

In light of the Legislature's amendment to section 1063.1(c)(8) removing from the definition of a covered claim section 5814 penalties incurred by an insolvent insurer, we agree with the WCAB's decision to rescind the penalties previously awarded by the WCJ. Accordingly, we deny the petition for writ of review.

DISPOSITION

The petition for writ of review is denied. This opinion is final forthwith as to this court... .

Footnote 1. The current petition was properly filed in this appellate district because Petitioners reside in Merced County. (Lab. Code, § 5950; Gov. Code, § 69100, subd. (e).)

Footnote 2. In 2003, section 5814 provided: "When payment of compensation has been unreasonably delayed or refused, either prior to or subsequent to the issuance of an award, the full amount of the order, decision, or award shall be increased by 10 percent. Multiple increases shall not be awarded for repeated delays in making a series of payments due for the same type or specie of benefit unless there has been a legally significant event between the delay and the subsequent delay in payments of the same type or specie of benefits. The question of delay and the reasonableness of the cause therefor shall be determined by the appeals board in accordance with the facts. This delay or refusal shall constitute good cause under Section 5803 to rescind, alter, or amend the order, decision, or award for the purpose of making the increase provided for herein."

Footnote 3. While not relevant here, the WCAB also invited further arguments related to another recent en banc WCAB decision, *Leinon v. Fisherman's Grotto* (2004) 69 Cal. Comp. Cases 995 [Appeals Board en banc opinion], addressing a self–imposed 10 percent penalty under section 4650, subdivision (d).

Duty to Defend an Employee's Civil Action

While an insurance company's duty to defend a civil action may be quite broad, even encompassing lawsuits with a new potential for coverage, CIGA's obligation to defend is more limited.

CIGA does not stand in the shoes of an insolvent carrier for all purposes. In *Waite v. CIGA* (2006) 71 Cal. Comp. Cases 591, the Court of Appeal, Second District, in an unpublished opinion stated, in part:

Appellants Mary Lou Waite, Emerson Hess, Earl Soller, William M. Morrow and Morite of California (appellants) appeal from a judgment entered following a court trial in favor of respondent California Insurance Guarantee Association (CIGA) on appellants' action for declaratory relief and breach of statutory obligation. We affirm the judgment of the trial court.

CONTENTIONS

Appellants contend that the trial court erred in determining that CIGA is not obligated to pay for the defense of a lawsuit brought against appellants by a former employee, Danielle N. Macomber (Macomber), which appellants' insolvent former insurance company, Reliance Insurance Company (Reliance), refused to fund.

Specifically, appellants contend that CIGA's obligation to pay the costs appellants incurred defending the Macomber lawsuit is coextensive with Reliance's duty to defend the lawsuit.

In support of their argument that Reliance had a duty to defend the lawsuit, appellants argue (1) that Macomber's false imprisonment claim was potentially covered by their Reliance insurance policies; (2) that, because the Macomber first amended complaint contained a cause of action for false imprisonment, appellants had a reasonable expectation that Reliance would defend the Macomber action; and (3) that Macomber's claim for assault and battery resulting in bodily injury was potentially covered by their Reliance insurance policies.

FACTS AND PROCEDURAL HISTORY

From June 1996 to April 1999, Macomber worked as a waitress at a Red Robin restaurant in Clovis, California. Beginning in late January 1999, Macomber was the victim of sexual harassment by her supervisor, Bill Vidana. The harassment began on Super Bowl Sunday of 1999, when Vidana told Macomber a sexually explicit story. Over the following six weeks, Macomber was subject to numerous incidents of harassment, including improper touching and inappropriate comments. The sexual harassment ended on or about March 15, 1999, after Vidana threw a ketchup bottle at Macomber after she refused to go out on a date with him. A month later, Macomber was terminated from employment for failing to show up for work.

In August 1999, Macomber filed a lawsuit against Red Robin International and Bill Vidana (Macomber action). Her initial complaint for damages alleged violations of the California Fair Employment and Housing Act (FEHA), wrongful termination, assault and battery, and intentional infliction of emotional distress. Two months later, on September 27, 1999, Macomber filed a first amended complaint which added appellants Morite of California, which owns the Red Robin restaurant, and its partners, Mary Lou Waite, Emerson Hess, Earl Soller, and William M. Morrow, as defendants. The first amended complaint reiterated the allegations of violations of FEHA, wrongful termination, assault and battery, intentional and negligent infliction of emotional distress, and added a cause of action for false imprisonment. Additionally, the first amended complaint added an allegation that the assault and battery cause of action resulted in bodily injury.

Appellants had purchased two insurance policies from Reliance: a commercial general liability (CGL) policy and an excess umbrella (umbrella) policy. The CGL policy provided for coverage for bodily injury, which was defined to encompass bodily injury arising out of false imprisonment. However, it provided an express exclusion for bodily injury to an employee of the insured arising out of and in the course of employment. The CGL policy further contained an express exclusion for any obligation of the insured under any workers' compensation law and a specific employment–related practices exclusion. The umbrella policy also provided for coverage for bodily injury, including injury arising out of false imprisonment, but also contained an express exclusion for employment–related practices and any obligation under a workers' compensation law.

Appellants notified Reliance of the Macomber action on or about October 18, 1999. By letter dated December 10, 1999, Reliance denied coverage because the employment–related practices exclusion specifically excluded coverage for the allegations raised in the Macomber action. On December 27, 1999, appellants asked Reliance to reconsider its denial. Reliance reopened its investigation, but by letter dated May 5, 2000, reaffirmed its denial.

The Macomber action went to trial in June 2000. Macomber voluntarily dismissed her causes of action for wrongful termination, assault and battery, intentional infliction of emotional distress, and false imprisonment on July 5, 2000. On July 26, 2000, the jury returned a verdict in favor of Macomber on the sexual harassment cause of action only. The jury awarded Macomber $11,760, which the trial court subsequently reduced to $10,000. The court denied Macomber's motion for attorney fees. On November 3, 2000, Macomber filed an appeal from the judgment. The Court of Appeal dismissed the appeal in an unpublished decision dated October 25, 2002.

On February 21, 2001, appellants filed this action against Reliance for breach of written contract and bad faith. After Reliance appeared in the action, it became insolvent. Reliance filed a notice of an order of liquidation dated October 3, 2001, from the Commonwealth Court of Pennsylvania. On or about November 19, 2001, appellants wrote to CIGA seeking reimbursement of defense costs it incurred defending themselves and Vidana in the Macomber action. CIGA denied appellants' request pursuant to Insurance Code section 1063.1(c)(1)(i) (Footnote 1) because there was no coverage for the Macomber action under the terms of the Reliance CGL or umbrella policies. On August 16, 2002, appellants amended their complaint to name CIGA in place of Doe 1. On November 6, 2002, appellants again amended their complaint to add causes of action for declaratory relief and breach of statutory duty against CIGA.

A court trial was conducted based on stipulated facts, exhibits and trial briefs on January 12, 2004 and February 9, 2004. On March 30, 2004, the trial court issued its statement of decision wherein it ruled that the claim presented by appellants was not a "covered claim" under section 1063.1 and, therefore, that CIGA had no obligation to pay for any of appellants' defense costs. Appellants filed a timely notice of appeal on June 10, 2004.

DISCUSSION

In interpreting the scope of CIGA's obligations under the statutory scheme by which it was created, we keep in mind that "[t]he legislative intent [for creating CIGA] was to [ensure] protection for the public against insolvent insurers when no secondary insurer is available." (*Bunner*

v. Imperial Ins. Co. (1986) 181 Cal. App. 3d 14, 20 [225 Cal. Rptr. 912].) "A remedial or protective statute should be liberally construed to promote the underlying public policy." (*Id.* at p. 21.) And, although CIGA's interpretation of the statute may be entitled to great weight, the ultimate responsibility for the interpretation of the law rests with the courts. (*Id.* at p. 22.)

II. The nature and purpose of CIGA

CIGA was created in 1969 as a compulsory association of state–regulated insurance companies. (*R. J. Reynolds Co. v. California Ins. Guarantee Assn.* (1991) 235 Cal. App. 3d 595, 599 [1 Cal. Rptr. 2d 405].) Its purpose is to provide against loss arising from the failure of an insolvent insurer to discharge its obligations under its insurance policies. (*Middleton v. Imperial Ins. Co.* (1983) 34 Cal. 3d 134, 137 [666 P.2d 1, 193 Cal. Rptr. 144].) CIGA assesses its members when another member becomes insolvent, thereby establishing a fund from which insureds whose insurers become insolvent can obtain financial and legal assistance. (*Isaacson v. California Ins. Guarantee Assn.* (1988) 44 Cal. 3d 775, 784 [750 P.2d 297, 244 Cal. Rptr. 655].) Member insurers then recoup assessments paid to CIGA by means of a surcharge on premiums to their policyholders. (*R. J. Reynolds Co. v. California Ins. Guarantee Assn., supra,* at p. 600.) In this way, the insolvency of one insurer does not impact a small segment of insurance consumers, but is spread throughout the insurance–consuming public, which in effect subsidizes CIGA's continued operation. (*Ibid.*)

While CIGA's general purpose is to pay the obligations of an insolvent insurer, it is not itself an insurer. (*R. J. Reynolds Co. v. California Ins. Guarantee Assn., supra,* 235 Cal. App. 3d at p. 600.) "CIGA is *not* in the 'business' of insurance . . . . CIGA issues no policies, collects no premiums, makes no profits, and assumes no contractual obligations to the insureds." (*Isaacson v. California Ins. Guarantee Assn., supra,* 44 Cal. 3d at p. 787.) Rather, it is authorized by statute to pay only covered claims of an insolvent insurer, those determined by the Legislature to be in keeping with the goal of providing protection for the insured public. (*R. J. Reynolds Co. v. California Ins. Guarantee Assn., supra,* at p. 600.)

III. CIGA's obligation is not coextensive with Reliance's duty to defend

Appellants contend that Macomber's first amended complaint contained causes of action which created the *potential* that the Macomber action would be covered by the Reliance policies. According to appellants, this potential for coverage was enough to trigger Reliance's duty to defend the lawsuit. Appellants cite *Gray v. Zurich Insurance Co.* (1966) 65 Cal. 2d 263, 275 [419 P.2d 168, 54 Cal. Rptr. 104] for the proposition that an insurance carrier has a broad obligation to defend its insured against a claim which *"potentially* seeks damages within the coverage of the policy."

However, Reliance made an initial determination that the Macomber lawsuit was outside of the scope of appellants' coverage and thus that it had no duty to defend. Appellants have set forth extensive argument as to why Reliance's determination was incorrect. In doing so, appellants ask us to adopt the following logic: because Reliance had a duty to defend the Macomber lawsuit, CIGA necessarily must reimburse appellants for the money they expended defending the lawsuit. Appellants' position is grounded on the premise that CIGA's obligation to pay for the costs of defending a lawsuit is coextensive with an insurance company's duty to defend.

We disagree with this premise. The question of an insurance company's duty to defend a lawsuit is answered by a different analysis from that which must be undertaken to determine CIGA's obligation to pay policyholders of insolvent insurance companies. While an insurance company's duty to defend may be quite broad – encompassing lawsuits with a mere *potential* for coverage – CIGA's obligation is more limited. Since "[t]he role of CIGA differs from that of the ordinary insurer," CIGA cannot and does not " 'stand in the shoes' of the insolvent insurer for all purposes." (*Biggs v. California Ins. Guarantee Assn.* (1981) 126 Cal. App. 3d 641, 645 [179 Cal. Rptr. 16].) CIGA does not have the obligation, nor the authority, to provide benefits beyond what is specifically outlined in the statutory scheme by which it was created.

We find that we need not address the question of whether Reliance's initial determination of its obligation to defend the Macomber lawsuit was correct. Instead, the question we must analyze is whether the claim that appellants tendered to CIGA on or about November 19, 2001, was a covered claim under section 1063.1, subdivision (c)(1).

IV. The trial court correctly determined that the defense of the Macomber lawsuit was not a covered claim under section 1063.1, subdivision (c)(1)

As set forth above, CIGA is authorized only to "pay and discharge covered claims." (§ 1063.2, subd. (a).) It is only "in connection therewith" that CIGA is to "pay for or furnish loss adjustment services and defenses of claimants when required by policy provisions . . . ." (*Ibid.*) Thus, [i]t is unequivocally clear [that] the scope of CIGA's rights and duties turns on the definition of 'covered claim.' " (*Saylin v. California Ins. Guarantee Assn.* (1986) 179 Cal. App. 3d 256, 262 [224 Cal. Rptr. 493] (*Saylin*).)

Section 1063.1, subdivision (c)(1) defines covered claims as "the obligations of an insolvent insurer . . . (i) imposed by law and within the coverage of an insurance policy of the insolvent insurer; (ii) which were unpaid by the insolvent insurer; (iii) which are presented as a claim to the . . . association . . . (v) for which the assets of the insolvent insurer are insufficient to discharge in full." The remainder of subdivision (c) enumerates nine separate categories of claims clearly "arising out of an insurance policy of an insolvent insurer" which nevertheless are not covered claims. (*Saylin v. California Ins. Guarantee Assn., supra*, 179 Cal. App. 3d at p. 262.)

Appellants' arguments that the Macomber lawsuit was potentially within the coverage of the Reliance policies are grounded on two causes of action set forth in Macomber's first amended complaint: (1) false imprisonment; and (2) assault and battery resulting in bodily injury. However, in analyzing whether appellants' defense of the Macomber action constituted a covered claim, CIGA was not limited to consideration of the first amended complaint. Instead, as set forth in *Saylin*, CIGA's analysis was properly carried out by a review of all the facts available at the time that the claim was tendered to CIGA.

In *Saylin*, an attorney was insured under a professional malpractice policy when he was sued for malpractice. The attorney's insurance company defended the malpractice action for two and one–half years before becoming insolvent. When the matter was tendered to CIGA, CIGA considered the deposition of the plaintiff, in which the plaintiff had testified that she did not receive legal advice from the insured attorney during the time period covered by the professional malpractice policy. Thus, the plaintiff's deposition established that the underlying malpractice lawsuit was not a covered claim. Division One of this court held that CIGA properly considered the deposition, which was available at the time the claim was tendered to CIGA, in determining whether the malpractice lawsuit was a covered claim. (*Saylin v. California Ins. Guarantee Assn., supra*, 179 Cal. App. 3d at pp. 262–264.)

When CIGA acquired the duty to determine whether appellants had presented a covered claim, CIGA knew that Macomber had voluntarily dismissed the false imprisonment and assault and battery causes of action at an early stage of trial. Furthermore, CIGA knew that the jury ultimately found in Macomber's favor only on the sexual harassment cause of action, which appellants do not contend was covered under the Reliance policies. Thus, on the date that appellants tendered their claim regarding the Macomber lawsuit to CIGA, November 19, 2001, CIGA had ample information confirming that the Macomber action was not within the coverage of the Reliance insurance policies. Because, on these facts, appellants had not tendered an obligation "imposed by law and within the coverage of an insurance policy" of Reliance (§ 1063.1, subd. (c)(1)(i)), CIGA was well within its rights in denying appellants' request for reimbursement of their defense costs. (*Saylin v. California Ins. Guarantee Assn., supra*, 179 Cal. App. 3d at p. 264.)

Appellants seek to distinguish *Saylin* by arguing that it does not stand for the proposition that CIGA is relieved of paying for a defense owed by the insolvent insurer. Appellants point out that in *Saylin*, the insolvent insurer had faithfully provided a defense to the insured until the insurer became insolvent. The difference, therefore, is that in *Saylin*, the insurance company made an initial determination to provide coverage. In contrast, Reliance refused to provide coverage for the Macomber action.

This distinction does not change the outcome. Regardless of whether the insurance company makes a decision to defend the underlying lawsuit or not, CIGA's duty is to determine independently whether the claim is a covered claim based on the facts available to it at the time the claim is tendered. (Footnote 2)(*Saylin v. California Ins. Guarantee Assn.*, supra, 179 Cal. App. 3d at p. 264.)

Appellants have provided no authority – nor have we found any – for their contention that CIGA has an obligation to cover expenses incurred in defending a lawsuit because, at some point in the past, there was a potential that the lawsuit might be within the coverage of a policy issued by the insolvent insurance company. In fact, appellants' argument that CIGA's obligation encompasses a situation where there is a mere potential for coverage under an insurance policy is directly contradicted by the language of the statute, which specifies that in order to qualify as a covered claim, the obligation must be "within the coverage of an insurance policy of the insolvent insurer." (§ 1063.1, subd. (c)(1)(i).) Based on the facts available to it at the time, CIGA properly determined that appellants' defense of the Macomber action was not a covered claim.

V. CIGA's additional defenses

CIGA sets forth additional arguments in an effort to limit its obligation. First, CIGA argues that, even if CIGA were forced to pay for the defense of the trial, there was no coverage for the Macomber appeal under the Reliance policies. Further, CIGA argues that the claims of two of the appellants are barred by section 1063.2, subdivision (c)(1) because the two individuals are residents of Pennsylvania.

Because we hold that CIGA properly determined that it has no obligation to compensate appellants for the defense of the Macomber action, we need not discuss these defenses.

DISPOSITION

The judgmentis affirmed. Appellants shall bear the costs of appeal... .

Footnote 1. All further statutory references are to the Insurance Code.

Footnote 2. At oral argument, counsel for both appellants and respondent addressed the argument first raised in appellants' reply brief that Macomber's bodily injury claim was not necessarily barred by the workers' compensation exclusions in the Reliance insurance policies because Macomber was the initial physical aggressor in the incident which resulted in Vidana throwing a ketchup bottle at Macomber. Preliminarily, because this argument was first raised in appellants' reply brief, we will not consider it. (*Reichardt v. Hoffman* (1997) 52 Cal. App. 4th 754, 764 [60 Cal. Rptr. 2d 770].) Further, because the bodily injury cause of action had been dismissed by the time the claim was tendered to CIGA, the argument is irrelevant.

Longshore and Harbor Loorken Compensation Act Claims

Longshore and Harbor Workers' Compensation Act claims are excluded from CIGA liability. *CIGA et. al. v. WCAB (Badenhop)* (2006) 71 Cal. Comp. Cases 1150.

Changing Administration

The Appeals Board has the power to appoint a solvent insurer administrator of a claim thereby relieving CIGA of the responsibility. Commenting on this in *IVAC Corporation, et. al. v. WCAB (Coronado)* (2006) 71 Cal. Comp. Cases 1878, the Court of Appeal, Fourth District, in upholding a Board decision relieving CIGA as administrator stated, in part:

On June 12, 2006, One Beacon Insurance and Commercial Union Insurance Company (Commercial Union) filed a petition for reconsideration with the Workers Compensation Appeals Board (WCAB), challenging a decision by the Workers' Compensation Judge (WCJ) appointing Commercial Union administrator of a workers' compensation award that California Insurance Guaranty [*sic*] Association (CIGA) had been administering after the bankruptcy of Reliance Insurance Company (Reliance). On October 29, 1997, Commercial Union and Reliance stipulated Commercial Union would pay 25 percent of the award and Reliance 75 percent. Reliance administered the award until 2001. In its petition, Commercial Union contended the WCJ erred in shifting responsibility for administrating the award from CIGA to Commercial Union, pointing out a new cumulative trauma claim against a subsequent employer/carrier and a petition to reopen for new and further disability were filed in 1998, complicating the case. It argued the stipulations of liability are poorly drafted making it virtually impossible to adjust the award; changing administrators has the effect of changing the division of liability agreed to by the parties; and the WCAB did not have jurisdiction to alter the award.

The WCJ issued a report recommending denial of the petition for reconsideration, reasoning all liability under the stipulated award had been paid except for ongoing medical treatment, and Commercial Union would not be involved in the new cumulative trauma claim, but would be involved in defense of the petition to reopen whether or not it were administrator. The WCJ concluded it is likely the applicant will not prosecute the new and further disability claim and reasoned the vagueness in the stipulations is cured by the agreement as to the proportionate share of liability agreed to for each carrier. It further concluded that appointing Commercial Union as administrator would not cause it undue disadvantage. The Workers' Compensation Appeals Board (WCAB) denied the petition for reconsideration, adopting the reasoning in the WCJ's report.

In the present petition, Commercial Union contends the WCAB has misinterpreted and misapplied the law. It argues under the reasoning of *California Ins. Guarantee Assn. v. Workers' Comp. Appeals Bd. (Argonaut)* (2005)

128 Cal. App. 4th 569 [27 Cal. Rptr. 3d 205, 70 Cal. Comp. Cases 551], and *California Ins. Guarantee Assn. v. Workers' Comp. Appeals Bd. (American Motors)* (2005) 128 Cal. App. 4th 307 [26 Cal. Rptr. 3d 845, 70 Cal. Comp. Cases 556], changing administrators from CIGA to Commercial Union affects the overall liability of the claim because if Commercial Union is administrator it will not have the right to seek contribution from CIGA. Therefore, instead of being liable for 25 percent of the award as agreed, it will be liable for 100 percent. It argues this result violates Labor Code section 5804, which requires an award not be rescinded, altered or amended after five years following the date of the injury.

Review of a decision of the WCAB is limited to whether the WCAB acted without or in excess of its powers, and whether the order, decision or award was unreasonable, not supported by substantial evidence, or procured by fraud. (Lab. Code, § 5952.) We cannot say the WCAB acted unreasonably or in excess of its powers by denying reconsideration. Commercial Union is jointly liable for the entire award and the change in administrator does not change that liability. The WCJ did not abuse its [*sic*] discretion in appointing Commercial Union as administrator.

Intentionally blank

Appendix A

● Pre–Designation of Personal Physician; Request for Change of Physician; Reporting Duties of Primary Treating Physician; Petition for Change of Primary Treating Physician.

Article 5. Predesignation of Personal Physician; Request for Change of Physician; Reporting Duties of the Primary Treating Physician; Petition for Change of Primary Treating Physician

§ 9780. Definitions

As used in this Article:
(a) "Claims Administrator" means a self–administered insurer providing security for the payment of compensation required by Divisions 4 and 4.5 of the Labor Code, a self–administered self–insured employer, a self–administered joint powers authority, a self–administered legally uninsured, or a third–party claims administrator for a self–insured employer, insurer, legally uninsured employer, or joint powers authority.
(b) "Emergency health care services" means health care services for a medical condition manifesting itself by acute symptoms of sufficient severity such that the absence of immediate medical attention could reasonably be expected to place the patient's health in serious jeopardy.
(c) "Facility" means a hospital, clinic or other institution capable of providing the medical, surgical, chiropractic or hospital treatment which is reasonably required to cure or relieve the employee from the effects of the injury.
(d) "First aid" is any one–time treatment, and a follow–up visit for the purpose of observation of minor scratches, cuts, burns, splinters, etc., which do not ordinarily require medical care. Such one–time treatment and follow–up visit for the purpose of observation, is considered first aid, even though provided by a physician or registered professional personnel.
(e) "Nonoccupational group health coverage" means coverage for nonoccupational health care that the employer makes available to the employee, including, but not limited to, a Taft Hartley or Employee Retirement Income Security Act

(ERISA) trust, or a health plan negotiated between a union or employee's association and the employer or employer's association.

(f) (1) "Personal Physician" means the employee's regular physician and surgeon, licensed pursuant to Chapter 5 (commencing with section 2000) of Division 2 of the Business and Professions Code, (2) who has been the employee's primary care physician, and has previously directed the medical treatment of the employee, and (3) who retains the employee's medical records, including the employee's medical history.

(g) "Primary Care Physician" means a physician who has the responsibility for providing initial and primary care to patients, for maintaining the continuity of patient care, and for initiating referral for specialist care. A primary care physician shall be either a physician who has limited his or her practice of medicine to general practice or who is a board–certified or board–eligible internist, pediatrician, obstetrician–gynecologist, or family practitioner.

(h) "Reasonable geographic area" within the context of Labor Code section 4600 shall be determined by giving consideration to:

   (1) The employee's place of residence, place of employment and place where the injury occurred; and

   (2) The availability of physicians in the fields of practice, and facilities offering treatment reasonably required to cure or relieve the employee from the effects of the injury;

   (3) The employee's medical history;

   (4) The employee's primary language.

NOTE: Authority cited: Sections 59, 133 and 4603.5, Labor Code. Reference: Section 4600, Labor Code.

HISTORY

1. Repealer of Article 5 (Sections 9783–9785, 9787 and 9788) and new Article 5 (Sections 9780–9787) filed 1–28–76 as an emergency; effective upon filing (Register 76, No. 5). For prior history, see Register 70, No. 49, and Register 72, No. 51.
2. Certificate of Compliance filed 1–29–76 (Register 76, No. 5).
3. New subsections (f)–(i) filed 11–7–78; effective thirtieth day thereafter (Register 78, No. 45).
4. Repealer and new article 5 heading and amendment of section and Note filed 3–14–2006; operative 3–14–2006 pursuant to Government Code section 11343.4 (Register 2006, No. 11).
5. Editorial correction of subsection (f)(1) (Register 2007, No. 7).

§ 9780.1.   Employee's Predesignation of Personal Physician

(a) An employee may be treated for an industrial injury in accordance with section 4600 of the Labor Code by a personal physician that the employee predesignates prior to the industrial injury if the following three conditions are met:

   (1) Notice of the predesignation of a personal physician is in writing, and is provided to the employer prior to the industrial injury for which treatment by the personal physician is sought. The notice shall include the personal physician's name and business address. The employee may use the optional predesignation form (DWC Form 9783) in section 9783 for this purpose.

   (2) The employer provides: (i) nonoccupational group health coverage in a health care service plan, licensed pursuant to Chapter 2.2 (commencing with section 1340) of Division 2 of the Health and Safety Code, or (ii) nonoccupational health coverage in a group health plan or a group health insurance policy as described in section 4616.7 of the Labor Code. The employer's provision of health coverage as defined herein is sufficient to meet this requirement, regardless of whether the employee accepts or participates in this health coverage.

   (3) The employee's personal physician agrees to be predesignated prior to the injury. The personal physician may sign the optional predesignation form (DWC Form 9783) in section 9783 as documentation of such agreement. The physician may authorize a designated employee of the physician to sign the optional predesignation form on his or her behalf. If the personal physician or the designated employee of the physician does not sign a predesignation form, there must be other documentation that the physician agrees to be predesignated prior to the injury in order to satisfy this requirement.

(b) If an employee has predesignated a personal physician prior to the effective date of these regulations, such predesignation shall be considered valid if the conditions in subdivision (a) have been met.

(c) Where an employer or an employer's insurer has a Medical Provider Network pursuant to section 4616 of the Labor Code, an employee's predesignation which has been made in accordance with this section shall be valid and the employee shall not be subject to the Medical Provider Network.

(d) Where an employee has made a valid predesignation pursuant to this section, and where the employer or employer's insurer has a Medical Provider Network, any referral to another physician for other treatment need not be within the Medical Provider Network.

(e) An employer who qualifies under (a)(2) of this section shall notify its employees of all of the requirements of this section and provide its employees with an optional form for predesignating a personal physician, in accordance with section 9880. The employer may use the predesignation form (DWC Form 9783) in section 9783 for this purpose.

(f) Unless the employee agrees, neither the employer nor the claims administrator shall contact the predesignated personal physician to confirm predesignation status or contact the personal physician regarding the employee's medical information or medical history prior to the personal physician's commencement of treatment for an industrial injury.

(g) Where the employer has been notified of an employee's predesignation of a personal physician in accordance with this section and where the employer becomes liable for an employee's medical treatment, the claims administrator shall:

    (1) authorize the predesignated physician to provide all medical treatment reasonably required to cure or relieve the injured employee from the effects of his or her injury;

    (2) furnish the name and address of the person to whom billing for treatment should be sent;

    (3) where there has been treatment of an injury prior to commencement of treatment by the predesignated physician, arrange for the delivery to the predesignated physician of all medical information relating to the claim, all X–rays, the results of all laboratory studies done in relation to the injured employee's treatment; and

    (4) provide the physician with (1) the fax number, if available, to be used to request authorization of treatment plans; (2) the complete requirements of section 9785; and (3) the forms set forth in sections 9785.2 and 9785.4. In lieu of providing the materials required in (2) and (3) immediately above, the claims administrator may refer the physician to the Division of Workers' Compensation's website where the applicable information and forms can be found at http://www.dir.ca.gov/DWC/dwc_home_page.htm.

(h) Notwithstanding subdivision (g), the employer shall provide first aid and appropriate emergency health care services reasonably required by the nature of the injury or illness. Thereafter, if further medical treatment is reasonably required to cure or relieve the injured employee from the effects of his or her injury, the claims administrator shall authorize treatment with the employee's predesignated personal physician in accordance with subdivision (g).

(i) If documentation of a physician's agreement to be predesignated has not been provided to the employer as of the time of injury, treatment shall be provided in accordance with Labor Code section 4600, or Labor Code section 4616, if the employer or insurer has established a Medical Provider Network, as though no predesignation had occurred. Upon provision of the documented agreement that was made prior to injury that meets the conditions of Labor Code section 4600(d), the employer or claims administrator shall authorize treatment with the employee's predesignated physician as set forth in subdivision (g).

NOTE: Authority cited: Sections 59, 133 and 4603.5, Labor Code. Reference: Sections 3551, 4600 and 4616, Labor Code.

HISTORY

1. New section filed 11–7–78; effective thirtieth day thereafter (Register 78, No. 45).
2. Amendment of section heading, repealer and new section and amendment of Note filed 3–14–2006; operative 3–14–2006 pursuant to Government Code section11343.4 (Register 2006, No. 11). 8 CA ADC s 9780.1

§ 9780.2. Employer's Duty to Provide First Aid and Emergency Treatment

NOTE: Authority cited: Sections 124, 127, 133, 138.2, 138.3, 138.4, 139, 139.5, 139.6, 4600, 4601, 4602, 4603, 4603.2, 4603.5, 5307.3, 5450, 5451, 5452, 5453, 5454, and 5455, Labor Code. Reference: Chapters 442, 709, and 1172, Statutes of 1977; Chapter 1017, Statutes of 1976.

HISTORY

1. New section filed 11–7–78; effective thirtieth day thereafter (Register 78, No. 45).
2. Repealer filed 3–14–2006; operative 3–14–2006 pursuant to Government Code section 11343.4 (Register 2006, No. 11).

§ 9781. Employee's Request for Change of Physician

(a) This section shall not apply to self–insured and insured employers who offer a Medical Provider Network pursuant to section 4616 of the Labor Code.

(b) Pursuant to section 4601 of the Labor Code, and notwithstanding the 30 day time period specified in subdivision (c), the employee may request a one time change of physician at any time.

    (1) An employee's request for change of physician pursuant to this subdivision need not be in writing. The claims administrator shall respond to the employee in the manner best calculated to inform the employee, and in no event later than 5 working days from receipt of said request, the claims administrator shall provide the employee an alternative physician, or if the employee so requests, a chiropractor or acupuncturist.

    (2) Notwithstanding subdivision (a) of section 9780.1, if an employee requesting a change of physician pursuant to this subdivision has notified his or her employer in writing prior to the date of injury that he or she has either a personal chiropractor or a personal acupuncturist, and where the employee so requests, the alternative physician tendered by the claims administrator to the employee shall be the employee's personal chiropractor or personal acupuncturist as defined in subdivisions (b) and (c), respectively, of Labor Code section 4601. The notification to the employer must include the name and business address of the chiropractor or acupuncturist. The employer shall notify its employees of the requirements of this subdivision and provide its employees with an optional form for notification of a personal

chiropractor or acupuncturist, in accordance with section 9880. DWC Form 9783.1 in section 9783.1 may be used for this purpose.

    (3) Except where the employee is permitted to select a personal chiropractor or acupuncturist as defined in subdivisions (b) and (c), respectively, of Labor Code section 4601, the claims administrator shall advise the employee of the name and address of the alternative physician, or chiropractor or acupuncturist if requested, the date and time of an initial scheduled appointment, and any other pertinent information.

(c) Pursuant to section 4600, after 30 days from the date the injury is reported, the employee shall have the right to be treated by a physician or at a facility of his or her own choice within a reasonable geographic area.

    (1) The employee shall notify the claims administrator of the name and address of the physician or facility selected pursuant to this subdivision. However, this notice requirement will be deemed to be satisfied if the selected physician or facility gives notice to the claims administrator of the commencement of treatment or if the claims administrator receives this information promptly from any source.

    (2) If so requested by the selected physician or facility, the employee shall sign a release permitting the selected physician or facility to report to the claims administrator as required by section 9785.

(d) When the claims administrator is notified of the name and address of an employee–selected physician or facility pursuant to subdivision (c), or of a personal chiropractor or acupuncturist pursuant to paragraph (2) of subdivision (b), the claims administrator shall:

    (1) authorize such physician or facility or personal chiropractor or acupuncturist to provide all medical treatment reasonably required pursuant to section 4600 of the Labor Code;

    (2) furnish the name and address of the person to whom billing for treatment should be sent;

    (3) arrange for the delivery to the selected physician or facility of all medical information relating to the claim, all X–rays and the results of all laboratory studies done in relation to the injured employee's treatment; and

    (4) provide the physician or facility with (1) the fax number, if available, to be used to request authorization of treatment plans; (2) the complete requirements of section 9785; and (3) the forms set forth in sections 9785.2 and 9785.4. In lieu of providing the materials required in (2) and (3) immediately above, the claims administrator may refer the physician or facility to the Division of Workers' Compensation's website where the applicable information and forms can be found at http://www.dir.ca.gov/DWC/dwc_home_page.htm.

NOTE: Authority cited: Sections 133 and 4603.5, Labor Code. Reference: Sections 3551, 4600 and 4601, Labor Code.

HISTORY

1. Repealer and new section filed 11–9–77; effective thirtieth day thereafter (Register 77, No. 46).

2. Repealer and new section and amendment of Note filed 3–14–2006; operative 3–14–2006 pursuant to Government Code section 11343.4 (Register 2006, No.11).

§ 9782.   Notice to Employee of Right to Choose Physician

(a) Except for an employer who has established a Medical Provider Network, or an employer whose insurer has established a Medical Provider Network, every employer shall advise its employees in writing of an employee's right (1) to request a change of treating physician if the original treating physician is selected initially by the employer pursuant to Labor Code section 4601, and (2) to be treated by a physician of his or her own choice 30 days after reporting an injury pursuant to subdivision (c) of Labor Code 4600.

(b) Every employer shall advise its employees in writing of an employee's right to predesignate a personal physician pursuant to subdivision (d) of Labor Code section 4600, and section 9780.1.

(c) The notices required by this section shall be provided in accordance with section 9880 and posted in accordance with section 9881.

NOTE: Authority cited: Sections 133 and 4603.5, Labor Code. Reference: Sections 3550, 3551, 4600, 4601 and 4616, Labor Code.

HISTORY

1. Repealer and new section filed 11–9–77; effective thirtieth day thereafter (Register 77, No. 46).

2. Repealer and new section filed 11–7–78; effective thirtieth day thereafter (Register 78, No. 45).

3. Amendment of section and Note filed 3–14–2006; operative 3–14–2006 pursuant to Government Code section 11343.4 (Register 2006, No. 11).

§ 9783. DWC Form 9783 Predesignation of Personal Physician

NOTICE OF PREDESIGNATION OF PERSONAL PHYSICIAN

In the event you sustain an injury or illness related to your employment, you may be treated for such injury or illness by your personal medical doctor (M.D.) or doctor of osteopathic medicine (D.O.) if:

- your employer offers group health coverage;
- the doctor is your regular physician, who shall be either a physician who has limited his or her practice of medicine to general practice or who is a board–certified or board–eligible internist, pediatrician, obstetrician–gynecologist, or family practitioner, and has previously directed your medical treatment, and retains your medical records;
- prior to the injury your doctor agrees to treat you for work injuries or illnesses;
- prior to the injury you provided your employer the following in writing: (1) notice that you want your personal doctor to treat you for a work–related injury or illness, and (2) your personal doctor's name and business address. You may use this form to notify your employer if you wish to have your personal medical doctor or a doctor of osteopathic medicine treat you for a work–related injury or illness and the above requirements are met.

NOTICE OF PREDESIGNATION OF PERSONAL PHYSICIAN

Employee: Complete this section.

To:

_____
(name of employer)
If I have a work–related injury or illness, I choose to be treated by:

_____
(name of doctor)(M.D., D.O.)

_____
(street address, city, state, ZIP)

_____
(telephone number)

Employee Name (please print):

_____

Employee's Address:

_____
_____

Employee's Signature: _____Date: _____

Physician: I agree to this Predesignation:
Signature: _____
Date: _____

(Physician or Designated Employee of the Physician)

The physician is not required to sign this form, however, if the physician or designated employee of the physician does not sign, other documentation of the physician's agreement to be predesignated will be required pursuant to Title 8, California Code of Regulations, section 9780.1(a)(3).

Title 8, California Code of Regulations, section 9783. (Optional DWC Form 9783 – Effective date March 2006)

NOTE: Authority cited: Sections 133, 4603.5 and 5307.3, Labor Code. Reference: Section 4600, Labor Code

HISTORY
1. Amendment filed 11–11–78; effective thirtieth day thereafter (Register 78, No. 45).
2. Repealer and new section heading, section and Note filed 3–14–2006; operative 3–14–2006 pursuant to Government Code section 11343.4 (Register 2006, No. 11).

§ 9784.   Duties of the Employer

NOTE: Authority cited: Sections 124, 127, 133, 138.2, 138.3, 138.4, 139, 139.5, 139.6, 4600, 4601, 4602, 4603, 4603.2, 4603.5, 5307.3, 5450, 5451, 5452, 5453, 5454, and 5455, Labor Code. Reference: Chapters 442, 709, and 1172, Statutes of 1977; Chapter 1017, Statutes of 1976.

HISTORY
1. Repealer and new section filed 11–9–77; effective thirtieth day thereafter (Register 77, No. 46).
2. Amendment filed 11–11–78; effective thirtieth day thereafter (Register 78, No. 45).
3. Repealer filed 3–14–2006; operative 3–14–2006 pursuant to Government Code section 11343.4 (Register 2006, No. 11).

§ 9785.   Reporting Duties of the Primary Treating Physician

(a) For the purposes of this section, the following definitions apply:
   (1) The "primary treating physician" is the physician who is primarily responsible for managing the care of an employee, and who has examined the employee at least once for the purpose of rendering or prescribing treatment and has monitored the effect of the treatment thereafter. The primary treating physician is the physician selected by the employer, the employee pursuant to Article 2 (commencing with section 4600) of Chapter 2 of Part 2 of Division 4 of the Labor Code, or under the contract or procedures applicable to a Health Care Organization certified under section 4600.5 of the Labor Code, or in accordance with the physician selection procedures contained in the medical provider network pursuant to Labor Code section 4616.
   (2) A "secondary physician" is any physician other than the primary treating physician who examines or provides treatment to the employee, but is not primarily responsible for continuing management of the care of the employee.
   (3) "Claims administrator" is a self–administered insurer providing security for the payment of compensation required by Divisions 4 and 4.5 of the Labor Code, a self–administered self–insured employer, or a third–party administrator for a self–insured employer, insurer, legally uninsured employer, or joint powers authority.
   (4) "Medical determination" means, for the purpose of this section, a decision made by the primary treating physician regarding any and all medical issues necessary to determine the employee's eligibility for compensation. Such issues include but are not limited to the scope and extent of an employee's continuing medical treatment, the decision whether to release the employee from care, the point in time at which the employee has reached permanent and stationary status, and the necessity for future medical treatment.
   (5) "Released from care" means a determination by the primary treating physician that the employee's condition has reached a permanent and stationary status with no need for continuing or future medical treatment.
   (6) "Continuing medical treatment" is occurring or presently planned treatment that is reasonably required to cure or relieve the employee from the effects of the injury.
   (7) "Future medical treatment" is treatment which is anticipated at some time in the future and is reasonably required to cure or relieve the employee from the effects of the injury.
   (8) "Permanent and stationary status" is the point when the employee has reached maximal medical improvement, meaning his or her condition is well stabilized, and unlikely to change substantially in the next year with or without medical treatment.
(b) (1) An employee shall have no more than one primary treating physician at a time.
   (2) An employee may designate a new primary treating physician of his or her choice pursuant to Labor Code §§4600 or 4600.3 provided the primary treating physician has determined that there is a need for:
      (A) continuing medical treatment; or
      (B) future medical treatment. The employee may designate a new primary treating physician to render future medical treatment either prior to or at the time such treatment becomes necessary.
   (3) If the employee disputes a medical determination made by the primary treating physician, including a determination that the employee should be released from care, or if the employee objects to a decision made pursuant to Labor Code section 4610 to modify, delay, or deny a treatment recommendation, the dispute shall be resolved under the applicable procedures set forth at Labor Code sections4061 and 4062. No other primary treating physician shall be designated by the employee unless and until the dispute is resolved.
   (4) If the claims administrator disputes a medical determination made by the primary treating physician, the dispute shall be resolved under the applicable procedures set forth at Labor Code sections 4610, 4061 and 4062.
(c) The primary treating physician, or a physician designated by the primary treating physician, shall make reports to the claims administrator as required in this section. A primary treating physician has fulfilled his or her reporting duties under this section by sending one copy of a required report to the claims administrator. A claims administrator may designate any person or entity to be the recipient of its copy of the required report.
(d) The primary treating physician shall render opinions on all medical issues necessary to determine the employee's eligibility for compensation in the manner prescribed in subdivisions (e), (f) and (g) of this section. The primary treating

physician may transmit reports to the claims administrator by mail or FAX or by any other means satisfactory to the claims administrator, including electronic transmission.

(e) (1) Within 5 working days following initial examination, a primary treating physician shall submit a written report to the claims administrator on the form entitled "Doctor's First Report of Occupational Injury or Illness," Form DLSR 5021. Emergency and urgent care physicians shall also submit a Form DLSR 5021 to the claims administrator following the initial visit to the treatment facility. On line 24 of the Doctor's First Report, or on the reverse side of the form, the physician shall (A) list methods, frequency, and duration of planned treatment(s), (B) specify planned consultations or referrals, surgery or hospitalization and (C) specify the type, frequency and duration of planned physical medicine services (e.g., physical therapy, manipulation, acupuncture).

(2) Each new primary treating physician shall submit a Form DLSR 5021 following the initial examination in accordance with subdivision (e)(1).

(3) Secondary physicians, physical therapists, and other health care providers to whom the employee is referred shall report to the primary treating physician in the manner required by the primary treating physician.

(4) The primary treating physician shall be responsible for obtaining all of the reports of secondary physicians and shall, unless good cause is shown, within 20 days of receipt of each report incorporate, or comment upon, the findings and opinions of the other physicians in the primary treating physician's report and submit all of the reports to the claims administrator.

(f) A primary treating physician shall, unless good cause is shown, within 20 days report to the claims administrator when any one or more of the following occurs:

(1) The employee's condition undergoes a previously unexpected significant change;

(2) There is any significant change in the treatment plan reported, including, but not limited to, (A) an extension of duration or frequency of treatment, (B) a new need for hospitalization or surgery, (C) a new need for referral to or consultation by another physician, (D) a change in methods of treatment or in required physical medicine services, or (E) a need for rental or purchase of durable medical equipment or orthotic devices;

(3) The employee's condition permits return to modified or regular work;

(4) The employee's condition requires him or her to leave work, or requires changes in work restrictions or modifications;

(5) The employee is released from care;

(6) The primary treating physician concludes that the employee's permanent disability precludes, or is likely to preclude, the employee from engaging in the employee's usual occupation or the occupation in which the employee was engaged at the time of the injury, as required pursuant to Labor Code Section 4636(b);

(7) The claims administrator reasonably requests appropriate additional information that is necessary to administer the claim. "Necessary" information is that which directly affects the provision of compensation benefits as defined in Labor Code Section 3207.

(8) When continuing medical treatment is provided, a progress report shall be made no later than forty–five days from the last report of any type under this section even if no event described in paragraphs (1) to (7) has occurred. If an examination has occurred, the report shall be signed and transmitted within 20 days of the examination.

Except for a response to a request for information made pursuant to subdivision (f)(7), reports required under this subdivision shall be submitted on the "Primary Treating Physician's Progress Report" form (Form PR–2) contained in Section 9785.2, or in the form of a narrative report. If a narrative report is used, it must be entitled "Primary Treating Physician's Progress Report" in bold–faced type, must indicate clearly the reason the report is being submitted, and must contain the same information using the same subject headings in the same order as Form PR–2. A response to a request for information made pursuant to subdivision (f)(7) may be made in letter format. A narrative report and a letter format response to a request for information must contain the same declaration under penalty of perjury that is set forth in the Form PR–2: "I declare under penalty of perjury that this report is true and correct to the best of my knowledge and that I have not violated Labor Code §139.3."

By mutual agreement between the physician and the claims administrator, the physician may make reports in any manner and form.

(g) When the primary treating physician determines that the employee's condition is permanent and stationary, the physician shall, unless good cause is shown, report within 20 days from the date of examination any findings concerning the existence and extent of permanent impairment and limitations and any need for continuing and/or future medical care resulting from the injury. The information may be submitted on the "Primary Treating Physician's Permanent and Stationary Report" form (DWC Form PR–3 or DWC Form PR–4) contained in section 9785.3 or section 9785.4, or in such other manner which provides all the information required by Title 8, California Code of Regulations, section 10606. For permanent disability evaluation performed pursuant to the permanent disability evaluation schedule adopted on or after January 1, 2005, the primary treating physician's reports concerning the existence and extent of permanent impairment shall describe the impairment in accordance with the AMA Guides to the Evaluation on Permanent Impairment, 5th Edition (DWC Form PR–4). Qualified Medical Evaluators and Agreed Medical Evaluators may not use DWC Form PR–3 or DWC Form PR–4 to report medical–legal evaluations.

(h) Any controversies concerning this section shall be resolved pursuant to Labor Code Section 4603 or 4604, whichever is appropriate.

(i) Claims administrators shall reimburse primary treating physicians for their reports submitted pursuant to this section as required by the Official Medical Fee Schedule.

NOTE: Authority cited: Sections 133, 4603.5 and 5307.3, Labor Code. Reference: Sections 4061, 4061.5, 4062, 4600, 4600.3, 4603.2, 4636, 4660, 4662, 4663 and 4664, Labor Code.

HISTORY

1. Amendment filed 11–9–77; effective thirtieth day thereafter (Register 77, No. 46).
2. Amendment of subsection (b) filed 11–11–78; effective thirtieth day thereafter (Register 78, No. 45).
3. Amendment of subsections (c) and (d) and new subsection (e) filed 7–11–89; operative 10–1–89 (Register 89, No. 28).
4. Amendment of section and Note filed 8–31–93; operative 8–31–93. Submitted to OAL for printing only pursuant to Government Code section 11351 (Register 93, No. 36).
5. New subsection (e) and subsection relettering filed 3–27–95; operative 3–27–95. Submitted to OAL for printing only pursuant to Government Code section 11351 (Register 95, No. 13).
6. Repealer and new section filed 11–9–98; operative 1–1–99 (Register 98, No. 46).
7. Amendment of subsections (e)(1), (f)(8) and (g) filed 12–22–2000; operative 1–1–2001 pursuant to Government Code section 11343.4(d) (Register 2000, No. 51).
8. Amendment of section and Note filed 5–20–2003; operative 6–19–2003 (Register 2003, No. 21).
9. Amendment of subsections (a)(1), (a)(8), (b)(3)–(4) and (g) and amendment of Note filed 12–31–2004 as an emergency; operative 1–1–2005 (Register 2004, No. 53). A Certificate of Compliance must be transmitted to OAL by 5–2–2005 or emergency language will be repealed by operation of law on the following day.
10. Certificate of Compliance as to 12–31–2004 order, including further amendment of subsections (a)(1) and (g), transmitted to OAL 4–29–2005 and filed 6–10–2005 (Register 2005, No. 23).

§ 9785.2. Form PR–2 "Primary Treating Physician's Progress Report"

9785.2 Form PR–2 "Primary Treating Physician's Progress Report" [Form PR–2 attached]

NOTE: Authority cited: Sections 133, 4603.5 and 5307.3, Labor Code. Reference: Sections 4061.5, 4600, 4603.2, 4610, 4636, 4660, 4662, 4663 and 4664, Labor Code.

HISTORY

1. New section filed 11–9–98; operative 1–1–99 (Register 98, No. 46).
2. Repealer and new form filed 12–22–2000; operative 1–1–2001 pursuant to Government Code section 11343.4(d) (Register 2000, No. 51).
3. Amendment of form filed 5–20–2003; operative 6–19–2003 (Register 2003, No. 21).
4. Amendment of section and Note filed 12–31–2004 as an emergency; operative 1–1–2005 (Register 2004, No. 53). A Certificate of Compliance must be transmitted to OAL by 5–2–2005 or emergency language will be repealed by operation of law on the following day.

§ 9785.3. Form PR–3 "Primary Treating Physician's Permanent and Stationary Report"

9785.3 Form PR–3 "Primary Treating Physician's Permanent and Stationary Report" [Form PR–3 attached]

NOTE: Authority cited: Sections 133, 4603.5 and 5307.3, Labor Code. Reference: Sections 4061.5, 4600, 4603.2, 4636, 4660, 4662, 4663 and 4664, Labor Code.

HISTORY

1. New section filed 11–9–98; operative 1–1–99 (Register 98, No. 46).
2. Change without regulatory effect amending DWC Form PR–3, page 3, last sentence in the "Precipitating activity" narrative under the "Subjective Findings" section filed 12–30–98 pursuant to section 100, title 1, California Code of Regulations (Register 99, No. 1).
3. Repealer and new form filed 12–22–2000; operative 1–1–2001 pursuant to Government Code section 11343.4(d) (Register 2000, No. 51).
4. Amendment of form filed 5–20–2003; operative 6–19–2003 (Register 2003, No. 21).
5. Amendment of section and Note filed 12–31–2004 as an emergency; operative 1–1–2005 (Register 2004, No. 53). A Certificate of Compliance must be transmitted to OAL by 5–2–2005 or emergency language will be repealed by operation of law on the following day.

§ 9785.4. Form PR–4 "Primary Treating Physician's Permanent and Stationary Report"

9785.4 Form PR–4 "Primary Treating Physician's Permanent and Stationary Report" [Form PR–4 attached]

NOTE: Authority cited: Sections 133 and 5307.3, Labor Code. Reference: Sections 4600, 4061.5, 4603.2, 4636, 4660, 4662, 4663 and 4664, Labor Code.

HISTORY
1. New section filed 12–31–2004 as an emergency; operative 1–1–2005 (Register 2004, No. 53). A Certificate of Compliance must be transmitted to OAL by 5–2–2005 or emergency language will be repealed by operation of law on the following day.

§ 9785.5. Primary Treating Physician (Repealed)

HISTORY
1. New section filed 12–31–93; operative 1–1–94. Submitted to OAL for printing only pursuant to Government Code section 11351 (Register 93, No. 53).
2. Amendment of subsection (d) filed 3–27–95; operative 3–27–95. Submitted to OAL for printing only pursuant to Government Code section 11351 (Register 95, No. 13).
3. Repealer filed 11–9–98; operative 1–1–99 (Register 98, No. 46).

§ 9786. Petition for Change of Primary Treating Physician

(a) A claims administrator desiring a change of primary treating physician pursuant to Labor Code Section 4603 shall file with the Administrative Director a petition, verified under penalty of perjury, on the "Petition for Change of Primary Treating Physician" form (DWC–Form 280 (Part A)) contained in Section 9786.1.

   The petition shall be accompanied by supportive documentary evidence relevant to the specific allegations raised. A proof of service by mail declaration shall be attached to the petition indicating that (1) the completed petition (Part A), (2) the supportive documentary evidence and (3) a blank copy of the "Response to Petition for Change of Primary Treating Physician", (DWC–Form 280 (Part B)), were served on the employee or, the employee's attorney, and the employee's current primary treating physician.

(b) Good cause to grant the petition shall be clearly shown by verified statement of facts, and, where appropriate, supportive documentary evidence. Good cause includes, but is not limited to any of the following:
   (1) The primary treating physician has failed to comply with Section 9785, subdivisions (e), (f)(1–7), or (g) by not timely submitting a required report or submitting a report which is inadequate due to material omissions or deficiencies;
   (2) The primary treating physician has failed to comply with subdivision (f)(8) of Section 9785 by failing to submit timely or complete progress reports on two or more occasions within the 12–month period immediately preceding the filing of the petition;
   (3) A clear showing that the current treatment is not consistent with the treatment plan submitted pursuant to Section 9785, subdivisions (e) or (f);
   (4) A clear showing that the primary treating physician or facility is not within a reasonable geographic area as determined by Section 9780(e).
   (5) A clear showing that the primary treating physician has a possible conflict of interest, including but not limited to a familial, financial or employment relationship with the employee, which has a significant potential for interfering with the physician's ability to engage in objective and impartial medical decision making.

(c) (1) Where good cause is based on inadequate reporting under subdivisions (b)(1) or (b)(2), the petition must show, by documentation and verified statement, that the claims administrator notified the primary treating physician or facility in writing of the complete requirements of Section 9785 prior to the physician's failure to properly report.
   (2) Good cause shall not include a showing that current treatment is inappropriate or that there is no present need for medical treatment to cure or relieve from the effects of the injury or illness. The claims administrator's contention that current treatment is inappropriate, or that the employee is no longer in need of medical treatment to cure or relieve from the effects of the injury or illness should be directed to the Workers' Compensation Appeals Board, not the Administrative Director, in support of a Petition for Change of Primary Treating Physician.
   (3) Where an allegation of good cause is based upon failure to timely issue the "Doctor's First Report of Occupational Injury or Illness," Form DLSR 5021, within 5 working days of the initial examination pursuant to Section 9785(e)(1) or (e)(2), the petition setting forth such allegation shall be filed within 90 days of the initial examination.
   (4) The failure to verify a letter response to a request for information made pursuant to Section 9785(f)(7), failure to verify a narrative report submitted pursuant to Section 9785(f)(8), or failure of the narrative report to conform to the format requirements of Section 9785(f)(8) shall not constitute good cause to grant the petition unless the claims

administrator submits documentation showing that the physician was notified of the deficiency in the verification or reporting format and allowed a reasonable time to correct the deficiency.

(d) The employee, his or her attorney, and/or the primary treating physician may file with the Administrative Director a response to said petition, provided the response is verified under penalty of perjury and is filed and served on the claims administrator and all other parties no later than 20 days after service of the petition. The response may be accompanied by supportive documentary evidence relevant to the specific allegations raised in the petition. The response may be filed using the "Response to Petition for Change of Primary Treating Physician" form (DWC–Form 280 (Part B)) contained in Section 9786.1. Where the petition was served by mail, the time for filing a response shall be extended pursuant to the provisions of Code of Civil Procedure Section 1013. Unless good cause is shown, no other document will be considered by the Administrative Director except for the petition, the response, and supportive documentary evidence.

(e) The Administrative Director shall, within 45 days of the receipt of the petition, either:

(1) Dismiss the petition, without prejudice, for failure to meet the procedural requirements of this Section;

(2) Deny the petition pursuant to a finding that there is no good cause to require the employee to select a primary treating physician from the panel of physicians provided in the petition;

(3) Grant the petition and issue an order requiring the employee to select a physician from the panel of physicians provided in the petition, pursuant to a finding that good cause exists therefore;

(4) Refer the matter to the Workers' Compensation Appeals Board for hearing and determination by a Workers' Compensation Administrative Law Judge of such factual determinations as may be requested by the Administrative Director; or

(5) Issue a Notice of Intention to Grant the petition and an order requiring the submission of additional documents or information.

(f) The claims administrator's liability to pay for medical treatment by the primary treating physician shall continue until an order of the Administrative Director issues granting the petition.

(g) The Administrative Director may extend the time specified in Subsection (e) within which to act upon the claims administrator's petition for a period of 30 days and may order a party to submit additional documents or information.

NOTE: Authority cited: Sections 133, 139.5, 4603, 4603.2, 4603.5 and 5307.3, Labor Code. Reference: Sections 4600, 4603 and 4603.2, Labor Code.

HISTORY

1. Repealer and new section filed 11–9–77; effective thirtieth day thereafter (Register 77, No. 46).
2. Amendment of subsections (a), (c), (d)(4), (e), and (f) filed 11–11–78; effective thirtieth day thereafter (Register 78, No. 45).
3. Amendment of subsection (a) filed 8–9–84; effective thirtieth day thereafter (Register 84, No. 35).
4. Change without regulatory effect of subsection (c) filed 7–11–86; effective upon filing (Register 86, No. 28).
5. Amendment of section and Note filed 8–31–93; operative 8–31–93. Submitted to OAL for printing only pursuant to Government Code section 11351 (Register 93, No. 36).
6. Amendment of subsections (b)(5), (d), and (g) filed 3–27–95; operative 3–27–95. Submitted to OAL for printing only pursuant to Government Code section 11351 (Register 95, No. 13).
7. Editorial correction of subsection (h) (Register 95, No. 29).
8. Editorial correction of inadvertently omitted subsection (d)(2) (Register 96, No. 52).
9. Amendment of subsection (f) and repealer and new subsection (g) filed 12–27–96; operative 12–27–96. Submitted to OAL for printing only pursuant to Government Code section 11351 (Register 96, No. 52).
10. Amendment of section heading and section filed 12–22–2000; operative 1–1–2001 pursuant to Government Code section 11343.4(d) (Register 2000, No. 51).
11. Amendment filed 5–20–2003; operative 6–19–2003 (Register 2003, No. 21).

§ 9786.1. Petition for Change of Primary Treating Physician; Response to Petition for Change of Primary Treating Physician DWC Form 280 (Parts A and B)

NOTE: Authority cited: Sections 133, 139.5, 4603, 4603.2, 4603.5, and 5307.3, Labor Code. Reference: Sections 4600, 4603 and 4603.2, Labor Code.

HISTORY

1. New section (DWC form 280) filed 12–22–2000; operative 1–1–2001 pursuant to Government Code section 11343.4(d) (Register 2000, No. 51).

§ 9787. Appeal from Administrative Director's Order Granting or Denying Petition for Change of Primary Treating Physician

Any order denying or granting the claims administrator's petition whether issued with or without hearing, shall be final and binding upon the parties unless within 20 days from service thereof the aggrieved party petitions the Workers' Compensation Appeals Board for relief in the manner prescribed by Section 10950 of the Board's Rules of Practice and Procedure.

NOTE: Authority cited: Sections 133, 139.5, 4603.2, 4603.5 and 5307.3, Labor Code. Reference: Sections 4600, 4603 and 4603.2, Labor Code.

HISTORY
1. Repealer and new section filed 11–9–77; effective thirtieth day thereafter (Register 77, No. 46).
2. Amendment of section heading and section filed 12–22–2000; operative 1–1–2001 pursuant to Government Code section 11343.4(d) (Register 2000, No. 51).
3. Amendment of section and new Note filed 5–20–2003; operative 6–19–2003 (Register 2003, No. 21).

Intentionally blank

Forms

Intentionally blank

For DWC only: MPN Approval Number	Date Application Received: / /

Cover Page for Medical Provider Network Application

1. Name of MPN Applicant _____

2. Address

3. Tax Identification Number

_____   _____-_____

_____

4. Type of MPN Applicant

☐ Self-Insured Employer   ☐ Group of Self-Insured Employers

☐ Self-Insured Security Fund   ☐ Joint Powers Authority   ☐ State   ☐ Insurer

5. Name of Medical Provider Network(s), if applicable:

6. If the medical provider network is one of the following deemed entities, check the appropriate box:

☐ Health Care Organization (HCO)
☐ Health Care Service Plan
☐ Group Disability Insurer
☐ Taft-Hartley Health and Welfare Trust Fund

7. Name of entity, administrator or other third-party who prepared MPN Application on behalf of MPN applicant (if applicable): _____

8. Signature of authorized individual: "I, the undersigned officer or employee of the MPN Applicant, have read and signed this application and know the contents thereof, and verify that, to the best of my knowledge and ability, the information included in this application is true and correct."

_____

Name of Authorized Individual   Title   Phone/Email

_____

Signature of Authorized Individual   Date Signed

9. Authorized Liaison to DWC:

_____

Name   Title   Organization   Phone/Email

_____

Address   Fax number

Submit an original Cover Page for Medical Provider Network Application with original signature, an original Application with the information required by Title 8, California Code of Regulations, section 9767.3 and a copy of the Cover Page and Application to the Division of Workers' Compensation. Mailing address: DWC, MPN Application, P.O. Box 71010, Oakland, CA 94612.

[DWC Mandatory Form – section 9767.4 – May 2007]

Intentionally blank

For DWC only: MPN Approval Number	Date Application Received: / /

Notice of Medical Provider Network Plan Modification §9767.8

1. Name of MPN Applicant _____

2. Address   3. Tax Identification Number

_____   _____-_____

_____

4. Type of MPN Applicant

      ☐ Self-Insured Employer   ☐ Group of Self-Insured Employers

      ☐ Self-Insured Security Fund   ☐ Joint Powers Authority   ☐ State   ☐ Insurer

5. Name of Medical Provider Network(s), if applicable:

6. Date of initial application approval and MPN approval number: _____

7. Dates of prior plan modifications approvals: _____

8 If the medical provider network is one of the following deemed entities, check the appropriate box:

      ☐ Health Care Organization (HCO)
      ☐ Health Care Service Plan
      ☐ Group Disability Insurer
      ☐ Taft-Hartley Health and Welfare Trust Fund

9. Name of entity, administrator or other third-party who prepared MPN Application on behalf of MPN applicant (if applicable): _____

10 Signature of authorized individual: "I, the undersigned officer or employee of the MPN Applicant, have read and signed this application and know the contents thereof, and verify that, to the best of my knowledge and ability, the information included in this application is true and correct."

_____

Name of Authorized Individual	Title	Phone/Email

_____

Signature of Authorized Individual	Date Signed

11. Authorized Liaison to DWC:

_____

Name	Title	Organization	Phone/Email

_____

Address	Fax number

Please give a short summary of the proposed modifications in the space provided below and place a check mark against the box that reflects the proposed modification. Please explain whether the modification will adversely affect the ability of the MPN to meet the regulatory and statutory MPN requirements.

☐ Change in Service Area: Provide documentation in compliance with section 9767.5.

☐ Change of MPN name: Provide new MPN name.

☐ Change of Division Liaison: Provide the name and contact information.

☐ Change of 10% or more in the number or specialty of Network Providers since the approval date of the previous MPN Plan application or modification: Provide the name, license number, and location of each physician by specialty type or name provider, if other than physician.

☐ Change of 25% or more in the number of covered employees since the approval date of the previous MPN Plan application or modification.

☐ Change in continuity of care policy: Provide a copy of the revised written continuity of care policy.

☐ Change in transfer of care policy: Provide a copy f the revised written transfer of care policy.

☐ Change in Economic Profiling: Provide a copy of the revised policy or procedure.

☐ Change in how the MPN complies with the access standards: Explain what change has been made and describe how the MPN still complies with the access standards.

☐ Change of employee notification materials: Provide a copy of the revised notification materials.

☐ Other (please describe): Attach documentation.

Submit an original Notice of MPN Plan Modification with original signature, any necessary documentation, and a copy of the Notice and documents to the Division of Workers' Compensation. Mailing address: DWC, MPN Application, P.O. Box 71010, Oakland, CA 94612.

PREDESIGNATION OF PERSONAL PHYSICIAN

In the event you sustain an injury or illness related to your employment, you may be treated for such injury or illness by your personal medical doctor (M.D.), doctor of osteopathic medicine (D.O.) or medical group if:

- your employer offers group health coverage;
- the doctor is your regular physician, who shall be either a physician who has limited his or her practice of medicine to general practice or who is a board-certified or board-eligible internist, pediatrician, obstetrician-gynecologist, or family practitioner, and has previously directed your medical treatment, and retains your medical records;
- your "personal physician" may be a medical group if it is a single corporation or partnership composed of licensed doctors of medicine or osteopathy, which operates an integrated multispecialty medical group providing comprehensive medical services predominantly for nonoccupational illnesses and injuries;
- prior to the injury your doctor agrees to treat you for work injuries or illnesses;
- prior to the injury you provided your employer the following in writing: (1) notice that you want your personal doctor to treat you for a work-related injury or illness, and (2) your personal doctor's name and business address.

You may use this form to notify your employer if you wish to have your personal medical doctor or a doctor of osteopathic medicine treat you for a work- related injury or illness and the above requirements are met.

NOTICE OF PREDESIGNATION OF PERSONAL PHYSICIAN

Employee: Complete this section.

To: _____ (name of employer)   If I have a work-related injury or illness, I choose to be treated by:

_____
(name of doctor)(M.D., D.O., or medical group)

_____(street address, city, state, ZIP)

_____(telephone number)

Employee Name (please print): _____

Employee's Address:
_____

Employee's
Signature_____Date:_____

Physician: I agree to this Predesignation:

Signature:_____Date:_____
(Physician or Designated Employee of the Physician or Medical Group)

The physician is not required to sign this form, however, if the physician or designated employee of the physician or medical group does not sign, other documentation of the physician's agreement to be predesignated will be required pursuant to Title 8, California Code of Regulations, section 9780.1(a)(3).

Title 8, California Code of Regulations, section 9783.
(Optional DWC Form 9783 March 1, 2007)

Intentionally blank

DESIGNACIÓN PREVIA DE MÉDICO PARTICULAR

En caso de que usted sufra una lesión o enfermedad relacionada con su empleo, usted puede recibir tratamiento médico por esa lesión o enfermedad de su médico particular (M.D.), médico osteópata (D.O.) o grupo médico si:

- su empleador le ofrece un plan de salud grupal
- el médico es su médico familiar o de cabecera, que será un médico que ha limitado su práctica médica a medicina general o que es un internista certificado o elegible para certificación, pediátra, gineco-obstreta, o médico de medicina familiar y que previamente ha estado a cargo de su tratamiento médico y tiene su expediente médico
- su "médico particular" puede ser un grupo médico si es una corporación o sociedad o asociación compuesta de doctores certificados en medicina u osteopatía, que opera un integrado grupo médico multidisciplinario que predominantemente proporciona amplios servicios médicos para lesiones y enfermedades no relacionadas con el trabajo.
- antes de la lesión su médico está de acuerdo a proporcionarle tratamiento médico para su lesión o enfermedad de trabajo
- antes de la lesión usted le proporcionó a su empleador por escrito lo siguiente: (1) notificación de que quiere que su médico particular le brinde tratamiento para una lesión o enfermedad de trabajo y (2) el nombre y dirección comercial de su médico particular.

Puede usar este formulario para notificarle a su empleador que desea que su médico particular o médico osteópata le proporcione tratamiento médico para una lesión o enfermedad de trabajo y que los requisitos mencionados arriba han sido cumplidos.

NOTICIA DE DESIGNACIÓN PREVIA DE MÉDICO PARTICULAR

Empleado: Rellene esta sección.

A: _____ (nombre del empleador) Si sufro una lesión o enfermedad de trabajo, yo elijo recibir tratamiento médico de:

_____
(nombre del médico)(M.D., D.O., o grupo médico)

_____ (dirección, ciudad, estado, código postal)

_____ (número de teléfono)

Nombre del Empleado (en letras de molde, por favor):

_____

Domicilio del Empleado:

_____

Firma del
Empleado _____ Fecha: _____

Médico: Estoy de acuerdo con esta Designación Previa:

Firma: _____ Fecha: _____
(Médico o Empleado designado por el Médico o Grupo Médico)

El médico no está obligado a firmar este formulario, sin embargo, si el médico o empleado designado por el médico o grupo médico no firma, será necesario presentar documentación sobre el consentimiento del médico de ser designado previamente de acuerdo al Código de Reglamentos de California, Título 8, sección 9780.1(a)(3).

Código de Reglamentos de California, Título 8, sección 9783.
(Formulario Opcional 9783 de la DWC 1 de marzo 2007)

Intentionally blank

NOTICE OF PERSONAL CHIROPRACTOR OR PERSONAL ACUPUNCTURIST

If your employer or your employer's insurer does not have a Medical Provider Network, you may be able to change your treating physician to your personal chiropractor or acupuncturist following a work-related injury or illness. In order to be eligible to make this change, you must give your employer the name and business address of a personal chiropractor or acupuncturist in writing prior to the injury or illness. Your claims administrator generally has the right to select your treating physician within the first 30 days after your employer knows of your injury or illness. After your claims administrator has initiated your treatment with another doctor during this period, you may then, upon request, have your treatment transferred to your personal chiropractor or acupuncturist.

You may use this form to notify your employer of your personal chiropractor or acupuncturist.

Your Chiropractor or Acupuncturist's Information:

_____

(name of chiropractor or acupuncturist)

_____

(street address, city, state, zip code)

_____

(telephone number)

Employee Name **(please print)**:

_____

Employee's address:

_____

Employee's
Signature_____Date:_____

DWC FORM 9783.1 (March 14, 2006)

Intentionally blank

NOTICIA DE QUIROPRÁCTICO PERSONAL O ACUPUNTOR
PERSONAL

Si su empleador o la compañía de seguros de su empleador no tiene una Red de Proveedores Médicos establecida, puede cambiar su médico que le esté proporcionando tratamiento médico a su quiropráctico o acupuntor personal después de una lesión o enfermedad de trabajo. Para ser elegible a hacer este cambio, usted debe antes de la lesión o enfermedad darle por escrito a su empleador el nombre y la dirección comercial de un quiropráctico o acupuntor personal. Generalmente, su administrador de reclamos tiene el derecho de elegir al médico que le proporcionará el tratamiento dentro de los primeros 30 días después de que su empleador sabe de su lesión o enfermedad. Después de que su administrador de reclamos haya iniciado su tratamiento con otro médico durante este tiempo, usted puede, bajo petición, transferir su tratamiento a su quiropráctico o acupuntor personal.

Puede usar este formulario para notificarle a su empleador sobre su quiropráctico o acupuntor personal.

Información sobre su Quiropráctico o Acupuntor:

_____

(nombre del quiropráctico o acupuntor)

_____

(dirección, ciudad, estado, código postal)

_____

(número de teléfono)

Nombre del Empleado (en letras de molde, por favor):

_____

Domicilio del Empleado:

_____

Firma del
Empleado_____Fecha:_____

Código de Reglamentos de California, Título 8, sección 9783.1.
(Formulario DWC 9783.1-Fecha de vigencia: marzo 2006)

Intentionally blank

PRIMARY TREATING PHYSICIAN'S PROGRESS REPORT (PR-2)

Check the boxes which indicate why you are submitting a report at this time. If the patient is "Permanent and Stationary" (i.e., has reached maximum medical improvement), do not use this form. You may use DWC Forms PR-3 or PR-4.

☐ Periodic Report   (required 45 days after last report) ☐ Change in treatment plan ☐ Released from care

☐ Change in work status   ☐ Need for referral or consultation ☐ Response to request for information

☐ Change in patient's condition ☐ Need for surgery or hospitalization ☐ Request for authorization

☐ Other:

Patient:
Last _____ First _____ M.I. _____ Sex _____
Address_____ City_____ State _____ Zip_____
Date of Injury_____ Date of Birth_____
Occupation_____ SS # _____ - _____ - _____ Phone (___)_____
Claims Administrator:
Name_____ Claim
Number_____
Address_____ City_____ State_____ Zip_____
Phone (___)_____ FAX (_____)_____

_____
Employer name: Employer Phone (____)
The information below must be provided. You may use this form or you may substitute or append a narrative report.
Subjective complaints:

Objective findings: (Include significant physical examination, laboratory, imaging, or other diagnostic findings.)

Diagnoses:
1. _____ ICD-9 _____
2. _____ ICD-9 _____
3. _____ICD-9 _____

Treatment Plan: (Include treatment rendered to date. List methods, frequency and duration of planned treatment(s). Specify consultation/referral, surgery, and hospitalization. Identify each physician and non-physician provider. Specify type, frequency and duration of physical medicine services (e.g., physical therapy, manipulation, acupuncture).   Use of CPT codes is encouraged. Have there been any **changes** in treatment plan? If so, why?

PRIMARY TREATING PHYSICIAN'S PROGRESS REPORT (PR-2)

<u>Work Status:</u> This patient has been instructed to:

☐ Remain off-work until_____.

☐ Return to *modified* work on_____ with the following limitations or restrictions
    (List all specific restrictions re: standing, sitting, bending, use of hands, etc.):
☐ Return to full duty on _____with no limitations or restrictions.

<u>Primary Treating Physician:</u> (original signature, do not stamp)   Date of exam: _____

I declare under penalty of perjury that this report is true and correct to the best of my knowledge and that I have not violated Labor Code § 139.3.

Signature: _____ Cal. Lic. # _____
Executed at: _____ Date: _____
Name:_____ Specialty: _____
Address:_____ Phone:_____

Division of Workers' Compensation
PRIMARY TREATING PHYSICIAN'S PERMANENT AND STATIONARY REPORT (PR-3)

> This form is required to be used for ratings prepared pursuant to the 1997 Permanent Disability Rating Schedule. It is designed to be used by the primary treating physician to report the initial evaluation of permanent disability to the claims administrator. It should be completed if the patient has residual effects from the injury or may require future medical care. In such cases, it should be completed once the patient's condition becomes permanent and stationary.
>
> **This form should not be used by a Qualified Medical Evaluator (QME) or Agreed Medical Evaluator (AME) to report a medical-legal evaluation.**

Patient:

Last Name _____ Middle Initial _____ First Name _____ Sex___ Date of Birth _____

Address _____ City _____ State _____ Zip _____

Occupation _____ Social Security No. _____ Phone No._____

Claims Administrator/Insurer:

Name _____ Claim No. _____ Phone No._____

Address _____ City _____ State _____ Zip _____

Employer:

Name _____ Phone No. _____

Address _____ City _____ State _____ Zip _____

> You must address each of the issues below. You may substitute or append a narrative report if you require additional space to adequately report on these issues.

Date of Injury_____ Last date _____ Date of current _____ Permanent & _____

            Date   worked   Date   examination   Date   Stationary date   Date

Description of how injury/illness occurred (e.g. Hand caught in punch press; fell from height onto back; exposed 25 years ago to asbestos):

Patient's Complaints:

Division of Workers' Compensation
PRIMARY TREATING PHYSICIAN'S PERMANENT AND STATIONARY REPORT (PR-3)

<u>**Relevant Medical History:**</u>

<u>**Objective Findings:**</u>

Physical Examination: (Describe all relevant findings; include any specific measurements indicating atrophy, range of motion, strength, etc.; include bilateral measurements - injured/uninjured - for upper and lower extremity injuries.)

Diagnostic tests results (X-ray/Imaging/Laboratory/etc.)

Diagnoses (List each diagnosis; ICD-9 code must be included)   ICD-9

1. _____   _____
2. _____   _____
3. _____   _____
4. _____   _____

	Yes	No	Cannot Determine
Can this patient now return to his/her usual occupation?	☐	☐	☐
If not, can the patient perform another line of work?	☐	☐	☐

DWC Form PR-3
(Rev. 06-05)

2

Division of Workers' Compensation
PRIMARY TREATING PHYSICIAN'S PERMANENT AND STATIONARY REPORT (PR-3)

Subjective Findings: Provide your professional assessment of the subjective factors of disability, based on your evaluation of the patient's complaints, your examination, and other findings. List specific symptoms (e.g. pain right wrist) and their frequency, severity, and/or precipitating activity using the following definitions:

Severity: Minimal pain - an annoyance, causes no handicap in performance.
        Slight pain - tolerable, causes some handicap in performance of the activity precipitating pain.
        Moderate pain - tolerable, causes marked handicap in the performance of the activity precipitating pain.
        Severe pain - precludes performance of the activity precipitating pain.

Frequency: Occasional - occurs roughly one fourth of the time.
        Intermittent - occurs roughly one half of the time.
        Frequent - occurs roughly three fourths of the time.
        Constant - occurs roughly 90 to 100% of time.

Precipitating activity: Description of precipitating activity gives a sense of how often a pain is felt and thus may be used with or without a frequency modifier. If pain is constant during precipitating activity, then no frequency modifier should be used. For example, a finding of "moderate pain on heavy lifting" connotes that moderate pain is felt whenever heavy lifting occurs. In contrast, "intermittent moderate pain on heavy lifting" implies that moderate pain is only felt half the time when engaged in heavy lifting.

	Yes	No	Cannot determine
Pre-Injury Capacity Are there any activities at home or at work that the patient cannot do as well now as could be done prior to this injury or illness?	☐	☐	☐

If yes, please describe pre-injury capacity and current capacity (e.g. used to regularly lift a 30 lb. child, now can only lift 10 lbs.; could sit for 2 hours, now can only sit for 15 mins.)

1.

2.

3.

4.

Division of Workers' Compensation
PRIMARY TREATING PHYSICIAN'S PERMANENT AND STATIONARY REPORT (PR-3)

<u>Preclusions/Work Restrictions</u>

	Yes	No	Cannot determine
Are there any activities the patient cannot do?	☐	☐	☐

If yes, please describe all preclusions or restrictions related to work activities (e.g. no lifting more than 10 lbs. above shoulders; must use splint; keyboard only 45 mins. per hour; must have sit/stand workstation; no repeated bending). Include restrictions which may not be relevant to current job but may affect future efforts to find work on the open labor market (e.g. include lifting restriction even if current job requires no lifting; include limits on repetitive hand movements even if current job requires none).

1.

2.

3.

4.

5.

6.

<u>Medical Treatment</u>: Describe any continuing medical treatment related to this injury that you believe must be provided to the patient. ("Continuing medical treatment" is defined as occurring or presently planned treatment.) Also, describe any medical treatment the patient may require in the future. ("Future medical treatment" is defined as treatment which is anticipated at some time in the future to cure or relieve the employee from the effects of the injury.) Include medications, surgery, physical medicine services, durable equipment, etc.

<u>Comments:</u>

Division of Workers' Compensation
PRIMARY TREATING PHYSICIAN'S PERMANENT AND STATIONARY REPORT (PR-3)

Apportionment:

Effective April 19, 2004, apportionment of permanent disability shall be based on causation. Furthermore, any physician who prepares a report addressing permanent disability due to a claimed industrial injury is required to address the issue of causation of the permanent disability, and in order for a permanent disability report to be complete, the report must include an apportionment determination. This determination shall be made pursuant to Labor Code Sections 4663 and 4664 set forth below:

Labor Code Section 4663. Apportionment of permanent disability; Causation as basis; Physician's report; Apportionment determination; Disclosure by employee

(a) Apportionment of permanent disability shall be based on causation.

(b) Any physician who prepares a report addressing the issue of permanent disability due to a claimed industrial injury shall in that report address the issue of causation of the permanent disability.

(c) In order for a physician's report to be considered complete on the issue of permanent disability, it must include an apportionment determination. A physician shall make an apportionment determination by finding what approximate percentage of the permanent disability was caused by the direct result of injury arising out of and occurring in the course of employment and what approximate percentage of the permanent disability was caused by other factors both before and subsequent to the industrial injury, including prior industrial injuries. If the physician is unable to include an apportionment determination in his or her report, the physician shall state the specific reasons why the physician could not make a determination of the effect of that prior condition on the permanent disability arising from the injury. The physician shall then consult with other physicians or refer the employee to another physician from whom the employee is authorized to seek treatment or evaluation in accordance with this division in order to make the final determination.

(d) An employee who claims an industrial injury shall, upon request, disclose all previous permanent disabilities or physical impairments.

Labor Code section 4664. Liability of employer for percentage of permanent disability directly caused by injury; Conclusive presumption from prior award of permanent disability; Accumulation of permanent disability awards

(a) The employer shall only be liable for the percentage of permanent disability directly caused by the injury arising out of and occurring in the course of employment.

(b) If the applicant has received a prior award of permanent disability, it shall be conclusively presumed that the prior permanent disability exists at the time of any subsequent industrial injury. This presumption is a presumption affecting the burden of proof.

(c)(1) The accumulation of all permanent disability awards issued with respect to any one region of the body in favor of one individual employee shall not exceed 100 percent over the employee's lifetime unless the employee's injury or illness is conclusively presumed to be total in character pursuant to Section 4662. As used in this section, the regions of the body are the following:

(A) Hearing.

(B) Vision.

(C) Mental and behavioral disorders.

(D) The spine.

(E) The upper extremities, including the shoulders.

(F) The lower extremities, including the hip joints.

(G) The head, face, cardiovascular system, respiratory system, and all other systems or regions of the body not listed in subparagraphs (A) to (F), inclusive.

(2) Nothing in this section shall be construed to permit the permanent disability rating for each individual injury sustained by an employee arising from the same industrial accident, when added together, from exceeding 100 percent.

	Yes	No
Is the permanent disability directly caused, by an injury or illness arising out of and in the course of employment?	☐	☐
Is the permanent disability caused, in whole or in part, by other factors besides this industrial injury or illness, including any prior industrial injury or illness?	☐	☐

If the answer to the second question is "yes," provide below: (1) the approximate percentage of the permanent disability that is due to factors other than the injury or illness arising out of and in the course of employment; and (2) a complete narrative description of the basis for your apportionment finding. If you are unable to include an apportionment determination in your report, state the specific reasons why you could not make this determination. You may attach your findings and explanation on a separate sheet.

Division of Workers' Compensation

PRIMARY TREATING PHYSICIAN'S PERMANENT AND STATIONARY REPORT (PR-3)

List information you reviewed in preparing this report, or relied upon for the formulation of your medical opinions:

Medical Records:

Written Job Description:

Other:

Division of Workers' Compensation
PRIMARY TREATING PHYSICIAN'S PERMANENT AND STATIONARY REPORT (PR-3)

Primary Treating Physician (original signature, do not stamp)

I declare under penalty of perjury that this report is true and correct to the best of my knowledge, and that I have not violated Labor Code §139.3.

Signature: _____ Cal. Lic. # : _____

Executed at: _____ Date: _____
(County and State)

Name (Printed): _____ Specialty: _____

Address: _____ City: _____ State: _____ Zip: _____

Telephone: _____

Division of Workers' Compensation
PRIMARY TREATING PHYSICIAN'S PERMANENT AND STATIONARY REPORT (PR-4)

This form is required to be used for ratings prepared pursuant to the 2005 Permanent Disability Rating Schedule and the AMA Guides to the Evaluation of Permanent Impairment (5th Ed.). It is designed to be used by the primary treating physician to report the initial evaluation of permanent impairment to the claims administrator. It should be completed if the patient has residual effects from the injury or may require future medical care. In such cases, it should be completed once the patient's condition becomes permanent and stationary.

This form should not be used by a Qualified Medical Evaluator (QME) or Agreed Medical Evaluator (AME) to report a medical-legal evaluation.

Patient:

Last Name_____ Middle Initial ____ First Name _____ Sex ____ Date of Birth _____

Address _____City _____ State _____ Zip _____

Occupation _____ Social Security Number _____ Phone No. _____

Claims Administrator/Insurer:

Name _____ Phone Number _____

Address _____City _____ State _____ Zip _____

Employer:

Name _____ Phone Number _____

Address _____City _____ State _____ Zip _____

Treating Physician:

Name _____ Phone Number _____

Address _____City _____ State _____ Zip _____

You must address each of the issues below. You may substitute or append a narrative report if you require additional space to adequately report on these issues.

Date of Injury_____ Last date _____ Permanent & _____ Date of current _____
  Date   worked _Date_   Stationary _Date_   examination _Date_

Description of how injury/illness occurred (e.g. Hand caught in punch press; fell from height onto back; exposed 25 years ago to asbestos):

Patient's Complaints:

Division of Workers' Compensation
PRIMARY TREATING PHYSICIAN'S PERMANENT AND STATIONARY REPORT (PR-4)

Relevant Medical History:

Objective Findings:

Physical Examination: Describe all relevant findings as required by the AMA Guides, 5th Edition. Include any specific measurements indicating atrophy, range of motion, strength, etc. Include bilateral measurements - injured/uninjured - for injuries of the extremities.

Diagnostic tests results (X-ray/Imaging/Laboratory/etc.)

Diagnoses (List each diagnosis; ICD-9 code must be included)   ICD-9

1. _____   _____

2. _____   _____

3. _____   _____

4. _____   _____

Impairment Rating:
Report the whole person impairment (WPI) rating for each impairment using the AMA Guides, 5th Edition, and explain how the rating was derived. List tables used and page numbers.

Impairment   WPI%   Table #(s).   Page #(s)

Explanation

Impairment   WPI%   Table #(s).   Page #(s)

Explanation

Impairment   WPI%   Table #(s).   Page #(s)

Explanation

Impairment   WPI%   Table #(s).   Page #(s)

Explanation

Pain assessment:

If the burden of the worker's condition has been increased by pain-related impairment in excess of the pain component already incorporated in the WPI rating under Chapters 3-17 of the AMA Guides, 5th Edition, specify the additional whole person impairment rating (0% up to 3% WPI) attributable to such pain. For excess pain involving multiple impairments, attribute the pain in whole number increments to the appropriate impairments. The sum of all pain impairment ratings may not exceed 3% for a single injury.

Apportionment:

Effective April 19, 2004, apportionment of permanent disability shall be based on causation. Furthermore, any physician who prepares a report addressing permanent disability due to a claimed industrial injury is required to address the issue of causation of the permanent disability, and in order for a permanent disability report to be complete, the report must include an apportionment determination. This determination shall be made pursuant to Labor Code Sections 4663 and 4664 set forth below:

Labor Code section 4663. Apportionment of permanent disability; Causation as basis; Physician's report; Apportionment determination; Disclosure by employee

(a) Apportionment of permanent disability shall be based on causation.

(b) Any physician who prepares a report addressing the issue of permanent disability due to a claimed industrial injury shall in that report address the issue of causation of the permanent disability.

(c) In order for a physician's report to be considered complete on the issue of permanent disability, it must include an apportionment determination. A physician shall make an apportionment determination by finding what approximate percentage of the permanent disability was caused by the direct result of injury arising out of and occurring in the course of employment and what approximate percentage of the permanent disability was caused by other factors both before and subsequent to the industrial injury, including prior industrial injuries. If the physician is unable to include an apportionment determination in his or her report, the physician shall state the specific reasons why the physician could not make a determination of the effect of that prior condition on the permanent disability arising from the injury. The physician shall then consult with other physicians or refer the employee to another physician from whom the employee is authorized to seek treatment or evaluation in accordance with this division in order to make the final determination.

(d) An employee who claims an industrial injury shall, upon request, disclose all previous permanent disabilities or physical impairments.

Labor Code section 4664. Liability of employer for percentage of permanent disability directly caused by injury; Conclusive presumption from prior award of permanent disability; Accumulation of permanent disability awards

(a) The employer shall only be liable for the percentage of permanent disability directly caused by the injury arising out of and occurring in the course of employment.

(b) If the applicant has received a prior award of permanent disability, it shall be conclusively presumed that the prior permanent disability exists at the time of any subsequent industrial injury. This presumption is a presumption affecting the burden of proof.

(c)(1) The accumulation of all permanent disability awards issued with respect to any one region of the body in favor of one individual employee shall not exceed 100 percent over the employee's lifetime unless the employee's injury or illness is conclusively presumed to be total in character pursuant to Section 4662. As used in this section, the regions of the body are the following:

A) Hearing.

(B) Vision.

(C) Mental and behavioral disorders.

(D) The spine.

(E) The upper extremities, including the shoulders.

(F) The lower extremities, including the hip joints.

(G) The head, face, cardiovascular system, respiratory system, and all other systems or regions of the body not listed in subparagraphs (A) to (F), inclusive.

(2) Nothing in this section shall be construed to permit the permanent disability rating for each individual injury sustained by an employee arising from the same industrial accident, when added together, from exceeding 100 percent.

	Yes	No
Is the permanent disability directly caused, by an injury or illness arising out of and in the course of employment?	☐	☐
Is the permanent disability caused, in whole or in part, by other factors besides this industrial injury or illness, including any prior industrial injury or illness?	☐	☐

If the answer to the second question is "yes," provide below: (1) the approximate percentage of the permanent disability that is due to factors other than the injury or illness arising out of and in the course of employment; and (2) a complete narrative description of the basis for your apportionment finding. If you are unable to include an apportionment determination in your report, state the specific reasons why you could not make this determination. You may attach your findings and explanation on a separate sheet.

Division of Workers' Compensation
PRIMARY TREATING PHYSICIAN'S PERMANENT AND STATIONARY REPORT (PR-4)

Future Medical Treatment: Describe any continuing medical treatment related to this injury that you believe must be provided to the patient. ("Continuing medical treatment" is defined as occurring or presently planned treatment.) And describe any medical treatment the patient may require in the future. ("Future medical treatment" is defined as treatment which is anticipated at some time in the future to cure or relieve the employee from the effects of the injury.) Include medications, surgery, physical medicine services, durable equipment, etc.

Comments:

Functional Capacity Assessment:

Note: The following assessment of functional capacity is to be prepared by the treating physician, solely for the purpose of determining a claimant's ability to return to his or her usual and customary occupation, and will not to be considered in the permanent impairment rating.

Limited, but retains MAXIMUM capacities to LIFT (including upward pulling) and/or CARRY:

[ ] 10 lbs. [ ] 20 lbs. [ ] 30 lbs. [ ] 40 lbs. [ ] 50 or more lbs.

FREQUENTLY LIFT and/or CARRY:

[ ] 10 lbs. [ ] 20 lbs. [ ] 30 lbs. [ ] 40 lbs. [ ] 50 or more lbs.

OCCASIONALLY LIFT and/or CARRY:

[ ] 10 lbs. [ ] 20 lbs. [ ] 30 lbs. [ ] 40 lbs. [ ] 50 or more lbs.

STAND and/or WALK a total of:

[1 Less than 2 HOURS per 8 hour day
[ ] Less than 4 HOURS per 8 hour day
[ ] Less than 6 HOURS per 8 hour day
[ ] Less than 8 HOURS per 8 hour day

SIT a total of:

[1 Less than 2 HOURS per 8 hour day
[ ] Less than 4 HOURS per 8 hour day
[ ] Less than 6 HOURS per 8 hour day
[ ] Less than 8 HOURS per 8 hour day

PUSH and/or PULL (including hand or foot controls):

[ ] UNLIMITED

[ ] LIMITED (Describe degree of limitation)

Division of Workers' Compensation

PRIMARY TREATING PHYSICIAN'S PERMANENT AND STATIONARY REPORT (PR-4)

ACTIVITIES ALLOWED:

	Frequently	Occasionally	Never
Climbing	[ ]	[ ]	[ ]
Balancing	[ ]	[ ]	[ ]
Stooping	[ ]	[ ]	[ ]
Kneeling	[ ]	[ ]	[ ]
Crouching	[ ]	[ ]	[ ]
Crawling	[ ]	[ ]	[ ]
Twisting	[ ]	[ ]	[ ]
Reaching	[ ]	[ ]	[ ]
Handling	[ ]	[ ]	[ ]
Fingering	[ ]	[ ]	[ ]
Feeling	[ ]	[ ]	[ ]
Seeing	[ ]	[ ]	[ ]
Hearing	[ ]	[ ]	[ ]
Speaking	[ ]	[ ]	[ ]

Describe in what ways the impaired activities are limited:

Environmental restrictions (e.g. heights, machinery, temperature extremes, dust, fumes, humidity, vibration etc.)

	Yes	No
Can this patient now return to his/her usual occupation?	☐	☐

List information you reviewed in preparing this report, or relied upon for the formulation of your medical opinions:

Medical Records:

Written Job Description:

Division of Workers' Compensation
PRIMARY TREATING PHYSICIAN'S PERMANENT AND STATIONARY REPORT (PR-4)

Other:

Primary Treating Physician (original signature, do not stamp)

I declare under penalty of perjury that this report is true and correct to the best of my knowledge, and that I have not violated Labor Code §139.3.

Signature: _____   Cal. Lic. # : _____

Executed at: _____   Date: _____
                (County and State)

Name (Printed): _____   Specialty: _____

Intentionally blank

STATE OF CALIFORNIA
DEPARTMENT OF INDUSTRIAL RELATIONS
DIVISION OF WORKERS' COMPENSATION
ADMINISTRATIVE DIRECTOR
Post Office Box 420603
San Francisco, CA 94142

PETITION FOR CHANGE OF PRIMARY TREATING PHYSICIAN
(LABOR CODE § 4603 & TITLE 8, CALIFORNIA CODE OF REGULATIONS, § 9786)

(Print or Type Names and Addresses)

WCAB Case Nos. (If any):_____

EMPLOYEE: _____

EMPLOYEE'S ADDRESS:_____

EMPLOYEE'S ATTORNEY: _____

EMPLOYEE'S ATTORNEY'S ADDRESS_____

EMPLOYER:_____

EMPLOYER'S ADDRESS:_____

CLAIMS ADMINISTRATOR:_____

CLAIMS ADMINISTRATOR'S ADDRESS:_____

CLAIMS ADMINISTRATOR'S CLAIM NUMBER(S):_____

NAME OF PRIMARY TREATING PHYSICIAN _____

PRIMARY TREATING PHYSICIAN'S ADDRESS:_____

PHYSICIAN PANEL: List below the **NAMES, ADDRESSES and MEDICAL SPECIALTIES** (e.g.-orthopedics, cardiology, etc.) of a panel of FIVE (5) physicians (to include one chiropractor if the employee is being treated by a chiropractor) available to provide treatment of the employee's injury in the event this petition is granted.

1._____

2._____

3._____

4._____

5._____

PART A　　　　　　　　　　1　　　　　　DWC Form 280 (Part A) (1/01)

Petitioner states that the following constitutes good cause for issuance of an *Order Granting Petition For Change Of Primary Treating Physician:* (Additional sheets may be attached if necessary)

NOTE: Attach to this Petition any supportive evidence (medical reports, declarations, etc.) that establishes good cause for the Petition to be granted. (See Title 8, California Code of Regulations, Section 9786)

VERIFICATION

I declare under penalty of perjury under the laws of the State of California that the foregoing is true and correct.

EXECUTED AT _____, CALIFORNIA ON _____
 (City)   (Date)

BY: _____ // _____
 Original Signature of Petitioner's Representative   // Name of Petitioner's Representative Preparing the Petition
 Preparing the Petition   (Print or type)

_____
(Address of Petitioner)

_____

YOU MUST ATTACH A PROOF OF SERVICE BY MAIL DECLARATION INDICATING THAT: (1) PART A (PETITION FOR CHANGE OF PRIMARY TREATING PHYSICIAN) *AND* PART B (RESPONSE TO PETITION FOR CHANGE OF PRIMARY TREATING PHYSICIAN) OF THIS FORM AND (2) ALL SUPPORTIVE EVIDENCE WERE MAILED TO THE EMPLOYEE OR THE EMPLOYEE'S ATTORNEY, AND THE PRIMARY TREATING PHYSICIAN.

Notice to Employee/Employee's Attorney and Primary Treating Physician:

Pursuant to Title 8, California Code of Regulations, Section 9786(d), you may file with the Administrative Director a RESPONSE to this petition within <u>20 days</u> from the date the petition was served on you. Your Response must be submitted using the *Response to Petition for Change of Treating Physician* form which is contained in Part B on Pages 3 and 4 of this form. You may attach additional sheets as needed to the Response form.

STATE OF CALIFORNIA
DEPARTMENT OF INDUSTRIAL RELATIONS
DIVISION OF WORKERS' COMPENSATION
ADMINISTRATIVE DIRECTOR
Post Office Box 420603
San Francisco, CA 94142

RESPONSE TO PETITION FOR CHANGE OF PRIMARY TREATING PHYSICIAN
(LABOR CODE § 4603 & TITLE 8, CALIFORNIA CODE OF REGULATIONS, § 9786(d))

(Print or type names and addresses)

WCAB Case Nos. (If any):_____

EMPLOYEE: _____

EMPLOYEE'S ATTORNEY_____

EMPLOYER:_____

CLAIMS ADMINISTRATOR:_____

CLAIMS ADMINISTRATOR'S CLAIM NUMBER:_____

NAME OF PRIMARY TREATING PHYSICIAN _____

The petition filed by or on behalf of the Claims Administrator does not establish good cause for the issuance of an *Order Granting Petition For Change Of Primary Treating Physician based on the following:* (additional sheets may be attached if necessary)

IMPORTANT: Attach to this Response any supportive documentary evidence (medical reports, affidavit and declaration, etc.) which establishes that there is not good cause for the Administrative Director to grant the Petition for Change of Primary Treating Physician. (See *Title 8, California Code of Regulations, § 9786*)

VERIFICATION

I declare under penalty of perjury under the laws of the State of California that the foregoing is true and correct.

EXECUTED AT _____, CALIFORNIA ON _____
          (City)   (Date)

BY: _____ // _____
    Original Signature of Person Preparing the Response // Name of Person Preparing the Response (Print or type)

Address:

_____

NOTICE TO EMPLOYEE/EMPLOYEE'S ATTORNEY: THE PROOF OF SERVICE BY MAIL DECLARATION BELOW MUST BE COMPLETED INDICATING A COPY OF THIS RESPONSE HAS BEEN MAILED TO THE CLAIMS ADMINISTRATOR OR ITS ATTORNEY, AND THE PRIMARY TREATING PHYSICIAN.

NOTICE TO PRIMARY TREATING PHYSICIAN: THE PROOF OF SERVICE BY MAIL DECLARATION BELOW MUST BE COMPLETED INDICATING A COPY OF THIS RESPONSE HAS BEEN MAILED TO THE CLAIMS ADMINISTRATOR OR ITS ATTORNEY, AND THE EMPLOYEE OR THE EMPLOYEE'S ATTORNEY.

PROOF OF SERVICE BY MAIL

On _____I served a copy of this Response to Petition for Change of Treating Physician on
      (date)

_____ at _____and
(Claims Administrator or its Attorney)   *(address)*

_____ at _____by
(Primary Treating Physician or Employee/   *(address)*
Employee's Attorney)

placing a true copy enclosed in a sealed envelope, addressed as indicated above and with postage fully prepaid, in the U.S. Mail at_____, California. I declare under penalty of perjury under the laws of the State of California that the foregoing is true and correct.

_____ // _____
      Original Signature of Declarant   //   Name of Declarant (Print or Type)

Appendix B

• Medical Provider Network (MPN); Independent Medical Reviewer

Article 3.5. Medical Provider Network

§ 9767.1. Medical Provider Networks–Definitions

(a) As used in this article:

  (1) "Ancillary services" means any provision of medical services or goods as allowed in Labor Code section 4600 by a non–physician.

  (2) "Covered employee" means an employee or former employee whose employer has ongoing workers' compensation obligations and whose employer or employer's insurer has established a Medical Provider Network for the provision of medical treatment to injured employees unless:

(A) the injured employee has properly designated a personal physician pursuant to Labor Code section 4600(d) by notice to the employer prior to the date of injury, or;

(B) the injured employee's employment with the employer is covered by an agreement providing medical treatment for the injured employee and the agreement is validly established under Labor Code section 3201.5, 3201.7 and/or 3201.81.

(3) "Division" means the Division of Workers' Compensation.

(4) "Economic profiling" means any evaluation of a particular physician, provider, medical group, or individual practice association based in whole or in part on the economic costs or utilization of services associated with medical care provided or authorized by the physician, provider, medical group, or individual practice association.

(5) "Emergency health care services" means health care services for a medical condition manifesting itself by acute symptoms of sufficient severity such that the absence of immediate medical attention could reasonably be expected to place the patient's health in serious jeopardy.

(6) "Employer" means a self–insured employer, the Self–Insurer's Security Fund, a group of self–insured employers pursuant to Labor Code section 3700(b) and as defined by Title 8, California Code of Regulations, section 15201(s), a joint powers authority, or the state.

(7) "Group Disability Insurance Policy" means an entity designated pursuant to Labor Code section 4616.7(c).

(8) "Health Care Organization" means an entity designated pursuant to Labor Code section 4616.7(a).

(9) "Health Care Service Plan" means an entity designated pursuant to Labor Code section 4616.7(b).

(10) "Insurer" means an insurer admitted to transact workers' compensation insurance in the state of California, California Insurance Guarantee Association, or the State Compensation Insurance Fund.

(11) "Medical Provider Network" ("MPN") means any entity or group of providers approved as a Medical Provider Network by the Administrative Director pursuant to Labor Code sections 4616 to 4616.7 and this article.

(12) "Medical Provider Network Plan" means an employer's or insurer's detailed description for a medical provider network contained in an application submitted to the Administrative Director by a MPN applicant.

(13) "MPN Applicant" means an insurer or employer as defined in subdivisions (6) and (10) of this section.

(14) "MPN Contact" means an individual(s) designated by the MPN Applicant in the employee notification who is responsible for answering employees' questions about the Medical Provider Network and is responsible for assisting the employee in arranging for an independent medical review.

(15) "Nonoccupational Medicine" means the diagnosis or treatment of any injury or disease not arising out of and in the course of employment.

(16) "Occupational Medicine" means the diagnosis or treatment of any injury or disease arising out of and in the course of employment.

(17) "Physician primarily engaged in treatment of nonoccupational injuries" means a provider who spends more than 50 percent of his/her practice time providing non–occupational medical services.

(18) "Primary treating physician" means a primary treating physician within the medical provider network and as defined by section 9785(a)(1).

(19) "Provider" means a physician as described in Labor Code section 3209.3 or other provider as described in Labor Code section 3209.5.

(20) "Regional area listing" means either:

(A) a listing of all MPN providers within a 15–mile radius of an employee's worksite and/or residence; or

(B) a listing of all MPN providers in the county where the employee resides and/or works if
1. the employer or insurer cannot produce a provider listing based on a mile radius
2. or by choice of the employer or insurer, or upon request of the employee.

(C) If the listing described in either (A) or (B) does not provide a minimum of three physicians of each specialty, then the listing shall be expanded by adjacent counties or by 5–mile increments until the minimum number of physicians per specialty are met.

(21) "Residence" means the covered employee's primary residence.

(22) "Second Opinion" means an opinion rendered by a medical provider network physician after an in person examination to address an employee's dispute over either the diagnosis or the treatment prescribed by the treating physician.

(23) "Taft–Hartley health and welfare fund" means an entity designated pursuant to Labor Code section 4616.7(d).

(24) "Third Opinion" means an opinion rendered by a medical provider network physician after an in person examination to address an employee's dispute over either the diagnosis or the treatment prescribed by either the treating physician or physician rendering the second opinion.

(25) "Treating physician" means any physician within the MPN applicant's medical provider network other than the primary treating physician who examines or provides treatment to the employee, but is not primarily responsible for continuing management of the care of the employee.

(26) "Workplace" means the geographic location where the covered employee is regularly employed.

NOTE: Authority cited: Sections 133 and 4616(g), Labor Code. Reference: Sections 1063.1, 3208, 3209.3, 3209.5, 3700, 3702, 3743, 4616, 4616.1, 4616.3, 4616.5 and 4616.7, Labor Code; and California Insurance Guarantee Association v. Division of Workers' Compensation (April 26, 2005) WCAB No. Misc. #249.

HISTORY
1. New article 3.5 (sections 9767.1–9767.14) and section filed 11–1–2004 as an emergency; operative 11–1–2004 (Register 2004, No. 45). A Certificate of Compliance must be transmitted to OAL by 3–1–2005 or emergency language will be repealed by operation of law on the following day.
2. New article 3.5 (sections 9767.1–9767.14) and section refiled 2–28–2005 as an emergency; operative 3–1–2005 (Register 2005, No. 9). A Certificate of Compliance must be transmitted to OAL by 6–29–2005 or emergency language will be repealed by operation of law on the following day.
3. New article 3.5 (sections 9767.1–9767.14) and section refiled 6–20–2005 as an emergency; operative 6–29–2005 (Register 2005, No. 25). A Certificate of Compliance must be transmitted to OAL by 10–27–2005 or emergency language will be repealed by operation of law on the following day.
4. Certificate of Compliance as to 6–20–2005 order, including amendment of section and Note, transmitted to OAL 7–29–2005 and filed 9–9–2005 (Register 2005, No. 36).

§ 9767.2. Review of Medical Provider Network Application

(a) Within 60 days of the Administrative Director's receipt of a complete application, the Administrative Director shall approve or disapprove an application based on the requirements of Labor Code section 4616 et seq. and this article. An application shall be considered complete if it includes information responsive to each applicable subdivision of section 9767.3. Pursuant to Labor Code section 4616(b), if the Administrative Director has not acted on a plan within 60 days of submittal of a complete plan, it shall be deemed approved.

(b) The Administrative Director shall provide notification(s) to the MPN applicant: (1) setting forth the date the MPN application was received by the Division; and (2) informing the MPN applicant if the MPN application is not complete and the item(s) necessary to complete the application.

(c) No additional materials shall be submitted by the MPN applicant or considered by the Administrative Director until the MPN applicant receives the notification described in (b).

(d) The Administrative Director's decision to approve or disapprove an application shall be limited to his/her review of the information provided in the application.

(e) Upon approval of the Medical Provider Network Plan, the MPN applicant shall be assigned a MPN approval number.

NOTE: Authority cited: Sections 133 and 4616(g), Labor Code. Reference: Section 4616, Labor Code.

HISTORY
1. New section filed 11–1–2004 as an emergency; operative 11–1–2004 (Register 2004, No. 45). A Certificate of Compliance must be transmitted to OAL by 3–1–2005 or emergency language will be repealed by operation of law on the following day.
2. New section refiled 2–28–2005 as an emergency; operative 3–1–2005 (Register 2005, No. 9). A Certificate of Compliance must be transmitted to OAL by 6–29–2005 or emergency language will be repealed by operation of law on the following day.
3. New section refiled 6–20–2005 as an emergency; operative 6–29–2005 (Register 2005, No. 25). A Certificate of Compliance must be transmitted to OAL by 10–27–2005 or emergency language will be repealed by operation of law on the following day.
4. Certificate of Compliance as to 6–20–2005 order, including new subsection (c) and subsection relettering, transmitted to OAL 7–29–2005 and filed 9–9–2005 (Register 2005, No. 36).

§ 9767.3. Application for a Medical Provider Network Plan

(a) As long as the application for a medical provider network plan meets the requirements of Labor Code section 4616 et seq. and this article, nothing in this section precludes an employer or insurer from submitting for approval one or more medical provider network plans in its application.

(b) Nothing in this section precludes an insurer and an insured employer from agreeing to submit for approval a medical provider network plan which meets the specific needs of an insured employer considering the experience of the insured employer, the common injuries experienced by the insured employer, the type of occupation and industry in which the insured employer is engaged and the geographic area where the employees are employed.

(c) All MPN applicants shall submit an original Cover Page for Medical Provider Network Application with original signature, an original application, and a copy of the Cover Page for Medical Provider Network and application to the Division.

(1) A MPN applicant may submit the provider information and/or ancillary service provider information required in section 9767.3(a)(8)(C) and (D) on a computer disk(s) or CD ROM(s). The information shall be submitted as a Microsoft Excel spread sheet or as a Microsoft Access File unless an alternative format is approved by the Administrative Director.

(2) If the network provider information is submitted on a disk(s) or CD ROM(s), the provider file must have at a minimum five columns. These columns shall be: (1) physician name (2) license number (3) the taxpayer identification number (4) specialty and (5) location of each physician.

(3) If the ancillary service provider information is submitted on a disk(s) or CD ROM(s), the file must have at a minimum five columns. The columns shall be (1) the name of the each ancillary provider (2) license number (3) the taxpayer identification number (4) specialty or type of service and (5) location of each ancillary service provider.

(d) If the network is not a Health Care Organization, Health Care Service Plan, Group Disability Insurance Policy, or Taft–Hartley Health and Welfare Fund, a Medical Provider Network application shall include all of the following information:

(1) Type of MPN Applicant: Insurer or Employer.

(2) Name of MPN Applicant.

(3) MPN Applicant's Taxpayer Identification Number.

(4) Name of Medical Provider Network, if applicable.

(5) Division Liaison: Provide the name, title, address, e–mail address, and telephone number of the person designated as the liaison for the Division, who is responsible for receiving compliance and informational communications from the Division and for disseminating the same within the MPN.

(6) The application must be verified by an officer or employee of the MPN applicant authorized to sign on behalf of the MPN applicant. The verification shall state: "I, the undersigned officer or employee of the MPN applicant, have read and signed this application and know the contents thereof, and verify that, to the best of my knowledge and belief, the information included in this application is true and correct."

(7) Nothing in this section precludes a network, entity, administrator, or other third–party, upon agreement with an MPN applicant, from preparing an MPN application on behalf of an insurer or employer.

(8) Description of Medical Provider Network Plan:

(A) State the number of employees expected to be covered by the MPN plan;

(B) Describe the geographic service area or areas within the State of California to be served;

(C) The name, license number, taxpayer identification number, specialty, and location of each physician as described in Labor Code Section 3209.3, or other providers as described in Labor Code Section 3209.5, who will be providing occupational medicine services under the plan. Alternatively, if the physicians are also part of a medical group practice, the name and taxpayer identification number of the medical group practice shall be identified in the application. By submission of the application, the MPN applicant is confirming that a contractual agreement exists with the physicians, providers or medical group practice in the MPN to provide treatment for injured workers in the workers' compensation system and that the contractual agreement is in compliance with Labor Code section 4609, if applicable.

(D) The name, license number (if required by the State of California), taxpayer identification number, specialty or type of service and location of each ancillary service, other than a physician or provider covered under subdivision (d)(8)(C), who will be providing medical services within the medical provider network. By submission of the application, the MPN applicant is confirming that a contractual agreement exists between the MPN and these ancillary services in the MPN or the MPN applicant and these ancillary services in the MPN;

(E) Describe how the MPN complies with the second and third opinion process set forth in section 9767.7;

(F) Describe how the MPN complies with the goal of at least 25% of physicians (not including pediatricians, OB/GYNs, or other specialties not likely to routinely provide care for common injuries and illnesses expected to be encountered in the MPN) primarily engaged in the treatment of nonoccupational injuries;

(G) Describe how the MPN arranges for providing ancillary services to its covered employees. Set forth which ancillary services, if any, will be within the MPN. For ancillary services not within the MPN, affirm that referrals will be made to services outside the MPN;

(H) Describe how the MPN complies with the access standards set forth in section 9767.5 for all covered employees;

(I) Describe the employee notification process, and attach an English and Spanish sample of the employee notification material described in sections 9767.12(a) and (b);

(J) Attach a copy of the written continuity of care policy as described in Labor Code section 4616.2;

(K) Attach a copy of the written transfer of care policy that complies with section 9767.9;

(L) Attach any policy or procedure that is used by the MPN applicant to conduct "economic profiling of MPN providers" pursuant to Labor Code section 4616.1 and affirm that a copy of the policy or procedure has been provided to the MPN providers or attach a statement that the MPN applicant does not conduct economic profiling of MPN providers;

(M) Provide an affirmation that the physician compensation is not structured in order to achieve the goal of reducing, delaying, or denying medical treatment or restricting access to medical treatment; and

(N) Describe how the MPN applicant will ensure that no person other than a licensed physician who is competent to evaluate the specific clinical issues involved in the medical treatment services, when these services are within the scope of the physician's practice, will modify, delay, or deny requests for authorization of medical treatment.

(e) If the entity is a Health Care Organization, a Medical Provider Network application shall set forth the following:

    (1) Type of MPN Applicant: Insurer or Employer

    (2) Name of MPN Applicant

    (3) MPN Applicant's Taxpayer Identification Number

    (4) Name of Medical Provider Network, if applicable.

    (5) Division Liaison: Provide the name, title, address, e–mail address, and telephone number of the person designated as the liaison for the Division, who is responsible for receiving compliance and informational communications from the Division and for disseminating the same within the MPN.

    (6) The application must be verified by an officer or employee of the MPN applicant authorized to sign on behalf of the MPN applicant. The verification shall state: "I, the undersigned officer or employee of the MPN applicant, have read and signed this application and know the contents thereof, and verify that, to the best of my knowledge and belief, the information included in this application is true and correct."

    (7) Nothing in this section precludes a network, entity, administrator, or other third–party, upon agreement with an MPN applicant, from preparing an MPN application on behalf of an insurer or employer.

    (8) Describe how the MPN complies with the second and third opinion process set forth in section 9767.7;

    (9) Confirm that the application shall set forth that at least 25% of the network physicians are primarily engaged in nonoccupational medicine;

    (10) Describe the geographic service area or areas within the State of California to be served and affirm that this access plan complies with the access standards set forth in section 9767.5;

    (11) Describe the employee notification process, and attach an English and Spanish sample of the employee notification material described in sections 9767.12(a) and (b);

    (12) Attach a copy of the written continuity of care policy as described in Labor Code section 4616.2;

    (13) Attach a copy of the written transfer of care policy that complies with section 9767.9 with regard to the transfer of on–going cases from the HCO to the MPN;

    (14) Attach a copy of the policy or procedure that is used by the MPN applicant to conduct "economic profiling of MPN providers" pursuant to Labor Code section 4616.1 and affirm that a copy of the policy or procedure has been provided to the MPN providers or attach a statement that the MPN applicant does not conduct economic profiling of MPN providers; and

    (15) Describe the number of employees expected to be covered by the MPN plan and confirm that the number of employees is within the approved capacity of the HCO.

    (16) By submission of the application, the MPN applicant is confirming that a contractual agreement exists with the physicians, providers or medical group practice in the MPN to provide treatment for injured workers in the workers' compensation system and that the contractual agreement with the providers is in compliance with Labor Code section 4609, if applicable.

(f) If the entity is a Health Care Service Plan, Group Disability Insurance Policy, or Taft–Hartley Health and Welfare Fund, in addition to the requirements set forth in subdivision (e) [excluding (e)(9) and (e)(15)], a Medical Provider Network application shall include the following information:

    (1) The application shall set forth that the entity has a reasonable number of providers with competency in occupational medicine.

        (A) The MPN applicant may show that a physician has competency by confirming that the physician either is Board Certified or was residency trained in that specialty.

        (B) If (A) is not applicable, describe any other relevant procedure or process that assures that providers of medical treatment are competent to provide treatment for occupational injuries and illnesses.

(g) If the MPN applicant is providing for ancillary services within the MPN that are in addition to the services provided by the Health Care Organization, Health Care Service Plan, Group Disability Insurance Policy, or Taft–Hartley Health and Welfare Fund, it shall set forth the ancillary services in the application.

(h) If a Health Care Organization, Health Care Service Plan, Group Disability Insurance Policy, or Taft–Hartley Health and Welfare Fund has been approved as a MPN, and the entity does not maintain its certification or licensure or regulated status, then the entity must file a new Medical Provider Network Application pursuant to section 9767.3 (d).

(i) If a Health Care Organization, Health Care Service Plan, Group Disability Insurance Policy, or Taft–Hartley Health and Welfare Fund has been modified from its certification or licensure or regulated status, the application shall comply with subdivision (d).

NOTE: Authority cited: Sections 133 and 4616(g), Labor Code. Reference: Sections 3209.3, 4609, 4616, 4616.1, 4616.2, 4616.3, 4616.5 and 4616.7, Labor Code.

HISTORY

1. New section filed 11–1–2004 as an emergency; operative 11–1–2004 (Register 2004, No. 45). A Certificate of Compliance must be transmitted to OAL by 3–1–2005 or emergency language will be repealed by operation of law on the following day.

2. New section refiled 2–28–2005 as an emergency; operative 3–1–2005 (Register 2005, No. 9). A Certificate of Compliance must be transmitted to OAL by 6–29–2005 or emergency language will be repealed by operation of law on the following day.
3. New section refiled 6–20–2005 as an emergency; operative 6–29–2005 (Register 2005, No. 25). A Certificate of Compliance must be transmitted to OAL by 10–27–2005 or emergency language will be repealed by operation of law on the following day.
4. Certificate of Compliance as to 6–20–2005 order, including amendment of section and Note, transmitted to OAL 7–29–2005 and filed 9–9–2005 (Register 2005, No. 36).

§ 9767.4.   Cover Page for Medical Provider Network Application

NOTE: Authority cited: Sections 133 and 4616(g), Labor Code. Reference: Sections 3700, 3743, 4616, 4616.5 and 4616.7, Labor Code.

HISTORY
1. New section filed 11–1–2004 as an emergency; operative 11–1–2004 (Register 2004, No. 45). A Certificate of Compliance must be transmitted to OAL by 3– 1–2005 or emergency language will be repealed by operation of law on the following day.
2. New section refiled 2–28–2005 as an emergency; operative 3–1–2005 (Register 2005, No. 9). A Certificate of Compliance must be transmitted to OAL by 6– 29–2005 or emergency language will be repealed by operation of law on the following day.
3. New section refiled 6–20–2005 as an emergency; operative 6–29–2005 (Register 2005, No. 25). A Certificate of Compliance must be transmitted to OAL by 10– 27–2005 or emergency language will be repealed by operation of law on the following day.
4. Certificate of Compliance as to 6–20–2005 order, including amendment of section and Note, transmitted to OAL 7–29–2005 and filed 9–9–2005 (Register 2005, No. 36).
5. Change without regulatory effect amending section filed 5–23–2007 pursuant to section 100, title 1, California Code of Regulations (Register 2007, No. 21).

§ 9767.5.   Access Standards

(a) A MPN must have at least three physicians of each specialty expected to treat common injuries experienced by injured employees based on the type of occupation or industry in which the employee is engaged and within the access standards set forth in (b) and (c).
(b) A MPN must have a primary treating physician and a hospital for emergency health care services, or if separate from such hospital, a provider of all emergency health care services, within 30 minutes or 15 miles of each covered employee's residence or workplace.
(c) A MPN must have providers of occupational health services and specialists within 60 minutes or 30 miles of a covered employee's residence or workplace.
(d) If a MPN applicant believes that, given the facts and circumstances with regard to a portion of its service area, specifically rural areas including those in which health facilities are located at least 30 miles apart, the accessibility standards set forth in subdivisions (b) and/or (c) are unreasonably restrictive, the MPN applicant may propose alternative standards of accessibility for that portion of its service area. The MPN applicant shall do so by including the proposed alternative standards in writing in its plan approval application or in a notice of MPN plan modification. The alternative standards shall provide that all services shall be available and accessible at reasonable times to all covered employees.
(e) (1) The MPN applicant shall have a written policy for arranging or approving non–emergency medical care for: (A) a covered employee authorized by the employer to temporarily work or travel for work outside the MPN geographic service area when the need for medical care arises; (B) a former employee whose employer has ongoing workers' compensation obligations and who permanently resides outside the MPN geographic service area; and (C) an injured employee who decides to temporarily reside outside the MPN geographic service area during recovery.
    (2) The written policy shall provide the employees described in subdivision (e)(1) above with the choice of at least three physicians outside the MPN geographic service area who either have been referred by the employee's primary treating physician within the MPN or have been selected by the MPN applicant. In addition to physicians within the MPN, the employee may change physicians among the referred physicians and may obtain a second and third opinion from the referred physicians.
    (3) The referred physicians shall be located within the access standards described in paragraphs (c) and (d) of this section.
    (4) Nothing in this section precludes a MPN applicant from having a written policy that allows a covered employee outside the MPN geographic service area to choose his or her own provider for non–emergency medical care.

(f) For non–emergency services, the MPN applicant shall ensure that an appointment for initial treatment is available within 3 business days of the MPN applicant's receipt of a request for treatment within the MPN.

(g) For non–emergency specialist services to treat common injuries experienced by the covered employees based on the type of occupation or industry in which the employee is engaged, the MPN applicant shall ensure that an appointment is available within 20 business days of the MPN applicant's receipt of a referral to a specialist within the MPN.

(h) If the primary treating physician refers the covered employee to a type of specialist not included in the MPN, the covered employee may select a specialist from outside the MPN.

(i) The MPN applicant shall have a written policy to allow an injured employee to receive emergency health care services from a medical service or hospital provider who is not a member of the MPN.

NOTE: Authority cited: Sections 133 and 4616(g), Labor Code. Reference: Sections 4616 and 4616.3, Labor Code.

HISTORY

1. New section filed 11–1–2004 as an emergency; operative 11–1–2004 (Register 2004, No. 45). A Certificate of Compliance must be transmitted to OAL by 3–1–2005 or emergency language will be repealed by operation of law on the following day.

2. New section refiled 2–28–2005 as an emergency; operative 3–1–2005 (Register 2005, No. 9). A Certificate of Compliance must be transmitted to OAL by 6–29–2005 or emergency language will be repealed by operation of law on the following day.

3. New section refiled 6–20–2005 as an emergency; operative 6–29–2005 (Register 2005, No. 25). A Certificate of Compliance must be transmitted to OAL by 10–27–2005 or emergency language will be repealed by operation of law on the following day.

4. Certificate of Compliance as to 6–20–2005 order, including amendment of section, transmitted to OAL 7–29–2005 and filed 9–9–2005 (Register 2005, No. 36).

§ 9767.6.   Treatment and Change of Physicians Within MPN

(a) When the injured covered employee notifies the employer or insured employer of the injury or files a claim for workers' compensation with the employer or insured employer, the employer or insurer shall arrange an initial medical evaluation with a MPN physician in compliance with the access standards set forth in section 9767.5.

(b) Within one working day after an employee files a claim form under Labor Code section 5401, the employer or insurer shall provide for all treatment, consistent with guidelines adopted by the Administrative Director pursuant to Labor Code section 5307.27 or, prior to the adoption of these guidelines, the American College of Occupational and Environmental Medicine's Occupational Medicine Practice Guidelines (ACOEM), and for all injuries not covered by the ACOEM guidelines or guidelines adopted by the Administrative Director, authorized treatment shall be in accordance with other evidence based medical treatment guidelines generally recognized by the national medical community and that are scientifically based. The Administrative Director incorporates by reference the American College of Occupational and Environmental Medicine's Occupational Medicine Practice Guidelines (ACOEM), 2nd Edition (2004), published by OEM Press. A copy may be obtained from OEM Press, 8 West Street, Beverly Farms, Massachusetts 01915 (www.oempress.com).

(c) The employer or insurer shall provide for the treatment with MPN providers for the alleged injury and shall continue to provide the treatment until the date that liability for the claim is rejected. Until the date the claim is rejected, liability for the claim shall be limited to ten thousand dollars ($10,000).

(d) The insurer or employer shall notify the employee of his or her right to be treated by a physician of his or her choice within the MPN after the first visit with the MPN physician and the method by which the list of participating providers may be accessed by the employee.

(e) At any point in time after the initial medical evaluation with a MPN physician, the covered employee may select a physician of his or her choice from within the MPN. Selection by the covered employee of a treating physician and any subsequent physicians shall be based on the physician's specialty or recognized expertise in treating the particular injury or condition in question.

(f) The employer or insurer shall not be entitled to file a Petition for Change of Treating Physician, as set forth at section 9786, if a covered employee is treating with a physician within the MPN.

NOTE: Authority cited: Sections 133 and 4616(g), Labor Code. Reference: Sections 4604.5, 4616, 4616.3, 5307.27 and 5401, Labor Code.

HISTORY

1. New section filed 11–1–2004 as an emergency; operative 11–1–2004 (Register 2004, No. 45). A Certificate of Compliance must be transmitted to OAL by 3–1–2005 or emergency language will be repealed by operation of law on the following day.

2. New section refiled 2–28–2005 as an emergency; operative 3–1–2005 (Register 2005, No. 9). A Certificate of Compliance must be transmitted to OAL by 6–29–2005 or emergency language will be repealed by operation of law on the following day.

3. New section refiled 6–20–2005 as an emergency; operative 6–29–2005 (Register 2005, No. 25). A Certificate of Compliance must be transmitted to OAL by 10–27–2005 or emergency language will be repealed by operation of law on the following day.

4. Certificate of Compliance as to 6–20–2005 order, including amendment of section, transmitted to OAL 7–29–2005 and filed 9–9–2005 (Register 2005, No. 36).

§ 9767.7.   Second and Third Opinions

(a) If the covered employee disputes either the diagnosis or the treatment prescribed by the primary treating physician or the treating physician, the employee may obtain a second and third opinion from physicians within the MPN. During this process, the employee is required to continue his or her treatment with the treating physician or a physician of his or her choice within the MPN.

(b) If the covered employee disputes either the diagnosis or the treatment prescribed by primary treating physician or the treating physician, it is the employee's responsibility to: (1) inform the person designated by the employer or insurer that he or she disputes the treating physician's opinion and requests a second opinion (the employee may notify the person designated by the employer or insurer either in writing or orally); (2) select a physician or specialist from a list of available MPN providers; (3) make an appointment with the second opinion physician within 60 days; and (4) inform the person designated by the employer or insurer of the appointment date. It is the employer's or insurer's responsibility to (1) provide a regional area listing of MPN providers and/or specialists to the employee for his/her selection based on the specialty or recognized expertise in treating the particular injury or condition in question and inform the employee of his or her right to request a copy of the medical records that will be sent to the second opinion physician; (2) contact the treating physician, provide a copy of the medical records or send the necessary medical records to the second opinion physician prior to the appointment date, and provide a copy of the records to the covered employee upon request; and (3) notify the second opinion physician in writing that he or she has been selected to provide a second opinion and the nature of the dispute with a copy to the employee. If the appointment is not made within 60 days of receipt of the list of the available MPN providers, then the employee shall be deemed to have waived the second opinion process with regard to this disputed diagnosis or treatment of this treating physician.

(c) If, after reviewing the covered employee's medical records, the second opinion physician determines that the employee's injury is outside the scope of his or her practice, the physician shall notify the person designated by the employer or insurer and employee so the employer or insurer can provide a new list of MPN providers and/or specialists to the employee for his/her selection based on the specialty or recognized expertise in treating the particular injury or condition in question.

(d) If the covered employee disagrees with either the diagnosis or treatment prescribed by the second opinion physician, the injured employee may seek the opinion of a third physician within the MPN. It is the employee's responsibility to: (1) inform the person designated by the employer or insurer that he or she disputes the treating physician's opinion and requests a third opinion (the employee may notify the person designated by the employer or insurer either in writing or orally); (2) select a physician or specialist from a list of available MPN providers; and (3) make an appointment with the third opinion physician within 60 days; and (4) inform the person designated by the employer or insurer of the appointment date. It is the employer's or insurer's responsibility to (1) provide a regional area listing of MPN providers and/or specialists to the employee for his/her selection based on the specialty or recognized expertise in treating the particular injury or condition in question and inform the employee of his or her right to request a copy of the medical records that will be sent to the third opinion physician; and (2) contact the treating physician, provide a copy of the medical records or send the necessary medical records to the third opinion physician prior to the appointment date, and provide a copy of the records to the covered employee upon request; and (3) notify the third opinion physician in writing that he or she has been selected to provide a third opinion and the nature of the dispute with a copy to the employee. If the appointment is not made within 60 days of receipt of the list of the available MPN providers, then the employee shall be deemed to have waived the third opinion process with regard to this disputed diagnosis or treatment of this treating physician.

(e) If, after reviewing the covered employee's medical records, the third opinion physician determines that the employee's injury is outside the scope of his or her practice, the physician shall notify the person designated by the employer or insurer and employee so the MPN can provide a new list of MPN providers and/or specialists to the employee for his/her selection based on the specialty or recognized expertise in treating the particular injury or condition in question.

(f) The second and third opinion physicians shall each render his or her opinion of the disputed diagnosis or treatment in writing and offer alternative diagnosis or treatment recommendations, if applicable. Any recommended treatment shall be in accordance with Labor Code section 4616(e). The second and third opinion physicians may order diagnostic testing if medically necessary. A copy of the written report shall be served on the employee, the person designated by the employer or insurer, and the treating physician within 20 days of the date of the appointment or receipt of the results of the diagnostic tests, whichever is later.

(g) The employer or insurer shall permit the employee to obtain the recommended treatment within the MPN. The covered employee may obtain the recommended treatment by changing physicians to the second opinion physician, third opinion physician, or other MPN physician.

(h) If the injured covered employee disagrees with the diagnosis or treatment of the third opinion physician, the injured employee may file with the Administrative Director a request for an Independent Medical Review.

NOTE: Authority cited: Sections 133 and 4616(g), Labor Code. Reference: Sections 4616(a) and 4616.3, Labor Code.

HISTORY

1. New section filed 11–1–2004 as an emergency; operative 11–1–2004 (Register 2004, No. 45). A Certificate of Compliance must be transmitted to OAL by 3–1–2005 or emergency language will be repealed by operation of law on the following day.

2. New section refiled 2–28–2005 as an emergency; operative 3–1–2005 (Register 2005, No. 9). A Certificate of Compliance must be transmitted to OAL by 6–29–2005 or emergency language will be repealed by operation of law on the following day.

3. New section refiled 6–20–2005 as an emergency; operative 6–29–2005 (Register 2005, No. 25). A Certificate of Compliance must be transmitted to OAL by 10–27–2005 or emergency language will be repealed by operation of law on the following day.

4. Certificate of Compliance as to 6–20–2005 order, including amendment of section, transmitted to OAL 7–29–2005 and filed 9–9–2005 (Register 2005, No. 36).

§ 9767.8.   Modification of Medical Provider Network Plan

(a) The MPN applicant shall serve the Administrative Director with an original Notice of MPN Plan Modification with original signature, any necessary documentation, and a copy of the Notice and any necessary documentation before any of the following changes occur:

    (1) A change of 10% or more in the number or specialty of providers participating in the network since the approval date of the previous MPN Plan application or modification.

    (2) A change of 25% or more in the number of covered employees since the approval date of the previous MPN Plan application or modification.

    (3) A material change in the continuity of care policy.

    (4) A material change in the transfer of care policy.

    (5) Change in policy or procedure that is used by the MPN to conduct "economic profiling of MPN providers" pursuant to Labor Code section 4616.1.

    (6) Change in the name of the MPN.

    (7) Change in geographic service area within the State of California.

    (8) Change in how the MPN complies with the access standards.

    (9) A material change in any of the employee notification materials required by section 9767.12.

(b) The MPN applicant shall serve the Administrative Director with a Notice of MPN Plan Modification within 5 business days of a change of the DWC liaison.

(c) The modification must be verified by an officer or employee of the MPN authorized to sign on behalf of the MPN applicant. The verification shall state: "I, the undersigned officer or employee of the MPN applicant, have read and signed this notice and know the contents thereof, and verify that, to the best of my knowledge and belief, the information included in this notice is true and correct."

(d) Within 60 days of the Administrative Director's receipt of a Notice of MPN Plan Modification, the Administrative Director shall approve or disapprove the plan modification based on information provided in the Notice of MPN Plan Modification. The Administrative Director shall approve or disapprove a plan modification based on the requirements of Labor Code section 4616 et seq. and this article. If the Administrative Director has not acted on a plan within 60 days of submittal of a Notice of MPN Plan Modification, it shall be deemed approved. Except for (a)(6) and (b), modifications shall not be made until the Administrative Director has approved the plan or until 60 days have passed, which ever occurs first. If the Administrative Director disapproves of the MPN plan modification, he or she shall serve the MPN applicant with a Notice of Disapproval within 60 days of the submittal of a Notice of MPN Plan Modification.

(e) A MPN applicant denied approval of a MPN plan modification may either:

    (1) Submit a new request addressing the deficiencies; or

    (2) Request a re–evaluation by the Administrative Director.

(f) Any MPN applicant may request a re–evaluation of the denial by submitting with the Division, within 20 days of the issuance of the Notice of Disapproval, a written request for a re–evaluation with a detailed statement explaining the basis upon which a re–evaluation is requested. The request for re–evaluation shall be accompanied by supportive documentary material relevant to the specific allegations raised and shall be verified under penalty of perjury. The MPN application and modification at issue shall not be refiled; they shall be made part of the administrative record by incorporation by reference.

(g) The Administrative Director shall, within 45 days of the receipt of the request for a re–evaluation, either:

    (1) Issue a Decision and Order affirming or modifying the Notice of Disapproval based on a failure to meet the procedural requirements of this section or based on a failure to meet the requirements of Labor Code section 4616 et seq. and this article; or

    (2) Issue a Decision and Order revoking the Notice of Disapproval and issue an approval of the modification;

(h) The Administrative Director may extend the time specified in subdivision (h) within which to act upon the request for a re–evaluation for a period of 30 days and may order a party to submit additional documents or information.

(i) A MPN applicant may appeal the Administrative Director's decision and order regarding the MPN by filing, within twenty (20) days of the issuance of the decision and order, a petition at the district office of the Workers' Compensation Appeals Board closest to the MPN applicant's principal place of business, together with a Declaration of Readiness to Proceed. The petition shall set forth the specific factual and/or legal reason(s) for the appeal. A copy of the petition and of the Declaration of Readiness to Proceed shall be concurrently served on the Administrative Director.

(j) The MPN applicant shall use the following Notice of MPN Plan Modification form:

    Submit an original Notice of MPN Plan Modification with original signature, any necessary documentation, and a copy of the Notice and documents to the Division of Workers' Compensation.

    Mailing address: DWC, MPN Application, P.O. Box 71010, Oakland, CA 94612.
    [DWC Mandatory Form – Section 9767.8 – May 2007]

NOTE: Authority cited: Sections 133, 4616(g) and 5300(f), Labor Code. Reference: Sections 3700, 3743, 4616, 4616.2 and 4616.5, Labor Code.

HISTORY

1. New section filed 11–1–2004 as an emergency; operative 11–1–2004 (Register 2004, No. 45). A Certificate of Compliance must be transmitted to OAL by 3– 1–2005 or emergency language will be repealed by operation of law on the following day.

2. New section refiled 2–28–2005 as an emergency; operative 3–1–2005 (Register 2005, No. 9). A Certificate of Compliance must be transmitted to OAL by 6– 29–2005 or emergency language will be repealed by operation of law on the following day.

3. New section refiled 6–20–2005 as an emergency; operative 6–29–2005 (Register 2005, No. 25). A Certificate of Compliance must be transmitted to OAL by 10– 27–2005 or emergency language will be repealed by operation of law on the following day.

4. Certificate of Compliance as to 6–20–2005 order, including amendment of section and Note, transmitted to OAL 7–29–2005 and filed 9–9–2005 (Register 2005, No. 36).

5. Change without regulatory effect amending form filed 5–23–2007 pursuant to section 100, title 1, California Code of Regulations (Register 2007, No. 21).

§ 9767.9.   Transfer of Ongoing Care into the MPN

(a) If the injured covered employee's injury or illness does not meet the conditions set forth in (e)(1) through (e)(4), the injured covered employee may be transferred into the MPN for medical treatment.

(b) Until the injured covered employee is transferred into the MPN, the employee's physician may make referrals to providers within or outside the MPN.

(c) Nothing in this section shall preclude an insurer or employer from agreeing to provide medical care with providers outside of the MPN.

(d) If an injured covered employee is being treated for an occupational injury or illness by a physician or provider prior to coverage of a medical provider network, and the injured covered employee's physician or provider becomes a provider within the MPN that applies to the injured covered employee, then the employer or insurer shall inform the injured covered employee and his or her physician or provider if his/her treatment is being provided by his/her physician or provider under the provisions of the MPN.

(e) The employer or insurer shall authorize the completion of treatment for injured covered employees who are being treated outside of the MPN for an occupational injury or illness that occurred prior to the coverage of the MPN and whose treating physician is not a provider within the MPN, including injured covered employees who pre–designated a physician and do not fall within the Labor Code section 4600(d), for the following conditions:

    (1) An acute condition. For purposes of this subdivision, an acute condition is a medical condition that involves a sudden onset of symptoms due to an illness, injury, or other medical problem that requires prompt medical attention and that has a duration of less than 90 days. Completion of treatment shall be provided for the duration of the acute condition.

    (2) A serious chronic condition. For purposes of this subdivision, a serious chronic condition is a medical condition due to a disease, illness, catastrophic injury, or other medical problem or medical disorder that is serious in nature and that

persists without full cure or worsens over 90 days and requires ongoing treatment to maintain remission or prevent deterioration. Completion of treatment shall be authorized for a period of time necessary, up to one year: (A) to complete a course of treatment approved by the employer or insurer; and (B) to arrange for transfer to another provider within the MPN, as determined by the insurer or employer. The one year period for completion of treatment starts from the date of the injured covered employee's receipt of the notification, as required by subdivision (f), of the determination that the employee has a serious chronic condition.

(3) A terminal illness. For purposes of this subdivision, a terminal illness is an incurable or irreversible condition that has a high probability of causing death within one year or less. Completion of treatment shall be provided for the duration of a terminal illness.

(4) Performance of a surgery or other procedure that is authorized by the insurer or employer as part of a documented course of treatment and has been recommended and documented by the provider to occur within 180 days from the MPN coverage effective date.

(f) If the employer or insurer decides to transfer the covered employee's medical care to the medical provider network, the employer or insurer shall notify the covered employee of the determination regarding the completion of treatment and the decision to transfer medical care into the medical provider network. The notification shall be sent to the covered employee's residence and a copy of the letter shall be sent to the covered employee's primary treating physician. The notification shall be written in English and Spanish and use layperson's terms to the maximum extent possible.

(g) If the injured covered employee disputes the medical determination under this section, the injured covered employee shall request a report from the covered employee's primary treating physician that addresses whether the covered employee falls within any of the conditions set forth in subdivisions (e)(1–4). The treating physician shall provide the report to the covered employee within twenty calendar days of the request. If the treating physician fails to issue the report, then the determination made by the employer or insurer referred to in (f) shall apply.

(h) If the employer or insurer or injured covered employee objects to the medical determination by the treating physician, the dispute regarding the medical determination made by the treating physician concerning the transfer of care shall be resolved pursuant to Labor Code section 4062.

(i) If the treating physician agrees with the employer's or insurer's determination that the injured covered employee's medical condition does not meet the conditions set forth in subdivisions (e)(1) through (e)(4), the transfer of care shall go forward during the dispute resolution process.

(j) If the treating physician does not agree with the employer's or insurer's determination that the injured covered employee's medical condition does not meet the conditions set forth in subdivisions (e)(1) through (e)(4), the transfer of care shall not go forward until the dispute is resolved.

NOTE: Authority cited: Sections 133, 4616(g), and 4062, Labor Code. Reference: Sections 4616 and 4616.2, Labor Code.

HISTORY

1. New section filed 11–1–2004 as an emergency; operative 11–1–2004 (Register 2004, No. 45). A Certificate of Compliance must be transmitted to OAL by 3–1–2005 or emergency language will be repealed by operation of law on the following day.

2. New section refiled 2–28–2005 as an emergency; operative 3–1–2005 (Register 2005, No. 9). A Certificate of Compliance must be transmitted to OAL by 6–29–2005 or emergency language will be repealed by operation of law on the following day.

3. New section refiled 6–20–2005 as an emergency; operative 6–29–2005 (Register 2005, No. 25). A Certificate of Compliance must be transmitted to OAL by 10–27–2005 or emergency language will be repealed by operation of law on the following day.

4. Certificate of Compliance as to 6–20–2005 order, including amendment of section, transmitted to OAL 7–29–2005 and filed 9–9–2005 (Register 2005, No. 36).

§ 9767.10. Continuity of Care Policy

(a) At the request of a covered employee, an insurer or employer that offers a medical provider network shall complete the treatment by a terminated provider as set forth in Labor Code sections 4616.2(d) and (e).

(b) An "acute condition," as referred to in Labor Code section 4616.2(d)(3)(A), shall have a duration of less than ninety days.

(c) "An extended period of time," as referred to in Labor Code section 4616.2(d)(3)(B) with regard to a serious and chronic condition, means a duration of at least ninety days.

(d) The MPN applicant's continuity of care policy shall include a dispute resolution procedure that contains the following requirements:

(1) Following the employer's or insurer's determination of the injured covered employee's medical condition, the employer or insurer shall notify the covered employee of the determination regarding the completion of treatment and whether or not the employee will be required to select a new provider from within the MPN. The notification shall be sent to the covered employee's residence and a copy of the letter shall be sent to the covered employee's primary

treating physician. The notification shall be written in English and Spanish and use layperson's terms to the maximum extent possible.

(2) If the terminated provider agrees to continue treating the injured covered employee in accordance with Labor Code section 4616.2 and if the injured covered employee disputes the medical determination, the injured covered employee shall request a report from the covered employee's primary treating physician that addresses whether the covered employee falls within any of the conditions set forth in Labor Code section 4616.2(d)(3); an acute condition; a serious chronic condition; a terminal illness; or a performance of a surgery or other procedure that is authorized by the insurer or employer as part of a documented course of treatment and has been recommended and documented by the provider to occur within 180 days of the contract's termination date. The treating physician shall provide the report to the covered employee within twenty calendar days of the request. If the treating physician fails to issue the report, then the determination made by the employer or insurer referred to in (d)(1) shall apply.

(3) If the employer or insurer or injured covered employee objects to the medical determination by the treating physician, the dispute regarding the medical determination made by the treating physician concerning the continuity of care shall be resolved pursuant to Labor Code section 4062.

(4) If the treating physician agrees with the employer's or insurer's determination that the injured covered employee's medical condition does not meet the conditions set forth in Labor Code section 4616.2(d)(3), the employee shall choose a new provider from within the MPN during the dispute resolution process.

(5) If the treating physician does not agree with the employer's or insurer's determination that the injured covered employee's medical condition does not meet the conditions set forth in Labor Code section 4616.2(d)(3), the injured covered employee shall continue to treat with the terminated provider until the dispute is resolved.

NOTE: Authority cited: Sections 133 and 4616(g), Labor Code. Reference: Section 4616.2, Labor Code.

HISTORY

1. New section filed 11–1–2004 as an emergency; operative 11–1–2004 (Register 2004, No. 45). A Certificate of Compliance must be transmitted to OAL by 3– 1–2005 or emergency language will be repealed by operation of law on the following day.

2. New section refiled 2–28–2005 as an emergency; operative 3–1–2005 (Register 2005, No. 9). A Certificate of Compliance must be transmitted to OAL by 6– 29–2005 or emergency language will be repealed by operation of law on the following day.

3. New section refiled 6–20–2005 as an emergency; operative 6–29–2005 (Register 2005, No. 25). A Certificate of Compliance must be transmitted to OAL by 10– 27–2005 or emergency language will be repealed by operation of law on the following day.

4. Certificate of Compliance as to 6–20–2005 order, including amendment of section, transmitted to OAL 7–29–2005 and filed 9–9–2005 (Register 2005, No. 36).

§ 9767.11. Economic Profiling Policy

(a) An insurer's or employer's filing of its economic profiling policies and procedures shall include:

(1) An overall description of the profiling methodology, data used to create the profile and risk adjustment;

(2) A description of how economic profiling is used in utilization review;

(3) A description of how economic profiling is used in peer review; and

(4) A description of any incentives and penalties used in the program and in provider retention and termination decisions.

NOTE: Authority cited: Sections 133 and 4616(g), Labor Code. Reference: Section 4616.1, Labor Code.

HISTORY

1. New section filed 11–1–2004 as an emergency; operative 11–1–2004 (Register 2004, No. 45). A Certificate of Compliance must be transmitted to OAL by 3– 1–2005 or emergency language will be repealed by operation of law on the following day.

2. New section refiled 2–28–2005 as an emergency; operative 3–1–2005 (Register 2005, No. 9). A Certificate of Compliance must be transmitted to OAL by 6– 29–2005 or emergency language will be repealed by operation of law on the following day.

3. New section refiled 6–20–2005 as an emergency; operative 6–29–2005 (Register 2005, No. 25). A Certificate of Compliance must be transmitted to OAL by 10– 27–2005 or emergency language will be repealed by operation of law on the following day.

4. Certificate of Compliance as to 6–20–2005 order transmitted to OAL 7–29–2005 and filed 9–9–2005 (Register 2005, No. 36).

§ 9767.12. Employee Notification

(a) An employer or insurer that offers a Medical Provider Network Plan under this article shall notify each covered employee in writing about the use of the Medical Provider Network 30 days prior to the implementation of an approved MPN, at the time of hire, or when an existing employee transfers into the MPN, whichever is appropriate to ensure that the employee has received the initial notification. The notification shall also be sent to a covered employee at the time of injury. The notification(s) shall be written in English and Spanish. The initial written notification shall include the following information:

  (1) How to contact the person designated by the employer or insurer to be the MPN contact for covered employees. The employer or insurer shall provide a toll free telephone number of the MPN geographical service area includes more than one area code;

  (2) A description of MPN services;

  (3) How to review, receive or access the MPN provider directory. Nothing precludes an employer or insurer from initially providing covered employees with a regional area listing of MPN providers in addition to maintaining and making available its complete provider listing in writing. If the provider directory is also accessible on a website, the URL address shall be listed;

  (4) How to access initial care and subsequent care, and what the access standards are under section 9767.5;

  (5) How to access treatment if (A) the employee is authorized by the employer to temporarily work or travel for work outside the MPN's geographical service area; (B) a former employee whose employer has ongoing workers' compensation obligations permanently resides outside the MPN geographical service area; and (C) an injured employee decides to temporarily reside outside the MPN geographical service area during recovery;

  (6) How to choose a physician within the MPN;

  (7) What to do if a covered employee has trouble getting an appointment with a provider within the MPN;

  (8) How to change a physician within the MPN;

  (9) How to obtain a referral to a specialist within the MPN or outside the MPN, if needed;

  (10) How to use the second and third opinion process;

  (11) How to request and receive an independent medical review;

  (12) A description of the standards for transfer of ongoing care into the MPN and a notification that a copy of the policy shall be provided to an employee upon request; and

  (13) A description of the continuity of care policy and a notification that a copy of the policy shall be provided to an employee upon request.

(b) At the time of the selection of the physician for a third opinion, the covered employee shall be notified about the Independent Medical Review process. The notification shall be written in English and Spanish.

(c) Covered employees shall be notified 30 days prior to a change of the medical provider network. If the MPN applicant is an insurer, then a copy of the notification shall be served on the insured employer. The notification shall be written in English and Spanish.

NOTE: Authority cited: Sections 133 and 4616, Labor Code. Reference: Sections 4616, 4616.2 and 4616.3, Labor Code.

HISTORY

1. New section filed 11–1–2004 as an emergency; operative 11–1–2004 (Register 2004, No. 45). A Certificate of Compliance must be transmitted to OAL by 3–1–2005 or emergency language will be repealed by operation of law on the following day.

2. New section refiled 2–28–2005 as an emergency; operative 3–1–2005 (Register 2005, No. 9). A Certificate of Compliance must be transmitted to OAL by 6–29–2005 or emergency language will be repealed by operation of law on the following day.

3. New section refiled 6–20–2005 as an emergency; operative 6–29–2005 (Register 2005, No. 25). A Certificate of Compliance must be transmitted to OAL by 10–27–2005 or emergency language will be repealed by operation of law on the following day.

4. Certificate of Compliance as to 6–20–2005 order, including amendment of section, transmitted to OAL 7–29–2005 and filed 9–9–2005 (Register 2005, No. 36).

§ 9767.13. Denial of Approval of Application and Reconsideration

(a) The Administrative Director shall deny approval of a plan if the MPN applicant does not satisfy the requirements of this article and Labor Code section 4616 et seq. and shall state the reasons for disapproval in writing in a Notice of Disapproval, and shall transmit the Notice to the MPN applicant by U.S. Mail.

(b) An MPN applicant denied approval may either:

  (1) Submit a new application addressing the deficiencies; or

  (2) Request a re–evaluation by the Administrative Director.

(c) Any MPN applicant may request a re–evaluation by submitting with the Division, within 20 days of the issuance of the Notice of Disapproval, a written request for re–evaluation with a detailed statement explaining the basis upon which a re–evaluation is requested. The request for a re–evaluation shall be accompanied by supportive documentary material relevant to the specific allegations raised and shall be verified under penalty of perjury. The MPN application at issue shall not be re–filed; it shall be made part of the administrative record by incorporation by reference.

(d) The Administrative Director shall, within 45 days of the receipt of the request for a re–evaluation, either:

    (1) Issue a Decision and Order affirming or modifying the Notice of Disapproval based on a failure to meet the procedural requirements of this section or based on a failure to meet the requirements of Labor Code section 4616 et seq. and this article; or

    (2) Issue a Decision and Order revoking the Notice of Disapproval and issue an approval of the MPN.

(e) The Administrative Director may extend the time specified in subdivision (d) within which to act upon the request for a re–evaluation for a period of 30 days and may order a party to submit additional documents or information.

(f) A MPN applicant may appeal the Administrative Director's decision and order regarding the MPN by filing, within twenty (20) days of the issuance of the decision and order, a petition at the district office of the Workers' Compensation Appeals Board closest to the MPN applicant's principal place of business, together with a Declaration of Readiness to Proceed. The petition shall set forth the specific factual and/or legal reason(s) for the appeal. A copy of the petition and of the Declaration of Readiness to Proceed shall be concurrently served on the Administrative Director.

NOTE: Authority cited: Sections 133, 4616(g) and 5300(f), Labor Code. Reference: Section 4616, Labor Code.

HISTORY

1. New section filed 11–1–2004 as an emergency; operative 11–1–2004 (Register 2004, No. 45). A Certificate of Compliance must be transmitted to OAL by 3–1–2005 or emergency language will be repealed by operation of law on the following day.

2. New section refiled 2–28–2005 as an emergency; operative 3–1–2005 (Register 2005, No. 9). A Certificate of Compliance must be transmitted to OAL by 6–29–2005 or emergency language will be repealed by operation of law on the following day.

3. New section refiled 6–20–2005 as an emergency; operative 6–29–2005 (Register 2005, No. 25). A Certificate of Compliance must be transmitted to OAL by 10–27–2005 or emergency language will be repealed by operation of law on the following day.

4. Certificate of Compliance as to 6–20–2005 order, including amendment of section heading, section and Note, transmitted to OAL 7–29–2005 and filed 9–9–2005 (Register 2005, No. 36).

§ 9767.14.   Suspension or Revocation of Medical Provider Network Plan; Hearing

(a) The Administrative Director may suspend or revoke approval of a MPN Plan if:

    (1) Service under the MPN is not being provided according to the terms of the approved MPN plan.

    (2) The MPN fails to meet the requirements of Labor Code section 4616 et seq. and this article.

    (3) False or misleading information is knowingly or repeatedly submitted by the MPN or a participating provider or the MPN knowingly or repeatedly fails to report information required by this article.

    (4) The MPN knowingly continues to use the services of a provider or medical reviewer whose license, registration, or certification has been suspended or revoked or who is otherwise ineligible to provide treatment to an injured worker under California law.

(b) If one of the circumstances in subdivision (a) exists, the Administrative Director shall notify the MPN applicant in writing of the specific deficiencies alleged. The Administrative Director shall allow the MPN applicant an opportunity to correct the deficiency and/or to respond within ten days. If the Administrative Director determines that the deficiencies have not been cured, he or she shall issue a Notice of Action to the MPN applicant that specifies the time period in which the suspension or revocation will take effect and shall transmit the Notice of Action to the MPN applicant by U.S. Mail.

(c) A MPN applicant may request a re–evaluation of the suspension or revocation by submitting to the Administrative Director, within 20 days of the issuance of the Notice of Action, a written notice of the request for a re–evaluation with a detailed statement explaining the basis upon which a re–evaluation is requested. The request for a re–evaluation shall be accompanied by supportive documentary material relevant to the specific allegations raised and shall be verified under penalty of perjury. The MPN application at issue shall not be re–filed; it shall be made part of the administrative record and incorporated by reference.

(d) The Administrative Director shall, within 45 days of the receipt of the request for a re–evaluation, either:

    (1) Issue a Decision and Order affirming or modifying the Notice of Action based on a failure to meet the procedural requirements of this section or based on a failure to meet the requirements of Labor Code section 4616 et seq. and this article;

    (2) Issue a Decision and Order revoking the Notice of Action;

(e) The Administrative Director may extend the time specified in subdivision (d) within which to act upon the request for a re-evaluation for a period of 30 days and may order a party to submit additional documents or information.

(f) A MPN applicant may appeal the Administrative Director's decision and order regarding the MPN by filing, within twenty (20) days of the issuance of the decision and order, a petition at the district office of the Workers' Compensation Appeals Board closest to the MPN applicant's principal place of business, together with a Declaration of Readiness to Proceed. The petition shall set forth the specific factual and/or legal reason(s) for the appeal. A copy of the petition and of the Declaration of Readiness to Proceed shall be concurrently served on the Administrative Director.

NOTE: Authority cited: Sections 133, 4616(g) and 5300(f), Labor Code. Reference: Section 4616, Labor Code.

HISTORY
1. New section filed 11–1–2004 as an emergency; operative 11–1–2004 (Register 2004, No. 45). A Certificate of Compliance must be transmitted to OAL by 3–1–2005 or emergency language will be repealed by operation of law on the following day.
2. New section refiled 2–28–2005 as an emergency; operative 3–1–2005 (Register 2005, No. 9). A Certificate of Compliance must be transmitted to OAL by 6–29–2005 or emergency language will be repealed by operation of law on the following day.
3. New section refiled 6–20–2005 as an emergency; operative 6–29–2005 (Register 2005, No. 25). A Certificate of Compliance must be transmitted to OAL by 10–27–2005 or emergency language will be repealed by operation of law on the following day.
4. Certificate of Compliance as to 6–20–2005 order, including amendment of section, transmitted to OAL 7–29–2005 and filed 9–9–2005 (Register 2005, No. 36).

§ 9767.15.   Compliance with Permanent MPN Regulations

a. This section applies to MPNs that were approved by the Administrative Director pursuant to the emergency Medical Provider Network regulations effective November 1, 2004

b. Employers or insurers whose MPNs were approved pursuant to the emergency Medical Provider Network regulations are not required to submit a Notice of MPN Plan Modification to comply with the new or revised sections of the permanent regulations, including:
   1. Section 9767.3(d)(8)(C) or Section 9767.3(d)(16) regarding the contractual agreements contained in the Application for a Medical Provider Network Plan provisions.
   2. Sections 9767.5(e)(1), (e)(2), (e)(3), (e)(4), 9767.5(h) and 9767.5(i) of the Access Standards provisions.
   3. Section 9767.9(g) provision providing a timeline for the treating physician's report and what happens if the treating physician fails to issue a timely report contained in the Transfer of Ongoing Care into the MPN provisions.
   4. Section 9767.10(b)(c) and (d) of the Continuity of Care provisions.
   5. Section 9767.12(a), (a)(1), (a)(2), (a)(3), (a)(4) and (a)(5) of the Employee Notification provisions.

c. At the time an employer or insurer with an approved MPN pursuant to the emergency Medical Provider Network regulations submits a Notice of MPN Plan Modification, the employer or insurer shall be required to verify compliance with the sections of the MPN permanent regulations listed in subdivision (b) above.

NOTE: Authority cited: Sections 133, 4616(g) and 5300(f), Labor Code. Reference: Sections 4609, 4616, 4616.2 and 4616.3, Labor Code.

HISTORY
1. New section filed 9–9–2005; operative 9–9–2005 (Register 2005, No. 36).

Intentionally blank

Article 3.6. Independent Medical Review

§ 9768.1.   Definitions

(a) As used in this article, the following definitions apply:

(1) "American College of Occupational and Environmental Medicine's Occupational Medicine Practice Guidelines" ("ACOEM") means the American College of Occupational and Environmental Medicine's Occupational Medicine Practice Guidelines, 2nd Edition (2004), published by OEM Press. The Administrative Director incorporates ACOEM by reference. A copy may be obtained from OEM Press, 8 West Street, Beverly Farms, Massachusetts 01915 (www.oempress.com).

(2) "Appropriate specialty" means a medical specialty in an area or areas appropriate to the condition or treatment under review.

(3) "Independent Medical Reviewer" ("IMR") means the physician who is randomly selected pursuant to subdivision (b) of Labor Code section 4616.4.

(4) "In–person examination" means an examination of an injured employee by a physician which involves more than a review of records, and may include a physical examination, discussing the employee's medical condition with the employee, taking a history and performing an examination.

(5) "Material familial affiliation" means a relationship in which one of the persons or entities listed in section 9768.2 is the parent, child, grandparent, grandchild, sibling, uncle, aunt, nephew, niece, spouse, or cohabitant of the Independent Medical Reviewer.

(6) "Material financial affiliation" means a financial interest (owns a legal or equitable interest of more than 1% interest in the party, or a fair market value in excess of $2000, or relationship of director, advisor, or active participant) in any person or entity listed in section 9768.2. It also means any gift or income of more than $300 in the preceding year except for income for services as a second opinion physician, third opinion physician, treating physician, Agreed Medical Evaluator, Qualified Medical Evaluator, or Independent Medical Reviewer.

(7) "Material professional affiliation" means any relationship in which the Independent Medical Reviewer shares office space with, or works in the same office of, any person or entity listed in section 9768.2.

(8) "Medical emergency" means a medical condition manifesting itself by acute symptoms of sufficient severity such that the absence of immediate medical attention could reasonably be expected to place the patient's health in serious jeopardy.

(9) "Medical Provider Network Contact" ("MPN Contact") means the individual(s) designated by the MPN Applicant in the employee notification who is responsible for answering employees' questions about the Medical Provider Network and is responsible for assisting the employee in arranging for an Independent Medical Review.

(10) "Panel" means the contracted providers in a specific specialty.

(11) "Relevant medical records" means all information that was considered in relation to the disputed treatment or diagnostic service, including: (A) a copy of all correspondence from, and received by, any treating physician who provided a treatment or diagnostic service to the injured employee in connection with the injury; (B) a complete and legible copy of all medical records and other information used by the physicians in making a decision regarding the disputed treatment or diagnostic service; (C) the treating physician's report with the disputed treatment or diagnosis; and (D) the second and third opinion physicians' reports.

(12) "Residence" means the covered employee's primary residence.

NOTE: Authority cited: Sections 133 and 4616, Labor Code. Reference: Section 4616.4, Labor Code.

HISTORY

1. New article 3.6 (sections 9768.1–9768.17) and section filed 12–31–2004 as an emergency; operative 1–1–2005 (Register 2004, No. 53). A Certificate of Compliance must be transmitted to OAL by 5–2–2005 or emergency language will be repealed by operation of law on the following day.

2. Certificate of Compliance as to 12–31–2004 order, including amendment of section, transmitted to OAL 4–29–2005 and filed 6–10–2005 (Register 2005, No. 23).

§ 9768.2   Conflicts of Interest

(a) The IMR shall not have any material, professional, familial, or financial affiliation with any of the following:

(1) The injured employee's employer or employer's workers' compensation insurer;

(2) Any officer, director, management employee, or attorney of the injured employee's medical provider network, employer or employer's workers' compensation insurer;

(3) Any treating health care provider proposing the service or treatment;

(4) The institution at which the service or treatment would be provided, if known;

(5) The development or manufacture of the principal drug, device, procedure, or other therapy proposed for the injured employee whose treatment is under review; or

(6) The injured employee, the injured employee's immediate family, or the injured employee's attorney.

(b) The IMR shall not have a contractual agreement to provide physician services for the injured employee's MPN if the IMR is within a 35 mile radius of the treating physician.

(c) The IMR shall not have previously treated or examined the injured employee.

NOTE: Authority cited: Sections 133 and 4616, Labor Code. Reference: Section 4616.4, Labor Code.

HISTORY

1. New section filed 12–31–2004 as an emergency; operative 1–1–2005 (Register 2004, No. 53). A Certificate of Compliance must be transmitted to OAL by 5–2–2005 or emergency language will be repealed by operation of law on the following day.

2. Certificate of Compliance as to 12–31–2004 order transmitted to OAL 4–29–2005 and filed 6–10–2005 (Register 2005, No. 23).

§ 9768.3   Qualifications of Independent Medical Reviewers

(a) To qualify to be on the Administrative Director's list of Independent Medical Reviewers, a physician shall file a Physician Contract Application pursuant to section 9768.5 that demonstrates to the satisfaction of the Administrative Director that the physician:

(1) Is board certified. For physicians, the Administrative Director shall recognize only specialty boards recognized by the appropriate California licensing board.

(2) Has an unrestricted license as a physician in California under the appropriate licensing Board;

(3) Is not currently under accusation by any governmental licensing agency for a quality of care violation, fraud related to medical practice, or felony conviction or conviction of a crime related to the conduct of his or her practice of medicine;

(4) Has not been terminated or had discipline imposed by the Industrial Medical Council or Administrative Director in relation to the physician's role as a Qualified Medical Evaluator; is not currently under accusation by the Industrial Medical Council or Administrative Director; has not been denied renewal of Qualified Medical Evaluator status, except for non–completion of continuing education or for non–payment of fees; has neither resigned nor failed to renew Qualified Medical Evaluator status while under accusation or probation by the Industrial Medical Council or Administrative Director or after notification that reappointment as a Qualified Medical Evaluator may or would be denied for reasons other than non–completion of continuing education or non–payment of fees; and has not filed any applications or forms with the Industrial Medical Council or Administrative Director which contained any untrue material statements;

(5) Has not been convicted of a felony crime or a crime related to the conduct of his or her practice of medicine; and

(6) Has no history of disciplinary action or sanction, including but not limited to, loss of staff privileges or participation restrictions taken or pending by any hospital, government or regulatory body.

NOTE: Authority cited: Sections 133 and 4616, Labor Code. Reference: Section 4616.4, Labor Code.

HISTORY

1. New section filed 12–31–2004 as an emergency; operative 1–1–2005 (Register 2004, No. 53). A Certificate of Compliance must be transmitted to OAL by 5–2–2005 or emergency language will be repealed by operation of law on the following day.

2. Certificate of Compliance as to 12–31–2004 order, including amendment of subsections (a) and (a)(3), transmitted to OAL 4–29–2005 and filed 6–10–2005 (Register 2005, No. 23).

§ 9768.4.   IMR Contract Application Procedures

(a) A physician seeking to serve as an Independent Medical Reviewer shall:

(1) Apply to the Administrative Director on the Physician Contract Application set forth in section 9768.5.

(2) Furnish a certified copy of his or her board certification, a copy of his or her current license to practice medicine, and submit other documentation of his or her qualifications as the Administrative Director may require.

(3) Designate specialties based on each of his or her board certifications.

(4) Designate the address(es) of the physician's office with necessary medical equipment where in–person examinations will be held.

(5) Agree to see any injured worker assigned to him or her within 30 days unless there is a conflict of interest as defined in section 9768.2.

(6) During the application process and after being notified by the Administrative Director that the contract application has been accepted, the physician shall keep the Administrative Director informed of any change of address, telephone, email address or fax number, and of any disciplinary action taken by a licensing board.

(b) The contract application, completed by the physician, and any supporting documentation included with the contract application, shall be filed at the Administrative Director's office listed on the form. The contract application submitted by the physician may be rejected if it is incomplete, contains false information or does not contain the required supporting documentation listed in this section.

(c) The Administrative Director shall maintain a list of physicians who have applied, and whom the Administrative Director has contracted with to conduct Independent Medical Reviews under Labor Code section 4616.4.

(d) The IMR contract term is two years. A physician may apply to serve for subsequent two year terms by following the procedure set forth in subdivision (a).

NOTE: Authority cited: Sections 133 and 4616, Labor Code. Reference: Section 4616.4, Labor Code.

HISTORY

1. New section filed 12–31–2004 as an emergency; operative 1–1–2005 (Register 2004, No. 53). A Certificate of Compliance must be transmitted to OAL by 5–2–2005 or emergency language will be repealed by operation of law on the following day.

2. Certificate of Compliance as to 12–31–2004 order, including amendment of subsections (a) and (c), transmitted to OAL 4–29–2005 and filed 6–10–2005 (Register 2005, No. 23).

§ 9768.5.   Physician Contract Application Form

Physician application contract DWC form 9768.5 (pdf)

Note to physicians: please use three letter specialty code when completing block 3 of application form)

SPECIALTY CODES

Code	Specialty	Code	Specialty
MAI	Allergy and Immunology	MPO	Occupational Medicine
MAA	Anesthesiology	MOP	Opthalmology
MRS	Colon & Rectal Surgery	MOSG	Orthopaedic Surgery (General)
MDE	Dermatology	MOSS	Orthopaedic – Shoulder
MEM	Emergency Medicine	MOSK	Orthopaedic – Knee
MFP	Family Practice	MOSB	Orthopaedic – Spine
MPM	General Preventive Medicine	MOSF	Orthopaedic – Foot and ankle
MOSU	Hand – Orthopaedic Surgery, Plastic Surgery, General Surgery	MTO	Otolaryngology
MMM	Internal Medicine	MAP	Pain Management – Psychiatry and Neurology, Physical Medicine and Rehabilitation, Anesthesiology
MMV	Internal Medicine – Cardiovascular Disease	MHA	Pathology
MME	Internal Medicine – Endocrinology Diabetes and Metabolism	MEP	Pediatrics
MMG	Internal Medicine – Gastroenterology	MPR	Physical Medicine & Rehabilitation
MMH	Internal Medicine – Hematology	MPS	Plastic Surgery
MMI	Internal Medicine – Infectious Disease	MPD	Psychiatry
MMO	Internal Medicine – Medical Oncology	MSY	Surgery
MMN	Internal Medicine – Nephrology	MSG	Surgery – General Vascular
MMP	Internal Medicine – Pulmonary Disease	MTS	Thoracic Surgery
MMR	Internal Medicine – Rheumatology	MTO	Toxicology – Preventive Medicine, Pediatrics, Emergency
MPN	Neurology	MUU	Urology
MNS	Neurological Surgery	MRD	Radiology
MNM	Nuclear Medicine	POD	Podiatry
MOG	Obstetrics and Gynecology		

DWC Form 9768.5 11/2006

NOTE: Authority cited: Sections 133 and 4616, Labor Code. Reference: Section 4616.4, Labor Code.Authority cited: Sections 133 and 4616, Labor Code. Reference: Section 4616.4, Labor Code.

HISTORY

1. New section filed 12–31–2004 as an emergency; operative 1–1–2005 (Register 2004, No. 53). A Certificate of Compliance must be transmitted to OAL by 5–2–2005 or emergency language will be repealed by operation of law on the following day.

2. Certificate of Compliance as to 12–31–2004 order, including amendment of section, transmitted to OAL 4–29–2005 and filed 6–10–2005 (Register 2005, No. 23).

3. Change without regulatory effect amending form filed 10–18–2006 pursuant to section 100, title 1, California Code of Regulations (Register 2006, No.42).

§ 9768.6. Administrative Director's Action on Contract Application Submitted by Physician

(a) After reviewing a completed contract application submitted by a physician, if the Administrative Director finds that the physician meets the qualifications, he/she shall accept the contract application made by the physician to be an Independent Medical Reviewer by executing the IMR contract, notify the physician by mail, and add the physician's name to the list of Independent Medical Reviewers. The contract term shall be for a two–year term beginning with the date of acceptance by the Administrative Director.

(b) If the Administrative Director determines that a physician does not meet the qualifications, he/she shall notify the physician by mail that the physician's contract application is not accepted and the reason for the rejection.

(c) A physician whose contract application has not been accepted may reapply.

(d) If the Administrative Director denies a physician's contract application following at least two subsequent submissions, the physician may seek further review of the Administrative Director's decision by filing an appeal with the Workers' Compensation Appeals Board, and serving a copy on the Administrative Director, within twenty days after receipt of the denial.

NOTE: Authority cited: Sections 133 and 4616, Labor Code. Reference: Sections 4616.4 and 5300(f), Labor Code.

HISTORY
1. New section filed 12–31–2004 as an emergency; operative 1–1–2005 (Register 2004, No. 53). A Certificate of Compliance must be transmitted to OAL by 5–2–2005 or emergency language will be repealed by operation of law on the following day.
2. Certificate of Compliance as to 12–31–2004 order, including amendment of subsection (a), transmitted to OAL 4–29–2005 and filed 6–10–2005 (Register 2005, No. 23).

§ 9768.7. IMR Request to Be Placed on Voluntary Inactive Status

A physician may request to be placed on the inactive list during the IMR contract term. The physician shall submit the request to the Administrative Director and specify the time period that he or she is requesting to be on voluntary inactive status. The two–year contract term is not extended due to a physician's request to be placed on voluntary inactive status.

NOTE: Authority cited: Sections 133 and 4616, Labor Code. Reference: Section 4616.4, Labor Code.

HISTORY
1. New section filed 12–31–2004 as an emergency; operative 1–1–2005 (Register 2004, No. 53). A Certificate of Compliance must be transmitted to OAL by 5–2–2005 or emergency language will be repealed by operation of law on the following day.
2. Certificate of Compliance as to 12–31–2004 order transmitted to OAL 4–29–2005 and filed 6–10–2005 (Register 2005, No. 23).

§ 9768.8. Removal of Physicians from Independent Medical Reviewer List

(a) The Administrative Director may cancel the IMR contract and remove a physician from the Independent Medical Reviewer list if the Administrative Director determines based upon the Administrative Director's monitoring of reports:
  (1) That the physician, having been notified by the Administrative Director of the physician's selection to render an Independent Medical Review, has not issued the Independent Medical Review report in a case within the time limits prescribed in these regulations on more than one occasion; or
  (2) That the physician has not met the reporting requirements on more than one occasion; or
  (3) That the physician has at any time failed to disclose to the Administrative Director that the physician had a conflict of interest pursuant to section 9768.2; or
  (4) That the physician has failed to schedule appointments within the time frame required by these regulations on more than one occasion; or
  (5) That the physician has failed to maintain the confidentiality of medical records and the review materials consistent with the applicable state and federal law.

(b) The Administrative Director shall cancel the IMR contract and remove a physician from the Independent Medical Reviewer list if the Administrative Director determines:
  (1) That the physician no longer meets the qualifications to be on the list; or

(2) That the physician's contract application to be on the list contained material statements which were not true.

(c) The Administrative Director shall place a physician on an inactive list for up to the end of the two year contract term whenever the Administrative Director determines that the appropriate licensing Board from whom the physician is licensed has filed an accusation for a quality of care violation, fraud related to medical practice, or conviction of a felony crime or a crime related to the conduct of his or her practice of medicine against the physician or taken other action restricting the physician's medical license. If the accusation or action is later withdrawn, dismissed or determined to be without merit during the two year contract term, the physician shall advise the Administrative Director who will then remove the physician's name from the inactive list. If the accusation or action is withdrawn, dismissed or determined to be without merit after the expiration of the two year contract term, the physician may reapply to serve as an Independent Medical Reviewer pursuant to section 9768.4.

(d) Upon removal of a physician from the Independent Medical Reviewer list or placement on the inactive list, the Administrative Director shall advise the physician by mail of the removal or placement on the inactive list, the Administrative Director's reasons for such action, and the right to request a hearing on the removal from the IMR list or placement on the inactive list.

(e) A physician who has been mailed a notice of removal from the list or placement on the inactive list, may, within 30 calendar days of the mailing of the notice, request a hearing by filing a written request for hearing with the Administrative Director. If a written request for hearing is not received by the Administrative Director within 30 calendar days of the mailing of the notice, the physician shall be deemed to have waived any appeal or request for hearing.

(f) Upon receipt of a written request for hearing, the Administrative Director shall prepare an accusation and serve the applicant physician with the accusation, as provided in Government Code section 11503.

(g) Hearings shall be held by the Administrative Director or his or her designee under the procedures of Chapter 5 of Part 1 of Division 3 of Title 2 of the Government Code (commencing with section 11500) and the regulations of the Office of Administrative Hearings (Title 1, California Code of Regulations, section 1000 et seq.).

(h) Failure to timely file a notice of defense or failure to appear at a noticed hearing or conference shall constitute a waiver of a right to a hearing.

(i) A physician who has been removed from the list may petition for reinstatement after one year has elapsed since the effective date of the Administrative Director's decision on the physician's removal. The provisions of Government Code section 11522 shall apply to such petition.

NOTE: Authority cited: Sections 133 and 4616, Labor Code; and Section 11400.20, Government Code. Reference: Section 4616.4, Labor Code; and Sections 11415.10, 11503 and 11522, Government Code.

HISTORY
1. New section filed 12–31–2004 as an emergency; operative 1–1–2005 (Register 2004, No. 53). A Certificate of Compliance must be transmitted to OAL by 5–2–2005 or emergency language will be repealed by operation of law on the following day.
2. Certificate of Compliance as to 12–31–2004 order, including amendment of section, transmitted to OAL 4–29–2005 and filed 6–10–2005 (Register 2005, No. 23).

§ 9768.9. Procedure for Requesting an Independent Medical Review

(a) If a covered employee disputes the diagnostic service, diagnosis, or medical treatment prescribed by the second opinion physician, the injured employee may seek the opinion of a third physician in the MPN. The covered employee and the employer or insurer shall comply with the requirements of section 9767.7(d). Additionally, at the time of the selection of the physician for a third opinion, the MPN Contact shall notify the covered employee about the Independent Medical Review process and provide the covered employee with an "Independent Medical Review Application" form set forth in section 9768.10. The MPN Contact shall fill out the "MPN Contact Section" of the form and list the specialty of the treating physician and an alternative specialty, if any, that is different from the specialty of the treating physician.

(b) If a covered employee disputes either the diagnostic service, diagnosis or medical treatment prescribed by the third opinion physician, the covered employee may request an Independent Medical Review by filing the completed Independent Medical Review Application form with the Administrative Director. The covered employee shall complete the "employee section" of the form, indicate on the form whether he or she requests an in–person examination or record review, and may list an alternative specialty, if any, that is different from the specialty of the treating physician.

(c) The Administrative Director shall select an IMR with an appropriate specialty within ten business days of receiving the Independent Medical Review Application form. The Administrative Director's selection of the IMR shall be based on the specialty of the treating physician, the alternative specialties listed by the covered employee and the MPN Contact, and the information submitted with the Independent Medical Review Application.

(d) If the covered employee requests an in–person examination, the Administrative Director shall randomly select a physician from the panel of available Independent Medical Reviewers, with an appropriate specialty, who has an office located within thirty miles of the employee's residence address, to be the Independent Medical Reviewer. If there is only one physician with an appropriate specialty within thirty miles of the employee's residence address, that physician shall be selected to be the Independent Medical Reviewer. If there are no physicians with an appropriate specialty who have offices located within thirty miles of the employee's residence address, the Administrative Director shall search in increasing five mile increments, until one physician is located. If there are no available physicians with this appropriate specialty, the Administrative Director may choose another specialty based on the information submitted.

(e) If the covered employee requests a record review, then the Administrative Director shall randomly select a physician with an appropriate specialty from the panel of available Independent Medical Reviewers to be the IMR. If there are no physicians with an appropriate specialty, the Administrative Director may choose another specialty based on the information submitted.

(f) The Administrative Director shall send written notification of the name and contact information of the IMR to the covered employee, the employee's attorney, if any, the MPN Contact and the IMR. The Administrative Director shall send a copy of the completed Independent Medical Review Application to the IMR.

(g) The covered employee, MPN Contact, or the selected IMR can object within 10 calendar days of receipt of the name of the IMR to the selection if there is a conflict of interest as defined by section 9768.2. If the IMR determines that he or she does not practice the appropriate specialty, the IMR shall withdraw within 10 calendar days of receipt of the notification of selection. If this conflict is verified or the IMR withdraws, the Administrative Director shall select another IMR from the same specialty. If there are no available physicians with the same specialty, the Administrative Director may select an IMR with another specialty based on the information submitted and in accordance with the procedure set forth in subdivision (d) for an in–person examination and subdivision (e) for a record review.

(h) If the covered employee requests an in–person exam, within 60 calendar days of receiving the name of the IMR, the covered employee shall contact the IMR to arrange an appointment. If the covered employee fails to contact the IMR for an appointment within 60 calendar days of receiving the name of the IMR, then the employee shall be deemed to have waived the IMR process with regard to this disputed diagnosis or treatment of this treating physician. The IMR shall schedule an appointment with the covered employee within 30 calendar days of the request for an appointment, unless all parties agree to a later date. The IMR shall notify the MPN Contact of the appointment date.

(i) The covered employee shall provide written notice to the Administrative Director and the MPN Contact if the covered employee decides to withdraw the request for an Independent Medical Reviewer.

(j) During this process, the employee shall remain within the MPN for treatment pursuant to section 9767.6.

NOTE: Authority cited: Sections 133 and 4616, Labor Code. Reference: Sections 4616.3 and 4616.4, Labor Code.

HISTORY

1. New section filed 12–31–2004 as an emergency; operative 1–1–2005 (Register 2004, No. 53). A Certificate of Compliance must be transmitted to OAL by 5–2–2005 or emergency language will be repealed by operation of law on the following day.
2. Certificate of Compliance as to 12–31–2004 order, including amendment of section, transmitted to OAL 4–29–2005 and filed 6–10–2005 (Register 2005, No. 23).

§ 9768.10. Application for Independent Medical Review (Form)

NOTE: Authority cited: Sections 133 and 4616, Labor Code. Reference: Sections 4616.3 and 4616.4, Labor Code.

HISTORY

1. New section filed 12–31–2004 as an emergency; operative 1–1–2005 (Register 2004, No. 53). A Certificate of Compliance must be transmitted to OAL by 5–2–2005 or emergency language will be repealed by operation of law on the following day.
2. Certificate of Compliance as to 12–31–2004 order, including amendment of section heading and section, transmitted to OAL 4–29–2005 and filed 6–10–2005 (Register 2005, No. 23).
3. Change without regulatory effect amending form filed 10–18–2006 pursuant to section 100, title 1, California Code of Regulations (Register 2006, No.42).

§ 9768.11. In–Person Examination or Record Review IMR Procedure

(a) The MPN Contact shall send all relevant medical records to the IMR. The MPN Contact shall also send a copy of the documents to the covered employee. The employee may furnish any relevant medical records or additional materials to the Independent Medical Reviewer, with a copy to the MPN Contact. If an in–person examination is requested and if a special form of transportation is required because of the employee's medical condition, it is the obligation of the MPN Contact to arrange for it. The MPN Contact shall furnish transportation and arrange for an interpreter, if necessary, in advance of the in–person examination. All reasonable expenses of transportation shall be incurred by the insurer or employer pursuant to Labor Code section 4600. Except for the in–person examination itself, the Independent Medical Reviewer shall have no ex parte contact with any party. Except for matters dealing with scheduling appointments, scheduling medical tests and obtaining medical records, all communications between the Independent Medical Reviewer and any party shall be in writing, with copies served on all parties.

(b) If the IMR requires further tests, the IMR shall notify the MPN Contact within one working day of the appointment. All tests shall be consistent with the medical treatment utilization schedule adopted pursuant to Labor Code section 5307.27 or, prior to the adoption of this schedule, the ACOEM guidelines, and for all injuries not covered by the medical treatment utilization schedule or the ACOEM guidelines, in accordance with other evidence based medical treatment guidelines generally recognized by the national medical community and that are scientifically based.

(c) The IMR may order any diagnostic tests necessary to make his or her determination regarding medical treatment or diagnostic services for the injury or illness but shall not request the employee to submit to an unnecessary exam or procedure. If a test duplicates a test already given, the IMR shall provide justification for the duplicative test in his or her report.

(d) If the employee fails to attend an examination with the IMR and fails to reschedule the appointment within five business days of the missed appointment, the IMR shall perform a review of the record and make a determination based on those records.

(e) The IMR shall serve the report on the Administrative Director, the MPN Contact, the employee and the employee's attorney, if any, within 20 days after the in–person examination or completion of the record review.

(f) If the disputed health care service has not been provided and the IMR certifies in writing that an imminent and serious threat to the health of the injured employee exists, including, but not limited to, the potential loss of life, limb, or bodily function, or the immediate and serious deterioration of the injured employee, the report shall be expedited and rendered within three business days of the in–person examination by the IMR.

(g) Subject to approval by the Administrative Director, reviews not covered under subdivision (f) may be extended for up to three business days in extraordinary circumstances or for good cause.

(h) Extensions for good cause shall be granted for:
(1) Medical emergencies of the IMR or the IMR's family;
(2) Death in the IMR's family; or
(3) Natural disasters or other community catastrophes that interrupt the operation of the IMR's office operations.

(i) Utilizing the medical treatment utilization schedule established pursuant to Labor Code section 5307.27 or, prior to the adoption of this schedule, the ACOEM guidelines, and taking into account any reports and information provided, the IMR shall determine whether the disputed health care service is consistent with the recommended standards. For injuries not covered by the medical treatment utilization schedule or by the ACOEM guidelines, the treatment rendered shall be in accordance with other evidence–based medical treatment guidelines which are generally recognized by the national medical community and scientifically based.

(j) The IMR shall not treat or offer to provide medical treatment for that injury or illness for which he or she has done an Independent Medical Review evaluation for the employee unless a medical emergency arises during the in–person examination.

(k) Neither the employee nor the employer nor the insurer shall have any liability for payment for the Independent Medical Review which was not completed within the required timeframes unless the employee and the employer each waive the right to a new Independent Medical Review and elect to accept the original evaluation.

NOTE: Authority cited: Sections 133 and 4616, Labor Code. Reference: Sections 4616.4 and 5307.27, Labor Code.

HISTORY
1. New section filed 12–31–2004 as an emergency; operative 1–1–2005 (Register 2004, No. 53). A Certificate of Compliance must be transmitted to OAL by 5–2–2005 or emergency language will be repealed by operation of law on the following day.
2. Certificate of Compliance as to 12–31–2004 order, including amendment of subsections (a), (e), (j) and (k), transmitted to OAL 4–29–2005 and filed 6–10–2005 (Register 2005, No. 23).

§ 9768.12.   Contents of Independent Medical Review Reports

(a) Reports of Independent Medical Reviewers shall include:
(1) The date of the in–person examination or record review;
(2) The patient's complaint(s);
(3) A listing of all information received from the parties reviewed in preparation of the report or relied upon for the formulation of the physician's opinion;
(4) The patient's medical history relevant to the diagnostic services, diagnosis or medical treatment;
(5) Findings on record review or in–person examination;
(6) The IMR's diagnosis;

(7) The physician's opinion whether or not the proposed treatment or diagnostic services are appropriate and indicated. If the proposed treatment or diagnostic services are not appropriate or indicated, any alternative diagnosis or treatment recommendation consistent with the medical treatment utilization schedule shall be included;

(8) An analysis and determination whether the disputed health care service is consistent with the medical treatment utilization schedule established pursuant to Labor Code section 5307.27 or, prior to the adoption of this schedule, the ACOEM guidelines. For injuries not covered by the medical treatment utilization schedule or by the ACOEM guidelines, an analysis and determination whether the treatment rendered is in accordance with other evidence–based medical treatment guidelines which are generally recognized by the national medical community and scientifically based; and

(9) The signature of the physician.

(b) The report shall be in writing and use layperson's terms to the maximum extent possible.

(c) An Independent Medical Reviewer shall serve with each report the following executed declaration made under penalty of perjury:

"I declare under penalty of perjury that this report is true and correct to the best of my knowledge and that I have not violated Labor Code section 139.3.

_____
Date

_____ "
Signature

NOTE: Authority cited: Sections 133 and 4616, Labor Code. Reference: Sections 139.3, 4616.4 and 5307.27, Labor Code.

HISTORY

1. New section filed 12–31–2004 as an emergency; operative 1–1–2005 (Register 2004, No. 53). A Certificate of Compliance must be transmitted to OAL by 5–2–2005 or emergency language will be repealed by operation of law on the following day.

2. Certificate of Compliance as to 12–31–2004 order, including amendment of subsections (a) and (c), transmitted to OAL 4–29–2005 and filed 6–10–2005 (Register 2005, No. 23).

§ 9768.13.   Destruction of Records by the Administrative Director

The Administrative Director may destroy any forms or documents submitted to the Administrative Director as part of the IMR process two years after the date of receipt.

NOTE: Authority cited: Sections 133 and 4616, Labor Code. Reference: Section 4616.4, Labor Code.

HISTORY

1. New section filed 12–31–2004 as an emergency; operative 1–1–2005 (Register 2004, No. 53). A Certificate of Compliance must be transmitted to OAL by 5–2–2005 or emergency language will be repealed by operation of law on the following day.

2. Certificate of Compliance as to 12–31–2004 order transmitted to OAL 4–29–2005 and filed 6–10–2005 (Register 2005, No. 23).

§ 9768.14.   Retention of Records by Independent Medical Reviewer

Each Independent Medical Reviewer shall retain all comprehensive medical reports completed by the Independent Medical Reviewer for a period of five years from the date of the IMR report.

NOTE: Authority cited: Sections 133 and 4616, Labor Code. Reference: Section 4616.4, Labor Code.

HISTORY

1. New section filed 12–31–2004 as an emergency; operative 1–1–2005 (Register 2004, No. 53). A Certificate of Compliance must be transmitted to OAL by 5–2–2005 or emergency language will be repealed by operation of law on the following day.

2. Certificate of Compliance as to 12–31–2004 order, including amendment of section, transmitted to OAL 4–29–2005 and filed 6–10–2005 (Register 2005, No. 23).

§ 9768.15.   Charges for Independent Medical Reviewers

(a) Payment for the services of the Independent Medical Reviewers shall be made by the employer or insurer.
(b) The fee shall be based on the Official Medical Fee Schedule using confirmatory consultation codes (99271 through 99275 for in–person examinations or 99271 through 99273 for evaluations not requiring an in–person examination), 99080 for reports, and 99358 for record reviews, and any other appropriate codes or modifiers.
(c) An IMR shall not accept any additional compensation from any source for his or her services as an IMR except for services provided to treat a medical emergency that arose during an in–person examination pursuant to section 9768.11(j).

NOTE: Authority cited: Sections 133 and 4616, Labor Code. Reference: Section 4616.4, Labor Code.

HISTORY
1. New section filed 12–31–2004 as an emergency; operative 1–1–2005 (Register 2004, No. 53). A Certificate of Compliance must be transmitted to OAL by 5–2–2005 or emergency language will be repealed by operation of law on the following day.
2. Certificate of Compliance as to 12–31–2004 order, including amendment of subsections (a) and (b), transmitted to OAL 4–29–2005 and filed 6–10–2005 (Register 2005, No. 23).

§ 9768.16.   Adoption of Decision

(a) The Administrative Director shall immediately adopt the determination of the Independent Medical Reviewer and issue a written decision within 5 business days of receipt of the report.
(b) The parties may appeal the Administrative Director's written decision by filing a petition with the Workers' Compensation Appeals Board and serving a copy on the Administrative Director, within twenty days after receipt of the decision.

NOTE: Authority cited: Sections 133 and 4616, Labor Code. Reference: Sections 4616.4 and 5300(f), Labor Code.

HISTORY
1. New section filed 12–31–2004 as an emergency; operative 1–1–2005 (Register 2004, No. 53). A Certificate of Compliance must be transmitted to OAL by 5–2–2005 or emergency language will be repealed by operation of law on the following day.
2. Certificate of Compliance as to 12–31–2004 order, including amendment of subsection (a), transmitted to OAL 4–29–2005 and filed 6–10–2005 (Register 2005, No. 23).

§ 9768.17.   Treatment Outside the Medical Provider Network

(a) If the IMR agrees with the diagnosis, diagnostic service or medical treatment prescribed by the treating physician, the covered employee shall continue to receive medical treatment from physicians within the MPN.
(b) If the IMR does not agree with the disputed diagnosis, diagnostic service or medical treatment prescribed by the treating physician, the covered employee shall seek medical treatment with a physician of his or her choice either within or outside the MPN. If the employee chooses to receive medical treatment with a physician outside the MPN, the treatment is limited to the treatment recommended by the IMR or the diagnostic service recommended by the IMR.
(c) The medical treatment shall be consistent with the medical treatment utilization schedule established pursuant to Labor Code section 5307.27 or, prior to the adoption of this schedule, the ACOEM guidelines. For injuries not covered by the medical treatment utilization schedule or by the ACOEM guidelines, the treatment rendered shall be in accordance with other evidence–based medical treatment guidelines which are generally recognized by the national medical community and scientifically based.
(d) The employer or insurer shall be liable for the cost of any approved medical treatment in accordance with Labor Code section 5307.1 or 5307.11.

NOTE: Authority cited: Sections 133 and 4616, Labor Code. Reference: Sections 4616.4, 5307.1, 5307.11 and 5307.27, Labor Code.

HISTORY
1. New section filed 12–31–2004 as an emergency; operative 1–1–2005 (Register 2004, No. 53). A Certificate of Compliance must be transmitted to OAL by 5–2–2005 or emergency language will be repealed by operation of law on the following day.
2. Certificate of Compliance as to 12–31–2004 order, including amendment of Note, transmitted to OAL 4–29–2005 and filed 6–10–2005 (Register 2005, No. 23).

Intentionally blank

Forms

Intentionally blank

PHYSICIAN CONTRACT APPLICATION
(INDEPENDENT MEDICAL REVIEWER)
For the Department of Industrial Relations
Division of Workers' Compensation
P.O. Box 71010
Oakland, CA 94612

FOR OFFICE USE ONLY
NO.:
INPUT DATE:
INPUT BY:

BLOCK 1

PLEASE TYPE OR PRINT LEGIBLY

Please list your primary location. **DO NOT USE P.O. BOX. You may provide additional office addresses at which you may schedule appointments, on a separate sheet.**

LAST NAME | FIRST NAME | MI | JR/SR

BUSINESS ADDRESS | CITY | ZIP+4

MAILING ADDRESS, if different from above | CITY | ZIP+4

E-MAIL ADDRESS

(AREA CODE) PHONE NO. | (AREA CODE) FAX NO. | CAL. PROFESSIONAL LICENSE NUMBER | EXPIRATION (MM/YY)

BLOCK 2

MEDICAL/GRADUATE SCHOOL

CITY | STATE | DEGREE | DATE OF DEGREE

ALL PHYSICIANS are to furnish their board certification and current hospital privileges, if applicable.
PLEASE LIST:

Hospital/Facility	Location (City/State)	Type	From	To
Hospital/Facility	Location (City/State)	Type	From	To

BLOCK 3   PHYSICIANS MUST MEET THE FOLLOWING REQUIREMENTS   Yes No

1) I am board certified in a specialty recognized by the appropriate California licensing Board. ☐ ☐
List name(s) of board: _____

2) Date of expiration of board certification, if applicable _____

3) List the requested specialty codes using the three digit specialty codes listed on page 5 _____

BLOCK 4

Physicians are prohibited from serving as an IMR in cases in which they have a material professional, familial, or financial affiliation with any of the parties or companies involved. YOU are responsible for determining whether you have one of these affiliations in any particular case, and for recusing yourself, although the Administrative Director will attempt to screen out any cases in which a conflict of interest is apparent from the names of all companies with which you have a material professional, familial or financial affiliation, as defined in the Regulations. **Please list entities with which you have an affiliation, and respond "not applicable" if appropriate.**

Workers' Compensation Insurance Companies

1.	3.
2.	4.

Workers' Compensation Third Party Administrators

1.	3.
2.	4.

Utilization Review Companies

1.	3.
2.	4.

Medical Provider Networks (Name or MPN number)

1.	3.
2.	4.

Hospitals or Ambulatory Surgery Centers (Please include the address(es) of the facility)

1.	3.
2.	4.

Drugs, Devices, Procedures or Therapies

1.	3.
2.	4.

** PROVIDE ADDITIONAL SHEETS WHEN NECESSARY**

BLOCK 5   PLEASE CHECK:

1) That the physician sections of this contract are fully completed, dated and signed with an original signature. We will not accept faxed applications.
2) That all necessary documentation is attached:
   - ❖ A Copy of your current California Professional License.
   - ❖ A Copy of your board certification(s).
   - ❖ Certification of your current hospital privileges, if applicable.

IMPORTANT: Your contract application to be an Independent Medical Review Physician shall be returned if it incomplete, and it must be submitted prior to obtaining your appointment.

	Yes	No

License Status

Have you ever been formally disciplined by any State Medical Licensing Board? ☐ ☐
*If the answer is "Yes", please furnish full particulars on a separate sheet.

Is any accusation by any State medical licensing board for a quality of care violation, ☐ ☐
fraud related to medical practice, or felony conviction or conviction of a crime related
to the conduct of your practice of medicine currently pending against you?
*If the answer is "Yes", please furnish full particulars on a separate sheet.

Have you ever lost hospital staff privileges? ☐ ☐
*If the answer is "Yes", please furnish full particulars on a separate sheet.

My license to practice medicine is active and is neither restricted nor encumbered by ☐ ☐
suspension, interim suspension or probation.
*If the answer is "No", please furnish full particulars on a separate sheet.

I agree to notify the Administrative Director if my license to practice medicine is placed on ☐ ☐
suspension, interim suspension, probation or is restricted by my licensing agency,
if my Board Certification is revoked, if my hospital staff privileges are revoked, or if I am
convicted of a felony crime or a crime related to the conduct of my practice of medicine.

Verification

I understand that by submitting this contract application, I am offering to be an Independent Medical Reviewer. I have used reasonable diligence in preparing and completing this contract application. I have reviewed this completed contract application and to the best of my knowledge the information contained herein and in the attached supporting documentation is true, correct and complete. I understand that if this contract application is accepted that I will be placed on the list of eligible Independent Medical Reviewers. I understand that the Title 8, California Code of Regulations, sections 9768.1 et seq. set forth requirements that I must comply with and I agree to comply with those requirements. I understand that I must maintain the confidentiality of medical records and the rview materials consistent wit the applicable state and federal law. I confirm that I am familiar with the *American College of Occupational and Environmental Medicine's Occupational Medicine Practice Guidelines*, 2nd Edition (2004), published by OEM Press. If the Administrative Director adopts a medical treatment utilization schedule pursuant to Labor Code section 5307.27 during the two-year term of this contract, I agree to become familiar with that schedule no later than its effective date. I understand that this contract application is not accepted by the Administrative Director of the Division of Workers' Compensation until is it signed by the Administrative Director. I declare under penalty of perjury under the laws of the state of California that the foregoing is true and correct.

Executed on _____ at _____, CA _____
 (MM/DD/YY)   County   Applicant's Signature

A PUBLIC DOCUMENT

PRIVACY NOTICE – The Information Practices Act of 1977 and the Federal Privacy Act Require the Administrative Director to provide the following notice to individuals who are asked by a governmental entity to supply information for appointment as an Independent Medical Reviewer physician.

The California Labor Code provides for physicians and surgeons to participate in the workers' compensation Independent Medical Reviewer program. The Division of Workers' Compensation has adopted regulations which require applicants under this program to provide: name; business address, professional education, training, license number, board certifications, fellowships, conflicts of interest, and documents deemed necessary by the Administrative Director of the Division of Workers' Compensation. It is mandatory to furnish all the appropriate information requested by the Administrative Director. This contract may not be accepted if all the requested information is not provided.

The principal purpose for requesting information from physicians and surgeons is to administer the Independent Medical Review program within the California workers' compensation system. Additional information may be requested.

As authorized by law, information furnished on this form may be given to: you, upon request; the public pursuant to the Public Records Act; a governmental entity, when required by state of federal law; to any person pursuant to a subpoena or court order or pursuant to any other exception in Civil Code § 1798.24.

An individual has a right of access to records containing his/her personal information that are maintained by the Administrative Director. An individual may also amend, correct, or dispute information in such personal records. (Civil Code § 1798.34-1798.37.)
Requests should be sent to:

> Division of Workers' Compensation – Medical Unit
> P.O. Box 71010
> Oakland, CA 94612

Copies of all records are ten cents ($0.10) per page, payable in advance. (Civil Code § 1798.33.)

ACCEPTANCE OF CONTRACT APPLICATION BY ADMINISTRATIVE DIRECTOR

The Administrative Director of the Division of Workers' Compensation accepts this contract application and agrees to add this physician's name to the list of eligible Independent Medical Reviewers for a two year term beginning with the date this contract is executed.

Executed on _____ at _____, CA _____
             (MM/DD/YY)   County   Administrative Director

(Note to physicians: please use three letter specialty code when completing block 3 of application form)

SPECIALTY CODES

AI	Allergy and Immunology
AA	Anesthesiology
RS	Colon & Rectal Surgery
DE	Dermatology
EM	Emergency Medicine
FP	Family Practice
PM	General Preventive Medicine
OSU	Hand – Orthopaedic Surgery, Plastic Surgery, General Surgery
MM	Internal Medicine
MV	Internal Medicine – Cardiovascular Disease
ME	Internal Medicine – Endocrinology Diabetes and Metabolism
MG	Internal Medicine – Gastroenterology
MH	Internal Medicine – Hematology
MI	Internal Medicine – Infectious Disease
MO	Internal Medicine – Medical Oncology
MN	Internal Medicine - Nephrology
MP	Internal Medicine – Pulmonary Disease
MR	Internal Medicine – Rheumatology
PN	Neurology
NS	Neurological Surgery
NM	Nuclear Medicine
OG	Obstetrics and Gynecology
PO	Occupational Medicine
OP	Opthalmology
OSG	Orthopaedic Surgery (General)
OSS	Orthopaedic –Shoulder
OSK	Orthopaedic –Knee
OSB	Orthopaedic –Spine
OSF	Orthopaedic –Foot and ankle
TO	Otolaryngology
AP	Pain Management –Psychiatry and Neurology, Physical Medicine and Rehabilitation, Anesthesiology
HA	Pathology
EP	Pediatrics
PR	Physical Medicine & Rehabilitation
PS	Plastic Surgery
PD	Psychiatry
SY	Surgery
SG	Surgery – General Vascular
TS	Thoracic Surgery
TO	Toxicology – Preventive Medicine, Pediatrics, Emergency
UU	Urology
RD	Radiology
OD	Podiatry

WC Form 9768.5   5
May 2007

Independent Medical Review Application
(Division of Workers' Compensation – 8 CCR §9768.10 Mandatory Form)

yee Section: The Employee shall complete this section and send the completed form to the Administrative Director. g address: Dept. of Industrial Relations, Division of Workers' Compensation, P.O. Box 71010, Oakland, CA 94612.

| yee Name | Employee Phone Number / Fax | Employee's Address |

| vee's Attorney's Name, if applicable | Attorney's Phone Number / Fax | Attorney's Address |

ant to Labor Code section 4616.4, I request that the Administrative Director set an Independent Medical Review 30 days from receipt of this Application.

one: ☐ Request for In-Person Examination   ☐ Request for Record Review (no In-Person Examination)

preter needed for exam? _____ If yes, language: _____

be diagnosis and part of body affected: _____

n for request for Independent Medical Review. Please explain if the dispute involves the diagnosis, treatment or a test additional page or additional materials, such as medical records, if necessary):

_____

an alternative specialty, other than specialty of treating physician, if any, from the list on the instructions for this form:

_____

se: I, _____ (injured employee or person authorized pursuant to law to act on behalf of the injured yee), authorize the release of relevant medical records to the Independent Medical Reviewer.

| re of injured employee or authorized person | Date |

al Provider Network Contact Section: The MPN Contact shall complete this section and send the form to the employee.

| yee | Employer |

| | Claim Number |

| l Provider Network | Date of Injury |

| g Physician | Specialty | Address |

| pinion Physician and specialty | 3rd Opinion Physician and specialty |

an alternative specialty other than specialty of treating physician, if any, from the list on the back of this form:

_____

re under penalty of perjury that I mailed a copy of the Application for IMR to the above named Employee on

| Signature | Phone number, fax, and email of MPN Contact |

| of MPN Contact | Address |

Instructions for Independent Medical Review Application Form

Instructions for MPN Contact: At the time of the selection of the physician for a third opinion, you are required to notify the covered employee about the Independent Medical Review process and provide the covered employee with this "Independent Medical Review Application" form. You are required to fill out the "MPN Contact section" of the form. You must then send the form to the employee, who will fill out the top section of the form and send it to the Division of Workers' Compensation. The DWC will send you written notification of the name and contact information of the Independent Medical Reviewer. You must then send the employee's relevant medical records as defined by section 9768.1(a)(11) to the Independent Medical Reviewer. A copy of the medical reports must also be sent to the employee.

Instructions for Injured Employee: This application is being sent to you because you have requested a third opinion to address your dispute with your treating doctor's diagnosis, suggested test, or suggested medical treatment. **Please wait until you read the report from the third opinion doctor before you fill out this form.** If the report resolves your dispute, then you do not need to fill out this form. If you still have a dispute with your treating doctor, then you may request an Independent Medical Review by completing this form and sending it to:

Dept. of Industrial Relations
Division of Workers' Compensation
P.O. Box 71010
Oakland, CA 94612.

An Independent Medical Review is done by a physician who does not work directly with your doctor. You can visit the doctor and be examined or you can choose to have the doctor review your records. Indicate on the form whether you want to be examined (in-person examination) or if you only want to have your records reviewed.

The specialty of the doctor will be the same as the specialty of your treating physician, if possible. Not all types of doctors can be an Independent Medical Reviewer. You may select another type of doctor in case your doctor's specialty is not available. To do this, look at the list of specialists below and chose one type. Indicate this choice on the application. You will receive the name and contact information of the Independent Medical Reviewer from the Division of Workers' Compensation. When you receive the name of the Independent Medical Reviewer, you must make an appointment within 60 days. The Independent Medical Reviewer is required to schedule an appointment with you within 30 days. If you fail to make the appointment with the Independent Medical Reviewer within 60 days, you will not be allowed to have an Independent Medical Review on this dispute. **Written notice must be made to the Administrative Director and MPN Contact if you wish to withdraw the request for an Independent Medical Review after this form has been submitted.**

SPECIALTY CODES

MAI	Allergy and Immunology	**MAA**	Anesthesiology
MRS	Colon & Rectal Surgery	**MDE**	Dermatology
MEM	Emergency Medicine	**MFP**	Family Practice
MPM	General Preventive Medicine	**MHD**	Hand – Orthopaedic Surgery, Plastic Surgery, General Surgery
MMM	Internal Medicine	**MMV**	Internal Medicine – Cardiovascular Disease
MME	Internal Medicine – Endocrinology Diabetes and Metabolism	**MMG**	Internal Medicine - Gastroenterology
MMH	Internal Medicine – Hematology	**MMI**	Internal Medicine – Infectious Disease
MMO	Internal Medicine – Medical Oncology	**MMN**	Internal Medicine - Nephrology
MMP	Internal Medicine – Pulmonary Disease	**MMR**	Internal Medicine – Rheumatology
MPN	Neurology	**MNS**	Neurological Surgery
MNM	Nuclear Medicine	**MOG**	Obstetrics and Gynecology
MPO	Occupational Medicine	**MOP**	Ophthalmology
MOS	Orthopaedic Surgery	**MTO**	Otolaryngology
MAP	Pain Management –Psychiatry and Neurology, Physical Medicine and Rehabilitation, Anesthesiology	**MHA**	Pathology
MEP	Pediatrics	**MPR**	Physical Medicine & Rehabilitation
MPS	Plastic Surgery	**MPD**	Psychiatry
MRD	Radiology	**MSY**	Surgery
MSG	Surgery – General Vascular	**MTS**	Thoracic Surgery
MTX	Toxicology – Preventive Medicine, Pediatrics, Emergency	**MUU**	Urology
POD	Podiatry		

Appendix C

● Utilization Review Standards (UR)

Article 5.5.1. Utilization Review Standards

§ 9792.6.   Utilization Review Standards

As used in this Article:

(a) "ACOEM Practice Guidelines" means the American College of Occupational and Environmental Medicine's Occupational Medicine Practice Guidelines, Second Edition.

(b) "Authorization" means assurance that appropriate reimbursement will be made for an approved specific course of proposed medical treatment to cure or relieve the effects of the industrial injury pursuant to section 4600 of the Labor Code, subject to the provisions of section 5402 of the Labor Code, based on the Doctor's First Report of Occupational Injury or Illness," Form DLSR 5021, or on the "Primary Treating Physician's Progress Report," DWC Form PR–2, as contained in section 9785.2, or in narrative form containing the same information required in the DWC Form PR–2.

(c) "Claims Administrator" is a self–administered workers' compensation insurer, an insured employer, a self–administered self–insured employer, a self–administered legally uninsured employer, a self–administered joint powers authority, a third–party claims administrator or other entity subject to Labor Code section 4610. The claims administrator may utilize an entity contracted to conduct its utilization review responsibilities.

(d) "Concurrent review" means utilization review conducted during an inpatient stay.

(e) "Course of treatment" means the course of medical treatment set forth in the treatment plan contained on the "Doctor's First Report of Occupational Injury or Illness," Form DLSR 5021, or on the "Primary Treating Physician's Progress Report," DWC Form PR–2, as contained in section 9785.2 or in narrative form containing the same information required in the DWC Form PR–2.

(f) "Emergency health care services" means health care services for a medical condition manifesting itself by acute symptoms of sufficient severity such that the absence of immediate medical attention could reasonably be expected to place the patient's health in serious jeopardy.

(g) "Expedited review" means utilization review conducted when the injured worker's condition is such that the injured worker faces an imminent and serious threat to his or her health, including, but not limited to, the potential loss of life, limb, or other major bodily function, or the normal timeframe for the decision–making process would be detrimental to the injured worker's life or health or could jeopardize the injured worker's permanent ability to regain maximum function.

(h) "Expert reviewer" means a medical doctor, doctor of osteopathy, psychologist, acupuncturist, optometrist, dentist, podiatrist, or chiropractic practitioner licensed by any state or the District of Columbia, competent to evaluate the specific clinical issues involved in the medical treatment services and where these services are within the individual's scope of practice, who has been consulted by the reviewer or the utilization review medical director to provide specialized review of medical information.

(i) "Health care provider" means a provider of medical services, as well as related services or goods, including but not limited to an individual provider or facility, a health care service plan, a health care organization, a member of a preferred provider organization or medical provider network as provided in Labor Code section 4616.

(j) "Immediately" means within 24 hours after learning the circumstances that would require an extension of the timeframe for decisions specified in subdivisions (b)(1), (b)(2) or (c) and (g)(1) of section 9792.9.

(k) "Material modification" is when the claims administrator changes utilization review vendor or makes a change to the utilization review standards as specified in section 9792.7.

(l) "Medical Director" is the physician and surgeon licensed by the Medical Board of California or the Osteopathic Board of California who holds an unrestricted license to practice medicine in the State of California. The Medical Director is responsible for all decisions made in the utilization review process.

(m) "Medical services" means those goods and services provided pursuant to Article 2 (commencing with Labor Code section 4600) of Chapter 2 of Part 2 of Division 4 of the Labor Code.

(n) "Prospective review" means any utilization review conducted, except for utilization review conducted during an inpatient stay, prior to the delivery of the requested medical services.

(o) "Request for authorization" means a written confirmation of an oral request for a specific course of proposed medical treatment pursuant to Labor Code section 4610(h) or a written request for a specific course of proposed medical treatment. An oral request for authorization must be followed by a written confirmation of the request within seventy–two (72) hours. Both the written confirmation of an oral request and the written request must be set forth on the "Doctor's First Report of Occupational Injury or Illness," Form DLSR 5021, section 14006, or on the Primary Treating Physician Progress Report, DWC Form PR–2, as contained in section 9785.2, or in narrative form containing the same information required in the PR–2 form. If a narrative format is used, the document shall be clearly marked at the top that it is a request for authorization.

(p) "Retrospective review" means utilization review conducted after medical services have been provided and for which approval has not already been given.

(q) "Reviewer" means a medical doctor, doctor of osteopathy, psychologist, acupuncturist, optometrist, dentist, podiatrist, or chiropractic practitioner licensed by any state or the District of Columbia, competent to evaluate the specific clinical issues involved in medical treatment services, where these services are within the scope of the reviewer's practice.

(r) "Utilization Review plan" means the written plan filed with the Administrative Director pursuant to Labor Code section 4610, setting forth the policies and procedures, and a description of the utilization review process.

(s) "Utilization Review process" means utilization management functions that prospectively, retrospectively, or concurrently review and approve, modify, delay, or deny, based in whole or in part on medical necessity to cure or relieve, treatment recommendations by physicians, as defined in Labor Code section 3209.3, prior to, retrospectively, or concurrent with the provision of medical treatment services pursuant to Labor Code section 4600. Utilization Review does not include determinations of the work–relatedness of injury or disease, or bill review for the purpose of determining whether the medical services were accurately billed.

(t) "Written" includes a facsimile as well as communications in paper form.

NOTE: Authority cited: Sections 133, 4603.5 and 5307.3, Labor Code. Reference: Sections 3209.3, 4062, 4600, 4600.4, 4604.5 and 4610, Labor Code.

HISTORY

1. New section filed 7–20–95; operative 7–20–95. Submitted to OAL for printing only pursuant to Government Code section 11351 (Register 95, No. 29).

2. Amendment of subsections (a)(4), (c)(1), (c)(3)(iii)–(iv) and (c)(4)(i)–(iii) filed 11–9–98; operative 1–1–99 (Register 98, No. 46).

3. New article 5.5.1 (sections 9792.6–9792.11) and repealer and new section filed 12–9–2004 as an emergency; operative 12–13–2004 (Register 2004, No. 50). A Certificate of Compliance must be transmitted to OAL by 4–12–2005 or emergency language will be repealed by operation of law on the following day.

4. New article 5.5.1 (sections 9792.6–9792.11) and repealer and new section refiled 4–6–2005 as an emergency; operative 4–12–2005 (Register 2005, No. 14). A Certificate of Compliance must be transmitted to OAL by 8–10–2005 or emergency language will be repealed by operation of law on the following day.

5. Certificate of Compliance as to 4–6–2005 order, including amendment of section and Note, transmitted to OAL 8–10–2005 and filed 9–22–2005 (Register 2005, No. 38).

§ 9792.7. Utilization Review Standards–Applicability

(a) Effective January 1, 2004, every claims administrator shall establish and maintain a utilization review process for treatment rendered on or after January 1, 2004, regardless of date of injury, in compliance with Labor Code section 4610. Each utilization review process shall be set forth in a utilization review plan which shall contain:

    (1) The name, address, phone number, and medical license number of the employed or designated medical director, who holds an unrestricted license to practice medicine in the state of California issued pursuant to section 2050 or section 2450 of the Business and Professions Code.

(2) A description of the process whereby requests for authorization are reviewed, and decisions on such requests are made, and a description of the process for handling expedited reviews.

(3) A description of the specific criteria utilized routinely in the review and throughout the decision–making process, including treatment protocols or standards used in the process. A description of the personnel and other sources used in the development and review of the criteria, and methods for updating the criteria. Prior to and until the Administrative Director adopts a medical treatment utilization schedule pursuant to Labor Code section 5307.27, the written policies and procedures governing the utilization review process shall be consistent with the recommended standards set forth in the American College of Occupational and Environmental Medicine's Occupational Medicine Practice Guidelines, Second Edition. The Administrative Director incorporates by reference the American College of Occupational and Environmental Medicine's Occupational Medicine Practice Guidelines (ACOEM), Second Edition (2004), published by OEM Press. A copy may be obtained from OEM Press, 8 West Street, Beverly Farms, Massachusetts 01915 (www.oempress.com). After the Administrative Director adopts a medical treatment utilization schedule pursuant to Labor Code section 5307.27, the written policies and procedures governing the utilization review process shall be consistent with the recommended standards set forth in that schedule.

(4) A description of the qualifications and functions of the personnel involved in decision–making and implementation of the utilization review plan.

(5) A description of the claims administrator's practice, if applicable, of any prior authorization process, including but not limited to, where authorization is provided without the submission of the request for authorization.

(b) (1) The medical director shall ensure that the process by which the claims administrator reviews and approves, modifies, delays, or denies requests by physicians prior to, retrospectively, or concurrent with the provision of medical services, complies with Labor Code section 4610 and these implementing regulations.

(2) A reviewer who is competent to evaluate the specific clinical issues involved in the medical treatment services, and where these services are within the reviewer's scope of practice, may, except as indicated below, delay, modify or deny, requests for authorization of medical treatment for reasons of medical necessity to cure or relieve the effects of the industrial injury.

(3) A non–physician reviewer may be used to initially apply specified criteria to requests for authorization for medical services. A non–physician reviewer may approve requests for authorization of medical services. A non–physician reviewer may discuss applicable criteria with the requesting physician, should the treatment for which authorization is sought appear to be inconsistent with the criteria. In such instances, the requesting physician may voluntarily withdraw a portion or all of the treatment in question and submit an amended request for treatment authorization, and the non–physician reviewer may approve the amended request for treatment authorization. Additionally, a non–physician reviewer may reasonably request appropriate additional information that is necessary to render a decision but in no event shall this exceed the time limitations imposed in section 9792.9 subdivisions (b)(1), (b)(2) or (c). Any time beyond the time specified in these paragraphs is subject to the provisions of subdivision (g)(1)(A) through (g)(1)(C) of section 9792.9.

(c) The complete utilization review plan, consisting of the policies and procedures, and a description of the utilization review process, shall be filed by the claims administrator, or by the external utilization review organization contracted by the claims administrator to perform the utilization review, with the Administrative Director. In lieu of filing the utilization review plan, the claims administrator may submit a letter identifying the external utilization review organization which has been contracted to perform the utilization review functions, provided that the utilization review organization has filed a complete utilization review plan with the Administrative Director. A modified utilization review plan shall be filed with the Administrative Director within 30 calendar days after the claims administrator makes a material modification to the plan.

(d) Upon request by the public, the claims administrator shall make available the complete utilization review plan, consisting of the policies and procedures, and a description of the utilization review process.

(1) The claims administrator may make available the complete utilization review plan, consisting of the policies and procedures and a description of the utilization review process, through electronic means. If a member of the public requests a hard copy of the utilization review plan, the claims administrator may charge reasonable copying and postage expenses related to disclosing the complete utilization review plan. Such charge shall not exceed $0.25 per page plus actual postage costs.

NOTE: Authority cited: Sections 133, 4603.5 and 5307.3, Labor Code. Reference: Sections 4062, 4600, 4600.4, 4604.5 and 4610, Labor Code.

HISTORY

1. New section filed 12–9–2004 as an emergency; operative 12–13–2004 (Register 2004, No. 50). A Certificate of Compliance must be transmitted to OAL by 4–12–2005 or emergency language will be repealed by operation of law on the following day.

2. New section refiled 4–6–2005 as an emergency; operative 4–12–2005 (Register 2005, No. 14). A Certificate of Compliance must be transmitted to OAL by 8–10–2005 or emergency language will be repealed by operation of law on the following day.

3. Certificate of Compliance as to 4–6–2005 order, including amendment of section, transmitted to OAL 8–10–2005 and filed 9–22–2005 (Register 2005, No. 38).

§ 9792.8.   Utilization Review Standards–Medically–Based Criteria

(a) (1) The criteria shall be consistent with the schedule for medical treatment utilization adopted pursuant to Labor Code section 5307.27. Prior to adoption of the schedule, the criteria or guidelines used in the utilization review process shall be consistent with the American College of Occupational and Environmental Medicine's (ACOEM) Practice Guidelines, Second Edition. The guidelines set forth in the ACOEM Practice Guidelines shall be presumptively correct on the issue of extent and scope of medical treatment until the effective date of the utilization schedule adopted pursuant to Labor Code section 5307.27. The presumption is rebuttable and may be controverted by a preponderance of the scientific medical evidence establishing that a variance from the guidelines is reasonably required to cure or relieve the injured worker from the effects of his or her injury.

(2) For all conditions or injuries not addressed by the ACOEM Practice Guidelines or by the official utilization schedule after adoption pursuant to Labor Code section 5307.27, authorized treatment shall be in accordance with other evidence–based medical treatment guidelines that are generally recognized by the national medical community and are scientifically based. Treatment may not be denied on the sole basis that the treatment is not addressed by the ACOEM Practice Guidelines until adoption of the medical treatment utilization schedule pursuant to Labor Code section 5307.27. After the Administrative Director adopts a medical treatment utilization schedule pursuant to Labor Code section 5307.27, treatment may not be denied on the sole basis that the treatment is not addressed by that schedule.

(3) The relevant portion of the criteria or guidelines used shall be disclosed in written form to the requesting physician, the injured worker, and if the injured worker is represented by counsel, the injured worker's attorney, if used as the basis of a decision to modify, delay, or deny services in a specific case under review. The claims administrator may not charge an injured worker, the injured worker's attorney or the requesting physician for a copy of the relevant portion of the criteria or guidelines used to modify, delay or deny the treatment request.

(4) Nothing in this section precludes authorization of medical treatment not included in the specific criteria under section 9792.8(a)(3).

NOTE: Authority cited: Sections 133, 4603.5 and 5307.3, Labor Code. Reference: Sections 4062, 4600, 4600.4, 4604.5 and 4610, Labor Code.

HISTORY

1. New section filed 12–9–2004 as an emergency; operative 12–13–2004 (Register 2004, No. 50). A Certificate of Compliance must be transmitted to OAL by 4–12–2005 or emergency language will be repealed by operation of law on the following day.

2. New section refiled 4–6–2005 as an emergency; operative 4–12–2005 (Register 2005, No. 14). A Certificate of Compliance must be transmitted to OAL by 8–10–2005 or emergency language will be repealed by operation of law on the following day.

3. Certificate of Compliance as to 4–6–2005 order, including amendment of section, transmitted to OAL 8–10–2005 and filed 9–22–2005 (Register 2005, No. 38).

§ 9792.9.   Utilization Review Standards–Timeframe, Procedures and Notice Content

(a) The request for authorization for a course of treatment as defined in section 9792.6(e) must be in written form.

(1) For purposes of this section, the written request for authorization shall be deemed to have been received by the claims administrator by facsimile on the date the request was received if the receiving facsimile electronically date stamps the transmission. If there is no electronically stamped date recorded, then the date the request was transmitted. A request for authorization transmitted by facsimile after 5:30 PM Pacific Time shall be deemed to have been received by the claims administrator on the following business day as defined in Labor Code section 4600.4 and in section 9 of the Civil Code. The copy of the request for authorization received by a facsimile transmission shall bear a notation of the date, time and place of transmission and the facsimile telephone number to which the request was transmitted or be accompanied by an unsigned copy of the affidavit or certificate of transmission which shall contain the facsimile telephone number to which the request was transmitted. The requesting physician must indicate the need for an expedited review upon submission of the request.

(2) Where the request for authorization is made by mail, and a proof of service by mail exists, the request shall be deemed to have been received by the claims administrator five (5) days after the deposit in the mail at a facility regularly maintained by the United States Postal Service. Where the request for authorization is delivered via certified mail, return receipt mail, the request shall be deemed to have been received by the claims administrator on the receipt date

entered on the return receipt. In the absence of a proof of service by mail or a dated return receipt, the request shall be deemed to have been received by the claims administrator on the date stamped as received on the document.

(b) The utilization review process shall meet the following timeframe requirements:

(1) Prospective or concurrent decisions shall be made in a timely fashion that is appropriate for the nature of the injured worker's condition, not to exceed five (5) working days from the date of receipt of the written request for authorization.

(2) If appropriate information which is necessary to render a decision is not provided with the original request for authorization, such information may be requested by a reviewer or non–physician reviewer within five (5) working days from the date of receipt of the written request for authorization to make the proper determination. In no event shall the determination be made more than 14 days from the date of receipt of the original request for authorization by the health care provider.

(A) If the reasonable information requested by the claims administrator is not received within 14 days of the date of the original written request by the requesting physician, a reviewer may deny the request with the stated condition that the request will be reconsidered upon receipt of the information requested.

(3) Decisions to approve a physician's request for authorization prior to, or concurrent with, the provision of medical services to the injured worker shall be communicated to the requesting physician within 24 hours of the decision. Any decision to approve a request shall be communicated to the requesting physician initially by telephone or facsimile. The communication by telephone shall be followed by written notice to the requesting physician within 24 hours of the decision for concurrent review and within two business days for prospective review.

(4) Decisions to modify, delay or deny a physician's request for authorization prior to, or concurrent with the provision of medical services to the injured worker shall be communicated to the requesting physician initially by telephone or facsimile. The communication by telephone shall be followed by written notice to the requesting physician, the injured worker, and if the injured worker is represented by counsel, the injured worker's attorney within 24 hours of the decision for concurrent review and within two business days of the decision for prospective review. In addition, the non–physician provider of goods or services identified in the request for authorization, and for whom contact information has been included, shall be notified in writing of the decision modifying, delaying, or denying a request for authorization that shall not include the rationale, criteria or guidelines used for the decision.

(5) For purposes of this section "normal business day" means a business day as defined in Labor Code section 4600.4 and Civil Code section 9.

(c) When review is retrospective, decisions shall be communicated to the requesting physician who provided the medical services and to the individual who received the medical services, and his or her attorney/designee, if applicable, within 30 days of receipt of the medical information that is reasonably necessary to make this determination. In addition, the non–physician provider of goods or services identified in the request for authorization, and for whom contact information has been included, shall be notified in writing of the decision modifying, delaying, or denying a request for authorization that shall not include the rationale, criteria or guidelines used for the decision.

(d) Failure to obtain prior authorization for emergency health care services shall not be an acceptable basis for refusal to cover medical services provided to treat and stabilize an injured worker presenting for emergency health care services. Emergency health care services, however, may be subjected to retrospective review. Documentation for emergency health care services shall be made available to the claims administrator upon request.

(e) Prospective or concurrent decisions related to an expedited review shall be made in a timely fashion appropriate to the injured worker's condition, not to exceed 72 hours after the receipt of the written information reasonably necessary to make the determination. The requesting physician must indicate the need for an expedited review upon submission of the request. Decisions related to expedited review refer to the following situations:

(1) When the injured worker's condition is such that the injured worker faces an imminent and serious threat to his or her health, including, but not limited to, the potential loss of life, limb, or other major bodily function, or

(2) The normal timeframe for the decision–making process, as described in subdivision (b), would be detrimental to the injured worker's life or health or could jeopardize the injured worker's permanent ability to regain maximum function.

(f) The review and decision to deny, delay or modify a request for medical treatment must be conducted by a reviewer, who is competent to evaluate the specific clinical issues involved in the medical treatment services, and where these services are within the scope of the individual's practice.

(g) (1) The timeframe for decisions specified in subdivisions (b)(1), (b)(2) or (c) may only be extended by the claims administrator under the following circumstances:

(A) The claims administrator is not in receipt of all of the necessary medical information reasonably requested.

(B) The reviewer has asked that an additional examination or test be performed upon the injured worker that is reasonable and consistent with professionally recognized standards of medical practice.

(C) The claims administrator needs a specialized consultation and review of medical information by an expert reviewer.

(2) If subdivisions (A), (B) or (C) above apply, the claims administrator shall immediately notify the requesting physician, the injured worker, and if the injured worker is represented by counsel, the injured worker's attorney in writing, that the claims administrator cannot make a decision within the required timeframe, and specify the

information requested but not received, the additional examinations or tests required, or the specialty of the expert reviewer to be consulted. The claims administrator shall also notify the requesting physician, the injured worker, and if the injured worker is represented by counsel, the injured worker's attorney of the anticipated date on which a decision will be rendered. This notice shall include a statement that if the injured worker believes that a bona fide dispute exists relating to his or her entitlement to medical treatment, the injured worker or the injured worker's attorney may file an Application for Adjudication of Claim and Request for Expedited Hearing, DWC Form 4, in accordance with sections 10136(b)(1), 10400, and 10408. In addition, the non–physician provider of goods or services identified in the request for authorization, and for whom contact information has been included, shall be notified in writing of the decision to extend the timeframe and the anticipated date on which the decision will be rendered in accordance with this subdivision. The written notification shall not include the rationale, criteria or guidelines used for the decision.

(3) Upon receipt of information pursuant to subdivisions (A), (B), or (C) above, and (b)(2)(A), the claims administrator shall make the decision to approve, and the reviewer shall make a decision to modify or deny the request for authorization within five (5) working days of receipt of the information for prospective or concurrent review. The decision shall be communicated pursuant to subdivisions (b)(3) or (b)(4).

(4) Upon receipt of information pursuant to subdivisions (A), (B), or (C) above, the claims administrator shall make the decision to approve, and the reviewer shall make a decision to modify or deny the request for authorization within thirty (30) days of receipt of the information for retrospective review.

(h) Every claims administrator shall maintain telephone access from 9:00 AM to 5:30 PM Pacific Time, on normal business days, for health care providers to request authorization for medical services. Every claims administrator shall have a facsimile number available for physicians to request authorization for medical services. Every claims administrator shall maintain a process to receive communications from health care providers requesting authorization for medical services after business hours. For purposes of this section "normal business day" means a business day as defined in Labor Code section 4600.4 and Civil Code section 9. In addition, for purposes of this section the requirement that the claims administrator maintain a process to receive communications from requesting physicians after business hours shall be satisfied by maintaining a voice mail system or a facsimile number for after business hours requests.

(i) A written decision approving a request for treatment authorization under this section shall specify the specific medical treatment service approved.

(j) A written decision modifying, delaying or denying treatment authorization under this section shall be provided to the requesting physician, the injured worker, and if the injured worker is represented by counsel, the injured worker's attorney and shall contain the following information:

(1) The date on which the decision is made.

(2) A description of the specific course of proposed medical treatment for which authorization was requested.

(3) A specific description of the medical treatment service approved, if any.

(4) A clear and concise explanation of the reasons for the claims administrator's decision.

(5) A description of the medical criteria or guidelines used pursuant to section 9792.8, subdivision (a)(3).

(6) The clinical reasons regarding medical necessity.

(7) A clear statement that any dispute shall be resolved in accordance with the provisions of Labor Code section 4062, and that an objection to the utilization review decision must be communicated by the injured worker or the injured worker's attorney on behalf of the injured worker to the claims administrator in writing within 20 days of receipt of the decision. It shall further state that the 20–day time limit may be extended for good cause or by mutual agreement of the parties. The letter shall further state that the injured worker may file an Application for Adjudication of Claim and Request for Expedited Hearing, DWC Form 4, showing a bona fide dispute as to entitlement to medical treatment in accordance with sections 10136(b)(1), 10400, and 10408.

(8) Include the following mandatory language:

Either

"If you want further information, you may contact the local state Information and Assistance office by calling [enter district I & A office telephone number closest to the injured worker] or you may receive recorded information by calling 1–800–736–7401.

Or

"If you want further information, you may contact the local state Information and Assistance office closest to you. Please see attached listing (attach a listing of I&A offices and telephone numbers) or you may receive recorded information by calling 1–800–736–7401."

And

"You may also consult an attorney of your choice. Should you decide to be represented by an attorney, you may or may not receive a larger award, but, unless you are determined to be ineligible for an award, the attorney's fee will be deducted from any award you might receive for disability benefits. The decision to be represented by an attorney is yours to make, but it is voluntary and may not be necessary for you to receive your benefits."

In addition, the non–physician provider of goods or services identified in the request for authorization, and for whom contact information has been included, shall be notified in writing of the decision modifying, delaying, or denying a request for authorization that shall not include the rationale, criteria or guidelines used for the decision.

(9) Details about the claims administrator's internal utilization review appeals process, if any, and a clear statement that the appeals process is on a voluntary basis, including the following mandatory statement:

"If you disagree with the utilization review decision and wish to dispute it, you must send written notice of your objection to the claims administrator within 20 days of receipt of the utilization review decision in accordance with Labor Code section 4062. You must meet this deadline even if you are participating in the claims administrator's internal utilization review appeals process."

(k) The written decision modifying, delaying or denying treatment authorization provided to the requesting physician shall also contain the name and specialty of the reviewer or expert reviewer, and the telephone number in the United States of the reviewer or expert reviewer. The written decision shall also disclose the hours of availability of either the review, the expert reviewer or the medical director for the treating physician to discuss the decision which shall be, at a minimum, four (4) hours per week during normal business hours, 9:00 AM to 5:30 PM., Pacific Time or an agreed upon scheduled time to discuss the decision with the requesting physician. In the vent the reviewer is unavailable, the requesting physician may discuss the written decision with another reviewer who is competent to evaluate the specific clinical issues involved in the medical treatment services.

(l) Authorization may not be denied on the basis of lack of information without documentation reflecting an attempt to obtain the necessary information from the physician or from the provider of goods or services identified in the request for authorization either by facsimile or mail.

NOTE: Authority cited: Sections 133, 4603.5 and 5307.3, Labor Code. Reference: Sections 4062, 4600, 4600.4, 4604.5 and 4610, Labor Code.

HISTORY
1. New section filed 12–9–2004 as an emergency; operative 12–13–2004 (Register 2004, No. 50). A Certificate of Compliance must be transmitted to OAL by 4–12–2005 or emergency language will be repealed by operation of law on the following day.
2. New section refiled 4–6–2005 as an emergency; operative 4–12–2005 (Register 2005, No. 14). A Certificate of Compliance must be transmitted to OAL by 8–10–2005 or emergency language will be repealed by operation of law on the following day.
3. Certificate of Compliance as to 4–6–2005 order, including amendment of section, transmitted to OAL 8–10–2005 and filed 9–22–2005 (Register 2005, No. 38).

§ 9792.10.   Utilization Review Standards–Dispute Resolution

(a) (1) If the request for authorization of medical treatment is not approved, or if the request for authorization for medical treatment is approved in part, any dispute shall be resolved in accordance with Labor Code section 4062.

(2) An objection to a decision disapproving in whole or in part a request for authorization of medical treatment, must be communicated to the claims administrator by the injured worker or the injured worker's attorney in writing within 20 days of receipt of the utilization review decision. The 20–day time limit may be extended for good cause or by mutual agreement of the parties.

(3) Nothing in this paragraph precludes the parties from participating in an internal utilization review appeal process on a voluntary basis provided the injured worker and if the injured worker is represented by counsel, the injured worker's attorney have been notified of the 20–day time limit to file an objection to the utilization review decision in accordance with Labor Code section 4062.

(4) Additionally, the injured worker or the injured worker's attorney may file an Application for Adjudication of Claim, and a Request for Expedited Hearing, DWC Form 4, in accordance with sections 10136(b)(1), 10400, and 10408, and request an expedited hearing and decision on his or her entitlement to medical treatment if the request for medical treatment is not authorized within the time limitations set forth in section 9792.9, or when there exists a bona fide dispute as to entitlement to medical treatment.

(b) The following requirements shall be met prior to a concurrent review decision to deny authorization for medical treatment and to resolve disputes:

(1) In the case of concurrent review, medical care shall not be discontinued until the requesting physician has been notified of the decision and a care plan has been agreed upon by the requesting physician that is appropriate for the medical needs of the injured worker. In addition, the non–physician provider of goods or services identified in the request for authorization, and for whom contact information has been included, shall be notified in writing of the decision modifying, delaying, or denying a request for authorization that shall not include the rationale, criteria or guidelines used for the decision.

(2) Medical care provided during a concurrent review shall be medical treatment that is reasonably required to cure or relieve from the effects of the industrial injury.

NOTE: Authority cited: Sections 133, 4603.5 and 5307.3, Labor Code. Reference: Sections 4062, 4600, 4600.4, 4604.5 and 4610, Labor Code.

HISTORY

1. New section filed 12–9–2004 as an emergency; operative 12–13–2004 (Register 2004, No. 50). A Certificate of Compliance must be transmitted to OAL by 4–12–2005 or emergency language will be repealed by operation of law on the following day.

2. New section refiled 4–6–2005 as an emergency; operative 4–12–2005 (Register 2005, No. 14). A Certificate of Compliance must be transmitted to OAL by 8–10–2005 or emergency language will be repealed by operation of law on the following day.

3. Certificate of Compliance as to 4–6–2005 order, including amendment of subsection (b)(1), transmitted to OAL 8–10–2005 and filed 9–22–2005 (Register 2005, No. 38).

§ 9792.11.   Utilization Review Standards–Penalties

(a) To carry out the responsibilities mandated by Labor Code Section 4610(i), the Administrative Director, or his or her designee, shall investigate the utilization review process of any employer, insurer or other entity subject to the provisions of section 4610. The investigation shall include, but not be limited to, review of the practices, files, documents and other records, whether electronic or paper, of the claims administrator, and any other person responsible for utilization review processes for an employer. As used in sections 9792.11 through 9792.15, the phrase 'utilization review organization' includes any person or entity with which the employer, or an insurer, or third party administrator, contracts to fulfill part or all of the employer's utilization review responsibilities under Labor Code section 4610 and Title 8 of the California Code of Regulations, sections 9792.6 through 9792.15.

(b) Notwithstanding Labor Code section 129(a) through (d) and section 129.5 subdivisions (a) through (d), the Administrative Director, or his or her designee, may conduct a utilization review investigation pursuant to Labor Code section 4610, which may include, but is not limited to, an audit of files and other records.

(c) The Administrative Director, or his or her designee, may conduct a utilization review investigation at any location where Labor Code Section 4610 utilization review processes occur, as follows:

(1) For utilization review organizations:

(A) A Routine Investigation shall be initiated at each known utilization review organization at least once every three (3) years. The investigation shall include a review of a random sample of requests for authorization, as defined by section 9792.6(o), received by the utilization review organization during the three most recent full calendar months preceding the date of the issuance of the Notice of Utilization Review Investigation. The investigation may also include a review of any credible complaints received by the Administrative Director since the time of the previous investigation. If there has not been a previous investigation, the investigation may include a review of any credible complaints received by the Administrative Director since the effective date of sections 9792.11 through 9792.15.

(B) Target Investigations:

1. A Return Target Investigation of the same investigation subject shall be conducted within 18 months of the date of the previous investigation if the performance rating was less than eighty–five percent.

2. A Special Target Investigation may be conducted at any time based on credible information indicating the possible existence of a violation of Labor Code section 4610 or sections 9792.6 through 9792.12.

3. The Return Target Investigation and the Special Target Investigation may include: (i) a review of the requests for authorization previously investigated which contained violations; (ii) a review of the file or files pertaining to the complaint or possible violation; (iii) a random sample of requests for authorization received by the utilization review organization during the three most recent full calendar months preceding the date of the issuance of the Notice of Utilization Review Investigation; (iv) a sample of a specific type of request for authorization; and (v) any credible complaints received by the Administrative Director since the time of any prior investigation. If there has not been a previous investigation, the investigation may include a review of any credible complaints received by the Administrative Director since the effective date of sections 9792.11 through 9792.15.

(2) For a claims administrator:

(A) A Routine Investigation shall be initiated at each claims adjusting location at least once every five (5) years concurrent with the profile audit review done pursuant to Labor Code sections 129 and 129.5. The investigation shall include a review of a random sample of requests for authorization, as defined by section 9792.6(o), received by the claims administrator during the three most recent full calendar months preceding the date of the issuance of the Notice of Utilization Review Investigation. The investigation may also include a review of any credible complaints received by the Administrative Director since the time of the previous investigation. If there has not been a previous investigation, the investigation may include a review of any credible complaints received by the Administrative Director since the effective date of sections 9792.11 through 9792.15.

(B) Target Investigations:

1. A Return Target Investigation of the same investigation subject shall be conducted within 18 months of the date of any previous investigation if the performance rating was less than eighty–five percent.

2. A Special Target Investigation may be conducted at any time based on credible information indicating the possible existence of a violation of Labor Code section 4610 or sections 9792.6 through 9792.12.

3. The Return Target Investigation and the Special Target Investigation may include: (i) a review of the requests for authorization previously investigated which contained violations; (ii) a review of the file or files pertaining to the complaint or possible violation; (iii) a random sample of requests for authorization received by the claims administrator during the three most recent full calendar months preceding the date of the issuance of the Notice of Utilization Review Investigation; (iv) a sample of a specific type of request for authorization; and (v) any credible complaints received by the Administrative Director since the time of any prior investigation. If there has not been a previous investigation, the investigation may include a review of any credible complaints received by the Administrative Director since the effective date of sections 9792.11 through 9792.15.

(d) The number of requests for authorization randomly selected for investigation shall be determined based on the following table:

Population of requests for authorization received during a three month calendar period

Sample Size

5 or less	all
6–10	1 less than total
11–13	2 less than total
14–16	3 less than total
17–18	4 less than total
19–20	5 less than total
21–23	6 less than total
24	17
25–26	18
27–29	19
30–31	20
32–33	21
34–36	22
37–39	23
40–41	24
42–44	25
45–48	26
49–51	27
52–55	28
56–58	29
59–62	30
63–67	31
68–72	32
73–77	33
78–82	34
83–88	35
89–95	36
96–102	37
103–110	38
111–119	39
120–128	40
129–139	41
140–151	42
152–164	43
165–179	44
180–197	45
198–217	46
218–241	47
242–269	48
270–304	49
305–346	50
347–399	51
400–468	52
469–562	53
563–696	54
697–905	55
906–1,272	56
1,273–2,091	57
2,092–5,530	58
5,531 +	59

(e) Complaints concerning utilization review procedures may be submitted with any supporting documentation to the Division of Workers' Compensation using the sample complaint form that is posted on the Division's website at: http://www.dir.ca.gov/dwc/FORMS/UtilizationReviewcomplaintform.pdf

Complaints should be mailed to DWC Medical Unit–UR, P.O. Box 71010, Oakland, CA 94612, attention UR Complaints or emailed to DWCManagedCare@dir.ca.gov. Complaints received by the Division of Workers' Compensation will be reviewed and investigated, if necessary, to determine if the complaints are credible and indicate the possible existence of a violation of Labor Code section 4610 or sections 9792.6 through 9792.12.

(f) Administrative penalties may be assessed for any failure to comply with Labor Code section 4610, or sections 9792.6 through 9792.12 of Title 8, California Code of Regulations, except that the penalties listed in section 9792.12(a)(6) through (14) and (b) shall only be imposed if the request was subject to the Labor Code section 4610 utilization review process.

(g) In the event an investigation of utilization review processes is done at the claims administrator's adjusting location, concurrent with a profile audit review done pursuant to Labor Code section 129 or 129.5, the administrative penalty amounts for each violation of Labor Code section 4610 or sections 9792.6 through 9792.12 of Title 8, California Code of Regulations, shall be governed by sections 9792.11 through 9792.15. Any such administrative penalty for utilization review process violations shall apply in lieu of the administrative penalty amount allowed under the audit regulations at section 10111.2(b)(8)[vi] of Title 8, California Code of Regulations. In addition, any report of findings from the investigation and any Order to Show Cause re: Assessment of Administrative Penalties prepared by the Administrative Director, or his or her designee, based on violations of Labor Code section 4610 or sections 9792.6 through 9792.12 of Title 8, California Code of Regulations, shall be prepared separately from any audit report or assessment of administrative penalties made pursuant to Labor Code section 129 and 129.5. The Order to Show Cause re: Assessment of Administrative Penalties for violations of sections 9792.6 et seq of Title 8 of the California Code of Regulations shall be governed by sections 9792.11 through 9792.15.

(h) The Administrative Director, or his or her designee, may also utilize the provisions of Government Code sections 11180 through 11191 to determine whether any violations of the requirements in Labor Code section 4610 or sections 9792.6 through 9792.12 of Title 8, California Code of Regulations, have occurred.

(i) Sections 9792.11 through 9792.15 of Title 8 of the California Code of Regulations shall apply to any Labor Code section 4610 utilization review investigation conducted on or after the effective date of sections 9792.11 through 9792.15 and for conduct which occurred on or after the effective date of sections 9792.11 through 9792.15.

(j) Unless the Administrative Director in his or her discretion determines that advance notice will render a Special Target or Return Target Investigation less useful, the claims administrator or utilization review organization shall be notified of its selection for an Investigation. Claims administrators and utilization review organizations shall be sent a Notice of Utilization Review Investigation. The Notice of Utilization Review Investigation shall require the investigation subject to provide the following:

(1) A description of the system used to identify each request for authorization (if applicable). To the extent the system identifies any of the following information in an electronic format, the claims administrator or utilization review organization shall provide in an electronic format a list of each and every request for authorization received at the investigation site during a three month calendar period specified by the Administrative Director, or his or her designee, and the following data elements: i) a unique identifying number for each request for authorization if one has been assigned; ii) the name of the injured worker; iii) the claim number used by the claims adjuster; iv) the initial date of receipt of the request for authorization; v) the type of review (expedited prospective, prospective, expedited concurrent, concurrent, retrospective, appeal); vi) the disposition (approve, deny, delay, modify, withdrawal); and, vii) if applicable, the type of person who withdrew the request (requesting physician, claims adjuster, injured employee or his or her attorney, or other person). In the event the claims administrator or utilization review organization is not able to provide the list in an electronic format, the list shall be provided in such a form that the listed requests for authorization are sorted in the following order: by type of utilization review, type of disposition, and date of receipt of the initial request;

(2) A description of all media used to transmit, share, record or store information received and transmitted in reference to each request, whether printed copy, electronic, fax, diskette, computer drive or other media;

(3) A legend of any and all numbers, letters and other symbols used to identify the disposition (e.g. approve, deny, modify, delay or withdraw), type of review (expedited prospective, prospective, expedited concurrent, concurrent, retrospective, appeal), and other abbreviations used to document individual requests for authorization and a data dictionary for all data elements provided;

(4) A description of the methods by which the medical director for utilization review ensures that the process by which requests for authorization are reviewed and approved, modified, delayed, or denied is in compliance with Labor Code section 4610 and sections 9792.6 through 9792.10, as required by sections 9792.6(l) and 9792.7(b) of Title 8 of the California Code of Regulations; and

(5) The following additional information, may be requested by the Administrative Director or his or her designee, as applicable to the type of entity investigated: i) whether utilization review services are provided externally; ii) the

name(s) of the utilization review organization(s); iii) the name and address of the employer; and iv) the name and address of the insurer.

(k) The utilization review organization or claims administrator shall provide the requested information listed in subdivision (j) within fourteen (14) calendar days of receipt of the Notice of Utilization Review Investigation. Based on the information provided, the Administrative Director, or his or her designee, shall provide the claims administrator or utilization review organization with a Notice of Investigation Commencement, which shall include a list of randomly selected requests for authorization from a three month calendar period designated by the Administrative Director and complaint files (if applicable) for investigation.

(l) For utilization review organizations: Within fourteen (14) calendar days of receipt from the Administrative Director, or his or her designee, of the Notice of Investigation Commencement, the utilization review organization shall deliver to the Administrative Director, or his or her designee, a true and complete copy of all records, whether electronic or paper, for each request for authorization listed. Copies of the records shall be delivered with a statement signed under penalty of perjury by the custodian of records for the location at which the records are held, attesting that all of the records produced are true, correct and complete copies of the originals, in his or her possession. After reviewing the records, the Administrative Director, or his or her designee, shall determine if an onsite investigation is required. If an onsite investigation is required, fourteen (14) calendar days notice shall be provided to the utilization review organization.

(m) For claims administrators: The Notice of Investigation Commencement shall be provided to the claims administrator at least fourteen (14) calendar days prior to the commencement of the onsite investigation. The claims administrator shall produce for the Administrative Director, or his or her designee, on the first day of commencement of the onsite investigation, the true, correct and complete copies, whether electronic or paper, whether located onsite or offsite, of each request for authorization identified by the Administrative Director or his or her designee, together with a statement signed under penalty of perjury by the custodian of records for the location at which the records are held, attesting that all of the records produced are true, correct and complete copies of the originals.

(n) In the event the Administrative Director, or his or her designee, determines additional records or files are needed for review during the course of an onsite investigation, the claims administrator or utilization review organization shall produce the requested records in the manner described by subdivision 9792.11(k), within one (1) working day when the records are located at the site of investigation, and within five (5) working days when the records are located at any other site. Any such request by the Administrative Director or his or her designee also may include records or files pertaining to any complaint alleging violations of Labor Code sections 4610 or sections 9792.6 through 9792.12 of Title 8 of the California Code of Regulations. The Administrative Director or his or her designee may extend the time for production of the requested records for good cause.

(o) If the date or deadline in sections 9792.9(b) and 9792.9(c) of Title 8 of the California Code of Regulations to perform any act related to utilization review practices falls on a weekend or holiday, for the purposes of assessing penalties, the act may be performed on the next normal business day, as defined by Labor Code section 4600.4 and Civil Code section 9. This subdivision shall not apply in cases involving concurrent or expedited review. The timelines in sections 9792.9(b) of Title 8 of the California Code of Regulations shall only be extended as provided under section 9792.9(g) of that title.

(p) If the claims administrator or utilization review organization does not record the date a document is received, it shall be deemed received by using the method set out in section 9792.9(a)(2), except that:

(1) where the request for authorization is made by mail through the U.S. postal service and no proof of service by mail exists, the request shall be deemed to have been received by the claims administrator, or utilization review organization on whichever date is earlier, either the receipt date stamped by the addressee or within five (5) calendar days of the date stated in the request for authorization or where the addressee can show a delay in mailing by the postmark date on the mailing envelope then: (A) within five (5) calendar days of the postmark date, if the place of mailing and place of address are both within California; (B) within ten (10) calendar days if the place of address is within the United States but outside of California; or (C) within twenty (20) calendar days if the place of address is outside of the United States; and

(2) where the request for authorization is made by express mail, overnight mail or courier without any proof of service, the request shall be deemed received by the addressee on the date specified in any written confirmation of delivery.

(q) Upon initiating a Special Target Investigation, the Administrative Director, or his or her designee, shall provide to the claims administrator or the utilization review organization a written description of the factual information or of the complaint containing factual information or a copy of the complaint that triggered the utilization review investigation, unless the Administrative Director or his or her designee determines that providing the information would make the investigation less useful. The claims administrator or utilization review organization shall have ten (10) business days upon receipt of the written description or copy of the complaint to provide a written response to the Administrative Director or his or her designee. After reviewing the written response, the Administrative Director, or his or her designee, shall either close the investigation without the assessment of administrative penalties or conduct further investigation to determine whether a violation exists and whether to impose penalty assessments.

(r) For utilization review organizations: The files and other records, whether electronic or paper, that pertain to the utilization review process shall be retained for at least three (3) years following either: (1) the most recent utilization review decision for each injured employee, or (2) the date on which any appeal from the assessment of penalties for violations of Labor Code section 4610 or sections 9792.6 through 9792.12 is final, whichever date is later. Claims administrators shall retain their claim files as set forth in section 10102 of Title 8 of the California Code of Regulations.

(s) Upon receipt of a notice of Routine or Target Investigation or any other request from the Administrative Director, or his or her designee, to review all files and other records pertaining to the employer's utilization review process, whether electronic or paper, that are created or held outside of California, the claims administrator or utilization review organization shall either deliver all such requested files and other records to an address in California specified by the Administrative Director, or his or her designee, or reimburse the Administrative Director for the actual expenses of each investigator who travels outside of California to the place where the records are held, including the per diem expenses, travel expenses and compensated overtime of the investigators.

(t) A preliminary investigation report will be provided to the claims administrator or utilization review organization. The preliminary investigation report shall consist of the preliminary notice of utilization review penalty assessments, the performance rating, and may include one or more requests for additional documentation or compliance. A conference to discuss the preliminary investigation report shall be scheduled, if necessary, within twenty–one calendar days from the issuance of the preliminary findings. Following the conference, the Administrative Director or his or her designee shall issue an Order to Show Cause Re: Assessment of Administrative Penalty (which shall include the final investigation report), as set forth in section 9792.15.

(u) The claims administrator or utilization review organization may stipulate to the allegations and final report set forth in the Order to Show Cause.

(v) Within forty–five (45) calendar days of the service of the Order to Show Cause Re: Assessment of Administrative Penalties, if no answer has been filed, or within 15 calendar days after any and all appeals have become final, the claims administrator or utilization review organization shall provide the following:

(1) A notice, which shall include a copy of the final investigation report, the measures actually implemented to abate such conditions, and the website address for the Division where the performance rating and summary of violations is posted. If a hearing was conducted under section 9792.15, the notice shall include the Final Determination in lieu of the final investigation report.

(2) For utilization review organizations: the notice must be served on any employer or third party claims administrator that contracted with the utilization review organization and whose utilization review process was assessed with a penalty pursuant to section 9792.12, and any insurer whose utilization review process was assessed with a penalty pursuant to section 9792.12.

(3) For claims administrators: the notice must be served on any self–insured employer and any insurer whose utilization review process was assessed with a penalty pursuant to section 9792.12.

(4) The notice shall be served by certified mail.

(5) Documentation of compliance with this section shall be served on the Administrative Director within thirty calendar days from the date the notice was served.

NOTE: Authority cited: Sections 11180–11191, Government Code; and Sections 133, 4610 and 5307.3, Labor Code. Reference: Sections 129, 129.5, 4062, 4600, 4600.4, 4604.5, 4610 and 4614, Labor Code.

HISTORY

1. New section filed 6–7–2007; operative 6–7–2007 pursuant to Government Code section 11343.4 (Register 2007, No. 23). For prior history, see Register 2005, No. 38

§ 9792.12. Administrative Penalty Schedule for Labor Code section 4610 Utilization Review Violations

(a) Mandatory Administrative Penalties. Notwithstanding Labor Code section 129.5(c)(1) through (c)(3), the penalty amount that shall be assessed for each failure to comply with the utilization review process required by Labor Code section 4610 and sections 9792.6 through 9792.12 of Title 8 of the California Code of Regulations, is:

(1) For failure to establish a Labor Code section 4610 utilization review plan: $50,000;

(2) For failure to include all of the requirements of section 9792.7(a) in the utilization review plan: $5,000;

(3) For failure to file the utilization review plan or a letter in lieu of a utilization review plan with the Administrative Director as required by section 9792.7(c): $10,000;

(4) For failure to file a modified utilization review plan with the Administrative Director within 30 calendar days after the claims administrator makes a material modification to the plan as required by section 9792.7(c): $5,000;

(5) For failure to employ or designate a physician as a medical director, as defined in section 9792.6(l), of the utilization review process, as required by section 9792.7(b): $50,000;

(6) For issuance of a decision to modify or deny a request for authorization regarding a medical treatment, procedure, service or product where the requested treatment, procedure or service is not within the reviewer's scope of practice (as set forth by the reviewer's licensing board): $25,000;

(7) For failure to comply with the requirement that only a licensed physician may modify, delay, or deny requests for authorization of medical treatment for reasons of medical necessity to cure or relieve, except as provided for in Labor Code section 4604.5(d) and section 9792.9(b)(2) and (3): $25,000;

(8) For failure of a non–physician reviewer (person other than a reviewer, expert reviewer or medical director as defined in section 9792.6 of Title 8 of the California Code of Regulations), who approves an amended request to possess an amended written request for treatment authorization as provided under section 9792.7(b)(3) when a physician has voluntarily withdrawn a request in order to submit an amended request: $1,000;

(9) For failure to communicate the decision in response to a request for an expedited review, as defined in section 9792.6(g), in a timely fashion, as required by section 9792.9: $15,000;

(10) For failure to approve the request for authorization solely on the basis that the condition for which treatment was requested is not addressed by the medical treatment utilization schedule adopted pursuant to section 5307.27 of the Labor Code: $5,000;

(11) For failure to discuss or document attempts to discuss reasonable options for a care plan with the requesting physician as required by Labor Code section 4610(g)(3)(B), prior to denying authorization of or discontinuing medical care, in the case of concurrent review: $10,000;

(12) For failure to respond to the request for authorization by the injured employee's requesting treating physician, in the case of a non–expedited concurrent review: $2,000;

(13) For failure to respond to the request for authorization by the injured employee's requesting treating physician, in the case of a non–expedited prospective review: $1,000;

(14) For failure to respond to the request for authorization by the injured employee's requesting treating physician, in the case of a retrospective review: $500;

(15) For failure to disclose or otherwise to make available, if requested, the Utilization Review criteria or guidelines to the public, as required by Labor Code section 4610, subdivision (f)(5) and section 9792.7(d) of Title 8 of the California Code of Regulations: $100.

(16) For failure to timely serve the Administrative Director with documentation of compliance pursuant to section 9792.11(v)(5): $500.

(17) For failure to timely comply with any compliance requirement listed in the Final Report if no timely answer was filed or any compliance requirement listed in the Determination and Order after any and all appeals have become final: $500.

(b) Additional Penalties and Remediation.

(1) After conducting a Routine or Return Target Investigation, the Administrative Director, or his or her designee, shall calculate the investigation subject's performance rating based on its review of the randomly selected requests. The investigation subject's performance rating may also be calculated after conducting a Special Target Investigation. The performance rating will be calculated as follows:

(A) The factor for failure to make and/or provide a timely response to a request for authorization shall be determined by dividing the number of randomly selected requests with violations involving failure to make or provide a timely response to a request for authorization by the total number of randomly selected requests.

(B) The factor for notice(s) with faulty content shall be determined by dividing the number of requests involving notice(s) with faulty content by the total number of randomly selected requests.

(C) The factor for failure to issue notice(s) to all appropriate parties shall be determined by the number of requests involving the failure to issue notice(s) to all appropriate parties by the total number of randomly selected requests.

(D) The investigation subject's investigation performance rating will be determined by adding the factors calculated pursuant to subsections (b)(1)(A) through (b)(1)(C), dividing the total by three, subtracting from one, and multiplying by one–hundred.

(E) If the investigation subject's performance rating meets or exceeds eighty–five percent, the Administrative Director, or his or her designee, shall assess no penalties for the violations listed in this subdivision. If the performance rating is less than eighty–five percent, the violations shall be assessed as set forth below in (b)(2) through (b)(5):

(2) For the types of violations listed below in (b)(4) and (b)(5), each violation shall have a penalty amount, as specified of $100 in (b)(4) or $50 in (b)(5). The penalty amount specified in (b)(4) and (b)(5) shall be waived if the investigation subject's performance rating meets or exceeds eighty–five percent, or if following a Routine Investigation the claims administrator or utilization review organization agrees in writing to:

(A) Deliver to the Administrative Director, or his or her designee, within no more than thirty (30) calendar days from the date of the agreement or the number of days otherwise specified, written evidence, tendered with a declaration made under penalty of perjury, that explains or demonstrates how the violation has been abated in compliance with the applicable statute or regulations and the terms of abatement specified by the Administrative Director; and

(B) Grant the Administrative Director, or his or her designee, entry, upon request and within the time frame specified in the agreement, to the site at which the violation was found for a Return Target Investigation for the purpose of verifying compliance with the abatement measures reported in subdivision 9792.12(b)(1)(A) above and agree to a review of randomly selected requests for authorization; and

    (C) Reinstatement of the penalty amount previously waived for each such instance, in the event the violative condition is not abated within the time period specified by the Administrative Director, or his or her designee, or in the event that such abatement measures are not consistent with abatement terms specified by the Administrative Director, or his or her designee.

(3) In the event the Administrative Director, or his or her designee, returns for a Return Target Investigation, after the initial violation has become final, and the subject fails to meet the performance standard of 85%, the amount of penalty shall be calculated as described below and in no event shall the penalty amount be waived:

    (A) The penalty amount for each violation shall be multiplied by two for a second investigation, but in no event shall the total penalties for the violations exceed $100,000;

    (B) The penalty amount for each violation shall be multiplied by five for a third investigation, but in no event shall the total penalties for the violations exceed $200,000;

    (C) The penalty amount for each violation shall be multiplied by ten for a fourth investigation, but in no event shall the total penalties for the violations exceed $400,000.

(4) For each of the violations listed below, the penalty amount shall be $100.00 for each instance found by the Administrative Director, or his or her designee:

    (A) For failure to immediately notify all parties in the manner described in section 9792.9(g)(2) of the basis for extending the decision date for a request for medical treatment;

    (B) For failure to document efforts to obtain information from the requesting party prior to issuing a denial of a request for authorization on the basis of lack of reasonable and necessary information;

    (C) For failure to make a decision to approve or modify or deny the request for authorization, within five (5) working days of receipt of the requested information for prospective or concurrent review, and to communicate the decision as required by section 9792.9(g)(3);

    (D) For failure to make and communicate a retrospective decision to approve, modify, or deny the request, within thirty (30) working days of receipt of the information, as required by section 9792.9(g)(4);

    (E) For failure to include in the written decision that modifies, delays or denies authorization, all of the items required by section 9792.9(j);

    (F) For failure to disclose or otherwise to make available, if requested, the Utilization Review criteria or guidelines, to the injured employee whose case is under review, as required by Labor Code section 4610(f)(5) and section 9792.8(a)(3) Title 8 of the California Code of Regulations.

(5) For each of the violations listed below, the penalty amount shall be $50.00 for each instance found by the Administrative Director, or his or her designee:

    (A) For failure by a non–physician or physician reviewer to timely notify the requesting physician, as required by section 9792.9(b)(2), that additional information is needed in order to make a decision in compliance with the timeframes contained in section 9792.9(b);

    (B) For failure to communicate the decision to approve to the requesting physician in the case of prospective or concurrent review, by phone or fax within 24 hours of the decision, as required by Labor Code section 4610(g)(3)(A) and in accordance with section 9792.9(b)(3) of Title 8 of the California Code of Regulations;

    (C) For failure to send a written notice of the decision to modify, delay or deny to the requesting party, and to the injured employee and to his or her attorney if any, within twenty four (24) hours of making the decision for concurrent review, or within two business days for prospective review, as required by Labor Code section 4610(g)(3)(A) and section 9792.9(b)(4) of Title 8 of the California Code of Regulations;

    (D) For failure to communicate a decision in the case of retrospective review as required by section 9792.9(c) within thirty (30) days of receipt of the medical information that was reasonably necessary to make the determination;

    (E) For failure to provide immediately a written notice to the requesting party that a decision on the request for authorization cannot be made within fourteen (14) days for prospective and concurrent reviews, or within thirty (30) days for retrospective in accordance with section 9792.9(g)(2);

    (F) For failure to document that one of the following events occurred prior to the claims administrator providing written notice for delay under Labor Code section 4610(g)(5):

        (1) the claims administrator had not received all of the information reasonably necessary and requested;

        (2) the employer or claims administrator has requested a consultation by an expert reviewer;

        (3) the physician reviewer has requested an additional examination or test be performed;

    (G) For failure to explain in writing the reason for delay as required by section 9792.9(g)(2) of Title 8 of the California Code of Regulations when the decision to delay was made under one of the circumstances listed in section 9792.9(g)(1).

(6) After the time to file an answer to the Order to Show Cause Re: Assessment of Administrative Penalties has elapsed and no answer has been filed or after any and all appeals have become final, the Administrative Director, or his or her designee, shall post on the website for the Division of Workers' Compensation the performance rating and summary of violations for each utilization review investigation.

(c) The penalty amounts specified for violations under subsection 9792.12(a) and (b) above may, in the discretion of the Administrative Director, be reduced after consideration of the factors set out in section 9792.13 of Title 8 of the California Code of Regulations. Failure to abate a violation found under section 9792.12(b)(4) and (b)(5), in the time period or in a manner consistent with that specified by the Administrative Director, or his or her designee, shall result in the assessment of the full original penalty amount proposed by the Administrative Director for that violation.

NOTE: Authority cited: Sections 133, 4610 and 5307.3, Labor Code. Reference: Sections 129, 129.5, 4062, 4600, 4600.4, 4604.5, 4610 and 4614, Labor Code.

HISTORY

1. New section filed 6–7–2007; operative 6–7–2007 pursuant to Government Code section 11343.4 (Register 2007, No. 23).

§ 9792.13.   Assessment of Administrative Penalties – Penalty Adjustment Factors

(a) In any investigation that the Administrative Director deems appropriate, the Administrative Director, or his or her designee, may mitigate a penalty amount imposed under section 9792.12 after considering each of these factors:
   (1) The medical consequences or gravity of the violation(s);
   (2) The good faith of the claims administrator or utilization review organization. Mitigation for good faith shall be determined based on documentation of attempts to comply with the Labor Code and regulations and shall result in a reduction of 20% for each applicable penalty;
   (3) The history of previous penalties;
   (4) The frequency of violations found during the investigation giving rise to a penalty;
   (5) Penalties may be mitigated outside the above mitigation guidelines in extraordinary circumstances, when strict application of the mitigation guidelines would be clearly inequitable; and
   (6) In the event an objection or appeal is filed pursuant to subsection 9792.15 of these regulations, whether the claims administrator or utilization review organization abated the alleged violation within the time period specified by the Administrative Director or his or her designee.
(b) The Administrative Director, or his or her designee, may assess both an administrative penalty under Labor Code section 4610 and a civil penalty under subdivision (e) of Labor Code section 129.5 based on the same violation(s).
(c) The Administrative Director, or his or her designee, shall not collect payment for an administrative penalty under Labor Code section 4610 from both the utilization review organization and the claims administrator for an assessment based on the same violation(s).
(d) Where an injured worker's or a requesting provider's refusal to cooperate in the utilization review process has prevented the claims administrator or utilization review organization from determining whether there is a legal obligation to perform an act, the Administrative Director, or his or her designee, may forego a penalty assessment for any related act or omission. The claims administrator or utilization review organization shall have the burden of proof in establishing both the refusal to cooperate and that such refusal prevented compliance with the relevant applicable statute or regulation.

NOTE: Authority cited: Sections 133, 4610 and 5307.3, Labor Code. Reference: Sections 129, 129.5, 4062, 4600, 4600.4, 4604.5, 4610 and 4614, Labor Code.

HISTORY

1. New section filed 6–7–2007; operative 6–7–2007 pursuant to Government Code section 11343.4 (Register 2007, No. 23).

§ 9792.14.   Liability for Penalty Assessments

(a) If more than one claims administrator or utilization review organization has been responsible for a claim file, utilization review file or other file that is being investigated, penalties may be assessed against each such entity for the violation(s) that occurred during the time each such entity had responsibility for the file or for the utilization review process.
(b) The claims administrator or utilization review organization is liable for all penalty assessments made against it, except that if the subject of the investigation is acting as an agent, the agent and the principal are jointly and severally liable for all penalty assessments resulting from a given investigation. This paragraph does not prohibit an agent and its principal from allocating the administrative penalty liability between them. Liability for civil penalties assessed pursuant to Labor Code section 129.5(e) for violations under Labor Code section 4610 or sections 9792.6 through 9792.10 of Title 8 of the California Code of Regulations shall not be allocated.
(c) Successor liability may be imposed on a claims administrator or utilization review organization that has merged with, consolidated, or otherwise continued the business of a corporation, other business entity or other person that was cited by the Administrative Director for violations of Labor Code section 4610 or sections 9792.6 through 9792.12. The surviving entity or person responsible for administering the utilization review process for an employer, shall assume and be liable for all the liabilities, obligations and penalties of the prior corporation or business entity. Successor liability will be imposed if

there has been a substantial continuity of business operations and/or the new business uses the same or substantially the same work force.

NOTE: Authority: Sections 133, 4610 and 5307.3, Labor Code. Reference: Sections 129, 129.5, 4062, 4600, 4600.4, 4604.5, 4610 and 4614, Labor Code.

HISTORY

1. New section filed 6–7–2007; operative 6–7–2007 pursuant to Government Code section 11343.4 (Register 2007, No. 23).

§ 9792.15. Administrative Penalties Pursuant to Labor Code section 4610 – Order to Show Cause, Notice of Hearing, Determination and Order, and Review Procedure

(a) Pursuant to Labor Code section 4610(i), the Administrative Director shall issue an Order to Show Cause Re: Assessment of Administrative Penalty when the Administrative Director, or his or her designee (the investigating unit of the Division of Workers' Compensation), has reason to believe that an employer, insurer or other entity subject to Labor Code section 4610 has failed to meet any of the requirements of this section or of any regulation adopted by the Administrative Director pursuant to the authority of section 4610.

(b) The order shall be in writing and shall include all of the following:

 (1) Notice that an administrative penalty may be assessed;

 (2) The final investigation report, which shall consist of the notice of utilization review penalty assessment, the performance rating, and may include one or more requests for documentation or compliance;

(c) The order shall be served personally or by registered or certified mail.

(d) Within thirty (30) calendar days after the date of service of the Order to Show Cause Re: Assessment of Administrative Penalties, the claims administrator or utilization review organization may pay the assessed administrative penalties or file an answer as the respondent with the Administrative Director, in which the respondent may:

 (1) Admit or deny in whole or in part any of the allegations set forth in the Order to Show Cause;

 (2) Contest the amount of any or all proposed administrative penalties;

 (3) Contest the existence of any or all of the violations;

 (4) Set forth any affirmative and other defenses;

 (5) Set forth the legal and factual bases for each defense.

(e) Any allegation and proposed penalty stated in the Order to Show Cause that is not contested shall be paid within thirty (30) calendar days after the date of service of the Order to Show Cause.

(f) Failure to timely file an answer shall constitute a waiver of the respondent's right to an evidentiary hearing. Unless set forth in the answer, all defenses to the Order to Show Cause shall be deemed waived. If the answer is not timely filed, within ten (10) days of the date for filing the answer, the respondent may file a written request for leave to file an answer. The respondent may also file a written request for leave to assert additional defenses, which the Administrative Director may grant upon a showing of good cause.

(g) The answer shall be in writing and signed by, or on behalf of, the claims administrator or utilization review organization and shall state the respondent's mailing address. It need not be verified or follow any particular form.

 (1) The respondent must file the original and one copy of the answer on the Administrative Director and concurrently serve one copy of the answer on the investigating unit of the Division of Workers' Compensation (designated by the Administrative Director). The original and all copies of any filings required by this section shall have a proof of service attached.

(h) Within sixty (60) calendar days of the issuance of the Order to Show Cause Re: Assessment of Administrative Penalty, the Administrative Director shall issue the Notice of the date, time and place of a hearing. The date of the hearing shall be at least ninety calendar days from the date of service of the Notice. The Notice shall be served personally or by registered or certified mail. Continuances will not be allowed without a showing of good cause.

(i) At any time before the hearing, the Administrative Director may file or permit the filing of an amended complaint or supplemental Order to Show Cause. All parties shall be notified thereof. If the amended complaint or supplemental Order to Show Cause presents new charges, the Administrative Director shall afford the respondent a reasonable opportunity to prepare its defense, and the respondent shall be entitled to file an amended answer.

(j) At the Administrative Director's discretion, the Administrative Director may proceed with an informal pre–hearing conference with the respondent in an effort to resolve the contested matters. If any or all of the violations or proposed penalties in the Order to Show Cause, the amended Order or the supplemental Order remain contested, those contested matters shall proceed to an evidentiary hearing.

(k) Whenever the Administrative Director's Order to Show Cause has been contested, the Administrative Director may designate a hearing officer to preside over the hearing. The authority of the Administrative Director or the designated hearing officer shall include, but is not limited to: conducting a pre–hearing settlement conference; setting the date for an evidentiary hearing and any continuances; issuing subpoenas for the attendance of any person residing anywhere within the state as a witness or party at any pre–hearing conference and hearing; issuing subpoenas duces tecum for the production of documents and things at the hearing; presiding at the hearings; administering oaths or affirmations and certifying official acts; ruling on objections and motions; issuing pre–hearing orders; and preparing a Recommended Determination and Opinion based on the hearing.

(l) The Administrative Director or the designated hearing officer shall set the time and place for any pre–hearing conference on the contested matters in the Order to Show Cause, and shall give sixty (60) calendar days written notice to all parties.

(m) The pre–hearing conference may address one or more of the following matters:

(1) Exploration of settlement possibilities;

(2) Preparation of stipulations;

(3) Clarification of issues;

(4) Rulings on the identity of witnesses and limitation of the number of witnesses;

(5) Objections to proffers of evidence;

(6) Order of presentation of evidence and cross–examination;

(7) Rulings regarding issuance of subpoenas and protective orders;

(8) Schedules for the submission of written briefs and schedules for the commencement and conduct of the hearing;

(9) Any other matters as shall promote the orderly and prompt conduct of the hearing.

(n) The Administrative Director or the designated hearing officer shall issue a pre–hearing order incorporating the matters determined at the pre–hearing conference. The Administrative Director or the designated hearing officer may direct one or more of the parties to prepare the pre–hearing order.

(o) Not less than thirty (30) calendar days prior to the date of the evidentiary hearing, the respondent shall file and serve the original and one copy of a written statement with the Administrative Director or the designated hearing officer specifying the legal and factual bases for its answer and each defense, listing all witnesses the respondent intends to call to testify at the hearing, and appending copies of all documents and other evidence the respondent intends to introduce into evidence at the hearing. A copy of the written statement and its attachments shall also concurrently be served on the investigating unit of the Division of Workers' Compensation. If the written statement and supporting evidence are not timely filed and served, the Administrative Director or the designated hearing officer shall dismiss the answer and issue a written Determination based on the evidence provided by the investigating unit of the Division of Workers' Compensation. Within ten (10) calendar days of the date for filing the written statement and supporting evidence, the respondent may file a written request for leave to file a written statement and supporting evidence. The Administrative Director or the designated hearing officer may grant the request, upon a showing of good cause. If leave is granted, the written statement and supporting evidence must be filed and served no later than ten (10) calendar days prior to the date of the hearing.

(p) Oral testimony shall be taken only on oath or affirmation.

(q) (1) Each party shall have these rights: to call and examine witnesses, to introduce exhibits; to cross–examine opposing witnesses on any matter relevant to the issues even though that matter was not covered in the direct examination; to impeach any witness regardless of which party first called him or her to testify; and to rebut the evidence.

(2) In the absence of a contrary order by the Administrative Director or the designated hearing officer, the investigating unit of the Division of Workers' Compensation shall present evidence first.

(3) The hearing need not be conducted according to the technical rules relating to evidence and witnesses, except as hereinafter provided. Any relevant evidence shall be admitted if it is the sort of evidence on which responsible persons are accustomed to rely in the conduct of serious affairs, regardless of the existence of any common law or statutory rule which might make the admission of the evidence improper over objection in civil actions.

(4) Hearsay evidence may be used for the purpose of supplementing or explaining other evidence but upon timely objection shall not be sufficient in itself to support a finding unless it would be admissible over objection in civil actions. An objection is timely if made before submission of the case to the Administrative Director or to the designated hearing officer.

(r) The written affidavit or declaration of any witness may be offered and shall be received into evidence provided that (i) the witness was listed in the written statement pursuant to section 9792.15(n); (ii) the statement is made by affidavit or by declaration under penalty of perjury; (iii) copies of the statement have been delivered to all opposing parties at least twenty (20) days prior to the hearing; and (iv) no opposing party has, at least ten (10) days before the hearing, delivered to the proponent of the evidence a written demand that the witness be produced in person to testify at the hearing. The Administrative Director or the designated hearing officer shall disregard any portion of the statement received pursuant to this regulation that would be inadmissible if the witness were testifying in person, but the inclusion of inadmissible matter does not render the entire statement inadmissible. Upon timely demand for production of a witness in lieu of admission of an affidavit or declaration, the proponent of that witness shall ensure the witness appears at the scheduled hearing and the proffered declaration or affidavit from that witness shall not be admitted. If the Administrative Director or the designated hearing officer determines that good cause exists that prevents the witness from appearing at the hearing, the declaration may be introduced in evidence, but it shall be given only the same effect as other hearsay evidence.

(s) The Administrative Director or the designated hearing officer shall issue a written Determination and Order Assessing Penalty, if any, including a statement of the basis for the Determination and each penalty assessed, within sixty (60) days of the date the case was submitted for decision, which shall be served on all parties. This requirement is directory and not jurisdictional.

(t) The Administrative Director shall have sixty (60) calendar days to adopt or modify the Determination and Order Assessing Penalty issued by the Administrative Director or the designated hearing officer. In the event the recommended Determination and Order of the designated hearing officer is modified, the Administrative Director shall include a statement of the basis for the Determination and Order Assessing Penalty signed and served by the Administrative Director, or his or her designee. If the Administrative Director does not act within sixty (60) calendar days, then the recommended Determination and Order shall become the Determination and Order on the sixty–first calendar day.

(u) The Determination and Order Assessing Penalty shall be served on all parties personally or by registered or certified mail by the Administrative Director.

(v) The Determination and Order Assessing Penalty, if any, shall become final on the day it is served, unless the aggrieved party files a timely Petition Appealing the Determination of the Administrative Director. All findings and assessments in the Determination and Order Assessing Penalty not contested in the Petition Appealing the Determination of the Administrative Director shall become final as though no petition were filed.

(w) At any time prior to the date the Determination and Order Assessing Penalty becomes final, the Administrative Director or designated hearing officer may correct the Determination and Order Assessing Penalty for clerical, mathematical or procedural error(s).

(x) Penalties assessed in a Determination and Order Assessing Penalty shall be paid within thirty (30) calendar days of the date the Determination and Order became final. A timely filed Petition Appealing the Determination of the Administrative Director shall toll the period for paying the penalty assessed for the item appealed.

(y) All appeals from any part or the entire Determination and Order Assessing Penalty shall be made in the form of a Petition Appealing the Determination of the Administrative Director, in conformance with the requirements of chapter 7, part 4 of Division 4 of the Labor Code. Any such Petition Appealing the Determination of the Administrative Director shall be filed at the Appeals Board in San Francisco (and not with any district office of the Workers' Compensation Appeals Board), in the same manner specified for petitions for reconsideration.

NOTE: Authority cited: Sections 133, 4610 and 5307.3, Labor Code. Reference: Sections 129, 129.5, 4062, 4600, 4600.4, 4604.5, 4610, 4614 and 5300, Labor Code.

HISTORY

1. New section filed 6–7–2007; operative 6–7–2007 pursuant to Government Code section 11343.4 (Register 2007, No. 23).

Appendix C

Intentionally blank

Forms

Intentionally blank

Utilization Review (UR) Complaint Form
State of California
Division of Workers' Compensation Medical Unit

Utilization review complaint form

What it is and how to use it

Utilization review (UR) is the process used by employers or insurance companies to review treatment to determine if it is medically necessary. All employers or the insurance companies handling workers' compensation claims are required by law to have a UR program. This program will be used to decide whether or not to approve medical treatment recommended by a physician.

The UR process is governed by Labor Code section 4610 and regulations written by the CA Division of Workers' Compensation (DWC). The DWC regulations are contained in Title 8, California Code of Regulations, sections 9792.6 et seq.

Medical providers, injured workers or others who find that UR is not being done according to the regulations can file a complaint with the DWC. The attached form may be used to register a complaint regarding UR services connected with workers' compensation injuries and treatment.

Injured workers may also benefit from reading the UR fact sheet (A) at http://www.dir.ca.gov/dwc/iwguides.html.

Please fill out the form as completely as possible, checking all complaint boxes that apply. Please include any additional information or documentation required to clarify the details of your complaint.

Completed complaint forms can be sent by U.S. mail, fax or e-mail to the address provided at the bottom of the form.

Glossary of terms:

Supporting documentation:	All written material related to the complaint(s), including letters or faxes regarding modification, delay or denial of specific treatment request(s).
COEM:	The American College of Occupational and Environmental Medicine. The state of California is currently using the ACOEM Practice Guidelines, Second Edition, as its medical treatment guidelines.

Utilization Review (UR) Complaint Form
State of California
Division of Workers' Compensation Medical Unit

Please fill out this form as completely as possible. This information will remain confidential, except to the extent necessary to investigate the complaint. If information is not known, leave item blank.

Today's date: _____ Name of person making complaint: _____ Ph #: _____

Address: _____ City: _____ ZIP Code _____

Person making complaint (check one):
☐ Injured worker   ☐ Attorney   ☐ Provider   ☐ Other: _____

_____   ___/___/___   _____
Name of injured worker   Date of injury   Claim number

_____   _____   _____
Physician/ Provider   Provider phone number   UR company

_____   _____
Name of insurance co. or claims administrator   Name & phone number of claims adjuster

Nature of complaint (check all that apply):

☐ Decision to modify, delay, or deny treatment was made by a non-physician

☐ Inadequate explanation of the reasons for UR decision

☐ Medical criteria or guidelines used to make decision were not disclosed

☐ UR decisions were not made within required time limits

☐ Treatment denied solely because the condition was not addressed by the ACOEM Practice Guidelines.

☐ No statement in decision that dispute shall be resolved in accordance with Labor Code section 4062

☐ Payment denied even though service was authorized

☐ Requested services denied for lack of information, but the reviewer did not request additional information

☐ Other _____

If you had trouble contacting the UR reviewer (check all that apply):

☐ Modification, delay or denial (MDD) letter did not contain the reviewer's contact information

☐ Failure to specify in MDD letter a four hour time block when reviewer available

☐ Unable to reach reviewer to discuss treatment decisions

☐ Failure to maintain telephone access for UR authorization from 9 a.m. to 5:30 p.m. PST on normal business days

☐ Unable to leave a message after business hours

☐ UR reviewer calls you after CA business hours

Please provide a brief description of the complaint and attach all supporting documentation.
If necessary, add extra pages for description:

To submit this complaint to the DWC Medical Unit, either:
1. Print this form and mail or fax it to: DWC Medical Unit-UR, PO Box 71010, Oakland, CA 94612—Attn: UR Complaints. **Fax: (510) 286-0686**
2. Save the completed form to your computer and e-mail it to: DWCManagedCare@dir.ca.gov. Please put "UR complaint" in th subject line.
However you submit this form, be sure to keep a copy for your records.

DWC UR complaint form 1

DWC Medical Unit
P.O. Box 71010
Oakland, CA 94612
Report of Suspected Medical Care Provider Fraud

Labor Code section 3823 requires any insurer, self-insured employer, third-party administrator, workers' compensation administrative law judge, audit unit, attorney, or other person that believes that a fraudulent claim has been made by any person or entity providing medical care, as described in Labor Code section 4600, to report the apparent fraudulent claim in the manner prescribed by the reporting protocols adopted by the administrative director of the Division of Workers' Compensation.

Complaining party (Please check the box that best describes you. Insurers, self-insured employers or third-party administrators should not use this form. These entities should use the Department of insurance suspected fraudulent claim referral form (FD-1).):

Person submitting the complaint:

☐ Injured worker ☐ Attorney ☐ Physician ☐ Other

Name: _____

Company: _____

Address: _____

City: _____ State: _____ Zip Code: _____

Home telephone number: ( ) _____

Work telephone number: ( ) _____

E-mail: _____

Preferred place to contact you: (check one) Home_____ Work_____

Complaint against (If more than one provider is involved, please attach additional sheets identifying each one):

Name: _____

Company: _____

Address: _____

City: _____ State: _____ Zip Code:_____

Type of health care provider: _____

DWC Form SMBFR 1115 (Rev.3/2006)

Description of the alleged fraudulent activity: Please provide as much detail as possible, including the nature of the unlawful act, why you believe that the activity you are reporting constitutes fraud, names, dates and documents. Please attach additional sheets if necessary and provide a copy of any relevant documentation you have. *PLEASE DO NOT ATTACH ORIGINAL DOCUMENTS*.

DWC Form SMBFR 1115 (Rev.3/2006)

Claim information (If more than one injured worker's care is involved, please attach additional sheets):

Date of injury: _____ WCAB case number(s) (if known): _____

Name of injured worker: _____

Address: _____

City: _____ State: _____ Zip Code: _____

Injured worker's Social Security number (if known): _____

Injured worker's date of birth (if known): _____

Name of employer at date of injury: _____

Address: _____

City: _____ State: _____ Zip Code: _____

Location where injury occurred:_____

Name of insurer or third party administrator: _____

Address:_____

City: _____ State: _____ Zip Code: _____

Claims administrator's claim number (if known): _____

Reports to other agencies Has the suspected fraudulent activity been reported to any law enforcement or professional licensing board? If so, please identify the agency, contact person and telephone number.

Report submitted by

Signature: _____ Date: _____

Please print your name: _____

Where to report (Send this completed form and photocopies of relevant supporting documents to):

Division of Workers' Compensation-Medical Unit
P.O. Box 71010
Oakland, CA 94612

DWC Form SMBFR 1115 (Rev.3/2006)

Intentionally blank

Appendix D

● Medical Treatment Utilization Schedule

Article 5.5.2. Medical treatment utilization schedule

§ 9792.20 Medical Treatment Utilization Schedule –Definitions

(a) "American College of Occupational and Environmental Medicine (ACOEM)" is a medical society of physicians and other health care professionals specializing in the field of occupational and environmental medicine, dedicated to promoting the health of workers through preventive medicine, clinical care, research, and education.

(b) "ACOEM Practice Guidelines" means the American College of Occupational and Environmental Medicine's Occupational Medicine Practice Guidelines, 2nd Edition (2004). The Administrative Director incorporates the ACOEM Practice Guidelines by reference. A copy may be obtained from the American College of Occupational and Environmental Medicine, 25 Northwest Point Blvd., Suite 700, Elk Grove Village, Illinois, 60007–1030 (www.acoem.org).

(c) "Claims administrator" is a self–administered workers' compensation insurer, a self–administered self–insured employer, a self–administered legally uninsured employer, a self–administered joint powers authority, a third–party claims administrator, or the California Insurance Guarantee Association.

(d) "Evidence–based " means based, at a minimum, on a systematic review of literature published in medical journals included in MEDLINE.

(e) "Functional improvement" means either a clinically significant improvement in activities of daily living or a reduction in work restrictions as measured during the history and physical exam, performed and documented as part of the evaluation and management visit billed under the Official Medical Fee Schedule (OMFS) pursuant to Sections 9789.10–9789.111; and a reduction in the dependency on continued medical treatment.

(f) "Medical treatment" is care which is reasonably required to cure or relieve the employee from the effects of the industrial injury consistent with the requirements of sections 9792.20–9792.23.

(g) "Medical treatment guidelines" means the most current version of written recommendations revised within the last five years which are systematically developed by a multidisciplinary process through a comprehensive literature search to assist in decision–making about the appropriate medical treatment for specific clinical circumstances.

(h) "MEDLINE" is the largest component of PubMed, the U.S. National Library of Medicine's database of biomedical citations and abstracts that is searchable on the Web. Its website address is www.pubmed.gov.

(i) "Nationally recognized" means published in a peer–reviewed medical journal; or developed, endorsed and disseminated by a national organization with affiliates based in two or more U.S. states; or currently adopted for use by one or more U.S. state governments or by the U.S. federal government; and is the most current version.

(j) "Peer reviewed" means that a medical study's content, methodology and results have been evaluated and approved prior to publication by an editorial board of qualified experts.

(k) "Scientifically based" means based on scientific literature, wherein the body of literature is identified through performance of a literature search in MEDLINE, the identified literature is evaluated, and then used as the basis for the guideline.

(l) "Strength of Evidence" establishes the relative weight that shall be given to scientifically based evidence.

NOTE: Authority: Sections 133, 4603.5, 5307.3 and 5307.27, Labor Code. Reference: Sections 77.5, 4600, 4604.5 and 5307.27, Labor Code.

HISTORY

1. New article 5.5.2 (sections 9792.20–9792.23) and section filed 6–15–2007; operative 6–15–2007 pursuant to Government Code section 11343.4 (Register 2007, No. 24).

§ 9792.20 Medical Treatment Utilization Schedule

(a) The Administrative Director adopts the Medical Treatment Utilization Schedule consisting of Sections 9792.20 through Section 9792.23. The Administrative Director adopts and incorporates by reference the following medical treatment guidelines into the Medical Treatment Utilization Schedule:

(1) The American College of Occupational and Environmental Medicine's Occupational Medicine Practice Guidelines (ACOEM Practice Guidelines), Second Edition (2004). A copy may be obtained from the American College of Occupational and Environmental Medicine, 25 Northwest Point Blvd., Suite 700, Elk Grove Village, Illinois, 60007–1030 (www.acoem.org).

(2) Acupuncture Medical Treatment Guidelines.

The Acupuncture Medical Treatment Guidelines set forth in this subdivision shall supersede the text in the ACOEM Practice Guidelines, Second Edition, relating to acupuncture, except for shoulder complaints, and shall address acupuncture treatment where not discussed in the ACOEM Practice Guidelines.

(A) Definitions:

(i) "Acupuncture" is used as an option when pain medication is reduced or not tolerated, it may be used as an adjunct to physical rehabilitation and/or surgical intervention to hasten functional recovery. It is the insertion and removal of filiform needles to stimulate acupoints (acupuncture points). Needles may be inserted, manipulated, and retained for a period of time. Acupuncture can be used to reduce pain, reduce inflammation, increase blood flow, increase range of motion, decrease the side effect of medication–induced nausea, promote relaxation in an anxious patient, and reduce muscle spasm.

(ii) "Acupuncture with electrical stimulation" is the use of electrical current (micro–amperage or milli–amperage) on the needles at the acupuncture site. It is used to increase effectiveness of the needles by continuous stimulation of the acupoint. Physiological effects (depending on location and settings) can include endorphin release for pain relief, reduction of inflammation, increased blood circulation, analgesia through interruption of pain stimulus, and muscle relaxation. It is indicated to treat chronic pain conditions, radiating pain along a nerve pathway, muscle spasm, inflammation, scar tissue pain, and pain located in multiple sites.

(iii) "Chronic pain for purposes of acupuncture" means pain that persists for at least 30 days beyond the usual course of an acute disease or a reasonable time for an injury to heal or that is associated with a chronic pathological process that causes continuous pain (e.g., reflex sympathetic dystrophy). The very definition of chronic pain describes a delay or outright failure to relieve pain associated with some specific illness or accident.

(B) Indications for acupuncture or acupuncture with electrical stimulation include the following presenting complaints in reference to the following ACOEM Practice Guidelines Chapter Headings:

(i) Neck and Upper Back Complaints

(ii) Elbow Complaints

(iii) Forearm, Wrist, and Hand Complaints

(iv) Low Back Complaints

(v) Knee Complaints

(vi) Ankle and Foot Complaints

(vii) Pain, Suffering, and the Restoration of Function

(C) Frequency and duration of acupuncture or acupuncture with electrical stimulation may be performed as follows:

(i) Time to produce functional improvement: 3 to 6 treatments.

(ii) Frequency: 1 to 3 times per week

(iii) Optimum duration: 1 to 2 months

(D) Acupuncture treatments may be extended if functional improvement is documented as defined in Section 9792.20(e).

(b) The Medical Treatment Utilization Schedule is intended to assist in the provision of medical treatment by offering an analytical framework for the evaluation and treatment of injured workers and to help those who make decisions regarding the medical treatment of injured workers understand what treatment has been proven effective in providing the best medical outcomes to those workers, in accordance with section 4600 of the Labor Code.

(c) Treatment shall not be denied on the sole basis that the condition or injury is not addressed by the Medical Treatment Utilization Schedule. In this situation, the claims administrator shall authorize treatment if such treatment is in accordance with other scientifically and evidence–based, peer–reviewed, medical treatment guidelines that are nationally recognized by the medical community, in accordance with subdivisions (b) and (c) of section 9792.22, and pursuant to the Utilization Review Standards found in Section 9792.6 through Section 9792.10.

(E) It is beyond the scope of the Acupuncture Medical Treatment Guidelines to state the precautions, limitations, contraindications or adverse events resulting from acupuncture or acupuncture with electrical stimulations. These decisions are left up to the acupuncturist.

NOTE: Authority: Sections 133, 4603.5, 5307.3 and 5307.27, Labor Code. Reference: Sections 77.5, 4600, 4604.5 and 5307.27, Labor Code.

HISTORY
New section filed 6–15–2007; operative 6–15–2007 pursuant to Government Code section 11343.4 (Register 2007, No. 24).

§ 9792.22 Presumption of Correctness, Burden of Proof and Strength of Evidence

(a) The Medical Treatment Utilization Schedule is presumptively correct on the issue of extent and scope of medical treatment and diagnostic services addressed in the Medical Treatment Utilization Schedule for the duration of the medical condition. The presumption is rebuttable and may be controverted by a preponderance of scientific medical evidence establishing that a variance from the schedule is reasonably required to cure or relieve the injured worker from the effects of his or her injury. The presumption created is one affecting the burden of proof.

(b) For all conditions or injuries not addressed by the Medical Treatment Utilization Schedule, authorized treatment and diagnostic services shall be in accordance with other scientifically and evidence–based medical treatment guidelines that are nationally recognized by the medical community.

(c) (1) For conditions or injuries not addressed by either subdivisions (a) or (b) above; for medical treatment and diagnostic services at variance with both subdivisions (a) or (b) above; or where a recommended medical treatment or diagnostic service covered under subdivision (b) is at variance with another treatment guideline also covered under subdivision (b), the following ACOEM's strength of evidence rating methodology is adopted and incorporated as set forth below, and shall be used to evaluate scientifically based evidence published in peer–reviewed, nationally recognized journals to recommend specific medical treatment or diagnostic services:

(A) Table A – Criteria Used to Rate Randomized Controlled Trials

Studies shall be rated using the following 11 criteria. Each criterion shall be rated 0, 0.5, or 1.0, thus the overall ratings range from 0–11. A study is considered low quality if the composite rating was 3.5 or less, intermediate quality if rated 4–7.5, and high quality if rated 8–11

Criteria	Rating Explanation
Randomization: Assessment of the degree that randomization was both reported to have been performed and successfully* achieved through analyses of comparisons of variables between the two groups.*Simply allocating individuals to groups does not constitute sufficient grounds to assess the success of randomization. The groups must be comparable; otherwise, the randomization was unsuccessful.	Rating is "0" if the study is not randomized or reports that it was and subsequent analyses of the data/tables suggest it either was not randomized or was unsuccessful. Rating is "0.5" if there is mention of randomization and it appears as if it was performed, however there are no data on the success of randomization, it appears incomplete, or other questions about randomization cannot be adequately addressed. Rating is "1.0" if randomization is specifically stated and data reported on subgroups suggests that the study did achieve successful randomization.
Treatment Allocation Concealed: Concealment of the allocation scheme from all involved, not just the patient.	Rating is "0" if there is no description of how members of the research team or subjects would have not been able to know how they were going to receive a particular treatment, or the process used would not be concealed. Rating is "0.5" if the article mentions how allocation was concealed, but the concealment was either partial involving only some of those involved or other questions about it are unable to be completely addressed. Rating is "1.0" if there is a concealment process described that would conceal the treatment allocation to all those involved.
Baseline Comparability: Measures how well the baseline groups are comparable (e.g., age, gender, prior treatment).	Rating is "0" if analyses show that the groups were dissimilar at baseline or it cannot be assessed. Rating is "0.5" if there is general comparability, though one variable may not be comparable. Rating is "1.0" if there is good comparability for all variables between the groups at baseline.
Patient Blinded	Rating is "0" if there is no mention of blinding of the patient. Rating is "0.5" if it mentions blinding, but the methods are unclear. Rating is "1.0" if the study reports blinding, describes how that was carried out, and would plausibly blind the patient.
Provider Blinded	Rating is "0" if there is no mention of blinding of the provider. Rating is "0.5" if it mentions blinding, but the methods are unclear. Rating is "1.0" if the study reports blinding, describes how that was carried out and would plausibly blind the provider.

Assessor Blinded	Rating is "0" if there is no mention of blinding of the assessor. Rating is "0.5" if it mentions blinding, but the methods are unclear. Rating is "1.0" if the study reports blinding, describes how that was carried out and would plausibly blind the assessor.
Controlled for Co–interventions: The degree to which the study design controlled for multiple interventions (e.g., a combination of stretching exercises and anti–inflammatory medication or mention of not using other treatments during the study).	Rating is "0" if there are multiple interventions or no description of how this was avoided. Rating is "0.5" if there is brief mention of this potential problem. Rating is "1.0" if there is a detailed description of how co–interventions were avoided.
Compliance Acceptable: Measures the degree of non–compliance.	Rating is "0" if there is no mention of non–compliance. Rating is "0.5" if non–compliance is briefly addressed and the description suggests that there was compliance, but a complete assessment is not possible. Rating is "1.0" if there are specific data and the non–compliance rate is less than 20%.
Dropout Rate: Measures the drop–out rate.	Rating is "0" if there is no mention of drop–outs or it cannot be inferred from the data presented. Rating is "0.5" if the drop–out issue is briefly addressed and the description suggests that there were few drop–outs, but a complete assessment is not possible. Rating is "1.0" if there are specific data and the drop–out rate is under 20%.
Timing of Assessments: Timing rates the timeframe for the assessments between the study groups.	Rating is "0" if the timing of the evaluations is different between the groups. Rating is "0.5" if the timing is nearly identical (e.g., one day apart). Rating is "1.0" if the timing of the assessments between the groups is identical.
Analyzed by Intention to Treat: This rating is for whether the study was analyzed with an intent to treat analysis.	Rating is "0" if it was not analyzed by intent to treat. Rating is "0.5" if there is not mention of intent to treat analysis, but the results would not have been different (e.g., there was nearly 100% compliance and no drop–outs). Rating is "1.0" if the study specifies analyses by intention to treat.
Lack of Bias: This rating does not enter into the overall rating of an article. This is an overall indication of the degree to which biases are felt to be present in the study.	Rating is "0" if there are felt to be significant biases that are uncontrolled in the study and may have influenced the study's results. Rating is "0.5" if there are felt to be some biases present, but the results are less likely to have been influenced by those biases. Rating is "1.0" if there are few biases, or those are well controlled and unlikely to have influenced the study's results.

(B) Table B – Strength of Evidence Ratings

Levels of evidence shall be used to rate the quality of the body of evidence. The body of evidence shall consist of all studies on a given topic that are used to develop evidence–based recommendations. Levels of evidence shall be applied when studies are relevant to the topic and study working populations. Study outcomes shall be consistent and study data shall be homogeneous.

A	**Strong evidence–base**: One or more well–conducted systematic reviews or meta–analyses, or two or more high–quality studies.
B	**Moderate evidence–base**: At least one high–quality study, a well–conducted systematic review or meta–analysis of lower quality studies or multiple lower–quality studies relevant to the topic and the working population.
C	**Limited evidence–base**: At least one study of intermediate quality.
I	**Insufficient Evidence**: Evidence is insufficient or irreconcilable.

(2) Evidence shall be given the highest weight in the order of the strength of evidence.

NOTE: Authority: Sections 133, 4603.5, 5307.3 and 5307.27, Labor Code. Reference: Sections 77.5, 4600, 4604.5 and 5307.27, Labor Code.

HISTORY

1. New section filed 6–15–2007; operative 6–15–2007 pursuant to Government Code section 11343.4 (Register 2007, No. 24).

§ 9792.23.   Medical Evidence Evaluation Advisory Committee.

(a) (1) The Medical Director shall create a medical evidence evaluation advisory committee to provide recommendations to the Medical Director on matters concerning the medical treatment utilization schedule. The recommendations are advisory only and shall not constitute scientifically based evidence.

    (A) If the Medical Director position becomes vacant, the Administrative Director shall appoint a competent person to temporarily assume the authority and duties of the Medical Director as set forth in this section, until such time that the Medical Director position is filled.

  (2) The members of the medical evidence evaluation advisory committee shall be appointed by the Medical Director, or his or her designee, and shall consist of 17 members of the medical community holding the following licenses: Medical Doctor (M.D.) board certified by an American Board of Medical Specialties (ABMS) approved specialty board; Doctor of Osteopathy (D.O.) board certified by an ABMS or American Osteopathic Association (AOA) approved specialty board; M.D. board certified by a Medical Board of California (MBC) approved specialty board; Doctor of Chiropractic (D.C.); Physical Therapy (P.T.); Occupational Therapy (O.T.); Acupuncture (L.Ac.); Psychology (PhD.); or Doctor of Podiatric Medicine (DPM), and representing the following specialty fields:

    (A) One member shall be from the orthopedic field;

    (B) One member shall be from the chiropractic field;

    (C) One member shall be from the occupational medicine field;

    (D) One member shall be from the acupuncture medicine field;

    (E) One member shall be from the physical therapy field;

    (F) One member shall be from the psychology field;

    (G) One member shall be from the pain specialty field;

    (H) One member shall be from the occupational therapy field;

    (I) One member shall be from the psychiatry field;

    (J) One member shall be from the neurosurgery field;

    (K) One member shall be from the family physician field;

    (L) One member shall be from the neurology field;

    (M) One member shall be from the internal medicine field;

    (N) One member shall be from the physical medicine and rehabilitation field;

    (O) One member shall be from the podiatrist field;

    (P) Two additional members shall be appointed at the discretion of the Medical Director or his or her designee.

  (3) In addition to the seventeen members of the medical evidence evaluation advisory committee appointed under subdivision (a)(2) above, the Medical Director, or his or her designee, may appoint an additional three members to the medical evidence evaluation advisory committee as subject matter experts for any given topic.

(b) The Medical Director, or his or her designee, shall serve as the chairperson of the medical evidence evaluation advisory committee.

(c) To evaluate evidence when making recommendations to revise, update or supplement the medical treatment utilization schedule, the members of the medical evidence evaluation advisory committee shall:

  (1) Apply the requirements of subdivision (b) of Section 9792.22 in reviewing medical treatment guidelines to insure that the guidelines are scientifically and evidence–based, and nationally recognized by the medical community;

  (2) Apply the ACOEM's strength of evidence rating methodology to the scientific evidence as set forth in subdivision (c) of Section 9792.22 after identifying areas in the guidelines which do not meet the requirements set forth in subdivision (b) of Section 9792.22;

  (3) Apply in reviewing the scientific evidence, the ACOEM's strength of evidence rating methodology for treatments where there are no medical treatment guidelines or where a guideline is developed by the Administrative Director, as set forth in subdivision (c) of Section 9792.22.

(d) The members of the medical evidence evaluation advisory committee, except for the three subject matter experts, shall serve a term of two year period, but shall remain in that position until a successor is selected. The subject matter experts shall serve as members of the medical evidence evaluation advisory committee until the evaluation of the subject matter guideline is completed. The members of the committee shall meet as necessary, but no less than four (4) times a year.

(f) The Administrative Director, in consultation with the Medical Director, may revise, update, and supplement the medical treatment utilization schedule as necessary.

NOTE: Authority: Sections 133, 4603.5, 5307.3 and 5307.27, Labor Code. Reference: Sections 77.5, 4600, 4604.5 and 5307.27, Labor Code.

HISTORY

1. New section filed 6–15–2007; operative 6–15–2007 pursuant to Government Code section 11343.4 (Register 2007, No. 24).

No Forms

Intentionally blank

Appendix E

● Spinal Surgery Second Opinion Procedure

Article 5.1. Spinal Surgery Second Opinion Procedure

§ 9788.01. Definitions

As used in this Article:

(a) "Agreed second opinion physician" is a physician agreed upon by an employer and represented employee pursuant to Labor Code Section 4062 subdivision (b).

(b) "Completion of the second opinion process" occurs on the forty–fifth day after the receipt of the treating physician's report by the employer, unless the time has been extended by mutual written consent of the parties as provided in these regulations, or unless the time has been extended as provided in these regulations because the employee failed to attend an examination with the second opinion physician or agreed second opinion physician.

(c) "CPTã" means the procedure codes set forth in the American Medical Association's Physicians' Current Procedural Terminology (CPT) 1997, copyright 1996, American Medical Association.

(d) "Income" of a person includes the income of that person's business partner, physician member of the office of a group practice as defined in Labor Code section 139.3, spouse, cohabitant, and immediate family. Income of a second opinion physician does not include income from employment which had terminated prior to the time the physician was selected as a second opinion physician where there is no reasonable prospect of future employment.

(e) "Material familial affiliation" means a relationship in which one of the persons or entities listed in subdivision (c) of Labor Code section 4062 is the parent, child, grandparent, grandchild, sibling, uncle, aunt, nephew, niece, spouse, or cohabitant of the second opinion physician. For entities of the employer, insurer, physician, medical group, independent practice association, administrator, utilization review entity, facility, or institution mentioned in subdivision (c) of Labor Code section 4062, which are not persons, the familial affiliation shall be determined by considering the relationship of all of the officers, directors, owners and management employees, and individual claims administrators and supervisors to the second opinion physician.

(f) "Material financial affiliation" includes all of the following financial relationships between the second opinion physician and another person or entity listed in subdivision (c) of Labor Code section 4062, or parent or subsidiary or otherwise related business entity of a person or entity:

(1) One has a direct or indirect investment worth two thousand dollars or more in the other;

(2) One is a director, officer, partner, trustee, employee, or holds any position of management in the other;

(3) One has a direct or indirect interest worth two thousand dollars or more in fair market value in an interest in real estate owned or controlled by the other;

(4) One has received income of any kind, including gifts, from the other, aggregating three hundred dollars or more within the twelve months prior to the time of selection as a second opinion physician, except that the following income shall not be counted for this purpose:

    A. income for services as a second opinion physician;

    B. income for services as a treating physician;

    C. income for services as an agreed medical examiner;

    D. income for services as a panel Qualified Medical Evaluator selected for unrepresented employees;

    E. income from services as a Qualified Medical Evaluator for represented employees.

    F. income for services as a Qualified Medical Evaluator for an employer from the first five cases in any twelve month period for the same employer, carrier, or administration.

(5) One has an employment or promise of employment relationship with the other.

(g) "Material professional affiliation" is any relationship in which the second opinion physician shares office space with, or works in the same office of, any of the other persons or entities listed in subdivision (c) of Labor Code section 4062.

(h) "Parent, subsidiary, and otherwise related business entity" have the same meanings as in Section 18703.1, Title 2, Division 6 of the California Code of Regulations.

(i) "Receipt of the treating physician's report" is the day it was first received by the employer, insurance carrier, or administrator.

(j) "Retired spinal surgeon" is a physician currently licensed in the State of California who once had, but no longer has, hospital privileges to perform spinal surgery described in Section 9788.2(c)(2). "Retired spinal surgeon" does not include a physician whose hospital privileges to perform spinal surgery were either surrendered by the physician or were terminated or not renewed by the hospital, after disciplinary charges were filed or after a disciplinary investigation was commenced.

(k) "Second opinion physician" is the physician who is randomly selected pursuant to subdivision (b) of Labor Code section 4062 to render the second opinion on a treating physician's recommendation of spinal surgery.

(l) "Spinal surgery" includes:

(1) any of the procedures listed in the Official Medical Fee Schedule denominated by the following CPTR procedure code numbers: 22100, 22101, 22102, 22103, 22110, 22112, 22114, 22116, 22210, 22212, 22214, 22216, 22220, 22222, 22224, 22226, 22548, 22554, 22556, 22558, 22585, 22590, 22595, 22600, 22610, 22612, 22614, 22630, 22632, 22800, 22802, 22804, 22808, 22810, 22812, 22830, 22840, 22841, 22842, 22843, 22844, 22845, 22846, 22847, 22848, 22849, 22850, 22851, 22852, 22855; 22899; 62287, 62292, 63001 through 63615; and,

(2) any other procedure, which is not listed in subdivision (l)(1), which is a non–diagnostic invasive procedure to the spine or associated anatomical structures to perform an operative or curative procedure which is not primarily an analgesic procedure; and,

(3) any procedure which involves the introduction of energy, a foreign substance, or a device that destroys tissue in the spine and/or associated structures, including nerves and disks, or involves the implantation of devices into the spine and associated structures, including nerves and disks, and which is not primarily an analgesic procedure;

(4) Notwithstanding subdivisions (1) through (3), "spinal surgery" does not include penetration of the body by needles in the performance of acupuncture by a practitioner whose license permits the performance of acupuncture, nor does "spinal surgery" include surgery which is required because of a bona fide medical emergency.

NOTE: Authority cited: Sections 133, 5307.1 and 5307.3, Labor Code. Reference: Sections 4062(b) and 4600, Labor Code.

HISTORY

1. New article 5.1 (sections 9788.01–9788.91) and section filed 7–2–2004 as an emergency; operative 7–2–2004 (Register 2004, No. 27). A Certificate of Compliance must be transmitted to OAL by 11–1–2004 or emergency language will be repealed by operation of law on the following day.

2. Certificate of Compliance as to 7–2–2004 order, including amendment of subsection (l)(1), transmitted to OAL 11–1–2004 and filed 12–15–2004 (Register 2004, No. 51).

§ 9788.1. Employer's Objection To Report Of Treating Physician Recommending Spinal Surgery

(a) An objection to the treating physician's recommendation for spinal surgery shall be written on the form prescribed by the Administrative Director in Section 9788.11. The employer shall include with the objection a copy of the treating physician's report containing the recommendation to which the employer objects. The objection shall include the employer's reasons, specific to the employee, for the objection to the recommended procedure. The form must be executed by a principal or employee of the employer, insurance carrier, or administrator.

(b) Declarations.

(1) Declaration as to receipt of treating physician's recommendation.

The employer's objection shall include one of two versions of a declaration made under penalty of perjury regarding the date the report containing the treating physician's recommendation was first received by the employer, employer's insurance carrier, or administrator, in the format of the form prescribed by Section 9788.11.

Version A of the declaration shall be used if the declarant has personal knowledge of all the facts. Version B of the declaration may be used if the recipient employer, insurance carrier or administrator has a written policy of date–stamping every piece of mail on the date it was delivered to its office, this policy is consistently followed, the declarant is knowledgeable about the policy, and the report bears a legible date stamp showing when it was received in the office.

The declaration must be executed by a principal or employee of the employer, insurance carrier, or administrator.

(2) Declaration as to service of objection.

The employer's objection shall include a declaration made under penalty of perjury, in the format of the form prescribed by Section 9788.11 as to the date and time the objection was served, and the manner in which the objection was served.

The declaration must be executed by a principal or employee of the employer, insurance carrier, or administrator.

(c) Service of Objection.

(1) The employer shall serve the objection and the report containing the treating physician's recommendation on the Administrative Director, the employee, the employee's attorney, if any, and on the treating physician within 10 days of receipt of the treating physician's report containing the recommendation. An objection which is mailed to the Administrative Director and is received more than ten days after the date of receipt of the treating physician's report is untimely unless it bears a postmark date no later than the tenth day after the date of receipt of the treating physician's report. The employer shall serve the original of the objection on the Administrative Director.

(2) Service on the Administrative Director shall be by mail or physical delivery. Service on the employee, employee's attorney, and treating physician shall be by mail or physical delivery or, if prior consent has been obtained from the recipient to be served by fax, may be by fax.

(d) If after an employer has served the objection on the Administrative Director, either the employer and a represented employee agree to an agreed second opinion physician or the employer withdraws its objection to the treating physician's recommendation for spinal surgery, the employer shall notify the Administrative Director within one working day of the agreement or withdrawal of objection. This notification may be by fax.

NOTE: Authority cited: Sections 133 and 5307.3, Labor Code. Reference: Sections 4062(b) and 4600, Labor Code.

HISTORY

1. New section filed 7–2–2004 as an emergency; operative 7–2–2004 (Register 2004, No. 27). A Certificate of Compliance must be transmitted to OAL by 11–1–2004 or emergency language will be repealed by operation of law on the following day.

2. Certificate of Compliance as to 7–2–2004 order, including amendment of section, transmitted to OAL 11–1–2004 and filed 12–15–2004 (Register 2004, No. 51).

§ 9788.11. Form for Employer's Objection To Report Of Treating Physician Recommending Spinal Surgery

DWC form 233 (.pdf document)

This form, together with the report of the treating physician containing the recommendation for treatment which is objected to, is to be mailed to the Administrative Director, Medical Unit, P.O. Box 8888, San Francisco, CA 94128–8888, and copies served by mail or physical delivery or fax on the employee, employee's attorney, and treating physician. The objection form and report may be served on the employee, employee's attorney, and treating physician by fax, but only if prior consent has been obtained from the recipient to be served by fax. This form may not be served on the Administrative Director by fax. This Objection must be sent within ten (10) days of the first receipt by any of the employer, insurance carrier, or administrator, of the treating physician's report containing the recommendation.

Declarations

The form contains two declarations to be signed under penalty of perjury. The first is a declaration specifying the date that the report containing the treating physician's recommendation was first received by the employer, insurance carrier, or administrator. The second declaration specifies the date and manner of serving of the objection.

The form includes two versions of the declaration specifying the date of receipt of the report. Only one version needs to be completed. Version A shall be completed by an employee having personal knowledge of the facts of when the report was received, such as the person who opened the mail. Version B shall be completed by an employee who knows from the date stamp when the report was received, if all mail to the firm is date–stamped on the date it is received, the signer is readily knowledgeable about the policy, the policy is consistently followed, and the report bears a legible date stamp.

The declaration regarding service of the objection must be signed by the person having knowledge of how the report was served.

NOTE: Authority cited: Sections 133 and 5307.3, Labor Code. Reference: Sections 4062(b) and 4600, Labor Code.

HISTORY

1. New section filed 7–2–2004 as an emergency; operative 7–2–2004 (Register 2004, No. 27). A Certificate of Compliance must be transmitted to OAL by 11–1–2004 or emergency language will be repealed by operation of law on the following day.
2. Certificate of Compliance as to 7–2–2004 order, including repealer and new form, transmitted to OAL 11–1–2004 and filed 12–15–2004 (Register 2004, No. 51).

§ 9788.2. Qualifications of Spinal Surgery Second Opinion Physicians

(a) An agreed second opinion physician may be any California licensed board–certified or board–eligible orthopaedic surgeon or neurosurgeon.

(b) The Administrative Director shall maintain a list of qualified surgeons who have applied, and whom the Administrative Director has found to be eligible to give second opinions under Labor Code § 4062 (b) after random selection by the Administrative Director.

(c) To apply to be on the Administrative Director's list, a physician shall demonstrate to the satisfaction of the Administrative Director that the physician:

    (1) Is currently board certified either as a neurosurgeon by the American Board of Neurological Surgery or the American Osteopathic Board of Surgery, or as an orthopaedic surgeon by either the American Board of Orthopaedic Surgery or the American Osteopathic Board of Orthopedic Surgery;

    (2) Has current hospital privileges in good standing at an accredited hospital in California to perform spinal surgery without proctoring;

    (3) Has an unrestricted license as a physician and surgeon in California;

    (4) Has no record of previous discipline by any governmental physician licensing agency, and is not then under accusation by any governmental physician licensing agency;

    (5) Has not been terminated or had discipline imposed by the Industrial Medical Council or Administrative Director in relation to the physician's role as a Qualified Medical Evaluator; is not then under accusation by the Industrial Medical Council or Administrative Director; has not been denied renewal of Qualified Medical Evaluator status, except for non–completion of continuing education or for non–payment of fees; has neither resigned nor failed to renew Qualified Medical Evaluator status while under accusation or probation by the Industrial Medical Council or Administrative Director or after notification that reappointment as a Qualified Medical Evaluator may or would be denied for reasons other than non–completion of continuing education or non–payment of fees; and has not filed any applications or forms with the Industrial Medical Council or Administrative Director which contained any untrue material statements; and

    (6) Has not been convicted of any crime involving dishonesty or any crime of moral turpitude.

(d) The Administrative Director may also accept to be on the list a retired spinal surgeon who does not meet the qualifications of subdivision (c)(2), but who does meet the qualifications of subdivisions (c)(1), (c)(3), (c)(5), (c)(6), and either (c)(4) or (e), if the retired spinal surgeon met the qualifications of subdivision (c)(2) within three years of application. The qualification of such physician shall not extend longer than three years from the last time the physician met the requirements of subdivision (c)(2).

(e) The Administrative Director may also accept to be on the list a physician who does not meet the qualifications of subdivision (c)(4), but who does meet the qualifications of subdivisions (c)(1), (c)(2), (c)(5), (c)(6), and either (c)(3) or (d), if at least five years have elapsed since discipline was imposed, the physician is not currently the subject of a discipline accusation, and the Administrative Director finds that the physician has been rehabilitated.

NOTE: Authority: Sections 133 and 5307.3, Labor Code. Reference: Sections 4062(b) and 4600, Labor Code.

HISTORY

1. New section filed 7–2–2004 as an emergency; operative 7–2–2004 (Register 2004, No. 27). A Certificate of Compliance must be transmitted to OAL by 11–1–2004 or emergency language will be repealed by operation of law on the following day.
2. Certificate of Compliance as to 7–2–2004 order transmitted to OAL 11–1–2004 and filed 12–15–2004 (Register 2004, No. 51).

§ 9788.3. Application Procedures

Physicians seeking to serve as a second opinion physician shall:

(a) Make application to the Administrative Director on the form prescribed by the Administrative Director in Section 9788.31.

(b) Furnish certified copies of their board certification and hospital privileges, and shall submit other documentation of their qualifications as the Administrative Director may require.

(c) Both after making application, and after being notified by the Administrative Director that the application has been accepted, the physician shall keep the Administrative Director informed of any change of address, telephone, or fax number.

(d) The physician shall also notify the Administrative Director within 10 days, if the California Medical Board, or any other state medical board from whom the physician is licensed, files any accusation or charges against the physician, or imposes any discipline.

NOTE: Authority cited: Sections 133 and 5307.3, Labor Code. Reference: Sections 4062(b) and 4600, Labor Code.

HISTORY
1. New section filed 7–2–2004 as an emergency; operative 7–2–2004 (Register 2004, No. 27). A Certificate of Compliance must be transmitted to OAL by 11–1–2004 or emergency language will be repealed by operation of law on the following day.
2. Certificate of Compliance as to 7–2–2004 order, including new subsection (d), transmitted to OAL 11–1–2004 and filed 12–15–2004 (Register 2004, No. 51).

§ 9788.31.   Application Form

DWC form 232 (.pdf document)

NOTE: Authority cited: Sections 133 and 5307.3, Labor Code. Reference: Sections 4062(b) and 4600, Labor Code

HISTORY
1. New section filed 7–2–2004 as an emergency; operative 7–2–2004 (Register 2004, No. 27). A Certificate of Compliance must be transmitted to OAL by 11–1–2004 or emergency language will be repealed by operation of law on the following day.
2. Certificate of Compliance as to 7–2–2004 order transmitted to OAL 11–1–2004 and filed 12–15–2004 (Register 2004, No. 51).
3. Change without regulatory effect amending form filed 10–18–2006 pursuant to section 100, title 1, California Code of Regulations (Register 2006, No.42).

§ 9788.32.   Administrative Director's Action on Application

(a) After reviewing a completed application, if the Administrative Director finds that the applicant meets the qualifications, he/she shall notify the applicant by mail, and add the applicant's name to the list of second opinion physicians.

(b) If a physician applicant does not qualify only because the physician has a record of previous discipline by a governmental physician licensing agency and if at least five years have elapsed since discipline was imposed, the Administrative Director shall notify the physician that the physician may within ninety days submit written evidence of the physician's rehabilitation from the offenses or inadequacies for which discipline was imposed. If no evidence is submitted within that time period, the Administrative Director shall reject the application. If the physician submits evidence, the Administrative Director shall consider any written evidence submitted by the physician along with any other evidence the Administrative Director may obtain through investigation. The Administrative Director shall make a finding as to whether the physician has been rehabilitated from the offenses or inadequacies for which discipline was imposed. If the Administrative Director does not find that the physician has been rehabilitated, the Administrative Director shall reject the application.

(c) If the Administrative Director finally determines that an applicant does not meet the qualifications, he/she shall notify the applicant by mail that the application is rejected.

(d) An applicant whose application has been rejected may, within 30 days of the mailing of the notice of rejection, request a hearing by filing a written request for hearing with the Administrative Director. If a written request for hearing is not received by the Administrative Director within 30 days of the mailing of the notice of rejection, the applicant shall be deemed to have waived any appeal or request for hearing.

(e) Upon receipt of a written request for hearing, the Administrative Director shall serve a statement of issues, as provided in Government Code section 11504.

(f) Hearings shall be held under the procedures of Chapter 5 of Part 1 of Division 3 of Title 2 of the Government Code (commencing with section 11500) and the regulations of the Office of Administrative Hearings (California Code of Regulations, Title 1, Division 2).

(g) Failure to file timely a mailed notice of defense or failure to appear at a noticed hearing or conference shall constitute a waiver of a right to a hearing.

(h) An applicant whose application has been rejected may reapply after:
 1. one year has elapsed from the date his application was rejected; or

2. the time when the deficiencies which were the reasons for rejection have been corrected; whichever occurs first.

NOTE: Authority cited: Sections 133 and 5307.3, Labor Code; and Sections 11400.20 and 11415.10, Government Code. Reference: Sections 4062(b) and 4600, Labor Code.

HISTORY
1. New section filed 7–2–2004 as an emergency; operative 7–2–2004 (Register 2004, No. 27). A Certificate of Compliance must be transmitted to OAL by 11–1–2004 or emergency language will be repealed by operation of law on the following day.
2. Certificate of Compliance as to 7–2–2004 order transmitted to OAL 11–1–2004 and filed 12–15–2004 (Register 2004, No. 51).

§ 9788.4. Removal of Physicians from the Spinal Surgery Second Opinion Physician List

(a) The Administrative Director may remove from the list any physician whenever the Administrative Director learns:
   (1) That the physician no longer meets the qualifications to be on the list; or
   (2) That the California Medical Board, or any other state medical board from whom the physician is licensed, has filed any accusation against the physician; or
   (3) That the physician, having been notified by the Administrative Director of the physician's selection to render a second opinion in any case, has not served the second opinion report in that case within forty–five days after the receipt of the treating physician's report by the employer, unless the employee failed to attend an examination; or
   (4) That the physician's application to be on the list contained statements which were not true; or
   (5) That the physician has at any time failed to disclose to the Administrative Director that the physician had a material professional, familial, or financial affiliation with any of the persons or entities listed in subdivision (c) of Labor Code section 4062 in any case in which the physician had been selected as a second opinion physician.
   (6) That the physician has declined to accept assignment as a second opinion physician at any time except during a period for which the physician had notified the Administrative Director of unavailability per Section 9788.45.
   (7) That the physician has filed notifications of unavailability for more than 120 days of any one year period. The first one year period shall commence with the date the physician was added to the list of spinal surgery second opinion physicians by the Administrative Director.
(b) Upon removal of a physician from the list, the Administrative Director shall advise the physician by mail of the removal, the Administrative Director's reasons for removal, and the right to request a hearing on the removal.
(c) A physician who has been mailed a notice of removal from the list may, within 30 days of the mailing of the notice of removal, request a hearing by filing a written request for hearing with the Administrative Director. If a written request for hearing is not received by the Administrative Director within 30 days of the mailing of the notice of removal, the physician shall be deemed to have waived any appeal or request for hearing.
(d) Upon receipt of a written request for hearing, the Administrative Director shall serve an accusation, as provided in Government Code section 11503.
(e) Hearings shall be held under the procedures of Chapter 5 of Part 1 of Division 3 of Title 2 of the Government Code (commencing with section 11500) and the regulations of the Office of Administrative Hearings (California Code of Regulations, Title 1, Division 2).
(f) Failure to file timely a mailed notice of defense or failure to appear at a noticed hearing or conference shall constitute a waiver of a right to a hearing.
(g) A physician who has been removed from the list may petition for reinstatement after one year has elapsed since the effective date of the decision on the physician's removal. The provisions of Government Code section 11522 shall apply to such petition.

NOTE: Authority cited: Sections 133 and 5307.3, Labor Code; and Sections 11400.20, 11415.10 and 11522, Government Code. Reference: Sections 4062(b) and 4600, Labor Code.

HISTORY
1. New section filed 7–2–2004 as an emergency; operative 7–2–2004 (Register 2004, No. 27). A Certificate of Compliance must be transmitted to OAL by 11–1–2004 or emergency language will be repealed by operation of law on the following day.
2. Certificate of Compliance as to 7–2–2004 order, including amendment of section, transmitted to OAL 11–1–2004 and filed 12–15–2004 (Register 2004, No. 51).

§ 9788.45.   Unavailability of Second Opinion Physician

A physician who will be unavailable to accept assignments for a period of 30 days or more for any reason, shall, at least 30 days prior to a period of unavailability, notify the Administrative Director in writing of the dates of the physician's unavailability.

NOTE: Authority cited: Sections 133 and 5307.3, Labor Code. Reference: Sections 4062(b) and 4600, Labor Code.

HISTORY
1.   New section filed 12–15–2004; operative 12–15–2004 (Register 2004, No. 51).

§ 9788.5.   Random Selection of Second Opinion Physician

(a)   Within five (5) working days of the Administrative Director's receipt of an objection to a recommendation for spinal surgery, the Administrative Director shall randomly select a physician from those listed physicians located within a thirty (30) mile radius of the employee's address, provided that six physicians are located within that radius; and if six are not located within that radius, using ever increasing radii, until at least six (6) physicians are located from which a random selection may be made. The Administrative Director shall not include among the six physicians any physician that the Administrative Director has determined, from the information submitted to the Administrative Director by the physician and by the employer objecting to the treating physician's recommendation, has a material affiliation prohibited by subdivision (c) of Labor Code section 4062. The selected second opinion physician shall notify the Administrative Director if he/she has a material professional, familial, or financial affiliation with any of the persons or entities listed in subdivision (c) of Labor Code section 4062, within five working days of the physician's receipt of notification of selection. Upon such notification, the Administrative Director shall immediately select a replacement second opinion physician.

(b)   Until the Administrative Director shall have a computerized system for random selection of physicians, the Administrative Director shall manually make random selections as in subdivision (a), except that instead of using an initial thirty mile radius, the Administrative Director shall select from those physicians located within the same zipcode as the employee's address, or if there are not at least six physicians located within that zipcode, then additional adjacent zipcodes shall be used until there are at least six physicians found within the geographic area of selection.

(c)   Upon selection by the Administrative Director, the second opinion physician shall, unless the physician notifies the Administrative Director of a material professional, familial, or financial affiliation, notify the parties within five working days of the physician's receipt of notification of selection of the date and time of any appointment for examination of the employee. If the physician arranges an appointment with the employee by telephone, the physician shall thereafter send the employee a written notice containing the details of the appointment.

(d)   Within ten days of the selection of a second opinion physician, either the employer or the employee may object to the selection on the basis that the second opinion physician has a material professional, familial, or financial affiliation with any of the persons or entities listed in subdivision (c) of Labor Code section 4062, by filing a written objection with the Administrative Director and serving the other parties. The Administrative Director may either sustain the objection, in which case a new selection shall be made, or deny the objection.

(e)   The Administrative Director shall exclude from the selection process any physician who has notified the Administrative Director of unavailability pursuant to Section 9788.45.

NOTE: Authority cited: Sections 133 and 5307.3, Labor Code. Reference: Sections 4062(b) and 4600, Labor Code.

HISTORY
1.   New section filed 7–2–2004 as an emergency; operative 7–2–2004 (Register 2004, No. 27). A Certificate of Compliance must be transmitted to OAL by 11–1–2004 or emergency language will be repealed by operation of law on the following day.
2.   Certificate of Compliance as to 7–2–2004 order, including amendment of subsection (c) and new subsection (e), transmitted to OAL 11–1–2004 and filed 12–15–2004 (Register 2004, No. 51).

§ 9788.6.   Examination by Second Opinion Physician or Agreed Second Opinion Physician

(a)   The second opinion physician or agreed second opinion physician may physically examine the patient–employee, if the second opinion physician or agreed second opinion physician determines in his or her sole discretion that an examination of the patient–employee is required, but nevertheless must physically examine the patient–employee before finally rendering a second opinion in all cases in which the second opinion physician or agreed second opinion physician disagrees with the recommendation of the treating physician. If there is to be a physical examination of the patient–employee, the second opinion physician or agreed second opinion physician shall schedule the examination, and shall, at least ten days in advance of the scheduled examination, send written notice of the date, time, and place of the examination to the employee, the employee's attorney, if any, and the party who objected to the recommended surgery.

(b) The employer shall, and the employee may, furnish all relevant medical records to the second opinion physician or agreed second opinion physician, including x–ray, MRI, CT, and other diagnostic films, and any medical reports which describe the employee's current spinal condition or contain a recommendation for treatment of the employee's spinal diagnoses. The employer shall serve all reports and records on the employee, except for x–ray, MRI, CT and other diagnostic films and for other records which have been previously served on the employee. If a special form of transportation is required because of the employee's medical condition, it is the obligation of the employer to arrange for it. The employer shall furnish transportation expense in advance of the examination. Except for during the examination, a second opinion physician or agreed second opinion physician shall have no ex parte contact with any party.

(1) In the case of a represented employee, except for matters dealing with the scheduling of appointments, missed appointments, the furnishing of records and reports, and the availability of the report, all communications between a second opinion physician or agreed second opinion physician and any party shall be in writing, with copies served on the other parties.

(2) In the case of an unrepresented employee, except for during the examination and for matters dealing with the scheduling of appointments, missed appointments, the furnishing of records and reports, and the availability of the report, there shall be no communications between any party and a second opinion physician until after the report has been served.

(c) If the employee fails to attend an examination with a second opinion physician or agreed second opinion physician, and the physician is unable to reschedule the employee's appointment before the 35th day after receipt of the treating physician's report, the time to complete the second opinion process shall be extended for an additional 30 days. If a second opinion physician is unable to schedule another examination within the 30 additional days, the Administrative Director, upon request, will select another second opinion physician.

NOTE: Authority cited: Sections 133 and 5307.3, Labor Code. Reference: Sections 4062(b) and 4600, Labor Code.

HISTORY

1. New section filed 7–2–2004 as an emergency; operative 7–2–2004 (Register 2004, No. 27). A Certificate of Compliance must be transmitted to OAL by 11–1–2004 or emergency language will be repealed by operation of law on the following day.

2. Certificate of Compliance as to 7–2–2004 order, including amendment of section, transmitted to OAL 11–1–2004 and filed 12–15–2004 (Register 2004, No. 51).

§ 9788.7.   Contents Of Second Opinion and Agreed Second Opinion Physician Reports

(a) If the second opinion physician or agreed second opinion physician disagrees with the recommendation of the treating physician, the second opinion physician's or agreed second opinion physician's report may include a recommendation for a different treatment or therapy.

(b) Reports of second opinion physicians and agreed second opinion physicians shall include, where applicable:

(1) The date of the examination;

(2) The patient's complaints;

(3) A listing of all information received from the parties reviewed in preparation of the report or relied upon for the formulation of the physician's opinion;

(4) The patient's medical history relevant to the treatment determination;

(5) Findings on record review or examination;

(6) The relevant diagnosis;

(7) The physician's opinion whether or not the proposed spinal surgery is appropriate or indicated, and any alternate treatment recommendations;

(8) The reasons for the opinion, including a reference to any treatment guidelines referred to or relied upon in assessing the proposed medical care;

(9) The signature of the physician.

(c) Second opinion physicians and agreed second opinion physicians shall serve with each report the following executed declaration made under penalty of perjury:

"In connection with the preparation and submission of the attached report of second opinion on recommended spinal surgery, I declare, on the date next written, under penalty of perjury of the laws of the State of California, that I have no material familial affiliation, material financial affiliation, or material professional affiliation prohibited by Labor Code Section 4062, subdivision (c).

_____   _____

date   signature"

NOTE: Authority cited: Sections 133 and 5307.3, Labor Code. Reference: Sections 4062(b) and 4600, Labor Code.

HISTORY

1. New section filed 7–2–2004 as an emergency; operative 7–2–2004 (Register 2004, No. 27). A Certificate of Compliance must be transmitted to OAL by 11–1–2004 or emergency language will be repealed by operation of law on the following day.
2. Certificate of Compliance as to 7–2–2004 order transmitted to OAL 11–1–2004 and filed 12–15–2004 (Register 2004, No. 51).

§ 9788.8.   Time Limits For Providing Reports

Second opinion physicians and agreed second opinion physicians shall simultaneously serve the report on the Administrative Director, the employer, the employee, and the employee's attorney, if any, as soon as possible, but in any event within forty–five days of receipt of the treating physician's report (as defined herein), unless the parties have agreed in writing to extend the time to a later date.

NOTE: Authority cited: Sections 133 and 5307.3, Labor Code. Reference: Sections 4062(b) and 4600, Labor Code

HISTORY

1. New section filed 7–2–2004 as an emergency; operative 7–2–2004 (Register 2004, No. 27). A Certificate of Compliance must be transmitted to OAL by 11–1–2004 or emergency language will be repealed by operation of law on the following day.
2. Certificate of Compliance as to 7–2–2004 order, including amendment of section, transmitted to OAL 11–1–2004 and filed 12–15–2004 (Register 2004, No. 51).

§ 9788.9.   Charges for Services of Second Opinion Physician and Agreed Second Opinion Physician

Payment for the services of the second opinion physician shall be made by the employer. The fee shall be:

(a) if the physician examines the injured worker, the same as the fee allowed under Section 9795 for a Basic Comprehensive Medical–Legal Evaluation, without modifiers which might otherwise be allowed under Section 9795(d); or,
(b) if the physician does not examine the injured worker, one half of the fee allowed under Section 9795 for a Basic Comprehensive Medical–Legal Evaluation, without modifiers which might otherwise be allowed under Section 9795(d).

NOTE: Authority cited: Sections 133 and 5307.3, Labor Code. Reference: Sections 4062(b) and 4600, Labor Code.

HISTORY

1. New section filed 7–2–2004 as an emergency; operative 7–2–2004 (Register 2004, No. 27). A Certificate of Compliance must be transmitted to OAL by 11–1–2004 or emergency language will be repealed by operation of law on the following day.
2. Certificate of Compliance as to 7–2–2004 order transmitted to OAL 11–1–2004 and filed 12–15–2004 (Register 2004, No. 51).

§ 9788.91.   Filing of a Declaration of Readiness to Proceed

(a) If the report of the second opinion physician or agreed second opinion physician concurs with the treating physician's recommendation for surgery, the employer shall authorize the surgery and communicate that authorization to the treating physician within three working days of receipt of the second opinion physician's report.
(b) If the report of the second opinion physician or agreed second opinion physician does not concur with the treating physician's recommendation for surgery, the employer shall file a declaration of readiness to proceed within 14 days of receipt of the second opinion physician's report, unless the parties agree with the determination of the second opinion physician or agreed second opinion physician, or unless the employer has authorized the surgery.

NOTE: Authority cited: Sections 133 and 5307.3, Labor Code. Reference: Sections 4062(b) and 4600, Labor Code.

HISTORY

1. New section filed 7–2–2004 as an emergency; operative 7–2–2004 (Register 2004, No. 27). A Certificate of Compliance must be transmitted to OAL by 11–1–2004 or emergency language will be repealed by operation of law on the following day.
2. Certificate of Compliance as to 7–2–2004 order, including amendment of section, transmitted to OAL 11–1–2004 and filed 12–15–2004 (Register 2004, No. 51).

Intentionally blank

Forms

Intentionally blank

State of California
Department of Industrial Relations
Division of Workers' Compensation

OBJECTION TO TREATING PHYSICIAN'S
RECOMMENDATION FOR SPINAL SURGERY

EMPLOYEE

Last Name	First Name	Other names/initials	Social Security Number	Date of Injury

W.C.A.B. Case No.	Claim No. (If Available)	Telephone (If Available)	Fax No. (If Available)

RESIDENCE ADDRESS: Street	City	State	Zip Code

EMPLOYER

Name

MAILING ADDRESS: Street	City	State	Zip Code

Insurance Carrier:

Claims Administrator:

Company providing utilization review:

Employer health care provider:

EMPLOYEE'S ATTORNEY

Name

MAILING ADDRESS: Street	City	State	Zip Code

Telephone:	Fax Number:

TREATING PHYSICIAN

Last Name:	First Name:	Other names/initials:

MAILING ADDRESS: Street	City	State	Zip Code

Telephone:	Fax Number:	E-mail:

Physician's Medical Group:

Independent Practice Association:

Exact procedure which is being objected to:

Name of facility or institution at which the proposed procedure is to be performed:

Name of facility or institution at which an alternative procedure (if any) recommended by the employer, employer health care provider, carrier, or administrator is proposed to be performed:

Date that the treating physician's recommendation for this procedure was first received by any of employer, insurance carrier, administrator:

Name of entity which received it on that date:

Type of entity (employer, insurance carrier, or administrator):

NAME OF PERSON SIGNING THIS OBJECTION:			
Name:	Company:		
MAILING ADDRESS: Street	City	State	Zip Code
Telephone:	Fax Number:	E-mail:	

Reason(s) for this objection, specific to this employee:

Declaration Regarding Receipt of Report – SEE INSTRUCTIONS

Version A

I declare under penalty of perjury of the laws of the State of California that:

1. I am employed by _____.
2. The enclosed physician's report was first received by the employer, insurance carrier or administrator, the name of which firm is _____, on _____.
                                                                                (date)
3. I have personal knowledge of the above facts.

_____   _____
(Signature of Declarant)   (date)

Version B

I declare under penalty of perjury of the laws of the State of California that:

1. I am employed by _____.
2. The enclosed physician's report was first received by the employer, insurance carrier or administrator, the name of which firm is _____, on _____.
                                                                                (date)
3. The firm stated in (2), above, has a written policy of date-stamping every piece of mail on the date it is delivered to its office; this policy is consistently followed; I am knowledgeable about this policy, and the report bears a date stamp showing that it was received in the firm's office on _____.
                                                                  (date)

I have personal knowledge of the facts in (1) and (3), above, and as to the facts in (2), above, I am informed and believe them to be true.

_____   _____
(Signature of Declarant)   (date)

_____   _____   _____
(Signature of Person Executing Form)   (Title)   (date)

Declaration Regarding Service of Objection

I declare under penalty of perjury of the laws of the State of California that:

1. I am employed by _____.

2. On _____, I served the enclosed objection on the persons/firms served,
   (date)

and on the Administrative Director, and by the means of service, indicated in the box below. If service is by mail, I further declare that I am readily familiar with the practice of the office stated in (1), above, of collection and processing of correspondence for mailing. Under that practice it would be deposited with the U.S. Postal Service on that same day with postage fully prepaid at _____ California, in the ordinary course of business. I further declare that if served by mail, I either deposited the objection personally in the U.S. Mails, or that I placed it for normal collection with the office stated in (1), in time for collection and processing that same day. If service is by fax, I further declare that I transmitted a true copy to the fax numbers stated in the box below pursuant to oral and/or written agreement by the recipient to receive by fax. If service is by delivery, I further declare that I am familiar with the practice of the office stated in (1), above for messenger delivery, and I caused the objection in a sealed envelope to be delivered to a courier employed by _____ who was to personally deliver each such envelope within two working days to the office of the address at the place and on the date indicated in the box below:

Person/Firm served and Address	Means of service: e.g. mail/certified mail/fax/FedEx Fax number, if by fax	(time, if by fax)
ADMINISTRATIVE DIRECTOR		Cannot fax to Administrative Director

_____   _____

(Signature of Declarant)   (date)

INSTRUCTIONS

Signing and Serving

The declarations and this form must be signed by Principals or Employees of the employer, insurance carrier, or administrator.

This form, together with the report of the treating physician containing the recommendation for treatment which is objected to, is to be mailed to the Administrative Director, Medical Unit, P.O. Box 71010, Oakland, CA 94612, and copies served by mail or physical delivery or fax on the employee, employee's attorney, and treating physician. The objection form and report may be served on the employee, employee's attorney, and treating physician by fax, but only if prior consent has been obtained from the recipient to be served by fax. This form may not be served on the Administrative Director by fax. This Objection must be sent within ten (10) days of the first receipt by any of the employer, insurance carrier, or administrator, of the treating physician's report containing the recommendation.

Declarations

The form contains two declarations to be signed under penalty of perjury. The first is a declaration specifying the date that the report containing the treating physician's recommendation was first received by the employer, insurance carrier, or administrator. The second declaration specifies the date and manner of serving of the objection.

The form includes two versions of the declaration specifying the date of receipt of the report. Only one version needs to be completed. Version A shall be completed by an employee having personal knowledge of the facts of when the report was received, such as the person who opened the mail. Version B shall be completed by an employee who knows from the date stamp when the report was received, if all mail to the firm is date-stamped on the date it is received, the signer is readily knowledgeable about the policy, the policy is consistently followed, and the report bears a legible date stamp.

The declaration regarding service of the objection must be signed by the person having knowledge of how the report was served.

APPLICATION FOR SPINAL SURGERY 2ND OPINION PHYSICIAN LIST
For the Department of Industrial Relations
Division of Workers' Compensation
P.O. Box 71010
Oakland, CA 94612

FOR OFFICE USE ONLY
NO.:
INPUT DATE:
INPUT BY:

BLOCK 1 (FOR BOTH NEUROSURGEONS & ORTHOPAEDISTS) PLEASE TYPE OR PRINT LEGIBLY

Please list your primary location. DO NOT USE P.O. BOX. You may provide additional office addresses at which you may schedule appointments on a separate sheet.

LAST NAME	FIRST NAME	MI	JR/SR

BUSINESS ADDRESS	CITY	ZIP + 4

MAILING ADDRESS, if different from above	CITY	ZIP + 4

(AREA CODE) PHONE NO.	(AREA CODE) FAX NO.	CAL. PROFESSIONAL LICENSE NUMBER	EXPIRATION (MM/YY)

BLOCK 2 ALL APPLICANTS

MEDICAL SCHOOL

CITY	STATE	DEGREE	YEAR COMPLETED

ALL APPLICANTS are to furnish their board certification and current hospital privileges.

PLEASE LIST:

Hospital/Facility	Location (City/State)	Type	From	To

Hospital/Facility	Location (City/State)	Type	From	To

DWC Form 232
Title 8, CCR § 9788.31
May 2007

BLOCK 3   APPLICANT MUST MEET ONE OF THE FOLLOWING REQUIREMENTS   YES   NO

1) I am board certified in neurosurgery by the American Board of Neurological Surgery. ☐ ☐
2) I am board certified in orthopaedics by the American Board of Orthopaedic Surgery. ☐ ☐
3) I am board certified in orthopaedics by the American Osteopathic Board of Orthopaedic Surgery. ☐ ☐
4) I am certified in neurosurgery by the American Osteopathic Board of Orthopaedic of Surgery. ☐ ☐

Date of expiration of board certification:_____

BLOCK 4   ALL APPLICANTS   YES   NO

1) Have you ever been formally disciplined by a State Medical Licensing Board?

   * If the answer is "Yes", please furnish full particulars on a separate sheet. ☐ ☐
2) Is any accusation by any State medical licensing board currently pending against you?

   * If the answer is "Yes", please furnish full particulars on a separate sheet. ☐ ☐

3) Do you currently have hospital privileges in spinal surgery? ☐ ☐
3a) If the answer is NO, have you had privileges in spinal surgery in the past? ☐ ☐

4) Have you ever been convicted of a crime?

   * If the answer is YES, please furnish all particulars on a separate sheet. ☐ ☐
5) Have you ever applied to the Industrial Medical Council or Administrative Director to be a Qualified Medical Evaluator?

   * If the answer is NO, please skip to Questions in BLOCK 5. ☐ ☐

6) If the Answer to Question 5 is YES: Has the Industrial Medical Council or the Administrative Director ever denied appointment for a reason other than for failing to pass the Qualified Medical Evaluator examination, informed you that it would deny appointment for a reason other than for failing to pass the Qualified Medical Evaluator examination, or filed a statement of issues in regard to your application for appointment?

   * If the answer is YES, please furnish all particulars on a separate sheet. ☐ ☐

7) If the Answer to Question 5 is YES: Have you ever filed an application or official form with the Industrial Medical Council or Administrative Director which contained an untrue material statement? ☐ ☐

8) If the Answer to Question 5 is YES: Have you ever been appointed as a Qualified Medical Evaluator? ☐ ☐

9) If the Answer to Question 8 is YES: Has the Industrial Medical Council or the Administrative Director ever suspended or terminated your appointment as a Qualified Medical Evaluator, placed you on probation, filed an accusation against you, denied reappointment, informed you that it would deny reappointment, or filed a statement of issues in regard to your appointment or reappointment?

   * If the answer is YES, please furnish all particulars on a separate sheet. ☐ ☐

BLOCK 5   (FOR ALL APPLICANTS)
Most recent hospital privileges in spinal surgery.

Hospital/Facility	Date

LOCK 6 ALL APPLICANTS

ysicians may not serve in cases in which they have a material professional, familial or financial affiliation with any of the parties or mpanies involved. YOU are responsible for determining whether you have one of these affiliations in any particular case, and for :using yourself, although the Administrative Director will attempt to screen out any cases in which a conflict of interest is apparent from e names of the parties involved. So that the Administrative Director can do this screening, please list the names of all companies with ich you have a material professional, familial or financial affiliation, as defined in the Regulations.

orkers' Compensation Insurance Companies

1.	3.
2.	4.

orkers' Compensation Third Party Administrators

1.	3.
2.	4.

ilization Review Companies

1.	3.
2.	4.

oup Health Plans

1.	3.
2.	4.

edical Group(s). (Please include the address(es) of the group)

1.	3.
2.	4.

dependent Practice Association(s). (Please include the address(es) of the association)

1.	3.
2.	4.

ospital or Ambulatory Surgery Centers. (Please include the address(es) of the facility)

1.	3.
2.	4.

inal Surgery Related Drugs, Devices, Procedures or Therapies.

1.	3.
2.	4.

*PROVIDE ADDITIONAL SHEETS WHEN NECESSARY**

BLOCK 7   ALL APPLICANTS - PLEASE CHECK:

1) That your application is fully completed, dated and signed with an original signature.
We will not accept faxed applications.

2) That all necessary documentation is attached:
   ❖ A copy of your current California Professional License.
   ❖ A copy of your board certification(s).
   ❖ Certification of your current hospital privileges.

IMPORTANT: Your application for appointment as a Second Opinion Surgeon shall be returned if it is incomplete, and it must be submitted prior to obtaining your appointment.

BLOCK 8   ALL APPLICANTS
License Status

A. My license to practice medicine is active and is neither restricted nor encumbered by suspension, interim suspension or probation.

B. I agree to notify the Administrative Director if my license to practice medicine is placed on suspension, interim suspension, probation or is restricted by my licensing agency, or if any State Medical Licensing Board files an accusation against me.

Verification

I have used all reasonable diligence in preparing and completing this application. I have reviewed this completed application and to the best of my knowledge the information contained herein and in the attached supporting documentation is true, correct and complete. I declare under penalty of perjury under the laws of the State of California that the foregoing is true and correct.

Executed on _____ **at** _____ **, CA** _____
   (MM/DD/YY)   **County**   **Applicant's Signature**

A PUBLIC DOCUMENT

PRIVACY NOTICE - The Information Practices Act of 1977 and the Federal Privacy Act require the Administrative Director to provide the following notice to individuals who are asked by a governmental entity to supply information for appointment as a Qualified Medical Evaluator (QME).

The principal purpose for requesting information from QMEs is to administer the QME program within the California workers' compensation system. Additional information may be requested if your application is denied and/or a disciplinary action is taken.

The California Labor Code requires every QME physician to meet certain statutory requirements. Physicians are required by the Labor Code to provide: name; business address/addresses; professional education; training; license number; year entered practice and other requirements deemed necessary by the Administrative Director. It is mandatory to furnish all the appropriate information requested by the Administrative Director. Failure to provide all of the requested information may result in the denial of the application.

As authorized by law, information furnished on this form may be given to: you, upon request; the public, pursuant to the Public Records Act; a governmental entity, when required by state or federal law; to any person, pursuant to a subpoena or court order or pursuant to any other exception in Civil Code § 1798.24.

An individual has a right of access to records containing his/her personal information that are maintained by the Administrative Director. An individual may also amend, correct, or dispute information in such personal records (Civil Code § 1798.34-1798.37).

Requests should be sent to: Division of Workers' Compensation-Medical Unit
                                   P.O. Box 71010
                                   Oakland, CA 94612
                                   (510) 286-3700 or (800) 794-6900
                                   Fax: (510) 622-3467

You may request a copy of the Division of Workers' Compensation policy and procedures for inspection of records at the above address. Copies of the procedures and all records are ten cents ($0.10) per page, payable in advance. (Civil Code § 1798.33).

Appendix F

● Administrative Penalties Pursuant To Labor Code section 5814.6

Article 1.   Administrative Penalties Pursuant To Labor Code section 5814.6

§ 10225.   Definitions

As used in this article:

(a) "Adjusting location" means the office where claims are administered. Separate underwriting companies, employers that are both self–administered and self–insured, and/or third–party administrators operating at one location shall be combined as one adjusting location only if claims are administered under the same management at that location. Where claims are administered from an office that includes a satellite office at another location, claims administered at the satellite office(s) will be considered as part of the single adjusting location for investigation and auditing purposes under this article when it is demonstrated that the claims are under the same immediate management.

(b) "Administrative Director" means the Administrative Director of the Division of Workers Compensation, including his or her designee.

(c) "Claim" means a request for compensation, or record of an occurrence in which compensation reasonably would be expected to be payable for an injury arising out of and in the course of employment.

(d) "Claim file" means a record in paper or electronic form, or any combination, containing all of the information specified in section 10101.1 of Title 8 of the California Code of Regulations and all documents or entries related to the provision, payment, delay, or denial of benefits or compensation under Divisions 1, 4 or 4.5 of the Labor Code.

(e) "Claims administrator" means a self–administered workers' compensation insurer; a self–administered self–insured employer; a self–administered legally uninsured employer; a self–administered joint powers authority; or a third–party claims administrator for an insurer, a self–insured employer, a legally uninsured employer or a joint powers authority.

(f) "Compensation" means every benefit or payment, including vocational rehabilitation, supplemental job displacement benefits, medical treatment, medical and medical–legal expenses, conferred by Divisions 1 and 4 of the Labor Code on an injured employee or the employee's dependents.

(g) "Compensation order" means any award, order or decision issued by the Workers' Compensation Appeals Board or the Division of Workers' Compensation vocational rehabilitation unit by which a party is entitled to payment of compensation.

(h) "Concurrent medical treatment authorization" means authorization requested or provided during an inpatient stay.

(i) "Determination and Order" means Determination and Order in re Labor Code s 5814.6 Administrative Penalties.

(j) "Employee" means every person in the service of another, as defined under Article 2 of Chapter 2 of Part 1 of Division 4 of the Labor Code (Sections 3350 et seq.), or in the case of the employee's death, his or her dependent, as each is defined in Division 4 of the Labor Code, or the employee's or dependent's agent or attorney.

(k) "Employer" shall have the same meaning as the word 'employer' as defined in Division 4 of the Labor Code (sections 3300 et seq.).

(l) "General business practice" means a pattern of violations of Labor Code section 5814 at a single adjusting location that can be distinguished by a reasonable person from an isolated event. The pattern of violations must occur in the handling of more than one claim. The pattern of violations may consist of one type of act or omission, or separate, discrete acts or omissions in the handling of more than one claim. However, where a claim file with a violation of Labor Code section 5814 has been adjusted at multiple adjusting locations, that claim file may be considered when determining the general business practice of any of the adjusting locations where the conduct that caused the violation occurred even if the file has been transferred to a different adjusting location.

(m) "Indemnity" means payments made directly to an eligible person as a result of a work injury and as required under Division 4 of the Labor Code, including but not limited to temporary disability indemnity, salary continuation in lieu of temporary disability indemnity, permanent disability indemnity, vocational rehabilitation temporary disability indemnity, vocational rehabilitation maintenance allowance, life pension and death benefits.

(n) "Insurer" means any company, group, or entity in, or which has been in, the business of transacting workers' compensation insurance for one or more employers subject to the workers' compensation laws of this state. The term insurer includes the State Compensation Insurance Fund.

(o) "Investigation" means the process used by the Administrative Director, or his or her designee, pursuant to Section 10225.1 and/or Government Code sections 11180 through 11191, to determine whether a violation of Labor Code section 5814.6 has occurred, including but not limited to reviewing, evaluating, copying and preserving electronic and paper records, files, accounts and other things, and interviewing potential witnesses.

(p) "Joint powers authority" means any county, city, city and county, municipal corporation, public district, public agency, or political subdivision of the state, but not the state itself, included in a pooling arrangement under a joint exercise of powers agreement for the purpose of securing a certificate of consent to self–insure workers' compensation claims under Labor Code Section 3700(c).

(q) "Knowingly" means acting with knowledge of the facts of the conduct at issue. For the purposes of this article, a corporation has knowledge of the facts an employee receives while acting within the scope of his or her authority. A corporation has knowledge of information contained in its records and of the actions of its employees performed in the scope and course of employment. An employer or insurer has knowledge of information contained in the records of its third–party administrator and of the actions of the employees of the third–party administrator performed in the scope and course of employment.

(r) "Notice of Assessment" means Notice of Labor Code s 5814.6 Administrative Penalty Assessment.

(s) "Penalty award" means a final order or final award by the Workers' Compensation Appeals Board to pay penalties due to a violation of section 5814 of the Labor Code.

(t) "Petition Appealing Determination and Order" means Petition Appealing Determination and Order of the Administrative Director in re Labor Code s 5814.6 Administrative Penalties.

(u) "Proof of service" means an affidavit or declaration made under penalty of perjury and filed with one or more documents required to be filed, setting out a description of the document(s) being served, the names and addresses of all persons served, whether service was made personally or by mail, the date of service, and the place of service or the address to which mailing was made.

(v) "Prospective medical treatment authorization" means authorization requested or provided prior to the delivery of the medical services.

(w) "Recommended Determination and Order" means Recommended Determination and Order in re Labor Code s 5814.6 Administrative Penalties.

(x) "Retrospective medical treatment authorization" means authorization requested or provided after medical services have been provided and for which services approval has not already been given.

(y) "Salary continuation" means payment made to an injured employee as provided under Division 4 of the Labor Code.

(z) "Serve" means to file or deliver a document or to cause it to be delivered to the Administrative Director or his or her designee, or to such other person as is required under this article.

(aa) "Stipulated Order" means a Notice of Assessment that was timely paid.

(bb) "Supplemental job displacement benefits" means benefits as described under Labor Code section 4658.5 and sections 10133.50–10133.59 of Title 8 of the California Code of Regulations.

(cc) "Third–party administrator" means an agent under contract to administer the workers' compensation claims of an insurer, a self–insured employer, a legally uninsured employer, a self–insured joint powers authority or on behalf of the California Insurance Guarantee Association. The term third–party administrator includes the State Compensation Insurance Fund for locations that administer claims for legally uninsured and self–insured employers, and also includes managing general agents.

(dd) "Utilization Review files" means those files, documents or records, whether paper or electronic, containing information that documents an employer or insurer utilization review process required under Division 4 of the Labor Code.

(ee) "Workers' Compensation Appeals Board" means the Appeals Board, commissioners, deputy commissioners, presiding workers' compensation judges and workers' compensation administrative law judges.

NOTE: Authority cited: Sections 133, 5307.3 and 5814.6, Labor Code. Reference: Sections 129.5, 139.48, 5814 and 5814.6, Labor Code.

HISTORY
1. New subchapter 1.8.1 (sections 10225–10225.2) and section filed 4–26–2007; operative 5–26–2007 (Register 2007, No. 17).

§ 10225.1. Schedule of Administrative Penalties Pursuant to Labor Code section 5814.6

(a) Administrative penalties shall only be imposed under this section based on violations of Labor Code section 5814, after more than one penalty award has been issued by the Workers' Compensation Appeals Board on or after June 1, 2004 based on conduct occurring on or after April 19, 2004 for unreasonable delay or refusal to pay compensation within a five year time period. The five year period of time shall begin on the date of issuance of any penalty award not previously subject to an administrative penalty assessment pursuant to Labor Code section 5814.6.

(b) The Division of Workers' Compensation shall at least monthly submit copies of WCAB decisions, findings, and/or awards issued pursuant to Labor Code section 5814 to the Audit Unit.

(c) The Audit Unit shall obtain monthly Labor Code section 5814 activity reports and shall determine if the decisions, findings, and/or awards are final. If more than one final penalty award has been issued on or after June 1, 2004 against a claims administrator at a single adjusting location, the Audit Unit may proceed with an investigation.

(d) To determine whether a violation described in Labor Code section 5814.6 has occurred, and notwithstanding Labor Code section 129(a) through (d) and section 129.5 subdivisions (a) through (c) and sections 10106, 10106.1, 10107 and 10107.1 of Title 8 of the California Code of Regulations, the Administrative Director, or his or her designee, may conduct an investigation, which may include but is not limited to an audit of claims and/or utilization review files. The investigation may be independent of, or may be conducted concurrently with, an audit conducted pursuant to Labor Code section 129 and 129.5.

(e) The Administrative Director, or his or her designee, may also utilize the provisions of Government Code sections 11180 through 11191 to carry out the responsibilities mandated by Labor Code section 5814.6.

(f) The Administrative Director may issue a Notice of Assessment under this article in conjunction with an order to show cause pursuant to section 10113 of Title 8 of the California Code of Regulations, charging both an administrative penalty under this section and a civil penalty under subdivision (e) of Labor Code section 129.5 in the same pleading, however only one penalty may be imposed by the Administrative Director following the hearing on such charges.

(g) Pursuant to Labor Code section 5814.6, the Administrative Director, or his or her designee, shall issue a Notice of Assessment for administrative penalties against an employer and/or insurer as follows:

  (1) $100,000 for when the Administrative Director, or his or her designee, has evidence to support a finding that an employer or insurer knowingly violated Labor Code section 5814 with a frequency that indicates a general business practice, and additionally for each applicable penalty award, the following;

  (2) $30,000 for each penalty award by the Workers' Compensation Appeals Board for a violation of Labor Code section 5814 for an unreasonable delay or refusal to comply with an existing compensation order;

  (3) For each penalty award by the Workers' Compensation Appeals Board for a violation of Labor Code section 5814 for an unreasonable delay or refusal to make a payment of temporary disability benefits or salary continuation payments in lieu of temporary disability; vocational rehabilitation maintenance allowance, life pension, or death benefits:
    (A) $5,000 for 14 days or less of indemnity benefits;
    (B) $10,000 for 15 days through 42 days of indemnity benefits;
    (C) $15,000 for more than 42 days of indemnity benefits.

  (4) For each penalty award by the Workers' Compensation Appeals Board for a violation of Labor Code section 5814 for an unreasonable delay or refusal to provide authorization for medical treatment:
    (A) $1,000 for retrospective medical treatment authorization;
    (B) $5,000 for prospective or concurrent medical treatment authorization;
    (C) $15,000 for prospective or concurrent medical treatment authorization when the employee's condition is such that the employee faces an imminent and serious threat to his or her health.

  (5) For each penalty award by the Workers' Compensation Appeals Board for a violation of Labor Code section 5814 for an unreasonable delay or refusal to reimburse an employee for self–procured medical treatment costs:
    (A) $1,000 for medical treatment costs of $100 or less, excluding interest and penalty;
    (B) $2,000 for medical treatment costs of more than $100 to $300, excluding interest and penalty;
    (C) $3,000 for medical treatment costs of more than $300 to $500, excluding interest and penalty;
    (D) $5,000 for medical treatment costs of more than $500, excluding interest and penalty.

  (6) $2,500 for each penalty award by the Workers' Compensation Appeals Board for a violation of Labor Code section 5814 for an unreasonable delay or refusal to provide the the supplemental job displacement benefit, as required by section 10133.51(b) and section 10133.56(c), respectively, of Title 8 of the California Code of Regulations.

  (7) $2,500 for each penalty award by the Workers' Compensation Appeals Board for a violation of Labor Code section 5814 for an unreasonable delay or refusal to make payment to an injured worker as reimbursement for payment for services provided for a supplemental job displacement benefit voucher, or where the unreasonable delay or refusal to pay the training provider causes an interruption in the employee's retraining.

  (8) For each penalty award by the Workers' Compensation Appeals Board for a violation of Labor Code section 5814 for an unreasonable delay or refusal to make a payment of permanent disability indemnity benefits:
    (A) $1,000 for 15 weeks or less of indemnity benefits;
    (B) $5,000 for more than 15 but not more than 50 weeks of indemnity benefits;

    (C) $7,500 for more than 50 but not more than 95 weeks of indemnity benefits;

    (D) $15,000 for more than 95 weeks of indemnity benefits.

  (9) $2,500 for any other penalty award by the Workers' Compensation Appeals Board pursuant to Labor Code section 5814 not otherwise specified in this section.

(h) In cases that the Administrative Director deems appropriate, the Administrative Director, or his or her designee, may mitigate a penalty imposed under this section after considering each of these factors:

  (1) The consequences and gravity of the violation(s).

  (2) The good faith of the claims administrator.

  (3) The history of previous penalty awards under Labor Code section 5814.

  (4) The number and type of the violations.

  (5) The time period in which the violations occurred.

  (6) The size of the claims adjusting location.

(i) Each administrative penalty assessed under this section shall be doubled upon a second Order (which may be a Stipulated Order or a final Determination and Order) by the Administrative Director under Labor Code s 5814.6 against the same employer or insurer within a five (5) year period. Each administrative penalty under this section shall be tripled upon a third Order (which may be a Stipulated Order or a final Determination and Order) by the Administrative Director under Labor Code s 5814.6 against the same employer or insurer within the same five (5) year period.

(j) In no event shall the administrative penalties assessed against a single employer or insurer in a single Stipulated Order or final Determination and Order after doubling or tripling exceed $400,000.

NOTE: Authority cited: Sections 133, 5307.3 and 5814.6, Labor Code. Reference: Sections 129.5, 139.48, 5814 and 5814.6, Labor Code; and Sections 11180–11191, Government Code.

HISTORY

1. New section filed 4–26–2007; operative 5–26–2007 (Register 2007, No. 17).

§ 10225.2. Notice of Administrative Penalty Assessment, Appeal Hearing Procedures and Review

(a) Pursuant to Labor Code section 5814.6, the Administrative Director shall issue a Notice of Assessment when the Administrative Director, or his or her designee (the investigating unit of the Division of Workers Compensation), has evidence to support a finding that an employer or insurer has knowingly violated section 5814 with a frequency that indicates a general business practice.

(b) Successor liability may be imposed on a corporation or other business entity that has merged with, consolidated with, or otherwise continued the business of an employer or insurer that is subject to penalties under Labor Code section 5814.6. The surviving entity shall assume and be liable for all the liabilities, obligations and penalties of the prior employer or insurer. Successor liability will be imposed if there has been a substantial continuity of business operations and/or the new business uses the same or substantially the same work force.

(c) The Notice of Assessment shall be in writing and shall contain all of the following:

  (1) The basis for the penalty assessment, including a statement of the alleged violations and the amount of each proposed penalty;

  (2) A description of the methods for paying or appealing the penalty assessment.

(d) The Notice of Assessment shall be served personally or by registered or certified mail.

(e) Within thirty (30) calendar days after the date of service of the Notice of Assessment, the employer or insurer may pay the penalties as assessed or file an appeal with the Administrative Director.

(f) If the employer or insurer pays the penalties within thirty (30) calendar days, the Notice of Assessment shall be deemed a Stipulated Order.

(g) If the employer or insurer files an appeal of the Notice of Assessment with the Administrative Director, the appeal shall:

  (1) Admit or deny, in whole or in part any of the allegations set forth in the Notice;

  (2) Appeal the existence of any or all of the alleged violations;

  (3) Appeal the amount of any or all the penalties assessed;

  (4) Set forth any affirmative and other defenses;

  (5) Set forth the legal and factual bases for each defense and each ground for appeal. Any item listed in the Notice of Assessment but not appealed shall be paid within thirty (30) calendar days after the date of service of the Notice of Assessment.

(h) Failure to timely file an appeal shall constitute a waiver of the appellant's right to an evidentiary hearing. Unless set forth in the appeal, all defenses to the Notice of Assessment shall be deemed waived. The appellant may also file a written request for leave to assert additional defenses which the Administrative Director may grant upon a showing of good cause.

(i) The appeal shall be in writing signed by, or on behalf of, the employer or insurer, and shall state the appellant's mailing address. The appeal shall be verified, under penalty of perjury, by the employer or insurer. If the appellant is a corporation, the verification may be signed by an officer of the corporation. In the event the appellant is not the employer, the employer's address shall be provided and the employer shall be included on the proof of service.

(1) The appellant shall file the original and one copy of the appeal on the Administrative Director and concurrently serve one copy of the appeal on the investigating unit of the Division of Workers Compensation designated by the Administrative Director. The original and all copies of any filings required by this section shall have a proof of service attached.

(j) At any time before the hearing, the Administrative Director may file or permit the filing of an amended Notice of Assessment. All parties shall be notified thereof. If the amended Notice of Assessment presents new allegations or new penalties, the Administrative Director shall afford the Appellant a reasonable opportunity to prepare its defense, and the Appellant shall be entitled to file an amended appeal.

(k) At the Administrative Director's discretion, the Administrative Director may proceed with an informal pre–hearing conference with the appellant in an effort to resolve the contested matters. If any or all of the proposed penalties in Notice of Assessment or the amended Notice of Assessment remain contested, those contested matters shall proceed to an evidentiary hearing.

(l) Whenever the Administrative Director's Notice of Assessment has been contested, the Administrative Director may designate a hearing officer to preside over the hearing. The authority of the Administrative Director or any designated hearing officer includes, but is not limited to: conducting a prehearing settlement conference; setting the date for an evidentiary hearing and any continuances; issuing subpoenas for the attendance of any person residing anywhere within the state as a witness or party at any pre–hearing conference and hearing; issuing subpoenas duces tecum for the production of documents and things at the hearing; presiding at hearings; administering oaths or affirmations and certifying official acts; ruling on objections and motions; issuing prehearing orders; and preparing a Recommended Determination and Order based on the hearing.

(m) The Administrative Director, or the designated hearing officer, shall set the time and place for any prehearing conference on the contested matters in a Notice of Hearing and shall give sixty (60) calendar days written notice to all parties.

(n) The prehearing conference may address one or more of the following matters:

(1) Exploration of settlement possibilities.
(2) Preparation of stipulations.
(3) Clarification of issues.
(4) Rulings on identity and limitation of the number of witnesses.
(5) Objections to proffers of evidence.
(6) Order of presentation of evidence and cross–examination.
(7) Rulings regarding issuance of subpoenas and protective orders.
(8) Schedules for the submission of written briefs and schedules for the commencement and conduct of the hearing.
(9) Any other matters as shall promote the orderly and prompt conduct of the hearing.

(o) The Administrative Director, or the designated hearing officer, shall issue a prehearing conference order incorporating the matters determined at the prehearing conference. The Administrative Director, or the designated hearing officer, may direct one or more of the parties to prepare the prehearing conference order.

(p) Not less than 30 calendar days prior to the date of the pre–hearing conference, or if no pre–hearing conference is set, not less than 30 calendar days prior to the date of the evidentiary hearing, the Appellant shall file and serve the original and one copy of a written statement with the Administrative Director, or the designated hearing officer, specifying the legal and factual bases for its appeal and each defense, listing all witnesses the Appellant intends to call to testify at the hearing, and appending copies of all documents and other evidence the Appellant intends to introduce into evidence at the hearing. A copy of the written statement and its attachments shall also concurrently be served on the investigating unit of the Division of Workers' Compensation. If the Appellant's written statement and supporting evidence are not timely filed and served, the Administrative Director, or the designated hearing officer, shall dismiss the appeal and the violations and penalties as stated in the Notice of Assessment shall be final, due and payable. Within ten (10) calendar days of the date for filing the written statement and supporting evidence, the Appellant may file a written request for leave to file a written statement and supporting evidence. The Administrative Director, or the designated hearing officer, may grant the request, upon a showing of good cause. If leave is granted, the written statement and supporting evidence must be filed and served no later than ten (10) calendar days prior to the date of the hearing.

(q) Oral testimony shall be taken only on oath or affirmation.

(r) (1) Each party shall have these rights: to call and examine witnesses, to introduce exhibits; to cross–examine opposing witnesses on any matter relevant to the issues even though that matter was not covered in the direct examination; to impeach any witness regardless of which party first called him or her to testify; and to rebut the evidence.

(2) In the absence of a contrary order by the Administrative Director, or the designated hearing officer, the investigating unit of the Division of Worker's Compensation shall present evidence first.

(3) The hearing need not be conducted according to the technical rules relating to evidence and witnesses, except as hereinafter provided. Any relevant evidence shall be admitted if it is the sort of evidence on which responsible persons are accustomed to rely in the conduct of serious affairs, regardless of the existence of any common law or statutory rule which might make improper the admission of the evidence over objection in civil actions.

(4) Hearsay evidence may be used for the purpose of supplementing or explaining other evidence but over timely objection shall not be sufficient in itself to support a finding unless it would be admissible over objection in civil actions. An objection is timely if made before submission of the case to the Administrative Director, or to the designated hearing officer.

(s) The written affidavit or declaration of any witness may be offered and shall be received into evidence provided that (i) the witness was listed in the written statement pursuant to section 10225.2(p), (ii) the statement is made by affidavit or by declaration under penalty of perjury, (iii) copies of the statement have been delivered to all opposing parties at least 20 calendar days prior to the hearing, and (iv) no opposing party has, at least 10 calendar days before the hearing, delivered to the proponent of the evidence a written demand that the witness be produced in person to testify at the hearing. The Administrative Director, or the designated hearing officer, shall disregard any portion of the statement received pursuant to this regulation that would be inadmissible if the witness were testifying in person, but the inclusion of inadmissible matter does not render the entire statement inadmissible. Upon timely demand for production of a witness in lieu of admission of an affidavit or declaration, the proponent of that witness shall ensure the witness appears at the scheduled hearing and the proffered declaration or affidavit from that witness shall not be admitted. If the Administrative Director, or the designated hearing officer, determines that good cause exists that prevents the witness from appearing at the hearing, the declaration may be introduced in evidence, but it shall be given only the same effect as other hearsay evidence.

(t) The Administrative Director, or the designated hearing officer, shall issue a written Recommended Determination and Order, granting or denying the appeal, in whole or part, and affirming or amending the penalty assessment(s). The Recommended Determination and Order shall include a statement of the basis for the decision and each penalty assessed. It shall be served on all parties within sixty (60) calendar days of the date the case was submitted for determination. This requirement is directory and not jurisdictional.

(u) The Administrative Director shall have up to sixty (60) calendar days to adopt or modify the Recommended Determination and Order issued by the Administrative Director or the designated hearing officer. In the event the Recommended Determination and Order is modified, the Administrative Director shall include a statement of the basis for the Determination and Order. If the Administrative Director does not act within sixty (60) calendar days, then the Recommended Determination and Order shall become the Determination and Order on the sixty–first calendar day.

(v) The Determination and Order shall be served on all parties personally or by registered or certified mail by the Administrative Director.

(w) The Determination and Order, if any, shall become final on the date it was served, unless the aggrieved party files a timely Petition Appealing Determination and Order within twenty (20) days. A timely filed Petition Appealing the Determination and Order tolls the period for paying any disputed penalty. All findings and assessments in the Determination and Order that are not contested in the Petition Appealing Determination and Order shall become final as though no such petition was filed.

(x) At any time prior to the date the Determination and Order becomes final, the Administrative Director may correct the Determination and Order for clerical, mathematical or procedural error.

(y) Penalties assessed in a Determination and Order shall be paid within thirty (30) calendar days of the date the Determination and Order has been served, if no Petition Appealing Determination and Order has been filed. The penalties shall be deposited into the Return–to–Work–Fund.

(z) All appeals from any part or the entire Determination and Order shall be made in the form of a Petition Appealing the Determination and Order, in conformance with the requirements of chapter 7, part 4 of Division 4 of the Labor Code. Any such Petition Appealing the Determination and Order shall be filed at the Workers' Compensation Appeals Board in San Francisco (and not with any district office of the Workers' Compensation Appeals Board), in the same manner specified for petitions for reconsideration.

NOTE: Authority cited: Sections 133, 5307.3 and 5814.6, Labor Code. Reference: Sections 129.5, 139.48, 5300, 5814, 5814.6 and 5900 et seq., Labor Code.

HISTORY

1. New section filed 4–26–2007; operative 5–26–2007 (Register 2007, No. 17).

No Forms

Intentionally blank

Appendix G

● Medical–Legal Expenses and Comprehensive Medical–Legal Evaluations

Article 5.6.   Medical–Legal Expenses and Comprehensive Medical–Legal Evaluations

§ 9793.   Definitions

As used in this article:

(a) "Claim" means a claim for compensation as evidenced by either the filing of a claim form pursuant to Section 5401 of the Labor Code or notice or knowledge of an injury under Section 5400 or 5402 of the Labor Code.

(b) "Contested claim" means any of the following:

(1) Where the claims administrator has rejected liability for a claimed benefit.

(2) Where the claims administrator has failed to accept liability for a claim and the claim has become presumptively compensable under Section 5402 of the Labor Code.

(3) Where the claims administrator has failed to respond to a demand for the payment of compensation after the expiration of any time period fixed by statute for the payment of indemnity benefits, including where the claims administrator has failed to either commence the payment of temporary disability indemnity or issue a notice of delay within 14 days after knowledge of an employee's injury and disability as provided in Section 4650 of the Labor Code.

(4) Where the claims administrator has accepted liability for a claim and a disputed medical fact exists.

(c) "Comprehensive medical–legal evaluation" means an evaluation of an employee which (A) results in the preparation of a narrative medical report prepared and attested to in accordance with Section 4628 of the Labor Code, any applicable procedures promulgated under Section 139.2 of the Labor Code, and the requirements of Section 10606 and (B) is either:

(1) performed by a Qualified Medical Evaluator pursuant to subdivision (h) of Section 139.2 of the Labor Code, or

(2) performed by a Qualified Medical Evaluator, Agreed Medical Evaluator, or the primary treating physician for the purpose of proving or disproving a contested claim, and which meets the requirements of paragraphs (1) through (5), inclusive, of subdivision (g).

(d) "Claims Administrator" means a self–administered insurer providing security for the payment of compensation required by Divisions 4 and 4.5 of the Labor Code, a self–administered self–insured employer, a group self–insurer, or a third–party claims administrator for a self–insured employer, insurer, legally uninsured employer, group self–insurer, or joint powers authority.

(e) "Disputed medical fact" means an issue in dispute, including an objection to a medical determination made by a treating physician under Section 4062 of the Labor Code, concerning (1) the employee's medical condition, (2) the cause of the employee's medical condition, (3) treatment for the employee's medical condition, (4) the existence, nature, duration or extent of temporary or permanent disability caused by the employee's medical condition, or (5) the employee's medical eligibility for rehabilitation services.

(f) "Follow–up medical–legal evaluation" means an evaluation which includes an examination of an employee which (A) results in the preparation of a narrative medical report prepared and attested to in accordance with Section 4628 of the Labor Code, any applicable procedures promulgated under Section 139.2 of the Labor Code, and the requirements of Section 10606, (B) is performed by a qualified medical evaluator, agreed medical evaluator, or primary treating physician within nine months following the evaluator's examination of the employee in a comprehensive medical–legal evaluation and (C) involves an evaluation of the same injury or injuries evaluated in the comprehensive medical– legal evaluation.

(g) "Medical–legal expense" means any costs or expenses incurred by or on behalf of any party or parties, the administrative director, or the appeals board for X–rays, laboratory fees, other diagnostic tests, medical reports, medical records, medical testimony, and as needed, interpreter's fees, for the purpose of proving or disproving a contested claim. The cost of medical evaluations, diagnostic tests, and interpreters is not a medical–legal expense unless it is incidental to the production of a comprehensive medical–legal evaluation report, follow–up medical–legal evaluation report, or a supplemental medical–legal evaluation report and all of the following conditions exist:

(1) The report is prepared by a physician, as defined in Section 3209.3 of the Labor Code.

(2) The report is obtained at the request of a party or parties, the administrative director, or the appeals board for the purpose of proving or disproving a contested claim and addresses the disputed medical fact or facts specified by the party, or parties or other person who requested the comprehensive medical–legal evaluation report. Nothing in this paragraph shall be construed to prohibit a physician from addressing additional related medical issues.

(3) The report is capable of proving or disproving a disputed medical fact essential to the resolution of a contested claim, considering the substance as well as the form of the report, as required by applicable statutes, regulations, and case law.

(4) The medical–legal examination is performed prior to receipt of notice by the physician, the employee, or the employee's attorney, that the disputed medical fact or facts for which the report was requested have been resolved.

(5) In the event the comprehensive medical–legal evaluation is served on the claims administrator after the disputed medical fact or facts for which the report was requested have been resolved, the report is served within the time frame specified in Section 139.2(j)(1) of the Labor Code.

(h) "Medical–legal testimony" means expert testimony provided by a physician at a deposition or workers' compensation appeals board hearing, regarding the medical opinion submitted by the physician.

(i) "Medical research" is the investigation of medical issues. It includes investigating and reading medical and scientific journals and texts. "Medical research" does not include reading or reading about theGuides for the Evaluation of Permanent Impairment (any edition), treatment guidelines (including guidelines of the American College of Occupational and Environmental Medicine), the Labor Code, regulations or publications of the Division of Workers' Compensation (including thePhysicians' Guide), or other legal materials.

(j) "Primary treating physician" is the treating physician primarily responsible for managing the care of the injured worker in accordance with subdivision (a) of Section 9785.

(k) "Reports and documents required by the administrative director" means an itemized billing, a copy of the medical–legal evaluation report, and any verification required under Section 9795(c).

(l) "Supplemental medical–legal evaluation" means an evaluation which (A) does not involve an examination of the patient, (B) is based on the physician's review of records, test results or other medically relevant information which was not available to the physician at the time of the initial examination, (C) results in the preparation of a narrative medical report prepared and attested to in accordance with Section 4628 of the Labor Code, any applicable procedures promulgated under Section 139.2 of the Labor Code, and the requirements of Section 10606 and (D) is performed by a qualified medical evaluator, agreed medical evaluator, or primary treating physician following the evaluator's completion of a comprehensive medical–legal evaluation.

NOTE: Authority cited: Sections 133, 4627, 5307.3 and 5307.6, Labor Code. Reference: Sections 4061, 4061.5, 4062, 4620, 4621, 4622, 4625, 4628, 4650, 5307.6 and 5402, Labor Code.

HISTORY

1. New article 5.6 (sections 9793–9795) filed 1–10–85; designated effective 3–1–85 (Register 85, No. 2).
2. Change without regulatory effect filed 7–11–86; effective upon filing (Register 86, No. 28).
3. Repealer and new section filed 8–3–93; operative 8–3–93. Submitted to OAL for printing only pursuant to Government Code section 11351 (Register 93, No. 32).
4. Amendment of article heading, section and Notefiled 12–31–93; operative 1–1–94. Submitted to OAL for printing only pursuant to Government Code section11351 (Register 93, No. 53).
5. Change without regulatory effect amending subsections (f) and (i) filed 6–12–2002 pursuant to section 100, title 1, California Code of Regulations (Register 2002, No. 24).
6. Amendment of subsections (a) and (b)(3), new subsection (i), subsection relettering and amendment of newly designated subsection (j) filed 6–30–2006; operative 7–1–2006. Submitted to OAL for filing with the Secretary of State and printing only pursuant to Government Code section 11340.9(g) (Register 2006, No. 26).

§ 9794.   Reimbursement of Medical–Legal Expenses

(a) The cost of comprehensive, follow–up and supplemental medical–legal evaluation reports, diagnostic tests, and medical–legal testimony, regardless of whether incurred on behalf of the employee or claims administrator, shall be billed and reimbursed as follows:

(1) X–rays, laboratory services and other diagnostic tests shall be billed and reimbursed in accordance with the official medical fee schedule adopted pursuant to Labor Code Section 5307.1. In no event shall the claims administrator be liable for the cost of any diagnostic test provided in connection with a comprehensive medical–legal evaluation report unless the subjective complaints and physical findings that warrant the necessity for the test are included in the

medical–legal evaluation report. Additionally, the claims administrator shall not be liable for the cost of diagnostic tests, absent prior authorization by the claims administrator, if adequate medical information is already in the medical record provided to the physician.

(2) The cost of comprehensive, follow–up and supplemental medical–legal evaluations, and medical–legal testimony shall be billed and reimbursed in accordance with the schedule set forth in Section 9795.

(b) All medical–legal expenses shall be paid within 60 days after receipt by the employer of the reports and documents required by the administrative director unless the claims administrator, within this period, contests its liability for such payment.

(c) A claims administrator who contests all or any part of a bill for medical–legal expense, or who contests a bill on the basis that the expense does not constitute a medical–legal expense, shall pay any uncontested amount and notify the physician or other provider of the objection within sixty days after receipt of the reports and documents required by the administrative director. Any notice of objection shall include or be accompanied by all of the following:

(1) An explanation of the basis for the objection to each contested procedure and charge. The original procedure codes used by the physician or other provider shall not be altered. If the objection is based on appropriate coding of a procedure, the explanation shall include both the code reported by the provider and the code believed reasonable by the claims administrator, and shall include the claim's administrator's rationale as to why its code more accurately reflects the service provided. If the claims administrator denies liability for the entire medical–legal expense, the objection shall set forth the legal, medical or factual basis for the denial.

(2) If additional information is necessary as a prerequisite to payment of the contested bill or portions thereof, a clear description of the information required.

(3) The name, address, and telephone number of the person or office to contact for additional information concerning the objection.

(4) A statement that the physician or other provider may adjudicate the issue of the contested charges before the Workers' Compensation Appeals Board. A form objection which does not identify the specific deficiencies of the report in question shall not satisfy the requirements of this subdivision.

(d) All reports and documents required by the administrative director shall be included in or attached to the medical–legal report when it is filed and served on the parties pursuant to Section 10608 or served on the parties pursuant to Section 4061 or 4062 of the Labor Code.

(e) Physicians shall keep and maintain for three years, and shall make available to the administrative director by date of examination upon request, copies of all billings for medical–legal expense.

(f) A physician may not charge, nor be paid, any fees for services in violation of Section 139.3 of the Labor Code or subdivision (d) of Section 5307.6 of the Labor Code;

(g) Claims administrator shall retain, for three years, the following information for each comprehensive medical evaluation for which the claims administrator is billed:

(1) name and specialty of medical evaluator;

(2) name of the employee evaluated;

(3) date of examination;

(4) the amount billed for the evaluation;

(5) the date of the bill;

(6) the amount paid for the evaluation, including any penalties and interest;

(7) the date payment was made.

This information may be stored in paper or electronic form and shall be made available to the administrative director upon request. This information shall also be made available, upon request, to any party to a case, where the requested information pertains to an evaluation obtained in the case.

NOTE: Authority cited: Sections 133, 4627, 5307.3 and 5307.6, Labor Code. Reference: Sections 4620, 4621, 4622, 4625, 4626, 4628 and 5307.6, Labor Code.

HISTORY

1. Repealer and new section filed 8–3–93; operative 8–3–93. Submitted to OAL for printing only pursuant to Government Code section 11351 (Register 93, No. 32).

2. Amendment of subsections (a)–(c)(1) and (e), and new subsections (f)–(h) filed 12–31–93; operative 1–1–94. Submitted to OAL for printing only pursuant to Government Code section 11351 (Register 93, No. 53).

3. Repealer of subsection (h) filed 2–14–96; operative 2–14–96. Submitted to OAL for printing only pursuant to Government Code section 11351 (Register 96, No. 7).

4. Editorial correction of subsection (a) (Register 2001, No. 22).

§ 9795. Reasonable Level of Fees for Medical–Legal Expenses, Follow–up, Supplemental and Comprehensive Medical–Legal Evaluations and Medical–Legal Testimony

(a) The schedule of fees set forth in this section shall be prima facie evidence of the reasonableness of fees charged for medical–legal evaluation reports, and fees for medical–legal testimony.

Reports by treating or consulting physicians, other than comprehensive, follow–up or supplemental medical–legal evaluations, regardless of whether liability for the injury has been accepted at the time the treatment was provided or the report was prepared, shall be subject to the Official Medical Fee Schedule adopted pursuant to Labor Code Section 5307.1 rather than to the fee schedule set forth in this section.

(b) The fee for each evaluation is calculated by multiplying the relative value by $12.50, and adding any amount applicable because of the modifiers permitted under subdivision (d). The fee for each medical–legal evaluation procedure includes reimbursement for the history and physical examination, review of records, preparation of a medical–legal report, including typing and transcription services, and overhead expenses. The complexity of the evaluation is the dominant factor determining the appropriate level of service under this section; the times to perform procedures is expected to vary due to clinical circumstances, and is therefore not the controlling factor in determining the appropriate level of service.

(c) Medical–legal evaluation reports and medical–legal testimony shall be reimbursed as follows:

CODE   B.R.   PROCEDURE DESCRIPTION
ML100   Missed Appointment for a Comprehensive or Follow–Up Medical–Legal Evaluation. This code is designed for communication purposes only. It does not imply that compensation is necessarily owed.

CODE   RV   PROCEDURE DESCRIPTION
ML101   5   Follow–up Medical–Legal Evaluation. Limited to a follow–up medical–legal evaluation by a physician which occurs within nine months of the date on which the prior medical–legal evaluation was performed. The physician shall include in his or her report verification, under penalty of perjury, of time spent in each of following activities: review of records, face–to–face time with the injured worker, and preparation of the report. Time spent shall be tabulated in increments of 15 minutes or portions thereof, rounded to the nearest quarter hour. The physician shall be reimbursed at the rate of RV 5, or his or her usual and customary fee, whichever is less, for each quarter hour.

CODE   RV   PROCEDURE DESCRIPTION
ML102   50   Basic Comprehensive Medical–Legal Evaluation. Includes all comprehensive medical–legal evaluations other than those included under ML 103 or ML 104.

CODE   RV   PROCEDURE DESCRIPTION
ML103   75   Complex Comprehensive Medical–Legal Evaluation. Includes evaluations which require three of the complexity factors set forth below. In a separate section at the beginning of the report, the physician shall clearly and concisely specify which of the following complexity factors were required for the evaluation, and the circumstances which made these complexity factors applicable to the evaluation. An evaluator who specifies complexity factor (3) must also provide a list of citations to the sources reviewed, and excerpt or include copies of medical evidence relied upon:

(1) Two or more hours of face–to–face time by the physician with the injured worker;

(2) Two or more hours of record review by the physician;

(3) Two or more hours of medical research by the physician;

(4) Four or more hours spent on any combination of two of the complexity factors (1)–(3), which shall count as two complexity factors. Any complexity factor in (1), (2), or (3) used to make this combination shall not also be used as the third required complexity factor;

(5) Six or more hours spent on any combination of three complexity factors (1)–(3), which shall count as three complexity factors;

(6) Addressing the issue of medical causation, upon written request of the party or parties requesting the report, or if a bona fide issue of medical causation is discovered in the evaluation;

(7) Addressing the issue of apportionment, when determination of this issue requires the physician to evaluate the claimant's employment by three or more employers, three or more injuries to the same body system or body region as delineated in the Table of Contents of Guides to the Evaluation of Permanent Impairment (Fifth Edition), or two or more or more injuries involving two or more body systems or body regions as delineated in that Table of Contents. The Table of Contents of Guides to the Evaluation of Permanent Impairment (Fifth Edition), published by the American Medical Association, 2000, is incorporated by reference.

(8) Addressing the issue of medical monitoring of an employee following a toxic exposure to chemical, mineral or biologic substances;

(9) A psychiatric or psychological evaluation which is the primary focus of the medical–legal evaluation.

(10) Addressing the issue of denial or modification of treatment by the claims administrator following utilization review under Labor Code section 4610.

CODE RV   PROCEDURE DESCRIPTION

ML104 5   Comprehensive Medical–legal Evaluation Involving Extraordinary Circumstances. The physician shall be reimbursed at the rate of RV 5, or his or her usual and customary hourly fee, whichever is less, for each quarter hour or portion thereof, rounded to the nearest quarter hour, spent by the physician for any of the following:

(1) An evaluation which requires four or more of the complexity factors listed under ML 103; In a separate section at the beginning of the report, the physician shall clearly and concisely specify which four or more of the complexity factors were required for the evaluation, and the circumstances which made these complexity factors applicable to the evaluation. An evaluator who specifies complexity factor (3) must also provide a list of citations to the sources reviewed, and excerpt or include copies of medical evidence relied upon.

(2) An evaluation involving prior multiple injuries to the same body part or parts being evaluated, and which requires three or more of the complexity factors listed under ML 103, including three or more hours of record review by the physician;

(3) A comprehensive medical–legal evaluation for which the physician and the parties agree, prior to the evaluation, that the evaluation involves extraordinary circumstances. When billing under this code for extraordinary circumstances, the physician shall include in his or her report (i) a clear, concise explanation of the extraordinary circumstances related to the medical condition being evaluated which justifies the use of this procedure code, and (ii) verification under penalty of perjury of the total time spent by the physician in each of these activities: reviewing the records, face–to–face time with the injured worker, preparing the report and, if applicable, any other activities.

CODE RV   PROCEDURE DESCRIPTION

ML105 5   Fees for medical–legal testimony. The physician shall be reimbursed at the rate of RV 5, or his or her usual and customary fee, whichever is less, for each quarter hour or portion thereof, rounded to the nearest quarter hour, spent by the physician. The physician shall be entitled to fees for all itemized reasonable and necessary time spent related to the testimony, including reasonable preparation and travel time. The physician shall be paid a minimum of one hour for a scheduled deposition.

CODE RV   PROCEDURE DESCRIPTION

ML106 5   Fees for supplemental medical–legal evaluations. The physician shall be reimbursed at the rate of RV 5, or his or her usual and customary fee, whichever is less, for each quarter hour or portion thereof, rounded to the nearest quarter hour, spent by the physician. Fees will not be allowed under this section for supplemental reports following the physician's review of (A) information which was available in the physician's office for review or was included in the medical record provided to the physician prior to preparing the initial report or (B) the results of laboratory or diagnostic tests which were ordered by the physician as part of the initial evaluation.

(d) The services described by Procedure Codes ML101 through ML106 may be modified under the circumstances described in this subdivision. The modifying circumstances shall be identified by the addition of the appropriate modifier code, which is reported by a two–digit number placed after the usual procedure number separated by a hyphen. The modifiers available are the following:

–92 Performed by a primary treating physician. This modifier is added solely for identification purposes, and does not change the normal value of the service.

–93 Interpreter needed at time of examination, or other circumstances which impair communication between the physician and the injured worker and significantly increase the time needed to conduct the examination. Requires a description of the circumstance and the increased time required for the examination as a result. Where this modifier is applicable, the value for the procedure is modified by multiplying the normal value by 1.1. This modifier shall only be applicable to ML 102 and ML 103.

–94 Evaluation and medical–legal testimony performed by an Agreed Medical Evaluator. Where this modifier is applicable, the value of the procedure is modified by multiplying the normal value by 1.25. If modifier –93 is also applicable for an ML–102 or ML–103, then the value of the procedure is modified by multiplying the normal value by 1.35.

–95 Evaluation performed by a panel selected Qualified Medical Evaluator. This modifier is added solely for identification purposes, and does not change the normal value of any procedure.

(e) Requests for duplicate reports shall be in writing. Duplicate reports shall be separately reimbursable and shall be reimbursed in the same manner as set forth in the Official Medical Fee Schedule adopted pursuant to Labor Code Section 5307.1.

(f) This section shall apply to medical–legal evaluation reports where the examination occurs on or after the effective date of this section. The 2006 amendments to this section shall apply to: (1) medical–legal evaluation reports where the medical examination to which the report refers occurs on or after the effective date of the 2006 amendments; (2) medical–legal testimony provided on or after the effective date of the 2006 amendments; and (3) supplemental medical legal reports that are requested on or after the effective date of the 2006 amendments regardless of the date of the original examination.

NOTE: Authority cited: Sections 133, 4627, 5307.3 and 5307.6, Labor Code. Reference: Sections 139.2, 4061, 4061.5, 4062, 4620, 4621, 4622, 4625, 4626, 4628, 5307.6 and 5402, Labor Code.

HISTORY

1. Repealer and new section filed 8–3–93; operative 8–3–93. Submitted to OAL for printing only pursuant to Government Code section 11351 (Register 93, No. 32).

2. Change without regulatory effect amending subsection (a) and subsection (c)medical–legal evaluation procedure code ML104 filed 8–27–93 pursuant to section 100, title 1, California Code of Regulations (Register 93, No.35).

3. Amendment of section heading, section and Notefiled 12–31–93; operative 1–1–94. Submitted to OAL for printing only pursuant to Government Code section11351 (Register 93, No. 53).

4. Amendment filed 2–24–99; operative 4–1–99 (Register 99, No. 9).

5. Change without regulatory effect amending subsections (b) and (d) filed 6–12–2002 pursuant to section 100, title 1, California Code of Regulations (Register 2002, No. 24).

6. Amendment of section and Notefiled 6–30–2006; operative 7–1–2006. Submitted to OAL for filing with the Secretary of State and printing only pursuant to Government Code section 11340.9(g) (Register 2006, No. 26).

No Forms

Intentionally blank

Appendix H

• Return to Work

Article 12.   Return To Work

§ 10001.   Definitions

(a) "Alternative work" means work (1) offered either by the employer who employed the injured worker at the time of injury, or by another employer where the previous employment was seasonal work, (2) that the employee has the ability to perform, (3) that offers wages and compensation that are at least 85 percent of those paid to the employee at the time of injury, and (4) that is located within a reasonable commuting distance of the employee's residence at the time of injury.

(b) "Claims Administrator" means a self–administered insurer providing security for the payment of compensation required by Divisions 4 and 4.5 of the Labor Code, a self–administered self–insured employer, a self–administered joint powers authority, a self–administered legally uninsured, or a third–party claims administrator for a self–insured employer, insurer, legally uninsured employer, or joint powers authority.

(c) "Modified Work" means regular work modified so that the employee has the ability to perform all the functions of the job and that offers wages and compensation that are at least 85 percent of those paid to the employee at the time of injury, and located within a reasonable commuting distance of the employee's residence at the time of injury.

(d) "Permanent and stationary" means the point in time when the employee has reached maximal medical improvement, meaning his or her condition is well stabilized, and unlikely to change substantially in the next year with or without medical treatment, based on (1) an opinion from a treating physician, AME, or QME; (2) a judicial finding by a Workers' Compensation Administrative Law Judge, the Workers' Compensation Appeals Board, or a court; or (3) a stipulation that is approved by a Workers' Compensation Administrative Law Judge or the Workers' Compensation Appeals Board.

(e) "Regular Work" means the employee's usual occupation or the position in which the employee was engaged at the time of injury and that offers wages and compensation equivalent to those paid to the employee at the time of injury, and located within a reasonable commuting distance of the employee's residence at the time of injury.

(f) "Seasonal Work" means employment as a daily hire, a project hire, or an annual season hire.

NOTE: Authority cited: Sections 133, 139.48 and 5307.3, Labor Code. Reference: Sections 139.48 and 4658.1, Labor Code; Henry v. WCAB(1998) 68 Cal.App.4th 981.

HISTORY

1. New section filed 6–30–2006; operative 7–1–2006. Submitted to OAL for filing with the Secretary of State and printing only pursuant to Government Code section 11340.9(g) (Register 2006, No. 38). For prior history, see Register 96, No. 52.

§ 10002.   Offer of Work; Adjustment of Permanent Disability Payments

(a) This section shall apply to all injuries occurring on or after January 1, 2005, and to the following employers:

   (1) Insured employers who employed 50 or more employees at the time of the most recent policy inception or renewal date for the insurance policy that was in effect at the time of the employee's injury;

   (2) Self–insured employers who employed 50 or more employees at the time of the most recent filing by the employer of the Self–Insurer's Annual Report that was in effect at the time of the employee's injury; and

   (3) Legally uninsured employers who employed 50 or more employees at the time of injury.

(b) Within 60 calendar days from the date that the condition of an injured employee with permanent partial disability becomes permanent and stationary:

   (1) If an employer does not serve the employee with a notice of offer of regular work, modified work or alternative work for a period of at least 12 months, each payment of permanent partial disability remaining to be paid to the employee from the date of the end of the 60 day period shall be paid in accordance with Labor Code section 4658(d)(1) and increased by 15 percent.

   (2) If an employer serves the employee with a notice of offer of regular work, modified work or alternative work for a period of at least 12 months, and in accordance with the requirements set forth in paragraphs (3) and (4), each payment of permanent partial disability remaining to be paid from the date the offer was served on the employee shall be paid in accordance with Labor Code section 4658(d)(1) and decreased by 15 percent, regardless of whether the employee accepts or rejects the offer.

   (3) The employer shall use Form DWC–AD 10133.53 (Section 10133.53) to offer modified or alternative work, or Form DWC–AD 10003 (Section 10003) to offer regular work. The claims administrator may serve the offer of work on behalf of the employer.

   (4) The regular, alternative, or modified work that is offered by the employer pursuant to paragraph (2) shall be located within a reasonable commuting distance of the employee's residence at the time of the injury, unless the employee waives this condition. This condition shall be deemed to be waived if the employee accepts the regular, modified, or alternative work, and does not object to the location within 20 calendar days of being informed of the right to object. The condition shall be conclusively deemed to be satisfied if the offered work is at the same location and the same shift as the employment at the time of injury.

(c) If the claims administrator relies upon a permanent and stationary date contained in a medical report prepared by the employee's treating physician, QME, or AME, but there is subsequently a dispute as to an employee's permanent and stationary status, and there has been a notice of offer of work served on the employee in accordance with subdivision (b), the claims administrator may withhold 15% from each payment of permanent partial disability remaining to be paid from the date the notice of offer was served on the employee until there has been a final judicial determination of the date that the employee is permanent and stationary pursuant to Labor Code section 4062.

   (1) Where there is a final judicial determination that the employee is permanent and stationary on a date later than the date relied on by the employer in making its offer of work, the employee shall be reimbursed any amount withheld up to the date a new notice of offer of work is served on the employee pursuant to subdivision (b).

   (2) Where there is a final judicial determination that the employee is not permanent and stationary, the employee shall be reimbursed any amount withheld up to the date of the determination.

   (3) The claims administrator is not required to reimburse permanent partial disability benefit payments that have been withheld pursuant to this subdivision during any period for which the employee is entitled to temporary disability benefit payments.

(d) If the employee's regular work, modified work, or alternative work that has been offered by the employer pursuant to paragraph (1) of subdivision (b) and has been accepted by the employee, is terminated prior to the end of the period for which permanent partial disability benefits are due, the amount of each remaining permanent partial disability payment from the date of the termination shall be paid in accordance with Labor Code section 4658 (d) (1), as though no decrease in payments had been imposed, and increased by 15 percent. An employee who voluntarily terminates his or her regular work, modified work, or alternative work shall not be eligible for the 15 percent increase in permanent partial disability payments pursuant to this subdivision.

(e) Nothing in this section shall prevent the parties from settling or agreeing to commute the permanent disability benefits to which an employee may be entitled. However, if the permanent disability benefits are commuted by a Workers' Compensation Administrative Law Judge or the Workers' Compensation Appeals Board pursuant to Labor Code section

5100, the commuted sum shall account for any adjustment that would have been required by this section if payment had been made pursuant to Labor Code section 4658.

(f) When the employer offers regular, modified or alternative work to the employee that meets the conditions of this section and subsequently learns that the employee cannot lawfully perform regular, modified or alternative work, the employer is not required to provide the regular, modified or alternative work.

(g) If the employer offers regular, modified, or alternative seasonal work to the employee, the offer shall meet the following requirements:

   (1) the employee was hired for seasonal work prior to injury;

   (2) the offer of regular, modified or alternative seasonal work is of reasonably similar hours and working conditions to the employee's previous employment, and the one year requirement may be satisfied by cumulative periods of seasonal work;

   (3) the work must commence within 12 months of the date of the offer; and

   (4) The offer meets the conditions set forth in this section.

NOTE: Authority cited: Sections 133, 139.48 and 5307.3, Labor Code. Reference: Sections 139.48 and 4658, Labor Code;Del Taco v. WCAB(2000) 79 Cal.App.4th 1437;Anzelde v. WCAB(1996) 61 Cal. Comp. Cases 1458 (Writ denied); and Henry v. WCAB(1998) 68 Cal.App.4th 981.

HISTORY
1. New section filed 6–30–2006; operative 7–1–2006. Submitted to OAL for filing with the Secretary of State and printing only pursuant to Government Code section 11340.9(g) (Register 2006, No. 38). For prior history, see Register 96, No. 52

§ 10003. Form [DWC AD 10003 Notice of Offer of Work]

DWC AD 10003 Notice of Offer of Work

NOTE: Authority cited: Sections 133, 139.48 and 5307.3, Labor Code. Reference: Sections 139.48 and 4658, Labor Code.

HISTORY
1. New section filed 6–30–2006; operative 7–1–2006. Submitted to OAL for filing with the Secretary of State and printing only pursuant to Government Code section 11340.9(g) (Register 2006, No. 38). For prior history, see Register 96, No. 52.

§ 10004. Participation Not Required

(a) This section shall apply to injuries occurring on or after July 1, 2004;

(b) An "Eligible Employer" means any employer, except the state or an employer eligible to secure the payment of compensation pursuant to subdivision (c) of Section 3700, who, based on the employer's payroll records or other equivalent documentation or evidence, employed 50 or fewer full–time employees on the date of injury.

(c) "Full–time employee" means an employee who, during the period of his or her employment within the year preceding the injury, worked an average of 32 or more hours per week.

(d) The Return to Work Program is administered by the Administrative Director for the purpose of promoting the employee's early and sustained return to work following a work–related injury or illness.

(e) This program shall be funded by the Return to Work Fund, which shall consist of all penalties collected pursuant to Labor Code section 5814.6 and transfers made to this fund by the Administrative Director from the Workers' Compensation Administrative Revolving Fund established pursuant to Labor Code section 62.5. The reimbursement offered to eligible employees as set forth in this section shall be available only to the extent funds are available.

(f) An eligible employer shall be entitled to reimbursement through this program for expenses incurred to make workplace modifications to accommodate an employee's return to modified or alternative work, up to the following maximum amounts:

   (1) $1,250 to accommodate each temporarily disabled employee, for expenses incurred in allowing such employee to perform modified or alternative work within physician–imposed temporary work restrictions; and

   (2) $2,500 to accommodate each permanently disabled employee, for expenses incurred in returning such employee to sustained modified or alternative work within physician–imposed permanent work restrictions; however, if an employer who has received reimbursement for a temporarily disabled employee under paragraph (1) is also requesting reimbursement for the same employee for accommodation of permanent disability, the maximum available reimbursement is $2,500. For the purpose of this subdivision, "sustained modified or alternative work" is work anticipated to last at least 12 months.

(g) Reimbursement shall be provided for any of the following expenses, provided they are specifically prescribed by a physician or are reasonably required by restrictions set forth in a medical report:

   (1) modification to worksite;

   (2) equipment;

    (3) furniture;

    (4) tools; or

    (5) any other necessary costs reasonably required to accommodate the employee's restrictions.

(h) An eligible employer seeking reimbursement pursuant to subdivision (d) shall submit a "Request for Reimbursement of Accommodation Expenses" (Form DWC AD 10005, section 10005) to the Division of Workers' Compensation Return to Work Program within ninety (90) calendar days from the date of the expenditure for which the employer is seeking reimbursement. As a condition to reimbursement, the expenditure shall not have been paid or covered by the employer's insurer or any source of funding other than the employer. The filing date may be extended upon a showing of good cause for such extension. The employer shall attach to its request copies of all pertinent medical reports that contain the work restrictions being accommodated, any other documentation supporting the request, and all receipts for accommodation expenses. Requests should be sent to the mailing address for the Division of Workers' Compensation Return to Work Program that is listed in the web site of the Division of Workers' Compensation, at: http://www.dir.ca.gov/

(i) The Administrative Director or his or her designee shall review each "Request for Reimbursement of Accommodation Expenses," and within sixty (60) business days of receipt shall provide the employer with notice of one of the following:

    (1) that the request has been approved, together with a check for the reimbursement allowed, and an explanation of the allowance, if less than the maximum amounts set forth in subdivision (d); or

    (2) that the request has been denied, with an explanation of the basis for denial; or

    (3) that the request is deficient or incomplete and indicating what clarification or additional information is necessary.

(j) In the event there are insufficient funds in the Return to Work Fund to fully reimburse an employer or employers for workplace modification expenses as required by this section, the Administrative Director shall utilize the following priority list in establishing the amount of reimbursement or whether reimbursement is allowed, in order of decreasing priority as follows:

    (1) Employers who have not previously received any reimbursement under this program;

    (2) Employers who have not previously received any reimbursement under this program for the employee who is the subject of the request;

    (3) Employers who are seeking reimbursement for accommodation required in returning a permanently disabled employee to sustained modified or alternative work; and,

    (4) Employers who are requesting reimbursement for accommodation required by a temporarily disabled employee.

(k) An eligible employer may appeal the Administrative Director's notice under subdivision (i) by filing a Declaration of Readiness to Proceed with the local district office of the Workers' Compensation Appeals Board within twenty calendar days of the issuance of the notice, together with a petition entitled "Appeal of Administrative Director's Reimbursement Allowance," setting forth the basis of the appeal. A copy of the Declaration of Readiness to Proceed and the petition shall be concurrently served on the Administrative Director.

NOTE: Authority cited: Sections 133, 139.48 and 5307.3, Labor Code. Reference: Sections 62.5, 139.48 and 5814.6, Labor Code.

HISTORY

1. New article 12 (sections 10004–10005) and section filed 7–19–2006; operative 8–18–2006 (Register 2006, No. 29). For prior history of article 12 (sections 10001–10021), see Register 88, No. 21; Register 95, No. 7 and Register 96, No. 52.

§ 10005.   Reporting Requirements

Form DWC AD 10005 – Request for Reimbursement of Accommodation Expenses For injuries on or after July 1, 2004

NOTE: Authority cited: Sections 133, 139.48 and 5307.3, Labor Code. Reference: Sections 62.5, 139.48 and 5814.6, Labor Code.

HISTORY

1. New section filed 7–19–2006; operative 8–18–2006 (Register 2006, No. 29). For prior history, see Register 96, No. 52.

§ 10006.   Notice to Employee

NOTE: Authority cited: Sections 133, 138.4, 139.5 and 5307.3, Labor Code. Reference: Chapter 1435, 1974 Stats.

HISTORY

1. Repealer and new section filed 5–17–88; operative 7–1–88 (Register 88, No. 21). For prior history, see Register 83, No. 30.

2. Repealer of section filed 12–27–96; operative 12–27–96. Submitted to OAL for printing only pursuant to Government Code section 11351 (Register 96, No. 52).

§ 10007. Reports to Bureau

NOTE: Authority cited: Sections 133, 138.4, 139.5 and 5307.3, Labor Code. Reference: Chapter 1435, 1974 Stats.

HISTORY
1. Repealer and new section filed 5–17–88; operative 7–1–88 (Register 88, No. 21). For prior history, see Register 83, No. 30.
2. Repealer of section filed 12–27–96; operative 12–27–96. Submitted to OAL for printing only pursuant to Government Code section 11351 (Register 96, No. 52).

§ 10007.1. Entitlement Issues

NOTE: Authority cited: Section 139.5, Labor Code. Reference: Section 133, Labor Code.

HISTORY
1. New section filed 6–15–81; effective thirtieth day thereafter (Register 81, No. 25).
2. Repealer filed 5–17–88; operative 7–1–88 (Register 88, No. 21).

§ 10008. Identification of Need for Vocational Rehabilitation Services

NOTE: Authority cited: Sections 133, 138.4, 139.5 and 5307.3, Labor Code. Reference: Chapter 1435, 1974 Stats.

HISTORY
1. Repealer and new section filed 5–17–88; operative 7–1–88 (Register 88, No. 21). For prior history, see Register 83, No. 30.
2. Repealer of section filed 12–27–96; operative 12–27–96. Submitted to OAL for printing only pursuant to Government Code section 11351 (Register 96, No. 52).

§ 10009. Initiation of Vocational Rehabilitation Services

NOTE: Authority cited: Sections 133, 138.4, 139.5 and 5307.3, Labor Code. Reference: Chapter 1435, 1974 Stats.

HISTORY
1. Repealer and new section filed 5–17–88; operative 7–1–88 (Register 88, No. 21). For prior history, see Register 79, No. 30.
2. Repealer of section filed 12–27–96; operative 12–27–96. Submitted to OAL for printing only pursuant to Government Code section 11351 (Register 96, No. 52).

§ 10010. Independent Vocational Evaluators

NOTE: Authority cited: Sections 133, 138.4, 139.5 and 5307.3, Labor Code. Reference: Chapter 1435, 1974 Stats.

HISTORY
1. Repealer and new section filed 5–17–88; operative 7–1–88 (Register 88, No. 21). For prior history, see Register 75, No. 1.
2. Repealer of section filed 12–27–96; operative 12–27–96. Submitted to OAL for printing only pursuant to Government Code section 11351 (Register 96, No. 52).

§ 10011. Vocational Rehabilitation Plans

NOTE: Authority cited: Sections 133, 138.4, 139.5 and 5307.3, Labor Code. Reference: Chapter 1435, 1974 Stats.

HISTORY
1. Repealer and new section filed 5–17–88; operative 7–1–88 (Register 88, No. 21). For prior history, see Register 83, No. 30.
2. Repealer of section filed 12–27–96; operative 12–27–96. Submitted to OAL for printing only pursuant to Government Code section 11351 (Register 96, No. 52).

§ 10012. Plan Approval

NOTE: Authority cited: Sections 133, 138.4, 139.5 and 5307.3, Labor Code. Reference: Chapter 1435, 1974 Stats.

Appendix H

HISTORY
1. Repealer and new section filed 5–17–88; operative 7–1–88 (Register 88, No. 21). For prior history, see Register 79, No. 30.
2. Repealer of section filed 12–27–96; operative 12–27–96. Submitted to OAL for printing only pursuant to Government Code section 11351 (Register 96, No. 52).

§ 10013.   Entitlement Issues

NOTE: Authority cited: Sections 133, 138.4, 139.5 and 5307.3, Labor Code. Reference: Chapter 1435, 1974 Stats.

HISTORY
1. Repealer and new section filed 5–17–88; operative 7–1–88 (Register 88, No. 21). For prior history, see Register 83, No. 30.
2. Repealer of section filed 12–27–96; operative 12–27–96. Submitted to OAL for printing only pursuant to Government Code section 11351 (Register 96, No. 52).

§ 10014.   Bureau Resolution of Disputes

NOTE: Authority cited: Sections 133, 138.4, 139.5 and 5307.3, Labor Code. Reference: Chapter 1435, 1974 Stats.

HISTORY
1. Repealer and new section filed 5–17–88; operative 7–1–88 (Register 88, No. 21). For prior history, see Register 79, No. 30.
2. Repealer of section filed 12–27–96; operative 12–27–96. Submitted to OAL for printing only pursuant to Government Code section 11351 (Register 96, No. 52).

§ 10015.   Interruption of Services

§ 10016.   Conclusion of Vocational Rehabilitation Services

NOTE: Authority cited: Sections 133, 138.4, 139.5 and 5307.3, Labor Code. Reference: Chapter 1435, 1974 Stats.

HISTORY
1. Repealer and new section filed 5–17–88; operative 7–1–88 (Register 88, No. 21). For prior history, see Register 83, No. 30.
2. Repealer of section filed 12–27–96; operative 12–27–96. Submitted to OAL for printing only pursuant to Government Code section 11351 (Register 96, No. 52).

§ 10017.   Reinstatement of Vocational Rehabilitation Benefits

NOTE: Authority cited: Sections 133, 138.4, 139.5 and 5307.3, Labor Code. Reference: Chapter 1435, 1974 Stats.

HISTORY
1. Repealer and new section filed 5–17–88; operative 7–1–88 (Register 88, No. 21). For prior history, see Register 83, No. 30.
2. Repealer of section filed 12–27–96; operative 12–27–96. Submitted to OAL for printing only pursuant to Government Code section 11351 (Register 96, No. 52).

§ 10018.   Vocational Rehabilitation Temporary Disability Indemnity

NOTE: Authority cited: Sections 133, 138.4, 139.5 and 5307.3, Labor Code. Reference: Chapter 1435, 1974 Stats.

HISTORY
1. New section filed 5–17–88; operative 7–1–88 (Register 88, No. 21).
2. Repealer of section filed 12–27–96; operative 12–27–96. Submitted to OAL for printing only pursuant to Government Code section 11351 (Register 96, No. 52).

§ 10019.   Bureau File Retention

NOTE: Authority cited: Sections 133, 138.4, 139.5 and 5307.3, Labor Code. Reference: Chapter 1435, 1974 Stats.

HISTORY
1. New section filed 5–17–88; operative 7–1–88 (Register 88, No. 21).
2. Renumbering and amendment of former section 10019 to section 10134 filed 2–16–95; operative 2–16–95. Submitted to OAL for printing only pursuant to Government Code § 11351 (Register 95, No. 7).

§ 10020.   Enforcement of Notice and Reporting Requirements

NOTE: Authority cited: Sections 133, 138.4, 139.5 and 5307.3, Labor Code. Reference: Chapter 1435, 1974 Stats.

HISTORY
1. New section filed 5–17–88; operative 7–1–88 (Register 88, No. 21).
2. Repealer of section filed 12–27–96; operative 12–27–96. Submitted to OAL for printing only pursuant to Government Code section 11351 (Register 96, No. 52).

§ 10021.   Rehabilitation of Industrially Injured Inmates

NOTE: Authority cited: Sections 133, 138.4, 139.5 and 5307.3, Labor Code. Reference: Chapter 1435, 1974 Stats.

HISTORY
1. New section filed 5–17–88; operative 7–1–88 (Register 88, No. 21).
2. Renumbering of former section 10021 to new section 10133.4 filed 12–27–96; operative 12–27–96. Submitted to OAL for printing only pursuant to Government Code section 11351 (Register 96, No. 52).

Intentionally blank

Forms

Intentionally blank

DWC-AD 10003 NOTICE OF OFFER OF REGULAR WORK
For injuries occurring on or after 1/1/05

THIS SECTION TO BE COMPLETED BY EMPLOYER OR CLAIMS ADMINISTRATOR:

Claims Administrator:_____ Claim Number:_____
(Name of Claims Administrator)

Based on the opinion of___ treating physician   QME   AME _____, you are able to return to
(Name of Physician)

your usual occupation or the position you held at the time of your injury on_____.
(Date)

Date you are eligible to return to job:_____(as stated in the above physician's report)

Employer:_____
(Name of Firm)

Job Title:_____

Starting Date:_____

__ This position is at the same location and shift as your pre-injury position.

__ This position is at a different location than your pre-injury position, as follows:_____

_____

__ This position is for a different shift than your pre-injury position, as follows:_____
(start time)   (end time)

You may contact _____concerning this position. Phone No.:_____
(Name of Contact Person)

You must return the completed form to the employer or claims administrator listed here:

_____
(Name of Employer or Claims Administrator)   (Mailing address)

This position is expected to last for a total of at least 12 months of work. If this position does not last for a total of at least 12 months of work, you may be entitled to an increase in your permanent disability benefit payments.

This position provides wages and compensation of $_____, that are equivalent to or more than the wages and compensation paid to you at the time of your injury.

I,_____, have obtained the above job offer information from your employer.
(Name of Claims Administrator)

If the job offered is at a different location than the job you held at the time of your injury, and you believe the commuting distance to this job from the residence where you lived at the time of your injury is not reasonable, you may object to the job offer as not being within a reasonable commuting distance. You may also waive this commuting distance requirement. You will be considered to have waived this requirement if you accept the above offer of work or do not reject the offer within twenty calendar days of receipt of this notice.

THIS SECTION TO BE COMPLETED BY EMPLOYEE: Claim Number_____

The employee must accept, reject, or object to this offer for regular work and return this form to the employer or claims administrator listed on page one within 20 calendar days of receipt of the offer or it will be deemed that the employee has waived the right to object to the location or shift. The employee should keep a copy of this form for his or her records.

Name of employee:_____   Date offer received:_____

I understand that if my disability is permanent and stationary and the employer has fulfilled its legal obligations related to this offer, my remaining permanent disability payments will be decreased by 15% whether I accept or reject this offer.

Offer of Regular Work at Same Location and/or Shift

__   I accept this offer of regular work.

__   I reject this offer of work. Reason:_____

Note: If either party has a dispute or objection regarding the offer of regular work, or if the employee rejects the offer regular work, that party may file a Declaration of Readiness with the local district office of the Workers' Compensation Appeals Board (WCAB).

Offer of Regular Work at a Different Location and/or Shift

I understand that I have the right to object to a work offer when the location or shift is different than what I had at the time of my injury.

__   I accept the offer and waive my right to object to the job location or shift as not being within a reasonable commuting distance from the residence where I lived at the time of my injury.

__   I reject this offer of work. Reason: _____

__   I object to this offer because the job location that has been offered is different than the job location I held at the time of my injury, and I do not believe this job allows a reasonable commute from my residence. I understand if the claims administrator does not agree with this objection, my remaining permanent disability weekly benefit payment may be decreased by 15%.

__   I object to this offer because the job shift that has been offered is different than the job shift I held at the time of my injury. I understand if the claims administrator does not agree with this objection, my remaining permanent disability weekly benefit payment may be decreased by 15%.

Note: If either party has a dispute or objection regarding the offer of regular work, or if the employee rejects the offer regular work, that party may file a Declaration of Readiness with the local district office of the Workers' Compensation Appeals Board (WCAB).

_____   Date: _____
                    Signature

Proof of Service By Mail or Hand Delivery

I am a resident of the County of _____. I am over the age of eighteen years and not a party to the within matter. My business address is:

_____.

On _____, I served the **Notice of Offer of Regular Work** on the party/parties listed
    below by either method of service described below:

    A. Placing a true copy of the **Notice of Offer of Regular Work** in a sealed envelope with
    postage fully prepaid addressed to each person whose name and address is given below
    by depositing the envelope in the United States mail.

Or

    B. Personally serving a true copy of the **Notice of Offer of Regular Work** on each person
    whose name and address is given below.

Enter the name of the party and indicate the type of service in the box (either A or B as described above.)

Name of Party: Type of Service

_____   ☐

_____   ☐

_____   ☐

_____   ☐

I declare under penalty of perjury under the laws of the State of California that the foregoing is true and correct.

Executed at

_____on _____.

Signature:_____

Intentionally blank

DWC-AD 10003 NOTICIA DE OFERTA DE TRABAJO REGULAR
Para lesiones ocurriendo el o después del 1/1/05

ESTA SECCIÓN DEBE SER RELLENADA POR EL EMPLEADOR O ADMINISTRADOR DE RECLAMOS:

Administrator de Reclamos:_____Número de Reclamo:_____
(Nombre del Administrador de Reclamos)

Basada en la opinion del___médico que lo atendió   QME   AME_____, usted puede regresar a
(Nombre del Médico)

su ocupación usual o al puesto que tuvo a la hora de su lesión el_____.
(Fecha)

Fecha en que es elegible para regresar a su trabajo:_____(como está indicado en el informe del médico)

Empleador:_____
(Nombre de la empresa)

Puesto:_____

Fecha de Comienzo:_____

__ Este puesto está ubicado en el mismo lugar y turno que el puesto que ocupó antes de la lesión.

__ Este puesto está ubicado en una localidad diferente a la del puesto que ocupó antes de la lesión, por lo siguiente:

_____

__ Este puesto es un turno diferente al que ocupó antes de la lesión, por lo siguiente:_____
(empieza)   (termina)

Puede contactar a _____sobre este puesto. No.de teléfono:_____
(Nombre del contacto)

Debe de regresar el formulado rellenado al empleador o administrador de reclamos indicado aquí:

_____
(Nombre del Empleador o Administrador de Reclamos)   (Dirección postal)

Se espera que este puesto dure por lo menos un total de 12 meses de trabajo. Si este puesto no dura por lo menos un total de 12 meses de trabajo, usted puede tener derecho a un aumento en los pagos del beneficio de incapacidad permanente.

Este puesto proporciona un sueldo y compensación de $_____, que son equivalente a o más que el sueldo y compensación que le pagaron a la hora de su lesión.

Yo,_____, he obtenido la información sobre la oferta de trabajo antedicha
(Nombre del Administrador de Reclamos)
de su empleador.

Si el trabajo ofrecido está ubicado en un lugar diferente al del trabajo que tuvo antes de su lesión y usted cree que la distancia de viajar de la residencia donde vivió a la hora de su lesión a este trabajo no es razonable, usted puede oponerse a la oferta de trabajo como no estando a una distancia de viaje razonable . También puede rechazar el requisito de viajar una distancia razonable. Le considerarán haber renunciado este requisito si usted acepta la oferta de trabajo antedicha o no rechaza la oferta dentro de viente días naturales a partir de recibir esta noticia.

<u>**ESTA SECCIÓN DEBE SER RELLENADA POR EL EMPLEADO:**</u>   **Número de Reclamo**_____

El empleado debe de aceptar, rechazar, u oponerse a esta oferta de trabajo regular y regresar este formulario al empleador o administrador de reclamos indicado en la primera página dentro de 20 días naturales de haber recibido oferta o se considerará que el empleado ha renunciado el derecho a oponerse a la ubicación o turno. El empleado debe guardar una copia de este formulario para su propio archivo.

Nombre del empleado:_____ Fecha de cuando la oferta fue recibida:_____

Entiendo que si mi incapacidad está permanente y estable y el empleador ha cumplido con las obligacio
legales relacionadas con esta oferta, mis pagos restantes de incapacidad permanente serán reducidos por 1
ya sea si acepto o rechazo esta oferta.

<u>**Oferta de Trabajo Regular en la Misma Ubicación y/o Turno**</u>

___ Acepto esta oferta de trabajo regular.

___ Rechazo esta oferta de trabajo. Razón:_____

Nota: Si cualquier parte tiene algun desacuerdo o objeción sobre la oferta de trabajo regular o si el empleado rechaz la oferta de trabajo regular, esa parte puede presentar una Declaración de Disposición con la oficina local de la Junt de Apelaciónes de Compensación de Trabajadores (WCAB).

<u>**Oferta de Trabajo Regular en una Diferente Ubicación y/o Turno**</u>

Entiendo que tengo el derecho de oponerme a una oferta de trabajo cuando la ubicación o turno es diferente a la que tuve a la hora de mi lesión.

___ Acepto la oferta y renuncioa mi derecho de oponerme a la ubicación o turno de trabajo como no estando a una distancia de viaje razonable de la residencia de donde viví a la hora de mi lesión .

___ Rechazo esta oferta de trabajo. Razón: _____

___ Me opongo a esta oferta porque el trabajo está ubicado en una localidad diferente a la del trabajo que tuve a la hora de mi lesión y no creo que la distancia de viajar de mi residencia a este trabajo es razonable. Entiendo que si e administrador de reclamos no está de acuerdo con esta objeción, mis pagos restantes del beneficio de incapacidad permanente pueden ser reducidos por 15%.

___ Me opongo a esta oferta porque el turno de trabajo que a sido ofrecido es diferente al que tuve a la hora de mi lesión. Entiendo que si el administrador de reclamos no está de acuerdo con esta objeción, mis pagos restantes del beneficio de incapacidad permanente pueden ser reducidos por 15%.

Nota: Si cualquier parte tiene algun desacuerdo o objeción sobre la oferta de trabajo regular o si el empleado rechaz la oferta de trabajo regular, esa parte puede presentar una Declaración de Disposición con la oficina local de la Junt de Apelaciónes de Compensación de Trabajadores (WCAB).

_____   Fecha: _____
                Firma

Prueba de Entrega Por Correo o Entrega Personal

Soy residente del Condado de _____. Tengo más de dieciocho años de edad y no soy parte de este caso. Mi dirección comercial es:

_____.

El _____, Entregué la **Noticia de Oferta de Trabajo Regular** a la parte/a las partes nombrada (s) a continuación ya sea por uno de los métodos de entrega descritos abajo:

    A. Poniendo una copia auténtica de la **Noticia de Oferta de Trabajo Regular** en un sobre sellado con el franqueo completamente pagado por adelantado y dirigido a cada persona cuyo nombre y dirección está nombrada a continuación y depositando el sobre en el correo de los Estados Unidos.

O

    B. Personalmente entregando una copia auténtica de la **Noticia de Oferta de Trabajo Regular** a cada persona cuyo nombre y dirección está nombrada a continuación.

Ponga el nombre de cada parte y indique la clase de entrega en la casilla (ya sea A o B como descrito arriba.)

Nombre de la Parte: Clase de Entrega

_____ ☐

_____ ☐

_____ ☐

_____ ☐

Declaro bajo pena de perjurio bajo las leyes del Estado de California que lo antedicho es verdadero y correcto.

Ejecutado en

_____el _____.

Firma:_____

Intentionally blank

Request for Reimbursement of Accommodation Expenses
For injuries on or after July 1, 2004
Form DWC AD 10005

Name of Employer: _____ Address of Employer: _____

_____

Phone Number: _____ Name of Injured Employee: _____

WCAB number (if applicable): _____ ____ Claim Number _____

Job Title (at time of injury): _____

Job Duties (attach job description if available): _____

_____

Date of Injury: _____

Reimbursement is requested for expenses to accommodate a:

_____ temporarily disabled employee ($1250 maximum)

_____ permanently disabled employee ($2500 maximum)

Employee's work restrictions and accommodation required (attach treating physician's, QME or AME report):

_____

_____

_____

Itemized list of costs for which reimbursement is requested (attach all receipts):

1. Modification to worksite (list all work done and total cost)   Cost

_____

_____

_____

_____

2. Equipment, furniture and/or tools (list each item and cost)   Cost

_____

_____

_____

_____

3. Any other accommodation expenses: Cost

_____

_____

_____

_____

(Attach additional sheets if necessary)

Total Costs: _____

The above costs have not been paid for and are not covered by the insurance carrier or any other source.

I declare that the information I have provided on this form is true and correct under penalty of perjury.

_____
Signature of employer or employer's representative   Date

MANDATORY FORMAT
STATE OF CALIFORNIA
8 CCR Section 10005

Intentionally blank

DWC-AD 10133.53 NOTICE OF OFFER OF MODIFIED OR ALTERNATIVE WORK
For injuries occurring on or after 1/1/04

THIS SECTION COMPLETED BY CLAIMS ADMINISTRATOR:

Employer (name of firm)_____ is offering you the position of a

(name of job) _____.

You may contact _____ concerning this offer.   Phone No.: _____

Date of offer: _____   Date job starts: _____.

Claims Administrator:_____Claim Number:_____

NOTICE TO EMPLOYEE   Name of employee: _____

Date of Injury:_____Date offer received: _____

You have 30 calendar days from receipt to accept or reject the attached offer of modified or alternative work. Regardless of whether you accept or reject this offer, the remainder of your permanent disability payments may be decreased by 15%. However, if you fail to respond in 30 days or reject this job offer, you will not be entitled to the supplemental job displacement benefit unless:

Modified Work ☐   **or   Alternative Work** ☐

A. You cannot perform the essential functions of the job; or
B. The job is not a regular position lasting at least 12 months; or
C. Wages and compensation offered are less than 85% paid at the time of injury; or
D. The job is beyond a reasonable commuting distance from residence at time of injury.

THIS SECTION TO BE COMPLETED BY EMPLOYEE

___   I accept this offer of Modified or Alternative work.

___   I reject this offer of Modified or Alternative work and understand that I am not entitled to the Supplemental Job Displacement

   Benefit.

I understand that if I voluntarily quit prior to working in this position for 12 months, I may not be entitled to the Supplemental Job Displacement Benefit.

_____   Date _____
Signature

I feel I cannot accept this offer because:

NOTICE TO THE PARTIES
If the offer is <u>not</u> accepted or rejected within 30 days of the offer, the offer is deemed to be rejected by the employee.

The employer or claims administrator must forward a completed copy of this agreement to the Administrative Director within 30 days of acceptance or rejection. (A.D., "SJDB," Division of Workers' Compensation, P.O. Box 420603, S.F., CA 94142-0603)
If a dispute occurs regarding the above offer or agreement, either party may request the Administrative Director to resolve the dispute by filing a Request for Dispute Resolution (Form DWC-AD 10133.55) with the Administrative Director.

DWC-AD 10133.53 NOTICE OF OFFER OF MODIFIED OR ALTERNATIVE WORK
For injuries occurring on or after 1/1/04

POSITION REQUIREMENTS

Actual job title:

Wages: $_____ per   Hour ___   Week ___   Month ___

Is salary of modified/alternative work the same as pre-injury job?   Yes ___   No ___

Is salary of modified/alternative work at least 85% of pre-injury job?   Yes ___   No ___

Will job last at least 12 months?   Yes ___   No ___

Is the job a regular position required by the employer's business?   Yes ___   No ___

Work location: _____

Duties required of the position:

Description of activities to be performed (if not stated in job description):

Physical requirements for performing work activities (include modifications to usual and customary job):

Name of doctor who approved job restrictions (optional):_____ Date of report::_____

Date of last payment of Temporary Total Disability:

Preparer's Name:

Preparer's Signature: Date

Form DWC-AD 10133.53 (August 18, 2006)   MANDATORY FORM (Page 2 of 3)
                                                   STATE OF CALIFORNIA
                                                   (08/06)

Proof of Service By Mail

I am a citizen of the United States and a resident of the County of _____. I am over the age of eighteen years and not a party to the within matter.

My business address is:

_____

On _____, I served the **Notice of Offer of Modified or Alternative Work** on the parties listed below by placing a true copy thereof enclosed in a sealed envelope with postage fully prepaid, and thereafter deposited in the U. S. Mail at the place so addressed.

I declare under penalty of perjury under the laws of the State of California that the foregoing is true and correct.

Executed at _____on _____.

Signature:_____

Copies Served On: _____

Intentionally blank

DWC-AD 10133.53 NOTICIA DE OFERTA DE TRABAJO MODIFICADO O ALTERNATIVO
Para lesiones ocurriendo el o después del 1/1/04

ESTA SECCIÓN DEBE SER RELLENADA POR EL ADMINISTRADOR DE RECLAMOS:

Empleador (nombre de la empresa)_____ le está ofreciendo el puesto de un/una

(nombre del trabajo) _____.

Puede contactar a _____ sobre esta oferta.   No. de teléfono: _____

Fecha de oferta: _____   Fecha de cuando empieza el trabajo: _____

Administrador de Reclamos:_____Número de Reclamo:_____

AVISO AL EMPLEADO   Nombre del empleado: _____

Fecha de lesión: :_____Fecha de cuando la oferta fué recibida:_____
_____

Usted tiene 30 días naturales de cuando recibe la oferta para aceptar o rechazar la oferta de trabajo modificado o alternativo que está adjunto. A pesar de que acepte o rechaze esta oferta, sus pagos restantes de incapacidad permanente pueden ser reducidos por un 15%. Sin embargo, si no responde dentro de 30 días o rechaza esta oferta de trabajo, no tendrá derecho a los beneficios suplementarios por desplazamiento de trabajo a menos que:

Trabajo Modificado ☐ o Trabajo Alternativo ☐

A. Usted no puede desempeñar las funciones esenciales del trabajo o
B. El trabajo no es un puesto regular que durará por lo menos 12 meses o
C. El sueldo y la compensación ofrecida son menos del 85% pagado a la hora de la lesión o
D. El trabajo es más allá de una distancia razonable de viaje de su residencia a la hora de la lesión.

ESTA SECCIÓN DEBE SER RELLENADA POR EL EMPLEADO

__ Acepto esta oferta de trabajo Modificado o Alternativo.

__ Rechazo esta oferta de trabajo Modificado o Alternativo y entiendo que no tengo derecho a los Beneficios Suplementarios

    por Desplazamiento de Trabajo.

Entiendo que si yo dejo el trabajo voluntariamente antes de haber trabajado en este puesto por 12 meses, tal vez no tendré derecho a los Beneficios Suplementarios por Desplazamiento de Trabajo.

_____   Fecha _____
Firma

Siento que no puedo aceptar esta oferta debido a que:

AVISO A LAS PARTES

Si la oferta <u>no</u> es aceptada o rechazada dentro de 30 diás de la oferta, la oferta será considerada rechazada por el empleado.

El empleador o administrador de reclamos debe remitir una copia de este acuerdo rellenado al Director Administrativo dentro de 30 diás de la aceptación o rechazo. (A.D., "SJDB," Division of Workers' Compensation, P.O. Box 420603, S.F., CA 94142-0603).

Si ocurre un desacuerdo sobre la oferta o el acuerdo descrito arriba, cualquier parte puede pedirle al Director Administrativo que resuelva el desacuerdo presentando una Resolución de Disputa (Formulario DWC-AD 10133.55) con el Director Administrativo.

DWC-AD 10133.53 NOTICIA DE OFERTA DE TRABAJO MODIFICADO O ALTERNATIVO
Para lesiones ocurriendo el o después del 1/1/04

REQUISITOS EXIGIDOS POR EL PUESTO

Título actual del puesto:

Sueldo: $ por   Hora ___   Semana ___   Mes ___

¿Es el salario del trabajo modificado/alternativo el mismo del trabajo antes de la lesión?   Sí ___   No ___

¿Es el salario del trabajo modificado/alternativo por lo menos el 85% del trabajo antes de la lesión?   Sí   No   ___   ___

¿Durará el trabajo por lo menos 12 meses?   Sí ___   No ___

¿Es el trabajo un puesto regular requerido por el negocio del empleador?   Sí ___   No ___

Ubicación del trabajo: _____

Tareas exigidas por el puesto:

Descripción de las actividades que deben ser realizadas (si es que no está indicado en la descripción de trabajo):

Requisitos físicos para realizar las actividades de trabajo (incluya las modificaciones al trabajo usual y de costumbre):

Nombre del médico que aprobó las restricciones de trabajo (opcional):_____ Fecha del informe:_____

Fecha del último pago de Incapacidad Temporal Total:

Nombre del Preparador:

Firma del Preparador: Fecha

Prueba de Entrega por Correo

Soy un/una ciudadano(a) de los Estados Unidos y residente del Condado de

_____. Tengo más de dieciocho años de edad y no soy parte de

este caso.

Mi dirección comercial es:

_____

El _____, Entregué la **Noticia de Oferta de Trabajo Modificado**

o Alternativo a las partes nombradas a continuación, poniendo una copia auténtica del mismo en un

sobre sellado con el franqueo completamente pagado por adelantado y depositado en un correo de

los Estados Unidos y con la dirección indicada así.

Declaro bajo pena de perjurio bajo las leyes del Estado de California que lo antedicho es verdadero y

correcto.

Ejecutado en _____el _____.

Firma:_____

Copias Fueron Entregadas A:_____

Appendix I

• Supplemental Job Displacement Benefit

Article 7.5.   Supplemental Job Displacement Benefit

§ 10133.50.   Definitions

(a) The following definitions apply for injuries occurring on or after January 1, 2004:

  (1) Alternative Work. Work that the employee has the ability to perform, that offers wages and compensation that are at least 85 percent of those paid to the employee at the time of injury, and that is located within reasonable commuting distance of the employee's residence at the time of injury.

  (2) Approved Training Facility. A training or skills enhancement facility or institution that meets the requirements of section 10133.58.

  (3) Claims Administrator. The person or entity responsible for the payment of compensation for a self–administered insurer providing security for the payment of compensation required by Divisions 4 and 4.5 of the Labor Code, a self–administered self–insured employer, or a third–party claims administrator for a self–insured employer, insurer, legally uninsured employer, or joint powers authority.

  (4) Employer. The person or entity that employed the injured employee at the time of injury.

  (5) Essential Functions. Job duties considered crucial to the employment position held or desired by the employee. Functions may be considered essential because the position exists to perform the function, the function requires specialized expertise, serious results may occur if the function is not performed, other employees are not available to perform the function or the function occurs at peak periods and the employer cannot reorganize the work flow.

  (6) Insurer. Has the same meaning as in Labor Code section 3211.

  (7) Modified Work. Regular work modified so that the employee has the ability to perform all the functions of the job and that offers wages and compensation that are at least 85 percent of those paid to the employee at the time of injury, and located within a reasonable commuting distance of the employee's residence at the time of injury.

  (8) Nontransferable Training Voucher. A document provided to an employee that allows the employee to enroll in education–related training or skills enhancement. The document shall include identifying information for the employee and claims administrator, specific information regarding the value of the voucher pursuant to Labor Code section 4658.5.

  (9) Notice. A required letter or form generated by the claims administrator and directed to the injured employee.

  (10) Offer of Modified or Alternative Work. An offer to the injured employee of medically appropriate employment with the date–of–injury employer in a form and manner prescribed by the Administrative Director.

  (11) Parties. The employee, the claims administrator and their designated representatives, if any.

  (12) Permanent Partial Disability Award. A final award of permanent partial disability determined by a Workers' Compensation Administrative Law Judge or the Workers' Compensation Appeals Board.

  (13) Regular Work. The employee's usual occupation or the position in which the employee was engaged at the time of injury and that offers wages and compensation equivalent to those paid to the employee at the time of injury, and located within a reasonable commuting distance of the employee's residence at the time of injury.

(14) Supplemental Job Displacement Benefit. An educational retraining or skills enhancement allowance for injured employees whose employers are unable to provide work consistent with the requirements of Labor Code section 4658.6.

(15) Vocational & Return to Work Counselor (VRTWC). A person or entity capable of assisting a person with a disability with development of a return to work strategy and whose regular duties involve the evaluation, counseling and placement of disabled persons. A VRTWC must have at least an undergraduate degree in any field and three or more years full time experience in conducting vocational evaluations, counseling and placement of disabled adults.

(16) Work Restrictions. Permanent medical limitations on employment activity established by the treating physician, Qualified Medical Examiner or Agreed Medical Examiner.

NOTE: Authority cited: Sections 133, 4658.5 and 5307.3, Labor Code. Reference: Sections 124, 4658.1, 4658.5 and 4658.6, Labor Code.

HISTORY
1. New article 7.5 (sections 10133.50–10133.60) and section filed 6–6–2005; operative 8–1–2005 (Register 2005, No. 23).

§ 10133.51. Notice of Potential Right to Supplemental Job Displacement Benefit

(a) This section and section 10133.52 shall only apply to injuries occurring on or after January 1, 2004.
(b) Within 10 days of the last payment of temporary disability, if not previously provided, the claims administrator shall send the employee, by certified mail, the mandatory form "Notice of Potential Right to Supplemental Job Displacement Benefit Form" that is set forth in Section 10133.52.

NOTE: Authority cited: Sections 133, 4658.5 and 5307.3, Labor Code. Reference: Section 4658.5, Labor Code.

HISTORY
1. New section filed 6–6–2005; operative 8–1–2005 (Register 2005, No. 23)

§ 10133.52. "Notice of Potential Right to Supplemental Job Displacement Benefit Form."

Notice of Potential Right to Supplemental Job Displacement Benefit Form (Mandatory Form)

If your injury causes permanent partial disability, which prevented you from returning to work within 60 days of the last payment of temporary disability, and the claims administrator has not provided you with a Form DWC–AD 10133.53 "Notice of Offer of Modified or Alternative Work," you may be eligible for a supplemental job displacement benefit in the form of a nontransferable voucher for education–related retraining or skill enhancement, or both, at state approved or accredited schools.

The amount of the voucher for the supplemental job displacement benefit will be as follows:

Up to four thousand dollars ($4,000) for a permanent partial disability award of less than 15%.
Up to six thousand dollars ($6,000) for a permanent partial disability award between 15 and 25%.
Up to eight thousand dollars ($8,000) for a permanent partial disability award between 26 and 49%.
Up to ten thousand dollars ($10,000) for a permanent partial disability award between 50 and 99%.

A permanent partial disability award is issued by a Workers' Compensation Administrative Law Judge or the Workers' Compensation Appeals Board. You may also settle your potential eligibility for a voucher as part of a compromise and release settlement for a lump sum payment. Any settlement must be reviewed and approved by a Workers' Compensation Administrative Law Judge.

The voucher may be used for payment of tuition, fees, books, and other expenses required by the school for retraining or skill enhancement. Not more than 10 percent of the voucher moneys may be used for vocational or return to work counseling. A list of vocational return to work counselors is available on the Division of Workers' Compensation's website www.dir.ca.gov or upon request.

If you are eligible, and you have not already settled the benefit, you will receive the voucher from the claims administrator within 25 calendar days from the date the permanent partial disability award is issued by the Workers' Compensation Administrative Law Judge or the Workers' Compensation Appeals Board.

If modified or alternative work is available, you will receive a Form DWC–AD 10133.53 "Notice of Offer of Modified or Alternative Work" from the claims administrator within 30 days of the termination of temporary disability indemnity payments. The claims administrator will not be required to pay for supplemental job displacement benefits if the offer for modified or alternative work meets the following conditions:

(1) You have the ability to perform the essential functions of the job provided;
(2) the job provided is in a regular position lasting at least 12 months;

(3) the job provided offers wages and compensation that are at least 85 percent of those paid to you at the time of the injury; and

(4) the job is located within reasonable commuting distance of your residence at the time of injury.

If there is a dispute regarding the Supplemental Job Displacement Benefit, the employee or claims administrator may file Form DWC–AD 10133.55 "Request for Dispute Resolution before the Administrative Director."

If you have a question or need more information, you can contact your employer or the claims administrator listed below. You can also contact a State Division of Workers' Compensation Information and Assistance Officer.

Date:
_____

Name of Claims Administrator:
_____

Phone No.:
_____

Address of Claims Administrator:
_____
_____

Email (optional):
_____

NOTE: Authority cited: Sections 133, 4658.5 and 5307.3, Labor Code. Reference: Section 4658.5, Labor Code.

HISTORY
1. New section filed 6–6–2005; operative 8–1–2005

§ 10133.53. Form DWC–AD 10133.53 "Notice of Offer of Modified or Alternative Work."

Form DWC–AD 10133.53

NOTE: Authority cited: Sections 133, 4658.5 and 5307.3, Labor Code. Reference: Sections 4658, 4658.1, 4658.5 and 4658.6, Labor Code.

HISTORY
1.   New section filed 6–6–2005; operative 8–1–2005 (Register 2005, No. 23).

§ 10133.54. Dispute Resolution

(a)   This section and section 10133.55 shall only apply to injuries occurring on or after January 1, 2004.

(b)   When there is a dispute regarding the Supplemental Job Displacement Benefit, the employee, or claims administrator may request the Administrative Director to resolve the dispute.

(c)   The party requesting the Administrative Director to resolve the dispute shall:

(1)   Complete Form DWC–AD 10133.55 "Request for Dispute Resolution before the Administrative Director;"

(2)   Clearly state the issue(s) and identify supporting information for each issue and position;

(3)   Attach all pertinent documents;

(4)   Submit the original request and all attached documents to the Administrative Director and serve a copy of the request and all attached documents on all parties; and

(5)   Sign and date the proof of service section of Form DWC–AD 10133.55 "Request for Dispute Resolution before the Administrative Director."

(d)   The opposing party shall have twenty (20) calendar days from the date of the proof of service of the Request to submit the original response and all attached documents to the Administrative Director and serve a copy of the response and all attached documents on all parties.

(e)   The Administrative Director or his or her designee may request additional information from the parties.

(f)   The Administrative Director or his or her designee shall issue a written determination and order based solely on the request, response, and any attached documents within thirty (30) calendar days of the date the opposing party's response and supporting information is due. If the Administrative Director or his or her designee requests additional information, the written determination shall be issued within thirty (30) calendar days from the receipt of the additional information. In the event no decision is issued within sixty (60) calendar days of the date the opposing party's response is due or within sixty (60) calendar days of the Administrative Director's receipt of the requested additional information, whichever is later, the request shall be deemed to be denied.

(g) Either party may appeal the determination and order of the Administrative Director by filing a written petition together with a Declaration of Readiness to Proceed pursuant to section 10414 with the local district office of the Workers' Compensation Appeals Board within twenty calendar days of the issuance of the decision or within twenty days after a request is deemed denied pursuant to subdivision (f). The petition shall set forth the specific factual and/or legal reason(s) for the appeal. A copy of the petition and a copy of the Declaration of Readiness to Proceed shall be concurrently served on the Administrative Director.

NOTE: Authority cited: Sections 133, 4658.5 and 5307.3, Labor Code. Reference: Sections 4658.5 and 4658.6, Labor Code.

HISTORY
1. New section filed 6–6–2005; operative 8–1–2005 (Register 2005, No. 23).

§ 10133.55. Form DWC–AD 10133.55 "Request for Dispute Resolution Before the Administrative Director."

Form DWC–AD 10133.55

NOTE: Authority cited: Sections 133, 4658.5 and 5307.3, Labor Code. Reference: Section 4658.5, Labor Code.

HISTORY
1. New section filed 6–6–2005; operative 8–1–2005 (Register 2005, No. 23).

§ 10133.56. Requirement to Issue Supplemental Job Displacement Nontransferable Training Voucher

(a) This section and section 10133.57 shall only apply to injuries occurring on or after January 1, 2004.
(b) The employee shall be eligible for the Supplemental Job Displacement Benefit when:
   (1) the injury causes permanent partial disability; and
   (2) within 30 days of the termination of temporary disability indemnity payments, the claims administrator does not offer modified or alternative work in accordance with Labor Code section 4658.6; and
   (3) either the injured employee does not return to work for the employer within 60 days of the termination of temporary disability benefits; or
   (4) in the case of a seasonal employee, where the employee is unable to return to work within 60 days of the termination of temporary disability benefits because the work season has ended, the injured employee does not return to work on the next available work date of the next work season.
(c) When the requirements under subdivision (b) have been met, the claims administrator shall provide a nontransferable voucher for education–related retraining or skill enhancement or both to the employee within 25 calendar days from the issuance of the permanent partial disability award by the Workers' Compensation Administrative Law Judge or the Workers' Compensation Appeals Board.
(d) The voucher shall be issued to the employee allowing direct reimbursement to the employee upon the employee's presentation to the claims administrator of documentation and receipts or as a direct payment to the provider of the education related training or skill enhancement and/or to the VRTWC.
(e) The voucher must indicate the appropriate level of money available to the employee in compliance with Labor Code section 4658.5.
(f) The mandatory voucher form is set forth in Section 10133.57.
(g) The voucher shall certify that the school is approved and if outside of California, approval is required similarly to the Bureau for Private Postsecondary (BPPVE).
(h) The claims administrator shall issue the reimbursement payments to the employee or direct payments to the VRTWC and the training providers within 45 calendar days from receipt of the completed voucher, receipts and documentation.

NOTE: Authority cited: Sections 133, 4658.5, 4658.6 and 5307.3, Labor Code. Reference: Sections 4658.5 and 4658.6, Labor Code.

HISTORY
1. New section filed 6–6–2005; operative 8–1–2005 (Register 2005, No. 23

§ 10133.57. Form DWC–AD 10133.57 "Supplemental Job Displacement Nontransferable Training Voucher Form."

Supplemental Job Displacement Nontransferable Training Voucher Form (Form DWC–AD 10133.57 – Mandatory Form) For injuries occurring on or after 1/1/04

You have been determined eligible for this nontransferable, Supplemental Job Displacement Voucher. This voucher may be used for the payment of tuition, fees, books, and other expenses required by a state approved or accredited school that you enroll in for the purpose of education related retraining or skill enhancement, or both.

The state approved or accredited school will be reimbursed upon receipt of a documented invoice for tuition, fees, books and other required expenses required by the school for retraining or skill enhancement. If you pay for the eligible expenses, you may be reimbursed for these expenses upon submission of documented receipts. No more than 10 percent of the value of this voucher may be used for vocational or return to work counseling. If you decide to voluntarily withdraw from a program, you may not be entitled to a full refund of the voucher amount utilized.

Please present this original letter to the state approved or accredited school and/or the Vocational & Return to Work Counselor of your choice, chosen from the list developed by the Division of Workers' Compensation's Administrative Director, in order to initiate your training and return to work counseling. A list of Vocational & Return to Work Counselors is available on the Division of Workers' Compensation's website www.dir.ca.gov or upon request. The school and/or counselor should contact me regarding direct payment from your supplemental job displacement benefit.

Injured Employee Information: Upon completing the voucher form the injured employee must return the form with receipts and documentation to the claims administrator immediately for reimbursement. (The claims administrator must complete Nos. 1–8 of this voucher form prior to sending it to the injured employee.)

1. Injured Employee Name _____

2. Address _____
    City _____ State _____
    Zip Code _____

3. Claim Number _____
    Phone Number _____
    Claims Administrator

4. Name _____

5. Claims Mailing Address _____

6. City _____ State _____
    Zip Code _____

7. Claims Representative _____
    Phone Number _____

8. $ _____ is available to the injured employee based on _____% of Permanent Partial Disability Award
    The injured employee must complete Nos. 9–19 and sign and date this voucher form.
    (VRTWC) Vocational Return to Work Counselor (if any)

9. Name _____
    Phone Number _____

10. Address _____

11. City _____ State _____
    Zip Code _____

12. Funds used for vocational and return to work counseling $_____ (10% maximum of voucher value)
    Training Provider Details (Attach additional pages for each provider if necessary.)

13. Provider Name _____

14. Provider Address _____
    Phone Number _____

15. City _____ State _____
    Zip Code _____

16. Provider approval number _____

17. Expiration Date _____

18. Provider Contact Name _____

19. Training Cost _____
    Injured Employee Signature _____
    Date _____

Note to Claims Administrator: Upon receipt of voucher, receipts and documentation from the employee, reimbursement payments to the employee or direct payments to VRTWC and training providers must be made within 45 calendar days.

NOTE: Authority cited: Sections 133, 4658.5 and 5307.3, Labor Code. Reference: Section 4658.5, Labor Code.

HISTORY

1. New section filed 6–6–2005; operative 8–1–2005 (Register 2005, No. 23). 8 CA ADC s 10133.57

§ 10133.58. State Approved or Accredited Schools

(a) This section shall only apply to injuries occurring on or after January 1, 2004.

(b) Private providers of education–related retraining or skill enhancement selected to provide training as part of a supplemental job displacement benefit shall be:

　(1) approved by the Bureau for Private Postsecondary and Vocational Education (www.bppve.ca.gov), or a California state agency that has an agreement with the Bureau for the regulation and oversight of non–degree–granting private postsecondary institutions;

　(2) accredited by one of the Regional Associations of Schools and Colleges authorized by the United States Department of Education; or

　(3) certified by the Federal Aviation Administration.

(c) Any training outside of California must be approved by an agency in that state similar to the Bureau for Private Postsecondary and Vocational Education.

NOTE: Authority cited: Sections 133, 4658.5 and 5307.3, Labor Code. Reference: Section 4658.5, Labor Code.

HISTORY

1. New section filed 6–6–2005; operative 8–1–2005 (Register 2005, No. 23).

§ 10133.60. Termination of Claims Administrator's Liability for the Supplemental Job Displacement Benefit

(a) For injuries occurring on or after January 1, 2004, the claims administrator's liability to provide a supplemental job displacement voucher shall end if either (a)(1) or (a)(2) occur:

　(1) the claims administrator offers modified or alternative work to the employee, meeting the requirements of Labor Code §4658.6, on DWC–AD Form 10133.53 "Notice of Offer of Modified or Alternative Work";

　　(A) If the claims administrator offers modified or alternative work to the employee for 12 months of seasonal work, the offer shall meet the following requirements:

　　　1. the employee was hired on a seasonal basis prior to injury; and

　　　2. the offer of modified or alternative work is on a similar seasonal basis to the employee's previous employment;

　(2) the maximum funds of the voucher have been exhausted.

NOTE: Authority cited: Sections 133 and 5307.3, Labor Code. Reference: Sections 4658.1, 4658.5, 4658.6 and 5410, Labor Code; and Henry v. WCAB (1998) 68 Cal.App.4th 981.

HISTORY

1. New section filed 6–6–2005; operative 8–1–2005 (Register 2005, No. 23)

Forms

Intentionally blank

DWC-AD 10133.53 NOTICE OF OFFER OF MODIFIED OR ALTERNATIVE WORK
For injuries occurring on or after 1/1/04

THIS SECTION COMPLETED BY CLAIMS ADMINISTRATOR:

Employer (name of firm)_____ is offering you the position of a

(name of job) _____.

You may contact _____ concerning this offer.   Phone No.: _____

Date of offer: _____   Date job starts: _____.

Claims Administrator:_____Claim Number:_____

NOTICE TO EMPLOYEE   Name of employee: _____

Date of Injury:_____Date offer received: _____

You have 30 calendar days from receipt to accept or reject the attached offer of modified or alternative work. Regardless of whether you accept or reject this offer, the remainder of your permanent disability payments may be decreased by 15%. However, if you fail to respond in 30 days or reject this job offer, you will not be entitled to the supplemental job displacement benefit unless:

Modified Work ☐ or **Alternative Work** ☐

A. You cannot perform the essential functions of the job; or
B. The job is not a regular position lasting at least 12 months; or
C. Wages and compensation offered are less than 85% paid at the time of injury; or
D. The job is beyond a reasonable commuting distance from residence at time of injury.

THIS SECTION TO BE COMPLETED BY EMPLOYEE

___ I accept this offer of Modified or Alternative work.

___ I reject this offer of Modified or Alternative work and understand that I am not entitled to the Supplemental Job Displacement
       Benefit.

I understand that if I voluntarily quit prior to working in this position for 12 months, I may not be entitled to the Supplemental Job Displacement Benefit.

_____   Date _____
Signature

I feel I cannot accept this offer because:

NOTICE TO THE PARTIES
If the offer is _not_ accepted or rejected within 30 days of the offer, the offer is deemed to be rejected by the employee.

The employer or claims administrator must forward a completed copy of this agreement to the Administrative Director within 30 days of acceptance or rejection. (A.D., "SJDB," Division of Workers' Compensation, P.O. Box 420603, S.F., CA 94142-0603)
If a dispute occurs regarding the above offer or agreement, either party may request the Administrative Director to resolve the dispute by filing a Request for Dispute Resolution (Form DWC-AD 10133.55) with the Administrative Director.

Form DWC-AD 10133.53 (August 18, 2006)   MANDATORY FORM (Page 1 of 3)
STATE OF CALIFORNIA
(08/06)

DWC-AD 10133.53 NOTICE OF OFFER OF MODIFIED OR ALTERNATIVE WORK
For injuries occurring on or after 1/1/04

POSITION REQUIREMENTS

Actual job title:

Wages: $ _____ per Hour ___ Week ___ Month ___

Is salary of modified/alternative work the same as pre-injury job?   Yes ___ No ___

Is salary of modified/alternative work at least 85% of pre-injury job?   Yes ___ No ___

Will job last at least 12 months?   Yes ___ No ___

Is the job a regular position required by the employer's business?   Yes ___ No ___

Work location: _____

Duties required of the position:

Description of activities to be performed (if not stated in job description):

Physical requirements for performing work activities (include modifications to usual and customary job):

Name of doctor who approved job restrictions (optional):_____ Date of report::_____

Date of last payment of Temporary Total Disability:

Preparer's Name:

Preparer's Signature: Date

Form DWC-AD 10133.53 (August 18, 2006)   MANDATORY FORM (Page 2 of 3)
                                                      STATE OF CALIFORNIA
                                                            (08/06)

DWC-AD 10133.53 NOTICE OF OFFER OF MODIFIED OR ALTERNATIVE WORK
For injuries occurring on or after 1/1/04

Proof of Service By Mail

I am a citizen of the United States and a resident of the County of

_____. I am over the age of eighteen years and not a party to the

within matter.

My business address is:

_____

On _____, I served the **Notice of Offer of Modified or**

Alternative Work on the parties listed below by placing a true copy thereof enclosed in a sealed

envelope with postage fully prepaid, and thereafter deposited in the U. S. Mail at the place so

addressed.

I declare under penalty of perjury under the laws of the State of California that the foregoing is true

and correct.

Executed at _____on _____.

Signature:_____

Copies Served On: _____

Intentionally blank

DWC-AD 10133.53 NOTICIA DE OFERTA DE TRABAJO MODIFICADO O ALTERNATIVO
Para lesiones ocurriendo el o después del 1/1/04

ESTA SECCIÓN DEBE SER RELLENADA POR EL ADMINISTRADOR DE RECLAMOS:

Empleador (nombre de la empresa)_____ le está ofreciendo el puesto de un/una

(nombre del trabajo) _____.

Puede contactar a _____ sobre esta oferta.   No. de teléfono: _____

Fecha de oferta: _____   Fecha de cuando empieza el trabajo: _____

Administrador de Reclamos:_____Número de Reclamo:_____

AVISO AL EMPLEADO   Nombre del empleado: _____

Fecha de lesión: :_____Fecha de cuando la oferta fué recibida:_____

_____

Usted tiene 30 días naturales de cuando recibe la oferta para aceptar o rechazar la oferta de trabajo modificado o alternativo que está adjunto. A pesar de que acepte o rechaze esta oferta, sus pagos restantes de incapacidad permanente pueden ser reducidos por un 15%. Sin embargo, si no responde dentro de 30 días o rechaza esta oferta de trabajo, no tendrá derecho a los beneficios suplementarios por desplazamiento de trabajo a menos que:

Trabajo Modificado ☐ o Trabajo Alternativo ☐

A. Usted no puede desempeñar las funciones esenciales del trabajo o
B. El trabajo no es un puesto regular que durará por lo menos 12 meses o
C. El sueldo y la compensación ofrecida son menos del 85% pagado a la hora de la lesión o
D. El trabajo es más allá de una distancia razonable de viaje de su residencia a la hora de la lesión.

ESTA SECCIÓN DEBE SER RELLENADA POR EL EMPLEADO

__ Acepto esta oferta de trabajo Modificado o Alternativo.

__ Rechazo esta oferta de trabajo Modificado o Alternativo y entiendo que no tengo derecho a los Beneficios Suplementarios

   por Desplazamiento de Trabajo.

Entiendo que si yo dejo el trabajo voluntariamente antes de haber trabajado en este puesto por 12 meses, tal vez no tendré derecho a los Beneficios Suplementarios por Desplazamiento de Trabajo.

_____   Fecha _____
              Firma

Siento que no puedo aceptar esta oferta debido a que:

AVISO A LAS PARTES

Si la oferta <u>no</u> es aceptada o rechazada dentro de 30 diás de la oferta, la oferta será considerada rechazada por el empleado.

El empleador o administrador de reclamos debe remitir una copia de este acuerdo rellenado al Director Administrativo dentro de 30 diás de la aceptación o rechazo. (A.D., "SJDB," Division of Workers' Compensation, P.O. Box 420603, S.F., CA 94142-0603).

Si ocurre un desacuerdo sobre la oferta o el acuerdo descrito arriba, cualquier parte puede pedirle al Director Administrativo que resuelva el desacuerdo presentando una Resolución de Disputa (Formulario DWC-AD 10133.55) con el Director Administrativo.

DWC-AD 10133.53 NOTICIA DE OFERTA DE TRABAJO MODIFICADO O ALTERNATIVO

Para lesiones ocurriendo el o después del 1/1/04

REQUISITOS EXIGIDOS POR EL PUESTO

Título actual del puesto:

Sueldo: _____ $ _____ por Hora ___ Semana ___ Mes ___

¿Es el salario del trabajo modificado/alternativo el mismo del trabajo antes de la lesión? Sí ___ No ___

¿Es el salario del trabajo modificado/alternativo por lo menos el 85% del trabajo antes de la lesión? Sí ___ No ___

¿Durará el trabajo por lo menos 12 meses? Sí ___ No ___

¿Es el trabajo un puesto regular requerido por el negocio del empleador? Sí ___ No ___

Ubicación del trabajo: _____

Tareas exigidas por el puesto:

Descripción de las actividades que deben ser realizadas (si es que no está indicado en la descripción de trabajo):

Requisitos físicos para realizar las actividades de trabajo (incluya las modificaciones al trabajo usual y de costumbre):

Nombre del médico que aprobó las restricciones de trabajo (opcional):_____ Fecha del informe:_____

Fecha del último pago de Incapacidad Temporal Total:

Nombre del Preparador:

Firma del Preparador: _____ Fecha

Prueba de Entrega por Correo

Soy un/una ciudadano(a) de los Estados Unidos y residente del Condado de

_____. Tengo más de dieciocho años de edad y no soy parte de

este caso.

Mi dirección comercial es:

_____

El _____, Entregué la **Noticia de Oferta de Trabajo Modificado**

o Alternativo a las partes nombradas a continuación, poniendo una copia auténtica del mismo en un

sobre sellado con el franqueo completamente pagado por adelantado y depositado en un correo de

los Estados Unidos y con la dirección indicada así.

Declaro bajo pena de perjurio bajo las leyes del Estado de California que lo antedicho es verdadero y

correcto.

Ejecutado en _____el _____.

Firma:_____

Copias Fueron Entregadas A:_____

DWC-AD 10133.55 Request for Dispute Resolution Before the Administrative Director (For injuries occurring on or after 1/1/04) ___Original ___Response	Has employer accepted this claim? ___ Yes ___ No Has liability for injury been found by the WCAB? ___ Yes ___ No Has it been more than 60 days since TTD ended? ___ Yes ___ No Has PPD award been stipulated, issued/approved? ___ Yes ___ No	DWC Use Only

Social Security Number	WCAB Number	DWC Unit Number

Employee Name (Last)	(First)	(MI) Phone	Date of Birth

Address (Street)	(City)	(State)	(Zip)

Employer Name	Phone	Insurance Company Name; Or, if Self-Insured, Certificate Name
Address		Adjusting Agency Name (if adjusted)
City, State, Zip		Claims Mailing Address

Date of Injury	Claim Number	City, State, Zip	Phone No.

Employee Representative (if any)	Employer Representative
Firm Name	Firm Name
Address	Address
City, State, Zip Phone No.	City, State, Zip Phone No.

Vocational & Return to Work Counselor (if applicable)

Firm Name	Representative Name
Address (Street, City, State, Zip	Phone No.

The Administrative Director is requested to resolve the following dispute because the parties disagree on: (Please describe and attach all pertinent documents)

Summary of Parties' Informal Efforts to Resolve this Dispute	Proof of Service: I declare under penalty of perjury under the laws of the State of California that on the date written below, I mailed a copy of this request with a copy of any documents included with this request to the following parties at the following addresses: **Administrative Director, (SJDB), Division of Workers' Compensation, P.O. Box 420603, San Francisco, CA 94142-0603**

Name of Requester	Date	Signature	Date

Form DWC-AD 10133.55 (August 18, 2006)

Intentionally blank

Supplemental Job Displacement
Nontransferable Training Voucher Form
(Form DWC-AD 10133.57 – Mandatory Form)
For injuries occurring on or after 1/1/04

You have been determined eligible for this nontransferable, Supplemental Job Displacement Voucher. This voucher may be used for the payment of tuition, fees, books, and other expenses required by a state approved or accredited school that you enroll in for the purpose of education related retraining or skill enhancement, or both.

The state approved or accredited school will be reimbursed upon receipt of a documented invoice for tuition, fees, books and other required expenses required by the school for retraining or skill enhancement. If you pay for the eligible expenses, you may be reimbursed for these expenses upon submission of documented receipts. No more than 10 percent of the value of this voucher may be used for vocational or return to work counseling. If you decide to voluntarily withdraw from a program, you may not be entitled to a full refund of the voucher amount utilized.

Please present this original letter to the state approved or accredited school and/or the Vocational & Return to Work Counselor of your choice, chosen from the list developed by the Division of Workers' Compensation's Administrative Director, in order to initiate your training and return to work counseling. A list of Vocational & Return to Work Counselors is available on the Division of Workers' Compensation's website www.dir.ca.gov or upon request. The school and/or counselor should contact me regarding direct payment from your supplemental job displacement benefit.

Injured Employee Information: Upon completing the voucher form the injured employee must return the form with receipts and documentation to the claims administrator immediately for reimbursement. (The claims administrator must complete Nos. 1 – 8 of this voucher form prior to sending it to the injured employee.)

1. Injured Employee Name_____

2. Address_____

   City_____ State_____ Zip Code_____

3. Claim Number_____ Phone Number_____

Claims Administrator

4. Name _____

5. Claims Mailing Address_____

6. City _____ State _____ Zip Code _____

7. Claims Representative _____ Phone Number _____

8. $_____ is available to the injured employee based on _____% of Permanent Partial Disability Award

The injured employee must complete Nos. 9 – 19 and sign and date this voucher form.

(VRTWC) Vocational Return to Work Counselor (if any)

9. Name _____ Phone Number _____

10. Address _____

11. City _____ State _____ Zip Code _____

12. Funds used for vocational and return to work counseling $_____ (10% maximum of voucher value)

Training Provider Details (Attach additional pages for each provider if necessary.)

13. Provider Name _____

14. Provider Address _____ Phone Number _____

15. City _____ State _____ Zip Code _____

16. Provider approval number _____

17. Expiration Date _____

18. Provider Contact Name _____

19. Training Cost _____

Injured Employee Signature _____ **Date** _____

Note to Claims Administrator: Upon receipt of voucher, receipts and documentation from the employee, reimbursement payments to the employee or direct payments to VRTWC and training providers must be made within 45 calendar days.

Appendix J

● Notices for Injuries Involving Loss of Time from Work or Denial of Claim

Article 8.   Notices for Injuries Involving Loss of Time or Denial of Claim

§ 9810.   General Provisions

(a) This Article applies to benefit notices prepared on or after its effective date. Amendments to this Article filed with the Secretary of State in January, 1994 shall become effective for notices required to be sent on or after April 1, 1994.

(b) The Administrative Director may, at his or her discretion, issue and revise from time to time a Benefit Notice Instruction Manual as a guide for completing and serving the notices required by this Article.

(c) Benefit notice letters may be produced on the claims administrator's letterhead. The notice letters shall identify the employee's name, employer's name, the claim number, the date the notice was sent to the employee, and the date of injury. All notices shall clearly identify the name and telephone number and address of the person responsible for the payment and adjusting of the claim, and shall clearly state that additional information may be obtained from an Information and Assistance officer with the Division of Workers' Compensation. If the employer offers additional disability benefits in addition to those provided by law under workers' compensation, the claims administrator may incorporate the information within the notices required by these regulations. A single benefit notice may encompass multiple events.

(d) The claims administrator shall make available to the employee, upon request, copies of medical reports other than psychiatric reports which the physician has recommended not be provided to the employee.

(e) The claims administrator shall send a copy of each benefit notice, and any enclosures not previously served on the attorney (except benefit notice pamphlets), concurrently to the attorney of any represented employee.

(f) Any deadline for reply which is measured from the date a notice is sent, and all rights protected within the deadline, are extended if the notice is sent by mail, as follows: by 5 days if the place of mailing and the place of address are in the same state of the United States; by 10 days if the place of mailing and the place of address are in different states of the United States; by 20 days if the place of mailing is in and the place of address is outside the United States. All notices shall be mailed from the United States.

(g) Copies of all benefit notices sent to injured workers shall be maintained by the claims administrator in paper or electronic form.

NOTE: Authority cited: Sections 59, 133, 138.3, 138.4, 139.5(a)(2), 4061(a), (b), (d) and 5307.3, Labor Code. Reference: Sections 138.4, 139.5(a)(3), 4061 and 4650(a) through (d), Labor Code.

HISTORY

1. Repealer of article 8 (sections 9810–9878, not consecutive) and new article 8 (sections 9810–9817) filed 7–15–83; effective thirtieth day thereafter (Register 83, No. 30). For prior history, see Registers 81, No. 42; 79, No. 30; 78, No. 45; 73, Nos. 51 and 38; 72, No. 51; and 66, No. 20.

2. Editorial correction of 7–15–83 order redesignating effective date to 8–1–83 pursuant to Government Code section 11346.2(d) filed 7–19–83 (Register 83, No. 30).

3. Editorial correction of 7–15–83 order filed 8–11–83 (Register 83, No. 33).

4. Amendment of article heading, section and Note filed 1–7–94; operative 1–7–94. Submitted to OAL for printing only pursuant to Government Code section 11351 (Register 94, No. 1).
5. Repealer of subsection (d) and subsection relettering filed 7–7–2004; operative 8–1–2004 pursuant to Government Code section 11343.4 (Register 2004, No. 28).

§ 9811.   Definitions

As used in this Article:
(a) "Claims Administrator" means a self–administered insurer providing security for the payment of compensation required by Divisions 4 and 4.5 of the Labor Code, a self–administered self–insured employer, or a third–party claims administrator for a self–insured employer, insurer, legally uninsured employer, or joint powers authority.
(b) "Date of knowledge of injury" means the date the employer had knowledge of a worker's injury or claim of injury.
(c) "Date of knowledge of injury and disability" means the date the employer had knowledge of (1) a worker's injury or claim of injury, and (2) the worker's inability or claimed inability to work because of the injury.
(d) "Duration" means any known period of time for which benefits are to be paid, or, where benefits will continue for an unknown period of time the event that will occur which will determine when benefits will terminate.
(e) "Employee" includes dependent(s) in the event of any injury which results in death.
(f) "Employee's (or claimant's) remedies", of which an employee or claimant shall be informed in benefit notices when specified in these regulations, means the right to disagree with the decision; to consult with an Information and Assistance Officer; to consult with and be represented by an attorney; to apply to the Workers' Compensation Appeals Board, or in the case of a vocational rehabilitation dispute to the Rehabilitation Unit, to resolve a dispute.
(g) "Employer" means any person or entity defined as an employer by Labor Code Section 3300.
(h) "Injury" means any injury as defined in Labor Code Section 3208 which results in lost time beyond the date of injury, medical treatment beyond first aid, or death.

NOTE: Authority cited: Sections 59, 133, 138.3, 138.4 and 5307.3, Labor Code. Reference: Sections 138.4, 139.5(c), (d), 3208, 3300, 3351, 3351.5, 3700, 3753, 4635(a), 4650(a) through (d), 4653, 4654, 4700 and 4701, Labor Code; Sections 11651 and 11652, Insurance Code; Sections 2330 and 2332, Civil Code.

HISTORY
1. Amendment of section and Note filed 1–7–94; operative 1–7–94. Submitted to OAL for printing only pursuant to Government Code section 11351 (Register 94, No. 1).

§ 9812.   Benefit Payment and Notice

(a) Temporary Disability Notices. When an injury causes or is claimed to cause temporary disability:
  (1) Notice of First Temporary Disability Indemnity Payment. The first time the claims administrator pays temporary disability indemnity, the claims administrator shall advise the employee of the amount of temporary disability indemnity due, how it was calculated, and the duration and schedule of indemnity payments. The notice shall be sent no later than the 14th day after the employer's date of knowledge of injury and disability.
  (2) Notice of Delay in Any Temporary Disability Indemnity Payment. If the employee's entitlement to any period of temporary disability indemnity cannot be determined within 14 days of the date of knowledge of injury and disability, the claims administrator shall advise the employee within the 14–day period of the delay, the reasons for it, the need, if any, for additional information required to make a determination, and when a determination is likely to be made. The claims administrator shall send an additional notice or notices within 5 days after the determination date it specified, to advise of any further delay. The additional delay notices shall include the employee's remedies and shall comply with all requirements for an original delay notice.
  (3) Notice of Denial of Any Temporary Disability Indemnity Payment.
(a) If the claims administrator denies liability for the payment of any period for which an employee claims temporary disability indemnity, the notice shall advise the employee of the denial, the reasons for it, and the employee's remedies. The notice shall be sent within 14 days after the determination to deny was made.
(b) Notice of Resumed Benefit Payments (TD, SC, PD, VRTD/VRMA). If the payment of temporary disability indemnity, salary continuation, permanent disability indemnity, or vocational rehabilitation temporary disability indemnity or maintenance allowance is resumed after terminating any of these benefits, the claims administrator shall advise the employee of the amount of indemnity due and the duration and schedule of payments. Notice shall be sent within 14 days after the employer's date of knowledge of the entitlement to additional benefits.
(c) Notice of Changed Benefit Rate or Schedule (TD, SC, PD, VRTD/VRMA). When the claims administrator changes the benefit rate or benefit payment schedule for temporary disability indemnity, salary continuation, permanent disability indemnity, or vocational rehabilitation temporary disability indemnity or maintenance allowance, the claims administrator

shall advise the employee, as applicable, of the amount of the new benefit rate and the reason the rate is being changed, or of the new benefit payment schedule. Notice shall be given before or with the new payment.

(d) Notice that Benefits Are Ending (TD, SC, PD, VRTD/VRMA). With the last payment of temporary disability indemnity, permanent disability indemnity, salary continuation, or vocational rehabilitation temporary disability indemnity or maintenance allowance, the claims administrator shall advise the employee of the ending of indemnity payments and the reason, and shall make an accounting of all compensation paid to or on behalf of the employee in the species of benefit to which the notice refers, including the dates and amounts paid and any related penalties. If the decision to end payment of indemnity was made after the last payment, the claims administrator shall send the notice and accounting within 14 days of the last payment. The notice shall include the employee's remedies.

(e) Permanent Disability Notices For Injuries Which Occurred Prior To 1991. For injuries which occurred before January 1, 1991:

    (1) Existence and Extent of Permanent Disability is Known. Within 14 days after the claims administrator knows that the injury has caused permanent disability and knows the extent of that disability, the claims administrator shall advise the employee of the amount of the weekly permanent disability indemnity payment, how it was calculated, the duration and frequency of payments, the total amount to be paid, and the employee's remedies if he or she disagrees.

    (2) Existence of Permanent Disability is Known, Extent is Uncertain. If the claims administrator knows that the injury has caused permanent disability but cannot determine its extent within the 14 days after the last payment of temporary disability indemnity, or within 14 days after knowledge that the employee's injury has resulted in permanent disability if there was no compensable temporary disability, the claims administrator nevertheless shall make timely payment of permanent disability indemnity and shall advise the employee of the amount of the weekly permanent disability indemnity payment, how it was calculated, the duration and schedule of payments, and the claims administrator's reasonable estimate of the amount of permanent disability indemnity to be paid.

    The claims administrator shall notify the employee that his or her medical condition will be monitored until the extent of permanent disability can be determined and that the disability payments will be revised at that time if appropriate. Within 14 days after the claims administrator determines the extent of permanent disability indemnity benefits, the claims administrator shall notify the employee as provided by paragraph (1).

    (3) Existence of Permanent Disability is Uncertain. If the existence of permanent disability is uncertain, the claims administrator shall advise the employee within 14 days after the last payment of temporary disability indemnity, or within 14 days of receiving a claim or medical report alleging the existence of permanent disability if the claims administrator paid no temporary disability, that the claims administrator cannot yet determine whether the injury will cause permanent disability. The notice shall specify the reasons for the delay in determination, the need, if any, for additional information required to make a determination, and when the determination is likely to be made. The claims administrator shall send an additional notice or notices no later than 5 days after the determination date it specified, to advise of any further delay. The additional delay notices shall include the employee's remedies and shall comply with all requirements for an original delay notice. If the reason for the delay is that the employee's medical condition is not permanent and stationary, the claims administrator shall advise the employee that his or her medical condition will be monitored until it is permanent and stationary, at which time an evaluation will be performed to determine the amount of permanent disability indemnity, if any, due the employee. Within 14 days after the claims administrator determines that permanent disability exists, the claims administrator shall notify the employee of the commencement of permanent disability indemnity payments as provided by paragraph (1) or (2).

    (4) Notice That No Permanent Disability Exists. If the claims administrator alleges that the injury has caused no permanent disability, the claims administrator shall advise the employee within 14 days after the claims administrator determines that the injury has caused no permanent disability and shall include the employee's remedies.

(f) Permanent Disability Notices for Injuries Occurring in 1991, 1992, 1993.

    (1) Condition Not Permanent and Stationary (P & S), May Cause Permanent Disability–Notice of Monitoring Until P&S Date. If the injury has resulted or may result in permanent disability but the employee's medical condition is not permanent and stationary, the claims administrator shall advise the employee, together with the last payment of temporary disability indemnity, that permanent disability indemnity is or may be payable but that the amount cannot be determined because the employee's medical condition has not yet reached a stationary status. The notice shall advise the employee that his or her medical condition will be monitored until it is permanent and stationary, at which time a medical evaluation will be performed to determine the existence and extent of permanent impairment or limitations and the need for continuing medical care. The notice shall advise the employee of the estimated date when a determination is likely to be made, and the claimant's remedies. The claims administrator shall send an additional notice or notices within 5 days after the determination date it specified, to advise of any further delay. The additional delay notices shall include the employee's remedies and shall comply with all requirements for an original delay notice.

    (2) Condition Becomes Permanent and Stationary, May Cause Permanent Disability–Notice of Qualified Medical Evaluator (QME) Procedures. Within 5 working days after receiving information indicating that the employee's condition is permanent and stationary and has caused or may have caused permanent disability, the claims administrator shall advise the employee that his or her medical condition is permanent and stationary and of the

procedures for evaluating permanent disability and need for continuing medical care, and shall include the employee's remedies.

(3) Notice of Permanent Disability Indemnity Advances When Injury Causes Permanent Disability. If the claims administrator knows that the employee has sustained permanent disability, whether or not its extent is known and whether or not the employee's medical condition is permanent and stationary, the claims administrator shall advise the employee of the weekly permanent disability indemnity payment, how it was calculated, the duration and schedule of payments, and the claims administrator's reasonable estimate of permanent disability indemnity to be paid, within 14 days after knowledge that the employee's injury has resulted in permanent disability, whichever is later.

(4) Notice That No Permanent Disability Exists. If the claims administrator alleges that the injury has caused no permanent disability, the claims administrator shall advise the employee that no permanent disability indemnity is payable. This notice shall be sent within 14 days after the claims administrator determines that the injury has caused no permanent disability. The notice shall also advise the employee of the process to obtain a formal medical evaluation to contest the determination that the employee has no permanent disability and shall advise of the employee's remedies.

(g) Permanent Disability Notices For Injuries Occurring on or after 1/1/94. For injuries occurring on or after January 1, 1994:
All notices in this subdivision shall include the following mandatory language:

"Please call me if you have questions. If you want further information, you may contact the local state Information and Assistance office by calling [enter district I & A office telephone number closest to the injured worker] or you may receive recorded information by calling 1–800–736–7401.

You may also consult an attorney of your choice. Should you decide to be represented by an attorney, you may or may not receive a larger award, but, unless you are determined to be ineligible for an award, the attorney's fee will be deducted from any award you might receive for disability benefits. The decision to be represented by an attorney is yours to make, but it is voluntary and may not be necessary for you to receive your benefits".

(1) Condition Not Permanent and Stationary, May Cause Permanent Disability–Notice of Monitoring Until P&S Date. If the injury has resulted or may result in permanent disability but the employee's medical condition is not permanent and stationary, the claims administrator shall advise the employee together with the last payment of temporary disability indemnity, that permanent disability indemnity is or may be payable but that the amount cannot be determined because the employee's medical condition has not yet reached a stationary status. The notice shall advise the employee that his or her medical condition will be monitored until it is permanent and stationary, at which time a medical evaluation will be performed to determine the existence and extent of permanent impairment or limitations and the need for continuing medical care. The notice shall advise the employee of the estimated date when a determination is likely to be made. The claims administrator shall send an additional notice or notices no later than 5 days after the determination date it specified, to advise of any further delay. The additional delay notices shall include the employee's remedies and shall comply with all requirements for an original delay notice.

(2) Condition Becomes Permanent and Stationary, Causes Permanent Disability–Notice of QME Procedures. Together with the last payment of temporary disability or within 14 days of determining the amount of permanent disability payable, the claims administrator shall advise the employee of the claims administrator's determination of the amount of permanent disability indemnity payable, the basis for the determination, and whether there is need for continuing medical care. The notice shall include the employee's available remedies and:

(A) If the employee is unrepresented, the notice shall advise the employee that if either party disagrees with the treating physician's report, the worker must follow the procedures to request a comprehensive medical evaluation from a panel of Qualified Medical Evaluators supplied by the Industrial Medical Council. The notice shall include the claims administrator's decision on whether the claims administrator accepts or refutes the treating physician's evaluation of the employee's permanent impairment and shall be accompanied by the form prescribed by the Industrial Medical Council with which to request assignment of a panel of Qualified Medical Evaluators.

(B) If the employee is unrepresented and the claims administrator is not requesting a rating from the Disability Evaluation Unit, the notice shall also advise the worker that he or she may contact an Information and Assistance Officer to have the treating physician's evaluation reviewed and rated by the State of California Disability Evaluation Unit.

(C) If the employee is unrepresented and the claims administrator has or will be requesting a rating from the Disability Evaluation Unit on the treating physician's evaluation, the notice shall advise the employee that he or she will be receiving a rating based on the treating physician's evaluation from the Disability Evaluation Unit.

(D) If the employee is represented by an attorney, the notice shall advise the employee that he or she may obtain an additional medical evaluation by an Agreed Medical Examiner or, if no agreement on an Agreed Medical Examiner can be reached, by a Qualified Medical Evaluator of his or her choice, and that arrangements for this evaluation should be discussed with the employee's attorney. The notice shall also indicate whether or not the claims administrator disputes the treating physician's evaluation of the employee's permanent impairment and limitations.

(3) Notice That No Permanent Disability Exists. If the claims administrator alleges that the injury has caused no permanent disability, the claims administrator shall advise the employee that no permanent disability indemnity is payable. This notice shall be sent together with the last payment of temporary disability indemnity or within 14 days

after the claims administrator determines that the injury has caused no permanent disability. The notice shall include the employee's remedies and:

(A) If the employee is unrepresented, the notice shall advise the worker that if he or she disagrees with the treating physician's report on which the claims administrator's determination is made, he or she may request a comprehensive medical evaluation from a physician selected from a panel of Qualified Medical Evaluators supplied by the Industrial Medical Council. The notice shall also advise of the procedure for requesting the panel and shall be accompanied by the form prescribed by the Industrial Medical Council with which to request assignment of a panel of Qualified Medical Evaluators.

(B) If the employee is unrepresented, the notice shall also advise the worker that he or she may contact an Information and Assistance office to have the treating physician's evaluation review and rated by the State of California Disability Evaluation Unit.

(C) If the employee is unrepresented and the claims administrator has or will be requesting a rating from the Disability Evaluation Unit on the treating physician's report, the notice shall advise the employee that he or she will be receiving a rating based on the treating physician's evaluation from the Disability Evaluation Unit.

(D) If the employee is represented by an attorney, the notice shall advise the employee that an additional evaluation may be obtained from an Agreed Medical Evaluator or, if no agreement on an Agreed Medical Evaluator can be reached, by a Qualified Medical Evaluator of his or her choice and that arrangements for this evaluation should be discussed with the employee's attorney. The notice shall also indicate whether or not the claims administrator disputes the treating physician's evaluation of the employee's permanent impairment and limitations.

(4) Notice of Permanent Disability Indemnity Advances When Injury Causes Permanent Disability. If the claims administrator knows that the employee has sustained permanent disability, whether or not its extent is known and whether or not the employee's medical condition is permanent and stationary, the claims administrator shall advise the employee of the weekly permanent disability indemnity payment, how it was calculated, the duration and schedule of payments, and the claims administrator's reasonable estimate of permanent disability indemnity to be paid, within 14 days after the last payment of temporary disability indemnity, or within 14 days after knowledge that the employee's injury has resulted in permanent disability, whichever is later.

(h) Notices to Dependents in Death Cases. In a case of fatal injury which is or is claimed to be compensable under the workers' compensation laws of this state, or involving accrued compensation which was not paid to an injured employee before the employee's death, the claims administrator shall advise the dependent(s) of the status of any benefits to which they may be entitled or which they have claimed as a result of the employee's death. As used in this subsection, "dependent" includes any person who may be or has claimed to be entitled to workers' compensation benefits as the result of an employee's death (including compensation which was accrued and unpaid to an injured worker before his or her death), and also includes the parent or legal guardian of minor dependent children. The claims administrator shall send each dependent a copy of all notices concerning benefits claimed by, or which may be payable to, that dependent, including notices sent to a different dependent if the benefits paid to the different dependent affect the amount payable to the other claimant. If the claims administrator discovers a new dependent after having sent a notice, the claims administrator shall send copies of each prior notice which concerned benefits to which the newly-discovered dependent might be entitled, to that dependent.

(1) Benefit Payment Schedule. If the claims administrator pays death benefits (including compensation which was accrued and unpaid to an injured worker before his or her death), the claims administrator shall advise each affected dependent of the amount of the death benefit payable to the dependent, how it was calculated, the duration and schedule of payments and other pertinent information. Notice is required within 14 days after the claims administrator's date of knowledge both of the death and of the identity and address of the dependent.

(2) Notice of Changed Benefit Rate, Amount or Schedule or that Benefits are Ending. If the claims administrator changes the benefit rate, amount or payment schedule, or ends payment, of a death benefit to a dependent, the claims administrator shall advise the affected dependent of the change and the reason for it, or of the new payment schedule. A notice that benefits are ending shall include an accounting of all compensation paid to the claimant. A notice that payment is ending shall be sent with the last payment unless the decision to end payment was made after that payment; in that case it shall be sent within 14 days of the last payment. Other notices concerning changed payments shall be sent before or with the changed payment, but not later than 14 days after the last payment which was made before the change.

(3) Delay in Determining Benefits. If the claims administrator cannot determine entitlement to some or all death benefits, the claims administrator shall advise each affected dependent of the delay, the reasons for it, the need, if any, for additional information required to make a determination, and when a determination is likely to be made. Notice is required within 14 days after the claims administrator's date of knowledge of the death, the identity and address of the affected dependent, and the nature of the benefit claimed or which might be due. The claims administrator shall send an additional notice or notices no later than 5 days after the determination date it specified, to advise of any further delay. The additional delay notices shall include the employee's remedies and shall comply with all requirements for an original delay notice.

(4) Notices Denying Death Benefits. If the claims administrator denies liability for the payment of any or all death benefits, the claims administrator shall advise the claimant of the denial, the reasons for it, and the claimant's remedies. The notice shall be sent within 14 days after the determination to deny was made.

(i) Notice Denying Liability for All Compensation Benefits. If the claims administrator denies liability for the payment of all workers' compensation benefits for any claim except a claim for death benefits, including medical–only claims, the claims administrator shall advise the employee of the denial, the reasons for it, and the claimant's remedies. The notice shall be sent no later than 14 days after the determination to deny was made.

(j) Notice of Delay in Determining All Liability. If the claims administrator cannot determine whether the employer has any liability for an injury, other than an injury causing death, within 14 days of the date of knowledge of injury, the claims administrator shall advise the employee within the 14–day period of the delay, the reasons for it, the need, if any, for additional information required to make a determination, and when a determination is likely to be made. The claims administrator shall send an additional notice or notices no later than 5 days after the determination date it specified, to advise of any further delay. The additional delay notices shall include the employee's remedies and shall comply with all requirements for an original delay notice.

For injuries on or after January 1, 1990, if the claims administrator sends a notice of a delay in its decision whether to accept or deny liability for the claim, the notice shall include an explanation that the claim is presumed to be compensable if not denied within 90 days from the filing of the claim form, and that this presumption can be rebutted only with evidence discovered after the 90–day period.

NOTE: Authority cited: Sections 59, 133, 138.3, 138.4, 139.5(a)(2), 4636(d), 4637 and 5307.3, Labor Code. Reference: Sections 138.4, 139.5, 4061(a), (b), (d)(e)(f), 4650(a) through (d), 4661.5, 4700, 4701, 4702, 4703, 4703.5, 4903(a) and 5402, Labor Code.

HISTORY
1. Repealer and new section filed 7–11–89; operative 10–1–89 (Register 89 No. 28).
2. Amendment of section and Note filed 1–7–94; operative 1–7–94. Submitted to OAL for printing only pursuant to Government Code section 11351 (Register 94, No. 1).

§ 9813.   Vocational Rehabilitation Notices

(a) The following notices are applicable to all dates of injury unless otherwise specified:
   (1) Notice of First Payment. The first time the claims administrator pays vocational rehabilitation temporary disability or maintenance allowance, the claims administrator shall advise the employee of the amount of indemnity due, how it was calculated, and the duration and schedule of indemnity payments. The notice is due by the 14th day after the employee requested vocational rehabilitation services. The notice shall include, if applicable, the employee's option to add an amount from permanent disability benefits to increase the maintenance allowance payments to the temporary disability rate.
   (2) Delay in Providing Vocational Rehabilitation. If upon receipt of a medical report which indicates that an employee is likely to be precluded from his or her usual and customary occupation, or upon receipt of a request for vocational rehabilitation services the claims administrator cannot determine the employee's entitlement to vocational rehabilitation services, a notice of delay shall be sent. The notice shall be sent no later than 10 days from the date of receipt of the medical report or no later than 10 days from receipt of the employee's request for services.

   The delay notice shall explain the reason for delay, the need, if any, for additional information required to make a determination and the date by which a determination is likely to be made. The claims administrator shall send an additional notice or notices no later than 5 days after the determination date specified, to advise of any further delay. The additional delay notices shall include the employee's remedies and shall comply with all requirements for an original delay notice.
   (3) Denial of Vocational Rehabilitation Benefits. The claims administrator shall advise the employee of its determination that an employee is not a qualified injured worker, the reasons for it, enclosed a copy of the document in which the determination is based and the employee's remedies. The notice shall include a DWC Form RU 103 Request for Dispute Resolution and, if no Rehabilitation Unit case number exists, a DWC Form RU 101 Case Initiation Document. The notice is due within 10 days of either:
      (A) A request for vocational rehabilitation services; or
      (B) Receipt of a treating physician's final report determining medical eligibility subsequent to 90 days of aggregate total temporary disability; or
      (C) Receipt of the document upon which the claims administrator relied for its determination.
         If the claims administrator denies liability for rehabilitation services but remains liable for paying VRTD or VRMA benefits, the notice shall explain the distinction between the terminated and continuing rehabilitation benefits.

(4) Interruption or Deferral of Vocational Rehabilitation Services. Within 10 days after agreeing to interrupt or defer vocational rehabilitation services, the claims administrator shall advise the employee of the interruption and the dates it will be in effect. The claims administrator shall send a like notice within 10 days after agreeing to a new or extended period of interruption. The notice shall include an explanation of the specific steps he or she must take to notify the claims administrator that he or she is ready to resume participation (e.g., written or telephonic communication to the claims administrator, the agreed Qualified Rehabilitation Representative or the employee's representative), and information regarding the likely termination of the employee's rights to vocational rehabilitation should the employee fail to request services within 5 years from the date of injury.

If the parties agree to an interruption or deferral which extends beyond the statutory period, the notice shall advise the employee that failure to request services within the agreed upon time frame is likely to terminate the employee's rights to rehabilitation services.

For injuries occurring on or after 1/1/94 where an interruption occurs during a vocational rehabilitation plan, the notice shall explain that the plan must by law be completed within 18 months of approval.

(b) Vocational Rehabilitation Notices for Injuries Occurring Prior to 1990.

(1) Potential Eligibility for Rehabilitation. Within 10 days of receipt of a physician's report or knowledge of a physician's opinion indicating that an employee may be permanently precluded from his or her usual and customary occupation or the position in which he or she was engaged at the time of injury, or if the employee has been totally temporarily disabled for an aggregate of 180 days, the claims administrator shall notify the employee within 10 days of the 180th day of his or her potential eligibility for vocational rehabilitation services. The notice shall include all of the following information:

(A) An explanation of the vocational rehabilitation services and rehabilitation temporary disability benefits available to the employee;

(B) Instructions how the employee may apply for vocational rehabilitation (e.g., by written or telephonic communication to the claims administrator, the agreed Qualified Rehabilitation Representative or the employee's representative);

(C) Notice of the employee's right to participate in selecting an agreed rehabilitation counselor;

(D) Notice that vocational rehabilitation benefits may not be settled or otherwise converted to cash payments;

(E) Either an offer of vocational rehabilitation services, or notice of delay or denial notice in accordance with Section 9813(a)(2) or (3).

(c) Vocational Rehabilitation Notices for Injuries Occurring in 1990, 1991, 1992 or 1993.

(1) At 90 days of Aggregate Temporary Disability Benefits. The claims administrator shall notify the worker no later than 10 days after an employee has accrued 90 days of aggregate temporary total disability benefits of the assignment of the Qualified Rehabilitation Representative (QRR) for the purpose of explaining the employee's potential entitlement to vocational rehabilitation services. The notice shall include a statement that the QRR will be assisting the employee in the development of a job description to submit to the treating physician for an opinion regarding whether the employee may be released to his or her usual and customary occupation. The notice shall further state that the employee will be notified of the physician's opinion when available.

(2) Potential Eligibility for Rehabilitation. Within 10 days of receipt of a physician's report or knowledge of a physician's opinion indicating that an employee is medically eligible for vocational rehabilitation, or if prior notice has not been sent, within 10 days after the employee has been totally temporarily disabled for an aggregate of more than 365 days, the claims administrator shall notify the employee of his or her potential eligibility for vocational rehabilitation services. The notice shall include the following information:

(A) The "Help in Returning to Work" pamphlet published by the Division of Workers' Compensation;

(B) If the notice contains an offer of services, the notice shall include instructions on how to apply for vocational rehabilitation services (e.g., by written or telephonic communication to the claims administrator, the agreed Qualified Rehabilitation Representative or the employee's representative);

(C) If the notice contains an offer of services, the notice shall state that failure to apply within 90 days of receipt of this notice may terminate the employee's entitlement to vocational rehabilitation services;

(D) If the notice contains an offer of services, information on the employee's right to assist in the selection of an agreed upon Qualified Rehabilitation Representative;

(E) If the notice contains an offer of services, advice that the employee may request an evaluation of his or her ability to benefit from the provision of services prior to accepting or rejecting vocational rehabilitation services;

(F) The notice may include a statement from the claims administrator that every effort will be made to identify a modified or alternate job with the same employer to speed the employee's return to the labor market.

(G) Either an offer of vocational rehabilitation services, or a delay or denial notice in accordance with Section 9813(a)(2) or (3) of these regulations.

(3) Reminder of Potential Eligibility. If the employee has not requested vocational rehabilitation services after notification of medical eligibility, the claims administrator shall remind the employee of his or her right to vocational rehabilitation services. The notice shall be made not earlier than 45 nor later than 70 days after the employee's receipt of the Notice of Potential Eligibility.

(4) Intention to Withhold Maintenance Allowance for Failure to Cooperate. If the employee unreasonably fails to cooperate in the provision of vocational rehabilitation services, the claims administrator shall give the employee written notice of any intention to withhold payment of vocational rehabilitation maintenance allowance, the reasons, and the employee's right to object within 10 days of receiving the notice. The notice shall be made at least 15 days before ending payment of vocational rehabilitation maintenance allowance. The notice include a DWC Form RU 103 "Request for Dispute Resolution" and, if no Rehabilitation Unit case number exists, a DWC Form RU 101 Case Initiation Document.

(d) Vocational Rehabilitation Notices for Injuries Occurring in 1994 or later.

    (1) At 90 days of Aggregate Temporary Disability Benefits. The claims administrator shall notify the employee no later than 10 days after the employee accrues 90 days of aggregate temporary total disability benefits of the employee's potential rights to vocational rehabilitation. The notice shall include the "Help in Returning to Work–94" pamphlet published by the Division of Workers' Compensation.

    (2) Potential Eligibility for Rehabilitation. Within 10 days of receipt of a physician's report or knowledge of a physician's opinion indicating that an employee is medically eligible for vocational rehabilitation, or if prior notice has not been sent within 10 days after the employee has been totally temporarily disabled for an aggregate of 365 days, the claims administrator shall notify the employee of his or her potential eligibility for vocational rehabilitation services. The notice shall indicate the following information:

        (A) The "Help in Returning to Work–94" pamphlet published by the Division of Workers' Compensation;

        (B) If the notice contains an offer of services, the notice shall include instructions on how to apply for vocational rehabilitation services (e.g., by written or telephonic communication to the claims administrator, the agreed Qualified Rehabilitation Representative or the employee's representative);

        (C) If the notice contains an offer of services, the notice shall state that failure to apply within 90 days of receipt of this notice may terminate the employee's entitlement to vocational rehabilitation services;

        (D) If the notice contains an offer of services, information on the employee's right to assist in the selection of an agreed upon Qualified Rehabilitation Representative;

        (E) If the notice contains an offer of services, advice that the employee may request an evaluation of their ability to benefit from the provision of services prior to accepting or rejecting vocational rehabilitation services. The employee must further be advised that fees for such an evaluation are included within the forty–five hundred dollars ($4,500) maximum fees available for counseling services.

        (F) The notice shall include a statement from the claims administrator whether a modified or alternate job with the employer is available. In the event that additional investigation into the availability of alternate or modified work is required, a final notice regarding the availability of modified or alternate work shall be sent within 30 days. This time limit may be extended by agreement of the parties.

        (G) Either an offer of vocational rehabilitation services, or delay or denial notice in accordance with paragraph (2) or (3) of subdivision (a).

    (3) Reminder of Potential Eligibility. If the employee has not requested vocational rehabilitation services after notification of medical eligibility, the claims administrator shall remind the employee of his or her right to vocational rehabilitation services. The notice shall be made not earlier than 45 nor later than 70 days after the employee's receipt of the Notice of Potential Eligibility.

    (4) Intention to Withhold Maintenance Allowance for Failure to Cooperate. If the employee unreasonably fails to cooperate in the provision of vocational rehabilitation services, the claims administrator shall give the employee written notice of any intention to withhold payment of vocational rehabilitation maintenance allowance, the reasons, and the employee's right to object within 10 days of receiving the notice. The notice shall be made at least 15 days before ending payment of vocational rehabilitation maintenance allowance. The Notice shall include a DWC Form RU 103 "Request for Dispute Resolution" and, if no Rehabilitation Unit case number exists, a DWC Form RU 101 Case Initiation Document.

NOTE: Authority cited: Sections 59, 133, 138.3, 138.4, 139.5(a)(2), 4636(d), 4637 and 5307.3, Labor Code. Reference: Sections 138.4, 139.5, 4061(a), (b), (d), 4636, 4637, 4641, 4643, 4644, 4650(a) through (d), 4661.5, 4700, 4701, 4702, 4703, 4703.5, 4903(a) and 5402, Labor Code.

HISTORY

1. Repealer filed 7–11–89; operative 10–1–89 (Register 89, No. 28).
2. New section filed 1–7–94; operative 1–7–94. Submitted to OAL for printing only pursuant to Government Code section 11351 (Register 94, No. 1). For prior history, see Register 89, No. 28.
3. Amendment of subsections (a)(2)–(a)(3)(C), (c)(2), (c)(2)(B)–(E), (d)(2) and (d)(2)(B)–(E) filed 2–21–95; operative 2–21–95. Submitted to OAL for printing only pursuant to Government Code section 11351 (Register 95, No. 8).

§ 9814.   Salary Continuation

In relation to periods of temporary disability, where an employer provides salary or other payments in lieu of or in excess of temporary disability indemnity, the claims administrator or employer shall comply with the notice requirements of this article which apply to temporary disability. In addition, the claims administrator or employer shall include a full explanation of the salary continuation plan with the initial notice.

NOTE: Authority cited: Sections 59, 133, 138.4, 139.5(a)(2), 4637 and 5307.3, Labor Code. Reference: Sections 4650(a), (c), (d), (g), 4800, 4804.1, 4806, 4850–4850.7, Labor Code.

HISTORY
1. Amendment filed 7–11–89; operative 10–1–89 (Register 89, No. 28).
2. Amendment of section and Note filed 1–7–94; operative 1–7–94. Submitted to OAL for printing only pursuant to Government Code section 11351 (Register 94, No. 1).

§ 9815.   Corrected Notice

If information in any notice, or the action taken as reflected in the notice, was incorrect or incomplete, the claims administrator shall provide the employee with a corrected notice within 14 days of knowledge of the error or omission. The notice shall be identified as a "Corrected Notice" and explain the nature and reason for the correction. Any additional benefits due as a result of the error or omission shall be paid or provided with the notice, if not previously provided.

NOTE: Authority cited: Sections 59, 133, 138.4, 139.5(a)(2), 4637 and 5307.3, Labor Code. Reference: Sections 138.4, 139.5, 4061(a), (b), (d), 4636, 4637, 4641, 4643, 4644, 4650(a) through (d), 4661.5, 4700, 4701, 4702, 4703, 4703.5, 4903(a) and 5402, Labor Code.

HISTORY
1. Amendment of section and Note filed 1–7–94; operative 1–7–94. Submitted to OAL for printing only pursuant to Government Code section 11351 (Register 94, No. 1).

§ 9816.   Enforcement of Reporting Requirements. (Repealed)

NOTE: Authority cited: Sections 138.3 and 138.4, Labor Code. Reference: Sections 138.3, 138.4 and 5453, Labor Code.

HISTORY
1. Repealer filed 1–7–94; operative 1–7–94. Submitted to OAL for printing only pursuant to Government Code section 11351 (Register 94, No. 1).

§ 9817.   Destruction of Records. (Repealed)

NOTE: Authority cited: Sections 138.3 and 138.4, Labor Code. Reference: Sections 138.4, 4650, 4651, 4700–4703 and 5402, Labor Code.

HISTORY
1. Repealer filed 1–7–94; operative 1–7–94. Submitted to OAL for printing only pursuant to Government Code section 11351 (Register 94, No. 1).

Intentionally blank

No Forms

Intentionally blank

Appendix K

● Standards Applicable to Workers' Compensation Claims Adjusters and Medical Billing Entities and Certification of those Standards by Insurers

State of California
Department of Insurance
45 Fremont Street
San Francisco, California 94105
CALIFORNIA CODE OF REGULATIONS, TITLE 10
CHAPTER 5, SUBCHAPTER 3

ADOPT ARTICLE 20 TO READ:

Article 20. Standards Applicable to Workers' Compensation Claims Adjusters and Medical Billing Entities and Certification of those Standards by Insurers.

Section 2592   Authority and Purpose

These regulations are promulgated pursuant to authority granted to the Insurance Commissioner under the provisions of Section 11761 of the California Insurance Code. The purpose of these regulations is to set forth the minimum standards of training, experience, and skill that workers' compensation claims adjusters, including adjusters working for medical billing entities, must possess to perform their duties with regard to workers' compensation claims and to specify how insurers must meet those standards.

NOTE: Authority and reference cited: Section 11761 of the Insurance Code

Section 2592.01   Definitions

For purposes of these regulations:
(a) "Certify" means a written statement made under penalty of perjury.
(b) "Claims adjuster" means a person who, on behalf of an insurer, is responsible for determining the validity of a workers' compensation claim, including a "medical only" claim. The adjuster may also establish a case reserve, approve and process indemnity and medical benefits, may hire investigators, attorneys or other professionals and may negotiate settlements of claims. "Claims adjuster" also means a person who is responsible for the immediate supervision of a claims adjuster but does not mean an attorney representing the insurer or a person whose primary function is clerical.
(c) "Classroom" means any space sufficiently designed so that the instructor and students can communicate with a high degree of privacy and relative freedom from outside interference. The instructor may be physically present or may communicate with students by means of an electronic device.
(d) "Course" means any program of instruction taken or given to satisfy the requirements of Insurance Code Section 11761.
(e) "Curriculum" means a course of study that satisfies the requirements of Insurance Code Section 11761. The curriculum must provide sufficient content, including time allocated to each subject area, to enable claims adjusters to meet minimum standards of training, experience, and skill to perform their duties with regard to workers' compensation claims.

(f) "Experienced claims adjuster" means a person who has had at least five years within the past eight years of on–the–job experience adjusting California workers' compensation claims and has been certified as an experienced claims adjuster by an insurer. A person who has successfully completed the written examination specified by Title 8, Section 15452 of the California Code of Regulations is an experienced claims adjuster, provided that he or she has either worked as a workers' compensation claims adjuster continuously since passing the examination; had at least five years of experience working with California workers' compensation within the past eight years; or has passed the examination within the previous five years.

(g) "Experienced medical–only claims adjuster" means a person who has had at least three years within the past five years of on–the–job experience adjusting California workers' compensation medical–only claims and has been designated as an experienced medical–only claims adjuster by an insurer or a person meeting the training requirements of this regulation and certified by an insurer.

(h) "Instructor" means a person who conveys curriculum content to students on behalf of an insurer, a training entity, or a medical billing entity. An instructor shall have at least eight (8) years of experience in the workers' compensation system in the previous 12 years, including at least four years of experience with California workers' compensation. Persons knowledgeable about specific workers' compensation issues may train students under the supervision of an instructor.

(i) "Insurer" means an insurance company admitted to transact workers' compensation insurance in California, the State Compensation Insurance Fund, an employer that has secured a certificate of consent to self–insure from the Department of Industrial Relations pursuant to Labor Code Section 3700(b) or (c) or a third party administrator that has a secured a certificate of consent pursuant to Labor Code Section 3702.1.

(j) "Medical billing entity" means an entity that is not an insurer as defined herein that reviews or adjusts workers' compensation medical bills for an insurer.

(k) "Post–certification training" means a course of study provided to trained and/or experienced workers' compensation claims adjusters. Post–certification training also includes seminars, workshops, or other informational meetings pertaining to California workers' compensation.

(l) "Student" means an individual taking a course that is required for that person in order to be a workers' compensation claims adjuster.

(m) "Training" means to provide a course of instruction that includes the topics specified in Sections 2592.04 and 2592.05.

NOTE: Authority and reference cited: Section 11761 of the Insurance Code

Section 2592.02   Training Required For Claims Adjusters

(a) Every insurer shall require all claims adjusters who handle workers' compensation claims, other than those who are exempt from the requirement of such training pursuant to paragraph (f) and (g) of Section 2592.01, to be trained pursuant to this subparagraph:

 (1) The insurer shall require at least 160 hours of training for claims adjusters, at least 120 hours of which shall be conducted in a classroom with an instructor. The insurer shall require at least 120 hours of training for claims adjusters who adjust only claims where medical benefits and not indemnity benefits are provided or at issue, at least 80 hours of which shall be conducted in a classroom with an instructor. On the job training shall be done under the supervision of an instructor or an experienced claims adjuster.

 (2) A medical–only claims adjuster who has completed 120 hours of training pursuant this section may be certified as a claims adjuster upon completion of 40 additional hours of workers' compensation claims training, provided that such training is completed within six months of the claims adjuster beginning to adjust claims that include indemnity benefits.

(b) The training required by this section shall be completed within a twelve consecutive month period, during which time a claims adjuster trainee may adjust claims under the supervision of an experienced claims adjuster.

(c) Any classes or courses taken within two years before the effective date of these regulations that satisfy the curriculum requirement may be used to meet the hourly requirements upon verification by the student of the type of course taken, the course of study, the date or dates taken, the instructor or organization providing the class or course, and the number of hours taken.

(d) Beginning January 1, 2005, every insurer shall require a minimum of 30 hours of post–certification training every two years for all experienced claims adjusters and experienced medical only claims adjusters. Such post–certification training may include seminars, workshops, or other informational meetings pertaining to California workers' compensation.

(e) The insurer may provide the training directly or by sending its employees to be trained by another entity. A workers' compensation insurance company or self–insured employer shall certify that the course of instruction provided to its own staff or which is provided to the claims adjusters who work for a third party administrator which adjusts claims for the insurance company or self–insured employer meets all the requirements set forth in this Article and that all of the claims adjusters who adjust claims on behalf of the insurance company or self–insured employer have actually attended the training for the required number of hours.

(f) An adjuster who has been certified by an insurer as having completed the training required by this subchapter shall not be required to be re–trained and re–certified in order to adjust claims for a different insurer.

(g) An insurer may not employ an individual in the capacity of claims adjuster who has not been trained pursuant to this Article or who is not an experienced claims adjuster, except that an individual who is undergoing training may adjust claims under the direct supervision of an experienced claims adjuster.

NOTE: Authority and reference cited: Section 11761 of the Insurance Code

Section 2592.03   Curriculum

(a) The course of study required by Section 2592.02 for claims adjusters who handle claims that include both medical and indemnity benefits shall include but not be limited to the following topics:
1. Historical overview of the workers' compensation system.
2. Organizational structure of the system.
3. The workers' compensation insurance policy, its forms and endorsements, insurance principles of compensation.
4. Concepts and terminology.
5. Benefit provisions.
6. Compensability.
7. Notice requirements.
8. Temporary disability.
9. Permanent disability, including evaluation and rating.
10. Death benefits.
11. Return to work and vocational rehabilitation.
12. Cumulative trauma.
13. Serious and willful misconduct.
14. WCAB procedures, forms, hearings, and penalties.
15. Investigation.
16. Fraud.
17. Medical terminology.
18. Knowledge and use of utilization guidelines (American College of Occupational and Environmental Medicine or other guidelines approved by the Administrative Director of the Division of Workers' Compensation.)
19. Medical evidence.
20. Fee schedules.
21. Liens.
22. Apportionment.
23. Subrogation.
24. Reserving.
25. Ethical issues.

(b) The course of study required for the training of claims adjusters who adjust only claims where medical benefits and not indemnity benefits are provided or at issue, shall include, at a minimum, topics relevant to workers' compensation medical care and benefits.

(c) The course of study required by Section 2592.02(d) shall include changes in the law that affect workers' compensation claims and other topics relevant to the work of a trained and/or experienced claims adjuster.

NOTE: Authority and reference cited: Section 11761 of the Insurance Code

Section 2592.04   Training Required for Medical Bill Reviewers

Entities that review medical bills on behalf of an insurer shall require all personnel employed as bill reviewers to be trained. The medical bill review entity shall require at least 40 hours of training for medical bill reviewers, at least 30 hours of which shall be conducted in a classroom by an instructor. No more than 10 hours of training may be on–the–job training.

(a) The training required by this section shall be completed within a six month period, during which time a medical bill review trainee may review bills under appropriate supervision.

(b) Beginning January 1, 2005, every entity that reviews medical bills on behalf of an insurer shall require a minimum of 16 hours every year of post–certification training for all medical bill reviewers, including those who have been trained and certified pursuant to this chapter.

(c) The entity that reviews medical bills may provide the training directly or by sending its employees to be trained by another entity. The medical bill review entity shall certify that the course of instruction it provides or that is provided by another entity meets all the requirements set forth in this section and that all of its bill reviewers have actually attended the training.

(d) A medical bill reviewer who has been certified by a medical bill review entity as having completed the training required by this Article shall not be required to be re–trained and re–certified in order to review bills for a different medical bill review entity.

(e) The topics for the training of medical bill reviewers shall include but not be limited to the following topics:
 (1) the correct use of billing codes and detection of improper use of billing codes.
 (2) All fee schedules applicable to workers' compensation medical care.
 (3) Workers' compensation benefit provisions.
 (4) Cumulative trauma.
 (5) WCAB procedures, forms, hearings, and penalties.
 (6) Fraud.
 (7) Medical terminology.
 (8) Utilization guidelines (ACOEM or other AD–approved guidelines.)
 (9) Medical evidence.
 (10) Liens.
 (11) Ethical issues.

NOTE: Authority and reference cited: Section 11761 of the Insurance Code

Section 2592.05   Accreditation

(a) A Certificate of Completion in the form and manner determined by the commissioner shall be provided by the insurer or medical billing entity to any person who successfully completes the adjuster training, including the curriculum subjects required by section 2592.03 herein or the medical bill review training required by Section 2592.04, respectively.

(b) An Experienced Claims Adjuster Certificate in the form and manner determined by the commissioner shall be provided by the insurer or training entity sponsored by the insurer to any person who has at least five years of on–the–job experience of handling workers' compensation claims in California within the past eight years and has successfully completed the post–certification training including the curriculum subjects required by section 2592.03.
 (1) Failure of a claims adjuster described in Section 2592.01(f) to fulfill the requirement for post–certification training every two years shall result in that claims adjuster being no longer considered an experienced claims adjuster.
 (2) A person who had been an experienced claims adjuster but who had not fulfilled the post–certification training requirement may fulfill such requirement at any time within five years of having become an experienced claims adjuster and may thereafter be considered an experienced claims adjuster. The post–certification training required under this subparagraph is 30 hours for every two years subsequent to the time when the claims adjuster had become an experienced claims adjuster.

(c) Upon request by a policyholder or an injured worker whose claim is being adjusted by a claims adjuster, the insurer employing the claims adjuster shall provide a copy of the claims adjuster's Certificate of Completion or Experienced Claims Adjuster Certificate to the requesting policyholder or injured worker.

NOTE: Authority and reference cited: Section 11761 of the Insurance Code

Section 2592.06   Maintenance of Records

(a) An insurer shall maintain records pertaining to the training of the adjusters in its employ for whom training has been provided or sponsored, or who were trained by another insurer, for eight (8) years after the adjuster has completed the training. If the trained claims adjuster is employed by an insurer other than the insurer providing the training, the insurer that provided the training shall send copies of the adjuster's records pertaining to training to the insurer employing the adjuster within 20 days after a request for the records has been sent. The records which shall be kept in the form and manner specified by the commissioner shall contain the following information:
 (1) Name and address of adjuster.
 (2) Date training completed.
 (3) Name, address, and telephone number of training entity.

(b) All insurers shall maintain a record of all courses given to comply with this chapter. The record shall include:
 (1) The name and business address of all students, along with the beginning and ending date of the training of the student and a statement stating whether or not the student has completed the training in all topic areas required to be covered.
 (2) A complete description of the curriculum, including all topics covered with a detailed statement of how much time was spent training students in each topic.
(c) All records maintained pursuant to this Article shall be made available to the Insurance Commissioner and to the Administrative Director of the Division of Workers' Compensation.

NOTE: Authority and reference cited: Section 11761 of the Insurance Code

Section 2592.07   Submission of Documents

Insurers shall submit all documents described in Section 2592.07(b) under penalty of perjury to the commissioner. The commissioner shall publish on the Department of Insurance public web site sufficient information submitted pursuant to this subsection to allow policyholders to choose an insurer that has an adequately trained staff of claims adjusters.

NOTE: Authority and reference cited: Section 11761 of the Insurance Code

Intentionally blank

Appendix L

• Workers' Compensation Adjuster Training: Frequently Asked Questions

Workers' Compensation Adjuster Training: Frequently Asked Questions

1. When did the workers' compensation claims adjuster training take effect?

The regulations defining the minimum training requirements for workers' compensation claims adjusters and medical bill reviewers became effective on February 22, 2006.

2. What are the training requirements for a workers' compensation claims adjuster?

An individual can be designated a claims adjuster, medical–only claims adjuster or medical bill reviewer by meeting the experience or the training requirements. For those that do not meet the requisite experience requirements to be designated a claims adjuster, medical–only claims adjuster, or medical bill reviewer, the minimum number of hours of training in specified curriculum topics are as follows: Claims adjusters = 160 hours of training (120 hours in a classroom with an instructor). Medical–Only Claims Adjusters = 80 hours of training (50 hours in a classroom with an instructor). Medical Bill Reviewers = 40 hours of training (30 hours in a classroom with an instructor).

3. How do I qualify as an experienced claims adjuster or medical bill reviewer?

A person may be able to adjust workers' compensation claims or review medical bills based on their experience. An Experienced Claims Adjuster must meet one of the following requirements: Ø Have five (5) years in the last eight (8) years of on–the–job experience adjusting California workers' compensation claims; or supervising claims adjusters handling workers' compensation claims; or Ø Successfully completing the Self–Insurance Exam written examination (specified by Title 8, Section 15452 of the California Code of Regulations) and have either (1) worked as a claims adjuster or supervisor of workers' compensation claims continuously since passing the examination, or (2) passing the exam within the previous five years. An Experienced Medical–Only Claims Adjuster must meet the following requirements: Ø Have at least 3 years in the past 5 years of on–the–job experience adjusting California workers' compensation medical–only claims. An Experienced Medical Bill Reviewer must meet the following requirements: Have at least 3 years in the past 5 years of on–the–job experience adjusting California workers' compensation medical bills.

4. If a person has been a workers' compensation claims adjuster or a medical bill reviewer for many years, does that adjuster or medical bill reviewer need to complete the training?

It depends on whether or not they meet the experience requirements as outlined in the question above. If they do not meet the requisite experience criteria, they must complete the training. Once designated, they must continue to meet the post–designation training requirements to be able to continue to be authorized to adjust claims or review medical bills.

5. Are adjusters who are not licensed by the California Department of Insurance required to complete the adjuster training? If yes, what are the requirements?

Workers' compensation claims adjusters and medical bill reviewers are not licensed under these regulations. However, these regulations apply to all claims adjusters and medical bill reviewers who handle California workers' compensation claims.

6. Are claims adjusters required to complete workers' compensation training again if they leave the industry or haven't adjusted claims in a long time?

If they meet the requisite experience requirements, claims adjusters do not have to complete or repeat the training requirements. If they do not meet the requisite experience criteria, they must complete the training. Once designated, they must continue to meet the post–designation training requirements to be able to continue to be authorized to adjust claims.

7. How frequently does a claims adjuster or medical bill reviewer need to complete the training?

The claims adjuster or medical bill reviewer only needs to complete the initial training one time if they do not meet the experience requirements. However, they must continue to complete the post–designation training requirements.

8. Where can a claims adjuster or medical bill reviewer sign–up for the training?

The insurer is responsible for the initial training of claims adjusters and medical only claims adjusters and providing Designations. The insurer may also train and provide Designations to their medical bill reviewers or have a medical billing entity train and provide Designations. Post–Designation training can be taken through other entities that provide classes, seminars, or workshops, but it will be up to insurers to document the post–designation training and issue Post–Designation Training Forms once the requisite hours of post–designation training are completed. However, the adjuster should consult the insurer they work for as to their recommendation for training.

9. Does an insurer that employs adjusters or medical bill reviewers need to complete the certification to the Insurance Commissioner each year?

Yes. The statute and regulations specify that all insurers must certify annually to the Insurance Commissioner that those individuals adjusting claims and medical bills on their behalf have met the minimum training or experience requirements established by the Commissioner through the Regulations.

10. What does an insurer, self–insured employer, or third–party administrator who employs claims adjusters or medical bill reviewers have to do to meet the workers' compensation claims adjuster regulation requirements?

Train their claims adjusters and medical bill reviewers according to the regulations. Make sure they are appropriately designated. Maintain the documentation of training and designation. Certify annually to the Commissioner by July 1st regarding their compliance with the Regulations.

11. How long does an insurer have to maintain records of their employees?

Insurers must maintain copies of the Designation Forms of those adjusting claims or reviewing medical bills on their behalf for as long as those individuals work for them and for five years thereafter.

12. Should an insurer submit their Designation Forms to the Department of Insurance?

No. Insurers do not need to and should not submit the Designation Forms to the Department of Insurance. Insurers should only submit the Certification Form annually to the Insurance Commissioner by July 1st.

13. Where do the insurers submit the Annual Certification Forms?

They should submit them to: California Department of Insurance, Producer License Bureau – Education Section, Attention: Annual Certification of Claims Adjusters and Medical–Only Claims Adjusters (or Medical Bill Reviewers), 320 Capitol Mall, Sacramento, CA 95814. This information is found on the forms which are available on the Department of Insurance website.

Intentionally blank

Appendix M

● Defense Pro, Inc.
Charts

We thank Defense Pro, Inc., for permission to reprint their excellent charts.You may telephone them at (877) 374-3744 for further details and other information pertaining to their other excellent aids to the workers' compensation community.

Use our free calculator for all charts at www.getmedlegal.com/calculatorprog/WCCalculator.asp

%	Weeks 96-03	PD 7/1/96 to 12/31/02	PD 2003	2004 Weeks 2004	2004 PD 2004	%	Weeks 96-03	PD 7/1/96 to 12/31/02	PD 2003	2004 Weeks 2004	2004 PD 2004
1	3.00	420.00	555.00	4.00	800.00	51	274.25	46,622.50	50,736.25	294.00	58,800.00
2	6.00	840.00	1,110.00	8.00	1,600.00	52	282.25	47,982.50	52,216.25	302.00	60,400.00
3	9.00	1,260.00	1,665.00	12.00	2,400.00	53	290.25	49,342.50	53,696.25	310.00	62,000.00
4	12.00	1,680.00	2,220.00	16.00	3,200.00	54	298.25	50,702.50	55,176.25	318.00	63,600.00
5	15.00	2,100.00	2,775.00	20.00	4,000.00	55	306.25	52,062.50	56,656.25	326.00	65,200.00
6	18.00	2,520.00	3,330.00	24.00	4,800.00	56	314.25	53,422.50	58,136.25	334.00	66,800.00
7	21.00	2,940.00	3,885.00	28.00	5,600.00	57	322.25	54,782.50	59,616.25	342.00	68,400.00
8	24.00	3,360.00	4,440.00	32.00	6,400.00	58	330.25	56,142.50	61,096.25	350.00	70,000.00
9	27.00	3,780.00	4,995.00	36.00	7,200.00	59	338.25	57,502.50	62,576.25	358.00	71,600.00
10	30.25	4,235.00	5,596.25	40.25	8,050.00	60	346.25	58,862.50	64,056.25	366.00	73,200.00
11	34.25	4,795.00	6,336.25	45.25	9,050.00	61	354.25	60,222.50	65,536.25	374.00	74,800.00
12	38.25	5,355.00	7,076.25	50.25	10,050.00	62	362.25	61,582.50	67,016.25	382.00	76,400.00
13	42.25	5,915.00	7,816.25	55.25	11,050.00	63	370.25	62,942.50	68,496.25	390.00	78,000.00
14	46.25	6,475.00	8,556.25	60.25	12,050.00	64	378.25	64,302.50	69,976.25	398.00	79,600.00
15	50.25	8,040.00	9,296.25	65.25	13,050.00	65	386.25	65,662.50	71,456.25	406.00	81,200.00
16	54.25	8,680.00	10,036.25	70.25	14,050.00	66	394.25	67,022.50	72,936.25	414.00	82,800.00
17	58.25	9,320.00	10,776.25	75.25	15,050.00	67	402.25	68,382.50	74,416.25	422.00	84,400.00
18	62.25	9,960.00	11,516.25	80.25	16,050.00	68	410.25	69,742.50	75,896.25	430.00	86,000.00
19	66.25	10,600.00	12,256.25	85.25	17,050.00	69	418.25	71,102.50	77,376.25	438.00	87,600.00
20	70.50	11,280.00	13,042.50	90.25	18,050.00	70	426.50	98,095.00	98,095.00	446.25	111,562.50
21	75.50	12,080.00	13,967.50	95.25	19,050.00	71	435.50	100,165.00	100,165.00	455.25	113,812.50
22	80.50	12,880.00	14,892.50	100.25	20,050.00	72	444.50	102,235.00	102,235.00	464.25	116,062.50
23	85.50	13,680.00	15,817.50	105.25	21,050.00	73	453.50	104,305.00	104,305.00	473.25	118,312.50
24	90.50	14,480.00	16,742.50	110.25	22,050.00	74	462.50	106,375.00	106,375.00	482.25	120,562.50
25	95.75	16,277.50	17,713.75	115.50	23,100.00	75	471.50	108,445.00	108,445.00	491.25	122,812.50
26	101.75	17,297.50	18,823.75	121.50	24,300.00	76	480.50	110,515.00	110,515.00	500.25	125,062.50
27	107.75	18,317.50	19,933.75	127.50	25,500.00	77	489.50	112,585.00	112,585.00	509.25	127,312.50
28	113.75	19,337.50	21,043.75	133.50	26,700.00	78	498.50	114,655.00	114,655.00	518.25	129,562.50
29	119.75	20,357.50	22,153.75	139.50	27,900.00	79	507.50	116,725.00	116,725.00	527.25	131,812.50
30	126.00	21,420.00	23,310.00	145.75	29,150.00	80	516.50	118,795.00	118,795.00	536.25	134,062.50
31	133.00	22,610.00	24,605.00	152.75	30,550.00	81	525.50	120,865.00	120,865.00	545.25	136,312.50
32	140.00	23,800.00	25,900.00	159.75	31,950.00	82	534.50	122,935.00	122,935.00	554.25	138,562.50
33	147.00	24,990.00	27,195.00	166.75	33,350.00	83	543.50	125,005.00	125,005.00	563.25	140,812.50
34	154.00	26,180.00	28,490.00	173.75	34,750.00	84	552.50	127,075.00	127,075.00	572.25	143,062.50
35	161.00	27,370.00	29,785.00	180.75	36,150.00	85	561.50	129,145.00	129,145.00	581.25	145,312.50
36	168.00	28,560.00	31,080.00	187.75	37,550.00	86	570.50	131,215.00	131,215.00	590.25	147,562.50
37	175.00	29,750.00	32,375.00	194.75	38,950.00	87	579.50	133,285.00	133,285.00	599.25	149,812.50
38	182.00	30,940.00	33,670.00	201.75	40,350.00	88	588.50	135,355.00	135,355.00	608.25	152,062.50
39	189.00	32,130.00	34,965.00	208.75	41,750.00	89	597.50	137,425.00	137,425.00	617.25	154,312.50
40	196.00	33,320.00	36,260.00	215.75	43,150.00	90	606.50	139,495.00	139,495.00	626.25	156,562.50
41	203.00	34,510.00	37,555.00	222.75	44,550.00	91	615.50	141,565.00	141,565.00	635.25	158,812.50
42	210.00	35,700.00	38,850.00	229.75	45,950.00	92	624.50	143,635.00	143,635.00	644.25	161,062.50
43	217.00	36,890.00	40,145.00	236.75	47,350.00	93	633.50	145,705.00	145,705.00	653.25	163,312.50
44	224.00	38,080.00	41,440.00	243.75	48,750.00	94	642.50	147,775.00	147,775.00	662.25	165,562.50
45	231.00	39,270.00	42,735.00	250.75	50,150.00	95	651.50	149,845.00	149,845.00	671.25	167,812.50
46	238.00	40,460.00	44,030.00	257.75	51,550.00	96	660.50	151,915.00	151,915.00	680.25	170,062.50
47	245.00	41,650.00	45,325.00	264.75	52,950.00	97	669.50	153,985.00	153,985.00	689.25	172,312.50
48	252.00	42,840.00	46,620.00	271.75	54,350.00	98	678.50	156,055.00	156,055.00	698.25	174,562.50
49	259.00	44,030.00	47,915.00	278.75	55,750.00	99	687.50	158,125.00	158,125.00	707.25	176,812.50
50	266.25	45,262.50	49,256.25	286.00	57,200.00						

Permanent Disability 2005 - 2007

For instructions and authority see http://www.getmedlegal.com/wcbooks/PDChartExplain.pdf

%	Weeks 2005/2006	2005 PD 2005	2005 PD +15%	2005 PD -15%	2006 & 2007 PD 2006	2006 & 2007 PD +15%	2006 & 2007 PD -15%
1	3.00	660.00	660.00	561.00	690.00	690.00	586.50
2	6.00	1,320.00	1,320.00	1,122.00	1,380.00	1,380.00	1,173.00
3	9.00	1,980.00	1,994.14	1,683.00	2,070.00	2,084.79	1,759.50
4	12.00	2,640.00	2,753.14	2,244.00	2,760.00	2,878.29	2,346.00
5	15.00	3,300.00	3,512.14	2,805.00	3,450.00	3,671.79	2,932.50
6	18.00	3,960.00	4,271.14	3,366.00	4,140.00	4,465.29	3,519.00
7	21.00	4,620.00	5,030.14	3,927.00	4,830.00	5,258.79	4,105.50
8	24.00	5,280.00	5,789.14	4,488.00	5,520.00	6,052.29	4,692.00
9	27.00	5,940.00	6,548.14	5,049.00	6,210.00	6,845.79	5,278.50
10	30.25	6,655.00	7,370.39	5,656.75	6,957.50	7,705.41	5,913.88
11	34.25	7,535.00	8,382.39	6,404.75	7,877.50	8,763.41	6,695.88
12	38.25	8,415.00	9,394.39	7,152.75	8,797.50	9,821.41	7,477.88
13	42.25	9,295.00	10,406.39	7,900.75	9,717.50	10,879.41	8,259.88
14	46.25	10,175.00	11,418.39	8,648.75	10,637.50	11,937.41	9,041.88
15	50.50	11,110.00	12,493.64	9,443.50	11,615.00	13,061.54	9,872.75
16	55.50	12,210.00	13,758.64	10,378.50	12,765.00	14,384.04	10,850.25
17	60.50	13,310.00	15,023.64	11,313.50	13,915.00	15,706.54	11,827.75
18	65.50	14,410.00	16,288.64	12,248.50	15,065.00	17,029.04	12,805.25
19	70.50	15,510.00	17,553.64	13,183.50	16,215.00	18,351.54	13,782.75
20	75.50	16,610.00	18,818.64	14,118.50	17,365.00	19,674.04	14,760.25
21	80.50	17,710.00	20,083.64	15,053.50	18,515.00	20,996.54	15,737.75
22	85.50	18,810.00	21,348.64	15,988.50	19,665.00	22,319.04	16,715.25
23	90.50	19,910.00	22,613.64	16,923.50	20,815.00	23,641.54	17,692.75
24	95.50	21,010.00	23,878.64	17,858.50	21,965.00	24,964.04	18,670.25
25	100.75	22,165.00	25,206.89	18,840.25	23,172.50	26,352.66	19,696.63
26	106.75	23,485.00	26,724.89	19,962.25	24,552.50	27,939.66	20,869.63
27	112.75	24,805.00	28,242.89	21,084.25	25,932.50	29,526.66	22,042.63
28	118.75	26,125.00	29,760.89	22,206.25	27,312.50	31,113.66	23,215.63
29	124.75	27,445.00	31,278.89	23,328.25	28,692.50	32,700.66	24,388.63
30	131.00	28,820.00	32,860.14	24,497.00	30,130.00	34,353.79	25,610.50
31	138.00	30,360.00	34,631.14	25,806.00	31,740.00	36,205.29	26,979.00
32	145.00	31,900.00	36,402.14	27,115.00	33,350.00	38,056.79	28,347.50
33	152.00	33,440.00	38,173.14	28,424.00	34,960.00	39,908.29	29,716.00
34	159.00	34,980.00	39,944.14	29,733.00	36,570.00	41,759.79	31,084.50
35	166.00	36,520.00	41,715.14	31,042.00	38,180.00	43,611.29	32,453.00
36	173.00	38,060.00	43,486.14	32,351.00	39,790.00	45,462.79	33,821.50
37	180.00	39,600.00	45,257.14	33,660.00	41,400.00	47,314.29	35,190.00
38	187.00	41,140.00	47,028.14	34,969.00	43,010.00	49,165.79	36,558.50
39	194.00	42,680.00	48,799.14	36,278.00	44,620.00	51,017.29	37,927.00
40	201.00	44,220.00	50,570.14	37,587.00	46,230.00	52,868.79	39,295.50
41	208.00	45,760.00	52,341.14	38,896.00	47,840.00	54,720.29	40,664.00
42	215.00	47,300.00	54,112.14	40,205.00	49,450.00	56,571.79	42,032.50
43	222.00	48,840.00	55,883.14	41,514.00	51,060.00	58,423.29	43,401.00
44	229.00	50,380.00	57,654.14	42,823.00	52,670.00	60,274.79	44,769.50
45	236.00	51,920.00	59,425.14	44,132.00	54,280.00	62,126.29	46,138.00
46	243.00	53,460.00	61,196.14	45,441.00	55,890.00	63,977.79	47,506.50
47	250.00	55,000.00	62,967.14	46,750.00	57,500.00	65,829.29	48,875.00
48	257.00	56,540.00	64,738.14	48,059.00	59,110.00	67,680.79	50,243.50
49	264.00	58,080.00	66,509.14	49,368.00	60,720.00	69,532.29	51,612.00
50	271.25	59,675.00	68,343.39	50,723.75	62,387.50	71,449.91	53,029.38

2

Permanent Disability 2005 - 2007

For instructions and authority see http://www.getmedlegal.com/wcbooks/PDChartExplain.pdf

%	Weeks 2005/2006	PD 2005	PD +15%	PD -15%	PD 2006	PD +15%	PD -15%
			2005			**2006 & 2007**	
51	279.25	61,435.00	70,367.39	52,219.75	64,227.50	73,565.91	54,593.38
52	287.25	63,195.00	72,391.39	53,715.75	66,067.50	75,681.91	56,157.38
53	295.25	64,955.00	74,415.39	55,211.75	67,907.50	77,797.91	57,721.38
54	303.25	66,715.00	76,439.39	56,707.75	69,747.50	79,913.91	59,285.38
55	311.25	68,475.00	78,463.39	58,203.75	71,587.50	82,029.91	60,849.38
56	319.25	70,235.00	80,487.39	59,699.75	73,427.50	84,145.91	62,413.38
57	327.25	71,995.00	82,511.39	61,195.75	75,267.50	86,261.91	63,977.38
58	335.25	73,755.00	84,535.39	62,691.75	77,107.50	88,377.91	65,541.38
59	343.25	75,515.00	86,559.39	64,187.75	78,947.50	90,493.91	67,105.38
60	351.25	77,275.00	88,583.39	65,683.75	80,787.50	92,609.91	68,669.38
61	359.25	79,035.00	90,607.39	67,179.75	82,627.50	94,725.91	70,233.38
62	367.25	80,795.00	92,631.39	68,675.75	84,467.50	96,841.91	71,797.38
63	375.25	82,555.00	94,655.39	70,171.75	86,307.50	98,957.91	73,361.38
64	383.25	84,315.00	96,679.39	71,667.75	88,147.50	101,073.91	74,925.38
65	391.25	86,075.00	98,703.39	73,163.75	89,987.50	103,189.91	76,489.38
66	399.25	87,835.00	100,727.39	74,659.75	91,827.50	105,305.91	78,053.38
67	407.25	89,595.00	102,751.39	76,155.75	93,667.50	107,421.91	79,617.38
68	415.25	91,355.00	104,775.39	77,651.75	95,507.50	109,537.91	81,181.38
69	423.25	93,115.00	106,799.39	79,147.75	97,347.50	111,653.91	82,745.38
70	433.25	116,977.50	134,176.98	99,430.88	116,977.50	134,176.98	99,430.88
71	449.25	121,297.50	139,144.98	103,102.88	121,297.50	139,144.98	103,102.88
72	465.25	125,617.50	144,112.98	106,774.88	125,617.50	144,112.98	106,774.88
73	481.25	129,937.50	149,080.98	110,446.88	129,937.50	149,080.98	110,446.88
74	497.25	134,257.50	154,048.98	114,118.88	134,257.50	154,048.98	114,118.88
75	513.25	138,577.50	159,016.98	117,790.88	138,577.50	159,016.98	117,790.88
76	529.25	142,897.50	163,984.98	121,462.88	142,897.50	163,984.98	121,462.88
77	545.25	147,217.50	168,952.98	125,134.88	147,217.50	168,952.98	125,134.88
78	561.25	151,537.50	173,920.98	128,806.88	151,537.50	173,920.98	128,806.88
79	577.25	155,857.50	178,888.98	132,478.88	155,857.50	178,888.98	132,478.88
80	593.25	160,177.50	183,856.98	136,150.88	160,177.50	183,856.98	136,150.88
81	609.25	164,497.50	188,824.98	139,822.88	164,497.50	188,824.98	139,822.88
82	625.25	168,817.50	193,792.98	143,494.88	168,817.50	193,792.98	143,494.88
83	641.25	173,137.50	198,760.98	147,166.88	173,137.50	198,760.98	147,166.88
84	657.25	177,457.50	203,728.98	150,838.88	177,457.50	203,728.98	150,838.88
85	673.25	181,777.50	208,696.98	154,510.88	181,777.50	208,696.98	154,510.88
86	689.25	186,097.50	213,664.98	158,182.88	186,097.50	213,664.98	158,182.88
87	705.25	190,417.50	218,632.98	161,854.88	190,417.50	218,632.98	161,854.88
88	721.25	194,737.50	223,600.98	165,526.88	194,737.50	223,600.98	165,526.88
89	737.25	199,057.50	228,568.98	169,198.88	199,057.50	228,568.98	169,198.88
90	753.25	203,377.50	233,536.98	172,870.88	203,377.50	233,536.98	172,870.88
91	769.25	207,697.50	238,504.98	176,542.88	207,697.50	238,504.98	176,542.88
92	785.25	212,017.50	243,472.98	180,214.88	212,017.50	243,472.98	180,214.88
93	801.25	216,337.50	248,440.98	183,886.88	216,337.50	248,440.98	183,886.88
94	817.25	220,657.50	253,408.98	187,558.88	220,657.50	253,408.98	187,558.88
95	833.25	224,977.50	258,376.98	191,230.88	224,977.50	258,376.98	191,230.88
96	849.25	229,297.50	263,344.98	194,902.88	229,297.50	263,344.98	194,902.88
97	865.25	233,617.50	268,312.98	198,574.88	233,617.50	268,312.98	198,574.88
98	881.25	237,937.50	273,280.98	202,246.88	237,937.50	273,280.98	202,246.88
99	897.25	242,257.50	278,248.98	205,918.88	242,257.50	278,248.98	205,918.88

Permanent Partial Disability
Weekly Rate
Use our free calculator for all charts at www.getmedlegal.com/calculatorprog/WCCalculator.asp

Date of Injury (on or after)	Percentage Disability	Minimum		Maximum	
		Earnings	Rate	Earnings	Rate
1/1/84	1:0 - 99.75	105	70	210	**140**
1/1/91	1:0 - 24.75	105	70	210	**140**
	25:0 - 99.75	105	70	222	**148**
7/1/94	1:0 - 14.75	105	70	210	**140**
	15:0 - 24.75	105	70	222	**148**
	25:0 - 69.75	105	70	237	**158**
	70:0 - 99.75	105	70	252	**168**
7/1/95	1:0 - 14.75	105	70	210	**140**
	15:0 - 24.75	105	70	231	**154**
	25:0 - 69.75	105	70	246	**164**
	70:0 - 99.75	105	70	297	**198**
7/1/96	1:0 - 14.75	105	70	210	**140**
	15:0 - 24.75	105	70	240	**160**
	25:0 - 69.75	105	70	255	**170**
	70:0 - 99.75	105	70	345	**230**
1/1/03	1:0 - 69.75	150	100	277.50	**185**
	70:0 - 99.75	150	100	345	**230**
1/1/04	1:0 - 69.75	157.50	105	300	**200**
	70:0 - 99.75	157.50	105	375	**250**
1/1/05	1:0 - 69.75	157.50	105	330	**220**
	70:0 - 99.75	157.50	105	405	**270**
1/1/06	1:0 - 69.75	195	130	345	**230**
	70:0 - 99.75	195	130	405	**270**

- Permanent disability weekly payments are paid at 2/3 of weekly earnings -- not to exceed the above maximum rate and must be at least the minimum rate.
- Permanent disability weekly payments are paid for the number of week specified in the first table.
- PD is not increased by SAWW LC 4453(b)

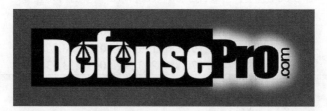

9108 Pittsburg Avenue, Suite 101
Rancho Cucamonga, CA 91730
(877) 877-3744 FAX   (888) 374-3749   Info@DefensePro.com
www.DefensePro.com

Life Pension

Use our free calculator for all charts at www.getmedlegal.com/calculatorprog/WCCalculator.asp

Disability %	Date of Injury (on or after)					
	4/1/74	7/1/94	7/1/95	7/1/96	1/1/03 *	1/1/06 *
70	16.15	23.65	31.15	38.65	38.65	77.31
71	17.77	26.02	34.27	42.52	42.52	85.04
72	19.38	28.38	37.38	46.38	46.38	92.77
73	21.00	30.75	40.50	50.25	50.25	100.50
74	22.61	33.11	43.61	54.11	54.11	108.23
75	24.23	35.48	46.73	57.98	57.98	115.96
76	25.85	37.85	49.85	61.85	61.85	123.69
77	27.46	40.21	52.96	65.71	65.71	131.42
78	29.08	42.58	56.08	69.58	69.58	139.15
79	30.69	44.94	59.19	73.44	73.44	146.88
80	32.31	47.31	62.31	77.31	77.31	154.61
81	33.92	49.67	65.42	81.17	81.17	162.34
82	35.54	52.04	68.54	85.04	85.04	170.08
83	37.15	54.40	71.65	88.90	88.90	177.81
84	38.77	56.77	74.77	92.77	92.77	185.54
85	40.38	59.13	77.88	96.63	96.63	193.27
86	42.00	61.50	81.00	100.50	100.50	201.00
87	43.61	63.86	84.11	104.36	104.36	208.73
88	45.23	66.23	87.23	108.23	108.23	216.46
89	46.85	68.60	90.35	112.10	112.10	224.19
90	48.46	70.96	93.46	115.96	115.96	231.92
91	50.08	73.33	96.58	119.83	119.83	239.65
92	51.69	75.69	99.69	123.69	123.69	247.38
93	53.31	78.06	102.81	127.56	127.56	255.11
94	54.92	80.42	105.92	131.42	131.42	262.84
95	56.54	82.79	109.04	135.29	135.29	270.57
96	58.15	85.15	112.15	139.15	139.15	278.31
97	59.77	87.52	115.27	143.02	143.02	286.04
98	61.38	89.88	118.38	146.88	146.88	293.77
99	63.00	92.25	121.50	150.75	150.75	301.50

Injury Date (on or after)	Weekly Earnings Maximum
1/1/84	107.69
7/1/94	157.69
7/1/95	207.69
7/1/96	257.69
1/1/03	257.69 *
1/1/06	515.38 *

* For injuries occurring on or after 1/1/03 commencing on 1/1/04 the payment is increased by State Average Weekly Wage (SAWW) percentage increase from prior year as reported by the US Department of Labor for California. LC §4659(c). This is not reflected in the above tables because life pension payments do not commence until permanent partial payments end. For a date of injury in 2003 with a permanent partial disability of 70% life pension payments would not start until 426.5 weeks after the permanent and stationary date. Payments would not begin until 8.17 years after the P&S date.

- When the permanent disability is 70 % or greater life pension weekly payments are made at the above rate depending the percentage of disability.
- Payments commence after the permanent disability weeks specified in the first table end.
- Formula: Life pension = (% - 60) x .015 x (Weekly Earnings within maximum)

Temporary Total Disability Weekly Payments in 2007

Use our free calculator for all charts at www.getmedlegal.com/calculatorprog/WCCalculator.asp

Dae of Injury	Average Weekly Earnings	Temporary Total Disability Payment
Any date of injury	Below 198.37 Above 1322.48	132.25 2/3 x Weekly Earnings **881.66**

Temporary disability payments are paid at 2/3 of the weekly earnings within the limits specified in the above table. LC §4653

Aggregate disability payments for a single injury occurring on or after 4/19/04 shall not extend for more than 104 compensable weeks within a period of two years from the date of commencement of TD. Certain acute or severe disabilities extend for 240 weeks. LC 4656(b)(2)

For injuries occurring on or after 1/1/05 commencing 1/1/07 the limits are increased annually by percentage increase of State Average Weekly Wage (SAWW). LC §4453(a)(10)

Temporary total disability payments made two years after the date of injury are paid at the current rate in effect when paid. LC §4661.5

Permanent Total Disability Weekly Payments in 2007

Date of Injury (on or after)	Average Weekly Earnings Limits in effect at DOI	Weekly Earnings Limits for 2007	Permanent Total Disability Min & Max Payment Commencing 1/1/07
1/1/03	189 to 903	189 to 903	140.26 2/3 x Weekly Earnings x 1.1132 **670.15**
1/1/04	189 to 1092	189 to 1092	140.26 2/3 x Weekly Earnings x 1.1132 **810.41**
1/1/05	189 to 1260	198.37 to 1322.48	**144.37** 2/3 x Weekly Earnings x 1.09166 **962.47**
1/1/06	189 to 1260	198.37 to 1322.48	**138.81** 2/3 x Weekly Earnings x 1.04959 **925.37**
1/1/07	198.37 to 1322.48	198.37 to 1322.48	132.25 2/3 x Weekly Earnings **881.65**

This table does not apply to injuries occurring before 1/1/03.

Payments: For injuries occurring on or after 1/1/03 payments are increased annually commencing on January 1 following the date of injury, and each year thereafter, based upon the percentage increase of the SAWW for the previous year. LC §4659(c)

Limits: For injuries occurring on or after 1/1/05 commencing 1/1/07 are increased annually by percentage increase of State Average Weekly Wage (SAWW). LC §4453(a)(10)

DefensePro

Death Benefits

Use our free calculator for all charts at www.getmedlegal.com/calculatorprog/WCCalculator.asp

Date of Injury (on or after)	Dependents Total	Dependents Partial	Benefit Maximum
1/1/84	1	0	70,000
	2 or more	NA	95,000
	1	1 or more	70,000 + 4 x annual support but not more than 95,000
	0	1 or more	4 x annual support but no more than 70,000
1/1/91	1	0	95,000
	2 or more	NA	115,000
	1	1 or more	95,000 + 4 x annual support but not more than 115,000
	0	1 or more	4 x annual support but not more than 95,000
7/1/94	1	0	115,000
	2	NA	135,000
	3 or more	NA	150,000
	1	1 or more	115,000 + 4 x annual support but not more than 125,000
	0	1 or more	4 x annual support but not more than 115,000
7/1/96	1	0	125,000
	2	NA	145,000
	3 or more	NA	160,000
	1	1 or more	125,000 + 4 x annual support but not more than 145,000
	0	1 or more	4 x annual support but not more than 125,000
1/1/06	1	0	250,000
	2	NA	290,000
	3 or more	NA	320,000
	1	1 or more	250,000 + 4 x annual support but not more than 290,000
	0	1 or more	8 x annual support but not more than 250,000

- Maximum burial expense $5,000.
- Death benefits are paid in payments at the same rate as temporary total disability unless otherwise ordered except the minimum payment is $224.00 per week. After two years from the date of death payments are increased to the temporary total disability rate currently in effect at the date of payment.
- Dependents conclusively presumed wholly dependent:
    (1) minor child or a child of any age found to be physically or mentally incapacitated from earning who was either living with deceased parent or the deceased parent is legally liable at the time of injury;
    (2) spouse earning less than $30,000 in the preceding 12 months at time of death.
- Where there is one or more totally dependent minor children, payments shall continue after the maximum is paid until the youngest child attains the age of 18 or until the death of a child physically or mentally incapacitated from earnings.
- Where there are two or more total dependents there is no increase for partial dependents.
- If there are no total dependents and one or more partial dependents, the partial dependents share in accordance with their relative extent of dependency.
- Temporary or permanent disability payments, if any, stop at death. Accrued and unpaid compensation is paid to the dependents. Accrued disability compensation is in addition to death benefits if the employment injury contributed to or caused the death.

Life Expectancy and Work Life Expectancy

Age	Male L.E.	PV $1 / Week	Work Life	Female L.E.	PV $1 / Week	Work Life
16	59.6	$1,420.59	36.6	64.8	$1,475.40	26.0
17	58.6	$1,411.30	36.3	63.8	$1,467.26	25.6
18	57.7	$1,402.00	35.9	62.8	$1,458.94	25.3
19	56.8	$1,392.87	35.5	61.9	$1,450.51	24.9
20	55.8	$1,383.64	35.2	60.9	$1,441.78	24.6
21	54.9	$1,374.18	34.8	59.9	$1,432.82	24.3
22	54.0	$1,364.44	34.5	58.9	$1,423.59	23.9
23	53.1	$1,354.45	34.1	58.0	$1,414.11	23.6
24	52.1	$1,344.06	33.8	57.0	$1,404.31	23.2
25	51.2	$1,333.32	33.4	56.0	$1,394.23	22.9
26	50.3	$1,322.18	32.6	55.1	$1,383.84	22.4
27	49.4	$1,310.73	31.8	54.1	$1,373.19	21.9
28	48.4	$1,298.88	31.0	53.1	$1,362.25	21.5
29	47.5	$1,286.64	30.2	52.2	$1,350.95	21.0
30	46.5	$1,274.08	29.4	51.2	$1,339.40	20.5
31	45.6	$1,261.18	28.6	50.2	$1,327.49	20.1
32	44.7	$1,247.89	27.8	49.3	$1,315.29	19.6
33	43.7	$1,234.31	27.0	48.3	$1,302.74	19.1
34	42.8	$1,220.30	26.3	47.3	$1,289.96	18.6
35	41.9	$1,205.95	25.5	46.4	$1,276.83	18.2
36	40.9	$1,191.31	24.6	45.4	$1,263.48	17.6
37	40.0	$1,176.38	23.8	44.5	$1,249.78	17.0
38	39.1	$1,161.13	23.0	43.5	$1,235.80	16.4
39	38.2	$1,145.53	22.2	42.6	$1,221.46	15.8
40	37.3	$1,129.68	21.4	41.6	$1,206.85	15.2
41	36.4	$1,113.54	20.5	40.7	$1,191.98	14.6
42	35.5	$1,097.16	19.7	39.7	$1,176.79	14.1
43	34.6	$1,080.53	18.9	38.8	$1,161.30	13.5
44	33.7	$1,063.54	18.1	37.9	$1,145.41	12.9
45	32.8	$1,046.36	17.3	37.0	$1,129.30	12.3
46	31.9	$1,028.81	16.5	36.0	$1,112.83	11.7
47	31.1	$1,011.20	15.7	35.1	$1,096.08	11.1
48	30.2	$993.31	14.9	34.2	$1,078.93	10.5
49	29.3	$975.12	14.1	33.3	$1,061.40	9.9
50	28.5	$956.71	13.3	32.4	$1,043.57	9.2
51	27.7	$938.05	12.5	31.5	$1,025.39	8.6
52	26.8	$919.09	11.7	30.6	$1,006.85	8.0
53	26.0	$899.89	10.9	29.7	$988.02	7.4
54	25.2	$880.14	10.1	28.9	$968.70	6.8
55	24.4	$860.45	9.3	28.0	$949.23	6.2
56	23.6	$840.26	8.6	27.1	$929.33	5.7
57	22.8	$820.25	7.9	26.3	$909.40	5.2
58	22.0	$799.23	7.2	25.4	$888.77	4.8
59	21.2	$778.58	6.5	24.6	$868.34	4.3
60	20.4	$757.88	5.8	23.8	$847.68	3.8
61	19.7	$737.35	5.1	22.9	$827.00	3.3
62	18.9	$716.24	4.4	22.1	$805.68	2.9
63	18.2	$695.53	3.7	21.3	$784.52	2.4
64	17.5	$674.47	3.0	20.5	$763.05	1.9
65	16.8	$653.48	2.3	19.8	$741.63	1.4
66	16.1	$632.33	2.2	19.0	$719.86	1.3
67	15.4	$611.16	2.0	18.2	$697.89	1.2
68	14.8	$590.16	1.8	17.5	$675.90	1.1
69	14.1	$569.06	1.6	16.8	$653.78	1.0
70	13.5	$548.33	1.5	16.0	$631.46	.9

PV column is a commutation of a payment of $1 for the remainder of the person's life at 3% interest. For example, a female age 53 with life pension of $490.00 P = 988.02 x 490 = $484,129.80. To commute an attorney fee where the payment is reduced divide the attorney fee by PV. For example, an attorney fee of $11,500: Reduction of payment = $11,500 / 988.02 = $11.64. Payment would be $490.00 – 11.64 = $478.36. This chart does not take into account cost of living increases, nor increases due to the changes in the State Average Weekly Wage (SAWW) over time. **Work Life expectancy values is reprinted with permission from The New Work Life Expectancy Tables 2006 by Vocational Economic, Inc. The Life Expectancy table is based on US Life Tables 2003.**

TABLE OF CASES

Intentionally blank

TABLE OF AUTHORITIES

REGULATIONS

INSURANCE CODE

LABOR CODE

SENATE BILL

CIVIL CODE

PENAL CODE

CODE OF CIVIL PROCEDURE

GOVERNMENT CODE

BUSINESS AND PROFESSIONS CODE

Intentionally blank

INDEX